Contemporary Marketing Research

THIRD EDITION

THIRD EDITION

Contemporary Marketing Research

Carl McDaniel, Jr.
University of Texas at Arlington

Roger Gates
University of Texas at Arlington

WEST PUBLISHING COMPANY
Minneapolis/St. Paul ■ New York ■ Los Angeles ■ San Francisco

Production Credits

COPYEDITING	Allen Gooch
COMPOSITION	Parkwood Composition
PHOTO RESEARCH	Dallas Chang
TEXT AND COVER DESIGN	K. M. Weber
COVER IMAGES	© 1995 PhotoDisc, Inc.
ILLUSTRATION	Randy Miyake
INDEX	Terry Casey

West's Commitment To The Environment

In 1906, West Publishing Company began recycling materials left over from the production of books. This began a tradition of efficient and responsible use of resources. Today, up to 95 percent of our legal books and 70 percent of our college and school texts are printed on recycled, acid-free stock. West also recycles nearly 22 million pounds of scrap paper annually—the equivalent of 181,717 trees. Since the 1960s, West has devised ways to capture and recycle waste inks, solvents, oils, and vapors created in the printing process. We also recycle plastics of all kinds, wood, glass, corrugated cardboard, and batteries, and have eliminated the use of Styrofoam book packaging. We at West are proud of the longevity and the scope of our commitment to the environment.

Production, printing, and binding by West Publishing Company.

 TEXT IS PRINTED ON 10% POST CONSUMER RECYCLED PAPER 

British Library Cataloguing-in-Publication Data. A catalogue record for this book is available from the British Library.

610 Opperman Drive
P.O. Box 64526
St. Paul, MN 55164-0526

Printed in the United States of America

03 02 01 00 99 98 97 96 8 7 6 5 4 3 2 1 0

Library of Congress Cataloging-in-Publication Data

McDaniel, Carl D.
Contemporary marketing research/Carl McDaniel, Roger Gates.
—3rd. ed.
p. cm.
Includes bibliographical references and index.
ISBN 0-314-06122-3 (alk. paper)
1. Marketing research. I. Gates, Roger H., 1942– . II. Title.
HF5415.2.M382 1996
658.8'3—dc20 95-8926
CIP

TO OUR CHILDREN

Mark and Chelley

CARL McDANIEL

Stephanie, Lara and Jordan

ROGER GATES

Contents in Brief

Contents

3 Who Does Marketing Research? 54

4 Ethics in Marketing Research 82

PART II

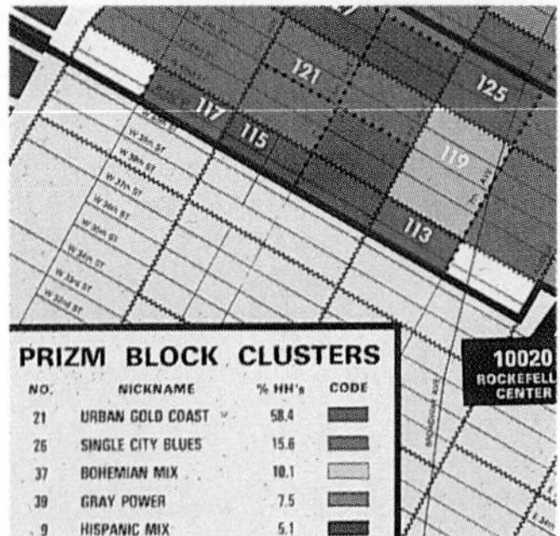
PRIZM BLOCK CLUSTERS
NO. NICKNAME % HH's CODE
21 URBAN GOLD COAST 58.4
26 SINGLE CITY BLUES 15.6
37 BOHEMIAN MIX 10.1
39 GRAY POWER 7.5
9 HISPANIC MIX 5.1
10020
ROCKEFELL
CENTER

PART III

Data Acquisition 336

10 Understanding Measurement 338

11 Attitude Measurement 364

PART IV

Data Analysis 500

15 Data Processing and Fundamental Data Analysis 502

16 Data Analysis: Statistical Testing of Differences 538

17 Data Analysis: Bivariate Correlation and Regression 575

18 Multivariate Data Analysis 596

Appendix 1 Comprehensive Cases 733

Appendix 2 Statistical Tables 775

Glossary G-1

Endnotes E-1

Index I-1

Preface

Successful contemporary marketing practices focus on quality and customer satisfaction. We have used these tenets to create every edition of *Contemporary Marketing Research.* The tremendous increase in sales from one edition to the next has been extremely gratifying. Our task is to continue to listen to both of you, the professor and the student, to create the finest marketing research text in the world. We will continue to do everything in our power to make certain that your trust and confidence in *Contemporary Marketing Research, 3rd Edition* is well placed.

The third edition is indeed a new text. We have made changes in every chapter and well over 100 significant changes in all. Many of these new features are based on feedback from our customer-satisfaction research. We have tried very hard to respond to *every* significant comment that was made. Perhaps you will notice how a certain point was changed or elaborated on based on your comments.

Roger Gates is the president of a major marketing research firm that is on the cutting edge of technology. Being active in the industry every day, he sees changes as they occur and trends as they develop. These are fully incorporated in the text. Thus, this text has not only the most current academic research in marketing, but unmatched industry perspective straight from the marketing research firing line. The third edition truly is *contemporary marketing research.*

We Have Retained the Features that Made the Second Edition a Best-Seller

There is probably no greater hindrance to learning than a dull textbook. With this in mind, we've strived to make *Contemporary Marketing Research, 3rd Edition* a truly pleasurable and captivating reading experience. This has been accomplished by:

- *Using a full color format throughout the text.* Ours was the first marketing research textbook ever produced in full color. Its purpose is to assist the student in understanding important concepts as well as being pleasurable to read. Color not only makes the text more interesting, it highlights key points by setting off certain sections of a chapter. An example of a color setoff is the "Global Marketing Research" features. Color also enhances the text photographs and makes them more lifelike.
- *Opening each chapter with a real-world marketing research example.* At the conclusion of each opening vignette, we post a few teaser questions designed to pique the students' interest in the material about to be covered.

- *Writing in a lively, informal style developed over the years by two highly experienced and successful authors.* Careful attention to language and sentence structure and the use of hundreds of "real-world" examples make *Contemporary Marketing Research, 3rd Edition* engrossing while at the same time rigorous.
- *Implementing a research user's orientation.* A number of features have been incorporated into the text to aid future managers in effectively utilizing marketing research. In Chapter 1, we offer an extensive discussion on when to conduct marketing research and when not to. Chapter 2 discusses not only the research process but also where and how managers get involved—i.e., the research request. Chapter 3 will help the future managers understand "the players" in the research industry. Chapter 19 tells the reader what to look for in a marketing research report and how to get managers to use marketing research data.

A Professional Learning Tool

Creating a book that's a pleasure to read is an important step in developing an effective learning tool. Still, pedagogical devices are necessary to complete the task. *Contemporary Marketing Research, 3rd Edition* offers:

- Chapter learning objectives that challenge the student to explain, discuss, understand, and clarify the concepts to be presented.
- An opening vignette, full-color photos and illustrations, and special in-text sections to amplify and clarify text material. See Mediamark Research, Inc. (Chapter 7) and Gold 'n' Plump chicken (Chapter 10)
- A comprehensive chapter summary.
- Key terms—bold faced in the text and listed at the end of the chapter, as well as defined in the margins.
- Review questions, recalling key points in the chapter.
- Discussion questions—probing, thought-provoking questions designed to stimulate class discussion.
- Two case studies per chapter–short, real-world, and written in a lively style to enhance student learning and enjoyment. See American Express (Case 3.2) and Black and Decker power tools (Case 8.1).
- Five comprehensive, real-world cases with accompanying data sets for student analysis. See Appendix A (Heritage Restaurants, Grocery Shopping Habits, and Rockingham National Banks.
- Ethics cases at the end of each part pose real-world ethical dilemmas faced by marketing researchers and managers.

A Model for the Text

The model for chapter sequence and topical coverage embodies a contemporary design to focus on understanding marketing research from a user's perspective. Part One begins with a short review of where marketing research fits into the marketing management process and when to conduct research. Next, the marketing research process is explained. The stage is then set for an overview of the research industry. Part One concludes with marketing research ethics, which explores ethical decision making in all phases of the research process.

The remainder of *Contemporary Marketing Research, 3rd Edition* follows in logical sequence:

PART TWO Creating a Research Design
PART THREE Data Acquisition
PART FOUR Data Analysis
PART FIVE Marketing Research Action

New for the Third Edition

Chapter 18 on multivariate data analysis has been completely rewritten. The Federal Communications Commission earned over $1 billion when it auctioned off previously restricted frequencies. This new "space" will be used by leading-edge companies to offer personal communication service (PCS), a much-advanced and cheaper form of cellular telephone service. In effect, your home will no longer be hardwired and all your telephones will be portable. The cutting-edge example for Chapter 18 is PCS. It begins with the chapter opening vignette and carries through multiple regression, discriminant analysis, cluster analysis, and factor analysis. The material on conjoint analysis is new as well. This chapter provides the clearest and most interesting explanation of multivariate data analysis on the market.

More emphasis on global marketing research. The coverage of international survey research in Chapter 7 has been further expanded from the second edition. Also, we doubled the number of "Global Marketing Research" in-chapter features. These stories offer tips on conducting research in the global marketplace and offer examples of how international marketing research is done. For example, in Chapter 3 we present a feature on how the North American Free Trade Agreement (NAFTA) is impacting marketing research. In Chapter 12 we offer tips on conducting marketing research in Asia.

We maintain the contemporary edge by replacing virtually all the chapter opening vignettes. Some examples of new opening vignettes include the stunning failure of Beech Aircraft's Starship, customer satisfaction research for Princess Cruise Line, and a new promotional theme for Keep America Beautiful.

You will read the latest about what today's marketing researchers are thinking and saying. Students and professors have told us how informative and interesting they find our in-chapter vignettes titled "A Professional Researcher's Perspective." These features allow researchers to "tell it like it is" in the real world of marketing research. We offer 17 new "Professional Researcher's Perspectives" in the third edition. Topics range from a discussion on respondent satisfaction to how to moderate focus groups.

The latest in marketing research techniques and practices are covered in the in-chapter stories called "Marketing Research in Practice." These were another popular feature of the second edition, and we present 12 new "Marketing Research in Practice" features in this edition. Examples include how Brawny Paper Towels' package was redesigned using marketing research to what multivariate statistics software packages researchers are using and how they rate them.

All the hottest topics in marketing research are covered:

- The role of marketing research in delivering quality and customer satisfaction.
- The future of marketing research.

- Strategic alliances.
- Certification of marketing researchers.
- The proactive role of the Council for Marketing and Public Opinion Research (CMOR).
- New database technologies.
- Low-incidence targeted samples.
- Using the Internet in marketing research.
- The importance of shifting demographics on survey research.
- Oversurveying key target groups.
- Latest scanner-based software.
- Using virtual reality in experimentation.
- The latest alternatives to test marketing.
- The trend toward field management companies.
- The latest on presentation software.

The most extensive appendices of any marketing research text on published secondary databases and databases of interest to marketers have been thoroughly revised by a professional business librarian. For example, we now include the American Marketing Association's *International Membership Directory and Marketing Services Guide* and up-to-date publications such as *Marketing Information: A Professional Reference Guide*, 1995.

The *third edition of Contemporary Marketing Research contains 12 new end-of-chapter cases and all new end-of-text comprehensive cases with databases.* The new end-of-chapter cases include Toyota, Hitachi, Panasonic, Blockbuster Video, Black and Decker, American Airlines, and more. The comprehensive database cases cover such topics as restaurant patronage and design; supermarket preferences, shopping habits, and perceptions; and credit card preferences of teachers. Comprehensive Case A, Heritage Restaurants, is short, with a limited number of variables, and serves as an excellent introduction to simple data analysis. The questionnaire is a screener for a much larger study. We recommend that this case be used after Chapter 15 to illustrate one-dimensional analysis and cross-tabulations. Comprehensive Case B continues the research on Heritage Restaurants with a large quantitative study. This data set lends itself to extensive analysis and is recommended to be used after Chapters 16 and 17. Comprehensive Case C is the final extension of Heritage Restaurants. The short questionnaire can be used for perceptual mapping and conjoint analysis. We recommend that this case be used after Chapter 18. Comprehensive Case D, grocery shopping habits survey, lends itself to both bivariate and multivariate statistical analyses. The case is rich in patronage data and demographics. Comprehensive Case E, the Visa card, deals with teachers' perceptions of new credit card features. The data set is amenable to a variety of statistical tests including multivariate statistics such as discriminant analysis.

Selected specific changes on a part-by-part basis are as follows:

PART ONE An Introduction to Marketing Research

- Heavier emphasis on the role of marketing research on quality and customer satisfaction—i.e., return on quality.
- The importance of keeping existing customers.
- The pros and cons of a career in marketing research.

- Extended example that carries throughout Chapter 2 on the Chrysler Minivan.
- Clearer presentation on temporal sequence and concomitant variation.
- Global marketing research expenditures.
- How NAFTA is impacting marketing research.
- Global marketing research trends.
- Marketing research practices around the world.
- Respondent satisfaction.
- The right to privacy.
- European protection of consumer rights.
- The Council for Marketing and Public Opinion Research (CMOR).
- The certification of marketing researchers.

PART TWO Creating a Research Design

- Database creation using Vons Supermarkets and Blockbuster as extended examples.
- Database technologies.
- How to search a database.
- Demographic databases offered by CompuServe and other on-line vendors.
- The Internet and how it can be used by marketing researchers.
- Geographic information systems.
- Why people participate in focus groups.
- Qualities of a well-trained focus group moderator.
- New excerpts from focus group discussions with college students on credit card usage.
- Nominal group sessions.
- Photo sorts.
- The importance of shifting demographics on survey research.
- New table describing emerging survey research techniques.
- Interactive voice response telephone surveys.
- Conducting surveys via CompuServe.
- Kiosk-based research.
- Interviewing children.
- Japanese marketing research.
- Shopper tracking devices.
- "Laskerville," a town where researchers go and "blend in" to the community to observe consumer behavior.
- Portable, passive people meter.
- Scanner-based software.
- The Info Scan Census.
- Virtual reality in experimentation.
- Alternatives to test marketing.

PART THREE Data Acquisition

- Administering scales to Asian Americans.
- The necessity of rotating items to control for position bias.
- Tips on questionnaire design.
- Field management companies.
- Perils of sample frame error.
- Low-incidence targeted samples.

PART FOUR Data Analysis

- Optical scanning of questionnaires.
- New material on evaluating differences and changes.
- New example of the Kolmogorov-Smirnov test.
- New example of computer output showing *P*-value calculation.
- New examples on bivariate regression.
- Multivariate statistics software packages.
- New examples on multiple regression, discriminant analysis, cluster

analysis, factor analysis, and conjoint analysis extended from the Chapter 18 opening vignette.
- Simulating buyer choice using conjoint analysis.

PART FIVE Marketing Research in Action

- Presentation software.
- Presentation software graphics.
- Problems with research reports.
- Key factors in the effective use of marketing research.
- The use of customer satisfaction research by marketing researchers for their own clients.
- New material on product positioning research.
- New material on forms of segmentation research.

New Supplements for the Third Edition

The Lipton Noodles Alfredo Case, by John F. Tanner, Jr., Baylor University. This extensive case is for those instructors who want students to spend less time doing fieldwork and more time learning about marketing research. Students perform limited fieldwork (just enough to get a feel for it) and conduct a focus group and an experiment. The case can be used in a quarter or a semester term.

The Marketing Research Workbook, by Chip Miller of Pacific Lutheran University. This workbook includes hands-on activities for most chapters of the text. The activities help students improve their research skills and managerial decision making, such as which market to target, when to make decisions, and what type of research to use.

ASTOUND Presentation Software. ASTOUND is a state-of-the-art presentation graphics program for Microsoft Windows or the Macintosh. This integrated program allows instructors to retrieve and work with any of the transparencies that accompany the book. Images can easily be edited, added, or deleted. The program includes over 500 pre-loaded slides with four-color graphics, key stroke control, and many animations. Other features of the system include the following:

- The instructor can present transparencies electronically in the classroom.
- Transparencies from the program can be printed in one or four colors.
- The instructor can edit and change any of the material included in the transparency set or add new material as needed.
- The instructor can animate and show a slide show with transition effect.
- We have created a full multimedia presentation for Case 17.2 on the ASTOUND disc. The presentation can be used as a self-running demonstration or you can customize the presentation to your own needs. This is an excellent example of how multimedia can be used to communicate research results in a corporate setting.

State of the Art Supplements Package

Our satisfaction marketing research told us that you believe we have created the most extensive and useful set of supplements ever created for the marketing research course. These supplements have been retained and updated. The key variables in creating a motivational and enthusiastic learning environment are the textbook, the instructor's lectures, and supplemental material used to augment and reinforce the textbook material. Because *Contemporary Marketing Research, 3rd Edition* is being used in the only marketing research course most students will ever take, we want to maximize the students' understanding and appreciation of marketing research. At the same time, we hope to minimize unnecessary classroom and project preparation time for the instructor. We would like to thank Glen Jarboe for creating the third edition of the Marketing Research Project Manual. Other supplements for *Contemporary Marketing Research, 3rd Edition* are:

- *The Marketing Research Project Manual, 3rd Edition.* This highly popular manual offers a detailed, step-by-step procedure for students to follow in the conducting of a market research project with an emphasis on survey research and data analysis. The third edition contains more vignettes about alternative projects and a complete data set keyed to the results reported in the manual. The SPSS has been rewritten for Windows software. Also, a new project is featured on creating a landscaping business. Instructors who require a real-world marketing research project have found that the manual saves valuable class time and provides lucid explanations of the research process.
- *Instructor's Manual with Video Guide.* Insightful comments from users have enabled us to create the most comprehensive instructor's manual available for the marketing research course. The complete lecture outline for each chapter with supplemental notes is designed so that instructors can use the material during class lectures and discussions. The manual also includes video summaries for the video library that includes a description, running times, key points, and discussion questions.
- *Test bank.* The new classroom-tested and validated test bank contains over 1,500 multiple choice, true/false, and case questions. The questions are designed to test the student's knowledge of the most salient points of each chapter. A computerized version, WESTEST, is also available.
- *Statistics by StatSoft.* This highly rated software package is an integrated statistical analysis, graphics, and database management system. The student edition features a wide array of basic and advanced analytical procedures such as regression analysis, factor analysis, discriminant function, analysis, and cluster analysis. This user-friendly package is available to accompany the text at a substantially discounted price.
- *Comprehensive Case Data Banks.* There are five comprehensive research cases at the end of the text. A complete data set of raw research results is available on diskette for each case.
- *Videos.* All videos in our existing video package will be offered in the third edition. Soon we will release three new videos featuring the Minnesota Twins baseball club, Promus Companies, and Price-Costco—a giant warehouse club chain. Existing videos include: *One on One: Getting It Right.* This tape deals with interviewing techniques used by marketing researchers. After each interviewing topic is discussed and illustrated on the tape, questions for discussion follow. *Focus Group on Women's Shoes.* A focus group conducted by a professional moderator trainer for Riva Marketing Research, Chicago. *Focus Group on a New Deodorant.* A focus group conducted by a professional moderator trainer for Riva Marketing Research, Chicago. *Marketing Research and the Interview.* This tape discusses and demonstrates proper marketing research interviewing tech-

niques. *Developing Crystal Pepsi.* This tape discusses and illustrates the research that went into the development of Crystal Pepsi. *A. C. Nielsen Grocery Category Management.* Illustrates grocery audits and information outputs from A. C. Nielsen 1991. *Chilton Research Services.* Tape illustrates the capabilities and resources of one of America's largest full service marketing research firms. *Behind the Scenes (Advertising Education Foundation).* Shows campaign development process and the role of marketing research in the process. Includes strategy/concept discussions and focus group shots. *Depth Interview with a Homemaker on Nutritious Snacks* (DDB Needham). Middle-class homemaker discusses products for her family as a part of a lifestyle study. *How to Conduct a Focus Group.* Professional moderator trainer explains how to conduct a focus group.

- Transparencies revised to enhance classroom utility. Approximately 100 transparency masters or key Astound slides are available separately. These include key figures from the text as well as alternate transparencies of new material. The Astound presentation files contain over 500 transparencies available for electronic presentation or as one-color or form-color print files.

Acknowledgments

A major text with many supplements, such as this, is always a team effort. We have no doubt that we are working with the finest people in both academia and publishing. We can't say enough good things about our production editor and project leader, Christine Hurney. We would not have a text or package without her encouragement, managerial people skills, and fortitude to "stay the course." Once again, Rick Leyh, our editor, proved that creativity and the highest standards in publishing will produce a textbook that delivers superior student and professor satisfaction. Alex von Rosenberg assisted in invaluable ways with the project's development. A special thanks goes to RoseAnn Reddick for typing the manuscript and the revisions. We are also indebted to David Andrus at Kansas State University for preparing the test bank and Shiva Nandan at Missouri Western State College for preparing the instructor's manual. The many changes in the third edition are the results of suggestions from our reviewers. The advice and counsel of the following individuals was deeply appreciated. We appreciate the conscientious reviewers on the third edition who helped to guide our discussion on important content questions. They are in our dept and include:

Rajshekhar Javalgi, Cleveland State University
Ellen Kennedy, University of Saint Thomas
Leigh Lawton, University of Saint Thomas
Linda Morris, University of Idaho
Joseph Orsini, California State University-Sacramento
Thomas Page, Michigan State University
Gordon Patzer, University of Northern Iowa
William Perttula, San Francisco State University
James Roberts, Baylor University
Joel Saegert, University of Texas at San Antonio
Peter Sanchez, Villanova University
Bruce Stern, Portland State University
John Summey, Southern Illinois University

Contemporary Marketing Research

THIRD EDITION

PART I

An Introduction to Market Research

Admit One
Admit One
Free Gift
New, improved . . .

CHAPTER 1

The Role of Marketing Research in Management Decision Making

LEARNING OBJECTIVES

1. To review the marketing concept and the marketing mix.
2. To comprehend the marketing environment within which managers must make decisions.
3. To define marketing research.
4. To understand the importance of marketing research in shaping marketing decisions.
5. To learn when marketing research should and should not be conducted.
6. To understand the history of marketing research

It was a bold concept—a sleek airplane made not from metal but from carbon-plastic, with startling L-shaped wings and twin turboprop engines mounted aft to push rather than pull. Raytheon Company's Beech unit invested a decade and a small fortune on it, called it Starship, and marketed it as a flashy but fuel-efficient alternative to the corporate jet.

But Starship has made a hard landing in the marketplace. In one of the most expensive flops in commercial aviation, Raytheon officials now concede that they have quietly written off much of the development cost of the plane, estimated by some analysts to approach $500 million. Only 23 Starships have been sold—fewer than half the 50 orders claimed by Raytheon before the first sale in 1990. Although Raytheon hasn't given up on Starship, the plane's dismal sales show how even a successful company can misjudge its customers and misread a changing market.

The latest Starship model has won some plaudits from pilots, who praise its stability, handling, avionics, and roomy interior. Raytheon is starting a new advertising campaign designed by TeamOne, the firm that handles the luxury Lexus automobile.

The Starship was a $500 million mistake because of a lack of marketing research.
SOURCE: ©1991 Russell Munson/The Stock Market.

"For the pilot and the passenger, it has really got everything," says Dennis Murphy, sales manager at Elliott Flying Services in Des Moines, Iowa. But "for the money, the performance isn't there," Murphy adds. "For $5 million, you can buy a jet. Starship just doesn't fit in today's market."

Raytheon counted on Starship's fuel efficiencies to attract frugal buyers, but as the plane developed, energy prices fell and became less of an issue. Starship's relative slowness as a nonjet became a liability since speed remained important for business buyers. Starship's space-age design also was thought of as an attraction for corporate chiefs. But it "turns out the older-generation CEO-level manager is very conservative—he doesn't want people pointing at him when he lands," a Raytheon executive says.

The new Starship model is now on sale, albeit with more modest expectations on the part of its makers. "We're aiming for the independent-minded entrepreneur who's been very successful and wants to make a statement when he lands somewhere, to turn heads when he taxis down the runway," says Max Bleck, president of Raytheon. "We recognize that's a limited market."[1]

The Starship story makes several important points about marketing research. First, executive intuition and a focus on "What can we do?" Instead of "What does the customer want?" can often be very costly. In the case of the Starship, about $500 million. A $250,000 or less marketing research project probably could have saved Raytheon about a half-billion dollars. Second, the longer management postpones marketing research, the more expensive it is to fix or resolve the problem. The Starship fiasco would have bankrupted all but America's largest companies. ■

In this chapter we begin by reviewing how and where marketing research fits into the overall marketing process. Next, the role of marketing research in management decision making is discussed. We then describe the various opportunities available in the research industry. The chapter concludes with a brief preview of the textbook.

The Nature of Marketing

marketing
The process of planning and executing the conception, pricing, promotion, and distribution of ideas, goods, and services to create exchanges that satisfy individual and organizational objectives.

marketing concept
A business philosophy based on consumer orientation, goal orientation, and systems orientation.

consumer orientation
Identification of and focus on the people or firms most likely to buy a product and production of a good or service that will meet their needs most effectively.

goal orientation
A focus on the accomplishment of corporate goals; a limit set on consumer orientation.

Marketing is the process of planning and executing the conception, pricing, promotion, and distribution of ideas, goods, and services to create exchanges that satisfy individual and organizational objectives.[2] The potential for exchange exists when there are at least two parties and each has something of potential value to the other. When the two parties can communicate and deliver the desired goods or services, exchange can take place. How do marketing managers attempt to stimulate exchange? They follow the "right" principle. They attempt to get the right goods or services to the right people at the right place at the right time at the right price using the right promotion techniques. This principle tells you that marketing managers control many factors that ultimately determine marketing success. To make the "right" decisions, management must have timely decision-making information. Marketing research is a primary channel for providing that information.

The Marketing Concept

To efficiently accomplish their goals, firms today have adopted the **marketing concept,** which requires (1) a consumer orientation, (2) a goal orientation, and (3) a systems orientation. **Consumer orientation** means that firms strive to identify the group of people (or firms) most likely to buy their product (the target market) and to produce a good or offer a service that will meet the needs of the target customers most effectively. The second tenet of the marketing concept is **goal orientation;** that is, a firm must be consumer oriented only to the extent that it also accomplishes corporate goals. These goals in profit-making firms usually center on financial criteria, such as a 15 percent return on investment.

The third component of the marketing concept is a **systems orientation.** A system is an organized whole—or a group of diverse units that form an integrated whole—functioning or operating in unison. It is one thing for a firm to say it is consumer oriented and another actually to be consumer oriented. Systems must be established first to find out what consumers want and to identify market opportunities. As you will see later, identifying target market needs and market opportunities are the tasks of marketing research. Next, this information must be fed back to the firm. Without feedback from the marketplace, a firm is not truly consumer oriented.

systems orientation
Creation of systems to monitor the external environment and deliver the marketing mix to the target market.

Researching the Marketing Mix

Establishing the marketing concept is the first step in developing a marketing-oriented organization. Within the marketing department, a **marketing mix,** based upon the marketing concept, must be created. This mix is the unique blend of product pricing, promotion, offerings, and distribution designed to reach a specific group of consumers.

marketing mix
The unique blend of product pricing, promotion, offerings, and distribution designed to meet the needs of a specific group of consumers.

Each element within the marketing mix can be controlled by the marketing manager. A strategy for each element must be uniquely constructed and blended with other elements by the marketing manager to achieve an optimum mix. Any mix is only as good as its weakest component. For example, a weak product with an excellent distribution system is often doomed to failure. Campbell Soup Company, for example, has an excellent distribution system that reaches over 95 percent of all retail grocers. Yet, its Red Kettle soups were an ill-conceived product that failed in the marketplace because of poor positioning. Marketing research can help find and eliminate "weak links" in the marketing mix. New product research, for example, could have evaluated the general concept of Red Kettle soups. Also, taste tests and packaging tests to evaluate the design, size, and color of the can should have been conducted.

The External Marketing Environment

Over time, the marketing mix must be altered because of changes in the environment in which consumers live, work, and make purchasing decisions. This means that some new consumers will become part of the target market, some others will drop out of the market, and those who remain may have different tastes, needs, incomes, lifestyles, and purchase habits than the original target consumers.

Although managers can control the marketing mix, they cannot control elements in the external environment that continually mold and reshape the target market. Unless management understands the external environment, the firm cannot intelligently plan its future. An organization is often unaware of the forces that influence its future. Marketing research is a key means for understanding the environment. Knowledge of the environment helps a firm not only to alter its present marketing mix, but also to identify new opportunities. For example, America's increasing propensity to "eat out" and the surging popularity of Italian food led Pillsbury to create the highly successful Olive Garden chain of restaurants.

The Role of Marketing Research in Decision Making

Marketing research plays two key roles in the marketing system. First, it is part of the marketing intelligence feedback process. It provides decision makers with data on the effectiveness of the current marketing mix and provides insights for necessary changes. Market research also is the primary tool for exploring new opportunities in the marketplace. Segmentation research and new product research help identify the most lucrative opportunities for marketing managers.

Marketing Research Defined

marketing research

The planning, collection, and analysis of data relevant to marketing decision making and the communication of the results of this analysis to management.

Now that you have an understanding of how **marketing research** fits into the overall marketing system, we can proceed with a formal definition of the term as specified by the American Marketing Association:

> Marketing research is the function which links the consumer, customer, and public to the marketer through information—information used to identify and define marketing opportunities and problems; generate, refine, and evaluate marketing actions; monitor marketing performance; and improve understanding of marketing as a process. Marketing research specifies the information required to address these issues; designs the method for collecting information; manages and implements the data collection process; analyzes the results; and communicates the findings and their implications.[3]

We like a shorter definition: marketing research is the planning, collection, and analysis of data relevant to marketing decision making and the communication of the results of this analysis to management.

The Importance of Marketing Research to Management

descriptive function

The gathering and presentation of statements of fact.

diagnostic function

The explanation of data or actions.

predictive function

Specification of how to use the descriptive and diagnostic research to predict the results of a planned marketing decision.

Marketing research can be viewed as playing three functional roles: descriptive, diagnostic, and predictive. Its **descriptive function** includes gathering and presenting statements of fact. For example, what is the historic sales trend in the industry? What are consumers' attitudes toward a product and its advertising? The second role of research is the **diagnostic function,** wherein data or actions are explained. What was the impact on sales when we changed the design on the package? The final role of research is the **predictive function.** How can the researcher use the descriptive and diagnostic research to predict the results of a planned marketing decision?

The Unrelenting Drive for Quality and Customer Satisfaction

Quality and customer satisfaction have become the key competitive weapons of the mid-1990s. Few organizations will prosper in today's environment without a focus on quality, continual improvement, and customer satisfaction. Corporations across the globe have implemented quality improvement and satisfaction programs in an effort to reduce costs, retain customers, increase market share, and, last but not least, improve the bottom line.

When total quality management swept through corporate America in the 1980s, the emphasis was strictly on product improvement. But product improvement per se wasn't the answer. Consider the case of Varian Associates Incorporated, a manufacturer of scientific equipment. The company put 1,000 of its managers through a four-day course on quality. The company's Silicon Valley headquarters buzzed with quality-speak. Talk of work teams and cycle times replaced discussion of electrons and X rays. Varian went about virtually reinventing the way it did business—with what seemed to be stunning results. A unit that makes vacuum systems for computer clean rooms boosted on-time delivery from 42 percent to 92 percent. The semiconductor unit cut the time it took to put out new designs by 14 days. However, producing quality products wasn't enough. Obsessed with meeting production schedules, the staff in that vacuum-equipment unit didn't return customers' phone calls, and the operation ended up losing market share. Radiation-repair people were so rushed to meet deadlines that they left before explaining their work to customers.

"All of the quality-based charts went up and to the right, but everything else went down," says Richard M. Levy, executive vice-president for quality.[4] The company actually lost money in the late 1980s.

The drive for quality, as demonstrated by Varian, was often a production-oriented, mechanistic exercise that proved meaningless to customers. And quality that means little to customers usually doesn't produce a payoff in improved sales, profits, or market share. It's wasted effort and expense. Today the new mantra is **return on quality.** This means two things: (1) that the quality being delivered is the quality desired by the target market and (2) that added quality

return on quality
Management objective based on the principles that the quality being delivered is the quality desired by the target market and that quality must have a positive impact on profitability.

UPS learned from marketing research that speed wasn't everything. Customers also wanted interaction with the drivers. SOURCE: © W. Eastep, Courtesy of United Parcel Service.

must have a positive impact on profitability. Today, for example, banking giant NationsBank Corporation measures every improvement in service, from adding more tellers to offering new mortgage products, in terms of added profitability.

The key to making "return on quality" work is marketing research. It is the mechanism that enables organizations to determine what types and forms of quality are important to the target market. And marketing research can sometimes force companies to abandon cherished beliefs. United Parcel Service Inc., for example, had always assumed that on-time delivery was the paramount concern of its customers. Everything else came second. Before long, UPS's definition of quality centered almost exclusively on the results of time-and-motion studies. Knowing the average time it took elevator doors to open on a certain city block and figuring how long it took people to answer their doorbells were critical parts of the quality equation. So was pushing drivers to meet exacting schedules. The problem was that UPS's marketing research was asking the wrong questions. Its survey asked customers if they were pleased with delivery time and whether they thought delivery could be even faster.

When UPS recently began asking broader questions about how it could improve service, it discovered that clients weren't as obsessed with on-time delivery as previously thought. The biggest surprise to UPS management: customers wanted more interaction with drivers—the only face-to-face contact any of them had with the company. If drivers were less harried and more willing to chat, customers could get some practical advice on shipping.

"We've discovered that the highest-rated element we have is our drivers," says Lawrence E. Farrel, UPS's service-quality manager.[5]

In a sharp departure, the company is encouraging its 62,000 delivery drivers to get out of their trucks and visit customers along with salespeople. It also allows drivers an additional 30 minutes a week to spend at their discretion to strengthen ties with customers and perhaps bring in new sales.

The Paramount Importance of Keeping Existing Customers An inextricable link exists between customer satisfaction and customer loyalty. Long-term relationships simply don't just happen but are grounded in the delivery of service and value by the firm. Customer retention pays big dividends for organizations. Powered by repeat sales and referrals, revenues and market share grow. Costs fall because firms spend less funds and energy attempting to replace defectors. Steady customers are easy to serve because they understand the modus operandi and make fewer demands on employees' time. Increased customer retention also drives job satisfaction and pride, which leads to higher employee retention. In turn, the knowledge employees acquire as they stay longer increases productivity. A Bain & Company study estimates that a decrease in the customer defection rate by 5 percent can boost profits by 25 percent to 95 percent.[6]

The ability to retain customers is based upon an intimate understanding of their needs. This knowledge comes primarily from marketing research. For example, British Airways recast its first-class transatlantic service based upon detailed marketing research. Most airlines stress top-of-the-line service in their transatlantic first-class cabins. British Air research found that most first-class passengers simply wanted to sleep. British Air now gives premium flyers the option of dinner on the ground, before takeoff, in the first-class lounge. Once on board,

Marketing research data told British Air that most transatlantic first-class passengers simply wanted to sleep. As a result, British Air began stressing excellent service before take off and after landing. SOURCE: Courtesy of Saatchi & Saatchi Advertising.

they can slip into British Air pajamas, put their heads on real pillows, slip under blankets, and then enjoy an interruption-free flight. On arrival, first-class passengers can have breakfast, use comfortable dressing rooms and showers, and even have their clothes pressed before they set off for business. These changes in British Air's first-class service were driven strictly by marketing research.[7]

Managers Must Understand the Ever-Changing Marketplace

Marketing research also helps managers understand what is going on in the marketplace. Historically, marketing research has been practiced for as long as marketing has existed. The early Phoenicians carried out market demand studies as they traded in the various ports of the Mediterranean Sea. Marco Polo's diary indicates he was performing a marketing research function as he traveled to China. There is even evidence that the Spanish systematically conducted "market surveys" as they explored the New World, and there are examples of marketing research conducted during the Renaissance. Today, a marketing manager might, for example, consider offering coupons with the introduction of a new frozen pastry. The coupon will be used along with network television advertising to induce trial of the new pastry. The question arises as to who should receive the coupons. The sales promotion expenditure will be more effective if coupons are mailed to those households most likely to redeem them. Previous experience with frozen pastry coupon redemptions suggests that heavy coupon users in general are most likely to redeem the new pastry coupons. The next logical question fot the marketing manager to ask would be, "Are there any identifiable demographic characteristics of heavy coupon users versus light users?" Market research revealed that the only statistically significant difference is that the female head of household is not employed full time (see Table 1.1). The marketing manager would then specify this characteristic when purchasing the mailing list for the new frozen pastry coupons.

The vice-president of marketing research for NBC explains how the company uses marketing research in "A Professional Researcher's Perspective" in this section of the chapter.

proactive management

Management philosophy that involves continuously altering the marketing mix to fit emerging patterns in economic, social, and competitive environments.

The Proactive Role of Marketing Research

Understanding the nature of the marketing system is a necessity for a successful marketing orientation. By having a thorough knowledge of factors that have an impact on the target market and the marketing mix, management can be proactive rather than reactive. A **proactive management** alters the marketing mix to fit newly emerging patterns in economic, social, and competitive environments

TABLE 1.1 Demographics of Heavy Coupon Users

	HEAVY (TOP 20%)	MEDIUM–LIGHT	NONUSER
Average Household Size	3.6	3.2	3.4
Average Age Female Head	43.1	45.2	41.9
Household Income ($000)	$30.9	$29.1	$28.7
Female Head Attended College	51%	50%	52%
Average Monthly Grocery Bill	$334	$292	$303
Female Head Does not Work Outside or Works Part Time	65%	61%	55%

A Professional Researcher's Perspective

NBC's research staff numbers about forty-five employees. Most of them are in New York City, but some—program researchers—are in California (Burbank), where most entertainment programs are produced and where programming decisions are made. The following areas within the Research Department are listed according to size.

1. Audience Research
2. Program Research
3. News Research
4. Affiliate Research/Owned Stations Research
5. Marketing and Sales Research
6. Social and Development Research
7. New Media Research

The activities of the seven areas are coordinated by the vice-president of marketing research, who reports to the head of the TV network.

AUDIENCE RESEARCH

The largest section within the Research Department is Audience Research, which seeks to answer the question, "How many people are watching?" As noted, it is crucial to document the size and also the nature of the audience because profits depend largely on audience size and composition. Audience measurement data are called *ratings.* In contrast to the use of the word in everyday English as well as in psychological research, television "ratings" are not evaluative measures; they are audience counts.

PROGRAM RESEARCH

Program Research provides information on entertainment programs. The research is designed to help programmers develop series and made-for-TV movies with audience appeal, to schedule them during the most advantageous time slots, and to provide guidance for the promotion of programs. Successful research contributes to profits, both by making programs attractive to larger audiences (thereby producing higher advertising revenue) and by reducing the cost of developing and scheduling programs that would otherwise turn out to be failures. To achieve these objectives, Program Research conducts the following kinds of studies.

Concept tests explore reactions of the potential audience to the program at the idea stage. This research helps sift through the hundreds of ideas submited to the network each season and prevents ideas with little audience appeal from being developed into "pilots." Phone surveys and focus groups are used.

"Pilot tests" provide research on a filmed prototype of a series. They are conducted before a series is scheduled. Obviously, a good test enhances a program's chances of being scheduled. Such research once was conducted in a movie theater with an invited audience who were asked to indicate with a hand-held dial how they liked or disliked the viewed material. NBC now prefers a test that more closely simulates home viewing conditions and is therefore more reliable. Selected

continues

cable subscribers are asked to watch a "special preview" in their homes and then answer questions about the program.

Series research is conducted after a series has been scheduled to identify its most successful elements and most appealing stories. This information is used to help the producers and programmers improve the program. Research is conducted among viewers by phone.

Scheduling research, usually called *competitives,* asks potential viewers whether they would watch a show if it were scheduled at the same time as a number of other shows. The purpose is to explore the strength of the show's appeal and to gather information on possible schedule changes. Such research has been found valuable in assessing how schedule changes (by NBC or by a competitor) will affect the ratings of a series.

Promotion research uses surveys and focus groups to explore which aspects of a program, especially a made-for-TV movie, are most appealing to the audience. The findings are used to help design the promotion for that program in print (such as in *TV Guide* and other TV magazines) and on the air.

NEWS RESEARCH

News Research is a separate department from Program Research, reflecting the fact that news and entertainment are very different kinds of programs and that the two areas report to different divisions within the organization. The News Division is distinct from the Entertainment Division, and the journalists who work on the news and informational programs are extremely protective of their editorial independence. However, News Research is useful in assessing people's interest in and understanding of different kinds of news presentations. It explores the appeal of news anchors and reporters and is an aid to promotion. It also helps with the development of new informational programs.

AFFILIATE RESEARCH/OWNED STATIONS RESEARCH

These research areas use ratings data almost exclusively but, in contrast to Audience Research, concentrate on local (i.e., station) ratings data. They help the individual stations improve their performance in both entertainment and news programming. To the extent that affiliates and owned stations are interested in other kinds of research, these departments also occasionally report on studies prepared by other research areas.

MARKETING AND SALES RESEARCH

With competition for advertising dollars increasing, the role of marketing has expanded and the tasks of sales have become more complex. The research function serving those departments has been strengthened to support their activities. Marketing and Sales Research is generally expected to continue to gain in importance. Marketing and Sales Research uses program ratings data frequently but also conducts primary research studies. An example follows.

Viewing by College Students. Many advertisers want to reach a young audience, especially one that is likely to be relatively affluent and whose members may function as trendsetters for certain products. College students certainly fit that description. Unfortunately, many of them do not live in homes that can be measured by ratings services, but rather in student housing. There were strong indications that some NBC programs had large followings on campus—but NBC was not getting credit (meaning advertiser payment) for that audience. Marketing and Sales Research designed a study to provide audience data on students that would be good enough to convince advertisers. (Despite the shortcomings of ratings, advertisers use them to determine what they will pay for commercials and usually are skeptical of viewing information that is not based on them.)

NBC commissioned an extensive study using complex sampling procedures and designs, which confirmed the initial impression: there was a sizable unmeasured audience and the widespread assumption that students do not watch television was inaccurate. Though students view less during the hours when most people watch (during the early evening), they view more at other times (during the day and especially late at night, after 11:00 P.M.).

SOCIAL AND DEVELOPMENT RESEARCH

This department monitors research on television's effect and to support NBC's self-regulatory activities. The department's responsibilities were expanded to include monitoring research on demographic, lifestyle, and attitudinal trends that help identify opportunities to attract more audience and increase sales. Examples include studies on working women, children as consumers, and zapping of commercials.

NEW MEDIA RESEARCH

This is the newest area in NBC's Research Department. Its main task is to analyze ratings for the various cable channels, but it also compiles other information on the so-called new media—that is, information about trends in basic and pay cable installation and subscription, pay-per-view, VCR usage, satellite TV, and alternate distribution systems.[8] ■

whereas a reactive management waits for change to have a major impact on the firm before deciding to take action. It is the difference between viewing the turbulent marketing environment as a threat (a reactive stance) or an opportunity (a proactive stance). Procter & Gamble Company, for example, was reactive in the 1980s in the disposable diaper market when it attempted to defend itself against environmentalist claims of nonbiodegradability. A proactive stance would have been to create a biodegradable diaper. Marketing research plays a key role in proactive management by anticipating changes in the market and consumer desires and then designing goods and services to meet those needs.

The proactive manager continually seeks new opportunities in the ever-changing marketplace. For example, even in today's slow-growth economy, some new consumers enter while others leave. The characteristics of new consumers vary widely by product category, but two groups are particularly important for a wide range of products: young people and immigrants (see Figure 1.1). Both groups are forming their preferences for numerous products and services and both will support the marketplace for decades after they make their initial choices.

In 1990, 24 million Americans were between the ages of 13 and 19. By 2040, this population will grow to nearly 34 million, according to Census Bureau projections. Eight percent of the U.S. population is foreign-born, and 24 percent of the foreign-born have entered the United States since 1985. The Census Bureau estimates that immigration will account for more than one-third of U.S. population growth over the next 50 years. This huge number of new consumers will need to become acquainted with brands, retail outlets, and service providers. The best way for a proactive company to get its share of these "new consumers" is to understand their needs and wants. This means marketing research.

marketing strategy
Guiding the long-run use of the firm's resources based on its existing and projected capabilities and on projected changes in the external environment.

A proactive manager not only examines emerging markets but also seeks, through strategic planning, to develop a long-run **marketing strategy** for the firm. A strategic plan guides the long-run use of the firm's resources based on the firm's existing and projected internal capabilities and on projected changes in the external environment. A good strategic plan is based upon good marketing research. It helps the firm meet long-run profit and market share goals. Poor strategic planning can threaten the survival of the firm. Montgomery Ward, floundering for almost a decade because of inadequate planning and lack of understanding of the marketplace, had to give up its once-dominant catalog sales division.

Applied Research versus Basic Research

Virtually all marketing research is conducted to better understand the marketplace, to find out why a strategy failed, or to reduce uncertainty in management

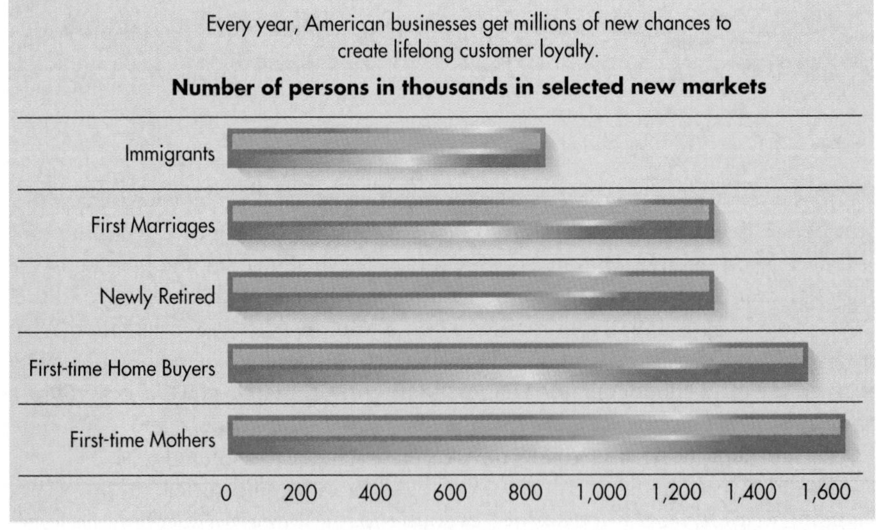

FIGURE 1.1
Emergent Markets
SOURCE: David W. Stewart, "Advertising In a Slow Growth Economy," *American Demographics* (September 1994), p. 42.

decision making. All research conducted for these purposes is called **applied research.** For example, should the price of frozen dinners be raised 40 cents? What name should Ford select for a new sedan? Which commercial has the highest level of recall: A or B? On the other hand, **basic,** or pure, **research** attempts to expand the frontiers of knowledge; it is research not aimed at a specific pragmatic problem. Basic research hopes to provide further confirmation to an existing theory or to learn more about a concept or phenomenon. For example, basic research might test a hypothesis on high-involvement decision making or consumer information processing. In the long run, basic research helps us understand more about the world in which we live. The findings of basic research usually cannot be implemented by managers in the short run. Most basic research is now conducted in universities. In contrast, most research undertaken by businesses is applied research because it must be cost-effective and of demonstrable value to the decision maker.

applied research

Research aimed at solving a specific, pragmatic problem—better understanding of the marketplace, determination of why a strategy or tactic failed, reduction of uncertainty in management decision making.

basic research

Research aimed at expanding the frontiers of knowledge rather than solving a specific, pragmatic problem.

Deciding Whether to Conduct Market Research

A manager who is faced with several alternative solutions to a particular problem should not instinctively call for applied marketing research. In fact, the first decision to be made is whether to conduct marketing research at all. In a number of situations, it is best not to conduct marketing research.

A Lack of Resources There are two situations when a lack of resources should preclude marketing research from being undertaken. First, an organization may lack the funds to do the research properly. If a project calls for a sample of 800 respondents but the budget allows for only 50 interviews, the quality of the information would be highly suspect. Second, funds may be available to do the research properly but insufficient to implement any decisions resulting from the research. Sometimes small organizations in particular lack the necessary resources to create an effective marketing mix. In one case, for example, the director of a performing arts guild was in complete agreement with the recommendations that resulted from a market research project. However, two years after the project was completed, nothing had been done because the money was not available.

Research Results Would Not Be Useful Some types of marketing research studies measure lifestyle and personality factors of customers and potential customers. Assume that a study finds introverted men with a poor self-concept yet a high need for achievement are most likely to patronize a discount brokerage service. Management of Charles Schwab discount brokerage might be hard-pressed to use this information.

Poor Timing in the Marketplace Marketing research should not be undertaken if the opportunity for successful entry into a market has already passed. If a product is in the late maturity or decline stage of the product life cycle, such as record turntables or console black and white television, it would be foolish to do research for new product entry. The same is true for markets rapidly approaching saturation, such as super premium ice cream; that is, Häagen-Dazs,

Ben and Jerrys, Schraffts, and Blue Bell. For products already in the market, however, research is needed to modify the products as tastes, competition, and other factors change.

The Decision Already Has Been Made In the real world of management decision making and company politics, marketing research has sometimes been used improperly. Several years ago a large marketing research study was conducted for a bank with over $300 million in deposits. The purpose of the research project was to guide top management in mapping a strategic direction for the bank during the next five years. After presenting the report to the president, he said, "I fully agree with your recommendations because that was what I was going to do anyway! I'm going to use your study tomorrow when I present my strategic plan to the board of directors." The question was then asked by the researcher, "What if my recommendations had been counter to your decision?" The bank president laughed and said, "They would have never known that I had conducted a marketing research study!" Not only was the project a waste of money, but it certainly raised a number of ethical questions in the researcher's mind.

When Managers Cannot Agree on What They Need to Know to Make a Decision Although it may seem obvious that research should not be undertaken until objectives are specified, it sometimes happens. Although preliminary or exploratory studies are commonly done to better understand the nature of the problem, a large, major research project should not be. It is faulty logic to say "Well, let's just go ahead and do the study and then we will better understand the problem and know what steps to take." The wrong phenomena might be studied or key elements needed for management decision making may not be included.

When Decision-Making Information Already Exists Some companies have been conducting research in certain markets for many years. They understand the characteristics of the target customers and what they like and dislike about existing products. Under these circumstances, further research would be redundant and a waste of money. Procter & Gamble, for example, has extensive knowledge of the coffee market. After it conducted initial taste tests, P&G went into national distribution with Folger's Instant Coffee without further research. The Sara Lee Corporation did the same thing with its frozen croissants, as did Quaker Oats with Chewy Granola Bars. This tactic, however, does not always work. P&G thought it understood the pain reliever market thoroughly, so it bypassed market research for Encaprin encapsulated aspirin. The product failed because it lacked a distinct competitive advantage over existing products and was withdrawn from the market.

When The Costs Of Conducting Research Outweigh the Benefits There are rarely situations in which a manager has such tremendous confidence in her judgment that additional information relative to a pending decision would not be accepted if it were available and free. The manager might have sufficient confidence to be unwilling to pay very much for it or wait long to receive it. Willingness to acquire additional decision-making information depends upon a manager's perception of its quality, price, and timing. The manager would be willing

TABLE 1.2 The Decision Whether to Conduct Market Research

MARKET SIZE	SMALL PROFIT MARGIN	LARGE PROFIT MARGIN
Small	Cost likely to be greater than benefit; e.g., eyeglasses replacement screw, tire valve extension	Possible benefits greater than cost, e.g., ultraexpensive Lambeggehni-type sportswear, larger specialized industrial equipment; e.g., Joy Manufacturing, computer-aided metal stamping machines
Large	Benefits likely to be greater than costs; e.g., Stouffers frozen entrees, Crest's tartar control toothpastes	Benefits most likely to be greater than costs; e.g., medical equipment like CAT scanners, Toshiba's high-definition television

NOTE: The decision on whether to conduct marketing research depends on whether the perceived cost is greater than the benefit. Two important determinants of potential benefit are profit margins and market size.

to pay more for perfect information, that is, data that left no doubt on which alternative to follow, than for information that left uncertainty as to what to do. In summary, research should be undertaken only when the expected value of the information is greater than the cost of obtaining the data.[9]

Generally speaking, potential new products with large profit margins are going to have greater potential benefit than products with smaller profit margins, assuming that both items have the same sales potential. Also, new product opportunities in large markets are going to offer greater potential benefits than those in smaller markets if competitive intensity is the same in both markets (see Table 1.2).

The History and Future of Marketing Research

The many benefits that accrue to management from using marketing research served as the initial impetus to begin conducting marketing research in the United States. One might imagine, because of the competitive advantage a company can gain from engaging in market research, that it has been used by businesses for centuries. Such is not the case. The industry did not move out of its embryonic years until 1900.

The Development of Market Research

The Inception—Pre-1900 The first recorded marketing research survey was taken in July 1824 by the *Harrisburg Pennsylvanian*. It was an election poll in which Andrew Jackson received 335 votes; John Quincy Adams, 169; Henry Clay, 29; and William H. Crawford, 9. Later the same year, another newspaper, the *Raleigh Star*, undertook to canvass political meetings held in North Carolina, "at which the sense of the people was taken." Perhaps the first research practitioner was John Jacob Astor when, in the 1790s, he employed an artist to sketch the hats worn by fashionable New York women so that he could keep abreast of fashion trends.

The first documented use of research to make informed marketing decisions was carried out by the advertising agency N. W. Ayer in 1879. That first systematic effort was a simple survey of state and local officials to determine expected

The first marketing researcher in America was John Jacob Astor, who hired an artist to sketch the hats worn by fashionable women. Mr. Astor wanted to keep up with the latest fashions.
SOURCE: The Bettmann Archive.

levels of grain production. The purpose of the research was to develop the scheduling of advertising for a producer of farm equipment. The second documented instance of marketing research appears to have been at E. I. du Pont de Nemours & Company around the turn of the century. It involved the systematic compilation of salespersons' reports on a variety of customer characteristics. The response to this second research effort was a harbinger of things to come. The salespersons who were responsible for obtaining and reporting the data were outraged because they didn't like the extra paperwork.

Academic researchers entered into marketing research about 1895, when Harlow Gale, a professor of psychology at the University of Minnesota, introduced the use of mail surveys to study advertising. He mailed 200 questionnaires and received 20 completed questionnaires, a 10 percent response rate. Gale's work was quickly followed by the pioneering work of Walter Dill Scott at Northwestern University. Scott introduced the use of experimentation and psychological measurement to the fledgling practice of advertising.

Early Growth—1900–1920 It was not until after the turn of the century that consumer demand surged and the growth of mass production meant larger and more distant markets. No longer was America characterized by cottage-shop industries with the craftsman-seller in daily contact with the marketplace. The need arose to understand consumers' buying habits and attitudes toward the manufacturers' wares. In response to this need, the first formal research department was established by the Curtis Publishing Company in 1911. The research focused primarily on the automobile industry as manufacturers had decided that everyone who had the money and inclination to buy a car had done so. The manufacturers were seeking a new group of consumers to which to target their promotions. A few years later, Daniel Starch pioneered recognition measures of advertising response, and E. K. Strong introduced recall measures and scaling to marketing.

The Adolescent Years—1920–1950 Percival White developed the first application of scientific research to commercial problems. White's words express his realization of the need for systematic and continual marketing research:

> Perhaps the greatest advantage of the company's having its own market analysis department is that the work then becomes a continuous process, or at least a process

> which is carried forward at periodic intervals, so that altered conditions in the market and in the industry at large are always kept in view. The necessity for regarding markets as constantly changing and not as fixed phenomena should not be lost sight of.[11]

White's book bore scant resemblance to this text. For example, the book avoided the use of statistics and mathematics except for a brief mention of the U.S. Census.

The 1930s saw widespread use of survey research. A. C. Nielsen entered the research business in 1922. He amplified on White's earlier work with the development of the "share of market" concept plus many other services that became the foundation for one of America's largest marketing research organizations. It was not until the late 1930s that formal courses in marketing research became common on college campuses; a substantial body of knowledge developed within both the practice and academic communities. Two events, the spread of broadcast media and World War II, helped the fledgling discipline coalesce into a well-defined profession. Social scientists found that broadcast media created interesting new phenomena and increased the variability of human behavior.

By the end of the 1930s, simple examinations of respondents' replies were becoming categorized and compared across groups classified by differences in income, gender, or family status. Simple correlation analysis came into use but was not widespread; those who would use it had to be able to go directly to the statistical sources for such techniques using texts by some of the pioneers in the field at this time, including G. Udney Yule, Mordecai Ezekiel, and Horace Sechrist, among others.

The requirements of the world war pressed social scientists into service on a number of fronts. Tools and methods that had been novelties before the war were adopted and adapted to study the consumer behavior of soldiers and of their families on the home front. Among those tools were experimental design, opinion polling, human factors research, and operations research techniques. In the 1940s, focus groups developed under the leadership of Robert Merton. During the late 1940s, the importance of random selection in sampling became widely recognized and major advances were made in sampling techniques and polling procedures. A small number of psychologists who had been assigned to work in the Army Quartermaster Corps found their way into industry, where they introduced techniques for consumer tests of products.[12]

The Maturing of Market Research—1950–Present The change from a seller's market to a buyer's market (resulting from World War II pent-up demand) necessitated better marketing intelligence. No longer could producers sell all of anything they produced. The rising costs of production "tooling up," advertising, inventories, and other factors made the price of failure much higher than it had been in the past. Now, marketing research first determines what the market wants and then goods are crafted to meet those needs.

The mid-1950s brought forth market segmentation, based largely on easily identifiable demographic characteristics of customers. The same period gave rise to motivation research with its emphasis on why consumers behave as they do. The underlying concepts of segmentation and motivation analysis, combined with the power of survey techniques, led to such innovations as psychographics and benefit segmentation. In the 1960s, mathematical models were developed for description and prediction—stochastic models, Markovian models, linear learning models. Even more significant was the rapid development of the computer during the early 1960s. These machines greatly enhanced the researcher's ability to quickly analyze, store, and retrieve large amounts of data.

Marketing Research Today and in the Future

Precisely where research will go in the future is difficult to foretell, but it is safe to predict that marketing research will greatly expand both quantitatively and qualitatively. More studies will be conducted and costs will definitely rise. At the same time, increasingly more sophisticated approaches will be adopted and refined. (Some of these trends will be highlighted in subsequent chapters as the topics come up.) There will be a greater emphasis on scanner-based research, database marketing, and customer satisfaction research, to name a few. Of greatest significance, however, is the fact that marketing research activities will grow in scope and extend into other arenas such as nonprofit organizations and government services. Also, fewer companies will be without formal market research departments.

A Preview of the Text

Now that you understand the role of marketing research in the management decision-making process, situations when research should be undertaken, and how the field has evolved, you are prepared to venture ahead in the book. You will find that every chapter is written from the perspective of a research user (a manager) rather than a technical market researcher. This approach is deliberate because most readers will never be researchers, but many will need to apply the results of marketing research in decision making. For those interested in pursuing a career in marketing research, an appendix to this chapter provides a description of various types of jobs available in the field. Chapter 2 explains the steps involved in conducting marketing research. Next, Chapter 3 describes the marketing research industry and the corporate marketing research department. Part One concludes with Chapter 4, Ethics in Marketing Research.

Part Two of the book focuses on developing a marketing research design. It begins in Chapter 5 with a description of the sources and uses of secondary data, computerized databases, and decision support systems. Chapter 6 explains the differences between quantitative and qualitative research and elaborates on various qualitative techniques. Chapter 7 describes the nature of survey research, which is the most popular means of gathering primary data. Chapter 8 examines collecting data through observation techniques. Part Two concludes with an explanation of simulation and experimentation in marketing research (Chapter 9).

Part Three describes primary data acquisition tactics. Measurement concepts are set forth in Chapter 10. Chapter 11 describes attitude scaling techniques and the nature of attitudes. Data collection forms and questionnaire design are demonstrated in Chapter 12. Chapters 13 and 14 detail basic sampling concepts and sample size determination.

Part Four of the text demonstrates various techniques for data analysis. Chapter 15 focuses on data processing and basic statistical analysis. Chapter 16 discusses statistical testing of differences; and Chapter 17 discusses measures of association. Chapter 18 concludes Part Four with multivariate analysis methodologies.

The fifth part of the text is devoted to other topics in marketing research. Communicating the results of marketing research is summarized in Chapter 19. Chapter 20 provides an overview of specific types of marketing research such as product, quality, and advertising research.

The text also offers two concluding appendices. Appendix One consists of five comprehensive cases with databases. The second appendix is a series of statistical tables.

Summary

Marketing is a process of planning and executing the conception, pricing, promotion, and distribution of ideas, goods, and services to create exchanges that satisfy individual and organizational objectives. Marketing managers attempt to get the right goods or services to the right people at the right place at the right time at the right price, using the right promotion technique. This may be accomplished by following the marketing concept. The marketing concept is based on consumer orientation, goal orientation, and systems orientation.

The marketing manager must work within an internal environment of the organization and understand the external environment over which he has little, if any, control. The primary variables over which the marketing manager has control are place, price, promotion, and product decisions. The unique combination of these four variables is called the *marketing mix.*

Marketing research plays a key part in providing the information for managers to shape the marketing mix. Marketing research has grown in importance because of management's focus on customer satisfaction and retention. It is also a key tool in proactive management. Marketing research should be undertaken only when the perceived benefits are greater than the costs.

Marketing research in the United States traces its roots back to 1824, when the first public poll was taken. The early growth period was from 1900 until 1920, characterized by the establishment of the first formal market research department. Next came the adolescent years, from 1920 until 1950. This era saw the widespread use of survey research. The maturing of marketing research began in 1950 and continues to the present. Today we are experiencing growth in the number and sophistication of both quantitative and qualitative marketing research techniques. This is further aided by the increasing sophistication of communication, scanner, and computer technology.

Key Terms

marketing
marketing concept
consumer orientation
goal orientation
systems orientation
marketing mix
marketing research
descriptive function
diagnostic function
predictive function
return on quality
proactive management
marketing strategy
applied research
basic research

Review and Discussion Questions

1. The role of marketing is to create exchanges. What role might marketing research play in the facilitation of the exchange process?
2. Marketing research has traditionally been associated with manufacturers of consumer goods. Today, we are experiencing an increasing number of organizations, both profit making and nonprofit, using marketing research. Why do you think this trend exists? Give some examples.
3. Explain the relationship between marketing research and the marketing concept.
4. Name two consumer goods, two services, and two nonprofit concepts that might have logically been developed with marketing research.
5. Comment on the following statement: "I own a restaurant in the downtown area. I see customers every day whom I know on a first-name basis. I understand their likes and dislikes. If I put something on the menu and it doesn't sell, I know that they didn't like it. I also read the magazine *Modern Restaurants,* so I know what the trends are in the industry. This is all of the marketing research I need to do."
6. Why is marketing research important to marketing executives? Give several reasons.
7. How do you think marketing research might differ between (a) a retailer, (b) a consumer goods manufacturer, (c) an industrial goods manufacturer, and (d) a charitable organization?
8. Ralph Moran is planning to invest $1.5 million in a new restaurant in Saint Louis. When Ralph applied for a construction financing loan, the bank officer asked whether he had conducted any research. Ralph replied, "I checked on research and a marketing research company wanted $20,000 to do the work. I decided that with all the other expenses of opening a new business, research was a luxury that I could do without." Comment.
9. What is meant by "return on quality"? Why do you think that the concept evolved? Give an example.
10. Give a personal example in which a company either retained your business or lost you as a customer because of service delivery.
11. Describe three situations in which marketing research should not be undertaken. Explain why this is true.
12. Give an example of (a) the descriptive role of marketing research, (b) the diagnostic role, and (c) the predictive function of marketing research.

CASE 1.1

Creating New Products at Toyota, Hitachi, and Panasonic

Many Japanese companies take a different tack from American firms when designing new products. Toyota USA employs a small team of anthropologists to study the cultural setting within which Americans choose to live. Using the California market as a leading indicator of lifestyle trends, the anthropologists observe people in their homes since that is where customers most obviously express their preferences for living conditions. They observe how loud the TV volume is set; whether multiple media are turned on simultaneously; the kind, brightness, colors, patterns, and degrees of lighting; spareness or clutter; how food and dishes are arranged in cabinets; and how individuals interact with one another.

What does this have to do with designing an automobile that will be released in five years? Toyota wants to anticipate the interior environment and exterior appearance that are most likely to delight the customer. It seeks a certain "touch" and "feel" that will be familiar and exciting to the customer. Only asking questions of the customer at the earliest stages of design is unlikely to yield useful information for a car that will not be released for several years.

Hitachi uses the same type of indirect analysis in identifying new product characteristics for its household appliances that will appeal to its Japanese customers. Hitachi's product designers observed that more Japanese women were joining the work force, and, thus, laundry would have to be done early in the morning or late in the evening. Hitachi subsequently designed a very quiet washing machine to introduce into a marketplace where noise was previously not a design consideration. A second observation that was key in the development of this quieter product was that clothes were not as soiled before washing as they once were. Many Japanese had changed from washing clothes when the clothes were dirty to when they had been worn only once to obtain a freshly washed feeling. Hitachi was successful in gaining significant market share with this product introduction before competing firms were able to redesign their product. Recognizing the change in lifestyle of working women that would make dryers more popular than hanging laundry to air dry and recognizing the limited living space of most customers, Hitachi developed a washer and dryer that used the same "container" to hold the clothes.

Matsushita, manufacturer of electronic devices sold under the Panasonic label in the United States, refined the function of its automatic bread-making machine by observing the "best" bread maker in Tokyo. Designers who were dissatisfied with the characteristics of the bread that the prototype machines produced made detailed observations of the techniques used by the baker of a well-known restaurant. The mechanisms for mixing ingredients and kneading dough and the baking temperature were each modified. The new product produced bread that met customer requirements more closely than did the prototype—and "delighted" customers by providing the ability to make high-quality fresh bread at home.

1. Are these Japanese firms conducting marketing research?
2. Do you think that other types of consumer information would be necessary before designing the car? washing machine? bread-making machine? If so, what is needed?
3. Once the products are on the market, is there a need for any other marketing research? Why? If so, what would be required?

CASE 1.2

The New American Man

Here's a portrait of the American man, circa 1996. He is romantic and self-centered, family oriented and individualistic, hardworking and leisure loving. In other words, he is a mass of contradictions. Men act as consumers in two ways—as individuals and as members of a household. These two levels of purchase behavior can become intertwined. For example, only 46 percent of men buy all their own personal items, according to a survey conducted by Maritz Marketing Research. Thirty-five percent of men buy half or most of their own things, and 18 percent buy just some or none. In contrast, 82 percent of women control all their personal purchases, and 10 percent buy most of their own goods.

Men shop almost as frequently as women, but their habits are different. They are slightly more likely than women to shop every day (11 percent do, versus 7 percent of women), and they are also more likely than women to shop less than once a week (28 percent versus 23 percent). The majority of both sexes go shopping at least once a week but not every day.

Men's living arrangements largely determine their consumer behavior. For example, men who live alone provide for all their daily needs. But single men do not act like women who live alone. Single men spend 61 percent of their food budgets away from home, compared with 41 percent for single women. Men have mixed feelings about all the changes going on in their lives. Some welcome the challenges and appreciate the choices, whereas others fight them. A *GQ* study divides men into different attitudinal groups based on their attitudes toward change. Men who like choices are called *Change Adapters*. They are younger, better educated, and more affluent than *Change Opposers*. These two groups shop for different items, and they shop in different ways. *Opposers* have less money than *Adapters*, so they are cautious spenders. They are more likely to shop at discount stores and to look for sales and imitation products. They are not greatly influenced by advertising.

The Roper Organization has dubbed today's young men as "new romantics," based on research it has done for *Playboy* magazine. Nearly 70 percent of men aged 18 to 29 consider themselves "romantic," although the definition of that term varies from person to person. Men and women in their 20s are most likely to agree on the timing of their most recent romantic interlude, according to Roper. This may point the way to increased harmony between the sexes, along with growing markets for clothing, jewelry, and other romantic items.[13]

1. Why would magazines like *Playboy* and *GQ* commission marketing research studies?
2. How might a large retail department store chain use the preceding information? a grocery chain?
3. Is the preceding research basic or applied? Why?

APPENDIX A

A Career in Marketing Research

Marketing research offers a variety of career paths depending upon one's education level, interests, and personality. Most jobs are to be found with either research suppliers (firms that conduct research for clients) or research users (corporations that depend on market research for decision-making guidance). A limited number of market research positions are also available with advertising agencies and various branches of government.

Positions with research suppliers tend to be concentrated in a few large cities; for example, New York, Chicago, Los Angeles, San Francisco, and Dallas. Although research suppliers are found throughout the country, a majority of the larger firms (and entry-level jobs) are found in these cities. Research users, on the other hand, tend to be more widely scattered and found in communities of various size; for example, General Mills in Minneapolis; Tyson Foods in Springdale, Arkansas.

Women have long been accepted as equals in the marketing research industry. Senior-level positions are increasingly filled by female executives. At the college entry-level position of junior analyst, women are twice as prevalent as men. Obviously, young women increasingly are recognizing the opportunities that await them in the exciting field of marketing research.

There was a time when a decision to go into marketing research represented a lifetime career commitment. Once you were a marketing researcher, there was a good chance you would always be a marketing researcher. Today this inflexibility is not so prevalent. Now it is more common to see people transfer into and out of the marketing research department as part of a career in marketing.

Table A.1 presents a comparative summary of career positions within the research industry. Not all companies have all positions, but you will find people with these titles across the industry. The table also lists the minimum experience and education typical for each position.

Positions within Supplier Organizations

Research suppliers offer a majority of the entry-level career positions in the market research field. Many of the newer firms are entrepreneurial in nature and are headed by a founder or partners. In smaller companies, the founder-owner not

TABLE A.1 Career Opportunities in Marketing Research: General Duties and Qualifications

POSITION	LEVEL OF RESPONSIBILITY	MINIMUM EXPERIENCE	MINIMUM EDUCATION
Director	Department Administration	10+ years	Graduate Degree
Assistant Director	Projects Administration	5+ years	Graduate Degree
Senior Analyst	Project Supervision	3–5 years	College Degree (may require Graduate Degree)
Analyst	Project Analysis and Expediting	2–4 years	College Degree (may require Graduate Degree)
Statistician	Statistical Analysis	0 years	College Degree (may require Graduate Degree)
Clerical Supervisor	Office Management	3–5 years	Vocational Degree
Junior Analyst	Project Assistance	0 years	College Degree
Field Director	Data Collection Supervisor	3–5+ years	High School
Librarian	Library Management	0 years	College Degree
Interviewer	Questionnaire Administration	0 years	Some High School
Tabulator and Clerk	Simple Tabulation, Filing, and Organizing	0 years	Some High School

only manages the company but typically is involved in selling and conducting research projects. Owners of larger supplier organizations perform basically the same functions as top managers in other large corporations, such as creating strategic plans and developing broad corporate policies. It is also common in large supplier organizations to have managers that specialize in either a specific industry or type of research; for example, manager of health care research, financial research, or political polling. Firms also may have a director of qualitative research or a director of multivariate studies. Nonmanagerial jobs found in supplier firms follow.

Statistician—Data Processing Specialist A person holding this position is viewed as internal expert on statistical techniques, sampling methods, and market research software programs such as SPSS, SAS, or UNCLE. Normally, a master's degree or even a Ph.D. is required and an undergraduate's degree is a minimum.

Senior Analyst A senior analyst is usually found in larger firms. The individual typically works with an account executive to plan a research project and then supervises several analysts who execute the projects. Senior analysts work with a minimal level of supervision themselves. They often work with analysts in developing questionnaires and may help in analyzing difficult data sets. The final report is usually written by an analyst but reviewed, with comments, by the senior analyst. This position is usually given budgetary control over projects and responsibility for meeting time schedules.

Analyst The analyst usually handles the bulk of the work required for executing research projects. An analyst normally reports to a senior analyst. She assists in questionnarie preparation and pretests, then does data analysis, and writes the preliminary report. Much of the secondary data work is performed by the analyst.

Junior Analyst This job is typically at the entry-level for a degreed person. A junior analyst works under close supervision on rather mundane tasks; for example, editing and coding questionnaires, performing basic statistical analysis, conducting secondary data searches, and writing rough draft reports on simple projects.

Account Executive An account executive is responsible for making sales to client firms and keeping client organizations satisfied enough to continue funneling work to the research supplier. An account executive works on a day-to-day basis with clients and serves as liaison between the client and the research organization. Account managers must understand each client's problems and know what research techniques should be employed to provide the right data. He must be able to explain to the client what research techniques are needed in a nontechnical manner. Moreover, the account executive must be able to sell the firm's services and abilities over competing suppliers. Account executives work hand in hand with the research analysts to develop the research methodology to solve the client's problems. This position often requires an MBA degree.

Field Work Director Most market research firms do not have their own interviewers. Instead, they rely on market research field services throughout the United States to conduct the actual interviews. Field services are the production line of the market research industry. They hire, train, and supervise interviewers within a specific geographic area. A field work director is responsible for obtaining completed interviews in the proper geographic area, using the specified sampling instructions, within a specified budget, and on time. Field work directors keep in close touch with field services throughout the United States. They know which field services have the best interviewers and can maintain time schedules. After a study has been fielded, the field service director obtains daily reports from the field service. Typical data reported include the number of completed interviews; the number of refusals; interviewing hours, travel time, and mileage; and problems, if any.

Clerical Supervisor Large research suppliers usually have a clerical supervisor. This person is in charge of the centralized handling and processing of statistical data. Duties includes scheduling work, maintaining accuracy, and supervising data entry clerks and other clerical help.

Positions Within Research Departments and Advertising Agencies

Only a handful of manufacturers and retailers have full-blown research departments. These companies, like Kraft General Foods, Sears, and Procter & Gamble, have organization structures similar to research suppliers. Often these departments compete against outside suppliers for the company's research work.

A new product manager at General Mills who finds that an outside supplier is cheaper or offers a superior methodology is usually free to award the contract to the supplier. In addition to the positions just listed, a full-service research department will have a research director and an assistant director.

Research Director The research director (sometimes vice-president of research) is responsible for the entire research program of the company. The director may conduct strategic research for top management or accept work from new product managers, brand managers, or other internal clients. In some cases, the director may initiate proposals for studies but typically responds to requests. She has full responsibility for the market research budget and, where resources are limited, may have to set priorities regarding projects undertaken. The director hires the professional staff and exercises general supervision of the research department. He normally presents the findings of strategic research projects to top management. This position often requires a master's degree and, in some companies, a Ph.D. The director often is viewed as the top technical expert in the department as well.

Theodore Dunn, research director of Benton & Bowles Advertising, one of the world's largest agencies, provides a glimpse of the job of ad agency researchers:

> Their job is to understand current and potential customer needs and to help translate it into advertising strategy. Then, through research, they provide creative information that helps in the creation of selling advertising. The effort is directed more against the development of the agency's product and less against the development of the client's product. In so doing, agency research departments are now better able to concentrate their efforts and then do it with fewer people.
>
> The staffs of agency research departments today are better trained in the social sciences. Their training better enables them to measure and understand consumer needs and reactions. But more important than their training, they are better integrated into the process of developing advertising than was true just five years ago. It's this integration of research into the agency process of developing advertising that makes for greater utility.
>
> At Benton & Bowles, we have a formal system for coordinating the various services in the agency. There are five associate research directors, each of whom is responsible for research on specific brands and assigned to a core group, for each of his or her accounts. The core group is made up of account management and an associate research director. The group is charged by our management with developing agency advertising and marketing strategies for its brand. Its purpose is not only to take advantage of the individual services input but also to profit by the interaction of all people involved.
>
> Because we have this system at B&B, the specific research tools we use are geared to the right problems. In fact, the creative person in the core group very often requests certain kinds of information from research which is needed to develop advertising. When he asks for a study, he is looking for information, and you can bet he'll use it and use it better than when someone just drops a research report on his desk, and that is the first he has ever heard of the project.
>
> What kinds of research does the core group want? They want to know all they can about their consumers. Who are their best customers? How do consumers feel about existing products and brands? What are they like demographically? What are they like psychographically? Socially? Does their product cater better to one demographic or psychographic subgroup? How do consumers use the product? With what frequency do they use it? Who accounts for what volume? What's the best position/promise for the brand?

From this they develop an advertising strategy. Creative people then use research to help guide them in making judgments about the best executions for the strategy. They want to know, for example, which of several initial executions on which they are working has the best chance of breaking through the mass of communications impinging on the consumer and being remembered. They want to know which best communicates what they want to say. Which does it most convincingly? Which best predisposes the consumer to buy? Sometimes they decide to combine elements of several commercials to develop a better one than any of their original alternatives. Sometimes they decide not to pursue another execution direction in favor of their original.[14]

Assistant Research Director This position is normally found only in large full-scale research departments. The person is second in command and reports to the research director. Senior analysts, statisticians, and data processing specialists usually report to the assistant director, who performs many of the same functions as the director.

Research Directors and Others in Limited Function Research Departments

Most research departments in corporations or advertising agencies are limited in their functions. Therefore, they do not conduct the research or analyze the data. Instead, they formulate requests for research proposals, analyze the proposals, award contracts to research suppliers, and evaluate the supplier's work. Internally, they work with brand managers and new product specialists in formulating research problems and interpreting and implementing the recommendations of the research reports provided by the suppliers.

The research director and assistant director (if any) function in a manner similar to their positions described earlier. Analysts formulate and evaluate proposals and the work of research suppliers. They also help implement the recommendations. With the exception of a secretary, there are usually no other personnel in a limited function research department.

A Career in Marketing Research at 3M

To gain an appreciation for a career in marketing research, we'll examine the career path in one company.

The challenges are tough and the opportunities available to marketing researchers at 3M are almost limitless. The biggest challenge is that each researcher has an annual goal of a set percentage of time that must be sold on approved projects. The opportunities presented by a large number of businesses, with thousands of products that need research information, are obvious.

The Corporate Marketing Research Department consists of about 29 people, organized as in Figure A.1. The marketing research project work is carried out by the analysts, senior analysts, supervisors, and the two research managers. (The research manager for Corporate Planning Services works solely for the Corporate Planning and Strategy Committee.) Projects are obtained through requests from marketing personnel in the operating units or from sales calls made by analysts and senior analysts. A sales call may be the result of follow-up from a previous project, introduction of a new research service, information on new or expanded

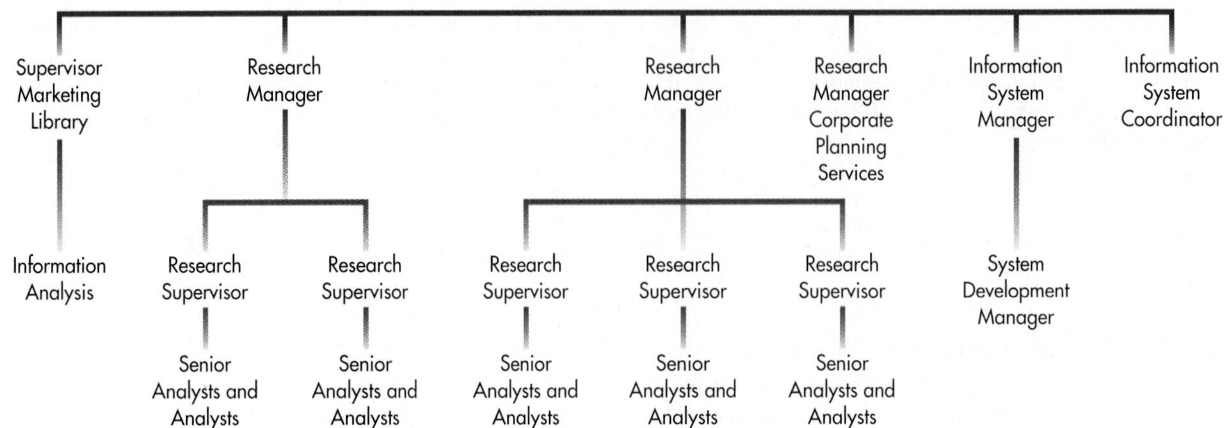

FIGURE A.1

Organization of Corporate Marketing Research Department at 3M

SOURCE: Joseph R. Kendall, "Corporate Marketing Research at 3M," *Marketing Research* (June 1991), pp. 4–6.

activity in the operating unit, or the introduction of a new analyst. All project requests take the form of a proposal that outlines the marketing situation, the information needed, how the information will be obtained, timing, and costs. The signed proposal, with an operating unit designated to be charged for the costs, is the authorization to proceed with the project.

The analysts are recruited from university MBA programs and from among 3M employees in other disciplines (i.e., engineering, laboratory, etc.) who have obtained an MBA while working at 3M and want to make a career change. The analysts' career goals are in marketing management but they are interested in, and have an aptitude for, spending three years in marketing research. Just about all of the analysts have postbaccalaureate business experience with 3M or other companies.

In the first year, about 60 percent of an analyst's time is spent on research projects for operating units. The remainder of the time is spent in development seminars and classes covering sampling, study design, questionnaire design, focus groups, and other relevant subjects. The classes taken depend on prior experience and aptitude. All analysts take sales training from one of 3M's divisional sales trainers. (They are expected to sell their time to cover their costs, so they are given sales training. Also, managers believe that sales training is very beneficial in developing the personal interviewing techniques required in many projects).

One year as an analyst, with good performance, qualifies a person for a position as a senior analyst. This is a promotion and the senior positions require selling close to 100 percent of one's time. The senior analyst is the workhorse of the project system, devoting time entirely to getting projects sold, completed, and reported.

The researchers' projects, for the most part, are divided along sector and group lines. Therefore, an individual's work will have an emphasis in a particular area such as industrial, health care, or imaging. However, if a project in one sector calls for an area of expertise that resides with someone assigned to another sector, that person can cross over for the project. Flexibility is an important element in the personal development of the analysts.

The senior analyst becomes a supervisor in about one year and is given one or two of the beginning analysts to develop into a competent researcher and future 3M marketer. The supervisor still does operating unit work, handling some of the more complex projects and selling time in the 60 percent to 80 percent range.

Supervisors will have developed a special rapport with several operating units over the years and will invariably be offered a marketing position in one of the line units at about the time three years have been completed. Alternatively, the managers of Corporate Marketing Research will be asked for a recommendation to fill an operating unit marketing position and the available supervisors will be recommended for interviews.[15]

A Professional Researcher's Perspective

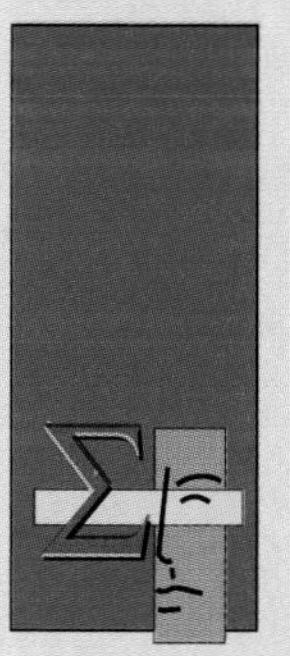

Richard Kitaeff, district manager, Market Research and Quality Measurements–AT&T, says that persons considering a career in marketing research need to know the pros and cons.

At a point early in a career as a researcher, one must decide whether one's loyalty is with the research profession or with moving up the career ladder within the corporation, because as a rule the two are incompatible. Although spending two or three years within a research group is viewed as a good broadening experience, a person who stays longer comes to be viewed as a technician. If that happens, with few exceptions, the person will be a career researcher. What this means is that a person can move up the research ladder within a corporation, but as a research specialist he generally is blocked from achieving a level beyond what might be called "upper middle management." So, in most cases, if a person wants to be a researcher and wants to stay within the corporation, she will probably not become an officer.

A second option can be exercised by persons who want to be researchers but who don't want the responsibility of management. Some individuals can be happy remaining at the "project leader" level without aspiring to or attaining a higher level. There is a niche in the corporate world for people with such a mind-set.

One can, however, stay in research, make a lot of money, and have the satisfaction of being an officer in a company by working for, buying into, or starting a research company. Working for a research company carries with it the burden not only of producing excellent research, but also of withstanding the often day-to-day insecurity of working for something less than a blue-chip company. Of course, buying

continues

into or starting a research company carries not only this burden, but also the responsibility of managing the nonresearch side of the business. Some individuals just don't have that knack, even during the best of economic times. Those who succeed, however, can find a financially and professionally rewarding career.

In contrast, one can choose the path that is more likely to lead to career growth. Researchers who dedicate themselves to moving up the corporate ladder should leave a research assignment after two years or so, before the "R" is forever burned into their forehead. In my experience, lower-level researchers are often sought to work in the organizations of the clients they serve. This is true for several reasons. First, researchers usually do not work for only one client organization. As a result, if they have done a good job, they are sought simply because of their broad exposure. Second, because they have conducted research studies for the client, they often are very conversant with the issues facing the client and can "hit the ground running." Third, by virtue of training, experience, and aptitude, researchers are usually well educated, knowledgeable, and intelligent people who would do a good job no matter what the assignment.

The organizations that typically raid the research organization are product management and marketing. But no matter what organization the researcher joins, it is important that it not be "support"—it must be mainstream or the individual will end up in the same situation as before.

To sum it all up, if a person wants to stay in research as a career, in most cases one of three things will happen. That person might manage other researchers and perhaps achieve an upper-middle-management level. He will remain a "working researcher," never getting to the top management level. Or the person might leave the world of the corporation and join a research firm, in which case she not only will practice research, but also will be subject to the risks and rewards of entrepreneurship. On the other hand, the person can leave research and stay within the corporate world. In this case, the sky is the limit.[16] ■

CHAPTER 2

The Marketing Research Process

LEARNING OBJECTIVES

1. To learn the steps involved in the marketing research process.
2. To understand the components of the research request.
3. To become familiar with the nature of management within a research department.
4. To learn the advantages and disadvantages of survey, observation, and experimental research techniques.

Honda uses all the standard research tools, including focus groups and customer surveys. The company even videotapes drivers as they test new cars. In response to all this customer input, Honda has made thousands of changes in the Accord since introducing it in 1976. The new wrinkles range from installing a suspension system used on racing cars for improved handling to changing the shape of the rear window so that a large soft drink can be passed into the car without spilling. In the process, Honda just happened to produce the best-selling car in America from 1989 until 1992, when the Ford Taurus edged it out. Says Ben Knight, vice-president for R&D of Honda North America: "We believe that the market and the customer will always find the truth."

SOURCE: Courtesy of American Honda.

Honda's manufacturing unit kicked off its most extensive customer research effort yet, the E. T. Phone Home Project. (The name and the notion were lifted from the film *E.T.*) Over a three-month period, factory workers who actually bolt and bang the Accord together called more than 47,000 recent Accord buyers, or about half the owners who had registered their cars with the company the previous spring. Honda's goal: to find out whether customers were happy with their autos and to get ideas for improvements.[1] ■

The process used by Honda to find out how well their cars are meeting customer needs and to get ideas for making changes and adding new features sounds pretty simple. The idea of having the factory workers who make the cars call recent purchasers is innovative and involves a direct dialogue between producers and consumers. More companies may adopt this approach. Yet, several logical steps in the research process have to be taken before reliable decision-making information can be obtained. What are the basic steps in the market research process? How is marketing research managed in a company like Honda? These are the issues we will address in Chapter 2.

The Research Process

The research process builds a foundation for the remainder of the text. Every subsequent chapter will examine some specific aspect of this procedure. The marketing research process is shown in Figure 2.1.

Problem/Opportunity Identification and Formulation

The research process begins with the recognition of a marketing problem or opportunity. As changes occur in the firm's external environment, marketing managers are faced with the questions, "Should we change the existing marketing mix?" and, if so, "How?" Marketing research may be used to evaluate product, promotion, distribution, or pricing alternatives. In addition, it is used to find and evaluate new market opportunities.

For example, Chrysler, the inventor of the minivan, created one of the most successful new automobile products in decades. Success, of course, invites mimicry. Although the market for minivans has continued to grow, so has the competition. Chrysler must do everything it can to understand the changing needs and wishes of the target market to maintain its market share. The problem in this case is to deliver exceptional value to the target customer to maintain and build market share and profits.

FIGURE 2.1
The Marketing Research Process

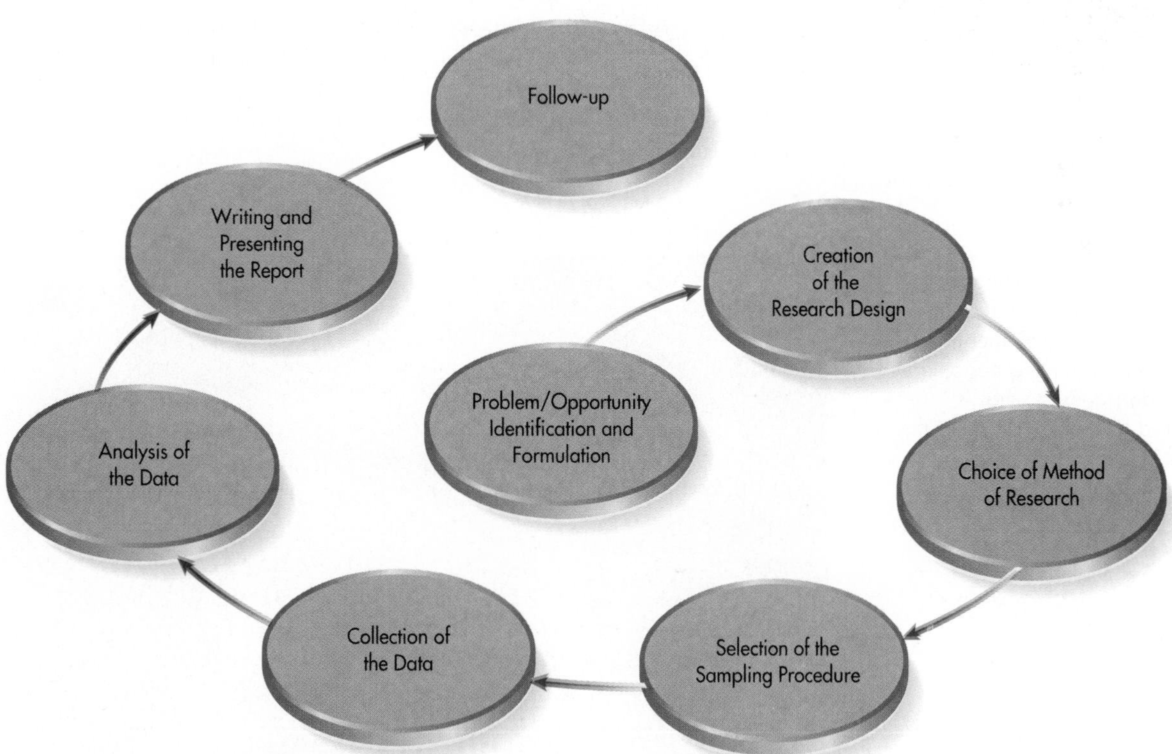

Once a problem has been sensed, the marketing researcher comes into the picture. The first responsibility of the researcher, whether from an internal staff or outside consulting firm, is to work with the marketing manager to precisely define or uncover the problem whose symptoms have been observed. Certainly, no area of marketing research requires more insight and creativity than the process of problem definition. It is the first step in arriving at a solution. It is also the most critical part of the marketing research process. Proper definition of a problem also provides guidance and direction for the entire research process. Truly, a well-defined problem is "half the battle" of conducting research.

Anthony Miles, vice-president of the Boston Consulting Group, discusses three key questions he always seeks to answer at the problem definition stage:

1. Why is the information being sought?
2. Does this information already exist?
3. Can the question really be answered?

Find Out Why the Information Is Being Sought Large amounts of money, effort, and time are wasted because requests for marketing information are poorly formulated or misunderstood. For example, managers may not have a clear idea of what they want or may not phrase the question properly. Therefore, the following activities may answer the first question:

- Discuss what the information is to be used for and what decisions might be made as a result. Go through examples in detail.
- Try to get the client or manager to set priorities among the questions. This helps sort out the central questions from those of incidental interest.
- Rephrase the questions in several slightly different forms and discuss the differences.
- Create sample data and ask if they would help answer the questions. Simulate the decision process.

Chrysler uses marketing research to learn what "exceptional value" means to its target car buying customers. By understanding what is desired, Chrysler can build the "right vehicle" with the corresponding "right level and type of service." SOURCE: Courtesy of Chrysler Corporation.

- Remember that the more clear-cut you think the questions are and the more quickly you come to feel that the question is straightforward, the more you should doubt that you have understood the real need.

Determine Whether the Information Already Exists It often seems easier and more interesting to develop new information than to delve through old reports and data files to see whether it already exists. There is a tendency to assume that current data are superior to data collected in the past.

Current data appear to be a "fix on today's situation." One has more control over the format and comprehensiveness of fresh data—they promise to be easier to work with.

Determine Whether the Question Really Can Be Answered In companies where research is in discredit, a frequent reason is that too much was promised from prior pieces of work. It is extremely important to avoid being impelled by overeagerness to please or by managerial macho into an effort that one knows has a limited probability of success. In most cases, it is possible to discern in advance the likelihood of success by identifying the following:

- Instances in which you know for certain that information of the type required exists or can be readily obtained.
- Situations in which you are fairly sure, but not fully certain, that the information can be gathered, based on similar prior experiences.
- Cases in which you know you are trying something quite new and in which there is a real risk of drawing a complete blank.

Using Exploratory Research to Define the Problem Once a problem is recognized, it is extremely important for the researcher to understand exactly what needs to be examined. Obviously, Chrysler is not going to change America's driving habits in any significant way. So, the firm is going to use marketing research to help guide its decision making. At this early stage of the research process, it is often necessary to conduct exploratory research. **Exploratory research** is usually small-scale research undertaken to define the exact nature of the problem and to gain a better understanding of the environment within which the problem has occurred. The Chrysler researcher, for example, might review several existing studies and articles on driving trends. Competing retail dealers could be visited to see which features they are promoting and how they are selling their minivans. A small-scale survey of consumers might be developed along with interviews of company executives. In addition, small groups of consumers may be brought together to discuss driving habits. This type of qualitative research is the subject of Chapter 6.

exploratory research
Preliminary research to clarify the exact nature of the problem to be solved.

Exploratory research tends to be highly flexible, with researchers following ideas, clues, and hunches as long as time and money constraints permit. Often ideas and clues can be obtained from so-called experts in the field. According to one industrial marketing research expert, "It is not uncommon to find that less than 1 percent of the 'knowledgeable' persons associated with an industrial market possess virtually all of the relevant information about the market . . . [therefore] careful attention should be given to the selection of knowledgeable persons." The researcher for Chrysler could seek out publishers of automotive magazines and researchers at the Department of Transportation. He should also seek information from persons within the firm who might have insight into automotive trends.

As the researcher moves through the exploratory research process, a list of problems and subproblems should be developed. The investigator should discern what all the probable factors are that seem to be somewhat related to the problem area. These are probable research topics. This stage of problem definition requires a brainstorming-type approach, but one guided by the previous stage's findings. All possibilities should be listed without regard to the feasibility of addressing them via research.

Unfortunately, given the natural desire of managers to get something going and the short time frame available for marketing research projects, the problem definition phase of the project is often not given proper attention. In many instances, this phase can be time-consuming and seem to be heading nowhere. The tendency to short-circuit problem definition is unfortunate, for it can be very costly. The value of this phase of the research process lies in getting efforts off on the right track. A considerable amount of time and effort can be wasted in pursuit of the wrong problem.

Definition of Research Objectives The culmination of the problem/opportunity formulation process is a statement of the research objectives. These objectives are stated in terms of the precise information necessary and desired to solve the marketing management problem.

Diane Schmalensee, director of research operations, Marketing Science Institute, offers the following insights on research objectives.

> Objectives guide the researcher in developing good research, and they help the client evaluate the final product. So the client should be convinced of the importance of objectives.
>
> Even when clients seem to know the objectives, keep digging until the true purpose of the project has been uncovered. Otherwise, the research method may be at odds with the research objective, resulting in off-target findings.
>
> Objectives must be specific. Clients frequently state objectives in vague, general terms, and they must be prodded into providing details. For example, a client may want to determine if its advertising has been effective. The researcher must learn what the client means by "effective" and the purpose of the advertising. Research mechanics will differ considerably between measuring brand awareness for a new line of cosmetics among women age 15–25 and convincing men age 18–40 that one's light beer has lusty flavor.
>
> Limit the number of objectives. The fewer the study objectives, the easier it is to keep track of them, make sure each is addressed fully, and determine the most appropriate methodology.
>
> Once the research objectives have been established, research design and analysis are fairly straightforward.[2]

Research Objectives Must Avoid the "Nice to Know" Syndrome
Even after conducting exploratory research, managers often tend to discuss research objectives in terms of broad areas of ignorance. They say, in effect, "Here are some things I don't know." Chrysler management might say, "I wonder if the target consumers are thinking about having larger families?" Managers are implicitly thinking, "When the research results come in, it will be nice to know more about the target market's trend in family size. Once I have more

knowledge, then I can make some decisions." Unfortunately, this scenario will usually lead to disappointment. There is nothing wrong with interesting findings, but they also must be "actionable." That is, the findings must provide decision-making information.

Accomplishment of a research objective must do more than reduce management's level of ignorance. Unless all the research is exploratory, it should lead to a decision. Perhaps the best way to assure actionable research is to determine how the research results will be implemented. In the case of Chrysler, assume that exploratory research uncovered a number of reports on middle class families with children (the primary target market). One such report described a satellite global positioning system now available on some cars in Japan. The system will essentially guide the driver from point "A" to point "B" using video maps. Other reports noted that families taking a vacation by car tend to bring "a lot of stuff" for over-the-road entertainment and consumption. This could have implications for storage space (perhaps either hot or cold), vehicle electronics and plug-ins, food holders, and so forth.

Management Decisions and Research Objectives Research objectives are basically a restatement of what management needs to know to make a decision in research terms. In the Chrysler case, the research objectives are

1. To determine the percentage of families who get lost at least once on a family driving vacation.
2. To determine the receptiveness of minivan owners to a satellite video mapping system at alternative price levels.
3. To determine the demand for a food warmer in the minivan.
4. To determine the demand for a refrigerator in the minivan.
5. To determine the demand for a built-in-VCR-player in the minivan.
6. To access the need for additional food/drink holders throughout the vehicle.

Research Objectives Stated as Hypotheses Often researchers state research objectives in the form of a hypothesis. A hypothesis is a conjectural statement about a relationship between two or more variables that can be tested with empirical data. Hypotheses are tentative statements that are considered to be plausible given the available information. A good hypothesis will contain clear implications for testing stated relationships. For example, based on exploratory research, a researcher might hypothesize that the addition of a satellite video mapping system as an exclusive Chrysler minivan option at a price of $2,000 will increase Chrysler's minivan market share by 4 percent. A second hypothesis might be that new minivan customers will be predominately families with adult heads of household between 28 and 45 years of age, with two children living at home, and a total family income of $55,000 to $90,000 annually. The development of research hypotheses sets the stage for creating the research design.

Creating the Research Design

research design
The plan to be followed to answer the research objectives; the structure or framework to solve a specific problem.

The **research design** is the plan to be followed to answer the research objectives or hypotheses. In essence, the researcher develops a structure or framework to solve a specific problem. There is no single, best research design. Instead, the investigator faces an array of choices, each with certain advantages and disadvantages. Ultimately, trade-offs are typically involved. A common trade-off is between research costs and the quality of decision-making information provided. Generally speaking, the more precise and error free the information obtained, the higher the cost. Another common trade-off is between time constraints and the type of research design selected. In summary, the researcher must attempt to provide management with the best information possible subject to the various constraints under which she must operate.

descriptive studies
These studies answer the questions who, what, when, where, and how.

Descriptive Studies The researcher's first task is to decide whether the research will be descriptive or causal. **Descriptive studies** are conducted to answer who, what, when, where, and how questions. Implicit in descriptive research is that management already knows or understands the underlying relationships of the problem area. Returning to our Chrysler example, it is assumed, based upon the exploratory research, that if Americans on vacation by car are getting lost with some degree of regularity, or would like to know where hotels, motels, and restaurants are located, they would be interested in a satellite video mapping system. Without knowledge of relationships, descriptive research would have little value for decision makers. For example, it would make no sense to do a research study in the northeast sector of the United States that provided age, income, family size, and educational levels of various geographic segments if Chrysler had no idea what relationship, if any, these variables had on the demand for a Chrysler minivan.

causal studies
These studies examine whether one variable causes or determines the value of another variable.

dependent variable
A symbol or concept expected to be explained or caused by the independent variable.

independent variable
The symbol of concept over which the researcher has some control or can manipulate to some extent and that is hypothesized to cause or influence the dependent variable.

Causal Studies In **causal studies** the researcher investigates whether one variable causes or determines the value of another variable. A variable is simply a symbol or concept that can assume any one of a set of values. An independent variable in a research project is a presumed cause of the dependent variable, the presumed effect. For example, does the level of advertising (independent variable) determine the level of sales (dependent variable) for Chrysler? A **dependent variable** is a variable expected to be predicted or explained. An **independent variable** is a variable in an experiment that the market researcher can, to some extent, manipulate, change, or alter. An independent variable is expected to influence the dependent variable. Descriptive research can tell us that two variables seem to be somehow associated, such as advertising and sales, but cannot provide reasonable proof that the high levels of advertising cause high sales. Because descriptive research can shed light on associations or relationships, it helps the researcher in selecting variables for a causal study. For example, without the descriptive data, the Chrysler researcher wouldn't know whether to examine age, occupation, income, or a host of other variables.

temporal sequence
Appropriate causal order of events.

A causal study for Chrysler might involve changing one independent variable (for example, the number of direct mailings over a six-month period to target customers) and then observing the effect on the dependent variable (minivan sales). Given that the minivan sales go up when the number of promotional mailings are increased, there is an appropriate causal order of events called **temporal sequence.** The concept of temporal sequence is one criterion for causality that must be met.

A second criterion for causality is the necessity of concomitant variation. The degree to which a cause (direct mail promotion) and effect (minivan sales) occur

Chrysler can use marketing research to assess the potential demand for a satellite video mapping system for its mini vans. SOURCE: Courtesy of Chrysler Corporation.

together or vary together is called **concomitant variation.** If direct mail promotions are considered a cause of increased sales, then when the number of direct mail promotions goes up, minivan sales should go up, and when the number of promotions falls, sales should fall to near the preincrease in direct promotion level. If, however, an increase in direct mail promotions does not result in an increase in minivan sales, the researcher must conclude that the hypothesis about the relationship between the increase in direct mail promotions and minivan sales is not correct.

concomitant variation
The degree to which a cause and effect occur or vary together.

An ideal situation would be one in which sales of minivans increased markedly every time Chrysler increases its direct mail promotions (up to a saturation level). But, alas, we live in a world where perfection is rarely achieved. One additional mailing might bring in a small increase in sales and the next mailing a larger increment, or vice versa. Also, in the next six-month period, an increase in direct mail promotion might produce no increase or even a decline in sales.

Remember, even perfect concomitant variation would not prove that *A* causes *B*. All that the researcher could say is that the association makes the hypothesis more likely but does not prove it.

The third issue of causality is to recognize the possibility of **spurious association.** This means that another variable or other variables might possibly cause changes in the dependent variable. The ideal situation would be one in which the researcher demonstrates that there is a total absence of other causal factors. In the real world of marketing research, it is very difficult to identify and control all other potential causal factors. Think for a moment of all the variables that could cause the sales of Chrysler minivans to increase or decrease.

spurious association
Another variable or variables may cause changes in the dependent variable.

The researcher may lower spurious associations by holding constant other factors that could influence sales of minivans: for example, prices, newspaper and television advertising, coupons, discounts, and dealer inventory levels. Alternatively, the researcher may look at changes in sales in similar socioeconomic areas.

Choosing a Basic Method of Research

A research design, either descriptive or causal, is chosen according to a project's objectives. The next step is to select a means of gathering data. There are three basic research methods: (1) survey, (2) observation, and (3) experiment. Survey research is often descriptive in nature but can be causal. Experiments are almost always causal, and observation research is typically descriptive.

survey research
Research in which an interviewer interacts with respondents to obtain facts, opinions, and attitudes.

Survey **Survey research** involves an interviewer (except in mail surveys) interacting with respondents to obtain facts, opinions, and attitudes. A questionnaire is used to provide an orderly and structured approach to data gathering. Face-to-face interviews may take place within the respondent's home, in a shopping mall, or in a place of business.

observation research
Descriptive research that monitors respondents' actions without direct interaction.

Observation The fastest growing form of **observation research** involves the use of cash registers with scanners, which read tags with bar codes to identify the item being purchased. The future of observation research is somewhat mind-boggling. For example, A. C. Nielsen has been using black boxes for years on television sets to silently siphon off information on a family's viewing habits. But what if the set is on and no one is in the room? To overcome that problem, researchers say TVs might be equipped with heat sensors that will feel when the viewer is watching. Or participants might wear rings or watches with a transmitter that would signal the presence of "person *A* in the room while the television is on." Some have even talked of surgically implanting a transmitter into the body of a test subject. Far-fetched? The technology is already available.[3]

experiments
Research to measure causality in which one or more variables are changed while observing the effect of the change on another variable.

Experiments **Experiments** are the third method researchers use to gather data. An experiment is distinguished by the researcher's changing one or more variables—price, package, design, shelf space, advertising theme, or advertising expenditures—while observing the effects of those changes on another variable (usually sales). The objective of experiments is to measure causality. The best experiments are those in which all factors are held constant except the ones being manipulated. This enables the researcher to observe that changes in sales, for example, can be caused by changes in the amount of money spent on advertising. Holding all other factors constant in the external environment is a monumental and costly, if not impossible, task. Factors such as competitors' actions in various markets, weather, and economic conditions are beyond the control of the researcher.

One way researchers attempt to control factors that might influence the dependent variable is to use a laboratory experiment; that is, an experiment conducted in a test facility rather than in the natural environment. Researchers sometimes create simulated supermarket environments, give consumers script (play money), and then ask them to shop as they normally would for groceries. By varying package design or color over several time periods, for example, the researcher can determine which package is most likely to stimulate sales. Although laboratory techniques can provide valuable information, one must realize that the consumer is not in a natural environment. How a person acts in a laboratory may be different from an actual shopping situation. Experiments are discussed in detail in Chapter 9.

Selecting the Sampling Procedure

The sample is actually part of the research design but is a separate step in the research process. A sample is a subset from a larger population. Several questions must be answered before a sampling plan is selected. First, the population or universe of interest must be defined. This is the group from which the sample will be drawn. It should include all the people whose opinions, behavior, preferences, attitudes, and so on will aid the marketer's decision making. An example would be all persons who eat Mexican food at least once every 60 days. After the population had been defined, the next question is whether to use a probability sample or a nonprobability sample.

Probability Versus Nonprobability Samples A **probability sample** is characterized by every element in the population having a known nonzero probability of being selected. Such samples allow the researcher to estimate how much sampling error is present in a given study. **Nonprobability samples** include all samples that cannot be considered probability samples. Specifically, any sample in which little or no attempt is made to ensure that a representative cross section of the population is obtained can be considered a nonprobability sample. The researchers cannot statistically calculate the reliability of the sample; that is, they cannot determine the degree of sampling error that can be expected. Sampling is the topic of Chapter 13.

probability samples
Subsets of a population that ensure a representative cross section by giving every element in the population a known nonzero chance of being selected.

nonprobability samples
Subsets of a population in which little or no attempt is made to ensure a representative cross section.

Collecting the Data

Most data collection is done by marketing research field services. Field service firms, found throughout the country, specialize in providing interviewing for data collection on a subcontract basis. A typical research study involves data collection in several cities and requires working with a comparable number of field service firms. To ensure that all subcontractors do everything exactly the same way, detailed field instructions should be developed for every job. Nothing should be left to chance; no interpretations of procedures should be left to the subcontractors.

Besides interviewing, field service firms provide group research facilities, mall intercept locations, test product storage, and kitchen facilities to prepare test food products. They also conduct retail audits (counting the amount of product sold from retail shelves). After an in-home interview has been completed, field service supervisors validate the survey by recontacting about 15 percent of the respondents to make sure certain responses were recorded properly and the person was actually interviewed.

Analyzing the Data

After the data have been collected, the next step in the research process is data analysis. The purpose of this analysis is to interpret and draw conclusions from the mass of collected data. The marketing researcher may use techniques beginning with simple frequency analysis and ultimately culminating in complex multivariate techniques. Data analysis will be discussed in Chapters 15 through 18.

Preparing and Writing the Report

After data analysis is completed, the researcher must prepare the report and communicate the conclusions and recommendations to management. This is a key step in the process because a marketing researcher who wants conclusions acted upon must convince the manager that the results are credible and justified by the data collected.

The researcher will ordinarily be required to present both written and oral reports on the project. The nature of the audience must be kept in mind when these reports are being prepared and presented. The reports should begin with a clear, concise statement of the research objectives, followed by a complete, but brief and simple, explanation of the research design or methodology employed. A summary of major findings should come next. The report should end with a presentation of conclusions and recommendations for management.

Because most people who enter marketing become research users rather than research suppliers, it is important to know what to look for in a report. Evaluating research will be a much greater portion of one's job than other aspects of marketing research. Like many other items we purchase, quality is not always readily apparent. Nor does a high price for the project necessarily guarantee superior quality. The basis for measuring quality is to return to the research proposal. Did the report meet the objectives established in the proposal? Was the methodology outlined in the proposal followed? Are the conclusions based on logical deductions from the data analysis? Do the recommendations seem prudent, given the conclusions?

Is the writing style crisp and lucid? It has been said that a reader who is offered the slightest opportunity to misunderstand probably will. The report should also be as concise as possible. It should follow the format outlined earlier so that important findings and recommendations can be found quickly and determined easily.

Follow-Up

After a company has spent a considerable amount of effort and money conducting marketing research and preparing a report, it is important for the findings to be used. Management should determine whether the recommendations were followed and why or why not. One way to help ensure that the research will be used is to minimize conflict between the marketing research department and other departments.

Management of Marketing Research

The Research Request

research request

Document used in large organizations that describes a potential research project, its benefits to the organization, and estimated costs. A project cannot begin until the research request has been formally approved.

Before conducting the research project, Chrysler might require approval of a formal **research request.** Moderate- and large-size retailers, manufacturers, and nonprofit organizations often use the research request as a basis for determining which projects will be funded. Typically, in larger organizations there are far more requests by managers for marketing research information than monies available to conduct such research. The research request step is a formalized approach to allocating scarce research dollars.

It is very important for the brand manager, new product specialist, or whoever is in need of research information to clearly state in the formal research request why the desired information is critical to the organization. Otherwise, the person with approval authority may fail to see why the research expenditure is necessary.

In smaller organizations, the communication link between the brand managers and the market researchers is much closer. The day-to-day contact often removes the need for a formal research request. Instead, decisions to fund research are made on an ad hoc basis by the marketing manager or the director of marketing research.

Completion and approval of the request represents a disciplined approach to identifying research problems and obtaining funding to solve them. The degree of effort expended at this step in the research process will be reflected in the quality of information provided the decision maker because it will guide the design, data gathering, analysis, and reporting of the research toward a highly focused objective. The components of a formal research request are as follows:

1. *Action.* The decision maker must describe the action to be taken on the basis of the research. This will help the decision maker focus on what information makes sense and guide the researcher in creating the research design and in analyzing the results.
2. *Origin.* This is a statement of the events that led to a need for a decision to act. It helps the researcher understand more deeply the nature of the research problem.
3. *Information.* The decision maker must list the questions that he needs to have answered to take the action. Carefully considering this area improves the efficiency of the research and ensures that the questions make sense in light of the action to be taken.
4. *Use.* This section explains how each piece of information will be used to help make the actual decision. It gives logical reasons for each piece of the research and ensures that the questions make sense in light of the action to be taken.
5. *Targets and subgroups.* This section describes from whom the information must be gathered for the action to be taken. This helps the researcher design the sample for the research project.
6. *Logistics.* Time and budget constraints always affect the research technique that is chosen for a project. For this reason, approximations of the amount of money required and the amount of time that exists before results are needed must be stated as a part of the research request.
7. *Comments.* Any other comments relevant to the research project must be stated so that, once again, the researcher can fully understand the nature of the problem.[4]

AT&T is an example of a large company that relies on a research request as a management tool. Once the request is approved at AT&T, it enters the "Project Log" as described in "A Professional Researcher's Perspective" by Richard Kitaeff, manager of marketing research and quality measurement at AT&T.

Manager-Researcher Conflict

Complaints about ineffectiveness, uselessness, and even interference in the decision process are all too common by product managers and corporate executives.[5] On the other hand, many researchers do not respect product managers because

A Professional Researcher's Perspective

In recent years, the workload of each of the research professionals reporting to me has increased. The result can be great confusion about "where we are" in each study. The large number of studies causes difficulty in being able to keep each study apart in our minds. To cope with this problem, I have developed the "Market Research Project Log" as an aid to me in organizing work flow and keeping track of the projects.

Operationally, as soon as a client requests a research study, I assign a number, name, and project leader. At that point, the project leader plans the flow of the project and establishes a time line so that the achievement dates of all key project elements are established.

At the beginning of a study, the log entry for a study could look like Table 2.1. When a particular phase of a study is complete, the project leader places an *X* in the column. Sometimes a particular step (e.g., a presentation) is not required, so *NA* goes in that box. Table 2.2 is an example of what a portion of a log might look like. When a project has been completed, it is removed from the log.

Probably the most important aspect of the log is how we use it. Once a week I meet with my project managers and review changes in the log and the new projects that have been added to it. By doing this, I can have a thorough understanding of the workload in my organization, a sense of the types of activities that are planned and under way, and an opportunity to adjust if one group is much busier than another.

This system of project management is one that works for me. The project components I track are ones that I have found to be on the critical path in my corporation in terms of project management (i.e., getting the work done) and importance to the client (i.e., due dates of receivables from us).[6] ■

TABLE 2.1 Log Entry at Beginning of Study

PROJECT NO.	PROJECT NAME	PROJECT LEADER	PROJECT DESIGN	PROJECT APPROVAL	FIELD-WORK START	FIELD-WORK END	ANALYSIS	PRESENTATION	FINAL REPORT
RK007	LD Usage	AB	3/11	3/18	3/25	4/8	4/22	4/29	5/13

TABLE 2.2 Part of a Market Research Project Log

PROJECT NO.	PROJECT NAME	PROJECT LEADER	PROJECT DESIGN	PROJECT APPROVAL	FIELD-WORK START	FIELD-WORK END	ANALYSIS	PRESENTATION	FINAL REPORT
RK007	LD Usage	AB	3/11	3/18	3/25	4/8	4/22	4/29	5/13
RK009	Winback	ML	3/15	3/18	NA	NA	4/13	4/13	NA
RK101	Impact Study	NC	X	X	4/10	4/30	5/7	5/7	5/21

they do not act on the researcher's recommendations. Some managers have research studies conducted because it is expected of them. Other managers are unsure of what to do so they request research to avoid or postpone a decision. New product managers will sometimes request a study and then publicize the results only if it confirms their preconceived notions about the product concept.

Resolution of these problems is not a simple task. The first step is a clear delineation of authority and responsibility. A researcher's job is to conduct research and provide information; a manager's job is to make decisions. Thus, researchers must recognize that their job is to provide actionable information to decision makers. In turn, the managers must clearly define what information is needed for strategy and tactics and what format will be most useful for decision making.[7]

Types of Decision-Making Information A marketing research department's mission can be classified in three broad categories: programmatic, selective, or evaluative.[8] **Programmatic research** is done to develop marketing options through market segmentation, market opportunity analysis, or consumer attitude and product usage studies. **Selective research** is used to test decision alternatives. Some examples are testing concepts for new products, advertising copy testing, and test marketing. **Evaluative research** is done to assess program performance. Illustrations include tracking advertising recall, organizational image studies, and examining customer attitudes on the quality of service that the firm is providing.

programmatic research

Research done to develop marketing options through market segmentation, market opportunity analysis, or consumer attitude and product usage studies.

selective research

Research to choose among several viable alternatives identified by programmatic research.

evaluative research

Research to determine the effectiveness and efficiency of specific programs.

Programmatic decision problems arise from management's need to obtain a market overview periodically. This usually is prompted by a feeling that the market is continually changing or by new marketing plans that call for the introduction of new products, ad campaigns, packaging, or whatever. Perhaps product management is concerned that the existing market information base is inadequate or outdated for present decision making. Current information is needed to develop viable marketing options. Typical questions include

- Does the market exhibit any segmentation opportunities?
- If so, what are the profiles of the various segments?
- Do some segments appear to be more likely candidates than others for the company's marketing efforts?
- What new product opportunities are in the various segments?
- What marketing program options should be considered in light of the segmentation analysis?

The marketing research department's role is to suggest a research program that will answer these questions within the firm's budgetary constraints.

Selective decision problems arise after several viable options have been identified by programmatic research. If no alternative is clearly superior to the others, product management normally will wish to test several alternatives. Selective research may be required at the concept stage or any other stage in the marketing process, such as when developing advertising copy, evaluating various product formulations, or assessing an entire marketing program, as in test marketing.

Evaluative decision problems arise when the effectiveness and efficiency of programs need evaluation. Evaluative research is closely related to programmatic research, often constituting an input into programmatic research when program changes or entirely new options are demanded because of present performance.

Global Marketing Research

In contrast to Western practice, Japanese executives don't give managers sole responsibility for a research area. They conduct research and make decisions by consensus, and they lean toward their intuitive judgment. Rarely do Japanese executives call in an outside professional, and when they do, they often disregard the consultant's report if it goes against their instincts about the best course of action. When Kozo Ohsone, the executive in charge of developing Sony's portable, compact Discman, heard that the company's marketing people were thinking about commissioning a research study, he told them not to waste their money.[9] ■

The response of the marketing research department to the need for evaluative information is often to conduct tracking studies.

Factors Influencing a Manager's Decision to Use Research Information Understanding a research department's role is a major step in reducing researcher-manager conflict. It is also important for a researcher to have knowledge of what factors influence a manager to use research data. These factors are (1) conformity to prior expectations; (2) clarity of presentation; (3) research quality; (4) political acceptability within the firm; and (5) challenge to the status quo.[10] Managers and researchers both agree that technical quality is the most important determinant of research use. However, managers are less likely to use research that does not conform to preconceived notions or is not politically acceptable.[11] This does not mean, of course, that researchers should alter their findings to meet management's preconceived notions. Also, marketing managers in industrial firms tend to use research findings more than do their counterparts in consumer goods organizations.[12] This is attributed to a greater exploratory objective in information collection, a greater degree of formalization of organizational structure, and a lesser degree of surprise in the information collection.

Summary

The steps in the market research process are

1. Identification and formulation of the problem/opportunity
2. Creation of the research design
3. Choice of the method of research
4. Selection of the sampling procedure
5. Collection of data
6. Analysis of data
7. Preparation of the research report
8. Follow-up

In larger organizations, it is often common to have a research request prepared after the definition of research objectives. The research request generally describes the action to be taken on the basis of the research, the reason for the need for the information, how the information will be used, the target groups from whom the information should be gathered, the amount of time and money needed to complete the research project, and any other information pertinent to the request.

In specifying a research design, the researcher must determine whether the research will be descriptive or causal. Descriptive studies are conducted to answer who, what, when, where, and how questions. Causal studies are those in which the researcher investigates whether one variable (independent) causes or determines the value of another variable (dependent). The next step in creating a research design is to select a research method: survey, observation, or experiment. Survey research involves an interviewer interacting with a respondent to obtain facts, opinions, and attitudes. Observation research, in contrast, does not rely on direct interaction with people. An experiment is distinguished by the researcher changing one or more variables while observing the effects of those changes on another variable (usually sales). The objective of most experiments is to measure causality.

A sample is a subset from a larger population. A probability sample is characterized by every element in the population having a known nonzero probability of being selected. Nonprobability samples include all samples that cannot be considered probability samples. Any sample in which little or no attempt is made to ensure that a representative cross section of the population is obtained can be considered a nonprobability sample.

A marketing research department's mission can be described as programmatic, selective, or evaluative. Programmatic research is done to develop marketing options through market segmentation, market opportunity analysis, or attitude and usage studies. Selective research is used to test decisional alternatives. Evaluative research is done to assess program performance.

Key Terms

exploratory research
research design
descriptive studies
causal studies
dependent variable
independent variable
temporal sequence
concomitant variation
spurious association
survey research
observation research
experiments
probability samples
nonprobability samples
research request
programmatic research
selective research
evaluative research

Review and Discussion Questions

1. The definition of the research problem is one of the most critical steps in the research process. Why? Who should be involved in this process?
2. What role does exploratory research play in the market research process? How does exploratory research differ from other forms of market research?
3. In the absence of company problems, is there any need to conduct marketing research?
4. Are there any situations in which it would be better to take a census of the population rather than a sample? Give several examples.

5. Critique the following methodologies and suggest more appropriate alternatives:
   a. A supermarket was interested in determining its image. It dropped a short questionnaire into the grocery bag of each customer before sacking the groceries.
   b. To assess the extent of its trade area, a shopping mall stationed interviewers in the parking lot every Monday and Friday evening. Interviewers walked up to persons after they had parked their cars and asked them for their zip codes.
   c. To assess the popularity of a new movie, a major studio invited people to call a 900 number and vote yes, they would see it again, or no, they would not. Each caller was billed a two-dollar charge.
6. You have been charged with determining how to attract more business majors to your school. Outline the steps you would take, including the sampling procedures, to accomplish the task.
7. What are the three alternative missions of marketing research departments? Give examples of each.
8. What are some sources of conflict between marketing researchers and other managers? How can these be minimized?
9. What are the conditions for causality? Discuss the criterion.
10. Do you think market researchers should always use probability samples? Why or why not?

CASE 2.1

Chevrolet Tries to Determine "Are We Almost There?"

Each year Chevrolet sponsors its "Discover America" tour in which families are loaned a redesigned Lumina sedan and are provided with money and trip destinations for a family vacation. Beta Research, an independent marketing research firm, surveyed 300 women in conjunction with the "Discover America" tour. Each respondent has at least one child between the ages of three and 11 years old and goes on family driving trips from time to time. A few of the survey findings are in Table 2.3.[13]

TABLE 2.3 Survey of Family Vacationers

Parental roles on the road:

37% said the husband and wife pack equally
68% said the husband does most of the driving
97% of families get lost at one time or another, but 56% of wives mostly ask for directions compared with 17% of husbands

What families bring:

71% of kids take activity/coloring and reading books
22% take handheld video games
18% take personal tape players or CD players
35% pack fruit or dried fruit
34% pack chips and popcorn

Most-heard comments from the back seat:

74% heard "Are we almost there?"
5% heard "He/she is bothering me."
5% heard "I need to use the bathroom."

1. Is this an exploratory study? If not, what are the research questions?
2. Do you think the research is causal or descriptive? Defend your answer.
3. In terms of decision-making information, is the research programmatic, selective, or evaluative? Why?

CASE 6.2

Pizza Heaven

Pizza Heaven is a small, West Coast, independent chain of pizza restaurants that caters primarily to college students. Accordingly, the restaurants are usually located near a campus and promote their offerings extensively in college newspapers. In the past year, Pizza Heaven sales have slipped, and management feels that the national chains such as Pizza Hut, Pizza Inn, and Domino's are making inroads into its market, along with single-store, independent pizza restaurants.

Pizza Heaven decided to conduct marketing research to determine its image among its customers and to see if the company needed to reposition itself. The first step was to do exploratory research. The exploratory research consisted of a pilot study with 40 students. According to the pilot study, the college students expected to find a dark, informal, fun atmosphere in a pizza restaurant. They did not want to see noisy games or movies at the restaurant. College students claimed they used coupons extensively. The respondents particularly liked the two-for-one coupons offered by Pizza Inn and Domino's. Pizza was considered an intermediate food—something between a fast hamburger and a formal restaurant. Study participants thought of pizza primarily as a group activity rather than a dating situation. They noted that pizza also was a mood or an impulse food because of its distinct taste. They enjoyed eating other foods at pizza restaurants. College students usually ate pizza with more than one person, and not everyone wanted pizza. Submarine sandwiches came up quite frequently as food that many ordered as an alternate. Convenience played a big part in where the students chose to eat pizza.

Naturally, the most important feature in a pizza restaurant was the quality of the pizza. A good pizza was defined as hot, with a lot of fresh ingredients. It should have a large quantity of cheese, sauce, and meat. Some students claimed they would drive farther to get a favorite pizza (which was usually produced by an independent pizza restaurant). They said the independent's pizza was typically thicker and had more ingredients for the same amount of money than the average chain pizza.

The college students were generally negative toward luncheon specials. They said the pizzas were usually cold and dry. Also, they noted that the selection was often poor. Many of them did not think of pizza for lunch.

1. Now that Pizza Heaven is armed with the information from the exploratory research, should it begin implementing the findings? Why or why not?
2. If additional research should be undertaken, what topics should be covered? Why?
3. Outline the procedure for implementing additional market research.

CHAPTER 3

Who Does Marketing Research?

LEARNING OBJECTIVES

1. To appreciate the structure of the marketing research industry.
2. To comprehend the nature of corporate marketing research departments.
3. To learn about the various types of firms and their functions in the market research industry.
4. To understand the functions of the advertising agency research department.

Princess Cruises' famous fleet of Love Boats sails to destinations around the world. The company is the third largest in the industry based on market share and carries approximately 450,000 passengers annually.

The company's market research department analyzes more than 185,000 customer satisfaction questionnaires each year. The onboard survey on the following page is distributed one per cabin before the last day of each cruise. Passengers are asked to place the surveys in a locked box when they are completed. The 45-question survey is very detailed, looking at opinions of precruise documents and logistics such as airport transfers to the ships, airline flights, and shore excursions. It also looks at presentation of food, quality of ingredients, variety of menu, and service areas such as stateroom service, housekeeping, and front desk performance. The surveys are distributed on every voyage of each of the nine ships in the Princess fleet.

SOURCE: © Porterfield/Chickering/Photo Researchers.

The market research department produces a monthly summary report that examines onboard performance by cruise destination and vessel and that identifies any specific problems that need to be addressed. For example, the ongoing survey has led to changes in the menu items and buffets.

Princess Cruises often turns to Pine Company, a Santa Monica, California, marketing research company, to conduct customized research studies. One recent study examined satisfaction with booking of shore excursions in two ways, either through a travel agent or Princess before the cruise or through the shore excursion office on each Princess vessel.

"From our standard onboard surveys, we've gotten some feedback that (the booking process) is one of our weaker areas. In response, we designed a survey that explained in detail the various attributes affecting shore excursions to try to remedy any problems we might be having." says Jaine Goldfarb, Ph.D., a manager of market analysis for Princess Cruises.[1] ■

Dear Princess Passenger,

In our continuous effort to provide the highest quality experience to our passengers, we periodically seek your opinions on specific areas of your cruise experience. This short questionnaire is designed to evaluate how our Shore Excursion Program has served you throughout your cruise. Please take a few moments to share your impressions with us, as your opinions are invaluable to us.

Please fill in circles as shown. Use pencil or blue or black ink. Correct ● Incorrect

I. PRE-CRUISE DOCUMENTS

1. Did you receive the "Adventures Ashore" shore excursion booklet prior to your cruise? *(If no, please skip to question 11)* Yes ○ No ○

2. How soon prior to your sailing date did you receive your pre-cruise document package (which included your Shore Excursion Booklet)?

a. Within one week ○
b. One to three weeks ○
c. Three to six weeks ○
d. Six weeks to three months ○
e. More than three months ○

3. Were these booklets received early enough so you could review them? Yes ○ No ○

4. Please rate the booklets on the following dimensions:

	Strongly Agree			Strongly Disagree	N/A
a. The presentation of information was very appealing.	○	○	○	○	○
b. Enough information was provided.	○	○	○	○	○
c. The information was useful.	○	○	○	○	○
d. The information was easy to understand.	○	○	○	○	○

5. Did you pre-reserve your shore excursions? *(If not, skip to question 11)* Yes ○ No ○

6. If yes, by which method

a. I mailed my reservation form to Princess. ○
b. My travel agent mailed my reservation form to Princess. ○
c. I FAXed my reservation form to Princess. ○
d. My travel agent FAXed my reservation form to Princess. ○
e. I called Princess directly. ○
f. My travel agent called Princess directly. ○

7. How easy did you find it to pre-reserve your excursions?

Very Easy			Very Difficult	N/A
○	○	○	○	○

8. Did you purchase the "Adventures Ashore" video to help you decide which excursions to take? Yes ○ No ○

V. OVERALL SHUTTLE BUS SERVICE

21. Please rate the shuttle bus service on the following:

	Excellent			Poor	N/A
a. quality	○	○	○	○	○
b. efficiency of dispatch	○	○	○	○	○

22. Please rate the shuttle bus coordinator on the following:

	Excellent			Poor	N/A
a. helpfulness	○	○	○	○	○
b. friendliness	○	○	○	○	○
c. knowledge	○	○	○	○	○

VI. MEAL/SHORE EXCURSION SCHEDULES

23. Did you find that meals and shore excursions were conveniently scheduled (ie., they did not conflict with each other?) Yes ○ No ○

24. If no, in which ports did you have a scheduling conflict?

____

VII. ADDITIONAL COMMENTS

25. What other information regarding shore excursions would you like to have had?

26. Please list any other comments regarding shore excursions.

Southern Caribbean/Shore Tour

Princess Cruise Line uses marketing research to measure customer satisfaction with all aspects of each cruise. Princess hopes to gain repeat customers by correcting any perceived service difficulties.

Princess Cruises' marketing research department and Pine Company are just two types of marketing research organizations in the industry. What types of companies conduct marketing research? What types of specialized services and support firms exist in the research industry? What are the basic characteristics of the industry today? We will examine these questions in this chapter.

The Evolving Structure of the Marketing Research Industry

Today, about $8.1 billion a year is spent on marketing/advertising/public opinion research services around the world, according to estimates developed by the European Society for Opinion and Marketing Research. That estimate puts U.S. spending at $2.9 billion.[2]

During the past two decades, the marketing research industry has become highly concentrated. About 39 percent of the world's spending for research services goes to just the 10 largest marketing research organizations. About 51 percent is held by the 25 largest worldwide organizations.[3] The other half is shared literally by a thousand or more small research firms.

This concentration is even more pronounced in the United States, where the 10 largest firms account for 59 percent of the total U.S. spending for marketing/advertising/public opinion research. The 20 largest firms account for 72 percent, and the top 30 account for 79 percent. If anything, this trend toward concentration continues, largely because of mergers. The wave of mergers in the late 1980s and early 1990s that resulted in the consolidation of marketing departments at top package goods companies has had an immediate impact on the competitive environment.

"When a Philip Morris absorbs a General Foods and then a Kraft, or when an R. J. Reynolds acquires a Nabisco, there's only a certain number of service companies and a certain amount of service those [conglomerates] are going to use," says David Learner, president of MRCA Information Services.[4] "One of the efficiencies of combining companies is the elimination of duplicate services, and the most damage that has been done to marketing research has been done [from mergers]," he says.

Corporate mergers, more than the economy, have spurred consolidations and alliances among research companies as they battle for business among a smaller client universe. This also intensified price competition among researchers, with earnings for some top companies sliding even as revenues grew.

"Research has been moving into a third phase that will be challenging, certainly, but also provide opportunities," says John Costello, president of Nielsen Marketing Research USA.[5] "The first phase was collecting information. The second was turning that information into insights. This third phase will be converting those insights into results."

Because of the competitiveness of markets in the 1990s, that third phase has been hastened along, Costello says. It has focused research user attention more on productivity and cost of sales than on pure growth.

The various types of organizations encountered in the research industry are summarized in Table 3.1. The structure of the marketing research industry is summarized in Figure 3.1 on page 60. This diagram shows the process for survey-based research operating at four levels. The diagram depicts companies at Levels 1 and 2 as the ultimate consumers of marketing research data, the information users. The information they need rests with individual consumers and those who make business purchase decisions, the respondents. Companies at Level 3 are the research designers and providers, and companies at Level 4 are the data collectors.

Thomas Dupont, president of D^{2}Research and chairman of the Council of American Survey Research Organizations (CASRO), sees a bright future for marketing research during the next decade. He explains why in "A Professional Researcher's Perspective" on page 58.

Level 1. Primary Information Users (Corporate Marketing Research Departments)

Level 1 organizations are the ultimate users of marketing research data provided by their marketing research departments. Their primary business is the sale of

A Professional Researcher's Perspective

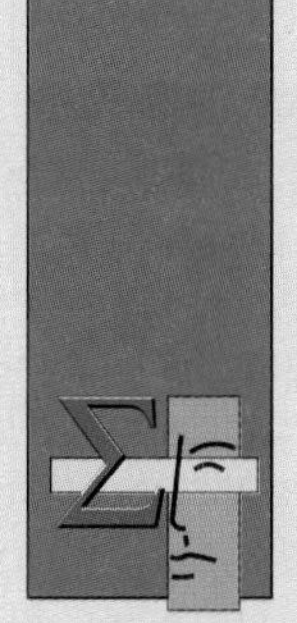

Marketing research will prosper in the coming years.

1. Some segments of the service industry have been heavy research users (particularly travel and financial services), whereas others (business and personal services, retail, restaurants) have been infrequent users of research. As a psychologist, I am particularly fascinated by the opportunities inherent in better understanding the interaction between the customer and the salesperson/service provider, and the resulting implications for employee selection and training.
2. Major changes in the way health care is delivered and paid for seem inevitable, and this should afford major opportunities for the marketing research industry. All providers—physicians, drug companies, hospitals, and laboratories—will have to become more efficient, perhaps banding together in larger groups than now. There will be a need for these new entities to differentiate themselves from the competition and woo customers—an unfamiliar concept for many in that industry. This represents a whole new class of customers for marketing research.
3. It is increasingly obvious that the introduction of new brands has become less and less profitable. There are many reasons for this, including the fragmentation of media, which makes mass marketing much more expensive than before, as well as the increasing willingness of retailers to act as gatekeepers. Whatever the reasons, the implications are that competition among established brands will become more and more intense (witness the unprecedented price cut that Philip Morris took on its flagship Marlboro brand). As this continues, manufacturers will be looking for ever more subtle advantages over the competition, advantages that will require careful and sensitive consumer survey research to ferret out.
4. As has always been true, new technologies will change behavior in unpredictable ways. Just as the "cocooning" phenomenon of the 1980s was in large part attributable to the proliferation of VCRs and other home entertainment advances, and new telecommunications devices (fax, cellular, beepers) are transforming communications and working patterns today, we can expect the next wave of technology to have a similar impact on our lives. As just one example, during the next 10 years, we will enter a new dimension of telecommunication/entertainment as our homes are wired with fiber-optic cable. There will be much more to this than picturephones and 500-channel cable TV, and survey research will be needed to understand who is using this new technology, how they are using it, and why.[6] ■

TABLE 3.1 General Categories of Institutions Involved in Marketing Research

INSTITUTION	ACTIVITIES, FUNCTIONS, AND SERVICES
Level 1. Corporate Marketing Research Departments	Marketing research departments in firms such as Kraft General Foods or Procter & Gamble
Level 2. Ad Agency Research Departments	Marketing research departments in advertising agencies such as J. Walter Thompson, Young and Rubicam, or Foote, Cone and Belding
Level 3. Custom or Ad Hoc Research Firms	Marketing research consulting firms such as Market Facts, Data Development, or MARC, which do customized marketing research projects addressing specific problems for individual clients
Level 3. Syndicated Service Firms	Marketing research data gathering and reporting firms like A. C. Nielsen, Arbitron, or Information Resources Incorporated, which collect data of general interest to many firms but for no one firm in particular; anyone can buy the data they collect; prominent in the media audience field and retail sales data
Level 4. Field Service Firms	Collect data only, on a subcontract basis for corporate marketing research departments, ad agency research departments, custom research firms, or syndicated research firms
Specialized Service Firms*	Provide specialized support service to the marketing research industry, such as SDR in Atlanta, which provides sophisticated quantitative analysis
Others*	Governmental agencies, university research bureaus, individual university professors, database providers, and others

*These organizations typically operate at Levels 1, 2, or 3.

products and services. They use marketing research data to support the marketing decision-making process. They need marketing research data on an ongoing basis to:

1. Determine how various target groups will react to alternative marketing mixes.
2. Evaluate the ongoing success of operational marketing strategies.
3. Assess changes in the external or uncontrollable environment and their implications for their product or service strategy.

Figure 3.1 shows that these companies, and their marketing research departments, may work with a combination of custom and syndicated research firms, go directly to ad agencies, or use all or some combination of these alternatives to satisfy their many marketing research needs.

Level 2. Information Users (Ad Agencies)

Ad agencies (Level 2) also are in the position of serving corporate clients, but they also may be ultimate consumers of marketing research data. Their main business is the development and execution of ad campaigns. To properly fulfill this role, they often need marketing research data. They may obtain data from custom and syndicated research firms or from field service firms, or they may use some combination of these alternatives.

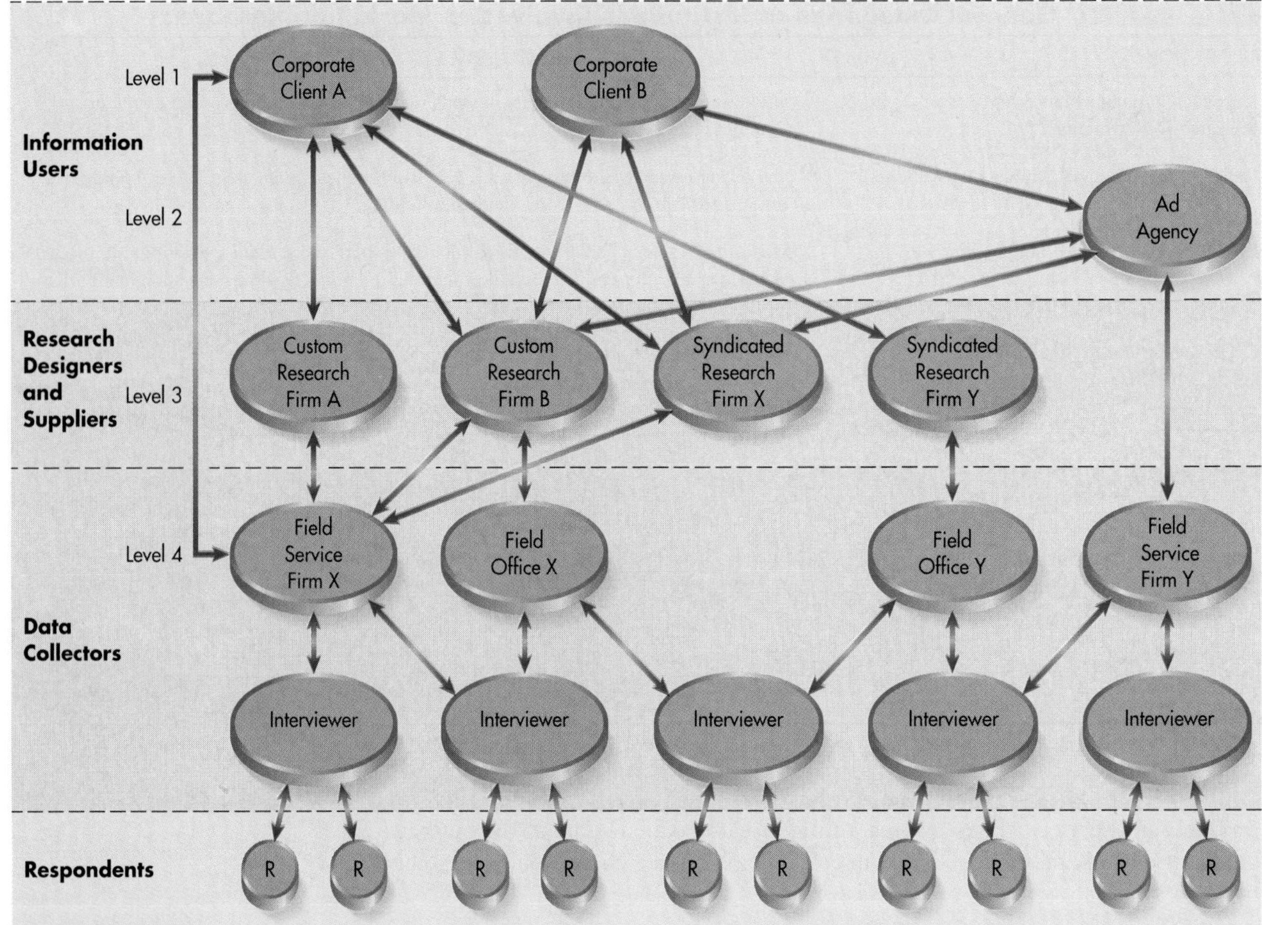

FIGURE 3.1
The Marketing Research Industry

Level 3. Research Designers and Suppliers

Custom and syndicated marketing research firms (Level 3) represent the front line of the research industry. They sell research services, design research studies, analyze the results, and make recommendations to their clients. They design research, manage its execution, and buy data collection and other services from firms down the line (see Figure 3.1).

Level 4. Data Collectors

Field service firms (Level 4) collect data for syndicated research firms, custom research firms, ad agencies, and corporations. Field offices are data collection operations run by custom or syndicated research firms; however, these are rare today. Most custom and many syndicated research firms depend on field services for their survey data collection needs.

At Level 4 are the interviewers who actually collect the data. They typically work on a part-time, as-needed basis and may work for several different field service firms, depending on the amount of business the various field services have at any given time.

Measurement of the opinions, preferences, intentions, behavior, and so on of respondents or potential buyers is the goal of the research process. What potential buyers feel, think, do, and intend to do are the focus of the entire marketing research industry.

Corporate Marketing Research Departments

Because corporations are the final consumers and the initiators of most marketing research, they are the logical starting point in developing an understanding of how the research industry operates. Most large corporations have a marketing research department. Some companies are melding marketing research and strategic planning, whereas others are combining marketing research and the customer satisfaction department. Virtually all consumer package goods manufacturers of any size have a marketing research department.

corporate marketing research departments

Departments of major firms that produce or oversee collection and analysis of information relevant to marketing the firm's present or future products or services.

The average size of marketing research departments is quite small. One recent study found that only 15 percent of the service companies such as Federal Express and Delta Airlines had marketing research departments with more than 10 employees.[7] Twenty-three percent of the manufacturers' research departments had more than 10 employees. The size of research departments has been trending downward because of mergers and reengineering. Few research managers expect the staff reduction to continue. On an encouraging note, about half the research managers expect their budgets to continue to grow.[8] As marketing research departments shrink in size and budgets continue to grow, the implica-

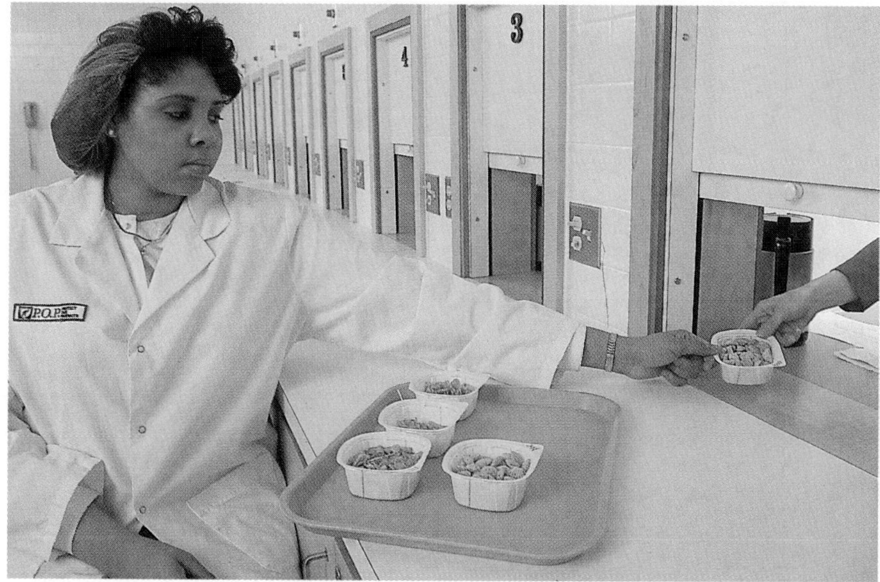

Most corporate marketing research departments are quite small. However, Kelloggs of Battle Creek, Michigan maintains an extensive test kitchen. SOURCE: © Seth Resnick/Stock Boston.

tion is clear. Companies are conducting less research internally and are outsourcing more to research suppliers.

Marketing research department managers believe that the industry is changing rapidly in the 1990s. Time pressures to "get information now" have significantly increased. The poverty of time also places demands on marketing researchers to communicate clearly and succinctly. Other changes voiced by the research managers are shown in Figure 3.2.

FIGURE 3.2

Marketing Research Department Managers' Perceptions of How the Research Industry Has Changed during the 1980s and 1990s

SOURCE: Jay Roth, "The Marketing Research Industry Monitor," *CASRO Journal* (1993), p. 25.

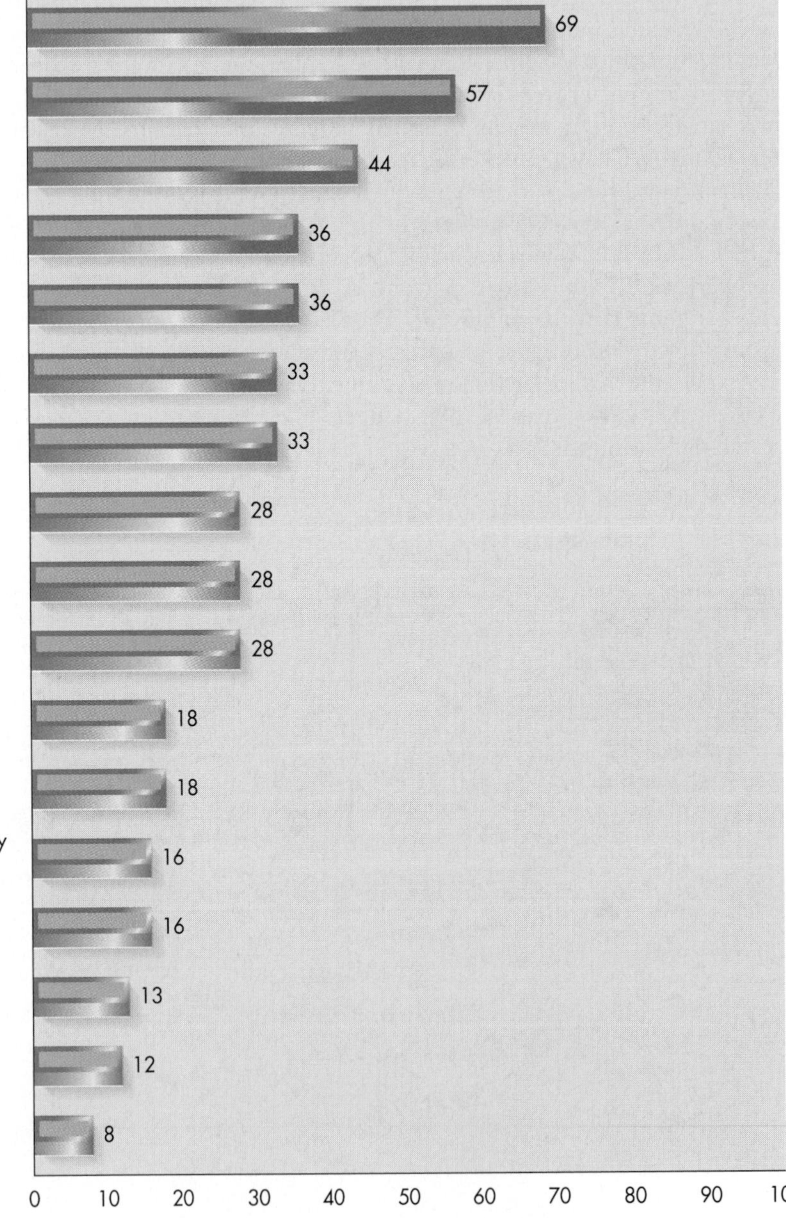

A Professional Researcher's Perspective

Stromberg-Carlson, based in Lake Mary, Florida, is the U.S. arm of GPT, a global telecommunications company. We design and build every component system in the digital communications network. We are best known for building switches, the highly sophisticated equipment that connects one telephone line to another.

At Stromberg-Carlson, the marketing group is responsible for market research, contract proposals and fulfillment, proposals and documentation, and, among other things, strategic planning. Importantly, we are also responsible for all communications, including advertising, public relations, sales promotion, and trade shows. All of our communications programs have their foundations in research.

Much of our marketing research in recent years has been devoted to finding out the industry's perception of our technical capabilities, how we compare with competitors, and our future capabilities. We depend on our marketing research to help us prioritize our markets.

Our positioning program grew out of basic market research into the Bell market. We studied each of the regional holding companies and developed extensive data on its networks. We learned that though the Bells were best known for their service to the large metropolitan centers, which require large switches, they also served suburban and rural areas, which might be an acceptable fit to the size of our switching system that typically handles 15,000 or fewer subscriber lines.

We found that more than 70 percent of the Bell company lines were connected to switching centers of fewer than 15,000 lines. These centers constituted about 85 percent of the end offices that the Bell companies operated. It was clear that the large suburban and rural service areas offered far greater potential than the smaller service areas dominated by corridors of major cities.

Using our extensive research as the base, we formulated a plan to focus on the Bell operating companies with the most extensive rural and suburban networks. Our plan took care to meet the needs of our current customers, the smaller independent telephone companies. It was our reputation with this group that we needed to build to a point in which our technology and products would be recognized industrywide.

Eventually, the Bell companies we had targeted began to take us seriously. We were given the chance to state our case and soon became the first company other than AT&T and Northern Telecom to win meaningful business from a Bell company. We succeeded in positioning ourselves as a first-rate supplier of small switching systems.[9] ■

How Corporate Marketing Research Departments Work

The previous discussion provided an overview of the corporate marketing research department. But what do marketing research departments actually do? Studies of the marketing research function in major corporations have determined that a wide variety of activities are performed. These activities are summarized in Table 3.2.[10]

Because different corporations have different information needs, marketing research departments are often quite different from company to company. Some departments, like the one at Delta Airlines, concern themselves almost exclusively with the analysis of internal operating data. Other departments, such as the one at American Airlines, are more concerned with collecting and analyzing customer and noncustomer data. Still other research departments, like the ones at Frito-Lay or Radio Shack, buy virtually all their survey and analysis work from outside suppliers. At the other end of the spectrum, companies such as Kraft General Foods, Procter & Gamble, Pillsbury, General Mills, and others, though purchasing many research services externally, have the capability to design and execute all phases of a marketing research project. The article in "A Professional Researcher's Perspective" on page 63 explains how one industrial goods manufacturer uses marketing research. The story is told by Roger Hall, director of marketing communications for Stromberg-Carlson.

Because we cannot deal with all types of marketing research departments, attention will be devoted to those found in the more sophisticated, larger companies. In these companies, research is a staff department and the director of the department will likely report to the top marketing executive. Although the research manager reports to a high-level marketing executive, most of the work of the department will be with product or brand managers, new product development managers, and other frontline managers. With the possible exception of various recurring studies that may be programmed into the firm's marketing information system, the marketing research department typically does not initiate studies. In fact, the research director may control little or no actual budget. Instead, line managers have funds in their budgets earmarked for research.

When brand managers perceive that they have a problem requiring research, they go to the marketing research department for help. Working with the marketing research manager or a senior analyst, they go through a series of steps that may lead to the design and execution of a marketing research project (see Chapter 2).

Jack Honomichl, a prolific writer about the marketing research industry and president of Marketing Aid Center, Incorporated, talks about the marketing research department of the future in "A Professional Researcher's Perspective" on page 66.

The Marketing Research Industry

Level 3. The Big Marketing Research Companies

Although the marketing research industry is characterized by hundreds of small firms, there are some giants in the industry. Table 3.3 shows 1993 sales for the 30 largest marketing research firms. The world's largest marketing research firm is D&B Marketing Information Services headquartered in Cham, Switzerland. The company is owned by Dun and Bradstreet Corporation of the United States. D&B Marketing's three largest subsidiaries also are American. The first is Nielsen Marketing Research, which was the largest research firm in America before being purchased by Dun and Bradstreet. Nielsen measures retail consumer

TABLE 3.2 **Research Activities of 587 Companies**

	DONE BY MARKET RESEARCH DEPT.	DONE BY ANOTHER DEPT.	DONE BY OUTSIDE FIRM	PERCENT DOING
A. Business/Economic and Corporate Research				
1. Industry/market characteristics and trends	66%	6%	14%	83%
2. Acquisitions/diversification studies	36	14	8	53
3. Market share analyses	64	6	11	79
4. Internal employee studies (morale, communication, etc.)	31	13	14	54
B. Pricing				
1. Cost analysis	31	24	3	60
2. Profit analysis	30	24	2	59
3. Price elasticity	31	12	5	45
4. Demand analysis:				
a. market potential	61	8	39	74
b. sales potential	53	12	4	69
c. sales forecasts	47	15	3	67
5. Competitive pricing analyses	46	16	4	63
C. Product				
1. Concept development and testing	50	6	17	68
2. Brand name generation and testing	30	5	14	38
3. Test market	34	8	10	45
4. Product testing of existing products	35	7	10	47
5. Packaging design studies	25	4	11	31
6. Competitive product studies	42	7	11	58
D. Distribution				
1. Plant/warehouse location studies	14	9	5	23
2. Channel performance studies	20	7	5	29
3. Channel coverage studies	18	6	5	26
4. Export and international studies	16	5	5	19
E. Promotion				
1. Motivation research	29	3	14	37
2. Media Research	30	9	22	57
3. Copy research	30	5	21	50
4. Advertising effectiveness	43	6	22	65
5. Competitive advertising studies	31	5	14	47
6. Public image studies	37	7	23	60
7. Sales force compensation studies	14	15	6	30
8. Sales force quota studies	14	14	6	26
9. Sales force territory structure	19	14	3	31
10. Studies of premiums, coupons, deals, etc.	28	5	7	36
F. Buying Behavior				
1. Brand preference	36	4	19	54
2. Brand attitudes	37	3	19	53
3. Product satisfaction	52	5	17	68
4. Purchase behavior	45	3	17	61
5. Purchase intentions	45	3	16	60
6. Brand awareness	41	3	20	59
7. Segmentation studies	45	3	18	60

Note that "Percent Doing" does not equal sum of "Done by" responses due to multiple responses in "Done by" categories.

SOURCE: Thomas C. Kinnear, *1988 Survey of Marketing Research* (Chicago: American Marketing Association, 1989), p. 43.

A Professional Researcher's Perspective

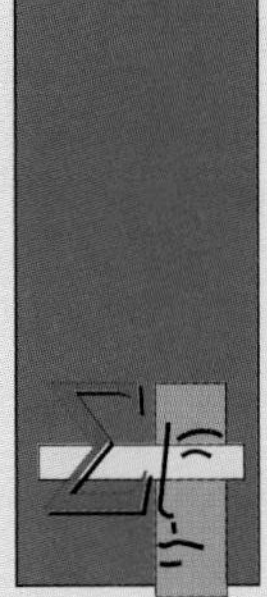

In enlightened companies, there will come to be a new corporate unit headed by a chief information officer. This CIO will rank right up there in the corporate hierarchy with the CFO and report to the CEO. This new corporate information unit will formalize top management's realization that timely, accurate information from the marketplace is a make-or-break proposition; what you don't know can kill you.

As differences between competing products narrow, profitable differentiation comes from an intimate (hopefully, real time) understanding of what's going on in the marketplace and the ability to capitalize on windows of opportunity. The CIO would coordinate all the corporation's information sources, distill and analyze the "findings," and continually brief the corporate CEO. The CIO's unit would have several deputy directors, depending on the corporation's main business activity. These could include the following:

- *Business intelligence officer:* Many corporations have one now. This unit's main function is to monitor closely anything a competitor does: personnel changes, new construction, financials, acquisitions, etc. Input comes most from public domain sources, and the concept is to know, and to try to understand, every move a competitor makes. A plant expansion, for example, might reveal plans a competitor has for a product.
- *Syndicated data source officer:* As appropriate for the corporation's industry, this unit would constantly monitor the syndicated marketing services available and make buy recommendations. Also, this unit would tap into corporate data sources (for example, factory shipments) and tailor them to meld with external data sources.
- *Management information systems officer:* This would be the same as what now exists in many corporations. Main function: systems and software that expedite the timely processing and distillation of data—from internal and external sources—and make them easily accessible to top operating management; makes relevant make or buy decisions regarding required software.
- *Customer satisfaction measurement officer:* Depending on the nature of the corporation's product or service, this would be a key member of the team. As top management realizes that the cost of obtaining new customers is very high, it is critical to prevent the loss of existing customers as much as possible.
- *Custom research officer:* This is a unit to design and conduct ad hoc research as required to obtain data unavailable from sources mentioned here. Test marketing would be the responsibility of this unit.[11] ■

purchases and related causal factors for manufacturers and retailers of grocery products, health and beauty aids, and other packaged durable goods. Nielsen Media Research, also part of Dun and Bradstreet, offers the Nielsen National Television Index, which measures television audience size and viewer characteristics. The third subsidiary is IMS International, Incorporated, which is a phar-

TABLE 3.3 Top 30 U.S. Research Organizations in 1993

1993 RANK	ORGANIZATION	HEADQUARTERS	TOTAL RESEARCH REVENUES (MILLIONS)	PERCENT REVENUES FROM OUTSIDE U.S.
1	D&B Marketing Information Services	Cham, Switzerland	$1,868.3	61.0%
2	Information Resources, Inc.	Chicago, IL	334.5	15.0
3	The Arbitron Co.	New York, NY	172.0	
4	Walsh International/PMSI	Phoenix, AZ	115.4	34.4
5	Westat, Inc.	Rockville, MD	113.1	
6	Maritz Marketing Research, Inc.	Saint Louis, MO	74.4	
7	The NPD Group	Port Washington, NY	66.0	23.8
8	NFO Research, Inc.	Greenwich, CT	51.9	
9	Elrick & Lavidge, Inc.	Atlanta, GA	47.1	
10	Market Facts, Inc.	Arlington Heights, IL	45.6	
11	The MARC Group	Las Colinas, TX	44.7	
12	Walker Group	Indianapolis, IN	38.1	1.9
13	Abt Associates, Inc.	Cambridge, MA	36.4	
14	MRB Group	London, England	35.0	
15	The National Research Group, Inc.	Los Angeles, CA	34.5	15.0
16	NOP Information Group	Livingston, NJ	33.0	
17	Intersearch Corp.	Horsham, PA	32.2	
18	The BASES Group	Covington, KY	31.0	5.0
19	Millward Brown, Inc.	Naperville, IL	29.0	
20	Opinion Research Corp.	Princeton, NJ	26.6	27.9
21	Burke Marketing Research	Cincinnati, OH	26.1	2.9
22	Roper Starch Worldwide, Inc.	Mamaroneck, NY	24.9	4.0
23	J. D. Power & Associates	Agoura Hills, CA	24.5	
24	Creative & Response Research Svcs.	Chicago, IL	23.8	
25	Research International USA	New York, NY	22.7	30.4
26	Louis Harris and Associates, Inc.	New York, NY	22.0	68.2
27	Chilton Research Services	Radnor, PA	22.0	
28	Mercer Mgt. Consulting/Decision Research	Lexington, MA	20.7	
29	Yankelovich Partners	Westport, CT	20.1	8.0
30	ASI Market Research	Stamford, CT	17.5	

SOURCE: "The Honomichl 50," *Marketing News* (June 6, 1994), p. H4.

maceutical industry marketing research organization. D&B Marketing Information Services, and Nielsen in particular, are growing rapidly in the global marketplace.

Level 3. Custom Research Firms

Custom, or ad hoc, marketing research firms, as noted earlier, are primarily in the business of executing custom, one-of-a-kind marketing research projects for corporate clients. If the corporation has a new product or service idea, packaging idea, ad concept, new pricing strategy, product reformulation, or other related marketing problems or opportunities that need to be dealt with, the custom research firm is the place to go for research help.

custom, or ad hoc, marketing research firms
Research companies that carry out customized marketing research to address specific projects for corporate clients.

There are thousands of custom marketing research firms in this country. However, the overwhelming majority of these firms are small, with billings of less than $1 million and fewer than 10 employees. They may serve clients only in their local areas. They may or may not specialize by type of industry or type of research.

Global Marketing Research

The passage of the North American Free Trade Agreement (NAFTA) in 1993 has focused increased attention on conducting marketing research in Mexico. About $5.5 million a year is spent on marketing research in Mexico. The Mexican subsidiary of Nielsen Marketing Research is, by far, the largest marketing research firm operating in Mexico, controlling about one-half of total research expenditures. Founded in 1967, Nielsen Mexico is a conglomerate with about 386 employees, plus interviewing staff.

In addition to continuous audits of product movement through samples or panels of retail stores (food, drug, liquor, etc.), Nielsen does surveys, ad hoc and omnibus, and operates consumer samples or panels whose members keep diaries of all their grocery purchases. Like all other Mexican research firms, it is headquartered in Mexico City.

After Nielsen, there is a sharp drop-off. The two largest survey research firms—Asesoria e Investigaciones Gamma and IMOP–Gallup Mexico—have annual revenues in the $4 million to $5 million range, and from there on a firm doing $1.5 million to $2 million a year is considered big in Mexico.

One of the first things U.S. researchers operating in Mexico will have to face up to is that they cannot rely on telephone and mail service for data collection. Most data collection is usually door-to-door and concentrated in three or four of the largest cities (markets), namely Matamoros, Monterrey, Guadalajara, and Mexico City, which—with a metropolitan population of 17 million—is the world's second largest city (after Tokyo) and home to one out of every five Mexicans.

Mexican research firms either have their own interviewers in such major markets or make use of local field services there. Even with diary panels, the normal operating procedure is to work with respondent households door-to-door, with drop-off and pickup, and to ensure compliance with data collection requests.[12] ■

Like other astute marketers, custom marketing research firms try to position themselves to differentiate their services from those of their competitors. Lynn Lin, president of Burke International of Covington, Kentucky, one of America's largest marketing research organizations, describes how he developed the BASES system (ranked number 18 in size) in "A Professional Researcher's Perspective" on pages 70–71.

Level 3. Syndicated Service Firms

syndicated service research firms

Companies that collect, package, and sell the same general market research data to many firms.

In sharp contrast to the custom research company example, **syndicated service research firms** collect and sell the same marketing research data to many firms. Anyone willing to pay the price can buy the data these firms collect, package, and sell. Syndicated service firms are relatively few in number and, in comparison to custom research firms, are relatively large. The four largest marketing research firms in America are primarily syndicated services. Syndicated service firms deal mostly with media audience and product movement data. Syndicated service firms are based on serving information needs that many companies have in common. For example, many companies advertise on network television. Their problem is to select shows that reach their target customers most efficiently. They need information on the size and demographic composition of the audiences for different television programs. It would be extremely inefficient for each firm to collect these data individually.

Audience Data Syndicated Services Two companies, Nielsen Media Research and Arbitron, collect television audience data and sell it to all those interested. The buyers of the data secure higher-quality information than they could afford if they had to collect it themselves, and they obtain it at a fraction of the cost.

audience data syndicated services

Companies that collect, package, and sell general data on media audiences to many firms.

Product Movement Data Syndicated Services The second major area of marketing research information where syndicated service firms maintain a strong position is in product movement data. Nielsen, IMS, and Information Resources enjoy high visibility in this area. **Product movement data syndicated services** are in the business of compiling and selling data that tell their subscribers how well their products and their competitors' products are selling at the retail level.

product movement data syndicated services

Companies that collect, package, and sell retail or wholesale sales data to many firms.

The traditional Nielsen Marketing Research service was built around retail grocery and drugstore shelf audit data where as Information Resources and a new Nielsen service depend on grocery store scanner data. In its traditional service, Nielsen actually sent auditors to do a national sample of drugstores to count products on the shelf. Today all of Nielsen's store data is gathered by scanner. Scanner-based research will be discussed in detail in Chapter 8.

Nielson Household Services Hand-Held Scanner. SOURCE: Courtesy of Nielson Household Services.

FEATURES

- User friendly
- Personalized; names of household members, stores shopped
- Personal prompts

FUNCTIONS

- Scanning shopping trips
- Transmitting information via telephone
- Responding to "bar-coded' surveys

INFORMATION CAPTURED FOR EACH SHOPPING TRIP

- Store or outlet where panelist shopped
- Age and sex of primary and secondary shopper
- Date of purchase
- Universal product code
- Number of units purchased
- Price paid
- Use of any consumer-perceived deals
- Total dollars spent per trip

A Professional Researcher's Perspective

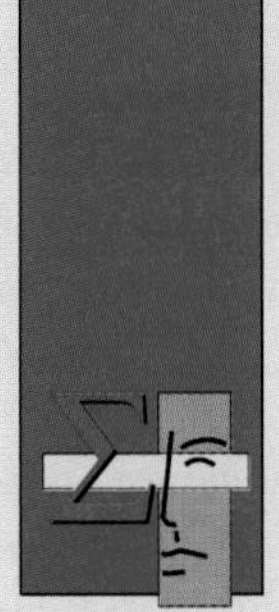

In the mid-1970s, Booz-Allen & Hamilton realized that there was a growing need for early evaluating of new products' sales potential prior to test marketing. Thus, I decided to use data from AdTel and Market Audits, other units within Booz-Allen & Hamilton, to

1. Calibrate the empirical weights of consumer purchase intention to a behavior conversion factor.
2. Quantify the effect of advertising and promotional supports on trial, repeat, purchase cycle, and purchase units.
3. Use the dynamic behavioral volumetric model that Gerald Eskin, Channing Stowell, and I worked out at Pillsbury under the watchful guidance of our boss, Dudley Ruch.

When BASES was launched in November 1977, the system consisted of

BASES I concept test to estimate early trial potential.

BASES II concept/in-home use test to evaluate all sales components plus sales volume for the first three years under each marketing scenario.

BASES III in-store test executed in actual supermarket or large drugstore with final packaging and commercial to evaluate the sales potential, usually used as a final disaster check prior to national or test market introduction.

BASES IV in-market monitoring and forecasting (also called Tel-Trac and now called Launch Control in the United States) to evaluate initial launch performance, sales effect of early marketing events, and the forecasting or simulations of the various marketing plans, and

BASES Awareness Estimation Model to estimate total brand awareness based on clients' marketing plans.

The uniqueness and flexibility of this system as compared with others at the time was that BASES could evaluate a new product's potential very early in the development process before a large investment on final packaging, final commercial copy, and final product formulation was spent. This is critical since after the BASES III stage, almost every investment for the new product

Level 4. Field Service Firms

field service firms
Companies that only collect survey data for corporate clients or research firms.

A true **field service firm** does nothing but collect survey data—no research design, no analysis. Field service firms are data collection specialists who collect data on a subcontract basis for corporate marketing research departments, custom research firms, syndicated service research firms, and ad agency research departments.

The following description of the sequence of activities undertaken by a typical field service company provides a good idea of how these firms operate:

Client Contact — Client custom research firm, syndicated research firm, corporate or ad agency research department) alerts field service firm that it has a particular type of study (telephone interview, mail interview, etc.), except advertising and in-market promotion spending are consummated. At this point it is nearly impossible to reverse the launching momentum that has been built up over the years of development.

Many new BASES services were also developed. These include

- PASS (Positioning Analysis & Segmentation Summary)
- SOVA (Source of Volume Analysis)
- BASES LX for five-types of line extensions
- BASES Restager for relaunch of existing product
- PLAN BASES (or BASES PLANNER) for evaluating the possible risk of entering into a new category before any consumer survey
- PRE-BASES to screen and evaluate early new product concepts
- Extension of BASES into durable goods and services.

Today, BASES enjoys a very significant position in the world of pretest market forecasting. In fact, it has been the world leader since the mid-1980s, with experience in 37 countries. Based on industry surveys and our own information, it appears that BASES currently has about 60 percent market share in the world's pretest market business.

BASES has been expanding, and will continue to expand, the system in two directions: new countries and new product categories. The developing countries/regions such as Pakistan, the Middle East, and Eastern Europe are of immediate interest. New product categories that we have been concentrating on lately are cigarettes, alcoholic beverages, automobiles (forecast from concept and car clinic data), and many other durable goods and services. Also, products and/or services that require forecasting potential subscription rates such as new magazines are of particular interest at the moment.

Increasingly, BASES is becoming a marketing consultant that clients rely upon to optimize their product mix, marketing plans, and strategic direction. This means that database maintenance, continual analysis of the effect of marketing variables, and training of consultants are of utmost importance. My conclusion is that a good model is essential for accurate forecasting, but quality data are still the king.[13] ■

	seeking a particular type of respondent (e.g., women with children between ages three and eight who have served a canned spaghetti product to their children in the past 30 days), for a particular date, requiring a certain number of interviews for a certain number of days
Estimate Cost Bid	The field service indicates that it can or cannot handle the job; it may be asked to provide a bid or cost estimate at this point
Interviewer Recruiting	The field service lines up interviewers from its pool to work on the particular job

Interviewer Training	The day the job is to begin, a briefing or training session is held to acquaint interviewers with the requirements of the particular job or questionnaire
Interviewing Status Reports	Daily reports are made to the client regarding progress, number of interviews completed, and costs, which permit the client to determine whether the job is on schedule and within budget; the field service can advise its client of problems in any areas
Quality Control	Interviewers bring in their completed assignments and the interviews are edited and validated (editing refers to checking interviews to see that they were completed correctly; validation entails calling a certain percentage of each interviewer's respondents to determine whether the interview took place and if it was done in the prescribed manner)
Ship to Client	Finally, the completed, edited, and validated interviews are shipped to the client

The field service provides interviewing and supervisory service. Most custom research firms rely on field services because it is uneconomical for them to handle the work themselves. There are too many cities to cover, and it is always uncertain as to which cities will be needed over time. On the other hand, field service firms in particular cities maintain a steady work flow by having many research firms and corporate and ad agency research departments as their clients.

Until about 20 years ago, most field service firms were operated by women out of their homes. Their major asset was typically a pool of a dozen or so interviewers available for assignment. Although field service firms of this type still exist, the trend is toward larger, more professional, and better equipped organizations.

The major field service firm of today has a permanent office. It probably has one or more permanent mall test centers, focus group facilities, a central location telephone interviewing facility, other specialized facilities and equipment, and possibly even WATS (wide area telephone service) lines for interviewing throughout the country from a single location. Another recent trend in the field service business is the emergence of multicity operations.

Specialized Service and Support Firms

specialized service or support firms

Companies that handle a specific facet of research, such as data processing or statistical analysis, for many corporate clients.

Finally, in the marketing research industry there are a number of very **specialized service or support firms**. These are firms that provide various types of support services to marketing research and other firms.

Data Processing First are those firms that offer various computer and data processing services. These firms take completed questionnaires and handle all editing and coding, do computer data entry, and run all tabulations and other analysis required by their clients.

Sample Generation A second realm where specialized service firms are found is in the sample generation area. Firms such as Survey Sampling, Inc., of Westport, Connecticut, provide samples of households and businesses to their clients. They maintain massive databases with information on millions of households and businesses from which they generate samples to their clients' specifications.

Secondary Data A third area of specialized service to the research industry is provided by firms providing access to specialized databases via computer. For example, no company needs to purchase all U.S. census tapes when it needs a demographic profile of a single metro area. The secondary data firms provide access to the data via on-line computer networks or provide the desired data on floppy diskettes so their clients can process it on their own PCs.

Statistical Analysis With the growing use of sophisticated statistical techniques, a new type of marketing research support firm, the data analysis specialist, has emerged. Firms such as Sophisticated Data Research in Atlanta provide sophisticated consulting services to marketing research firms and corporate marketing research departments regarding the selection and use of various statistical techniques for the analysis of marketing research data.

Other In addition to the four types of firms just discussed, a number of other assorted and miscellaneous types of specialized service or support firms are found in the marketing research industry. Each has found its niche through the cultivation of expertise in a very specific facet of the marketing research process where researchers are likely to seek outside assistance.

Ad Agency Research Department

Ad agency marketing research departments are a cross between the corporate marketing research department and the custom marketing research firm. They are similar to corporate marketing research departments in that they are parts of organizations (ad agencies) whose major business is something other than the sale of marketing research services. They are similar to custom research firms in the sense that they also do research for external clients.

ad agency marketing research departments

Departments of advertising agencies that produce or oversee research to support the development and evaluation of advertising for the agency's clients.

A check of the *Standard Directory of Advertising Agencies*[14] shows that over 93 percent of all agencies with billings of more than $10 million have a marketing research department. The major use of research by ad agencies is to support the development and evaluation of advertising for their clients. Different ideas or approaches to ad campaigns and rough, simulated commercials are tested. Various cuts of finished commercials are frequently evaluated, and ongoing campaigns are monitored via research. Although much ad agency research is oriented toward testing ads at various stages, agency research departments may initiate more fundamental types of research. For example, the agency may recommend that the client do market segmentation research through the agency to better identify advertising audiences so as to assist the agency in selecting media and the message.

An example of an ambitious form of basic research undertaken by an advertising agency is the annual lifestyle survey conducted by the DDB Needham Worldwide agency. In this survey, a representative national sample of several thousand consumers is interviewed. Each is administered a very lengthy questionnaire with detailed questions regarding his activities, interests, opinions, buying habits, and demographics. The results are compiled and translated into profiles of several lifestyle market segments. The agency has even gone so far as to hire actors to portray the "typical" person from each lifestyle segment. These videotapes are reviewed by the agency's copy writers and other creative personnel to help them gain a mental picture of the consumers they are communicating to for clients such as McDonald's and Bud Lite.

The scope of marketing research at some of the largest advertising agencies is changing. Traditionally, advertising agencies conducted "endless copy tests and endless group discussions." Today the focus is switching from evaluating output (finished advertisements) to guiding input (overall strategy development).

Most ad agencies (and their research departments) are relatively small. They, therefore, lean heavily on outside contractors to execute all or major parts of studies. The agency research people often work with their corporate clients to design the study and then contract out the interviewing to field service firms and data processing and tabulation to a tab house.[15] The agency research people complete the process by preparing a report. Another approach might involve farming out the entire study, once research objectives have been agreed upon, to a custom research firm, depending on the scope, complexity, and specialized nature of the project.

Other Organizations and Individuals

Finally, various other organizations and individuals, although not truly part of the marketing research industry, must be mentioned because of their special contribution to it. Included here are various government agencies at the federal, state, and local levels; university bureaus of business and economic research; individual university professors who serve as marketing research consultants; research units associated with various industry groups, database providers, and others. In the case of all but the university professors, these institutions serve primarily as sources of extremely valuable and useful data for the marketing research industry. Those university professors, primarily those in marketing departments, who also are marketing research consultants, provide a pool of sophisticated talent that is tapped on an as-needed basis by corporate marketing research departments, companies with no internal marketing research capabilities, custom research firms, and others. Database providers such as CompuServe, America Online, and Prodigy enable researchers to tap vast stores of secondary data. Moreover, the Internet provides data and software for countless research projects around the world.

The role of various government agencies is important, though they serve primarily as providers of secondary data. Specific examples of agencies and the types of data they provide are presented and discussed in Chapter 5.

The Growing Role of Strategic Partnering and Global Research

Marketing research is becoming a team effort. Under pressure from clients and the cost of increasingly sophisticated technology, research companies are forming strategic alliances, sharing data or capabilities as a cost-effective way to grow. The trend toward **strategic partnering**—even with competitors—will continue, industry executives say.

strategic partnering

Two or more marketing research firms with unique skills and resources form an alliance to offer a new service for clients, provide strategic support for each firm, or in some other manner create mutual benefits.

> "The '90s are the decade of the strategic alliance agreement," said Tom Daley, president of Spectra Marketing, Chicago. "The technology is so expensive and leadership positions so vulnerable that it's the way business has to go. It used to be that when you introduced a new [research] product or service, it was two or three years before everyone matched it. Now Nielsen can have it in the marketplace next week. So everyone's asking, 'How can I get smarter faster?' And strategic alliances are the answer."[16]

Spectra, a geodemographic research company founded in 1988, has been built through a series of strategic alliances. It has deals with several major companies, including Information Resources, Incorporated (IRI), Claritas Corporation, Market Facts, and Donnelly Marketing's Carol Wright unit. IRI has been one of the most active in forming alliances, having set deals with Arbitron Company, Citicorp, VideOCart, and Simmons Marketing Research in 1994. The latter partnership combines IRI's data on who buys what in the United States with *Simmons Magazine* readership data. This will enable the partnership to develop indices about what products appeal to magazine readers.[17] "In 1979 we introduced BehaviorScan on an investment of a few million dollars. You couldn't even begin to think of duplicating that system for anywhere near that cost," said IRI Chairman–CEO Gian Fulgoni. "The cost of doing business and the complexity of the business are driving the trend to strategic alliances."[18] Other recent examples of strategic partnering include

- Nielsen Marketing Research USA bought an interest in Market Simulations and then joined GTE Interactive Services to create and test Retail Alliance, and integrated service for retailers and manufacturers.
- Axiom Corporation, Conway, Arizona, formed a research and development alliance with Young & Rubicam, New York, providing the agency with database management services and direct marketing software.
- Market Facts, Chicago, and the M/A/R/C Group, Las Colinas, Texas, formed a strategic alliance covering consumer mail surveys. Market Facts will buy the mail panel operation of a M/A/R/C subsidiary, merging it with its larger, 360,000-household panel. M/A/R/C can use the combined panel for 10 years, but the two companies will design studies and analyze panel data independently.

There is no doubt that strategic partnering will continue to be an important trend in the marketing research industry throughout the 1990s.

In addition to research firms forming strategic partnerships, marketing research suppliers and other clients also are forming alliances. Typically, marketing research firms have operated in an environment in which client business is obtained on a project-by-project basis, through either competitive bidding or negotiated pricing. For many research clients, the standard procedure is to obtain multiple bids for each project. The reputation and quality of the research firm's work are considered, as well as price. Although a given firm may be used repeatedly, each project is treated as a stand-alone transaction, and future business is always at risk to a more competitive firm.

In a strategic partnership, the client and research firm work together on a forward-looking and ongoing basis. A partnering relationship would establish a defined set of activities for which a research firm would provide services without bidding project-by-project. Services provided may include data collection, product or customer tracking systems, or any research activity for which the firm may have special expertise or productive capability.

About half of all large marketing research departments engage in strategic partnering with research suppliers.[19] Partnering is most common in service companies and consumer package goods manufacturers. The advantages of this type of partnering is that it allows for better coordination of effort and increased productivity as the supplier develops intimate knowledge of the research user's needs and its customers. The research firm, in turn, can concentrate resources directly on the client's projects rather than on selling and making proposals.

Global Marketing Research Trends

Strategic partnering is not just an American phenomenon but is occurring all around the globe. The predominant buyers of global marketing research are the world's big multinational companies. As their organizations and strategies become increasingly global, they will require an ongoing strategic counseling relationship rather than one characterized by a string of individual projects. Research suppliers that hope to capitalize on global strategic partnerships will have to have offices in a number of countries (or at least a local presence). The suppliers also must have the personnel and expertise to conduct global research studies combined with a high level of technical expertise in the home office. Finally, a global marketing research supplier must have thorough knowledge in global marketing. Phillip Barnard, chairman of Research International, Great Britain's largest marketing research firm, discusses several trends he foresees in the following "Global Marketing Research" feature.

Summary

This chapter focuses on the types of firms that form the marketing research industry and the functions they perform. The research industry may be categorized as follows:

1. Corporate marketing research departments—marketing research departments in major firms such as Kraft General Foods and Ralston Purina.
2. Ad agency research departments—marketing research departments in advertising agencies such as J. Walter Thompson and Grey Advertising.
3. Custom or ad hoc research firms—firms that handle customized marketing research projects addressing specific problems for individual clients. Syndicated service firms—firms that collect data of general interest. Anyone can purchase the information. These are prominent in the media audience field and scanner data research.
4. Field service firms—data collection firms.

The structure of the research industry may be viewed as having four levels: the users of research data, ad agencies, custom and syndicated marketing research firms, and field service firms. A key trend in the research industry today is strategic partnering. Global trends include global partnering, enhanced tracking studies, more Total Quality research, greater qualitative/quantitative integration, and new forms of gathering marketplace information.

Global Marketing Research

Marketing research practice is evolving and maturing around the globe. In this period of change, there are new opportunities both for those in research companies and for corporate researchers. Expected global developments include:

1. *Enhanced tracking studies*—Tracking studies refer to measuring a phenomenon at different points in time (i.e., customer satisfaction, corporate image, advertising recall). Enhancement to tracking services will occur in at least three respects:
   - more multicountry tracking on a comparable basis
   - more and/or different measures in trackers; especially more emphasis on various types of brand equity measurement to be embedded in "advertising effectiveness" tracking
   - wider scope of tracking studies; we already track eight different areas of marketplace information for our clients:
   - advertising effectiveness
   - business efficiency
   - brand equity
   - corporate imagery
   - brand purchase/usage
   - product quality
   - brand imagery
   - customer satisfaction
2. *Business control monitors*—One particular form of tracking that we believe will become increasingly important is the "business control monitor" (BCM). This form of research service helps clients in the overall management of their businesses by tracking behavioral measures of efficiency or quality. Examples include:
   - the speed of transaction or response (e.g., serving time in a fast food outlet, speed of letter delivery, waiting time in a bank)
   - physical fulfillment (e.g., percentage of failures or damaged goods, reliability of durables)
   - after-sales performance (e.g., complaints handling; how many and how long to solve)
3. *Total Quality measures*—The adoption of Total Quality Management (TQM) by many major organizations brings the need for measurement to monitor its degree of success, both initially and via incremental improvement over time. As the concept of quality delivery becomes more widespread and is given political encouragement, new kinds of organizations will emerge as users of the services of market research companies. Typically, these new clients will have many thousands of employees and customers. They will need to measure, among internal as well as external customers, the effectiveness of their communications, customer satisfaction, and the overall effectiveness of their service delivery.

Apart from major corporations in the fully commercial sector, research companies will increasingly be working with central and local government (e.g., education,

continues

health, and Social Security providers); public utilities; and other regulated industries.

4. *Greater qualitative/quantitative integration*—A welcome fusion of these often separate traditions is being driven by clients' demands for business sector specialists to handle their research needs. Specialists in automotive research, the pharmaceutical market, or telecommunications will be expected to offer the full research toolbox. The most successful will be fluent and comfortable in both the qualitative and quantitative environment, integrating the full range of research inputs against the background of their own specialist knowledge and experience of the client's business sector.
5. *Survey research–marketplace information*—Taking a leaf from the Japanese book of gathering marketplace information, there will be greater integration of our "normal" survey-based data with such other market information sources as dealer visits and interviews, store observation, and personal contact with customers at retail outlets. In Japan, client marketing management rather than research companies tends to conduct such investigations.
6. *Corporate research opportunities*—Company researchers, particularly in the United States, are often seen by their top management as reactive and project-oriented, rather than the strategic thinking agents of change management would like them to be. The growing recognition of brands as a company's key assets gives the corporate researcher a new opportunity to move center stage as "guardian" of the company's brand equity. The role would be somewhat analogous to that of the advertising agency planner and would draw heavily on brand monitoring and similar inputs from the corporation's regular information flows, databases, and decision support systems.[20] ■

Key Terms

custom, or ad hoc, marketing research firms
syndicated service research firms
audience data syndicated services
product movement data syndicated services
field service firms
specialized service or support firms
ad agency marketing research departments
strategic partnering

Review and Discussion Questions

1. Compare and contrast custom and syndicated marketing research firms.
2. What is the role of field services in marketing research?
3. Discuss several types of support service firms in the research industry.
4. Describe the levels of the marketing research industry.
5. List several key characteristics of corporate marketing research departments.

6. Discuss the different "product offerings" of syndicated service firms.
7. Explain the role of ad agency research departments.
8. Define strategic partnering. Why has it become so prominent in the marketing research industry in America and globally?
9. Discuss the trends in global research and their impact on American research suppliers.

CASE 3.1

Anchor Marketing Research

Anchor Marketing Research is a custom marketing research firm in Detroit. Allen Mayberry, president, is concerned about a new type of strategic partnering that is occurring within the marketing research industry. Traditional strategic partnering occurs when two marketing research firms with unique skills and resources form an alliance to offer a new service for clients, provide strategic support for each partner, or in some other manner create mutual benefits. In the new form of strategic partnering, a large research user, such as Kraft General Foods, decides to work closely with a very limited number of custom and syndicated research firms rather than getting competitive bids from a large number of firms. Once a partnership is established, it is quite difficult for a new firm to break the bond between research supplier and user.

Anchor was founded in 1990 and has quickly grown to a $12-million-a-year firm. The firm's primary competitive advantage is its expertise in multivariate statistical techniques and mathematical modeling for new products. Allen Mayberry is concerned that despite Anchor's talents, it may have limited opportunity to showcase them because of the new type of strategic partnering. Currently, the firm is not engaged in strategic partnering. Allen decided that the best way to assess the situation is to do marketing research. Anchor interviewed 100 marketing research directors from large research user organizations. The sample consisted of consumer products companies—54 percent; service organizations—36 percent; and business-to-business firms—10 percent. The findings were as follows:

PARTNERING TRENDS (BASE = 100)	%
Partnering more now	59
Will partner more in future	38
Other companies will partner more	73

Three-fourths of all firms claim to be doing some kind of partnering. It is widespread among all types and sizes of companies, though particularly strong among the larger organizations. For those that are not partnering with their research firms, respondents say they don't need to or mention cost considerations.

REASONS NOT TO PARTNER (BASE = 25)	%
No need	60
Bid out projects	28
Depends on cost	20

The 25 firms not partnering are more sensitive to cost considerations, and they worry slightly more about giving the research firm too much power. The same does not seem to be true among the ones that are partnering, however.

ADVANTAGES OF PARTNERING (BASE = 75)	%
Know our needs	51
Replicate studies	45
Consistency—ongoing relationships	43
Saves money—more value	33
Faster turnaround	32
Provide expertise	21

RATINGS OF PARTNERING BENEFITS (5 = AGREE STRONGLY)

BENEFIT	NOW PARTNERING MEAN (BASE = 75)	NOT PARTNERING MEAN (BASE = 25)
Helps a research firm learn about the client's business	4.6	4.4
Makes it more efficient and simple to work with a research firm	4.7	3.8
Helps a research firm provide better design and analysis	4.3	3.8
Helps develop standard procedures and norms	4.3	3.7

Reasons to partner center on making client researchers more efficient and effective—research firms know their needs and can replicate studies, be more consistent, give faster turnaround, and provide expertise. Also, one-third of respondents believe they are getting a better value, so partnering works during budget crunches.

RATINGS OF PARTNERING DRAWBACKS (5 = AGREE STRONGLY)

DRAWBACK	NOW PARTNERING MEAN (BASE = 75)	NOT PARTNERING MEAN (BASE = 25)
Risks having the research firm overcharge the client	2.8	3.9
Risks making the research firm too powerful at the client company	2.8	3.4
Cannot work because the client and research firm have different goals	1.8	1.6

HOW PARTNERING WORKS (BASE = 75)	%
Informal agreement	71
Limited number of suppliers	37
Don't bid out	9
Contract	7

Very few clients and research firms have formal contracts—only 7 percent of those partnering. Most have an informal agreement or have decided on their own to limit the number of research firms with which they work.[21]

1. You are Allen Mayberry. Would you enter into strategic partnering?
2. If so, how would you go about it?

CASE 3.2

American Express Creates a New Product—the Optima True Grace Card

Following a yearlong effort to come up with a product that stands out in the increasingly competitive credit card wars, American Express Co. believe it finally has found the answer: the Optima True Grace Card. The card, developed with the help of close to 4,000 consumer interviews, is a response to complaints that most credit cards do not have grace periods. Although cardholders who pay their entire bills immediately don't pay any interest, users who carry balances generally are charged as soon as they make new purchases. The True Grace Card is far more generous: Its interest period won't start until 25 days after the close of each monthly account cycle, even if the cardholder carries over the balance.

The company's first credit card—the original Optima Card that was launched in 1987—was a disaster. Weak credit standards led to massive loan write-offs as well as skepticism about American Express's ability to compete in the tough world of credit cards. But experts say the company has no choice but to try again: Amex users accounted for just 19.5 percent of $439 billion in U.S. charges on Visa, MasterCard, and Amex cards in 1993. That's down from a 32.5 percent share of the $77 billion charged in 1983.

The new effort began during a meeting of American Express's top credit card executives in June 1993. It was there that Mr. Golub, Amex chief executive officer, pronounced that although the original Optima Card had recovered, the company had to develop a whole series of new cards. A couple of weeks later, Brian C. Kleinberg, a 37-year-old marketing executive, assembled a four-person team that quickly generated 15 potential card ideas. During August, the team conducted a dozen focus groups in New Jersey, Chicago, and San Francisco, where the original ideas were refined, and the number of ideas grew to more than 30. Further quantitative studies helped the team zero in on the "True Grace" concept.

During spring 1994, marketing executives began developing promotional materials, and the text was tested on groups of consumers. Kleinberg says the name of the new card grew out of a consumer's comment at one of those sessions. American Express executives readily agree that the Optima True Grace Card will not have the widespread appeal of the company's flagship charge card. Recognizing that American Express can no longer rely on a single card, Phillip Reise, president of American Express's Cardmember Financial Services, says, "This is not the silver bullet, but there aren't any silver bullets anymore."[22]

1. American Express did not conduct its research using its own personnel. What type or types of firms probably conducted the research?
2. Do you think that American Express would be a good candidate for strategic partnering? Why or why not?
3. One of the chapter's "Global Marketing Research" features mentioned the growth of tracking studies. How might American Express use tracking research?

CHAPTER 4

Ethics in Marketing Research

LEARNING OBJECTIVES

1. To understand the nature of ethics and the levels of moral development.
2. To become aware of some of the factors involved in making ethical decisions.
3. To review some unethical practices found among marketing research suppliers.
4. To gain insight into unethical practices among research clients.
5. To examine unethical practices among marketing research field services.
6. To become familiar with respondents' rights.
7. To review contemporary ethics in the marketing research industry.
8. To discover methods by which the level of professionalism in marketing research can be raised.

In the wildly insecure world of movie executives, Joseph Farrell soothes anxieties. National Research Group, Inc. (NRG), the company he founded and runs, dominates the field of motion-picture research. And such research plays an ever-increasing role in guiding the industry. NRG generates streams of data on everything from which films moviegoers plan to see to which movie ads are most effective. Almost every major film is screened several times in front of test audiences recruited by NRG, which then gathers, quantifies, and analyzes viewer reaction.

NRG research helps determine whether a movie gets promoted a lot or hardly at all. Film endings may be changed and scenes eliminated based on NRG findings. The smash hit *The Bodyguard,* for instance, was reworked to include more action footage with Kevin Costner after preview screening data from NRG showed that young males were less enthusiastic about the fim than were their female counterparts, according to the movie's director, Mick Jackson. The movie went on to gross more than $400 million for Warner Bros.

SOURCE: © David Young-Wolff/PhotoEdit.

Farrell's numbers seem to give Hollywood a rare solid scale of measurement, a touchstone of objectivity in a business where big financial decisions are often made on the basis of hype, sizzle, and politics.

"You nurture a project for a year or 18 months, and then you go to the first screening, and the lights come up and nobody looks at you. Everybody's looking at Joe Farrell," says Brandon Tartikoff, former chairman of Paramount Pictures.

But the relationship between NRG and the studios is a delicate and ambiguous one. Ask studio executives or movie producers if they are dependent on Farrell and they frequently run for cover. Many directors and writers quietly resent the sway that such a technocrat has gained over their creations. And even Hollywood tycoons want people to believe that they treat a movie like art rather than like a new brand of toothpaste. So Farrell and NRG keep a very low profile. In many ways, the company is Hollywood's little secret.

But there are claims that Farrell has been keeping a secret of his own. About two dozen former NRG employees—ranging from hourly workers to senior officials—say that the company's research data are sometimes falsified by Farrell or others at the firm. They say that they have witnessed or taken part in the doctoring or outright manufacturing of information that NRG sells to Hollywood studios, which pay NRG up to several million dollars a year.

"Joe described the changes as 'little white lies,'" says Eric Williams, a former NRG employee who analyzed movie-screening results. Two other former NRG employees say Farrell himself fabricated data or ordered it done. Several people say Farrell told them he manipulated data at the behest of studio officials or filmmakers.

Beside the allegations about Farrell, numerous former employees say data were fabricated by subordinates because of the sheer pressure to generate numbers quickly. NRG's corporate culture was such, they say, that when pushed to the wall, some employees felt that it was in their interest to fudge numbers rather than force NRG to tell a studio that a job wouldn't be finished on time. The former head of NRG's telephone research operation, responsible for the company's phone surveys, says she complained about doctoring by NRG employees to Farrell's co-chairperson, Catherine Paura, but no action was taken.

Why hoodwink Hollywood? The former employees and others cite several possible reasons besides tight deadlines. Sometimes, movie-screening scores have been manipulated upward because Farrell didn't want to be the bearer of bad news, and insecure executives want to feel as if they are making some progress, the former employees say. Other times, the doctoring may help justify changes that Farrell or his mogul clients previously suggested in a film, they say.[1] ■

Where does one draw the line between ethical and unethical decision making? How can marketing research employees learn to make ethical decisions? What are some of the ethical issues facing research suppliers and field service firms? What are the rights of a respondent? These are some of the questions that will be answered in Chapter 4.

Developing a Philosophy of Ethics

Ethics Defined

ethics
Moral principles or values generally governing the conduct of an individual or group.

morals
Judgments concerning the goodness or badness of human action or character.

Ethics refers to moral principles or values generally governing the conduct of an individual or group. **Morals** are often described in terms of good or bad. Good and bad can be thought of in different terms, including effective and ineffective, respectively. A good market research interviewer makes or exceeds the assigned quota. If the interviewer promises that the respondent will receive a free gift for participating in the survey (when the interviewer knows full well that no gift will be forthcoming), is she still a good interviewer? What if the interview enabled the interviewer to exceed quota at a below average cost-per-interview?

A second connotation of good or bad is deviant versus conforming behavior. Bad and good also are used to express the distinction between criminal and law-abiding behavior. And finally, the terms are defined by religions, which vary markedly on what is good or bad. A Muslim who eats pork would be bad, as would a fundamentalist Christian who drinks whiskey.

Levels of Moral Development

A marketing researcher must consider various ethical implications in the decision-making process. As you can easily see, ethics is very situation specific and time oriented. Nevertheless, all of us must have an ethical base that will serve us both in the world of research and in our personal lives. Moral development of individuals can be defined as having reached one of three levels: preconventional morality, conventional morality, and post conventional morality.[2] **Preconventional morality** is childlike in nature; it is calculating, self-centered, and even selfish, based upon what will be immediately punished or rewarded. Thus, an interviewer may decide not to make up an interview because if the falsified questionnaire is uncovered, it will result in immediate termination. The interviewer's behavior is not based upon a sense of what is right or wrong, but instead on the threat of punishment. **Conventional morality** moves from an egocentric viewpoint toward the expectations of society. Loyalty and obedience to the organization (or society) become paramount. At the conventional morality level, an ethical marketing research decision might be concerned with whether it is ethical to conduct a 45-minute mall intercept interview. **Postconventional morality** represents morality of the mature adult. At the postconventional level of morality, researchers are less concerned about how others might see them and more concerned about how they see and judge themselves over the long run. A marketing researcher who has attained this morality might ask, "Even though it is legal and will increase company profits, is it right in the long run? Might it do more harm than good in the end?"

preconventional morality
A childlike morality, based on immediate gratification or punishment.

conventional morality
Morality based on the expectations of society.

postconventional morality
Morality based on how one views and judges oneself in the long run.

Conventional Morality

Because marketing researchers (ideally) more often encounter individuals with conventional or postconventional levels of morality, we will examine these concepts in more detail. Conventional morality shifts the moral focus from self-centeredness toward the expectations of society. Loyalty, duty, and obedience become the central virtues. This form of morality is governed by the laws and expectations of the reference groups in which a person works and lives. Conventional morality makes the approval and disapproval of the group the norm of moral good and evil. Generally, *legal* means ethical and *illegal* means unethical. Also, selfishness is the root of evil. Selfish feelings are those not shared by the group—these feelings are individualistic. Thus, a researcher's selfish feelings are antisocial and immoral. The unethical researcher goes on his own tyrannical and arrogant way. A rule of thumb for a person practicing conventional morality would be: "Would I want my family, friends, and employers to see this decision and its consequences on television?" If the answer is yes, then go ahead. If the answer is no, then additional thought should be given to finding a more satisfactory decision.[3]

Postconventional Morality

Postconventional morality shifts in focus away from group expectations and back to the self. However, it is not a return to the self-centeredness of preconventional morality. Those who achieve postconventional morality are less concerned about how others see them and more concerned with how they view themselves.

A new product manager for a major pesticide manufacturer created a new type of fly trap. It consisted of two 3-inch plastic discs, one on top of the other, held apart by ¾-inch plastic pillars. The interior contained a pheromone to attract flies and a glue that remained sticky for up to six months. The trap was designed to work like the highly successful Roach Motel. The primary advantage of the fly trap was that it could be placed in a kitchen window (flies are attracted to kitchens because of minute quantities of decaying organic matter and warmth relative to the rest of a house) without the fear of pesticide poisoning.

Product placement tests were conducted in Tampa and Phoenix in early October, which was the end of the fly season. A follow-up questionnaire revealed a generally high level of satisfaction with the product. A great deal of the satisfaction was the result of consumer confusion. They had no flies in their home, so they assumed that the traps repelled flies! The traps were, of course, designed to attract flies. The few consumers who did have flies in their homes noted the traps were ineffective. The attractant was not strong enough to lure the flies to the glue. In short, the product did not work as designed.

Because most respondents didn't have any flies in their homes and the product concept was so intuitively appealing, overall planned purchase intent was high. The new product manager estimated that several million traps could be sold throughout the country before purchasers realized that the traps were ineffective. By creating a new brand name for the traps and providing them under a dummy corporation name, the successful consumer brands already offered by the manufacturer would not be associated with the traps. The company already produced similar products, thus new production equipment was not necessary. The new product manager recommended a go-ahead for the product. The marketing manager examined the recommendation and agreed that it was an opportunity to quickly bring in a hefty profit since the traps would sell for a premium price. She felt, however, that selling the products was morally wrong and rejected the project. The marketing manager was practicing postconventional morality.

Approaches to the Development of a Philosophy of Ethics

Morality of an individual is determined by that person's ethical philosophy. An individual's ethical philosophy consists of the rules he adopts to govern his conduct and the values that person deems worth pursuing in life.

philosophy

A systematic attempt to understand individual and collective human experience.

Philosophy, in its broadest sense, is a systematic attempt to understand our individual and collective human experience. Two basic approaches have prevailed in developing a philosophy of ethics. The first approach argues on the basis of consequences. This method of ethical reasoning, called a *teleological approach*, states that whether an action is right or wrong depends on the consequences of that action. This approach is exemplified by utilitarianism, which is discussed later. A second approach to moral reasoning, called *deontological* (from the Greek word *deon*, "that which is binding"), states that duty is the basic moral category, and duty is independent of consequences. An action is right if it has certain characteristics and wrong if it has other characteristics or is of another kind. The morality of an act does not depend on whether it produces good or bad consequences. Instead, we must act in a manner that is morally right and avoid that which is morally wrong, irrespective of the consequences. The traditional Judeo-Christian approach to morality is deontological. Perhaps the most eloquent spokesperson for this approach to ethical philosophy was Immanuel Kant.

Over the centuries a number of ethical philosophies have been put forth. Appendix A of this chapter provides a brief summary of the most popular philosophies of ethical behavior and offers marketing research applications.

Making Ethical Decisions

Fortunately, most marketing researchers have moved beyond the self-centered, manipulative theories of preconventional morality, yet many have not achieved postconventional morality. Business ethics will continue to move forward, but unless there is positive action, business ethics is nothing more than empty moralizing.

Today's business ethics is actually a subset of the values held by society as a whole. The values used by marketing people to make decisions have been acquired through family, educational, and religious institutions, as well as social movements (e.g., antinuclear, women's rights). A market researcher with a mature set of ethical values accepts personal responsibility for decisions that affect the full community, including responsibility for

1. Employees' needs and desires and the long-range best interests of the organization.
2. Persons directly affected by company activities and their long-range goodwill and best interests (this creates good publicity for the firm).
3. Social values and conditions for society at large that provide values, sanctions, and a social structure that enable the company to exist.

Because the players in the marketing research game (you and I) ultimately have to make the decisions and determine the rules, how do we do this in an ethical manner? Obviously, there is no cut-and-dried answer to this question. One structured way of examining the ethics of a business decision is to ask the 11 questions listed in Table 4.1. A yes answer to questions 1, 8, 9, and 10 is a good indication that the decision is ethical. Rational and fair answers to the remaining questions that produce no harm to other parties should confirm that an action is ethical.

The final question in Table 4.1 basically asks, "Where do you draw the line?" In a number of research firms (and many other businesses), it is customary to give a bottle of whiskey to a good account at Christmastime. But what about a case of whiskey? Is the gift a thank-you for past business or an inducement for future business? How will the gift be seen by others? Is it something that has to be concealed from others?

TABLE 4.1 Eleven Questions for Examining the Ethics of a Business Decision

1. Have you defined the problem accurately?
2. How would you define the problem if you stood on the other side of the fence?
3. How did this situation occur in the first place?
4. To whom and to what do you give your loyalty as a person and as a member of the corporation?
5. What is your intention in making this decision?
6. How does this intention compare with the probable results?
7. Whom could your decision or action injure?
8. Can you discuss the problem with the affected parties before you make your decision?
9. Are you confident that your position will be as valid over a long period of time as it seems now?
10. Could you disclose without qualm your decision or action to your boss, your CEO, the board of directors, your family, society as a whole?
11. Under what conditions would you allow exceptions to your stand?

SOURCE: Copyright 1981 by the President and Fellows of Harvard College; all rights reserved. Reprinted by permission of *Harvard Business Review*. Laura L. Nash, "Ethics without the Sermon," *Harvard Business Review* (November–December 1981), p. 81.

A Code of Ethics

code of ethics
Guidelines for making ethical decisions.

A **code of ethics** can serve as a guideline for making ethical decisions. The most detailed code of market research ethics has been established by the Council of American Survey Research Organizations (CASRO). The code covers: (1) responsibilities to respondents, (2) the importance of privacy and the avoidance of harassment, and (3) responsibilities to clients, responsibilities in reporting to clients and the public, and responsibilities to field service firms and interviewers. Most market research and survey research firms in the United States belong to CASRO. There is no overall agreement in the research industry on what a code of ethics should contain. Yet when comparing the code of ethics of CASRO, the American Marketing Association, and three other marketing research trade associations, five basic values stand out. These are keeping promises, serving others, not deceiving others, not harming others, and ensuring justice.[4] Some researchers contend that *any* code of ethics for marketing researchers is impractical because circumstances are so variable and individualized that they defy generalization.[5] This attitude of simply "throwing in the towel" is, in the authors' opinion, unacceptable.

Research Supplier Ethics

Unethical acts in marketing research can emanate from one of three basic sources: the research supplier, the research client, or the field service firm. Table 4.2 details some of the most common unethical practices in marketing research.

Low-Ball Pricing

low-ball pricing
Offering an unrealistically low price to attract customers.

A research supplier should quote a firm price based upon a specific incidence rate and questionnaire length. If either of the latter two items changes, then the client should expect a change in the contract price. **Low-ball pricing** in any form is unethical. In essence, low-ball pricing is quoting an unrealistically low price to

TABLE 4.2 Unethical Practices in Marketing Research

RESEARCH SUPPLIERS	RESEARCH CLIENTS	FIELD SERVICES
Low-ball pricing	Issuing bid requests when a supplier has been predetermined	Overreporting hours worked
Underpaying field services	Obtaining free advice and methodology via bid requests	Falsifying data
Lack of objectivity	Making false promises	Use of professional respondents
Abuse of respondents	Unauthorized requests for proposals	Lack of data validation
Selling unnecessary research		
Violating client confidentiality		

secure a firm's business and then using some means to substantially raise the price. For example, quoting a price based on an unrealistically high incidence rate (percentage of people in the sampling universe who qualify to participate in the survey) is a form of low-ball pricing. Offering to conduct small group qualitative research (discussed in detail in Chapter 6) at $3,000 a group and, after receiving a client commitment saying, "the respondent's fees for participating in the group discussion are, of course, 'extra'" is a form of low balling.

Underpaying Field Services

A number of large research organizations have acquired a reputation for "grinding down" field service fees. After a field service has completed the work and returned it to the supplier, it has almost no leverage to exact payment. Not only are field service bills cut, but payment periods of three to six months are not uncommon. These practices are patently unethical.

Lack of Objectivity

Biased sampling, misusing statistics, ignoring relevant data, or creating a research design with the objective of supporting a predetermined objective must be avoided by research suppliers. One of the fastest-growing areas of research today is so-called advocacy studies. These studies are commissioned by companies or industries for public-relations purposes or to advocate or "prove" a position. For example, Burger King once used the responses to the following question in an advocacy study in an attempt to justify the claim that its method of cooking hamburgers was preferred over McDonald's: "Do you prefer your hamburgers flame-broiled or fried?" Another researcher rephrased the question: "Do you prefer a hamburger that is grilled on a hot stainless-steel grill or cooked by passing the meat through an open gas flame?" The results were reversed; McDonald's was preferred to Burger King.[6]

Stated consumer preference for Burger King burgers over McDonald's can be reversed simply by changing the wording of the questions.

Kiwi Brands, a shoe polish company, commissioned a study on the correlation between ambition and shiny shoes. The study found that 97 percent of self-described "ambitious" young men believe polished shoes are important. In many cases, advocacy studies simply use samples that are not representative of the population. For example, "There's good news for the 65 million Americans currently on a diet," trumpeted a news release for a diet products company. Its study showed that people who lose weight can keep it off. The sample: 20 graduates of the company's program who endorse it in commercials.

Lengthy telephone surveys have resulted in more and more persons refusing to participate in marketing research interviews. SOURCE: © Rob Crandall/Stock Boston.

When studies are released to the news media, the methodology should be readily available to news reporters. Typically this is not the case, often on the ground that the material is proprietary. A survey done for a coupon redemption company, Carolina Manufacturer's Service, found that a "broad cross section of Americans find coupons to be true incentives for purchasing products." The description of the methodology was available only for a price: $2,000.[7]

Abuse of Respondents

Respondent abuse can take several forms. Perhaps the most common problem is lengthy interviews. Approximately 20 percent of the respondents participating in a "survey on surveys" said that interviews were too long.[8] A part of the problem stems from "as long as you're in the field" mentality of product managers. It is not uncommon for clients to request additional "nice-to-know" questions or even exploratory questions on an entirely separate project. This leads to ballooning the questionnaire, 30-minute telephone interviews, and 40-minute mall interviews. Some projects necessitate so much information that it leads to excessive interview lengths. Moniter, a twice-a-year survey on social change, often lasts at least two hours. As a result of long interviews and telephone sales pitches, more and more Americans are refusing to participate in survey research. Two-thirds of Americans consider surveys and telemarketing the same thing or "don't know" if they are different.[9] Today, at least one-third of people contacted refuse to participate in a survey.[10] This compares with 15 percent a decade ago.

A second form of abuse is overinterviewing a stratum of people or geographic area. For example, middle-class, younger (under 35) women are likely to be interviewed frequently.[11] Also, some geographic areas tend to be much more heavily surveyed than others. For example, no one has been able to adequately explain the intense popularity of Jackson, Michigan (see Table 4.3). Continual requests for interviews are viewed by some potential respondents as a form of abuse.

Interest in a product or service is often discerned in the interviewing process. The researcher knows the interviewees' potential purchasing power from asking income and other pertinent financial questions. Although the introduction phase of the questionnaire usually promises confidentiality, some researchers have sold names and addresses with this information to firms seeking sales leads. An individual willing to participate in the survey research process has a right to have her privacy protected. Yet, the president of a marketing research company recently wrote an article in a publication of the American Marketing Association advocating the sale of lead generation information![12]

Dick Whittington, vice-president of Marketing Research at American Express, recently wrote an open letter to his colleagues in the research industry regarding respondent satisfaction. A summary of his position is presented in "A Professional Researcher's Perspective" on pages 92–93.

Selling Unnecessary Research

A research supplier dealing with a client who has little or no familiarity with market research often has the opportunity to "trade the client up." For example, a project might call for four qualitative research discussion groups and a telephone survey of approximately 350 consumers. Yet, the research supplier sells eight groups and 500 door-to-door interviews with a 400-interview telephone follow-up in six months.

It is perfectly acceptable to offer a prospective client several research designs with several alternative prices when and if the situation warrants alternative designs. The supplier should point out the pros and cons of each method along with sample confidence intervals. The client, in consultation with the supplier, then can decide objectively which design best suits the company's needs.

Violating Client Confidentiality

Information about a client's general business activities or the results of a client's project should not be disclosed to a third party. A supplier should not even disclose the name of a client unless permission is received in advance.

TABLE 4.3 The 20 Most Heavily Surveyed Metropolitan Statistical Areas Per Capita in the United States

1. Jackson, MI	11. Cincinnati, OH-KY-IN PMSA
2. Boise, ID	12. Merced, CA
3. Sioux Falls, SD	13. Fort Worth-Arlington, TX PMSA
4. San Diego, CA	14. Portland-Vancouver, OR-WA PMSA
5. Akron, OH PMSA	15. Santa Fe, NM
6. Rochester, MN	16. Houston, TX PMSA
7. South Bend, IN	17. Canton-Massillon, OH
8. San Francisco, CA PMSA	18. Los Angeles-Long Beach, CA PMSA
9. Miami, FL PMSA	19. New Orleans, LA
10. Charleston, WV	20. Austin-San Marcos, TX

SOURCE: *Survey Sampling, Inc.*

A Professional Researcher's Perspective

In ever-increasing numbers, research respondents are telling us how dissatisfied they are with the interview process. We clearly have not met their expectations . . . and most of them blame the perceived client sponsor for these shortcomings. It is clearly time for a change. . . . If you doubt me, look at your latest completion incidences—which can range from 9 percent to 40 percent on the low end—talk to your favorite provider partners throughout the interview chain, and then spend some time with your own respondents. Stand back and listen. I have and I'm convinced.

Remember, respondents are people just like us. Their most valuable and precious commodity is time. Everyone has too much to do and too little time to do it. And knowing the pressures this puts on me, I'm very disturbed when large numbers of respondents volunteer that:

- Interviews are intrusive, inconvenient, and way too long
- They are boring and repetitive
- Many just plain don't make sense
- Interviewers mislead and manipulate . . . just to get completions and/or to get the specific responses they desire
- Many respondents are not even thanked and few feel adequately compensated for their time and efforts

The attitude of the research community seems to be, "The respondent doesn't know who I am so if I abuse them a bit, who cares?" And this attitude, together with its accompanying behavior, could very well kill the research business as we know it today.

Thinking about these issues, my priorities seem to coalesce on four main points:

1. It's time to quit pointing fingers at others and time to get our own house in order. If we eliminated all fraudulent telemarketing, successfully identified ourselves as an industry, got everyone educated and certified as professional researchers, and quieted all the privacy advocates, we would definitely have less to complain about, but we would still have a broken product and one that irritated and alienated respondents.
2. Respondents are our industry's only unique resource, and it's about time we started treating them as such. The respondent feedback I've summarized about says we face a serious customer satisfaction problem. And if we don't solve it, then the resultant defections will put us in a

The thorniest issue of confidentiality is one of where does "background knowledge" stop and conflict exist as a result of work with a previous client. One researcher put it this way:

> I get involved in a number of proprietary studies. The problem that often arises is that some studies end up covering similar subject matter as previous studies. Our code of ethics states that you cannot use data from one project in a related project for a competi-

resource management crisis.

3. According to respondents, the interview experience can and does affect brand and company perceptions. And most respondents feel that they know exactly who to blame for nearly every bad interview experience—the client, not the research provider. Maybe it's about time we started treating all respondents as if they knew exactly who sponsored every study.
4. Respondents are people like you and me, with similar time pressures and responsibilities. It's time we started recognizing this and showing that we respect and value them and their time as much as we respect and value the information they provide. Actually, this is just another form of the golden rule, and I don't believe we treat respondents as we would want to be treated.

These four reengineering priorities suggest a host of potential actions or solutions. I have compiled the following list; it's not exhaustive, but it's a great start.

- **Limit interview length** by staying single-minded and avoiding the nice-to-know.
- **Prerecruit** more often.
- **Confine use of** the more intrusive methods, days, and times to when they're really necessary.
- **Tell respondents** how long it will really take, even before they agree to participate.
- **Adequately compensate** them for their time and value.
- **Be honest,** no matter what.
- **Always say** thanks.
- **Require that interviewers** look and act professional at all times.
- **Train interviewers** in customer service and satisfaction.
- **Measure respondent** satisfaction and tie it to performance assessments and compensation for everyone in the research chain: interviewer, field service provider, and client manager.
- **Control recontact** frequency.
- **Represent respondent** needs and rights to your company and client. Learn to say "no" and make it stick.
- **Make interviews easier** and more convenient for the respondent.
- **Make them involving,** interesting, and yes, even fun.

Minimally, I expect this effort to result in a code of "Survey Research Standards and Practices" and a "Respondent Bill of Rights." We at American Express are already working on our own versions of these documents, and we will be happy to share them with anyone considering respondent satisfaction improvements.[13] ■

tor. However, since I often know some information about an area, I end up compromising my original client. Even though upper management formally states that it should not be done, they also expect it to be done to cut down on expenses. This conflict of interest situation is difficult to deal with. At least in my firm, I don't see a resolution to the issue. It is not a onetime situation, but rather a *process* that perpetuates itself. To make individuals redo portions of studies which have recently been done is ludicrous, and to forgo potential new business is almost impossible from a financial perspective.[14]

Research Client Ethics

Like research suppliers, clients (or users) also have a number of ethical "dos and don'ts." Some of the more common areas are discussed.

Issuing Bid Requests When a Supplier Has Been Predetermined

It is not uncommon for a client to prefer one research supplier over another. Such preference may be due to a good working relationship, cost considerations, ability to make deadlines, friendship, or quality of the research staff. Having a preference per se is not unethical. It is unethical, however, to predetermine which supplier will receive a contract and yet ask for proposals from other suppliers to satisfy corporate requirements. The time, effort, and expense required from the firms that have no opportunity to win the contract is very unfair.

Obtaining Free Advice and Methodology via Bid Requests

Client companies seeking bargain basement prices have been known to solicit detailed proposals, including complete methodology and a sample questionnaire from a number of suppliers. After "picking the brains" of the suppliers, the client assembles a questionnaire and then contracts directly with field services to gather the data. A variation of this tactic is to go to the cheapest supplier with the client's own proposal derived by taking the best ideas from the other proposals. The client then attempts to get the supplier to conduct the more elaborate study at the low-ball price.

Making False Promises

Another technique used by unethical clients to lower their research costs is to hold out the nonexistent carrot. For example, a client might say, "I don't want to promise anything, but we are planning a major stream of research in this area, and if you will give us a good price on this first study, we will make it up to you on the next one." Unfortunately, the next one never comes, or if it does, the same line is used on another unsuspecting supplier.

Unauthorized Request for Proposals

The following situations involve client representatives who have sought proposals without first receiving the authority to allocate the funds to implement them.

1. A client representative will ask for proposals and then go to management to find out whether she can get the funds to carry them out.
2. A highly regarded employee will make a proposal to management on the need for marketing research in a given area. Although management is not too enthused about the idea, it will tell the researcher to seek bids so as not to dampen his interest or miss a potentially (but in its view highly unlikely) good idea.

3. The client representative and her management have different ideas on what the problem is and how it should be solved. The research supplier is not informed of the management view, and even though the proposal meets the representative's requirements, it is rejected out-of-hand by management.
4. The representative will step out-of-bounds; for instance, a marketing research manager will ask for a proposal on analyzing present sales performance without prior consultation with the sales department. Through fear of negative feedback, corporate politics, or lack of understanding of marketing research, the sales department will block implementation of the proposal.[15]

Field Service Ethics

Market research field services are the production arm of the research industry. They are the critical link between the respondent and research supplier. It is imperative that information is properly recorded and sampling plans are carefully followed. Otherwise, the best research design still produces invalid information—garbage in and garbage out. Maintaining high ethical standards will aid a field service in procuring good raw data for the research firm.

Overreporting Hours Worked

Because field services are located hundreds, if not thousands, of miles away from the research suppliers, there is rarely any person-to-person contact between the two organizations. A lack of personal supervision of field services' data gathering by the research supplier tempts some field service managers to pad the number of hours worked by the interviewers. Field services usually are compensated by a commission based upon the number of interviewing hours. Thus, there is an implicit incentive to overreport hours worked or to use slow, inefficient interviews. Because of the widespread tendency to overreport interviewing hours, some research suppliers cut virtually every bill submitted by the field service. Other suppliers simply avoid field services that submit above-average bills on a consistent basis.

Falsifying Data

Because field services pay interviewers the minimum wage or only slightly above it, they do not always attract the highest caliber worker. Historically, field service managers have experienced problems with interviewer cheating. The cheating runs the gamut from sitting down at the kitchen table and filling out questionnaires to using telephone numbers of friends and pay phones to bypass the validation process. When the field service validator calls to validate an interview with a pay phone number, it rings but no one answers. An unsuspecting validator assumes that no one is at home and goes to the next questionnaire.

Good field service managers can weed out dishonest interviewers. There have been a few cases in which the field service manager works with the dishonest interviewers to provide phony interviews. A common ploy is to report that the work was properly validated when, in fact, the field service manager knew that the interviews were fake. Only further validation by the research supplier uncovered the ruse.

In other cases, dishonest field services have been pinpointed by the research client. Big users of market research, such as Kraft General Foods, maintain a data bank of respondents' names, addresses, and phone numbers. Kraft General Foods also uses a number of different research suppliers and has its own in-house research department. When a field service receives an interviewing assignment from Data Development Corporation, Walker Research, or any other research supplier, the field service rarely knows for whom the research supplier is working. An unscrupulous field service manager or interviewer might use the same pay telephone number on a project for, say, Data Development, and another questionnaire for Walker Research, yet the client in both cases was Kraft General Foods. By pulling together phone numbers of interviewees from several research suppliers, Kraft General Foods has been able to pinpoint both dishonest interviewers and field services.

Use of Professional Respondents

The problem of professional respondents arises most often in the recruitment of focus group participants. Virtually all field services maintain a database of people willing to participate in qualitative discussion groups and a list of their demographic characteristics. Maintaining such a list is good business and quite ethical. When qualifications for group participants are easy (e.g., pet owners, persons who drive station wagons), there is little temptation to use professional respondents. However, when a supplier wants persons who are heavy users of Oxydol detergent or own a Russian Blue cat, it is not unheard of for a group recruiter to call a professional respondent and say, "I can get you into a group tomorrow with a $40 respondent fee and all you need to say is that you own a Russian Blue cat."

Another common occurrence is that a research supplier will specify that the participant must not have been a member of a qualitative discussion group within the past six months. This is an attempt by the research company to weed out professional respondents. However, dishonest field services will simply tell the professional respondent to deny having participated within the past six months.

Lack of Data Validation

It is customary for field services to validate 15 percent of each interviewer's work to make certain that the proper person was interviewed and that the data was recorded accurately. Validation is one of the services provided in exchange for the field service's commission fee. Field services sometimes validate fewer than 15 percent of the interviews. Also, the field service may not validate any of the work of a trusted interviewer.

Respondent Rights

Respondents in a market research project typically are giving their time and opinions and receive little or nothing in return. These individuals, however, do have certain rights that should be upheld by all market researchers (see Figure 4.1).[16] All potential participants in a research project have the right to choose, the right to safety, the right to be informed, and the right to privacy.

The Right to Choose

Everyone has the right to determine whether to participate in a marketing research project. Some people may not fully understand this prerogative. For example, poorly educated individuals or children may not fully appreciate this privilege. Also, a person who would like to terminate an interview or experiment may give short, incomplete answers or even false data.

If a person consents to be a part of an experiment or to answer a questionnaire, this does not give the researcher carte blanche to do whatever he wants. The researcher still has an obligation to the respondent. For example, a person participating in a taste test involving a test product and several existing products prefers the test product. This does not give the researcher the right to use the respondent's name and address in a promotion piece saying that "Ms. Jones prefers new Sudsies to Brand X."

The Right to Safety

Research participants have the right to safety from physical or psychological harm. It is unusual for a respondent to be exposed to physical harm. There have been cases, however, of persons becoming ill in food taste tests. Also, on a more subtle level, it is rare for researchers to warn respondents that a test product contains, say, a high level of salt. An unwitting respondent with hypertension could be placed in physical danger if the test ran several weeks.

FIGURE 4.1
Respondents' Rights

It is much more common for a respondent to be placed in a psychologically damaging situation. Individuals might experience stress when an interviewer presses them to participate in a study. Others might feel stressful when they cannot answer questions or are given a time limit to complete a task (for example, "you have five minutes to browse through this magazine and then I will ask you a series of questions").

The Right to Be Informed

Research participants have the right to be informed of all aspects of a research task. By knowing what is involved, how long it will take, and what will be done with the data, a person can make an intelligent choice on whether to participate in the project.

Often it is necessary to disguise the name of the research sponsor to avoid biasing the respondent. For example, it is poor research practice to say, "We are conducting a survey for Pepsi; which brand of soft drink do you consume most often?" In cases in which disguising the sponsor is required, a debriefing following the completion of the interview should be used. The debriefing should provide information about the study's purpose, the sponsor, what happens next with the data, and any other pertinent information. A debriefing can aid in reducing respondent stress and building goodwill for the research industry. Unfortunately, taking the time to debrief a respondent is a cost that most companies are unwilling to incur.

A final aspect of being informed occurs in some business and academic research whereby the researcher offers to provide the respondent with a copy of the research results as an incentive to obtain participation in the project. When a commitment has been made to disseminate the findings to survey respondents, it should be fulfilled. On more than one occasion, the authors participated in academic surveys with the carrot of "research results" offered but never delivered.

The Right to Privacy

All consumers have the right to privacy. Consumer privacy can be defined in terms of two dimensions of control. The first dimension includes control of unwanted telephone, mail, or personal intrusion in the consumer's environment, and the second is concerned with control of information about the consumer. Consumer privacy can be viewed in the context of any interaction, profit or nonprofit, between marketer and consumer, including (but not limited to) credit and cash sales, consumer inquiries, and marketer-initiated surveys.[17] The very nature of the marketing research business requires interviewers to invade an individual's privacy. An interviewer calls or approaches strangers, asks them for a portion of their time—their limited, free time—and asks them to answer personal questions, sometimes very personal questions.

Perhaps the greatest privacy issue of consumers is marketing databases (see Chapter 5). The amount of information that industry is collecting is staggering. Insurance companies are reported to have health records on nine out of 10 working Americans. There are 1,200 credit bureaus in this country, which maintain files on 170 million people. About 500 million credit reports are sold annually. In

1992, 300 million credit cards were in circulation. Eighty-five federal databases exist, containing 288 million records on 114 million Americans. Personnel records; health benefit and worker's compensation claims; credit card purchase records; telephone, messaging, and information services; real estate transactions; magazine subscriptions; travel and entertainment records; and automobile registrations are all fertile sources of information about citizens' activities, habits, and thoughts. There are 20,000 mailing lists commercially available that can provide this information to both the public and private sectors.[18] The Standard Rate and Data Service mailing-list catalog, which is a standard industry tool, includes lists that reflect religion, sexual orientation, medical information, and political contributions.[19]

Companies use the information in the databases for market segmentation studies and a variety of other purposes. Perhaps the most common use is for direct marketing either by telephone or mail. Examples of database marketing abuses abound. For example, televangelist Oral Roberts mailed a six-page solicitation to lists of consumers with serious credit problems. In it, he invited them to send him a $100 "war-on-debt seed-faith gift." In return, Roberts would help these people pray their way out of their financial burdens. He would pray even harder if the recipient sent back information about the precise amounts owed on car loans, credit cards, school loans, mortgages, personal loans, and medical bills.[20]

A national opinion survey, "The Equifax Report on Consumers in the Information Age," found that 79 percent of the public is concerned about threats to personal privacy. Also, 55 percent of Americans feel that protection of information about consumers will get worse by the year 2000. Most Americans (67 percent) believe that "the present use of computers is an actual threat to personal privacy"—a dramatic increase from 1978 when 37 percent felt this way.[21]

One way information technology may invade privacy is through computer matching. This typically occurs when a manager accesses several large databases and matches data about an individual in one database with information about her in other databases. Usually the match is made on the Social Security number because it is included on most documents and records pertaining to individuals. By combining databases through matching, a more extensive profile of individuals is obtained and, in this way, the manager learns a great deal about an individual's shopping habits and personal characteristics—so that, ostensibly, better decisions can be made.[22]

Database marketers can provide information on temptingly specific markets. For example, marketers can rent the names, addresses, and phone numbers of 16,000 Jewish singles with incomes of $50,000-plus compiled by Jewish Introductions International. Or perhaps they want to target National Credit Database's 6.2 million bank and retail credit accounts that had fallen behind 60 days or target 80,000 purchasers of Omega Artificial Intelligence Software's "Eliza" psychotherapy software.[23]

The concerns about overcontacting the public, telephone abuses, and computer matching have caused some people to set up special interest and action groups. One such organization is Private Citizen, Inc., an Illinois-based privacy advocacy group that claims to have a membership of about 500 people, all of whom do not want to receive *any* unsolicited telephone calls. Private Citizen,

Inc., sends out a notice to businesses (telemarketing, charitable causes, services, survey research firms, etc.), along with a Private Citizen Directory. The notice states:

> Junk calls are a nuisance, an invasion of my privacy, and they interfere with the peaceful enjoyment of my property. . . . I am unwilling to allow use of my time or property for such calls without payment. . . . I offer to accept such calls for a $100 fee. . . . Each such call shall be an acceptance of this offer and upon its answer ratification. . . . Your junk call constitutes agreement to: the compensation's reasonableness, payment of all reasonable incurred collection and attorney's fees and your consent to have all related calls appropriately recorded as evidence of your agreement.[24]

Junk calls are defined as calls that are "intended to sell, rent, survey/poll, solicit information about, encourage donations to, generate/qualify sales leads for, create interest in or renew subscriptions for anything . . . of concern to the calling entity, whether such organization be of a commercial, nonprofit, survey research or political nature."[25]

Although many local businesses, such as carpet cleaners, pest control companies, and others use cold calling to generate sales leads, most national organizations do not. The reason is that cold calling and mass direct mailings are simply not economically efficient. Big companies use targeted marketing for telephone calls and mailings. Although no mechanism exists on the national level to eliminate unsolicited telephone calls, individual companies such as American Express and Eddie Bauer give their customers the option to have their names excluded when their customer lists are sold. The Direct Marketing Association's Mail Preference Service offers people the right to suppress all mailings. Mailing is no longer cheap. The average mailing costs 50 cents a piece. The Mail Preference Service eliminates 875 million names from mailing lists each year. By suppressing 875 million pieces of unwanted mail at 50 cents a piece, business saves more than $400 million.[26]

Companies like Eddie Bauer maintain huge databases which they often sell to others. Eddie Bauer gives customers the option to have their names deleted when they sell their lists.

Global Marketing Research

Concerns about restrictive government policies and regulations for the marketing research industry extend beyond U.S. borders. For example, the European Commission, a Pan-European governing body based in Brussels, issues what it terms "directives" that could come to prevail throughout the 12 EC member countries. One such directive, aimed at data privacy, decrees that repondents cannot be asked questions about "sensitive subjects" without the respondent's written permission.

In Ireland, the marketing research community is banding together to try to thwart a government ruling that political poll results could not be published during a specified time period (say, two weeks) immediately before an election. The polls can be conducted, but the findings can't be made known to the general public. Some other governments have toyed with the same restriction.

In the United Kingdom, there is the Data Protection Act, which is designed primarily to prevent abuse of household financial records and information stored by database marketers. But this also covers marketing research databases and records of all individual survey rspondents. It says a firm cannot gather data on individuals, coupled with their address, without written consent, and individuals have the right to see data on themselves in a database.

British research firms must be licensed (that is, registered) to collect data but can request an exemption to the written consent provision. That's what large British research firms do. Of course, there is always the possibility that a change of government might deny exemptions. ■

In addition to various activist groups, the federal government has begun to take an interest in the privacy issue. Congress introduces a number of bills each year that relate to access to database information and telephone solicitation. No privacy-related bills have passed so far. If the marketing research industry does not quickly establish a self-regulating body to monitor privacy abuses, federal legislation is only a matter of time.

Contemporary Marketing Research Ethics

A later survey of marketing researchers and marketing managers replicated a 1970 study on marketing ethics.[27] The two groups were chosen because it was felt that each would use a different approach to evaluating the ethics of a particular action. Marketing executives, it was assumed, would evaluate all actions based upon the attained results (gains or losses attained)—a teleological approach. On the other hand, market research activities require adherence to standards and rules (e.g., the steps in the market research process and of applying statistical formulas). Therefore, researchers were expected to follow a deontological approach to ethical actions.

TABLE 4.4 Comparison of Responses to the Ethical Scenarios (Items)

	PERCENTAGE OF DISAPPROVALS[a]			
	Marketing Researchers		*Marketing Executives*	
SCENARIO (ITEM)	*1970 Study (n = 259)*	*1989 Study (n = 205)*	*1970 Study (n = 142)*	*1989 Study (n = 215)*
Confidentiality				
1. Use of ultraviolet ink "A project director went to the Marketing Research Director's office and requested permission to use an ultraviolet ink to precode a questionnaire for a mail survey. The project director pointed out that although the cover letter promised confidentiality, respondent identification was needed to permit adequate tabulations of the data. The Marketing Research Director gave approval."	70	57[c]	77	69
2. Hidden tape recorders "In a study intended to probe deeply into the buying motives of a group of wholesale customers, the Marketing Research Director authorized the use of the department's special attache case equipped with hidden tape recorders to record the interviewers."	67	84[b]	71	81[d]
3. One-way mirrors "One of the products of X Company is brassieres. Recently, the company has been having difficulty making decisions on a new product line. Information was critically needed regarding how women put on their brassieres. The Marketing Research Director therefore designed a study in which two local stores agreed to put one-way mirrors in the foundations of their dressing rooms. Observers behind these mirrors successfully gathered the necessary information."	78	94[b]	82	97[b]
Research Integrity				
4. Fake research firm "In another study concerning consumers' magazine reading habits, the Marketing Research Director decided to contact a sample of consumers using the fictitious company name Media Research Institute. This successfully camouflaged the identity of X Company as the sponsor of the study."	13	30[b]	16	30[c]
5. Distortions by marketing vice-president "In the trial run of a major presentation of the Board of Directors, the marketing vice-president deliberately distorted some recent research findings. After some thought, the Marketing Research Director decided to ignore the matter since the vice-president obviously knew what he was doing."	87	88	86	89
Conflict of interest				
6. Possible conflict of interest "A market testing firm to which X Company gives most of its business recently went public. The Marketing Research Director of X Company had been looking for a good investment and proceeded to buy some $20,000 of its stock. The firm continues as X Company's leading supplier for testing."	57	56	38	44
Marketing Mix Issues				
7. Exchange of price data "X Company belongs to a trade association with an active marketing research subgroup. At the subgroup's meetings, the Marketing Research				

TABLE 4.4 Comparison of Responses to the Ethical Scenarios (Items)—*Continued*

SCENARIO (ITEM)	PERCENTAGE OF DISAPPROVALS[a]			
	Marketing Researchers		*Marketing Executives*	
	1970 Study (n = 259)	*1989 Study (n = 205)*	*1970 Study (n = 142)*	*1989 Study (n = 215)*
Director regularly exchanges confidential price information. The Marketing Research Director then turns the information over to the company's sales department but is careful not to let the marketing vice-president know about it. Profits are substantially enhanced, and top management is protected from charges of collusion."	89	89	82	87
8. Advertising and product misuse "A recent study showed that several customers of X Company were misusing Product B. Although this posed no danger, customers were wasting their money by using too much of the product at a time. But, yesterday, the Marketing Research Director saw final comps/sketches on Product B's new ad campaign which not only ignored the problem of misuse but actually seemed to encourage it. The Marketing Research Director quietly referred the advertising manager to the research results, well known to all of the people with product B's advertising, but did nothing beyond that."	58	39[b]	66	55[d]
Social Issues				
9. General trade data to center city group "The marketing research department of X Company frequently makes extensive studies of its retail customers. A federally supported minority group working to get a shopping center in its residential area wanted to know if it could have access to this trade information. Since the Marketing Research Director has always refused to share this information with trade organizations, the request was declined."	34	13[b]	25	10[b]
10. NMAC request for recent price study "The National Marketing Advisory Council (formed of top marketing executives and marketing educators to advise the Commerce Department) has a task force studying inner city prices. The head of this study group recently called to ask if the group could have a copy of a recent X Company study which showed that inner city appliance prices are significantly higher than in suburban areas. Since X Company sells appliances to these inner city merchants, the Marketing Research Director felt compelled to refuse the request."	39	20[b]	51	26[b]
11. Assigning personnel to an inner city planning group "A local Office of Economic Opportunity group recently called to ask the Marketing Research Director to assign an assistant to the planning group working on the inner city shopping center mentioned earlier. Since such a shopping center would force a good number of inner city retail customers of X Company out of business, the Marketing Research Director refused the request."	51	24[b]	57	24[b]

[a]To simplify the data, only disapproval rates ("disapprove somewhat" or "disapprove") are reported.

[b]Difference between the two studies significant at .001 level.

[c]Difference between the two studies significant at .01 level.

[d]Difference between the two studies significant at .05 level.

SOURCE: Merle C. Crawford, "Attitudes of Marketing Executives toward Ethics in Marketing Research," *Journal of Marketing Research* (April 1970):46–52; and Ishmael P. Akaah and Edward Riordan, "Judgment of Marketing Professionals about Ethical Issues in Marketing Research: A Replication and Extension," *Journal of Marketing Research* (February 1989): 112–120.

A number of scenarios were presented to 420 marketing executives and researchers. Each was evaluated on a five-point scale ranging from "disapprove" to "approve." The results are shown in Table 4.4. The researchers found 15 significant shifts (of a total of 22 comparisons) in research ethics judgments.

For some research ethics issues (use of hidden tape recorders to record interviews, use of one-way mirrors to gather research data, and use of fictitious company name as study sponsor), marketing professionals (both executives and researchers) express stronger disapproval in the newer study than was observed in 1970. For other issues ("soft" stand on the use of ad that reinforces product misuse and denial of research help to minority groups), marketing professionals (both executives and researchers) are more approving today than those in the earlier research. For use of ultraviolet ink to precode questionnaires, marketing researchers (in particular) show stronger approval of the practice than was found in 1970.

The other major finding in the 1989 study was that three corporate factors—extent of ethical problems within the organization, top management actions on ethics, and organizational role (executives versus researchers)—underlie differences in marketing professionals' research ethics judgments. Marketing professionals who perceive fewer ethical problems in their organizations tend to disapprove more strongly of "unethical" or questionable research practices than those who perceive more ethical problems.

The study also found that top managers can influence the behavior of marketing professionals by actions that encourage ethical behavior or discourage unethical behavior. The 1989 study also revealed that executives and researchers differed in terms of research ethics judgments: executives expressed stronger disapproval of two research ethics issues than did researchers and vice versa for a third research ethics issue. The findings did not give a clear indication of the relationship between research ethics judgments (researchers versus executives) and moral philosophy (teleological versus deontological). Finally, the 1989 study showed that a code of ethics, organizational rank, and industry category lacked significance as correlates of research ethics judgments.

Raising the Level of Professionalism in Marketing Research

Ethics and Professionalism

High standards of ethics and professionalism go hand in hand. Good ethics provides a solid foundation for professionalism, and striving for a lofty level of professionalism necessitates proper ethics on the part of researchers.

Indications of a Lack of Professionalism

Phone-In Polls There are numerous signs that professionalism has not reached a desired level in the marketing research industry. One example is the phone-in poll in which viewers or listeners are encouraged to volunteer their opinions by calling a toll-free (or nominal charge) number. In such surveys, sample selection based upon probability theory is nonexistent. One poll, for exam-

Call-in polls are not scientific, yet they are often assumed by the public to be representative.

ple, conducted by *USA Today* showed that Americans loved Donald Trump. A month later, *USA Today* reported that 5,640 of the 7,800 calls came from offices owned by one man, Cincinnati financier Carl Lindner. Lindner would not comment, but a spokesperson told *USA Today* that Lindner's employees admire Trump. *USA Today* says its call-in polls are not meant to be scientific and are "strictly for fun."[28] Yet, the information derived is widely reported by the media and is often assumed by the public to be representative.[29]

Sales Pitches Disguised as Research Another serious problem is the use of sales pitches disguised as marketing research. Although the latter problem is caused by persons outside the research industry, it still casts a negative light on legitimate researchers.

An example of selling disguised as research, discussed by Diane Bowers, executive director of the Council of American Survey Research Organizations (CASRO), is found in "A Professional Researchers Perspective" on pages 106–108. CASRO is a trade association representing approximately 130 full-service marketing research firms.

Proactive Efforts to Enhance the Level of Professionalism in the Market Research Industry

The Efforts of CASRO

Several positive steps have been taken recently to improve the level of professionalism in the marketing research industry. For example, CASRO has sponsored several symposia that deal with ethical issues in survey research. CASRO also has created a code of ethics that has been widely disseminated to research professionals. The CASRO board has worked with other groups such as the Marketing Research Association to provide input to legislatures considering antimarketing research legislation.

A Professional Researcher's Perspective

"You've got something that's worth $1,500 to me. . . . Your opinion is valuable. You've always given it away freely. But I'll reward you for it. I'll give you up to $1,500 worth of FREE gifts in exchange for your opinion of the TV programs that you watch." This is an excerpt from a direct mail letter soliciting "TV Raters" sent by John Westcott, vice-president of American Media Research Corporation (AMRC). It sounds wonderful, doesn't it?

And the more you read Westcott's letter, the more wonderful it sounds. All you have to do to receive up to $1,500 worth of free gifts is to fill out a "TV Survey" form every month for 36 months. Then, John Westcott writes, "We'll take your survey answers and match them up with similar responses from all over the country. This report, profiling the viewing habits and consumer preferences of our TV Raters, will be delivered to top executives in the Television, Entertainment, and Consumer Goods industries. This important data will be marketed to some of America's largest and most powerful media, mailing list, and consumer product companies."

Yes, this sounds great! Even the "small enrollment fee" of up to $20 and "a modest shipping and processing charge of about $2.00 or so each month" for the free gifts you get when you send in the monthly TV survey doesn't dampen your enthusiasm. *And* if you enroll within the next 11 days, you'll get a "Promptness Gift worth not $25, not $50, not $75, but $95!" If you're a bargain hunter and a public-spirited citizen, interested both in free gifts and in having your opinions count ("Your Answers May Affect Millions"), why not join up?

The scheme worked. People enrolled as "TV Raters" by the thousands. After all, to the inexperienced, unknowing eye, there doesn't seem to be anything wrong with this program—not really.

But there is a lot wrong with this scheme. And soon after this letter hit people's mailboxes, many questions and complaints were brought up by consumer and industry watchdogs, including the survey research industry, by the knowing public, *and* even by disillusioned "TV Raters" themselves.

Several times CASRO sent letters to AMRC asking about the TV Rater survey, explaining survey research industry standards on respondent confidentiality and protection from harassment and misrepresentation, and questioning the validity of the data being collected. Finally, CASRO received a response from Donald Pickman, president and CEO of American Media Research Corporation.

Pickman wrote, "We at American Media are definitely interested in structuring our business to maximize its potential to output the information contained in the database. It is my intention to further review with you any input you and your organization can provide that will help achieve our goals and not offend your standards of practice." I never did figure out what Pickman meant, though I suspect his intentions were as questionable as his sentence structure.

Within a week of receiving the letter from Pickman, I got a call from Stacy Ludwig, an attorney with the United States Postal Service. It seemed that the USPS had received a number of complaints from individuals and from organizations, including CASRO, questioning the legitimacy of the AMRC operation, both as a seller of "free" products and as a survey research company. CASRO was asked to participate in the USPS investigation of AMRC. Ludwig wanted to learn all about the research industry and how surveys are conducted.

Harry W. O'Neill, vice-chairman of The Roper Organization; David Lapovsky, vice-president of Arbitron Ratings Company; and I provided written affidavits on legitimate survey research and industry standards, and we were prepared to testify against AMRC before an administrative law judge in Washington, D.C. In his affidavit to the USPS, O'Neill described different types of survey research, sampling and statistical measures, and reporting arrangements. He also wrote:

The conduct of survey research has become more difficult in recent years because of such factors as (1) the increase of working women and families with both heads in the workforce, thereby making it harder to reach a respondent at a convenient time, (2) the increase in crime and dangerous neighborhoods, making door-to-door inverviewing less desirable for the interviewer and a cause for suspicion on the part of potential respondents, (3) the increase of telemarketing, which often is conducted by using research as a guise and, even when legitimate, competes for the time of potential survey respondents, and (4) the increase of mail solicitations for contributions using research as a guise. Given [these] problems, coupled with the increase in legitimate survey research, we are very sensitive to any activity that can cast a bad light on our industry. AMRC is such an activity, for the following reasons:

1. It charges respondents for participation—a practice no legitimate survey company engages in.
2. It leads respondents to believe their opinions are being sought by top executives in the entertainment and consumer products industries when the service has no clients.
3. It not only promises gifts for participation whose value falls short of that which is promised but also charges shipping and handling for the gifts. If a legitimate survey firm rewards a respondent with a gift, there is never a charge.
4. Most seriously, while claiming to be a survey research company, AMRC violates respondent anonymity. Respondent names are put into a direct marketing file and respondents obviously will be solicited at some future date. Legitimate research firms, on the contrary, assure respondents that survey participation never will result in a future sales

continues

contact. To the extent respondents are not treated well by AMRC, are told untruths, find their names on mailing lists—and all of this is associated with a company claiming to be a research company—the credibility of our industry will suffer.

On January 22, 1990, a Cease and Desist Order was signed by the USPS judicial officer. The Cease and Desist Order covered AMRC, its officers, directors, owners, and employees and extended to AMRC's promotional materials and "to any promotion that seeks to obtain remittances of money or property through the mail in connection with a survey." Furthermore, the order directed that "If any purpose of [the AMRC] program is to solicit money, to compile mailing lists or to sell products, [AMRC] is hereby further ordered not to represent, identify, or describe their promotion as a survey."[30] ■

The Creation of CMOR

In January 1992, research industry leaders decided to band together to address the critical issues of government affairs and respondent cooperation because no existing association could adequately move forward alone on either of these two initiatives. Further, it was clear that these issues required broad industry support and involvement and substantial funding. Separate fund-raising efforts for each initiative would seriously compromise the viability of both initiatives.

It became evident that the marketing and opinion research industry needed to take action to protect itself from unreasonable government prohibitions, to bolster its image among the public and legislators, to promote self-regulation, and to develop a means to differentiate the research industry from other industries that appear to be similar.

The January 1992 meeting of research professionals led to the creation of the Council for Marketing and Public Opinion Research (CMOR). The organization initially raised $500,000 to help meet the following objectives:

1. Establish a single, unified voice for the research industry to speak to respondents, legislators, and regulators. This unified voice would have three major characteristics: (1) be broad enough to be all-encompassing in terms of who it represents; (2) be focused in its objectives to remain solely dedicated to this mission, and (3) be nonpartisan to make it possible to speak for every facet of the industry.
2. Monitor state and federal legislation and lobby on behalf of the interests of the research industry to prevent passage of unnecessarily restrictive legislation.
3. Work proactively with government leaders to protect the industry from abuses of the research process.
4. Develop a means for the public to determine the legitimacy of a research interaction.
5. Differentiate the research industry from other kinds of unsolicited contacts with the public.
6. Create an educational platform that will strengthen and expand research industry alliances to increase and mobilize the support for CMOR.

7. Provide support to, and complement the efforts of, other industry associations.[31]

Since its founding, CMOR has met with several successes on the legislative front and made some significant progress regarding respondent cooperation as well. CMOR has successfully fought legislation that would require research supervisors to notify interviewers when they were monitoring telephone surveys. Monitoring is an important tool for controlling the quality of telephone interviewing. If interviewers knew exactly when they were being monitored, they could save their "best efforts" for those time periods.

CMOR has completed an educational brochure and a respondent thank-you card. CMOR also has set up a toll-free telephone number, (800) 887-CMOR, and has been responding regularly to abuses of research by suggers and fruggers (selling and fund-raising under the guise of research). A "Respondent Bill of Rights" has been published and has been distributed to the trade press, better business bureaus, chambers of commerce, and other public and consumer advocacy groups.[32]

Actions and Publications of ARF

The Advertising Research Foundation (ARF) has published a position paper, "Phony or Misleading Polls." The paper is a business-to-business document designed to alert nonresearch businesspersons to the serious problems of sales pitches disguised as survey research and phone-in polls. The position paper contrasts errant practices with accepted industry procedures, pointing out the ways in which these practices are unacceptable and misleading. It also discusses the implications of the practices, examined from the perspective of both businesses and society. The paper concludes with a suggestion that the solution to the problem lies in self-regulation as opposed to government regulation. Other ARF publications that provide general standards for research and practical guidelines for their implementation include *ARF Criteria for Marketing and Advertising Research* and *Guidelines for the Public Use of Market and Opinion Research*.[33]

A Need for Researcher Certification

Professors Bruce Stern and Terry Crawford argue that accountants, financial analysts, attorneys, and market researchers are all considered professionals with strong technical foundations.[34] Yet, all but market research have a program that certifies the competence of its practitioners. Stern notes that even insurance and real estate, which do not require their practitioners to have college degrees, have certification programs.

Today it is far too easy to begin practicing marketing research. We have seen several "fast-talkers" convince unwary clients that they are qualified researchers. Unfortunately, relying on poor information to make major decisions has resulted in loss of market share, profits, and, in some cases, bankruptcy. Stern and Crawford propose the certification process be structured as follows:

> Certification should be given to persons who have demonstrated competence on a multipart examination. Ideally, the exam should test them on secondary data sources, methodology for empirical research, data interpretation, and marketing basics.
>
> Passing all four parts of the examination will demonstrate a person's ability to use secondary data to satisfy information needs instead of relying totally on more expen-

> sive empirical techniques. When empirical research is needed, he will have demonstrated competence in problem definition, sampling, questionnaire design, choice of survey vehicles, experimentation, field operations, data analysis, interpretation of statistical output, and the ability to make sound marketing recommendations from the data.[35]

Certification has generated a great deal of debate among members of the marketing research industry. It should be noted that certification is not licensing. Licensing is a mandatory procedure administered by a governmental body that allows one to practice a profession. Certification is a voluntary program administered by a nongovernmental body that provides a credential for differentiation in the marketplace. The issue of certification is sensitive because it directly affects marketing researchers' ability to practice their profession freely. The arguments can be summed up as follows:[36]

CON There is no single criterion on which to judge a researcher. The profession is too diverse, so the exam would have to be very basic.

PRO It is not necessary to test every competency for every type of research. Other diverse groups such as the American Society of Interior design have a successful certification program.

CON Politics would play a big part in the process, it would be expensive and time-consuming, and there isn't a viable organization to oversee the process.

PRO Organizations are composed of members; members use their collective voice to create a certification program. Researchers could be certified through continuing education programs and phased listing.

CON Because certification is voluntary, there is no guarantee that poor researchers wouldn't continue to operate. Certification, therefore, would not legitimize the profession. Also, a certification program probably would require grandfathering in many current researchers. Thus some incompetent researchers probably would be certified.

PRO Certification would help to establish marketing research as a true profession. It demonstrates to government regulators that the industry is concerned about competency. The certification process would provide a forum for discussing what it takes to be professional.

CON There is no evidence that certification would create higher quality research.

PRO Certification would help the public distinguish between legitimate surveys and those done with a built-in bias. (Certified researchers would not conduct biased polls.) Certified researchers would be held more accountable through such things as mandatory methodology disclosures.

CON Because certification is voluntary, it never resolves ethical issues.

PRO Current organizational ethical codes have not been effective in preventing abuses. Self-regulation may forestall governmental regulation.

CON Certification can't guarantee competence.

PRO Certification would help protect consumers and clients because the research profession now suffers a multitude of poorly trained and inexperienced practitioners. Certification would at least provide research users with some assurance of knowledge, experience, and commitment to the profession.

As you can see, the issues of certification are complex and emotional. Not surprisingly, there is great diversity of opinion within the research industry. A recent study of almost 300 marketing research professionals found 17 percent strongly in favor of certification, 20 percent strongly opposed, and the remainder somewhere in the middle.[37] To date, no organization has taken action to begin a certification program.

Summary

Ethics refers to moral principles or values generally governing the conduct of an individual or group. Morals are often described in terms of good or bad. There are three levels of moral development: preconventional morality, conventional morality, and postconventional morality. Preconventional morality is childlike in nature: calculating, self-centered, and even selfish, based on what will be immediately punished or rewarded. Conventional morality moves from an egocentric viewpoint toward the expectations of society. Postconventional morality represents morality of the mature adult.

Some of the unethical practices by some market research suppliers include low-ball pricing, underpaying field services, lack of objectivity, abuse of respondents, sale of unnecessary research, and violation of client confidentiality. In contrast, unethical practices performed by some research clients are requests for bids when a supplier has been predetermined, bid requests to gain free advice on methodology, false promises, and unauthorized requests for proposals. Unethical practices of market research field services include overreported hours worked, falsified data, use of professional respondents, and lack of data validation.

Respondents have certain rights. These include the right to determine whether to participate in a marketing research project. Second, respondents have the right to safety from physical and psychological harm. Respondents also have the right to be informed of all the aspects of the research task. They should know what is involved, how long it will take, and what will be done with the data. Respondents also have the right to privacy. In the past 20 years, there has been a significant shift in ethics among market researchers.

The level of professionalism in the market research industry can be raised through the efforts of organizations like CASRO and CMOR and socially concerned marketing research firms. Researcher certification continues to be a highly controversial and emotional issue within the research community.

Key Terms

ethics
morals
preconventional morality
conventional morality
postconventional morality
philosophy
code of ethics
low-ball pricing

Review and Discussion Questions

1. Distinguish between preconventional, conventional, and postconventional morality, and give examples of each.
2. Turn to Table 4.4 and poll the class on the various scenarios to determine whether the students think they are ethical or unethical. Then ask students on either side of the issue to justify their logic.
3. Can an individual with high personal ethical standards make unethical decisions for the corporation to achieve its objectives? Why or why not?

4. What do you foresee as the role of a code of ethics within an organization? What can be done to ensure that employees follow this code of ethics?
5. Who would you say has the greatest responsibility within the marketing research industry to raise the standards of ethics—market research suppliers, market research clients, or field services?
6. What role should the federal government play in establishing ethical standards for the marketing research industry? How would this be enforced?
7. If respondents agree or consent to interviews after being told they will be paid $20 for their opinions, do they forfeit any respondent rights? If so, what rights have been forfeited?
8. What is the relationship between ethics and professionalism? What do you think can be done to raise the level of professionalism within the marketing research industry?

CASE 4.1

Century Cigarettes

Doug Hageman, a former R.J. Reynolds Tobacco Company employee, tells how the company used test marketing espionage by Philip Morris to completely mislead its competitor.

"Being first with a new product in the tobacco industry is the absolute key to marketing success," Hageman said. "RJR proved that with the introduction of More, a 120mm cigarette that looked like a skinny cigar. Even though all our competitors immediately broke with their own 120mm products, More wound up with 70 percent of the market. That made RJR very sensitive about being first with new products. We were working on the Century 25-pack, but we knew that Philip Morris was working on a 25-pack of its own and would have it to market ahead of us, unless we could get them sidetracked.

"We took Winston Light, put a different filter on it, packaged it in a spiffy black foil wrapper and called it Sterling. We hustled off to do 'test market studies' in Tulsa, a common test market, so no one was surprised by that choice. Although there are a lot of wholesalers in the tobacco business, only 'directs'—the licensed accounts that apply the local state's tax stamp—deal directly with the manufacturers. As such, it's easy to get a few direct accounts to let you see the real numbers they're buying of a particular product, so a reasonably accurate market share study can be compiled.

"RJR hired a firm from Los Angeles, sent them around to buy Sterling in big numbers at retail and warped the sales figures to a point where Philip Morris just couldn't stand it anymore. They back-burnered their 25-pack and broke with Players, which was just Marlboro Light with a 'cork' filter. Meanwhile, we came trotting out with Century 25s, a product made in complete secrecy in RJR's R&D department and shrink-wrapped until we had enough for a new brand kickoff. Philip Morris never suspected a thing we did, and we caused them to lay out around $125 million to break a brand that never did do anything in the market. It has to rank as one of the best marketing 'dirty tricks' ever pulled on a competitor."[38]

1. Philip Morris was obviously monitoring RJR's test marketing. Do you think this practice is unethical? Why or why not?

2. Do you think that RJR's "dirty trick" was unethical? Why or why not?
3. Where does one draw "the ethical line" when gathering competitive intelligence?

CASE 4.2

The Exxon Valdez Research

The Superior Court of Alaska, Third Judicial District, ordered John Petterson, principal of San Diego-based Impact Assessment, Inc., to turn raw data over to Exxon relating to a report he prepared for communities near the Exxon Valdez oil slick. The report covers behavior patterns of the residents. His study was commissioned by the "Oiled Mayors," the name pegged to the mayors of the towns affected by the spill. Through 600 household interviews, Petterson, an anthropologist, gathered demographic and health history information and more sensitive information about area residents' activities, including alcohol and drug abuse since the spill.

Diane Bowers, CASRO executive director, noted, "There was a comfort level in the past. The courts protected us. This is an exception." The scope of the Exxon litigation, which includes 200 lawsuits involving 5,300 individuals, also can be considered an exception. Petterson called the entire court proceedings "a joke."

Despite acquiring his files, "Neither the plaintiffs nor defendants . . . have knowledge of our methodology, interviewer training, or protocols to survey structuring," which he said are just as important as the information the court awarded to them. "There isn't any confidential information anymore," Petterson said. "Telling your respondents it's confidential is wrong. It's not. You're lying. If somebody out there wants your information badly enough, they can have it. If the issue is sufficiently important, and your information is unique, some attorney can always get it. You don't have to surrender it if no one important is after it. Exxon is important," he said. "We are nothing to the case."[39]

1. Do you agree or disagree with John Petterson? Why?
2. Do the courts have the right, in your opinion, to violate a respondent's right to privacy?
3. What can marketing researchers do to avoid giving raw survey data to the courts in the future?

APPENDIX A

Philosophies of Ethical Behavior with Marketing Research Applications

Ethical Relativism

Ethical relativism claims that when any two cultures, organizations, or people hold different moral views on an action, both can be right. Judgment of what is right and wrong is culturally determined. Thus, there are many moralities, each equally valid or good. Assume that two producers of hair conditioners analyzed customer use of their respective products and both firms found that customers were using too much conditioner with each application. Overuse was not harmful, but simply wasted the product and shortened the repurchase cycle. Manufacturer "A" did nothing, and both market researchers and manufacturers felt that their inaction was entirely ethical. Manufacturer "B" felt that the only ethical choice was to change the bottle label to discourage overuse. Ethical relativism would say that both decisions were ethical because they were based upon two distinct corporate cultures.

A problem with ethical relativism is that one can never disagree with anyone about the morality of an action. A moral judgment is based upon one's emotions, and emotions are not true or false. When two people have different emotions (which are not right or wrong), they are not disagreeing with each other. A second consequence, then, of ethical relativism is that people can never be mistaken in their moral judgment.[40]

Utilitarianism

The ethical philosophy of utilitarianism states that an action is right if it produces the greatest amount of good for the greatest number of people affected by the action; otherwise, it is wrong. In essence, morality of an action is a cost-benefit analysis for those affected by the action. It is a teleological approach to ethics.

Perhaps the biggest drawback of this approach is how one calculates consequence of acts on an a priori basis, particularly if one has never encountered the situation previously. For example, assume that a research supplier has a contract with a manufacturer to conduct a massive study during April and May. The project is so large that all the firm's personnel and resources must be devoted to it. Before beginning the study, an opportunity comes along for an even bigger study during April and May with twice the profit potential and the opportunity to hire more employees. Should the research supplier break the original contract? To be morally right, the action must produce the greatest good for the greatest number of people affected. The researcher must compare the good from breaking the contract with the total good from not breaking the contract. How is this determined? What if breaking the contract will put the first manufacturer at such a severe competitive disadvantage that it will go out of business? (An alternative interpretation of utilitarianism says that the course of action should be selected that produces more good than harm.)

Kantian Formalism

Immanuel Kant's ethical formalism is quite complex. We will focus on some of the major principles of formalism. First, Kant says that a moral action must be universal. If an action is moral for one person, it must be moral for everyone. Everyone is commanded to do what is morally right; therefore, any action taken must not interfere with others doing it. For example, if a rule was "kill people when you get mad at them," then, because everyone gets angry, everyone would die. The rule leads to its own demise. On the other hand, "respect human life" in a universal sense means that all respect each other's lives. Following the rule does not interfere with others doing it.

Kant's second principle is to treat others with respect and dignity. People are rational beings and rational beings are worthwhile, have dignity, and are worthy of respect. Thus, people have rights because of the kinds of beings they are. These rights include the right to live and own private property.

Kant also said that moral behavior is rational behavior. Morality is not imposed from the outside into a person; it is part of one's nature. Moral law is self-imposed and self-recognized. Animals are not rational beings because they cannot conceive of moral law nor can they choose whether to act in accordance with it. Humans, in contrast, have the freedom to act or not to act in accordance with moral law. As rational beings, people accept limitations on what they permit themselves to do, because they understand that they live and work in a community. All see the necessity of restricting their own actions—for example, not to lie, steal, or murder—just as they expect others to restrict their actions. The test of the morality of a rule is whether rational beings accept it. If they accept it regardless of whether they are the giver or the receiver of actions, it is a moral rule.

Recall that a deontological approach to philosophy says that what makes an action right is not the sum of its consequences but the fact that it conforms to moral law. The test of conformity to moral law is that the act has a certain form; hence, the name, *ethical formalism*. What is the required form? According to Kant, the act must be universal, respect rational beings, and be autonomous.

A problem with formalism arises when moral rules conflict. Assume that a young man just out of college goes to work for his father, who owns a marketing research firm. The son works with his father on a project and observes that his father fabricates about half the data. Upon completion of the project, the son is required to make a written and oral report to the client. After the report is made, the client confides in the young man that this project is critical to the survival of the firm. The client looks at the young man and asks, "Are you absolutely sure that this data is of the highest quality? If we made an incorrect decision based upon your research, we will probably go bankrupt and our 300 employees will lose their jobs!" Before leaving the research firm, the father had told the young man to "convince the client that they bought the best research that money can buy."

Thus, we have a moral conflict. Does the young man "honor thy father" or does he lie? One approach for resolving the dilemma is to make exceptions to the rule. Thus, one may be allowed to kill another person as a last resort in self-defense. A second approach is to carefully and rationally determine whether one rule can take precedence over another. By stating reasons for rank ordering the rules, the reasons can be analyzed as a justification for breaking a lower-ranking rule.

Social Darwinism

Social Darwinism is based upon Charles Darwin's evolutionary philosophy.[41] The businesses that survive over time do so because they are fit. Thus, the best businesses and the brightest minds survive and carry on the competitive battle. The root of evil is any attempt to interfere with this process of selective adaptation for survival. Why? Because this is the same as interfering with the progress and improvement of the American business system. Thus, government should adopt a hands-off policy regarding competition and the economy. Social Darwinism claims that one cannot fight evolution and its laws. Given this truism, there is no room for either moral good or evil. What happens, happens. Thus, social Darwinism is a no-ethics free-for-all.

Machiavellianism

Niccolo Machiavelli, the Renaissance statesman, once noted: "Any person who decides in every situation to act as a good man is bound to be destroyed in the company of so many men who are not good. Wherefore, if a Prince desires to stay in power, he must learn how to be not good and must avail himself of that ability, or not, as the occasion requires."[42] Thus, Machiavellian ethics claims that "is" takes precedence over "ought." On the one hand, there is the business world that we wish existed, a world of trust, loyalty, justice, and honesty . . . the way things ought to be. However, the world is filled with injustice, unfairness, dishonesty, and intolerance. According to Machiavellian philosophy, marketing researchers should make decisions based on the way things really are. Also, morality is for a person's private life; in the business world expediency prevails. Assume that a researcher anticipates a 5 percent probability that a job will be fielded on November 1 and a 95 percent probability that the job will be ready to go to the field on November 15. What alert date should be given to the field services that will handle the data collection? If the November 1 date is given and the job is ready to go on that date, the field work will be completed two weeks early. Or on the other hand, it is likely that the field services will turn down other work and lose revenue if the researcher's job is not fielded on November 1. If this pattern of giving alerts and then postponing jobs becomes a common phenomenon, then many of the field services would no longer accept the researcher's work. Therefore, the researcher decides on a November 15 alert date. Note that this Machiavellian decision has no basis in morality. The researcher cared little whether the field services would lose money. The primary concern was that, in the future, the field services would not accept the researchers' assignments.

To a Machiavellian, a "good" market researcher is a successful market researcher. A successful researcher is aware of the forces that move people to action and can manipulate them to their own ends.

Objectivism

Objectivism is an ethical philosophy espoused by the philosopher Ayn Rand. Recall that for Machiavelli, marketing research takes place in the world of "is"—the world of objective fact. Ethics is found in the world of "ought"—the never-never land of wishful thinking. For Machiavelli, ethics has nothing to do with market research. For Ayn Rand, market research also belongs in the world of "is," but the world of objective fact is the basis of ethics. The real world, according to Rand, is the lifeblood of ethics. Ethics should be based upon reality, not feelings. A research client may feel that a sample size of 300, in fact, should consist of 300 separate interviews—not 275 actual interviews and 25 random replications (replicating 25 questionnaires). But the fact remains that some researchers fill out a target sample size through random replication. This is reality! The research client should deal with this fact objectively, regardless of how distasteful it may be.

To Rand, the rational mind is one that gets fed the correct data about objective reality. It will yield productivity, value, and happiness. A person out of touch with objective reality is doomed to failure. By determining what "is" will yield guidelines for what one ought ethically to do. Moral good, according to Rand, is achieved by having a clear-eyed view of "what is" and productive work. Evil is survival by parasitism—living off the productivity of others. The penalty of immorality is that the person's fate is determined by the whims of others. Ethics, then, is a matter of rational self-interest.

PART I

ETHICAL DILEMMA

Syndicated Research by J. D. Power

In 1971, J. D. Power decided to create small-scale mail surveys that would focus on automobiles. The first consisted of the initial 1,000 buyers of the new Mazda rotary-engine vehicle. The second was a survey of the buyers of front-wheel drive passenger cars such as the Honda 600 and other entries from Saab, Renault, Peugeot, and Subaru. The studies were low cost, low priced, and an immediate success.

Mazda Motors of America did not subscribe to the first survey, but Mazda Japan did, as did General Motors, Ford, Chrysler, Volkswagen, and a host of other Japanese car manufacturers. At $1,800 per subscribing company, J. D. Power felt that he had the key to success, and he also sent out the first press release with topline results. Mazda Motors of America used the headline from the press release without attribution for a television commercial: "Nine out of 10 owners of Mazda rotary-engine cars would recommend them to their friends." This was J. D. Power's first indication that he was creating advertisable research. A year later, at the request of several subscribers to the first Mazda Rotary Engine Owner Survey, the company conducted another survey to gauge the acceptance of the product after a year of ownership. He also raised the price to $2,500.

The results of the follow-up survey revealed that one out of five owners experienced an "O" ring failure that resulted in the need for an engine overhaul. One of the Detroit-based subscribers leaked the findings to the *Wall Street Journal,* which confronted Mazda Motors of America. Mazda subscribed to the study and challenged J. D. Power's findings, methodology, and general capabilities to project from a sample of 500 returns. Within 24 hours, the story was in every newspaper throughout the world. The rest is history—all the other automobile manufacturers, including GM and Ford, scuttled their development work on rotary engines and Mazda went to work on correcting the deficiencies.

In the mid 1990s, J. D. Power and Associates was grossing more than $20 million per year. Now Power, who was 65 years old in 1995, wants to become the quality judge for everything from computers to airlines to phone companies. But his capricious management style has prompted several key employees to leave recently. And Power plays conflicting roles—providing advice to consumers while selling research and advertising claims to manufacturers—that could undermine the company's credibility.

Both problems were evident in the resignation of Christopher Cedergren, J. D. Power's chief market-competition analyst. Power told Cedergren, who is often quoted by auto writers, to stop publicly criticizing carmakers because he was upsetting clients. "We muzzled him," says Power bluntly. Because of that and other differences, Cedergren quit.

Power's methods were evident in his company's first survey of satisfaction among personal-computer users. Power officials phoned Dell Computer Corporation in Austin, Texas, with the good news that Dell had topped the Power computer survey. Then the Power people told Dell it would cost them $72,000 to buy the syndicated survey and another $40,000 to advertise its results. Dell paid up.

"One has to understand that a survey of this nature will pay for itself in a fairly short order of time," explains Barry Rumac, Dell's director of advertising. Indeed, Dell's computer sales quickly jumped an additional 10 percent.

Power perfected this formula in the auto industry. He charges automakers up to $130,000 for a major survey—notably the Customer Satisfaction Index, which tracks the experiences of car buyers during the year after their purchase, and the Initial Quality Survey, which measures defects in the first 90 days of a car's life. Then Power announces the top finishers—and charges them thousands of dollars more to advertise how well they did. The companies who do not do well can rest assured that Power will not publicly disclose their names. Instead, the company offers to sell them consulting advice—to help them do better on the next J. D. Power survey, of course. "We'll coach every company that wants us to coach them," Power declares.

Nobody questions the basic validity of J. D. Power's research. For the two major surveys, J. D. Power mails out about 80,000 questionnaires and gets back close to 30,000 responses. Power dismisses the notion that his methods lead to conflicts of interest. He views his surveys as "the voice of the consumer." Being a cheerleader instead of a critic allows him to be effective, he says. "Maybe it would be ideal to [release] the ratings on everybody," Power acknowledges. But that would require selling the surveys directly to consumers instead of to carmakers, he says. He adds, "We've done more for market research in the auto industry than anyone else—I, personally, and we, the company—by getting top management to focus on the consumer."

Automakers pay because the surveys can sound impressive—at times maybe too much so. In 1989, Power's quality survey named the Buick LeSabre the most trouble-free domestic model, with only 89 defects per 100 cars. Never mind that Ford's Crown Victoria had just 91 defects per 100 cars, a difference Power says was within the margin of error and statistically meaningless. Buick heavily advertised its victory, and Lesabre sales surged more than 40 percent.

In 1990, GM's Chevrolet division used the Power survey to tout its Lumina coupe as "the most trouble-free car in its class." But the class—midsize specialty cars—included only seven vehicles, all domestic. The Lumina coupe beat the other six but had more defects than the average for all cars. Criticism of the Chevy ad prompted Power to ban such "best of class" advertising this year.

1. Is it echical for J. D. Power to provide information to consumers about product quality while charging manufacturers to advertise J. D. Power survey results?
2. Discuss the ethical issues involved in J. D. Power's handling of Christopher Cedergren.
3. Are the actions that J. D. Power took when Dell computer finished at the top of the satisfaction survey ethical? Why or why not?
4. Should complete survey results be made public? Is it unethical to withhold such information?
5. Does the banning of "best of class" advertising by J. D. Power provide evidence that the company is one of high ethical standards?

SOURCE: This case was developed from Neal Templin, "Expanding Beyond Automobile Surveys, J. D. Power Defends Its Business Methods," The Wall Street Journal (September 5, 1991), pp. B1, B4; and "J. D. Power, A Different Kind of Marketing Research Firm," CASRO Journal (1991), pp. 75–78.

PART II

Creating a Research Design

CHAPTER 5

Published Secondary Data, Computerized Databases, and Decision Support Systems

LEARNING OBJECTIVES

1. To understand how to create an internal database.
2. To distinguish between primary and secondary data and understand the advantages and disadvantages of each.
3. To understand the growth and types of on-line databases.
4. To learn the nature of decision support systems.
5. In the appendixes, to learn the multitude of sources of secondary data.

The marketing research function at Samsonite Corporation combines traditional research methods with newer database-oriented approaches, all within a "customer-oriented" environment. Databases, 800 numbers, and consumer service provide unique marketing research tools to aid in decision making and help position Samsonite to cope with the challenges of retail consolidation, blurring of traditional distribution channels, development of new distribution channels, and better informed, proactive consumers.

Robert Bengen, director of Direct Marketing and Research at Samsonite, describes the role of Samsonite's database in its marketing research. "The consumer database is the main source of information about our consumers," Bengen says. "It is 'driven' by the consumer response card—asking for demographic, lifestyle, and purchase information—inserted into all Samsonite luggage and business cases. After about two years of operation [late 1993], we had nearly a half-million records, and the monthly numbers are increasing steadily.

SOURCE: Courtesy of the Samsonite Corporation.

"The consumer database has provided a wealth of information for marketing planning. By analyzing the characteristics of purchasers of our different products, say, Silhouette 5 products versus Ultralite 2 products, we have been able to target our products and our planning more exactly. Also, by examining our consumers against the population as a whole, we have been able to understand where we are *underrepresented* and have produced products for these targets. One good example of this is our Esteem luggage, which is targeted toward professional women.

"Second, our consumer and prospect databases also have aided our sales department in increasing sales to our retail accounts. For example, the Samsonite purchasers' profile shows that our consumers are nicely *overrepresented* in the key 25- to 54-year-old age group, are upscale, educated, active, and do lots of traveling, especially air travel and foreign travel. This profile is a very powerful one and has been used successfully by our salespeople to drive home the point to retailers that 'Samsonite's the type of business you want.'

"In addition, analyses of Samsonite purchasers in different retail accounts (account profiles) have enabled our salespeople to (1) understand our accounts better and work with them more effectively and (2) show accounts how taking on additional Samsonite luggage lines will target different shoppers. As one salesperson said, 'If we show that we know as much or more about the account than does the account itself, then we are in a great position to make additional sales.'

"One other thing we have done—and will do more of in the future—is retail trading area analyses. Using the OASYs database program, we have been able to profile both the census population and the Samsonite purchaser population around a store or group of stores so we can work cooperatively with accounts to develop highly targeted direct marketing programs to key target groups."[1] ■

Will databases, such as Samsonite's, eliminate the need for primary research? What are the advantages and pitfalls of secondary data? How are on-line databases affecting researchers? These are some of the questions we will address in Chapter 5.

The Nature of Secondary Data

secondary data

Data that have been previously gathered.

primary data

New data gathered to help solve the problem at hand.

internal database

Database developed from data within the organization.

Secondary data are pieces of information that have been gathered and only *might* be relevant to the problem at hand. **Primary data,** in contrast, are survey, observation, or experiment data collected to solve the particular problem under investigation. In other words, it is highly unlikely that any marketing research problem is entirely unique or has never occurred before. It also is probable that someone else has investigated this problem or one similar to it in the past. There are two basic sources of secondary data: the company itself **(internal databases)** and other organizations or persons (external databases).

Creating an Internal Database

For many companies, a computerized database containing information about customers and prospects has become an essential marketing tool. A database is simply a collection of related information. A good starting point for creating an internal secondary database is to pull information from the firm's sales or inquiry processing and tracking system. Typically, such a system is built upon a salesperson's "call report." Call reports provide a blueprint of a salesperson's daily activities. A report details the number of calls made, characteristics of each firm visited, sales activity resulting from the call, and information picked up regarding competitors such as price changes, new products, credit term modifications, and new features stressed by competitors.

Creating an internal marketing secondary database built upon sales results and customer preferences can be a powerful marketing tool. Catalog companies such as Speigel's and L. L. Bean have become masters at building and using internal databases. The story of how Cabela's, a major fishing tackle and outdoors products company, uses its database is presented in the following "Marketing Research in Practice."

Marketing Research in Practice

Cabela's depends on its database to control the distribution costs of its four-color catalogs. In a typical year, Cabela's sends out at least nine mailings of between 300,000 and three million catalogs each.

Cabela's constantly winnows out the people who do not respond. It also sends specific kinds of catalogs to buyers based on their purchasing patterns, says marketing director Sharon Robison. The company divides customers into 10 major categories, from the buyers of footwear to buyers of gifts and fishing and bow-hunting equipment. Cabela's gathers new names by sharing its mailing list with similar catalog companies such as Gander Mountain, by renting address lists from magazines, by advertising in hunting and fishing publications, and by soliciting new names from current catalog recipients.[2] ■

Keys to a Successful Internal Database

To achieve the levels of success that Cabela's and other organizations have with their internal databases, several steps must be taken. First, organizations must create a **database management system.** This involves capturing data on the computer, organizing them for effective use, updating and maintaining them, and being able to readily retrieve information from the system for marketing decision making. This is no simple task. With today's technology, storing data on a computer is trivial. Creating an internal secondary database system with the proper blend of experienced people, hardware, and software to make data usable is a complex task.

database management system
The system in which data are captured on the computer, organized for effective use, updated, and maintained to provide information for decision making.

Second, database users must be trained on how to retrieve information and how to manipulate the data using **database management software.** Some of the basic abilities a manager will acquire by using such software include

database management software
Computer programs for the retrieval and manipulation of data.

- Inputing: Adding new data to the database.
- Querying: Looking for specific pieces of information, such as sales prospects not called on in two years.
- Sorting: Taking an alphabetical list of sales prospects and sorting it by zip code for distribution to sales representatives in those regions for follow-up.
- Extracting: A researcher might want to evaluate the rough potential for a new product with the firm's current base of customers.

A researcher who believed that each employee in an office or plant would create a market for seven units of the new product per year could quickly determine the product's potential, by location, by extracting the key fields from the database—company name, location, number of employees—and inserting a column that multiplies each employee by a factor of seven.

A manager also would typically learn spreadsheet applications for the database. Spreadsheet software is designed to reflect the format of a standard business spreadsheet. Rows and columns of data, each with their applicable labels, can be added, subtracted, divided, multiplied, and formulated in as many ways as the user likes. The final tabulated results can be printed as a finished report. The software's obvious advantage is the incredible speed at which these calculations can be accomplished. Thus, a number of different scenarios can be postulated and their impacts examined. For example, Jim Clancy opened a small deli across the street from the college he is attending (see Table 5.1). Last quarter Jim had sales of $12,000, a gross profit margin of 15 percent, and a net profit of $720. Using an electronic spreadsheet, Jim can determine what will happen next quarter if sales increase 8 percent and his gross margin remains the same. Jim may be faced with an increase in meat costs that will cut his gross margin to 12 percent. However, he feels that advertising in the college newspaper may begin paying off so that sales could rise 11 percent over the previous quarter. Under this scenario, net profit will fall to $400.

Database technology, from a software perspective, has continued to improve. While most databases were based on a flat-file approach in the past, the current trend is toward the use of more sophisticated and powerful relational databases. The distinction between these two approaches to database design and implementation is discussed in detail in the following "A Professional Researcher's Perspective."

The Growing Importance of Internal Database Marketing

Perhaps the fastest-growing use of an internal database is database marketing. *Database marketing* is the creation of a large computerized file of customers' and potential customers' profiles and purchase patterns. Specifically, database marketing can

- Evaluate sales territories.
- Identify most profitable and least profitable customers.
- Identify most profitable market segments and target efforts with greater efficiency and effectiveness.

TABLE 5.1 How Electronic Spreadsheets Answer "What If?" Questions

	BASE		8% SALES INCREASE/15% GM		11% SALES INCREASE/12% GM	
Sales	12,000	100%	12,960	100%	13,320	100%
Cost of Sales	10,200	85%	11,016	85%	11,722	88%
Gross Profit	1,800	15%	1,944	15%	1,598	12%
Sales Expenses	600	5%	648	5%	666	5%
Administration	480	4%	518	4%	533	4%
Profit	720	6%	778	6%	400	3%

A Professional Researcher's Perspective

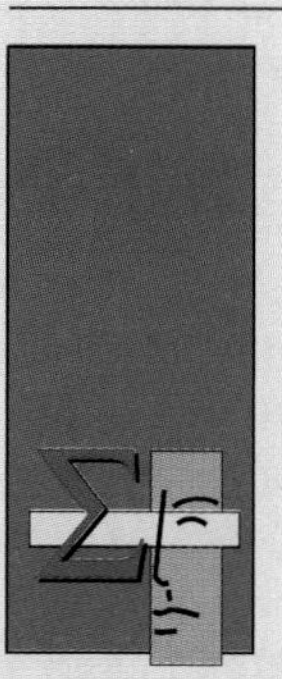

With an undergraduate degree in Computer Science and an MBA, Mike Foytik, senior vice-president for Information Science for DSS Research, exemplifies the new breed of managers in marketing services jobs with strong backgrounds in computers. He is a strong proponent of the use of *relational databases.* He has designed dozens for DSS clients in direct marketing and retailing.

He notes that there are many advantages to using a relational database compared with the *traditional database approach,* sometimes referred to as the *flat-file method.* In a relational database, data are stored in several small structures or files rather than in a single large one. Each of the small files in a relational database contains key information that allows individual records in the database to be linked to associated data in other individual files that make up the entire database structure.

For example, a customer database might contain one file that includes customer information such as name, mailing address, and Social Security number. This information needs to be updated occasionally. Products purchased by each customer would go into another file that is updated frequently (every time the customer buys something). The two files might be linked by the customer's Social Security number.

With each new order, a record will be created that included the product purchased, the price, other relevant information concerning the purchase, and the buyer's Social Security number. Under the traditional, flat-file approach, all this information, the product purchase information and the buyer's personal information, would have to be entered with each product purchase.

Relational databases have a number of distinct advantages:

- *Less data storage space required.* There is very little redundant information in a relational database. Data such as addresses are stored only once for each customer rather than being stored with every new purchase that is added. Foytik notes that "we have achieved 75 percent storage space reductions for some of our clients."
- *More flexible.* Relational databases offer much greater flexibility and efficiency regarding changes in the data to be stored and the way data are used in the future. With flat-file databases, every time a new data field is added to the database, the database must be recreated so that the new data field is added to every record in the database. With a relational database, new information would be stored in a new file and, therefore, has no effect on existing data in other files in the relational database.
- *Easier to restrict access to sensitive information.* Relational databases can be easily designed to restrict user access to certain areas of the database via the use of special passwords or codes while still allowing more general access to less sensitive areas. In flat-file databases, this sort of restricted access to some parts of the data-

continues

base is all but impossible. Users must have either total access or no access.

- *Can easily design the database to accommodate many users.* Foytik notes that "most of our clients have a number of different departments with very different informational needs accessing customer data." With flat-files, separate copies of the database must be created and modified to meet the needs of different users. With relational databases, the physical data remain unchanged while the data or reports seen by the different user groups (sometimes called the logical data) can be varied.

Finally, he notes, all these advantages come at some cost. First, relational databases require much more sophisticated software and more sophisticated people to program it. Second, relational databases require much more up-front planning if the company is to reap the full benefits of this type of data. Finally, relational databases tend to require more processor horsepower. This is becoming less of an issue with the price/performance ratio of computers constantly improving.[3] ■

- Aim marketing efforts to those products, services, and segments that require the most support.
- Increase revenue through repackaging and repricing products for various market segments.
- Evaluate opportunities for offering new products or services.
- Identify products or services that are best-sellers or most profitable.
- Evaluate existing marketing programs.

Some companies are successfully merging external marketing secondary data and the firm's internal database. One of the best examples is a power company based in Charlotte, North Carolina. Its experience is presented in the "Marketing Research in Practice" feature in this section.

Beginning in the 1950s, network television enabled advertisers to "get the same message to everyone simultaneously." Database marketing can get a customized, individual message to everyone simultaneously through direct mail. This is why database marketing is sometimes called "micro marketing." Database marketing can create a computerized form of the old-fashioned relationship that people used to have with the corner grocer, butcher, or baker. "A database is sort of a collective memory," says Richard G. Barlow, president of Frequency Marketing, Inc., a Cincinnati-based consulting firm. "It deals with you in the same personalized way as a mom-and-pop grocery store, where they knew customers by name and stocked what they wanted."[4]

The size of many databases is somewhat mind boggling: Ford Motor Company's is about 50 million names; Kraft General Foods, 30 million; Citicorp, 30 million; and Kimberly Clark, maker of Huggies diapers, 10 million new mothers. American Express, for example, can pull from its database all cardholders who made purchases at golf pro-shops in the past six months, or who attended sym-

Blockbuster uses its internal database to help customers select movies which they will enjoy.

phony concerts, or who traveled to Europe more than once in the past year, or the very few people who did all three activities.

A technique of growing popularity for building a database is the creation of "customer clubs." Kraft, for example, has been inviting kids to join the Cheese & Macaroni Club. For three proofs-of-purchase, $2.95, and a completed membership form with the child's (and, of course, Mom's) address, Kraft will send a painter's cap, bracelet, shoelaces, a book of stickers, and other goodies.[5] By requiring customers who respond to offers of free shirts, sleeping bags, or other merchandise to fill out detailed questionnaires, Philip Morris has built a database of about 26 million smokers.

Blockbuster Entertainment Corp. is using its database of 36 million households and two million daily transactions to help its video-rental customers select movies and steer them to other Blockbuster subsidiaries. In Richmond, Virginia, the company is testing a computerized system that recommends 10 movie titles based on a customer's prior rentals. The suggestions are printed on a card that also offers targeted promotions. Customers who have rented children's films, for example, might get a discount at Discovery Zone, Blockbuster's play-center subsidiary.

Vons Company, Southern California's largest supermarket chain, and ninth largest in America, has upgraded its check-approval card into a VonsClub card. The card was a foundation for creating a database that gave automatic discounts on items selected for promotion. Vons's objective was to build a comprehensive database of exactly what's in shoppers' baskets each time they leave the store. Using that data, Vons can understand consumer behavior better and send a monthly mailing of individually laser-printed discount coupons to each VonsClub member. Even food processors and manufacturers benefit from Vons's database. Beech-Nut, a maker of baby foods, has used the VonsClub mailer to identify every household that has purchased a baby product for the first time in the preceding eight weeks. Says Susan Widham, vice-president of Marketing at Beech-Nut, "This program enables me to target an offer specifically to a consumer

The Vons Club card enables the large supermarket chain to build a database which identifies everything in a specific shopper's basket every time they shop. SOURCE: Courtesy of the VONS Companies, Inc.

based on the type and quantity of a product they buy, the frequency they buy it, and whether they buy my product or my competitor's."[6] Under consideration, she says, is a 50-cent-off coupon—to hold on to Beech-Nut customers—and a $1-off coupon for Gerber Products Co. customers, to get them to switch brands.

Database Technologies As you can see, gathering data is not all that difficult. The big challenge has been making sense out of what has been gathered rather than not using the information. The amount of information in some databases is huge. American Express's database contains more than 500 billion bytes of data on how customers have used its 35 million green, gold, and platinum charge cards to spend $350 billion since 1991.[7] Fingerhut, a database firm, is expanding its collection of mail-order customer data from about 600 billion bytes to about two trillion, or two terabytes. This amount of information would choke a mainframe computer. Supercomputers are the only answer. Fingerhut uses a Sun Microsystems parallel processor, whereas American Express relies on Thinking Machines Corporation's supercomputers. Parallel processors use groups of microprocessors to scan huge volumes of data extremely fast. Database software, sold by Oracle, Sybase, IBM, Informix and others, cross-indexes data records into giant matrices. This makes finding specified records much easier.

Much more exciting is neural-network software. This software, available from HNC Software, Customer Insight, and others, designed after the pattern of cells in the human brain, can automatically "learn" from large sets of data on its own. By scanning thousands of data records again and again, the software can build a strong statistical model describing important relationships and patterns in the data. All that's required is a standard, high-end PC equipped with a plug-in neural-net "accelerator" board. Customer Insight has tailored HNC Software Database Mining Workstation software, based on neural-net techniques, just for database marketing.[8] Once a statistical model of the ideal customer, for example, is constructed, a supercomputer finds all the prospects matching the profile.

Renting Internal Databases Some companies rent their internal databases to obtain extra revenue. At times, this practice can raise important ethical questions. At one time Blockbuster planned to rent lists of customer rentals at its video stores. The plan was quickly dropped, however, when management found that federal law forbids video stores from disclosing information on movies that customers rent. Burger King doesn't rent its database. A spokesperson for the company noted, "We were concerned that if people knew their names would be sold, it would hamper participation in its Kid's Club.[9]

Under pressure from New York state authorities, American Express disclosed it was telling merchants more about its cardholders' spending habits than it had previously acknowledged. The company revealed that information about cardholders' lifestyles and spending habits was used to create joint marketing efforts with merchants. Previously, the company told cardholders that it merely provided merchants a mailing list for marketing or promotions based on information in the initial application for the card.

As a result of an agreement with the New York Attorney General's office, American Express had to notify more than 20 million cardholders nationwide that it compiles profiles of spending behavior and that it uses the information for "target marketing" purposes. The cardholders would then have the option of having their information excluded from any future marketing efforts.[10]

Published Secondary Data

Internal

Published secondary information originating within the company includes documents such as annual reports, reports to stockholders, product testing results perhaps made available to the news media, and house periodicals composed by the company's personnel for communication to employees, customers, or others. Often this information is incorporated into a company's internal database.

External

Innumerable outside sources of secondary information also exist, principally in the forms of government (federal, state, and local) departments and agencies that compile and publish summaries of business data. Trade and industry associations also provide published secondary data. Still another set is composed of all business periodicals and other news media that regularly publish studies and articles on the economy, specific industries, and even individual companies. The unpublished summarized secondary information from these sources corresponds to internal reports, memos, or special-purpose analyses with limited circulation. Economic considerations or priorities in the organization may preclude publication of these summaries. Finally, it is conceivable that pockets of raw data may reside in these organizations just as they occur in the marketing researcher's own (client) firm. It should be evident that each type of secondary information requires that unique tasks be performed to render it useful to the researcher. Appendix A provides a detailed list of many published secondary data.

Advantages of Secondary Data

Marketing researchers use secondary information because it can be obtained at a fraction of the cost, time, and inconvenience of primary data collection. Additional advantages for using secondary information include the following.

1. *Secondary information may help to clarify or redefine the definition of the problem as part of the exploratory research process.* As you learned in Chapter 3, secondary data plays a key role in exploratory research. A local YMCA was concerned about its stagnant level of membership and a lack of participation in many traditional YMCA programs. It decided to survey members and nonmembers. Secondary data revealed a tremendous influx of young, single persons into the target market while the number of "traditional families" remained constant. The problem was redefined to examine how the YMCA could attract a significant share of the young single adult market while maintaining its traditional family base.

2. *Secondary information may actually provide a solution to the problem.* It is highly unlikely that a problem faced by a manager and communicated to the marketing researcher will never before have been encountered; there is always a possibility that someone else has addressed the identical problem or a very similar one. Someone may have collected the precise information desired but not for the same purpose as the problem faced by the manager.

   Many states publish a directory of manufacturers that contains information on the location, markets, product lines, number of plants, names of key personnel, number of employees, and sales levels of companies. For example, a consulting company specializing in long-range strategic planning for members of the semiconductor industry desired a regional profile of its potential clients. Individual state directories were used to compile the profile. No primary data collection was necessary.
3. *Secondary information may provide primary data research method alternatives.* Each primary research endeavor is custom designed for the situation at hand; consequently, the marketing researcher should always be open to information that offers research alternatives. For example, the authors conducted a research project for a large southwestern city's convention and visitor's bureau. A research report prepared by *Meeting and Convention Planners* magazine was obtained before designing the questionnaire. The secondary report published by the magazine contained the original questionnaire. A series of scaling questions were used in the author's questionnaire. Not only were the scales well-designed, but results from the study could be compared with the magazine's data.
4. *Secondary information may alert the marketing researcher to potential problems or difficulties.* Apart from alternatives, secondary information may divulge potential dangers. Unpopular collection methods, sample selection difficulties, or respondent hostility may be uncovered. For example, examination of a study of anesthesiologists by a researcher planning to conduct a study to measure the level of satisfaction with certain existing drugs used in the profession uncovered a high refusal rate in a telephone survey. The researcher also had planned a telephone study but switched to a mail questionnaire with a response incentive.
5. *Secondary information may provide necessary background information and build creativity for the research report.* Secondary information can often provide a wealth of background data for planning a research project. It may offer a profile of potential buyers versus nonbuyers, industry data, new product features desired, language used by purchasers to describe the industry, and existing products and their advantages and disadvantages. Language used by target consumers can aid in phrasing questions that will be understood correctly and be meaningful to respondents. Background data also can often meet some research objectives, eliminating the need to ask the questions in a present study. Shorter questionnaires typically have higher completion rates. Secondary data can sometimes enrich research findings by providing additional insights into what the data mean or by corroborating current findings. Finally, secondary data can serve as a reference base for subsequent research projects.

Limitations of Secondary Data

Despite the many advantages of secondary data, they also pose some dangers and pitfalls. The disadvantages are lack of availability, lack of relevance, inaccuracy, and insufficiency.[11]

Lack of Availability

For some research questions there are simply no available data. If Kraft General Foods wants to evaluate the taste, texture, and color of three new gourmet brownie mixes, there are no secondary data that would answer these questions. Consumers must try each mix and then evaluate it. If McDonald's wants to evaluate its image in Phoenix, Arizona, it must gather primary data. If Ford wants to know the reaction of college students to a new two-seater sports car design, it must show prototypes to the students and evaluate their opinions. Of course, secondary data may have played a major role in the engineer's design plan for the car.

Lack of Relevance

It is not uncommon for secondary data to be expressed in units or measures that cannot be used by the researcher. For example, Joan Dermott is a retailer of oriental rugs who determined that the primary customers for her wares are families with total household incomes of $40,000 to $80,000. Higher-income consumers tend to purchase rugs beyond the price range carried by the dealer. In attempting to decide whether to open a store in another Florida city, she cannot find useful income data. One source offered class breakdowns from $30,000 to $50,000, $50,000 to $70,000, $70,000 to $90,000, and so forth. A second secondary source breaks down incomes as less than $15,000, $15,000 to $30,000, and more than $30,000. Even if the income brackets had met Joan's needs, she encountered another problem: lack of publication currency. One study was conducted in 1980 and the other in 1982. In Florida's dynamic markets, the percentages probably were no longer relevant. This is often the case with U.S. census data, which are historically nearly two years old before they are available in publications. However, computer disks for the 1990 census were available much sooner.

Inaccurate Data

Users of secondary data should always be suspicious of the accuracy of the data. There are a number of potential sources of error when a researcher gathers, codes, analyzes, and presents data. Any report that does not mention possible sources of error and ranges of error should be suspect.

Using secondary data does not relieve the researcher from attempting to assess their accuracy.[12] A few guidelines for determining secondary data accuracy are as follows.

1. *Who gathered the data?* The source of the secondary data is a key to accuracy. Federal agencies, most state agencies, and large commercial market research

firms generally can be counted on to have conducted their research as professionally as possible. One should always be on guard when examining data in which a hidden agenda might be present. A chamber of commerce, for instance, is always going to put its best foot forward. Similarly, trade associations often advocate one position or another.

2. *What was the purpose of the study?* Data are always collected for some reason. Understanding the motivation for the research can provide clues in assessing the quality of the data. A chamber of commerce study conducted to provide data that can be used to attract new industry to the area should be viewed with a great deal of scrutiny and caution. There have been situations in which advertising agencies were hired by their clients to assess the impact of their advertising programs. In other words, advertising agencies were asked to evaluate the quality of the job they were doing for their clients!
3. *What information was collected?* A researcher should always identify exactly what information was gathered. For example, in a dog food study, were purchasers of canned, dry, and semimoist food interviewed or just one or two types of dog food purchasers surveyed? In a voters' survey, were only Democrats or Republicans interviewed? Were the respondents qualified to make certain they are registered voters? Was any attempt made to ascertain the respondent's likelihood of voting in the next election? Were self-reported data used to infer actual behavior?
4. *When was the information collected?* A shopping mall study that surveyed shoppers only on weekends would not reflect the "typical" mall patrons. A telephone survey conducted from 9:00 A.M. to 5:00 P.M. would vastly underrepresent working persons. A survey of Florida visitors conducted during the summer probably would reveal different motivations and interests from winter visitors.
5. *How was the information obtained?* Were the data collected by mail, telephone, or personal interview? Each of these techniques offers advantages and disadvantages. What was the refusal rate? Were decision makers interviewed or a representative of the decision maker? In short, the researcher must attempt to discern the amount of bias injected into the data by the information-gathering process. A mail survey with a 1 percent response rate (where only 1 percent of those who received the survey mailed it back) probably contains a lot of self-selection bias.
6. *Is the information consistent with other information?* A lack of consistency between secondary data sets should serve as a caution sign. The researcher should delve into possible causes of the discrepancy. A different sample frame, time factor, sampling methodology, questionnaire structure, and other factors can lead to variations in studies. If possible, the researcher should assess the reliability of the studies as a basis of determining which, if any, study should be used for decision making.

Insufficient Data

A researcher may determine that data are available, relevant, and accurate but still are not sufficient to make a decision or bring complete closure to a problem. A manager for WalMart discount stores may have sufficient secondary data on incomes, family sizes, number of competitors, and growth potential to determine, among five Iowa towns with populations of less than 20,000, where to locate its next store. However, as no traffic counts exist for the selected town, primary data will have to be gathered to select a specific site for the store.

The New Age of Secondary Information—On-Line Databases

Gathering traditional secondary data was often an arduous task. It meant writing for government, trade association, or other reports—then waiting several weeks for a reply. Many times one or more trips to the library were required, and then needed reports may have been checked out or missing. Today, the rapid development of **on-line** computerized **databases** have alleviated much of the drudgery associated with gathering secondary data. An on-line database is a public information database accessible to anyone with proper communication facilities. With more than 10,000 databases available in 1995, virtually every topic of interest to a marketing researcher can be found in some database.[13]

on-line database
A public information database accessible to anyone with proper communication facilities.

Data communication requires a computer system on one end as the sender or receiver and either another computer system or terminal on the other. A modem is used to transfer data over telephone lines. At the receiving end another **modem** converts the sounds back into electrical impulses. Some day, a fiber optic telephone cable will be able to transmit 100 trillion bits per second!

Types of Databases

Databases cover a variety of different subjects, geographic areas, and frequency of updates. Databases can be divided into four major categories: numeric, bibliographic, directory, and full text.

Numeric databases contain original survey data such as the VALS2 database. More than 12,000 respondents are reported with data describing their attitudes, wants, and beliefs in the eight VALS (values and lifestyles) categories developed by the Stanford Research Institute. These data are melded with Mediamark Research Incorporated's study of 20,000 adults regarding magazines they read, the radio programs they listen to, and the television they watch. In addition, purchase habits on 5,700 individual brands are available.

numeric database
Database containing original survey data on a wide variety of general topics.

One of the most valuable **bibliographic databases** for marketing is FINDEX. More than 11,000 studies done by more than 500 research firms are indexed. The database offers instant access to citations of market research reports, consumer and product studies, store audit reports, subscription research services, and surveys of 55 industries worldwide.

bibliographic database
An index of published studies and reports, which may include explanation and analysis.

A popular **directory database** used to get a "quick picture" of a company is *Standard and Poor's Corporate Descriptions*. It contains information on 55,000 public and private U.S. corporations. Some of the information provided includes capital expenditures; number of employees, officers, and directors; names of principal stockholders; and two years of balance sheet data.

directory database
Data available through directories or indexes of directory-type data.

As the name implies, **full text databases** contain the complete text of the source documents making up the database. For example, the *Harvard Business Review Online* database contains the full text of articles from 1976 to the present.

full text database
Index containing the full text of source documents, such as articles.

Searches can be conducted in a number of ways: by subject, title, company, industry, product, service, and others.

On-Line Vendors

on-line vendor
An intermediary that acquires databases from a variety of database creators.

An **on-line** database **vendor** is an intermediary that acquires databases from a variety of database creators. Such databases offer electronic mail, news, finance, sports, weather, airline schedules, software, encyclopedias, bibliographies, directories, full text information, and numeric databases. Thus, a user can go to a single on-line vendor and gain access to a variety of databases. Billing is simplified because a single invoice covers the use of a variety of databases on the vendor's system. Also, searching is simplified because it is standardized for all databases offered by the vendor. On-line vendors also provide an index to assist the researcher in determining which databases will most likely meet the researcher's needs. Several of the most popular on-line databases are CompuServe, America Online, Prodigy, Dow Jones News/Retrieval Service, and DIALOG. CompuServe is a subsidiary of H&R Block. DIALOG, a subsidiary of Knight-Ridder, offers more than 400 different databases containing more than 150 million items of information. Selected databases offered by several major on-line vendors are shown in Table 5.2. The depth of the number and types of databases available is extraordinary. For example, CompuServe offers five U.S. demographics databases. A summary of each is detailed in Table 5.3

How to Search

On-line databases have two layers: individual records that make up the database and search software that picks out the records you want from the thousands or millions in the database. Think of search software as an idiot that works at the speed of light. If you type in a word or phrase, the software will find every occurrence of that word or phrase in the database, exactly as you typed it and regardless of context. The system will respond with the number of records in the database that match your search.[14]

Say you are interested in mentions of the president's home. A search of the phrase *white house* might retrieve 45 records—14 that pertain to 1600 Pennsylva-

TABLE 5.2 Selected Offerings of the Popular On-Line Vendors

DOW JONES	DIALOG	COMPUSERVE
Disclosure II	Disclosure II (business database)	Standard & Poor's General Information File
Dow Jones News	Management Contents	Washington Post
Current Quotes	Standard & Poor's Corporate Description	World Book Encyclopedia
Wall Street Journal	Books in Print	Microquote (stock information)
Academic American Encyclopedia	Electronic Yellow Pages	Business Information Wire
Cineman Movie Reviews	Magazine Index	AP News
AP News	AP News	Comp*U*Store
Comp*U*Store	OAG	OAG
OAG		

TABLE 5.3 American Demographic Databases Offered by CompuServe

- *Business Demographics* reports from Market Statistics are based on U.S. census information and are designed for business market analysis. Two types of reports are offered. The Business to Business Report includes information on all broad Standard Industrial Classification (SIC) categories, providing the total number of employees in each category for a designated geographical area. The Advertisers' Service Report offers data on businesses that constitute the SIC categories for Retail Trade. Each $10 report breaks down the total number of businesses for each specified geographical area in relation to company size. Both reports can be requested by zip code, county, state, metropolitan area, Arbitron TV markets, Nielsen TV markets, or the entire United States.
- *Cendata* offers U.S. census information directly from the U.S. Census Bureau, allowing you to spot patterns, trends, and correlations that make for informed decisions. This menu-based system offers several hundred thousand records culled from the censuses and surveys conducted by the Census Bureau for the entire United States, as well as specific states and counties, on such topics as agriculture, business, construction and housing, foreign trade, governments, manufacturing, population, and genealogy. Economic time-series data from the U.S. government are published on Cendata within an hour of its release to the media, offering users instant access to timely information on current economic developments. In addition to census reports, Cendata features explanatory articles that help make sense of the numerical data.
- *Neighborhood Demographic Reports* from CACI, Inc. provide basic demographic information by U.S. zip code. Four neighborhood reports are available: Demographics, Civic/Public Activity, Gift Idea, and Sports/Leisure Activity. Each report costs $10.
- *Supersite* from CACI allows you to narrow your search to specific and compact geographical areas. The reports are offered for the entire United States and every state, county, metropolitan area, Arbitron TV market, Nielsen TV market, place, census tract, minor civil division, and zip code in the country. Demographic reports are provided, covering general demographics, income, housing, education, employment, and current and projected-year forecasts. You can focus your search on one specific geographic area or enter more than one for a consolidated market report. Included are Demographic Reports based on the 1990 Census Profile, Update and Forecast Data, and Purchase Potential Reports, as well as ACORN Target Marketing, which analyzes and profiles consumers based on the type of residential area in which they live. Prices for reports range from $25 to $45.
- *US-State-County Reports* from CACI offer demographic information for the entire United States, any state or county, and include such data as total population, number of households, average age, average household income, type of households, occupations, race, and more. Each report costs $10.

SOURCE: CompuServe

nia Avenue, four on the coffee brand, one on Marin County (an area known for the predominantly white color of its houses), and 26 from the White House Publishing Company in New Delhi, India.

Marketing-Oriented Databases

Database needs of marketers run the gamut from simple mailing lists to detailed consumption patterns broken down by psychographic profiles. Attempting to list every database of interest to marketers would be an encyclopedic task. Moreover, new databases are coming on-line every day. A few of the most widely used databases and a brief description of each is provided in Appendix B.

Advantages of On-Line Databases

On-line databases provide a number of important advantages. First, the researcher has quick access to a much greater variety of information than ever before. Second, the efficient use of on-line search protocols helps the researcher quickly pinpoint relevant data. Third, the large in-house staffs formerly required to research and maintain files can be eliminated. This reduces labor costs and increases productivity. Finally, small firms can gain access to the same secondary data as large organizations and do it just as efficiently. This tends to make small firms competitive with big companies with huge libraries and large staffs.

Disadvantages of On-Line Databases

The immense variety of information available to the marketing researcher as shown by the description of key databases in Appendix B could engender a false sense of euphoria. On-line databases are no marketing research panacea. Like all tools of the researcher, this one has its drawbacks.

One potential disadvantage is that a person not skilled at "searching" a database may be deluged with data. The researcher must carefully select the search words used to locate appropriate citations, abstracts, and full text stories. Often this means researchers must familiarize themselves with an industry's terminology to narrow the search.

One novice researcher working for Ogilvy and Mather advertising agency in New York inadvertently punched in a command to call up all stories in their entirety. Once placed, the instruction could not be canceled. The result was a $700 bill for data and telephone time.

Some databases tend to have decision rules for what is included or excluded from the database but do not make this expressly known to the user. For example, one database that indexes news publications includes domestic news and international news but only international news relating to Europe. Thus, a researcher may inadvertently miss important secondary information even when using the proper search operators simply because certain documents were never added to the database.

Another complaint is that some databases do not keep their files up-to-date. It is not uncommon to find that the most current information is several months old. If current data are of critical importance, the researcher may still end up browsing through current periodicals at a local library.

On-line research is not necessarily cheap. Most vendors charge in fractions of hours. Hourly fees for databases can range from nominal ($20) to expensive ($200 plus). The network through which users call vendors usually charges by the hour, too, and the charge is roughly equivalent to what you might spend if you had to directly call the vendor's computer long-distance. Some vendors also charge for the actual information users retrieve. A bibliographic citation might be free, but the full text of an article might cost a few dollars, and a corporate financial report might run $100 or more. Users must be sure to know what costs they are facing before they request a lot of information.

Surfing the Internet

The global web of computer networks known as the Internet can be accessed through on-line vendors such as America Online, CompuServe, and Delphi Internet. The on-line world boasts of more than 60,000 public-access bulletin boards in North America alone.[15] These are the virtual equivalent of a clubhouse, an association, or even a neighborhood bar. Users exchange messages, ask questions, and swap useful software. An example of how to "surf the net" is given in "Marketing Research in Practice" on page 140.

Dell Computer Corp. has an Internet SWAT team. It peruses traffic for any mention of Dell products, ready to swoop into "threads" of conversations to help solve customer problems, change negative perceptions and protect the compa-

Dell Computer Corp. has a SWAT team that peruses the net looking for mentions of Dell to help solve customer problems and protect the Dell image.

ny's reputation. The Internet, say some company officials, enables them to learn more about customers electronically than through traditional marketing research surveys and telephone-service calls. "People can be pretty direct. You can be pretty cocky when you don't have to look someone in the eye," says Mal Ransom, Packard Bell Electronics Inc.'s marketing vice-president, who sometimes takes to Prodigy and CompuServe himself to answer customers.[16]

Spying on competitors isn't out of the question, either. Dell, Compaq Computer Corp., and others confess that they use the Internet and the other networks to check up on rival PC makers, looking for discussions of bugs, product delays, and red-hot products and ideas. "Our engineering teams constantly go through the Internet and get bits and pieces," says Compaq's Anthony Cyplik, manager of North American systems marketing.[17]

Opinions on the Internet weigh in from far and wide. On a recent day, a professor from the University of Sydney in Australia inquired about whether to buy a notebook computer from Dell or from Acer, Inc. in Taiwan. A University of Virginia professor polled opinions on Dell versus Gateway desktops. A Digital Equipment Corp. executive discussed how pleased he was with his Gateway purchase. Someone identified only as "Bill" from the Naval Surface Warfare Center inquired about Gateway complaints.

Marketing Research in Practice

The fastest growing part of the Internet is the World Wide Web (known as the Web). The Web has pictures, sound, and hyperlinks that—with the aid of a program called a browser—let you move effortlessly across the Internet from one document to another. Fax software and data communications programs round out the must-have software list for the serious communicator. Taking a cue from the major business software companies, which bundle their applications as a software suite, many developers now sell fax and data communications software in one box—think of it as a communications suite.

Using a Web browser you can access hyperlinked multimedia Web documents—also known as *pages* or *sites*—stored on Internet-connected computers around the world. Thanks to its ease of use, multimedia capabilities, and interactivity, the Web has been hailed by some as the most important advance in publishing since the printing press.

The Web connects more than 50,000 computer networks used by tens of millions of people worldwide. Analysts estimate that 2 million people now have access to the Web and that several million more will join them as the major online services—Prodigy, America Online, and CompuServe— roll out Web browsers of their own.

Assume that you, as a market researcher, wanted the most recent county population estimates for Georgia. One way is to e-mail the Public Affairs Office at the census bureau (pio@census.gov). A bureau employee will quickly fax back a geodemographic map of Georgia counties with the information requested or simply e-mail the numbers. Alternatively, a researcher can use the Internet. Assume you want to know the latest national population estimate. Simply enter the bureau's main data bank, select the Population menu, and ask for the "Popclock Projection." You'll get the best estimate of the nation's total population at the exact time of your request.

Are you more interested in statistics about states? Again, select "Enter the Main Data Bank" at the initial menu, then select "Statistical Abstract Summaries by States." Here you'll find a whole array of social and economic indicators on such topics as federal funds and social insurance programs, poverty, income, infant mortality, births and deaths, business failures, and even the number of hazardous-waste sites. They are taken from the *Statistical Abstract of the United States*, a venerable government publication now in its 114th year.

Another popular item at the bureau's Internet site is County Business Patterns, which contains state- and county-level data on employment, payrolls, and establishments. You can also get bureau news releases arranged by subject and date of release. Type in "California," for example, and you'll see all news releases with data for California. The stop labeled "News and Analysis from the Center for Economic Studies" is full of recent research papers with titles like "Gross Job Creation, Gross Job Destruction, and Employment."[18] ■

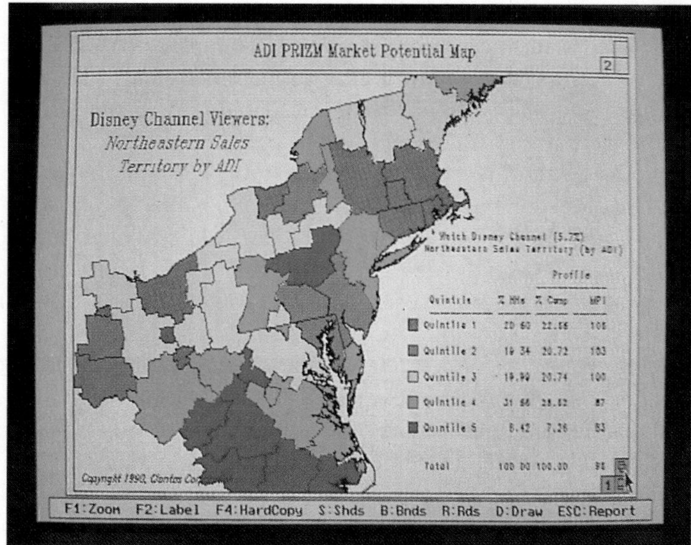

Computerized database packages assist researchers with segmentation and demographic studies and mapping. SOURCE: Courtesy of Claritas, Inc.

Computerized Database Packages

A number of companies are offering computerized database packages for personal computers. For example, the Claritas Corporation has created a package called Compass/Agency designed for advertising agencies and Compass/Newspaper for newspapers to do segmentation and demographic studies and mapping. Claritas recently added Arbitron ratings and data from Simmons Marketing Research Bureau and Mediamark on product usage to Compass/Agency. The Compass/Newspaper system contains more than 200 preformatted reports and maps. Users also can import data on subscribers, readership, or advertisers and display them as reports and maps or export data into other standard software packages, such as spreadsheets, word processing, and graphics applications.[19]

The Department of Commerce also has made 1990 census data available on CD-ROM for use on PCs. Information available includes 1,300 categories of population, education, marital status, number of children in the home, home value or monthly rent, and income. The bureau also offers TIGER files, which provide a digital street map of the entire United States. They include mapping files that identify the location of streets, highways, railroads, pipelines, power lines, and airports. Boundary files identify counties, municipalities, census tracts, census block groups, congressional districts, voter precincts, rivers, and lakes.[20]

Geographic Information Systems

A **geographic information system (GIS)** typically consists of a demographic database, digitized maps, a computer, and software that enables the user to add corporate data to the mix. The GIS isn't new: Utilities, oil companies, and governments have long used such systems to plot transmission routes, manage natural resources, and track pollution; the technology already accounts for $2.1. billion a year in hardware, software, and consulting sales.[21] But the cost of a GIS has

geographic information system
A business tool for interpreting data that consists of a demographic database, digitized maps, a computer, and software.

fallen so dramatically in recent years that the GIS is now on the verge of becoming one of the hottest business information tools. Companies as diverse as Cigna, Sears, Super Valu, the Gap, and Isuzu have adopted mapping as a down-to-earth way to interpret data that were previously available only in the form of numbingly complex printouts, spreadsheets, and charts. Maps offer researchers, managers, and clients an intuitive way to organize things. People remember things about space that they don't about any other way of organizing things.

Geographers talk about lines, points, and areas, while marketing researchers talk about roads, stores, and sales territories. But thinking in terms of lines, points, and areas is a good way to sort out the business uses of geovisual databases. Applications involving lines include finding the quickest truck routes for long-haul freight companies to calculating the shortest routes for local delivery trucks. Applications involving points include finding the best potential sites for retail bank branches and devising the best strategy for a network of warehouses. Applications involving areas range from finding the best markets for hardware sales or where to locate a new Taco Bell. GIS can also answer more detailed marketing questions. If a marketing researcher for Target wanted to know how many of the company's high sales performance stores have trading areas that overlap by at least 50 percent with the trading areas for WalMart, a geovisual system will perform a function geographers call spatial querying to answer it.

Applying a GIS Roasters (a hypothetical name but a true example) is a gourmet coffee retailer that was seeking ways to boost sales.[22] A GIS was used to increase store traffic and build nonstore sales through a home-delivery program. The opportunity to expand into home delivery was identified when it was discovered that although customers would make purchases of whole-bean or custom-ground gourmet coffees while at the mall, once the coffee had been consumed,

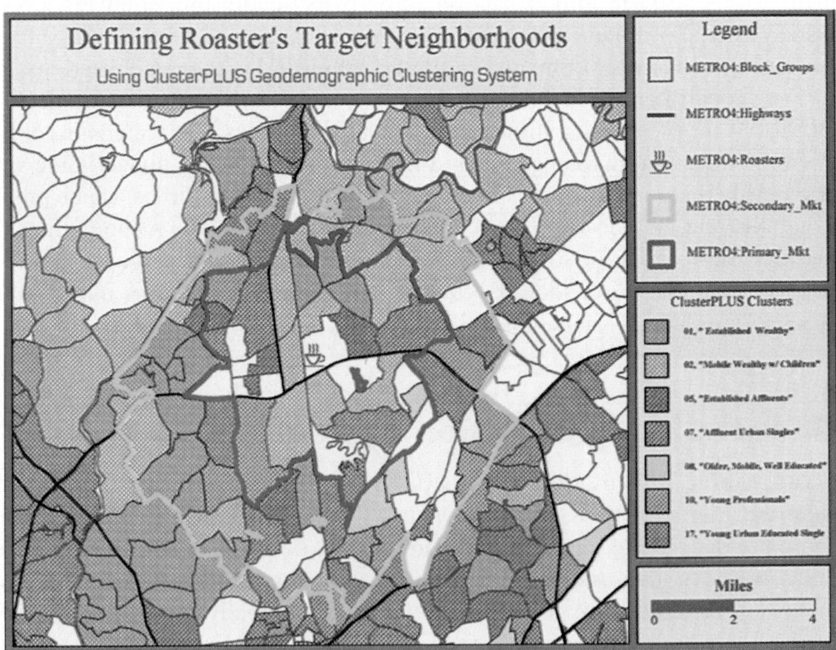

FIGURE 5.1

Customer Profile Map Created with Geographic, Information System Technology

With CIS and an enhanced profile of existing customers, Roasters was able to pinpoint neighborhoods containing the best prospects.

SOURCE: *Marketing Tools* magazine, © 1994. Reprinted with permission. Data from Conquest for Windows, map created with Atlas GIS: Strategic Mapping, Inc. Santa Clara, CA.

most customers went back to the brand they could buy more conveniently at the local grocery store.

Roaster's uses a Point-of-Sale (POS) register system that captures customer information and maintains it in a database. The database, which includes customer names, addresses, purchase history, and favorite blends of coffees, provided an abundance of data for the marketing project. Using the Atlas GIS from Strategic Mapping, Inc., a consultant address-matched the customer records to produce a map displaying the primary and secondary trade areas of the stores. The primary and secondary trade areas were defined for this retailer as the geographic areas containing 50 percent and 80 percent of the store's customers, respectively, as shown on the map. The purpose of defining the trade areas is to reveal where the core of the store's existing customers originates and to establish a geographic area to target with promotional materials (see Figure 5.1).

Realizing that not every household in the trade areas would represent a prime prospect, the consultant used another Strategic Mapping product, ClusterPLUS, to cluster-code Roaster's customer database and identify the dominant clusters. The majority of customers resided in one of the following clusters:

Established Wealthy
Mobile Wealthy with Children
Established Affluents
Affluent Urban Singles
Older, Mobile, Well Educated
Young Professionals
Young Urban Educated Singles

Having an enhanced profile of Roaster's customers, a map was created to reveal the neighborhoods within the trade areas that contained the desired clusters, as detailed on the map. This allowed Roaster's to target those neighborhoods with prospects most like the existing customers.

One of the goals of the project was to use direct mail to promote the home-delivery program, as well as build store traffic. Today's use of zip+4 postal code mailing lists will bring the researcher to within 250 feet or less of the actual address. The mailing lists Roaster's used also were input into the POS system and maintained as the prospect database. When the mailings result in store traffic or telephone orders for home delivery, the customer's name is automatically recategorized from "prospect" to "active" status within the database and the customer's purchase behavior analyzed.

The Atlas GIS system was used to identify the households in which the promotional mailings generated home-delivery accounts and, in a separate function, in which the mailings resulted in increased store traffic. After each mailing, Roaster's could visualize which neighborhoods responded well and which did not. Because the retailer knew how many households were in each block group, market penetration could be easily calculated.

The retailer also used in-store displays and registration forms to promote the home-delivery program. Once in-store customers had signed up for the home-delivery service, the GIS was used to identify the geographic areas where those accounts were located. This way, Roaster's could compare the results of the in-store promotions with the direct-mail campaign. Roaster's use of the GIS has been a major key to increased profitability.

Decision Support Systems

GIS, computerized databases, published secondary data, and internal databases are important parts of an organization's information system. Intelligent decision making is always predicated on having good information.

Information Management

Everyone who has been faced with a decision immediately comes to realize that information is the single most vital component to the quality of that decision. You need information to define the problem, to determine its scope and magnitude, to generate and evaluate alternatives, and so forth. Poor decisions are principally the result of lack of information, incorrect information, or invalid assumptions.

Today, most managers in large- and medium-size organizations and progressive smaller ones are bombarded with all kinds of information. The concern at firms such as American Airlines, Park-Davis Pharmaceuticals, and Citicorp has shifted from the generation of information to the shaping and evaluation of information so as to be useful to the decision maker.

Information management comes down to the development of a system for procuring, processing, and storing this information so that it can be retrieved when needed for management decision making. In other words, some type of marketing information system is needed. American Airlines foresees in the near future information systems that

> will drive the transition from corporate hierarchies to networks. Companies will become collections of experts who form teams to solve specific business problems and then disband. Information technology will blur distinctions between centralization and decentralization; senior managers will be able to contribute expertise without exercising authority.
>
> [Our information system] will allow senior executives to make their presence felt more deeply without requiring more day-to-day control. Eventually, executives should be able to practice selective intervention. The information system, by virtue of its comprehensiveness, will alert senior managers to pockets of excellence or trouble and allow them to take appropriate action more quickly. Over time, the role of management will change from overseeing and control to resolving important problems and transferring best practices throughout the organization.[23]

Evolution of Computer-based Information Systems

To better understand the nature of an information system, let us take a brief look at the history of computer-based information systems.

electronic data processing (EDP) systems

Information systems that manipulate raw data with little intrinsic meaning to reflect transactional relationships, such as declarative and summary reports.

EDP Systems The first type of information processing used by many firms was an **electronic data processing (EDP) system,**[24] commonly used during the 1960s and 1970s. EDP systems tended to be designed from a technical perspective that aimed at optimizing the performance of the computer hardware rather than satisfying any individual manager's needs. The output of the EDP system consisted mainly of declarative reports and summary reports. For example, accounts receivable listings and salespersons' expense reports were common forms of output from this system. An EDP system takes the raw data that have little intrinsic meaning and changes them to a form that reflects a transactional relationship. The output was presented in a rigid format.

Marketing Information Systems Because EDP systems failed to adequately address the needs of many managers, companies began developing **marketing information systems (MIS).** The evolution began in the early 1970s and still continues. An MIS involves the creation of data rather than just simple manipulation of data. For example, creation of a sales forecast versus compiling a sales expense report from existing data. An MIS focuses on putting the data in a form useful to a variety of people within the organization. The MIS is composed of standardized reports and forecasts.

marketing information systems (MIS)
These systems create rather than simply manipulate data, presenting data in a form useful to a variety of people within the organization.

The MIS report presents data in a general format and frequently provides the marketing decision maker with more information than is necessary. For example, to get a sales forecast for Chicago, one may receive a report that includes Chicago, Milwaukee, Detroit, and other large cities in the North Central Territory. At worst, the Chicago forecast may have to be dug out from a report that covers every major market in the United States! Thus, an MIS places the burden on the user to select the meaningful information and discard the remainder.

Decision Support Systems **Decision support systems (DSS)** began coming into vogue during the late 1970s. A DSS is designed from the individual decision maker's perspective. It tends to be relatively unstructured (in contrast to EDP systems and MIS) because system use must be initiated and controlled by the individual decision maker. Characteristics of a true DSS are as follows:

decision support systems (DSS)
An interactive, personalized MIS, designed to be initiated and controlled by individual decision makers.

1. *Interactive.* The manager gives simple instructions and sees results generated on the spot. The process is under the manager's direct control; no computer programmer is needed. No need to wait for scheduled reports.
2. *Flexible.* It can sort, regroup, total, average, and manipulate the data in a variety of ways. It will shift gears as the user changes topics, matching information to the problem at hand. For example, the chief executive can see highly aggregated figures, while the marketing analyst can view very detailed breakouts.
3. *Discovery oriented.* It helps managers probe for trends, isolate problems, and ask new questions.
4. *Easy to learn and use.* Managers need not be particularly computer knowledgeable. Novice users should be able to elect a standard, or "default," method of using the system, bypassing optional features to work with the basic system immediately and gradually learning its possibilities. This minimizes the frustration that frequently accompanies new computer software.

A diagram of a DSS is shown in Figure 5.2. Managers use DSS to conduct sales analyses, forecast sales, evaluate advertising, analyze product lines, and keep tabs on market trends and competitors' actions. In essence, a DSS is an interactive, personalized version of an MIS. A DSS not only allows managers to ask "what if?" questions, but also enables them to look at the data any way they want.

Decision Support Systems in Practice

More than 400 marketing professionals at Quaker Oats use the DSS daily. System usage can be grouped into three major categories: first, reporting and track-

FIGURE 5.2
A Decision Support System
SOURCE: Michael Dressler, Joquin Ives Brant, and Ronald Beall, *Industrial Marketing* (March 1983), p. 54.

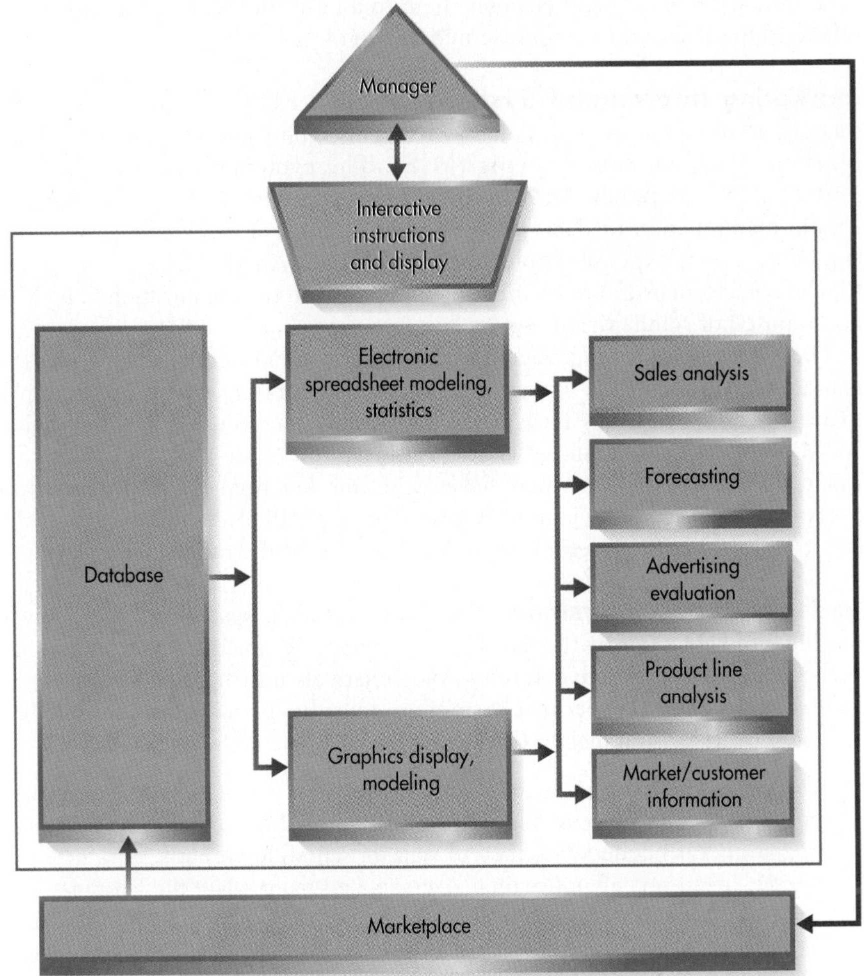

ing include running the standard reports; second, marketing planning is how Quaker Oats automates the brand planning and budgeting process by adding "what if?" analysis and marketing capabilities; and third, ad hoc queries elicit people's immediate answers to spontaneous marketing-based questions. Consider the examples in "A Professional Researcher's Perspective" on the next page.

Like Quaker Oats, other companies' successful use of DSS has resulted in a growing popularity of the sytsems.[25] K-mart, Northwestern Mutual Life, and 3M now find that their DSS provides an invaluable competitive advantage. Companies such as Federal Express, Avis, Otis Elevator, and Frito-Lay have increased the efficiency of gathering field reports by providing their employees with handheld computers.

Frito-Lay for instance, has given handheld computers to all its 11,000 delivery people. The data they collect feed a system that helps the company manage production, monitor sales, and guide promotional strategy. A delivery person can enter orders at each store in a minute or two, running through a programmed

A Professional Researcher's Perspective

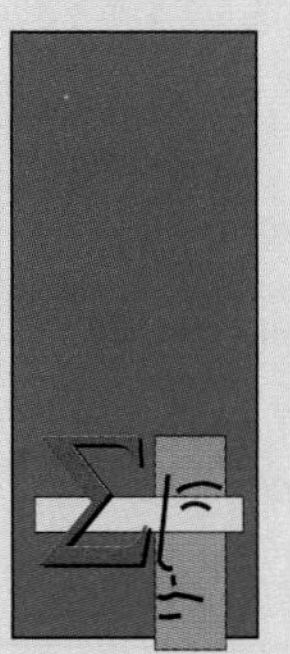

Nancy Bydalek, brand manager for Quaker's Van de Camp products, uses the DSS for compiling information needed for brand planning. "By running 'what if?' scenarios and marketing spreadsheets based on such considerations as forecasted volume, prices, and advertising spending," she says, "I get a national view of my business compared to the competition, so I can identify geographical areas that are doing well and not so well."

The system also helps Quaker sharpen its promotions. "When we plan a specific promotion," explains Greg Peterson, marketing manager of the Cornmeal brand, "we go back in time and see the bottom-line effect that different promotional events had on sales. We then plug in the cost of a planned promotion and see what the final effect is going to be on the brand's volume and profit."[26] ■

product list complete with prices. The machine plugs into a printer in the delivery truck to produce an itemized invoice. At day's end, it generates a sales report and, through a hookup in the local warehouse, transmits it in seconds to company headquarters in Dallas.[27]

Pros and Cons of MIS versus DSS

Each approach to automation has its advantages and disadvantages. A mainframe orientation makes for easy access to corporate data via terminals and better ensures the data's integrity. But because of backlogs, it can take months for users to get their company's data processing professionals to tailor programs to specific applications. Managers must also rely on calculators and scratch pads for departmental budgeting and scheduling. And if mainframes or other central computers "crash," terminals connected to the system go down, too.

A distributed approach (DSS) gives individual managers quick access to computing and the ability to handle a host of applications without time-sharing delays. But a lack of coordination among the many users can lead to security problems and duplication of effort. Personal computers can be relatively expensive and bothersome to maintain and upgrade.

The Move Toward DSS

Today thousands of smaller businesses also will have information systems more sophisticated than those that America's largest corporations had just a decade earlier. These systems, for the most part, resemble DSS rather than a traditional MIS.[28] A sampling of firms using DSS is shown in Table 5.4. The advantages of an effective DSS are immense, including the following.

1. *Substantial cost savings are realized.* One direct mail insurance company developed a simple method to compare past response rates of various market segments and thereby saved $40,000 that otherwise would have been wasted by

Progressive companies give handheld computers to their delivery personnel. The data they collect feed an information system that enables managers to alter production schedules to have the right inventory mix and guide promotional strategy.
SOURCE: © Ken Kerbs.

mailing to households with a low probability of response. A large industrial products firm, soon after implementation of a decision support system focusing on distribution, reported savings in the hundreds of thousands of dollars. Similarly, other companies can draw direct profitability from their DSS.

A DSS developed by Coca-Cola enables marketing managers interactively to determine profit and loss by brand, gross margin, and operating profit; it also helps managers examining gross profit changes and marketing and sales expense fluctuations. This DSS also allows interactive analysis of various profit-and-loss situations with differing performance levels through its interactive interrogation features. As DSS models are built, other areas of Coca-Cola are being targeted for support. Company-owned bottlers benefit from using models that evaluate financial alternatives for bottler plant expansions. Corporate planning develops models to review company sales, gross profit, and direct marketing expenses, as well as to analyze company and competitor shares of the market and advertising.

2. *Marketer's understanding of the decision environment is increased.* The decision maker is forced to view the decision and information environment within which she operates. This perception often leads to facing decision areas too often shoved under the carpet, as well as recognizing relationships between decisions and information flows that have never been noticed before.

A sales territory is a dynamic environment, constantly roiled by changes in customers, competitors, products, and sales force turnover. Although this cre-

TABLE 5.4 A Sample of Company DSS and How They Are Used

COMPANY	DSS USE
American Airlines	Price, Route Selection, and Aircraft Maintenance
American Petrofina	Corporate Planning and Forecasting
Central and Southwest Corporation	Corporate Planning and Forecasting
Champlin Petroleum	Corporate Planning and Forecasting
First United Bankcorporation	Investment Evaluation
Frito-Lay, Inc.	Price, Advertising, Distribution, and Promotion Selection
General Dynamics	Price Evaluation
Gifford-Hill and Company	Corporate Planning and Forecasting
Lear Petroleum	Evaluation of Potential Drilling Sites
Mercantile Texas Corporation	Corporate Planning and Forecasting
National Gypsum	Corporate Planning and Forecasting
Southern Railway	Train Dispatching and Routing
Texas–New Mexico Power	Corporate Planning and Forecasting
Texas Oil and Gas Corporation	Evaluation of Potential Drilling Sites
Texas Utilities Company	Corporate Planning and Forecasting
The Western Company	Corporate Planning and Forecasting

ates imbalanced workloads and potential sales, managers are reluctant to realign their territories to reflect such changes because of the time consumed in tedious calculations. Merrell Dow Pharmaceuticals put an end to such reluctance with a DSS. A manager enters his own criteria, such as potential and actual sales, doctor and pharmacy counts, and travel time. The DSS combines this business data with geographic features, road networks, and five-digit zip codes to come up with the optimal territory alignment.

The program was especially helpful when the company replaced its single sales force with two sales forces to get broader product coverage. A Merrell Dow sales force promotes prescription pharmaceuticals, and a Lakeside sales force sells over-the-counter drugs. In all, the United States had to be redrawn to create 400 Merrell Dow sales territories and 250 Lakeside territories.

3. *Decision-making effectiveness is upgraded.* Many companies can now retrieve and use information that was never accessible before. This replacement of facts for intuition in decision making has led to more effective and less "seat-of-the-pants" decision making than in the past. Jerome Chazen, executive vice-president of Liz Claiborne, Inc., notes that the firm's DSS has improved management decision making. Systematic Updated Retail Feedback (SURF) reports come in daily from 16 stores that represent a cross section of store sizes and geographical locations. Computer programs take the SURF data and "play with it in dozens of different ways to get a feeling for how the consumer is reacting to the merchandise we're shipping," Chazen says. "Most apparel manufacturers tend to identify the best-selling items in the line with how they're purchased by the retailer. We've discovered that there's often no relationship between what the retailer thinks and what the consumer buys."
4. *Information value is improved.* Tied to decision-making effectiveness, but worthy of its own note, is the improved quantity and quality of information provided to the marketing manager. Managers now have relevant, reliable, and timely information never before available. For example, Chuck Mitchell, district sales manager for Savin Business Machines, used to wade through reams

of data and then tenuously suggest, "I think you should try to arrange more product demos." Now, with the flexibility of a new DSS, Chuck can firmly declare to a sales representative, "I know that if you put on more demos you'll write more orders." He points to his terminal and tells the person, "All the information about your activities is there, and it shows that your bookings are down because you're not putting on as many demos as you used to."[29]

Problems in Implementing a Decision Support System

With all of the advantages, what seem to be the primary inhibitors to adopt a DSS? In a nutshell, it is a "people" problem. More specifically, the problem involves the following aspects.

1. *Many benefits are intangible.* The tangible benefits from a company's investment in its DSS are few relative to the intangibles. Much of the value of providing accurate, relevant, and timely information to marketing decision makers comes from more effective decision making. But, in some cases, top corporate executives cannot see profits directly attributable to the DSS. This usually lessens commitment by top management and leads to a diversion of funds and interest away from existing and planned computer systems. If a company is going to successfully launch a DSS, it is imperative that high-level managers are involved in developing, implementing, and operating the system. This promotes conceptions of the system's significance and furthers its integration into the organization.[30]
2. *Communication bridges must be built.* To develop an effective DSS, marketing managers and system designers must work closely to identify marketing problems, decision areas, information needs, and information sources. Historically, marketing practitioners and system designers have had great difficulty communicating, which led to sizable gaps in information needed and offered. The result has been an emphasis by system designers on data warehousing instead of matching user needs.
3. *Decision support system users must be trained.* Research has shown that the training of marketing managers as system users has not always been at an acceptable level. Decision makers can hardly be expected to use an information system if they do not understand what it can and cannot do.
4. *Managers are naive or suspicious of computer-based systems.* Closely allied to the preceding problem is the lack of experience and necessary background in many older marketing managers. Such individuals' formal education never provided them with a contemporary computer orientation. Furthermore, much of their on-the-job training has never exposed them to the potential benefits of using a computer, much less how to communicate with one. This lack of training often produced fear, the fear that the computer will make them look foolish or possibly result in the loss of their job. Consequently, they avoid its use and sometimes even express open hostility.

Summary

Secondary data are any pieces of information gathered and known to the marketing researcher but that only might be relevant to the problem at hand. Primary data are survey, observation, or experimental data collected to solve the particular problem under investigation. Secondary data can come from sources internal to the organization or external to it. A database is a collection of related data. The most common type of marketing internal database is founded on customer information. For example, a customer database will have demographic and perhaps psychographic information about existing customers and purchase data such as when the goods and services were bought, the types of merchandise procured, the dollar sales amount, and any promotional information associated with the sales. An internal database also may contain competitive intelligence, such as new products offered by competitors, price changes, and changes in competitors' service policies. A good internal database relies on a database management system. Also, the database users must be trained in how to manipulate the data and retrieve needed information.

There are several advantages to secondary data. First, secondary data may help to clarify or redefine the definition of the problem as part of the exploratory research process. Second, secondary information may actually provide a solution to the problem. Third, secondary information may provide primary data research method alternatives. Fourth, secondary data may alert the marketing researcher to potential problems and difficulties. And finally, secondary information may provide necessary background data and build credibility for the research report.

The disadvantages of secondary data are the lack of needed information, lack of relevance, inaccurate data, and insufficient information for decision making.

A tremendous growth in on-line databases has made access to secondary information much simpler. An on-line database is a public information database available to anyone with proper communication facilities. There are four major categories of on-line databases: numerical databases, bibliographic databases, directory databases, and full text databases. An on-line database vendor is an intermediary that acquires databases from a variety of database creators. Thus, a user can go to a single on-line vendor and gain access to a variety of databases. Some popular vendors are Dow Jones, Dialog, Prodigy, and CompuServe. The advantages of on-line databases are several. First, the researcher has quick access to a tremendous variety of information. Second, the efficient use of on-line search protocols helps quickly pinpoint relevant data. Third, the large in-house staff formerly required to research and maintain files can be eliminated. And finally, small firms can gain access to the same secondary data as large organizations and do it just as efficiently. The major disadvantage is that a person not skilled at searching through a database may be inundated with information. Sometimes this information can be very expensive.

A large secondary data bibliography is provided in the Appendix A to this chapter. It should be valuable to any student seeking published sources of information.

Computer-based information systems have evolved from EDP systems that tended to be designed from a technical perspective aimed at optimizing the performance of computer hardware rather than satisfying any individual manager's needs, unlike MIS and DSS. An MIS involves the creation of data rather than simple manipulation of data. It focuses on putting the data in a form useful to a variety of people within the marketing organization. Often MIS reports will present data in a general format and may provide the decision maker with more information than is necessary. Decision support systems are designed from the individual decision maker's perspective. A DSS is interactive, flexible, discovery oriented, and easy to learn. Companies today are still debating the merits of an MIS versus a DSS.

Key Terms

- secondary data
- primary data
- internal database
- database management system
- database management software
- on-line database
- modem
- numeric database
- bibliographic database
- directory database
- full text database
- on-line vendor
- geographic information system
- electronic data processing (EDP) systems
- marketing information systems (MIS)
- decision support systems (DSS)

Review and Discussion Questions

1. Why should companies consider creating a marketing internal database? Name some types of information that might be found in this database and sources of this information.
2. What are some of the keys to ensuring the success of an internal database?
3. Why is secondary data often preferred to primary data?
4. What pitfalls might a researcher encounter in using secondary data?
5. What are the major categories of on-line databases? Give examples of each.
6. If your college or university has access to several on-line vendors, determine the various types of information that can be obtained. If on-line access is not possible, go to the library and determine what information is available in DIALOG, Prodigy, CompuServe, and Dow Jones News Retrieval.
7. What are some of the advantages and pitfalls of on-line databases?
8. Assume that you are a brand manager for a line of facial tissues. Your sales have been growing at the rate of 4 percent per year for the past three years. What role might secondary data play in evaluating the market position of your brand?
9. In the absence of company problems, is there any need to conduct marketing research? develop a decision support system?
10. Compare and contrast an MIS and a DSS. Why do you think companies still have difficulty making the decision as to which system to install?

CASE 5.1

Blockbuster Video

When executives at Blockbuster Entertainment Corp.[31] wanted to put rental video games into the machines that kids across America had received during the 1993 holiday season, they tapped their expansive database. Of its 40 million customers, the company took aim at those with children and sent a direct mail promotion in January and February. The hope was to outperform the industry standard draw of 2 percent to 4 percent, said Robert L. Carberry, VP-technology. It worked even better than they expected, drawing a 30 percent redemption rate.

By going to the database to determine what titles and product features appealed to youngsters, Blockbuster was able to structure the promotion to meet existing user preferences. "That is a tremendous marketing tool," Carberry said of the company's database. It's an emerging tool that's growing daily. It currently stores information from about two billion transactions, he said, and grows by one million customer transactions each day.

The list of 40 million names is a rich and current resource Blockbuster has said it will share with no one. Information gathered each day is fed from every store into the company's Fort Lauderdale, Florida, mainframe computer, which then tabulates member preferences. The system will become especially potent for "just in time" electronic creation of video games for rental. The company's NewLeaf Entertainment system, which signed an agreement with Sega of America to produce games on demand, will allow individual stores to create product to meet orders.

However, building such a database can be difficult for other company venues, like its 529 retail music stores. Membership cards aren't needed for a purchase. But customers who do first show their cards or fill out a membership form at the stores' listening bars, where they can preview music, will strengthen its stock of information, Carberry said. That will allow Blockbuster to cross-promote merchandise between divisions.

Blockbuster recently entered into a joint venture with Sony Music Corp. and Pace Entertainment Corp. to build and manage amphitheaters across the nation. The result could be a promotion that would allow customers to rent a movie and get a discount on a concert or compact disc or vice versa—all the while providing the company with information on customer preferences. Tapping the database to determine a given market's taste for artists or styles would allow Blockbuster to tailor promotions.

1. Can you think of other ways that Blockbuster might use its database?
2. There is a federal law that video stores can't rent names and information from their databases. Why do you think this law was passed?
3. Blockbuster has recently entered into the production of movies and television films. Could the database be of value in this business? How?

CASE 5.2

American Gardener

Even with 88 million Americans shopping by mail, finding and filling a niche in the marketplace is harder than ever. Rising costs for producing, marketing, and mailing catalogs have made startups more difficult than ever. These facts have not been lost on Barbara Burt, who is considering opening a mail order gardening tools and accessories business.

Approximately 90 percent of the hundreds of mail order businesses that start in somebody's basement or kitchen fail, experts estimate. The competition for the $33 billion per year in catalog sales is growing at a staggering rate, with the number of small mail order companies up 47 percent since 1980. Although apparel and gift items remain the most popular catalog categories, entrepreneurs have created catalogs offering virtually every conceivable item for sale. Each is searching for that all-important unique niche. Burt plans to offer unusual garden tools that typically are not found in the everyday hardware store. Many of her items will be imported from Japan and Europe. In addition to tools, she plans to offer exotic vegetables and flower seeds, rare bulbs, and garden clothing.

1. Using the data sources suggested in Appendix A, identify at least six separate sources of information that might be of importance to Burt in making her go

or no-go decision and in developing a marketing strategy.

2. Go to the library and determine how many gardeners there are in the United States; break this information down further by types of equipment bought, types of vegetables and flowers grown, and socioeconomic characteristics of the gardeners.
3. Which states would contain the largest number of target consumers? Explain and describe the secondary sources from which you derived your conclusions.
4. How can she use secondary data to assess who her potential competitors might be?

APPENDIX A

Published Secondary Data[32]

I. General Marketing Sources

American Marketing Association Bibliography Series (Chicago). Issued irregularly. Contains a series of annotated bibliographies with emphasis on books and periodicals. Each covers a particular topic in some depth.

Communication Abstracts (Beverly Hills, Calif.: Sage Publications, Inc.). Issued bimonthly. Indexes and abstracts major communication-related articles, reports, and books. In addition to advertising and marketing, covers such topics as mass communication, small-group communication, the media, and public opinion.

Journal of Marketing, "Marketing Literature Review" (New York: American Marketing Association) Published quarterly by the American Marketing Association. Contains an annotated bibliography of articles published within the last year in major business, economic, and social science periodicals.

II. Advertising and Promotion Data

Advertising Age (Chicago: Crain Communications, Inc.). Selected special issues: "U.S. Advertising Agency Profiles," annual, April. Covers larger agencies. Each agency profile lists billings figure, accounts won and lost, billings breakdown by media, gross income. "Foreign Agency Income Reports," annual, April. Same data as in preceding are given, when available. Agencies arranged by country. "100 Leading National Advertisers," annual, September. For each, data on advertising expenditures, sales and profits, rank of leading product lines and brands, market share, sales, advertising personnel. Other issues published include "Top 100 Leading Markets" (published every three years) and "100 Leading Media Companies" (annual, August).

Broadcasting & Cable Market Place (New Providence, NJ: K.R. Bowker, annual). Formerly the *Broadcasting Yearbook*. Directory of U.S. and Canadian television and radio stations. Also includes television market data and additional industry-related information. A cable section includes information on cable systems in the United States and Canada. A related publication is *Television & Cable Factbook*

(Washington, D.C.: Warren Publishing). Annual. The *Stations* volume gives expanded information on television stations, including market data. Volume 2 covers cable; Volume 3 covers services.

Journal of Advertising Research (New York: Advertising Research Foundation). Bimonthly. This publication presents research studies, literature reviews, and listings.

Standard Directory of Advertisers (Skokie, Ill.: National Register Publishing Co.). Annual, plus supplements. Lists over 26,000 U.S. companies doing national or regional advertising. Data include company personnel, name of advertising agency, advertising budget figures, types of media used. Also a separate geographic index.

Standard Directory of Advertising Agencies (Skokie, Ill.: National Register Publication Co., Inc.). Issued three times yearly, plus supplements. Lists agency officers, accounts, and approximate annual billings of about 8,700 U.S. and foreign agencies.

Standard Rate and Data Service, Inc. (Skokie, Ill. Standard Rate & Data Service). Various titles, many issued monthly. Provides current advertising rates and related data for U.S. radio and TV stations, consumer magazines, business publications, newspapers, other media. Some market data included in the radio, TV, and newspaper volumes. The *SRDS* is considered the standard source of cost estimation for media planning.

Advertising Expenditure Around the World (New York: Starch INRA Hooper). Annual. Provides estimates of expenditures in various media categories, arranged by country.

III. Indexes

Adler, James B. *CIS Annual* (Washington, D.C.: Congressional Information Service). Published monthly with quarterly, 1970 to present. Basic source for working papers of Congress. Information is in the form of abstracts of congressional documents (microfiche of actual documents available) covering the entire range of congressional publications. Two sections—indexes and abstracts. The subject title indexes use entry number referrals.

Guide to U.S. Government Publications (McLean, Va.: Documents Index). Published annually, 1973 to present. Annotated guide to publications of the various U.S. government agencies. Volume 1 contains a list of publications in existence as of January 1973; Volume 2 covers publications of abolished agencies and discontinued publications; Volume 3 explains and outlines the Superintendent of Documents classification scheme, by which Volumes 1 and 2 are arranged. Agency and title index.

Business Service Check List (Washington, D.C.: Department of Commerce). Published biweekly. Serves as a guide to U.S. Department of Commerce publications and to key business indicators.

Robinson, Judith S. *Tapping the Government Grapevine: The User Friendly Guide to U.S. Government Information Systems*, 2nd ed. (Phoenix, AZ: Oryx Press, 1993). A guide and introduction to the many forms of information produced and distributed by the federal government. Covers print sources as well as the growing segment of electronic information created by government agencies in CD ROMS, electronic bulletin boards and databases.

The Federal Register (Washington, D.C.: Office of National Archives and Records Administration). Published daily. Contains all regulatory matter issued by all national agencies and governmental bodies. These listings are both complete and official, and they are indexed.

Census Data

The Bureau of the Census is by far the largest publisher of comprehensive statistical data. Its catalog, which is published monthly *(Monthly Product Announcements)* with annual cumulations *(Census Catalog and Guide)*, contains good, descriptive lists of all census publications. The Census Bureau publishes only its most widely used censuses and surveys. Much more information is available, usually on computer tapes. This information provides limitless possibilities for subject cross classifications or area tabulations. The following sampling of information available through the census surveys is divided into three parts: Census Data Index; Census of Population Data; and Specific Census Data Sources. Census data are now available on CD-ROM.

Census Data Index *Census Catalog and Guide* (Washington, D.C.: U.S. Department of Commerce, Bureau of the Census). Annual. Monthly supplements in *Monthly Product Announcements*. Complete index of Census Bureau data, including publications and unpublished materials. Main divisions are publications, data files, and special tabulations.

Census of Population Data *Census of Population and Housing* (Series PC) (Washington, D.C.: Department of Commerce, Bureau of the Census). Published every 10 years. Detailed characteristics of the population for states, counties, cities, and towns in a series of reports that give data on number of inhabitants, general population characteristics (age, sex, race, etc.), and general social and economic characteristics. Separate "Subject Reports," Series PC(2), cover statistics on ethnic groups, migration, fertility, marriage and living arrangements, education, employment, occupation and industry, and income. 1990 available on CD-ROM. Data detail to block level and zip code.

Specific Census Data Sources Produced and published to be used as major economic indicators.

Economic Census (Washington, D.C., Bureau of the Census). Published every five years. Multivolume. Tables. Contains statistical data on retail and wholesale trade and on selected service industries for the United States, Guam, and the Virgin Islands. Arranged geographically and by Standard Industrial Classification (SIC) codes with subject reports. Issued for years ending in "2" and "7," the census is supplemented by "Monthly Retail Trade," "Selected Services Receipts," and the "Monthly Wholesale Trade" series. 1992 available on CD-ROM. Data detail to zip code level.

Current Business Reports: Monthly Retail Trade, Sales and Inventories (Washington, D.C.: Bureau of the Census). Published monthly. Graphs, tables. Includes information on monthly sales for U.S. retail stores by kind of business, region, selected states, and Metropolitan Statistical Areas (MSAs). Also contains data on department stores and end-of-month accounts receivable. These reports are issued several weeks after the end of the month reported; a companion series, *Current Business Reports: Advance Monthly Retail Sales*, providing preliminary data, is issued one week after the month reported. These cumulate into an *Annual Retail Trade* series and finally into the quinquennial *Economic Census*.

Current Business Reports: Monthly Wholesale Trade, Sales and Inventories (Washington, D.C.: Bureau of the Census). Published monthly. Graphs, tables. Contains monthly figures for wholesale inventories and sales arranged by kinds of business and geographic divisions. The reports are issued several weeks after the end of the month reported and cumulate into the quinquennial *Economic Census*.

Census of Manufacturers (Washington, D.C.: Bureau of the Census). Published every five years. Supplies data on U.S. manufacturing firms.

County Business Patterns (Washington, D.C.: Department of Commerce, Bureau of the Census). Issued annually in paper or CD-ROM. Detailed SIC-level industry data on virtually all U.S. industries based on a complete count of all business conducted every March. Data show number of establishments, employment size and payroll. Geographic areas covered: U.S., states and counties. Essential source for measuring business activity at national and local levels.

Census of Retail Trade (Washington, D.C.: Bureau of the Census). Published every five years. Compiles data for states, SMSAs, counties, and cities with populations of 2,500 or more by type of business. Data include number of establishments, sales, payroll, and personnel. Available on CD-ROM.

Census of Service Industries (Washington, D.C.: Bureau of the Census). Published every five years. Includes data on hotels, motels, beauty parlors, barber shops, and other retail service organizations. Survey also includes information on number of establishments, receipts, payrolls for states, SMSAs, counties, and cities. Available on CD-ROM.

Census of Transportation (Washington, D.C.: Bureau of the Census). Published every five years. Tables. Compiled using data from mail survey of carriers and Census of Population data. Issued for years ending in "2" and "7." Provides travel data on the civilian populations, truck inventory and use, and shipment of commodities by manufacturers. Most of these data are not publicly available elsewhere. This work is the most important cumulative general source for U.S. transportation data. Available on CD-ROM.

Census of Wholesale Trade (Washington, D.C.: Bureau of the Census). Published every five years. Presents statistics for states, SMSAs, and counties on number of establishments, sales, payroll, and personnel for kind of business. Available on CD-ROM.

National Trade Data Bank (NTDB) (Washington, D.C.: Department of Commerce, Economics and Statistics Administration, Office of Business Analysis). Issued monthly on CD-ROM. A searchable full-text compilation of the best of import and export data and information, international trade promotion and economic data from 15 federal agencies. Selected government agency publications are included in full; agencies include the Bureau of Economic Analysis, Bureau of the Census, International Trade Administration and the International Trade Commission. Major international commerce publications such as *Foreign Economic Trends and their Implications for The United States* and *Overseas Business Reports* are no longer published in paper but are available exclusively from *NTDB*.

IV. Selected Sources of Data Generated by the Federal Government

Categories include statistical and national economic indicators, congressional developments, international commerce, domestic commerce, localized databases, consumer interests, and the environment. Pertinent publications for specific industries and activities are listed under "domestic commerce."

Statistical and Economic Indicators

American Statistics Index (Washington, D.C.: Congressional Information Service). Published monthly with annual cumulations, 1973 to present. Important source of identifying statistical publications published by the U.S. government. Indexes and abstracts statistics on numerous topics from the publications of many government agencies. Index volume contains four separate indexes that list publications by subject and name; by geographic, economic, and demographic categories; by title; and by agency report numbers. Abstract volume gives brief descriptions of the publications and their content.

O'Hara, Frederick and Sicignano, R. *Handbook of United States Economic and Financial Indicators* (Westport, CT: Greenwood Press, 1985). A finding guide to 200 economic indicators published by 55 governmental and private organizations. Indexed by topic or by indicator name, it defines each indicator and lists major publications and the frequency with which the indicator is announced.

Economic Report of the President transmitted to the Congress (together with the *Annual Report* of the Council of Economic Advisers) (Washington, D.C.: GPO). Published annually. The annual report of the CEA takes up the major portion of this publication. Discusses economic policy and outlook and economic trends of the year. Includes statistical tables relating to income, employment, and publication.

Economic Indicators (Washington, D.C.: Superintendent of Documents, GPO). Published monthly, 1953 to present. Charts, tables. A digest of current information on economic conditions of prices, wages, production, business activity, purchasing power, credit, money, and federal finance. Gives monthly figures for the past two years; frequently goes back as far as 1939.

Measuring Markets: A Guide to the Use of Federal and State Statistical Data (Washington, D.C.: Department of Commerce, GPO, 1979). Materials published by state and federal governments that are useful in marketing research. Sources for population, income, employment, sales statistics, and some state taxes are included. Examples demonstrate the use of federal statistics in market analysis.

Statistical Abstract of the United States (Washington, D.C.: Department of Commerce, Bureau of the Census, GPO). Published annually, 1879 to present. Tables. Arranged in 34 categories, it is a reliable source for statistical summaries of the economy, business, population, and politics. Emphasis is on information of national scope, plus tables for regions, states, and some local areas. Table of contents, introductory text to each section, source notes for each table, and bibliography of sources are extremely useful guides to additional material. Subject index.

Survey of Current Business (Washington, D.C.: Department of Commerce, Bureau of Economic Analysis, GPO). Published monthly, 1921 to present. Official source of gross national product, national income, and international balance of payments. Important reference for business statistics, including general economic and industrial statistics for specific products plus articles analyzing current business situations. Subject index. Statistics are indexed in *American Statistics Index* (see previously).

International Commerce

Business America (Washington, D.C.: Department of Commerce). Published monthly. Gives current information on commodities and foreign countries, especially those of interest to the foreign trader. Other phases covered include industrial developments, laws, and regulations of foreign countries.

Foreign Commerce Handbook: Basic Information and Guide to Sources (Washington, D.C.: U.S. Chamber of Commerce). Published irregularly. Useful guide to foreign commerce sources.

Foreign Economic Trends and Their Implications for the United States (Washington, D.C.: Bureau of International Commerce). Issued semiannually or annually for each country. Prepared by the U.S. Foreign Service/Embassies. Contains one summary table, a narrative of economic trends, and an analysis of possible implications of these trends for U.S. foreign trade. No longer published in paper; available only on National Trade Data Bank on CD-ROM.

Overseas Business Reports (Washington, D.C.: Bureau of International Commerce). Published annually. Compiled using data from the Office of International Marketing. Each report deals with a group of countries' basic economic structure, trade regulations, practices and policies, market potential, and investment laws. Designed to aid business in gaining access to, and increasing its share of, foreign markets. No longer published in paper; available only on National Trade Data Bank on CD-ROM.

Domestic Commerce

Classification Manual *Standard Industrial Classification Manual* (Washington, D.C.: U.S. Government Printing Office, 1987). A guide to a classification system that sorts establishments by type of activity in which engaged, to facilitate the collection, tabulation, presentation, and analysis of data, and to promote uniformity and comparability in presenting statistical data collected by various agencies of the U.S. government, state agencies, trade associations, and private research organizations. Covers entire range of economic activities. (Targeted for revision in 1997.)

Specific Industrial Information This section is a sampling of reports on industrial information by many departments, bureaus, agencies, and committees.

Federal Reserve Bulletin (Washington, D.C.: Board of Governors of the Federal Reserve System). Published monthly. A source of statistics on banking, deposits, loans and investments, money market rates, securities prices, industrial production, flow of funds, and various other areas of finance in relation to government, business, real estate, and consumer affairs.

Statistics of Communications Common Carriers (Washington, D.C.: Federal Communications Commission). Published annually. Graphs, tables. Compiled using data from monthly and annual reports filed with the FCC. Contains detailed financial and operating data, by company, for all telephone and telegraph companies and communications holding companies engaged in interstate and foreign communication service and for the U.S. Communication Satellite Corporation. Invaluable for information about specific utilities and the communications industry in general.

Small Business Bibliographies (Washington, D.C.: Small Business Administration). Published irregularly. Briefly describes particular business activities. Substantial bibliography includes federal, state, and nongovernment publications. Preface to each issue may be helpful to those seeking career information.

Index of Patents Issued from the U.S. Patent and Trademark Office (Washington, D.C.: U.S. Patent and Trademark Office). Published annually. Two volumes. Volume 1 indexes patents listed in the year's issues of the *Official Gazette* by name of patentee. Entries include a general designation of the invention, patent number, date of issue, and classification code. Volume 2 indexes patents by subject of invention as indicated by the classification code number identified in the *Manual of Classification.* A convenient appendix is a list of libraries receiving current issues of U.S. patents and of depository libraries receiving the *Official Gazette.*

Index of Trademarks Issued from the U.S. Patent and Trademark Office (Washington, D.C.: U.S. Patent and Trademark Office). Published annually. Alphabetically indexes registrants of trademarks issued or published in the *Official Gazette* of the U.S. Patent and Trademark Office during the calendar year.

V. General Reference Sources of Business Information and Ideas

Business Reference Librarian

The business reference librarian should be consulted as a timesaving first step in gathering business facts. This specialist has the best sources at her fingertips and can give expert guidance. She compiles book lists concerning specific areas, identifies special library collections, and is aware of books scheduled for publication. The business reference librarian is often a member of the Special Libraries Association, a national organization of librarians who meet monthly in local chapters, keeping abreast of the best reference material available. Through networking, the librarian is aware of the holdings in all business reference libraries in the general area and in university, public, and corporate libraries open to the public.

The business reference librarian can also tap into the interlibrary loan system—a free, cooperative exchange system of books and periodicals from member libraries across the country.

Encyclopedias

Encyclopedias compile information on a wide range of topics and answer the need for basic, concise data. Entries are signed articles with frequent illustrations, plates, diagrams, maps, bibliographies, and indexes.

Burek, Deborah, ed., *Encyclopedia of Associations* (Detroit: Gale Research Co.). Published annually. Guide to over 50,000 associations. Three volumes: Volume 1. *National Organizations of the United States* in three parts; Volume 2. *Geographic and Executive Indexes;* Volume 3. Supplement; also *Regional, State, and Local Organizations* (five regional volumes).

Exporters' Encyclopedia (New York: Dun and Bradstreet International). Published annually. Detailed facts on shipments to every country in the world. Covers regulations, types of communication and transportation available, foreign trade organizations, general export information, general reference tables, and listings of ports.

Novallo, Annette, ed. Information Industry Directory, 15th ed. (Detroit: Gale Research Co., 1995). Two volumes: Volume 1. describes companies that produce and provide electronic systems, services and products in the U.S. and 70 other countries. Volume 2 contains indexes.

Almanacs and Yearbooks

Almanacs are collections of current factual information covering a broad range of topics.

World Almanac and Book of Facts (New York: Press Pub. Co.). Published annually. Facts on many diverse subjects.

Yearbooks are fact books providing current information. They usually give more information than almanacs.

CRB Commodity Yearbook (New York: Knight-Ridder Financial). Published 3 times a year. Statistical yearbook with data on production, prices, stocks, exports, and imports for more than 100 commodities. Editorial comments on new developments affecting commodities.

VI. Specialized Sources of Specific Data

Bibliographies

Bibliographies, lists of printed sources of information on a topic, are the most important starting point for business facts. They can quickly lead the business executive or student to original available sources of information on a specific topic.

Bibliographic Index: A Cumulative Bibliography of Bibliographies (New York: H. W. Wilson Co.). Published twice a year. Annual cumulations. Lists, by subject, sources of bibliographies containing 50 or more citations of books, pamphlets, and periodicals.

Daniells, Lorna. *Business Information Sources,* 3d ed. (Berkeley: University of California Press, 1993). Selected and well-annotated business bibliography based on the collection at the Baker Library at the Harvard Business School. The marketing chapter covers handbooks, dictionaries, guides, periodicals and directories. Marketing topics include: consumer behavior, marketing channels, international marketing, pricing, sales, advertising and retailing.

Marketing Information: A Professional Reference Guide, 3d ed. Hiram Barksdale and Jack Goldstucker, eds. (Atlanta: Georgia State University Press, 1995). Annotated directory and guide to marketing handbooks, periodicals, bibliographies and other publications broken into topical areas such as: distribution, international marketing, industrial marketing, pricing, product management, sales promotion.

Service to Business and Industry (New York: Brooklyn Public Library, Business Library). Published 10 times each year. Annotated bibliographies covering current business topics.

What's New in Advertising and Marketing (New York: Special Libraries Association). Published 10 times a year. Used as a prime selection tool for library purchases of marketing-related monographs, reports, and periodicals.

Woy, James, ed. *Encyclopedia of Business Information Sources*, 10th ed. (Detroit: Gale Research Co., 1994). Quick survey of basic information sources covering 1,140 subjects. Provides specific citations, dealing with a single point, with the business manager in mind. Includes reference works, periodicals, trade associations, statistical sources, and on-line databases.

Periodical Directories, Periodical Indexes, Periodicals, Newsletter Directories, and Newspaper Indexes

Periodical directories are helpful reference tools for finding major industry publications relevant to a specific area.

Business Publication Rates and Data (Skokie, Ill.: Standard Rate & Data Service). Published monthly. Guide to business, trade, and technical publications arranged by "market served" classifications.

Periodical indexes are valuable sources of current information for a broad scope of subjects. Abstracts provide the added feature of descriptive notation.

Business Periodicals Index (New York: H.W. Wilson Co.). Published monthly with annual cumulations, 1958 to present. Cumulative subject index covering 270 business periodicals in the English language. Subject categories are very specific. Separate book review index follows subject index in the annual volume. Available in CD-ROM.

Predicasts F&S Index United States (Cleveland: Predicasts). Published weekly, with monthly, quarterly, and annual cumulations, 1960 to present. Index covering company, industry, and product information from 750 business-oriented periodicals and brokerage house reports in the United States. Information arranged by company name, expanded SIC number, and company according to expanded SIC groups. Now available in CD-ROM format.

Predicasts F&S Index International. Same as preceding, except that it gives information about the rest of the world, excluding Europe.

Predicasts F&S Index Europe. Same as *F&S International*, but with coverage of European continent only in journals and collective volumes.

Index of Economic Articles (Homewood, Ill.: Richard D. Irwin, Inc.). Published annually. Bibliographies from 200 English-language journals on articles, communications, papers, and proceedings discussions. Classified index and author index. Now available on CD-ROM as *EconLit.*

Management Contents (Northbrook, Ill.: Management Contents). Published biweekly. Reproduction of the tables of contents of a selection of 150 of the best business and management journals. Each issue can be scanned for significant articles. Now available as on-line database.

Directories

Directories provide brief data on companies, organizations, or individuals. They are used for a variety of purposes: to determine the manufacturer of a specific product; to check companies located in a particular area; to verify company names, addresses, and telephone numbers; and to identify company officers.

American Marketing Association International Membership Directory and Marketing Services Guide. (Chicago: The American Marketing Association). Published annually. Information on officers and branches of firms providing marketing services such as advertising and marketing research or consulting. Roster of AMA Members is indexed by company/organization affiliation.

Consultants and Consulting Organizations Directory, 14th ed. (Detroit: Gale Research Co., 1994). Indexes more than 20,000 firms, people, and organizations involved in consulting. Main arrangement is geographic, with subject, personal name, and organization name indexes.

Ethridge, James M., ed., *Directories in Print,* 12th ed. (Detroit: Gale Research Co., 1995). Nearly 16,000 informative, up-to-date listings of current directories. 2,100 subject headings and cross references.

Kruzas, Anthony T., and Robert C. Thomas, eds., *Business Organizations, Agencies and Publications Directory,* 8th ed. (Detroit: Gale Research Co., 1995). Supplies exact names to write, phone, or visit for current facts, figures, rulings, verifications, and opinions on business matters. Names agencies, associations, groups, federations, organizations, and, whenever possible, authorized contact people.

Million Dollar Directory (New York: Dun and Bradstreet). Published annually in five volumes. Lists 160,000 U.S. companies worth $750,000 or more. Gives officers and directors, products or services, SIC number, sales, and number of employees. Division, geographic, location indexes. Also available as on-line database.

National Trade and Professional Associations of the U.S. and Canada and Labor Unions (Washington, D.C.: Columbia Books, Inc.). Published annually. Listing of trade and professional organizations and labor unions with national memberships. Key work, geographic, and budget size indexes.

Research Services Directory, 6th ed. (Detroit: Gale Research Co., 1995). Lists for-profit organizations providing research services on a contract or fee-for-service basis to clients. Covered research activities include business, education, energy and the environment, agriculture, government, public affairs, social sciences, art and the humanities, physical and earth sciences, life sciences, and engineering and technology.

Standard and Poor's Corporation Records (New York: Standard and Poor's Corp.). Published semimonthly in loose-leaf format, 1925 to present. Corporate news and financial information on American, Canadian, and foreign companies. Provides company history, officers, and product data. *Daily News* covers current corporate developments. Indexes to main entry and subsidiaries.

Thomas Register of American Manufacturers (New York: Thomas Publishing Co.). Published annually. Comprehensive U.S. directory restricted to manufacturing firms. Volumes 1–16 are indexes to manufacturers by product; Volume 18 includes a list of trade names. Volumes 17–18 lists manufacturers by company name, including information similar to Standard & Poor's *Register.* Volumes 19–26 are compilations of manufacturers' catalogues.

Biographies

Biographical reference books are useful sources of information regarding people, living or deceased. They provide dates of birth and death, nationality, and information about occupations.

Reference Book of Corporate Managements (New York: Dun and Bradstreet). Published annually. Directory of top executives arranged by company, birthdate, college, and employment history.

Standard & Poor's Register of Corporations, Directors and Executives. (New York: Standard & Poor's). Published annually. Volume 2, *Directors and Executives,* gives biographical information on 70,000 corporate officers.

VII. Statistical Sources

Statistics are an absolute necessity for decision makers. They are becoming increasingly valuable and available through computer on-line databases. The more comprehensive compilations are provided by government agencies, universities, and trade associations. These statistics determine U.S. and regional business trends. Data are also gathered for specific industries. Examples are banking and monetary statistics; labor and marketing statistics; and plant and equipment expenditures studies. Other sources concentrate on important international statistics and foreign economic trends.

Statistical sources are divided into two major sections: indexes and selected statistical sources for general information, and international and industrial marketing statistics.

Indexes

Predicasts Forecasts (Cleveland: Predicasts, Inc.). Published quarterly, cumulated annually. Abstracts business and financial forecasts for specific U.S. industrial products and the general economy. Presents composite data for economic, construction, energy, and other indicators. Now available on CD-ROM.

O'Brien, Jacqueline and Wassermann, S.R., *Statistics Sources: A Subject Guide to Data on Industrial, Business, Social, Educational, Financial and Other Topics for the U.S. and Internationally,* 18th ed. (Detroit: Gale Research Co., 1994). Finding guide to statistics indexes information from domestic and international sources. Arranged dictionary style; includes selected bibliography of key statistical sources.

Selected Statistical Sources

Levine, Sumner N., ed., *Business One Irwin Business and Investment Almanac* (Homewood, Ill.: Business One Irwin). Published annually. Tables and graphs. Most basic, comprehensive statistical information on various aspects of business, finance, investments, and economics for recent trends. Includes articles on tax, accounting, and labor developments. Subject index.

Industry Many business projects involve gathering statistical or investment data on a particular industry. The following source provides useful statistics on leading industries and analyzes current trends and future projections.

Yearbook of Industrial Statistics (New York: United Nations). Published annually. Supplemented monthly in *Monthly Bulletin of Statistics.* Volume 1: *General*

Industrial Statistics. A body of international statistics on population, agriculture, mining, manufacturing, finance, trade, and education. Volume 2: *Commodity Production Data* supplies internationally comparable data on the production of industrial commodities internationally.

Marketing Access to current statistical data is essential to those engaged in market research. Marketing departments attempting to determine sales potential, set sales quotas, or establish effective sales territories are interested in details such as population, number of households, age, sex, marital status, occupation, education level, income, and purchasing power. Much of this information is available from U.S. government sources. Individual states also publish statistical series, often on a more timely basis than the federal government. Private companies also generate data applicable to marketing functions.

Rand McNally *Commercial Atlas and Marketing Guide* (Chicago: Rand McNally). Published annually, 1884 to present. Includes maps for each state in the United States and a section of maps of foreign countries. Marketing statistics for states and some worldwide data, such as airline and steamship distances, are provided. Also included are population statistics and figures for retail sales, bank deposits, auto registrations, etc., for principal cities.

Editor and Publisher Market Guide (New York: The Editor and Publisher). Published annually, 1884 to present. Market data are provided for more than 1,500 U.S. and Canadian cities in which newspapers are published. Included are figures for population, households, principal industries, and retail outlets. Estimates are given by county and newspaper city, and strategic market segment analysis is performed for such items as population and personal income. Total retail sales are arranged by state.

Market Share Reporter (Detroit: Gale Research). Published annually. Published market share data on over 4,000 companies and 2,500 products, facilities and brands. Each entry includes the market share data and cites the original source making it a good index to published sources of market data on specific products or specific markets.

Survey of Business Buying Power Data Service (New York: Sales & Marketing Management). Published annually, 1977 to present. A spin-off of the July and October statistical issues of *Sales & Marketing Management* magazine. Arranged in three volumes. Volume 1 lists county and city population characteristics, such as household distribution, effective buying income, total retail store sales, and various buying power indexes. Volume 2 includes retail sales by individual store groups and merchandise line categories for the current year. Volume 3 lists TV market data, metro area and county projections for population, effective buying income, and retail sales.

International Marketing Data & Statistics, 16th ed. (London, England: Euromonitor Publications, Ltd.). Annual. Provides a marketing profile of 142 nations. Data regarding transportation and utilities, credit, foreign trade outlook, investment, industry trends, distribution sales, advertising and research, trade regulations, and market profile.

APPENDIX B

Key Databases of Interest to Marketers[33]

Trademarkscan—Federal

On-line vendor: DIALOG

Produced by the oldest trademark search firm in the United States, Trademarkscan contains all active registered and pending trademarks on file with the U.S. Patent and Trademark Office. It also lists inactive trademarks back to 1984. This makes for a total of more than 1.2 million records, with about 1,500 new records and 4,000 revisions pouring in every week.

For each trademark, the database yields a classification number, a full description of the goods or services, a registration number and data, current status, and the owner's name and address.

PTS MARS (Marketing and Advertising Reference Service)

On-line vendor: DIALOG, Data-Star, NEXIS

Predicasts' Marketing and Advertising Reference Service (MARS) contains more than 150,000 citations, with abstracts, to literature on the advertising and marketing of consumer goods and services. The service reviews 140 publications, including such magazines as *Marketing Review, Variety, Advertising Age, Folio,* and *Adweek*, as well as newsletters, trade publications, journals, and relevant sections of major U.S. newspapers.

Specific or general searching can be done using Predicasts' product codes, expanded versions of the Standard Industrial Classification codes. Users can also search by type of information included in the abstract or by geographical location.

PTS PROMT

On-line vendors: Data-Star, DIALOG, NEXIS

Since 1972, Predicasts has offered its Overview of Markets and Technology, a comprehensive database of very informative, high-quality abstracts of business periodicals and magazines. More than 1,200 publications are covered; weekly updates add 2,500 entries to the more than 800,000 already on-line.

More than 200 of the abstracted publications are foreign, though all abstracts are in English.

Detailed company, product, or market information can be found here, including information on 120,000 companies—public or private, domestic or foreign, established or emerging.

Coverage includes new products, acquisitions, marketing, finance, foreign trade, manufacturing—virtually all industries and products.

VALS2

On-line vendor: Interactive Market Systems, Telmar Group

In this database, Mediamark classifies its survey respondent's into the nine VALS2 (values and lifestyles) types developed by the Stanford Research Institute. Based on their attitudes, wants, and beliefs, American consumers are grouped into three categories: need-driven, outer-directed, and inner-directed. These categories are then subdivided into the nine VALS2 types, each of which has distinct buying styles, media use patterns, and demography.

SUPERSITE

On-line vendor: CompuServe

CACI, Inc. puts 1960, 1970, 1980, and 1990 census data with current-year updates and five-year forecasts in this geographic database. For any area in the United States, from a certain radius around a specific street intersection to an entire state, CACI can provide demographic descriptions, sales potential estimates, or ACORN profiles.

For more than 60,000 census tracts and minor civil divisions, SuperSite yields such demographic information as population, income, prices of housing, occupation, automobiles, educational attainment, family composition, and household appliances.

Sales potential estimates are available for 165 lines of retail merchandise, 16 types of retail outlets, and three banking services.

ACORN (A Classification of Residential Neighborhoods) puts every U.S. census block group into one of 45 market segments. Each market segment is a profile: a description of that type of neighborhood's demography, economy, and housing.

Simmons Study of Media and Markets

On-line vendors: Simmons Market Research Bureau, Interactive Market Systems

The people at Simmons Market Research Bureau, Inc., annually question 13,000 American adults about their use of 3,900 brands of products in more than 800 categories. In the process, SMRB measures audiences for magazines, television, radio, newspapers, outdoor advertising, and Yellow Pages. And it collects demographic and psychographic information on the respondents, so the data can be linked to ClusterPLUS, PRIZM, and VALS categories.

Altogether, the database holds more than two million pieces of information. The 27 demographic categories include age, sex, income, education, occupation, marital status, number of children, geographic region, and value of residence.

Trade and Industry ASAP

On-line vendors: DIALOG, NEXIS, BRS, Data-Star

Sister database to Magazine ASAP, Trade and Industry ASAP focuses on business and trade publications. It supplies the full text of more than 200 magazines, along with press releases from PR Newswire.

Mediamark Research Data Base

On-line vendors: Interactive Market Systems, Telmar Group, MSA, CompuServe

Twice a year, Mediamark Research, Inc. asks 20,000 American adults about the magazines they read, the radio programs they listen to, and the television they watch. It also collects personal, demographic, and consumer information. It covers 250 magazines titles, with such information as where they are read, how long they are read, and what actions the reading leads to (e.g., buying a product or following a recipe). Television and radio audiences also are estimated.

MRI–Mediamarkets

On-line vendor: Interactive Market Systems, Telmar Group, MSA

This database holds media and marketing information on 10 major markets: New York, Los Angeles, Chicago, Philadelphia, San Francisco, Boston, Detroit, Washington, D.C., Cleveland, and Saint Louis.

MRI–Mediamarkets includes audience estimates for these cities' newspapers, radio stations, radio station formats (such as top 40 or country and western), and television news programs. It also includes the survey respondents' usage patterns for an array of products and brand names. And demographic data on the respondents is included, too.

MRI Business-to-Business

On-line vendors: Interactive Market Systems, Telmar Group, MSA

What do business professionals buy for their businesses? To answer this question, Mediamark Research Inc. interviews 3,800 professionals and managers every year about their purchases of business products and magazines. Thirty-five categories of purchases are covered, including office equipment, advertising, and banking services. MRI measures the professional audiences for more than 200 magazines.

The database also includes demographic information on the respondents, including age, type of company, size of company, and occupational characteristics.

FINDEX

On-line vendor: DIALOG

FIND/SVP is one of the largest information brokers in the world. This database corresponds to its annual publication, *FINDEX: The Directory of Market Research Reports, Studies and Surveys.* The directory will tell who has done a market study on a particular product but will not summarize the findings. More than 11,000 studies done by more than 500 research firms are indexed. For 70 of these publishers, FIND/SVP can supply copies of the reports. For the rest, ordering information is provided.

The database offers instant access to citations of market research reports, consumer and product studies, store audit reports, subscription research services, multiclient industry studies, and surveys of 55 industries worldwide.

Donnelley Demographics

On-line vendor: DIALOG

The official source of information on population studies, Donnelley Marketing Information Services provides selected demographic data from the 1990 census, plus its proprietary current-year and five-year projections.

The data can be viewed for the United States in total or by state, county, city, town, or zip code. In addition, population segmentation by Metropolitan Statistical Areas, Areas of Dominant Influence, A. C. Nielsen's Designated Market Areas, or Selling Areas can be searched in the database.

The demographics are broken down by age, sex, race, industry, occupation, marital status, families, mobility, households, education, housing, income, etc.

D&B—Dun's Market Identifiers

On-line vendor: DIALOG, Data-Star, Dow-Jones, News/Retrieval

Dun's Marketing Services compiled this directory of 7.5 million U.S. public and private businesses with 5 or more employees or more than $1 million in sales. Profiles on these companies are extensive and detailed, providing more than 30 searchable facts about each company.

These include the company's address, history, sales, volume, number of employees, corporate family affiliations, parent or subsidiary relationships, headquarters and branch locations, and executive names and titles.

Harvard Business Review Online

On-line vendor: BRS, DIALOG, Data-Star, NEXIS

Just a week after the *Harvard Business Review* is released in print, it appears online to join the more than 3,300 records already on file. The database for this noted bimonthly management periodical contains the full text of articles from 1976 to the present.

Management and Marketing Abstracts

On-line vendor: Pergamon InfoLine

This bibliography contains abstracts from more than 100 international journals. Monographs, books, published proceedings, conference papers, newsletters, and corporate reports also are summarized.

D&B—Dun's Electronic Business Directory

On-line vendor: DIALOG

Directory information for 8.9 million U.S. businesses. Entries include address, telephone, SIC code and number of employees. Users can create custom lists by specifying zip code, state, city, county, telephone area code, size of company or type of business.

Arbitron Radio and Arbitron TV Local Market Report

On-line vendor: Interactive Market Systems

Television and radio stations, advertisers and advertising agencies can gain a wide variety of marketing information through Arbitron Information on Demand.

This database features more than 210 television and more than 263 radio markets. Audience psychographics are recorded with yearly surveys, and a wide variety of information can be retrieved. Rather than applying a formula to audience estimates contained within the printed Arbitron diaries—from which the information is extracted—the database focuses on real reach and frequency so the user can examine the data beyond gross impressions and rating points.

International Business Clearing House

On-line vendor: AT&T FYI News, Barter Worldwide

International Business Clearinghouse is a worldwide bartering and brokerage service containing comprehensive listings of goods and services offered for sale or trade by companies around the world. An invaluable source of data for anyone involved in world trade, this database offers information on a variety of business enterprises ranging from media, computer companies, and manufacturers to distributors and service companies such as airlines and hotels.

CHAPTER 

Qualitative Research

LEARNING OBJECTIVES

1. To define qualitative research.
2. To explore the popularity of qualitative research.
3. To understand why qualitative research is not held in high esteem by some practitioners and academicians.
4. To learn about focus groups and their tremendous popularity.
5. To gain insight into conducting and analyzing a focus group.
6. To study other forms of qualitative research.

As most apartment dwellers know, tracking down the building manager or landlord when you have a problem is next to impossible. Maybe it's a leaky faucet or a noisy neighbor—whatever it is, he usually doesn't want to hear about it. Unless, that is, you live in a complex managed by Homecorp, in which case management may just come looking for you to find out if everything is all right.

The Montgomery, Alabama, firm manages more than 70 apartment communities nationwide—its strongest presence is in the Southeast—serving more than 15,000 residents. Its two-year-old customer satisfaction research effort, the Focus program, includes an annual survey and focus groups with residents.

Homecorp goes beyond the usual industry practice of surveying customers when they move in and move out, says Bryan J. Rader, general manager of Homecorp Services. "The Focus program came about when we realized that the rest of the industry was doing an inadequate job by measuring satisfaction at only two contact points, the move-in and move-out. If you focus on your customer only at those points, you will never satisfy them."

SOURCE: © Bill Horsman/Stock Boston.

The company strives to listen to its customers throughout their residence in a Homecorp community. (All research is done in-house, except data processing. Rader moderates all the focus groups with residents.) Homecorp sends a customer satisfaction survey to its residents each February. The survey results are presented to community managers in April.

"We want to have the information communicated to the entire property together in staff meetings so that everyone buys into the information and realizes that he or she has as much impact on satisfaction as the manager. We want a total buy-in and teamwork in addressing any challenges that come up. We also want them to share in the success."

Rader also moderates a focus group once a year at each of the communities. A random selection of residents is invited to the leasing office in the evening and asked to elaborate on issues raised in the larger survey. "We get a better definition of why they are happy or unhappy. We also ask them to propose solutions to any problems they're facing because often the best solutions come from our residents. We monitor the performance of our proposed solutions, and, if they work at one property, we may try them at another. If it's not working, we put plans in place to try something else. The program has been a huge success, has increased bottom-line profits significantly, reduced turnover, and we've seen satisfaction grow by property in the last two years dramatically."[1] ■

Homecorp conducts traditional customer satisfaction survey research and also focus groups. Focus groups are a form of qualitative research. What is qualitative research and how does it differ from quantitative research? How is it conducted? What makes focus groups so popular? What makes all qualitative research so controversial? These are some of the issues we will explore in Chapter 6.

The Nature of Qualitative Research

Qualitative Research Defined

qualitative research
Research data not subject to quantification or quantitative analysis.

quantitative research
Studies that use mathematical analysis.

Qualitative research is a loosely used term. It means that the research findings are not subject to quantification or quantitative analysis. A quantitative study's findings may determine that a heavy user of a brand of tequila is 21 to 35 years of age with an annual income of $18,000 to $25,000. **Quantitative research** can reveal statistically significant differences between heavy and light users. In contrast, qualitative research could be used to examine the attitudes, feelings, and motivations of the heavy user. Advertising agencies planning a campaign for tequila might employ qualitative techniques to learn how the heavy users express themselves, what language they use, and, essentially, how to communicate with them.

The qualitative approach flows from the work of the mid-18th-century historian Giambattista Vico. Vico wrote that only people can understand people and that they do this through a faculty called *intuitive understanding*. In sociology and other social sciences, the concept of *Verstehen*, or the intuitive experiment, and the use of empathy have been associated with major discoveries (and disputes) within the field.

The Qualitative versus Quantitative Controversy

Table 6.1 compares qualitative and quantitative research on several levels. Perhaps most significant to managers is that qualitative research typically is characterized by small samples, which has provided a focal point for the criticism of all qualitative techniques. In essence, many managers are reluctant to base important strategy decisions on small sample research because it relies so greatly on the subjectivity and interpretation of the researcher. They strongly prefer a large

TABLE 6.1 Qualitative versus Quantitative Research

COMPARISON DIMENSION	QUALITATIVE RESEARCH	QUANTITATIVE RESEARCH
Types of Questions	Probing	Limited Probing
Sample Size	Small	Large
Information per Respondent	Much	Varies
Administration	Requires interviewer with Special Skills	Fewer Special Skills Required
Type of Analysis	Subjective, Interpretive	Statistical, Summarization
Hardware	Tape Recorders, Projection Devices, Video, Pictures, Discussion Guides	Questionnaires, Computers, Printouts
Ability to Replicate	Low	High
Training of the Researcher	Psychology, Sociology, Social Psychology, Consumer Behavior, Marketing, Marketing Research	Statistics, Decision Models, Decision Support Systems, Computer Programming, Marketing, Marketing Research
Type of Research	Exploratory	Descriptive or Causal

sample with computer analysis, summarized into tables. Large samples and statistical significance levels are aspects of marketing research with which these managers feel very comfortable because the data are generated in a rigorous and scientific manner.

The Popularity of Qualitative Research

The popularity of qualitative research continues to grow unabated. Several reasons tend to account for its popularity.[2] First, qualitative research is usually much cheaper than quantitative research. Second, there is no better way than qualitative research to understand the in-depth motivations and feelings of consumers. Because product managers often unobtrusively conduct a popular form of qualitative research by observing from behind a one-way mirror, they obtain firsthand experiences with "flesh-and-blood" consumers. Rather than read a computer printout containing countless tables of numbers or reading a consultant's report that digests reams of numbers, the product manager and other marketing personnel observe the consumer's reactions to concepts and hear consumers discuss the manufacturers' and competitors' products at length using their own language. Sitting behind a one-way mirror can be a humbling experience to a new product development manager when the consumer begins to tear apart product concepts that were months in development in the sterile laboratory environment.

Consider, for example, the quotation by Stephen Wells, The Connexions Group—Great Britain, regarding qualitative research in the following "A Professional Researcher's Perspective."

A third reason that qualitative research is popular is that it can improve the efficiency of quantitative research. Volvo of America Corporation was concerned that the U.S. automotive market was undergoing vast changes that could affect its market share. Volvo decided that a major research study was needed to gain an

A Professional Researcher's Perspective

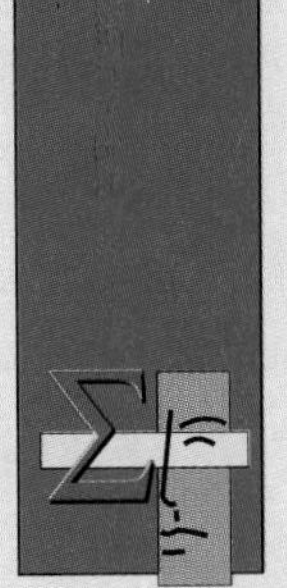

I do not accept that qualitative research is a science: it does not produce truths, factual, databased results; nor does it lend itself to being conducted in a series of clearly defined and separable steps—i.e., planning, data collection, analysis, interpretation—although this does not mean that it should not be conducted in a well-planned, systematic way. I see qualitative research as living and evolving, a source of insights and ideas, continuously arising, at any time. The currency of qualitative research being living, evolving ideas, not dry data. The search is for newness; new vision and insight.

A crucial role of qualitative research is to create the right environment in which ideas can arise and then develop and flourish. Every encouragement should be given for the unexpected to emerge. This can be achieved by setting up a tension: between, on the one hand, slavishly and meticulously going through everything respondents say and do, whilst, on the other, being alert to something quite new of which respondents are perhaps unaware at a conscious level.

I know that for qualitative research to deliver, the researcher must be committed to the point of obsession; manically curious, wildly inquisitive: with high energy levels being generated, either inner or outer directed according to the researcher's personality and with the researcher contributing this energy to the process.

A researcher must want to know *why*. Why do people think and behave as they do? Essentially what motivates them—makes them tick? Where are they coming from? What are they really like?[3] ■

appreciation of the changing marketplace. The project involved both a quantitative and a qualitative phase. The first phase of the project enabled the researchers to conduct a quantitative study that was both more insightful and less expensive because of a shorter questionnaire. Among the insights gained in the qualitative phase were the following: (1) Potential buyers considered Volvo in a number of different ways. Some considered Volvo very seriously and narrowed the choice of cars to Volvo and one other make. Others considered Volvo seriously, but it was not among the cars that survived the final decision. (2) Some considered Volvo seriously without ever visiting a showroom. (3) Despite Volvo's small share of the U.S. market, the qualitative information hinted at several important subsegments within the Volvo market.[4]

It is becoming more common for marketing researchers to combine qualitative and quantitative research into a single study or a series of studies. The Volvo example showed how qualitative research can be used subsequent to quantitative research; in other research designs, the reverse may be used. For instance, the patterns displayed in quantitative research can be enriched with the addition of qualitative information on the reasons and motivations of consumers. Thus, it is not a case of deciding which one is the right research strategy, but of determining where one is more appropriate. Or the situation may require using the two methodologies in conjunction with each other, if possible, to effect a better final research product. Perhaps the major argument for using qualitative research relates back to the scientific method itself. As noted by Bellenger and Greenberg:

> the research process and the decision-making process retain major subjective elements. The initial steps in the research process, that is, defining the problem and the information needs, formulating the hypotheses, and defining variables, are essentially subjective in nature. In addition, much of the research design stage, such as determining the type of research, sampling procedure and designing the measurement instrument, are also qualitative. Quantitative precision is meaningless if the wrong hypothesis is tested, the wrong variables are measured, or if the wrong instrument is chosen for a given problem. Even when these failings are avoided, the research results are subject to the judgmental interpretation of the researcher and of the ultimate decision maker. Clearly, the theoretical precision and objectivity of quantitative research can be substantially diluted by this array of subjective or qualitative factors. Thus the qualitative approach will still have merit in various subjective areas of marketing research even if the problems of accurate measurement can be overcome.[5]

In the final analysis, all research is undertaken to increase the effectiveness of marketing decision making. Qualitative research blends with quantitative measures by providing a more thorough understanding of consumer demand. Qualitative techniques involve open-ended questioning and probing. The data are rich, human, subtle, and often very revealing.

Limitations of Qualitative Research

Qualitative research can, and does, produce helpful and useful information. Yet it is held in disdain by many researchers. The first limitation relates to the fact that marketing successes and failures many times are based on small differences in a marketing mix. Qualitative research does not distinguish small differences as well as large-scale quantitative research does. We should note that qualitative research is sometimes superior in detecting problems that may escape notice in a quantitative study. For example, a major manufacturer of household cleaners conducted a large quantitative study in an effort to learn why its bathroom cleanser had lackluster sales. The manufacturer knew that the chemical compound was more effective than those used by leading competitors. The quantitative study provided no clear-cut answer. The frustrated product manager then turned to qualitative research. It was quickly uncovered that the muted pastel colors on the package did not connote "cleansing strength" to the shopper. Also, a number of women were using old toothbrushes to clean between the bathroom tiles. The package was redesigned with brighter colors and included a brush built into the top.

A second limitation of qualitative techniques is that qualitative studies are not necessarily representative of the population of interest to the researcher. One would be hard pressed to say that a group of 10 college students is representative of all college students, of college students at a particular university, of business majors at that university, or even marketing majors! Small sample sizes and free-flowing discussion can lead qualitative research projects down many paths. Also, people who are subjects of qualitative research are often free to tell us what interests them. A dominant individual in group discussion can lead a group into areas of only tangential interest to the researcher. It takes a highly skilled researcher to get the discussion back on track without stifling the group's interest, enthusiasm, and willingness to speak out.[6]

A final concern about qualitative research is the multitude of individuals who, without formal training, profess to be experts in the field. Because there is no certification body in marketing research, anyone can call herself a qualitative expert. Unfortunately, it is often difficult for the unsuspecting client to discern the researcher's qualifications or the quality of the research. On the other hand, to conduct a sophisticated quantitative study requires extensive training. It is extremely difficult, if not impossible, to bluff one's way through this type of project.

The Growing Role of Focus Groups

Focus Groups Defined

focus groups
Groups of eight to 12 participants who are led by a moderator in an in-depth discussion on one particular topic or concept.

group dynamics
The interaction among people in a group.

Focus groups had their beginnings in group therapy used by psychiatrists. Today, a **focus group** consists of eight to 12 participants who are led by a moderator in an in-depth discussion on one particular topic or concept. The goal of focus group research is to learn and understand what people have to say and why. The emphasis is on getting people talking at length and in detail about the subject at hand. The intent is to find out how they feel about a product, concept, idea, or organization, how it fits into their lives, and their emotional involvement with it.

Focus groups are much more than merely question-and-answer interviews. The distinction is made between "group dynamics" and "group interviewing." The interaction provided in **group dynamics** is essential to the success of focus group research; this interaction is the reason for conducting group rather than individual research. One of the essential postulates of group session usage is the idea that a response from one person may become a stimulus for another, thereby generating an interplay of responses that may yield more than if the same number of people had contributed independently.

The idea for group dynamics research in marketing came from the field of social psychology, where studies indicated that unknown to themselves, people of all walks of life and in all occupations will tell us more about a topic and do so in greater depth if they are encouraged to act spontaneously instead of reacting to questions. Normally, in group dynamics, direct questions are avoided. In their place are indirect inquiries that stimulate free and spontaneous discussions. The result is a much richer base of information of a kind impossible to obtain by direct interviews.

The Popularity of Focus Groups

Qualitative research and focus groups are often used as synonyms by marketing research practitioners. Popular writings abound with examples of researchers referring to qualitative research in one breath and focus groups in the next, even though, as discussed earlier, focus groups are but one aspect of qualitative research. Yet the overwhelming popularity of the technique has virtually overshadowed other qualitative tools.

How popular are focus groups? Most marketing research firms, advertising agencies, and consumer goods manufacturers use the technique. Today, more than $378 million a year is spent on focus group research by client firms.[7] Leo Burnett Company, for example, conducts more than 350 focus groups each year for clients. Focus groups tend to be used more extensively by consumer goods companies than by industrial goods organizations. The low incidence of use is understandable as industrial groups pose a host of problems not found in consumer research. For example, it is usually quite easy to assemble a group of 12 homemakers. However, putting together a group of 10 engineers, sales managers, or financial analysts is far more costly and time-consuming.

Types of Focus Groups

Bobby Calder, a noted scholar on qualitative research, has classified focus groups into three major groups: exploratory, clinical, and experiencing.[8] Table 6.2 compares the three types using seven areas of application.

Exploratory Groups

Exploratory focus groups are commonly used at the exploratory phase of the market research process to aid in the precise definition of the problem (see Chapter 2). They also can be viewed as pilot testing. Groups may be employed to test wording on a questionnaire or product placement instructions. Exploratory groups may have a more lofty goal of attempting to generate hypotheses for testing or concepts for further research. The research director of Time, Inc. says, "We use focus groups for fishing."[9] He then goes on to say that *fishing* means defining

exploratory focus groups
Focus groups that aid in the precise definition of the problem, in pilot testing, or in generating hypotheses for testing or concepts for further research.

TABLE 6.2 Types of Focus Groups and Their Applications

APPLICATIONS	EXPLORATORY	CLINICAL	EXPERIENCING
The approach should be used when the goal is to experience a "flesh and blood" consumer	No	No	Yes
Obtaining a high level of interaction among the group members is essential	Yes	Yes	Yes
A homogeneous group of people is necessary	No	No	Yes
The moderator's interviewing technique is crucial	No	Yes	No
The moderator must have scientific credentials	No	Yes	No
Observation by management is appropriate	No	No	Yes
Verbatim quotes should be emphasized in the report	No	No	Yes

SOURCE: Adapted from Bobby Calder, "Focus Groups and the Nature of Qualitative Marketing Research," *Journal of Marketing Research* 14 (August 1977): 353–364.

problems, generating hypotheses, exploring ideas, and preparing for quantitative research. One focus group came up with 166 new ways to prepare frozen chicken.[10] These ideas became the basis for further research.

Recently, Bausch & Lomb was in the process of exploring various interim packaging alternatives for its soft contact lens solutions. In focus groups conducted for the firm, product arrays were used to explore consumer reactions to current Bausch & Lomb and competitive products. Reactions to four proposed logos and seven proposed package designs were examined against a background of response to current packaging. Among the design elements analyzed were

- A white Bausch & Lomb logo (reverse type) on blue and green background colors. (Maintaining this reverse type and current colors was preferred and has the best brand association.)
- Color coding of the product types in the line was deemed more important than secondary brand names.
- Use of the "product type" color for package print.
- The use of numbers to designate heat (thermal) versus chemical (cold) systems was found to be inadequate and confusing. The specific words are being used instead.

The focus group information guided the package designers in creating new designs for test marketing.[11]

Clinical Focus Groups

clinical focus groups
Focus groups that explore subconscious motivation.

Clinical focus groups are qualitative research in its purest form. The research is conducted as a scientific endeavor, based upon the premise that a person's true motivations and feelings are subconscious in nature. What consumers say cannot be taken at face value; instead, the research must probe beneath the level of consciousness.

Obviously clinical groups require a moderator with expertise in psychology and sociology. It is assumed that a person's real motives must be uncovered using clinical judgment. Thus, the focus group becomes the data input source for clinical judgment. The moderator must be highly skilled to entice participants into revealing inner feelings and thoughts. The following example of clinical focus group research illustrates the concept.

> The group was conducted for the Parks and Recreation department of a large Eastern city. Group participants were teenagers with learning disabilities. The objective of the groups was to learn about disabled teens' need for, and potential use of, alternative forms of recreation.
>
> Before anyone could focus on recreation, it was important to get beyond the youths' anger and fear about being labeled as having a learning disability and needing special help. Getting the group members to talk about themselves and where they went to school broke the ice. It gave everyone a chance to see that all members were bright but in special programs at school because they had a learning hindrance.
>
> Once the common bond was established, each one began to look at the other as a potential friend. They identified possible activities that could be done in couples or as a group. The recreation department was eager to provide a normalizing experience and was planning to incorporate these teens into an existing program, which included competitive activities.
>
> The clinical focus group clearly demonstrated the inappropriateness of the department's planned approach. These teens did not want to be competitive and preferred

to make friends while playing alongside of, not with, peers. They were eager to develop noncompetitive skills within a group, such as horseback riding, swimming, and ice skating. This group planned a series of activities that were later incorporated into the roster of recreation programs. The members later assisted with recruiting other teens with learning disabilities.[12]

Because of the difficulty (if not impossibility) of validating findings from clinical groups and unskilled moderators attempting to conduct clinical groups, their popularity has markedly diminished. Perhaps when new psychoanalytic tools are developed and certification standards are developed for moderators, clinical groups will enjoy a resurgence.

Experiencing Focus Groups

A researcher who speaks of "doing a few groups" usually is referring to **experiencing focus groups.** Lewis Stone, former manager of Colgate-Palmolive's Research and Development Division, claims:

experiencing focus groups
Focus groups that enable a client to observe and listen to how consumers think and feel about products and services.

> If it weren't for focus groups, Colgate-Palmolive Co. might never know that some women squeeze their bottles of dishwashing soap, others squeeeeze them, and still others squeeeeeeeeeeze out the desired amount. Then there are the ones who use the soap "neat." That is, they put the product directly on a sponge or washcloth and wash the dishes under running water until the suds run out. Then they apply more detergent.
>
> Stone was explaining how body language, exhibited during focus groups, provides insights into a product that are not apparent from reading questionnaires on habits and practices. Focus groups represent a most efficient way of learning how one's products are actually used in the home. By drawing out the panelists to describe in detail how they do certain tasks . . . you can learn a great deal about possible need-gaps that could be filled by new or improved products, and also how a new product might be received.[13]

Thus, an experiencing approach represents an opportunity to "experience" a "flesh-and-blood" consumer. Reality in the kitchen or supermarket differs drastically from that of most corporate offices. It allows the researcher to experience the emotional framework in which the product is being used. In a sense, the researcher can go into a person's life and relive with him all the satisfactions, dissatisfactions, rewards, and frustrations experienced when the product is taken home.

A recent study has found that marketing research practitioners don't make the distinctions between focus group approaches in the same way that Calder does.[14] Moderators with different scientific orientations and training are equally likely to conduct focus groups with exploratory, experiencing, or clinical knowledge-gathering objectives. Also, research practitioners do not use the type of group to be conducted as a selection criterion when choosing a moderator.

Conducting Focus Groups

Now that you understand the types of focus groups, we can proceed to the process of conducting focus groups (see Figure 6.1). The space devoted to this topic is considerable because there is much potential for researcher error in conducting focus groups.

FIGURE 6.1
Steps in Conducting a Focus Group

Preparing for a Focus Group

The Setting Focus groups are usually held in a "**focus group facility.**" The setting is normally conference-room style with a large one-way mirror in one wall. Microphones are placed in an unobtrusive location (usually the ceiling) to record the discussion. Behind the mirror is the viewing room, which consists of chairs and note-taking benches or tables for the clients. The viewing room also houses the recording or videotape equipment. Figure 6.2 is an advertisement for a focus group facility and shows clients viewing a focus group behind a one-way mirror.

focus group facility
Facility consisting of conference or living room setting and a separate observation room. Facility also has audiovisual recording equipment.

Some research firms offer a living room setting as an alternative to the conference room. It is presumed that the informality of the living room will make the participants more at ease, as in a typical homelike setting. Another variation is to not use a one-way mirror but to televise the proceedings to a remote viewing room. This approach offers the advantage of clients being able to move around and speak in a normal tone of voice without being "heard" through the wall. On more than one occasion a client has lighted a cigarette while viewing a group, resulting in the flash being seen through the mirror.

Recruiting Participants Participants are recruited for focus groups from a variety of sources. Two common procedures are mall intercept interviews and random telephone screening. (Both methods are described in detail in the next chapter.) Researchers normally establish criteria for the group participants. For example, if Quaker Oats is researching a new cereal, it might request mothers with children ranging in age from seven to 12 years old who had served cold cereal, perhaps a specific brand, in the past three weeks.

Usually researchers strive to avoid repeat or "professional" respondents in focus groups. Professional respondents are viewed by many researchers as actors or at least persons who provide less than candid answers.[15] Questions also may be raised regarding who type of person will continually come to group sessions. Are they lonely? Do they really need the respondent fee that badly? It is highly unlikely the professional respondents are representative of many, if any, target

FIGURE 6.2

An Advertisement Illustrating a Focus Group in Progress

SOURCE: Courtesy of Focus Suites of Philadelphia.

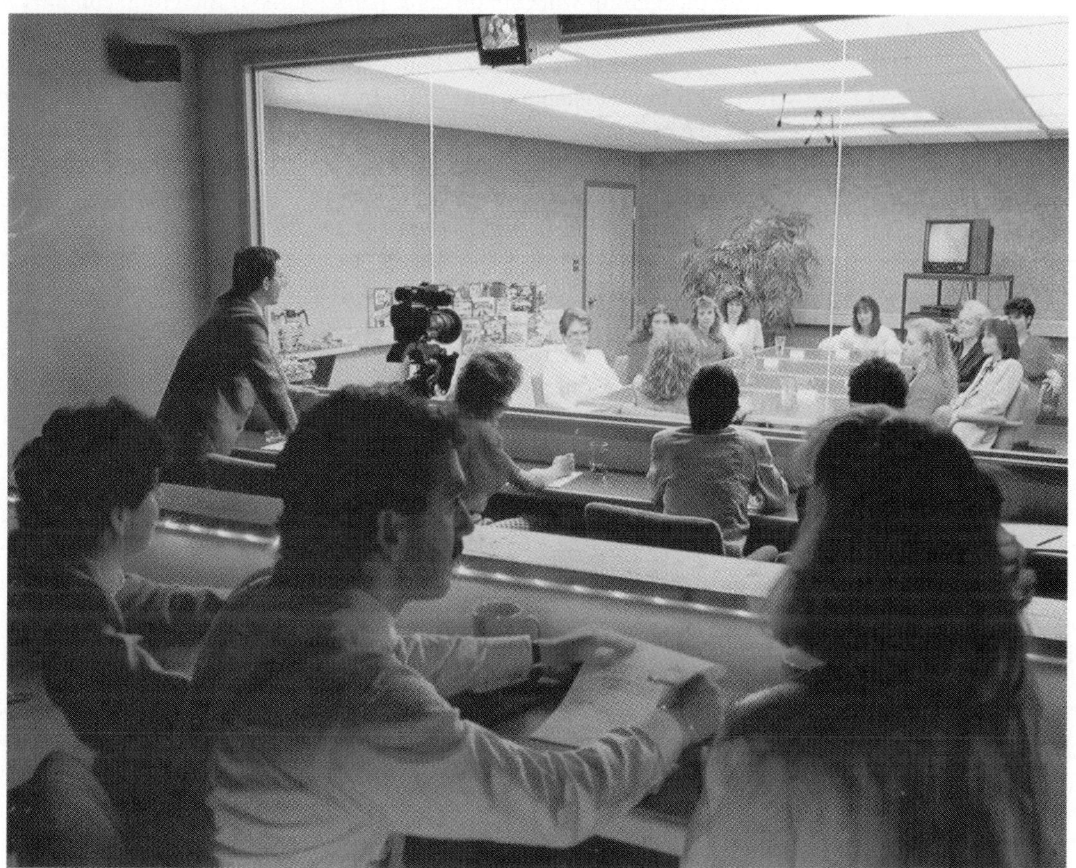

Find out what hundreds of researchers already know...

Focus Suites is like no other facility you've ever tried.

- The expertise of our professional recruiters is unsurpassed in this industry.
- We have three separate, totally private 3-room suites.
- These extraordinary suites are available for the same cost or less than that of an ordinary facility.

Call today for a competitive bid on your next qualitative research project.
Once you've tried us, you'll never be satisfied with an ordinary facility again.

The Right People... The Right Price... The Right Place

One Bala Plaza, Suite 622, 231 St. Asaphs Road,
Bala Cynwyd, PA 19004 (215) 667-1110

Circle No. 194 on Reader Card

markets. Unfortunately, field services find it much easier to use repeat respondents rather than recruit a fresh group each time. Most participate simply to get the respondent fee.[16]

A typical group will contain eight participants. If the group contains 10 people, there will be little time for the group members to express their opinions. Rarely will a group last more than two hours, with an hour and a half more common. The first 10 minutes is spent with introductions and an explanation of procedures. This leaves about 80 useful minutes in the session and up to 25 percent of that time is taken by the moderator. With 10 people in the group, it leaves an average of only six minutes per individual.

Yet, there is no ideal number of participants. If the topic is quite interesting or of a technical nature, fewer respondents are needed. The type of group will also affect the number recruited. More individuals should be recruited for an experiencing group than for a clinical group.

Why do people agree to participate in focus groups? Research shows that the number one reason is money.[17] Other motivations, in rank order, are: the topic was interesting, it was a convenient time, focus groups are fun, respondent knew a lot about the product, curiosity, and it offers an opportunity to express opinions. The study also found that participants who came only for the money were less committed to research and tended to fulfill their roles in a more perfunctory way.

Selecting the Moderator

focus group moderator
The person hired by the client to lead the focus group. This person may need a background in psychology or sociology or, at least, marketing.

Having qualified respondents and a good **focus group moderator** are the keys to successful focus groups. Regardless of the type of group conducted, a qualified moderator is essential. Qualifications, of course, depend on the type of group the researcher is conducting. A moderator of clinical groups should have extensive

A good moderator is an important key to a successful focus group.

training in psychology and social psychology. Although research has shown that this is not always the case. This individual is responsible not only for conducting the group but also for interpreting what the participants contribute to the discussion.

Considerable disagreement exists among researchers on educational requirements of exploratory and experiencing group moderators. One school of thought is that these individuals also should be trained in psychology or sociology. It is believed that this background is important to understand the nuances of human behavior. Exploratory moderators at the very least need solid training in marketing research. How else, it is argued, can the moderator develop hypotheses and a framework for quantitative research?

In the past few years there has been an increase in the number of formal moderator training courses offered by manufacturers with large market research departments, advertising agencies, and research firms. Most programs are strictly for employees, but a few are open to anyone. Table 6.3 on pages 186 and 187 lists the qualities that a well-trained moderator brings to a focus group. This list was developed by Naomi Henderson, president of RIVA Marketing Research, Inc., Bethesda, Maryland.

The second school of thought on moderator training maintains a different posture. It emphasizes personality, empathy, sensitivity, and good instincts. It assumes that some people just have a "feel" for conducting groups. Individuals who observe long enough and have these innate abilities can become good group moderators. Here, training consists of observing an established moderator conduct a few groups and then finding themselves in a room with eight or 10 people. Emerging an hour and a half later, they realize that they have conducted their first focus group.

A Discussion Guide Is Essential

Regardless of the type of training and personality a moderator possesses, a successful focus group requires a well-planned **discussion guide.** A discussion guide is an outline of the topics to be covered during the session. Usually the guide is generated by the moderator based on the research objectives and client information needs. It serves as a checklist to make certain that all salient topics are covered and in the proper sequence. For example, an outline might begin with attitudes and feelings toward eating out, then move to fast foods, and conclude with a discussion of food and decor of a particular chain. It is very important to get the research director and other client observers, such as a brand manager, to agree that the topics listed on the guide are the most important ones to be covered. It is not uncommon for a "team approach" to be used in generating a discussion guide.

discussion guide

A written outline of topics to cover during a focus group discussion.

The moderator's guide also tends to flow through three stages. In the first, rapport is established, the rules of group interaction are explained, and objectives are given. The second stage is characterized by the moderator attempting to provoke intensive discussion. The final stage is used for summarizing significant conclusions and testing limits of belief and commitment.

Table 6.4 on pages 188 and 189 shows an actual discussion guide (although more detailed than many guides) used by a moderator to explore the credit card usage of college students, their reactions to different tabletop concepts or displays

TABLE 6.3 Qualities that a Well-trained Moderator Brings to a Focus Group

1. Ability to design an appropriate research approach based on experience.
   - Can indicate when focus groups are not the right research tool.
   - Knows when in-depth interviews are needed rather than groups.
2. Ability to help the client establish appropriate and attainable research objectives.
   - Has experience in winnowing myriad objectives into the two or three that can be achieved in a qualitative study.
3. Objective, nonvested viewpoint.
   - As an "outsider," the trained moderator brings a fresh perspective to research objectives and their attainment.
4. Mastery of UPR.
   - "Unconditional positive regard" (UPR) is the ability to listen to viewpoints that are widely divergent from the thinking of the moderator and to hold those viewpoints as valid and appropriate because they comprise the belief system of the respondent.
   - UPR is also the ability to let respondents "be exactly the way they are" and to avoid the desire to educate or inform them when they speak in error.
5. Listening rather than "informing" attitude.
   - Allows respondents to tell moderator what moderator already knows.
   - Is trained to listen to what is said and what is not being said and to probe appropriately.
6. Ability to attend to various levels of nonverbal communication.
   - Can read the room—staying with people, not paper.
   - Uses visual cues as anchors for probing (e.g., eyes up = ask: "What picture did you make?").
7. Multiple techniques to handle group dynamics based on working models from different paradigms (e.g., NLP, psychology, sociology, anthropology).
   - NLP: neurolinguistic programming tools may include anchoring techniques/eye accessing cues/energy builders.
   - Psychology: effective group dynamic processes.
   - Sociology: knowing how people operate in group settings.
   - Anthropology: collecting data without disturbing belief systems.
8. Multiple skills to handle diverse opinions without becoming judgmental, evaluative, or threatening.
   - Working with hostile or diffident respondents.
   - Handling dominators/Milquetoasts.
   - Suppressing judgments.
   - Avoiding preconceptions.
   - Avoiding a "finger-pointing" voice tone.
9. Ability to allow for diverse opinions within the group and accept lack of consensus and closure.
   - Example: Two respondents have very different opinions and polarize the room. A trained moderator knows how to use the polarization as a "catalyst" for conversation.
10. Ability to handle logic tracking to make sure all key points have been explored and discussed in sufficient depth while staying inside time frame for data collection.
    - Reads the room like a clock face.
    - Remembers what's been said/not said, as in a poker game.
    - Uses good judgment and knows when to move on in an area so all key data are collected first.
    - Able to return to previous points, out of order.
    - Uses the "energy" in the room as catalyst to discussion rather than following the guide like a survey instrument.
11. Ability to elicit data by using various models/techniques appropriate to the respondents' frame of reference.
    - Treats each group as "unique," doesn't carry over from previous groups.
    - Varies approaches to groups on the basis of region, lifestyle, age, and other factors.
12. Ability to design a guide from the logic path of respondents.
    - Writes clear, logical questions that the respondents naturally want to answer.
    - Sees the research from the respondents' point of view, not just the viewpoint of the end user.

continues

TABLE 6.3 Qualities that a Well-trained Moderator Brings to a Focus Group—*Continued*

13. Ability to manage the following variables effectively on multiple levels.
    - Research models.
    - Client politics.
    - Field services.
    - Analysis.
14. Knowledge of key intervention techniques and ability to present stimuli to support the flow of conversation and open new areas of exploration.
    - Knows five to nine different interventions (e.g., for forecasting, "let's pretend," "build your own," "Board of Directors," obituary).
    - Knows quick, efficient, and different setups for TV spots, marker comps, radio spots, storyboards, etc.
15. Ability to create safe environment for respondents to deliver POBAs.
    - Can quickly create nonthreatening, nonevaluative, nonjudgmental settings.
16. Ability to "come down hard" when discussion gets out of hand or off track, without losing group affinity.
    - For example, uses verbal cues ("How does that relate to. . .") and nonverbal cues ("stop sign" hand gesture).
    - Is willing to eject a respondent so that others can provide the needed information.
17. Ability to cope with surprises, abrupt changes from group to group, and "gold mines" (unplanned for, but desirable, outcomes).
    - Can tolerate a continual state of "not knowing"—not knowing how things are going to turn out, whether what worked in the last group will work in the next, or what answer might come from a simple question.
    - Can accept the lack of closure and can realize that the "true findings" may not emerge until the analysis stage.
18. Ability to think fast, act independently, react quickly in dynamic situations, and relate to respondents without talking "up" or "down."
    - Knows when to let go and when to hang on like a terrier with a bone.
    - Learns to act independently of the "back room" and to be fully responsible for all aspects of the research process.
    - Learns to speak to respondents as life peers, not as a function of their education or ability level.
19. Ability to apply appropriate techniques to create an environment that elicits the fullest range of data from respondents.
    - Can quickly identify the right research tool/technique and apply it when needed.
20. Ability to create an environment that allows spontaneity, creative "bursts," and radical points to have same values as conservative points.
    - Can create an environment, a mood, or an atmosphere and shift it when necessary.
21. Ability to encourage group process within preestablished ground rules without resorting to rigid research formats or oppressive group control measures.
    - Within the bounds of the "sanctioned voyeurism" of focus group research, gives respondents seven to nine ground rules and gently reminds them when a ground rule is broken (e.g., "talk as loud as the moderator," "avoid side conversations," "have the courage of your convictions").
22. Ability to utilize "sophisticated naivete" to avoid leading respondents or to avoid having the moderator's personal viewpoint imbedded in the flow of discussion.
    - Resists providing verbal or nonverbal evidence of personal points of view.
    - Becomes skillful in seeming like a life peer in the experience of the respondents.
23. Ability to avoid second guessing respondents, provide feedback using the same words/tone as respondents, and pace and lead respondents as needed.
24. Ability to analyze subjective data with objective viewpoint.
25. Ability to draw trend lines across diverse levels of data and find common themes.

SOURCE: Naomi Henderson, "Trained Moderators Boost the Value of Qualitative Research," *Marketing Research* (June 1992), pp. 20–23.

TABLE 6.4 **Discussion Guide for College Student Credit Card Concepts Groups**

I. Warm-Up Explanation of Focus Groups/Rules (10–12 minutes)

A. Explain focus groups.
B. No correct answers—only your opinions. You are speaking for many other people like yourself.
C. Need to hear from everyone.
D. Some of my associates are watching behind mirror. They are very interested in your opinions.
E. Audiotapes—because I want to concentrate on what you have to say—so I don't have to take notes. Video, too.
F. Please—only one person talking at a time. No side discussions—I'm afraid I'll miss some important comments.
G. Don't ask me questions because what I know and what I think are not important—it's what you think and how you feel that are important. That's why we're here.
H. Don't feel bad if you don't know much about some of the things we'll be talking about—that's OK and important for us to know. If your view is different from that of others in the group, that's important for us to know. Don't be afraid to be different. We're not looking for everyone to agree on something unless they really do.
I. We need to cover a series of topics, so I'll need to move the discussion along at times. Please don't be offended.
J. *Any questions?*

II. Credit Card History. First of all, I am interested in your attitudes toward, and usage of, credit cards. (15 minutes)

A. How many have a major credit card? Which credit card/cards do you have? When did you acquire these cards?
B. Why/how did you get that credit card/cards?
C. Which credit card do you use most often? Why do you use that credit card most often? For what purpose/purposes do you use your credit card/cards most often?
D. Is it difficult for college students to get credit cards? Are some cards easier to get? Which ones? Is it difficult for college students to get a "good" or "desirable" credit card?
E. What is your current attitude toward credit cards and their use? Have your attitudes toward credit cards changed since you got one? How have they changed?

III. Tabletop Concepts. (25 minutes)

Now I am going to show you several concepts for tabletop displays for credit cards that might be set up on campus in places where students congregate, such as student union and student activities buildings. Each display would be one of several displays for different products and services. I am interested in your reactions to the different displays. After I show you each display, I would like for you to write down your initial reactions on this form (*show and pass out form*). I am interested in your initial reactions. After we take a minute for you to write down your reactions, we will discuss each concept in more detail.

A. SHOW FIRST CONCEPT.
   1. HAVE THEM WRITE FIRST REACTION.
   2. DISCUSSION
      a. What was your first reaction to this tabletop display? What, if anything, do you particularly *like* about this display? What, if anything, do you particularly *dislike* about this display?
      b. Would you stop to find out more? Are you drawn to this display? Why? Why not? What, if anything, is interesting about it?
      c. What is your reaction to ENVIRONMENTAL/EDUCATION/MUSIC OFFER? Likes/dislikes?
B. REPEAT FOR SECOND CONCEPT.

continues

TABLE 6.4 **Discussion Guide for College Student Credit Card Concepts Groups—*Continued***

C. REPEAT FOR THIRD CONCEPT.
D. SHOW ALL THREE CONCEPTS.
   1. Which of these concepts, if any, would be *most likely* to attract your attention? Get you to stop for more information? Why?
   2. Which one would be *least likely* to attract your attention? Get you to stop for more information? Why?

IV. Brochures and offers. (25 minutes)

Now I would like for you to see the credit card offers that might go with each of the displays we just discussed. First of all, I will show you a sample brochure and offer. Next, I would like for you to indicate your first reaction to the offer on the sheet provided. Finally, we will discuss your reactions to each offer.
A. SHOW FIRST BROCHURE AND OFFER.
   1. ASK THEM TO RECORD THEIR FIRST REACTION.
   2. DISCUSSION.
      a. What is your first reaction to this offer?
      b. What, if anything, do you particularly *like* about this offer? What, if anything, do you particularly *dislike* about this offer?
      c. Do you understand the offer?
      d. Do you feel it is an important benefit?
      e. Would you sign up for this offer? Why?
      f. Would this card displace an existing card?
      g. Would this be your card of choice?
      h. Would you continue to use this product after college?
      i. How does this card, described in this offer, compare with the card you use most frequently?
      j. How likely would you be to apply for this card? Why/why not? Would you plan to actually use this card, or just have it? Would you plan to keep it after college?
B. REPEAT FOR SECOND BROCHURE AND OFFER.
C. REPEAT FOR THIRD BROCHURE AND OFFER.
D. SHOW ALL THREE BROCHURES AND OFFERS.
   1. Which of these is the best offer? Why do you say that?
   2. Which, if any, of the cards described in these offers would you apply for? Why?

V. Designs. (10 minutes)

Finally, I would like for you to see three alternative designs for the credit card that would go with the environmental offer. As with the two previous sections of the discussion, I will show each design, ask for you to write down your initial reaction to the design, and then we will discuss each design. Please use the form provided earlier to write down your initial reactions.
A. SHOW FIRST DESIGN.
   1. ASK THEM TO WRITE DOWN FIRST REACTION.
   2. DISCUSSION.
      a. What is your first reaction to this design? Is there anything you particularly *like* about this design? *Dislike* about it?
      b. Is there anything about this design that would make you uncomfortable about using it while you are in college? How about after you get out of college?
B. REPEAT FOR SECOND DESIGN.
C. REPEAT FOR THIRD DESIGN.
D. SHOW ALL THREE DESIGNS.
   1. Which, if any, of these cards would you use? Prefer?
   2. Are there any of these cards you would not use? Why?

Thanks for your participation.

that might be used in student unions to entice students to sign up for cards, their reactions to different product concepts for credit cards, and, finally, their reactions to different designs for credit cards. The displays and offers are built around three concepts:

- CDs. A free CD to be chosen from a list when you sign up. Earn points toward free CDs via card usage.
- Environment. Card issuer donates money to plant a certain number of trees based on card usage. Money is given to an internationally recognized environmental organization.
- Credit Education. Educational material on credit use and abuse provided periodically. Credit reports provided free of charge once per year. Gold card provided after graduation if credit history is good.

The groups were conducted in several areas of the country with students from a variety of universities and colleges. In general, the Education approach was not attractive. Participants were split between a preference for the CD or the Environment concepts. However, none of the concepts tested really well. Excerpts from the discussions of the offers are provided in Appendix A on page 210.

Preparing the Focus Group Report

Typically, after the final group in a series is completed, there will be a moderator debriefing sometimes called an *instant analysis*. There are both pros and cons of this tradition. Arguments for employing instant analysis include (1) it provides a forum for combining the knowledge of the marketing specialists who viewed the group with that of the moderator, (2) getting an initial hearing of and reaction to the moderator's top-of-mind perceptions; and (3) using the heightened awareness and excitement of the moment to generate new ideas and implications in a brainstorming environment.[18]

The shortcomings include (1) biasing future analysis on the part of the moderator; (2) "hip-shooting commentary" without leaving time for reflecting on what transpired; (3) recency, selective recall, and other factors associated with limited memory capabilities; and (4) not being able to hear all that was said in a less than highly involved and anxious state. There is nothing wrong with a moderator debriefing as long as the moderator explicitly reserves the right to change her opinion after reviewing the tapes.

The formal written reports tend to follow several different patterns, depending upon the client's needs, the researcher's style, and what was formally agreed upon in the research proposal. At one extreme, the investigator can prepare a brief, impressionistic summary of the principal findings, relying mainly on memory. This form of report is most likely to be used with experiencing groups, where the primary goal is for the clients to "experience flesh-and-blood consumers." The client often retains the tape recordings of the sessions and listens to the groups several additional times to become immersed in what the consumers are saying.

At the other extreme, the researcher listens and relistens to the tapes, copying down salient quotes, and fitting the participant's thoughts into a more general scheme derived from the research objectives and the researcher's extensive training in the social sciences. In this setting, the respondent's comments make roughly the same contribution to the final report as a patient's free associations make to a psychoanalyst's case report. This style is found primarily in clinical group reports.

A method between the two extremes, and the most common, is often called the *cut and paste technique*. It lacks the in-depth psychological analysis of the clinical report but still requires considerable skill and insight on the part of the researcher. The first step is to have the group sessions transcribed. Next, the researcher reviews the transcripts looking for common threads or trends in response patterns. Similar patterns are then cut apart and matched between the groups. The researcher then ends up with folders containing relevant material by subject matter.

The last step is to write the actual report. It normally begins with an introduction describing the purpose of the research, the major questions the researcher sought to answer, the nature and characteristics of the group members, and how they were recruited. Next, it is common to present a two- or three-page summary of findings and recommendations and conclude with the main body of findings. If the group members' conversations have been well segmented and sorted, preparing the main body of the report will not be difficult. The first major topic is introduced and major points of the topic are summarized and then driven home with liberal use of actual respondent's remarks (verbatims). Subsequent topics are then covered in similar fashion.

Advantages and Disadvantages of Focus Groups

The advantages and disadvantages of qualitative research in general also apply to focus groups. Yet, focus groups also have some unique pros and cons that deserve mention.

Advantages of Focus Groups The interaction among respondents can stimulate new ideas and thoughts that might not arise during one-on-one interviews. And group pressure can help challenge respondents to keep their thinking more realistic. The energetic interaction among respondents also means that observation of a group generally provides "firsthand" consumer information to the client observers in a shorter amount of time and in a more interesting way than do individual interviews.

Another advantage focus groups offer is the opportunity to observe customers or prospects from behind a one-way mirror. In fact, there is growing use of focus groups to expose a broader range of employees to the customer comments and views. "We have found that the only way to get people to really understand what customers want is to let them see customers, but there are few people who actually come in contact with customers," says Bonnie Keith, corporate market research manager at Digital Equipment Corporation. "Right now, we are getting people from our manufacturing and engineering operations to attend and observe focus groups," says Keith.

Another advantage focus groups offer is that they often can be executed more quickly than many other research techniques. Too, findings from groups tend to be easier to understand and have a compelling immediacy and excitement. "I can get up and show a client all the charts and graphs in the world, but it has nowhere near the impact of showing eight or 10 customers sitting around a table and say-

A Professional Researcher's Perspective

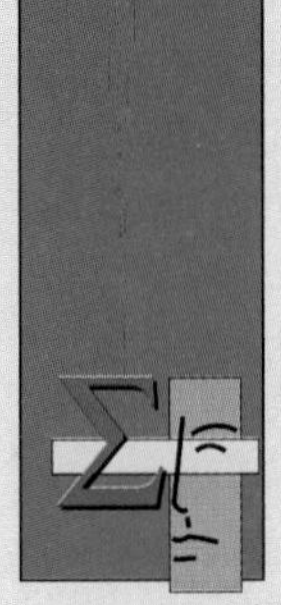

The following outlines what each person observing a session should do to ensure that he gets the most from the discussion.

- **Be totally familiar with the discussion guide before the groups begin.** This is important because you will understand the types of information the moderator will be seeking and the relative emphasis that will be placed on each topic before the discussion begins. As a result, you'll be able to concentrate on the discussion instead of your copy of the guide in order to figure out whether the moderator will cover a topic of interest later in the session.
- **Be sure you have agreed on an approach to communicating with the moderator during the group session.** Moderators have preferences for what works best for them. Many would prefer to walk back to the room to talk with the observers, finding that this is less distracting than receiving notes during the discussion. The important thing is that the clients have a chance to talk with the moderator a few times during the session to share ideas about the comments of the participants and to suggest new ways to approach a subject.
- **Before the group starts, write down the three to five most important things you want to learn from the participants.** Then, while the group is in progress, ensure that these topics are adequately covered by the moderator, along with ancillary material that needs to be discussed.
- **Ensure that the room is quiet while the group is in session.**

ing that the company's service isn't good," says Jean-Anne Mutter, director of marketing research at Ketchum Advertising.[19]

Thomas Greenbaum, president of Groups Plus, Incorporated, of Wilton, Connecticut, says that observing a focus group takes as much skill as moderating one. He discusses his idea in "A Professional Researcher's Perspective" on this page.

Disadvantages of Focus Groups Unfortunately, some of the very strengths of focus groups also can become disadvantages. For example, the immediacy and apparent understandability of focus group findings can mislead instead of inform. Jean-Anne Mutter says, "Even though you're only getting a very small slice, a focus group gives you a sense that you really understand the situation." She adds that focus groups can strongly appeal to "people's desire for quick, simple answers to problems, and I see a decreasing willingness to go with complexity and to put forth the effort needed to really think through the complex data that will be yielded by a quantitative study."[21]

The preceding sentiment is echoed by Gary Willets, director of marketing research for NCR Corporation. He notes, "What can happen is that you will do the focus group, and you will find out all of these details, and someone will say, 'OK, we've found out all that we need to know.' The problem is that what is said

It's difficult to concentrate on conversations in front of the mirror if observers talk and laugh.

- **Discipline yourself to focus on the big picture rather than on the comments of the minority.** The best way to listen is to concentrate on the sense of the discussion by the entire group, rather than on information generated by one or two dominant people who are the most positive or most negative speakers. It's very easy to reach a false sense of the group feeling because of aggressive behavior by one or two participants. Draw a diagram of the session room in your notepad and make brief notes about the comments by each participant.
- **Focus on the big issues, not the small ones.** Keep referring to the list of things you want to learn from the group to ensure that the moderator is addressing the real issues, rather than allowing the discussion to veer toward less important areas.
- **When the session ends, write a summary for yourself that outlines the most important things you learned, what you didn't learn that you'll need to get from subsequent sessions, and suggestions for changes in the discussion guide.** If each observer did this, the value of focus groups would improve dramatically.
- **Make sure the moderator conducts a brief postmortem after each group and a more in-depth one after all the sessions are completed.** The debriefing after each group is important to ensure good communication between the observers and the moderator about the quality and content of the group. It also helps ensure that any changes in the guide can be communicated in person to the moderator before the next session begins.[20] ■

in a focus group may not be all that typical. What you really want to do is do a qualitative study on the front end and follow it up with a quantitative study."[22] Focus groups, and qualitative research in general, is essentially inductive in its approach. The research is data-driven, with findings and conclusions being drawn directly from the information provided. In contrast, quantitative studies generally follow a deductive approach in which formulated ideas and hypotheses are tested with data collected specifically for that purpose.

Other disadvantages relate to the focus group process itself. For example, focus group recruiting is a problem if the type of person recruited responds differently to the issues being discussed than do other target segments. White middle-class individuals, for example, seem to participate in qualitative research in numbers that are disproportionate to their presence in the marketplace. Also, some focus group facilities create an impersonal feeling, making honest conversation unlikely. Corporate or formal decor with large boardroom tables and unattractive, plain, or gray decor may make it difficult for respondents to relax and share their feelings.

The greatest potential for distorting the focus group research is during the group interview itself. The moderator is part of the social interaction and must take care not to behave in ways that prejudice responses. The moderator's style

DILBERT reprinted by permission of UFS, Inc.

may contribute to bias. For example, an aggressive, confronting style may systematically lead respondents to say whatever they think the moderator wants them to say, to avoid attack. "Playing dumb" by the moderator may create perceptions that the moderator is insincere or phony, and this may cause respondents to withdraw.[23]

Respondents also can be a problem. Some individuals are simply introverted and do not like to speak out in group settings. Other people may attempt to dominate the discussion. These are people who know it all, or think they do, and who invariably answer every question first and do not give others a chance to speak. A dominating participant may succeed in swaying other group members. If a moderator is abrupt with a respondent, it can send the wrong message to other group members: "You'd better be cautious or I will do the same thing to you." Fortunately, a good moderator can stifle a dominant group member and not the rest of the group. Simple techniques used by moderators include avoiding eye contact with a dominant person, reminding the group that "we want to give everyone a chance to talk," saying "let's have someone else go first," or if someone else is speaking and the dominant person interrupts, the moderator should look at the initial speaker and say, "Sorry, I cannot hear you."[24]

Trends in Focus Groups

A number of fads have come and gone in focus group research in the past decade. No longer do we hear much about replicated groups, mega groups, multivariate groups, video thematic apperception test groups, or sensitivity groups.

What we are seeing is a continued growth in the use of focus groups. Although no reliable data exist, the authors guestimate that more than 50,000 focus groups are conducted in the United States annually. Commensurate with this is the expanding number (more than 700) and quality of focus group facilities in the United States. Most cities with more than 100,000 in population will have at least one group facility. Tiny viewing rooms with small one-way mirrors are rapidly disappearing. Instead, field services are installing plush two-tiered observation areas that wrap around the conference room to provide an unobstructed view of all respondents. Built-in counters for taking notes, padded chairs, and a fully stocked refreshment center are becoming commonplace (the latter can create problems).

telephone focus groups
Focus groups that are conducted via conference calling.

Telephone focus groups have recently emerged but may prove to be only a fad. The technique was developed because certain types of respondents, such as doctors, are always difficult to recruit. By using telephone conference calling, the need to travel to a group facility is eliminated. The moderator, who sits in front of a control console, knows who is talking because a light glows under the appropriate name tag when a participant speaks.[25] Visual aids can be mailed to the respondents in advance and opened only when instructed to do so by the moderator.

The disadvantages of this technique are many. The element of face-to-face group interaction is lost, and observation of facial expressions, eye movement, glances or gestures toward other participants, and other body language is impossible. Visual aids may not reach the respondents or they may be opened prematurely, thus losing the spontaneous response. In summary, the jury is still out on telephone focus groups.

A second trend is called **two-way focus groups.** The technique was developed by Bozell and Jacobs, Kenyon and Eckhardt, one of America's largest advertising agencies. It allows one target group to listen to and learn from a related group, as the following example shows.

two-way focus groups

A target focus group observes another focus group, then discusses what it learned through observing.

> Bozell and Jacobs was doing focus groups with physicians and patients related to the management of arthritis. Often, what patients think they are accomplishing by taking a medicine is different from the actual result. And physicians often do not know what their patients are thinking: how they feel about the medicine they are taking and what their emotional needs are, as opposed to physiological needs.
>
> We had the physicians observe a focus group of arthritis patients talking about their physicians and medications. We immediately followed the patient group with a focus group of the physicians who had observed the patients. The effect of the patient group on the physicians was startling. They emerged from behind the viewing room's one-way glass flushed and glassy-eyed. As they talked in their own group, with us observing, it became apparent they had little idea that patients would be taking as many as 10 to 15 medications at one time.
>
> Nor, it seems, had they really known the desperation their patients felt when their physicians didn't take the time to really talk with them; didn't take the time for them to feel they were being taken seriously. We knew we had a breakthrough technique when, observing the physician's group, we saw the transforming effect the patient group had on the physicians.[26]

Perhaps a third trend is represented by a new focus group television network entitled the FocusVision Network. Instead of flying from city to city, network clients can view the focus groups in their offices. Live focus groups are broadcast by video transmission from a nationwide network of independently owned focus facilities (see Figure 6.3). Clients view all the action on a 26-inch monitor and

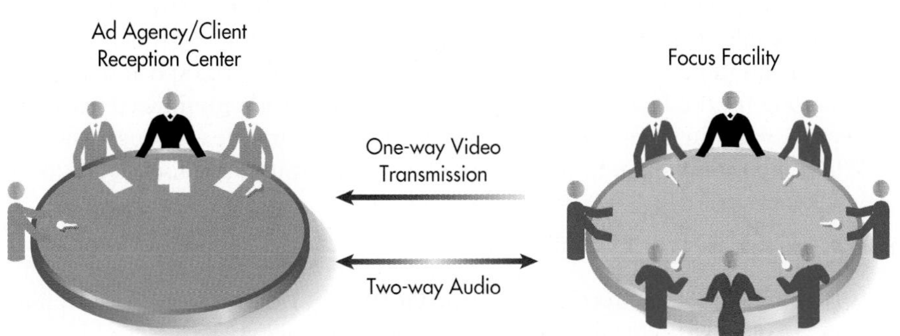

FIGURE 6.3
How the FocusVision Network Functions

control two cameras that allow a full group view, close-up, zoom, or pan. They can maintain audio contact with the moderator, videotape highlights or entire sessions, and hold "open mike" postgroup debriefings. Three-way interaction between the client office, a distant ad agency, and the transmitting facility is also available.

The moderator or a colleague behind the one-way mirror wears an earmold for input from the client. A remote control VCR is available for full or selected taping of the group. There is even an on-site fax machine so the client can immediately send new concepts, new copy, and moderator's guide changes. Clients for the new service are heavy focus group users including Ogilvy and Mather Advertising, Seagram Incorporated, Lintas Advertising, Johnson & Johnson, Ortho, and AT&T. Costs probably will prevent smaller firms from joining the network. The transmission fee is $1,450 per group in addition to standard respondent recruiting costs and fees, moderator charges, and written report. A FocusVision Reception Center costs $4,985 monthly and an installation charge of $6,220.[27] An advertisement for GroupNet Video, a lower-cost alternative to FocusVision Network, is shown in Figure 6.4.

nominal grouping session

Qualitative research method in which consumers, brought together in small groups, independently generate ideas about a subject and then discuss the ideas.

A final trend is the use of a **nominal grouping session (NGS)** as an alternative to focus groups in certain situations. NGSs are a first cousin of focus groups and are particularly useful for creating questionnaires and measurement scales (see Chapters 11 and 12). NGSs discover from, and explore with, targeted consumers the most important characteristics of the research problem, rather than forcing participants to discuss characteristics the researcher believes to be important. Table 6.5 illustrates a comparison between NGSs and focus groups. Some advantages of NGSs include:

- Some people are more comfortable reacting to others' ideas rather than generating their own. Thus, ideas introduced early in focus groups, which are usually the most obvious ones, tend to dominate group members' thoughts and discussions. In this way, more subtle and creative ideas often are suppressed. This does not happen in NGSs because participants generate ideas independently and then discuss them.
- Some people are more comfortable sharing only well-known ideas with a group because of group pressure for conformity. Thus, idea generation may be inhibited by the interaction among participants in focus groups. Written idea generation in NGSs minimizes this problem.
- Most people begin participation in groups quite uninvolved with the subject or problem, but involvement must be high to generate unique suggestions and insights. Seeing other NGS members actively listing ideas encourages each member to generate as many ideas as possible to avoid being viewed as inferior.
- Some people would prefer to remain primarily silent and let others carry the load. In addition, many of the same people find it difficult to speak in front of the group for the first time. Both of these limitations are minimized in NGSs because each member is required to introduce her own ideas in succession.
- When group members know one another, NGSs minimize domination by a few members.

Some drawbacks to NGSs include:

- It is not likely to be effective when the target population is inexpressive, illiterate, or otherwise unable to transfer thoughts adequately to paper.
- The researcher may need more knowledge about the product.

FIGURE 6.4

An Advertisement for GroupNet Video Conferencing

One trend in focus group research is linking remote viewing sites via television.

Just because you can't fly to the focus group, doesn't mean you can't attend.

Now, key people can attend a focus group and never leave town.

While the need for qualitative consumer information grows, demands on your time and resources also grow.

To solve this problem the VideoConferencing Alliance Network, a group of independently-owned, highly respected focus group facilities in major markets throughout the U.S., created GroupNet™ VideoConferencing.

GroupNet uses state-of-the-art PictureTel equipment, along with AT&T's technologically advanced network.

GroupNet™ VideoConferencing puts you there.

GroupNet's wide bandwidth transmissions allow for a high resolution picture and crystal clear sound. All sites provide fully interactive transmission, allowing observers in both transmitting and receiving sites to communicate with each other before, during, and after the groups.

There are no up-front investments, long-term contracts, or volume commitments to make — you pay only for what you use. All VideoConferencing Alliance Network members are capable of transmitting and receiving focus groups. So view from our sites or, if your company has compatible equipment, view from your own offices.

For a brochure or more information about GroupNet, call the VideoConferencing Alliance Network at 1-800-288-8226.

VIDEOCONFERENCING ALLIANCE NETWORK
1-800-288-8226

TABLE 6.5 Nominal Grouping Sessions versus Focus Groups

NOMINAL GROUPING SESSION PROCEDURES	FOCUS GROUP PROCEDURES
1. Individuals assigned to small groups (6–10) based on chosen/common characteristics.	Same.
2. Group members silently and independently generate ideas about a subject/problem.	Ideas generated during group interaction/ discussion.
3. Each member presents one idea to the group *without discussion* in an iterative fashion until all ideas are offered. All ideas are recorded on the board.	Ideas/items to be discussed are given by the researcher.
4. All ideas are discussed for clarification, combination, and evaluation. Expressions of the importance of ideas are encouraged, but criticisms of others' ideas are discouraged.	Same, but criticisms of ideas usually are accepted.
5. Each member privately rates or ranks the pooled ideas by importance.	Primarily unstructured discussion.
6. Discussion of the ratings by the group until consensus is reached on those ratings. This process generates the most important reasons for ratings.	Primarily unstructured discussion, which ends when the moderator/facilitator *believes* all important discussions have been completed.

SOURCE: Barry Langford, "Nominal Grouping Sessions," *Marketing Research* (Summer 1994), p. 17.

Other Qualitative Research Methodologies

Most of this chapter has been devoted to focus groups because of their pervasive use in marketing research. However, several other qualitative techniques are used, albeit on a much more limited basis.

Depth Interviews

depth interviews
One-on-one interviews that probe and elicit detailed answers to questions, often using nondirective techniques to uncover hidden motivations.

The term **depth interviews** has historically meant a relatively unstructured one-on-one interview. The interviewer is thoroughly trained in the skill of probing and eliciting detailed answers to each question. Sometimes psychologists are used as depth interviewers. They use clinical nondirective techniques to uncover hidden motivations.

The direction of a depth interview is guided by the responses of the interviewee. As the interview unfolds, the interviewer thoroughly probes each answer and uses the replies as a basis for further questioning. For example, a depth interview might begin with a discussion of snack foods. Each answer might follow with, "Can you tell me more?" "Would you elaborate on that?" "Is that all?" The interview might then move into pros and cons of various ingredients such as corn, wheat, potatoes. The next phase could delve into the sociability of the snack food. Are Fritos, for example, eaten alone or in a crowd? Are Wheat Thins usually reserved for parties? When should you serve Ritz crackers?

The advantages of depth interviews relative to focus groups are as follows:

1. Group pressure is eliminated so that each respondent reveals more honest feelings, not necessarily those considered most acceptable among peers.
2. The personal one-to-one situation gives the respondent the feeling of being the focus of attention, whose personal thoughts and feelings are important and truly wanted.
3. The respondent attains a heightened state of awareness in a personal interview because he is in constant rapport with the interviewer and there are no group members to hide behind.
4. The longer time devoted to individual respondents encourages the revelation of new information.
5. Respondents can be probed at length to reveal the feelings and motivations that underlie statements.
6. Without the restrictions of cultivating a group process, new directions of questioning can be improvised more easily. Individual interviews allow greater flexibility in exploring casual remarks and tangential issues, which may provide critical insights into the main issue.
7. The closeness of the one-to-one relationship allows the interviewer to become more sensitive to nonverbal feedback.
8. Depth interviews may be the only viable technique for certain situations in which competitors would otherwise be placed in the same room. For example, it might be very difficult to do a focus group on certain topics (e.g., systems for preventing bad checks) with managers from competing department stores or restaurants.

The disadvantages of depth interviews relative to focus groups are as follows:

1. Depth interviews are much more expensive than groups, particularly when viewed on a per-interview basis.

Depth interviews require the interviewer to thoroughly probe each response to reveal the respondent's feelings and motivations.

Global Marketing Research

The Japanese examine American consumers because they believe that the U.S. buyers are the world's trendsetters: what's popular here will soon be popular in the rest of the world. The Japanese track American pop culture to know which hot celebrities will be in demand for advertising. They study the way Americans shop to learn how to design stores. They dig into how buyers view themselves so they can design better-selling cars. Nissan researchers, for example, use qualitative research by asking dozens of consumers to cut out pictures from magazines and make a collage of "who you are." From that, Nissan gets a snapshot of market segments that traditional surveys cannot touch. People who paste up pictures of lobster dinners, American Express gold cards, and Porsche cars are labeled *showy sophisticates.* They're about 9 percent of the population. People who paste up Victoria's Secret ads and baby food jars are "self-sacrificing escapists"—11 percent of the population. By identifying such segments and learning what objects and images define the people in them, by using qualitative and quantitative techniques, Nissan can design cars to appeal to certain customers.[29] ■

2. Depth interviews *do not* generally get the same degree of client involvement as focus groups. If one of your objectives is to get the clients to view the research so they benefit firsthand from the information, it is difficult to convince most client personnel to sit through multiple hours of depth interviews.
3. Depth interviews are physically exhausting for the moderator, so it is difficult to cover as much ground in one day as it is with groups. Most moderators will not do more than four or five interviews in a day, yet in two focus groups they will cover 20 people.
4. Focus groups give the moderator an ability to leverage the dynamics of the group to obtain reaction from individuals that might not otherwise be generated in a one-on-one session.[30]

The success of any depth interview depends entirely on the interviewer. Good depth interviewers, whether psychologists or not, are hard to find and expensive. A second factor that determines the success of depth research is proper interpretation. The unstructured nature of the interview and the "clinical" nature of the analysis increases the complexity of the analysis. Small sample sizes, unstructured interviews that make intercomparisons difficult, interpretation that is subject to the nuances and frame of reference of the researcher, and high costs have all contributed to the lack of popularity of depth interviewing.

A few firms have found that depth interviews have an important role to play in qualitative research. N. W. Ayer, one of the nation's largest advertising agencies, had conducted several market segmentation studies of "baby boomers" but still felt that it lacked a good understanding of these consumers. Ayer's research director decided to conduct depth interviews.

The depth interviews generated four market segments: Satisfied Selves, who are optimistic and achievement-oriented; Contented Traditionalists, who are home-oriented and socially very conservative; Worried Traditionalists, anticipating disaster on all fronts; and '60s in the '90s, people who are aimless, unfulfilled, and have no direction in life.

Behavioral differences translated down to brand use. Using the category of alcohol, for example, Satisfied Selves use upscale brands and are the target for imported wine. Contented Traditionalists consume little alcohol, but when they drink they favor brown liquors, such as whiskey.

Worried Traditionalists drink at an average level, but their consumption levels are very different from the other segments. For each type of liquor there was a dual brand-use pattern; people in this segment reported using an upscale brand as well as a lower-priced one. "Maybe they have one brand on hand for when they entertain guests, the socially visible brands, and a cheaper brand they consume when home alone," the research director said. The members of the '60s in the '90s segment are heavy liquor consumers, especially of vodka and beer.[31]

Projective Techniques

projective techniques
Ways of tapping respondents' deepest feelings by having them "project" those feelings into an unstructured situation.

Projective techniques are sometimes incorporated into depth interviews. The origins of projective techniques lie in the field of clinical psychology. In essence, the objective of any projective test is to delve below surface responses to obtain true feelings, meanings, or motivations. The rationale behind projective tests comes from knowledge that people are often reluctant or cannot reveal their deepest feelings. In other instances, they are unaware of those feelings because of psychological defense mechanisms.

Projective tests are techniques for penetrating a person's defense mechanisms and allowing true feelings and attitudes to emerge. In general, a subject is presented with an unstructured and nebulous situation and asked to respond. Because the situation is ill-defined and has no true meaning, the respondent must use her own frame of reference to answer the question. In theory, the respondent "projects" her feelings into the unstructured stimulus. Because the subjects are not directly talking about themselves, defense mechanisms are purportedly bypassed. The interviewee is talking about something else or someone else, yet revealing her inner feelings.

Use of Projective Tests

Most projective tests are easy to administer and are tabulated like any other open-ended question. They are often used in conjunction with nonprojective open- and closed-ended questions. The projective test serves as a basis for gathering "richer" and perhaps more revealing data than standard questioning techniques. Projective techniques are often intermingled with image questionnaires, concept tests, and occasionally advertising pretests. It is also common to apply several projective techniques during a depth interview.

Types of Projective Tests

The most common forms of projective tests used in marketing research are word association, sentence and story completion, cartoon test, photo sorts, consumer drawings, and third-person techniques. Other techniques such as psychodrama tests and true TAT (Thematic Apperception Test) have been popular in treating psychological disorders but have been of less help in marketing research.

word association tests
Tests in which the interviewer says a word and the respondent must mention the first thing that comes to mind.

Word Association Tests Word association tests are among the most practical and effective projective tools for market researchers. An interviewer reads a word to a respondent and asks him to mention the first thing that comes into mind. Usually the consumer will respond with a synonym or an antonym. The list is read in quick succession to avoid time for defense mechanisms to come into play. If the respondent fails to answer within three seconds, some emotional involvement with the word is assumed.

Word association tests are used to select brand names, advertising campaign themes, and slogans. For example, a cosmetic manufacturer might ask consumers to respond to the following potential names for a new perfume:

infinity	flame	precious
encounter	desire	erotic

One of these words or a synonym suggested by the consumers might then be selected as the brand name.

sentence and story completion tests
Tests in which the respondents complete sentences or stories in their own words.

Sentence and Story Completion Sentence and story completion tests can be used in conjunction with word association tests. The respondent is furnished with an incomplete story or group of sentences and asked to complete them. A few examples follow:

1. Marshall Fields is . . .
2. The people who shop at Marshall Fields are . . .
3. Marshall Fields should really . . .
4. I don't understand why Marshall Fields doesn't . . .
5. Sally Jones just moved to Chicago from Los Angeles where she had been a salesperson for IBM. She is now a district manager for the Chicago area. Her neighbor, Rhonda Smith, has just come over to Sally's apartment to welcome her to Chicago. A discussion of where to shop ensues. Sally notes, "You know, I've heard some things about Marshall Fields . . ." What is Rhonda's reply?

As you can see, story completion simply provides a more structured and detailed scenario for the respondent. Again, the objective is for the interviewees to project themselves into the imaginary person mentioned in the scenario. Sentence completion and story techniques have been considered by some researchers to be the most useful and reliable of all the projective tests.

cartoon tests
Tests in which the respondent fills in the dialogue of one character in a cartoon.

Cartoon Tests Cartoon tests create a highly projective mechanism by means of cartoon figures or strips similar to those seen in comic books. The typical cartoon test consists of two characters—one balloon is filled with dialogue and the other balloon is blank. The respondent is then asked to fill in the blank balloon such as the example in Figure 6.5. Note that the figures are vague and without expression. This is done so that the respondent is not given "clues" regarding a suggested type of response. The ambiguity is designed to make it easier for the respondent to project in the cartoon.

Cartoon tests are extremely versatile. They can be used to obtain differential attitudes toward two types of establishments and the congruity, or lack of con-

FIGURE 6.5
Cartoon Test

gruity, between these establishments and a particular product. They can be used to measure the strength of an attitude toward a particular product or brand. They also can be used to ascertain what function is being performed by a given attitude.

Photo Sorts BBDO Worldwide, one of the country's largest advertising agencies, has developed a trademarked technique called *Photosort.* Consumers express their feelings about brands through a specially developed photo deck showing pictures of different types of people, from business executives to college students. Respondents connect the people with the brands they think they use. A **photo sort** conducted for General Electric found that consumers thought the brand attracted conservative, older, business types. To change that image, GE adopted the "Bring Good Things to Life" campaign. Another photo sort for Visa found the card had a wholesome, female, middle-of-the-road image in customers' minds. The "Everywhere You Want to Be" campaign was devised to interest more high-income men.[32]

photo sort
Respondent sorts photos of different types of people, identifying those photos that respondent feels would use the specified product or service.

BBDO interviewed 100 consumers who are the primary target market for beer: men, ages 21 to 49, who drink at least six beers weekly. Using Photosort, researchers showed each respondent 98 photographs and asked him to match each picture with the brand of beer that the photo subject probably drinks. A Bud drinker, as viewed by the respondents, is not exactly the corporate type: He appears tough, grizzled, blue collar. The Miller drinker, in contrast, comes off as light-blue collar, civilized, and friendly looking. Coors has a somewhat more feminine image—not necessarily a plus in a business in which 80 percent of the product gets consumed by men.[33]

Another photo sort technique was created by Grey Advertising, also a large New York advertising agency, entitled the *Pictured Aspirations Technique* (PAT). The device attempts to uncover how a product fits into a consumer's aspirations. Consumers sort a deck of photos according to how well the pictures describe their aspirations. In research done for Playtex's 18-hour bra, this technique revealed that the product was out of sync with the aspirations of potential customers. The respondents chose a set of pictures that expressed the "me they wanted to be" as very energetic, slim, youthful, and vigorous. But the pictures they used to express their sense of the product were a little more old-fashioned, a little stouter, less vital, and energetic looking. Out went the "Good News for Full-figured Gals" campaign with Jane Russell as spokesperson, and in came the more sexy, fashionable concept "Great Curves Deserve 18 Hours."

consumer drawings

Respondent draws what they are feeling or how they perceive an object.

Consumer Drawings Researchers sometimes ask consumers to draw what they are feeling or how they perceive an object. Sometimes **consumer drawings** can unlock motivations or express perceptions (see Case 6.2). For example, McCann-Erickson advertising agency wanted to find out why Raid roach spray outsold Combat insecticide disks in certain markets. In interviews, most users agreed that Combat is a better product because it kills roaches without any effort on the user's part. So the agency asked the heaviest users of roach spray—low-income southern women—to draw pictures of their prey (see Figure 6.6). The goal was to get at their underlying feelings about this dirty job.

All the 100 women who participated in the agency's interviews portrayed roaches as men. "A lot of their feelings about the roach were very similar to the feelings that they had about the men in their lives," said Paula Drillman, executive vice-president at McCann-Erickson. Many of the women were in common-law relationships. They said that the roach, like the man in their life, "only comes around when he wants food." The act of spraying roaches and seeing them die was satisfying to this frustrated, powerless group. Setting out Combat disks may have been less trouble, but it just didn't give them the same feeling. "These women wanted control," Drillman said. "They used the spray because it allowed them to participate in the kill."[34]

third-person techniques

Ways of learning respondents' feelings by asking them to answer for a third party: "your neighbor," "most people."

Third-Person Techniques Perhaps the easiest projective technique to apply, other than word association, are **third-person techniques.** Rather than asking someone directly what they think, it is couched as "your neighbor," or "most people" or some other third party. Rather than asking a person why she typically does not provide a nutritionally balanced breakfast, a researcher would ask, "Why don't many people provide their families nutritionally balanced breakfasts?" The third-person technique is often used to avoid issues that might be embarrassing or evoke hostility if answered directly by a respondent.

The Future of Qualitative Research

The rationale behind qualitative research tests is as follows:

1. The criteria employed and the evaluations made in most buying and usage decision have emotional and subconscious content.
2. This emotional and subconscious content is an important determinant of buying and usage decisions.
3. Such content is not adequately or accurately verbalized by the respondent through direct communicative techniques.
4. Such content is adequately and accurately verbalized by the respondent through indirect communicative techniques.[35]

To the extent that these tenets remain true or even partially correct, the demand for qualitative applications in marketing research will continue. But the problems

FIGURE 6.6

Consumer Drawings Can Reveal Purchasers' Motivations or Perceptions

SOURCE: Courtesy of McCann-Erickson New York.

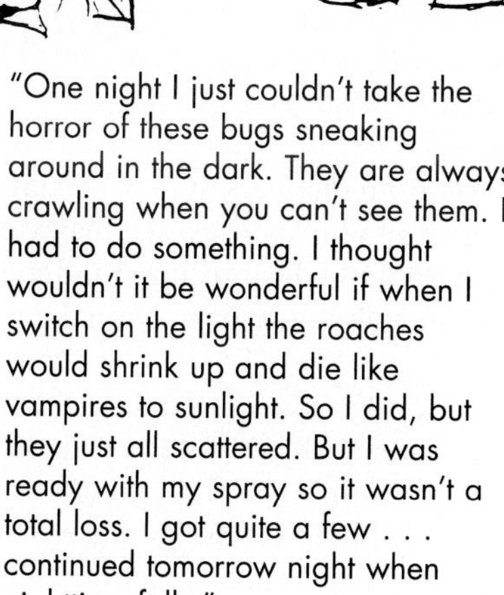

"One night I just couldn't take the horror of these bugs sneaking around in the dark. They are always crawling when you can't see them. I had to do something. I thought wouldn't it be wonderful if when I switch on the light the roaches would shrink up and die like vampires to sunlight. So I did, but they just all scattered. But I was ready with my spray so it wasn't a total loss. I got quite a few . . . continued tomorrow night when nighttime falls."

"A man likes a free meal you cook for him; as long as there is food he will stay."

"I tiptoed quietly into the kitchen, perhaps he wasn't around. I stretched my arm up to turn on the light. I hoped I'd be alone when the light went on. Perhaps he is sitting on the table I thought. You think that's impossible? Nothing is impossible with that guy. He might not even be alone. He'll run when the light goes on I thought. But what's worse is for him to slip out of sight. No, it would be better to confront him before he takes control and 'invites a companion'."

McCann-Erickson advertising agency asked users of roach spray to create drawings of their prey. From the drawings, the agency determined that roach spray sold better than insecticide disks since the users wanted control, and spray allowed them to actively kill the roaches.

of small sample sizes and subjective interpretation also will continue to plague some forms of qualitative research. Inability to validate and replicate qualitative research will further deter its growth.

On the positive side, the use of exploratory and experiencing focus groups will continue to grow. Focus group research can provide data and insight not available through any other techniques. Low cost and ease of application will provide even greater impetus for focus group use in this decade. Finally, clearly the qualitative-quantitative split will begin to close as adaptations and innovations are made on both sides to allow researchers to enjoy the advantages of both approaches simultaneously.

Summary

Qualitative research refers to research findings not subject to quantification or quantitative analysis. It is often used to examine attitudes, feelings, and motivations. Qualitative research, particularly focus groups, continues to grow in popularity for several reasons. First, qualitative research is usually cheaper than quantitative studies. Second, it is an excellent means to understand the in-depth motivation and feelings of consumers. Third, it can improve the efficiency of quantitative research.

Qualitative research is not without its disadvantages. One problem is that qualitative research sometimes will not distinguish small differences in attitudes or opinions as well as large-scale quantitative studies. Also, the respondents in qualitative studies are not necessarily representative of the population of interest to the researcher. Third, a number of individuals lack formal training yet profess to be experts in the field.

Focus groups typically consist of eight to 12 participants who are led by a moderator in an in-depth discussion on a particular topic or concept. The goal of the focus group is to learn and understand what people have to say and why. The emphasis is on getting people talking at length and in detail about the subject at hand. The interaction provided by group dynamics is essential to the success of focus group research. The idea is that a response from one person may become a stimulus for another, thereby generating an interplay of responses that may yield more information than if the same number of people had contributed independently to the discussion. Focus groups are the most popular type of qualitative research.

Focus groups can be divided into three major categories: exploratory, clinical, and experiencing. Exploratory focus groups are used at the exploratory phase of the market research process. They may attempt to clarify the problem or generate hypotheses for testing. A clinical focus group is based on the premise that a person's true motivations and feelings are subconscious in nature. Thus, such a group should be conducted by a moderator with expertise in psychology and sociology. It is assumed that a person's real motives must be uncovered using clinical judgment. Thus, the focus group data become the data input source for the clinical judgment. Experiencing focus groups are conducted to experience a so-called flesh-and-blood consumer. They are used by the researcher to experience the emotional framework in which a product is bought and consumed.

Most focus groups are held in a "group facility," which is typically set up conference-room style with a large one-way mirror in one wall. Microphones are placed in unobtrusive locations to record the discussion. Behind the mirror is a viewing room. Respondents are paid to participate. The moderator plays the critical role in determining the success or failure of the group.

A number of other qualitative research methodologies are used, but on a much more infrequent basis. One technique is depth interviews. Depth interviews historically are unstructured interviews. The interviewer is thoroughly trained in the skill of probing and eliciting detailed answers to each question. She often uses clinical nondirective techniques to uncover hidden motivations. Projective techniques are another form of qualitative research. The objective of any projective test is to delve below the surface responses to obtain true feelings, meanings, or motivations. Some common forms of projective tests are word association tests, sentence and story completion tests, cartoon tests, photo sorts, consumer drawings, and third-person techniques.

Key Terms

qualitative research
quantitative research
focus groups
group dynamics
exploratory focus groups
clinical focus groups
experiencing focus groups
focus group facility
focus group moderator
discussion guide
telephone focus groups
two-way focus groups
nominal grouping session
depth interviews
projective techniques
word association tests
sentence and story completion tests
cartoon tests
photo sorts
consumer drawings
third-person techniques

Review and Discussion Questions

1. What are the major differences between quantitative and qualitative research?
2. What are some of the possible disadvantages of using focus groups?
3. What differentiates exploratory, clinical, and experiencing groups from one another? Give examples of each.
4. What are some of the trends in focus group research? Why do you think these trends have evolved?
5. What is the purpose of projective techniques? What major factors are to be considered in conducting a projective test?
6. Conduct a focus group in your class on one of the following three topics:
   a. Student experiences at your student union
   b. Quality of frozen dinners and snacks and new items that would be desired.
   c. How students spend their entertainment dollars and what additional items of entertainment they would like to see offered.
7. Consumer drawing tests may ask study participants to draw the kind of person that would be consuming a particular product. Draw a typical Pepsi drinker versus a typical Coke drinker. What do the drawn images suggest about the participants' perceptions of Coke and Pepsi drinkers?
8. Write an obituary notice for a Milky Way bar, Dr. Pepper, Pepperidge Farm cookies, and Tony's frozen pizza.

CASE 6.1

Bickel & Brewer—Attorneys-at-Law

Bickel & Brewer uses qualitative research techniques to prepare for commercial litigation and major business cases. "Lawyers tend not to be good 'people' people," says William Brewer. "We spend most of our time sitting in plush offices. We need help keeping in touch."

Bickel & Brewer's offices have built-in mock courtrooms where attorneys are recorded and filmed as they present their cases to mock juries. The process mirrors focus group research, and for a good reason.

"Market researchers favor focus groups because they believe that group discussions reveal people's reactions to products in more depth and detail than standard interviews," write psychologists Valerie P. Hans and Neil Vidmar in their book *Judging the Jury.* "In the sense that attorneys are trying to sell a 'product,' that is, their 'brand' of the case as opposed to the competitor's brand, trial lawyers are confronted with a task similar to that of the market researcher: how to get the public, or the jury, to buy their goods."

"Madison Avenue is often able to guess what people will do," says Brewer. "That's my job, too. Most of the time, we can predict if a case is a winner or a loser and enhance the result. Why? Because we know what makes juries listen."

"Attorneys deal with a set of facts," says Mary Monroe, senior vice-president at the Gilmore Research Group, a Seattle-based market research firm. "They can't change the facts, but they can present them in a variety of different ways. We can help by letting attorneys test their arguments and find the best way of convincing the jury."

Gilmore runs mock trials for its attorney clients. After the "trials," the jurors are interviewed to determine how the attorney's presentation affected their decisions. "It's what we use a great deal with our advertiser clients," says Monroe. "It's slogans, campaigns, and packaging. It's the concept of watching people react to your product and tailoring your message to elicit the types of responses you want." The key to competing is winning cases. And to attorneys at Bickel & Brewer, the key to winning cases is similar to the way businesses win customers: knowing them better than the competition does.

"A lot of business is coming to firms like ours because we have invested heavily in the technological solutions that help us understand the jury process," says Brewer.[36]

1. Would you agree that a mock jury is "kind of a focus group?"
2. What other qualitative techniques could be used by lawyers to improve their effectiveness in the courtroom?
3. Do you see any ethical problems with lawyers using mock juries?

CASE 6.2

Pillsbury Cake Mixes

To learn more about its client's product, McCann-Erickson Advertising Agency decided to conduct some qualitative research. It brought 50 consumers into the agency and asked them to sketch likely buyers of two different brands of cake mixes. One cake mix was Pillsbury and the other was Duncan Hines. Examples of the sketches are shown in Figure 6.7. Consistently, the group portrayed Pillsbury customers as apron-clad, grandmotherly types, whereas they pictured Duncan Hines customers as svelte, contemporary women.

1. You are the account executive for Pillsbury. What kind of changes in its advertising program for cake mixes would you recommend? Why?
2. What other projective tests could have been used to ascertain consumers' perceptions of these two products? Pick at least one additional projective test and describe how it might be applied to explore images of Pillsbury and Duncan Hines cake mixes.
3. How might quantitative studies be used to confirm or disconfirm the findings of the qualitative research?

FIGURE 6.7
Who Baked the Cake?

APPENDIX A

Selected Excerpts from a Focus Group Conducted with College Students

Focus Group Comments on Education Offer

- I like the idea of the credit report. That's the best thing.
- I think it's good. Because otherwise you might have no idea, you may have done something where you weren't really aware that you had messed up.
- I think I like that offer the best because, for someone like me, I think I'm in the minority. I never had a credit card or knew anything about them until I moved away to school and my dad just handed me one with my name on it and said, "Don't ever use this unless you absolutely have to." So I never have. I use my own cash and my work money to support myself and buy all my gifts and whatever I wanted. So, I know nothing about it; I am thoroughly uneducated about it. So, I think if a person wants to get a credit card and wants to know about it, that's a really good way to help them along.
- You're being taught by the wrong people. You're being taught by the people who make the most of you making a mistake. I doubt I would read the material very much.
- I agree with what Steven said. I have a lot of friends who are in serious trouble with their credit cards and they always give them to me and say, "Cut that think up into a thousand pieces." I basically don't want much to do with them.
- I thought you were supposed to get gold cards when you have accumulated this grand credit. If you just get a gold card, it is going to take the whole idea of a gold card away.
- It should be like your bank statement; it should be part of the deal.
- You can get a copy of your credit report anyway on your own.
- I think getting an annual copy once a year is great.
- I think it is great if you get all that when you get your first credit card and this will teach you not to run it up.

Focus Group Comments on Environmental Offer

- Sounds kind of funny.
- I like it, but it sounds unlikely.
- That's a lot of trees.
- People just wouldn't take it seriously. I wouldn't. It seems like a game.
- It seems like the kind of thing that a credit card company would do and a couple of years later you would never hear of it again. I'm more worried about the trees that they are cutting down. I'm not saying that it's not important.
- I think that it's a little bit much. When you go down and you see all these trees that are planted for each year and every $100. But, I think that those who feel like they really haven't done anything for the environment might feel a little guilty and they might want to have at least one tree planted.
- What is the proof that they are really planting the trees? I want to know that.
- Definitely if it can be proved.
- The intent is not really there.
- They should plant a tree with the money they make, not on our spending.
- Why should we have to spend money for them to plant trees, plant trees anyway.
- It gives you an excuse to buy.
- I would rather have a percentage of my money to go to Arbor Alliance.

Focus Group Comments on CD Offer

- Outstanding.
- I think you would be getting a lot of idiots just applying for the card because of the CDs. You might not be getting people who are able to pay for it.
- I'd rather get a certificate and go to a record store.
- There are going to be a lot of cancellations though. Just get the CD and then cancel.
- It would not appeal to me that much. I would be thinking, "Where's the catch?"
- I guess I am stupid, but I thought it sounded good. With the price of CDs and I like to buy them.
- Most of the money that I spend on the credit card comes from compact discs.
- Are we talking about any CD? Are they going to send us a list? I want my own music.
- Buy CDs as LOW as $4.50, so that means $15.50 to $4.50.
- It is a bribe. Use my card and you can have a CD.

Focus Group Comments on CD Display

- Too gaudy.
- I like the CDs. They get my attention.
- I think the CD might. For the most part I guess my first reaction is, fortunately, general indifference. There is so much that we see constantly. I, for the most part, become pretty desensitized.

- I thought of a party, and I thought that might be a credit card that would give you cash back on buying CDs.
- I like the color of the banner. It's kind of a maroon color. It sticks in your head.
- I was just kind of turned off by the phrase, teasing you, the phrase, "that was music to your ears." That's just me.
- I'd stop because it was MasterCard.
- I would stop at it, but I probably wouldn't look very long just because I already have a card, and I'm happy with it. I'm not real picky about it. That's probably more because my mom has been paying the bill. I'm going to be soon. I would look at it if I didn't have a card. If I was looking for one.
- I think it's interesting, but it's pretty typical. Almost every kid I know has a CD player. If they didn't have one when they got to college, they have one now. Most kids buy them. I know a lot of my friends go spend their money on, as opposed to books, they'll buy CDs and buy used books from the bookstore or something.
- I didn't notice any black artists on there. So, to me that would be targeted at white kids, because the one thing that stuck out in my mind was Pearl Jam and that was all that I noticed on there when they named CDs. So maybe if there was Dr. Jay or something, it might have really stopped me. Now, there might be but I didn't notice it.
- It looks like one of those awful things you get in the mail, 25 CDs for a penny. It's too bright.
- Too busy.
- It lacks credibility. Credit cards are a big business; they are something you should take seriously.
- An MTV credit card.
- I think it's a worn out cliche, "music to your ears."
- A free CD? You can get 25 for a penny.

Focus Group Comments on Environmental Display

- Better.
- We're moving from the picture of CDs to the environment and, I think, I would look at that a little more readily than a free CD.
- I feel like every time I purchase something, there would be a percentage that would go to helping the environment. That would make me feel good.
- I was sort of put off at first because if it is a program like that, then I'd be much more for it, but I couldn't see what the card was trying to get at.
- I'd be interested to stop and see if the pamphlets are printed on recycled paper.
- Real iffy on it. I like it more, but I've seen a lot of things that supposedly help the environment. Twenty percent helps the environment, maybe one-half percent gets there. So I'm skeptical.
- It looks like money.
- I like it, I think it looks cool. Even though I probably would think after I stopped that it was some kind of terrible fraud or something, I would stop because I would think it was kind of cool.

- I wouldn't stop there because I think they should talk about the card instead of trees.
- If you were an environmentalist type, that would be right up your alley.
- I think that if somebody was environmentally conscious, they might go up and find out, "What's the deal, does a certain percentage go to a good cause?"
- I feel like turning plastic into trees is absurd, so I wouldn't stop.

Focus Group Comments on Education Display

- I don't like the cheesy frame.
- If I was a freshman, I don't like the phrase, "now even a freshman." I'd be insulted a little bit. And plus I thought the card on the cap, I mean, a credit card doesn't equal a degree.
- I think it would make you feel inclusive. I liked being called a freshman. I kind of felt left out, I know, because everybody already had their credit cards, and you didn't have one. Now I can have one, so I think I'd like that.
- But as a sophomore, I wouldn't even glance at it.
- I don't like that word Masters on there.
- I felt like they were trying to pick on the freshmen and suck them in.
- Being a senior or graduate student, you wouldn't want to walk up to a table like that.
- It would seem like they are giving me a chance to get a degree.
- I would stop and look at it, especially if I was a freshman.
- If I were just to read that, I wouldn't think that it would be a MasterCard booth.
- Even though I'm a senior I would stop, because I would think I want a Master's, because I want a master's degree, even though it's for a credit card it kind of plays on the finishing of your education.
- I think it's a little subdued as far as, when I see a picture of a mortarboard that happens to be a credit card, it's kind of a cool visual but it's not exactly jump out there and grab you.

CHAPTER 7

Primary Data Collection: Survey Research

LEARNING OBJECTIVES

1. To understand the reasons for the popularity of surveys.
2. To learn the types of errors in survey research.
3. To describe the types of surveys.
4. To gain insight into the factors that determine the choice of particular survey methods.
5. To realize the importance of the marketing research interviewer.
6. To appreciate the differences between domestic and international survey research.

If a researcher is looking for eager participants for a door-to-door survey, talk to western ranchers and southern country folk. But if you need to poll the rich or childless suburbanites, get ready for some hard work. Door-to-door surveys may yield an overall response rate of 70 percent, but the rate drops to 60 percent or less in these neighborhoods.

Knowing who will talk and who will refuse helps researchers design more accurate surveys. That's why Valentine Appel, senior vice-president of Backer Spielvogel Bates, and Julian Baim, director of research for Mediamark Research, Inc., analyzed the response rates of different socioeconomic groups. Their tool was PRIZM, a data product from Claritas that divides all Americans into 40 geodemographic clusters (with associated names). The four clusters most responsive to personal interviews were Tobacco Roads (92 percent response rate), Share Croppers (88 percent), Norma-Rae-Ville (83 percent), and Back Country Folks (82 percent). All are characterized as blue-collar and farmworkers living in small towns or rural areas of the South. The fifth-ranked cluster, Agri-Business (81 percent), is the wealthiest of this group and is the only one outside the South. This cluster is found in ranching, farming, lumbering, and mining areas of the Great Plains and Mountain states.

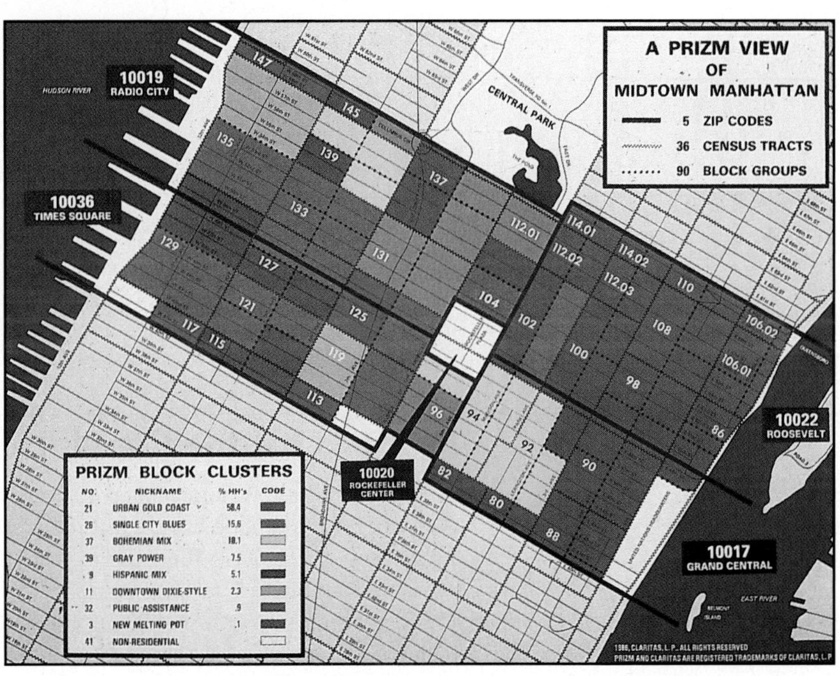

SOURCE: © 1995 Claritas, Inc., Arlington, VA.

The least responsive clusters tend to be wealthy, childless metropolitan residents. They include Urban Gold Coast (62 percent), Money and Brains (60 percent), Blue Blood Estates (59 percent), Gray Power (58 percent), and Bohemian Mix (56 percent). Urban Gold Coast has the highest concentration of one-person households living in high-rise apartment buildings. Money and Brains people tend to live in swank townhouses. Blue Blood Estates are CEOs and heirs to "old money." Gray Power includes nearly two million affluent retired people. Bohemian Mix is an integrated, singles-dominated, high-rise hodgepodge of white-collar workers, students, divorced persons, and artists.

Baim and Appel analyzed their list for demographic characteristics such as income, education, home value, household type, and race. They found only one significant correlation: responsiveness increases as median home values decrease. A higher proportion of retired and relatively well-off householders will lower a neighborhood's response rates.

Researchers at J. D. Power and Associates, a firm that specializes in measuring automobile purchaser satisfaction, have found that cluster responsiveness varies greatly for surveys taken by mail. Tobacco Road residents are among the least likely to respond to a mail survey, for example, while Gray Power residents are far more likely to participate by mail.[1] ■

Survey research is the use of a questionnaire to gather facts, opinions, and attitudes. It is the most popular way to gather primary data. What are the various types of survey research? Why are some more popular than others? As noted previously, not everyone is willing to participate in a survey. What kind of error problems does that create? What are the other types of errors encountered in survey research? These questions will be answered in Chapter 7.

Reasons for the Popularity of Surveys

About 126 million Americans have been interviewed at some point in their lives. Almost 72 million people were interviewed in 1990, 33 million more than in 1980. Americans spent 50 million hours responding to surveys in 1992. This is the equivalent of more than 15 minutes per adult per year.[2] Surveys have a high rate of usage in marketing research compared with other means of collecting primary data for some very good reasons.

1. *The need to know why.* In marketing research there generally is a critical need to have some idea about why people do or do not do something. For example, why did they buy or not buy our brand? What did they like or dislike about it? Who or what influenced them? We do not mean to imply that surveys can prove causation. Only that they can be used to develop some idea of the causal forces at work.
2. *The need to know how.* At the same time, the marketing researcher often finds it necessary to understand the process consumers go through before taking some action. How did they make the decision? What time period passed? What did they examine or consider? When and where was the decision made? What do they plan to do next?
3. *The need to know who.* The marketing researcher also needs to know who the person is from a demographic or lifestyle perspective. Information on age, income, occupation, marital status, stage in the family life cycle, education, and other factors is necessary to the identification and definition of market segments.

Marketing Research in Practice

JACKSON, MICHIGAN, IS MOST SURVEYED MARKET

There must be something very attractive about Jackson, Michigan, because researchers surveyed this market most frequently in 1994. Boise, Sioux Falls, San Diego, and Akron also seem to have a magical attraction, but Lima, Terre Haute, Wichita Falls, and Bryan-College Station do not.

The Jackson, Michigan, Metropolitan Statistical Area (MSA) has a population of about 152,300, a household count of 54,800, a median age of 34.0, and a median household effective buying income (EBI) of $32,752, according to 1993 Sales & Marketing Management's *Survey of Buying Power*. These statistics are close to the U.S. median figures; the U.S. median household EBI is $33,178, and the U.S. median age is 33.4.

HOW THE RANKS WERE DETERMINED

Each year, Survey Sampling, Inc. "marks" millions of numbers selected for survey research studies on its random digit sampling database. The distribution of the marked numbers from January through December 1993 was analyzed to determine the most popular survey research markets.[3]

Metro areas that have been most surveyed have changed dramatically over the past four years. Cincinnati and Kansas City are the only two markets that maintained a top 25 status since 1990. ■

SOURCE: Survey Sampling, Inc.

Types of Errors in Survey Research

When assessing the quality of information obtained from survey research, the manager must make some determination of the accuracy of those results. This requires careful consideration of the research methodology employed in relation to the various types of errors that might occur. The various types of errors that might be encountered in a survey are shown in Figure 7.1 on page 219.

Sampling Error

Two major types of errors may be encountered in connection with the sampling process. They are random error and systematic error, sometimes referred to as *bias*.

Surveys often attempt to obtain information from a representative cross section of a target population. The goal is to make inferences about the total population based on the responses given by respondents sampled. Even if all aspects of the sample are executed properly, the results are still subject to a certain amount of error **(random error** or **random sampling error)** because of chance variation. It is the difference between the sample value and the true value of the population mean. This error cannot be avoided, only reduced by increasing sample size. It is possible to estimate the range of random error at a particular level

random error or **random sampling error**
Error that results from chance variation.

TABLE 7.1 The Top 25 Most Surveyed Metropolitan Markets

1994	1992	1990
1. Jackson, MI	Midland, TX	Des Moines, IA
2. Boise, ID	Portland, ME	Milwaukee, WI
3. Sioux Falls, SD	Boulder-Longmont, CO	Indianapolis, IN
4. San Diego, CA	Grand Forks, ND-MN	Boulder-Longmont, CO
5. Akron, OH PMSA	Phoenix, AZ	Spokane, WA
6. Rochester, MN	Denver, CO	Fort Collins-Loveland, CO
7. South Bend, IN	Fargo-Moorhead, ND-MN	Pittsfield, MA
8. San Francisco, CA PMSA	Boise, ID	Seattle, WA
9. Miami, FL PMSA	Tucson, AZ	Sioux Falls, SD
10. Charleston, WV	Pittsfield, MA	Denver, CO
11. Cincinnati, OH-KY-IN PMSA	Duluth, MN	Santa Barbara-Santa Maria, CA
12. Merced, CA	Sherman-Denison, TX	Merced, CA
13. Fort Worth-Arlington, TX PMSA	Milwaukee, WI	Springfield, MO
14. Portland-Vancouver, OR-WA PMSA	Louisville, KY	Phoenix, AZ
15. Santa Fe, NM	Atlanta, GA	Louisville, KY
16. Houston, TX PMSA	Kansas City, MO-KS	Greeley, CO
17. Canton-Massillon, OH	San Diego, CA	Minneapolis-Saint Paul, MN-WI
18. Los Angeles-Long Beach, CA PMSA	Oxnard-Ventura, CA	Kansas City MO-KS
19. New Orleans, LA	Cincinnati, OH	Eugene-Springfield, OR
20. Austin-San Marcos, TX	Owensboro, KY	Cincinnati, OH
21. Santa Rosa, CA PMSA	Miami-Hialeah, FL	Rapid City, SD
22. Kansas City, MO-KS	Buffalo, NY	Albany-Schenectady, NY
23. Albany-Schenectady-Troy, NY	Cedar Rapids, IA	Saint Louis, MO-IL
24. Richmond-Petersburg, VA	San Francisco, CA	Tucson, AZ
25. Bridgeport-Stamford-Danbury, CT	San Jose, CA	Wilmington, DE

of confidence. Random error and the procedures for estimating it are discussed in detail in Chapters 13 and 14.

Systematic Error

systematic error
Error that results from the research design or execution

Systematic error, or bias, results from mistakes or problems in the research design or from flaws in the execution of the sample design. Systematic error, or bias, exists in the results of a sample if those results show a consistent tendency to vary in one direction (consistently higher or consistently lower) from the true value of the population parameter being estimated. Systematic error includes all sources of error except those introduced by the random sampling process. Therefore, systematic errors or bias are sometimes called *nonsampling errors*. The types of nonsampling errors that can systematically influence survey answers can be categorized as sample design error and measurement error. Sample design error is systematic error that results from an error in the sample design or sample procedures.

Sample design results may be biased for a number of reasons:

frame error
Error resulting from an inaccurate or incomplete sample frame.

- *Frame Error.* The sampling frame is the list of population elements or members from which units to be sampled are selected. **Frame error** results from using an incomplete or inaccurate sampling frame. The problem is that a sample drawn from a list that includes frame error may not be a true cross section of the target population. A common example of a situation that is likely to include frame error in marketing research involves the use of a published tele-

FIGURE 7.1
Total Survey Error and Its Components

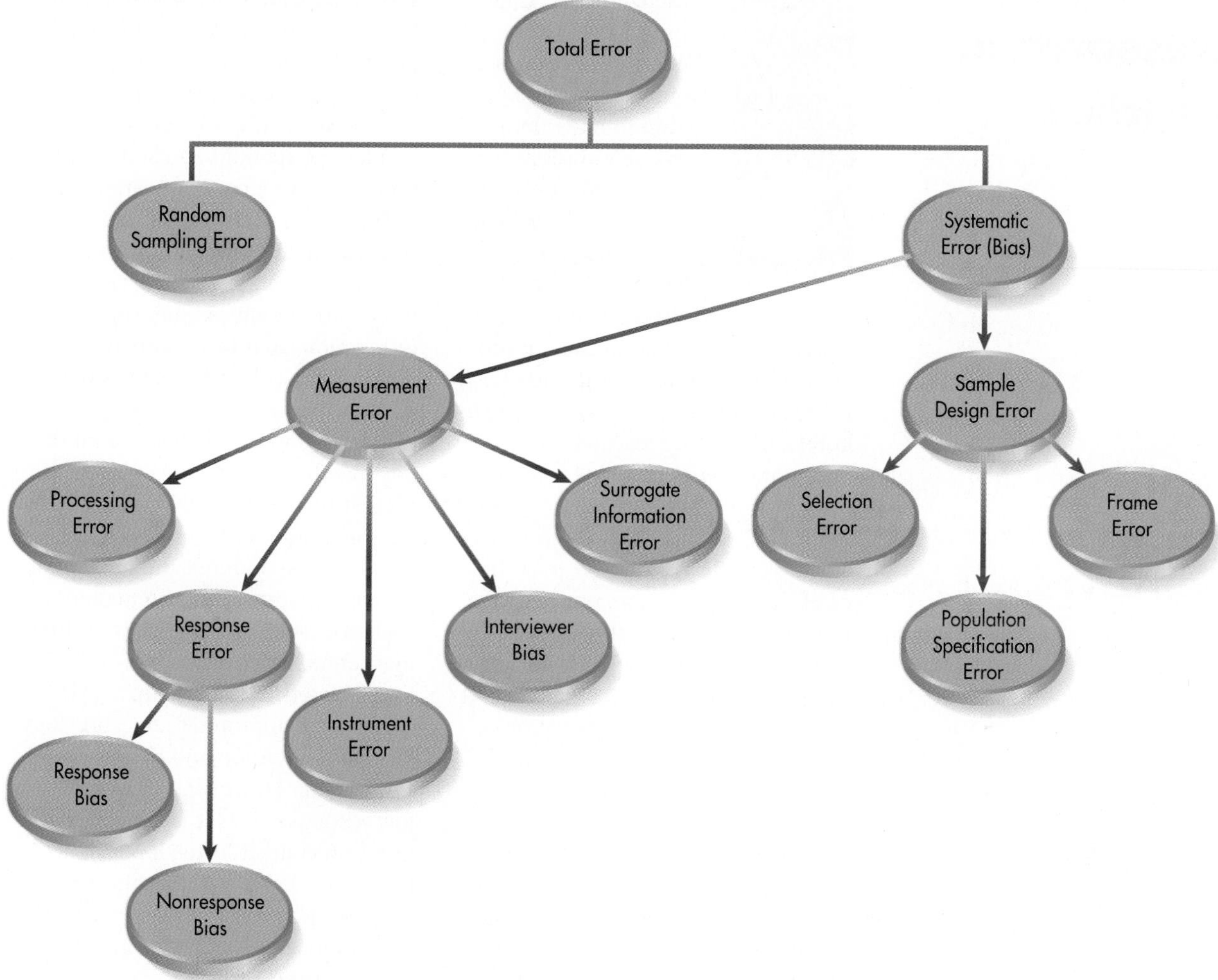

phone directory as a sample frame for a telephone survey. Many households are not listed or not listed accurately in the current telephone book because they do not want to be listed or because they have recently moved or changed their telephone number. Research has shown that those people who are listed in telephone directories are systematically different from those who are not listed in certain important ways.[4] This means that any study purporting to represent the opinions of all households in a particular area that is drawn from the current telephone directory is subject to frame error.

- *Population Specification Error*: **Population specification error** results from an incorrect definition of the universe or population from which the sample is to be selected. For example, we might define the population or universe for a study as people over the age of 35. It might later be determined that younger individuals should have been included and that the population should have

population specification error
Error that results from an incorrect definition of the universe, or population, from which the sample is chosen.

Marketing Research in Practice

One of the significant demographic changes in recent years has been the shift from a youth-oriented population to one oriented to people middle age or older. Not only are more Americans living longer, they also are living better. The 65-and-older population controls 50 percent of the discretionary income in the United States. This segment of the market is being courted increasingly by marketers. Marketing research plays an important role in understanding the desires, lifestyles, and values of this group. However, the research methods, tasks, and techniques must be carefully adapted to accommodate the characteristics of this market.

There are numerous physiological, cognitive, and social changes that take place during the aging process, which have marketing research implications. Farsightedness and other vision changes mean larger type on printed materials, additional lighting, or perhaps the use of contrasting colors. Diminished hearing means that special adjustments must be made for telephone and personal interviews to speak clearly and slowly, using interviewers with deep voices, or paying special attention to the delivery of the questions. To compensate for the diminished perception, learning, and information processing, questionnaire design should be simple and parsimonious. Visual aids should be used when possible. Mail questionnaires may be better because respondents can control the pace. If a telephone survey is selected, it could be used in conjunction with a paper questionnaire.

Interviewer training for personal interviews and telephone surveys is important. Data collection takes longer and involves more social interaction, so interviewers must be patient and as helpful as possible without biasing the results.

Changes in data collection methods may be necessary. In particular, pretesting is extremely important. Personal interviews are less stressful for older respondents and have higher response rates but also higher costs. Because of the abuses of direct marketers, older people are more likely to refuse to participate. Mail surveys are appropriate because they rely only on vision and they allow self-pacing. However, because of low response rates it is necessary to use a precontact letter, a personalized cover letter, a self-addressed and stamped return envelope, and a reminder card. Mall intercepts have many advantages but the special needs of older respondents must be taken into consideration. If focus groups are used, times as well as special transportation needs must be factored into the research design.[5] ■

been defined as those people 20 years of age or older. If those younger people who were excluded are significantly different in regard to the variables of interest, then the sample results will be biased.

selection error

Error that results from following incomplete or improper sampling procedures or not following proper ones.

■ *Selection Error.* **Selection error** can occur even when the analyst has a proper sample frame and has defined the population correctly. It occurs because of the use of incomplete or improper sampling procedures or when appropriate selection procedures are not properly followed. For example, door-to-door interviewers might decide to avoid houses that do not look neat and tidy because they think the people who live there will not be "pleasant." If people who live in houses that are not neat and tidy are systematically different from those in tidy houses, then selection error will be introduced into the results of the survey. Selection error is a much more serious problem in connection with nonprobability samples discussed in Chapter 13.

Measurement Error

Measurement error is often a much more significant threat to survey accuracy than random error. Frequently in the media, when the results of public opinion polls are quoted, and in professional marketing research reports, an error figure is reported (e.g., plus or minus 5 percent). The television viewer or the user of a marketing research study is left with the impression that this figure refers to total survey error. Unfortunately, this is not the case. This figure refers only to random sampling error. It does not include sample design error and speaks in no way to the measurement error that may exist in the research results. **Measurement error** occurs when there is a variation between the information being sought (true value) and the information obtained by the measurement process. For the most part, we are concerned with systematic measurement error. A number of types of errors may be caused by various deficiencies in the measurement process.

measurement error
Error that results from a variation between the information being sought and that actually obtained by the measurement process.

- *Surrogate Information Error.* **Surrogate information error** occurs when there is a discrepancy between the information actually required to solve a problem and the information being sought by the researcher. It is related to general problems in the research design, particularly failure to properly define the problem. A classic and well-known situation that involved surrogate information error relates to the New Coke fiasco. It has been reported that the research for New Coke focused on the taste of the product and failed to consider the attitudes of consumers toward a change in the product. The resulting failure of New Coke strongly suggests, as the producers of Coke should understand, that people purchase Coke for many reasons other than taste.

surrogate information error
Error that results from a discrepancy between the information needed to solve a problem and that sought by the researcher.

- *Interviewer Error.* **Interviewer error,** or interviewer bias, is due to interactions between the interviewer and the respondent. The interviewer may, consciously or unconsciously, influence respondents to give untrue or inaccurate answers. The interviewer's dress, age, gender, facial expressions, body language, or tone of voice may influence the answers given by some or all respondents. This type of error is caused by problems in the selection and training of interviewers or by the failure of interviewers to follow instructions. Interviewers must be properly trained and supervised to appear neutral at all times. In addition to the types of interviewer error discussed earlier is the problem of deliberate cheating. This is a significant problem in connection with door-to-door interviewing, where interviewers may be tempted to falsify interviews and get paid for work they did not actually do. The procedures developed by the researcher must include safeguards to make sure this problem will be detected (see Chapter 15).

interviewer error
Error that results from conscious or unconscious bias in the interviewer's interaction with the respondent.

- *Measurement Instrument Bias.* **Measurement instrument bias** is the result of problems with the measurement instrument or questionnaire (see Chapter 10). It can occur because of such problems as leading questions or by elements of the questionnaire design that make the recording of responses difficult and

measurement instrument bias
Error that results from the design of the questionnaire or measurement instrument.

prone to recording errors (see Chapter 12). Errors of this type are avoided by careful attention to detail in the questionnaire design phase of the research and by the use of questionnaire pretests before the start of field interviewing.

processing error

Error that results from incorrect transfer of information from the document to the computer.

- *Processing Error*: **Processing errors** are primarily caused by mistakes in the transfer of information from survey documents to the computer. For example, a data entry operator might enter the wrong response to a particular question. Errors of this type are avoided by the development and strict adherence to quality control procedures in the processing of survey results. This process is discussed in detail in Chapter 15.

nonresponse bias

Error that results from a systematic difference between those who do and do not respond to the measurement instrument.

- *Nonresponse Bias*. Ideally, if we select a sample of 400 people from a particular population, all 400 should be interviewed. As a practical matter, this will never happen. Response rates of 5 percent or less are not uncommon in mail surveys. The question is, "Are those who did respond to the survey systematically different in some important way from those who did not respond?" Such differences are called **nonresponse bias.** The authors recently examined the results of a study conducted among customers of a large savings and loan association. The response rate to the questionnaire, included in customer monthly statements, was slightly under 1 percent. Analysis of the occupations of those who responded revealed that the percentage of retired persons among respondents was 20 times higher than that percentage in the metropolitan area in question. This overrepresentation of retired individuals raised serious doubts in regard to the accuracy of the results.

Yet this experience may be the exception rather than the rule. One article reviewed 14 studies in which differences between respondents and nonrespondents (or early or later respondents) to mail surveys reportedly were found.[6] When the raw data were recalculated to address the question of whether differences between respondents and the entire sample are large enough to be meaningful, the less complete returns were found to approximate very closely the more complete returns. Of all the studies that have looked for such differences, none has been reported that found meaningful, practical differences between respondents and the entire sample or between early respondents and respondents as a whole.

Obviously, the higher the response rate, the less the possible impact of nonresponse because nonrespondents represent a smaller subset of the overall picture. If the decreases in bias associated with improved response rates are trivial, allocating resources to obtain higher response rates can be considered wasteful in studies in which the resources could be used for better purposes.

Thomas Danbury, chairman of Survey Sampling, reports that his firm conducted one study in which 65,000 telephone interviews were completed. Interviewers made up to seven attempts over a four-week period to reach each household and then up to seven more to interview a randomly selected adult. At the end, the researchers looked at what they would have found if only one attempt had been made, or two, all the way to seven. Danbury noted, "To our surprise, the results would have been very similar had we made no callbacks at all!"[7] Table 7.2 shows the incidence of several demographic characteristics measured by one attempt versus seven attempts. Despite the findings, Danbury still recommends three callback attempts.

Nonresponse error occurs (a) when a person cannot be reached at a particular time, (b) when a potential respondent is reached but cannot or will not participate at that time (for example, receiving a telephone request to participate in a

TABLE 7.2 Differences in Demographic Characteristics Based on One Callback Attempt versus Seven in a Survey of 65,000 Adults

DEMOGRAPHIC CHARACTERISTIC	ONE CALL	SEVEN CALLS
Income $50K+	45%	47%
Some college+	47%	49%
Employed full time	76%	78%
Married	65%	63%
Unlisted number	35%	37%
1–2 person household	52%	52%
Rent home	29%	30%
Moved in 5 years	48%	50%
Male	45%	46%

SOURCE: *Survey Sampling, Inc.*

survey just as the family sits down to dinner), and (c) when a person is reached but refuses to participate in a survey. The latter is the most serious problem because it may be possible to achieve future participation in the first two circumstances. In 1990, the refusal to participate rate rose to its highest level ever. Specifically, 36 percent of the respondents in the Walker Research industry image study refused to participate in a research study.[8] Fortunately, most of those people do not refuse 100 percent of the time. In fact, 84 percent of those who refused to participate in at least one study did participate in another study or studies. The three main reasons people refused to participate were[9]

inconvenience	64%
uninteresting subject matter	22%
fear of a sales pitch	13%

Other research on refusal rates suggests that the type of survey may influence whether the individual would participate. For example, consumers had a more favorable attitude toward participating in a door-to-door survey or mall interviews than other types of surveys.[10]

Julian Baim, vice-president of research, Mediamark Research, agrees that nonresponse may be due more to the types of survey than basic changes in consumers' attitudes. Baim feels that this is true throughout the world (see the "Global Marketing Research" on page 224).

- *Response Bias.* If there is a tendency for people to answer a particular question in a certain way, then we have **response bias.** Response bias can occur in two basic forms: deliberate falsification or unconscious misrepresentation. Deliberate falsification occurs when people deliberately give untrue answers to questions. There are many reasons why people might knowingly misrepresent information in a survey. They may wish to appear intelligent, not reveal information they feel is embarrassing, or conceal information that they consider to be personal For example, in a survey regarding fast food behavior, the respondent may have a fairly good idea of how many times he visited a fast food restaurant in the past month. However, he may not remember which fast food restaurants he visited or how many times he visited each restaurant. Rather than answering "Don't Know" in response to the question regarding which restaurants were visited, the respondent may simply guess.

response bias
error that results from the tendency of people to answer a question falsely, through deliberate misrepresentation or unconscious falsification.

Global Marketing Research

In comparing response rates around the world, with personal interviews, Julian Baim did not find a correlation between response rates and number of attempts or length of interview. There were substantial variations in response rates among countries, but no clear-cut culturally based explanation, Baim said.

The perception is that response rates are down in all countries except Norway, but that perception is not completely supported. The biggest drop is in the United Kingdom, leading to the conclusion that something is happening there, he said. Baim concluded that multinational nonresponse is not that different from the U.S. experience. Central cities pose the biggest nonresponse problem, he said, probably because of the inaccessibility of private residences (door attendants, etc.), interviewers' fear of crime in some areas, and the demographics of urban areas in general. There are more mail and phone interviews in the United States, and the problems associated with these methods are not yet being experienced by European researchers, who mainly conducted home and work personal interviews, he said.

In theory, nonresponse rates are higher in international marketing research for several reasons. First, cultural habits in many countries virtually prohibit communication with a stranger, particularly for women. For example, a researcher simply may not be able to speak on the phone with a housewife in an Islamic country to find out what she thinks of a particular brand. Second, in many societies, such matters as preferences for hygienic products and food products are too personal to be shared with an outsider. In many Latin American countries, a woman may feel ashamed to talk with a researcher about her choice of a brand of sanitary pad, hair shampoo, or perfume. Third, respondents in many cases may be unwilling to share their true feelings with interviewers because they suspect the interviewers may be agents of the government (for example, seeking information for imposition of additional taxes). Fourth, middle-class people, in developing countries in particular, are reluctant to accept their status and may make false claims to reflect the lifestyle of wealthier people. For example, in a study on the consumption of tea in India, more than 70 percent of the respondents from middle-income families claimed they used one of the several national brands of tea. This finding could not be substantiated since more than 60 percent of the tea sold nationally in India is unbranded, generic tea sold unpackaged. Fifth, many respondents, willing to cooperate, may be illiterate, so that even oral communication may be difficult.[11] ■

Unconscious misrepresentation occurs when the respondent is legitimately trying to be truthful and accurate but gives an inaccurate response. This type of bias may occur because of question format, question content, or various other reasons. Types of errors and strategies for minimizing errors are summarized in Table 7.3.

Types of Surveys

Asking people questions, is the essence of the survey approach. But what type of survey will be "best" in a given situation? The traditional survey alternatives discussed in this chapter are summarized in Table 7.4. Emerging approaches are summarized in Table 7.5.

TABLE 7.3 Types of Errors and Strategies for Minimizing Errors

I. RANDOM ERROR—RANDOM ERROR CAN BE REDUCED ONLY BY INCREASING SAMPLE SIZE.	
II. SYSTEMATIC ERROR—MINIMIZE SAMPLE DESIGN AND MEASUREMENT ERROR.	
A. Sample Design Error	
Frame Error	This error can be minimized by getting the best frame possible and doing preliminary quality control checks to evaluate the accuracy and completeness of the frame.
Population Specification Error	This error results from flaws in research design (e.g., incorrect definition of population of interest). It can be reduced or minimized only by means of more careful consideration and definition of the population of interest.
Selection Error	This error results from the use of incomplete or improper sampling procedures or when appropriate procedures are not followed. It can occur even if we have a good sample frame and an appropriate specification of the population. It is minimized by developing selection procedures that will ensure randomness and by developing quality control checks to make sure that these procedures are being followed in the field.
B. Measurement Error	
Surrogate Information Error	This error results from seeking and basing decisions on the wrong information. (The New Coke example was cited in the text.) It results from poor design and can be minimized only by paying more careful attention to specification of the types of information required to fulfill the objectives of the research.
Interviewer Error	This error occurs because of interactions between the interviewer and respondent that affect the responses given. It is minimized by more careful interviewer selection and training. In addition, quality control checks that involve unobtrusive monitoring of interviewers to ascertain whether prescribed behavior is being adhered to should be employed.
Measurement Instrument Bias	Also referred to as *questionnaire bias,* it is minimized only by careful questionnaire design and pretesting.
Nonresponse Bias	This error results from the fact that people chosen for the sample who actually respond are systematically different from those who are chosen and do not respond. It is particularly serious in connection with mail surveys. It is minimized by doing everything possible (e.g., shorten questionnaire, make questionnaire more respondent friendly, callbacks, incentives, contacting people when they are most likely to be at home, etc.) to encourage those chosen for the sample to respond.
Response Bias	Response bias occurs when something about a question leads people to answer it in a particular way. This type of error can be minimized by paying special attention to questionnaire design. In particular we must be sensitive to questions that are hard to answer, might make respondent look uninformed if she cannot answer, or deal with sensitive issues. Questions should be modified to deal with these problems (see Chapter 10).
Processing Error	These errors can occur in the process of transferring data from the questionnaires to the computer. This error is minimized by developing and following rigid procedures for transferring data and supporting quality control checks.

TABLE 7.4 Different Survey Approaches Commonly Used in Marketing Research

TYPE OF INTERVIEW	DESCRIPTION
Door-to-Door	Interviewer interviews consumer in consumer's home.
Executive Interview	Interview industrial product user (e.g., engineer, architect, doctor, executive) or decision maker at place of business regarding industrial product.
Mall Intercept	Interviewer interviews consumer in shopping mall or other high-traffic location. Interviews may be done in public areas of the mall or the respondent may be taken to a private test area.
Central Location Telephone Interview	Interviewing is conducted from a telephone facility set up for that purpose. These facilities typically have equipment that permits the supervisor to unobtrusively monitor the interviewing while it is taking place. Some of these facilities have Wide Area Telephone Service (WATS) to permit national sampling from a single location. An increasing number have computer-assisted interviewing capabilities. At these locations the interviewer sits in front of a computer terminal attached to a mainframe or a personal computer. The questionnaire is programmed into the computer. The interviewer enters responses directly.
Direct Computer Interview	Used increasingly, particularly in the mall environment. The consumer is seated at a computer terminal or personal computer. The questionnaire is programmed into the computer and the consumer is, in essence, interviewed by the computer.
Self-administered Questionnaires	Most frequently employed at high-traffic locations such as shopping malls or in captive audience situations such as classrooms and airplanes. Respondents are given general information on how to fill out the questionnaire and are left to fill it out on their own. Computers are being used in this area by sending software-driven questionnaires on diskettes to individuals who have personal computers.
Ad Hoc (one-shot) Mail Surveys	Questionnaires are mailed to a sample of consumers or industrial users. Instructions are included. Respondents are asked to fill out the questionnaire and return it via mail. Sometimes a gift or monetary incentive is provided. The same comment regarding computers under self-administered questionnaires applies here. We have not heard of questionnaires sent by fax, but why not?
Mail Panels	Several companies, including Market Facts, NPD Research, and National Family Opinion Research, operate large (more than 100,000 households) consumer panels. There are several important differences between mail panels and ad hoc mail surveys. First, people in the panel have been precontacted. The panel concept has been explained to them. They have agreed to participate for some period of time. In addition, participants are offered gratuities to participate in mail panels. Mail panels typically generate much higher response rates than do ad hoc mail surveys.

Door-to-Door Interviewing

door-to-door interviewing
Consumers are interviewed face to face in their homes.

Door-to-door interviewing in which consumers are interviewed in person in their homes, has traditionally been thought of as the best survey method. This conclusion was based on a number of factors. First, the door-to-door interview is a personal, face-to-face interview with all the attendant advantages—feedback from the respondent, the ability to explain complicated tasks, the ability to use special questionnaire techniques that require visual contact to speed up the interview or improve data quality, the ability to show the respondent product concepts and other stimuli for evaluation, and so on. Second, the consumer is seen as being at ease in a familiar, comfortable, secure environment.

The door-to-door interview remains the only viable way to do long depth interviews and certain in-home product tests. In addition, the door-to-door survey is

TABLE 7.5 Emerging Survey Approaches

APPROACH	DESCRIPTION AND COMMENTS
Point of Service Touch-Screen	Kiosks, equipped with touch-screen monitors, provide a new way to capture information from individuals in stores, health clinics, and other shopping or service environments. Although this approach is currently being used on a limited basis, little is known definitively about its advantages and disadvantages.[13]
Fax Surveys	This technique has emerged as a viable way to collect data from business firms in recent years. It has many of the same features of mail surveys. The major advantage is the speed with which information can be obtained in that the time required to get the survey in the hands of target respondents and to get it back from them is greatly reduced. There is some evidence that, in this early stage when the approach is still novel, response rates are higher than with mail surveys of comparable length.[14]
On-Line Surveys	Appeared for a time on America On-Line. Have recently disappeared from that venue. As the number of individuals connected to on-line services increases above the current estimates of nine to 10 million, we will see this approach become increasingly attractive. It is possible to administer fairly complex surveys via computer bulletin boards. This approach has been successfully used by DSS Research of Arlington, Texas, in a number of business applications.[15]
E-mail	There are a few reported instances of surveys being done via E-mail. Texas Instruments has used this approach for a number of employees. Unfortunately, current technology limits the types and complexity of information that can be obtained in this manner. This approach will become more widely used as E-mail platforms become more flexible and user-friendly.[16]
Voice Mail	Sophisticated IVR (interactive voice response) systems make it possible to complete automated surveys over the telephone by having respondents dial local or 800 numbers and respond to voice prompts (multiple-choice questions) by using the buttons on their touch-tone telephones. This approach has not been widely used. However, it has been successfully used with physicians and some other difficult-to-reach populations. This approach gives them the opportunity to call when it is convenient for them 24 hours per day, 365 days per year.[17]

the only way currently available to obtain anything approaching a probability sample in a study that involves showing concepts or other stimuli to consumers.

However, this approach to interviewing has a number of drawbacks that explain its declining use by commercial marketing researchers. Jerry Rosenkranz, chairman of Data Development, a large New York–based custom research firm, lists the difficulties associated with door-to-door interviewing.

- The growth of the two-adult working family and other changes in family composition mean less availability of potential respondents.
- Although response rates in-home cooperation rates were historically higher than for other approaches, they gradually are deteriorating.
- Unsafe (high crime) areas, distance, and lack of accessibility sometimes negated reaching the desired sample.
- The drop in qualified interviewing personnel, whether because of a drop in education or the increase in other options with better pay, has become a factor over time.
- The special characteristics required of a field interviewer, that is, the "chutzpah to make a cold call" limit the potential pool of interviews.
- The client and field service's unease due to the lack of "hands-on" control of a field force that is out there somewhere (in direct comparison to a permanent workforce in a centralized location under supervision—clocking in 9 to 5, etc.).
- The lack of communication between the home office, the field office, and the interviewing staff (except at the end of day) is a serious handicap if one wish-

Door-to-door interviewing is still done, but is extremely rare today. SOURCE: © Mary Kate Denny/PhotoEdit.

es to execute questionnaire changes, examine incidence rate, or hasten data retrieval.

- The effects of such old bugaboos as weather (too good or too bad), car problems, broken-in cars, sickness, etc.
- Cheating, fudging, or shortcutting by the interviewers, interviewing the wrong respondent, etc., promote high levels of validation. This post-field check may, be too late to permit us to replace the necessary data. In any case, it is very costly to go back for it.

The door-to-door approach to survey data collection is not likely to disappear from the marketing research scene. As noted earlier, it is the only viable data collection alternative in a number of situations. On the other hand, it is also unlikely that we will see this type of interviewing reassume the prominence it once enjoyed. Recent estimates (see Table 7.6) suggest that only about 15 percent of all persons interviewed in 1992 participated in a door-to-door interview.

Mall Intercept

mall intercept interviewing

Shoppers are intercepted in public areas of malls and interviewed face-to-face.

As the data in Table 7.6 indicate, **mall intercept interviewing** is a popular survey method. The approach is relatively simple. Shoppers are intercepted in the public areas of shopping malls and either interviewed in the mall or asked to come to a permanent interviewing facility in the mall. In 1996, approximately 500 malls throughout the country had permanent survey facilities operated by marketing research firms. An equal or greater number of malls permit market research firms to interview on a day-to-day basis. Many malls do not permit marketing research interviewing because they view it as an unnecessary nuisance to shoppers.

Mall interviewing is of relatively recent origin. The earliest permanent facilities date back less than 30 years with real growth in use of this technique coming during the 1970s. In general, the mall intercept interview is a low-cost sub-

TABLE 7.6 **Participation by Survey Type**

	PERCENTAGE PARTICIPATION*		
TYPE	1980	1986	1992
Mail	56	54	69
Telephone	75	76	68
Mall Intercept**	36	30	32
Door-to-Door	18	11	15

*Percentages are greater than 100 because of multiple responses

**Always a nonprobability sample whereas the other methods can be either a probability or a nonprobability sample.

SOURCE: *Walker 1992 Industry Image Study.*

stitute for the door-to-door interview. In fact, this approach probably has grown primarily at the expense of or as a replacement for door-to-door interviewing.

Mall surveys are less expensive than door-to-door interviews because respondents are coming to the interviewer rather than the other way around. Interviewers spend more of their time actually interviewing and less time hunting for someone to interview. Also, mall interviewers do not have the substantial travel time and mileage expenses associated with door-to-door interviewing. In addition to low cost, mall interviews have many of the advantages associated with door-to-door interviewing in that respondents can be shown various stimuli for their reactions and special questionnaire techniques can be used.[18]

Mall intercept surveys have largely replaced door-to-door interviewing. SOURCE: © Jeff Greenberg/PhotoEdit.

However, a number of serious disadvantages are associated with mall interviewing. First, it is virtually impossible to get a sample representative of a large metropolitan area from shoppers at a particular mall. Although they may be large, most malls draw from a relatively small area in proximity to the mall. In addition, a mall tends to attract a certain type of person based on the stores it contains. Studies also show that some people shop more frequently and therefore have a greater chance of being selected than others. Finally, many people refuse mall interviews. One study found that more than half of those approached refused either on initial contact or after they had been qualified.[19] By *qualified* we mean that responses to screening questions have indicated that the individual falls into a group in which the researcher is interested. In summary, mall interviewing cannot produce a good or representative sample except in the rare case where the population of interest is coincident with, or a subset of, the population of people who shop at the mall.

Second, the mall environment is not the comfortable home environment associated with the door-to-door interview. The respondent may be ill at ease, in a hurry, or preoccupied by various distractions outside the researcher's control. These factors may adversely affect the quality of the data obtained. The popularity of mall intercept interviews has held steady in recent years (see Table 7.6).

Executive Interviewing

Executive interviewing is used by marketing researchers to refer to the industrial equivalent of door-to-door interviewing. This type of survey involves interviewing businesspeople, at their offices, concerning industrial products or ser-

executive interviewing
The industrial equivalent of door-to-door interviewing.

vices. For example, if Hewlett-Packard wanted information regarding user preferences for different features that might be offered in a new line of computer printers, it would need to interview prospective user-purchasers of the printers. It is appropriate to locate and interview these people at their offices.

This type of interviewing is very expensive. First, individuals involved in the purchase decision for the product in question must be identified and located. Sometimes lists can be obtained from various sources, but more frequently screening must be conducted over the telephone. It may be likely that a particular company has individuals of the type being sought. However, locating those people within a large organization can be expensive and time-consuming. Once a qualified person is located, the next step is to get that person to agree to be interviewed and to set a time for the interview. This is not as hard as it might seem because most professionals seem to enjoy talking about topics related to their work.

Finally, an interviewer must go to the particular place at the appointed time. Long waits are frequently encountered; cancellations are not uncommon. This type of survey requires the very best interviewers because they are frequently interviewing on topics that they know very little about. Executive interviewing has essentially the same advantages and disadvantages as door-to-door interviewing.

Telephone Interviewing

As noted earlier, until 1990 telephone surveys were the most popular form of survey. The advantages of telephone interviewing are compelling. First, the telephone is a relatively inexpensive way to collect survey data. The major reason is that interviewer travel time and mileage are eliminated. A second advantage of the telephone interview is that it has the potential to produce a very high-quality sample. If proper sampling and callback procedures are employed, the telephone approach probably produces a better sample than any other survey procedure.[20] Random digit sampling or random digit dialing is a frequently used sampling approach (see Chapter 13). The basic idea is very simple. Instead of drawing the sample from the phone book or other directory, telephone numbers are generated via a random number procedure. This approach ensures that people with unlisted numbers and those who have moved or otherwise changed their telephone numbers since the last published phone book are included in the sample in their correct proportion.

The telephone survey approach has several inherent disadvantages. First, in the typical telephone interview of today, the respondent cannot be shown anything. Advanced cable TV systems and picture phones, which are expected to be in widespread use in the future, have the potential to overcome this limitation. This shortcoming ordinarily eliminates the telephone survey as an alternative in situations that require that the respondent be shown something—product concepts, advertisements, and the like.

Some have suggested that the telephone interview does not permit the interviewer to make various judgments and evaluations that can be made by the in-home interviewer—judgments regarding respondent income based on the home lived in and other outward signs of economic status. Granted, the interviewer does not have these cues in the telephone situation. However, in reality, the market research interviewer is almost never called upon to make such judgments. The reasons are spelled out in the section on marketing research interviewers.

A third disadvantage of the telephone interview is that it is more limited in regard to the quantity and types of information that can be obtained than is the door-to-door interview. First, some evidence suggests that the telephone interview must be shorter than the door-to-door interview. Respondent patience wears thin more easily, and it is easier to hang up the phone than throw an interviewer out of your living room. Second, the telephone is a poor choice for conducting the depth interview or the long interview with many open-ended questions.

A fourth disadvantage of telephone interviewing is the increased use of screening devices, such as CALLER ID, and screening via answering machines. Approximately 32 million U.S. households are equipped with telephone answering machines (up 52 percent in the past two years).[21] More than half of these households screen their calls at least some of the time. Call screening, of course, increases the nonresponse rate. Nonresponse rates are rising for telephone interviewing primarily because of telemarketing. A major survey found that 86 percent of the respondents would be more likely to participate in a telephone survey if they knew the call was to conduct a legitimate telephone survey, rather than to sell them something.[22]

Central Location Telephone Interviews

Central location telephone interviewing is conducted from a facility set up for that specific purpose. Nearly all telephone interviews are conducted from this type of environment today.

central location telephone interviewing

Interviewers make calls from a centrally located marketing research facility to reach and interview respondents.

The reasons for the prominence of the central location phone interview are fairly straightforward. Summarized in a single word, the main reason would be "con-

Callers at central telephone interviewing facilities collect data through phone surveys.

SOURCE: Courtesy of Mktg., Inc.

trol." First, the actual interviewing process can be monitored. Most central location telephone interviewing facilities have unobtrusive monitoring equipment that permits supervisors to listen in on interviews as they are actually being conducted. Interviewers who are not doing the interview properly can be corrected. Those who are incapable of conducting a proper interview can be eliminated. One supervisor may monitor from 10 to 20 interviewers. Ordinarily each interviewer is monitored at least once per shift. Second, completed interviews are edited on the spot as a further quality control check. Interviewers can be immediately informed of any deficiencies in their work. Finally, there is control over the hours that interviewers work. Interviewers report in and out and work regular hours.

Most national studies are conducted from a single facility. Without this capability, a study requiring, for example, 150 central location telephone interviews in Dallas, 150 in Washington, D.C., and 150 in Sacramento, California, would require the use of a field service firm in each of the three cities to conduct the interviewing. Sample data from such a study are shown in Table 7.7. The researcher faced with analyzing the data is confronted with the question of deciding whether differences in results for the three cities represent real differences or differences in the way the survey was administered in the three cities. If the interviewing had been conducted from a single facility, there would be no question. The analyst could feel relatively certain that consumers in Sacramento and Washington really liked the product better than did consumers in Dallas.

Computer-assisted Telephone Interviewing (CATI)

computer-assisted telephone interviewing

Central location telephone interviewing in which the interviewer enters answers directly into a computer.

Most research firms have computerized the central location telephone interviewing process. Each interviewer is seated in front of a computer terminal or a personal computer. When a qualified respondent gets on the line, the interviewer starts the interview by pressing a key or series of keys on the terminal or personal computer keyboard. The questions and multiple choice answers appear on the screen one at a time. The interviewer reads the question and enters the response, and the computer skips ahead to the appropriate next question. For example, we might ask whether the person has a dog. If the answer is "yes," there might be a series of questions regarding what type of dog food the person buys. If the answer is "no," these questions would be inappropriate. The com-

TABLE 7.7 Data from a Three-City Product Concept Test

	TOTAL	DALLAS	SACRAMENTO	WASHINGTON
Total	151 (100%)	50 (100%)	51 (100%)	50 (100%)
Definitely Purchase	39 (26%)	11 (22%)	15 (29%)	13 (26%)
Probably Purchase	40 (26%)	8 (16%)	15 (29%)	17 (34%)
Uncertain About	37 (25%)	13 (26%)	9 (18%)	15 (30%)
Probably Not Purchase	19 (13%)	10 (20%)	5 (10%)	4 (8%)
Definitely Not Purchase	16 (11%)	8 (16%)	7 (14%)	1 (2%)

NOTE: All percentages are computed with the column total as the base.

Global Marketing Research

In the United States, telephone interviewing is a well-established information gathering methodology of survey research. However, the use of the technique to gather information in foreign markets is still relatively new, especially in terms of telephone interviews originating in the United States but taking place with foreign consumers. To help researchers overcome residual language barriers, AT&T Co., New York, markets a service that features on-line interpreters fluent in 143 languages and dialects. Those specialists translate conversations into or out of English. Likewise, on a broader scale, the growth of global markets and the trend toward English as business's international language are breaking down cultural resistance Americans have met when conducting primary research in off shore markets.[23] ■

puter takes into account the answer to the dog ownership question and skips ahead to the next appropriate question.

In addition, the computer can help customize questionnaires. For example, in the early part of a long interview, we might ask respondents the years, makes, and models of all the cars they own. Later in the interview, questions might be asked about each specific car owned. The question might come up on the interviewer's screen as follows: "You said you own a 1992 Ford Taurus. Which family member drives this car most often?" Other questions about this car and others owned would appear in similar fashion. Questions like this can be handled in a traditional pencil and paper interview, but they are handled much more efficiently in the computerized version.

This approach eliminates the need for separate editing and data entry steps. There is no editing because there are no questionnaires. More to the point, in most computer systems it is not possible to enter an "impossible" answer. For example, if a question has three possible answers with codes A, B, C and the interviewer enters D, the computer will not accept it. It will ask that the answer be reentered. If a combination or pattern of answers is impossible, the computer will not accept the answer, and so on. Keypunching of completed questionnaires is eliminated because data are entered into the computer as interviews are completed.

Another advantage of computer interviewing is that computer tabulations can be run at any point in the study—after 200 people have been interviewed, after 400, or after any number. This luxury is not available with the pencil and paper interview. With the traditional interview, there may be a wait of a week or more after completion of all interviewing before detailed tabulations of the results are available. Instantaneous results available with computer-assisted telephone interviewing systems provide some real advantages. Based on preliminary tabulations, certain questions might be dropped, saving time and money in subsequent interviewing. If, for example, 98.3 percent of those interviewed answered a particular question in the same manner, there probably is no need to continue asking the question. Tabulations also may suggest the need to add questions to the survey. If an unexpected pattern of product use is uncovered in the early interviewing, questions can be added to further delve into this behavior. Finally, management may find the early reporting of survey results useful in preliminary planning and strategy development.

IVR Automated Telephone Surveys

A recent development that simplifies telephone surveys by using interactive voice response (IVR) technology to conduct interviews is called Completely Automated Telephone Surveys (CATS). Instead of using a human interviewer to read questions and key responses, CATS use the recorded voice of a professional interviewer to ask the questions. Respondents answer closed-ended questions by pushing numbers on their push-button phones. Open-ended responses are recorded on tape for verbatim transcription and coding.

There are two versions of CATS: outbound calling and inbound calling. Outbound calling requires an accurate list of respondents' telephone numbers because the computer dials a sample of phone numbers and a recording solicits participation from whomever answers. This method tends to get lower response rates because people find it easier to hang up on a machine. In the inbound calling version, respondents are given a phone number to call after they have been recruited, usually by mail.

Companies using CATS have found that they are getting quality data fast and at low cost. The system is flexible and can be adapted to particular research needs. It has been used for several different types of studies: customer satisfaction, service quality monitoring, product/warranty registration, in-home product test, and election day polls. Although CATS will never replace traditional methods, they offer researchers another choice.[24]

Direct Computer Interview

direct computer interviewing
Consumers are intercepted in a mall and interviewed by a computer that asks questions and accepts responses.

Direct computer interviewing differs from the type of computerized interviewing discussed previously in that instead of seating the interviewer at a terminal or personal computer, the respondent is seated in this position. This approach is currently being used in the mall environment by a number of firms. Consumers are intercepted and qualified in the mall and then brought to a test facility in the mall. They are seated at a personal computer, given some basic instruction on what to do, and the sequence to start the interview is entered by the administrator. The interview then proceeds in much the same way as the on-line telephone interview described earlier. The difference is that answers are entered by the respondent rather than by the interviewer.

Research conducted by the authors indicate that most adults have no trouble with the direct computer interview.[26] To respond, they simply enter the letter or number next to their choice. Most find the process interesting. In a study of computer interviewing conducted by the authors, 100 interviews were conducted face-to-face by interviewers and 100 interviews were administered by computer. The data produced by the two survey approaches were virtually identical. Respondents were equally likely to provide sensitive information whether interviewed in person or by computer. However, those interviewed by computer had a somewhat higher rate of nonresponse to individual questions. The level of validity (the degree to which a measurement accurately represents or measures

Marketing Research in Practice

How to find out what kids are thinking? This was the problem facing Karen Flischel, Nickelodeon's vice-president of research, in 1991. The programmers and marketers at the cable television network for kids wanted information from their young viewers that traditionally had been gathered via time-consuming focus groups and one-on-one interviews. It was the advent of E-mail that gave Flischel the idea to put kids on-line.

Nickelodeon put 70 viewers on-line via CompuServe. The kids use personal computers and modems to talk with Nickelodeon and with one another about a variety of topics. They can post notes on the computer bulletin board, and three times a week they log on for scheduled meetings. During these meetings, network researchers lead discussion on various topics. Specific network programs are discussed about a third of the time.

The kids who participate are, of course, CompuServe users. They range in age from eight to 12 and represent households with incomes ranging from $30,000 to $100,000. Half are minorities. The estimated annual maintenance for the system is $80,000 to $100,000, a fraction of what traditional research methods would cost.

Nickelodeon now gets more detailed data faster and cheaper than it could through traditional research methods. The kids provide instant feedback on programs. Other data come from responses to survey questions.

There are some who view this approach with skepticism and point out that it may be biased in favor of garrulous kids. Flischel points out that this system is a qualitative tool, and, as with any other qualitative research, the results cannot be projected to the national level.[25] ■

what it purports to measure), to the degree that it could be ascertained, was essentially the same for the two data collection approaches.

Because we are substituting machines (computers), which are becoming less expensive, for labor (interviewers), which is becoming more expensive, it is likely that in the future computers will be more widely used to collect survey data. Hardware and software developments continue to make this form of interviewing more feasible.

Self-administered Interview

The self-administered and mail survey methods discussed in this section have one thing in common. They differ from the other survey methods discussed in that no interviewer—human or computer—is involved.

The major disadvantage of the **self-administered questionnaire** approach is that no one is present to explain things to the respondent and clarify responses to open-ended questions. For example, if we ask people why they do not buy a particular brand of soft drink via an open-ended question, a typical answer would be something like "because I don't like it." From a managerial perspective this

self-administered questionnaire
A questionnaire filled out by the respondent with no interviewer.

Touch screen kiosks are being used to collect data in all types of environments.

answer is totally useless. It provides no information that can be used by management to alter the marketing mix and thereby make the product more attractive. If the survey were being conducted by an interviewer, she would be trained to "probe" for a response. This would mean that after receiving and recording the useless response, the interviewer would ask the respondent what it was he did not like about the product. The person being interviewed might then indicate a dislike for the taste. The interviewer would then ask what it was about the taste that the person did not like. Here we might finally get something useful with the respondent indicating that the product in question was, for example, too sweet. If many people give a similar response, management might elect to reduce the sweetness of the drink. The point is that without probing, you would have only the useless first response.

Some have argued that the absence of an interviewer is an advantage in that it eliminates one source of bias. There is no interviewer whose appearance, dress, manner of speaking, failure to follow instructions, and so on may influence answers to questions given by the respondent.

Self-administered interviews are often used in mall or other central locations where the researcher has access to a captive audience. Airlines, for example, often have programs in which questionnaires are administered in flight. Passengers are asked to rate various aspects of the airline's services. The results are used to track passenger perceptions of service over time. Many hotels, restaurants, and other service businesses provide brief questionnaires to patrons to find out how they feel about the quality of service provided (see Figure 7.2).

A recent development in the area of direct computer interviewing is kiosk-based computer interviewing. Kiosks are multimedia, touch-screen computers contained in freestanding cabinets. These computers can be programmed to administer complex surveys, show full-color scanned images (products, store layouts), play stereo sound clips, and show videos.

The kiosks have been used successfully at trade shows and conventions and are now being tried in retail environments where they have many applications. From a research standpoint, kiosk-based interviewing can be used in place of exit interviews to capture data on recent experiences. This form of interviewing tends to be less expensive. Kiosks have some definite advantages: People tend to give more honest answers than they would to a human interviewer, and internal control is higher because the survey is preprogrammed.[27]

Mail Surveys

ad hoc mail surveys

Questionnaires sent to selected names and addresses with no prior contact by the researcher.

mail panels

Participants are precontacted and screened, then periodically sent questionnaires.

There are two general types of mail surveys used in marketing research: ad hoc, or one-shot, mail surveys, and mail panels. In the case of **ad hoc,** or one-project, **mail surveys,** the researcher selects a sample of names and addresses from an appropriate source and mails a questionnaire to the people selected. Ordinarily there is no prior contact, and the sample is used only for the single project. However, the same questionnaire may be sent to nonrespondents several times to increase the overall response rate. In contrast, **mail panels** operate in the following manner:

1. A sample of people is precontacted by letter. In this initial contact the purpose of their participation in the panel is explained. People are usually offered a gratuity for participating in the panel for a period of time.

FIGURE 7.2

Self-administered Questionnaire

SOURCE: Courtesy of Accent Marketing & Research, Ltd., London.

Customer Survey

0 1 2 3 4 5 6 7 8 R
+ ☐☐☐☐☐☐☐☐☐☐

Please complete this questionnaire by ticking the appropriate boxes or by writing in your answer in the space provided. A separate questionnaire should be completed by EACH member of your travelling party aged 14 and over.

Veuillez compléter le questionnaire suivant en cochant les cases appropriées ou en écrivant votre réponse dans l'espace prévu. Un questionnaire séparé devrait être complété par CHAQUE membre de votre groupe de voyage âgé de 14 ans et au-delà.

Bitte füllen Sie den nachfolgenden Fragebogen durch Ankreuzen der entsprechendenb Kästchen bzw. schriftlich an den vorgesehenen Stellen aus. JEDES Mitglied Ihrer Reisegruppe über 14 Jahren sollte einen separaten Fragebogen ausfüllen.

Q1 Are you sitting in Club (1st) class or Express (2nd) class on this train?
Etes vous assis en classe Club (1ère) ou Express (2ème) dans ce train?
Sitzen Sie in der Club-Klasse (1. Kl) oder in der Express-Klasse (2. Kl) dieses Zuges?
Club (1st) ☐
Express (2nd) ☐

Q2 Are you flying or have you flown today?
Est-ce vous partez en voyage ou avez-vous voyagé par avion aujourd'hui?
Fliegen Sie heute oder Sie heute schon geflogen?
I will fly /*Je vais voyager par avion /Ich fliege* ☐
I have flown / *J'ai voyagé par avion /Ich bin geflogen* ☐
I am not flying (GO TO Q11) ☐
Je ne voyage pas par avion /Ich fliege nicht (ALLEZ A /WEITER ZU Q11)

Q3a Please write in the origin and destination of your flight and the scheduled arrival and departure times.
Veuillez inscrire l'origine et la destination de votre vol ainsi que les heures prévues de départ et d'arrivée.
Bitte geben Sie Ihren Abflug- und Zielort und die planmäßige Abflug- und Ankunftszeit an.
From /*De /Von* ....
To / *A /Zu* ....
Departure time / *Départ /Abflugzeit* ....
Arrival time /*Arrivée /Ankunftzeit* ....

Q3b Do you know your flight number?
Connaissez-vous le numéro de votre vol?
Wissen Sie Ihre Flugnummer?
If yes PLEASE WRITE IN ....

Q3c Which airline will/did you fly with?
Avec quelle compagnie aérienne volerez-vous/avez-vous volé?
Mit welcher Fluggesellschaft fliegen Sie/sind Sie geflogen?
....

OFFICE USE ONLY
0 1 2 3 4 5 6 7 8 9
☐☐☐☐☐☐☐☐☐☐ 1000
☐☐☐☐☐☐☐☐☐☐ 100
☐☐☐☐☐☐☐☐☐☐ 10
☐☐☐☐☐☐☐☐☐☐ 1

0 1 2 3 4 5 6 7 8 9
☐☐☐☐☐☐☐☐☐☐ 100
☐☐☐☐☐☐☐☐☐☐ 10
☐☐☐☐☐☐☐☐☐☐ 1

Q4 Are/were you on the outward or return leg of your air journey?
Outward ☐ Return ☐
Single leg journey ☐

Q5a Is/was this flight a direct one or will/did you change planes en route?
Direct flight (GO TO Q6) ☐
Will/did change planes en route ☐

Q5b Please write in your ultimate origin and ultimate destination airports of this trip.
Origin ☐ Destination ☐

Q6 What flight ticket type do/did you have?
Economy Full Fare ☐ First Class ☐
Stand-by/Apex ☐ Business/Club ☐
Staff-Discount ☐ Don't know ☐
Other discount ☐ Other ☐

Q7 What is the UK origin/destination of your journey today?
Central London ☐ Outer London (North) ☐
Outer London (South) ☐ Other South East ☐
East Anglia ☐ South West ☐
Midlands ☐ Northern England ☐
Scotland ☐ Wales ☐
N.Ireland ☐ Other ☐
Don't know ☐

Q8 What is your usual country of residence?
Mainland UK ☐ Northern Ireland/Eire ☐
Channel Islands ☐ Other ☐

Q9 How many **adults** are in your party (including yourself)?
One adult ☐ Two adults ☐
Three adults ☐ More than three adults ☐

PLEASE TURN OVER

continues

2. As part of the initial contact, consumers are asked to fill out a background data questionnaire on number of family members, ages, education, income, types of pets, types of vehicles and ages, types of appliances, and so forth.
3. After the initial contact, panel participants are sent questionnaires from time to time. The background data collected on initial contact enable researchers to send questionnaires only to appropriate households. For example, a survey regarding dog food usage and preferences would be sent only to dog owners.

A mail panel is a type of longitudinal study. A **longitudinal study** is one that questions the same respondents at different points in time.

longitudinal study
The same respondents are resampled over time.

FIGURE 7.2
Self-administered Questionnaire—*Continued*

Q10 How many **children** (aged 2-14) are in your party?
None ☐
One child ☐ Two children ☐
Three children ☐ More than three ☐

Q11 What is/was the nature of your journey today?
Flying on business ☐
Flying for a conference/trade fair/exhibition ☐
Flying for a holiday (package) ☐
Flying for a holiday (arranged independently) ☐
Flying to visit friends/relatives ☐
Flying to/from work ☐
Flying for other purposes ☐

Meeting friends/relatives at the airport ☐
Business at the airport ☐
Travel to/from work at the airport ☐
Travel to/from work in London ☐
Other reason, but not flying ☐

Q12 How many times in the last 12 months have you travelled by air? (PLEASE INCLUDE ALL YOUR FLIGHTS TO/FROM ANY AIRPORT)
None ☐ Once only ☐
2-3 times ☐ 4-5 times ☐
6-10 times ☐ 11-40 times ☐
41-50 times ☐ More than 50 times ☐

Q13 Where did you hear about Gatwick Express?
In Britain ☐ Outside Britain ☐

Q14 How did you **first** hear about the Gatwick Express? (TICK ONE BOX ONLY)
Advert in newspaper/magazine ☐
Poster/Leaflet ☐
Article in newspaper/magazine ☐
British Rail ☐
Word of mouth ☐
Signs at Gatwick Airport ☐
Signs at Victoria Station ☐
Travel guide ☐
Travel Agency information ☐
Airline leaflet or Airline Offices ☐
In-flight magazine ☐
In-flight announcement or flight staff ☐
Other ☐

Q15 Did you consider an alternative way of travelling between London and Gatwick Airport?
Yes ☐ No (GOTO Q17) ☐

Q16 Which alternative(s) did you consider?
(YOU MAY TICK MORE THAN ONE BOX)
Taxi ☐ Car ☐
Coach ☐ South Central Trains ☐
Thameslink Trains ☐ Other ☐

Q17 What was the **main** reason you chose to travel **by rail** to/from Gatwick for your journey today?
(TICK ONE BOX ONLY)
Speed ☐ Convenience ☐
Comfort ☐ Reliability ☐
Cost ☐ Other ☐

Q18 Why did you choose to travel **on the Gatwick Express** rather than any other train service between London and Gatwick Airport?
(YOU MAY TICK MORE THAN ONE BOX)
Speed ☐ Convenience ☐
Comfort ☐ Reliability ☐
Frequency ☐ Cost ☐
Always a train ready to join ☐
Didn't know about other train service ☐
Other ☐

Q19 What is your age?
Under 14 ☐ 14-17 ☐
18-24 ☐ 25-34 ☐
35-44 ☐ 45-54 ☐
55-64 ☐ 65 or over ☐

Q20 Are you male or female?
Male ☐ Female ☐

Q21 Do you have any other comments to make about the Gatwick Express service?

THANK YOU FOR YOUR COOPERATION, PLEASE HAND THIS QUESTIONNAIRE TO THE INTERVIEWER WHEN THEY RETURN OR LEAVE IT ON YOUR SEAT WHEN YOU LEAVE THE TRAIN.
MERCI DE VOTRE COOPERATION, VEUILLEZ REMETTRE CE QUESTIONNAIRE A L'ENQUETEUR A SON RETOUR OU LE LAISSER SUR VOTRE SIEGE AVANT DE SORTIR DU TRAIN.
WIR DANKEN IHNEN FÜR IHRE FREUNDLICHE HILFE. BITTE HÄNDIGEN SIE DIESEN FRAGEBOGEN AN DEN INTERVIEWER ZURÜCK, WENN DIESE/R ZU IHREM ABTEIL ZURÜCKKEHRT ODER LASSEN SIE IHN AUF DEM SITZ LIEGEN, WENN SIE SIE DEN ZUG VERLASSEN.

On first consideration, mail appears to be an attractive way to collect survey data. There are no interviewers to recruit, train, monitor, and pay. The entire study can be sent out and administered from a single location. Hard-to-reach respondents can be readily surveyed. Mail surveys appear to be convenient, efficient, and inexpensive.

Mail surveys of both types have the problems associated with not having an interviewer present, which were discussed in the section on self-administered questionnaires. No one is there to assist the respondent. In particular, no one is there to probe responses to open-ended questions, a real constraint on the types of information that can be sought and the interviewing techniques that can be employed. As a general rule, the length of the interview and consequently the quantity of information is more limited in the case of the mail survey than with survey methods involving interviewers.

TABLE 7.8 Tactics Employed to Increase Mail Survey Response Rates

Advance postcard or telephone call alerting respondent of survey
Follow-up postcard or phone call
Monetary incentives (nickel, dime, quarter, half-dollar)
Premiums (pencil, pen, keychain, etc.)
Postage stamps rather than metered envelopes
Self-addressed, stamped return envelope
Personalized address and well-written cover letter
Promise of contributions to favorite charity
Entry into drawings for prizes
Emotional appeals
Affiliation with universities or research institutions
Personally signed cover letter
Multiple mailings of the questionnaire
Bids for sympathy
Reminder that respondent participated in previous studies.

The ad hoc mail survey also suffers from the problem of a high rate of nonresponse and the attendant systematic error. Nonresponse in mail surveys is not a problem as long as everyone has an equal probability of not responding. However, numerous studies have shown that certain types of people—people with more education, higher-level occupations, women, those less interested in the topic, students, and others—have a greater probability of not responding.[28] Other types of people—generally the opposite of those just named—have a greater probability of responding. Response rates in ad hoc mail surveys may run anywhere from less than 10 percent to nearly 100 percent depending on length of questionnaire, content, group surveyed, incentives employed, and other factors.[29] Those who operate mail panels claim response rates as high as 70 percent.

To deal with the problem of low-response rates to mail surveys, many strategies designed to enhance response rate have been developed. Some of the more common ones are summarized in Table 7.8. The question always must be, "Is the cost of the particular strategy worth the increased response rate generated?" Unfortunately, there is no clear answer to this question that can be applied to all procedures in all situations.

Even with its shortcomings, mail remains a popular survey data collection technique in commercial marketing research. In fact, in 1992 more people participated in mail surveys than any other type of survey research (see Table 7.6).

Factors Determining Choice of Particular Survey Methods

A number of factors or considerations may affect the choice of a survey method in a given situation. The researcher should choose the survey method that will provide data of the desired types, quality, and quantity at the lowest cost. The major considerations in the selection of a survey method are summarized in Table 7.9 and discussed here.

TABLE 7.9 Factors That Determine the Selection of a Particular Survey Method

FACTOR	COMMENT
Sampling Precision	How accurate do the study results need to be? If the need for accuracy is not great, less rigorous and less expensive sampling procedures may be appropriate.
Budget Available	How much money is available for the interviewing portion of the study?
Need to Expose Respondent to Various Stimuli	Taste tests, product concept and prototype tests, ad tests, and the like require face-to-face contact, etc.
Quality of Data Required	How accurate do the results of the study need to be?
Length of Questionnaire	Long questionnaires are difficult to do by mail, over the phone, in a mall, etc.
Necessity of Having Respondent Perform Certain Specialized Tasks	Card sorts, certain visual scaling methods, and the like require face-to-face contact.
Incidence Rate	Are you looking for people who make up 1 percent of the total population or 50 percent of the population? If you are looking for a needle in a haystack, you need an inexpensive way to find it.
Degree of Structure of Questionnaire	Highly unstructured questionnaires may require data collection by the door-to-door approach.
Time Available to Complete Survey	Might not be able to use mail because you do not have time to wait for response.

Sampling Precision Required

The required level of sampling precision is an important factor in determining which survey method is appropriate in a given situation. Some projects by their very nature require a high level of sampling accuracy, whereas in others this may not be the overriding consideration. If sampling accuracy were the only criterion, the appropriate data collection technique probably would be central location telephone interviewing. The appropriate survey method for a project not requiring a high level of sampling accuracy might be the mail approach.

The trade-off between these two methods in regard to sampling precision is one of cost versus accuracy. The central location telephone survey method employing a random digit dialing sampling procedure will likely produce a better sample than the mail survey method. However, the mail survey will most likely cost less.

Mall surveys, as noted earlier, often produce poor samples. Other methods, such as door-to-door interviewing, have the potential to produce good samples if the interviewing process is carefully monitored and controlled.

Budget Available

The commercial marketing researcher frequently encounters situations in which the budget available for a study has a strong influence on the survey method used. Actually, budget usually is not the only factor affecting the choice of a survey method, but rather budget in combination with other considerations. For example, assume that for a particular study the budgetary constraint for interviewing is $10,000 and the sample size required for the necessary accuracy is 1,000. If we estimate that administering the questionnaire on a door-to-door basis will be $27.50 per interview and the cost of administering it via central location telephone will be $9.50 per interview, then the choice is fairly clear. This, of course, assumes that nothing about the survey absolutely requires face-to-face contact.

The Need to Expose the Respondent to Various Stimuli

In many studies, the marketing researcher needs to get respondent reactions to various marketing stimuli—product concepts, product components, and advertisements. In most cases, the need to get respondent reactions to stimuli implies personal contact between interviewer and respondent.

Non-face-to-face interviewing methods are generally out of the question for studies of this type. There are exceptions to this general rule that highlight the creativity of some researchers. Belden and Associates of Dallas developed a procedure built around sending respondents an envelope inside an envelope. The outer envelope contains an explanation of the study and a request that the inner envelope not be opened until the respondent is called on the phone by an interviewer. Researchers want to control respondent access to stimuli so that they can be sure of getting top-of-mind responses and be sure that all respondents have spent an equal amount of time examining materials. People who received envelopes are called on the telephone and told to open the inner envelope. They are then interviewed and their reactions to the stimuli (e.g., product concepts, ads, etc.) are sought.

The options are more limited in regard to taste tests, TV ad tests, and other similar types of tests. Taste tests typically require food preparation. This preparation must be done under controlled conditions so that the researcher can be certain that each person interviewed is responding to the same stimulus. The only viable survey alternative for tests of this type is the mall intercept approach or some variant. Variants include recruiting people to come to properly equipped central locations such as church community centers to sample products and be interviewed. For similar reasons, much TV ad testing is done via mall intercept. TV ad testing depends on use of videotaped prototypes of commercials. The equipment needed to show these tapes is expensive and not readily portable. Interviewing, therefore, must be conducted at malls and other central locations where the equipment can be set up.

Quality of Data Required

The quality of data required is an important determinant of which survey method to use. Data quality refers to the validity and reliability of the resulting data. These two concepts are discussed in greater detail in Chapter 10. However, validity is normally considered to refer to the degree to which a measure reflects only the characteristic of interest. In other words, a valid measure provides an accurate reading of the thing the researcher is trying to measure. Reliability refers to the consistency with which a measure produces the same results with the same or comparable populations.

Many factors other than the interviewing method affect data quality. Sampling methods used, questionnaire design, specific scaling methods employed, and interviewer training are a few of these factors. However, the various interviewing methods each have certain inherent strengths and weaknesses in regard to producing quality data. These strengths and weaknesses are summarized in Table 7.10.

The point is that the issue of data quality may override other considerations such as cost. For example, the researcher might estimate that it would be cheaper to conduct a long questionnaire with many open-ended questions via mall intercept. However, the data obtained by conducting the study in this manner might be so biased because of respondent fatigue, distraction, carelessness, and so on as to be worthless at best and misleading at worst. From a quality of information perspective, the study should have been conducted door-to-door.

Length of Questionnaire

As noted earlier, the length of the questionnaire—the amount of time that it takes the average respondent to complete the survey—is an important determinant of the appropriate survey method to use. If the questionnaire for a particular study takes an hour to complete, the choices of survey method are extremely limited. Telephone, mall intercept, and just about all other types of surveys except door-to-door interviews will not work. People shopping at a mall ordinar-

TABLE 7.10 Strengths and Weaknesses of Various Data Collection Techniques in Terms of Quality of Data Produced

METHOD	STRENGTH	WEAKNESS
Door-to-Door Executive	Respondent is at ease and secure in home; face-to-face contact; can observe respondent's home, etc.; interviewer can show, explain, probe, etc.	Cannot readily monitor interviewing process; may have distractions from other family members, telephone, etc.; greater chance for interviewer bias; sampling problems.
Mall Intercept	Interviewer can show, explain, probe like in door-to-door	May have many distractions inherent in mall environment; respondent may be in a hurry—not in proper frame of mind; more chance for interviewer bias; nonprobability sampling problems
Central Location Telephone	Can monitor the interviewing process readily; can have excellent sample; interviewers can explain and probe	Respondent may be distracted by things going on at the location; problems in long interviews and interviews with many open-ended questions
Self-administered	Elimination of interviewer and associated biases; respondent can complete the questionnaire when convenient; respondent also can look up certain information and work at own pace	No interviewer to show, explain, or probe; poor sample because of nonresponse; no control of who actually completes the questionnaire
Mail Questionnaire	Same as for self-administered	Same as for self-administered questionnaire; sample quality is better with mail panel

ily do not have an hour to spend being interviewed. Terminations increase and tempers flare when you try to keep respondents on the phone for an hour. Response rates plummet when we send people questionnaires through the mail that take an hour or more to complete. The trick is to match the survey technique to the length of the questionnaire.

Necessity of Having Respondent Perform Certain Specialized Tasks

Some surveys, require face-to-face interviewing because of the use of special measurement techniques or the need for specialized forms of information as input to quantitative techniques. They require face-to-face interviewing because the tasks are so complex that someone must be available to explain the task and to ascertain whether the respondent understands what is required.

Incidence Rate

Incidence rate is a term used to refer to the percentage of persons or households out of the general population that fit the qualifications of people to be interviewed in a particular study. For example, assume you are doing a taste test for a new Stovetop Stuffing mix. It has been decided that only those who have purchased a Stovetop Stuffing mix in the past 30 days should be interviewed. It is estimated that out of the general population, only 5 percent of all adults fall into this category. The incidence rate for this study is 5 percent. It is not unusual to

incidence rate
The percentage of people or households in the general population that fit the qualifications to be sampled.

The incidence rate for adult travel in the U.S. is quite high. A market researcher should not have trouble locating qualified respondents for a survey about traveling in the U.S. SOURCE: Ted Thai/Sygma.

Art collecting has a very low incidence rate. Door-to-door interviewing to locate art collectors for a survey would yield minimal results. A mail panel would be a lower cost alternative. SOURCE: D. Hudson/Sygma.

seek people with a 5 percent or lower incidence rate in marketing research. Actual survey incidence rates for a variety of factors are shown in Table 7.11.

Search costs, which are a function of the time spent trying to locate qualified respondents, frequently exceed interviewing costs (time spent actually interviewing). In those situations in which the researcher expects incidence rates to be low and search costs high, it is important that an interviewing method or combination of methods be employed that will provide the desired survey results at a reasonable cost.

Doing a low-incidence rate study on a door-to-door basis would, of course, be very expensive. This approach should be taken only if there is some compelling reason for using this approach, a long depth interview for example. The lowest-cost survey alternative for the low-incidence study is probably the mail panel. This assumes that the mail panel approach meets the other data collection requirements of the study. This is particularly true if the panel can be prescreened. As noted earlier, panel members are asked a number of questions, usu-

TABLE 7.11 Survey Research Incidence Rates

Financial	
Am Express Card	10.2% Adults
Annuities	3.1% Adults
Art or Antique Collecting	1.4% Adults
Discover Card	12.5% Adults
Auto and Boat	
Auto Insurance	79.7% Households
Motorcycles	7.3% Households
Powerboat	2.0% Households
Recreational Vehicles	1.9% Households
Hobbies and Interests	
Art or Antique Collecting	1.4% Adults
Bible or Devotional Reading	9.2% Adults
Casino Gambling	11.0% Adults
Diet or Keeping Thin	31.6% Adults
Dining out Frequently	53.4% Adults
Gardening	28.3% Adults
Gourmet Cooking	16.5% Adults
Needlecraft	17.8% Women
Performing Arts	12.7% Households
Pets—Cats	23.0% Homemakers
Pets—Dogs	30.0% Homemakers
Photography	12.5% Adults
Sewing	30.1% Women
Stamp or Coin Collecting	1.4% Adults
Wines	22.6% Adults
Home Improvement	
Deck	3.9% Households
Kitchen	4.1% Households
Landscaping	0.3% Households
Roof	3.6% Households
Travel and Tourism	
Current Passport	14.0% Adults
Frequent Flyer Club Member	6.8% Adults
Travel in the U.S.	56.1% Adults
Vacation—Air Travel	16.8% Adults
Vacation—Automobile	41.7% Adults
Vacation—Foreign Vacation	18.7% Adults
Sports	
Bicycling	15.3% Adults
Boat Owners	9.0% Households
Camping or Hiking	18.4% Adults
Fishing	21.3% Adults
Flying	0.5% Adults
Golfing	9.6% Adults
Hunting or Shooting	10.0% Adults
Running or Jogging	6.4% Adults
Snow skiing	5.7% Adults
Tennis	5.4% Adults
Walking for Health	28.4% Adults
Electronics	
Compact Disc Player	11.0% Households
Home Video Games	10.2% Adults
Home or Personal Computer	16.3% Households
Microwave Oven	55.5% Households
Smoke Detector	45.5% Households
VCR	55.4% Households
Video Camera	8.2% Households
Video Games	10.2% Adults

SOURCE: *The Frame*, published by Survey Sampling, Inc., July 1991.

Marketing Research in Practice

Survey research methods are becoming more creative, making them more adaptable to companies' specific needs. After tracking fashion trends in the youth market for a period of time, the Youthwear Division of Levi Strauss & Co. found that the interview was becoming more comprehensive and time-consuming. The problem was how to administer a 30- to 45-minute interview and still maintain the accuracy and integrity of the data as well as the attention and involvement of the boys who were ages nine to 14. Additionally, the company wanted to do the interviews in mall facilities across the country.

In conjunction with Touchstone Research, Brandon, Connecticut, and Analytical Computer Software (ACS), Levi Strauss designed a system involving an interviewer and a child. The interview format had a segment in which an interviewer entered data and a segment in which the children interacted with the computer. The system also included a videotape with explanations and instructions. Colors, sounds, and practice questions were included in the system to make it "kid friendly." There were also brief entertainment sections to give the boys a break during the questioning.

The computer-assisted interview was successful for several reasons. The boys seemed to be more comfortable interacting with the computer and were, therefore, more open and honest about their feelings. When interviews are done in several different markets, there is a risk that the differences in the quality of interviewing at the different locations will affect the accuracy of the data. The computer-assisted system provided continuity across markets.

The system simplified the interviewing process for the interviewers as well. A handbook was developed, which made the system relatively fail-safe for the interviewers. The software greatly reduced the number of tasks and the amount of paperwork interviewers had to handle.

This new technology is certainly not appropriate for all research situations, but it does have many applications. In particular, it seems to have many benefits in children's research, especially in tracking situations, concept testing, and similar situations in which complex information must be presented to the respondent and the measurements will be repeated.[30] ■

ally including some on product usage, when the panel is set up. If panel members had been asked if anyone in their household participated in downhill or Alpine snow skiing, the mail panel operator could pull out only those households with one or more skiers for a survey of Alpine skiers at very low cost.

Telephone interviewing offers the next most efficient device to screen for the low-incidence consumer. Sometimes two or more survey methods may be combined to deal more efficiently with the problem of locating low-incidence consumers. For example, we might screen for people who meet our qualifications over the telephone and then send someone to interview them in person. This approach can dramatically reduce costs in comparison to doing the study totally on a door-to-door basis.

Degree of Structure of the Questionnaire

In addition to length of questionnaire, degree of structure of the questionnaire may be a factor in determining which survey method is most appropriate for a given study. By structure we mean the extent to which the questionnaire follows a set sequence or order, follows a set wording of questions, and relies primarily on closed-ended (multiple-choice) questions. A questionnaire that does all these things would be a "structured" questionnaire. One that deviates from these set patterns would be considered "unstructured." A questionnaire with little structure is likely to require a face-to-face interview. Very brief, highly structured questionnaires do not ordinarily require face-to-face contact between interviewer and respondent. For studies of this type, mail, telephone, and self-administered questionnaires become viable options.

The Marketing Research Interviewer

No discussion of survey research in marketing can be considered complete without taking a look at the person who actually does the interviewing. As noted in Chapter 3, most marketing research interviewing is done under the direct supervision of field service firms. The actual interviewing is conducted, to a large extent, by individuals who work on a part-time basis for relatively low wages. The brand new, totally inexperienced interviewer works at a rate somewhere around minimum wage plus 20 percent. It is unusual to find even the most experienced interviewers earning more than minimum wage plus 50 percent. The pay is not good, and fringe benefits are usually nonexistent—no retirement benefits, no insurance, no extras.

Prospective interviewers are ordinarily sent on assignment with only a minimum of training. There is a high failure rate among first-time interviewers. It is strictly a "survival of the fittest" system. Somehow, this system produces a core of competent and dedicated interviewers. Questionnaires should be designed with the presumption that the capabilities of those who will administer them are limited. In general, the interviewer is treated as an automaton—ask questions exactly as written, record exactly what the respondent said, and so on. In general, questionnaires and interviewer instructions are set up with this principle in mind. Little or no discretion is left to the interviewer. The sample interviewer instructions and questionnaire shown in Chapter 12 illustrate these points.

Ordinarily, an interviewer's involvement with an interviewing assignment begins when he is asked to work on the particular job by a supervisor at a field service firm. If the interviewer accepts the assignment, he will be given a date and time for a briefing or training session on the job. At the briefing, the questionnaire for the study and all deadlines and requirements for the job will be discussed. Interviewers may be asked to bring in their first day's work (if interviewing is being conducted off-premises) to be checked to make sure there have been no misunderstandings and that everything is being done correctly. Ultimately, all interviews will be checked and a certain percentage, usually 10 percent to 20 percent, of the people interviewed by each interviewer will be recontacted to make certain they were actually interviewed before the completed questionnaires are sent to the client.

It would appear, given the above discussion, that interviewers do not play a major role in the marketing research process. However, interviewers are typically the main interface with consumers and are, therefore, a vital link to consumer cooperation. This is an area of concern now being addressed by the Marketing Research Association in conjunction with its Consumer Advocacy Council. They suggest several steps that should be used to develop and strengthen interviewers' consumer interaction skills: good training programs that include consumer rapport elements and a basic understanding of "cooperation turning points," frequent monitoring of interviewers' interaction skills to evaluate their impact on consumer cooperation, and feedback on monitoring results.

The importance of interviewers has been echoed by industry leaders. According to Howard Gershowitz, senior vice-president MKTG, "Companies that are succeeding right now realize that the interviewers are the key to their success."[31]

Survey Research in the International Market

The total marketing research expenditures for the world are estimated at $5.4 billion. Of the research, 40 percent is conducted in Western Europe and 39 percent in the United States. Japan accounts for only 9 percent of the research expenditures.[32] In Europe, most of the research is done in Germany, France, Italy, the United Kingdom, and Spain. Approximately 40 million interviews a year are carried out in all of Europe. Data collection methods vary substantially from country to country as shown in Table 7.12.

European Marketing Research

In terms of cost, European countries can be examined by quantitative and qualitative methods. In quantitative studies, the five most expensive countries are Germany, Switzerland, Italy, France, and Norway; Greece is the cheapest. For qualitative research, Norway is the most expensive, followed by France, Italy, Germany, and the Netherlands. About 25,000 people are employed professionally in European market research, with well over 100,000 interviewers.

Asian Marketing Research

In Asia, many countries have the capability of conducting some kinds of Western-style marketing research. Japan, Hong Kong, Singapore, and the Philippines have fairly advanced research industries. Japan has its own unique methodology in gathering secondary information. On the basis of highly developed networks of industry contacts, some Japanese research companies use "groupthink" technique studies to develop accurate market share estimates and competitive assessment information.

Although Japanese managers attach great importance to market information, they spend little on research relative to the United States and the United Kingdom. Japanese companies view the research business as just one aspect of a broad program of customer and retail intelligence. The marketing management within client companies is the main resource.

TABLE 7.12 European Data Collection Methods (Percent of Use)

	FRANCE	THE NETHERLANDS	SWEDEN	SWITZERLAND	UNITED KINGDOM
Mail	4	33	23	8	9
Telephone	15	18	44	21	16
Central location/streets	52	37	—	—	—
Home/work	—	—	8	44	54
Groups	13	—	5	6	11
Depth interviews	12	12	2	8	—
Secondary	4	—	4	8	—
Other	0	0	14	5	10

Japanese companies rarely base marketing decisions solely on primary data from consumer surveys. Instead they use the survey findings in conjunction with hard data based on detailed shipment information and audits of channels of distribution.

Until recently, the face-to-face personal interview was the dominate form of data collection in Japan. However, other methods are beginning to increase in significance while the use of face-to-face interviewing has dropped by at least a third. The use of mail surveys is on the increase, but there is low growth in telephone interviewing. Qualitative research is growing in importance.[33]

The governments in some Asian countries such as Taiwan and Japan release enough census data on individuals to make sample building easier and more accurate than it is in most Western countries. When a household moves in these countries, it is required to submit up-to-date information to a centralized government agency before any family member can use communal services like water, gas, electricity, and education.

Other countries in Asia such as China, South Korea, Indonesia, and India have research capabilities, but they are so underdeveloped as to require special supervision. Asia also has fewer marketing research firms that can act as data "translators," people who can transform computer tables and research results into specific marketing directions.

Marketing Research in the Independent Federation of States (Formerly USSR)

Opinion and market research in the Soviet Union dates back to the 1960s, during a brief thaw in the political and economic climate under Khrushchev.[35] For instance, large-scale youth surveys were conducted under the direction of Dr. Boris Grushin, then head of the Soviet Institute of Public Opinion at the *Komsomolskaya Pravda* newspaper. VNIIKS, All-Union Institute for Market Research, attached to the Ministry of Home Trade, also started doing research on issues of supply and demand around the same time. Much of VNIIKS's early work was "industrial research," in which it used a network of expert correspondents and informants throughout the Soviet Union.

With a few exceptions, most of the opinion surveys conducted before 1985 were designed to bolster the party line, not to determine truth. Usually, only pos-

Global Marketing Research

In a 1991 study, the Coca-Cola Co. compared marketing research prices across 13 Pacific Rim countries. The countries covered in the research were Australia, China (Shanghai only), Hong Kong, Indonesia, Japan, Malaysia, New Zealand, Pakistan, the Philippines, Singapore, South Korea, Sri Lanka, and Thailand. The results indicated that the Philippines, Japan, and China have the highest relative research prices and Sri Lanka and Singapore have the lowest. To develop comparisons, price quotations were obtained for 10 different research studies, all relating to soft drinks.

The average price for participating countries was first calculated for each study. Then each of these averages was set at an index of 100 to calculate the 10 separate price indices.

The study looked at two main categories of research: quantitative and qualitative. The relationship between the two differs widely by country. The most dramatic rank differences occur in the Philippines and Singapore.

Quantitative research in Singapore is expensive but qualitative research is average. Both Japan and Sri Lanka have comparatively stable index figures and rankings for both types of studies.

To develop an overall rating, the researchers calculated an index for each country using a simple arithmetic mean of available indices from the 10 for that country. Below are the overall ratings:

Japan	269
South Korea	137
Singapore	124
China	122
Hong Kong	117
Malaysia	104
Australia	90
Thailand	75
Indonesia	66
Philippines	65
New Zealand	61
Pakistan	42
Sri Lanka	21

The Coca-Cola Co. previously had conducted an identical study in 1990 in selected Latin American countries. In addition, the European Society for Opinion and Marketing Research (ESOMAR) had conducted a series of similar surveys in selected European countries. Average research prices in the three studies provided a basis for constructing overall price indices. These comparisons are based on the prices quoted for four projects found in all three studies.

Several conclusions can be drawn from the data:

- European marketing research is a third more expensive than Pacific Rim research and twice as expensive as Latin American research.
- Pacific Rim research is two-thirds more expensive than research in Latin America.

Research pricing indices are a useful tool for defining preliminary budgets when conducting multicountry research.[34] ■

itive and favorable findings were published. In addition, little concern was given to proper sampling procedures and interview techniques. Most of this early research was based on self-administered questionnaires distributed at respondents' places of work, which provided respondents little faith in the promise of anonymity.

Glasnost and the disintegration of the Russian state have proved to be a boon for the marketing research industry as the independent states struggle toward capitalism. Today, there are basically three types of research organizations in the former Soviet Union. The first type conducts marketing research projects almost exclusively. It includes groups that at one time or another were affiliated with government industry and trade agencies and new joint ventures with foreign partners, such as VNIIKS (affiliated with a Finnish research institute) and INFOMARKET (owned by the Russian Ministry of Metallurgy and a Dutch research company).

The second type has a more scholarly orientation, concentrating on public opinion research and social trends. Examples are the Institute of Sociology and the Institute of Applied Social Research, both of the Academy of Sciences. Universities such as Moscow State University and the University of Vilnius have also started centers of public opinion research.

The third type of research organization seeks to combine marketing and opinion research. Its clientele is diverse, ranging from independent news agencies to government and legislative branches, Western media, government agencies, research institutes, advertising agencies, and corporations. The Center for Public Opinion and Market Research and Vox Populi (VP), headed by Boris Grushin, are typical, and two of the best known, of this kind.

Taken together, currently available research services include individual-republic omnibuses, consumer panels, opinion leader panels, and ad hoc studies covering a wide range of social, economic, political, and marketing or business-related topics. Data collection techniques include face-to-face interviewing, surveys by mail, and even telephone interviewing among elites or opinion leaders.

Random sampling can be carried out using relatively accurate and comprehensive address lists. Largely because of the government's rigid control of society and the lack of population mobility, household rosters and voter registration lists are fairly up-to-date and comprehensive, covering about 95 percent of the population. Reputable survey organizations usually have no difficulty gaining access to these lists. As private housing and employment in the private sector become more commonplace, however, it may be increasingly difficult to update these lists, which, for now, provide an excellent source of sampling.

Much of the personal-interview research carried out to date has focused on key states; that is, Russia, the Ukraine, and the Baltic States—and these studies generally are considered to be more accurate and reliable than those purporting to cover the entire former Russian nation. Typically, field work is carefully controlled. For a new custom research study, supervisors from the various areas to be sampled assemble in Moscow for a briefing session, going over the questionnaire and sampling specifications in great detail. These supervisors, or "team leaders," are responsible for recruiting and training interviewers. The supervisors are often highly educated and usually have other professional jobs. For example, one study included a teacher of Russian literature, who could recite Pushkin forward and backward, and a professor of engineering from a local college. Regional offices validate 10 percent of all interviews. The level of participation in these surveys can make any Western researcher envious. Refusal rates are commonly less than 10 percent and the number of unsuccessful contacts and inaccessible locations (e.g., upscale apartment buildings) is also fairly low.

Conducting International Survey Research

Before conducting survey research, an international market researcher should first examine relevant secondary data. Secondary data have the same advantages and disadvantages in the international market as they do in the United States. They are relatively inexpensive and can usually be obtained more rapidly than primary data. National economic statistics and industry analyses published by the U.S. Department of Commerce are excellent sources of secondary information.

A number of countries gather census data much as in the United States. European countries such as Switzerland and Germany print a good deal of information on noncitizens. Canada collects data on religion. Both of these topics are ignored in U.S. censuses.

A marketing researcher cannot expect to find the same range of data topics from one country to the next, and this can complicate your life enormously. Consider income data, the lifeblood of most U.S. segmentation studies. Most nations do not include an income question in their censuses. Britain does not, Japan does not, nor do France, Spain, and Italy. Among the few countries that have asked about income are Canada, Australia, New Zealand, Mexico, Sweden, and Finland.

Willingness to Participate International marketing research uses the same tools, techniques, and theory as does domestic research. Yet it is done in vastly different environments. In some countries, a woman would never consider being interviewed by a man. A French-Canadian woman does not like to be questioned and is likely to be reticent; she prefers privacy for herself and her family. In some societies, a man would consider it beneath his dignity to discuss shaving habits or brand preference in personal clothing with anyone—and certainly not with a woman. In South Korea, for example, businesspeople are reluctant to answer any survey questions about their companies—it is considered disloyal to divulge any type of information to "outsiders." And most Japanese businesspeople are hesitant to take part in surveys during business hours—taking time away from your work for a survey is like "stealing" from your employer.[36] The growing resistance to surveys everywhere is a result of the misuse of interviewing by door-to-door salespeople claiming to be doing marketing research when, in fact, they are selling household items.

Although cultural differences may make survey research more difficult to conduct, it is possible. In some communities, it is necessary to enlist the aid of locally prominent people to open otherwise closed doors; in other situations, professional people and local students have been used as interviewers because of their knowledge of the market. As with most of the problems of collecting primary data, the difficulties are not insurmountable to a researcher aware of their existence.

Language and Comprehension

The most universal survey sampling problem in foreign countries is the language barrier.[37] Differences in idiom and the difficulty of exact translation create problems in eliciting the specific information desired and interpreting respondents' answers. Equivalent concepts may not exist in all languages. *Family*, for example, has different connotations in different countries. In the United States, it generally means only the parents and children. In Italy and many Latin countries, it could mean the parents, children, grandparents, uncles, aunts, cousins, and so forth. The meaning of names for family members can have different meanings depending on the context within which they are used. In the Indian culture, uncle and aunt are different for the maternal and paternal sides of the family. Also, in India, for example, 14 official languages are spoken in different parts of the country, and most government and business affairs are conducted in English. Similarly, in Switzerland, German is used in some areas and French in others. In the Republic of Congo, the official language is French, but only a small part of the population is fluent in French. Unfortunately, translating a questionnaire from one language to another is far from easy. Translating "out of sight, out of mind" from English to Danish became "invisible things are insane."

Resolving the Problems

There are no foolproof methods to take care of all the problems just discussed. The following suggestions, however, may help to eliminate some of the problems.[38]

International marketing research should be undertaken in conjunction with a reputable local firm. Such a firm may be a foreign office of a U.S. advertising firm like J. Walter Thompson, a U.S. accounting firm like Price Waterhouse, or a locally owned firm belonging to a third country like a Japanese advertising agency in Italy. The resources of the cooperating firm will be invaluable; for example, its knowledge of local customs, including things like the feasibility of interviewing housewives while husbands are at work; its familiarity with local environment, including modes of transportation available for personal interviews in smaller towns; and its contact in different parts of the country as sources for drawing a sample.

From the beginning, a person who has a grasp of both sound marketing research procedures and the local culture should be involved in all phases of the research design. Such a person can recommend the number of languages in which the questionnaire should be printed and the cultural traits, habits, customs, and rituals to keep in mind in different phases of the research.

The questionnaire may first be written in English, and then a native fluent in English can translate it into the local language(s). A third person should retranslate it into English. This retranslated version can then be compared with the original English version. The three people involved should work together to eliminate differences in the three versions of the questionnaire by changing phrases, idioms, and words. Ultimately, the questionnaire in the local language should accurately reflect the questions in the original English questionnaire.

Despite the difficulties often faced in conducting international research, some information is always better than none. Sunbeam, for example, failed to do research and only after lack of sales of its toaster in Italy found that although most

Europeans eat toast, Italians do not. Sunbeam also was first in the Italian market with an electric shaver for women. Again no research was done (after all, it was a high-quality product and sold well in the United States). The shaver bombed. Sunbeam later learned that Italian men like women with hair on their legs.

Summary

Surveys are popular for several reasons. First is the need by managers to know why people do or do not do something. Second, managers need to know how decisions are made. Third, managers need to know what kind of person, from a demographic or lifestyle perspective, is making the decision to buy or not buy a product.

There are two major categories of errors in survey research: random sampling error and systematic error or bias. Systematic error can be further broken down into measurement error and sample design error. Sample design error is composed of selection, population specification, and frame error. Frame error results from the use of an incomplete or inaccurate sampling frame. Population specification error results from an incorrect definition of the universe or population from which the sample is to be selected. Selection error results from using incomplete or improper sampling procedures or when appropriate selection procedures are not properly followed.

The second major category of systematic error is measurement error. Measurement error occurs when there is a discrepancy between the information being sought (the true value) and the information obtained by the measurement process. Measurement error can be created by a number of factors, including surrogate information error, interviewer error, measurement instrument bias, processing error, nonresponse bias, or response bias. Surrogate information error results from a discrepancy between the information actually required to solve a problem and the information sought by the researcher. Interviewer error occurs because of interactions between the interviewer and the respondent. Measurement instrument bias is caused by problems within the questionnaire itself. Processing error results from mistakes in the transfer of information from survey documents to the computer. Nonresponse bias occurs when a particular individual in a sample cannot be reached or refuses to participate in the survey. Response bias means that interviewees answer questions in a particular way. It may be deliberate falsification or unconscious misrepresentation.

There are several popular types of surveys. Door-to-door interviewing is the traditional method of interviewing individuals in their homes or apartments. Mall intercept interviewing contacts shoppers in public areas of shopping malls, either interviewing them in the mall or asking them to come to a permanent interviewing facility within the mall. Executive interviewing is the industrial equivalent of door-to-door interviewing; it involves interviewing professional people at their offices, typically concerning industrial products or services. Central location telephone interviewing is interviewing from a facility set up for the specific purpose of conducting telephone survey research. Computer-assisted telephone interviewing is associated with the central location interviewing process. Each interviewer is seated in front of a computer terminal or personal computer. The computer guides the interviewer and the interviewing process by having the questionnaire on the computer screen. The data are entered into the computer as the interview takes place. Direct computer interviewing takes place when the respondent sits at a computer terminal and responds to questions using a keyboard. This type of interviewing is limited to mall facilities. A self-administered interview is a survey questionnaire filled out by the respondent. The big disadvantage of this approach is that probes cannot be used to clarify responses. Mail surveys can be divided into ad hoc, or one-shot, surveys and mail panels. In ad hoc mail survey, questionnaires are mailed to potential respondents without prior contact. The sample is used only for the single survey project. In a mail panel, consumers are precontacted by letter and are offered an incentive for participating in the panel for a period of time. If they agree, they fill out a background data questionnaire. Then periodically panel participants are sent questionnaires.

The factors that determine which survey method will be used include sampling precision, budget availability, the need to expose respondents to various stimuli, quality of data required, length of questionnaire, the necessity of having the respondent perform certain specialized tasks, the incident rate sought, the degree of structure of the questionnaire, and the time available to complete the survey.

The key individual in survey research is the marketing research interviewer. For the most part, interviewing is conducted by individuals who work on a part-time basis for relatively low wages. The job not only is low-paying, but also is devoid of fringe benefits. Interviewers are often provided only a minimum of training. Also, because of the high failure rate, it is a survival of the fittest system. Yet, somehow this system tends to produce a core of competent and dedicated interviewers.

International survey research faces many of the same problems and opportunities as domestic research. In addition, international research faces cultural differences that may lower the participation rate and language and comprehension problems. In spite of these barriers, the cost of conducting international survey research is usually less than the benefits.

Key Terms

random error or random sampling error
systematic error
frame error
population specification error
selection error
measurement error
surrogate information error
interviewer error
measurement instrument bias
processing error
nonresponse bias
response bias
door-to-door interviewing
mall intercept interviewing
executive interviewing
central location telephone interviewing
computer-assisted telephone interviewing
direct computer interviewing
self-administered questionnaire
ad hoc mail surveys
mail panels
longitudinal study
incidence rate

Review and Discussion Questions

1. The owner of a hardware store in Eureka, California, is interested in determining demographic characteristics of people who shop at his store versus competing stores. He also wants to know what his image is relative to competing hardware stores. He would like to have the information within three weeks and is working on a limited budget. Which survey method would you recommend? Why?

2. Your supervisor has asked you to recommend which type of telephone interviewing your company should purchase from a survey research organization. Which would you recommend? Why?
3. The critical function within the survey research process is performed by the interviewer. Yet interviewers are typically paid minimum wage. If interviewers are so important, why is this true? What do you think should be done to raise the quality of survey research?
4. "A mall intercept interview is representative only of persons who shop in that particular mall. Therefore, only surveys that relate to shopping patterns of consumers within that mall should be conducted in a mall intercept interview." Discuss.
5. A colleague is arguing that the best way to conduct a study of attitudes toward city government in your community is through a mail survey because it is cheapest. How would you respond to your colleague? Assume that time is not a critical factor in your decision. Would this change your response? Why?
6. Discuss the various sources of sample design error and give examples of each.
7. Why is it important to consider measurement error in survey research? Why is this typically not discussed in professional market research reports?
8. What types of error might be associated with the following situations?
   a. Conducting a survey about attitudes toward city government using the telephone directory as a sample frame.
   b. Interviewing respondents only between 8:00 A.M. and 5:00 P.M. on features they would like to see in a new condominium development.
   c. Asking people if they have visited the public library in the past two months.
   d. Asking people how many tubes of toothpaste they used in the past year.
   e. Telling interviewers they can probe using any particular example they wish to make up.
9. Discuss some of the unique problems a researcher faces in conducting international survey research.

CASE 7.1

Your Personal Consultant, Inc.: A Consultant on a Disk

Like a genie in a bottle or a janitor in a drum, management support software captures a consultant on a floppy disk. By using a computer program to simulate a discussion with a human expert, a user can pick up negotiating tips, forecast a financial future, or devise a marketing strategy. These software productivity tools often are loosely grouped into two categories: decision support and expert systems. Decision support software addresses the individual situation with prepackaged responses culled from the experience of experts. Expert systems offer a blend of enlightened guidance and subjective judgment that allows you to arrive at your own answers. Your Personal Consultant, Inc. was organized in October 1995 as a $500,000 research and development limited partnership. The five founders kicked in $230,000 more, raised an additional $500,000 through a private placement, and netted $1.5 million in a public offering. Their first product, an expert system for picking a store location, went to market in January of the following year.

Gaining visibility in this market will not be easy. Major distributors are not interested in carrying a lot of additional software lines. Big advertising campaigns are beyond the means of this start-up operation. With approximately 100 companies already in the field, a shake out is bound to occur. At this point in time, Your Personal Consultant, Inc. could use a consultant of its own! It has no marketing plan per se.

1. What marketing problems are facing Your Personal Consultant, Inc., and what are its informational needs?
2. Can survey research be of benefit to the organization? If so, what survey methodology would you recommend?
3. What sources of survey error might be encountered in the type of survey methodology you recommended? Why?
4. What can be done to help minimize the possibility of this survey error?

CASE 7.2

J. C. Penney

J. C. Penney traditionally positioned itself as a mass merchandiser serving the needs of middle-class Americans. Its major competitors were other mass merchandisers such as Sears Roebuck. However, two decades ago, prompted in large part by demographic change as increasing numbers of women entered the workforce, J. C. Penney decided to change its positioning. Penney's mission statement no longer places it in competition with such mass merchandisers as Sears Roebuck; its new competitors are upscale department stores such as Macy's.

Because J. C Penney has been positioned as a mass merchandiser to middle America for many more decades than it has been positioned as an upscale department store, Penney's perception of its repositioning and new competitors may not mirror the consumers' perception of Penney. Possibly consumers do not yet totally perceive Penney as an upscale department store. A study therefore was conducted to determine Penney's progress toward its repositioning strategy. How do consumers view J. C. Penney? Do consumers perceive Penney as an upscale department store or does the traditional positioning still dominate?

A J. C. Penney store in Florin Mall, a major shopping mall in Sacramento, California, was selected for the study. Sears Roebuck and Mervyn's were selected to represent Penney's previous mass merchandiser positioning. Macy's of California and Weinstock's were selected to represent Penney's current repositioning as an upscale department store. The Sears Roebuck, Weinstock's, and Penney stores are all in the same mall; the other two stores, Mervyn's and Macy's, are located in the same geoeconomic area. Thus all five stores were equally accessible to the geographic customer base.

A visual display of women's clothing was selected to represent the position of the five stores selected for study, in large part because J. C. Penney has made a major effort to target professional working women. Pictures were taken of the five store's displays of women's clothing. Managers at the stores identified the displays they believed were most representative of their store. From the initial set of pictures, the researchers selected one display to represent each store.

On a Saturday, 165 female consumers participated in a survey taken at Florin Mall. To obtain a representative sample, the researchers were stationed at three mall entry locations, which coincidentally also were the locations of the Penney, Sears, and Weinstock's stores. Participants were asked to complete a matching task and a sorting task. The same pictures were used in both tasks.

In the matching task, participants were shown pictures of five displays of women's clothing, labeled *P*, *Q*, *R*, *S*, and *T*, and were asked to match the pictures with the list of stores on the survey form: Sears, Mervyn's, Macy's, Penney, and Weinstock's. In the sorting task, participants were given a stack of the five pictures of the displays and were instructed to sort them into piles according to their similarity. They were told that they were free to establish as many or as few piles as they wanted. After the matching and sorting tasks, each participant answered a brief questionnaire that provided store patronage patterns and demographic information.

RESULTS

The demographic characteristics of the sample are representative of J. C. Penney's target market, professional working women. Of the sample of women, 48 percent were between the ages of 22 and 35, 58 percent reported household income between $15,001 and $50,000, 56 percent were married, 68 percent were employed in the professions, and 61 percent were Caucasian.

Figure 7.3 shows the results of the sorting task. Customers perceived Penney's display as similar to those of the upscale department stores. Macy's of California and Weinstock's. They did not perceive Penney's display as similar to those of the mass merchandisers, Sears and Mervyn's.

Figure 7.4 shows the results of the matching task. Customers identified Penney's display as belonging to Macy's or Weinstock's. They did not identify Pen-

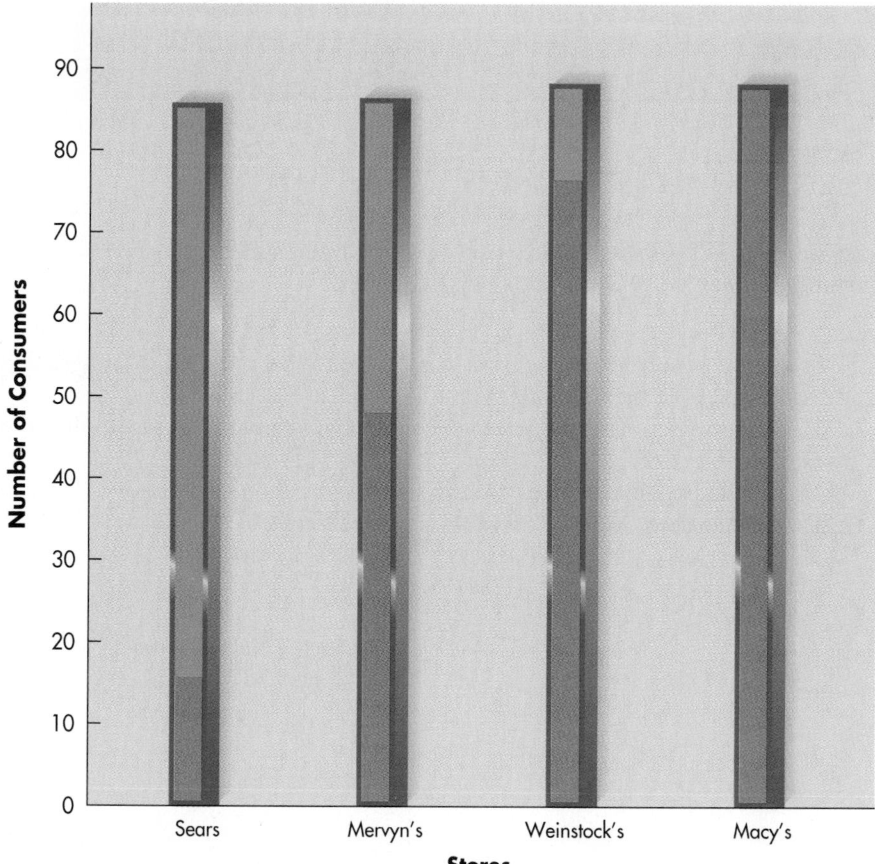

FIGURE 7.3
Number of Consumers Who Grouped Penney with Other Stores

FIGURE 7.4
Number of Consumers Who Identified the Store Displays as Belonging to Penney

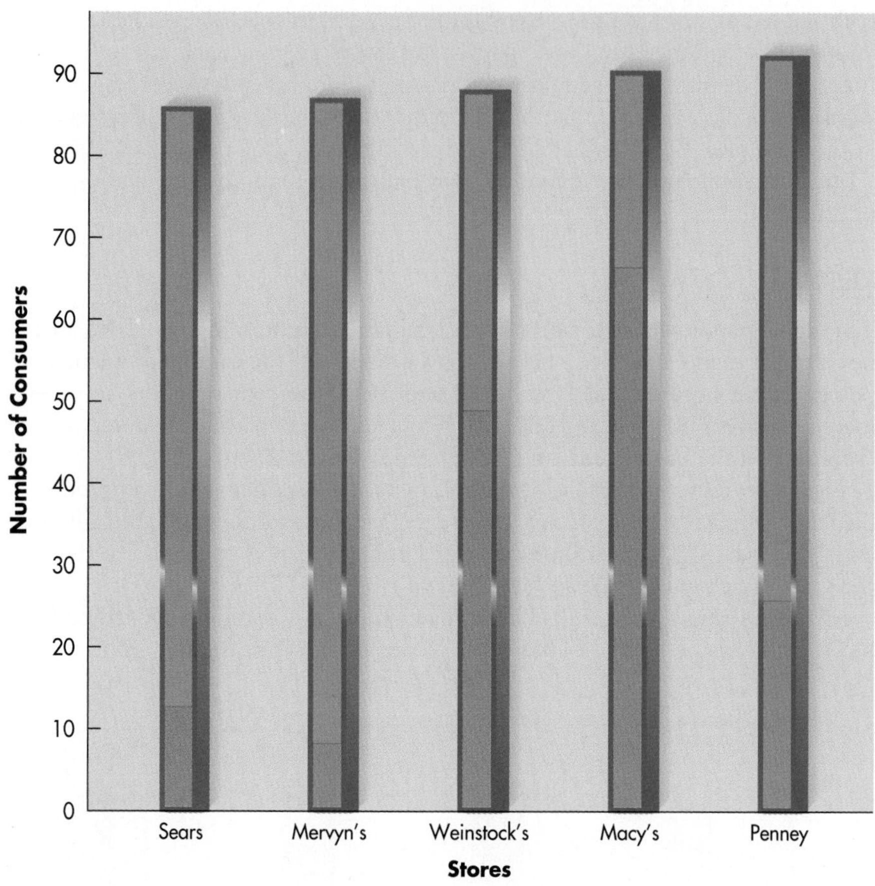

ney's display as belonging to Sears or Mervyn's. Interestingly, consumers did not identify Penney's display as belonging to Penney.[39]

1. What type of survey research was conducted? What are the advantages and disadvantages of the method?
2. What other types of survey research could have been used to accomplish the research objective?
3. Discuss the potential sources of error with the methodology used.
4. What conclusions could be drawn from the research.

CHAPTER 8

Primary Data Collection: Observation

LEARNING OBJECTIVES

1. To develop a basic understanding of observation research.
2. To learn the approaches to observation research.
3. To understand the advantages and disadvantages of observation research.
4. To explore the types of human observation.
5. To describe the types of machine observation and their advantages and disadvantages.
6. To explore the tremendous impact scanner research has had on the marketing research industry in the past few years.

Tracking consumers' every move is giving retailers both revealing statistical detail and new insights. The research efforts also have turned up some surprises:

- By peering from the catwalks at 1,600 shoppers, researchers for Marsh Supermarkets unearthed a troubling trend. People heavily shopped the periphery of the store—the produce, dairy, and meat sections—but frequently circumvented the core dry-goods section that takes up the bulk of store space. The Indiana store chain's inner aisles drew only 13 percent to 30 percent of the traffic, while the periphery accounted for as much as 80 percent.

SOURCE: Jose Fernandez/Woodfin Camp & Associates, Inc.

- VideOcart, Inc., a Chicago company that uses infrared sensors in store ceilings to track shopping carts, has spotted a lot of "dippers." These shoppers park their carts at the ends of aisles and then walk down, filling their arms with items from the shelves as they go. Retailers figure such shoppers probably buy less because they are limited by what they can carry.
- Certain departments draw huge numbers of people, but that doesn't guarantee proportionate sales, a study by the Food Marketing Institute trade group shows. By retracing the steps of 2,400 shoppers and checking what ended up in their grocery carts, the institute learned, for instance, that 77 percent of people walked through the bakery department but that only a third actually bought anything there.
- A study of Procter & Gamble Co. products in K Mart Corp. stores found that sales rose sharply when items like coffee and toothpaste were placed outside their normal aisles on display racks. With no coupons or price cuts, sales of the newly located toothpaste rose as much as 119 percent over a three-week test period, while coffee sales soared more than 500 percent. ■

The examples cited in the opening passage are forms of observation research. What is observation research? What are its advantages and limitations? Are other mechanical devices used in observation research? These are some of the questions we will answer in Chapter 8.

The Nature of Observation Research

Observation Research Defined

Instead of asking people questions as in the case of a survey, observation depends on watching what people do. Specifically, **observation research** can be defined as the systematic process of recording the behavioral patterns of people, objects, and occurrences without questioning or communicating with them. A market researcher using the observation technique witnesses and records information as events occur or compiles evidence from records of past events. Carried a step further, observation may involve watching people or phenomena and may be conducted by human observers or machines. Examples of these various observational situations are shown in Table 8.1.

observation research
Recording behavioral patterns without verbal communication.

Conditions for Using Observation

Three conditions must be met before observation can be successfully used as a data collection tool for marketing research. First, the needed information must be observable or inferable from behavior that can be observed. For example, if a researcher wants to know why an individual purchased a new Jeep rather than an Explorer, observation research will not provide the answer. Second, the behavior of interest must be repetitive, frequent, or predictable in some manner. Otherwise, the costs of observation make the approach prohibitively expensive. Finally, the behavior of interest must be of relatively short duration. Observation of the entire decision-making process for purchasing a new home, which might take several weeks or months, is not feasible.

Approaches to Observation Research

The researcher has a variety of observational approaches to choose from. The question is one of choosing the most effective approach from the standpoint of

TABLE 8.1 Observational Situations

SITUATION	EXAMPLE
People Watching People	Observers stationed in supermarkets watch consumers select frozen Mexican dinners. The purpose is to see how much comparison shopping people do at the point of purchase.
People Watching Phenomena	Observer stationed at an intersection counts traffic moving in various directions.
Machines Watching People	Movie or videotape cameras record behavior as in people watching people example.
Machines Watching Phenomena	Traffic counting machines monitor traffic flow.

cost and data quality for a particular research problem. The five dimensions along which observational approaches vary are (1) natural versus contrived situations, (2) disguised versus undisguised situations, (3) structured versus unstructured observation, (4) human versus machine observers, and (5) direct versus indirect observation.

Natural Versus Contrived Situations Counting how many people use the drive-in window at a particular bank during certain hours is a good example of a completely natural situation. The observer is playing no role in the behavior of interest. Those being observed should have no idea they are under observation. At the other extreme, we might recruit people to do their shopping in a simulated supermarket (rows of stocked shelves set up in a market research field service's mall facility is commonly used) so that we can carefully observe their behavior. In this case, it is necessary that the recruited people have at least some idea that they are participating in a study. The participants might be given grocery carts and told to browse the shelves and pick out items that they might normally use. The researchers might use alternative point-of-purchase displays for several products under study. The observers would note how long the shopper poised in front of the test displays and how often the product was actually selected, thus getting an idea of the effectiveness of the various displays.

A contrived environment better enables the researcher to control extraneous influencers that might have an impact on a person's behavior or the interpretation of that behavior. Also, a simulated environment tends to speed up the observation data gathering process. The researcher does not have to wait for natural events to occur but instead instructs the participants to perform certain actions. Because more observations can be collected in the same length of time, the result will be either a larger sample or a target sample size collected faster. The latter should lower the costs of the project.

The primary disadvantage of a contrived setting is that it is artificial and the observed behavior may be different from what would occur in a real-world situation. The more natural the setting, the more likely the behavior will be normal for the individual being observed.

open observation
The process of monitoring people who know they are being watched.

disguised observation
The process of monitoring people, objects, or occurrences that do not know they are being watched.

structured observation
A study in which the observer fills out a questionnairelike form or counts the number of times an activity occurs.

unstructured observation
A study in which the observer simply makes notes on the behavior being observed.

Open Versus Disguised Observation Does the person being observed know that he is being observed? It is well known that the presence of an observer may have an influence on the phenomena being observed.[2] Two general mechanisms work to bias the data. First, if people know they are being observed (as in **open observation**), they may behave differently. Second, the appearance and behavior of the observer offers a potential for bias similar to that associated with the presence of an interviewer in survey research.

A common form of **disguised observation** is the "mystery shopper." Department stores and chains, such as Sears, will send employees to competitors' stores and ask them to pretend to be shopping. The disguised observers check prices, point-of-purchase displays, and other factors.

Structured Versus Unstructured Observation can be structured or unstructured much in the same manner as surveys. In the **structured observation,** the observer fills out a questionnairelike form on each person observed. In the totally **unstructured observation,** the observer simply makes notes on the behavior being observed. In general, the same considerations that determine whether a survey should be structured or unstructured determine whether an observation should be structured or unstructured. If you already know a good deal about the behavior of interest, it probably makes more sense to do structured observations. If you know very little, unstructured observation is the proper approach, or at least an appropriate preliminary approach.

Structured observation often consists of simply counting the number of times a particular activity occurs. For example, the researcher may be interested in testing two sets of instructions on a new cake mix recipe. To develop a baseline of behavior, the researcher could have the participants prepare their own favorite recipes using the cake mix. One half of the group would get one set of instructions and the remainder the other set. Activities counted might be things such as number of times the instructions were read, number of trips to the cabinet to retrieve bowls and other instruments, number of strokes that the mix is beaten, oven temperatures, and so forth.

A device that can facilitate structured observation is the DataMyte 801 Performance Analyzer, manufactured by DataMyte Corp., Minnetonka, Minnesota. It enables the researcher to assign up to 20 different behaviors to various keys (e.g., smiled, frowned, tasted the product). The summary calculations provided by the DataMyte include the sequencing of the behaviors, the total number of occurrences for each, and the time taken for those behaviors. The result is a stream of data that effectively measures a behavioral process. Of course, to increase the reliability of the procedure, it is reasonable to use more than one observer.[3]

Human Versus Machine Observers In some situations it may be possible and even desirable to replace human observers with machines. In certain situations machines may do the job less expensively, more accurately, or more readily. Traffic counting devices probably are more accurate, definitely cheaper, and certainly more willing than human observers. It would not be feasible, for example, for A. C. Nielsen to have human observers in people's homes to record television viewing habits. Movie cameras and audiovisual equipment record behavior much more objectively and in greater detail than human observers ever could. Finally, the electronic scanners found in a growing number of retail stores provide more accurate and timely data on product movement than human observers ever could.

Direct Versus Indirect Observation Most of the observation done in marketing research is direct observation; that is, directly observing current behavior. However, in some cases past behavior must be observed. To do this, it is necessary to turn to some record of the behavior. Archaeologists dig up sites of old settlements and attempt to determine the nature of life in old civilizations from the physical evidence they find. **Garbologists** sort through people's garbage to analyze household consumption patterns. Marketing research usually is much more mundane. In a product prototype test it may be important for us to know how much of the test product actually was used. The most accurate way to find this out is to have the respondent return the unused product so that the researcher can observe how much actually was used. If a laundry soil and stain remover was placed for in-home use, it would be important to know how much of the product each respondent actually used. All their answers to other questions would be considered from this usage perspective.

garbologists

Researchers who sort through people's garbage to analyze household consumption patterns.

Marketing Research in Practice

Laskerville is a code-named small town outside Chicago. Researchers from Foote Cone & Belding (FCB), one of America's largest advertising agencies, have been slipping into the place, named for Albert Lasker, a founder of the Chicago ad agency, regularly since 1989. They do not identify themselves or the reason they are there, which is to study life in the town. At Laskerville, researchers conduct sophisticated marketing research that includes eavesdropping, reading local newspapers, and even attending funerals.

The Laskerville project is "an ongoing clandestine study about what people are thinking and doing in a small Midwestern town," said Karen Randolph, senior vice-president at FCB. FCB's clients include Coors, Kleenex, Raid, and Payless Shoes—"Heartland products that play a role in everyday lives," she said. Although most of FCB's clients are big brands, "they grew big with plain-speaking ads." FCB wanted to develop better ways to research trends and values among its clients' consumers, hence the birth of Laskerville, she said.

When FCB was determining which town actually would be Laskerville, Randolph said, potential candidates had to meet several criteria. The ideal Laskerville needed a population between 8,000 and 10,000, its own economic base, its own newspaper, and the presence of some national retailers, and it had to be within 120 miles of Chicago.

Three main areas of importance to Laskerville citizens:

- Children, who are central to the community, as well as a desire by residents to keep them there once they've grown. The high school is one of the town's main focal points, with sports and other events being big draws.
- The future of the town itself. "There is a strong sense that though things are tight economically, the people of Laskerville will pull through," Randolph said.
- Helping neighbors, which they "do without agonizing and do without self-congratulation," she said. In Laskerville, there are always raffles, blood drives, pancake breakfasts, and other fund-raisers to help people out. Many self-help groups are available, and residents show much respect for the church and church leaders.[4] ■

Advantages of Observation Research

The idea of watching what people actually do rather than depending on their reports of what they did has one very significant and obvious advantage: we see what people actually do rather than having to rely on what they say they did.[5] This approach can avoid much of the biasing factors caused by the interviewer and question structure associated with the survey approach. The researcher is not subject to problems associated with the willingness and ability of respondents to answer questions. Finally, some forms of data are gathered more quickly and accurately by observation. Rather than ask people to enumerate every item in their grocery bags, it is much more efficient to let a scanner record it. Alternatively, rather than asking young children which toys they like, the major toy manufacturers invite target groups of children into a large playroom and observe via a one-way mirror which toys are chosen and how long each holds the child's attention.

Computer manufacturers often send out mystery shoppers to check knowledge of sales people and sales practices at the retail level. SOURCE: © Michael Newman/PhotoEdit.

Disadvantages of Observation Research

The primary disadvantage of observation research is that only behavior and physical personal characteristics usually can be examined. The researcher does not learn about motives, attitudes, intentions, or feelings. Also, only public behavior is observed; private behavior, such as dressing for work, committee decisions of a company, and family activities at home, is beyond the scope of the researcher. A second problem is that present observed behavior may not be projectable to the future. Purchasing a certain brand of milk after examining several alternatives may hold in one time period, but not in the future.

Observation research can be time-consuming and costly if the observed behavior occurs rather infrequently. For example, if an observer in a supermarket is waiting to observe purchase behavior of persons selecting Lava soap, it may be a long wait. If the consumers chosen to be observed are selected in a biased pattern (for example, shoppers who go grocery shopping after 5:00 P.M.), distorted data may be obtained.

Human Observation

As noted in Table 8.1, people can be used to watch other people or certain phenomena. For example, people can be used as mystery shoppers, observers behind one-way mirrors, or to record shopper traffic and behavior patterns. Researchers also conduct retail and wholesale audits and do content analysis, which also are types of observation research.

Mystery Shoppers

As mentioned earlier, retailers send employees out to shop at competitive stores or company stores. Sears personnel, for example, regularly visit J. C. Penney and other large retailers to observe fixture layouts, merchandise displays, store traffic, and special promotions. McDonald's sends specially trained employees to its various restaurants to pose as customers. The **mystery shoppers** observe how long it takes to receive their order, courtesy of the counter clerks, whether the food was properly prepared, and cleanliness of the restaurants. Sometimes mystery shoppers are used not only to evaluate the quality of service but also to motivate employees. RCA's Consumer Electronics Division used mystery shoppers to evaluate sales performance and point-of-purchase assistance. A salesperson who asks the mystery shopper the "right questions" and behaves according to a checklist of criteria is rewarded on the spot with a check for $50. Subway Sandwiches also uses mystery shoppers as a motivational tool. One franchisee

mystery shoppers

People employed to pose as consumers and shop at the employer's competitors or their own stores to compare prices, displays, and the like.

installed signs behind the counter where only employees could see them. The signs read: "Is this the mystery shopper?"

The authors helped pay for our college educations by working as mystery shoppers for Hallmark Card Shops, Woolworths, and American Express. Thus, a mystery shopper not only observes a shopping environment, but also observes how employees react and behave based upon the shopper's action. For American Express, we would travel to a distant city (sometimes outside the United States), go to the local American Express Office, and tell them our card had been lost or stolen. We then asked for emergency cash and made a variety of other requests.

The largest mystery shopper organization in the United States is the Atlanta-based Shop'n Chek Incorporated. It has 16,000 part-time mystery shoppers with clients such as Sears, Wendy's, United Airlines, RCA, and General Motors. Fees range from $20 to $1,000 for each shopping trip, depending on how much information is gathered.[6]

One-Way Mirror Observations

The discussion of focus groups in Chapter 6 noted that focus group facilities almost always include an observation room with a one-way mirror. This allows clients to observe the group discussion as it unfolds. New product development managers, for example, can note consumers' reactions to various package prototypes as they are demonstrated by the moderator. The clients also can observe the degree of emotion exhibited by the consumer as she speaks. As mentioned

Child psychologists and toy designers can observe children from behind a one-way mirror at Fisher-Price's Play Laboratory to determine what toys the children choose and how they play with them. SOURCE: Courtesy of Fisher-Price, Inc.

earlier, **one-way mirror observations** are sometimes used by child psychologists and toy designers to watch children at play. One researcher spent 200 hours watching mothers change diapers to help with redesign of disposable diapers.

one-way mirror observations
The practice of watching unseen from behind a one-way mirror.

To properly use an observation room, the lighting level must be very dim relative to the actual focus group room. Otherwise, the focus group participants can see into the observation room. Several years ago, the authors were conducting a focus group using orthopedic surgeons in St. Louis. One physician arrived approximately 20 minutes early and was ushered into the group room. A young assistant product manager for the pharmaceutical manufacturer was already seated in the observation room. The physician, being alone in the group room, decided to take advantage of the large framed mirror on the wall for some last-minute grooming. He walked over to the mirror and began combing his hair . . . at the same time the assistant product manager, sitting about a foot away on the other side of the mirror, decided to light a cigarette. As the doctor combed his hair, there was suddenly a bright flash of light and another face appearing through the mirror. What happened next goes beyond the scope of this text. In recent years the trend has been to inform participants of the one-way mirror and to explain who is in the other room watching and why.

Shopper Patterns

As the opening piece described, **shopper pattern** studies are used by retailers to trace the flow of shoppers through a store. Normally, the researcher uses a diagram of the aisles and uses a pen to trace the footsteps of the shopper. By comparing the flows of a representative sample of shoppers, the store managers can determine where best to place such items as impulse goods. Alternatively, the store can change layouts over time and see how this modifies shopping patterns. Generally speaking, retailers want shoppers to be exposed to as much merchandise as possible while in the store. Supermarkets, for example, typically place necessities toward the rear of the store hoping that shoppers will place more items in their baskets on impulse as they move down the aisle to reach the milk, bread, or other necessities.

shopper patterns
Drawings that record the footsteps of a shopper through a store.

Shopper pattern studies help managers reposition merchandise to increase sales.
SOURCE: © Michael Newman/PhotoEdit.

A variant of shopper patterns studies have been conducted on how music influences shopping behavior. One study found that slow tempo music slowed the pace of shopping in a grocery store and significantly increased the size of the grocery bill.[7] In a study conducted in a restaurant, a researcher observed patrons consuming more alcoholic beverages and staying longer but consuming about the same amount of food when slow tempo music was played rather than tunes with a fast tempo.[8]

Content Analysis

content analysis

A technique used to study written material (usually advertising copy) by breaking it into meaningful units, using carefully applied rules.

Content analysis is an observation technique used to analyze written material (usually advertising copy) into meaningful units using carefully applied rules.[9] It is an objective, systematic description of the communication's content. These communications can be analyzed at many levels, such as image, words, or roles depicted. Thus, a researcher using content analysis attempts to determine what is being communicated to a target audience.

One study, for example, noted that the Federal Trade Commission had adopted an advertising substantiation program.[10] The goals of the program were to provide information that might aid consumers in making rational choices, and to provide evidence that would enhance competition by encouraging competitors to challenge advertising claims. Content analysis was used to measure the change in the content of advertisements before and after the substantiation program. In this case, the researchers looked at product attributes and claims, the level of verification in the ads, and how informative the ads were. The study found that the number of claims had declined and the level of verification had increased. The general level of informativeness did not change.

Another study hypothesized that because of the growing number of elderly Americans, advertisers would use more elderly models in their promotions. The researchers found there was, in fact, a significant increase in the use of the elderly in advertisements over the past three decades. The research also found that the elderly were often portrayed in relatively prestigious work situations and that older men were used much more frequently in ads than were older women.[11]

Humanistic Inquiry

humanistic inquiry

A research method in which the researcher is immersed in the system or group under study.

A new to marketing and controversial research method that relies heavily on observation is **humanistic inquiry.**[12] The humanistic approach advocates immersing the researcher in the system under study rather than the traditional scientific method, in which the researcher stands apart from the system being studied. Thus, the traditional researcher might conduct a large-scale survey or experiment to test a hypothesis, whereas the humanist engages in "investigator immersion." That is, the researcher becomes part of the group he is studying.

One humanist researcher was interested in interpreting the consumption values and lifestyles of old-line white, Anglo-Saxon Protestant (WASP) consumers. For 18 months the researcher engaged in field visits to Richmond, Virginia; Charleston, South Carolina; Wilton, Connecticut; and Kennebunkport, Maine. She participated in organizations and observed WASP consumers working, playing, eating dinner, attending church, discussing politics, and shopping in department stores and supermarkets.

Throughout the immersion process, the humanist researcher maintains two diaries or logs. One is a **theory-construction diary** that documents in detail the thoughts, premises, hypotheses, and revisions in thinking developed by the researcher. The theory-construction diary is vital to humanist inquiry because it shows the process by which the researcher has come to understand the phenomenon.

theory-construction diary
A journal that documents in detail the thoughts, premises, hypotheses, and revisions in thinking of a humanistic researcher.

The second set of notes maintained by the humanist researcher is a **methodological log.** In it are kept detailed and time-sequenced notes on the investigative techniques used during the inquiry, with special attention to biases or distortions a given technique may have introduced. The investigative techniques almost always include participant observation and may be supplemented by audiotape or videotape recordings, artifacts (e.g., shopping lists, garbage), and supplemental documentation (e.g., magazine articles, health records, survey data, census reports).

methodological log
A journal of detailed and time-sequenced notes on the investigative techniques used during a humanistic inquiry, with special attention to biases or distortions a given technique may have introduced.

To assess whether the interpretation is drawn in a logical and unprejudiced manner from the data gathered and the rationale employed, humanistic inquiry relies on the judgment of an outside auditor or auditors. These individuals should be researchers themselves, familiar with the phenomena under study. Their task is to review the documentation, field notes, methodological diary, and other supportive evidence gathered by the investigator to confirm (or disconfirm) that the conclusions reached do flow from the information collected.

Audits

Audits are another category of human observation research. An audit is examination and verification of the sale of a product. Audits generally fall into two categories: retail audits that measure sales to final consumers, and wholesale audits that determine the amount of product movement from warehouses to retailers. Wholesalers and retailers allow auditors into their stores and stockrooms and allow them to examine the company's sales and order records to verify product flows. In turn, the retailers and wholesalers receive cash compensation and basic reports about their operations from the audit firms.

audit
The examination and verification of the sale of a product.

Because of the availability of scanner-based data (discussed later in the chapter), physical audits at the retail level may someday all but disappear. Already the largest nonscanner-based wholesale audit company, SAMI, is out of business. Its client list was sold to Information Resources, Incorporated (IRI), a company that specializes in providing scanner data. Also, A. C. Nielsen, the largest retail audit organization, no longer uses auditors in grocery stores. The data is entirely scanner based. Nielsen uses both auditors and scanner data for other types of retail outlets. This probably will shift to scanner-only when a large majority of retailers within a store category (e.g., hardware stores, drugstores) install scanners.

A. C. Nielsen Retail Index

A. C. Nielsen conducts its audits at the retail level rather than the wholesale level. Nielsen claims the following disadvantages for wholesale auditing:

- Obviously such records do not measure *sales:* they report only movement of goods from one point in the distribution chain to another.

- They do not cover the entire *range* of movement; overlooked completely are goods shipped directly from manufacturers to retailers.
- They cannot possibly reflect product movement to the thousands of stores buying from warehouses that are unwilling or unable to provide information.
- They cannot contain the breadth of information available through on-the-scene, in-store measurements: price, distribution, out-of-stock, store promotion, display, and the like; information so important in evaluating the performance of new or existing products in national, regional, or test markets.[13]

Nielsen divides the 48 contiguous states into strata based on geography, population, store type, and sales volume. The following types of data are provided in the **A. C. Nielsen Retail Index.**

A. C. Nielsen Retail Index

Audit of food, household supplies, beauty aids, etc., at the retail level.

- *Sales to Consumers.* Company sales and sales' share, the same for competitors and total product class sales; reported nationally, by region, sales area, and store type.
- *Retailer Purchases.* Total merchandise purchased by retailers is reported in the same form as sales; that is, by brand, product class, major market divisions, and so on.
- *Retail Inventories.* Inventories are reported in the same manner as sales, but volume and share totals refer to the projected amount of unsold merchandise held by retailers. To complement volume information, Nielsen computes maximum distribution and out-of-stock for each brand on a store count basis, average inventories per store in stock, average monthly sales per store handling, and an index of a month's supply. These retail inventory data may enable management to assess retailer (sales) intentions toward a brand (and competitors) and evaluate inventory sufficiency relative to current and future sales rates.
- *Prices and Retailers' Gross Profit.* Provides the average price charged consumers for each brand, by size, type, and area, as well as the retailers' average margin of profit on each item for large independents. An analysis of the retail price structure of a brand (and its competitors) enables a manager to assess the impact of pricing policies on brand progress.
- *Distribution and Out-of-Stock.* Reflects the extent to which each major brand is exposed to all grocery activity based on the total sales of the stores handling each brand. Out-of-stock figures reveal the relative importance of stores without the item on the date of audit but handling the item during the two-month period between audits. These data, reported nationally and by market divisions, provide a revealing picture of sales success in getting distribution among important retail outlets.
- *Special Factory Packs.* Cents-off merchandise, banded combinations reflecting price reductions, and one-cent deals, for example, are reported separately for each listed brand to appraise its sales influence and impact.
- *Retailer Support.* Local advertising, in-store displays, and special prices are reported for each brand in terms of exposure to all-commodity sales nationally and by Nielsen territory. These data give a picture of the cooperation and support provided by retailers in response to trade deals, advertising allowances, and so on.[14]

Table 8.2 illustrates how a Nielsen auditor computes sales and inventories for each item audited. In the example, total sales of the item during the period

TABLE 8.2 Nielsen Retail Index Auditing

"ALPHA" BRAND OF SPOT REMOVER—3 OZ. IN SUPER X MARKET				
		FOR JUNE–JULY		
INVENTORY		PKGS.		VALUE
May 30	114 Pkgs.			
July 30	93 Pkgs.			
Change			21	
PURCHASES				
From Manufacturer (1 order)		12		$ 3.72
From wholesalers (4 orders)		48		15.00
Total			60	$18.72
CONSUMER SALES				
Packages			81	
Price, per pkg.				$ .39
Dollars, Total				$31.59
ADV. 1 2 3 4 5				
~~6~~ 7 8 9				
DISPLAY X				SELLING PRICE 39¢
				SPECIAL PRICE 35¢

SOURCE: A.C. Nielsen Company.

amounted to 81 units (a 21 unit change in inventory plus purchases of 60 units during the period). The brand was on display and had been advertised six separate times, by the retailer, during the period covered. The item was selling for 39 cents on the date of audit but had been advertised at a special price of 35 cents during the period, as noted. The Nielsen auditor, in recording inventories, separates the inventory of each item on a reserve versus forward basis. As a result, it is possible to break down the store inventories as to percentage in the selling area of the store (visible to customers) versus inventory in the reserve or storage areas.

The Importance of Audits to the Japanese

When Sony researched the market for a lightweight portable cassette player, results showed that consumers would not buy a tape player that did not record. Company chairman Akio Morita decided to introduce the Walkman anyway, and the rest is history. Today it is one of Sony's most successful products. Morita's disdain for large-scale consumer surveys and other scientific research tools is not unique in Japan. Matsushita, Toyota, and other well-known Japanese consumer goods companies are just as skeptical about the Western style of market research.

Machine Observation

The observation methods discussed so far have involved people observing things (audits) or consumers. Now we turn our attention to machines observing people and things.

Global Marketing Research

Japanese-style market research relies heavily on two kinds of information: "soft data" obtained from visits to dealers and other channel members and "hard data" about shipments, inventory levels, and retail sales. Japanese managers believe that these data better reflect the behavior and intentions of flesh-and-blood consumers. When Japanese managers want hard data to compare their products to competitors', they look at inventory, sales, and other information that show the items' actual movement through the channels. Then they visit channel members at both the retail and wholesale levels to analyze sales and distribution coverage reports, monthly product movement records (weekly for some key stores), plant-to-wholesaler shipment figures, and syndicated turnover and shipment statistics on competitors.

Japanese managers routinely monitor their markets at home and abroad this way. Consider how Matsushita dealt with the weak performance of its Panasonic distributor in South Africa. The sales figures he reported were reasonable, but he could not produce reliable data on sales and shares for the various types of stores or on inventory levels in the distribution chain.

A few years ago, three managers from the company's household electronics division paid a call on the South African distributor. Then they dropped in on the distributor's retail stores and wholesale facilities. After exchanging greetings and presenting a token gift from headquarters, they got right down to business. They asked to see inventory, shipment, and sales records as part of a complete store audit covering Matsushita and competitive products. Six weeks later, after analyzing all the data, they gave the incredulous distributor a complete picture of Panasonic's product movement and market share through the entire South African channel. They also told the distributor what figures he should collect and report to the home office in the future.[15] ■

Traffic Counters

traffic counters
Machines used to measure vehicular flow over a particular stretch of roadway.

Traffic counters are perhaps the most common and popular form of machine-based observation research (other than scanners). As the name implies, the machines are used to measure the vehicular flow over a particular stretch of roadway. Outdoor advertisers rely on traffic counts to determine the number of exposures per day to a specific billboard. Retailers use the information to ascertain where to place a particular type of store. Convenience stores, for example, require a moderately high traffic volume to reach target levels of profitability.

Physiological Measurement

When an individual is aroused or feels inner tension or alertness, his condition is referred to as *activation*.[16] Activation is stimulated via a subcortical unit, called

Marketing Research in Practice

Scientists believe that the brain's right hemisphere handles primarily spatial or musical tasks, while the left handles verbal and mathematical skills. Research on EEGs and advertising during the past decade or so has shown that emotional slice-of-life commercials tend to be processed mostly in the right portion of the brain. More logical ads, such as product demonstrations, are handled predominantly by the left part.

Such knowledge can help spot blunders that might turn an otherwise memorable commercial into a forgettable one. Neuro-Communication Research Laboratories, Inc., a Danbury, Connecticut, company that uses brain-wave analysis to evaluate ads, cites a commercial in which a father and daughter were speaking. The father's affection produced a high level of processing activity in the right side of the brain. But just as the viewer was being drawn into that emotional scene, the commercial quickly cut to product information. And, deep inside the brain, that caused trouble. The EEG showed the right hemisphere was still highly active, making it difficult for the brain to process words. Linguistic processing usually requires roughly equal activity in both the left and right hemispheres. In short, the timing may have muddled the message.

Commercials someday may be sliced into even smaller pieces for brain-wave analysis. Curt Weinstein, president of Neuro-Communication, hopes to begin analyzing the audio part of commercials apart from the video to determine how people may be responding to background music or narration, as opposed to the pictures they see. Then, he will be able to tell whether, for example, music is reinforcing a written message on the screen or whether it is detracting from it.[17] ■

the *reticular activation system* (RAS), located in the human brain stem. The sight of a product or advertisement, for example, can activate the RAS. As a result of directly provoking arousal processes in the RAS, there is an increase in the processing of information. Researchers have used a number of devices to measure the level of a person's activation.

EEG The **electroencephalogram (EEG)** is a machine that measures rhythmic fluctuations in the electric potential in the brain. It probably is the most versatile and sensitive procedure for detecting arousal but involves expensive equipment, a laboratory environment, and complex data analysis using special software programs. Researchers claim that EEG measures can be used to assess, among other effects, viewers' attention to an advertisement at specific points in time, the intensity of the emotional reactions elicited by specific aspects of the ad, and their comprehension and attention to the ad.[18] Other researchers have disputed the value of EEG for marketing research because of the cost of equipment and the special environment required.[19]

electroencephalogram (EEG)
A machine that measures the rhythmic fluctuations in electrical potential of the brain.

galvanic skin response (GSR)
The measurement of changes in the electric resistance of the skin associated with activation responses.

GSR The **galvanic skin response (GSR)**, also known as the *electrodermal response*, measures changes in the electric resistance of the skin associated with activation responses. A small electric current of constant intensity is sent into the skin through electrodes attached to the palmar side of the fingers. The changes in voltage observed between the electrodes indicate the level of stimulation. Because the equipment is portable and not expensive, the GSR is the most popular device for measuring activation. The GSR is used primarily to measure stimulus response to advertisements but is sometimes used in packaging research.

Inner Response, Incorporated uses the GSR to evaluate commercials. In one Eastman Kodak Company film-processing ad, Inner Response determined that the viewers' interest level built slowly in the opening scenes, rose when a snapshot of an attractive young woman was shown, but spiked highest when a picture appeared of a smiling, pigtailed girl. Kodak then knew which scenes had the highest impact and could retain them when making changes in the spot or cutting it to 15 seconds from 30.[20]

Global Marketing Research

Tony Siciliano, an American marketing researcher, has spent several years conducting research in France. He discusses here the use of the T-Scope in packaging research.

The tachistoscope, or T-Scope, is a slide projector with a timing device. It allows visual stimuli to be exposed at very fast and consistently accurate speeds. It was first used by psychologists and physiologists to measure visual acuity.

Siciliano notes: I moved to France to concentrate on providing research capabilities for American companies interested in European markets. Much to my surprise, the European clients of the French market research agency where I worked were keenly interested in the T-Scope techniques for testing packaging.

The best way to demonstrate a T-Scope technique is to cite an actual case history. We used the T-Scope for an infant's toiletry package that led to the development of a new package design. In tachistoscopic package testing, a complete package is shown at a high speed and respondents are asked to draw pictures of what they see. The product was a cotton-tipped stick used to clean infants' ears and eyes. The new package design had cotton sticks arranged in a cross-bow fashion (see illustration).

We found when women drew this design and were unaware of the brand (a leader in infant-care products), they would interpret it is something "poisonous," "dangerous," "to be kept away from children." Women who drew this design but knew the brand did not have these associations.

We realized from these findings that brand perception could be a serious impediment to analyzing a new package's performance. Thus, the cross-bow design was eliminated.[21] ■

Pupilometer The **pupilometer** measures changes in pupil dilation. The basic assumption is that increased pupil size reflects positive attitudes, interest, and arousal in an advertisement. The subjects view an advertisement while brightness and distance from the screen are held constant. The pupilometer has fallen from favor among many researchers because pupil dilation appears to measure some combination of arousal, mental effort, processing load, and anxiety.[22] Arousal alone is much better measured by means of GSR.

pupilometer
A machine that measures changes in pupil dilation.

Voice Pitch Analysis **Voice pitch analysis** examines changes in the relative vibration frequency of the human voice to measure emotion. In voice analysis, the normal or baseline pitch of an individual's speaking voice is charted by engaging the subject in an unemotional conversation. The greater the deviation from the baseline, the greater is said to be the emotional intensity of the person's reaction to a stimulus, such as a question. There are several advantages of voice pitch analysis over other forms of physiological measurement:

voice pitch analysis
The study of changes in the relative vibration frequency of the human voice to measure emotion.

- It records without physically connecting wires and sensors to the subject.
- The subject need not be aware of the record and analysis.
- The nonlaboratory setting overcomes the weaknesses of an artificial environment.
- It provides instantaneous evaluation of answers and comments.[23]

Voice pitch analysis has been used in package research, to predict consumer brand preference for dog food, and to determine which consumers from a target group would be most predisposed to try a new product.[24] Other research has applied voice analyses to measure consumers' emotional responses to advertising.[25] Validity of the studies to date have been subject to serious question.[26]

The devices just discussed are used to measure involuntary changes in an individual's physiological makeup. Arousal produces adrenaline, which enhances the activation process via a faster heart rate, increased blood flow, an increase in skin temperature and perspiration, pupil dilation, and an increase in brain-wave frequency. Researchers often impute information about attitudes and feelings based on these measures.

The People Reader lamp system inconspicuously records the reading habits of test subjects and measures the effectiveness of print advertisements. SOURCE: Courtesy of The Pretesting Company, Inc.

Opinion and Behavior Measurement

People Reader

A machine that simultaneously records the respondent's reading material and eye reactions.

People Reader The Pretesting Company has invented a device called the **People Reader.** The machine looks like a lamp and is designed so that when respondents sit in front of it they are not aware it is simultaneously recording both the reading material and their eyes. The self-contained unit is totally automatic and can record any respondent—with or without glasses—without the use of attachments, chin rests, helmets, or special optics. It allows respondents to read any size magazine or newspaper and lets them spend as much time as they need to go back and forth through the publication. Through the use of the People Reader and specially designed hidden cameras, the Pretesting Company has been able to document a number of pieces of information concerning both reading habits and the results of different size ads in terms of stopping power and brand-name recall. The company's research has found the following:

- Nearly 40 percent of all readers start from either the back of a magazine or "fan" a magazine for interesting articles and ads. Fewer than half the readers start from the very first page of a magazine.
- Rarely does a double-page ad provide more than 15 percent additional top-of-mind awareness than a single-page ad. Usually, the benefits of a double-page spread are additional involvement and communication, not top-of-mind awareness.
- In the typical magazine, nearly 35 percent of each of the ads receives less than two seconds' worth of voluntary examination.
- The strongest involvement power recorded for ads has been three or more successive single-page ads on the right-hand side of a magazine.
- Because most ads "hide" the name of the advertisers and do not show a close-up view of the product package, brand-name confusion is greater than 50 percent on many products such as cosmetics and clothing.
- A strong ad that is above average in stopping power and communication will work regardless of which section in the magazine it is placed. It will also work well in any type of ad or editorial environment. However, an ad that is below average in stopping power and involvement will be seriously affected by the surrounding environment.[27]

Pretesting has patented a watch that not only tells time but also records everything the wearer looks at on television, listens to on radio, or reads in magazines. The watch is designed to pick up nearly inaudible pulses emitted at regular intervals by televisions and radios. Magazines would have tiny transmitters hidden in the binding. The pulses act like the UPC bar codes on packaged goods and enable Pretesting to distinguish between the commercials you zapped and those you actually sat through. However, the advertising community was not ready for such a device.

The PreTesting Company decided to introduce its new patented technologies in a more acceptable format than the original watch. A new company was formed, Mediacheck, and the device consists of a white box, approximately the size of a small pocket novel, which sits near a television set. The equipment to detect the non-intrusive audio signal does not have to be hard wired into the television set. The code is detected by a small microphone which is placed close to the speaker of the television or radio. The audio code (which has already passed testing of compression, satellite uploading and accuracy in reading) is decoded by a device in the white box. The code is neither seen nor heard by the listener or viewer, and it is not stripable by a station or client that does not wish to be measured (see Figure 8.1).

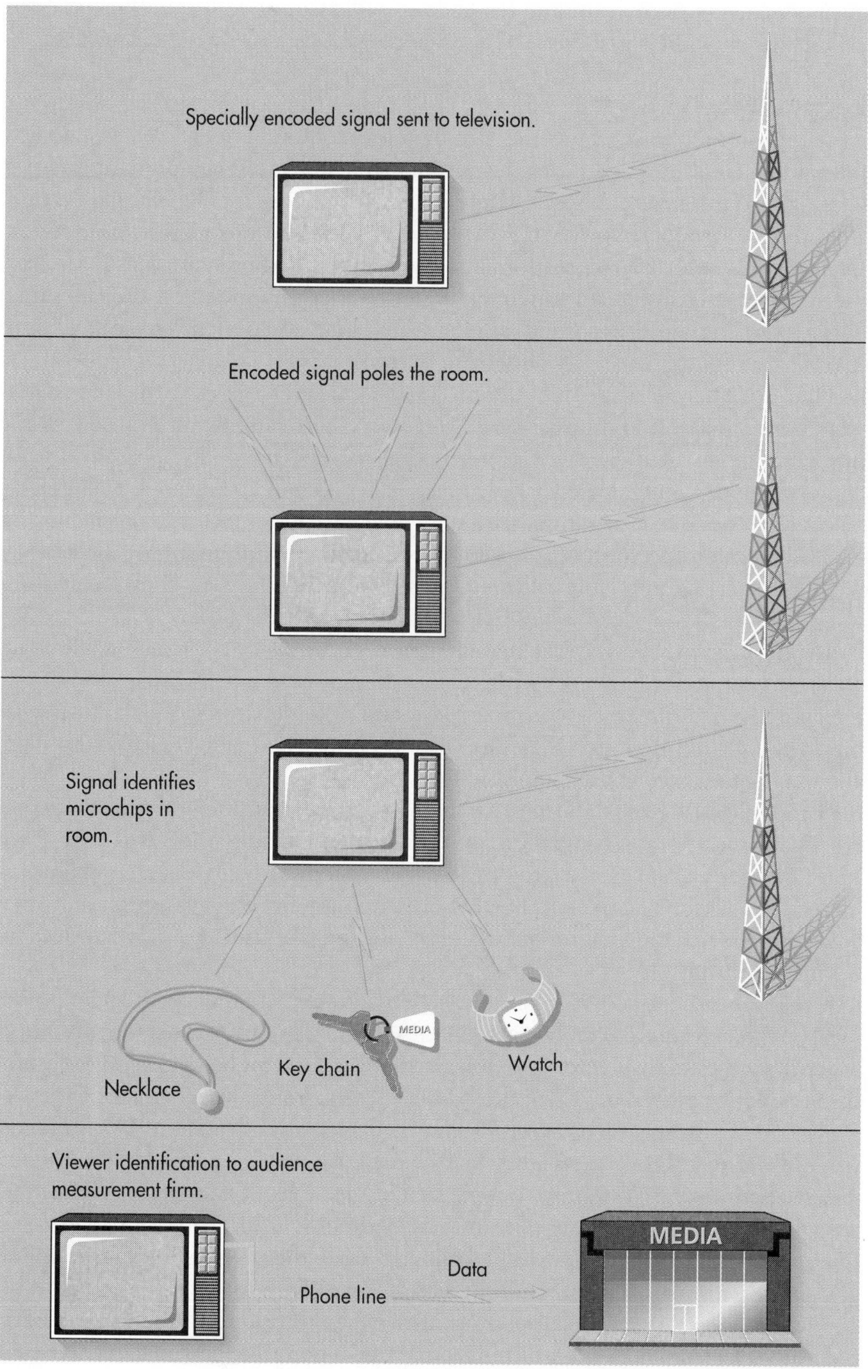

FIGURE 8.1

How PreTesting's New Audience Measurement System Works

SOURCE: Courtesy of The PreTesting Company, Inc.

Not only does the white box constantly register the different program and commercial code (and transmit its data by phone line to a central computer), but it constantly polls as to who is there in terms of the audience. Each member of the audience wears an ultra small microchip which can be placed inside a watch, pendant, bracelet or similar type of small, lightweight jewelry. The small device can even be clipped on to a garment. Whenever the set unit polls a room, these microchips respond, each with their unique RF code to tell the unit who is in the audience. All this information is gathered every three to five seconds by the set unit.[28]

people meter

A microwave computerized rating system that transmits demographic information overnight to measure national TV audiences.

People Meters Several years ago, A. C. Nielsen announced that it would use its **people meter** to measure the size of television audiences. The system is a microwave computerized rating system that transmits demographic information overnight to measure national TV audiences. It replaces the 30-year-old National Audience Composition (NAC) diary system used to record this information. The people meter provides information on what TV shows are being watched, the number of households watching, and which family members are watching. The type of activity is recorded automatically; household members merely have to indicate their presence by pressing a button.

The introduction of people meters caused considerable concern among networks, ad agencies, and advertisers who requested caution by Nielsen in the implementation of the device. The people meters, network research officials contend, gives younger viewers, who are less resistant to technology, a greater voice; older people, less patient with new devices and reluctant to press buttons, would be underrepresented. It is also contended that children under 10 years old will be especially unreliable button pushers. A recent study has shown that "button pushing fatigue" sets in before the end of two years.[29]

To offset the problems of the people meter, a new system has been made available to monitor viewers' faces with a cameralike device. The passive system uses a recorder programmed to recognize faces and note electronically when specific members of a family watch TV. The system notes when viewers leave the room and even when they avert their eyes from the screen.

Nielsen Media Research, the Dun and Bradstreet Corporation unit that compiles national TV ratings, worked jointly with the David Sarnoff Research Center of Princeton, New Jersey, to develop the system. Advertisers are demanding more proof of viewership, and the networks are under more pressure to show that advertising is reaching its intended targets. Ratings are used to help set prices for commercial time.

A Nielsen executive has said that a passive system should yield "even higher quality, more accurate data because the respondents don't have to do anything" other than "be themselves." The sensory equipment can be packaged to resemble a VCR and placed on top of the TV. It will electronically record the names of those it recognizes and the periods during which they watched TV. Strangers would be listed simply as visitors.[30] Already, however, the networks and advertisers are criticizing the passive people meter. One executive noted, "Who would want or allow one of those things in their bedroom?" Others claim that the system requires bright light to operate properly. Also, the box has limited peripheral vision, so it might not sense all the people in a given room.

Nielsen rival Arbitron Company thinks it has developed a better device to measure television ratings. Arbitron has created a portable, personal, passive people meter similar to the one created by MediaCheck. The Arbitron device won't be commercially available for several years and design plans are not yet final. However, it will be small enough to be carried or worn by each member of a household, perhaps in beeper, pin, or pendant form. More importantly, it would use a computer chip to measure both TV viewing and radio listening by a single consumer—offering advertisers, for the first time, an intimate peek into someone's combined media habits. Radio ratings today rely mostly on hand-scrawled diaries.

The new device would pick up audio signals encoded in the programs being watched or listened to, eliminating the risk that a lazy viewer would slack off and ignore punching in. Another prime advantage: It could stay with the roving viewer to measure radio habits in the car, TV habits at the local bar, and other out-of-home viewing that the people meter fails to pick up.[31] Data would be supplied to Arbitron either through a separate in-home modem or by mailing the meter back to the company.

Scanner-based Research

Two electronic monitoring tools create the scanner-based research system: television meters and laser **scanners,** which "read" the UPC codes on products and produce instantaneous information on sales. Separately, each monitoring device provides marketers with current information on the advertising audience and on sales and inventories of products. Together, television meters and scanners measure the impact of marketing. Has scanner-based research been of much benefit to marketers? The top executive of one manufacturer estimates that one-third to one-half of its gains in profitability in the past several years can be attributed to scanner-based research.[32]

scanners

Devices that read the UPC codes on products and produce instantaneous information on sales.

The development of scanner-based research has been slow for several reasons. One problem has been cost. An estimated $100 million has been spent on developing scanner-based systems, not easily justified in the market research industry obsessed with the bottom line. Cost justification, in terms of profit potential, has made the builders of these systems spread the risk by stretching out the development time. Technology is another problem. Hard technology adaptation to scanner-based research use has been slower than expected. Some of the technology is the nonpassive type, such as home scanners and people meters. This raises questions of bias, requiring validation, a time-consuming process. The soft technology development also has been slower than expected. The enormous computer capacity required to collect, process, and store the information databases has been consistently underestimated. Moreover, users of scanner data have been overwhelmed with the massive amounts of data. Marketing decision makers only need information if it can help them make decisions. Management needs decision-making information, not data. Therefore, suppliers of scanner data have created expert systems to give the data more utility for the managers (examples of these systems will be described later).

The marriage of scanners, database management, telecommunications, artificial intelligence, and computing gives hope for a "brave new world" of marketing. Discussions of this potential new world are presented in the following "A Professional Researcher's Perspective," first by a marketing researcher and then a major user of scanner data.

A Professional Researcher's Perspective

Walker Smith, vice-president of Marketing Spectrum, Atlanta, sees the marriage described in the text as leading to "real-time marketing."[33] As the gap in time between marketplace activity and marketplace response shrinks and disappears, marketing will become a real-time activity, no longer constrained to wait for batches of data before actions can be taken. Improvements in marketing strategy and tactics will be initiated the instant any weaknesses or opportunities become apparent and, in this world, advantage will accrue to firms with superior and more secure communications networks and to those with better ways of instantly evaluating, verifying, testing, and acting on marketplace data.

This scenario is not as far-fetched as it may seem. Already on Wall Street, real-time marketing is being implemented under the guise of program trading (an observation owed to Doug Haley of Yankelovich Clancy Shulman). In industries more dependent on physical distribution and delivery systems (as opposed to the electronic transfers possible in the financial industry), developments like just-in-time inventory are overcoming the barriers to real-time marketing.

Blair Peters, group research manager of Kraft General Foods Marketing Information Department, sees the future this way:

It does not take much imagination to weave a future scenario in which businesses base most of their decisions on robust and self-calibrating models. Such models will be robust in that the information takes into account every aspect of human behavior (e.g., purchasing, media) and product movement through the company's distribution channel (from plant, to warehouse, to store take-away). The models will be self-calibrating because of expert systems powered by artificial intelligence. This futuristic scenario is both exciting and frightening. It is exciting in that it represents a world that every information professional has dreamed about. Most problems could be analyzed. However, the scenario is frightening in that many people will be left behind in the wake of these changes. Professionals will have to retool in terms of their mind-set and technical skills or become obsolete.[33] ■

The two major scanner-based research suppliers are Information Resources, Incorporated (IRI) and A. C. Nielsen, a unit of Dun and Bradstreet Corporation; each has about half the market.[34] To gain an appreciation of scanner-based research, we will examine IRI in more detail.

BehaviorScan
A scanner-based research system that maintains a 3,000 household panel to record consumer purchases based upon manipulation of the marketing mix.

BehaviorScan IRI is the founder of scanner-based research. Its first product is called **BehaviorScan.**[35] A proprietary household panel of about 3,000 households has been recruited and maintained in each BehaviorScan minimarket. Panel members shop with an ID card, which is presented at checkout in scanner-

Scanner-based research has revolutionized the marketing research industry. SOURCE: © David Young-Wolff/PhotoEdit.

equipped grocery and drugstores, allowing IRI to electronically track each household's purchasing, item by item, over time. With such a measure of household purchasing, it is possible to manipulate marketing variables, such as TV advertising or consumer promotions, or introduce a new product and analyze real changes in consumer buying behavior.

For strategic tests of alternative marketing plans, the BehaviorScan household panels are split into two or more subgroups, perfectly balanced on past purchasing, demographics, and stores shopped. For advertising issues, commercials can be substituted at the individual household level, allowing one subgroup to view a test commercial, the other a control ad. This makes BehaviorScan the most effective means to evaluate changes in advertising weight, copy, and dayparts. In each market, IRI maintains permanent warehouse facilities and has an in-market staff to control distribution, price, and promotions. Competitive activity in all categories is monitored and a complete record of pricing, displays, and features permits an assessment of the promotion responsiveness to a brand.

The BehaviorScan markets are geographically dispersed cities: Pittsfield, Massachusetts; Marion, Indiana; Eau Claire, Wisconsin; Midland, Texas; Grand Junction, Colorado; and Cedar Rapids, Iowa. For testing consumer promotions such as coupons, sampling, or refund offers, balanced panel subsamples are created within each market. Then through direct mail or split newspaper-route targeting, a different treatment is delivered to each group. Both sales and profit are analyzed.

In-store variables also may be tested. Within the markets, split groups of stores are used to read the effect on sales of a change in packaging, shelf placement, or pricing. Tests are analyzed primarily on a store movement basis but analysis of purchasing by panel shoppers in the test and control stores is also possible. With the BehaviorScan system, it is possible to test alternative advertising levels while simultaneously varying in-store prices or consumer promotions, thereby testing a completely integrated marketing plan.

In summary, BehaviorScan allows marketing managers to answer critical marketing questions such as

- How many consumers try my brand and how many buy again?
- What volume level will my brand achieve in one year? In two years?
- Will my line extension "steal" share from its parent brand?
- What flavor mix will maximize trial?
- Does increased advertising or new copy increase sales?
- What are the implications of a change in price, package, or shelf placement?
- Who are my brand's buyers and what else do they buy?

InfoScan

A scanner-based tracking service for consumer packaged goods.

InfoScan IRI's most successful product, with sales of nearly $200 million per year, is **InfoScan.**[36] InfoScan is a scanner-based, national and local market tracking service for the consumer packaged goods industry. Retail sales, detailed consumer purchasing information (including measurement of store loyalty and total grocery basket expenditures), and promotional activity (trade and consumer) are monitored and evaluated for all UPC-coded products (see Figures 8.2 and 8.3). InfoScan collects weekly purchase data from 2,700 supermarkets, 500 drugstores, and 250 mass merchandisers. This results in a household panel of approximately 60,000 households. Over time, this has created a huge secondary database. IRI has taken the database and examined thousands of brands in more than 500 different packaged goods product categories. In such a database, IRI has what it refers to as thousands and thousands of "naturally occurring experiments." That is to say, hundreds of thousands of data points relating weekly sales to price reductions and merchandising activity. Using the database, the IRI researchers were able to look at a variety of marketing mixes and competitive situations and determine the results of managerial decision making. For example, using thousands of data points, IRI looked at the weekly sales response of an average brand to trade promotions (see Figure 8.4). The numbers are all expressed as a percentage over base sales (i.e., the sales level that one would observe with no trade support). IRI found that a 10 percent price reduction, on average, led to a 20 percent sales increase during the week of the price reduction. Adding a feature ad to the price reduction generated a 78 percent sales increase during the promoted week. An in-store display with a 10 percent price reduction doubled sales. An in-store display, coupled with a feature ad and a 10 percent price reduction, tripled sales. Further examination of the database produced other interesting results. These included the following:

1. *Advertising Weight Testing.* The traditional view of the impact of ad weight (advertising expenditures) would hold that increased weight could be expected to result in a sales increase, if one had good copy. In at least 50 percent of the tests involving increased weight, IRI found a significant sales increase. Not surprisingly, the absolute success levels were higher for new brands than for established brands. Presumably, this was because the job of advertising in generating sales increases is somewhat easier for new brands, where simply building awareness is often the key objective.
2. *Copy Testing.* The traditional view is that good copy can be expected to have a relatively immediate impact on sales. IRI completed a detailed analysis of all the copy tests that had been conducted in BehaviorScan with the objective of

FIGURE 8.2

How InfoScan Works

SOURCE: Information Resources, Inc.

UPC's for each grocery item are scanned at checkout. Information is sent from store to chain and on to IRI via telecommunication systems.

Household panel members present an identification card at that checkout which identifies and assigns items purchased to that household. Coupons are collected and matched to the appropriate UPC. Information is electronically communicated to IRI computers.

IRI field personnel visually surveys stores and all print media to record retailers' merchandising efforts, displays, and ad features. Field personnel also surveys retail stores for a variety of custom applications (e.g., average number of units per display, space allocated to specific sections, and number of facings). Results are electronically communicated to IRI computers.

Household panel members are selected for television monitoring and equipped with meters that automatically record the set's status every five seconds. Information is relayed back to IRI's computers.

Information is received at IRI and processed through the Neural Network (Artificial Intelligence) Quality Control System. The system approves the more than 35 million records obtained weekly for further data processing and identifies records that require further verification.

Completed databases are converted to the required client format, transferred to appropriate recording mediums . . . hard copy, mag tape, pc diskette, etc. . . . and sent to the subscriber.

understanding the speed with which the effect of copy on sales could be measured. Over two-thirds of the tests conducted in BehaviorScan revealed sales differences of at least 10 percent between the copy alternatives being tested within a three-month period. Approximately 75 percent of the tests showed at least a 10 percent sales difference within four months. And if a sales difference was generated initially, it almost invariably continued through the end of the test. This confirmed that a good creative effort could generate a sales increase—and maintain it.[37]

IRI's Software As mentioned previously, managers want decision making information, not data. The key to IRI's success is not the millions of new scanner records it obtains each week but the useful information derived from those records. Useful information for management is gleaned from powerful software.

FIGURE 8.3

InfoScan Data Collection

InfoScan provides scanner data derived from thousands of stores nationwide.

SOURCE: Information Resources, Inc.

FIGURE 8.4

Topical Report on Trade Promotions: Average Category Response to Trade Promotions

SOURCE: Information Resources, Inc.

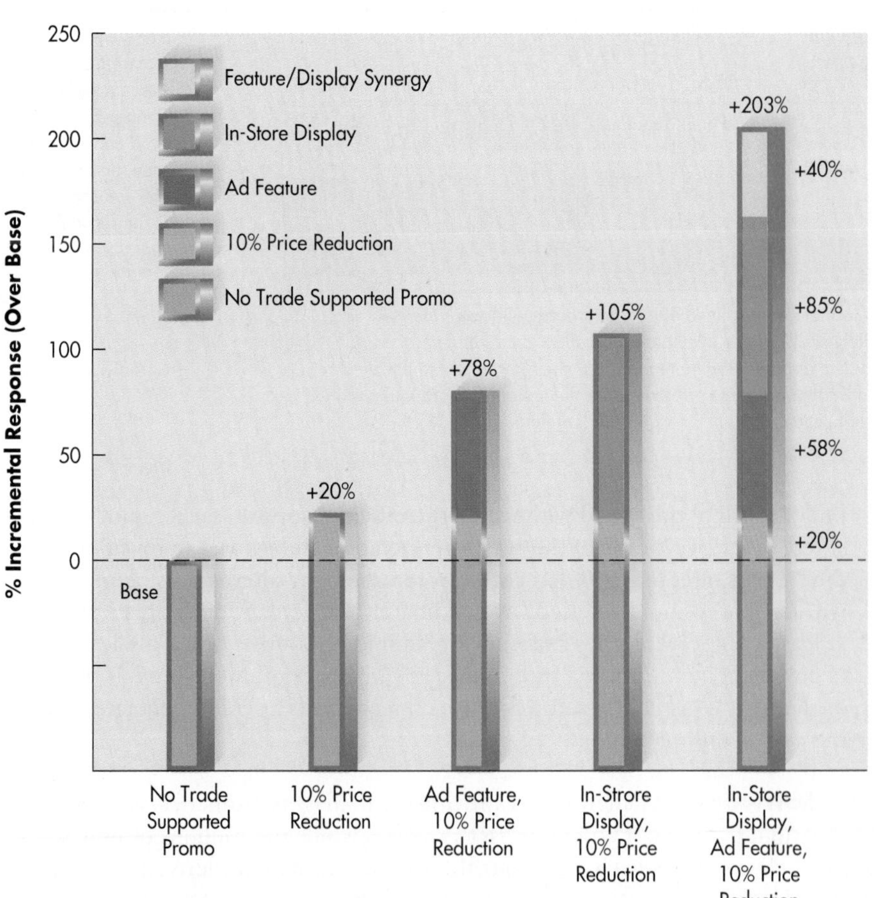

For example, IRI's Apollo Space Management Software helps answer one of the most fundamental questions faced by manufacturers and retailers: What is the most optimal use of retail shelf space—the most valuable asset in any store? Apollo analyzes scanner data from the InfoScan database to review the amount of shelf space, price, and profit components of product category shelf sets such as dishwashing soaps or cereals. It then provides actionable suggestions for optimizing shelf allocations for each item in the section. Apollo also can produce photo-quality schematics using its library of 120,000 product images and dimensions. Thus, the retailer gets a visual picture of what the shelf reallocation will look like (see Figure 8.5).

The Partners is an IRI expert software system designed to cut the mass of scanner data down to actionable pieces of information. The program flexibility allows for either a high-level, top-line approach to data analysis or an analysis-intensive exhaustive approach. Users choose whether to display information in prose, reports, or graphs. The Partners furnishes brand managers with insight into pricing and promotion data and their effect on sales, as well as in-depth knowledge on competitors' products. Key features of The Partners software are listed in Table 8.3. A sample report from The Partners is shown in Figure 8.6. The program also features presentation-quality graphics that can be used in making reports to management and clients.

The Partners
An expert software system designed to cut the mass of scanner data down to actionable pieces of information.

The Scanner Wars—IRI Versus Nielsen Like two heavyweight boxers, IRI and A. C. Nielsen are continually punching and counterpunching each other in the large and rapidly growing scanner data market. Each is seeking a competitive

TABLE 8.3 Key Features of The Partners Expert System Software

- Expediting Routine Analyses—Although business issues may change day-to-day, there are certain job functions that remain constant. To expedite these routine analyses, a user can create a folder for the purpose of "storing" her most frequently used reports, graphs, headlines, or presentations. The folder offers unlimited access to this information and can be viewed or printed in one step.

- Finding the News in the Data—You may begin your analysis by examining a Review. In the Review section, The Partners sifts through all the appropriate data available and uncovers current product performance and trend information. Looking at headlines, a user quickly gains an understanding of the important "news" in the data, including well and poorly performing products and competitors. Here managers also see the potential causes for changes in performance.

- Focusing Product Strategies—Upon identifying the issues of greatest concern, users now focus their analysis by taking the second step, Ranking. In this section, users work with ranking reports and quadrant analyses to better target strategies for distribution, promotion, pricing, and advertising. Using the quadrant analysis capabilities, a user gains a deeper understanding of recent developments by sorting products or geographics based on performance on two user-selected measures.

- Quantifying New Approaches—Next, an Opportunity Identification section allows users to determine the bottom-line effects of strengthening their weak spots and improving product performance. Results are quantified to show the impact of changing distribution, promotion, and pricing levels. Results are shown for both the retailer and the manufacturer, and specific next steps are recommended.

- Determining Profitable Strategies—Users can investigate the impact of new strategies in step four, Simulation. In this section a user takes this information a step further by discovering the implications of changing distribution, promotion, and other strategies. Using The Partners' "what-if?" simulation capabilities, a user can quickly evaluate various strategies. For example, a manager can manipulate promotional pricing and support and assess the increase to product sales and profits. Simulated scenarios are put into perspective by displaying real data from actual events alongside the simulated events.

SOURCE: Information Resources, Inc., 1994.

FIGURE 8.5

IRI's Apollo Space Management Software with Advanced Digitized Imaging Can Produce Photo-Quality Schematics of Optimal Shelf Allocations of Products

SOURCE: Information Resources, Inc.

advantage that will sway purchasers of scanner data (the most rapidly growing area of the marketing research industry). Scanner data revenues were more than $400 million in 1994.[38] Kraft General Foods alone spends more than $30 million a year for scanner data.[39]

A major difference between IRI and Nielsen is how the household level data are gathered. IRI scanner panel members present an ID card to the retailer, which is bar coded to identify the household making the purchase. Thus the data are captured at retail sites. Nielsen used a similar system consisting of 15,000 households until 1991. Nielsen phased out its in-store panel and substituted an in-home scanner panel. Nielsen households use a hand scanner, after shopping, to manually scan each purchase. In contrast, IRI's bar-coded identification card, which is used to scan the buyer's purchases, is a method of "passive collection." Several years ago, Nielsen increased its panel size to 40,000 households and IRI to 60,000. Approximately 4,500 panel members will be connected to Nielsen's Monitor Plus TV program for tracking viewing using the people meter. Nielsen claims its panel will measure all geographic locations. Also, by scanning at home, the system is not dependent on retailers that happen to be cooperating. Nielsen's panel covers about 1,147 counties, whereas IRI covers only 30 counties. Andy Tarshis, president of NPD/Nielsen says, "Can households in 30 counties be representative of the total United States?"[40] IRI executives counter Tarshis by asking, "How typical are households who agree to manually scan every item purchased after every shopping trip and then enter the price paid, coupon usage, and store name?" Tarshis also notes:

> "By increasing nearly threefold, our ability to do additional analysis increases may be tenfold," he said. "For example, warehouse clubs are becoming popular, but not everyone is a member. But by expanding to 40,000, the number of households buying at the clubs may be 5,000, which is a much more usable number than we get from 15,000 households."

FIGURE 8.6

Sample Report from The Partners

SOURCE: Information Resources, Inc., 1994.

SECRET's share has declined 0.7 points, from 11.1 to 10.4.

Among the components of SECRET, the top share gaine is SECRET STICK/SOLID (+0.7). The 2 products with the largest share loss are SECRET AEROSOL (–0.7) and SECRET ROLL-ON (–0.6).

Total US-Food's largest 3 share declines were posted in Boston, MA (–2.0), Los Angeles, CA (–1.3), and Detroit, MI (–1.2).

Among SECRET's major competitors, the 3 principal share gainers are MNEN LSpSt (+2.1), DEGREE (+0.9), and SUAVE (+0.5). The largest 3 share losses occurred for DRY IDEA (–1.5), BAN (–0.9), and SOFT & DRI (–0.9).

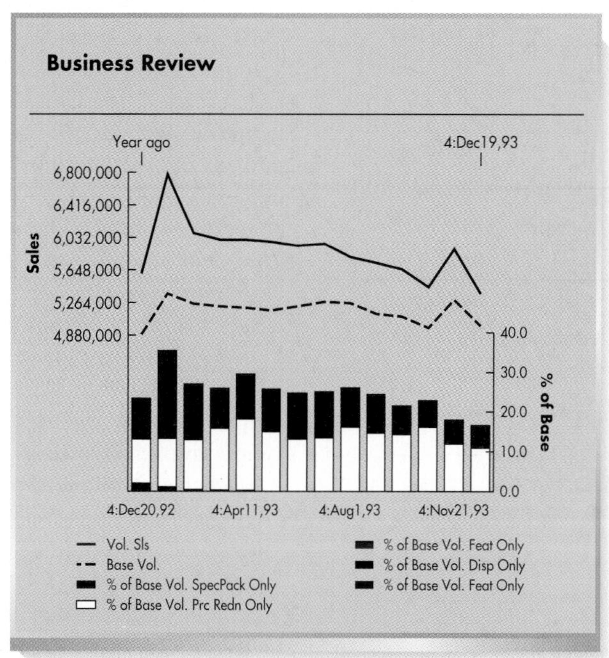

Sales Trend Review

	Volume Share		Base Volume Share		Incrm Volume Share	
	Current	Change	Current	Change	Current	Change
SECRET	10.4	-0.7	9.7	-1.0	0.8	-0.6
SECRET STICK/SOLID	5.5	0.7	4.8	0.7	0.7	-0.0
SECRET AEROSOL	3.2	-0.7	3.1	-0.4	0.0	-0.1
SECRET ROLL-ON	1.8	-0.6	1.7	-0.4	0.1	-0.2
Competitors						
MNEN LSpSt	5.3	2.1	4.2	1.4	1.2	0.7
DEGREE	4.5	0.9	4.1	0.8	0.4	0.0
SUAVE	4.9	0.5	4.6	0.6	0.3	-0.0
DRY IDEA	2.6	-1.5	2.2	-0.1	0.3	-0.5
BAN	4.3	-0.9	4.0	-0.9	0.3	-0.0
SOFT & DRI	4.6	-0.9	4.1	-0.8	0.5	-0.1
Total US—FOOD						
Boston, MA	10.4	-0.7	9.7	-0.1	0.8	-0.6
Los Angeles, CA	11.1	-0.2	9.5	-0.9	1.5	-1.1
Detroit, MI	8.8	-1.3	8.3	-1.4	0.5	0.1
	9.2	-1.2	8.5	-1.3	0.6	0.1

> The same is true for marketers interested in data from minorities. For example, 6 percent of the panel is Hispanic households; as the panel expands, that percentage becomes "a base large enough for us to do dramatically more analysis. We can compare Hispanic household trends on the East Coast vs. the West Coast or even look at a single market," Mr. Tarshis said. Nielsen intends to maintain at least 12 percent of the panel as black households, also enabling expanded analysis of that group.[41]

IRI's InfoScan was historically based upon cooperating supermarkets to supply scanner data. To counter Nielsen, IRI added 500 drugstores such as Walgreen's, Eckerd, and Drug Emporium. The company also added 250 mass merchandisers including Walmart, K Mart, and Target. This move was made because only 40 percent of health and beauty aid sales are realized in supermarkets. Another 40 percent is sold through drugstores, with the remaining 20 percent in mass merchandise outlets.[42] The new IRI sample, therefore, fills out the consumer package goods universe. In 1992 IRI provided its InfoScan panel members with a "keychain scanner," a portable, pocket-sized wand to register any product purchases made at nonscanner stores.[43]

In 1993, IRI introduced all-store, or "census-based," scanner data and created a service called InfoScan Census. Historically, data had been gathered from a sample of a few thousand of the nation's 15,000 plus supermarkets, a perfectly valid approach. However, by definition, a sample provides "estimates" that are subject to sampling error. Further, while a sample was able to measure sales in a city or even in a given grocery chain (i.e., Kroger), a sample could not pinpoint sales of each individual store in the chain. However, data from a "census" of all stores, as opposed to a sample, could.

Store-specific results are crucial information for a sales manager or any other manager seeking to implement micromarketing techniques. To illustrate, a sample might indicate that a brand's sales are up 10 percent in a particular chain; not a bad performance. However, since this is an average, based on a sample, there are some stores in which the brand's sales are up 20 percent and others in which sales are flat, or even declining. With census data it is now possible, for the first time, to identify which stores are underperforming and target them for special marketing attention. Just as electronically gathered scanner data were a major improvement over the old manual audit methodology, so too, are census data a great leap forward from "sample" data.

In 1994, IRI began tracking sales of household goods such as vacuum cleaners and coffee pots.[44] Its first major client was Helmac Products Corporation, a clothing-care products maker. Nielsen began tracking sales data for household goods marketers in 1992. Its major clients are Corning and Ekco Household. IRI will provide store-by-store data from certain retail chains and sample data from others. And so the battle continues.

Behavioral Research Versus Attitude Research—The Growing Chasm in Marketing Research The authors and a number of noted marketing research practitioners have observed a growing, and somewhat disturbing trend in large consumer package goods marketing research departments.[45] The controversy between attitude and behavioral research is not new in the academic world but has surfaced in the research industry with the advent of scanner data. In short, scanner research and survey research are not just two separate sets of research tools, they are becoming two separate sets of people. The scanner researchers (behavioralists) have a strong quantitative bent and are often mathematical modelers or statisticians. They begin and continue their careers by interacting with the scanner data supplier. They rarely, if ever, perform traditional survey research. The same is true in reverse for the survey researcher (attitude researcher).

Behavioralists are interested in what consumers actually do. This can be measured by the scanner data. They point out to the attitude researchers that "just because people tell you they are going to do something does not mean they will." Also, people do not always know or are not always willing to tell an interviewer what their motivations and feelings really are. The attitudinal researcher replies to the behavioralist that "scanner data are so sterile. You do not know feelings, how the products are used in their homes, or attitudes toward products, brands, or leading retailers. In fact, scanner research is like driving a car down the street but sitting backward in the driver's seat looking out the rear window. Regardless of how current, the scanner data look at past behavior while you (the company) attempt to move forward."

William Moult, president of ASI Marketing Research, New York, describes an imaginary dialog between the two groups in the following "A Professional Researcher's Perspective."

Marketing researchers need to be marketing oriented and not in one camp or another. The goal is to provide decision-making information to management. This means both types of data are needed.

Retailers Also Are Conducting Scanning Research

Retailers are not only purchasing scanner-based research from marketing researchers, they also are conducting their own tests.[46] With a better knowledge of what to stock, how to display it, and how to price and promote the brand for maximum profit, retailers can improve their profit margins and become less dependent on price-cutting promotions. Scanner-based research will help retailers kill off slow-moving brands and brands with poor profit margins.

Safeway Stores tests the effect of end-of-aisle displays on sales, even if such displays are not accompanied by price reductions or advertising. Scanner data can show, for example, whether multiproduct or single-product displays yield the most sales. Price elasticity also is tested. Safeway varies prices and display support and analyzes the results. "Although retailers are generally not fond of lowering prices drastically, we found that in some cases the volume of sales associated with the lower price ended up providing both the producer and the retailer with more profits that the 'normal' price," says Louise Booth, manager of scanner research, Safeway Stores.[47]

Safeway used scanner data to test alternative placements of products within a store. Results showed, for example, that foil-packaged sauce mixes should not be displayed together but spread around the store according to their contents (spaghetti sauce mix near bottled spaghetti cause, gravy mix near canned gravy, etc.). Another scanner test showed that sales increase 80 percent when candy bars are put on front-end racks near checkout stands. The finding led to a divisional policy change, Booth said.[48]

In 1990, Safeway created Safeway Scanner Marketing Research (SSMRS). Its first product is called StoreLab. Clients can test the effectiveness of off-shelf

A Professional Researcher's Perspective

The Scanner Researcher (notice the UPC symbol on his or her sweatshirt) would start by taking the position that "the cash register is the ultimate consumer voting machine."

The survey researcher (wearing his or her "your opinion counts" badge) responds by noting that "*listening* to your customer has always been a key to marketing success." It is worth mentioning that this is a point of view espoused by many CEOs as well.

But the scanner researchers insists that "*actions* speak louder than words." Now the survey researcher observes that "people can tell you *why* they buy certain products and how they *use* them." The scanner researcher reaffirms her commitment that "it is what the consumers *do* that counts." And the survey researcher's rebuttal is that "what consumers *think* and *feel* determines what they do."[49] ■

displays, shelf extenders, in-store signs, new package designs or sizes, and consumer bonus packages. Twenty Safeway stores, all equipped with scanners and all in the Denver metropolitan area, serve as StoreLab sites. SSMRS can match stores on category sales and provide aggregated data for clients in a customized format.[50]

The Future of Scanning The next generation of scanners, to be known as Scanner Plus, will have abilities far beyond those of today's machines. These scanners will be able to communicate with personal computers in homes. One function could be to analyze an individual household's consumption based on its prior purchase patterns and offer menu projections or product use suggestions with an associated shopping list. To encourage the use of that shopping list, special offers may be made on certain listed items. These special offers can be designed for each household rather than offering everyone the same promotion.

Scanner Plus also may keep track of each household's coupons and other special offers received directly from advertisers. These offers will simply be entered into the household's electronic account in both the household's personal computer as well as its "promotion" bank in Scanner Plus.

An example of a similar system already in use is the Vision Value card offered by Big Bear Supermarkets in Ohio. It combines scanning with the computerized equivalent of "green stamps" to provide consumers with coupons for products they actually use.

How will this new development affect marketing research? Advertisers will want to test the previously untestable, namely, how is a product's acceptance affected by a household's menu, or what is the optimum menu scenario for a product's particular set of attributes? Advertisers will want to test promotion values as a function of menu mix and repeat consumption rather than use today's criteria of covering the cost of the promotion.[51]

Summary

Observation research is the systematic process of recording the behavioral patterns of people, objects, and occurrences without questioning or communicating with them. To be successful, the needed information must be observable and the behavior of interest must be repetitive, frequent, or predictable in some manner. The behavior of interest also should be of a relatively short duration. There are five dimensions along which observational approaches vary: (1) natural versus contrived situations, (2) disguised versus undisguised situations, (3) structured versus unstructured observation, (4) human versus machine observers, and (5) direct versus indirect observation.

The biggest advantage of observation research is that we can see what people actually do rather than having to rely on what they say they did. Also some forms of data are more quickly and accurately gathered by observation. The primary disadvantage of this type of research is that the researcher learns nothing about motives, attitudes, intentions, or feelings.

People watching people can take the form of mystery shoppers; one-way mirror observations, such as child psychologists watching children play with toys; shopper patterns; content analysis; humanistic inquiry; and audits.

Machine observation includes traffic counters, physiological measurement devices, the People Reader, people meters, and scanners. The use of scanners in carefully controlled experimental settings enables the market researcher to accurately and objectively measure the direct causal relationship between different kinds of marketing efforts and actual sales. The leaders in this scanner-based research are Information Resources, Inc. and A. C. Nielsen.

Retailers, such as Safeway, are now offering their stores as testing laboratories for manufacturers. Packaged goods producers, such as Quaker Oats, can vary prices, promotion techniques, and package design and capture sales results via scanners. In the future, scanners will be able to communicate with personal computers in homes. One function may be to offer menu and product use suggestions.

Key Terms

observation research
open observation
disguised observation
structured observation
unstructured observation
mystery shoppers
one-way mirror observations
shopper patterns
content analysis
humanistic inquiry
theory-construction diary
methodological log
audit
A. C. Nielsen Retail Index
traffic counters
electroencephalogram (EEG)
galvanic skin response (GSR)
pupilometer
voice pitch analysis
People Reader
people meter
scanners
BehaviorScan
InfoScan
The Partners

Review and Discussion Questions

1. You are charged with the responsibility of determining whether men are brand conscious when shopping for racquetball equipment. Outline an observation research procedure for making that determination.

2. Fisher-Price has asked you to develop a research procedure for determining which of its prototype toys is most appealing to four- and five-year-olds. Suggest a methodology for making this determination.
3. What are the biggest drawbacks of observation research?
4. Compare and contrast the advantages and disadvantages of observation research versus survey research.
5. It has been said that "people buy things not for what they will do, but for what they mean." Discuss this statement in relation to observation research.
6. You are a manufacturer of a premium brand of ice cream. You want to know more about your market share, competitors' pricing, and types of outlets where your product is selling best. What kind of observational research data would you purchase? Why?
7. How might a mystery shopper be valuable to the following organizations: (a) Delta Airlines, (b) Marshall Field's, (c) H & R Block.
8. Why do you think that the research method of humanistic inquiry has caused such a controversy among social scientists? How does it differ from the traditional scientific method?
9. Compare and contrast people meters and the traditional diary approach to measuring audience sizes. What sources of bias might be found in people meter data?
10. Why has scanner-based research been seen as "the ultimate answer?" Do you see any disadvantages of this methodology?
11. If you were going to purchase scanner data, would you prefer IRI or Nielsen's methodology? Why?
12. Explain the attitudinal versus behavioralist controversy in the marketing research industry. Where do you stand?

CASE 8.1

Black & Decker Quantum Power Tools

You've seen this guy, and admit it, you hate him. He's the one who built that fancy new deck on the back of his house all by himself. A few months ago he finished off the basement, and lately he's been telling you that what he'd *really* love to do is blow out a wall and make the kitchen bigger. You, on the other hand, are still trying to change the switchplate in the den. Meet Mr. Super-Fixer-Upper, a growing breed in the ever-expanding, ever more sophisticated world of home improvement. This target market is called the "DIYer" in the trade. That is, a "do-it-yourselfer."

Black & Decker virtually stumbled across the opportunity in midpriced tools in summer 1991, a time when Japan's Makita and Sears's Craftsman line led the U.S. market. At that time Black & Decker was developing DeWalt, a pricey line of tools aimed at professional craftsmen and contractors. As Joseph Galli, 35, the energetic chief of the U.S. power tool division, relates: "We are finding in our research that a lot of nonprofessional consumers were really price-sensitive when it came to power tools. Sure, we know some serious DIYers were going to pay up and buy DeWalt. But others would just go elsewhere, and we're not a company that likes to leave business on the table for our competitors."

To gather intelligence on this new group, B&D gave Fieldwork Atlanta, an independent research firm, a tightly specified assignment: Find 50 male homeowners, ages 25 to 54, who own more than six power tools. The list arrived within two weeks. All 50—they included an airline pilot, a bank manager, a veterinarian, and, one of only two bachelors on the list, a teacher—were happy to be part of B&D's living laboratory.

From June to September, they were questioned about the tools they used and why they had picked particular brands. B&D marketing executives hung out with them in their homes and around their workshops. They watched how the 50 used their tools and asked why they liked or disliked certain ones, how the tools felt in their hands, and even how they cleaned up their work space when they were finished. The B&D people tagged along on shopping trips, too, monitoring what the DIYers bought and how much they spent. On occasion, executives even took an industrial psychologist with them on home visits, hoping this would tell even more about what the customer wanted.

By the end of 1991, Black & Decker had fortified its initial research by interviewing hundreds of Black & Decker customers who had mailed in warranty cards, asking them similar questions. The conclusion: Black & Decker could give these customers everything they wanted and more.

As they settled on the colors of the tools, team members turned to what to name their new line. Further customer research made the final decision easy: In tests, people liked Quantum. They said it sounded a step above other things, and they could pronounce it. Quantum it was. The name game wasn't quite over, however. The team had to decide whether to identify Black & Decker on the tools or the packaging. It does not appear on the DeWalt line because professional contractors had said they didn't consider Black & Decker tools sophisticated enough. In contrast, research showed that DIYers felt differently and had a lot of respect for the Black & Decker name. In fact, surveys by Landor Associates, a consulting firm, show it is the seventh most powerful brand in the United States. Says B&D exec Galli: "Since we were positioning Quantum as a step-up product for consumers, it made a lot of sense to have it carry the Black & Decker name, too."

In August 1993, the company began shipping a line of 18 new Quantum power tools to retailers. The launch was backed by a $10-million promotional budget.[52]

1. Would you say that "hanging around" with DIYers was observation research?
2. Spending time with the 50 DIYers gave Black & Decker a lot of information. Could researchers have skipped the quantitative study? Why?
3. What other forms of observation research might have been done in developing the Quantum line?

CASE 8.2

Sara Lee

Anita Scott has just been promoted to brand manager of frozen bakery products for Sara Lee. Her first new product introductions will be a line of frozen pastries. Currently, the company plans to introduce three flavors: chocolate, strawberry, and apricot. The pastries can be heated in a conventional oven or microwaved for quick preparation. Anita is considering using coupons in coordination with the introduction of the pastries. She has recently acquired some scanner data on coupon usage for new products. That information is presented in Tables 8.4 through 8.6 and in Figures 8.7 through 8.10.

1. After examining the scanner data, what kind of couponing strategy, including price, would you recommend for the pastry line?
2. What additional data would be useful to Anita in planning her couponing strategy?
3. What are some limitations that Anita should be aware of in using the scanner data?

TABLE 8.4 Coupon Usage on New Product Introductions

Issues
- Values versus Established Brands
- Use of Coupons on Trial versus Repeat Purchase
- Coupon-Related Purchases versus Other Purchases

THE DATA BASE

Markets: Evansville, IN
Portland, ME

Time Period: 39 Weeks from Introduction

Categories, Brands

Ready-to Eat Cereal	Cookies
Sun Flakes	Soft Batch
S'Mores	Duncan Hines
Fiber One	Puddin Creme
OJ's	Almost Home
Bran Muffin Crisp	Cereal Meal Bars
Almond Delight	S'Mores Chewy
Soluble Coffee	Dandy Bran
Classic	Rice Krispies
Silka	Whipps
Brava	Crackers
Decaf	Great Crisps
	Stone Creek

Sample Size: 3,912 Households

TABLE 8.5 Index of Coupon Triers to Noncoupon Triers

CATEGORY	VOLUME	PURCHASE OCCASIONS
Cereal	93%	91%
Soluble Coffee	76	77
Cookies	83	82
Cereal Meal Bars	97	95
Crackers	84	88
Average	87*	87*

NOTE: The buyer attracted by a coupon did not purchase as much or as often as a buyer that tried without a coupon. This is particularly true for the coffee brands studied.

*"The households that initially tried with a coupon purchased only 87 percent as much as the households that tried without a coupon. This is linked to the fact that triers with coupons purchased only on 87 percent as many occasions."

TABLE 8.6 **Summation**

Coupon values on new brands are slightly higher in absolute face value than coupons on established brands. The percentage discount spread is greater since the average dollar transaction on new products purchased with a coupon is lower.

Average Coupon Value

ESTABLISHED BRANDS		NEW BRANDS	
Value	% Redeemed	Value	% Redeemed
$.346	17.6%	$.380	22.0%

Average Retail Price

ESTABLISHED	NEW/COUPON REDEMPTION PURCHASE
$1.96	$1.73

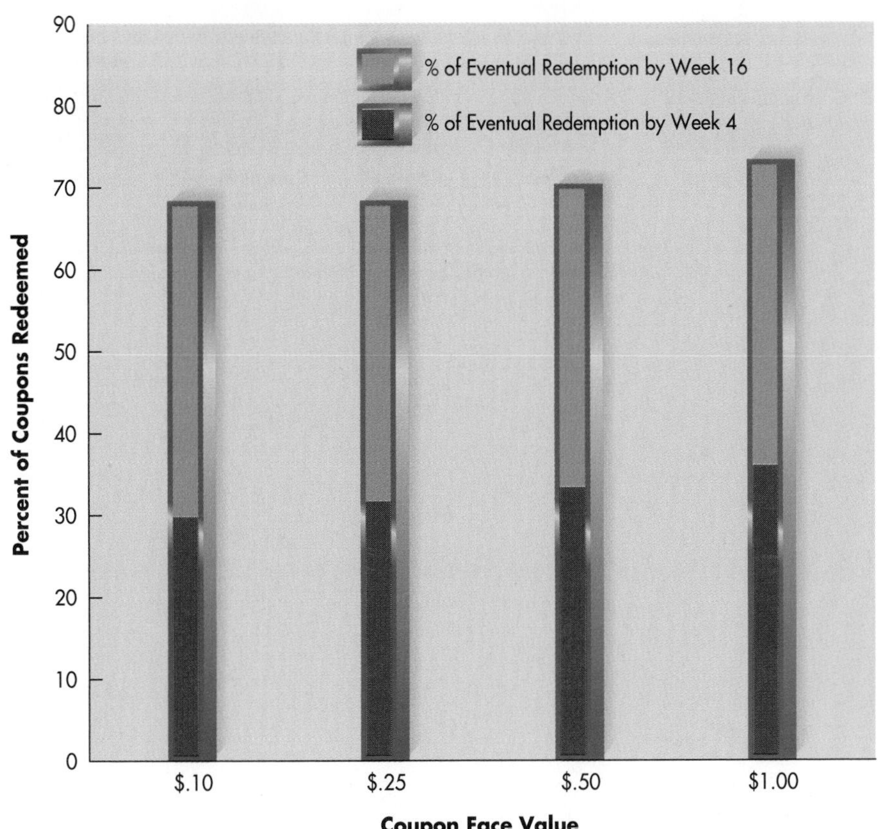

Note: Face value has no dffect on speed of redemption at sixteen weeks after the coupon drop. At four weeks post, higher value coupons have achieved only a slightly higher percentage of eventual redemption than do lower value coupons.

FIGURE 8.7
The Effect of Face Value on Speed of Redemption

FIGURE 8.8

Percent of Volume with Coupon Redemption

CATEGORY	ALL BRANDS	NEW BRANDS
Cereal	16.2%	24.8%
Soluble Coffee	30.5	17.8
Cookies	6.7	17.6
Cereal Meal Bars	13.0	18.1
Crackers	7.1	14.8
Average	14.7%	18.6%

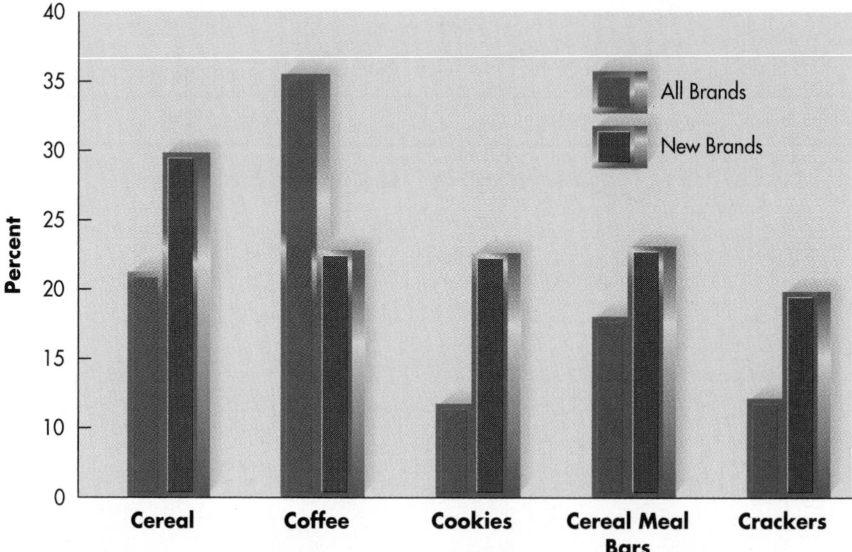

Note: For all new brands studied except soluble coffee, the percent of volume with redemption for new brands substantially exceeded existing brands. The relative difference is greatest in the cookie category.

FIGURE 8.9

Percent of Buying Households Redeeming Coupons

CATEGORY	ALL BRANDS	NEW BRANDS
Cereal	73.2%	45.8%
Soluble Coffee	57.4	37.1
Cookies	42.0	49.0
Cereal Meal Bars	41.8	38.8
Crackers	46.3	26.8
Average	52.1%	39.5%

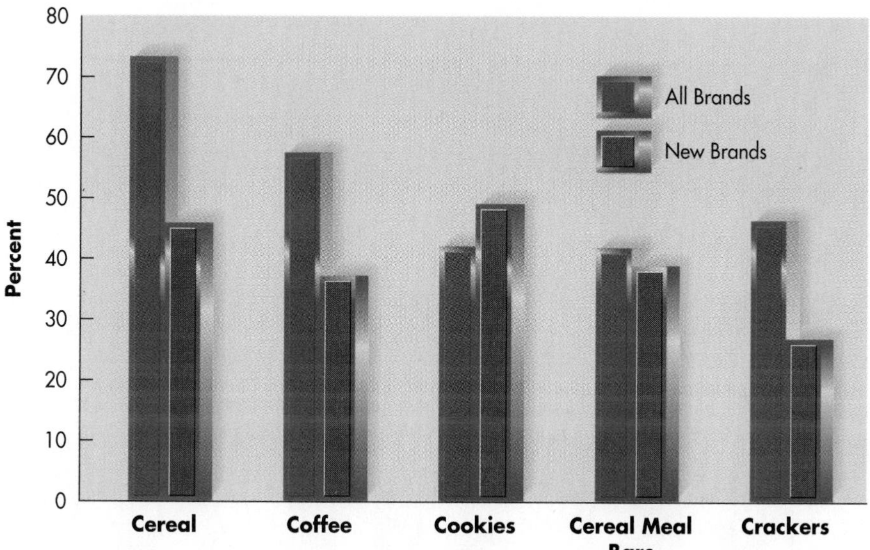

Note: For all new brands but cookies, a higher percentage of households buying on existing brands redeem coupons. This seeming discrepancy in cookies was probably caused by the coupon activity associated with the "Soft Cookie Wars."

FIGURE 8.10
All Brands

	Ounces (000)	Percent of Total Volume	Percent of Trial or Repeat Volume
Total Volume	414.7	100.0%	
Trial volume	145.8	35.1	
with coupon	29.6	7.1	20.2
without coupon	116.2	28.0	79.8
Repeat Volume	268.9	64.9	
with coupon	46.7	11.3	17.4
without coupon	222.2	53.6	82.6

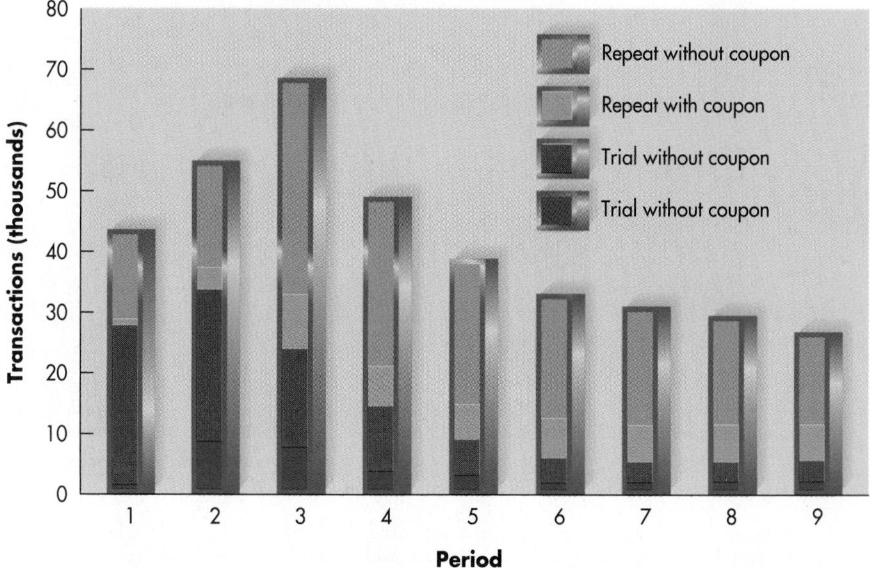

Note: When all brands are combined, coupon trial was 20 percent of total trial and peaked in period 2. Coupon repeat equals 17 percent of total repeat volume and grew consistently as a percent of total volume.

CHAPTER 9

Primary Data Collection: Experimentation

LEARNING OBJECTIVES

1. To understand the nature of experiments.
2. To gain insight into proving causation.
3. To learn about the experimental setting.
4. To examine experimental validity and the threats to validity.
5. To learn the disadvantages of experiments that limit their use in marketing research.
6. To compare preexperimental designs, true experimental designs, and quasi-experimental designs.
7. To gain insight into test marketing.

Grace Ingram is director of advertising for Taco Casita, a Mexican fast food restaurant chain with more than 400 outlets in Texas, New Mexico, Utah, Colorado, Louisiana, and Arkansas. The company has been in business for 15 years and experienced rapid growth over the first 10 years of that period. Sales for the past year exceeded $350 million. But the company has encountered a slower growth over the past two years and is considering major changes in its marketing strategy.

SOURCE: © Monkmeyer PhotoWorks.

Taco City is Taco Casita's major competitor in all markets. Taco City has 1,500 outlets throughout the United States and is a subsidiary of a major soft drink marketer. Taco Casita recently conducted a comprehensive marketing strategy evaluation that included focus groups and a large-scale telephone survey with Mexican food users throughout its market area. This evaluation and research pointed to a number of potential problems, but the one that Grace is most concerned with is the finding that Mexican fast food users think that Taco Casita's prices are too high. Taco Casita has positioned itself as the authentic Mexican fast food restaurant and has supported this position with the use of fresher, higher-quality ingredients than those used by its rivals. Grace is very concerned about the pricing issue because she knows that for Taco Casita to reduce its prices, the firm would have to make some reduction in the quality of the food it serves. She does not want to take this action unless she is very sure that the results for Taco Casita will be positive. She does not think that this question can be definitively answered by surveys, focus groups, or observation-based primary data collection. Grace is considering the possibility of testing a strategy change in the actual marketplace. However, she does not want to take the risk of testing a new "lower-price, somewhat-lower-quality" strategy throughout the entire area served by Taco Casita.

Taco Casita has four restaurants in the isolated market of Lubbock, Texas, and Grace is considering testing the new strategy in Lubbock for one year. At the end of this test, she will evaluate the results of the new strategy and make a recommendation to top managment regarding a possible change in the marketing strategy for Taco Casita.

Grace is concerned about a number of factors. First, is Lubbock a good place to conduct the test? Second, is one year long enough, or longer than necessary? Finally, what factors should she consider when evaluating the results of the Lubbock test? The issues confronting Grace Ingram are related to the main topic of this chapter, which pertains to experimental research. When is experimental research appropriate? How does one go about evaluating the results of an experiment? What are the inherent advantages and disadvantages of the experimental approach? Why conduct a field experiment rather than a laboratory experiment? These and a number of other questions will be considered in this chapter. After you have had an opportunity to read it, reconsider the questions raised by Grace's predicament to see whether you can make recommendations to her. ■

What Is an Experiment?

Research based on experimentation is fundamentally different from research based on survey or observation[1]. In the case of both survey and observation, the researcher is, in essence, a passive assembler of data. The researcher asks people questions or observes what they do. In the case of experiments, the situation is very different. The researcher becomes an active participant in the process.

In concept, an **experiment** is straightforward. The researcher changes or manipulates one thing, called an *explanatory, independent,* or *experimental variable,* to observe what effect this change has on something else, referred to as a *dependent variable.* In marketing experiments, the dependent variable is frequently some measure of sales, such as total sales, market share, or the like, and the explanatory or experimental variables are typically marketing mix variables, such as price, amount or type of advertising, changes in product features, or the like.

experiment

Research approach in which one variable is manipulated and the effect on another variable observed.

Demonstrating Causation

Experimental research is often referred to as *causal* (not casual) *research.* It is called **causal research** because it is the only type of research that has the potential to demonstrate that a change in one variable causes some predictable change in another variable. To demonstrate causation, that A likely caused B, we must be able to show three things:

causal research

Research designed to determine whether a change in one variable likely caused an observed change in another.

1. Concomitant variation
2. Appropriate time order of occurrence
3. Elimination of other possible causal factors

Please note that as we talk about causation and causality, we are using those terms in the scientific sense.[2] The scientific view of causation is quite different from the way the term is used commonly. First of all, the popular view of the term *causation* implies that there is a single cause of an event. For example, if we say the X is the cause of some observed change in Y, this implies that X is the only cause of the observed change in Y. The scientific view holds that X is only one of a number of determining conditions that caused the observed change in Y. Second, the everyday view of causality tends to imply a completely deterministic relationship. On the other hand, the scientific view implies a probabilistic relationship. The popular view is that if X is the cause of Y, then X must always lead to Y. The scientific view holds that X can be a cause of Y if the presence of X makes the occurrence of Y more probable or likely. Finally, the scientific view is that we never definitively prove the X is a cause of Y, but only infer that a relationship exists. In other words, causal relationships are always inferred and never demonstrated conclusively beyond a shadow of a doubt. The three types of evidence just cited (concomitant variation, appropriate time order of occurrence, and elimination of other possible causal factors) are used to infer causal relationships.

Concomitant Variation

concomitant variation

A predictable statistical relationship between two variables.

To provide evidence that a change in A caused a particular change in B, we must first show that there is **concomitant variation** or correlation between A and B. In other words, that they vary together in some predictable fashion. This relationship might be positive or inverse. An example of two variables that are related in a positive manner might be advertising and sales. They would be positively related if sales increased by some predictable amount when advertising increased. An example of two variables that are related in an inverse manner might be price and sales. They would be inversely (negatively) related if sales increased when price decreased and decreased when price increased. The researcher can test for the existence and direction of statistical relationships by means of a number of statistical procedures. These procedures include chi-square analysis, correlation analysis, regression analysis, and analysis of variance. All these statistical procedures are discussed later in the text (chi-square in Chapter 16, correlation analysis in Chapter 17, regression analysis in Chapter 18, and analysis of variance in Chapter 18).

However, concomitant variation by itself does not prove causation. Simply because two variables happen to vary together in some predictable fashion does not prove that one causes the other. You might, for example, find that there is a high degree of correlation between sales of a product in the United States and GNP of Germany. This may be true simply because both variables happen to be increasing at a similar rate. Further examination and consideration might show that there is no true link between the two variables. To prove causation, you must be able to show correlation, but correlation alone is not proof of causation.

Appropriate Time Order of Occurrence

appropriate time order of occurrence

To be considered a likely cause of a dependent variable, a change in an independent variable must occur before an observed change in the dependent variable.

The second thing that you must show to demonstrate that a causal relationship likely exists between two variables is that there is an **appropriate time order of occurrence.** To demonstrate that A caused B, the researcher must be able to show that A occurred before B occurred. For example, to demonstrate that a price change had an effect on sales, you must be able to show that the price change occurred before the change in sales was observed. However, showing that *A* and *B* vary concomitantly and that *A* occurred before *B* still does not provide evidence that is strong enough to permit us to conclude that *A* is the likely cause of an observed change in *B*.

Elimination of Other Possible Causal Factors

To infer that a causal relationship likely exists between *A* and *B*, the most difficult thing to demonstrate in many marketing experiments is that the change in *B* was not caused by some factor other than *A*. For example, we might increase our advertising expenditures and observe a particular increase in the sales of our product. Correlation and appropriate time order of occurrence are present. But has a likely causal relationship been demonstrated? The answer is clearly "No." It is possible that the observed change in sales is due to some factor other than the increase in advertising. For example, at the same time advertising expenditures were increased, a major competitor might have decreased advertising expenditures, or increased price, or pulled out of the market. Even if the competitive environment did not change, one or a combination of other factors may have influenced sales. For example, the economy in the area might have received a major boost for some reason that has nothing to do with the experiment. For any of these reasons or for many other possible reasons, the observed increase in sales might have been caused by some other factor or some combination of factors rather than or in addition to the increase in advertising expenditures. Much of the discussion in this chapter is related to the question of designing experiments that enable us to eliminate or adjust for the effects of other possible causal factors.

The Experimental Setting—Laboratory or Field

Experiments can be conducted in a laboratory or in a field setting.[3] Most experiments in the physical sciences are conducted in a laboratory setting. The major advantage of conducting experiments in a laboratory is the ability to control many other causal factors—temperature, light, humidity and so on—and focus on the effect of a change in *A* on *B*. In the lab, the researcher can more effectively deal with the third element of proving causation (elimination of other possible causal factors) and focus on the first two (concomitant variation and appropriate time order of occurrence).

Laboratory experiments provide a number of important advantages.[4] The major advantage, referred to earlier, relates to the ability to control all variables other than the experimental variable in the laboratory setting. This means that our ability to infer that an observed change in the dependent variable was caused by a change in the experimental or treatment variable is much stronger. As a result, laboratory experiments generally are viewed as having greater internal validity (internal validity is discussed in greater detail later). On the other hand, the controlled and possible sterile environment of the laboratory may not be a good analog of the marketplace. Because of this, the findings of laboratory experiments sometimes do not hold up when we transfer them to the actual marketplace. Therefore, laboratory experiments are often seen as having greater

laboratory experiments
Experiments conducted in a controlled setting.

field experiments
Tests conducted outside the laboratory in an actual market environment.

problems with external validity (external validity is discussed in greater detail later). However, laboratory experiments have many advantages and are probably being used to a greater extent today than in the past. The use of laboratory experiments at Keebler, as described in the following "Marketing Research in Practice" feature, provides a good example of effective use of laboratory experiments in the business world.

Many marketing experiments are conducted as **field experiments.** This means that they are conducted outside the laboratory in an actual market environment.

Marketing Research in Practice

Pizzarias are just one of the new products that are turning what was once a small biscuit and cookie company into a formidable competitor in the salty snack business. Keebler has become a case study of how to flank the competition by creating new products that offer consumers truly unique features. In 1991, Keebler sold $1.5 billion worth of cookies, crackers, salty snacks, and other related products. Roughly half this amount is from products that did not exist 10 years ago. New lines such as Pizzarias, Wheatables, and O'Boises potato chips have distinctive flavors, textures, and appeal.

Keebler learned the advantages of a strong new-product strategy during the cookie wars of the mid-1980s. Procter & Gamble and Frito-Lay tried to break into the cookie business with soft cookies, and Keebler was forced to respond quickly with new formulations of its own.

Since then, Keebler has used new technology and management techniques to reduce the time required for new product development. In 1986 Keebler opened an $11-million pilot plant and laboratory testing center called the Product and Process Development Center or PPDC. This facility includes a new product testing laboratory and a scale replica of a Keebler factory production line. New product ideas are tested with consumers in the testing laboratory. Once these new product ideas have passed consumer screening, new product teams can work out kinks in mixing, baking, frying, and packaging on an assembly line before the product moves into full production. Keebler executives say the production line has enabled it to eliminate 65 percent to 70 percent of the disappointments in factory line start-ups. This also means that Keebler can get a new product concept from the laboratory to the retail store with tremendous efficiency. Once management approves a new product, Keebler can get 90 percent national distribution within four weeks.

Another benefit of the laboratory testing and pilot plant is secrecy. Keebler has not needed a real, live test market in 10 years. Because of the PPDC, it does not have to do a factory dry run. Taste tests can be done in-house. The benefit: "We don't have to tip off our competition to what we are doing."[5] ■

Test markets, discussed later in this chapter, are a frequently used type of field experiment. Field experiments solve the problem of the realism of the environment but open up a whole new set of problems. The major problem is that in the field the researcher cannot control all spurious factors that might influence the dependent variable. In the field, the researcher cannot control the actions of competitors, the weather, the economy, societal trends, the political climate, and the like. Therefore, field experiments have more problems related to internal validity, whereas lab experiments have more problems related to external validity.

Experimental Validity

Validity is defined in Chapter 10 as actually measuring what we attempt to measure. The validity of a measure refers to the extent to which the measure is free from both systematic and random error. In addition to the general concept of validity, in experimentation we also are interested in two specific kinds of validity: internal validity and external validity.

Internal and External Validity

In an experimental design, any extraneous variable that may interfere with our ability to make causal inferences is considered a threat to validity.

Internal validity refers to the extent to which competing explanations for the experimental results observed can be avoided. If the researcher can show that the experimental or treatment variable actually produced the differences observed in the dependent variable, then the experiment can be said to be internally valid. This kind of validity requires evidence to demonstrate that variation in the dependent variable was caused by exposure to the treatment conditions and not by other causal factors.

internal validity
The extent to which competing explanations for the experimental results observed can be avoided.

External validity refers to the extent to which the causal relationships measured in an experiment can be generalized to outside persons, settings, and times.[6] The issue here is, How representative are the subjects and the setting used in the experiment of other populations and settings to which we would like to project the results? In general, field experiments offer a higher degree of external validity and a lower degree of internal validity than do laboratory experiments.

external validity
The extent to which causal relationships measured in an experiment can be generalized to outside persons, settings, and times.

Experimental Notation

Further discussion of experiments will be facilitated by using a standard system of notation to describe experiments. This system is described as the following:[7]

- *X* is used to indicate the exposure of an individual or a group to an experimental treatment. The experimental treatment is the factor whose effects we want to measure and compare. Experimental treatments may be factors such as different prices, package designs, point-of-purchase displays, advertising approaches, or product forms. Possible experimental treatments would include all possible elements of the marketing mix.
- *O* (for observation) is used to refer to the process of taking measurements on the test units. Test units are individuals or groups of individuals or entities

Campbell Soup Company executives believed that Ragu increased advertising and coupon offers to encourage consumers to stock up on Ragu spaghetti sauce to deter the market testing of Prego's spaghetti sauce.

(retail stores) whose response to the experimental treatments is being tested. Test units might include individual consumers, groups of consumers, retail stores, total markets, or any other entities that might be the targets of a firms marketing program.

- Different time periods are represented by the horizontal arrangement of the *X*s and *O*s. For example,

$$O_1 \qquad X \qquad O_2$$

would describe an experiment in which a preliminary measurement was taken on one or more test units O_1, the one or more test units were exposed to the treatment or experimental variable X, and a measurement of the test units was taken after the exposure O_2. The *X*s and *O*s also can be arranged vertically to show simultaneous exposure and measurement of different test units. For example, we might have the following design

$$\begin{matrix} X_1 & O_1 \\ X_2 & O_2 \end{matrix}$$

This design shows two different groups of test units. It also shows that each group of test units received a different experimental treatment at the same time (X_1 and X_2). Finally, the design shows that the two groups were measured simultaneously (O_1 and O_2).

Extraneous Variables: Threats to Experimental Validity

In interpreting experimental results, we would like to be able to conclude that the observed response is due to the effect of the experimental or treatment variable. However, many things stand in the way of our ability to reach this conclusion. In anticipation of possible problems in interpretation, we need to design our experiment so that we can eliminate extraneous factors as possible causes of the observed effect. Examples of extraneous factors or variables follow.[8]

history
Things that happen or outside variables that change between the beginning and end of an experiment.

History History refers to any variable or event other than those manipulated by the researcher (experimental or treatment variable) that takes place between the beginning and end of the experiment and that might affect the value of the dependent variable. Early tests of Prego Spaghetti Sauce by the Campbell Soup Company provide an example of the possible problems with this type of extraneous variable. Campbell executives claim that Ragu greatly increased its advertising levels and use of cents-off deals during their test. They believe that this increased marketing activity was designed to get shoppers to increase their inventories of Ragu and make it impossible for Campbell to get an accurate reading of potential sales for its Prego product.

maturation
Changes in subjects that take place during the experiment that are not related to the experiment but may affect their response to the experimental factor.

Maturation Maturation refers to changes in subjects throughout the course of the experiment that are a function of time and include such things as getting older, hungrier, tired, and the like. As a result, the responses of people to a treatment variable throughout the course of an experiment may change because of these maturation factors and not because of the treatment or experimental variable. The likelihood that maturation will be a serious problem in a particular experiment depends on the length of the experiment. The longer the experiment runs, the more likely it is that maturation will present problems for interpreting the results.

Instrument Variation **Instrument variation** refers to any changes in measurement instruments that might explain differences in the measurements taken. This is a serious problem in many marketing experiments in which people are used as interviewers or observers to measure the dependent variable. Measurements on the same subject may be taken by different interviewers or observers at different points in time. Any differences between these measurements may reflect differences in the way the interviewing or observation was done by different interviewers or observers. On the other hand, the same interviewer or observer may be used to take measurements on the same subject over time. In this case, differences may reflect the fact that the particular observer or interviewer has become less interested and is doing a sloppier job over time.

instrument variation
Differences or changes in measurement instruments (e.g., interviewers or observers) that explain differences in measurements.

Selection Bias The threat to validity of **selection bias** is encountered in situations in which the experimental or test group is systematically different from the population to which we would like to project the experimental results or from a control group to which we would like to compare results.

In projecting the results to a population that is systematically different from the test group, we may get results very different from those we got in the test because of differences in the makeup of the two groups. In a similar manner, an observed difference between a test group and an untreated control group (not exposed to the experimental or treatment variable) may be due to differences in the two groups and not to the effect of the experimental or treatment variable. We can ensure equality of groups by either matching or randomization. Randomization involves assigning subjects to test groups and control groups at random. Matching involves what the name suggests—we make sure that there is a one-to-one match between people or other units (stores) in the test and control groups in regard to key characteristics (e.g., age).

selection bias
Systematic differences between the test group and control group because of a biased selection process.

Mortality **Mortality** refers to the loss of test units during the course of an experiment. This is a problem because there is no easy way to know whether the test units that we lost would have responded to the experimental or treatment variable in the same way as those units that continued throughout the entire experiment. An experimental group that was representative of the population or the same as a control group may become nonrepresentative because of the systematic loss of the subjects with certain characteristics. For example, in a study of music preferences of the population, if we lost nearly all the subjects under the age of 25 during the course of the experiment, then we are very likely to get a biased picture of music preferences at the end of the experiment. In this case, our results probably would lack external validity.

mortality
Loss of test units or subjects during the course of an experiment. The problem is that those lost may be systematically different from those who stay.

Testing Effect **Testing effects** result from the fact that the process of experimentation may produce its own effect on the responses we observe. For example, measuring attitude toward a product before exposing subjects to an ad may act as a treatment and influence perception of the ad. Testing effects come in two forms:

testing effect
An effect that is a by-product of the research process and not the experimental variable.

- Main testing effects are the possible effects of earlier observations on later observations. For example, students taking the GMAT for the second time tend to do better than those taking the test for the first time. This is true even though students have no information about the items they actually missed on the first test. This effect also can be reactive in the sense that responses to the first administration of an attitude test have some actual effect on the attitudes of subjects that is reflected in subsequent applications of the same test.
- Interactive testing effect refers to the effect of a prior measurement on a subject's response to a later measurement. For example, if we ask subjects about their awareness of advertising for various products (preexposure measurement) and then expose them to advertising for one or more of these products (treatment variable), then postmeasurements are likely to reflect the joint effect of the preexposure and the treatment condition.

regression to the mean
Tendency for behavior of subjects to move toward the average for that behavior during the course of an experiment.

Regression To The Mean **Regression to the mean** refers to the observed tendency of subjects with extreme behavior to move toward the average for that behavior during the course of an experiment. Test units may exhibit extreme behavior because of chance, or, in some cases, they may have been specifically chosen because of their extreme behavior. You may, for example, have chosen people for an experimental group because they are extremely heavy users of a particular product or service. It has been observed that in these situations, it is likely for these extreme cases to move toward the average during the course of an experiment. The problem is that this movement toward the average, which has nothing to do with the treatment or experimental variable, may be interpreted to have been caused by the experimental or treatment variable.

Experimentation: Summary of Basic Issues

Experimental Design and Treatment

experimental design
A test in which the researcher has control over one or more independent variables and manipulates them.

In an **experimental design,** the researcher has control over one or more independent variables and manipulates one or more independent variables. In the experiments we discuss, typically only one independent variable is manipulated. Nonexperimental designs involve no manipulation and typically are referred to as *ex post facto* (after the fact) *research.* In this type of research, an effect is observed and then some attempt is made to attribute this effect to some causal factor. An experimental design includes four factors:

1. The *treatment* or experimental variable (independent variable) to be manipulated
2. The *subjects* to participate in the experiment
3. A *dependent variable* to measure
4. Some *plan or procedure* for dealing with extraneous causal factors

treatment
The independent variable that is manipulated in an experiment.

The **treatment** is the independent variable that is manipulated. *Manipulation* refers to the process in which the researcher sets the levels of the independent variable to test a particular causal relationship. To test the relationship between price (independent variable) and sales of a product (dependent variable), a researcher might expose subjects to three different levels of price and record the level of purchases under each level. Price is the variable that will be manipulat-

Students taking the GMAT exam usually improve on their second try even though they aren't given information about the items they missed on the first test. This is an example of the testing effect. SOURCE: © Mark Richards/PhotoEdit.

ed; price is the single treatment factor, with three treatment conditions or levels of price.

An experiment may include a test or treatment group and a control group. A *control group* is a group in which the independent variable is not changed during the course of the experiment. A *test group* is a group that is exposed to a manipulation (change) of the independent variable.

Experimental Effects

experimental effect
The effect of the treatment variable on the dependent variable.

The term **experimental effect** refers to the effect of the treatment variables on the dependent variable. The goal is to determine the effect of each treatment condition (level of treatment variable) on the dependent variable. For example, suppose that three different markets are selected to test three different prices or treatment conditions. Each price will be tested in each market for three months. In market one, a price 2 percent lower than existing prices for the product is tested; in market two, a price 4 percent lower is tested; and in market three, a price 6 percent lower is tested. At the end of the three-month test, sales in market one are observed to have increased by less than 1 percent over sales for the preceding three-month period. In market two, sales increased by 3 percent; and in market three, sales increased by 5 percent. The change in sales observed in each market would be the experimental effect.

The Control of Other (Extraneous) Causal Factors

Other (extraneous) causal factors are variables that can affect the dependent variable and should be controlled in some manner to establish a clear picture of the effect of the manipulated variable on the dependent variable. Extraneous causal factors are ordinarily referred to as *confounding variables* because they confound the treatment condition, making it impossible to determine whether changes in the dependent variable are due solely to the treatment conditions.

Four basic approaches are used to control extraneous factors: randomization, actual physical control, experimental design control, and statistical control.

randomization

The random assignment of subjects to treatment conditions to ensure equal representation of subject characteristics in all groups.

physical control

Holding the value or level of extraneous variables constant throughout the course of an experiment.

design control

Use of the experimental design to control extraneous causal factors.

statistical control

Adjusting for the effects of confounded variables by statistically adjusting the value of the dependent variable for each treatment condition.

Randomization involves randomly assigning subjects to treatment conditions so that we can reasonably assume that extraneous causal factors related to subject characteristics will be represented equally in each treatment condition, thus canceling out extraneous effects.

Physical control of extraneous causal factors involves somehow holding the value or level of the extraneous variable constant throughout the experiment. Another approach to physical control is *matching*. Under this approach, respondents are matched in regard to important personal characteristics (e.g., age, income, lifestyle) before being assigned to different treatment conditions. The goal is to make sure there are no important differences between characteristics of respondents in the test and control groups. Specific matching procedures are discussed later in this chapter.

Design control refers to the control of extraneous causal factors by means of specific types of experimental designs developed for this purpose. These designs will be discussed later in this chapter.

Finally, **statistical control** procedures can account for extraneous causal factors if they can be identified and measured throughout the course of the experiment. These procedures (e.g., analysis of covariance) can be used to adjust for the effects of a confounded variable on the dependent variable by statistically adjusting the value of the dependent variable within each treatment condition.

Why Are Experiments Not Used More Often?

The preceding discussion shows that experiments are an extremely powerful form of research—the only type of research that can truly explore the existence and nature of causal relationships between variables of interest. Given these obvious advantages over other research designs for primary data collection, you might ask why experimental research is not used more often. There are many reasons for this, including the cost of experiments, the issue of security, problems associated with implementing experiments, and the dynamic nature of the marketplace.

The High Cost of Experiments

To some degree, when making comparisons of the costs of experiments with the costs of survey or observation-based research, we are comparing apples to oranges. It is clear that experiments can be very costly in both money and time. In many cases, managers may anticipate that the costs of doing an experiment will exceed the value of the information gained. Consider, for example, the costs of testing three alternative advertising campaigns in three different geographic areas. Three different campaigns must be produced; airtime must be purchased in all three markets; the timing in all three markets must be carefully coordinated; some system must be put into place to measure sales before, during, and after the test campaigns have run; measurements of other extraneous variables must be made; extensive analysis of the results must be performed; and a variety of other tasks must be completed to execute the experiment. All of this may well cost more than $1 million.

Security Issues

A field experiment or test market involves exposing a marketing plan or some key element of a marketing plan in the actual marketplace. Undoubtedly, competitors will find out what is being considered well in advance of full-scale market introduction. This advance notice gives competitors an opportunity to decide if and how to respond. In any case, the element of surprise is lost. In some instances, competitors have actually "stolen" concepts that were being tested in the marketplace and gone into national distribution before the company testing the product or strategy element completed the test market.

Implementation Problems

A number of problems may be encountered that will hamper the implementation of experiments. These include the following: the difficulty of gaining cooperation within the organization, contamination problems, differences between test markets and the total population, and the lack of a group of people or geographic area available as a control group.

It may be extremely *difficult to obtain cooperation* within the organization in regard to executing certain types of experiments. For example, a regional marketing manager might be very reluctant to permit her market area to be used as a test market for a reduced level of advertising or a higher price. Quite naturally, there would be concern that the experiment might lower sales for the area.

Contamination refers to the fact that buyers from outside the test area may come into the area to top purchase the product because of the experiment. These purchases by outsiders will distort the results of the experiment. Outside buyers might live on the fringes of the test market area and receive TV advertisements intended only for those in the test area that offer a lower price, a special rebate, or some other incentive to buy a product. Their purchases would tend to indicate that the particular sales-stimulating factor being tested was more effective than actually was the case.

contamination
The inclusion of a group of respondents in a test who are not normally there; for example, outside buyers who see an advertisement intended only for those in the test area and enter the area to purchase the product being tested.

A third problem relates to the fact that in some cases *test markets may be so different* and the behavior of consumers in those markets so different that it is difficult to detect a relatively small experimental effect. This problem can be dealt with by careful matching of test markets and other strategies designed to ensure a higher degree of equivalency of test units.

Finally, in some situations no geographic area or group of people may be available to serve as a control group. This may be the case when dealing with industrial products, in which a very small number of purchasers are concentrated geographically. An attempt to test a new product among a subset of such purchasers would almost certainly be doomed to failure.

Selected Experimental Designs

In the following section, examples of preexperimental, true experimental, and quasi-experimental designs are discussed.[9] In outlining these experimental designs, we use the system of notation introduced earlier.

Three Preexperimental Designs

preexperimental design
A design that offers little or no control over extraneous factors.

Studies using **preexperimental designs** generally are difficult to interpret. This is because they offer little or no control over the influence of extraneous factors and, as a result, often are not much better than descriptive studies when it comes to making causal inferences. With these designs, the researcher has little control over aspects, such as to whom and when, of exposure to the treatment variable and measurements. However, these designs frequently are used in commercial marketing research because they are simple and inexpensive. They are useful for suggesting new hypotheses but do not offer strong tests of hypotheses. The reasons for this will be clear after you review the discussion that follows.

one-shot case study
Preexperimental design with no control group and an after measurement only.

The One-Shot Case Study The **one-shot case study** involves exposing test units (people or test market) to the treatment or experimental variable for some period of time and then taking a measurement of the dependent variable. Symbolically, the design is shown as

$$X \qquad O_1$$

There are two basic weaknesses in this design. No pretest observations are made of the test units that will receive the treatment, and no control group of test units that did not receive the treatment is observed. As a result of these deficiencies, the design does not deal with the effects of any of the extraneous variables discussed previously. Therefore, the design lacks internal validity and, most likely, external validity as well. This design is useful for suggesting causal hypotheses but does not provide a strong test of these hypotheses. Many test markets for new products (not previously on the market) are based on this design. Examples of this and other preexperimental designs are shown in Table 9.1.

one-group pretest-posttest design
Preexperimental design with pre- and postmeasurements but no control group.

The One-Group Pretest-Posttest Design The **one-group pretest-posttest design** is the design employed most frequently for test markets that involve testing changes in established products or marketing strategies. The fact that the product was on the market before the change provides the basis for the pretest measurement (O_1). The design is shown symbolically as

$$O_1 \qquad X \qquad O_2$$

Pretest observations are made on a single group of subjects or a single test unit (O_1) that later receives the treatment. Finally, a posttest observation is made (O_2). The treatment effect is estimated by $O_2 - O_1$.

History is a threat to the internal validity of this design because an observed change in the dependent variable might be caused by an event outside the experiment that took place between the pretest and posttest measurements. In laboratory experiments, this threat can be controlled by insulating respondents from outside influences. Unfortunately, this type of control is impossible in field experiments.

Maturation is another threat to this type of design. An observed effect might be caused by the fact that subjects have grown older, smarter, more experienced, or the like between the pretest and the posttest.

This design has only one pretest observation. As a result, we know nothing of the pretest trend in the dependent variable. The posttest score may be higher

TABLE 9.1 Examples of Preexperimental Designs

Situation

Blue Cross/Blue Shield is in the process of instituting a new sales training program for its existing sales force. The program is designed to increase the productivity of individual salespersons and, thus, the entire sales force.

Butler Moore, vice-president in charge of sales, wants to do a small-scale research project to determine whether the course is producing the desired results.

Billy Marion, director of marketing research, has proposed three preexperimental designs as outlined in the following.

One-Shot Case Study Design

This design would have the following features:

Basic design: $X\ O_1$

Sample: Ask for volunteers from among those who have taken the course.

Treatment (X): Taking the course.

Measurement $(O)_1$: Actual sales performance for the six-month period after the course.

Weaknesses: No conclusive inferences can be drawn from the results.

The posttest measurement of sales may be the result of many uncontrolled factors. It cannot be judged better or worse in the absence of a pretreatment of observation of sales performance.

There is no control group of salespersons who did not receive the treatment (take the course).

Static-Group Comparison

This design has the following features:

Basic design:

Experimental group $X\ O_1$

Control group O_2

Sample: Volunteers for both test and control groups.

Treatment: Same as previous.

Measurements (O_1, O_2): O_1 actual sales performance of experimental group for six months after the course; O_2 same for control group that did not take course (treatment).

Weaknesses:

No pretest measure to help us deal with threats such as history and maturation discussed earlier. Because subjects were not assigned to the two groups at random, differences in performance between the two groups may be attributed to differences in the groups (one group had more good salespersons to begin with) rather than the sales training course.

One-Group Pretest-Posttest Design

This is a somewhat better design.

Basic design: $O_1\ X\ O_2$

Sample: Same as previous.

Treatment: Same as previous.

Measurement (O_1, O_2): O_1 actual sales performance for the six months prior to course; O_2 actual sales performance for the six months after the course.

Comparison: Same as the previous design except a pretest, measure of sales performance (O_2) is taken.

Weaknesses: Better than one-shot case study design but still has many serious problems

Difference between pretest and posttest measures may be attributable to a number of things other than the sales training course.

These other things (extraneous factors) include

Economic conditions (better or worse conditions) may have contributed to the observed change in the dependent variable (history threat).

Salesperson may have matured (gotten better) in ways that had nothing to do with the course over the period (maturation).

The pretest measure and the fact that the sales force knew its performance was being monitored may have affected the performance (testing effect).

Some salespersons may have dropped out (left the company) over the period (mortality).

because of the increasing trend of the dependent variable in a situation in which this effect is not the treatment of research interest.

The Static-Group Comparison The **static-group comparison** design uses two treatment groups, one (experimental group) is exposed to the treatment and one (control group) is not. The two groups must be considered as nonequivalent because subjects are not randomly assigned to the groups. The design can be shown symbolically as follows:

Experimental Group	X	O_1
Control Group		O_2

static-group comparison
Preexperimental design that uses an experimental and a control group. However, subjects or test units are not randomly assigned to the two groups and no premeasurements are taken.

The treatment effect is estimated as $O_1 - O_2$. The most obvious flaws in this design are the absence of pretests and the fact that any posttest differences between the groups may be due to the treatment effect, selection differences between the nonequivalent groups, or many other reasons.

Three True Experimental Designs

true experimental design

Research using an experimental group and a control group, and assignment of test units to both groups is randomized.

In a **true experimental design,** the experimenter randomly assigns treatments to randomly selected test units. The random assignment of test units to treatments is denoted by (*R*) in our notation system. Randomization is an important mechanism that makes the results of true experimental designs better (more valid) than the results from preexperimental designs. True experimental designs are superior to preexperimental designs because randomization takes care of many extraneous variables. The principal reason for choosing to conduct randomized experiments over other types of research design is that they make causal inference clearer.[10] Three true experimental designs are discussed in this section.

before and after with control group

True experimental design that includes random assignment of subjects or test units to experimental and control groups and premeasurement of both groups.

Before and After With Control Group The **before and after with control group** can be presented symbolically as

Experimental Group	(*R*)	O_1	X	O_2
Control Group	(*R*)	O_3		O_4

Because the test units in this design are randomly assigned to the experimental and the control groups, the two groups can be considered equivalent. Therefore, they are likely to be subject to the same extraneous factors except for the treatment of research interest in the experimental group. For this reason, the difference between the pre- and postmeasurements of the control group $(O_4 - O_3)$ should provide a good estimate of the effect of all the extraneous influences experienced by each group. To get the true impact of the treatment variable X, the extraneous influences must be removed from the difference between the pre- and postmeasurements of the experimental group. Thus, the true impact of X is estimated by $(O_2 - O_1) - (O_4 - O_3)$. This design generally controls for all but two major threats to validity: mortality and history.

Mortality will be a problem if certain units drop out during the study and if the units dropping out differ systematically from the ones that remain. This results in a selection bias because the experimental and control groups are composed of different subjects at the posttest than they were at the pretest. History will be a problem in those situations in which events other than the treatment variable affect the experimental group but not the control group, or vice versa. Examples of this and other true experimental designs are provided in Table 9.2.

Solomon four-group design

Research using two experimental groups and two control groups to control for all extraneous variable threats.

The Solomon Four-Group Design The **Solomon four-group design** is similar to the previous design, however, a second set of experimental and control groups is added to control for all extraneous variable threats to internal validity and the interactive testing effect. This design is presented symbolically as follows.

Experimental Group 1:	(*R*)	O_1	X	O_2
Control Group 1:	(*R*)	O_3		O_4
Experimental Group 2:	(*R*)		X	O_5
Control Group 2:	(*R*)			O_6

TABLE 9.2 **Examples of True Experimental Designs**

Situation	
A shampoo marketer wants to measure the sales effect of a point-of-purchase display. The firm is considering two true experimental designs.	
After-Only with Control Group Design	Before and After with Control Group Design
This design would have the following features. Basic design: Experimental Group (R) X O_1 Control group (R) O_2 Sample: Random sample of stores that sell shampoo. Stores are randomly assigned to test and control groups. Groups can be considered equivalent. Treatment (X): Placing the point-of-purchase display in stores in the experimental group for one month. Measurements (O_1, O_2): Actual sales of company's brand during the period that the point-of-purchase displays are in the test stores. Comments: Because of random assignment of stores to groups, the test group and control group can be considered equivalent. Measure of the treatment effect of X is $O_1 - O_2$. If O_1 = 125,000 units and O_2 = 113,000 units, then the treatment effect = 12,000 units.	This design would have the following features. Basic design: Experimental Group (R) O_1 X O_2 Control Group (R) O_3 O_4 Sample: Same as previous. Treatment (X): Same as previous. Measurements (O_1 to O_4): O_1 and O_2 pre- and postmeasurements for the experimental group; O_3 and O_4 same for control group. Results: O_1 = 113,000 units O_2 = 125,000 units O_3 = 111,000 units O_4 = 118,000 units Comments: Random assignment to groups means that they can be considered equivalent. Because groups are equivalent, it is reasonable to assume that they will be equally affected by the same extraneous factors. The difference between the pre- and postmeasurements for the control group ($O_4 - O_3$, provides a good estimate of the effects of all extraneous factors on both groups. Based on these results, $O_4 - O_3$ = 7,000 units). The estimated treatment effect is $(O_2 - O_1) - (O_4 - O_3)$, (125,000 − 113,000) − (118,000 − 111,000) = 5,000 units.

The second experimental group receives no pretest but is otherwise identical to the first experimental group. The second control group receives only a posttest measurement.

This design provides several measures of the experimental treatment effect of X. They are $(O_2 - O_1) - (O_4 - O_3)$, $(O_6 - O_5)$, and $(O_2 - O_4)$. If there is agreement among these measures, the inferences that you can make about the effect of the treatment can be much stronger. In addition, with this design it is possible to directly measure the interaction of the treatment and before measure effects $[(O_2 - O_4) - (O_5 - O_6)]$.

after-only with control group True experimental design that involves random assignment of subjects or test units to experimental and control groups but no premeasurement of the dependent variable.

The After-Only With Control Group The **after-only with control group** design differs from the static-group comparison design (with nonequivalent groups) discussed earlier in regard to the assignment of the test units. In the earlier design, the test units were not randomly assigned to treatment groups. As a result, it was possible for the groups to differ in regard to the dependent variable before presentation of the treatment. This design deals with this shortcoming and can be shown symbolically as

$$\begin{array}{rccc} \text{Experimental Group:} & (R) & X & O_1 \\ \text{Control Group:} & (R) & & O_2 \end{array}$$

Essentially, it consists of the last two groups of the Solomon four-group design.

You will notice that the test units are randomly (R) assigned to experimental and control groups. This random assignment of test units to the groups should produce experimental and control groups that are approximately equal in regard to the dependent variable before presentation of the treatment to the experimental group. In addition, you also can reasonably assume that test unit mortality (one of the threats to internal validity) will affect each group in the same way.

Considering this design in the context of the shampoo example described in Table 9.2, we can see a number of problems. Events other than the treatment may have occurred during the experimental period in one or a few stores in the experimental group. If a particular store in the experimental group ran a sale on certain other products and, as a result, had a larger (more than average) number of customers in the store, shampoo sales might be increased because of the heavier traffic. Events such as these, which are store specific (history), may distort the overall treatment effect. Also, there is a possibility that a few stores may drop out during the experiment (mortality threat), resulting in a selection bias because the stores in the experimental group will be different at the posttest.

If the experimenter added second experimental and control groups, and the stores in the second experimental group were subjected to the new point-of-sale advertising campaign, then the design would become a Solomon four-group design. Posttest measures of shampoo sales for stores in the second experimental and control group would be taken (O_5, and O_6).

If the marketer observed an agreement between the measures $[(O_2 - O_1) - (O_4 - O_2)]$, $(O_6 - O_5)$, and $(O_2 - O_4)$, then the inference about the effects of point-of-sale advertising campaign will be much more conclusive.

Quasi-Experiments

When designing a true experiment, the researcher often must create artificial environments to control independent and extraneous variables. Because of this artificiality, questions are raised about the external validity of the experimental findings. **Quasi-experimental designs** have been developed to deal with this problem. They generally are more feasible in field settings than are true experiments.

quasi-experiments
Studies in which the researcher lacks complete control over the scheduling of treatment or must assign respondents to treatment in a nonrandom manner.

In quasi-experiments, the researcher lacks complete control over the scheduling of treatments or must assign respondents to treatments in a *nonrandom* fashion. These designs frequently are used in marketing research studies because cost and field constraints often do not permit the researcher to exert direct control over the scheduling of treatments and the *randomization* of respondents. Selected examples of these types of designs follow.

interrupted time-series design
Research in which the treatment "interrupts" ongoing repeated measurements.

Interrupted Time-Series Designs **Interrupted time-series designs** involve repeated measurement of an effect both before and after a treatment is introduced and "interrupts" previous data patterns. Interrupted time-series experimental designs can be shown symbolically as

$$O_1 \quad O_2 \quad O_3 \quad O_4 \qquad X \qquad O_5 \quad O_6 \quad O_7 \quad O_8$$

A common example of this type of design in marketing research involves the use of consumer purchase panels. You might use a panel to make periodic measures of consumer purchase activity (the *O*s). We might introduce a new promotional campaign (the *X*) and examine the panel data for an effect. The researcher has control over the timing of the promotional campaign but cannot be sure when the panel members were exposed to the campaign or if they were exposed at all.

This design is very similar to the one-group pretest-posttest design, $O_1\ X\ O_2$. However, time-series experimental designs have greater interpretability than the one group pretest-posttest design because the many pretest-posttest measurements taken provide more understanding of extraneous variables. If, for example, sales of a product were on the rise and a new promotional campaign was introduced, the true effect of this campaign cannot be estimated if a pretest and posttest design is used. However, the rising trend in sales would be obvious if a number of pretest and posttest observations had been made. The time-series design helps in determining the underlying trend of the dependent variable and provides better interpretability in regard to the treatment effect.

There are two fundamental weaknesses of this design. The primary weakness is the experimenter's *inability to control history.* Although maintaining a careful log of all possible relevant external happenings can reduce this problem, the experimenter has no way of determining the appropriate number and timing of pretest and posttest observations.

The other weakness of this design comes from the possibility of *interactive effects of testing* and evaluation apprehension resulting from the repeated measurements taken on test units. For example, panel members may become "expert" shoppers or become more conscious of their shopping habits. Under these circumstances, it may be inappropriate to make generalizations to other populations.

Multiple Time-Series Designs In some studies, based on time-series designs, we are able to find a group of test units to serve as a control group. If a control group can be added to the straight time-series design, then we can be more certain in our interpretation of the treatment effect. This design, called the **multiple time-series design,** can be shown symbolically as

$$\begin{array}{rccccccc} \text{Experimental Group:} & O_1 & O_2 & O_3 & X & O_4 & O_5 & O_6 \\ \text{Control Group:} & O_1 & O_2 & O_3 & & O_4 & O_5 & O_6 \end{array}$$

multiple time-series design
An interrupted time-series design with a control group.

The researcher must take care in selecting the control group. For example, an advertiser might test a new advertising campaign in a test city. That city would constitute the experimental group, and another city that was not exposed to the new campaign would be chosen as the control group. It is important that the test and control cities be roughly equivalent in regard to characteristics related to the sale of the product (e.g., competitive brands available).

Test Markets

Test Markets Defined

The term **test market** is used by marketing researchers rather loosely to refer to any research that[11]

- Involves testing a new product or any change in an existing marketing strategy (e.g., product, price, place promotion) in a single market, a group of markets, or a region of the country
- Involves the use of experimental procedures.

test market
Testing of a new product or some element of the marketing mix using experimental or quasi-experimental designs.

Test Market Usage and Objectives

New product introductions play a key role in shaping a firm's financial success or failure. The conventional wisdom in the corporate world is that new products will have to contribute more profits in the future than in the past because of higher levels of competition and a faster pace of change. However, the estimated failure rate of new products varies greatly; the rate can be anywhere from 66 percent to almost 90 percent. The results of a 1991 survey by Weston (Connecticut) Researcher Group EFO, Ltd. indicate that marketers expected 86 percent of their new products to fail. The estimate in 1984 was 80 percent.[12] In addition, data reported by Burke Marketing Research Services indicate that 65 percent of all new product dollars are spent on marginal or losing brands. To make up for the failures and maintain corporate profitability at necessary levels, those products that succeed must produce a return on investment averaging greater than 30 percent.

As you probably already recognize, test market studies have the goal of helping marketing managers make better decisions about new products and additions or changes to existing products or marketing strategies. Test market studies do this by providing a real-world test for evaluating products and marketing programs. Marketing managers use test markets to evaluate proposed national programs with all their separate elements on a smaller, less costly scale. The basic idea is to make a determination of whether the estimated profits that will result

Thousands of new consumer package goods products are test marketed in the United States each year. SOURCE: © Mark Richards/PhotoEdit.

if the product is rolled out on a national basis justify the potential risks. Test market studies are designed to provide information in regard to following issues:

- Estimate of market share and volume that can be projected to the total market.
- The effect that the new product will have on the sales of similar products (if any) already marketed by the company. The extent to which the new product takes business away from the company's existing products is referred to as the *cannibalization rate.*
- Characteristics of consumers who buy the product. Demographic data will almost surely be collected, and lifestyle, psychographic, and other types of classification data may be collected. This information will be useful in helping the firm refine the marketing strategy for the product. For example, knowing the demographic characteristics of likely purchasers will help in developing a media plan that will more effectively and efficiently reach target customers. Knowing the psychographic and lifestyle characteristics of target customers will provide valuable insights into how to position the product and the types of promotional messages that will appeal to them.
- The behavior of competitors during the test may provide some indication of what they will do if the product is introduced nationally.

In addition to traditional test markets, we also will discuss the growing area of **simulated test markets (STM)** as an alternative. STMs use survey data and mathematical models to simulate test market results at a much lower cost. Details of how STMs are actually conducted are provided later.

simulated test market (STM)
Alternative to traditional test market; survey data and mathematical models are used to simulate test market results at a much lower cost.

Test markets are, of course, discussed in this chapter because they employ experimental designs. Traditional test markets, by definition, are field experiments, whereas STMs tend to rely on a laboratory approach. Traditional test markets rely almost exclusively on preexperimental and time-series designs. STMs use preexperimental, time-series, and, in some cases, true experimental designs.

Costs of Test Marketing

Test marketing is expensive. It is estimated that a simple two-market test can cost \$300,000 to 400,000 and that a long-running, complex test in four or more markets can cost more than \$1 million. These estimates refer only to *direct costs,* which can include[13]

- Production of commercials
- Payments to advertising agency for services
- Media time at a higher rate because of low volume
- Syndicated research information
- Customized research information and associated data analysis
- Point-of-purchase materials
- Coupons and sampling
- Higher trade allowances to obtain distribution.

Also many possible *indirect costs* are associated with test marketing, including the following:

- Cost of management time spent on the test market
- Diversion of sales activity from existing products

- Possible negative impact of a test market failure on other products with the same family brand
- Possible negative trade reactions to your products if you develop a reputation of not doing well
- Cost of letting your competitors know what you are doing, allowing them to develop a better strategy or beat you to the national market.

The cost of test markets are high, and, as a result, they should be used only as the last step in a research process that has shown the new product or strategy to have considerable potential. In some situations, it may be cheaper to go ahead and launch the product, even if it fails.

Deciding Whether to Conduct a Test Market

Based on the preceding discussion, you can see that test markets offer at least two important benefits to the firm conducting the test.[14]

- First and foremost, the test market provides a vehicle by which the firm can obtain a good estimate of a product's sales potential under realistic market conditions. On the basis of these test results, the researcher can develop estimates of the product's national market share and use this figure to develop estimates of financial performance for the product.
- Second, the test should identify weaknesses of the product and the proposed marketing strategy for the product and give management an opportunity to correct any weaknesses. It will be much easier and less expensive to correct these problems at the test market stage than to correct them after the product has gone into national distribution.

On the other hand, these benefits must be weighed against a number of costs and other negatives associated with test markets.[15] The financial costs of test markets were discussed previously and are not insignificant. Another problem with test markets is that they give competitors an early indication of what you are planning to do. This gives them an opportunity to make adjustments in their marketing strategy, or, if your idea is easily copied and not legally protected, they may be able to emulate your idea and move into national distribution faster than you can. It has been suggested that four major factors should be taken into account in determining whether to conduct a test market.[16]

- First, you should weigh the cost and risk of failure against the probability of success and associated profits. If estimated costs are high and you are very uncertain about the likelihood of success, then you should lean toward doing a test market. On the other hand, if expected costs are low and the risk of product failure is also low, then an immediate national rollout without a test market may be the appropriate strategy.
- As suggested earlier, the likelihood and speed with which your competitors can copy your product and introduce it on a national basis also must be considered. If it can be easily copied, then it may be appropriate to go ahead and introduce the product without a test market.
- Consider the investment required to produce the product for the test market versus the investment required to produce the product in the quantities nec-

essary for a national rollout. In some cases, the difference in investment required may be very small. In these cases, it may make sense to introduce the product nationally without a test market. However, in those cases in which there is a very large difference between the investment required to produce the product for test market and the investment required to produce the product for a national rollout, conducting a test market before making a decision to introduce the product nationally makes good sense.

- The final consideration relates to the damage that an unsuccessful new product launch can inflict on a company's reputation. Failure may hurt the company's reputation with other members of the channel of distribution (retailers) and damage the company's ability to gain their cooperation in future product launches. In those cases in which this is a particular concern, test marketing is called for.

Steps In a Test Market Study

Once we have decided to conduct a test market, a number of steps must be carried out if we are to achieve a satisfactory result.

Define the Objective As always, with these kinds of lists, the first step in the process is to define the objectives of the test. Typical test market objectives are to

- Develop share and volume estimates
- Determine the characteristics of people who are purchasing the product
- Determine frequency and purpose of purchase
- Determine where (retail outlets) purchases are made
- Measure effect of sales of the new product on sales of the similar existing products in your line.

Select a Basic Approach After we have specified the objectives of the test market exercise, the next step is to decide on the type of test market method that is appropriate given the stated objectives. Three basic approaches are available. Each of these approaches is discussed in greater detail later in this chapter.

- *Simulated test market:* As noted earlier, STMs do not involve actual testing in the marketplace. Under this approach, we expose a sample of individuals, representative of the target group, to various stimuli (new product concepts) and have them make simulated purchase choices among these stimuli. These results are used as input to mathematical models to make projections of how the new product will sell if available nationally.
- *Standard test market:* As noted earlier, this approach involves an actual market test on a limited basis.
- *Controlled test market:* Under this approach the test market will be handled by an outside research company such as Information Resources, Inc. (see Chapter 8 for a more detailed discussion). This approach uses minimarkets operated by the testing company, as well as controlled store panels. The companies handling the test typically guarantee the distribution of the new product in stores that cover some percentage of the minimarkets. They typically provide

warehouse facilities and have their own field representatives to sell the product to retailers. They also are typically responsible for stocking shelves and tracking sales either manually or electronically.

Develop Detailed Procedures for the Test After we have developed the objectives and a basic approach for the test, then it is a question of developing a detailed plan for conducting the test. Manufacturing and distribution decisions must be made to ensure that adequate product is available and that it is available in most stores of the type that sell the particular product. In addition, the detailed marketing plan to be used for the test must be specified. The basic positioning approach must be selected, the execution of that approach in terms of actual commercials must be developed, a pricing strategy must be chosen, a media plan must be developed, and various promotional activities must be specified.

Select Markets for the Test The selection of markets for the test is an important decision. A number of factors must be taken into account when making this decision.[17]

- The market should not be overtested. Markets that have been used extensively by other companies for testing purposes may not respond in the same way as if they had not been used.
- The market should have normal development in the particular class. Sales in the market of the particular product should be typical, not unusually high or unusually low.
- Markets with unusual demographic profiles should be avoided. For example, college towns and retirement areas are not particularly good areas for testing most new products.
- Cities selected should reflect significant regional differences. If we find that sales of the product type vary significantly by region, then all the major regions should be represented by at least one city in the test.
- The markets chosen should have little media spillover into other markets and receive relatively little media from outside the area. For example, if the television stations in a particular market reach a very large area outside that market, the advertising used for the test product may pull in a large number of consumers from outside the market. This eventuality will make the product appear to be more successful than it really is.
- Media usage patterns for the market should be similar to national norms. For example, television viewership should not differ significantly from national patterns. This might bias the estimates that we make for the national market.
- The markets chosen should be big enough to provide meaningful results but not so big that testing becomes too expensive.
- Distribution channels in the chosen markets should reflect national patterns. For example, all the types of stores that sell the particular product should be present in the market and in their approximate national proportions.
- The competitive situation in the markets chosen should be similar to the national situation for the product category. For example, we would not want to use a market in which one or more of our national competitors are not present.
- The demographic profiles of the cities used should be similar to one another and similar to the national demographic profile.

As you can see by examining this list, many of the criteria relate to using cities that are microcosms of the country or a region of the country where the product ultimately will be sold. The basic motivation for taking this approach is to make sure that the test market results can be projected to the total area where the product will be sold. This is critical if we are to meet one of our important objectives: developing reliable estimates of sale of the new product from the test market. A list of the most typical metropolitan areas in the United States prepared by *American Demographics* is provided in Table 9.3.[18] The cumulative index in the table is an index of similarity to the national market considering housing value, age, and race characteristics of the market simultaneously. A value of 0.0 indicates a prefect match to the national market on these characteristics.

Execute the Plan Now that we have a plan in place, we can begin the execution of that plan. As we begin the test, a key decision that will have to be made is how long the test should run. The average test runs for six to 12 months. However, shorter and longer tests are not uncommon. The test must run long enough for an adequate number of repeat purchase cycles to be observed. This provides a measure of the "staying power" of a new product or marketing program. The shorter the average period is, the shorter the test needs to be. Cigarettes, soft drinks, and packaged goods are purchased every few days, while shaving cream, toothpaste, and so on are purchased only every few months. The latter types of products would require a longer test. Regardless of the product type, we need to

TABLE 9.3 Most Typical Metropolitan Areas

RANK	METROPOLITAN AREA	1990 POPULATION	CUMULATIVE INDEX	HOUSING VALUE INDEX	AGE INDEX	RACE INDEX
1	Detroit, MI	4,382,000	22.8	11.8	1.5	9.5
2	St. Louis, MO-IL	2,444,000	22.8	15.1	1.6	6.2
3	Charlotte-Gastonia Rock Hill, NC-SC	1,162,000	24.1	13.5	2.7	7.9
4	Forth Worth-Arlington, TX	1,332,000	25.1	17.0	5.9	2.2
5	Kansas City, MO-KS	1,566,000	25.4	17.9	2.7	4.8
6	Indianapolis, IN	1,250,000	25.5	16.7	2.4	6.3
7	Philadelphia, PA-NJ	4,857,000	26.7	18.0	1.7	7.1
8	Wilmington, NC	120,000	27.2	15.1	4.1	8.0
9	Cincinnatti, OH-KY-IN	1,453,000	27.2	19.1	1.6	6.6
10	Nashville, TN	985,000	27.6	18.5	2.9	6.2
11	Dayton-Springfield, OH	951,000	27.6	19.5	1.9	6.2
12	Jacksonville, FL	907,000	27.6	17.2	2.5	7.9
13	Toledo, OH	614,000	27.9	20.0	2.4	5.5
14	Greensboro-Winston-Salem-High Point, NC	942,000	27.8	17.6	2.9	7.3
15	Columbus, OH	1,377,000	28.4	19.0	3.8	5.7
16	Charlottesville, VA	131,000	28.5	16.9	6.3	5.2
17	Panama City, FL	127,000	28.6	20.1	2.6	6.0
18	Pensacola, FL	344,000	28.7	21.8	2.2	4.7
19	Milwaukee, WI	1,432,000	28.8	23.4	1.4	4.1
20	Cleveland, OH	1,831,000	28.9	18.2	3.4	7.4

Judith Waldrop, "All American Markets," *American Demographics* (January 1992): 27.

continue our test until the repeat purchase rate stabilizes. There is a tendency for the percentage of people making repeat purchases to drop for some period of time before reaching a level that remains relatively constant. Repeat purchase rate is very critical to the process of estimating ultimate sales of the project. If we end our test too soon, then we will overestimate sales.

Two other considerations relate to the expected speed of competitor reaction and the costs of running the test. If we have reason to expect that competitors will react quickly to what we are doing (introduce their own versions of the new product), then the test should be as short as possible. By minimizing the length of the test, we reduce the amount of time, they have to react. Finally, we must consider the value of additional information to be gained from the test against the cost of continuing to run the test. At some point, the value of additional information will be outweighed by its cost.

Analyze the Test Results Although we should have been evaluating the data produced by our experiment as we went along, after completion of the experiment we must make a more careful and thorough evaluation of the data. This analysis will focus on four areas:

- *Purchase Data.* This is often the most important data produced by the experiment. The levels of initial purchase (trial) throughout the course of the experiment provide an indication of how well our advertising and promotion program worked. The repeat rate (percentage of initial triers who made second and subsequent purchases) provides an indication of how well the product met the expectations created through advertising and promotion. Of course, the trial and repeat purchase results provide the basis for estimating sales and market share for the product if it were distributed nationally.
- *Awareness Data.* How effective were the media weight and media plan in creating awareness of the product? Do consumers know how much our product costs? Do they know its key features?
- *Competitive Response.* Ideally, we monitored the response of competitors during the period of the test market. For example, competitors may try to distort our test results by offering special promotions, price deals, quantity discounts, and the like. This may provide some indication of what they will do when we move into national distribution and will provide some basis for estimating the effect of these actions on their part.
- *Source of Sales.* Assuming this is a new entry in an existing product category, it is important to determine where our sales are coming from. In other words, which brands did the people who purchased our test product previously purchase? This gives us a true indication of real competitors and, if we have an existing brand in the market, tells us to what extent our new product will take business from our existing brands and from the competition.

Based on our evaluation, we will decide to go back and improve the product or marketing program, decide to drop the product, or decide to move into national or regional distribution.

Simulated Test Markets We briefly mentioned simulated test markets (sometimes referred to as *pretest markets*) earlier. Although there has been a decline in the use of traditional test markets, like the ones described earlier in

Marketing Research in Practice

Although it wasn't developed with marketing applications in mind, **Virtual Reality (VR)** is one of the latest technologies to be applied as a tool in experimentation. VR users are able to participate directly in real-time 3-D environments generated by computers. Simulation Research, Inc., in Manetta, Georgia, has used VR in the development of a system called Visionary Shopper®, which provides a simulated shopping environment and an experience as close to the real thing as possible.

In place of the helmet, gloves, and bodysuit associated with VR, Visionary Shopper uses a video screen to display very sharp 3-D color images of a simulated retail shelf. On the shelf is a complete set of products within a product category, arranged as it would be in a grocery store, with prices below the brands and promotions highlighted by shelf markers. As consumers use a trackball to "walk down" the aisle of a store, they can observe the brands on the shelf. The can touch a product on the screen and it will become larger and cover most of the screen. The consumer can then examine it on all sides as its price and other characteristics are displayed on the screen. Another touch of the screen returns it to the shelf or puts it into a shopping basket.

Visionary Shopper tests any marketing product variable that can be changed at the shelf. It also has applications for product concept testing because it shows a product as it would appear on the shelf.

The system can be found at various mall locations geographically dispersed throughout the United States as well as in many other countries around the world. Once recruited, shoppers participate in a 30-minute session. When needed, additional questions can be asked. Multiple shopping trips are compressed into one setting.

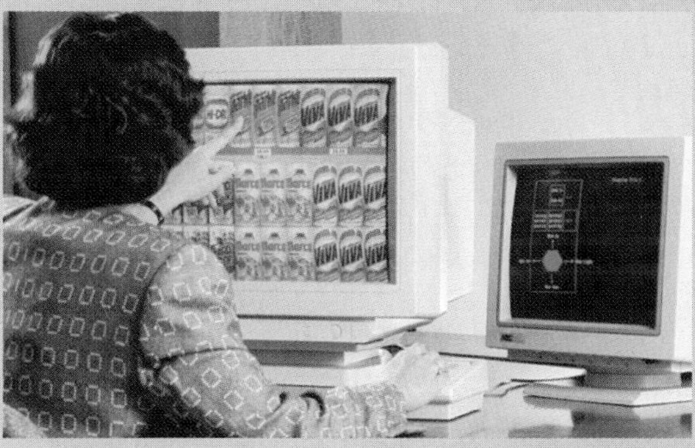

The visionary shopper uses a computerized simulated retail shelf to enable consumers to simulate the shopping experience. SOURCE: Courtesy of Simulation, Inc.

The goal of a simulation is realism, and it is the realism of both the shelf environment and the shopping scenario that makes Visionary Shopper so promising. The real power of the system is generating data for input into models for forecasting, including concept tests and concept/product tests.[19] ■

the chapter, there has been a corresponding increase in the use of STMs. STMs do not involve actual test markets; they rely on laboratory approaches and mathematical modeling. Under the STM approach, a model of consumer response to a new product is developed. This model is used to develop volume estimates and to provide information for evaluating features of the product and the anticipated marketing mix.[20] The typical STM includes the following steps:

- Intercept consumers at shopping malls (the mall intercept approach is discussed in Chapter 7).

virtual reality (VR)
An artificial environment that is experienced through sensory stimuli provided by a computer; it is one of the latest technologies to be applied as a tool in experimentation.

- Screen them for category use or target market membership. This is achieved via screening questions on a separate questionnaire or as the initial questions on the main questionnaire.
- Those who qualify are exposed to the new product concept or prototype and, in many cases, prototype advertising for the new product.
- Participants are given an opportunity to buy the new product in a real or laboratory setting.
- Interview those who purchased the new product after an appropriate time interval to determine their assessment of it and their likelihood to make further purchases.
- The trial and repeat purchase estimates, developed previously, provide the input for a mathematical model that is used to project share or volume for the product if it were distributed on a national basis. In addition, management must supply information regarding proposed advertising, distribution and other elements of the proposed marketing strategy for the new product.

Several STM systems are currently in widespread use. The four most popular STMs and the companies offering them are LTM (Yankelovich, Clancy, Shulman), ASSESSOR (M/A/R/C), BASES (Burke Marketing Services), and COMP (Elrick and Lavidge).

There are four major reasons for the growing popularity of STMs. First, they are relatively surreptitious. Given the fact that laboratory designs are employed, competitors are unlikely to know you are conducting the test or to know any of the details of the test or the nature of the new product you are testing. Second, they can be done more quickly than standard test markets. STMs usually can be completed in a maximum of three to four months. Standard test markets almost always take longer. Third, STMs are much cheaper than standard test markets. A typical STM can be conducted for $50,000 to $100,000. Cost of a typical standard test market may approach $1 million. Finally, and perhaps most important, evidence has been provided to show that STMs can be very accurate. For example, on the basis of a published validation study, ASSESSOR has been shown to produce predictions of market share that are, on average, within 0.8 share points of the actual shares achieved for the products.[21] In terms of the variance of the estimates produced by ASSESSOR, this study shows that 70 percent of the predictions fell within 1.1 share points of actual results.

Other Alternatives to Test Marketing

In addition to traditional test marketing and STMs, there are other alternatives by which companies can gauge a product's potential. One alternative is a "rolling rollout," which usually follows a pretest. A product is launched in a certain region rather than in one or two cities. Within a matter of days, scanner data can provide information on how the product is doing. The product can then be launched in additional regions, fixing ads and promotions along the way to a national introduction. General Mills has used this approach for products like Multi-Grain Cheerios.

Yet another alternative is to try a product out in a foreign market before rolling it out globally. Specifically, one or a few countries serve as a test market for a continent or even the world. This type of "lead country" strategy has been used by

A Professional Researcher's Perspective

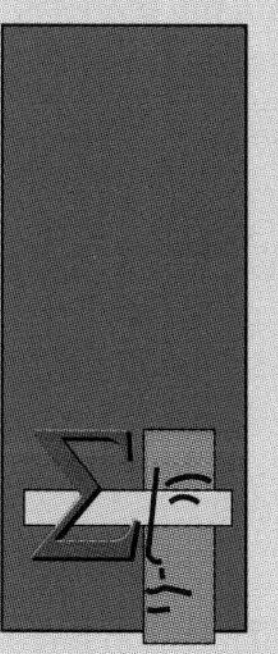

Test marketing is "the most difficult and abused variety of marketing research," but it is also the most valuable, said Doss Struse, director of marketing research services for General Mills, Minneapolis.

Companies will use almost every methodology and experimental design in their tests, "including many which are pretty poor from the standpoint of science." The role of marketing has become a specialized practice in controlled experiments, Struse said, usually when large marketing expenses are incurred in a business or a high risk in capital investment or marketing expense. "Over the years as marketing research has striven to mature as a scientific discipline, we have sought to gain more control over the testing environment. Marketing researchers have adopted each wave of innovation offering more control."

But greater control does not necessarily lead to better accuracy and validity, he warned. Many other elements of a test are just as important:

- In projecting results, one has to take the outcome of the test and figure out how to properly transfer it to another context in the future.
- Virtually every test market involves the notion of time. Yet, the analytic models researchers use to decipher the results are relatively weak.
- Developing the appropriate statistical controls by selecting matched panels of consumers or shares of market is considerably trickier in practice than in theory, and it generally is done incorrectly throughout the industry.
- Almost all the tests run by marketing researchers have an incredible confounding of effects.

In addition to these technical issues, there are numerous implementation issues. Four stand out among them.

First, when researchers run a test using paid media, they must appropriately represent what they would do on a broader scale. Second, they have to cope with how to translate promotion events from a continuing national scale to a test area. Third, researchers arrange or are forced to arrange tests that never can be duplicated in the "real world." Fourth, researchers often base their selection of tools on what is popular rather than on what will give appropriate results. "We've been guilty of buying high-tech tools which turn out to be unrealistic and underpowered statistically for the problem at hand," Struse said.[22] ■

Colgate-Palmolive Company. In 1991, the company launched Palmolive Optims shampoo and conditioner in the Philippines, Australia, Mexico, and Hong Kong. Later, the products were rolled out in Europe, Asia, Latin America, and Africa.

There are those marketers who think that classic test marketing may make a comeback. It may be that for totally new products, more thorough testing will be necessary, whereas for other types of introductions, such as line extensions, an alternative approach will be more appropriate.[23]

Summary

Experimental research provides evidence of whether the change in an independent variable causes some predictable change in a dependent variable. To show that a change in *A* likely caused an observed change in *B*, we must show three things: correlation, appropriate time order of occurrence, and the elimination of other possible causal factors. Experiments can be conducted in a laboratory or in a field setting. The major advantage of conducting experiments in a laboratory is that in this environment the researcher can control extraneous factors. However, in market research, laboratory settings often do not appropriately replicate the marketplace. Experiments conducted in the marketplace are called *field experiments*. The major difficulty with field experiments is that the researcher cannot control all the other factors that might influence the dependent variable.

In experimentation, we are concerned with internal and external validity. *Internal validity* refers to the extent to which competing explanations of the experimental results observed can be avoided. *External validity* refers to whether the causal relationships measured in an experiment can be generalized to other settings. *Extraneous variables* are other independent variables that may affect the dependent variable. They stand in the way of our ability of being able to conclude that an observed change in the dependent variable was due to the effect of the experimental or treatment variable. Extraneous factors discussed include history, maturation, instrument variation, selection bias, mortality, testing effects, and statistical regression.

In an experimental design, the researcher has control over one or more independent variables and manipulates one or more independent variables. Nonexperimental designs involve no manipulation and are referred to as *ex post facto research*. An experimental design includes four elements: the treatment, subjects, a dependent variable that will be measured, and a plan or procedure for dealing with extraneous causal factors. An experimental, or treatment, effect refers to the effect of a treatment variable on the dependent variable. Four basic approaches are used to control extraneous factors: randomization, actual physical control, experimental design control, and statistical control.

Experiments have an obvious advantage in that they are the only type of research that can demonstrate the existence and nature of causal relationships between variables of interest. Yet the amount of actual experimentation done in marketing research is limited because of the high cost of experiments, security issues, and implementation problems. There is evidence to suggest that the use of experiments in marketing research is growing.

Preexperimental designs offer little or no control over the influence of extraneous factors and are thus generally difficult to interpret. Examples include the one-shot case study, the one-group pretest-posttest design, and the static-group comparison. In a true experimental design, the researcher is able to eliminate all extraneous variables as competitive hypotheses to the treatment. Examples of true experimental design are the before and after with control group design, the Solomon four-group design, and after-only with control group design.

In quasi-experimental designs, the researcher has control over data collection procedures but lacks complete control over the scheduling of treatments. The treatment groups in a quasi-experiment normally are formed by assigning respondents to treatments in a nonrandom fashion. Examples of quasi-experimental designs are the interrupted time-series design and multiple time-series design.

Test marketing involves testing a new product or some element of the marketing mix by using experimental or quasi-experimental designs. Test markets are field experiments, and they are extremely expensive to conduct. The steps in conducting a test market study include defining the objectives for the study, selecting a basic approach to be used, developing detailed procedures for the test, selecting markets for the test, and analyzing the test results.

Key Terms

experiment
causal research
concomitant variation
appropriate time order of occurrence
laboratory experiments
field experiments
internal validity
external validity
history
maturation
instrument variation
selection bias
mortality
testing effect
regression to the mean
experimental design
treatment
experimental effect
randomization
physical control
design control
statistical control
contamination
preexperimental design
one-shot case study
one-group pretest-posttest design
static-group comparison
true experimental design
before and after with control group
Solomon four-group design
after-only with control group
quasi-experiments
interrupted time-series design
multiple time-series design
test market
simulated test market (STM)
virtual reality (VR)

Review and Discussion Questions

1. Ralston-Purina has developed a new frozen dog food. One simply heats it and serves it in the tray to the dog. Ralston-Purina is considering skipping test marketing and going directly into a national rollout. What are the advantages of doing so, given that Ralston-Purina is a major marketer of dog food? What are the disadvantages of not test marketing?
2. You are getting ready to test market a new shampoo for elderly consumers. How might you select test cities for this product? What are some cities that you would choose?
3. Why is experimentation best suited for determining causation?
4. Describe some independent and dependent variables that could be used in consumer goods experiments.
5. The student center at your university or college is considering three alternative brands of hot dogs to be offered on the menu. Design an experiment to determine which brand of hot dogs the students prefer.
6. The night students at the university or college are much older than day students. Introduce an explicit control for day versus night students in the preceding experiment.
7. Why are quasi-experiments much more popular in marketing research than true experiments?

8. How does the history effect differ from the maturation effect?
9. The manufacturer of microwave ovens has designed an improved model that will reduce energy costs and cook food evenly throughout. However, this new model will increase the product's price by 30 percent because of extra components and engineering design changes. The company wants to ascertain whether and to what extent the new model will affect sales of its microwave ovens. Propose an appropriate experimental design that can provide the information for management. Why was this design selected?
10. Discuss various methods by which extraneous causal factors can be controlled.
11. Explain how various measurements of the experimental effect in a Solomon four-group design can provide estimates of the effects of certain extraneous variables.
12. Discuss test marketing. Explain the advantages, disadvantages, and alternatives to traditional test marketing.

CASE 9.1

Market Analysts and Promotional Specialists, Inc.

Market Analysts and Promotional Specialists, Inc. (M.A.P.S.) is a marketing consulting firm that specializes in the development of promotional campaigns. The firm was formed five years ago by two young marketing graduate students, David Roth and Lisa Ryan. The students soon overcame their initial lack of experience and since have become known for their innovativeness and creativity. Their clients include industrial wholesalers, retail product manufacturers, food brokers, and distributors, as well as retail outlets.

In 1994, Dixie Brewing company enlisted M.A.P.S. to develop a new promotional campaign for its line of beers. At the time, Dixie was the last of the microbreweries in New Orleans and distributed its products within a 200-mile radius of the city. The company had enjoyed a good reputation for a number of years but recently tarnished its image by accidentally distributing a shipment of bad beer. Dixie also was losing market share because of increased competition from national brewers. Recently Miller High Life purchased Cresent Distributors, a large liquor distributor in the New Orleans area, and was beginning to implement aggressive promotional tactics in the local market.

Dixie was concerned primarily with its retail merchandising methods. M.A.P.S. immediately began to study Dixie's product line and the present shelf-space allocations in various stores throughout the market area. Because of M.A.P.S.'s previous work with food brokers, it realized that proper shelf placement was extremely important in supermarket merchandising.

The company's product line consisted of two beers, Dixie and Dixie Light. Both beers were sold in 32-ounce glass bottles, 12-ounce glass bottle six-packs, and 12-ounce can six-packs.

In New Orleans, beer may be purchased in supermarkets and convenience stores. Also, in most stores, beer can be purchased either warm or cold. In studying the refrigerated closets holding beverages, M.A.P.S. noticed that most were small, eight to 12 feet in length, and usually had glass doors on the front. Because of the relatively small size of the entire cold beer display, David and Lisa believed that the typical consumer would view the case from left to right. As such, they believed Dixie should place its products on the extreme left side of all cold beer cases.

Warm beer was displayed in a much different manner. Most stores displayed beverage products in bulk and usually devoted an entire aisle for such displays. David and Lisa reasoned that the normal consumer could not view all the brands at once and would thus have to "shop" or walk into the aisle. For this reason, they recommended that Dixie place its beer in the middle of the other brands.

Because Dixie Light was produced in response to Miller Lite, David and Lisa recommended that it be placed to the left of Miller Lite in both warm and cold beer displays. Traditionally, Dixie Light had been placed next to its standard beer brand. Dixie had noticed a significant decrease in its regular brand's market share on the introduction of Dixie Light.

To test its theories, M.A.P.S. selected a convenience store located in a suburb of New Orleans. The store contained both warm and cold beer displays. This store was then used in an experiment to measure the effect of shelf placement on beer sales. One treatment consisted of setting up the displays as they were currently being used in stores across town. The second treatment arranged the displays according to the New M.A.P.S. plan. All other factors such as price, number of bottles, and so forth were held constant throughout the experiment. The first version of the setup was used for the first two weeks in April, and the second treatment was run for the last two weeks.

The following statistics show the percentage of beer purchased by brand for each treatment:

	TREATMENT #1	TREATMENT #2
Dixie	18%	23%
Miller	18%	15%
Bud	19%	18%
Coors	13%	13%
Dixie Light	10%	8%
Miller Lite	13%	14%
Coors Light	9%	9%

1. Critique the research design with respect to internal and external validity considerations.
2. Discuss the advantages and disadvantages of using the convenience store in this experiment.
3. Based on the information given, what conclusions can be made regarding the M.A.P.S. plan?
4. Recommend a research design that would produce more interpretable results.

CASE 9.2

Laboratory Test Market

Yankelovich, Clancy, Shulman is a large marketing research firm headquartered in Connecticut. One of the many services provided by the firm is its LTM service for laboratory test markets. As suggested in the text, the laboratory or simulated test market provides a way of reducing the costs and time required to execute test markets. The LTM approach provides predictions of how a new product might perform, information regarding how the product might be changed to improve its chances of success, and overall performance in the marketplace. In addition, the LTM approach provided by Yankelovich, Clancy, Shulman provides information to help the marketer understand the behavioral and attitudinal factors that affect trial and repeat purchase decisions for a particular product concept.

Sales volume predictions are developed under the LTM approach by means of the following steps:

1. The first step is to recruit a representative sample of consumers from the target market for the new product to participate in a series of exercises. The consumers are recruited to come to a facility where the exercises or experiments are to be conducted. At the facility, they are taken into a testing room where they are asked to complete a questionnaire that seeks data on their demographic characteristics, purchase practices, and behavior in regard to the product category for the new product.
2. In the second phase of the test, consumers view test commercials for the new product in a competitive environment. After they have completed the questionnaire (step one) they are shown an actual TV program that includes a number of commercials for current brands in the product category, along with commercials for products and services in other categories. The goal is to make the viewing situation as realistic as possible in a test setting. Not every brand in the category in question will be covered. However, it is important to make sure that leading brands with heavy advertising weight are included.
3. In the third step, test participants are taken in small groups to a simulated store. This store is stocked with the brands that they have just seen in the program they viewed and other competing brands that may not have been included in the viewing exercise. They are provided with a certain amount of money with which to make purchases from the "store." They are given an amount of money less than the purchase price of the test product. They are then asked to make a purchase or not according to their preference. Obviously, making a purchase requires that they use at least some of their own money. This adds an element of realism to the otherwise contrived exercise in that only those individuals who are particularly attracted by a specific brand's features or benefits will spend some of their own money.
4. The fourth step involves discussion of their choices and the reasons for those choices and the completion of structured questionnaires covering the same issues. After completion of the discussion and the questionnaires covering the reasons for the choices, consumers go home and use the product they purchased as they normally would use such a product.
5. The fifth step involves calling the test participants at home after a sufficient amount of time has elapsed for them to have been likely to have used the test product. They were not told that they would be recontacted. The purpose of the follow-up telephone interview is to find out:

   - How they feel about the product they chose.
   - How other family members reacted to the product (if it is a product that is likely to be used, consumed, or noticed by other family members).
   - Their degree of satisfaction with the product.
   - Their reasons for the level of satisfaction.
   - Their comparisons of the product they chose with other products/brands in the category that they have used.
   - The amount of the product they used.

- Whether they have purchased more of the product, if it is available in the market, and/or their likelihood of purchasing more of the product in the future.

The data described here are collected, tabulated, and analyzed for all brands that were sold in the contrived environment test store. This permits the researchers to study results for the test product in relation to results for the other brands. This approach enables them to determine the test product's relative strengths and weaknesses.[23]

1. Critique the LTM approach.
2. What appear to be the major advantages of the LTM approach over the more traditional approach to test marketing?
3. What limitations do you see in the LTM approach.

PART II

ETHICAL DILEMMA

Mission Bell Field Services

Mission Bell Field Services, of Marina Del Rey, California, is like no other marketing research field service in the nation. Founded by Mary Ann Stubbs in 1984, its purpose is not to earn a profit, but to provide funding for two charities. The organization provides all the financing for the Marina Del Rey Home for Battered Women and 25 percent of the budget for a local homeless shelter. Stubbs founded the home for abused women after a close friend was killed by an abusive husband. Currently, the home provides meals, a place to stay, and counseling for an average of three women a week plus their children. Stubbs has used her country club and junior league connections to recruit volunteer interviewers. These women, and a few men, conduct marketing research interviews but donate their salaries to the company. Thus, Mission Bell not only earns a profit but also keeps the interviewers' salaries as well.

Despite this unique situation, Stubbs is not meeting her budget projections. The home for battered women is facing an $80,000 shortfall for the final quarter of the year, and the homeless shelter is expecting a $25,000 contribution from Mission Bell Field Services, yet no funds are available.

Stubbs is desperate. She is strongly considering "puffing up" the number of hours worked by 20 percent. Some marketing research companies pay field services based on hours worked, travel time, and mileage, plus a commission. Stubbs justifies her actions to herself by claiming that the big New York marketing research firms will not notice a small increase in reported hours worked, and they can afford it. Also, rather than all the money going into a rich New Yorker's pocket (the marketing research company's owners) a small amount of the potential profit will go to two worthwhile California charities.

Stubbs currently has three people in her office that do nothing but validate interviewers' work. Fifteen percent validation is an industry standard. Stubbs has recruited only socially prominent people to be her volunteer interviewers. They are doing the interviewing strictly for charity and certainly would not cheat. Stubbs decides that she will put the validators to work as interviewers to help increase total revenues.

Recently, Mission Bell conducted a major central location telephone study of 10,000 interviews on planned durable goods purchases within the next two years. The survey was conducted for the California Department of Economic Affairs to use as input in its econometrics forecasting model. The department is responsible for forecasting economic activity for the state government that, in turn, uses the data for revenue and spending projections for state agencies. Stubbs realized that she had a gold mine of information. She had a huge list of names, addresses, and telephone numbers of Californians who planned to purchase automobiles, homes, major appliances, and electronics over the next two years. A Japanese automobile manufacturer had already approached her about buying the names of potential new car buyers. A quick financial projection by Stubbs showed that by selling the names to 10 manufacturers of various consumer durable goods, she could cover her financial shortfall for the homeless shelter and reduce the deficit of the home for battered women. Selling people's names is a harmless act and the introductory remarks of the survey never mentioned confidentiality. Besides, a person does not have to buy something from the manufacturer.

1. Would you advise Stubbs not to "puff" the interviewers' hours? Are her actions nothing more than a small, involuntary contribution to her charities by some rich New Yorkers?
2. Since Stubbs uses unpaid volunteers as interviewers, is it not rather ridiculous to validate their work? Is this not particularly true as the validators could be bringing in additional revenue as interviewers?
3. Is it unethical for Stubbs to sell the names of the respondents? Is the "greater good" not being served by keeping the two charities in full operation? No one is going to be hurt by Stubbs's actions, and the respondents were not explicitly promised confidentiality.
4. Using Table 4.2 as a guide, identify any unethical practices you think Stubbs is committing.
5. Which level of moral development do you think Stubbs has achieved as a marketing researcher?
6. Which practice do you think is Stubbs's worst breach of research supplier ethics? Defend your answer.

PART III

Data Acquisition

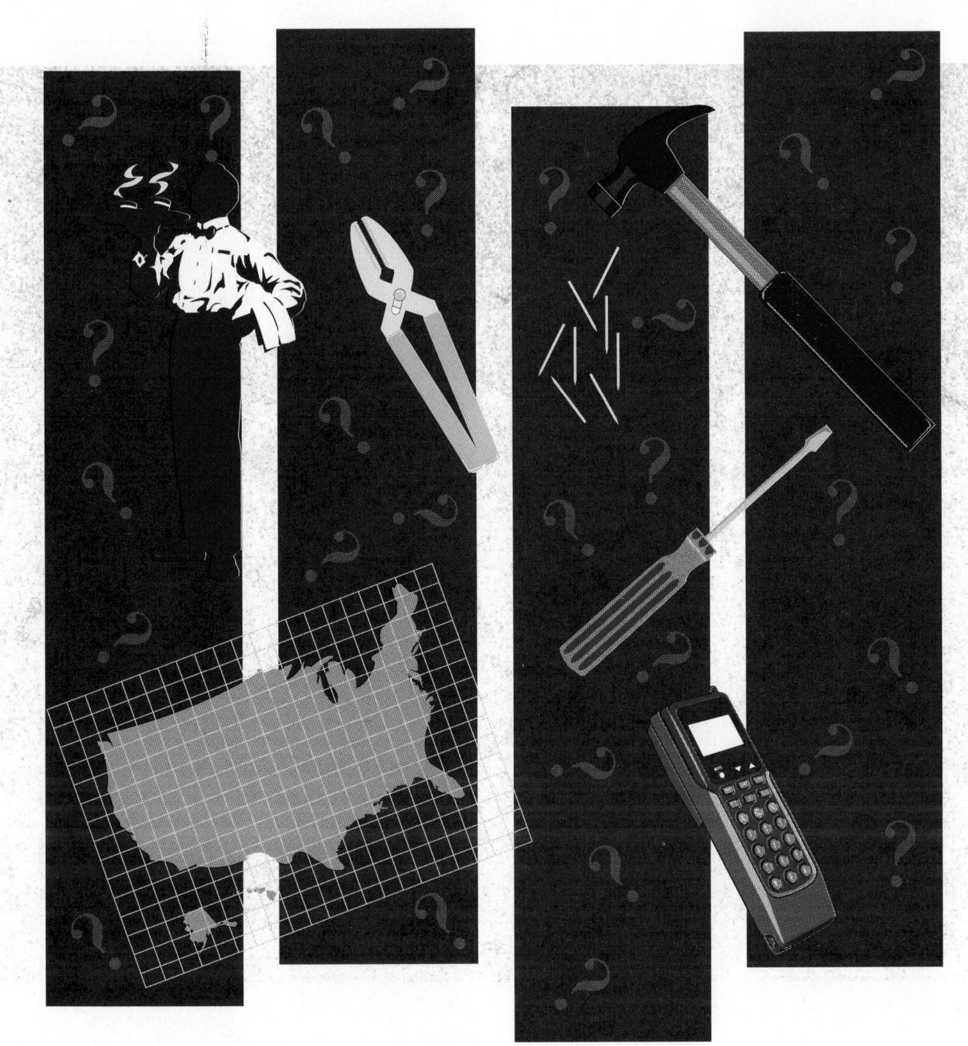

CHAPTER 10

Understanding Measurement

LEARNING OBJECTIVES

1. To understand the concept of measurement.
2. To learn about the measurement process and how to develop a good measurement.
3. To understand the four levels of scales and their typical usage.
4. To become aware of the concepts of reliability and validity.

Like many companies, Gold'n Plump Chicken, a regional processor and marketer of fresh chickens in Saint Cloud, Minnesota, found that its competitors were getting increasingly aggressive. Many years ago, Gold'n Plump Chicken had successfully branded what had been considered a commodity product but now realized the risk of consumers being seduced by lower-priced competitors. Gold'n Plump recognized the importance of protecting its dominance as a premium price, higher-quality product. Unfortunately, Gold'n Plump also had a limited marketing budget.

It's hard to find a point of difference in what is often seen as a commodity category. However, previous research had shown that Gold'n Plump was perceived by consumers as the more "thoroughly cleaned" chicken. Consumers were surprised and disappointed to find competitive chicken had extra fat or skin "hidden" under the chicken in the package. This was true of cut-up chicken as well as whole. In the previous research, consumers accepted competitive chicken for what it was—a product of "OK" quality. At the same time, they perceived Gold'n Plump as a better, cleaner chicken. The challenge was to communicate Gold'n Plump's unique difference to consumers and get them to define and to demonstrate exactly what "thoroughly cleaned" meant to them.

SOURCE: Courtesy of Gold'n Plump.

Three rough commercials connoting "thoroughly cleaned" were prepared. Neither client nor agency had the time or the money to produce expensive testing materials. In the past, respondents had been shown actual storyboards and probed for their reactions. One problem with testing storyboards was that the interviewer was relied upon to "walk" the respondent through the commercial. The advertising agency's own validation studies had shown that storyboards presented by "livelier" interviewers garnered higher scores. In this case there were no storyboards, but there were rough sketches—and a creative team. Putting those two together, videotapes were made of the copywriter explaining the sketches. Three separate videotapes were made, all using the same presenter. Each video was approximately two minutes long.

As expected, in response to all the concepts, respondents talked about how "thoroughly cleaned" meant that Gold'n Plump had the "excess fat removed," "no pinfeathers" and was "already trimmed." However, in-depth probing uncovered that one concept also had communicated to twice as many people that "thoroughly cleaned" meant that Gold'n Plump chicken was "convenient":

> "I thought it was a good presentation. It made you think about the chicken you bought in the past and how much cleaning and preparation it took and compare it to the Gold'n Plump Chicken. This is more convenient to fix."

The in-depth probing during the interview "sessions" also revealed that this particular concept—in which a hungry fox chooses a package of Gold'n Plump Chicken over a live hen standing next to him—was communicating that Gold'n Plump was "Fresh—Good as live chicken." When the concept was conceived, nobody had ever imagined that this message would be communicated:

Marketing research revealed that this advertisement conveyed the idea that Gold'n Plump was as fresh as a live chicken. SOURCE: Courtesy of Gold'n Plump Chicken.

"The fox is hungry, sees a live chicken. It appears he will eat the chicken. Then the hand reaches in with Gold'n Plump Chicken. This causes the fox to decide what chicken he wants. He decides he wants the chicken that is already cleaned up. 'Gold'n Plump—it's as fresh as live chicken."

Finally, from this one execution, many more consumers took away the idea that Gold'n Plump chicken also was healthier. Again, this was not one of the messages that was originally intended to be communicated (in fact, it was never even imagined):

"It is hassle-free. It saves you lots of effort and you don't have to worry about a lot of waste. It's convenient. It's fresher, therefore it's healthier. A fox, being a clever animal, knows a good deal when he sees one."

Follow-up telephone tracking revealed a significant increase in advertising awareness for Gold'n Plump Chicken. More importantly, despite the fact that the television campaign ran only three months, attribute scores of Gold'n Plump's competitors actually declined.[1] ■

SOURCE: Copy courtesy of Tim Huberty. Tim Huberty is Vice President, Account Planner at the Campbell Mithun Esty Advertising Agency in Minneapolis, Minnesota. He also teaches at the Graduate School of Business at the University of St. Thomas in St. Paul, Minnesota.

Data regarding the concept of "thoroughly cleaned" were based upon measurement, as was the information about increased awareness for Gold'n Plump and the decline of competitor's attribute scores. How does a researcher go about measuring a construct? How does one determine the reliability and validity of the information? These are some of the issues we will explore in Chapter 10.

The Concept of Measurement

Measurement is the process of assigning numbers or labels to objects, persons, states, or events in accordance with specific rules to represent quantities or qualities of attributes. Measurement then, is a procedure used to assign numbers that reflect the amount of an attribute possessed by an event, person, or object. Note that the event, person, or object is not being measured, but rather its attributes are. A researcher, for example, does not measure a consumer but measures attitudes, income, brand loyalty, age, and other relevant factors.

measurement
Process of assigning numbers or labels to things in accordance with specific rules to represent quantities or qualities of attributes.

Another key aspect of measurement is the concept of rules. A **rule** is a guide, a method, or a command that tells a researcher what to do. For example, a rule might say "assign the numbers *1* through *5* to people according to their disposition to do household chores. If they are extremely willing to do any and all household chores, assign them a *1*. If they are not willing to do any household chores, assign them a *5*." Equally, specific rules would be stated for assigning a *2*, *3*, or *4*.

rule
A guide, a method, or a command that tells a researcher what to do.

A problem often encountered with rules is a lack of clarity or specificity. Some things are easy to measure because rules are easy to create and follow. The measurement of gender, for example, is quite simple and concrete criteria can be offered to determine sex. The researcher is then told to assign a *1* for male and a *2* for female. Unfortunately, many characteristics of interest to a market researcher such as brand loyalty, purchase intent, or total family income are much more difficult to measure because it is difficult to devise rules to measure the true value of these consumer attributes. Let us examine how a researcher should measure a phenomenon.

The Measurement Process

Step One: Identify the Concept of Interest The measurement process is shown in Figure 10.1. Measurement begins by identifying a concept of interest for study. A concept is an abstract idea generalized from particular facts. A concept is a category of thought, or a category for grouping sense data together "as if they were all the same." All perceptions regarding a stoplight at South and Main streets is a category of thought, although a relatively narrow one. All stoplights, regardless of location, become a broader concept. Thus, a concept is a category of thought.

construct
Specific types of concepts that exist at higher levels of abstraction.

Step Two: Develop a Construct **Constructs** are specific types of concepts that exist at higher levels of abstraction. Constructs are invented for theoretical use. Not only are constructs more abstract than everyday concepts, but also they

FIGURE 10.1
The Measurement Process

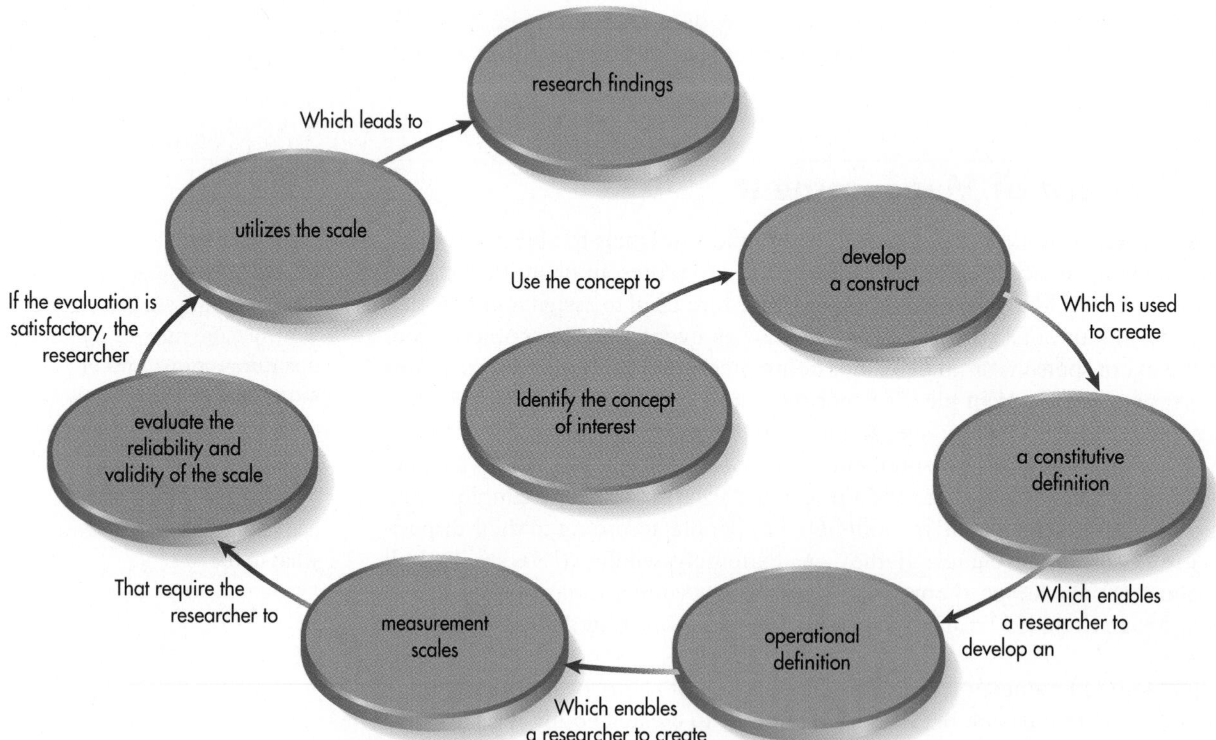

are likely to cut across various preexisting categories of thought. The value of specific constructs depends on how useful they are in explaining, predicting, and controlling phenomena, just as the value of everyday concepts depends on how much they assist us in everyday affairs. Generally, constructs are not directly observable. Instead, they are inferred by some indirect method such as findings on a questionnaire. Examples of marketing constructs include brand loyalty, high-involvement purchasing, social class, personality, and channel power. Constructs aid researchers by simplifying and integrating the complex phenomena found in the marketing environment.

Steps Three and Four: Define the Concept Both Constitutively and Operationally The third and fourth steps in the research process are to first define the concept constitutively and then operationally. A **constitutive** (or theoretical or conceptual) **definition** defines a concept with other concepts and constructs, establishing boundaries for the construct under study; it states the central idea or concept under study. Constructs of a scientific theory may be defined constitutively. All constructs, to be scientifically useful, must possess constitutive meaning. This means that they must be capable of being used in theories. A constitutive definition also is like a dictionary definition. A constitutively defined concept should fully distinguish the concept under investigation from all other concepts. Therefore, the study concept should be readily discernible from very similar but different concepts. A vague constitutive definition can lead to the incorrect research question being addressed. For instance, to say that we are interested in studying marital roles is so general as to be meaningless. Even to say that we want to examine marital roles of newlyweds (married less than 12 months) 24 to 28 years of age with four years of college may not suffice. One researcher may be interested in communication patterns as partners assume certain roles, while a second researcher may be interested in parenting roles.

constitutive definition
Defines a concept with other concepts and constructs, establishing boundaries for the construct under study and stating the central idea or concept under study.

A precise constitutive definition makes the operational definition task much easier. An **operational definition** defines which observable characteristics will be measured and the process for assigning a value to the concept. In other words, it assigns meaning to a construct in terms of the operations necessary to measure it in any concrete situation.

operational definition
Defines which observable characteristics will be measured and the process for assigning a value to the concept.

Because it is overly restrictive in marketing to insist that all variables be operationally defined in directly measurable terms, we find that many variables are defined in more abstract terms and measured indirectly, based on theoretical assumptions about their nature. For example, it is impossible to measure an attitude directly, because an attitude is an abstract concept referring to things that exist inside a person's mind. It is possible, nonetheless, to give a clear theoretical definition of an attitude as an enduring organization of motivational, emotional, perceptual, and cognitive processes with respect to some aspect of our environment. On the basis of this definition, instruments have been developed for measuring attitudes indirectly, by asking questions about how a person feels, what the person believes, and how the person intends to behave.

In summary, an operational definition serves as a bridge between a theoretical concept and real-world events or factors. Concepts such as "attitude" or "high-involvement purchasing" are abstractions that cannot be observed. Operational definitions transform such concepts into observable events. In other words, they define or give meaning to a concept by spelling out what the researcher must do to measure it. There are many different potential operational definitions for any single concept, regardless of how exact the constitutive definition may be. The researcher must choose the operational definition that fits most appropriately with the objectives of the research.

An example of a constitutive definition, a corresponding operational definition, and a resultant measurement scale are shown in Table 10.1. The operational definition of role ambiguity was developed by two marketing professors for use with salespeople and customer service personnel. The theoretical notion is that role ambiguity leads to job stress and impedes a worker's ability to improve performance and obtain job-based rewards. This leads to job dissatisfaction.

The Problem of Construct Equivalence Construct equivalence deals with how researchers, subjects, and others see, understand, and develop measurements of a particular phenomenon. The problem confronting the global marketing researcher is that because of sociocultural, economic, and political differences, construct perspectives may not be either identical or equivalent. The examples in the "Global Marketing Research" feature in this section of the

TABLE 10.1 Constitutive and Operational Definitions of Role Ambiguity

Constitutive Definition
Role ambiguity is a direct function of the discrepancy between the information available to the person and that which is required for adequate performance of a role. It is the difference between a person's actual state of knowledge and that which provides adequate satisfaction of one's personal needs and values.
Operational Definition
The amount of uncertainty (ranging from very uncertain to very certain on a five-point scale) an individual feels regarding job role responsibilities and expectations from other employees and customers.
Measurement Scale
The measurement scale consists of a 45-item scale with each item assessed by a five-point scale with category labels *1* = very certain, *2* = certain, *3* = neutral, *4* = uncertain, *5* = very uncertain. A sample of the 45 items are How much freedom of action I am expected to have How I am expected to handle nonroutine activities on the job The sheer amount of work I am expected to do To what extent my boss is open to hearing my point of view How satisfied my boss is with me How managers in other departments expect me to interact with them What managers in other departments think about the job I perform How I am expected to interact with my customers How I should behave (with customers) while on the job If I am expected to lie a little to win customer confidence If I am expected to hide my company's foul-ups from my customers About how much time my family feels I should spend on the job To what extent my family expects me to share my job-related problems How my coworkers expect me to behave while on the job How much information my coworkers expect me to convey to my boss

SOURCE: Adapted from Jagdip Singh and Gary K. Rhoads, "Boundary Role Ambiguity in Marketing-Oriented Positions: A Multidimensional Multifaceted Operationalization," *Journal of Marketing Research* 28 (August 1991): 328–338.

Global Marketing Research

Examples of construct equivalence problems include:

FUNCTIONAL EQUIVALENCE

In England, Germany, and Scandinavia, beer is generally perceived as an alcoholic beverage. In Mediterranean lands, however, beer is considered akin to soft drinks. Therefore, a study of the competitive status of beer in Northern Europe would have to build in questions on wine and liquor. In Italy, Spain, or Greece, the comparison would have to be with soft drinks.

In Italy, it's common for children to have a bar of chocolate between two slices of bread as a snack. In France, bar chocolate is often used in cooking. But a German housewife would be revolted by either practice.

CONCEPTUAL EQUIVALENCE

Were a researcher to use the concepts "out-group" and "in-group" in the United States and Greece, two different groups would be included. In the United States, the in-group includes people from one's own country and the out-group includes foreigners. In Greece, the out-group includes countrymen with whom the person is not closely associated.

Personality traits such as aggressiveness or assertiveness may not be relevant in all countries or cultures. The concept may be absent from the culture and language or may take on an entirely different meaning. For example, when Athenians were asked to help fellow Greeks and foreigners mail letters, the Greeks received worse treatment than did the foreigners.

As a final example, the Japanese and Western concepts of decisionmaking differ considerably. Whereas the Western sees decisionmaking as a discrete event, the Japanese cannot make that distinction.

DEFINITIONAL EQUIVALENCE

In France, fragrance is measured on a hot-cold continuum. In the United States and the United Kingdom, this is not an attribute assigned to fragrances. That is, the attribute used to categorize product classes may vary from one country or culture to another.

The beer example cited under functional equivalence provides another example of the problems in achieving definitional equivalence. In the United Kingdom, beer would be classified as an alcoholic drink. In Mediterranean cultures it should be classified as a soft drink.[2] ■

chapter highlight the construct equivalence problem faced by global marketing researchers.

Step Five: Develop a Measurement Scale Note in Table 10.1 that a scale has been developed ranging from "very certain" to "very uncertain." A **scale** is a set of symbols or numbers so constructed that the symbols or numbers can be assigned by a rule to the individuals (or their behaviors or attitudes) to

scale
A set of symbols or numbers so constructed that the symbols or numbers can be assigned by a rule to the individuals (or their behaviors or attitudes) to whom the scale is applied.

whom the scale is applied. The assignment on the scale is indicated by the individual's possession of whatever the scale is supposed to measure. Thus, a salesperson in Table 10.1 who feels she knows exactly how she is supposed to interact with customers would mark *very certain* on the scale.

Creating a measurement scale begins with determining the level of measurement desirable or possible. Table 10.2 describes the four basic levels of measurement, which are nominal, ordinal, interval, and ratio. These four levels lead to the four kinds of scales discussed in the following paragraphs.

nominal scales
Scales that partition data into mutually exclusive and collectively exhaustive categories.

Nominal Scales **Nominal scales** are one of the most common in marketing research. A nominal scale partitions data into categories that are mutually exclusive and collectively exhaustive. This implies that every bit of data will fit into one and only one category and all data will fit somewhere in the scale. The term *nominal* means "namelike," implying that the numbers assigned to objects or phenomena are naming or classifying but have no true number meaning; the numbers cannot be ordered, added, or divided. The numbers are simply labels or identification numbers and nothing else. Examples of nominal scales are

Sex	(1) Male	(2) Female	
Geographic area	(1) Urban	(2) Rural	(3) Suburban

The only quantification in numerical scales are the number and percentages of objects in each category; for example, 50 males (48.5 percent) and 53 females (51.5 percent). Computing a mean, for example, of 2.4 for geographic area would

TABLE 10.2 The Four Major Levels of Measurement

LEVEL	DESCRIPTION*	BASIC EMPIRICAL OPERATIONS	TYPICAL USAGE	TYPICAL DESCRIPTIVE STATISTICS
Nominal	Uses numerals to identify objects, individuals, events, or groups	Determination of equality/inequality	Classification (male/female; buyer/nonbuyer)	Frequency counts, percentages/modes
Ordinal	In addition to identification, the numerals provide information about the relative amount of some characteristic posed by an event, object, etc.	Determination of greater or less	Rankings/ratings (preferences for hotels, banks, etc., social class; ratings of foods based upon fat content, cholesterol)	Median (mean and variance metric)
Interval	Possesses all the properties of nominal and ordinal scales plus the intervals between consecutive points are equal	Determination of equality of intervals	Preferred measure of complex concepts/constructs (temperature scale; air pressure scale; level of knowledge about brands)	Mean/variance
Ratio	Incorporates all the properties of nominal, ordinal, and interval scales plus it includes an absolute zero point	Determination of equality of ratios	When precision instruments are available (sales; number of on-time arrivals; age)	Geometric mean/harmonic mean

*Because higher levels of measurement contain all the properties of lower levels, we can convert higher level scales into lower level ones (i.e., ratio to interval or ordinal or nominal; or interval to ordinal or nominal; or ordinal to nominal).

SOURCE: Adapted from S. S. Stevens, "On the Theory of Scales of Measurement," *Science* 103 (June 7, 1946), pp. 677–680.

be meaningless; only the mode, the value that appears most often, would be appropriate.

Ordinal Scales **Ordinal scales** maintain the labeling characteristics of nominal scales plus an ability to order data. Ordinal measurement is possible when the transitivity postulate can be applied. A postulate is an assumption that is an essential prerequisite to carrying out an operation or line of thinking. The transitivity postulate may be described by the notion that "if *a* is greater than *b*, and *b* is greater than *c*, then *a* is greater than *c*." Other terms that can be substituted are *is preferred to*, *is stronger than*, or *precedes*. An example of an ordinal scale is

ordinal scales

Nominal scales that can order data.

Please rank the following airlines from *1* to *5* with *1* being the most preferred and *5* the least preferred.

Delta ____
American ____
United ____
USAir ____
Northwest ____

Ordinal numbers are used strictly to indicate rank order. The numbers do not indicate absolute quantities, nor do they imply that the intervals between the numbers are equal. For example, the person ranking the airlines might like American only slightly more than USAir and perceive Northwest as totally unacceptable. Such information would not be obtained from an ordinal scale.

Because ranking is the objective of an ordinal scale, any rule prescribing a series of numbers that preserves the ordered relationship is satisfactory. In other words, American could have been assigned a value of 12; USAir, 17; Delta, 20; United, 25; and Northwest, 26; or any other series of numbers as long as the basic ordering is preserved. Common arithmetical operations such as addition or multiplication cannot be used with ordinal scales. The appropriate measure of central tendency is the mode and the median. A percentile or quartile measure is used for measuring dispersion.

A controversial (yet rather common) use of ordinal scales is to rate various characteristics. In this case, the researcher assigns numbers to reflect the relative ratings of a series of statements, then uses these numbers to interpret relative distance. Recall that our market researchers examining role ambiguity used a scale ranging from *very certain* to *very uncertain*. Note that the following values had been assigned:

(1)	(2)	(3)	(4)	(5)
Very Certain	Certain	Neutral	Uncertain	Very Uncertain

If a researcher can justify the assumption that the intervals are equal within the scale, then the more powerful parametric statistical tests can be applied. Parametric statistical tests will be discussed in Chapters 16 and 17. Indeed, some measurement scholars argue that we should normally assume equal intervals.

> The best procedure would seem to be to treat ordinal measurements as though they were interval measurements but to be constantly alert to the possibility of *gross* inequality of intervals. As much as possible about the characteristics of the measuring tools should be learned. Much useful information has been obtained by this approach,

Ordinal scales can be used to rank airline preferences. SOURCE: © Arthur Telley/FPG.

with resulting scientific advances in psychology, sociology, and education. In short, it is unlikely that researchers will be led seriously astray by heeding this advice, if they are careful in applying it.[3]

interval scales

Ordinal scales with equal intervals between points to show relative amounts; may include an arbitrary zero point.

Interval Scales **Interval scales** contain all the features of ordinal scales with the added dimension that the intervals between the points on the scale are equal. The concept of temperature is based upon equal intervals. Market researchers often prefer to use interval scales over ordinal scales because they can measure how much of a trait one consumer has (or does not have) over another. Interval scales enable a researcher to discuss differences separating two objects. The scale possesses properties of order and difference but with an arbitrary zero point; for example, Fahrenheit and centigrade scales. Thus, the freezing point of water is zero on one scale and 32 degrees on the other.

The arbitrary zero point of interval scales restricts the statements that a researcher can make about the scale points. One can say that 80°F is hotter than 32°F or that 64°F is 16° cooler than 80°F. However, one cannot say that 64°F is twice as warm as 32°F. Why? Because the zero point on the Fahrenheit scale is arbitrary. To prove our point, consider the transformation of the two temperatures to Celsius using the formula Celsius = (F—32)(5/9). Thus, 32°F equals 0°C and 64°F equals 17.8°C. Our previous statement for Fahrenheit (64° is twice as warm as 32°) does not hold for Celsius. The same would be true if we were evaluating airlines on which factors were liked the most on an interval scale. If American Airlines is given a 20 and USAir a 10, we cannot say that American is liked twice as much as USAir This is because a zero point defining the absence of liking has not been identified and assigned a value of zero on the scale.

Interval scales are amenable to computation of an arithmetic mean, standard deviation, and correlation coefficients. The more powerful parametric statistical tests such as *t*-tests and *F*-tests can be applied. In addition, researchers can take a more conservative approach and use nonparametric tests if there is concern about the equal intervals assumption.

Ratio Scales **Ratio scales** have all the powers of those previously discussed as well as a meaningful absolute zero or origin. Because there is universal agreement as to the location of the zero point, comparisons among the magnitudes of ratio-scaled values are acceptable. Thus, a ratio scale reflects the actual amount of a variable. Physical characteristics of a respondent such as age, weight, or height are examples of ratio-scaled variables. Other ratio scales are based on area, distance, money values, return rates, population counts, and lapsed periods of time.

ratio scales
Interval scales with a meaningful zero point so that magnitudes can be compared arithmetically.

Because some objects have none of the property being measured, a ratio scale originates at zero, thus having an absolute empirical meaning. For example, an investment (albeit a poor one) can have no rate of return, or a census tract in New Mexico could be devoid of any persons. Also, an absolute zero implies that all arithmetic operations are possible, including multiplication and division. Numbers on the scale indicate the actual amounts of the property being measured; that is, a large bag of McDonald's french fries weighs eight ounces and a regular bag at Burger King weighs four ounces. Thus, a large McDonald's bag of fries weighs twice as much as a regular Burger King bag.

Step Six: Evaluate the Reliability and Validity of the Measurement

Sources of Measurement Differences

An ideal market research study would provide information that is accurate, precise, lucid, and timely. Accurate data implies accurate measurement, or $M = A$, where M refers to measurement and A stands for complete accuracy. In market research, this ideal is rarely, if ever, obtained. Instead we have

$$M = A + E, \quad \text{where } E = \text{errors}$$

Errors can be either random or systematic, as noted in Chapter 7. **Systematic error** is error that results in a constant bias in the measurements. The bias results from faults in the measurement instrument or process. For example, if we are using a faulty ruler (one inch is actually one and a half inches) in Pillsbury's test kitchens to measure the height of chocolate cakes using alternative recipes, all cakes will be recorded below their actual height. **Random error** also influences the measurements but not systematically. Thus, random error is transient in nature and does not occur in a consistent manner. A person may not answer a question truthfully because he is in a bad mood that day.

systematic error
Error that results in a constant bias in the measurements.

random error
Error that affects measurement in a transient, inconsistent manner.

Two scores on a measurement scale can differ for a number of reasons.[4] Only the first reason listed does not involve error. You should determine whether the remaining seven sources of measurement differences are random error or systematic error.

1. A true difference in the characteristic being measured. A perfect measurement difference would be solely the result of actual differences. If John rates McDonald's service as *1* (excellent) and Sandy rated service as *4* (average), then the difference is due only to actual attitude differences.
2. Differences due to stable characteristics of individual respondents, such as personality, values, and intelligence. Sandy has an aggressive, rather critical personality and he gives no one and nothing the benefit of a doubt. He actu-

The way John answers questions on a survey for McDonald's may vary due to short-term personal factors. SOURCE: © Mary Kate/ PhotoEdit.

ally was quite pleased with the service he received at McDonald's, but he expects such service and so gave it an average rating.

3. Differences due to short-term personal factors, such as temporary mood swings, health problems, time constraints, fatigue, or other transitory factors. Earlier today, John won $400 in a "Name That Tune" contest on a local radio station. He stopped by McDonald's for a burger after he had picked up his winning check. His reply on the service quality questionnaire might have been quite different if he had been interviewed yesterday.
4. Differences caused by situational factors such as distractions or others present in the interview situation. Sandy is giving his replies while trying to watch his four-year-old nephew, who is running amok on the McDonald's playground; John had his new fiancee along when he was interviewed. Replies of both men might have been different if they had been interviewed at home while no other friend or relative was present.
5. Differences resulting from variations in administering the survey. Interviewers can ask questions with different voice inflections causing response variation. Different interviewers can cause responses to vary. This may be due to rapport, manner of dress, sex, race, or a host of other factors. Interviewer bias can be as subtle as the nodding-of-the-head. One interviewer who tended to nod unconsciously was found to bias some respondents. They thought that the interviewer was agreeing with them when it was in fact a way of saying, "OK, I'm recording what you say—tell me more."
6. Differences due to the sampling of items included in the questionnaire. When researchers attempt to measure the quality of service at McDonald's, the scales and other questions used represent only a portion of items that could have been used. The scales created by the researchers reflect their interpretation of the construct (service quality) and the way it is measured. If the researchers had used different words or items had been added or

removed, then the outcome with respect to scale values reported by John and Sandy might have been different.

7. Differences due to a lack of clarity in the measurement instrument. A question may be ambiguous, complex, or incorrectly interpreted. A question asking, "How far do you live from McDonald's?" with answers such as (1) less than five minutes, (2) five to 10 minutes, and so forth, is ambiguous. If someone is walking, it is undoubtedly longer than a person driving a car or riding a bike. This topic is covered in much greater detail in Chapter 11.
8. Differences due to mechanical or instrument factors. Blurred questionnaires, lack of space to fully record an answer, missing pages in a questionnaire, or a balky pen can result in differences in responses.

Reliability

A measurement scale that provides consistent results over time is reliable. If a ruler consistently measures a chocolate cake as nine inches high, then the rule is said to be reliable. Reliable scales, gauges, and other measurement devices can be used with confidence and with the knowledge that transient and situational factors are not interfering with the measurement process. Reliable instruments provide stable measures at different times under different conditions. A key question regarding reliability is, "If we measure some phenomenon over and over again with the same measurement device, will we get the same or highly similar results?" If the answer is affirmative, the device is reliable.

Therefore, **reliability** is the degree to which measures are free from random error and, therefore, provide consistent data. The less error there is, the more reliable the observation, so that a measurement that is free of error is a correct measure. Therefore a measurement is reliable if the measurement does not change when the concept being measured remains constant in value. However, if the concept being measured does change in value, the reliable measure will indicate that change. How can a measuring instrument be unreliable? If your weight stays constant at 150 pounds but repeated measurements on your bathroom scale show your weight to fluctuate, the lack of reliability may be due to a weak spring inside the scale.

reliability
Measures that are consistent from one administration to the next.

There are three ways to assess reliability: test-retest, equivalent forms, and internal consistency (see Table 10.3).

test-retest reliability
The ability of the same instrument to produce consistent results when used a second time under conditions as nearly the same as possible.

Test-Retest Reliability Test-retest reliability is obtained by repeating the measurement using the same instrument under as nearly the same conditions as possible. The theory behind test-retest is that if random variations are present,

TABLE 10.3 Assessing the Reliability of a Measurement Instrument

1. Test-Retest Reliability: Use the same instrument a second time under nearly the same conditions as possible.
2. Equivalent Form Reliability: Use two instruments that are as similar as possible to measure the same object during the same time period.
3. Internal Consistency Reliability: Compare different samples of items being used to measure a phenomenon during the same time period.

A Professional Researcher's Perspective

Martin Weinberger is executive vice-president of Oxtoby-Smith, Inc., New York, one of America's largest and oldest marketing research companies. His 25 years of experience in the research industry has led him to develop several perspectives regarding measurement in consumer research.

1. Sometimes Consumers Don't Tell the Truth; Sometimes They Are Willing to Reveal It

Several years ago, a major catalog company was having trouble with its boys' slacks—it was getting an unusually large number of returns. Consumers were writing that the reason for the return was that the slacks did not fit properly. On the basis of that information, the catalog sales company believed something must be wrong with the diagrams and instructions it provided to consumers for ordering the right size slacks. Oxtoby-Smith was asked to find out what was wrong with the diagrams or the instructions so the client could fix them. We were given the names of consumers who had returned the boys' slacks.

We sent our interviewers into the field, carrying the heavy catalog, with the diagrams and the instructions. What we found was not what we had expected to find. The consumers told us the slacks had fit perfectly well. The mothers had ordered three or four pairs of slacks for their teenage sons in the hope that the son would find *one* pair he would be willing to wear. Then the mother had to face returning the other two or three pairs. The mothers felt uncomfortable giving any explanation for the return of the slacks other than "poor fit." This finding indicated that the diagrams were not the problem. The instructions were not the problem.The catalog company had to learn to live with the returns in the same way the mothers had to live with the habits of their teenage sons.

2. Sometimes Consumers Claim More Than They Know; Sometimes They Are Just Confused

It has been well established that consumers sometimes claim awareness of brands that do not exist. That is why it is important to

stability
Lack of change in results from test to retest.

they will be revealed by variations in the scores between the two tests. **Stability** means that very few differences in scores are found between the first and second administration of the tests; the measuring instrument is said to be stable. For example, assume that a 30-item department store image measurement scale was administered to the same group of shoppers at two points in time. If the correlation between the two measurements was high, the reliability would be assumed to be high.

There are several problems with test-retest reliability. First, it may be very difficult to locate and gain the cooperation of respondents for a second testing. Second, the first measurement may alter the person's response on the second measurement. Third, environmental or personal factors may change, causing the second measurement to change.

include fictitious brand names in studies of brand awareness to see how much claiming is going on. In fact, I have done a study in which a fictitious brand name had *more* brand awareness than the client's brand and the client considered changing the name of its brand to the fictitious brand name!

3. Sometimes Consumers Don't Know Why They Buy the Brands They Buy

This section could be subtitled, "Why you should not ask why." I have conducted a large number of studies asking consumers, at the client's request, *why* they buy the products they buy, and I have looked at their answers to that question. At the same time, I have looked at their answers to other questions. I have found that consumers often do not really *know* why they buy the brands they buy.

A simple case in point is a food or beverage product. Ask consumers why they buy a brand, and they usually will tell you "because it tastes good." If you give a consumer a blind product test, you may find out that this individual cannot differentiate between his or her preferred Brand X and Brand Y. If you use a double-blind paired comparison, in one paired blind test a consumer will prefer X and in another paired blind test the same individual will prefer Y.

4. Consumers Not Only Have Opinions, They Have Passions

Generally, consumers are very cooperative. They will answer almost any questions you ask them. But, my experience teaches me that you need to know more than just their opinions; you need to know their passions.

For example, a manufacturer of toilet paper that is thinking of introducing a scented version might ask us to find out which of a series of scents is preferred by consumers. We could test the scents and tell them scent A is more widely preferred than scent B. However, we would be remiss in our job if we failed to find out whether consumers would be disposed toward toilet paper *with any scent at all* and what the scent preferences are of those who *like* the idea of scented toilet paper. Possibly those who are interested in toilet paper with scents prefer scent B over scent A, whereas scent A appeals to those who, in the marketplace, would be buying *unscented* paper.[5] ■

Equivalent Form Reliability The problems of the test-retest approach can be avoided by creating equivalent forms of a measurement instrument. For example, assume that the researcher is interested in identifying inner-directed versus outer-directed lifestyles. Two questionnaires can be created containing measures of inner-directed behavior and outer-directed behavior. Further, these measures should receive about the same emphasis on each questionnaire. Thus, although the questions used to ascertain the lifestyles are different on each questionnaire, the same number of questions used to measure each lifestyle should be approximately equal. The recommended interval for administering the second equivalent form is two weeks, although in some cases they are given one after the other or simultaneously. **Equivalent form reliability** is determined by measuring the correlation of the scores on the two instruments.

equivalent form reliability
The ability to produce similar results using two instruments as similar as possible to measure the same object.

There are two problems with equivalent forms that should be noted. First, it is very difficult and perhaps impossible to create two totally equivalent forms. Second, if equivalence can be achieved, it may not be worth the time, trouble, and expense involved. The theory behind the equivalent forms approach to reliability assessment is the same as test-retest. The primary difference between the test-retest and the equivalent forms methods is the testing instrument itself. Test-retest uses the same instrument, whereas equivalent form uses a different, but highly similar, measuring instrument.

internal consistency reliability
Ability to produce the similar results using different samples to measure a phenomenon during the same time period.

split-half technique
A method of assessing the reliability of a scale by dividing into two the total set of measurement items and correlating the results.

Internal Consistency Reliability The **internal consistency** measure of **reliability** assesses the ability to produce the similar results using different samples to measure a phenomenon during the same time period. The theory of internal consistency rests on the notion of equivalence. Equivalence is concerned with how much error may be introduced by different samples of items being used to measure a phenomenon. It is concerned with variations at one point in time among samples of items. A researcher can test for item equivalence by assessing the homogeneity of a set of items. The total set of items used to measure a phenomenon, such as inner-directed lifestyles, is divided into two halves; the total score of the two halves is then correlated (see Table 10.4). Use of the **split-half technique** typically calls for scale items to be randomly assigned to one half or the other. The problem with this method, however, is that the estimate of the coefficient of reliability is totally dependent upon how the items were split. Different splits result in different correlations but should not.

TABLE 10.4 Statements Used to Measure Inner-directed Lifestyles

I often don't get the credit I deserve for things I do well.
I try to get my own way regardless of others.
My greatest achievements are ahead of me.
I have a number of ideas that someday I would like to put into a book.
I am quick to accept new ideas.
I often think about how I look and what impression I am making on others.
I am a competitive person.
I feel upset when I hear that people are criticizing or blaming me.
I'd like to be a celebrity.
I get a real thrill out of doing dangerous things.
I feel that almost nothing in life can substitute for great achievement.
It's important for me to be noticed.
I keep in close touch with my friends.
I spend a good deal of time trying to decide how I feel about things.
I often think I can feel my way into the innermost being of another person.
I feel that ideals are powerful motivating forces in people.
I think someone can be a good person without believing in God.
The Eastern religions are more appealing to me than Christianity.
I feel satisfied with my life.
I enjoy getting involved in new and unusual situations.
Overall, I'd say I'm happy.
I feel I understand where my life is going.
I like to think I'm different from other people.
I adopt a commonsense attitude toward life.

To overcome the split-halves problems, many researchers now use the Cronbach Alpha. This technique computes the mean reliability coefficient estimates for all possible ways of splitting a set of items in half. A lack of correlation of an item with other items in the scale is evidence that the item does not belong in the scale and should be omitted. One limitation of the Cronbach Alpha is that the scale items require equal intervals. If this criteria cannot be met, another test called the KR-20 can be used. The KR-20 technique is applicable for all dichotomous or nominally scaled items.

Validity

Recall that the second characteristic of a good measurement device is validity. **Validity** addresses the issue of whether what we tried to measure was actually measured. When Coke first brought out "new Coke," it had conducted more than 5,000 interviews that purported to show new Coke was favored over original Coke. Unfortunately, its measurement instrument was not valid. This led to one of the greatest marketing debacles of all time! The validity of a measure refers to the extent to which the measurement instrument and procedure are free from both systematic and random error. Thus, a measuring device is valid if differences in scores solely reflect true differences on the characteristic we seek to measure rather than systematic or random error. You should realize that a necessary precondition for validity is that the measuring instrument is reliable. An instrument that is not reliable will not yield consistent results when measuring the same phenomenon over time.

validity
Whether what we tried to measure was actually measured.

A scale or other measuring device is basically worthless to a researcher if it lacks validity because it is not measuring what it is supposed to. On the surface, this seems like a rather simple notion, yet validity often is based on subtle distinctions. Assume that your teacher gives an exam that he has constructed to measure marketing research knowledge, and the test consists strictly of applying a number of formulas to simple case problems. A friend receives a low score on the test and protests to the teacher that she "really understands marketing research." Her position, in essence, is that the test was not valid. Rather than measuring knowledge of marketing research, it measured memorization of formulas and the ability to use simple math to find solutions. The teacher could repeat the exam only to find that student scores still fall in the same order. Does this mean that the protesting student was incorrect? Not necessarily; the teacher may be systematically measuring the ability to memorize rather than a true understanding of marketing research.

Unlike the teacher, who was attempting to measure market research knowledge, a brand manager is more interested in successful prediction. The manager, for example, wants to know if a purchase intent scale successfully predicts trial purchase of a new product. Thus, validity can be examined from a number of different perspectives, including face, content, criterion-related, and construct (see Table 10.5).

Face Validity **Face validity** is the weakest form of validity. It is concerned with the degree to which a measurement "looks like" it measured what it is supposed to. It is a judgment call by the researcher, made as the questions are designed. Thus as each question is scrutinized, there is an implicit assessment of

face validity
A measurement seems to measure what it is supposed to measure.

TABLE 10.5 Assessing the Validity of a Measurement Instrument

Face Validity	Researchers judge the degree to which a measurement instrument seems to measure what it is supposed to.
Content Validity	The degree to which the instrument items represent the universe of the concept under study.
Criterion-related Validity	The degree to which a measurement instrument can predict a variable that is designated a criterion. a. Predictive validity: The extent to which a future level of a criterion variable can be predicted by a current measurement on a scale. b. Concurrent validity: The extent to which a criterion variable measured at the same point in time as the variable of interest can be predicted by the measurement instrument.
Construct Validity	The degree to which a measure confirms a hypothesis created from a theory based upon the concepts under study. a. Convergent validity: The degree of association among different measurement instruments that purport to measure the same concept. b. Discriminant validity: The lack of association among constructs that are supposed to be different.

its face validity. Revisions enhance the face validity of the question until it passes the researcher's subjective evaluation. Alternatively, *face validity* can refer to the subjective agreement of researchers, experts, or people familiar with the market, product, or industry that a scale logically appears to be accurately reflecting what it is supposed to measure. A straightforward question such as "What is your age?" followed by a series of age categories generally is agreed to have face validity. Most scales used in market research attempt to measure attitudes or behavioral intentions, which are much more elusive.

content validity

The degree to which the instrument items represent the universe of the concept under study.

Content Validity Content validity is the representativeness or sampling adequacy of the content of the measurement instrument. In other words, does the scale provide adequate coverage of the topic under study? Say that McDonald's has hired you to measure the image of the company among adults 18 to 30 years of age who eat fast food hamburgers at least once a month. You devise a scale that asks consumers to rate the following:

modern building	1	2	3	4	5	old-fashioned building
beautiful landscaping	1	2	3	4	5	poor landscaping
clean parking lots	1	2	3	4	5	dirty parking lots
attractive signs	1	2	3	4	5	unattractive signs

A McDonald's executive would quickly take issue with this scale, claiming that a person could evaluate McDonald's on this scale either good or bad and never have eaten a McDonald's burger. In fact, the evaluation can be made simply by driving past a McDonald's. The executive could further argue that the scale lacks content validity because many important components of image such as the quality of the food, cleanliness of the eating area and restrooms, and promptness and courtesy of service had been omitted.

The determination of content validity is not always a simple matter. It is very difficult and perhaps impossible to identify all the facets of McDonald's image. Content validity ultimately becomes a judgmental matter. One can approach content validity by first carefully defining precisely what is to be measured. Second, an exhaustive literature search and focus groups can be conducted to identify all possible items for inclusion on the scale. Third, a panel of experts can be asked their opinions on whether an item should be included. Finally, the scale could be pretested and also an open-ended question asked that might identify other items to be included. For example, after a more refined image scale for McDonald's has been administered, a follow-up question could be, "Do you have any other thoughts about McDonald's that you would like to express?" Answers to this pretest question may provide clues for other image dimensions not previously covered.

Criterion-Related Validity **Criterion-related validity** examines the ability of a measuring instrument to predict a variable that is designated a criterion. To illustrate, assume that we wish to devise a test to identify marketing researchers who are exceptional at moderating focus groups. We begin by having impartial marketing research experts determine from a directory of marketing researchers who they judge to be best at moderating focus groups. We then construct 300 items to which group moderators are asked to reply yes or no, such as "I believe it is important to compel shy group participants to speak out" and "I like to interact with small groups of people." We then go through the responses and select the items that the good focus group moderators answered one way and the remainder the other way. Assume that this process produces 84 items, which we put together to form what we shall call the Test of Effectiveness in Focus Group Moderating (TEFGM). We feel that this test will identify good focus group moderators. The criterion of interest here is the ability to conduct a good focus group. We might explore further the criterion-related validity of TEFGM by administering it to a new group of moderators that has been previously divided into those who are good moderators and those who are not. Then we could determine how well the test identifies the group to which each marketing researcher is assigned. Thus criterion-related validity is concerned with detecting the presence or absence of one or more criteria considered to represent constructs of interest.

criterion-related validity
The degree to which a measurement instrument can predict a variable that is designated a criterion.

Two subcategories of criterion-related validity are predictive validity and concurrent validity. **Predictive validity** is the extent to which a future level of a criterion variable can be predicted by a current measurement on a scale. A voter-motivation scale, for example, is used to predict the likelihood of a person voting in the next election. A savvy politician is not interested in what the community as a whole perceives as important problems but only in what persons who are likely to vote perceive as important problems. These are the issues that the politician would address in speeches and advertising. Another example of predictive validity is the extent to which a purchase intent scale for a new Pepperidge Farm pastry predicts actual trial of the product.

predictive validity
The degree to which the future level of a criterion can be forecast by a current measurement scale.

Concurrent validity is concerned with the relationship between the predictor variable and the criterion variable, both of which are assessed at the same point in time; for example, the ability of a home pregnancy test to accurately determine whether a woman is pregnant right now. Such a test with low concurrent validity could cause a lot of undue stress.

concurrent validity
The degree to which a variable, measured at the same point in time as the variable of interest, can be predicted by the measurement instrument.

Construct Validity **Construct validity,** although often not consciously addressed by many market researchers on a day-to-day basis, is extremely important to marketing scientists. It involves understanding the theoretical foundations

construct validity
The degree to which a measurement instrument represents and logically connects, via the underlying theory, the observed phenomenon to the construct.

underlying the obtained measurements. A measure has construct validity if it behaves according to the underlying theory. Instead of addressing the major issue of interest to the brand manager (e.g., whether the scale adequately predicts whether a consumer will try my new brand), construct validity is concerned with the theory behind the prediction. Purchase behavior is something we can observe directly; someone either buys product A or does not. Yet scientists have developed constructs on lifestyles, involvement, attitude, and personality that help understand why someone purchases something or does not. These constructs are largely unobservable. We can observe behavior related to the constructs—that is, buying a product. We cannot observe the constructs themselves—such as an attitude. Constructs help scientists communicate and build theories to explain phenomena.

convergent validity
The degree of association among different measurement instruments that purport to measure the same concept.

discriminant validity
The lack of association among constructs that are supposed to be different.

Two statistical approaches for assessing construct validity are convergent and discriminant validity. **Convergent validity** is the degree of correlation among different measures that purport to measure the same construct. **Discriminant validity** is the lack of, or low correlation among, constructs that are supposed to be different. Assume that we develop a multi-item scale that measures the propensity to shop at discount stores. Our theory suggests that this propensity is caused by four personality variables: high level of self-confidence, low need for status, low need for distinctiveness, and high level of adaptability. Further, our theory suggests that propensity to shop at discount stores is not related to brand loyalty or high-level aggressiveness.

Evidence of construct validity would exist if our scale

- Correlates highly with other measures of propensity to shop at discount stores, such as reported stores patronized and social class (convergent validity)
- Has a low correlation with the unrelated constructs of brand loyalty and a high level of aggressiveness (discriminant validity).

Relating the Measures to Assess Validity All the types of validity discussed here are somewhat interrelated in both theory and practice. Predictive validity is obviously very important on a scale to predict whether a person will shop at a discount store. A researcher developing a discount store patronage scale probably would first attempt to understand the constructs that provide the basis for prediction. The researcher would put forth a theory about discount store patronage that, of course, is the foundation of construct validity. Next, the researcher would be concerned with which specific items to include on the discount store patronage scale and whether these items relate to the full range of the construct. Thus, the researcher would ascertain the degree of content validity. The issue of criterion-related validity can be addressed in a pretest by measuring scores on the discount store patronage scale and actual store patronage.

Reliability and Validity—A Concluding Comment

The concepts of reliability and validity are illustrated conceptually in Figure 10.2. Situation 1 shows holes all over the target. It could be due to the use of an old rifle, being a poor shot, or many other factors. This complete lack of consistency means there is no reliability. Because the instrument lacks reliability, thus creating huge errors, it cannot be valid. Measurement reliability is a necessary condition for validity.

FIGURE 10.2
Illustrations of Possible Reliability and Validity Situations in Measurement

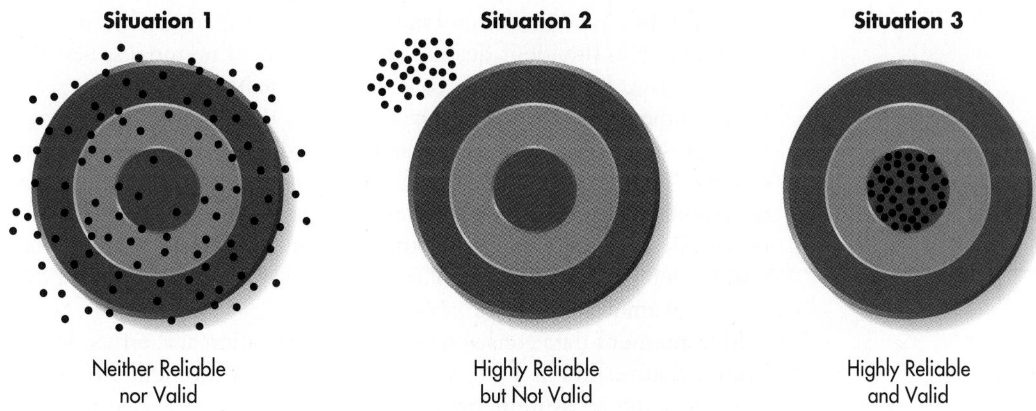

The second target denotes a very tight pattern (consistency) but is far removed from the bull's-eye. This illustrates that we can have a high level of reliability in an instrument (little variance) that lacks validity. The instrument is consistent, but it does not measure what it is supposed to measure. The shooter has a steady eye, but the sights are not adjusted properly. Situation 3 shows the criteria that researchers strive to achieve in a measurement instrument that is reliable, consistent, and valid (on target with what we are attempting to measure).

Despite the critical importance of assessing the reliability and validity of measurement instruments, most research articles written by marketing academics avoid the issue. Of all articles published from 1980 to 1990 in the *Journal of Marketing, Journal of Marketing Research*, and the *Journal of Consumer Research* that used survey research measures, only 40 percent reported reliability and validity estimates.[6] Although an improvement over the previous decade, more researchers and practitioners must address measurement issues. This is a necessary requirement to improve the decision-making information provided to management and to advance the science of marketing.

Summary

Measurement consists of using rules to assign numbers to objects in such a way as to represent quantities of attributes. Thus, it is a procedure used to assign numbers that reflect the amount of attributes possessed by an event, person, or object. A measurement rule is a guide, a method, or command that tells the researcher what to do. Accurate measurement requires rules that are both clear and specific.

The measurement process is as follows: identify the concept of interest, develop a construct, define the concept constitutively and operationally, develop a measurement scale, evaluate the reliability and validity of the scale, and then use the scale. A constitutive definition defines concepts with other concepts or constructs, establishing boundaries for the concept under study. It states the central idea or concept under study. An operational definition defines which observable characteristics will be measured and the process for assigning a value to the concept.

There are four basic levels of measurement: nominal, ordinal, interval, and ratio. A nominal scale partitions data into categories that are mutually exclusive and collectively exhaustive. The numbers assigned to objects or phenomena are numerical but have no number meaning; the numbers are simply labels. Ordinal scales maintain the identification characteristics of nominal scales plus an ability to order data. Interval scales contain all the features of ordinal scales with the added dimension that the interval between the points on the scale are equal. Interval scales enable the researcher to discuss differences separating two objects. They are amenable to computation of an arithmetic mean, standard deviation, and correlation coefficients. Ratio scales have all the powers of those previously discussed scales plus the concept of an absolute zero or origin, which enables comparison of the absolute magnitude of the numbers and which reflects the actual amount of the variable.

Measurement data consist of accurate information and errors. Systematic error is error that results in a constant bias in the measurements. Random error also influences the measurements but is not systematic; it is transient in nature and does not occur in a consistent manner. Reliability is the degree to which measures are free from random error and therefore provide consistent data. There are three ways to assess reliability: test-retest, internal consistency, and use of equivalent forms. *Validity* refers to the notion of actually measuring what we are attempting to measure. The validity of a measure refers to the extent to which the measurement device or process is free from both systematic and random error. Concepts of validity include face, content, criterion, and construct validity.

Key Terms

measurement
rule
construct
constitutive definition
operational definition
scale
nominal scales
ordinal scales
interval scales
ratio scales
systematic error
random error
reliability
test-retest reliability
stability
equivalent form reliability
internal consistency reliability
split-half technique
validity
face validity
content validity
criterion-related validity
predictive validity
concurrent validity
construct validity
convergent validity
discriminant validity

Review and Discussion Questions

1. What is measurement?
2. Differentiate between the four types of measurement scales, and discuss the types of information contained in each.
3. How does reliability differ from validity? Give examples of each.
4. Give an example of a scale that would be reliable but not valid. Also give an example of a scale that would be valid but not reliable.
5. What are three methods of assessing reliability?
6. What are three methods of assessing validity?

7. Give one conceptual definition and two or more operational definitions for each of the following concepts:
   a. convenience store
   b. brand loyalty
   c. inadequate customer service
   d. convenient location
8. You have just read a marketing research report on the testing of a new chewy candy. What indicators of measurement accuracy would you use in evaluating the quality of the data?
9. What are the permissible descriptive statistics used with nominal, ordinal, and interval scales? What are permissible inferential statistics used for these scales?

CASE 10.1

Traveling Asians

Asians typically have deep off-shore roots. Their sense of family and community consists of more than a small geographic area, as a look at a typical domestic and international long-distance bill attests. Studies have shown that Asians have friends and family throughout the United States and the entire world whom they treasure and want to visit. Their social and business networks are equally far-reaching.

For example, one recent travel study showed that among a particular Asian group living in Los Angeles:

- 80 percent had flown in the past five years;
- 70 percent had flown to Asia in the past five years;
- 61 percent have done both, i.e., flown at least once in the past five years, and plan to fly again in the very near future.

The number of Asian business travelers has been growing, and will continue to grow, in importance for travel industry revenue. An excellent example of that is what the Chinese refer to as "astronauts," or *tai kong ren* in Mandarin. These are Chinese men, typically with businesses in Hong Kong and Taiwan and wives and children in the United States or Canada. Besides the fact that these men spend so much time in the air that they are like astronauts, the sound of the Mandarin word is very similar to the word meaning "without wife."

Las Vegas is a favorite destination for many Asians, and the lure of that city can shed light on the need for culturally sensitive marketing. The Mirage has opened a permanent home for le Cirque du Soleil, a unique, nonverbal international circus that draws huge numbers of Asians—who face no language barriers for this entertainment.

Las Vegas promoters also realize that the Japanese enjoy visiting theme parks like Disneyland and that many of them love golf. With the opening of MGM's theme park, Treasure Island, and with several more golf facilities in the works, there has been a new boom in Japanese visits to that gambling oasis.

For Chinese visitors from Taiwan and Hong Kong, Las Vegas is a popular destination because of the casinos. The motivation for the majority of those who visit Las Vegas to gamble is the same—they go with the mind-set of winning a fortune. Las Vegas also is extremely popular with many Koreans.

1. Create a constitutive definition of the concept that Japanese love theme parks.
2. Now, define the construct operationally.
3. The frequency of flight information is scaled data. What level of measurement is it?
4. Illustrate how each level of measurement (see Table 10.2, page 346) could be used in a survey of Japanese vacationers in Las Vegas.

CASE 10.2

Evaluating Service Quality

The service industry accounts for 70 percent of the gross national product, absorbing approximately 72 percent of the total workforce, and is responsible for more than one-half of all consumer spending. The *Atlanta Journal* and the *Atlanta Constitution* invited its readers to fill out a questionnaire printed in the papers regarding service quality. A total of 610 readers filled out and mailed the newspaper questionnaire. The results were as follows:

	ATLANTA READERS BELIEVE SERVICE IS . . .		
INDUSTRY	Good	Bad	No Response
Airlines	55.7%	16.2%	28.0%
Auto dealers	15.6	52.1	32.3
Auto service	8.7	71.5	19.8
Banks	44.6	36.4	19.0
Brokerage firms	20.3	13.8	65.9
Car rental	27.2	16.2	56.4
Department stores	29.3	46.2	24.4
Discount brokers	18.0	50.5	31.3
Doctor/dentist	47.9	26.6	25.6
Dry cleaning	47.9	15.9	36.2
Electric hookup	23.9	12.6	63.4
Fast food	35.1	36.1	28.9
Grocery stores	45.4	25.6	29.0
Hospitals	27.1	34.4	38.5
Insurance companies	19.8	44.3	35.9
Local governments	9.0	59.3	31.5
Motels/hotels	44.4	16.7	38.9
Newspapers	49.7	20.0	30.3
Restaurants	35.9	27.2	36.9
Small appliance repair	9.2	29.7	61.2
Telephone hookup	26.1	30.0	43.9

SOURCE: The *Atlanta Journal* and *Atlanta Constitution*.

1. What are the constructs? What are the constitutive definitions in this case? Are they sufficient? If not, what are the implications?

2. What kind of scale probably was used? What is the highest level of scaling that could have been used? Give an example.
3. Describe four possible sources of error in the data.
4. Do you think that the scale is reliable? Why or why not? What could be done to test for reliability?
5. Is the scale valid in your opinion? Why? How might you determine validity?

CHAPTER 11

Attitude Measurement

LEARNING OBJECTIVES

1. To understand the nature of attitudes.
2. To become familiar with the concept of scaling.
3. To learn about the various types of attitude scales.
4. To realize the importance of purchase intent scales in marketing research.
5. To examine some basic considerations when selecting a type of scale.

Campbell Soup Company sells a lot of food products for children. Segmenting a market in which the customer who is buying the product isn't necessarily the one eating it is not always easy. Campbell does a lot of within-household segmentations to explore the constant food fight between parents and kids. Kids would be perfectly happy to live on Twinkies, Coca-Cola, and Gummi Worms if parents let them. But the parents' role is to be a gatekeeper and role model for their children's food choices. And as marketers, Campbell's role is to develop nutritious food that children will enjoy eating but that parents won't feel bad about buying. Thank goodness for Campbell, and for parents, that kids do like stuff that comes in cans.

When someone is researching a children's product, he must ask parents and kids to determine purchase interest, preferences, and attribute ratings. Often, there is a lot of variation. Campbell tested a canned pasta and sauce product and found that 56 percent of kids rated the product high on the liking scale, but that only 11 percent or 12 percent of mothers agreed. Fewer than half of moms indicated definite purchase intent, while more than 70 percent of kids wanted their mothers to buy the product for them. Campbell also found that these products appeal most to the under-six age group and that interest declined with age. This kind of research shows how to market the product. In this case, it shows that the ads must assure parents of quality while communicating children's positive purchase desire.[1] ■

Campbell's segmentation research is based upon the concept of measurement; for example, product attribute ratings. Campbell's research also encompassed several different types of attitude scales. What are the components of attitudes? What tools are available for measuring attitudes? What factors should be considered when selecting an attitude scale? These are the topics of Chapter 11.

The Nature of Attitudes

As discussed in Chapter 10, an **attitude** is an enduring organization of motivational, emotional, perceptual, and cognitive processes with respect to some aspect of our environment. It is a learned predisposition to respond in a consistently favorable or unfavorable manner toward an object. Attitudes tend to be long lasting and consist of clusters of interrelated beliefs. Attitudes also encompass our value systems, which represent our standards of good and bad, right and

attitude

An enduring organization of motivational, emotional, perceptual, and cognitive processes with respect to some aspect of our environment.

wrong, and so forth. Thus, you may have a specific attitude toward Disney World, based on beliefs about need for entertainment, cartoon characters, fantasy, crowds of people, waiting in lines, and many other things. Disney World also may be highly valued by you as good, clean, wholesome fun.

Attitudes and Behavior

The link between attitudes and behavior is complex. The prediction of future behavior for a group of consumers tends to be higher than the prediction of behavior for a single consumer.[2] Specifically, researchers have found the following:

1. The more favorable the attitude of consumers, the higher is the incidence of product usage.
2. The less favorable the attitude, the lower is the incidence of usage.
3. The more unfavorable people's attitudes are toward a product, the more likely they are to stop using it.
4. The attitudes of people who have never tried a product tend to be distributed around the mean in the shape of a normal distribution.[3]
5. When attitudes are based on actually trying and experiencing a product, attitudes predict behavior quite well. Conversely, when attitudes are based on advertising, attitude behavior consistency is significantly reduced.[4]

Components of Attitudes

Attitudes may be thought of as having three components: cognitive, affective, and behavioral (see Figure 11.1). Each component is of great interest to marketing decision makers.

cognitive component of attitudes

An individual's knowledge and beliefs about an object.

The Cognitive Component The **cognitive component of attitudes** is a person's knowledge and beliefs about an object. For example, David Johnson might believe that a BMW M series:

- contains a powerful engine
- is a prestigious vehicle
- is a good value for the money
- is excellent at cornering at high speeds

These beliefs represent the cognitive component of David's attitude toward the BMW M series. These beliefs may or may not be true, but they represent reality to David. The more positive beliefs associated with a product and the more positive each belief is, the more favorable the overall cognitive component is presumed to be. And, as all the components of an attitude generally are consistent, the more favorable is the overall attitude.

affective component of attitudes

An individual's feelings or emotional reactions about an object.

The Affective Component An individual's feelings or emotional reactions to an object represent the **affective component of attitudes.** If David claims "I love BMWs" or "Japanese can make middle- and low-priced cars but are not competent to make luxury cars," he is expressing his emotional feelings or the affective component of an attitude. David's overall feelings toward BMWs may

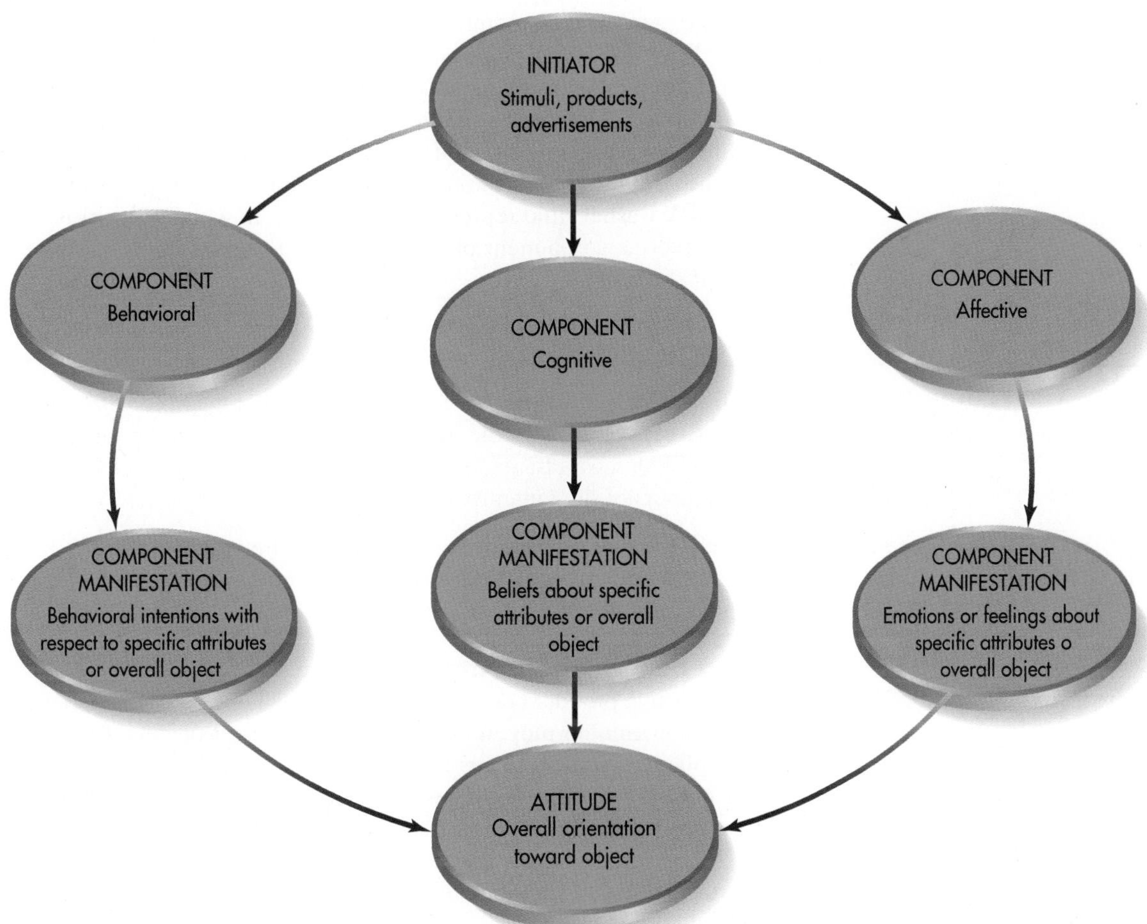

FIGURE 11.1
Attitude Components and Manifestations

be based on years of satisfied experience as a BMW owner. Conversely, his attitude toward Japanese auto manufacturers may be developed with little cognitive information. David's attitude may change as he encounters more cognitive data about Japanese luxury cars; for example, advertisements, automobile showrooms, and test drives.

A specific cognitive belief may be shared by two or more individuals, yet one person may have a positive affective response and the other a negative affective response. Consider the belief that "BMWs have powerful engines." David may view this product attribute in a very positive manner; for example, "I can go from 0 to 60 mph in 5.2 seconds and top out at 140 mph." David's spouse may think, "He will spend a fortune on gas and may kill himself with that powerful car."

The Behavioral Component The decision by David to purchase yet another BMW would represent the **behavioral component of an attitude.** The behavioral component may be represented by future intentions: "I plan to buy a Passport radar detector for my new BMW." Intentions usually are limited to a

behavioral component of attitudes
An individual's intentions to act in some manner based on attitudes about an object.

specific time period. A recommendation also is a behavioral component. For example, "Why don't you purchase Michelin radial tires." Behavior usually is directed toward a total product and is less likely to be attribute specific like cognitions and beliefs. However, variations can exist. David, for example, may purchase all his replacement parts and fluids from the BMW dealer except windshield washer fluid. He buys the fluid at Chief Auto Parts. For David, acquiring genuine BMW washer fluid represented a situation in which value was less than costs. His affective component of attitude toward washer fluids was that "they are all about the same."

Changing Attitudes

A marketing manager whose products are not meeting profit goals or market share objectives is faced with the necessity of boosting sales or perhaps dropping the products. The most efficient way to increase sales may be to change attitudes held by members of the target market. This can be accomplished in three ways:

1. Changing the belief(s) about the attributes of the brand.
2. Changing the relative importance of these beliefs.
3. Adding new beliefs.

Changing Beliefs About Attributes The first technique involves taking neutral or negative product or company attribute beliefs and trying to make them positive. It is a common ploy in many large cities for car dealers, furniture dealers, and appliance retailers to advertise "the world's worst location" when their stores are not on main thoroughfares. The idea is "yes, we have a terrible location, therefore we have really got to give you a good deal to entice you to drive out here." The retailer hopes that by changing the consumer's belief, the individual's attitude toward shopping there will be more favorable, and therefore the consumer will be more likely to patronize the store.

Changing Attitudes by Changing the Importance of Beliefs The second approach to attitude modification is to change the relative importance of a person's beliefs toward an attribute. For years, consumers have known that Post's Bran Flakes were high in natural fiber. The primary belief associated with this attribute was that the high fiber tended to act as a mild natural laxative. Today, however, the high fiber content of Bran Flakes is promoted as a possible factor in preventing colon cancer. The promotion campaign has resulted in an increase in profits and market share.

Adding New Beliefs The third approach is to add new beliefs. Blue Nun has promoted the idea that its white wine goes with just about anything—that it is not limited to fowl and fish. Chrysler tells us that the Jeep Wagoneer is not simply for the outdoor enthusiast but its roominess makes it a great family car. Toyota's Lexus ads claim "Our car looks like art." To distance Lexus from other Toyotas, the company required dealers to build new, separate showrooms. The showrooms feature Japanese-style screens, natural materials, stone floors, and even waterfalls in some locations. Floor space that would usually hold 12 cars showcases only four.

Examining the Link Between Measurements of Beliefs and Feelings and Actual Behavior

It is frustrating to marketers that there is often a limited relationship between the findings of an attitude study and actual consumer behavior. Yet, at least seven factors can reduce the consistency between measures of beliefs and feelings and observations of behavior.[5]

1. A favorable attitude requires a need or motive before it can be translated into action. Thus, a consumer may not feel a need for a BMW or might already own an acceptable, though less preferred, brand.
2. Translating favorable beliefs and feelings into ownership requires ability. A person simply may not be able to afford a BMW.
3. A study often measures attitudes toward one concept such as cars. Purchases often involve trade-offs both within and between product categories. The buyer might be able to afford a BMW but instead selects a Suzuki and uses the savings to go to graduate school and buy a new stereo system.
4. If the cognitive and affective components are weakly held, when the consumer obtains additional information while shopping, the initial attitudes may give way to new ones.
5. Market research typically measures the attitudes of one person in a family. The shopper may be strongly influenced by her spouse to buy a different car. A mother of three small children may insist that the husband forgo the new BMW for a Ford station wagon.
6. Researchers generally measure brand attitudes independent of the purchase situation. However, many items are purchased for, or in, specific situations. A person may be intent on buying a BMW, yet on the day of purchase Mercedes runs a full page ad in the newspaper offering $8,000 off list for all first-time Mercedes purchasers. Our consumer decides it is too good a deal to pass up.
7. It is difficult to measure all relevant aspects of an attitude. Survey respondents may be unwilling or unable to espouse all their feelings and beliefs about various products or brands. Alternatively, the researcher's measurement instrument may not cover certain aspects of consumers' attitudes.

Attitude Scales

As can be seen from the preceding discussion, marketing strategies often depend upon understanding attitudes of target consumers and, when necessary, attempting to change or modify those attitudes. Measurement of attitudes is much more difficult and uses less precise scales than those found in the physical sciences. As noted earlier, an attitude is a construct that exists in the minds of the consumer and is not directly observable unlike, for example, weight in the physical sciences. Attitude scaling is based on various operational definitions created to measure the attitude construct. In many cases, attitudes are measured at the nominal or ordinal level. Some more sophisticated scales enable the market researcher to measure at the interval level. One must be careful not to attribute the more powerful properties of an interval scale to the lower level nominal or ordinal scales.

Scaling Defined

scaling
Procedures for assignment of numbers (or other symbols) to a property of objects to impart some of the characteristics of numbers to the properties in question.

unidimensional scaling
Procedures designed to measure only one attribute of a respondent or object.

multidimensional scaling
Procedures designed to measure several dimensions of a concept or object.

The term **scaling** refers to procedures for attempting to determine quantitative measures of subjective and sometimes abstract concepts. It is defined as a procedure for the assignment of numbers (or other symbols) to a property of objects to impart some of the characteristics of numbers to the properties in question. A scale is a measurement tool. Thus, we assign a number scale to the various levels of heat and cold and call it a thermometer, as you recall from Chapter 10. Actually, we assign numbers to indicants of the properties of objects. The rise and fall of mercury in a glass tube is an indicant of temperature variations.

Scales are either unidimensional or multidimensional. **Unidimensional scaling** is designed to measure only one attribute of a respondent or object. Thus, we may create a scale to measure consumers' price sensitivity. We may use several items to measure price sensitivity, but we will combine them into a single measure and place all interviewees along a linear continuum, called *degree of price sensitivity.* **Multidimensional scaling** recognizes that a concept or object might be better described using several dimensions rather than one. For example, target customers for Jaguar automobiles may be defined in three dimensions: level of wealth, degree of price sensitivity, and appreciation of fine motor cars.

FIGURE 11.2
Three Types of Graphic Rating Scales

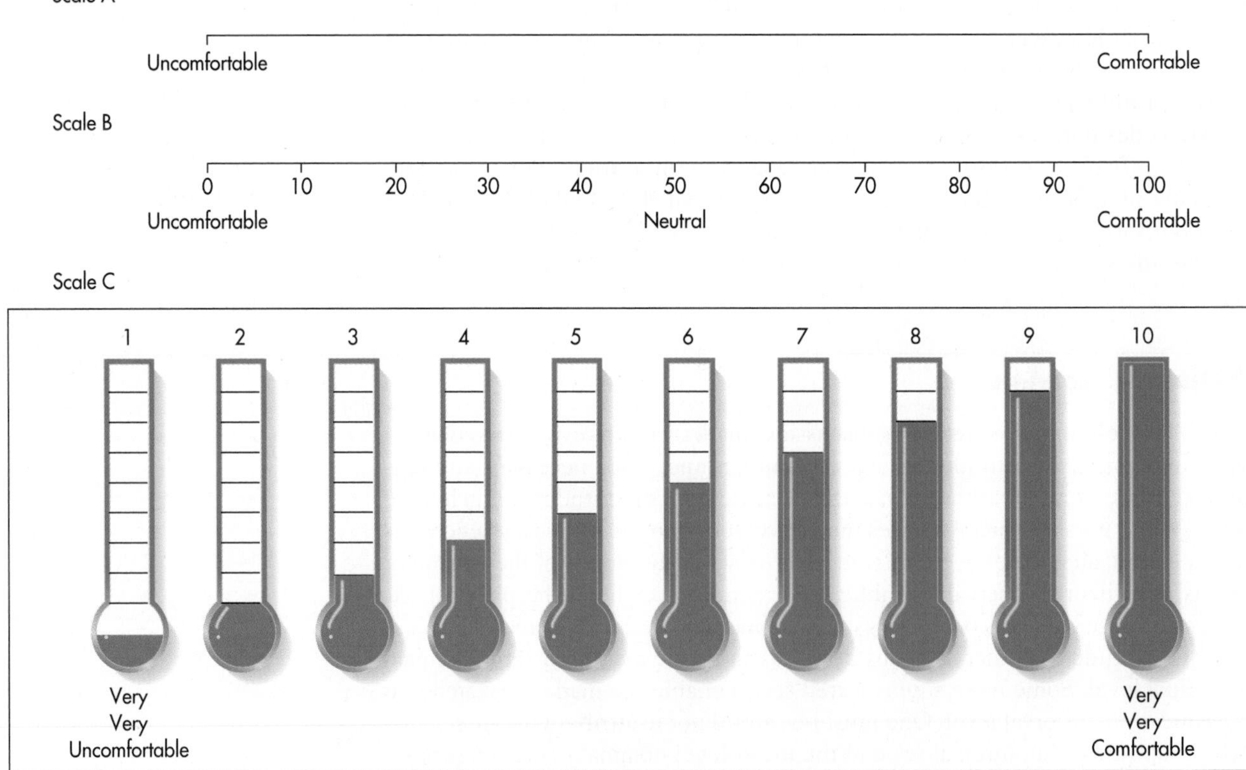

Graphic Rating Scales

Graphic rating scales present respondents with a graphic continuum typically anchored by two extremes. Figure 11.2 depicts three types of graphic rating scales that might be used to evaluate La-Z-Boy recliners. Scale A represents the simplest form of a graphic scale. Respondents are instructed to check their response along the continuum. After a check mark is made, a score is assigned by dividing the line into as many categories as desired and assigning the score based upon the category into which the mark has been placed. For example, if the line is six inches long, every inch could represent a category. Scale B offers the respondent slightly more structure by assigning numbers along the scale.

graphic rating scales
Graphic continuums anchored by two extremes presented to respondents for evaluation of a concept or object.

Graphic rating scales are not limited to simply placing a check mark along a continuum, as illustrated by scale C. Scale C has been used successfully by many researchers to speed up the interviewing process. The interviewer has the scale mounted on a card that is held in front of the respondent. Respondents are asked to touch the thermometer that best depicts their feelings.

Graphic ratings scales can be constructed easily and are simple to use. They also enable a researcher to discern fine distinctions, assuming that the rater has adequate discriminatory abilities. Numerical data obtained from the scales are typically treated as interval data.

One disadvantage of the scale is that if the ancors are too extreme, it tends to force respondents toward the middle of the scale. Also, one study has suggested that graphic rating scales are not as reliable as itemized rating scales.

Itemized Rating Scales

Itemized rating scales are very similar to graphic rating scales, except that respondents must select from a limited number of ordered categories rather than placing a check mark on a continuous scale (purists would argue that scale C in Figure 11.2 is an itemized ratings scale). Table 11.1 illustrates itemized ratings scales taken from nationwide market research surveys. As you can see, researchers often hand a copy of the basic scale to the respondent and ask for a rating after the interviewer reads off a characteristic. Starting points are rotated on each questionnaire to eliminate order bias. That is, starting with the same characteristic each time may act as a source of bias.

itemized rating scales
Scales in which the respondent selects an answer from a limited number of ordered categories.

Scale A was part of a questionnaire used to evaluate watches with a Sears logo. Scale B was on a screening questionnaire used for in-home placements of a new shampoo concept. The manufacturer wanted an equal number of users in each hair condition category. Scale C also was part of an in-home product test. It was administered after the teenager had used the sample product for two weeks. Scale D was used in a study of children's TV ads. Examples of other itemized rating categories are shown in Table 11.2.

Itemized ratings scales are easy to construct and administer but do not allow for the fine distinctions that can be achieved in a graphics rating scale. Yet the definitive categories found in itemized ratings scales usually produce more reliable ratings. Researchers must be careful when itemized or graphic rating scales are administered to Asian Americans and other immigrant market segments. Michael Halberstam, president of Interviewing Services of America, points out

TABLE 11.1 Itemized Rating Scales Used in National Surveys

SCALE A

Now, I'd like to ask you about just two watches specifically. The first one is the SEARS watch. I'm going to mention some characteristics of watches, and, as I mention each one, please tell me whether you think the SEARS watch is (HAND RESPONDENT RATING CARD) excellent, very good, good, fair, or poor.

. . . for the particular characteristic?

The first characteristic is (READ CHARACTERISTIC CIRCLED BELOW). Do you feel that the SEARS watch is excellent, very good, good, fair, or poor for (CHARACTERISTIC)?

(CONTINUE FOR *ALL* CHARACTERISTICS BELOW)

STARTING POINT		EXCELLENT	VERY GOOD	GOOD	FAIR	POOR
X	Value for the money	☐ 5	☐ 4	☐ 3	☐ 2	☐ 1
X	Brand name	☐ 5	☐ 4	☐ 3	☐ 2	☐ 1
Ⓧ	Accuracy	☐ 5	☐ 4	☐ 3	☐ 2	☐ 1
X	Durability	☐ 5	☐ 4	☐ 3	☐ 2	☐ 1
X	Manufacturer's reputation	☐ 5	☐ 4	☐ 3	☐ 2	☐ 1
X	After-sales service	☐ 5	☐ 4	☐ 3	☐ 2	☐ 1
X	Styling	☐ 5	☐ 4	☐ 3	☐ 2	☐ 1

SCALE B

9. Which statement on this card (HAND RESPONDENT CARD B) best describes the present condition of your hair?

1 ( ) Very damaged
2 ( ) Somewhat damaged
3 ( ) Slightly damaged
4 ( ) Not at all damaged

continues

the importance of understanding inherent differences in Asian American marketing research in "A Professional Researcher's Perspective" on page 376.

Rank-Order Scale

noncomparative

A judgment made without reference to another object, concept, or person.

rank-order scales

Scales in which the respondent compares one item with another or a group of items against each other and ranks them.

comparative scales

A judgment comparing one object, concept, or person against another on a scale.

Itemized and graphic scales are **noncomparative** because the respondent makes a judgment without reference to another object, concept, or person. **Rank-order scales,** on the other hand, are **comparative** because the respondent is asked to judge one item against another. Rank-order scales are widely used in market research for several reasons. They are easy to use and form an ordinal scale of the items evaluated. Instructions are easy to understand and the process typically moves at a steady pace. Some researchers claim that it forces respondents to evaluate concepts in a realistic manner. For example, Table 11.3 illustrates a series of rank-order scales taken from a study on eye shadows.

Rank-order scales also possess several disadvantages. If all the alternatives in a respondent's choice set are not included, the results could be misleading. For example, a respondent's first choice on all dimensions in the eye shadow study might have been Max Factor, which was not included. A second problem is that the concept being ranked may be completely outside a person's choice set, thus

TABLE 11.1 Itemized Rating Scales Used in National Surveys—*Continued*

SCALE C

Now, I would like to get your opinion on Stridex Cleansing Pads on some characteristics. (HAND RATING CARD) Using the phrases on this card, please tell me which one best indicates how much you agree or disagree that Stridex Cleansing Pads . . . (START WITH CHECKED CHARACTERISTICS AND CONTINUE UNTIL ALL ARE ASKED)

START		AGREE STRONGLY	AGREE SOMEWHAT	DISAGREE SOMEWHAT	DISAGREE STRONGLY
( )	Help prevent blemishes	___ 9-4	___ –3	___ –2	___ –1
( )	Help to clear up blemishes	___ 10-4	___ –3	___ –2	___ –1
( )	Are convenient to use	___ 11-4	___ –3	___ –2	___ –1
(✓)	Are not irritating	___ 12-4	___ –3	___ –2	___ –1
( )	Leave face feeling fresh	___ 13-4	___ –3	___ –2	___ –1
( )	Make you feel confident you are doing everything you can to help your skin look good	___ 14-4	___ –3	___ –2	___ –1

SCALE D

Very Very Good | | Very Very Poor

SOURCE: Scale D is adapted from Fred Cutler, "To Meet Criticisms of TV Ads, Researchers Find New Ways to Measure Children's Attitudes," *Marketing News* (January 27, 1978), p. 16, published by the American Marketing Association.

producing meaningless data. Perhaps a respondent doesn't use eye shadow and feels that the product isn't appropriate for any woman. A final limitation is that the scale gives the researcher only ordinal data. Nothing is learned about how far apart the items stand or how intense a person feels about the ranking of an item. Finally, we don't know why the items were ranked as they were.

Q-Sorting

Q-sorting
A sophisticated form of rank ordering using card sorts.

Q-sorting is basically a sophisticated form of rank ordering. A set of objects—verbal statements, slogans, product features, potential customer services, and so forth—is given to an individual to sort into piles according to specified rating categories (see Table 11.2). For example, the cards may each have a feature on them that can be designed into a new automobile. The respondents could then be asked to sort the cards according to how well they like the potential feature. With a large number of cards—Q-sorts usually contain from 60 to 120 cards—it would be very difficult to rank order them. For statistical convenience, the sorter is instructed to put varying numbers of cards in several piles, the whole making up a normal statistical distribution.

Here is a Q-sort distribution of 90 items:

TABLE 11.2 Selected Itemized Rating Scales

		PURCHASE INTENT		
Definitely will buy	Probably will buy		Probably will not buy	Definitely will not buy
		LEVEL OF AGREEMENT		
Strongly agree	Somewhat agree	Neither agree nor disagree	Somewhat disagree	Strongly disagree
		QUALITY		
Very good	Good	Neither good nor bad	Fair	Poor
		DEPENDABILITY		
Completely dependable	Somewhat dependable		Not very dependable	Not dependable at all
		STYLE		
Very stylish	Somewhat stylish		Not very stylish	Completely unstylish
		SATISFACTION		
Completely satisfied	Somewhat satisfied	Neither satisfied nor dissatisfied	Somewhat dissatisfied	Completely dissatisfied
		COST		
Extremely expensive	Expensive	Neither expensive nor inexpensive	Slightly inexpensive	Very inexpensive
		EASE OF USE		
Very easy to use	Somewhat easy to use		Not very easy to use	Difficult to use
		COLOR BRIGHTNESS		
Extremely bright	Very bright	Somewhat bright	Slightly bright	Not bright at all
		MODERNITY		
Very modern	Somewhat modern	Neither modern nor old-fashioned	Somewhat old-fashioned	Very old-fashioned

Excellent Feature										**Poor Feature**
3	4	7	10	13	16	13	10	7	4	3
10	9	8	7	6	5	4	3	2	1	0

This is a rank-order continuum from *Excellent Feature* to *Poor Feature,* with varying degrees of approval and disapproval between the extremes.

The numbers 3, 4, 7, . . ., 7, 4, 3 are the numbers of cards to be placed in each pile. The numbers below the line are the values assigned to the cards in each pile. That is, the three cards at the left, *Excellent Feature,* are each assigned 10, the four cards in the next pile are assigned 9, and so on through the distribution to the three cards at the extreme right, which are assigned 0. The center pile is a neutral pile. The respondent is told to put cards into the neutral pile that are left over after other choices have been made, cards that seem ambiguous or about which he cannot make a decision. In brief, this Q distribution has 11 piles with

TABLE 11.3 A Series of Rank-Order Scales Used to Evaluate Eye Shadows

Please rank the following eye shadows with 1 being the brand that best meets the characteristic being evaluated and 6 the worst brand on the characteristic being evaluated. The six brands are listed on card C. (HAND RESPONDENT CARD C.) Let's begin with the idea of having high-quality compacts or containers. Which brand would rank as having the highest-quality compacts or containers? Which is second? (RECORD BELOW.)

	Q.48 HAVING HIGH-QUALITY CONTAINER	Q.49 HAVING A HIGH-QUALITY APPLICATOR	Q.50 HAVING A HIGH-QUALITY EYE SHADOW
Avon	______	______	______
Cover Girl	______	______	______
Estee Lauder	______	______	______
Maybelline	______	______	______
Natural Wonder	______	______	______
Revlon	______	______	______

Card C		
Avon	Cover Girl	Estee Lauder
Maybelline	Natural Wonder	Revlon

varying numbers of cards in each pile, the cards in the piles being assigned values from 0 through 10. A Q-sort scale can be used to determine the relative ranking of items by individuals and to derive clusters of individuals who exhibit the same preferences. These clusters of people may then be analyzed as a potential basis for market segmentation. Factor analysis, discussed in Chapter 18, is used to analyze the responses to identify clusters of individuals. Thus, Q-sorting has a much different objective from other types of scaling. The goal is to uncover groups of individuals who possess similar attitudes on the ranking of eye shadows.

Rank order scales can be used to determine consumer preferences for brands of eye shadow.

A Professional Researcher's Perspective

Today we are able to effectively survey in 11 Asian languages and dialects including Cambodian, Cantonese, Hindi, Japanese, Korean, Laotian, Malay, Mandarin, Tagalog, Thai, and Vietnamese. One of the most astounding things we first learned in this business was these communities' interest in participating in surveys. Their desire to participate is driven by wanting to become a larger part of the American mainstream without losing their cultural identity. This is why we use bilingual Asian employees, many of whom were born outside the United States, to survey respondents in their native language.

The value of native-language interviewing can be seen with open-ended questions in which respondents tend to provide longer-than-normal answers that must be recorded in the native language to get the full flavor of the response.

Another important consideration in surveying Asians revolves around using numerical rating scales versus verbal rating scales. Using words like "excellent," "very good," "good," etc., doesn't work in these communities because there is no conceptual way to translate or make respondents understand the difference that mainstream Americans make between "very good" and "excellent" or "not very good" and "poor."[6] ■

Paired Comparisons

paired comparison scales
Scales that ask the respondent to pick one of two objects in a set based on some stated criteria.

Paired comparison scales ask a respondent to pick one of two objects from a set based upon some stated criteria. The respondent, therefore, makes a series of paired judgments between objects. Table 11.4 shows a paired comparison scale used in a national study for suntan products. Only part of the scale is shown, as the data collection procedure typically requires the respondent to compare all possible pairs of objects.

Paired comparisons overcome several problems of traditional rank-order scales. First, it is easier for people to select one item from a set of two than to rank a large set of data. Second, the problem of order bias is overcome. That is, a pattern in the ordering of items or questions may create a source of bias. On the negative side, because all possible pairs are evaluated, as the number of objects to be evaluated increases arithmetically, the number of paired comparisons increases geometrically. Thus, the number of objects to be evaluated should remain fairly small to prevent interviewee fatigue.

Constant Sum Scales

constant sum scales
Scales that ask the respondent to divide a given number of points, typically 100, among two or more attributes based on their importance to the person.

Constant sum scales are used more often by market researchers than paired comparisons because the long list of paired items is avoided. This technique requires the respondent to divide a given number of points, typically 100, among two or more attributes based on their importance to the person. This scale

TABLE 11.4 **A Paired Comparison Scale for Suntan Products**

14. Thinking about sun products in general, here are some characteristics used to describe them. Please tell me which characteristic in each pair is more important to you when selecting a sun care product.

a. Tans evenly	b. Tans without burning
a. Prevents burning	b. Protects against burning and tanning
a. Good value for the money	b. Goes on evenly
a. Not greasy	b. Does not stain clothing
a. Tans without burning	b. Prevents burning
a. Protects against burning and tanning	b. Good value for the money
a. Goes on evenly	b. Tans evenly
a. Prevents burning	b. Not greasy

requires that respondents value each individual item relative to all other items. The number of points allocated to each alternative indicates the ranks assigned to it by the respondent. The values assigned also are indicative of the relative magnitudes of each alternative as perceived by the respondent. A constant sum scale used in a national study of tennis sportswear is shown in Table 11.5. An additional advantage of the constant sum scale over a rank-order or paired comparison scale is that if two characteristics are perceived to have equal value, it can be so indicated.

A major disadvantage of this scale is that as the number of characteristics or items increases, it may confuse the respondent. That is, the respondent may have difficulty allocating the points to total 100. Most researchers feel that 10 items is the outer limit on a constant sum scale.

TABLE 11.5 **A Constant Sum Scale Used in a Tennis Sportswear Study**

Below are seven characteristics of women's tennis sportswear. Please allocate 100 points among the characteristics such that the allocation represents the importance of each characteristic to you. The more points that you assign to a characteristic, the more important it is. If the characteristic is totally unimportant, you should not allocate any points to it. When you've finished, please double-check to make sure that your total adds to 100.

CHARACTERISTICS OF TENNIS SPORTSWEAR	NUMBER OF POINTS
Is comfortable to wear	______
Is durable	______
Is made by well-known brand or sports manufacturers	______
Is made in the U.S.A.	______
Has up-to-date styling	______
Gives freedom of movement	______
Is a good value for the money	______
	100 points

The Semantic Differential

The semantic differential was developed by Charles Osgood, George Suci, and Percy Tannenbaum.[7] The focus of the original research was on the measurement of meaning of an object to a person. Thus, the object might be a savings and loan association and the meaning the image of the association to a certain group.

semantic differential

A method of examining the strengths and weaknesses of a product or company versus the competition by having respondents rank it between dichotomous pairs of words or phrases that could be used to describe it; the mean of the responses is then plotted in a profile or image.

The construction of a **semantic differential** scale begins with the determination of a concept to be rated, such as a company, brand, or store image. The researcher selects dichotomous (opposite) pairs of words or phrases that could be used to describe the concept. Respondents then rate the concept on a scale (usually 1–7). The mean of these responses for each pair of adjectives is computed and plotted as a "profile" or image.

Figure 11.3 is an actual image profile of an Arizona savings and loan association as perceived by noncustomers with family incomes of $45,000 and above. A quick glance shows that the firm is viewed as somewhat old-fashioned with rather plain facilities. It is viewed as well-established, reliable, successful, and probably very nice to deal with. The institution has parking problems and perhaps entry and egress difficulties. Its advertising is viewed as dismal.

The semantic differential is a quick and efficient means of examining the strengths and weaknesses of a product or company image versus the competition. More important, however, the semantic differential has been shown to be sufficiently reliable and valid for decision making and prediction in marketing and the behavioral sciences.[8] Also, the semantic differential has proved to be statistically robust (applicable) from one group of subjects to another when applied to corporate image research.[9] This makes possible the measurement and comparison of images held by interviewees with diverse backgrounds.

FIGURE 11.3 A Semantic Differential Profile of an Arizona Savings and Loan Association

ADJECTIVE 1	MEAN OF EACH ADJECTIVE PAIR							ADJECTIVE 2
	1	2	3	4	5	6	7	
Modern	*	*	*	*	*	*	*	Old-fashioned
Aggressive	*	*	*	*	*	*	*	Defensive
Friendly	*	*	*	*	*	*	*	Unfriendly
Well-established	*	*	*	*	*	*	*	Not well-established
Attractive exterior	*	*	*	*	*	*	*	Unattractive exterior
Reliable	*	*	*	*	*	*	*	Unreliable
Appeal to small companies	*	*	*	*	*	*	*	Appeal to big companies
Makes you feel at home	*	*	*	*	*	*	*	Makes you feel uneasy
Helpful services	*	*	*	*	*	*	*	Indifferent to customers
Nice to deal with	*	*	*	*	*	*	*	Hard to deal with
No parking or transportation problems	*	*	*	*	*	*	*	Parking or transportation problems
My kind of people	*	*	*	*	*	*	*	Not my kind of people
Successful	*	*	*	*	*	*	*	Unsuccessful
Ads attract a lot of attention	*	*	*	*	*	*	*	Haven't noticed ads
Interesting ads	*	*	*	*	*	*	*	Uninteresting ads
Influential ads	*	*	*	*	*	*	*	Not influential

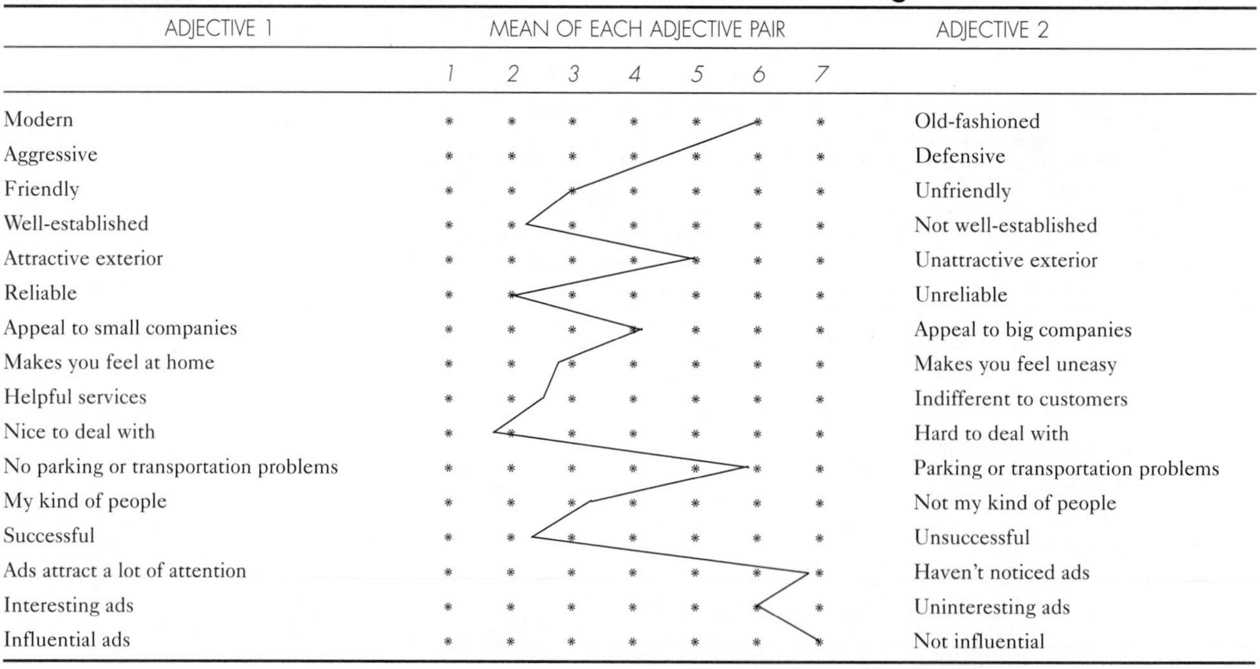

Global Marketing Research

Sabra Brock, vice-president of Citicorp, notes that devising scales and other types of questions requires careful planning when conducting marketing research in Asia. In Asia, many countries have the capability of conducting some kinds of Western-style marketing research. Japan, Hong Kong, Singapore, and the Philippines have fairly advanced research industries. Other countries in Asia such as China, South Korea, Indonesia, and India have research capabilities, but they are so underdeveloped as to require special supervision. Asia also has fewer research and marketing firms that can act as data "translators," people who can transform computer tables and research results into specific marketing directions.

Attitudes toward research vary from country to country in Asia, as do reactions to pricing, distribution, and promotion strategies. Most Asians respond differently to being interviewed than Americans. They frequently have less patience with the abstract and rational phrasing commonly used in questionnaires, particularly where literacy rates are low.

The interpretation of research tools like scales is different among educated Asians. The Japanese desire not to contradict, for example, makes for more yea-saying and upward scale bias than in a Western culture.

Apart from the varying reactions to research, there also are design implications to the distinct pricing and distribution strategies employed in Asia. For example, when querying Asians about pricing, the researcher must realize that they are especially prone to equating high price with high quality. In countries where imports are restricted or highly taxed, like South Korea and the Philippines, "imported" and especially "made in USA" are strong product claims.

Among the Chinese countries in Asia, many distinct dialects are spoken. A Hong Kong native speaks the Cantonese dialect and must study Mandarin to communicate easily in Taiwan. These language dissimilarities are critical in questionnaire development. In Hong Kong, written and oral Cantonese are different enough to necessitate rewriting a questionnaire when the methodology changes from self-administered to interviewer-read.[10] ■

Although these advantages have led many researchers to use the semantic differential as an image measurement tool, it is not without disadvantages. First, there is a lack of standardization. The semantic differential is a highly generalized technique that must be adapted for each research problem. There is no single set of standard scales, and hence the development of these becomes an integral part of the research.

The number of divisions on the semantic differential scale also presents a problem. If too few divisions are used, the scale is crude and lacks meaning; if too many are used, the scale goes beyond the ability of most people to discriminate. Researchers have found the seven-point scale to be the most satisfactory.

Another disadvantage of the semantic differential is the "halo effect." The rating of a specific image component may be dominated by the interviewee's overall impression of the concept being rated. This may be a significant bias if the image is hazy in the respondent's mind. To partially counteract the halo effect, the scale adjectives should be randomly reversed so all the "good" phrases are not placed on one side of the scale and the "bad" on the other. This forces the interviewee to evaluate the adjectives before responding. To facilitate analysis after the data have been gathered, all the "good adjectives" are placed on one side and the negative ones on the other.

Another problem occurs when analyzing a seven-point semantic differential scale in that care must be taken in interpreting a score of 4. A response of 4 will indicate one of two things—the respondent is either unable to relate the given pair of adjectives to the concept (they do not know) or simply may be neutral or indifferent. In many image studies, there frequently will be a large number of 4 responses. This phenomenon tends to pull the profiles toward the neutral position. Thus, the profiles lack clarity and little distinction appears.

Stapel Scale

Stapel scale

A scale, ranging from +5 to -5, that requires the respondent to rate how close and in what direction a descriptor adjective fits a given concept.

The **Stapel scale** is a modification of the semantic differential. A single adjective is placed in the center of the scale. Typically it is designed as a 10-point scale ranging from +5 to –5. The technique is designed to measure both the direction and intensity of attitudes simultaneously. The semantic differential, on the other hand, reflects how close the descriptor adjective fits the concept being evaluated. An example of a Stapel scale is shown in Figure 11.4.

The primary advantage of the Stapel scale is that it enables the researcher to avoid the arduous task of creating bipolar adjective pairs. It is also claimed that the scale permits finer discrimination in measuring attitudes. On the negative side is the problem that descriptor adjectives can be phrased in a positive, neutral, or a negative vein. The choice of phrasing has been shown to affect the scale results and the person's ability to respond.[11] The popularity of the semantic differential has declined extensively in the 1990s, primarily because of the increase in telephone interviewing. The Stapel scale has never had much popularity in commercial research and is used less than the semantic differential.

Likert Scales

Likert scale

A scale in which the respondent specifies a level of agreement or disagreement with statements that express a favorable or unfavorable attitude toward the concept under study.

The **Likert scale** also avoids the problem of developing pairs of dichotomous adjectives. The scale consists of a series of statements that express either a favorable or an unfavorable attitude toward the concept under study. The respondent is asked the level of agreement or disagreement with each statement. Each respondent is then given a numerical score to reflect how favorable or unfavorable her attitude is toward each statement. The scores are then totaled to measure the respondent's attitude.

Table 11.6 shows a Likert scale for persons who have admitted on a screening questionnaire that they have a foot odor problem but have not tried Johnson's Odor-Eaters Insoles. The scale is taken from a national study on the product.

The Likert scale only requires the respondent to consider one statement at a time with the scale running from one extreme to another. A series of statements

FIGURE 11.4 Example of a Stapel Scale

+5	+5
+4	+4
+3	+3
+2	+2
+1	+1
Friendly Personnel	Competitive Loan Rates
–1	–1
–2	–2
–3	–3
–4	–4
–5	–5

Select a *plus* number for words that you think describe the savings and loan accurately. The more accurately you think the word describes the company, the larger the plus number you should choose. Select a *minus* number for words you think do not describe the savings and loan accurately. The less accurately you think the word describes the institution, the larger the minus number you should choose; therefore, you can select any number from +5 for words that you think are very accurate all the way to –5 for words that you think are very inaccurate.

(attitudes) can be examined, yet there is only a single set of uniform replies for the respondent to give.

Rensis Likert created his scale to measure a person's attitude toward concepts (i.e., unions), activities (i.e., swimming), and so forth. He recommended the following steps in building the scale:

1. The researcher identifies the concept to be scaled. Let us assume that it is snow skiing.
2. The researcher assembles a large number (e.g., 75 to 100) of statements concerning the public's sentiments toward snow skiing.
3. Each test item is classified by the researcher as generally "favorable" or "unfavorable" with regard to the attitude under study. No attempt is made to scale the items; however, a pretest is conducted that involves the full set of statements and a limited sample of respondents.
4. In the pretest the respondent indicates agreement (or not) with *every* item, checking one of the following direction-intensity descriptors:
    a. Strongly agree
    b. Agree
    c. Undecided
    d. Disagree
    e. Strongly disagree
5. Each response is given a numerical weight (e.g., 5, 4, 3, 2, 1).

TABLE 11.6 A Likert Scale for Persons with Foot Odor Problems Who Have Not Tried Johnson's Odor-Eaters

(SHOW CARD J) Now I would like to find out your impressions about Johnson's Odor-Eaters, which you said you were familiar with but had not tried. As I read each characteristic, please tell me, using the statements on this card, if you strongly agree, agree, neither agree nor disagree, disagree, or strongly disagree.

	STRONGLY AGREE	AGREE	NEITHER AGREE NOR DISAGREE	DISAGREE	STRONGLY DISAGREE
They might make my feet feel hot	5	4	3	2	1
I am satisfied with what I am using	5	4	3	2	1
My problem is not serious enough	5	4	3	2	1
Too much trouble to cut them to fit to size	5	4	3	2	1
Price is too expensive	5	4	3	2	1
Might make my shoes too tight	5	4	3	2	1
I'm embarrassed to buy them	5	4	3	2	1
The advertising has not convinced me that the product is effective	5	4	3	2	1
Other insoles I've tried didn't work	5	4	3	2	1
Foot sprays work better	5	4	3	2	1
Foot powders work better	5	4	3	2	1
I've never used an insole	5	4	3	2	1
Wouldn't last more than a couple of weeks	5	4	3	2	1
Would look unattractive in my shoes	5	4	3	2	1
Would have to buy more than one pair	5	4	3	2	1
Would have to move them from one pair of shoes to another	5	4	3	2	1
No product for foot odor works completely	5	4	3	2	1
They might get too wet from perspiration	5	4	3	2	1
Don't know what an insole would feel like in my shoe	5	4	3	2	1

Card J

Strongly Agree	Agree	Neither Agree nor Disagree	Disagree	Strongly Disagree

6. The individual's *total-attitude score* is represented by the algebraic summation of weights associated with the items checked. In the scoring process, weights are assigned so that the direction of attitude—favorable to unfavorable—is consistent over items. For example, if 5 were assigned to "strongly approve" for favorable items, 5 should be assigned to "strongly disapprove" for unfavorable items.
7. After seeing the results of the pretest, the analyst selects only those items that appear to discriminate well between high and low *total* scorers. This may be done by first finding the highest and lowest quartiles of subjects on the basis of *total* score. Then, the mean differences on each *specific* item are compared between these high and low groups (excluding the middle 50 percent of subjects).
8. The 20 to 25 items finally selected are those that have discriminated "best" (i.e., exhibited the greatest differences in mean values) between high versus low total scorers in the pretest.
9. Steps 3 through 5 are then repeated in the main study.[12]

Likert created his scale so that a researcher could look at a summed score and tell whether a person's attitude toward a concept is positive or negative. For example, the maximum favorable score on a 20-item scale would be 100, therefore a person scoring 92 would be presumed to have a favorable attitude. Of course two people could both score 92 and yet have rated various statements differently. Thus, specific attitudes toward components of their overall attitude could differ markedly. For example, respondent A might strongly agree (5) that a bank has good parking and strongly disagree (1) that its loan programs are the best in town. Respondent B could have the exact opposite attitude, yet both summed scores would be 6.

In the world of commercial market research, Likert-like scales are very popular. They are quick and easy to construct and can be administered over the phone, or a respondent can be given a "reply category" card and be asked to call out an answer. Commercial researchers rarely follow the textbooklike process just outlined. Instead, the scales usually are developed jointly by a client project manager and a researcher. Many times the scales are created after a focus group.

Most important, the commercial researcher usually has a totally different motivation for using the scale. Instead of trying to discern positive and negative attitudes of individual respondents, he is more interested in attitudes toward the various components of the scale! Thus, referring back to the Odor-Eaters scale, the company was interested in determining what factors were causing target customers not to purchase Odor-Eaters. It was not really concerned whether respondent A had a positive or negative attitude toward Odor-Eaters. This notion also is often true for the semantic differential.

Purchase Intent Scales

purchase intent scales
Scales used to measure a respondent's intention to buy or not buy a product.

Perhaps the single scale used most often in commercial market research is the **purchase intent scale.** The ultimate issue for marketing managers is, Will they buy the product or not? If so, what percentage of the market can I expect to

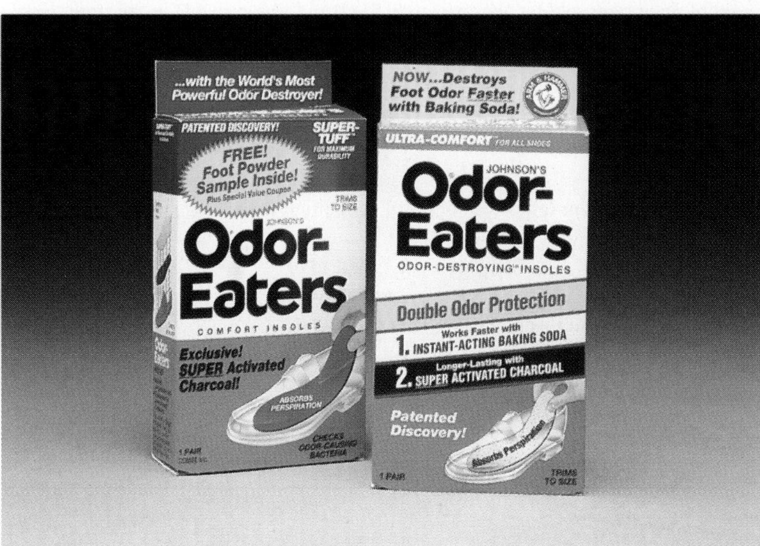

Johnson's used a Likert scale to conduct a study to determine what factors were causing target consumers not to purchase Odor-Eaters.

obtain? The purchase intent question normally is asked for all new products and services, product modifications, new services or service modifications by a retailer, and even by nonprofit organizations.

During new product development, the purchase intent question is asked during concept testing to get a rough idea of demand. The manager wants to quickly eliminate potential turkeys, take a careful look at those in which purchase intent is moderate, and push forward the projects that seem to have star potential. At this stage, investment is minimal and product modification or repositioning the concept is an easy task. As the product moves through development, the product itself, promotion strategy, price levels, and distribution channels become more concrete and focused. Purchase intent is evaluated at each stage of development and demand estimates are refined. The crucial go–no go decision for national or regional rollout typically comes after test marketing. Immediately before test marketing, commercial researchers have another critical stage of evaluation. Here the final, or near final, version of the product is placed in consumers' homes in test cities around the country. After a period of in-home use (usually two to six weeks), a follow-up survey is conducted among participants to find out their likes, dislikes, how it compares with what they use now, and what they would pay for it. The critical question near the end of the questionnaire is purchase intent.

Table 11.7, question 21, is a purchase intent question taken from a follow-up study on in-home placement of a fly trap. The trap consisted of two three-inch discs held about one-quarter inch apart by three plastic pillars looking somewhat like a large, thin yo-yo. The trap worked on the same principle as the Roach Motel. It contained a pheramone to attract the flies and a glue that would remain sticky for six months. Supposedly, the flies flew in but never out! Centered on the backside of one of the discs was an adhesive tab so that the disc could be attached to a kitchen window. The concept was to eliminate flies in the kitchen

TABLE 11.7 Purchase Intent Scale and Related Questions for an In-Home Product Placement of Fly Traps

21. If a set of three traps sold for approximately $1.00 and was available in the stores where you normally shop, would you:

	(51)
definitely by the set of traps	1
probably buy	2
probably not buy—SKIP TO Q23	3
definitely not buy—SKIP TO Q23	4

22. Would you use the traps (a) instead of or (b) in addition to existing products?

	(52)
instead of	1
in addition to	2

23. Would you recommend this product to your friends?

	(53)
definitely	1
probably	2
probably not	3
definitely not	4

area without resorting to a pesticide. Question *22* in Table 11.7 was designed to aid in positioning the product, and question 23 traditionally was used by the manufacturer as a double check on purchase intent. That is, if 60 percent of the respondents claimed that they definitely would buy the product and 90 percent said they definitely would not recommend the product to their friends, the researcher would question the validity of the purchase intent.

The purchase intent scale has been found to be a good predictor of consumer choice of frequently purchased and durable consumer products.[13] The scale is very easy to construct and consumers are simply asked to make a subjective judgment on their likelihood of buying a new product. From past experience in the product category, a marketing manager can translate consumer responses on the scale to estimates of purchase probability. Obviously, everyone who claims that she "definitely will buy" the product will not do so; in fact, a few who state that they definitely would not buy, will buy the product. The manufacturer of the fly trap is a major producer of both pesticide and nonpesticide pest control products. Assume that, based upon historical follow-up studies, the manufacturer has learned the following about purchase intent of nonpesticide home-use pest-control products:

- 63 percent of the "definitely will buy" actually purchase within 12 months
- 28 percent of the "probably will buy" actually purchase within 12 months
- 12 percent of the "probably will not buy" actually purchase within 12 months
- 3 percent of the "definitely will not buy" actually purchase within 12 months.

Suppose that the fly trap study resulted in the following:

- 40 percent—definitely will buy
- 20 percent—probably will buy
- 30 percent—probably will not buy
- 10 percent—definitely will not buy

Assuming that the sample is representative of the target market, then:

$$(.4)(63\%) + (.2)(28\%) + (.3)(12\%) + (.1)(3\%) = 34.7\% \text{ market share}$$

Most marketing managers would be deliriously happy at a market share prediction this high for a new product. Unfortunately, the fly trap prediction was high but because of consumer confusion the product was killed after the in-home placement (see the ethics discussion in Chapter 4).

It is not uncommon for market research firms to conduct studies containing a purchase intent scale, but the client does not have historical data to use as a basis for weighing the data. A reasonable but conservative estimate would be 70 percent of the "definitely will buy," 35 percent of the "probably will buy," 10 percent of the "probably will not buy," and zero for the "definitely will not buy."[14] Higher weights are common in the industrial market.

Some companies use the purchase intent scale to make go–no go decisions in product development without reference to market share. Typically, the managers simply add the "definitely will buy" and "probably will buy" and use that against a predetermined go–no go threshold. One consumer goods manufacturer, for example, requires a combined score of 80 percent or higher at the concept testing stage and 65 percent for a product to move from in-home placement tests to test marketing.

Global Marketing Research

Tony Siciliano is vice-president–director of International Research, A&G Research, New York. He has devised what he thinks is a more realistic scenario for respondents than the traditional five-point scale when they are asked to indicate their purchase intent. Here he describes his technique and a global application.

The "partial-payment coupon" is the one technique with which I've had the most success in measuring realistic purchase intent. It is administered like this: "We have coupons that are worth one-third the purchase price of a 16-ounce loaf of bread. With this coupon, you'll be paying $1 instead of the store price of $1.50. Which one-third off coupon do you want—Brand A, Brand B, etc.?" (It's not necessary to have coupons; after respondents make their choice, they are given cash.)

The most dramatic case history involving this technique occurred in France on a product test for the leading chewing gum. The brand had nearly a 70 percent market share, and a pricing decision had to be made when the cost of the ingredient chicle rose significantly. The client suspected competitors would *not* raise prices if his price went up because this would afford them a chance to erode the brand's enormous market share. Another solution was sought.

The standard size pack had 11 sticks of gum. The client decided to reduce the pack to 10 sticks and keep the price the same. A product test was conducted with two cells: 11 sticks at the current price and 10 sticks at the current price. No standard measurement in this test revealed any problem in reducing the pack from 11 sticks to 10. The five-point buying intent results corroborated this (see Table 11.8). I convinced the client to include the partial-payment coupon as the very last question. The rationale was that it could do nothing to bias the standard results and might reveal a problem not detected by the standard questioning. The hunch was right, as shown in Table 11.9.

Some Basic Considerations When Selecting a Scale

With the exception of purchase intent, for most nonimage studies, the question arises as to which scale to use. We have presented the most commonly used scales and the advantages and disadvantages of each.

Selecting a Rating, Ranking, Sorting, or Purchase Intent Scale

Most commercial researchers lean toward scales that can be administered over the telephone to save interviewing expense. Ease of administration and development also are important considerations. For example, a rank-order scale can be quickly created, whereas a semantic differential (rating scale) is often a long and tedious process. Decision-making needs of the client are always of paramount importance. Can the decision be made using ordinal data or must we have interval information? Researchers also must consider the respondents who usually prefer nominal and ordinal scales because of their simplicity. Ultimately, the

One explanation for the large difference between the five-point scale and the partial-payment coupon results is that people don't like to give the impression that they are "cheap" or "mercenary." In effect, this is what respondents would be doing if they admitted to interviewers that they would switch from their favorite brand if the pack size was reduced and yet cost the same.

This is the danger of a hypothetical buying-intention situation: For any number of reasons, respondents can mask their true feelings. The partial-payment coupon eliminates much of these masked or gratuitous responses because it's a close simulation of the actual buying experience. When a respondent selects the coupon, she does so with the realization that she will have to use some of her own money when making the purchase. A coupon that gives the product away free doesn't have the same effect because there is no risk if you're getting something for nothing.[15] ■

TABLE 11.8 Buying-Intent Results

	11 STICKS	10 STICKS
Definitely	86%	82%
Probably	6%	10%
Might/might not	8%	8%
Probably not	—	—
Definitely not	—	—
Base: (Test brand users)		

TABLE 11.9 Partial-Payment Coupon Results

	11 STICKS	10 STICKS
Test Brand	84%	53%
Other Brand	16%	47%

choice of which type of scale to use will depend upon the problem at hand and the questions that must be answered. It is not uncommon to find several types of scales in one research study. For example, an image study for a grocery chain might have a ranking scale of competing chains and a semantic differential to examine components of the chain's image.

Balanced Versus Nonbalanced Alternatives A **balanced scale** has the same number of positive and negative categories; a **nonbalanced scale** is weighted toward one end or the other. If the researcher expects a wider range of opinions, then a balanced scale probably is in order. If past research or a preliminary study has determined that most opinions are positive, then the scale should contain more positive gradients than negative. This would enable the researcher to ascertain the degree of positiveness toward the concept being researcher. The authors have conducted a series of studies for the YMCA and know that the

balanced scales

Scales with the same number of positive and negative categories.

nonbalanced scales

Scales weighted toward one end or the other.

overall image of the institution is positive. In tracking the YMCA's image, the following categories are used: (1) outstanding, (2) very good, (3) good, (4) fair, (5) poor.

Number of Categories The number of categories to be included in a scale is another question that must be resolved by the market researcher. If the number of categories is too small—for example, good, fair, poor—the scale is crude and lacks richness. A three-category scale does not reveal the intensity of feeling that, say, a 10-category scale offers. Yet, a 10-category scale may go beyond a person's ability to accurately discriminate from one category to another. Research has shown that rating scales typically should have from five to nine categories.[16] When a scale is being administered over the telephone, five categories seems to be the most that respondents can adequately handle.

Odd or Even Number of Scale Categories An even number of scale categories means that there is no neutral point. Without a neutral point, respondents are forced to indicate some degree of positive or negative feelings on an issue. Persons who are truly neutral are not allowed to express this feeling. On the other hand, some commercial market researchers say that putting a neutral point on a scale gives the respondent an easy way out. Assuming that he has no really strong opinion, the person does not have to concentrate on his actual feelings and can easily say that he is neutral. However, researchers also point out that it is rather unusual to be highly emotional about a new flavor of salad dressing, a package design, or a test commercial for a pickup truck.

Forced Versus Nonforced Choice A consideration, mentioned in our discussion of the semantic differential, is that if a neutral category is included, it typically will contain those who are neutral and those who lack knowledge to answer the question. Some researchers have resolved this issue by adding a "don't know" response as an additional category. For example, a semantic differential might be set up as follows:

Friendly 1 2 3 4 5 6 7 Unfriendly Don't Know
Unexciting 1 2 3 4 5 6 7 Exciting Don't Know

Adding a *don't know* option, however, can be an easy out for the lazy respondent.

A neutral point on a scale without a *don't know* option does not force a respondent to give a positive or negative opinion. A scale without a neutral point or a *don't know* forces even those persons with no information about an object to state an opinion. The argument for forced choice is the same as for a scale with an even number of categories. The arguments against forced choice are that inaccurate data are recorded or respondents refuse to answer the question. A questionnaire that continues to require respondents to provide an opinion when, in fact, they lack information to make a decision can create ill will and result in termination of the interview.

Summary

An attitude is an enduring organization of motivational, emotional, perceptual, and cognitive processes with respect to some aspect of our environment. It is a learned predisposition to respond in a consistently favorable or unfavorable manner toward an object. Attitudes can be changed through one of three ways: changing the beliefs about the attributes of a brand, changing the relative importance of those beliefs, or adding new beliefs.

Scaling refers to procedures for attempting to determine quantitative measures of subjective and sometimes abstract concepts. It is a procedure for the assignment of numbers or other symbols to a property of objects to impart some of the characteristics of the numbers to the properties in question. Scales are either unidimensional or multidimensional. A unidimensional scale is designed to measure only one attribute of a respondent or object. Multidimensional scaling recognizes that a concept or object might be better described using several dimensions rather than one.

One type of scale is called a graphic rating scale. Respondents are presented with a graphic continuum typically anchored by two extremes. Itemized rating scales are very similar to graphic rating scales except that respondents must select from a limited number of categories rather than placing a check mark on a continuous scale. A rank-order scale is comparative because respondents are asked to judge one item against another. A Q-sort is a sophisticated form of rank ordering. Respondents are asked to sort a large number of cards into piles or predetermined size. Paired comparison scales present two objects from a set and ask the respondent to pick one based on some stated criteria. Constant sum scales ask the respondent to divide a given number of points, typically 100, among two or more attributes based upon their importance to the person. This scale requires the respondent to value each individual item relative to all other items. The number of points allocated to each alternative indicates the ranks assigned it by the respondent.

The semantic differential was developed to measure the meaning of an object to a person. The construction of a semantic differential scale begins with a determination of the concept to be rated, such as a brand, and then the researcher selects dichotomous pairs of words or phrases that could be used to describe the concept. Respondents then rate the concept on a scale, usually 1–7. The mean of these responses for each pair of adjectives is computed and plotted as a profile or image. The Stapel scale is one in which a single adjective is placed in the center of the scale. Typically, it is designed to simultaneously measure both the direction and intensity of attitudes. The Likert scale also avoids the problem of developing pairs of dichotomous adjectives. The scale consists of a series of statements that express either a favorable or unfavorable attitude toward the concept under study. The respondent is asked the level of agreement or disagreement with each statement. Each respondent is then given a numerical score to reflect how favorable or unfavorable her attitude is toward each statement. Scores are then totaled to measure the respondent's attitude.

The scale used most often and perhaps most important to market researchers is the purchase intent scale. The purchase intent scale is used to measure a respondent's intention to buy or not buy a product. The purchase intent question usually asks a person to state whether he would: Definitely buy, Probably buy, Probably not buy, or Definitely not buy the product under study. The purchase intent scale has been found to be a good predictor of consumer choice of frequently purchased consumer durable goods.

When attempting to select a particular scale for a study, several factors should be considered. The first is whether to use a rating, ranking, or choice scale. Next, consideration must be given to the use of a balanced scale versus nonbalanced scale. The number of categories also must be determined. Another factor is whether to use an odd or even number of scale categories. Finally, the researcher must consider whether to use forced versus nonforced choice sets.

Key Terms

attitude
cognitive component of attitudes
affective component of attitudes
behavioral component of attitudes
scaling
unidimensional scaling
multidimensional scaling
graphic rating scales
itemized rating scales
noncomparative
rank-order scales
comparative scales
Q-sorting
paired comparison scales
constant sum scales
semantic differential
Stapel scale
Likert scale
purchase intent scales
balanced scales
nonbalanced scales

Review and Discussion Questions

1. Discuss some of the considerations in selecting a rating, ranking, or purchase intent scale.
2. What are some of the arguments for and against having a neutral point on a scale?
3. Compare and contrast the semantic differential, Stapel scale, and Likert scale. Under what conditions would a researcher use each one?
4. The local department store in your hometown has been besieged by competition from the large national chains. What are some ways that target customers' attitudes toward the store can be changed?
5. Develop a Likert scale to evaluate the parks and recreation department in your city.
6. Develop a purchase intent scale for students eating at the university's cafeteria. How might the reliability and validity of this scale be measured? Why do you think purchase intent scales are so popular in commercial marketing research?
7. What are the three components of attitudes? Give examples of each.
8. When might a researcher use a graphic rating scale rather than an itemized rating scale?
9. What are the disadvantages of a graphic rating scale?
10. Develop a rank-order scale for beer preferences of college students. What are the advantages and disadvantages of this type of scale?
11. What are some adjective pairs or phrases that could be used in a semantic differential to measure the image of your college or university?

CASE 11.1

Diamond Interstate Bank Tower

Portofino Management Company supervises the prestigious Diamond Interstate Bank Tower, a 1.2 million square foot commercial office building in Houston, Texas. High tenant satisfaction and resultant retention of the customer are of utmost importance to Portofino. The company decided that the best way to gauge customer satisfaction was through survey research. TFR Research interviewed 500 of the 3,500 tenants of the building, using the following questionnaire.

DIAMOND INTERSTATE BANK TOWER TENANT SURVEY

Thank you for participating in our survey. Every effort has been made to keep it as short as possible while still obtaining the essential information that will help the building managers provide you the very best level of property management service. For each question I read, tell me the number that most closely describes how you feel.

1. On a scale of 1 to 5, please rate the following aspects of the building.

1 = POOR 2 = FAIR 3 = GOOD 4 = EXCELLENT 5 = OUTSTANDING					
Personal safety	1	2	3	4	5
Parking	1	2	3	4	5
Office cleanliness	1	2	3	4	5
Rest room cleanliness	1	2	3	4	5
Window cleaning	1	2	3	4	5
City bus service	1	2	3	4	5
Highway access	1	2	3	4	5
Climate control	1	2	3	4	5
Lighting	1	2	3	4	5
Corridor cleanliness	1	2	3	4	5
Corridor decor	1	2	3	4	5
Corridor lighting	1	2	3	4	5
Elevator speed	1	2	3	4	5
Elevator frequency	1	2	3	4	5
Lobby area	1	2	3	4	5
Courtyard area	1	2	3	4	5
Building maintenance	1	2	3	4	5
Building attractiveness	1	2	3	4	5
Building neatness	1	2	3	4	5
Prestige of building	1	2	3	4	5

2. How many people work in your company?
   fewer than 10   10 to 25   26 to 50
   51 to 75   76 to 100   101 to 200
   over 200
3. What company do you work for? ______________________________
4. Approximately what is the distance from your home to the Diamond Interstate Bank Tower in miles? _______
5. Approximately how many times per month do you work in the building after normal working hours or on weekends? _______
6. How would you rate the traffic flow in the parking areas?
   1 = Poor   2 = Fair   3 = Good
   4 = Excellent   5 = Outstanding
7. If you have ever eaten your lunch in the courtyard area, please rate the availability of the tables and chairs.
   1 = Available none of the time   2 = Available some of the time
   3 = Available most of the time   4 = Available nearly all of the time
   5 = Have never eaten lunch in courtyard area
8. Please rank the following items in terms of their importance to you in choosing a restaurant for an every day meal. (1 is the most important, 6 is least important).
   Healthy choices _______
   Menu variety _______
   Price _______
   Quality of food _______
   Service _______
   Speed _______

9. Approximately how many times per month do you go to:
   Garden Room ________
   The Old Marketplace ________
   Mac's Steakhouse ________
10. On a scale of 1 to 5 please rate the following characteristics of the restaurants in the building.

1 = POOR   2 = FAIR   3 = GOOD   4 = EXCELLENT   5 = OUTSTANDING

	GARDEN ROOM				
Speed of service	1	2	3	4	5
Quality of food	1	2	3	4	5
Prices	1	2	3	4	5
Variety of menu	1	2	3	4	5
	THE OLD MARKETPLACE				
Speed of service	1	2	3	4	5
Quality of food	1	2	3	4	5
Prices	1	2	3	4	5
Variety of menu	1	2	3	4	5
	MAC'S STEAKHOUSE				
Speed of service	1	2	3	4	5
Quality of food	1	2	3	4	5
Prices	1	2	3	4	5
Variety of menu	1	2	3	4	5

11. How would you rate the selection of restaurants that are outside of the building but easily accessible by walking or riding the courtesy bus?
    1 = Poor   2 = Fair   3 = Good
    4 = Excellent   5 = Outstanding
12. Do you ever ride the shuttle bus to the Galleria area?
    Yes   No
13. If you answered YES to question 12 approximately how many times per month do you ride the shuttle bus? ________
14. Would you like the shuttle bus to go to the Galleria area on some scheduled days of the week?
    1 = Definitely Not   2 = Probably Not   3 = Might
    4 = Probably   5 = Definitely
15. How important to you is the availability of a shuttle bus service?
    1 = Not important   2 = Somewhat Important
    3 = Very Important   4 = Highly Important
16. Do you ever participate in various activities offered by the Diamond Interstate Bank Tower?
    Yes   No
17. If you answered NO to question 16, could you tell us why you have not participated in the activities?

    ____

    ____
18. On a scale of 1 to 5, please rate the following activities that you may have attended. (If not attended, leave blank.)

1 = POOR   2 = FAIR   3 = GOOD   4 = EXCELLENT   5 = OUTSTANDING

a. Parties on the plaza/Parties in the lobby.
1   2   3   4   5

b. Tenant nights at other establishments.
1   2   3   4   5

c. Seminars
1   2   3   4   5

19. Would you ever participate in brown-bag lunch seminars if the topics were of interest to you?
Yes No
20. If you answered YES to question 19, what seminar topics would you like to see presented?
____
____
21. Are there any other activities you would like to see offered by Diamond Interstate Bank Tower?
____
____
22. How often do you use the concierge service offered in the building?
1 = Once per week or more often 2 = One to three times per month
3 = Several times per year 4 = Less than once per year
5 = Have never used the concierge service
23. If you have ever used the concierge service, how would you rate it?
1 = Poor 2 = Fair 3 = Good
4 = Excellent 5 = Outstanding
24. What other services would you like to see offered by the concierge?
____
____
25. Are you satisfied with the retail services, other than the restaurants, within the building?
1 = Dissatisfied 2 = Somewhat Dissatisfied
3 = Somewhat Satisfied 4 = Mostly Satisfied
5 = Very Satisfied
26. What other types of retail services would you like to see in the building?
____
____
27. Are you aware of the recycling program in the building?
Yes No
28. How many of the last six issues of the building newsletter have you read?
____
29. If you have ever read the building newsletter, how would you rate it?
1 = Poor 2 = Fair 3 = Good
4 = Excellent 5 = Outstanding 6 = Don't read
30. Would you like to see the newsletter contain a classified section that might include job opportunities, items for sale, etc.?
Yes Indifferent No
31. What other topics would you like to see covered in the newsletter?
____
____
32. How long have you been working at the Diamond Interstate Bank Tower?
_______ Years _______ Months
33. What is your sex? Male Female
34. What is your age?
Under 21 21 to 25 26 to 35
36 to 49 50 to 69 over 70
35. What is your marital status?
1 = Single never married 2 = Married
3 = Separated/Divorced/Widowed
36. What is the highest level of education you have completed?
1 = Less than high school 2 = High School
3 = Vocational/technical/trade school 4 = Some College
5 = College degree 6 = Graduate school
37. Where do you normally park?
1 = Underground parking
2 = Outside lot on the building premises
3 = Paid parking off the building premises

38. Is there anything you would like brought to the attention of the building management?

____

____

____

1. Describe the type or types of scales being used in the questionnaire.
2. What types of data (i.e., nominal, ordinal, etc.) are being gathered from the scales?
3. What other types of scales could have been used to measure tenant satisfaction? Give some examples.

CASE 11.2

Frigidaire Refrigerators

Frigidaire was interested in comparing its image with a number of other appliance corporations. Some of the questions used on the questionnaire follow.

Q.1 We are interested in your overall opinion of five companies that manufacture refrigerators. Please rank them from 1 to 5 with 1 being the best and 5 the worst (READ LIST. BEGIN WITH COMPANY ( ) AND WRITE IN NUMBER GIVEN FOR *EACH* COMPANY LISTED. BE SURE *ONE* ANSWER IS RECORDED FOR EACH COMPANY.)

COMPANIES	RANK
General Electric	____
Westinghouse	____
Frigidaire	____
Sears	____
Whirlpool	____

Q.2 Now, I would like to have your opinion on a few statements that could be used to describe Frigidaire and the refrigerators it makes.

For each statement I read, please tell me how much you *agree* or *disagree* with the statement about Frigidaire. If you *agree completely* with the statement made, you should give it a *10* rating. If you *disagree completely* with the statement made, you should give it a *0* rating. Or, you can use any number in between which best expresses your opinion on each statement about Frigidaire. (READ LIST. BEGIN WITH STATEMENT CHECKED AND WRITE IN NUMBER GIVEN FOR *EACH* STATEMENT LISTED. BE SURE ONE ANSWER IS RECORDED FOR EACH.)

STATEMENTS	RATING
( ) They are a modern, up-to-date company	____
( ) Their refrigerators offer better value than those made by other companies	____
( ) Their refrigerators last longer than those made by other companies	____
( ) They are a company that stands behind their products	____
(✓) Their refrigerators have more special features than those made by other companies	____

( ) They are a well-established, reliable company ______
( ) Their refrigerators are more dependable than those made by other companies ______
( ) Their refrigerators offer higher-quality construction than those made by other companies ______
( ) Their refrigerators have a better guarantee or warranty than those made by other companies ______

Q.3 If you were buying a (READ APPLIANCE) today, what make would be your first choice? Your second choice? Your third choice? (DO *NOT* READ LIST. CIRCLE NUMBER BELOW APPROPRIATE APPLIANCE.)

Begin with appliance checked

	( ) Refrigerator			(✓) Electric Range		
BRANDS	FIRST CHOICE	SECOND CHOICE	THIRD CHOICE	FIRST CHOICE	SECOND CHOICE	THIRD CHOICE
General Electric	1	1	1	1	1	1
Westinghouse	2	2	2	2	2	2
Frigidaire	3	3	3	3	3	3
Sears	4	4	4	4	4	4
Whirlpool	5	5	5	5	5	5
Other (SPECIFY)						

Q.4 If you were in the market for a refrigerator today, how interested would you be in having the 1997 Frigidaire refrigerator that was described in the commercial in your home?

Would you say you would be . . . (READ LIST)

	Very interested	1
(CIRCLE	Somewhat interested	2
ONE	Neither interested or disinterested	3
NUMBER)	Somewhat disinterested, or	4
	Very disinterested	5

Q.5 Why do you feel that way? (PROBE FOR COMPLETE AND MEANINGFUL ANSWERS.)

____
____
____
____
____

Q.6 Now, I would like to ask you a few questions for statistical purposes only:

(A) Do you currently own any major appliances made by Frigidaire?

(CIRCLE ONE NUMBER)	Yes	1
	No	2

(B) Is the head of household male or female?

(CIRCLE ONE NUMBER)	Male	1
	Female	2

(C) Which letter on this card corresponds to your age group?

	A. Under 25	1
(CIRCLE	B. 25 to 34	2
ONE	C. 35 to 44	3
NUMBER)	D. 45 to 54	4
	E. 55 and Over	5

1. What types of scales are represented in the questionnaire? What is the purpose of each scale? What other scales could have been substituted to obtain the same data?
2. Could a semantic differential have been used in this questionnaire? If so, what are some of the adjective pairs that might have been used?
3. Do you think the managers of Frigidaire have the necessary information now to evaluate their competitive position as perceived by consumers? If not, what additional questions should be asked?

CHAPTER 12

Questionnaire Design

LEARNING OBJECTIVES

1. To learn the objectives of questionnaire design.
2. To understand the role of the questionnaire in the data collection process.
3. To become familiar with the criteria for a good questionnaire.
4. To learn the process for questionnaire development.
5. To become knowledgeable of the three basic forms of questions.
6. To learn the necessary procedures for successful implementation of a survey.

If they ever build a TV commercial Hall of Fame, there surely will be a space reserved for Iron Eyes Cody. Cody—you may remember him as the "Crying Indian"—was the "star" of the long-running public service announcement for Keep America Beautiful, Inc. (KAB) that ran on TV stations across the country during the past decade. Few who saw the commercial could forget its image of a single tear crawling down Cody's face as he reacted to the actions of litterbugs.

Effective though the spot was, it became outdated as the larger issue of waste management eclipsed littering in the public consciousness as the nation's top garbage-related problem. When Keep America Beautiful—a national non-profit organization dedicated to improving waste handling practices in American communities—set to developing a new PSA (public service announcement) to address the problem of waste management, it had to answer the question: How do you duplicate the impact of the "Crying Indian" spot? With the help of research, KAB and the Stamford, Connecticut-based ad agency Rotando, Lerch & Lafeliece developed a spot that just might do that.

Michael Douglas voiceover with *America the Beautiful* under: For future generations, our country is leaving behind our knowledge, our technologies, our values...

and 190 million tons of garbage every year! Recycling alone just can't do it. Keep America Beautiful is an organization that can do something.

We have solutions that have worked in cities and towns across the country.

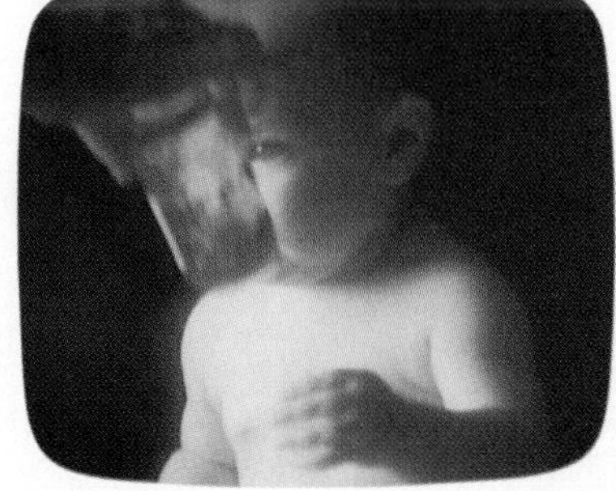

What can you do?

SOURCE: Courtesy of Keep America Beautiful, Inc.

The central image of the new KAB spot is a shot of a baby surrounded by mounds of garbage. The commercial begins with a close-up of the baby and pulls back to a wide shot as actor Michael Douglas narrates over the strains of "America the Beautiful": "For future generations, our country is leaving behind our knowledge, our technologies, our values. . . and 190 million tons of garbage every year. Recycling alone just can't do it. Keep America Beautiful is an organization that can do something. We have solutions that have worked in cities and towns across the country. What can you do? More than you think!"

Viewers are then invited to contact KAB for a free booklet. One version asks them to write to the address on the screen, the other flashes a toll-free number.

Using a detailed questionnaire to test the ad concept, KAB found that the image had broad appeal, says Jeff Francis, director of communications, Keep America Beautiful. "We showed them a tape of the idea and then conducted an interview. We found that the baby appealed to everyone. It was an image that, no matter what your age, your sex, if you have children or not, no matter what category you fall into, there was an emotional attachment to that child; which was good because we wanted this ad to be very broad based and hit as many constituency groups as possible. The interviews helped make up our minds about using the baby and the fact that it did appeal to everybody."

The interviews lasted about 30 minutes and included discussion of the ad concept and the issue of waste management. Since the ad was targeted at a broad cross section of people, the respondents came from a variety of backgrounds.[1] ■

The heart and soul of the advertising concept test, or any form of survey research, is the questionnaire. If the questions are poorly worded, the information gathered will be misleading. A faulty questionnaire design can lead to interviewer frustration and a confused respondent. This, in turn, leads to interviews terminated by the respondent. What is required for a good questionnaire? What steps are involved in questionnaire development? We will explore these and other issues in Chapter 12.

You will learn the vital role played by the questionnaire and the primary considerations to be held in mind when a researcher develops a questionnaire. Next, a step-by-step procedure for designing a questionnaire is presented. Within this procedure are descriptions of guidelines for evaluating individual questions for appropriateness, as well as an overview of alternative questions forms. We then describe the instructions for supervisors and interviewers that must accompany the questionnaire. Finally, the differences between observation forms and questionnaires are explained.

The Role of a Questionnaire

Questionnaire Defined

Every form of survey research relies on the use of a questionnaire. The questionnaire is the common thread for almost all data collection methods. A **questionnaire** is a set of questions designed to generate the data necessary for accomplishing the objectives of the research project. It is a formalized schedule for collecting information from respondents. Probably you have seen one or even filled one out recently. Creating the "right questionnaire" requires both hard work and creativity.

questionnaire
A set of questions designed to generate the data necessary for accomplishing the objectives of the research project.

A questionnaire provides standardization and uniformity in the data gathering process. It standardizes the wording and sequencing of the questions. Every respondent sees or hears the same words and questions; every interviewer asks identical questions. Without such, every interviewer could ask whatever she felt at the moment, and the researcher would be left with the question of whether respondents' answers were a consequence of interviewer influence, prompting, or interpretation. A valid basis for comparing respondents' answers would not exist. The jumbled mass of data would be unmanageable from a tabulation standpoint. In a very real sense, then, the questionnaire is a control device, but it is a very unique device as you will see.

The questionnaire (sometimes referred to as an *interview schedule* or *survey instrument*) plays a critical role in the data collection process. An elaborate sampling plan, well-trained interviewers, proper statistical analysis techniques, and good editing and coding are all for naught if the questionnaire is poorly designed. Improper design can lead to incomplete information, inaccurate data, and, of course, higher costs. The questionnaire and the interviewer are the production line of marketing research. It is here that the product, be it good or bad, is created. The questionnaire is the workers' (interviewers') tool that creates the basic product (respondent information).

The Critical Link

Figure 12.1 illustrates the pivotal role of the questionnaire. It is positioned between the survey objectives (drawn from the manager's problem) and the respondent's information. In this capacity it must translate the objectives into specific questions to solicit the information from the respondent. Assume that Timex is considering the development of a child's wristwatch. The timepiece would be made of plastic casing with printed circuits inside. The engineering staff believes that it can come up with a watch that will withstand the potential abuse of the normal activities of a child between eight and 13 years old. Preliminary market research is called for to determine the acceptability of the watch to the market. One objective would be to determine children's reaction to the watch. A child of eight cannot respond to questions that use words such as *acceptability*, *efficiency*, and *likelihood of purchase.*

The marketing researchers must translate the objectives into language understandable to the child as a respondent. The process illustrates the pivotal role of the questionnaire: it must translate the survey objectives into a form understandable to respondents and "pull" the requisite information from them. At the same time, it must recover their responses in a form easily tabulated and translated into findings and recommendations that satisfy the manager's information requirements.

Criteria For A Good Questionnaire

To design a good questionnaire, a number of considerations must be kept in mind: Does it provide the necessary decision-making information for management, does it consider the respondent, and does it meet editing, coding, and data processing requirements?

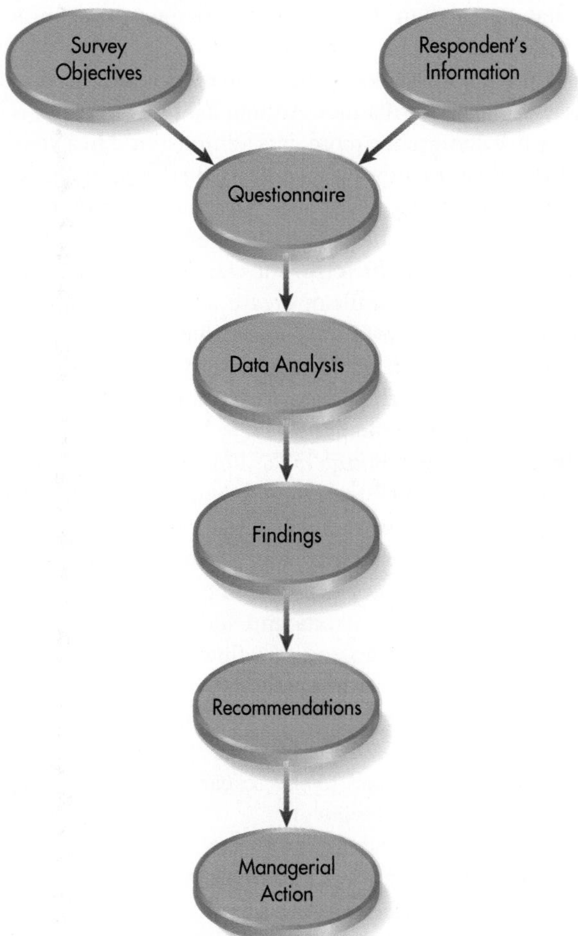

FIGURE 12.1
The Questionnaire's "Position" in the Research Process

Does It Provide the Necessary Decision-Making Information?

The primary role of any questionnaire is to provide the required information for management decision making. Any questionnaire that fails to provide important insights for management or decision-making information should be discarded or revised. This means that managers who will be using the data should always approve the questionnaire. By signing off on the questionnaire, the manager is implying, "Yes, this instrument will supply the data I need to reach a decision." If the manager does not sign off, then the marketing researcher will continue to make revisions to the questionnaire.

Consider the Respondent

As companies have recognized the importance of marketing research, the number of surveys taken annually has mushroomed. Poorly designed, confusing, and lengthy surveys have literally "turned off" thousands of potential respondents. It is estimated that more than 40 percent of all persons contacted refuse to participate in surveys.

To gather completed interviews, a questionnaire should be concise, interesting, and flow in a logical, clear-cut manner. Although a questionnaire is constructed at a person's desk or in a conference room, it is administered in a variety of situations and environments. Busy or otherwise preoccupied respondents will terminate uninteresting interviews. Some are conducted while a person is eager to get back to the television; others are done with a shopper who is in a hurry to finish his chores; and still others are conducted while the respondent's child is clinging to the harried parent. Length alone can create a dull interview. One New York company administers a social attitudes study that typically takes three to four-and-one-half hours to complete. The researcher who is designing the questionnaire must consider not only the type of respondent but also the interviewing environment and questionnaire length as well.

Sometimes brand managers engage in "as long as you're out there asking questions, it would be nice to know" false logic. "Nice to know" questions are those that seem interesting but convey no managerially useful information. By tacking on additional questions not related to the original purpose of the survey, two problems emerge. First, the interview becomes disjointed. A person is being questioned about soap purchase habits and suddenly the interviewer is asking about wine consumption. This destroys the flow and continuity of the questionnaire. The second problem is additional questionnaire length. Generally the longer the interview, the more difficult it is to find cooperative survey participants, and terminations also rise. Usually an interview that is only partially completed (a termination) is worthless to the researcher. It also is time-consuming, costly, and frustrating to the interviewer.

Fitting the Questionnaire to the Respondent A questionnaire should be designed explicitly for the intended respondent. Although a parent typically is the purchaser of cold cereals, the child, either directly or indirectly, often makes the decision as to which brand. Thus, a taste test questionnaire for children should be formulated in children's language. On the other hand, an interview schedule for the adult purchaser would be worded in language suitable for the adult interviewee. One of the most important tasks of questionnaire design is to "fit" the questions to the prospective respondent. The questionnaire designer must strip away the marketing jargon and business terminology that may be misunderstood by the respondent. In fact, it is best to use simple, everyday language, as long as the result is not insulting or demeaning to the respondent.

Editing, Coding, and Data Processing Requirements

editing

Going through the questionnaire to ensure the skip patterns were followed and the required questions filled out.

coding

The process of grouping and assigning numeric codes to the various responses to a question.

Once the information is gathered, it must be edited. **Editing** refers to going through the questionnaire to make certain the "skip patterns" are followed and required questions are filled out. A *skip pattern* is the sequence in which questions are asked. Table 12.1 denotes a skip pattern from 4a to 5a for persons who answered no to question 4a.

After editing, the questionnaire is coded for data processing. **Coding** is the conversion of interviewees' answers to numerical values or symbols easy to work with. Table 12.2 depicts a well-designed questionnaire that minimizes coding

TABLE 12.1 A Questionnaire Skip Pattern

4a. Do you usually use a cream rinse or a hair conditioner on your child's hair?
(1) No (SKIP TO 5A) (2) (ASK Q 4B)

4b. Is that a cream rinse that you pour on or a cream rinse that you spray on?
(1) ( ) Cream rinse that you pour on
(2) ( ) Cream rinse that you spray on

4c. About how often do you use a cream rinse or a hair conditioner on your child's hair? Would you say less than once a week, once a week, or more than once a week?
(1) ( ) Less than once a week
(2) ( ) Once a week
(3) ( ) More than once a week

5a. Thinking of the texture of your child's hair, is it. . . (READ LIST)
1 ( ) Fine 2 ( ) Course 3 ( ) Regular

5b. What is the length of your child's hair? (READ LIST)
1 ( ) Long 2 ( ) Medium 3 ( ) Short

effort. In recording the answer, the interviewer is indicating the questionnaire code for all questions except the one on occupation (question 18). Today, central location telephone interviewing is frequently conducted by an interviewer sitting at a computer terminal. The interviewer enters the response directly into the computer. Computer-assisted interviewing provides many advantages and also some new tasks.

Carefully examine the layout of the questionnaire in Table 12.2. Note that the interviewer or data terminal operator can look down the right-hand margin of the page and quickly and easily enter the data. The computer column number 57 is listed so that the operator will know exactly where she is at the beginning of the page. The questionnaire in Table 12.1 is an invitation to data entry error. The operator must convert closed-ended questions from alpha to numeric data and remember the columns that correspond to a given question. The operator's eyes also must shift from one side of the page to the other, further slowing the data entry process.

All "open-ended" questions are recorded verbatim by the interviewer. An open-ended question is one that does not contain prerecorded possible responses. Open-ended questions are sometines coded by listing the answers from a number of randomly selected completed questionnaires. If at all possible, the open-ended questions should be precoded. Those responses with the greatest frequency are then listed on a coding sheet such as that in Table 12.3. The editor uses the coding sheet to code the response to the open-ended question. Today, sophisticated neural network systems software is decreasing the necessity of manually coding open-ended questions. This will be explored in more detail in Chapter 15.

A Questionnaire Serves Many Masters

In summary, a questionnaire serves many masters. First, it must accommodate all the research objectives in sufficient depth and breadth to satisfy the information requirements of the manager. Next, it must "speak" to the respondent in understandable language and at the appropriate intellectual level. Furthermore, it must be convenient for the interviewer to administer, and it must allow the interviewer

TABLE 12.2 A Questionnaire Designed for Simplified Data Processing

Now I have just a few more questions for classification purposes.

		Col.
16. Are you employed outside your home? (CIRCLE)		57–
CONTINUE WITH Q. 17	Yes	1
SKIP TO Q. 21	No	2
17. If you were to purchase this new communications service, where would you be most likely to use it, in your home, office, or both? (CHECK ONE)		
	_______ Home	1
	_______ Office	2
	_______ Both	3
18. What is your occupation? (TYPE OF WORK, NOT PLACE OF EMPLOYMENT) ________________		
19. Are you in a management related position? (CIRCLE)		
CONTINUE WITH Q. 20	Yes	1
SKIP TO Q. 21	No	2
20. Is that upper, middle, or lower management? (CHECK ONE)		
	_______ Upper	1
	_______ Middle	2
	_______ Lower	3
21. What was the last grade of school you completed? (HAND CARD C TO RESPONDENT: CIRCLE RESPONSE.)		
	A. Some high school or less	1
	B. Completed high school	2
	C. Some college	3
	D. Completed college	4
	E. Graduate school	5
	F. Other education beyond high school (business, nursing, etc.)	6

to quickly record the respondent's answers. At the same time, it must be easy and fast to edit and check for completeness. It also should facilitate coding and data entry. Finally, the questionnaire must be translatable back into findings that respond to the manager's original questions.

The Questionnaire Development Process

Designing a questionnaire involves a logical series of steps, as shown in Figure 12.2 on page 406. The steps may vary slightly from researcher to researcher, but all tend to follow the same general sequence. Committees and lines of authority can complicate the questionnaire design process. It is often wise to clear each step of the design process with the individual who has the ultimate project authority. This is particularly true for step one, determining the decision-making information needed. Many work hours have been wasted on questionnaire design when a researcher developed a questionnaire to answer one type of question and the "real" decision maker wanted something entirely different.

It also should be noted that the design process itself, such as question wording and format, can raise additional issues or unanswered questions. This, in turn,

TABLE 12.3 Coding Sheet for Occupation Question from Questionnaire in Table 12.2

CATEGORY	CODE
Professional/Technical	1
Manager-Official-Self Employed	2
Clerical-Sales	3
Skilled Worker	4
Service Worker	5
Unskilled Laborer	6
Farm Operator or Rancher	7
Unemployed or Student	8
Retired	9

can send the researchers back to step one for a clearer delineation of the information sought.

Step One: Determine Survey Objectives, Resources, and Constraints

The research process often begins when a marketing manager, brand manager, or new product development specialist has a need for decision-making information that is not available. In some firms it is the responsibility of the manager to evaluate all secondary sources to make certain that the needed information has not already been gathered. In other companies, the manager leaves all research activities, primary and secondary, to the research department. The discussion of the research process in Chapter 2 covers this issue in more detail.

Although a brand manager may initiate the research request, everyone affected by the project, such as the assistant brand manager, group product manager, and even the marketing manager, should provide input into exactly what data are needed. **Survey** (information) **objectives** should be spelled out as clearly and precisely as possible. If this step is completed in a thorough fashion, the rest of the process will follow more smoothly and efficiently.

survey objectives
The decision-making information sought through the questionnaire.

Too much emphasis cannot be placed upon having empathy with the respondent. This is the place to make sure that other projects are not "tagged on" to the study objectives. It also is the point to "hash out" budget constraints versus information needs. If, for example, a consumer needs to be shown several package styles and logos, a personal interview is mandatory. Given a limited budget, it probably means that a mall intercept study is dictated. A mall intercept interview should almost always be kept to 15 minutes or less. Thus, the brand manager (or project initiator) is quite limited in the quantity of data that can be gathered. Picture yourself standing in a mall or sitting at an interview station for 20 minutes or more. Tempers and terminations begin to rise. If the interview is completed, the quality of data toward the end of the interview is often suspect.

Step Two: Determine the Data Collection Method

Chapter 7 discussed the variety of ways that survey data can be gathered, such as in-person, telephone, mail, or self-administration. Each method will have an

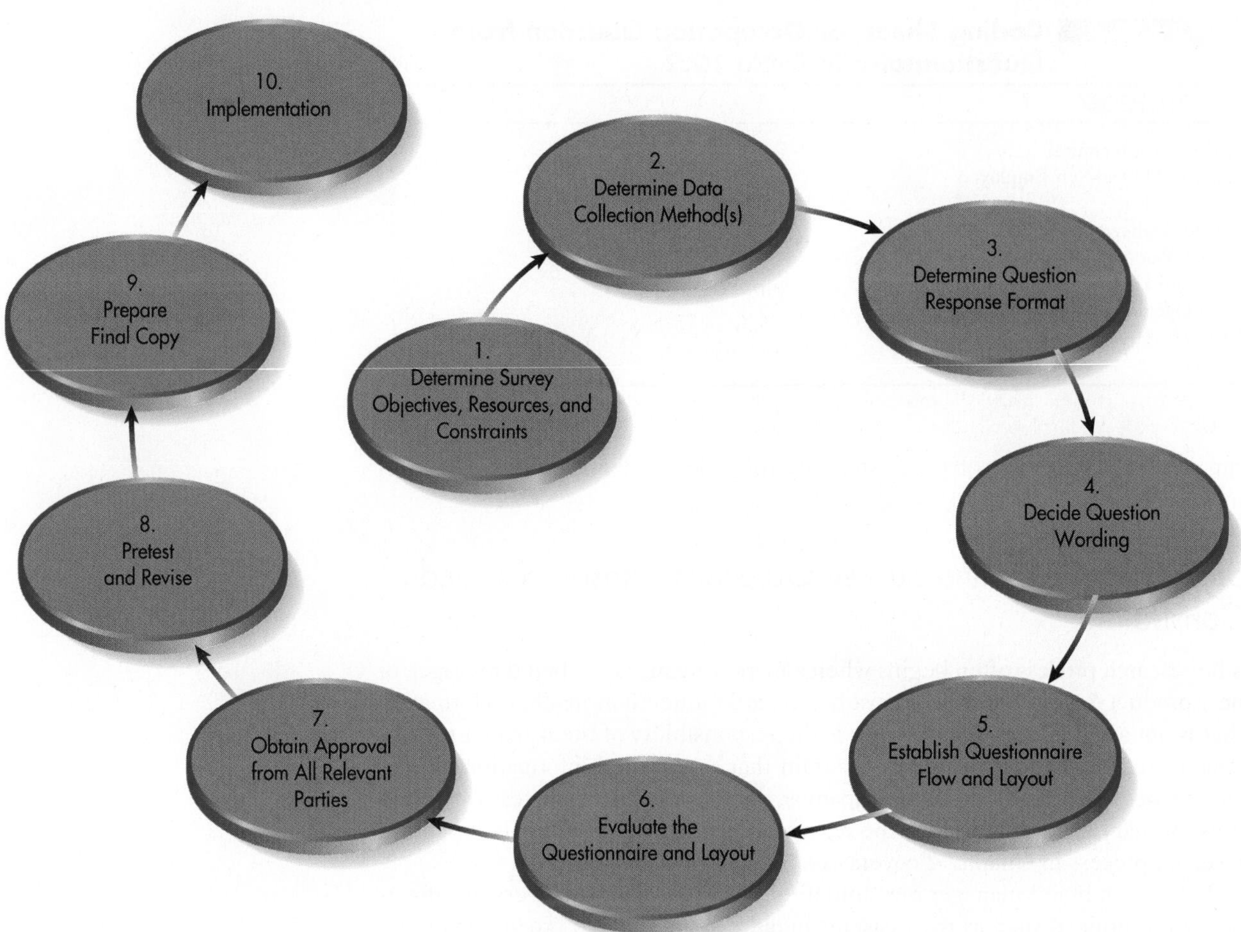

FIGURE 12.2
The Questionnaire Development Process

impact on questionnaire design. In fact, an in-person questionnaire in a mall will have constraints not found in an in-home interview. A mall interview, for example, faces the time limitation just discussed. A self-administered questionnaire must be very explicit and usually rather short. Because no interviewer will be present, opportunities to clarify a question will be lacking. A telephone interview often requires a rich verbal description of a concept to make certain the respondent understands the idea being discussed. In contrast, in a personal interview an interviewer can show the respondent a picture or demonstrate the concept.

Step Three: Determine the Question Response Format

Once the data collection method has been determined, the actual questionnaire design process begins. The first phase in the process concerns itself with the types of questions to be used in the survey. Three major types of question response formats are used in marketing research: open-ended, closed-ended, and scale-response questions.

Open-ended Questions Open-ended questions are those in which the respondent can reply in her own words. In other words, the researcher does not limit the response choices.

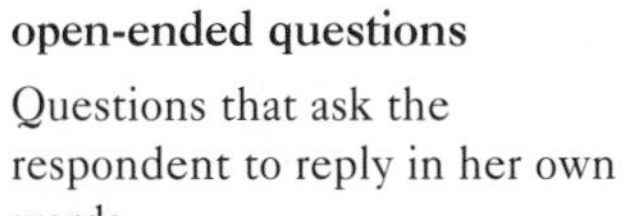

open-ended questions
Questions that ask the respondent to reply in her own words.

Often open-ended questions require "probes" from the interviewer. A *probe* is encouragement from the interviewer for the respondent to elaborate or continue the discussion. The interviewer may say, "Is there anything else?" or "Would you elaborate on that?" Probes aid in clarifying the respondent's interests, attitudes, and feelings. Computers are playing an increasingly important role in analyzing and recording probes to open-ended questions.

Open-ended questions offer several advantages to the researcher. They enable respondents to give their general reactions to questions like

1. What advantages, if any, do you think ordering from a mail order catalog company offers compared with local retail outlets? (*probe:* What else?)
2. Why do you have one or more of your rugs or carpets professionally cleaned rather than you or someone else in the household clean them?
3. What is there about the *color* of Product____that makes you like it the best? (*probe with:* What color is that?)
4. Why do you say that brand (you use most often) is better?

Each of these was taken from a different nationwide survey covering four products and services. Note that in questions 2 and 4, the open-ended question is part of a skip pattern. In question 2, for example, the respondents have already indicated that they use a professional carpet cleaning service and do not depend on members of the household.

Open-ended questions give a respondent the opportunity to answer in her own words.

Another advantage of open-ended responses is that they can provide the researcher with a rich array of information. The respondent is answering from his own frame of reference. Advantages are described in "real world" terminology rather than laboratory or marketing jargon. Often this is helpful in designing promotion themes and campaigns. It enables copywriters to use the consumer's language. This rich array of information can now be captured even in computer-assisted interviews.

The inspection of open-ended data also can serve as a means of interpreting closed-ended questions. This analysis often sheds additional light on the motivations or attitudes behind the closed-ended response patterns. It is one thing to know that color ranks second in importance out of five product attributes. But it might be much more valuable to know why color is important. For example, a recent study on mobile home park residents uncovered a great deal of dissatisfaction with the trash pick up service, but further inspection of the open-ended responses uncovered the reason: neighbors' dogs were allowed to run free and were overturning the receptacles.

Similarly, open-ended questions may suggest additional alternatives not listed in a closed-ended question. For example, a previously unrecognized advantage of using a mail order catalog might be uncovered from question 1. This advantage would have been omitted from a closed-ended question on the same subject.

One manufacturer that the authors consult with always ends a product placement questionnaire with the following: "Is there anything else that you would like to tell us about the product that you have tried during the past three weeks?" This seeks any final tidbit of information that might provide additional insight for the researcher.

Open-ended questions are not without their problems. One factor is the time-and-money-consuming process of editing and coding. Editing open-ended responses requires collapsing the many response alternatives into some reasonable number. If too many categories are used, data patterns and response frequencies may be difficult for the researcher to interpret. If the categories are too broad, the data are too general and important meaning may be lost. Even if a proper number of categories are used, editors may have to interpret what the interviewer has recorded and force the data into a category. Assume that the question was asked in a food study, "What, if anything, do you normally add to a taco that you have prepared at home, besides meat?" The question, of course, is open-ended and the coding categories might be as follows:

RESPONSE	CODE
Avocado	1
Cheese (Monterey Jack, Cheddar)	2
Guacamole	3
Lettuce	4
Mexican hot sauce	5
Olives (black or green)	6
Onions (red or white)	7
Peppers (red or green)	8
Pimento	9
Sour cream	0
Other	X

A Professional Researcher's Perspective

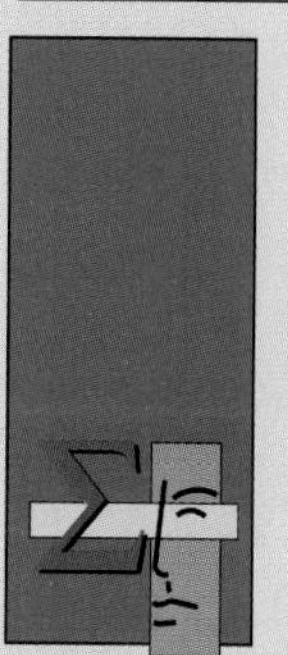

According to Dr. Charles Cleveland, president of Communication Development Company, there are about 600,000 words in the English language, but 50 words account for 40 percent of usage. Further 16,000 words account for 99 percent usage.

Communication Development Company (CDC) offers a variety of service that makes use of computer content analysis. CDC analyzes words collected from phone or in-person interviews, focus groups, written responses to questions, advertisements, speeches, and any source of spoken or written words. For example, in a service called *Q'cept*, CDC mails out a new product concept and about 24 hours later it calls the recipients for a 20-minute or so telephone interview about elements of the concept. CDC's interviewers are given "active listening" training, which they use to probe for a full "language picture" of what is going on in the respondent's mind. The entire interview is tape-recorded to be analyzed later.

When a respondent says, "I like it," the rest of what that person says about the concept could indicate that she really does or does not. At least the other language used might indicate what subparts of the concept could be improved—the picture, the name, certain descriptions in the body copy of the concept, and so on.

CDC reports to have the world's largest database of word meaning (e.g., all the words that co-occur with the word "comfort"). It goes beyond looking at the frequency of occurrence of a word and looks at its relative occurrence—how often it occurs versus how often it is expected to occur. With a service called Quester (the original name of the Communication Development Company), it reports to be able to tell marketers what thoughts (words) about a product may be so negative that they could *block* its purchase, what thoughts *support* the purchase, and which absent thoughts (*gaps*) might be added to help sell the product.

CDC's services are expensive on a per-respondent basis. For example, a *Q'cept* study for a single picture concept is $7,500 for 20 respondents. CDC maintains that 99 percent of the range of responses to the concept actually will come from 18 respondents. In other words, it does not need a large sample to perform its language analysis.[2] ■

What if an editor find the following response, "I usually add a green, avocado-tasting hot sauce." How would you code it? Or, "I cut up a mixture of lettuce and spinach." Or, "I'm a vegetarian; I don't use meat at all, my taco is filled only with guacamole."

Thus, a basic problem with open-ended questions lies in the interpretation-processing area. In fact, a two-phase judgment must be made. First, the researcher must decide on the proper set of categories and then each response must be evaluated as to which category it falls into.

Marketing Research in Practice

Adults and Surveys has developed a system called A&S Voice/CATI. When an open-ended question comes up on the screen, the interviewer has the capability to record the entire response in the respondent's own voice onto PC disk rather than a tape recorder. The assumption is that the interview is taking place via PC rather than a dumb terminal. The system affords some important new benefits for analysts of open-ended responses:

- By recording the entire open-ended response, the interviewer does not break spontaneity by interrupting to clarify and write or type the response.
- How a thing is said is captured along with what is said.
- It's even possible to record how the interviewers ask the questions and the give-and-take between the interviewer and the respondent.

The system stores the response on a computer as a digital file on hard disk or floppies. Hence, the verbatim response can be sorted like any other computer file. The data can be transmitted via telephone lines like any other data or the floppies can be mailed to researchers at the client firm.

In analyzing a customer satisfaction study, for example, the analyst can sort respondents who are satisfied and those who are dissatisfied and listen to each group's actual comments as to "why." During analysis and report presentation or preparation, actual-voice, open-ended responses can be sorted by answers to any other question in the questionnaire and by traditional classification questions (sex, age, income, etc.).[3] ■

A related problem of open-ended questions is interviewer bias. Although training sessions continually stress the importance of verbatim recording of open-ended questions, it is often not practiced in the field. Also, slow writers may unintentionally miss important comments. Good probes that ask, "Can you tell me a little more?" or "Is there anything else?" generally have better quality answers than poor probers.

These problems can be partially overcome by precoding open-ended questions. For example, possible answers to the taco question could have been listed on the questionnaire. A space would have been provided to write in any nonconforming reply in the "other" category. In a telephone interview, the question would still qualify as open-ended because the respondent would not see the categories, and the interviewer would be instructed not to divulge them. Precoding necessitates sufficient familiarity with previous studies of a similar nature to anticipate respondents' answers. Otherwise, a pretest with a fairly large sample is needed.

Open-ended questions also may be biased toward the articulate interviewee. A person with elaborate opinions and the ability to express them may have much greater input than a shy, inarticulate, or withdrawn respondent. Yet, they could be equally likely prospects for a product.

A final difficulty with open-ended questions is their inappropriateness on some self-administered questionnaires. If no interviewer is there to probe, a shallow, incomplete, or unclear answer may be recorded. If the taco question had appeared on a self-administered interview schedule without precoded choices, answers might read, "I use a little bit of everything," or "the same things they use in restaurants." These answers would have virtually no value to a researcher.

Closed-ended Questions A **closed-ended question** is one that requires the respondent to make a selection from a list of responses. The primary advantage of closed-ended questions is simply the avoidance of many of the problems of open-ended questions. Interviewer and coder bias are removed because the interviewer is simply checking a box, circling a category, recording a number, or punching a key. Reading response alternatives may jog a person's memory and provide a more realistic response. Also, because the option of expounding on a topic is not given to a respondent, there is no bias toward the articulate. Finally, the coding and data entry process is greatly simplified.

closed-ended questions
Questions that ask the respondent to choose from a list of answers.

One should realize the difference between a precoded open-ended question and a multiple-choice question. An open-ended question allows the respondent to answer in a freewheeling format. The interviewer simply checks the points on the prerecorded answers as they are given. Probing is used, but a list is *never* read. If an answer is given that is not precoded, it is written verbatim in the "other" column. In contrast, the closed-ended question *requires* that alternatives be read or shown to the respondent.

Traditionally, marketing researchers have separated the two-item response option from the many-item type. A two-choice question is called *dichotomous* and the many-item type is often called *multiple choice* or *multichotomous.* With the dichotomous closed-ended question, the response categories are sometimes implicit. For instance, how would you respond to the following question: "Did you buy gasoline for your automobile in the last week?" Obviously, the implicit options are "Yes" or "No." Regardless of the fact that a respondent may say, "I rented a car last week, and they filled it up for me. Does that count?" the questions would still be classified as dichotomous closed-ended.

Dichotomous Questions The simplest form of a closed-ended question is the dichotomous choice. A few examples are

1. Did you heat the Danish roll before serving it?
   Yes 1
   No 2
2. The federal government doesn't care what people, like me, think.
   Agree 1
   Disagree 2
3. Do you think that inflation will be greater or less than last year?
   Greater than 1
   Less than 2

Note that the respondent is limited to two fixed alternatives. It is easy to administer and usually evokes rapid response. Many times a neutral or no opinion/don't know is added to dichotomous questions to take care of those situations. Sometimes interviewers will jot down DK for "Don't know" or NR for "No response" if the neutral option is omitted from the questionnaire.

dichotomous questions

Questions that ask the respondent to choose between two answers.

Dichotomous questions are prone to a large amount of measurement error. Because alternatives are polarized, the wide range of possible choices between the poles is omitted. Thus, question wording is very critical to obtain accurate responses. Questions phrased in a positive form may well result in answers opposite from those expressed in a negative format. In the third question, response may vary depending upon whether *greater than* or *less than* is listed first. These problems can be overcome using a split ballot technique. One-half of the questionnaires are worded with *greater than* listed first and the other half with *less than* first. This procedure will aid in reducing potential bias.

multiple-choice questions

Questions that ask a respondent to choose among a list of more than two answers.

Multiple-Choice Questions **Multiple-choice questions** have about the same advantages and disadvantages as those given in the general discussion of closed-ended questions. Replies do not have to be coded like an open-ended question but limited information is provided. The interviewee is asked to give one alternative that correctly expresses his opinion or, in some instances, to indicate all alternatives that apply. Some examples of multiple choice questions follow:

1. I'd like you to think back to the last footwear of any kind that you bought. I'll read you a list of descriptions and would like for you to tell me which category it falls into. (READ LIST AND CHECK THE PROPER CATEGORY)
   Dress and/or Formal 1
   Casual 2
   Canvas-Trainer-Gym Shoes 3
   Specialized Athletic Shoes 4
   Boots 5
2. (HAND RESPONDENT CARD) Please look at this card and tell me the letter that indicates the age group you belong to:
   A. Under 17 1
   B. 17–24 Years 2
   C. 25–34 Years 3
   D. 35–49 Years 4
   E. 50–64 Years 5
   F. 65 and Over 6
3. In the *last three months,* have you used Noxzema Skin Cream: (CHECK ALL THAT APPLY)
   as a facial wash 1
   for moisturizing the skin 2
   for treating blemishes 3
   for cleansing the skin 4
   for treating dry skin 5
   for softening skin 6
   for sunburn 7
   for making the facial skin smooth 8

Question 1 may not cover all possible alternatives and, thus, would not capture a true response.[4] Where, for example, would an interviewer record work shoes? The same thing can be said for question 3. Not only are all possible alternatives not included, but also there is no possibility for respondents to elaborate or qualify their answers. Part of the problem can be easily overcome by adding an "Any other use?—RECORD VERBATIM" alternative to the questions.

Disadvantages of Closed-ended Questions Each type of closed-ended question represents unique disadvantages. For the dichotomous question form, the researcher finds that frequently the responses fail to communicate any

To determine how consumers use Noxzema Skin Cream, a multiple choice question could give respondents several alternatives to select.

intensity of feeling from the respondent. In some cases, the matter of intensity does not apply, as for the previous example on gasoline purchasing. But instances do arise in which the respondent feels very strongly about an issue but the intensity is lost in the dichotomous response form. If that interview had continued with this question, "Would you purchase gasoline priced $1.00 above current prices but which would guarantee twice the miles per gallon?" there is a high likelihood that the responses might range in intensity as observed in the following quotes: "No. Absolutely not"; "Gee, I doubt it"; "Well, I might try it"; or "You bet!"

The multiple response close-ended question has two additional disadvantages. First, the researcher must spend time generating the list of possible responses. This phase may require intensive analysis of focus group tapes, brainstorming, or secondary data investigation. In any case, it requires more time and effort than the open-ended alternative or the dichotomous form. Another problem with closed-ended multiple response questions is the range of possible answers. If the list is too long, the respondent may become confused or disinterested. One way to help overcome this problem is to show the interviewee a card and read down the list with her. A related problem with any list is position bias. Respondents typically will choose from among the first and last alternatives, all other things being equal.[5] Position bias can be overcome by marking an alternative with an *X* and instructing the interviewer to begin reading the list at the *X*'ed alternative instead of at the beginning of the list. The first question is marked with an *X* at alternative one, the second question at alternative two, and so forth.

scaled-response questions
Multiple-choice questions in which the choices are designed to capture the intensity of the respondent's answer.

Scaled-Response Questions The last response format to be considered is **scaled-response questions.** Consider the following two question forms.

Marketing Research in Practice

Recently a study was conducted (and the results here are disguised) in which 200 respondents were asked to rate a product on 10 attributes on 10-point scales—the type of thing market researchers request people to do every day. The results looked something like this:

SCALE	MEAN
Easy to open	3.62
Tastes good	6.54
For children	5.62
For adults	5.89
Good value	7.77
Easy to prepare	9.21
Attractive packaging	5.18
Sweetness	7.21
Reputable manufacturer	8.94
Nutritious	4.85

Now, in a vacuum, there's nothing at all unsettling about these results. But this particular test actually was a pretest of a new product evaluation system that was under consideration. In fact, since these scales were a small portion of a much larger, more elaborate questionnaire and the pretest was of an entirely new methodology, the scales weren't rotated—intentionally so, not as an indication of bad research design. When the order of asking is tacked on to these results, we see something a little different.

SCALE	MEAN	ORDER
Easy to prepare	9.21	First
Reputable manufacturer	8.94	Second
Good value	7.77	Third
Sweetness	7.21	Fourth
Tastes good	6.54	Fifth
For children	5.62	Sixth
For adults	5.89	Seventh
Attractive packaging	5.18	Eighth
Nutritious	4.85	Ninth
Easy to open	3.62	Tenth

These results were, as you might imagine, quite unnerving. With one exception, the means decrease uniformly by question order. So these data illustrate yet again the necessity of rotating items to control for position bias.[6] ■

1. Now that you have used the product, would you say that you would buy it or not? (CHECK ONE)
_______ Yes, would buy it
_______ No, would not buy it

2. Now that you have used the product, would you say that you would . . . (CHECK ONE)
_______ Definitely buy it
_______ Probably buy it
_______ Might or might not buy it
_______ Probably would not buy it
_______ Definitely would not buy it

The first question fails to capture intensity. It determines the direction (Yes versus No), but it cannot compare with the second one for completeness or sensitivity of response. The latter also is ordinal in nature.

A primary advantage of scaled-response questions is that scaling permits the measurement of the intensity of respondents' answers. Another advantage is that many scaled-response forms incorporate numbers, and these numbers may be used directly as codes. Finally, the marketing researcher is allowed to use much more powerful statistical tools with some scaled-response questions as discussed in Chapter 11.

The most significant problems of scaled-response questions evolve from respondent misunderstanding. Scaled questions sometimes tax respondents' abilities to remember and answer. First, the questionnaire must explain the response category options, then the respondent must translate these into his own frame of reference. To overcome the first problem, interviewers usually are provided with a detailed description of the response categories allowed and even instructed to elicit a "Yes" as to understanding the scale from the respondent before asking the questions. Take a look at Table 12.4 for examples of a telephone interviewer's instructions for scaled response questions. In the case of self-administered questionnaires, the researcher often presents an example of responding to a scale as part of the instructions.

Step Four: Decide the Question Wording

Once the marketing researcher has decided on the specific types of questions and the response formats, the next task is the actual writing of the questions. The wording of specific questions always poses significant time investment for the

TABLE 12.4 Sample Telephone Interviewer Instructions for a Scaled-Response Question Form

EXAMPLE #1

I have some statements which I will read to you. For each one, please indicate whether you "strongly agree," "agree," "disagree," "strongly disagree," or have no opinion. I will read the statement, and you indicate *your* opinion as accurately as possible. Are the instructions clear?

(IF THE RESPONDENT DOES NOT UNDERSTAND, REPEAT RESPONSE CATEGORIES. GO ON TO READ STATEMENTS AND RECORD RESPONSES. CIRCLE RESPONDENT'S OPINION IN EACH CASE.)

EXAMPLE #2

4. Now I'm going to read you a list of statements that may or may not be important to you in deciding where to shop for stereo equipment. Let's use your telephone dial as a scale. #1 would mean "definitely disagree" and #6 would mean "definitely agree." Or you can pick any number in between that best expresses your feelings.

Let's begin. To what extent do you agree or disagree that (INSERT STATEMENT) is an important aspect when deciding where to shop for stereo equipment?

EXAMPLE #3

Now I shall read a list of statements about automotive servicing which may or may not be *important* to you when servicing your car.

Let's use your telephone dial as a scale. . . .

Number 1 would mean you *disagree completely* with the statement.
Number 2 would mean you *disagree* with the statement.
Number 3 would mean you *somewhat disagree* with the statement.
Number 4 would mean you *somewhat agree* with the statement.
Number 5 would mean you *agree* with the statement.
Number 6 would mean you *agree completely* with the statement.

Do you have any questions about the scale?

1) To what extent do you agree or disagree that 1
(FILL IN THE STATEMENT) is a feature you consider 2
when selecting a place to have your car serviced? 3

marketing researcher. It is a skill developed over time and subject to constant improvement. Four general guidelines are useful to bear in mind during the wording and sequencing of each question.

1. *The wording must be clear.* If the researcher decides that a question is absolutely necessary, that question must be stated so that it means the same thing to all respondents. Ambiguous terminology should be avoided, such as "Do you live within five minutes of here?" or "Where do you usually shop for clothes?" The first example depends on mode of transportation (maybe the respondent walks), driving speed, perceived elapsed time, and other factors. It normally would be prudent to show the respondent a map with certain areas delineated and ask whether she lives within the area. The second question depends on the type of clothing, the occasion, the member of the family, and the meaning of the word *where.*

   Clarity also implies the use of reasonable terminology. A questionnaire is not a vocabulary test. Jargon should be avoided and verbiage should be geared to the target audience. A question such as "State the level of efficacy of your preponderant dishwasher liquid" probably would be greeted by a lot of blank stares. It would be much simpler to say "Are you (1) very satisfied, (2) somewhat satisfied, or (3) not satisfied with your current brand of dishwasher liquid?" It is best to use words that have precise meanings, universal usage, and minimal connotative confusion. When respondents are uncertain of what a question means, the incidence of "no response" increases.[7]

   Every prospective respondent represents a separate frame of reference. That is, each person is unique in personality, mental ability, experiences, education, and views of the world. The marketing manager's and the marketing researcher's frames of reference have much compatibility, but they may differ from those of consumer-respondents. Consequently, the questionnaire designer must use terminology native to the target respondent group and not use research jargon. The first task of wording questions, then, is to translate questions into everyday language.

   A further complication of this translation is to custom-tailor the wording to the target respondent group. If, for example, lawyers are to be interviewed, the wording should be appropriate. If construction laborers are to be questioned, the terminology must be modified appropriately. This advice is painfully obvious, but there are instances in which the failure to relate to respondents' frames of reference has been disastrous. A case in point is the use of the word *bottles* (or *cans*) in this question, "How many bottles of beer do you drink in a normal week?" In some southern states, beer is sold in 32, 12, 8, 7, 6, and even 4 ounce bottles. So a "heavy" drinker of eight bottles may consume only 32 ounces per week (8 x 4 oz.); in contrast a "light" drinker might only consume three bottles but 96 ounces (3 x 32 oz.).

   Clarity also can be improved at the beginning of the interview by stating the purpose of the survey. Usually, the respondent should understand the nature of the study and what is expected but not necessarily know who is sponsoring the project. This aids the interviewee in placing the questions in the proper perspective.

   A final aspect of clarity is the avoidance of two questions in one, sometimes called a *double-barreled question.* For example, "How did you like the taste and

Beer is sold in bottles and cans of varying sizes. In classifying respondents by the number of bottles they drink in a week, an inaccurate reading of the market may result.

texture of the coffee cake?" This should be broken into two questions: one concerning taste and the other texture. Each question should address only one aspect of evaluation.

2. *Select words so as to avoid biasing the respondent.* A question such as, "Do you often shop at lower-class stores like K Mart?" evokes an obvious response. Similarly, "Have you purchased any high-quality Black & Decker tools in the past six months?" also biases respondents. Questions can be leading, such as, "Weren't you pleased with the good service you received last night at the Holiday Inn?" These examples are quite obvious. Unfortunately, bias may be much more subtle than is illustrated in these examples.

   Sponsor identification too early in the interviewing process also can distort answers.[8] It does not take long, for example, for a person to recognize that a survey is being conducted for Miller beer if, after the third question, every question is related to this product. Or an opening statement such as "We are conducting a study on the quality of banking for Northeast National Bank and would like to ask you a few questions." Sometimes, of course, the true purpose of the study must be disguised to obtain an unbiased response. For example, a major food processor developed a package that would enable liquids, such as milk, to be kept without refrigeration for several weeks as long as the carton was unopened. This new process would save untold millions in refrigeration expenses, yet it goes against everything Americans were ever taught about food sanitation and refrigeration. Thus, the study was disguised as an orange juice taste test. One-half of the consumers were given cartons of the product to take home and told that refrigeration was unnecessary; the other half were told to refrigerate the product. Subsequent call-back interviews revealed a significant difference in the perceived quality of the identical product. The manufacturer concluded that cultural taboos were too strong at that time to overcome.

Global Marketing Research

Question context is very important when conducting Asian marketing research. Asian respondents often need to understand the context of a question before they can fully respond. The respondents use context as a filter through which they structure their "reality." If researchers don't provide a recognizable context, the respondents will redirect the question, answer in ways that give no real information, or create a context in order to respond. The obvious danger is that researchers may get information that reflects issues other than those sought.

Short and abrupt answers in themselves do not necessarily mean respondents are unwilling to engage in discussion. The respondents may, in fact, be signaling you that they can't relate to the framework as presented. The researcher needs to be perceptive enough to realize when his cultural construct or template has no meaning—or a significantly different meaning—for the respondents. Furthermore, the same cultural template may have different meanings among the subsegments of the same ethnic group.

Let's say you are preparing research on behavioral patterns of parents' leisure time with children. One widespread American assumption is that people value spending time with their families on their

3. *Consider the ability of the respondent to answer the question.* In some cases a respondent may have never acquired the information to answer the question. Asking a husband which brand of sewing thread is most preferred by his wife would often fall into this category. Asking respondents about a brand or store that they have never encountered creates the same problem. When a question is worded in such a manner that it implies that the respondent should be able to answer it, then often a reply will be forthcoming, but it will be nothing more than a wild guess. This creates measurement error, since uninformed opinions are being recorded.

   A second problems is forgetfulness. For example, "What was the name of the last movie you saw in a theater?" "Who were the stars?" "Did you have popcorn?" "How many ounces were in the container?" "What price did you pay for the popcorn?" "Did you purchase any other snack items?" "Why or why not?" You probably cannot remember the answers to all these questions. The same is true for the typical respondent. Yet a brand manager for Mars, Incorporated, wants to know what brand of candy you purchased last; what alternative brands were considered; and what factors led to the brand selected. Because brand managers want answers to these questions, market researchers ask them. This, in turn, also creates measurement error. Often respondents will give the name of a well-known brand, like Milky Way or Hershey. In other cases, respondents will mention a brand that they often purchase, but it may not be the last brand purchased.

days off from work. The interpretation of "spending time with family" means passing time with one's spouse and children. Another assumption is that "good" parents are involved in their children's extracurricular activities. A common scenario has the parents taking their kids to a Little League game, then barbecuing at home with a few friends and their children.

This American cultural construct has different degrees of relevance to various subgroups of the Asian segment. Although the more acculturated Asian-American families can relate comfortably to this concept, it's quite unfamiliar to many Asian families. If your target audience is Asian, but your research design is based on the aforementioned assumptions, you would be presenting a cultural construct that's not relevant to your intended audience. "Spending time with the family" holds a very different meaning for many Chinese. They would more likely interpret this concept as getting together socially with members of their extended families (parents, siblings, aunts, uncles, cousins, etc.) than to doing things with just their spouse and children. Moreover, the concept of "good parenting" for many Chinese parents does not include involvement in their children's sports activities. Many of them regard children's play and adult leisure as distinct activities, to be done separately or in parallel, rather than together.[9] ■

To avoid the problem of a respondent's inability to recall, time periods should be kept relatively short. For example, "Did you purchase a candy bar within the past seven days? If the reply is "yes," then brand and purchase motivation questions can be asked. Alternatively, a poor question would be, "How many movies have you rented in the past year to view at home on your VCR?" Instead, the researcher might ask:

a. How many movies have you rented in the past month to view on your VCR?
b. Would you say that in the last month, you rented more movies, fewer movies, or about the average number of movies you rent per month? (IF "MORE" OR "LESS" ASK:)
c. What would you say is the typical number of movies you rent per month?

4. *Consider the willingness of the respondent to answer the question.* The memory of a respondent may be totally clear, yet the respondent may not be willing to give a truthful reply. Reporting of an event is likely to be distorted in a socially desirable direction. If the event is perceived as embarrassing, sensitive in nature, threatening, or divergent from one's self-image, it is likely either not to be reported at all or to be distorted in a desirable direction.[10]

Calvin Hodock, senior vice-president of Comart/KLP, New York, cautions researchers about interpreting responses to marketing research questionnaires in "A Professional Researcher's Perspective" on pages 422–423.

Perhaps the question that interviewers dislike asking more than others and researchers are most dubious of is the income question. One study on savings revealed that small account balances were overreported and large savings balances were underreported.[11]

Embarrassing topics that deal with things such as borrowing money, personal hygiene, sexual activities, and criminal records must be phrased in a careful manner to minimize measurement error. One technique is to ask the question in the third person. For example, "Do you think that most people charge more on their credit cards than they should? Why?" By asking about "most people" rather than themselves, researchers may be able to learn more about the individual's attitude about credit and debt.

A third method for soliciting embarrassing information is to state that the behavior or attitude is not unusual prior to asking the question. For example, "Millions of Americans suffer from hemorrhoids; do you or any member of your family suffer from this problem?" This technique is called using counterbiasing statements and makes it less intimidating for the respondent to discuss embarrassing topics.

Step Five: Establish Questionnaire Flow and Layout

After the questions have been properly formulated, the next step is to sequence them and develop a layout for the questionnaire. Questionnaires are not constructed haphazardly. There is a logic to the positioning of each section of the questionnaire, and this logic is depicted in Table 12.5. Experienced marketing researchers are well aware that questionnaire development is the key to obtaining interviewer-interviewee rapport. The greater the rapport, the more likely the interviewer will obtain a completed interview. Also, the respondent's answers probably will be more carefully thought out and detailed. Researcher wisdom has developed the following general guidelines concerning questionnaire flow.

TABLE 12.5 How a Questionnaire Should Be Organized

LOCATION	TYPE	EXAMPLES	RATIONALE
Screeners	Qualifying questions	"Have you been snow skiing in the past 12 months?" "Do you own a pair of skis?"	To identify target respondents. Survey of ski owners who have skied in the past year.
First few questions	Warm-ups	"What brand of skis do you own?" "How many years have you owned them?"	Easy to answer shows respondent that survey is simple.
First third of questions	Transitions	"What features do you like best about the skis?"	Relate to research objectives, slightly more effort needed to answer.
Middle half of second third	Difficult and complicated	Following are 10 characteristics of snow skis. Please rate your skis on each characteristic using the scale below.	Respondent has committed to completing questionnaire and can see that just a few questions are left.
Last section	Classification and demographic	"What is the highest level of education you have attained?"	Some questions may be considered "personal" and respondent may leave them blank, but they are at the end of the survey.

1. *Use the screener questions to identify qualified respondents.* Most market research employs some variation of quota sampling. Only qualified respondents are interviewed, and specific minimum numbers (quotas) of various types of qualified respondents may be desired. A study on food products generally has quotas of users of specific brands, a magazine study screens for readers, a cosmetic study screens for brands awareness, and so forth.

   The **screeners** (screen questions) may be on the questionnaire, or, in many cases, a "screening questionnaire" may be provided. In this instance, a screener is filled out for everyone interviewed. Thus, any demographics obtained provide a basis for comparison against persons who qualify for the full study. A long screener can significantly increase the cost of the study. It means that you are obtaining more information from every contact with a respondent. Short screeners such as the one in Table 12.6 quickly eliminate unqualified persons and enable the interviewer to move immediately to the next potential respondent. Yet a longer screener can provide important information on the nature of nonusers, nontriers, or persons unaware of the product or service being researched.[12]

   Most important, screeners provide a basis for estimating the costs of a survey. A survey for which everyone qualified to be interviewed is going to be much cheaper than one with a 5 percent incidence rate, all else being equal. Many surveys are placed with field services at a flat rate per completed questionnaire. The rate is based on a stated "average interview time" and incidence rate. The screener is used to determine whether, in fact, the incidence rate holds true in a particular city. If it does not, the flat rate is adjusted accordingly.

screeners
Questions used to screen for appropriate respondents.

2. *After obtaining a qualified respondent, begin with a question that obtains a respondent's interest.* After introductory comments and screens to find a qualified respondent, the initial questions should be simple, interesting, and non-

TABLE 12.6 A Screening Questionnaire That Seeks Men 15 Years of Age and Older Who Shave at Least Three Times a Week with a Blade Razor

Hello. I'm from Data Facts Research. We are conducting a survey among men, and I'd like to ask you a few questions.

1. Do you or does any member of your family work for an advertising agency, market research firm, or a company that manufactures or sells shaving products?

(TERMINATE AND RECORD ON CONTACT RECORD SHEET)	Yes ( )
(CONTINUE WITH Q. 2)	No ( )

2. How old are you? Are you . . . (READ LIST)

(TERMINATE AND RECORD ON CONTACT RECORD SHEET) CHECK QUOTA CONTROL FORM—IF QUOTA GROUP FOR WHICH THE RESPONDENT QUALIFIES *IS NOT* FILLED, CONTINUE—IF QUOTA GROUP *IS* FILLED, THEN—TERMINATE AND RECORD)	Under 15 Yrs. Old ( ) 15 to 34 Yrs. Old ( ) Over 34 Yrs. Old ( )

3. The last time you shaved, did you use an electric razor or a razor that uses blades?

(TERMINATE AND RECORD ON CONTACT RECORD SHEET)	Electric Razor ( )
(CONTINUE WITH Q. 4)	Blade Razor ( )

4. How many times have you shaved in the past seven days?

   (IF LESS THAN THREE TIMES, TERMINATE AND RECORD ON CONTACT RECORD SHEET. IF THREE OR MORE TIMES, CONTINUE).

A Professional Researcher's Perspective

I must introduce you to Cohen's Law. It was developed by Dr. Louis Cohen, a man who is a "researcher's researcher" but unfortunately a bit obscure—not unlike Deming before the Japanese discovered his statistical theories for product quality. I offer you his research law only half-jokingly because I believe it is a major underlying dynamic of incorrect findings in marketing research. Cohen's Law states: "If you ask a question, you'll get an answer." The answer may be right, wrong, or somewhere in between, but you will always get an answer.

For example, ask consumers in a telephone interview whether they want nutritious snacks. Many will answer "yes" while munching on a chocolate-covered taco chip. Cohen's Law has real validity and operates every day in our research lives.

Cohen correctly pointed out, "Somehow, we feel that if a substantial number of respondents tell us what's important in buying a product, then the response is like money in the bank. After all, the responses came from consumers, those who 'vote' in the marketplace with their dollars." We have become absolutely convinced that consumers always have the right answers to the questions in our long, boring questionnaires. Do we really believe that respondents can rate four different brands on 40 attributes? Respondents couldn't care less by the time they get to rating the third or fourth brand. The whole experience for them is boring as well as exhausting.

Among the many demons in the art of asking questions is cognitive dissonance, which means that people cannot accept two psychological-

threatening. To open a questionnaire with an income or age question might be disastrous. These are often considered threatening and immediately put the respondent on the defensive. The initial question should be easy to answer without much forethought.

3. *Ask general questions first.* Once the interview proceeds beyond the opening "warm-up" questions, the questionnaire should proceed in a logical fashion. General questions are covered first to get the person thinking about a concept, company, or type of product, and then the questionnaire moves to the specifics. For example, a questionnaire on shampoo might begin with "Have you purchased a hair spray, hair conditioner, or hair shampoo within the past six weeks?" Then it would ask about the frequency of shampooing, brands purchased in the past three months, satisfaction and dissatisfaction with brands purchased, repurchase intent, characteristics of an "ideal" shampoo, respondent's hair characteristics, and finally demographics.

   The flow in the preceding example is logical. It initiates consumer thoughts on shampooing as it moves through the questionnaire and concludes with personal data. The shampoo format was taken from an actual questionnaire by a leading manufacturer. The interview lasted approximately 20 minutes. By the time the interviewer reached the personal data, the respondent ly conflicting thoughts, and the probability is high that they will dispose of the one that bothers them more. Gillette had lots of research indicating men were highly satisfied with Gillette Blue Blades. In reality, men were walking around with nicks, cuts, and scratches on their faces. It was only when they saw alternative, stainless steel blades from Wilkinson that the complaints about Blue Blades surfaced.

Remember Cohen's Law. Ask a question. Get an answer. Gillette asked lots of questions about Blue Blades. Nowhere in its research files was there any indication of dissatisfaction with Blue Blades. As Cohen noted, "Many product dissatisfactions and unsatisfied needs are hidden or camouflaged by cognitive dissonance. Most people would rather not go through life with problems and complaints on their minds." Do we really understand this observation in designing and thinking about marketing research?

About 10 years ago, General Foods did a study in which it asked children entering school and husbands going to work what they had eaten for breakfast. The interviewers then telephoned the mothers and wives of the respondents and asked them what they had served their families for breakfast that morning. There was a low correlation between the two groups. People lie to us when we ask questions, depending upon the circumstances of the interview and the subject.

Are we cognizant of these question pitfalls? Do we ever think about them? Or is our primary focus simply to ask questions, get answers, and run with numbers? There is inherent danger in talking to consumers. Our fixed way of doing things is kind of scary.[13] ■

was conditioned to answering questions. That is, a question-answer dialogue had been in progress for approximately 17 minutes; thus, the respondent continued to answer partially because of conditioning. Also, rapport had been established. By this time the respondent realized that it was definitely a legitimate request for information and not a sales pitch. Trust had been established and the interviewee is less reluctant to offer personal information.

4. *Ask questions that require "work" in the middle of the questionnaire.* Initially, the respondent is only vaguely interested and understanding of the nature of the survey. As the interest-building questions transpire, the interview process builds momentum and commitment to the interview. When the interviewer shifts to questions with scaled-response formats, the respondent must be motivated to understand the response categories and options. Alternatively, there might be questions that necessitate some recall or opinion formation on the part of the respondent. The interest, commitment, and rapport built up sustain the respondent in this part of the interview. Even if the self-administered method is used, the approach is the same: build interest and commitment early to motivate the respondent to finish the rest of the questionnaire.
5. *Insert "prompters" or strategic points.* Good interviewers can sense when a respondent's interest and motivation sag and will attempt to build them back

up. However, it is always worthwhile for the questionnaire designer to insert short encouragements at strategic locations in the questionnaire. These may be simple statements such as, "I only have a few more questions to go," or "This next section will be easier." On the other hand, they may be inserted as part of an introduction to a section, "Now that you have helped us with those comments, we would like to ask a few more questions"

6. *Position sensitive, threatening, and demographic questions at the end.* As mentioned earlier, occasions sometimes arise when the objectives of the study necessitate questions on topics about which respondents may feel uneasy. Embarrassing topics should be covered near the end of the questionnaire. Placing these questions at the end of the survey ensures that most of the questions will be answered before the respondent becomes defensive or breaks off the interview. Moreover, rapport has been established between the respondent and the interviewer by this time, increasing the likelihood of obtaining an answer. Another argument for placing sensitive questions toward the end is that by the time sensitive questions are asked, interviewees have been conditioned to respond. In other words, a pattern has been repeated many times. The interviewer asks a question and the respondent gives an answer. By the time embarrassing questions are asked, the respondent has become conditioned to reply.

Step Six: Evaluate the Questionnaire

Once a rough draft of the questionnaire has been designed, the marketing researcher is obligated to take a step back and critically evaluate it. This phase may seem redundant, given all the careful thought that went into each question. But recall the crucial role played by the questionnaire. At this point in the questionnaire development, the following items should be considered: (1) Is the question necessary? (2) Is the survey too long? and (3) Will the questions provide the answers to the survey objectives?

Is the Question Necessary? Perhaps the most important criterion for this phase of questionnaire development is ascertaining the necessity for a given question. Sometimes researchers and brand managers want to ask questions because "they were on the last survey we did like this," or because "it would be nice to know." Excessive demographics questions are very common. Education data, number of children in multiple age categories, and extensive demographics on the spouse are simply not warranted by the nature of many studies.

Each question must serve a purpose. It must be a screener, an interest generator, a required transition, or it must be directly and explicitly related to the stated objectives of this particular survey. Any question that fails to satisfy at least one of these criteria should be omitted.

Is the Questionnaire Too Long? At this point the researcher should role-play the questionnaire with volunteers acting as respondents. Although there is no magic number of interactions, the length of time it takes to complete the questionnaire should be averaged over a minimum of five trials. Any questionnaire to be administered in a mall or over the telephone that averages longer than 20 minutes should be a candidate for cutting. Sometimes mall interviews can run

A Professional Researcher's Perspective

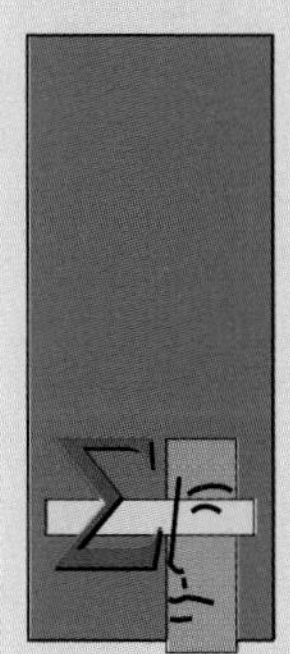

Susan Carroll, president of Words & Numbers Research Incorporated, offers the following tips on questionnaire design to improve both the response rate and data quality.

First, use nontraditional ways to structure questions on the questionnaire. The information you seek on the questionnaire should be like a wolf in sheep's clothing: simple in appearance, but sophisticated. This means that items on the questionnaire should be developed strategically. For example, instead of using the traditional rating scale for measuring importance of product features, ask respondents to divide 100 points among all the features, reflecting importance levels.

Second, mix up the response formats on items you ask respondents to complete. A survey that consists of all agree/disagree statements is like watching the same program on TV for five nights in a row. It is a sedative. Although there is no research on this, it is likely that questionnaires with the same types of response formats throughout get placed aside on the "to do" pile more often than those with variety built in. The respondent gets bored and puts off completion until later, which never comes.

Third, questionnaires should have specific sets of directions for each group or section of items. Do not assume that respondents know what you want them to do. Be clear in stating directions. There is nothing more aggravating than getting through half a questionnaire and being confused in the middle. Now you want to toss the questionnaire out even though you have wasted some of your time.

Fourth, pay attention to visual appearances of questionnaires. How many times do we receive questionnaires in which the appearance gets an "F" in Communications 101? Questionnaires that are black on white with no shading are difficult for the eye to follow. The same goes for using italics throughout a questionnaire; save it for wedding invitations. Type that is too small to read without a magnifying glass reflects poor judgment all the time, not just when you are surveying an aging population.

Important decisions such as putting boxes around groups of questions; using dark ink (preferably black) on light stock; shading multiple-response questions in the layout; selecting clean, clear typeface; having a short, attractive cover letter; and using lines to take the respondent's eye from question to response make a difference in whether the respondent will respond.

Fifth, number all sections, and number all items in each section. When the respondent sees that section one has items one through five, she is more likely to do all five. It is easy for the eye to miss a question because it is not numbered. For example, if you present the questions like this, you might get that important clarification you need:

4. Has our company improved, stayed the same, or declined?
5. How?

These five pointers may make a difference in boosting return rates, and higher return rates mean better information for strategic planning and action.[14] ■

slightly longer if an incentive is provided to the respondent. In-home interviews that last more than 45 minutes also should offer the respondent some incentive.

Common incentives are movie tickets, pen and pencil sets, and cash or checks. The use of incentives often actually lowers the survey costs because response rates increase and terminations during the interview decrease. If checks are used instead of cash, the canceled checks can be used to create a list of survey participants for follow-up purposes.

Will the Questions Provide the Desired Information to Accomplish the Research Objectives? The researcher must make certain that a sufficient number and type of questions are contained within the questionnaire to meet the decision-making needs of management. A suggested procedure is to carefully review the written objectives for the research project. Next, the researcher should go down the questionnaire and write each question number next to the objective that the particular question will help accomplish. For example, question 1 applies to objective 3, question 2 to objective 2, and so forth. If a question cannot be tied to an objective, the researcher should determine whether the list of objectives is complete. If the list is sufficient, the question should be omitted. Also, if after going through the entire questionnaire there is an objective with no questions listed beside it, appropriate questions should be added to the questionnaire.

Some very good advice on evaluating questionnaires comes from a woman who has evaluated thousands over the years. Joan Fredericks, president of Joan Fredericks Field Service, offers "dos" and "don'ts" in the "Marketing Research in Practice" feature on pages 428–429.

The objective of a good questionnaire layout is to make the tasks of the interviewer and respondent as clear, logical, and simple as possible. Several key considerations of layout and design follow.

Appearances of Mail and Self-Administered Questionnaires The appearance of a questionnaire that will be filled in by the respondent is a major determinant of the response rate. The questionnaire should be as professional looking as possible. It should be printed on high-quality paper and have a "typeset" appearance. If the questionnaire is four pages or longer, the researcher should consider putting it in a booklet format. Booklets are easy to use, look professional, and, when stapled, minimize the problems of lost pages.

Avoid a Cluttered Look The questionnaire should allow for plenty of open space. Rows and columns of answers should be spread far enough apart so that the interviewer or respondent can easily pick the proper row or column. A questionnaire that attempts to cram as much material on a page as possible appears busy, complex, and difficult. Crowded questionnaires lead to more incorrect replies being recorded. Naturally, if a questionnaire looks difficult and foreboding, it will have a negative effect on a person's willingness to participate in the study.

A mistake that is often made by novice questionnaire designers is to try to reduce the number of pages of a questionnaire by cramming material together. It is preferable by far to have a questionnaire that runs one or two pages longer and has an open, inviting format than a shorter, cluttered appearance.

Allow Plenty of Space for Open-ended Responses An open-ended question that allows half a line for a reply usually will receive a reply of that length and nothing more. Generally speaking, three to five lines (using 8½-inch-wide paper) are deemed sufficient for open-ended replies. The researcher must use his judgment on how much detail is desirable for an open-ended reply. Answer space for "Which department store did you visit most recently?" requires much less space. However, a follow-up question that asks, "What factors were most important in your decision to go to (Name of department store)?" requires substantially more lines for the response.

Consider Color Coding the Questionnaires If the research project is based upon interviewing specific groups of respondents, it is desirable to color code the questionnaires. For example, a racket manufacturer has placed a prototype racket (made of a new alloy) with 300 people who play racket sports at least twice a week. The sample consists of three groups of 100 each: racquetball players, tennis players, and squash players. Although the questionnaire focuses on the prototype racket, the questions vary somewhat depending upon the sport being played. To avoid confusion among the interviewers, the tennis questionnaires are green, the racquetball questionnaires are blue, and the squash questionnaires are white.

Instructions Printed Within the Questionnaire Should be in Capital Letters To avoid confusion and to clarify what is a question and what is an instruction, all instructions should be in capital letters. Capitalizing helps bring the instructions to the interviewers' or respondents' attention. For example, "IF 'YES' TO QUESTION 13, SKIP TO QUESTION 17."

Step Seven: Obtain Approval of All Relevant Parties

At this point in the questionnaire design process, the first draft of the questionnaire has been completed. Copies of it should be distributed to all parties that have direct authority over the project. Practically speaking, managers may step in at any time in the design process with new information, requests, or concerns. Wherever this arises, revisions are often necessitated. It is still important to get final approval of the first draft even if managers have already interceded in the development process.

Managerial approval commits management to obtaining a body of information via a specific instrument (questionnaire). If the question is not asked, the data will not be gathered. Thus, questionnaire approval tacitly reaffirms what decision-making information is needed and how it will be obtained. For example, assume that a new product questionnaire asks about shape, material, end use, and packaging. Once the form is approved, the new product development manager is implying that "I know what color the product will be" or "Is it not important to determine color at this time."

Step Eight: Pretest and Revise

When final managerial approval has been obtained, the questionnaire must be pretested. No survey should be taken without a pretest. Moreover, a **pretest** does

pretest
A trial run of a questionnaire.

Marketing Research in Practice

The ideal questionnaire doesn't exist. What suits the purpose of one study often proves wrong for another.

The first three dos are basic rules that can provide a solid foundation on which to build your questionnaire.

1. A questionnaire must be written as a conversation *with—not an interrogation of*—a respondent.
2. It must be arranged in a logical sequence, not in a maze apt to confuse and puzzle respondents, embarrassing them in efforts to extricate themselves, or to say it in researchese, answering just anything to get out.
3. At the beginning of each questionnaire, briefly do provide respondents with the purpose of being asked for information. Respondents are entitled to know. Put additional explanations in parentheses to use when needed.
4. Do use proper punctuation marks. They separate sentences, independent clauses, and parenthetical phrases. They may be used to make meanings more clearly understood, to emphasize, or to give pause for absorption of one part of your communication before moving to the next. Also of help are all capitalized letters, underlining, etc.
5. Do allow for "don't knows." Many authors leave "don't knows" off a questionnaire. If respondents have never seen or heard of "Whatchamacallit," why force them into a "cooperative," friendly, but meaningless reply? Also, remember that too many "don't knows," can be a problem because you don't obtain meaningful information.
6. Do provide pronunciations in brackets for words that differ in

not mean that one researcher should administer the questionnaire to another researcher. Ideally, a pretest is done by the best interviewers who will ultimately be working on the job and is administered to target respondents for the study. They are told to look for misinterpretations by respondents, lack of continuity, poor skip patterns, additional alternatives for precoded and closed-ended questions, and general respondent reaction to the interview. The pretest also should be conducted in the same mode as the final interview. If the study is to be door to door, then the pretest should be the same.

Researchers should consider coding and tabulating the pretest data. The data should be put into tabular form and simple cross tabulations and other statistical routines carried out where possible. This will give the researcher a rough notion of the type of output that will be generated from the study and its adequacy to answer the study objectives. Also, the hypothetical tables will confirm the need for various sets of data. If there is no place to put the responses to a question, either the data are superfluous or some contemplated analysis was omitted. If various parts of the country. If you've been met anywhere with "Oh, we call that. . .," then you know already that proper research prior to writing a questionnaire will help in preventing embarrassment on all sides.

Now for the don'ts:

1. Don't begin with, "I would like to ask you. . . " Who are you? Speaking on what authority? Far better to say "We," and even that shouldn't be overdone. On a five-page questionnaire, it was found 11 times. A bit overwhelming right? Why not simply say, "Now the next question. . ." and say it quickly. They know you didn't come to play bridge.
2. Don't say, "Would you mind. . ." Why should they? Why enter a negative thought? In the same vein, rule out "Can you" and "Could you." Why deflate a respondent's ego and self-confidence.
3. Don't use lengthly, unfamiliar words unless they justified the topic of study. Why use "conversely" rather than "on the contrary?" Why use "noxious" rather than "hurtful"? Why use "pernicious" rather than "harmful"? There's always the danger a respondent might pretend, or honestly believe, to understand and offer completely irrelevant answers.
4. Don't use words that could sound like something else.
5. Don't preface sentences with "You might want to. . ." or "You might not want to. . ." These might influence respondents in having to make a certain choice. If a respondent doesn't like the flow of the copy—or the interviewer—the outcome may differ radically from expectations due to such negative influences. Watch behavioral attitudes.[15] ■

some part of a table remains empty, a necessary question may have been omitted. Trial tabulations show, as no previous method can, that all data collected will be put to use, and that all necessary data will be obtained.[16]

After completion of the pretest, any necessary changes should be made. Approval should then be reobtained before going into the field. If the pretest resulted in extensive design and question alterations, a second pretest would be in order.

Step Nine: Prepare Final Questionnaire Copy

Even the final copy phase does not allow the researcher to relax. Precise typing instructions, spacing, numbering, and precoding must be set up, monitored, and proofread. In some instances the questionnaire may be photoreduced to save space, or it even may be specifically folded and stapled. In general, the quality of copying and the paper used is a function of who will see the questionnaire. In a mail survey, compliance and subsequent response rates may be affected positively by a professional appearance. For telephone interviews, in contrast, the quality is of much less importance; the copy simply must be readable.

Step Ten: Implementing the Survey

The completion of the questionnaire establishes the basis for obtaining the desired decision-making information from the marketplace. A series of forms and procedures also must be issued with the questionnaire to make certain that the data are gathered correctly, efficiently, and at a reasonable cost. Depending on the data collection method, these include supervisor's instructions, interviewer instructions, screeners, call record sheets, and visual aids.

Supervisor's Instructions

As discussed in Chapter 3, most research interviewing is conducted by field services. It is the service's job to complete the interviews and send them back to the researcher. In essence, field services are the production line of the marketing research industry.

supervisor's instructions
Written directions to the field service on how to conduct the survey.

Supervisor's instructions inform them of the nature of the study, start and completion dates, quotas, reporting times, equipment and facility requirements, sampling instructions, number of interviewers required, and validation procedures. In addition, detailed instructions are required for any taste test that involves food preparation. Quantities typically are measured and cooked using rigorous measurement techniques and devices.

The supervisor's instructions are a vitally important part of any study. They establish the parameters under which the research is conducted. Without clear instructions, the interview may be conducted 10 different ways in 10 cities. A sample page from a set of supervisor's instructions is shown in Table 12.7.

Interviewer's Instructions

interviewer's instructions
Written directions to the interviewer on how to conduct the interview.

Interviewer's instructions cover many of the same points as supervisor's instructions but are geared to the actual interview. The nature of the study is explained, sampling methodology is given, and reporting forms and times are given. Often a sample interview is included with detailed instructions on skip patterns, probing, and quotas. A sample page of interviewer's instructions is shown in Table 12.8.

Interviewer Training in the United Kingdom More survey research is conducted in the United States and the United Kingdom than in any other countries. Yet the survey research industries are quite different in the two countries. For example, the average length of employment of an interviewer with a field service in England is five years, compared with 14 months in the United States. This is probably because of higher relative pay in the United Kingdom and fewer alternative employment opportunities. The biggest difference between the two countries, however, is the amount of control and influence the Market Research Society (MRS) has over survey research in the United Kingdom. Its organizational counterpart in the United States, the Marketing Research Association (MRA), has relatively little influence and control over survey research. The influ-

TABLE 12.7 A Sample Page of Supervisor's Instructions for a Diet Soft Drink Taste Test

Purpose	To determine from diet soft drink users their ability to discriminate among three samples of Diet Dr. Pepper and give opinions and preferences between two of the samples.
Staff	3–4 experienced interviewers per shift.
Location	One busy shopping center in a middle to upper-middle socioeconomic area. The center's busiest hours are to be worked by a double shift of interviewers. In the center, 3–4 private interviewing stations are to be set up and a refrigerator and good counter space made available for product storage and preparation.
Quota	192 completed interviews broken down as follows: A minimum of 70 Diet Dr. Pepper users A maximum of 122 other diet brand users
Project Materials	For this study, you are supplied the following: 250 Screening Questionnaires 192 Study Questionnaires 4 Card A's
Product/Preparation	For this study, our client shipped to your refrigerated facility 26 cases of soft drink product. Each case contains 24 10-oz. bottles—312 coded with an *F* on the cap, 312 with an *S*. Each day, you are to obtain from the refrigerated facility approximately 2–4 cases of product—1–2 of each code. Product must be transported in coolers and kept refrigerated at the location. It should remain at approximately 42°F. In the center, you are to take one-half of the product coded *F* and place the #23 stickers on the bottles. The other half of the *F* product should receive #46 stickers. The same should be done for product *S*—one-half should be coded #34, the other half #68. A supervisor should do this task before interviewing begins. Interviewers will select product by *code number*. Code number stickers are enclosed for this effort. Each respondent will be initially testing three product samples as designated on the questionnaire. Interviewers will come to the kitchen, select the three designated bottles, open and pour 4 oz. of each product into its corresponding coded cup. The interviewer should cap and *refrigerate* leftover product when finished pouring and take only the three *cups* of product on a tray to respondent.

ence and control over survey research by the MRS is through its Interviewer Quality Control Scheme (IQCS). Although only 19 percent of the marketing research firms and field services in the United Kingdom are part of the IQCS, the organizations are by far the largest in the industry and account for most of the research revenues.

Call Record Sheets

Call record sheets are used to measure the efficiency of the interviewers. The form normally indicates the number of contacts and the results of the contact (see Table 12.9). A supervisor can examine calls per hour, contacts per completed interview, average time per interview, and similar measures to analyze an interviewer's efficiency. If, for example, contacts per completed interview are high, the field supervisor should examine the reasons behind it. Perhaps the interviewer is not using a proper approach or the area may be difficult to cover.

call record sheets
Interviewers' logos listing the number and results of a contact.

A researcher can use aggregated data for all interviewers of a field service to measure field service efficiency. A high cost per interview for a field service might be traced to a large number of contacts per completed interview. This, in turn, may be due to poor interviewer selection and training by the field service.

TABLE 12.8 A Sample Page of Interviewer Instructions for a Magazine Readership Study

Purpose	The purpose of this study is to determine a relationship between people's attitudes and the magazines they read regularly.
Method	All interviewing is to be conducted by telephone within your local dialing area. We will neither use nor pay for any work not conducted in exact accordance with our job instructions.
When to Interview	Begin interviewing immediately. All interviewing is to be conducted from 5:30 P.M. to 9:30 P.M. weekdays and all day Saturday. You also may interview on Sunday. All work is to be completed by Sunday, November 5.
Sample Lists	You have been provided with Sample Lists. You are to interview the person in the household who reads the magazine and is a qualified respondent. Use the Sample Lists and try to complete interviews with subscribers or readers of affluent publications.
Eligible Respondents	A respondent is eligible if 1. The total annual family income is above $25,000 and 2. He or she is employed in one of the prelisted categories in Q. B.
Quota	You are to complete a total of 13 interviews.
Call Record Sheets	You are to use the Call Record Sheet to list the name and telephone number of each call you make. All telephone numbers and listings are to be done during the interviewing hours. We *will not* pay for additional time for looking up numbers and listings. Record the outcome of each call you make.
Validation Forms	We have included Validation Forms on which you must list information about completed interviews. A properly filled out Validation Form must accompany each delivery of work you make to your supervisor. Fill in all the information required at the top of the form. Then, fill in the following: ■ Under "Quota Group", name of magazine. ■ Under "Sex", sex of respondent. ■ Under "Respondent Name", write in the full name. ■ Under "Telephone Number", write in the phone number.

Visual Aids and Other Supplements

Many studies use visual aids to facilitate the interviewing process. These range from simple "show cards" that enumerate alternatives to closed-ended questions to videotape players that show test commercials or a product in use. In product studies, a test product or products are often left with the respondent. This can present logistics difficulties if weight or perishability is a problem. Consider, for example, a door-to-door ice cream study in the summertime in which each respondent is given a half gallon of three different test products. In this case, the product was packed in Styrofoam containers of 15 half gallons. Each box contained dry ice, thus avoiding the melting problem. However, the boxes were so large that most interviewers could get only one or two in their car. There was a tremendous increase in interviewer mileage and travel time over a typical study because of the continual return to the frozen food locker for additional product. As you can see by now, the researcher's job is just beginning when the questionnaire design is completed.

field management companies

Firms that provide support services such as questionnaire formatting, screener writing, and data collection to full-service research companies.

Field Management Companies

Conducting fieldwork is much easier today than in years past. The stereotypical "kitchen table" field service is passing into history. In its place are companies that specialize in field management.[17] **Field management companies** such as

TABLE 12.9 The Call Record Sheet for a Deodorant Study

	DATE	DATE	DATE	DATE
Total Completions	______	______	______	______
Quota A	______	______	______	______
Quota B	______	______	______	______
Terminate at	______	______	______	______
Q. A	______	______	______	______
Q. B.	______	______	______	______
Q. C—No deodorant/antiperspirant	______	______	______	______
Q. D—No Roll-On	______	______	______	______
Q. E—Ban Full	______	______	______	______
Q. E—"Other" Full	______	______	______	______
Q. F—Refusal	______	______	______	______
Q. G—No Telephone	______	______	______	______
Total Incomplete Contacts	______	______	______	______
No One Home	______	______	______	______
No Woman Available	______	______	______	______
Refused	______	______	______	______
Language/Hearing	______	______	______	______
Respondent Break-Off	______	______	______	______
Knows Respondent	______	______	______	______
Other	______	______	______	______
Briefing Hours	______	______	______	______
Interviewing Hours	______	______	______	______
Travel Hours	______	______	______	______
Mileage	______	______	______	______

QFact, On-Line Communications, and Direct Resource generally provide questionnaire formatting, screener writing, development of instructional and peripheral materials, shipping departments, field auditing, and all coordination of data collection, coding, and tab services required for the project. Upon study completion, they typically provide a single, consolidated invoice for the project. Generally lean on staff, these companies are designed to provide the services clients need without attempting to compete with the design and analytical capabilities of full-service companies and ad agency research staffs.

In fact, a number of full-service companies and qualitative professionals also have discovered that field management can cost-effectively increase their productivity by allowing them to take on more projects using fewer of their internal resources.

One example of this is the newly formed business relationship between Heakin Research and M/A/R/C, which hired Heakin to handle field management on particular types of studies. Likewise, several qualitative researchers have developed ongoing relationships with field management companies who function as extensions of the consultant's staff, setting up projects and freeing up the researcher to conduct groups, write reports, and consult with clients.

Of course, like any other segment of the research industry, field management does have its limitations. By definition, field management companies generally do not provide design and analytical capabilities. This means that their clients may, on occasion, need to seek other providers to meet their full-service needs.

A Professional Researcher's Perspective

Quite simply, field management is not for everyone. However, if one or more of the following conditions exist in your company or department, it may be right for you:

- You design and analyze or moderate some or all of your own research
- Your staff is stretched to the limit
- Your time is better spent dealing with clients than handling the details of fielding custom projects
- You demand value for your research dollar.

Once you've made the decision to try field management, it is important to select the company that best meets the specific needs of your organization. Consider the following factors when selecting a field management company:

EXPERIENCE

How long has the company provided field management service? For what types of companies has the company worked? What is the company's track record on the types of projects or with the types of respondents you need most often?

SPECIALIZATION

Many field management companies specialize in particular methodologies or study types such as large, difficult, or ongoing projects. Some have international expertise, others don't. Make certain that you get the most qualified company by probing their areas of expertise.

DATA COLLECTION SUPPLIERS

Some field management companies also operate their own data collection or qualitative facilities. Although this is neither good nor bad by definition, the slight edge goes to those who operate well-regarded facilities since they know what it takes to accomplish projects accurately and often provide more realistic expectations and more effective troubleshooting.

Additionally, as a relatively new segment of the industry, experience, services, and standards vary tremendously from firm to firm. It's advisable to carefully screen prospective companies and check references.

These limitations notwithstanding, field management provides a way for researchers to increase their productivity while cost-effectively maintaining the quality of the information on which their company's decisions and commitments are made.

Maura Isaacs, of QFact Marketing Research of Cincinnati, discusses some factors to consider when choosing a field management company in "A Professional Researcher's Perspective" feature in this section.

Summary

This chapter examines the objectives of the questionnaire, as well as its construction and evaluation. After defining a questionnaire and explaining its role in the data collection process, the criteria for a good questionnaire are established. These criteria are categorized into the following topic areas:

Additionally, probe their criteria for selecting the data collection companies to whom they field out work. Although your specific experience with various firms may be different from theirs, try to understand their basis for selection. Also, ask them how often and on what basis they review these suppliers.

STAFF

The backgrounds of the staff and principals may be very telling. Probing length of time both in research and with the current firm may either be reassuring or send up red flags.

RESOURCES

Make certain that the firm you select has the resources you most need in-house. Examples of this might include an inbound 800 number for status reports, sizable storage space and a fully equipped shipping department for product storage, or experienced field auditors on staff. Over the long run, your costs will be lower given in-house availability of the services and facilities you most need. In addition, in-house resources may indicate the true volume of a particular type of project in which the company has indicated specialization.

INTANGIBLES

Are you looking for a research partner, an extension of your company or department, or a supplier? How do the companies you interview view client relationships? What is the business philosophy of the companies you talk with? Is that philosophy compatible with your own? What are the operating standards and quality control procedures? How much effort does each company put forth to answer your questions? What is their level of detail orientation? And, most importantly, are you comfortable with the people you interview?[18] ■

1. Achieving the goals of the study
2. Fitting the questionnaire to the respondent
3. Editing, coding, and data processing

The bulk of this chapter is devoted to the process of developing a questionnaire. This process is addressed in a sequential format beginning with survey objectives, resources, and constraints. The process continues with these steps:

1. Determine data collection method
2. Determine question response format
3. Decide question wording
4. Establish questionnaire flow and layout
5. Evaluate the questionnaire
6. Obtain approval from all relevant parties
7. Pretest and revise questionnaire
8. Prepare final copy
9. Implement questionnaire

Specific attention is paid to distinguishing among the three different types of questions (open ended, closed ended, and scaled response) and the advantages and disadvantages of each. In addition, guidelines are introduced to facilitate the proper wording and positioning of questions within the questionnaire.

This chapter concludes with special procedures necessary for successful implementation of the survey. These steps are used to ensure that the data are gathered properly. Supervisor's instructions, interviewer's instructions, call record sheet, and visual aids are discussed within this context. We also note that many research organizations are now turning to field management companies to actually conduct the interviews.

Key Terms

questionnaire
editing
coding
survey objectives
open-ended questions
closed-ended questions
dichotomous questions
multiple-choice questions
scaled-response questions
screeners
pretest
supervisor's instructions
interviewer's instructions
call record sheets
field management companies

Review and Discussion Questions

1. Explain the role of the questionnaire in the research process.
2. How do respondents influence the design of a questionnaire? Suggest some examples, such as questionnaires designed for engineers, welfare recipients, baseball players, generals in the army, and migrant farmworkers.
3. Discuss the advantages and disadvantages of open-ended questions and closed-ended questions.
4. Outline the procedure for developing a questionnaire. Assume that you are developing a questionnaire for a new sandwich for McDonalds. Use this situation to discuss the questionnaire development.
5. Give examples of poor questionnaire wording. What is wrong with each of these questions?
6. Once a questionnaire is developed, what other factors need to be considered before putting the questionnaire into the hands of interviewers?
7. Why is pretesting a questionnaire important? Are there some situations in which pretesting can be forgone?
8. Design three open-ended and three closed-ended questions to measure consumers' attitudes toward BMW automobiles.
9. What's wrong with the following questions?
   a. How do you like the flavor of this high-quality Maxwell House coffee?
   b. What do you think of the taste and texture of this Sara Lee coffee cake?
   c. We are conducting a study for Bulova watches. What do you think of the quality of Bulova watches?
   d. How far do you live from the closest mall?
   e. Who in your family shops for clothes?
   f. Where do you buy most of your clothes?
10. What do you see as the major advantages of using a field management company? What about drawbacks?

CASE 12.1

American Airlines

American Airlines, like most service businesses today, is interested in building and maintaining long-term relationships with its customers by providing excellent customer service. Marketing research is a key link in the customer service process. It is the feedback mechanism that allows management to evaluate and control the level of service it is providing. Sometimes the airline also will evaluate other factors such as attitudes toward the economic environment. American Airlines surveys its passengers on selected flights. The following questionnaire was administered on one of these flights.

AMERICAN AIRLINES PASSENGER SURVEY

1. What is this Flight Number? ______________________ Date __________
2. In which cabin are you seated? 25
   First Class. . . ______ 1 Business Class. . . ______ 2 Coach. . . ______ 3
3. All things considered, what is your overall opinion of this flight? 26
   Excellent. . . ______ 1 Good. . . ______ 2 Fair. . . ______ 3 Poor. . . ______ 4
4. Are you flying on a discount fare today?
   Yes. . . ______ 1 No. . . ______ 2 27
5. What is (was) the principal reason for your taking this trip?
   (Please check the *one* most compelling.) 28–29

Primary Business		Primarily Personal/Pleasure	
Standard business trip	______ 01	Visit Friends/relatives	______ 06
Convention, trade show, etc.	______ 02	Sightsee, visit resort, cruise	______ 07
Company training/sales meeting	______ 03	Personal emergency	______ 08
Military duty	______ 04	Moving residence/going to or from school	______ 09
Other	______ 05	Other	______ 10

   Combination
   Accompanying family member/friend on their business trip ______ 11
   Equally compelling business and personal/pleasure reasons ______ 12
6. Have you ever flown on a commercial airline before this trip? 30
   Yes ______ 1 No ______ 2
7. Of all the airline trips you made during the past 12 months, how many were for: (COUNT A ROUND TRIP AS ONE TRIP)

	Number of Trips	
Pleasure or personal reasons	______	31–32
Business reasons	______	33–34
None in past 12 months	______	35
		36

8. Do you expect to use a commercial airline more, or less, during the next 12 months than during the past 12 months for:

	More 1	Less 2	About the same 3	Don't Know 4	
Pleasure or personal reasons	______	______	______	______	37
Business reasons	______	______	______	______	38
					39–42

   To help us plan our own development programs, we would like to have your general impressions of the economic conditions in the country as a whole. 49
9. How do you think business conditions are today? 43
   Good ______ 1 Mixed, Some Good and Some Bad ______ 2 Bad ______ 3
10. How do you expect business conditions in this country to be during the next 12 months? 44
    Better ______ 1 About the same ______ 2 Worse ______ 3
11. Do you feel that this is a good time, or a bad time, for people like yourself to make major purchases for their home or family (such things as major appliances, furniture, or home renovations)? 45

A Good Time to Buy ______ 1 Uncertain, It Depends ______ 2
A Bad Time to Buy ______ 3

12. The one most important factor in determining your response to 11 was: 46
Interest rates ______ 1
Prices ______ 2
Purchase necessity ______ 3
Personal circumstances ______ 4
General feeling about the economy, the government, or business conditions ______ 5
Other ______ 6 47–48

13a. Do you expect the rate of inflation in the next 12 months to: 49
Increase ______ 1 Remain about the Same ______ 2 Decrease ______ 3

b. Do you expect unemployment in the next 12 months to: 50
Increase ______ 1 Remain about the Same ______ 2 Decrease ______ 3

14. Do you think stock prices, on the average, will be higher or lower six months from now?
Higher ______ 1 About the Same ______ 2 Lower ______ 3

We also are interested in your general impressions of how you feel you are getting along these days.

15a. Compared with a year ago, would you say that you are now financially: 52
Better Off ______ 1 About the Same ______ 2 Worse Off ______ 3

b. How about a year from now, do you expect to be financially: 53
Better Off ______ 1 About the Same ______ 2 Worse Off ______ 3

c. Compared with a year ago, would you say your current rate of savings is: 54
Greater ______ 1 About the Same ______ 2 Worse Off ______ 3

16. All things considered, how would you describe the value of the transportation and service received on today's flight in relation to your fare? 55
A Real Bargain ______ 1 Priced about Right ______ 2 Priced Too High______ 3 56–64

17. What is your occupation? 65–66
Executive or managerial ______ 01
Professional ______ 02
Teacher or professor ______ 03
Sales representative/agent ______ 04
Government or military ______ 05
Secretarial, clerical, office worker, sales clerk ______ 06
Craftsman, mechanic, serviceworker, operative ______ 07
Homemaker ______ 08
Airline employee/Travel agent ______ 09
Student ______ 10
Retired ______ 11
Other ______ 12

18. Your total annual family income before taxes: (Estimate in U.S. Dollars) 67
Under $20,000 ______ 1
$20,000–$29,000 ______ 2
$30,000–$39,000 ______ 3
$40,000–$49,000 ______ 4
$50,000–$59,000 ______ 5
$60,000–$69,000 ______ 6
$70,000–$79,000 ______ 7
$80,000–$89,000 ______ 8
$90,000–$99,000 or more ______ 9
$100,000 or more ______ 0

19. What is the highest level of academic study you have completed? 68
Less than high school ______ 1
High school ______ 2
Junior college/trade school ______ 3
Some college ______ 4
College Graduate ______ 5
Postgraduate degree ______ 6

20. Your Age: 69
18–21 years ______ 1
22–29 years ______ 2
30–39 years ______ 3
40–49 years ______ 4
50–59 years ______ 5
60–64 years ______ 6
65–69 years ______ 7
70 or older ______ 8

21. Your sex: Male: ______ 1 Female: ______ 1 70

22. Your marital status: 71
Single: ______ 1 Married: ______ 2 Widowed: ______ 3

23. If you live in a U.S. postal area, what is your zip code? 72–76

____
zip code

Thank you for your cooperation.

1. What do you think were the objectives of this research?
2. Critique the questionnaire flow.
3. How would the questionnaire have been different if it had been a telephone survey? Be specific.

CASE 12.2

Arrow Cleaners

S. T. Arrow owned a chain of dry cleaners in Portland, Oregon. Competition from One-Hour Martinizing and a regional chain had lowered Arrow's market share from 14 percent to 12 percent. Moreover, his overall profits had fallen 11 percent from the previous year. Arrow decided that an aggressive marketing strategy was in order. Before establishing such a strategy, he felt that a thorough study of the dry cleaning market was needed. The following questionnaire was created by Arrow and was given to each customer as he left one of his stores.

DRY CLEANING QUESTIONNAIRE

Name ______

Address ______

Phone Number ______

Where do you take your dry cleaning and laundry?

______

How much do you spend on dry cleaning/laundry? ______

Sex: Male ______ Female ______

Age Group: Under 30 ______ 30–40 ______ 40–50 ______ 50–60 ______ Over 60 ______

Marital Status: Single ______ Married ______

Income: Under $5,000 ______ $5,000–25,000 ______ $25,000–60,000 ______ Over $60,000 ______

Number living in home: Alone ______ 2 people ______ 3 people ______ 4 people ______ 5 people or more ______

Home: ______ Rent ______ Own ______ What type of housing? ______

Education: High School Graduate ______ Associate Degree ______ Bachelor's Degree ______ Master's Degree ______ More ______

1. How long have you been using your dry cleaner? ______
2. How would you rate it? Great ______ Good ______ OK ______ Not Too Good ______ Bad ______

4. The Dry Cleaning Establishment	I now use offers	I would like to use would offer
Convenience		
— All work done on premises	______	______
— Wash'n'wear cleaning services	______	______
— Pressing 'while you wait'	______	______
— Washing 'while you wait'	______	______
— A drive-through window	______	______
— Computerized receipts and organization	______	______
— Shirt laundry service	______	______
— An outlet for drop off/pick up	______	______
— Machines to pick up/drop off after hours	______	______
— A special for people moving into a new location where the cleaners pick up, clean, and deliver rugs and drapes for new home	______	______
5. Services		
— Shoe repair	______	______
— Shoe shining	______	______
— Mending	______	______
— Altering and tailoring	______	______
— Hand pressing	______	______
— Dyeing	______	______
— Summer/winter clothing storage	______	______
— Hand laundering	______	______
— Sponged and pressed	______	______
— Fur storage	______	______
6. For Sale		
— Ties and other accessories	______	______
— Spot removers, lint brushes, etc.	______	______
— Buttons, thread, zippers, etc.	______	______
— Woolite	______	______

7. Who in your home drops off/picks up the dry cleaning/laundry?

— Wife/mother/self	______	______
— Husband/father/self	______	______
— Each decides their own clothing is ready	______	______
— We take turns	______	______

8. Who within the household decides that the clothing is in need of dry cleaning?

— Wife/mother/self	______	______
— Husband/father/self	______	______
— Each decides their own clothing is ready	______	______
— Other family member/self	______	______

9. Please check one for each topic.

	A) I am this type	B) I would like to remain as this type
— 'I hate housework. I just hate having to do it.'	______	______
— 'I'd rather pay more to enjoy more. It's easier to pay someone to clean my home and clothes so I'm free to do what I want to do.'	______	______
— 'I enjoy being at home. I was brought up believing a woman's place is in the home and that's where I'm happy.'	______	______
— 'I like cleaning my home. It gives me a good feeling.'	______	______
— 'Since I have small children, I'm at home, so I clean. But if I were working, it would be easier to have someone come in.'	______	______
— 'I don't feel right having someone else cleaning up after me. I find myself cleaning before they come and after they leave. They don't clean the way I do.'	______	______

10. Check the phrase in each group that best describes (Check one for each column)

	Your present dry cleaner	The way you would like your dry cleaner to be or remain as
A) Makes me feel like an intruder	______	______
Keeps me waiting	______	______
Businesslike	______	______
Always has a friendly word	______	______
B) Gives the feeling he's too busy for me	______	______
Forgets my name when they're crowded	______	______
Always says hello even when they're busy	______	______
Takes the time to treat me individually no matter what	______	______
C) There's a chemical odor and the posters are outdated and curled at the ends	______	______
There's nothing noticeable about the shop good or bad	______	______
The shop smells clean, the clothes are scientifically racked, and the posters are helpful	______	______
D) Standardized service	______	______
Efficient, but distant	______	______
Interested in personal requirements	______	______
Goes out of their way to please	______	______
E) The shop leaves an unkempt impression	______	______
Neat, but cluttered store	______	______
There is space to move around	______	______
The shop has a warm, cared-for look	______	______
F) The store could use a thorough cleaning	______	______
The shop is acceptably clean	______	______

Assuringly sanitary store	______	______
G) There's never an answer to questions	______	______
I must point out spots, belts, loose buttons	______	______
We discuss whether it can be cleaned	______	______
The dry cleaner explains particular processes and new chemicals	______	______

1. Critique S. T. Arrow's questionnaire.
2. What additional topics should have been covered?
3. Discuss the sampling procedure.
4. Did S. T. Arrow develop his questionnaire in a scientific manner?

CHAPTER 13

Basic Sampling Issues

LEARNING OBJECTIVES

1. To understand the concept of sampling.
2. To learn the steps in developing a sampling plan.
3. To distinguish between probability samples and nonprobability samples.
4. To understand the concepts of sampling error and nonsampling error.
5. To review the types of probability sampling methods.
6. To gain insight into nonprobability sampling methods.

Adele Johnson is marketing director for Citycell. Citycell provides cellular telephone service in a large California metropolitan area. Based on careful analysis of Citycell subscribers and other marketing research, Johnson has developed a very good profile of her target customer. She is preparing a $2-million advertising campaign for the coming year and is uncertain about two different creative approaches suggested by Citycell's advertising agency. Before selecting one of the approaches and giving the agency approval to produce commercials, Johnson feels that she needs to do some marketing research.

She is currently considering a marketing research proposal prepared by a research firm that she has worked with in the past. She has considerable confidence in the competence of the research supplier. The research firm has suggested two alternative approaches for collecting the necessary data. The first approach is built around telephone interviewing. The firm has suggested that telephone numbers be generated at random, that all interviewing be conducted from its central location telephone facility, and that a sample size of 400 be employed for the study. The firm has indicated that a sample of this size will provide estimates of consumer sentiment that are within plus or minus 5 percent of true values with 95 percent confidence. Although the firm suggested the telephone approach, it has expressed some misgivings about this approach to obtaining consumer reactions to the different advertising concepts.

SOURCE: © Stewart Cohen/Tony Stone Images.

As an alternative, the supplier suggested that the data be collected via mall intercept interviewing. It reasons that the mall intercept approach will provide a better environment in which to expose consumers to the test commercials. Consumers will be exposed to a tape that includes simulated radio spot commercials. The research company is concerned that it will be much more difficult to simulate the commercials over the phone than in the mall environment. On the other hand, the proposal indicates that because the mall intercept sample will be a quota sample, the results will not be projectable to the total market. The firm has also recommended a sample size of 400 for the mall survey.

The bid for the survey based on a telephone approach is $10,500 and the bid for the mall intercept approach is $15,000. The mall approach is more expensive and may well generate a more valid response from individual consumers, but because all the interviewing will be conducted at a single mall location, it cannot produce a sample that is representative of the entire population of target customers in the market. The telephone survey will be cheaper and will involve a truly representative sample of target consumers. However, there is concern that consumer reactions to the ads will not be as valid as those obtained in a mall intercept situation. Johnson is weighing the alternatives and trying to arrive at the best decision. ■

The issues confronting Adele Johnson are related to the central topic of this chapter. The question is one of choosing the "best" approach, in a given situation, for selecting a sample of people from whom to collect data. As this example suggests, different alternatives have different costs, data quality levels, and levels of sampling accuracy associated with them. The challenge, as always, is to obtain the required information at the appropriate level of quality at the lowest possible cost. These issues are covered in this chapter. After you have had an opportunity to read this chapter, review Adele Johnson's situation, and see what choice you would make between the two alternatives.

Definition of Important Terms

Population or Universe

population or universe
The total group of people from whom information is needed.

In the area of sampling, the terms **population** and **universe** are used interchangeably.[1] In this discussion, we will use the term *population*. The population or population of interest is the total group of people from whom we need to obtain information. One of the first things the analyst must do is to define the population of interest. This often involves defining the target market for the product or service in question.

For example, a researcher conducting a product concept test for a new nonprescription cold symptom relieving product, such as Contac, might take the position that the population of interest includes everyone because everyone suffers from colds from time to time. However, although everyone suffers from colds from time to time, not everyone buys a nonprescription cold symptom relieving product. In this case, the first task would probably be to ask people whether they had purchased or used one or more of a number of competing brands during some time period. Only those who had purchased or used one of these brands would be included in the population of interest.

Defining the population of interest is a key step in the sampling process. The issue is, Whose opinions are needed to fulfill the objectives of the research?

There are no specific rules to follow in defining the population of interest. It requires the researcher to apply good logic and judgment. Often the definition of the population is based on the characteristics of current or target customers.

Sample versus Census

The term **census** is used to refer to those situations in which data are obtained from or about every member of the population of interest. Censuses are not often employed in marketing research. In most marketing research situations, the population includes many thousands, hundreds of thousands, or millions of individuals. The cost and time required to take a census of population of this magnitude are so great as to preclude the possibility of its use.

census
Data obtained from every member of the population of interest.

It has been demonstrated time and time again that a relatively small but carefully chosen **sample** can quite accurately reflect the characteristics of the population from which it is drawn. A sample is nothing more than a subset of the population. Information is obtained from or about a subset of the population to make estimates about various characteristics of the total population. Ideally, the subset of the population from or about which information is obtained should be a representative cross section of the total population.

sample
A subset of the population of interest.

Although, as we noted earlier, censuses are not often used in marketing research, there are instances in which they are appropriate and feasible. For example, censuses may be appropriate and feasible in industrial products settings in which a particular firm may have only a small number of customers for the highly specialized products it sells. In these situations, it may be possible to obtain information from the entire population of customers.

Finally, though the idea of a census may be a very appealing in that there is a general perception that a census is more accurate than a sample, this is not necessarily true. Particularly when we are trying to do a census of a human population, there are many impediments to actually obtaining information from every member of the population. For example, we may not be able to obtain a complete and accurate list of all the members of the population or certain members of the population may refuse to provide information to us. Because of these impediments, the ideal of a census is seldom attainable even if we are dealing with relatively small populations. The problems of achieving the goal of a census of a large human population are formidable. You may have read or heard about these types of problems in connection with the 1990 U.S. Census of Population.[2] (See Figure 13.1. on pages 446 and 447)

Steps in Developing a Sampling Plan

The process of developing an operational sampling plan can be separated into seven steps, which are summarized in Figure 13.2 on page 448. Each step in the process is discussed here.

Defining the Population of Interest

The basic issue is to specify the characteristics of those individuals or things (e.g., companies, stores, etc.) from whom information is needed to meet the objectives

FIGURE 13.1

U.S. Population Census Short Form

The 1990 U.S. Population Census consisted of a short form sent to 5 in every 6 households which contained the 7 population questions and 7 household questions shown here. The long form included additional questions on citizenship, education, employment, housing, income, etc.

	PERSON 1	PERSON 2
Please fill one column ➡ for each person listed in Question 1a on page 1.	Last name First name Middle initial	Last name First name Middle initial
2. How is this person related to PERSON 1? Fill ONE circle for each person. If **Other relative** of person in column 1, fill circle and print exact relationship, such as mother-in-law, grandparent, son-in-law, niece, cousin, and so on.	START in this column with the household member (or one of the members) in whose name the home is owned, being bought, or rented. If there is no such person, start in this column with any adult household member.	If a RELATIVE of Person 1: ○ Husband/wife ○ Brother/sister ○ Natural-born or adopted son/daughter ○ Father/mother ○ Grandchild ○ Other relative ○ Stepson/stepdaughter If NOT RELATED to Person 1: ○ Roomer, boarder, or foster child ○ Unmarried partner ○ Housemate, roommate ○ Other nonrelative
3. Sex Fill ONE circle for each person.	○ Male ○ Female	○ Male ○ Female
4. Race Fill ONE circle for the race that the person considers himself/herself to be. If **Indian (Amer.)**, print the name of the enrolled or principal tribe. → If **Other Asian or Pacific Islander (API)**, print one group, for example: Hmong, Fijian, Laotian, Thai, Tongan, Pakistani, Cambodian, and so on. → If **Other race**, print race. →	○ White ○ Black or Negro ○ Indian (Amer.) (Print the name of the enrolled or principal tribe.) ○ Eskimo ○ Aleut Asian or Pacific Islander (API) ○ Chinese ○ Japanese ○ Filipino ○ Asian Indian ○ Hawaiian ○ Samoan ○ Korean ○ Guamanian ○ Vietnamese ○ Other API ○ Other race (Print race)	○ White ○ Black or Negro ○ Indian (Amer.) (Print the name of the enrolled or principal tribe.) ○ Eskimo ○ Aleut Asian or Pacific Islander (API) ○ Chinese ○ Japanese ○ Filipino ○ Asian Indian ○ Hawaiian ○ Samoan ○ Korean ○ Guamanian ○ Vietnamese ○ Other API ○ Other race (Print race)
5. Age and year of birth **a.** Print each person's age at last birthday. Fill in the matching circle below each box. **b.** Print each person's year of birth and fill the matching circle below each box.	a. Age: 0 ○ 0 ○ 0 ○; 1 ○ 1 ○ 1 ○; 2 ○ 2 ○; 3 ○ 3 ○; 4 ○ 4 ○; 5 ○ 5 ○; 6 ○ 6 ○; 7 ○ 7 ○; 8 ○ 8 ○; 9 ○ 9 ○ b. Year of birth: 1 ● 8 ○ 0 ○ 0 ○; 9 ○ 1 ○ 1 ○; 2 ○ 2 ○; 3 ○ 3 ○; 4 ○ 4 ○; 5 ○ 5 ○; 6 ○ 6 ○; 7 ○ 7 ○; 8 ○ 8 ○; 9 ○ 9 ○	a. Age: 0 ○ 0 ○ 0 ○; 1 ○ 1 ○ 1 ○; 2 ○ 2 ○; 3 ○ 3 ○; 4 ○ 4 ○; 5 ○ 5 ○; 6 ○ 6 ○; 7 ○ 7 ○; 8 ○ 8 ○; 9 ○ 9 ○ b. Year of birth: 1 ● 8 ○ 0 ○ 0 ○; 9 ○ 1 ○ 1 ○; 2 ○ 2 ○; 3 ○ 3 ○; 4 ○ 4 ○; 5 ○ 5 ○; 6 ○ 6 ○; 7 ○ 7 ○; 8 ○ 8 ○; 9 ○ 9 ○
6. Marital status Fill ONE circle for each person.	○ Now married ○ Separated ○ Widowed ○ Never married ○ Divorced	○ Now married ○ Separated ○ Widowed ○ Never married ○ Divorced
7. Is this person of Spanish/Hispanic origin? Fill ONE circle for each person. If **Yes, other Spanish/Hispanic**, print one group. →	○ No (not Spanish/Hispanic) ○ Yes, Mexican, Mexican-Am., Chicano ○ Yes, Puerto Rican ○ Yes, Cuban ○ Yes, other Spanish/Hispanic (Print one group, for example: Argentinean, Colombian, Dominican, Nicaraguan, Salvadoran, Spaniard, and so on.)	○ No (not Spanish/Hispanic) ○ Yes, Mexican, Mexican-Am., Chicano ○ Yes, Puerto Rican ○ Yes, Cuban ○ Yes, other Spanish/Hispanic (Print one group, for example: Argentinean, Colombian, Dominican, Nicaraguan, Salvadoran, Spaniard, and so on.)
FOR CENSUS USE ⟶	○ ○	○ ○

FIGURE 13.1

U.S. Population Census Short Form—*Continued*

H1a. Did you leave anyone out of your list of persons for Question 1a on page 1 because you were not sure if the person should be listed — for example, someone temporarily away on a business trip or vacation, a newborn baby still in the hospital, or a person who stays here once in a while and has no other home?

○ Yes, please print the name(s) and reason(s). ○ No

b. Did you include anyone in your list of persons for Question 1a on page 1 even though you were not sure that the person should be listed — for example, a visitor who is staying here temporarily or a person who usually lives somewhere else?

○ Yes, please print the name(s) and reason(s). ○ No

H2. Which best describes this building? Include all apartments, flats, etc., even if vacant.

○ A mobile home or trailer
○ A one-family house detached from any other house
○ A one-family house attached to one or more houses
○ A building with 2 apartments
○ A building with 3 or 4 apartments
○ A building with 5 to 9 apartments
○ A building with 10 to 19 apartments
○ A building with 20 to 49 apartments
○ A building with 50 or more apartments
○ Other

H3. How many rooms do you have in this house or apartment? Do NOT count bathrooms, porches, balconies, foyers, halls, or half-rooms.

○ 1 room ○ 4 rooms ○ 7 rooms
○ 2 rooms ○ 5 rooms ○ 8 rooms
○ 3 rooms ○ 6 rooms ○ 9 or more rooms

H4. Is this house or apartment —

○ Owned by you or someone in this household with a mortgage or loan?
○ Owned by you or someone in this household free and clear (without a mortgage)?
○ Rented for cash rent?
○ Occupied without payment of cash rent?

If this is a ONE-FAMILY HOUSE —

H5a. Is this house on ten or more acres?

○ Yes ○ No

b. Is there a business (such as a store or barber shop) or a medical office on this property?

○ Yes ○ No

Answer only if you or someone in this household OWNS OR IS BUYING this house or apartment —

H6. What is the value of this property; that is, how much do you think this house and lot or condominium unit would sell for if it were for sale?

○ Less than $10,000	○ $70,000 to $74,999
○ $10,000 to $14,999	○ $75,000 to $79,999
○ $15,000 to $19,999	○ $80,000 to $89,999
○ $20,000 to $24,999	○ $90,000 to $99,999
○ $25,000 to $29,999	○ $100,000 to $124,999
○ $30,000 to $34,999	○ $125,000 to $149,999
○ $35,000 to $39,999	○ $150,000 to $174,999
○ $40,000 to $44,999	○ $175,000 to $199,999
○ $45,000 to $49,999	○ $200,000 to $249,999
○ $50,000 to $54,999	○ $250,000 to $299,999
○ $55,000 to $59,999	○ $300,000 to $399,999
○ $60,000 to $64,999	○ $400,000 to $499,999
○ $65,000 to $69,999	○ $500,000 or more

Answer only if you PAY RENT for this house or apartment —

H7a. What is the monthly rent?

○ Less than $80	○ $375 to $399
○ $80 to $99	○ $400 to $424
○ $100 to $124	○ $425 to $449
○ $125 to $149	○ $450 to $474
○ $150 to $174	○ $475 to $499
○ $175 to $199	○ $500 to $524
○ $200 to $224	○ $525 to $549
○ $225 to $249	○ $550 to $599
○ $250 to $274	○ $600 to $649
○ $275 to $299	○ $650 to $699
○ $300 to $324	○ $700 to $749
○ $325 to $349	○ $750 to $999
○ $350 to $374	○ $1,000 or more

b. Does the monthly rent include any meals?

○ Yes ○ No

FOR CENSUS USE

A. Total persons

0 1 2 3 4 5 6 7 8 9

B. Type of unit

Occupied: ○ First form ○ Cont'n
Vacant: ○ Regular ○ Usual home elsewhere

C1. Vacancy status

○ For rent ○ For sale only ○ Rented or sold, not occupied
○ For seas/rec/occ ○ For migrant workers ○ Other vacant

C2. Is this unit boarded up?

○ Yes ○ No

D. Months vacant

○ Less than 1 ○ 1 up to 2 ○ 2 up to 6
○ 6 up to 12 ○ 12 up to 24 ○ 24 or more

E. Complete after

○ LR ○ TC ○ QA JIC 1 ○
○ P/F ○ RE ○ I/T
○ MV ○ ED ○ EN

○ P0 ○ P3 ○ P6 JIC 2 ○
○ P1 ○ P4 ○ IA
○ P2 ○ P5 ○ SM

F. Cov.

○ 1b ○ 1a ○ 7 ○ H1

G. DO **ID**

0 1 2 3 4 5 6 7 8 9

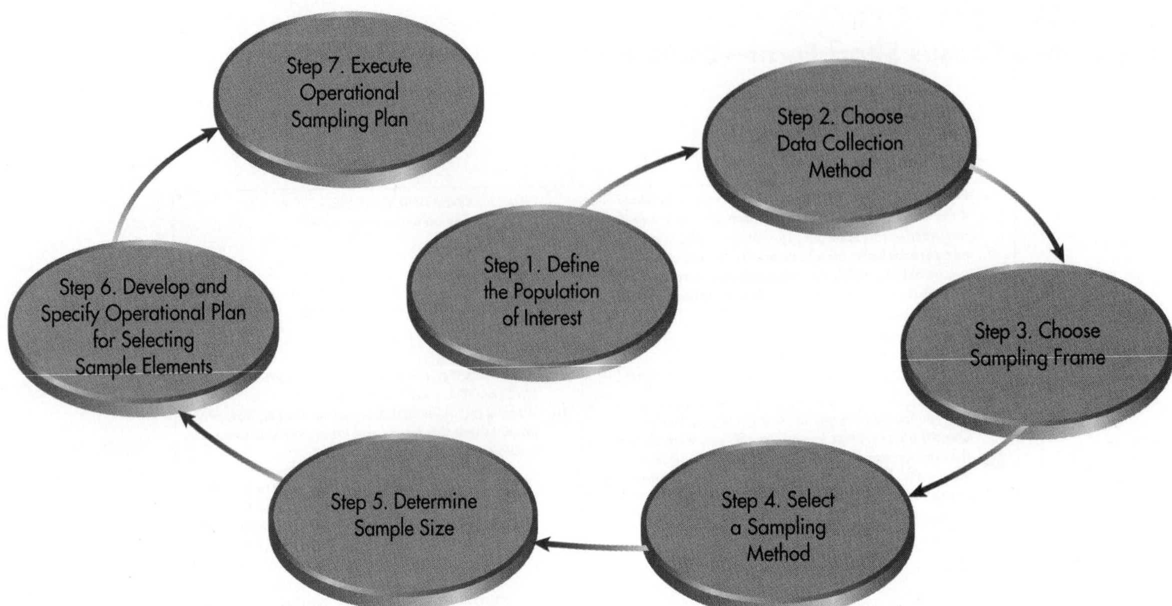

FIGURE 13.2
Steps in Developing a Sampling Plan

of the research. The population of interest is often specified in terms of some combination of the following characteristics: geography, demographic characteristics, product or service use characteristics, or awareness measures. These bases for population definition are discussed in Table 13.1. In surveys, the question of whether a particular individual does or does not belong to the population of interest is often dealt with by means of screening questions at the beginning of the questionnaire. Even if we have a list of the population and sample from that list, screening questions are still used to qualify the potential respondent. A sample sequence of screening questions is provided in Table 13.2.

TABLE 13.1 **Some Bases for Defining the Population of Interest**

BASIS	DISCUSSION
Geography	What geographic area is to be sampled? Usually a question of a client's scope of operation. Could be a city, county, metropolitan area, state, group of states, the entire United States, or a number of countries.
Demographics	Given the objectives of the research and the target market for the product, whose opinions, reactions, and so on are relevant. Are we interested in getting information from women over 18; women 18–34; women 18–34 with household incomes over $35,000 per year, who work, and have preschool children?
Use	In addition to the preceding, the population of interest frequently is defined in terms of some product or service use requirement. This is usually stated in terms of some use versus nonuse or use of some quantity of the product or service on some period of time. The following examples of use screening questions illustrate the point: ■ Do you drink five or more cans, bottles, or glasses of diet soft drinks in a typical week? ■ Have you traveled to Europe for vacation or business purposes in the past two years? ■ Have you or has anyone in your immediate family been in a hospital for an overnight or extended stay in the past two years?
Awareness	We may be interested in surveying those individuals who are aware of the company's advertising to explore what the ad communicated to them about the characteristics of the product or service.

In addition to defining who will be included in the population of interest, it is sometimes important also to define who will be excluded. Most commercial marketing research surveys exclude certain individuals for so-called security reasons. Very frequently the first question on a questionnaire will ask whether the individual or anyone in the household works in marketing research, advertising, or in the product or service area dealt with in the survey (see question 5 in Table 13.2). If the individual indicates that she or someone in the household works in one of these industries, the interview is terminated. This is referred to as a security question because individuals in the industries in question are viewed as security risks. They may be competitors or work for competitors, and we do not want to give them some indication of what we may be planning to do.

There may be reasons to exclude individuals for other reasons. For example, Coca-Cola might wish to do a survey among individuals who drink five or more cans, bottles, or glasses of soft drink in a typical week but who do not drink Coca-Cola because they are interested in developing a better understanding of heavy

TABLE 13.2 **Example of Screening Question Sequence to Determine Population Membership**

Hello. I'm _________ with _________ Research. We're conducting a survey about products used in the home. May I ask you a few questions?

1. Have you been interviewed about any products or advertising in the past 3 *months*?

Yes		TERMINATE AND TALLY
No	→	*CONTINUE*

2. Which of the following hair care products, if any, have you used in the past month? (HAND PRODUCT CARD TO RESPONDENT. CIRCLE ALL MENTIONS.)

   1 Regular Shampoo

   2 Dandruff Shampoo

   3 Cream Rinse/Instant Conditioner

   4 "Intensive" Conditioner

INSTRUCTIONS: *IF "4" IS CIRCLED—SKIP TO Q. 4 AND CONTINUE FOR "INTENSIVE" QUOTA*
IF "3" IS CIRCLED *BUT NOT 4*—ASK Q. 3 AND CONTINUE FOR "INSTANT" QUOTA

3. You said that you have used a creme rinse/instant conditioner in the past month. Have you used either a creme rinse or an instant conditioner in the past week, or not?

Yes (used in the past week)	→	*CONTINUE FOR "INSTANT" QUOTA*
No (not used in past week)	→	TERMINATE AND TALLY

4. Into which of the following groups does your age fall? (READ LIST, CIRCLE AGE.)

X	Under 18	→	CHECK AGE QUOTAS
1	8–24		
2	25–34		
3	35–44		
X	45 or over		

5. Previous surveys have shown that people who work in certain jobs may have different reactions to certain products. Now, do you or does any member of your immediate family work for an advertising agency, a market research firm, a public relations firm, or a company that manufactures or sells personal care products?

Yes		TERMINATE AND TALLY
No	→	*CONTINUE*

IF RESPONDENT QUALIFIES, INVITE HER TO PARTICIPATE AND COMPLETE NAME GRID BELOW.)

soft drink users who do not drink Coke. Therefore, researchers might wish to exclude those individuals who indicate they have drunk one or more cans, bottles, or glasses of Coca-Cola in the past week.

The results to the Gallup survey, described in Figure 13.3, suggest how the definition of the population might influence the overall results. How would the overall results have looked if men had been excluded in the definition of the population of interest? Is there a correct definition of the population of interest for this study? If so, what is the correct definition of the population?

Marketing Research in Practice

"A New Technique for Objective Methods for Measuring Reader Interest in Newspapers" was the title of George Gallup's Ph.D. thesis at the University of Iowa. Working with the *Des Moines Register and Tribune* and the 200-year-old statistical theory probabilities of Swiss mathematician Jakob Bernoulli, Gallup developed "sampling" techniques. He showed that you did not have to talk to everybody as long as you randomly selected respondents according to a sampling plan that takes into account whatever diversity was relevant in the universe of potential respondents—geographic, ethnic, economic. Although not everybody understood or believed his ideas then—or now—this intellectual invention was a big deal.

On many occasions, Gallup used a particular example to explain what he was talking about and doing. "Suppose there are 7,000 white beans and 3,000 black beans well churned in a barrel. If you scoop out 100 of them, you'll get approximately 70 white beans and 30 black beans in your hand, and the range of your possible error can be computed mathematically. As long as the barrel contains many more beans than your handful, the proportion will remain within that margin of error 997 times out of 1,000."

In the early 1930s, George Gallup was in great demand around the country. He became head of the journalism department at Drake University and then switched to Northwestern. During this period he was doing readership surveys for newspapers throughout the northeastern United States. In the summer of 1932, a new advertising agency, Young and Rubicam, invited him to New York to create a research department and procedures for evaluating the effectiveness of advertising. In that same year, he used his polling techniques to help his mother-in-law get elected secretary of state of Iowa. Based on this experience, he was confident that his sampling methodology was valid not only for beans and newspaper readers but for voters also. As long as you understood the sampling universe—white, black, male, female, rich, poor, urban, rural, Republican, Democratic—you could predict elections or calculate public attitudes on public opinion questions by interviewing a relatively small number of people as long as that small number of people was representative of that total population from which they were drawn. Gallup proved that population values could be accurately estimated by means of scientific samples and made a fortune in the process.[3] ■

FIGURE 13.3

An Example of a Gallup Poll Newsletter

SOURCE: Courtesy of Gallup Polls.

The GALLUP POLL

NEWS SERVICE

Volume 56, No. 42c. Friday, March 13, 1992

Public Divided On Implant Restrictions

By Larry Hugick

PRINCETON, NJ — Americans are divided over whether access to silicone gel breast implants should be restricted because of concerns about safety. According to a recent Gallup poll, public opinion splits three ways on implants: more than a third (37%) of adults aware of the controversy believe that implant surgery should be available to all women who request it; about three in ten (29%) feel the procedure should be available only on a limited basis; and another three in ten (31%) feel it should be banned entirely because of safety concerns.

Last month a federal advisory panel took a middle position on access to implants. The Food and Drug Administration panel recommended allowing women who have had cancer surgery to get them, but restricting access for otherwise healthy women seeking to increase their breast size.

Opinion Divides By Gender and Age

Women and older people are most likely to favor a total ban on silicone gel breast implant surgery. Men and younger people are most likely to feel there should be no restrictions on access. The gender gap is especially wide among the better-educated. While over half (53%) of college-educated men say implants should be available to all women who want them, only about a third (32%) of college-educated women agree.

Who's to Blame: Not Just the Manufacturers

While Dow Corning and other manufacturers have been most widely criticized in the media coverage of this controversy, the public tends to spread the blame around for problems that may have resulted from implants. Manufacturers are most often singled out for blame, but even so, less than half (40%) of aware Americans find the companies producing the product to be at fault. Three in ten (30%) blame women too eager to change their physical appearance and another 30% hold government regulators of public health and safety responsible. Doctors and the medical profession are least likely to be seen as culpable (18%).

Methodology

The results are based on telephone interviews with a randomly selected national sample of 1,001 adults, 18 years and older, conducted February 28-March 1, 1992. For results based on samples of this size, one can say with 95 percent confidence that the error attributable to sampling and other random effects could be plus or minus 3 percentage points. In addition to sampling error, question wording and practical difficulties in conducting surveys can introduce error or bias into the findings of public opinion polls.

Have you heard or read about the recent controversy over the safety of silicone breast implants?

	Total	Women	Men
Yes	92%	93%	91%
No	8	7	9
No opinion	*	*	*
	100%	100%	100%

* Less than 0.5%

continues

FIGURE 13.3

An Example of a Gallup Poll Newsletter—*Continued*

Do you think silicone breast implants should be legally available to all women who want them, legally available only in special circumstances — such as when a woman has had a mastectomy, or should silicone breast implants be banned entirely because of safety concerns? (Based on those who have heard or read about the recent controversy, 931 respondents)

	Total	Women	Men
Legally available to all women who want them	37%	31%	44%
Legally available only in certain circumstances	29	31	27
Banned entirely	31	36	24
No opinion	3	2	5
	100%	100%	100%
(Number of interviews)	(931)	(472)	(459)

Which of the following do you blame for the current problems over silicone breast implants? (Based on those who have heard or read about the recent controversy)

	Total	Women	Men
Companies that make the implants	40%	40%	41%
Women who were too eager to change their physical appearance	31	30	31
Government agencies which regulate public health and safety	26	30	21
The medical profession and doctors	19	18	20
No opinion	3	3	3
None of the above	2	1	2

Note: totals add to more than 100% due to multiple responses

Choose Data Collection Method

The selection of a data collection method, as indicated in the opening vignette about Adele Johnson, has considerable impact on the nature of the sampling process. Subsequent steps in the sampling process will be influenced by the data collection method to be used. As noted in the vignette, for example, telephone interviewing has certain inherent advantages and mall intercept interviewing has certain inherent disadvantages in regard to sampling.

Choose Sampling Frame

sampling frame
List of population elements from which we select units to be sampled.

The third step in the process is to identify the **sampling frame.** Previously, we defined the *sampling frame* as a list of the population elements or members from which we select units to be sampled. In the ideal situation, we have such a list and it is complete and accurate. Unfortunately, all too often, we have no such list. For example, the population for a particular study may be defined to include those individuals who have played three or more rounds of 18 holes of golf in the past 30 days. There is obviously no list that provides a complete enumeration of these individuals. In these instances, instead of a sample frame in the traditional sense, we will have to reflect the sample frame in some procedure that will produce a representative sample of individuals with the desired characteristics. For example, a telephone book might be the sample frame for a telephone survey sample. This example also illustrates that there seldom is a perfect correspondence between the sampling frame and the population of interest. The population of interest might be all households in the city in question. However, the telephone book would not include those households that do not have telephones and those with unlisted numbers.

Unfortunately, there is substantial evidence that those with listed numbers and those with no listing are significantly different in regard to a number of important characteristics. It has been shown that voluntarily unlisted subscribers are more likely to be renters, live in the central city, have recently moved, have larger families, have younger children, and have lower incomes than their counterparts with listed numbers.[4] There are also significant differences between the two groups in terms of purchase, ownership, and usage patterns of certain products.

Unlisted numbers are more prevalent in the West, in metropolitan areas, and among nonwhites and those in the 18-to-34 age group.[5] These findings have been confirmed in a number of studies.[6] The implications are clear; if representative samples are to be obtained in telephone surveys, sampling procedures that include an appropriate proportion of households with unlisted numbers must be employed.

The extent of the problem is suggested by the data in Table 13.3. In such cases, a procedure may be used to generate a list of the elements of the population to be sampled. **Random digit dialing,** described in Table 13.4, involves generating lists

random digit dialing
Method of generating lists of telephone numbers at random.

TABLE 13.3 The 1994 20 Metropolitan Statistical Areas with the Highest Incidence of Unlisted Phones

MSA[a] NAME	TOTAL MSA HOUSEHOLDS	PERCENT HOUSEHOLDS WITH PHONES	PERCENT ESTIMATED UNLISTED HOUSEHOLDS	MSA RANK BASED ON PERCENT UNLISTED HOUSEHOLDS
Sacramento, CA PMSA[b]	554,876	97.5	68.3	1
Oakland, CA PMSA	810,042	98.0	67.3	2
Fresno, CA	275,265	95.6	67.0	3
Los Angeles-Long Beach, CA PMSA	3,066,785	96.7	66.7	4
San Jose, CA PMSA	532,580	98.8	66.6	5
San Diego, CA	941,365	97.8	65.0	6
Orange County, CA PMSA	871,081	98.5	62.8	7
Riverside-San Bernardino, CA PMSA	987,309	96.0	62.3	8
San Francisco, CA PMSA	662,913	98.3	61.3	9
Bakersfield, CA	205,719	94.8	61.2	10
Ventura, CA PMSA	226,001	98.4	60.4	11
Las Vegas, NV-AZ	417,940	95.8	59.6	12
Jersey City, NJ PMSA	210,884	93.5	48.0	13
Tacoma, WA PMSA	239,190	97.1	44.5	14
Portland-Vancouver, OR-WA PMSA	659,017	97.2	44.1	15
Detroit, MI PMSA	1,615,658	96.7	41.1	16
Tucson, AZ	285,849	94.2	39.8	17
Honolulu, HI	280,953	98.0	39.7	18
El Paso, TX	197,062	91.6	39.3	19
Phoenix-Mesa, AZ	929,991	94.3	37.8	20

SOURCE: Courtesy of Survey Sampling, Inc. © Copyright Survey Sampling, Inc., 1994.

[a]Metropolitan Statistical Area
[b]Primary Metropolitan Statistical Area

of telephone numbers at random. Developing an appropriate sampling frame is often one of the most challenging problems facing the researcher in the area of sampling.[7]

TABLE 13.4 Random Digit Dialing Procedure

The only solution to the problems of unlisted telephone numbers is to generate phone numbers by some random process. This practice, referred to as random digit dialing (RDD), is simple in theory—phone numbers are generated at random. However, practical considerations complicate the picture greatly. The first and foremost of these is the relatively small proportion of working numbers among all possible 10-digit telephone numbers. Only about 1 in 170 of all possible telephone numbers (9,999,999,999 possible) are actually in use (60,000,000 residential numbers). The proportion of working residential numbers in RDD samples can be increased dramatically by selecting from only the 103 working area codes (first three digits). This approach yields approximately one working residential number for every 17 randomly generated. From a cost standpoint this rate is still too low, entailing too many unproductive dialings. The question at this point is, What type of RDD system will simultaneously cut the proportion of unproductive dialings while including a proportionate number of unlisted phone homes in the sample? There are three alternative approaches that meet these two objectives to varying degrees: the four-digit approach, three-digit approach, and approaches built around the use of a telephone book.

Four-Digit Approach

Taking the four-digit approach, the researcher must, in addition to restricting the sample to the 103 working area codes, select numbers only from working central offices or exchanges. The last four digits of the number are generated via some process that approaches randomness. These are approximately 30,000 working exchanges in the continental United States or about 300 million possible numbers. This approach will, therefore, yield approximately one working number for every five generated randomly. Problems with this approach relate to the fact that all exchanges have an equal probability of being selected while some have a high proportion of all possible numbers in service and others have only a small proportion in service.

Three-Digit Approach

The next logical progression in RDD technology is the three-digit approach. The three-digit method increases the proportion of working numbers to better than one in three. This is possible because the phone company does not assign numbers from a particular exchange at random but from within working banks of 1,000 numbers. Consulting the section of a crisscross directory where phone numbers are listed numerically will show that within a particular exchange certain sequences of 1,000 numbers (000–999) are totally unused while other groups of 1,000 are, for example, 70 percent in use. Employing the three-digit option, the user must specify area codes, exchanges, and "working banks" (fourth digit) of numbers within exchanges. Working banks may be identified from a crisscross directory or selected via probability sample from the telephone book. A bank with no working listed numbers has no chance of being selected, while a bank with 60 percent of its numbers listed has twice as much chance of being selected as one with only 30 percent listed. The final step of the three-digit approach is to generate the last three digits of each working area code/exchange/bank by means of some random process.

The three-digit method is more efficient in eliminating nonworking numbers, but increases bias due to missing (from the directory) new working banks that have been activated. The four-digit method is safer from the standpoint of avoiding bias, but more expensive due to the greater number of calls that must be made. It is suggested that the three-digit method is most appropriate when the directory or directories for the area of interest are relatively current or when there has been little growth in the area since the publication of the most recent directory. In other cases the four-digit method should be given serious consideration.

Using Telephone Books

RDD samples can also be generated from the telephone book. In general, this is accomplished by selecting numbers at random from the book and adding a random number to the sixth or seventh digits. Somewhere between one in two and one in three of the numbers generated will be working residential numbers. This is a viable approach because all exchanges and banks are proportionately represented in the book. Generally, the phone book is recommended as a RDD sample source only in those cases where the appropriate computer hardware and software are not available. There are two major reasons for making this recommendation. First, the construction of a sample by this approach is fairly time-consuming and expensive whether it is done for or by the interviewers. Second, if the interviewers are given directions and left to generate the numbers themselves, the researcher loses all control over the validity of the sample.

Computer programs can incorporate three- or four-digit approaches and generate RDD samples at very low cost. In addition, the printout can set up to capture additional data and to help the researcher control field costs and proper execution of the sampling plan.

SOURCE: Roger Gates and Bob Brobst, "RANDIAL: A Program for Generating Random Telephone Numbers," *Journal of Marketing Research* 14 (May 1977): 240.

Marketing Research in Practice

Fish, Barnes, and Banahan provide two interesting examples of sample frame error. The first example involves a poll conducted by the *Literary Digest* in 1936. This publication predicted that Alf Landon would win the election over Franklin Roosevelt on the basis of the results of a very large (more than two million) sample of voters chosen from telephone directories and automobile ownership lists. Unfortunately, the sample frames used (telephone directories and automobile lists) were not representative of the population of American voters in 1936. Many people did not have telephones, and many did not have cars. These individuals tended to have lower incomes. Therefore, the frames chosen were heavily weighted in favor of the affluent who were more likely to vote Republican (for Landon). The *Literary Digest* went out of business shortly after the election because of the severe loss of credibility associated with its erroneous prediction.

The case of a dog food manufacturer who conducted extensive market research among dog owners provides a more humorous example. The manufacturer made demand estimates, tested the packaging style and size, and designed and tested an advertising campaign—all with dog owners. The product was launched with a big campaign and experienced tremendous initial sales. However, a few months later sales came to a virtual standstill. The company brought in a consultant who took the dog food out to the local dog pound and put it in front of the dogs. They did not touch it. Despite all the marketing research with dog owners, the manufacturer did not see the potential for sample frame error.[8] ■

Selecting a Sampling Method

The fourth step in the process involves the selection of a sampling method. The selection of a particular sampling method will depend on the objectives of the study, the financial resources available, time limitations, and the nature of the problem under investigation. The major alternative sampling methods can be grouped under two headings: probability sampling methods and nonprobability sampling methods. A number of alternatives are available under each of these headings.

probability samples
Samples in which every element of the population has a known, nonzero probability of selection.

Probability samples must be selected in such a way that every element of the population has a known, nonzero probability of selection.[9] The simple random sample is the best known and most widely used probability sampling method. The simple random sample must be selected in such a way that every member or element of the population has a known and equal probability of being selected. Under probability sampling, the researcher must closely adhere to precise selection procedures that avoid arbitrary or biased selection of elements. When these procedures are followed strictly, the laws of probability are in effect. This allows calculation of the extent to which a sample value can be expected to differ from a population value. This difference is referred to as *sampling error*.

nonprobability samples

Samples that include the selection of specific elements from the population in a nonrandom manner.

Nonprobability samples include the selection of specific elements from the population in a nonrandom manner. Nonrandomness occurs due to accident when population elements are selected on the basis of convenience—because they are easy or inexpensive to reach. Purposeful nonrandomness would involve a sampling plan that systematically excluded or overrepresented certain subsets of the population. For example, a sample designed to represent the opinions of all women over the age of 18 that was based on a telephone survey conducted during the day on weekdays would systematically exclude working women.

Probability samples offer several advantages, including the following:[10]

- The researcher can be sure of obtaining information from a representative cross section of the population of interest.
- Sampling error can be computed.
- The survey results are projectable to the total population. For example, if 5 percent of the individuals sampled in a research project based on a probability sample gave a particular response, the researcher can project this percentage, plus or minus the sampling error, to the total population.

On the other hand, certain disadvantages are associated with probability samples:

- They are more expensive than nonprobability samples of the same size in most cases. A certain amount of professional time must be spent in developing the sample design.
- Probability samples take more time to design and execute than nonprobability samples. The procedures that must be followed in the execution of the sampling plan will increase the amount of time required to collect data.

The disadvantages of nonprobability samples are essentially the reverse of the advantages of probability samples:

- Sampling error cannot be computed.
- The researcher does not know the degree to which the sample is representative of the population from which it was drawn.
- The results of nonprobability samples cannot be projected to the total population.

Given the disadvantages of nonprobability samples, one may wonder why they are used. In fact they are used frequently by marketing researchers. The reasons for their use relate to their inherent advantages:

- Nonprobability samples cost less than probability samples. This characteristic of nonprobability samples may have considerable appeal in those situations in which accuracy is not of the utmost importance. Exploratory research is an example of this type of situation.
- Nonprobability samples ordinarily can be conducted more quickly than probability samples. The reasons for this were discussed earlier.
- Nonprobability samples can produce samples of the population that are reasonably representative if executed properly.

Reprinted from Advertising Age. Courtesy of Bill Whitehead.

Issues related to beliefs of the public in regard to sampling issues are summarized in the Marketing Research in Practice feature on 900 number polls.

In addition to choosing between probability and nonprobability samples, the researcher must chose between a number of types of samples under each of these major categories. These are summarized in Figure 13.4. These options are discussed in greater detail later in the chapter.

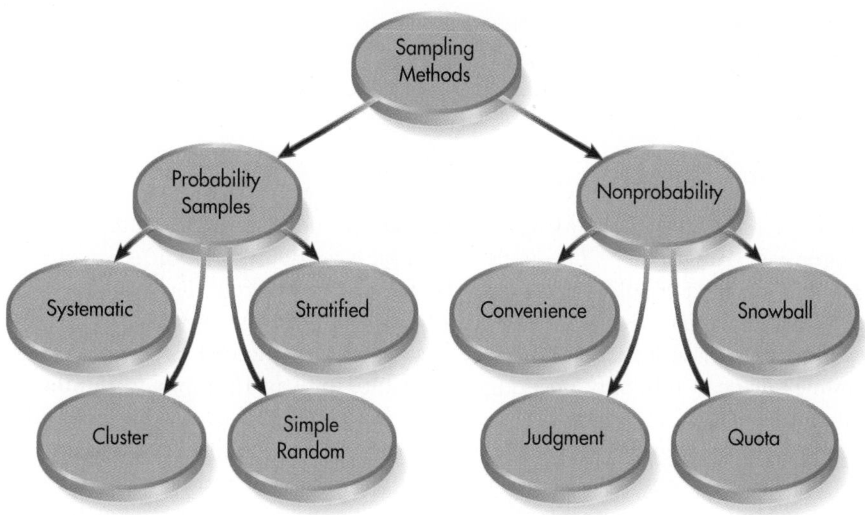

FIGURE 13.4
Classification of Sampling Methods

Marketing Research in Practice

We have all seen the 900 number telephone polls on CNN and other news programs. These polls violate all the statistical principles on which legitimate research surveys are based. The responses from self-selection 900 number polls are not projectable to any definable population group because they are biased due to the fact that they are based on responses from only those aware of the poll, interested enough to respond, willing and able to pay to respond, and able to reach the given number. There is also the possibility that a given individual may make multiple calls to such a 900 number poll.

Although these polls are clearly not representative, a recent poll conducted by the R. H. Bruskin Company based on a national telephone probability survey of 1,000 adults indicates that substantial proportions of the general population believe these polls are legitimate and representative in certain respects:

- 45 percent believe that the results of these call-in polls are believable.
- 40 percent believe that the results of these polls should be believed because thousands of people participated in the poll.
- 40 percent believe that those who call in on these kinds of polls have the same opinions as those who do not call in.
- 38 percent believe that those who respond to these kinds of polls are typical of the entire U.S. population.
- 36 percent believe that the results of these polls would not be reported if they were not accurate.
- 34 percent believe that the results of these polls should be believed because they are sponsored by major television, newspaper, or magazine organizations.
- 24 percent believe that these polls are scientific.
- 24 percent believe that the results of these polls accurately represent what the country as a whole thinks.[11] ■

Determine Sample Size

Once we have chosen the sampling method, the next step is to determine the appropriate sample size. The issue of sample size determination is covered in detail in the next chapter. In Chapter 14, we discuss the role that available budget, various rules of thumb, the number of subgroups to be analyzed, and traditional statistical methods play in this process. In the case of nonprobability samples, we can rely only on budget available, rules of thumb, and number of subgroups to be analyzed in determining sample size, However, with probability samples, formulas are used to calculate the sample size required given target levels of acceptable error (difference between sample result and population value) and levels of confidence (likelihood that the confidence interval which is the sample result plus or minus the acceptable error will take in the true population value). As noted earlier, the ability to make statistical inferences about population values based on sample results is a major advantage of probability samples.

Development of Operational Procedures for Selecting Sample Elements

The operational procedures to be used in the selection of sampling elements in the data collection phase of a project should be developed and specified whether a probability or nonprobability sample is being used.[12] The procedures are much more critical to the successful execution of a probability sample. In regard to probability samples, the procedures should be detailed, clear, and unambiguous and should take all discretion regarding the selection of specific sample elements away from the interviewer. Failure to develop a proper operational plan for selecting sample elements can jeopardize the entire sampling process. An example of an operational sampling plan is provided in Table 13.5.

Execution of the Sampling Plan

The final step in the sampling process involves the execution of the operational sampling plan discussed in the previous step. It is important that this step include adequate checking to make sure that specified procedures are adhered to.

TABLE 13.5 Example of Operational Sampling Plan

In the instructions that follow, reference is made to follow your route around a "block." In cities this will be a city block. In rural areas, a "block" is a segment of land surrounded by roads.

1. If you come to a dead end along your route, proceed down the opposite side of the street, road, or alley, traveling in the other direction. Continue making right turns, where possible, calling at every third occupied dwelling.
2. If you go all the way around a block and return to the starting address without completing four interviews in listed telephone homes, attempt an interview at the starting address. (This should seldom be necessary.)
3. If you work an entire block and do not complete the required interviews, proceed to the dwelling on the opposite side of the street (or rural route) that is *nearest* the starting address. Treat it as the next address on your Area Location Sheet and interview that house only if the address appears next to an "X" on your sheet. If it does not, continue your interviewing to the left of that address. Always follow the right turn rule.
4. If there are no dwellings on the street or road opposite the starting address for an area, circle the block opposite the starting address, following the right turn rule. (This means that you will circle the block following a clockwise direction.) Attempt interviews at every third dwelling along this route.
5. If, after circling the adjacent block opposite the starting address, you do not complete the necessary interviews, take the next block found, *following a clockwise direction*.
6. If the third block does not yield the dwellings necessary to complete your assignment, proceed to as many blocks as necessary to find the required dwellings; these blocks follow a clockwise path around the primary block.

SOURCE: Reprinted from interviewer guide by permission of Belden Associates, Dallas, Texas. The complete guide was over 30 pages long and contained maps and other aids for the interviewer.

Sampling and Nonsampling Errors

Consider a situation in which our goal is to determine the average age of the members of a particular population.[13] If we can obtain accurate information about all members of the population, we can compute the population parameter average age. A population parameter is a value that defines a true characteristic of a total population. Assume that μ (population parameter or average age) is 36.3 years. As already noted, it is almost always impossible to measure the entire population. Instead, the researcher takes a sample and makes inferences about population parameters from sample results. In regard to the problem of computing average age, the analyst might take a sample of 400 from a population of 250,000. An estimate of the average age of the members of the population (X) would be calculated from the sample values. Assume the average age of the sample members is 35.8 years. A second random sample of 400 might be drawn from the same population and the average again computed. In the second case, the average might be 36.8 years. Additional samples might be chosen and means computed for the various samples. The researcher would find that the means computed for the various samples would in most cases be fairly close but not identical to the true population value.

The accuracy of sample results is affected by two general types of error: sampling error and nonsampling (measurement) error. The following formula portrays the effect of these two types of error on the problem of estimating a population mean:

$$\overline{X} = \mu \pm \epsilon_s \pm \epsilon_{ns}$$

$\overline{X}$ = sample mean
μ = true population mean
ϵ_s = sampling error
ϵ_{ns} = nonsampling or measurement error

Sampling error is the error that results when the sample selected is not perfectly representative of the population. There are two types of sampling error: random and administrative. Administrative error relates to the problems in the administration or execution of the sample. That is, there are flaws in the design or execution of the sample that cause it to be not representative of the population. These types of error can be avoided or minimized by careful attention to the design and execution of the sample. Random sampling error is due to chance and cannot be avoided. This type of error can only be reduced by increasing sample size.

Measurement or nonsampling error includes everything other than sampling error that can cause inaccuracy and bias in the study results.

Probability Sampling Methods

Simple Random Sampling

simple random sample

Sample selected in such a way that every element of the population has a known and equal probability of inclusion in the sample.

Simple random sampling is considered to be the purest form of probability sample. As mentioned earlier, a probability sample is a sample in which every element of the population has a *known* and *equal* probability of being selected into the sample. For a simple random sample, that known and equal probability is computed as follows:

$$\text{Probability of Selection} = \frac{\text{Sample Size}}{\text{Population Size}}$$

For example, if the population size is 10,000 and the sample size is 400, then the probability of selection is 4 percent. It is computed as follows:

$$.04 = \frac{400}{10{,}000}$$

If a sampling frame (listing of all the elements of the population) is available, the researcher can select a simple random sample as follows:

1. Assign a number to each element of the population. A population of 10,000 elements would be numbered from 1 to 10,000.
2. Using a table of random numbers (see Table 1 in Appendix Two, "Statistical Tables"), you would begin at some arbitrary point and move up, down or across until 400 (sample size) five-digit numbers between 00001 and 10,000 are chosen.
3. The numbers selected from the table identify specific population elements to be included in the sample.

Simple random sampling is appealing because it seems simple and meets all necessary requirements of a probability sample. It guarantees that every member of the population has a known and equal chance of being selected for the sample. Simple random samples begin with a complete listing of the population. Complete listings that are current are extremely difficult and often impossible to obtain. It can be employed quite successfully in telephone surveys through the use of random digit dialing. Finally, simple random sampling can be used to select respondents from computer files. Computer programs are available or can be readily written to select random samples from computer files such as customer lists.

Systematic Sampling

systematic sampling
Probability sampling in which the entire population is numbered, and elements are drawn using a skip interval.

Systematic sampling is often used as a substitute for simple random sampling. Its popularity is based on its simplicity. Systematic sampling produces samples that are almost identical to those generated via simple random sampling.

To use this approach, it is necessary to obtain a listing of the population, just as in simple random sampling. The researcher must determine a *skip interval* and select names based on this skip interval. This interval can be computed very simply through the use of the following formula:

$$\text{Skip Interval} = \frac{\text{Population Size}}{\text{Sample Size}}$$

For example, if you were using the local telephone director and computed a skip interval of 100, every 100th name would be selected for the sample. The use of this formula ensures that the entire list will be covered.

A random starting point should be used in systematic sampling. For example, if you were using a telephone directory, it would be necessary to draw a random number to determine the page on which to start. Suppose page 53 is drawn. Another random number would be determined to decide the column on that page. Assume the third column is drawn. A final random number would be drawn to determine the actual starting position in that column; say, the 17th name. From that beginning point, the skip interval would be employed.

The main advantage of systematic sampling over simple random sampling is economy. It is often simpler, less time-consuming, and less expensive to use systematic sampling than simple random sampling. The greatest danger in the use of systematic sampling lies in the listing of the population. Some populations may contain hidden patterns that the researcher may inadvertently pull into the sample. However, this danger is remote when alphabetical listings are used.

Stratified Samples

stratified samples
Probability samples that force sample to be more representative.

Stratified samples are probability samples that are distinguished by the following procedural steps:

- First, the original or parent population is divided into two or more mutually exclusive and exhaustive subsets (e.g., male and female).
- Second, simple random samples of elements from the two or more subsets are chosen independently from each other.

Although some authors go to great pains to point out that the requirements for a stratified sample do not specify the bases that should be used to separate the original or parent population into subsets, common sense dictates that the population be divided on the basis of factors that can be shown to be related to the characteristic of the population we are really interested in measuring. For example, if you are doing a political poll to predict the outcome of an election and can show that there is a significant difference in the way men are likely to vote and the way women are likely to vote, then gender would be an appropriate basis for stratification. If you do not do stratified sampling in this manner, then you do not get the benefits of stratified sampling, and you have expended additional time, effort, and resources for no benefit. In the preceding example, gender is the basis for stratification, and we will have one stratum made up of men and one stratum made up of women. These strata are mutually exclusive and exhaustive in that every population element can be assigned to one and only one stratum (male or female) and no population elements are unassignable. The second stage in the process involves drawing simple random samples independently from each stratum.

Stratified samples are used rather than simple random samples because of their potential for greater statistical efficiency.[14] This means that if we have two samples from the same population, one a properly stratified sample and the other a simple random sample, the stratified sample will have a smaller sampling error. If, on the other hand, the goal is to attain a certain target level of sampling error, it can be achieved with a smaller stratified sample. Stratified samples are statistically more efficient because one source of variation has been eliminated. How this is achieved is explained in greater detail later.

You might ask the question, "If stratified samples are statistically more efficient, why are they not used all the time?" There are two reasons:

1. Frequently the information necessary to *properly* stratify the sample is not available. For example, little may be known about the demographic characteristics of the consumers of a particular product. Note that we said *properly* stratify the sample. To properly stratify the sample and to get the benefits of

stratification, you must pick bases for stratification where there are significant differences between the members of the two or more strata in regard to the measurement of interest.

2. Even if the necessary information is available, the time or costs of stratification may not be warranted from a cost versus value of information perspective.

In the case of a simple random sample, the researcher depends entirely on the laws of probability to generate a representative sample of the population. In the case of a stratified sample, the researcher, to some degree, forces the sample to be representative by making sure that important or salient dimensions of the population are represented in the sample in their true population proportions. For example, the researcher may know that although men and women are equally likely to be users of a particular product, women are much more likely to be heavy users of that product. In a study designed to analyze consumption patterns of the product, failure to properly represent women in the sample will result in a biased view of consumption patterns. Assume that women make up 60 percent of the population of interest and men account for 40 percent of the population. A simple random sample of the population, even if everything were done absolutely correctly, might result in a sample that is made up of 55 percent women and 45 percent men. This would be due to sampling fluctuations. This is the kind of error we get when we flip a coin 10 times. The correct result would be five heads and five tails, but more than half the time we would get a result other than five heads and five tails. In similar fashion, even a properly drawn and executed simple random sample will seldom generate a sample made up of 60 percent women and 40 percent men from a population made up of 60 percent women and 40 percent men. However, in the case of a stratified sample, the researcher will force the sample to have 60 percent women and 40 percent men.

As noted, the added precision of a stratified sample comes at some cost. Three steps are involved in implementing a properly stratified sample:

1. Identify salient (important) demographic or classification factors—factors that are correlated with the behavior of interest. For example, in a study of consumption rates for a particular product, there may be reason to believe that men and women have different average consumption rates. To use gender as a basis for meaningful stratification, the researcher must be able to show with actual data that there are significant differences in the consumption levels of men and women. In this manner, various salient factors are identified. Research indicates that after the six most important salient factors have been identified, the identification of additional salient factors adds little in the way of additional sampling efficiency.[15]
2. Next, determine what proportions of the population fall into the various subgroups under each stratum (e.g., if gender has been determined to be a salient factor, what proportion of the population is male and what proportion is female?). Using these proportions you can determine how many respondents are required from each subgroup. However, before making a final determination, a decision must be made as to whether to use proportional allocation or disproportional or optimal allocation.[16]
   - Under **proportional allocation,** the number of elements selected from a stratum is directly proportional to the size of the stratum in relation to the

proportional allocation
Sampling in which the number of elements selected from a stratum is directly proportional to the size of the stratum relative to the population.

size of the population. With proportional allocation, the proportion of elements to be taken from each stratum is given by the formula n/N, where n = the size of the stratum and N = the size of the population.

disproportional or optimal allocation

Sampling in which the number of elements taken from a given stratum is proportional to the relative size of the stratum and the standard deviation of the characteristic under consideration.

- **Disproportional or optimal allocation** produces the most efficient samples and provides the most precise or reliable estimates for a given sample size. This approach requires a *double weighting scheme.* Under this double weighting scheme, the number of sample elements to be taken from a given stratum is proportional to the relative size of the stratum and the standard deviation of the distribution of the characteristic under consideration for all elements in the stratum. This is done for two reasons. First, the size of a stratum is important because those strata with a larger number of elements are more important in determining the population mean. Therefore, these strata are more important in deriving estimates of population parameters. Second, it also makes sense that relatively more elements should be drawn from those strata having larger standard deviations (more variation) and relatively fewer elements should be drawn from those strata having smaller standard deviations. By allocating relatively more of our sample to those strata where the potential for sampling error is greatest (largest standard deviation), we get more bang for our buck and improve the overall accuracy of our estimates. There is no difference between proportional allocation and disproportional allocation if the distributions of the characteristic under consideration have the same standard deviations from stratum to stratum.

3. Finally, the researcher would select separate simple random samples from each strata. Actually, this process will be implemented somewhat differently in reality. Assume that our stratified sampling plan requires that 240 women and 160 men be interviewed. We will sample from the total population including both men and women and keep track of the number of men and women interviewed during the process. Let us say, for example, that at some point in the process we have interviewed 240 women and 127 men. From that point on, we will interview only men until we have reached the target of 160 men. In this manner, the process would generate a sample in which the proportion of men and women in the sample is as required by the allocation scheme in Step 2.

Stratified samples are not used as often as one might expect in marketing research. The problem is that the researcher frequently does not have, in advance, the information necessary to properly stratify the sample. Stratification cannot be based on guesses or hunches but must be based on hard data regarding the characteristics of the population and the relationship between these characteristics and the behavior under investigation. Stratified samples are frequently used in political polling and media audience research. In those areas, the researcher is much more likely to have the information necessary to implement the stratification process just described.

cluster samples

Sampling approach used with door-to-door interviewing in which the sampling units are selected in groups to reduce data collection costs.

Cluster Samples

The types of samples discussed until now have all been single unit samples, in which each sampling unit is selected separately. In the case of **cluster samples,** the sampling units are selected in groups.[17] There are two basic steps in cluster sampling:

- First, the population of interest is divided into mutually exclusive and exhaustive subsets.
- Second, a random sample of the subsets is selected.

If the researcher samples all the elements in the subsets selected, the procedure is a one-stage cluster sample. However, if a sample of elements is selected in some probabilistic manner from the selected subsets, then the procedure is a two-stage cluster sample. Both stratified and cluster sampling involve dividing the population into mutually exclusive and exhaustive subgroups. However, the issue that distinguishes the two is that in the case of stratified samples, a sample of elements is selected from each subgroup. In the case of cluster sampling, the researcher selects a sample of subgroups and then either collects data from all the elements in the subgroup (one-stage cluster sample) or from a sample of the elements (two-stage cluster sample).

All the probability sampling methods discussed to this point require sample frames that list or provide some organized breakdown of all the elements in the target population. Under cluster sampling, the researcher develops sample frames that include groups or clusters of elements of the population without actually listing individual elements. Sampling is executed with such frames by taking a sample of the clusters in the frame and generating lists or other breakdowns for only those clusters that have been selected for the sample. Finally, a sample is selected from the elements of the clusters selected.

The area sample, in which the clusters are units of geography (e.g., city blocks), is the most popular type of cluster sample. A researcher, conducting a

If market researchers choose this area of Chicago as their only area for cluster sampling they will not get a heterogeneous sample typical of the metropolitan area. SOURCE: © Doris DeWitt/ Tony Stone Images.

Marketing Research in Practice

When studies of national scope are involved, Opinion Research Corporation (ORC) probability sampling plans are developed in the context of their national probability sample. This is a permanent sampling framework that eliminates the need and expense of repeating some of the basic and most complex steps in drawing a sample in such assignments.

1. *Step 1. Selecting Counties.* The first step in developing the national probability sample used by ORC in nationwide studies is to list the approximately 3,000 counties in the United States. The list is grouped on the basis of the nine U.S. Census Bureau regions. Within each region, the list is ordered by size of population. Counties are selected from the list so that each county has a probability of being selected proportionate to its population.
2. *Step 2. Towns.* Within each county selected, all minor civil divisions (e.g., towns or cities) are then listed in order of population, and the selection procedure described previously for selecting counties is repeated. That is, each town has a probability of selection proportionate to its population.
3. *Step 3. Actual Interviewing Locations.* Once the towns are selected, starting points for the interviews are selected. These starting points are determined from telephone directories covering the towns selected.
4. *Step 4. Individual Households.* The households to be surveyed within a town are determined by selecting one or more telephone numbers at random from the local telephone book. Because some people have listed telephones and others do not, the actual interviewing starts next door to the address of the telephone number selected. In this way, every household in the United States can enter into the sample.
5. *Step 5. Individual Respondents.* The selection of individual respondents is also completely predesignated by the sampling plan. When the study requires that information be obtained from a particular person in a household such as a man or a woman, that person is specified. In other cases, when any of a number of persons in a household might be eligible (e.g., the study might require interviews with persons 21 and over), random methods are used to preselect the person to be interviewed.

In this situation, the interviewer lists on a form all the residents of a household and their ages in a predetermined order (e.g.,, from oldest to youngest). Each individual is assigned a number. Finally, the interviewers refers to a selection table to determine which person to interview.[18] ■

door-to-door survey in a particular metropolitan area, might randomly choose a sample of city blocks from that metropolitan area. After selecting a sample of clusters, a sample of consumers would be interviewed from each cluster. All interviews would be conducted in the clusters selected and none in other clusters. By interviewing only within the cluster selected, the researcher would dramatically reduce interviewer travel time and expenses. Cluster sampling is considered to be a probability sampling technique because of the random selection of clusters and the random selection of elements within each cluster selected.

Under cluster sampling, it is assumed that the elements in a cluster are just as heterogeneous as the total population. If the characteristics of the elements of a cluster are very similar, then that assumption is violated and the researcher has a problem. In the example just described, there may be little heterogeneity within clusters because the residents of clusters are very similar to each other and different from those in other clusters. Typically, this potential problem is dealt with in the sample design by selecting a large number of clusters into the sample and sampling a relatively small number of elements from each cluster.

This type of cluster sample is a two-stage cluster sample. Stage one involves the selection of clusters, and stage two involves the selection of elements from within clusters. Multistage area sampling or multistage area probability samples involve three or more steps.[19] These types of samples are used for national surveys or surveys that cover large regional areas. Under samples of this type, the researcher randomly selects geographic areas in progressively smaller units. For example, a statewide door-to-door survey might include the following steps:

1. Choose counties within the state to make sure that different areas are represented in the sample. Counties within the state should be selected with a probability proportional to the number of sampling units (households) within the county. Counties with a larger number of households would have a higher probability of selection than counties with a smaller number of households.
2. Select residential blocks within the selected counties.
3. Select households within the residential blocks selected.

A more detailed example is provided in the Marketing Research in Practice feature on Opinion Research Corporation on page 466.

From the standpoint of statistical efficiency, cluster samples are generally less efficient than other types of probability samples. In other words, a cluster sample of certain size will have a larger sampling error than a simple random sample or a stratified sample of that same size. To illustrate the greater cost efficiency and lower statistical efficiency of a cluster sample, consider the following example. We need to select a sample of 200 households in a particular city for in-home interviews. If these 200 households were selected via a simple random sample, they would be scattered across the city. A cluster sample might be implemented in this situation by selecting 20 residential blocks in the city and randomly selecting 10 households within each block to be interviewed. It is easy to see that interviewing costs will be dramatically reduced under the cluster sampling approach. Interviewers would not have to spend as much time traveling and would dramatically reduce their mileage and travel time. In regard to sampling error, we can see that the advantage would go to the simple random sample. Interviewing 200 households scattered across the city would increase the chance of getting a representative cross section of respondents. If all the interviewing is conducted in 20 randomly selected city blocks within the city, it is possible that certain ethnic, social, or economic groups could be missed or over- or underrepresented.

As noted previously, cluster samples are, in nearly all cases, statistically less efficient than simple random samples. It is possible to view a simple random sample as a special type of cluster sample, in which the number of clusters is equal to the total sample size, and we select one sample element per cluster. At this point, the statistical efficiency of the cluster sample and the simple random sample are equal. From this point on, as we decrease the number of clusters and increase the number of sample elements per cluster, the statistical efficiency of the cluster sample declines. At the other extreme, we might select a single cluster and select all the sample elements from that cluster. For example, we might select one relatively small geographic area in the city where you live and interview 200 people from that area. How comfortable would you be that a sample selected in this manner would be representative of the entire metropolitan area where you live?

Nonprobability Sampling Methods

In a general sense, any sample that does not meet the requirements of a probability sample is, by definition, a nonprobability sample. We have already noted that a major disadvantage of nonprobability samples is the inability to calculate sampling error. This suggests the even greater difficulty of evaluating the overall quality of nonprobability samples. We know that they do not meet the standard required of probability samples, but the question is, How far do they deviate from that standard? The user of the data from a nonprobability sample must make this assessment. The assessment must be based on a careful evaluation of the methodology used to generate the nonprobability sample. Is it likely that the methodology employed would generate a reasonable cross section of target population? Or is the sample hopelessly biased in some particular direction? These are the assessments that must be made. Four types of nonprobability samples are frequently used: convenience, judgment, quota, and snowball samples.

Convenience Samples

convenience samples
Samples used primarily for reasons of convenience.

Convenience samples are samples used, as their name implies, for reasons of convenience. Companies like Frito Lay often do preliminary tests of new product formulations developed by their R&D departments using employees. At first, this may seem to be a highly biased approach to the problem. However, they are not asking employees to evaluate their existing products or to compare their products with competitive products. They are asking employees only to provide gross sensory evaluations of new product formulations (e.g., saltiness, crispiness, greasiness). In situations like this, convenience samples may represent an efficient and effective means of obtaining the required information. This is particularly true if we are dealing with an exploratory situation, where there is a pressing need to get an approximation of the true value inexpensively.

Reports from the industry indicate that the use of convenience sampling is growing at a faster rate than the growth of probability sampling. The reason for this, as suggested in the Marketing Research in Practice feature on SSI-LITe, is the growing availability of databases of consumers in low incidence and hard to find categories. For example, if a company has developed a new athlete's foot remedy and needs to conduct a survey among people who suffer from the malady, it would find that these individuals make up only 4 percent of the population. This means that in a telephone survey, researchers would have to actually talk with 25 people before finding one individual who suffers from the problem. An attractive alternative is to purchase a list of individuals known to suffer from the problem. The cost of the survey and the time necessary to complete it can be dramatically reduced. Although the list was developed from individuals who had used coupons when purchasing the product or who had sent in for manufacturers' rebates and was therefore, not a perfectly representative sample frame, companies are increasingly willing to make the trade-off of lower cost and faster turnaround for a lower-quality sample. Examples of some of the more than 1,500 lists available from Survey Sampling, Inc. are provided in Table 13.6.

Judgment Samples

The term **judgment sample** is applied to any situation in which the researcher is attempting to draw a representative sample based on judgmental selection criteria. Most test markets and many product tests conducted in shopping malls are essentially judgmental samples. In the case of test markets, one or a few markets are selected based on the judgment that they are representative of the population as a whole. Malls are selected for product taste tests based on the researcher's judgment that the particular mall attracts a reasonable cross section of consumers who fall into the target group for the product being tested.

judgment samples
Samples in which the selection criteria are based on personal judgment that the element is representative of the population under study.

TABLE 13.6 Survey Sampling SSI-LITe Category

CATEGORY	DESCRIPTION	COUNT
Art/Antiques	interest in clothing	call for count
Astrology/Occult	interest in reading about	call for count
Beer	by usage and by brand	call for count
Bible/Devotional Reading		5,562,000
CD Player	own	7,373,000
Cellular Phone	own	564,000
Cordial/Liqueur Drinkers	by frequency use	call for count
Crossword Puzzles		2,004,000
Dog Owners	by size of dog	6,804,000
Expecting Child	by date of birth	call for count
Fine Arts/Antiques	interest in	2,945,000
Hemorrhoid Remedy	by frequency of use	call for count
IRA Investment	want	call for count
Mayonnaise	by brand use	call for count
Mouthwash	by brand use	call for count
Plaque Rinse	by frequency use	call for count
Recreational Vehicles		2,513,000
Students, College	by class year	call for count
Suffers From	back pain	460,170

SOURCE: Courtesy of Survey Sampling, Inc. © Copyright Survey Sampling, Inc., 1994.

Marketing Research in Practice

SSI-LITe (SSI's Low Incidence Targeted samples) sales increased by nearly 50 percent in 1993. SSI-LITe is a form of convenience sampling, which the research industry can use to assist in screening for low incidence segments of the population. To the degree that SSI's sampling services act as a barometer of research activity, SSI-LITe sales suggest that the use of convenience samples is growing at a faster rate than the use of probability samples.

Probability sampling in the strictest sense allows each potential respondent an opportunity to be selected for a study. The probabilities of selection can be controlled and calculated as a result of sample selection. Research results can serve both enumerative as well as analytical purposes. This is not the case when a subjective selection of respondents is used, as with SSI-LITe and other nonprobability samples. Yet the practical constraints of time and budgets clearly make a case for the use of nonprobability samples.

When less than 1 percent of U.S. households purchase a certain brand, research options may become quite limited and targeted samples, such as SSI-LITe, provide researchers with the opportunity to gain an understanding of attitudes and behaviors that they could not otherwise gain. The problem occurs when the researcher or research user attempts to project the findings to the total population, which can lead to costly wrong decisions. The researcher must understand the limitations when the research design employs anything other than a probability sample. ■

SOURCE: Courtesy of Survey Sampling, Inc.

Quota Samples

quota samples

Samples in which quotas are established for population subgroups. Selection is by nonprobability means.

Because **quota samples** are typically selected in such a way that demographic characteristics of interest to the researcher are represented in the sample in the same proportions as they are in the population, it is easy to understand how quota samples and stratified samples might be confused. There are, however, two key differences between a quota sample and a stratified sample. First of all, respondents for a quota sample are not selected on a random basis, as they must be for a stratified sample. Second, in a stratified sample, the classification factors used for stratification must be selected on the basis of the existence of a correlation between the classification factor and the behavior of interest. There is no such requirement in the case of a quota sample. The demographic or classification factors of interest in a quota sample are selected on the basis of researcher judgment.

Snowball Sampling

snowball samples

Samples in which selection of additional respondents is based on referrals from the initial respondents.

Snowball samples use sampling procedures that involve the selection of additional respondents on the basis of referrals from the initial respondents. This procedure is used to sample from low incidence or rare populations.[21] By *low incidence* or *rare populations*, we are referring to populations that make up a very small percentage of the total population. The costs of finding members of these rare populations may be so great as to force the researcher to use a technique like snowball sampling for cost efficiency. For example, an insurance company might be interested in obtaining a national sample of individuals who have switched from the indemnity form of health care coverage to a health maintenance organization in the past six months. It would be necessary to sample an extremely large number of consumers nationally to locate 1,000 consumers who fall into this population. It would be far more economical to conduct an initial sample to identify 200 people who fall into the population of interest and obtain the names of an average of four other people from each of the respondents to the initial survey to complete the sample of 1,000.

The main advantages of snowball sampling relate to the dramatic reduction in search costs. However, this advantage comes at some cost. The total sample is likely to be biased because the individuals whose names were obtained from those sampled in the initial phase are likely to be very similar to those initially sampled. As a result, the resulting sample may not be a good cross section of the total population. There should be some limits on the number of respondents obtained through referral, though there are no specific rules regarding what these limits should be. Finally, this approach may be hampered by the fact that respondents may be reluctant to give referrals.

Summary

The population, or universe, is the total group of people in whose opinions one is interested. A census involves collecting desired information from all the members of the population of interest. A sample is simply a subset of a population. The steps in developing a sampling plan are as follows: define the population of interest, choose the data collection method, choose the sampling frame, select the sampling method, determine sample size, develop and specify an operational plan for selecting sampling elements, and execute the operational sampling plan. The sampling frame is the means of listing the elements of the population from which the sample will be drawn or the specification of a procedure for generating the elements of the population to be sampled.

Probability sampling methods are selected in such a way that every element of the population has a known, nonzero probability of selection. Nonprobability sampling methods include all methods that select specific elements from the population in a nonrandom manner. Probability samples have several advantages over nonprobability samples, including reasonable certainty that information will be obtained from a representative cross section of the population, a sampling error that can be computed, and survey results that can be projected to the total population. However, probability samples are more expensive than nonprobability samples and usually take much more time to design and execute. Recent evidence indicates that convenience samples are growing in popularity.

The accuracy of sample results is affected by sampling error and nonsampling error. Sampling error is the error that results because the sample selected is not perfectly representative of the population. There are two types of sampling error: random and administrative. Random sampling error is due to chance and cannot be avoided.

Probability sampling methods include simple random samples, systematic sampling, stratified samples, and cluster samples. Nonprobability sampling techniques include convenience samples, judgment samples, quota samples, and snowball samples.

Key Terms

Population or universe
Census
Sample
Sampling frame
Random digit dialing
Probability samples
Nonprobability samples
Simple random sampling
Systematic sampling
Stratified samples
Proportional allocation
Disproportional or optimal allocation
Cluster samples
Convenience samples
Judgment samples
Quota samples
Snowball samples

Review and Discussion Questions

1. Describe five distinct populations at your university.
2. What are some situations in which a census would be better than a sample? Why are samples usually taken rather than censuses?
3. Develop a sampling plan for examining undergraduate business students' attitudes toward children's advertising.
4. Give an example of a perfect sample frame. Why is a telephone directory often not an acceptable sample frame of a particular city?
5. Distinguish between probability and nonprobability samples. What are the advantages and disadvantages of each? Why are nonprobability samples so popular in marketing research?
6. Distinguish among a systematic sample, cluster sample, and stratified sample. Cite examples of each.
7. What is the difference between a stratified sample and a quota sample?
8. American National Bank has 1,000 customers. The manager wishes to draw a sample of 100 customers. How would this be done using systematic sampling? What impact would it have on the technique, if any, if the list were ordered by average size of deposit?
9. Simple random samples are rarely used for door-to-door interviewing. Why do you think this is true?
10. Do you see any problem with drawing a systematic sample from a telephone book, assuming that the telephone book is an acceptable sample frame?
11. Define a snowball sampling. Give an example.
12. Name some possible sampling frames for the following:
    a. Patrons of sushi bars
    b. Owners of hamsters.
    c. Racquetball players.
    d. Fly rod owners.
    e. Retailers of Silly Putty.
    f. Emigrants to the United States of less than two years
    g. Persons with acne.
    h. Women wearing size 4 dresses.

13. Identify the following sample designs:
    a. The names of 20 patrons of a bingo parlor are drawn out of a hat and a questionnaire is administered to them.
    b. A radio talk show host invites listeners to call in and vote yes or no on banning nuclear weapons.
    c. A dog food manufacturer wants to test a new dog food. It decides to select 100 dog owners who feed their dogs canned food, 100 who feed their dogs dry food, and 100 who feed their dogs semimoist food.
    d. All members of Alpha Beta fraternity are questioned regarding their satisfaction with the last Spring Dinner.

CASE 13.1

Data Perspectives

Data Perspectives, a custom marketing research firm in Chicago, has been retained by Pillsbury to conduct an in-home use test for a new line of frozen, deep dish pizzas. Laboratory tests have suggested that the formulation developed for the crust of the new product produces a cooked crust that is not too soggy and not too crispy. This is the type of crust that those who prefer deep dish pizzas said they want in focus groups and mall intercept taste tests.

The purpose of the study is to find out whether consumers get the same results as achieved in the lab when they prepare the product at home. This is necessary because home ovens do not produce the precise temperatures produced with ovens in the lab and consumers may cook the product after various degrees of defrosting.

In market segmentation studies, the client has found that there are five regional markets in terms of pizza preferences. It has identified the following metropolitan areas to represent each market:

- Boston—Northeast.
- Chicago—Midwest.
- Atlanta—Southeast.
- Phoenix—Southwest.
- Los Angeles—West Coast.

The sampling method given to each interviewer is provided in Figure 13.5 and 13.6 on page 474.

1. How would you describe the sampling methodology?
2. What are the advantages and disadvantages of this type of sampling method?

FIGURE 13.5

Interviewer Instructions for Selecting Sampling Blocks

The interviewer is to *select* the block or sampling area for this group of interviews.

You are to first find a map of this town (usually a gas station is the best place). Start in the upper left-hand corner (northwest corner) of the map and begin counting the blocks until you reach block number ________. This block will be the block marked with an *X* on the sampling sheet (S-1) attached to this folder.

If the number given above is greater than the actual number of blocks in this town, you should simply continue your count after the last block, again beginning with the first block on the upper left-hand corner.

For example, if the number listed above were 25 and there were only 10 blocks in this particular town (Town A), you would select the block to interview in as follows:

You would begin counting with the block in the upper left-hand corner, counting across to your right. In this case there are only 10 blocks, so you begin with number 11 at the first block again, etc. In this case the fifth block is selected because the number 25 falls on that block.

The fifth block here then becomes the block marked *X* on the sampling sheet. You are to begin interviewing at the corner designated on that sheet and follow the instructions listed there. Please list the street boundaries of the block you have selected on the sampling sheet also.

Note: In the preceding case, if the number were 5 or 15 or 25 or 35 or 45, and so on, the fifth block would still be selected in each of these cases.

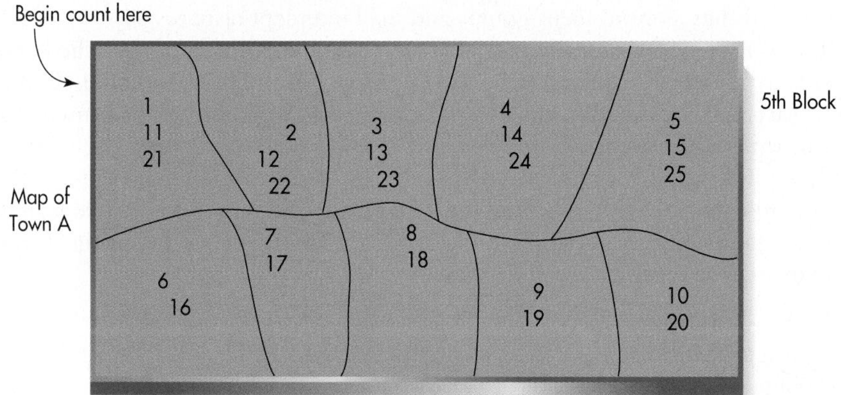

FIGURE 13.6

Sampling Plan

You are to complete 10 interviews in the primary sampling block *X*. Do not make any callbacks. If you have not completed 10 interviews when you return to the starting point, go to *A* block and continue to interview. Start at the same point as you did on the primary sampling block. If you have not completed your 10 interviews when you return to the starting point on block *A*, proceed to block *B* and follow the same procedure. If you still have not completed 10 interviews, go to block *C* and then *D*. If, after interviewing around block *D* you still have not completed 10 interviews, call your supervisor immediately.

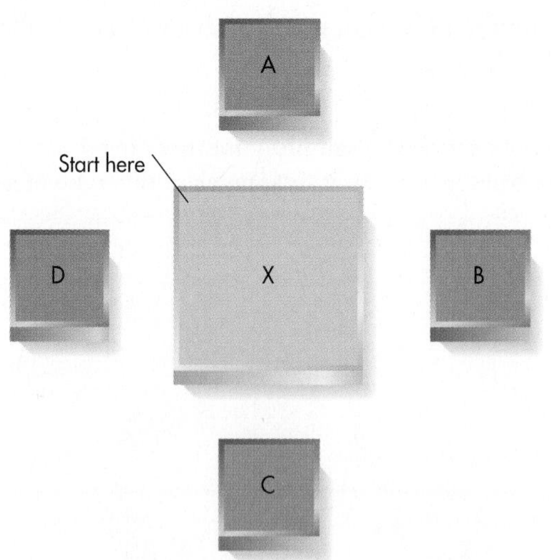

CASE 13.2

The Data Group

The Data Group has been hired by the National Furniture Dealers Association to determine the following: What specific factors motivate people to purchase furniture? How do these factors differ between purchasing furniture for initial household setup and purchasing furniture for redecoration? Why do people select one furniture brand over another? Why do people select one furniture store over another? Do consumers know or care whether a furniture store is a member of the National Furniture Dealers Association? What value-added services would furniture purchasers like to have available at furniture stores (e.g., consultation on decorating plan)?

The Data Group underbid three other research companies to obtain the contract from the National Furniture Dealers Association. In fact, its bid was almost 40 percent lower than the next lowest bid. The primary way in which the data group was able to provide the lowest bid related to its sampling methodology. In its proposal, the Data Group specified that college students would be used to gather the survey data. Its plan called for randomly selecting 20 colleges from across the country, contacting the chairperson of the marketing department and asking her to submit a list of 10 students who would be interested in earning extra money. Finally, the Data Group would contact the students individually with the goal of identifying five students at each school who would ultimately be asked to complete 10 interviews. Students would be paid $10 for each completed survey. The only requirement imposed in regard to selecting potential respondents was that they had to have purchased $200 worth of furniture in the past two years. The Data Group proposal suggested that the easiest way to do this would be to go to the student union or student center during the lunch hour and go from table to table asking those at each table whether they might be interested in participating in the survey.

1. How would you describe this sampling methodology?
2. What problems do you see arising from this technique?
3. Suggest an alternative sampling method that might give the National Furniture Dealers Association a much better picture of the information it desired.

CASE 13.3

New Mexico National Bank

New Mexico National Bank (NMNB) operates branches in 43 cities and towns throughout New Mexico. The bank offers a complete range of financial services, including Visa and Mastercard credit cards. NMNB has 62,500 people in the state using its credit cards. From the original application, it has certain information about these individuals, including name, address, zip code, telephone number, income, education, and assets. NMNB is interested in determining whether there is a relationship between the volume of purchases charged on credit cards and demographic characteristics of the individual cardholder. For example, are individuals in certain parts of the state more or less likely to be heavy users of the card? Is there a relationship between the person's income and his level of card usage? Is there a relationship between the person's level of education and card usage? Norman Robbins is research director for NMNB, and he is currently in the process of developing a design for the research. If you were Robbins, how would you answer the following questions.

1. How would you define the population of interest for the study?
2. What sample frame would you use for the project?
3. What procedure would you use to select a simple random sample from the sampling frame you chose above?
4. How would you approach the process of drawing a stratified sample from the sampling frame you chose?
5. Could you use your sample frame to draw a cluster sample? How would you go about it?
6. Which of the three probability sampling methods, just covered, would you choose for this study? Why would you choose that particular procedure?

CHAPTER 14

Sample Size Determination

LEARNING OBJECTIVES

1. To learn the financial and statistical issues in the determination of sample size.
2. To discover the methods for determining sample size.
3. To gain an appreciation of a normal distribution.
4. To understand population, sample, and sampling distribution.
5. To distinguish between point and interval estimates.
6. To recognize problems involving sampling means and proportions.

Handy Dan's is a chain of home improvement centers operating in several Southwest states. Handy Dan's wants to develop information about the characteristics of its current customer base. However, it cannot afford to hire a commercial marketing research firm to do the research. It has contacted Dr. Lara Gates, who teaches the marketing research course at a local university, and they have reached an agreement whereby her class will do the research project.

Lara has created teams responsible for executing different aspects of the research. Jeff Rayburn is a member of the team responsible for developing the sample plan. The team has decided, after an initial meeting with the marketing director at Handy Dan's, that a simple random sample is the appropriate type of sample for the project. Jeff is responsible for determining how large the sample should be. He recognizes that a major goal of the research is to estimate the proportions or percentages of Handy Dan's customers that fall into various demographic groups. In addition, he has determined that Handy Dan's believes that it needs estimates of population values that are within ± 5.0 percent of the true values. He remembers, from an earlier statistics course, that you can make such inferences about sample results but you can make them only with some level of confidence, never with certainty. Referring to the statistics book from his earlier course, he has determined that the team can make inferences such as "We are 95 percent confident that the true population value is wihin ± 5.0 percent of the estimates based on our sample."

SOURCE: © Bob Daemmrick/Stock Boston.

He has discussed the matter with other members of his team and with the marketing manager at Handy Dan's. Both his team and the marketing manager agree that an error of ± 5.0 percent with 95 percent confidence is acceptable. He is now trying to figure out how to calculate the sample size necessary to meet these requirements. After reading this chapter, you should know how to approach the sample size calculation problem that Jeff is currently considering.[1] ■

Consider the issues that Jeff and his team are facing. As you read this chapter, answers to the various questions will be presented. When you finish the chapter, you should be prepared to answer all the questions presented in the opening vignette. In particular, you should be able to make the necessary sample size calculation.

Determining Sample Size for Probability Samples

Financial, Statistical, and Managerial Issues

The process of determining sample size for probability samples involves financial, statistical, and managerial issues. Other things being equal, the larger the sample, the less the sampling error. However, larger samples cost more money, and the funds available for a particular project are always limited. In addition, though the costs of larger samples tend to increase on a linear basis, the level of sampling error decreases at a rate only equal to the square root of the relative increase in sample size. In other words, if sample size is quadrupled, data collection costs will be quadrupled, but the level of sampling error will be reduced by only one-half. Finally, managerial issues must be reflected in sample size calculations. How accurate do our estimates need to be and how confident do we need to be that true population values are taken in by the chosen confidence interval? As you will see later in the chapter, there are a number of possibilities. In some cases, there is a need to be very precise (small sampling error) and very confident that population values fall in the small range of sampling error (confidence interval). In other cases, you may not need to be as precise or confident.

Methods for Determining Sample Size

Budget Available

Frequently, the sample size for a project is determined by the budget available. Sample size, in essence, is frequently determined backward. A brand manager may have $20,000 available in the budget for a particular marketing research project. After deducting other project costs (e.g., research design, questionnaire development, data processing, analysis, etc.), the remainder determines the size of the sample that can be surveyed. There are limits, of course. If the dollars available are enough for only a clearly inadequate sample, a decision must be made. Either additional funds must be found or the project should be canceled.

Although this approach may seem highly unscientific and arbitrary, it is a fact of life in a corporate environment based on the budgeting of financial resources. Financial constraints challenge the researcher to develop research designs that will generate data of adequate quality for decision-making purposes with limited resources. This "budget available" approach forces the researcher to carefully consider the value of information in relation to its cost.

Rules of Thumb

Potential clients may specify in RFPs (requests for proposals) that they want a sample of 200, 400, 500, or some other specific size. Sometimes this number is based on some consideration of sampling error, and in other cases it is based on nothing more than past experience and sample sizes used in the past for similar studies. The justification for the specified sample size may boil down to nothing more than the "gut feel" that it is an appropriate sample size.

It may be that the sample size requested is judged to be adequate to support the objectives of the proposed research. In other cases, the researcher may determine that the sample size requested is not adequate. In these instances, the researcher should present arguments for a larger sample size to the client and let the client make the final decision. If the arguments for a larger sample size fall on deaf ears, the researcher may decline to submit a proposal in the belief that the sample size is so inadequate as to fatally cripple the research effort.

Number of Subgroups to Be Analyzed

In any sample size determination problem, serious consideration must be given to the number and anticipated size of various subgroups of the total sample about which there will be a need to make statistical inferences. For example, we might decide that a sample of 400 is quite adequate on an overall basis. However, if male and female respondents must be analyzed separately and the sample is expected to be 50 percent male and 50 percent female, then the expected sample size for each subgroup is only 200. Is this number adequate to permit the analyst to make the desired statistical inferences about the characteristics of the two groups? If, in addition, the results are to be analyzed by both sex and age, the problem gets even more complicated. Assume that it is important to analyze four subgroups of the total sample as follows:

- Men under 35
- Men 35 and over
- Women under 35
- Women 35 and over

If each group is expected to make up about 25 percent of the total sample, then there will be only 100 respondents in each subgroup. Is this an adequate number to permit us to make the kinds of statistical inferences about these groups that the objectives of the research require?

Other things being equal, the larger the number of subgroups that need to be analyzed, the larger the required total sample size. It has been suggested that the sample should be large enough so that there will be 100 or more respondents in each major subgroup and a minimum of 20 to 50 respondents in each of the less important subgroups.

Traditional Statistical Methods

You probably have been exposed to traditional approaches for determining sample size for simple random samples. These approaches are reviewed in this chapter. Three pieces of information are required to make the necessary calculations when using a sample result:

- An estimate of the population standard deviation.
- The acceptable level of sampling error.

- The desired level of confidence that the sample result will fall within a certain range (result ± sampling error) of true population values.

With these three pieces of information, we can calculate the size of the simple random sample required.

The Normal Distribution

General Properties

The concept of a **normal distribution** is crucial to classical statistical inference. There are several reasons for its importance. First, many variables encountered by marketers have probability distributions that are close to the normal distribution. Examples include the number of cans, bottles, or glasses of soft drink consumed by soft drink users; the number of times that people who eat at fast food restaurants go to restaurants of this type in an average month; and the average hours per week spent viewing television. Second, the normal distribution is useful for a number of theoretical reasons; one of the more important of these relates to the central limit theorem. According to the **central limit theorem,** for any population (regardless of its distribution), a distribution of samples means ($\bar{X}$) approaches a normal distribution as the sample size increases. The importance of this factor will become clear later in the chapter. Third, the normal distribution is a useful approximation of many discrete probability distributions.

normal distribution

A continuous distribution that is bell shaped and symmetrical about the mean—mean, median and mode are equal. Sixty-eight percent of the observations fall within plus or minus one standard deviation of the mean, approximately 95 percent fall within plus or minus two standard deviations, and approximately 99.5 fall within plus or minus three standard deviations.

central limit theorem

A distribution of a large number of sample means or sample proportions will approximate a normal distribution regardless of the actual distribution of the population from which they were drawn.

If, for example, we were to measure the heights of a large sample of men in the United States and plot those values on a graph, a distribution similar to the one shown in Figure 14.1 would result. This distribution is a normal distribution that has a number of important characteristics, including the following:

1. The normal distribution is bell-shaped and has only one mode. The mode is a measure of central tendency and is the particular value that occurs most frequently. A bimodal (two modes) distribution would have two peaks or humps.

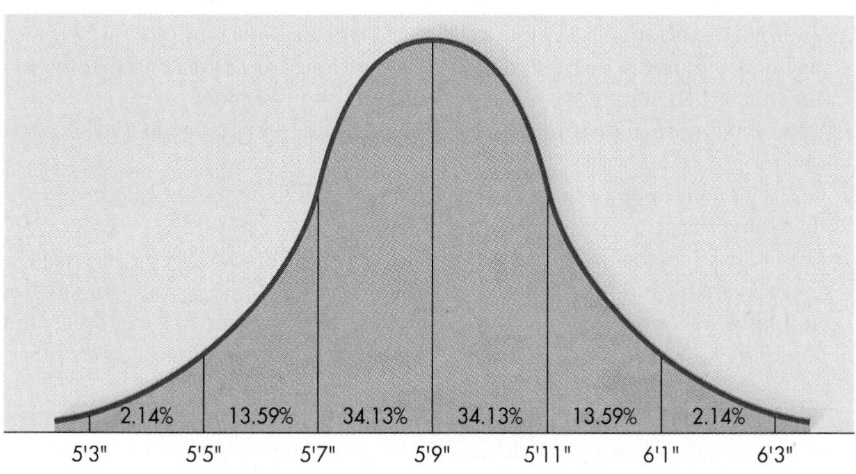

FIGURE 14.1

Distribution of the Heights of Men in the United States Based on a Large Sample

A Professional Researcher's Perspective

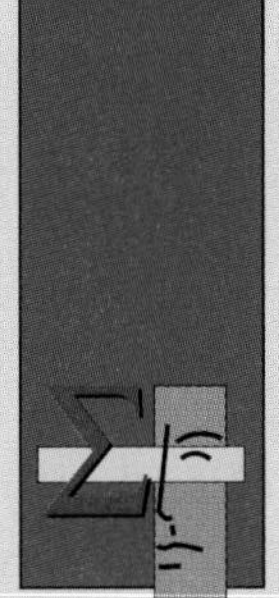

Marketers, all too often, try to save a few bucks on sample size and risk millions in opportunity loss. This is according to Thomas Semon, expert columnist for *Marketing News*. He noted that an ad agency that he once worked for bragged about using samples of 120 for copy research. Samples of this size can be fine in some cases but not in others. There is not a one-size-fits-all sample size for any type of research. The really critical factor is the size of the expected difference or change to be measured—the smaller that is, the larger the sample must be, squared.

In testing two versions of an ad, a current or control version and a new version, we might adopt the rule that the new version will be adopted if it scores significantly higher than the current or control version. "Significance" might be set at either the 90 percent or 95 percent confidence level.

This type of decision criterion protects against the risk that random sampling error results in an overestimate of the favorable response and leads to the false conclusion that the new version should be adopted. However, the opposite problem (underestimate of the favorable response, leading to the false conclusion that the new version should be rejected) is just as likely and the decision criterion specified does not protect against this possibility. In this example, a sample size of 120 does not have the statistical power to protect against the opportunity loss that may result from a failure to recognize superiority of the new version.

When the effect size, the needed or expected difference, is large (e.g., more than 10 percentage points), then statistical power is typically not a problem. However, very small effect sizes (e.g., 2 percentage points) may require such large sample sizes as to be impractical from a cost perspective.[2] ■

2. A normal distribution is symmetric about its mean. This is another way of saying that it is not skewed and that the three measures of central tendency (mean, median, and mode) are all equal to the same value.
3. A particular normal distribution is uniquely defined by its mean and standard deviation.
4. The total area under a normal curve is equal to one, meaning that it takes in all observations.
5. The area of a region under the normal distribution curve between any two values of a variable equals the probability of observing a value in that range when randomly selecting an observation from the distribution. For example, on a single draw there is a 34.13 percent chance of selecting a man between 5'7" and 5'9" in height from the distribution shown in Figure 14.1
6. The normal distribution has the feature that the area between the mean and a given number of standard deviations from the mean is the same for all normal distributions. In other words, the area between the mean and plus or

minus one standard deviation takes in 68.26 percent of the area under the curve or 68.26 percent of the observations. This is called the *proportional property* of the normal distribution. This feature provides the basis for much of the statistical inference that we will discuss in this chapter.

The Standard Normal Distribution

Any normal distribution can be transformed into what is known as a **standard normal distribution.** The standard normal distribution has the same features as any normal distribution. However, the mean of the standard normal distribution is always equal to zero and the standard deviation is always equal to one. The probabilities provided in Table 2 in Appendix Two are based on a standard normal distribution. A simple transformation formula can be used to transform any value X from any normal distribution to its equivalent value Z for a standard normal distribution. This transformation is based on the proportional property of the normal distribution:

standard normal distribution

A normal distribution with a mean of zero and a standard deviation of one.

$$Z = \frac{\text{value of variable} - \text{mean of the variable}}{\text{standard deviation of the variable}}$$

Symbolically, the formula can be stated as

$$Z = \frac{X - \mu}{\sigma}$$

where

X = value of the variable
μ = mean of the variable
σ = standard deviation of the variable

The areas under (percent of all observations) a standard normal distribution for various Z values **(standard deviations)** are shown in Table 14.1. The standardized normal distribution is shown in Figure 14.2.

standard deviation

A measure of dispersion calculated by subtracting the mean of a series from each value in a series, squaring each result, summing them, dividing the sum by the number of items minus one, and taking the square root of this value.

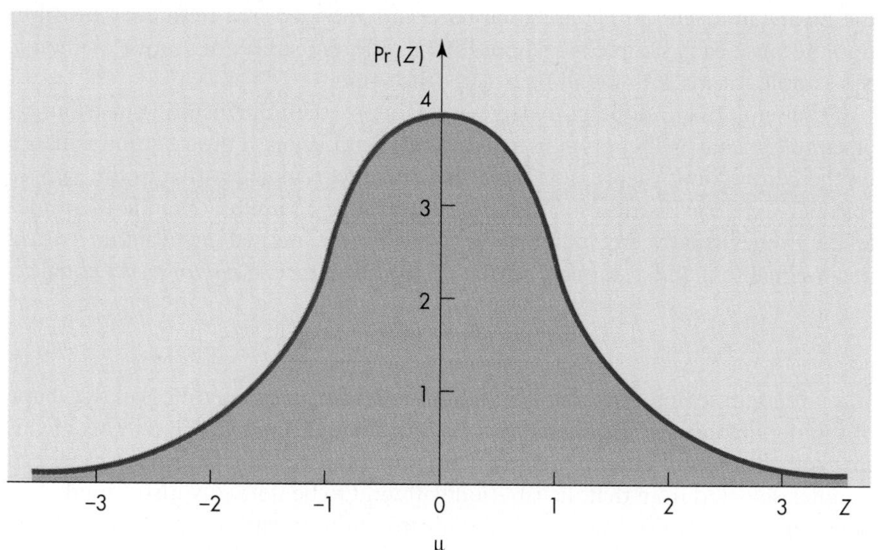

FIGURE 14.2

Standardized Normal Distribution

NOTE: The term Pr(Z) is read "the probability of Z."

TABLE 14.1 Area Under Standard Normal Curve for Z Values (standard deviations) of 1, 2, and 3

Z VALUES (STANDARD DEVIATION)	AREA UNDER STANDARD NORMAL CURVE (%)
1	68.26
2	95.44
3	99.74

Population, Sample, and Sampling Distributions

The purpose of conducting a survey based on a sample is to make inferences about the population, not to describe the sample. The population, as defined earlier, includes all possible individuals or objects from whom or about which we might collect information to meet the objectives of the research. A sample is a subset of the total population.

population distribution
A frequency distribution of all the elements of a population.

sample distribution
A frequency distribution of all the elements of an individual sample.

sampling distribution of sample means
A frequency distribution of the means of many samples drawn from a particular population. It is normally distributed.

A **population distribution** is a frequency distribution of all the elements of the population. This frequency distribution has a mean, usually represented by the Greek letter μ, and a standard deviation, usually represented by the Greek letter σ. A **sample distribution** is a frequency distribution of the elements of an individual (single) sample. In a sample distribution, the mean is usually represented by $\bar{x}$ and the standard deviation is usually represented by S.

At this point, it is necessary to introduce a third distribution, the sampling distribution of the sample mean. Understanding this distribution is crucial to understanding the basis for our ability to compute sampling error in simple random samples. The **sampling distribution of the sample mean** is a conceptual and theoretical probability distribution of the means of all possible samples of a given size drawn from a particular population. Although this distribution is seldom calculated, its known properties have tremendous practical significance. To actually derive a distribution of sample means, a large number of simple random samples (e.g., 25,000) of a certain size are drawn from a particular population. Then, the means for each sample are computed and arranged in a frequency distribution. Because each sample is composed of a different subset of sample elements, the sample means will not all be exactly the same.

If the samples are sufficiently large and random, then the resulting distribution of sample means will approximate a normal distribution. This assertion is based on the central limit theorem. Once again, this theorem states that as the sample size increases, the distribution of the means of a large number of random samples taken from virtually any population approaches a normal distribution with a mean equal to μ and a standard deviation (referred to as *standard error*) equal to

$$S_{\bar{x}} = \frac{\sigma}{\sqrt{n}} \qquad \text{where } n = \text{sample size}$$

It is important to note that the central limit theorem holds regardless of the shape of the population distribution from which the samples are selected. This means that regardless of the distribution of the population, a distribution of means of samples selected from that distribution will tend to be normally distributed. The notation ordinarily used to refer to the means and standard deviations of population, sample, and sampling distributions is summarized in Table 14.2.

TABLE 14.2 Symbols Used for Means and Standard Deviations of Various Distributions

DISTRIBUTION	MEAN	STANDARD DEVIATION
Population	μ	σ
Sample	$\bar{X}$	S
Sampling	$\mu_{\bar{x}} = \mu$	$S_{\bar{x}}$

The **standard error of the mean** ($S_{\bar{x}}$) is computed as indicated earlier because the variance or dispersion within a particular distribution of sample means will be smaller if it is based on larger samples. Common sense tells us that individual sample means will, on the average, be closer to the population mean with larger samples. The relationships among the population distribution, sample distribution, and sampling distributions of the mean are shown graphically in Figure 14.3. The sampling distribution of the mean is discussed further and another concept, the sampling distribution of the proportion, is introduced in the following sections.

standard error of the mean
The standard deviation of a distribution of sample means.

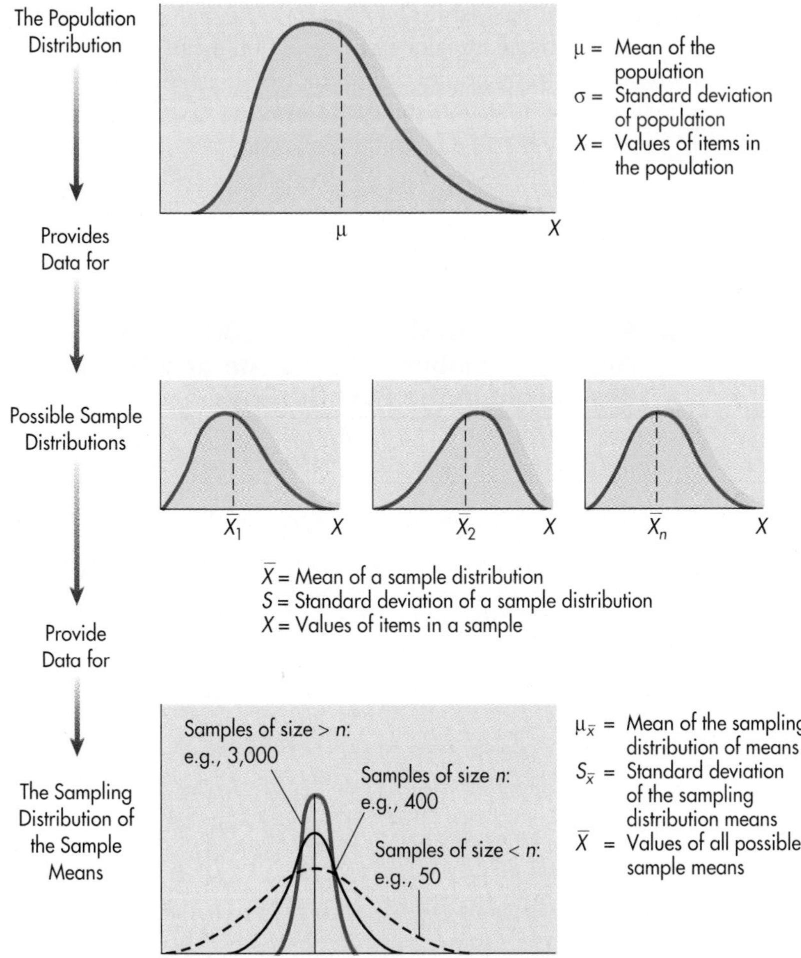

FIGURE 14.3

Relationships of the Three Basic Types of Distribution

SOURCE: Adapted from D. H. Sanders, A. F. Murphy, and R. J. Eng, *Statistics: A Fresh Approach*, p. 123, © 1980 McGraw-Hill.

Sampling Distribution of the Mean

Basic Concepts

Consider a sampling exercise in which a researcher takes 1,000 simple random samples of size 200 from the population of all consumers who have eaten at a fast food restaurant at least once in the past 30 days to estimate the average number of times these individuals eat at a fast food restaurant in an average month.

If the researcher computes the mean number of visits for each of the 1,000 samples and sorts them into intervals based on their relative values, the frequency distribution shown in Table 14.3 might be the result. These frequencies are shown in a histogram in Figure 14.4. In addition, a normal curve has been superimposed on this histogram. As you can see, the histogram closely approximates the shape of a normal curve. If we drew a large enough number of samples of size 200, computed the mean of each sample, and plotted those means, then the resulting distribution will be a normal distribution. The normal curve shown in Figure 14.4 is the sampling distribution of the mean for this particular problem. The sampling distribution of the mean for simple random samples that are large (30 or more observations) has the following characteristics:

1. The distribution is a normal distribution.
2. The distribution has a mean equal to the population mean.
3. The distribution has a standard deviation, referred to as the *standard error of the mean,* equal to the population standard deviation divided by the square root of the sample size:

$$\sigma_{\bar{x}} = \frac{\sigma}{\sqrt{n}}$$

TABLE 14.3 Frequency Distribution of 1,000 Sample Means: Average Number of Times Ate at a Fast Food Restaurant in the Past 30 Days

CATEGORY—NUMBER OF TIMES	FREQUENCY OF OCCURRENCE
2.6–3.5	8
3.6–4.5	15
4.6–5.5	29
5.6–6.5	44
6.6–7.5	64
7.6–8.5	79
8.6–9.5	89
9.6–10.5	108
10.6–11.5	115
11.6–12.5	110
12.6–13.5	90
13.6–14.5	81
14.6–15.5	66
15.6–16.5	45
16.6–17.5	32
17.6–18.5	16
18.6–19.5	9
Total	1,000

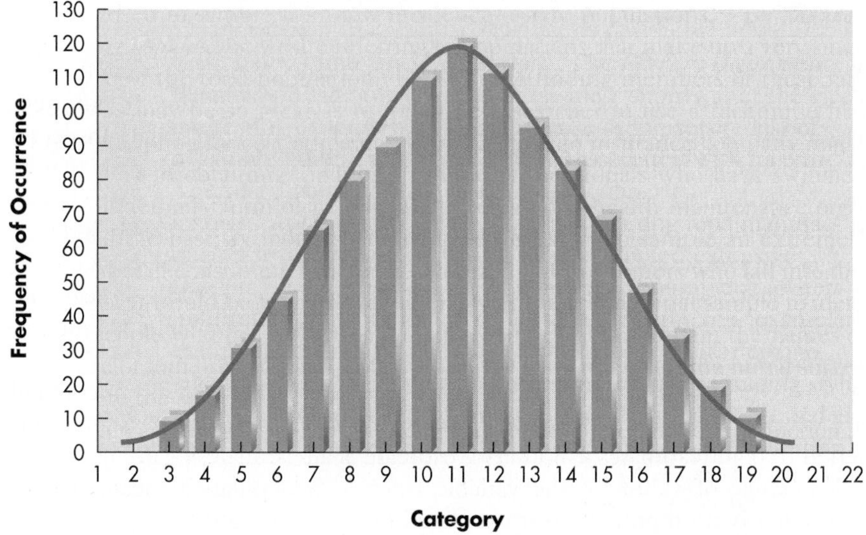

NOTE: Category is number of times person ate at a fast food restaurant in past 30 days, with a normal distribution superimposed.

FIGURE 14.4

Actual Sampling Distribution of Means

This statistic is referred to as the *standard error of the mean* instead of the standard deviation to indicate that it applies to a distribution of sample means rather than to the standard deviation of a sample or a population. Keep in mind, as noted earlier, that this calculation applies only to a simple random sample and not to other types of samples. Other types of probability samples (e.g., stratified samples and cluster samples) use more complex formulas for computing standard error.

Making Inferences on the Basis of a Single Sample

In practice we are not interested in taking all possible random samples from a particular population and generating a frequency distribution like the one shown in Table 14.3 and a histogram like the one shown in Figure 14.4. Normally, we want to take one simple random sample and make some statistical inference about the population from which the sample was drawn. The question is, What is the probability that any one simple random sample of a particular size will produce an estimate of the population mean that is within one standard error (plus or minus) of the true population mean? The answer, based on the information provided in Table 14.1, is that there is a 68 percent probability that any one sample from a particular population will produce an estimate of the population mean that is within plus or minus one standard error of the true value, because 68 percent of all sample means will fall in this range. There is a 95 percent probability that any one simple random sample of a particular size from a given population will produce a value that is within plus or minus two standard errors of the true population mean and a 99.7 percent probability that such a sample will produce an estimate of the mean that is within plus or minus three standard errors of the population mean.

Point and Interval Estimates

point estimates
Inferences regarding the sampling error associated with a particular estimate of a population value.

When using the results of a sample to make estimates of a population mean, two kinds of estimates can be generated: point and interval estimates. In **point estimates,** the sample mean is the best estimate of the population mean. Inspection of the sampling distribution of the mean shown in Figure 14.4 suggests that it is likely that a particular sample result will produce a mean that is relatively close to the population mean. However, the mean of a particular sample could be any one of the sample means shown in the distribution. A small percentage of these sample means are a considerable distance from the true population mean. The distance between the sample mean and the true population mean is called the *sampling error.*

interval estimates
Inferences regarding the likelihood that a population value will fall within a certain range.

confidence level
The probability that a particular confidence interval will include the true population value.

Given that point estimates based on sample results are exactly correct in only a small percentage of all possible cases, **interval estimates** generally are preferred to point estimates. An interval estimate is an estimate regarding an interval or range of values of the variable, such as a population mean, that the researcher is attempting to estimate. In addition to stating the size of the interval, it is customary to state the probability that the interval will take in the true value of the population mean. This probability normally is referred to as the *confidence coefficient* or **confidence level,** while we refer to the interval as the *confidence interval.*

Interval estimates of the mean are derived as follows. A random sample of a given size is drawn from the population of interest and the mean of that sample is calculated. This particular sample mean is known to lie somewhere within the sampling distribution of all possible sample means but exactly where this particular mean falls in that distribution is not known. In addition, there is a 68 percent probability that this particular sample mean lies within one standard error (plus or minus) of the true population mean. Based on this information, the statement can be made that the researcher is 68 percent confident that the true population value is equal to the sample value plus or minus one standard error. Symbolically, this statement would be stated as follows:

$$\overline{X} - 1\sigma_{\overline{x}} \leq \mu \leq \overline{X} + 1\sigma_{\overline{x}}$$

Using this same logic, the statement can be made that the researcher is 95 percent confident that the true population value is equal to the sample estimate plus or minus two standard errors (technically 1.96, but 2 is often used for convenience in calculation); and 99.7 percent confident that the true population value falls within the interval defined by the sample value plus or minus three standard errors.

All this assumes that the standard deviation of the population is known. In most situations, this is not the case. If the standard deviation of the population were known, by definition the mean of the population also would be known, and there would be no need to take a sample in the first place. Lacking information on the standard deviation of the population, its value is estimated based on the standard deviation of the sample.

Sampling Distribution of the Proportion

Marketing researchers frequently are interested in estimating proportions or percentages rather than or in addition to estimating means. Common examples include the following:

- The percent of the population that are aware of a particular ad.
- The percent of the population who will buy a new product.
- The percent of the population of all individuals who have visited a fast food restaurant in the past 30 days, who have visited a fast food restaurant four or more times during that period.
- The percent of the population who subscribe to a particular newspaper.

In situations like these, in which a population proportion or percentage is of interest, we shift to the sampling distribution of the proportion.

The **sampling distribution of the proportion** is a relative frequency distribution of the sample proportions of a large number of random samples of a given size drawn from a particular population. The sampling distribution of a proportion has the following characteristics:

sampling distribution of the proportion
A frequency distribution of the proportions of many samples drawn from a particular population. It is normally distributed.

1. It approximates a normal distribution.
2. The mean proportion for all possible samples is equal to the population proportion.
3. The standard error of a sampling distribution of proportion can be computed with the following formula:

$$S_p = \sqrt{\frac{P(1-P)}{n}}$$

where

S_p = standard error of sampling distribution of proportion
P = estimate of population proportion
n = sample size

Consider the need to estimate the percentage of all fast food users who have visited a fast food restaurant four or more times in the past 30 days. As when generating a sampling distribution of the mean, 1,000 random samples of size 200 might be selected from the population of all fast food users, and the proportion of users who have visited a fast food restaurant four or more times in the past month for all 1,000 samples computed. These values can then be plotted in a frequency distribution, and this frequency distribution will approximate a normal distribution. The estimated standard error of the proportion for this distribution is computed using the formula for the standard error of a proportion provided earlier.

For reasons that, we hope, will be clear after you read the next section, marketing researchers have a tendency to cast sample size problems as problems of estimating proportions rather than means.

A distribution of sample means for average number of visits to fast food restaurants will be normally distributed.

Sample Size Determination

Problems Involving Means

Consider the previous example that involved estimating how many times the average fast food restaurant user visits a fast food restaurant in an average month. Management needs an estimate of the average number of visits to make a decision regarding a new promotional campaign currently under consideration. To make this estimate, the marketing research manager for the firm intends to survey a simple random sample of all fast food users. The question is, What information is necessary to determine the appropriate sample size for the project? First of all, the formula for calculating the required sample size for problems that involve the estimation of a mean is as follows:

$$n = \frac{Z^2 \sigma^2}{E^2}$$

where

Z = level of confidence expressed in standard errors
σ = population standard deviation
E = acceptable amount of sampling error

allowable sampling error The amount of sampling error the researcher is willing to accept.

population standard deviation The standard deviation of a variable for the entire population.

Three pieces of information are needed to compute the sample size required.

1. Specification of the acceptable or **allowable** level of **sampling error** (E).
2. Specification of the acceptable level of confidence in standard errors or Z values. In other words, how confident do you want to be that the specified confidence interval takes in the population mean.
3. Finally, an estimate of the **population standard deviation** (σ) is required.

The level of confidence (Z) and the amount of error (E) to be used must be set by the researcher. As noted earlier, the level of confidence and amount of error are set based not only on statistical criteria, but also on financial and managerial criteria. In an ideal world, we would like to always set the level of confidence at a very high level and the amount of error at a very small level. However, because this is a business decision, cost must be considered. An acceptable trade-off between accuracy, level of confidence, and cost must be determined. In some situations, the need for precision and a high level of confidence may be less than in others. For example, in an exploratory study you may be interested in developing a basic sense of whether attitudes toward your product generally are positive or negative. Precision may not be critical. However, in a product concept test you may need to make a much more precise estimate of sales for a new product to make a potentially costly and risky decision to introduce a new product.

The third item on the list of required information, an estimate of the population standard deviation, presents a more serious problem. As noted earlier, if the population standard deviation were known, the population mean also would be known (the population mean is needed to compute the population standard deviation). There would be no need to draw a sample. The question is, How can the researcher estimate the population standard deviation before selecting the sample? One or some combination of four approaches can be used to deal with this problem:

1. *Use results from a prior survey*. In many cases, the firm may have conducted a prior survey dealing with the same or a similar issue. In this situation, the most obvious solution to the problem would be to use the results of the prior survey as an estimate of the population standard deviation in this situation.
2. *Conduct a pilot survey*. If this is to be a large scale project, it may be possible to devote some time and some resources to a small scale pilot survey of the population. The results of this pilot survey can be used to develop an estimate of the population standard deviation that can be used in the sample size determination formula.
3. *Use secondary data*. In some cases, secondary data may be available that can be used to develop an estimate of the population standard deviation.
4. *Use judgment*. If all else fails, an estimate of the population standard deviation can be developed based solely on judgment. This process may be implemented by seeking judgments from a variety of managers who would be in a position to make educated guesses regarding the required population parameters.

It should be noted that after the survey has been conducted and the sample mean and sample standard deviation have been calculated, the researcher is in a position to assess the accuracy of the estimate of the population standard deviation used to calculate the required sample size. At this time, if it is deemed appropriate, adjustments can be made in the initial estimates of sampling error.

Consider the problem involving estimation of the average number of fast food visits made in an average month by users of fast food restaurants. The values to be substituted into the formula follow:

- After consultation with managers in the company, the marketing research manager determines that it is necessary to produce an estimate of the average number of times that fast food users visit fast food restaurants. She further determines that managers believe that a high degree of accuracy is needed and translates this to mean that the estimate should be within 0.10 (one-tenth) of a visit of the true population value. This value (0.10) should be substituted into the formula for the value of E.

- In addition, the marketing research manager has decided that, all things considered, she needs to be 95 percent confident that the true population mean falls into the interval defined by the sample mean plus or minus E (as just defined). Two standard errors (technically 1.96) are required to take in 95 percent of the area under a normal curve; therefore, a value of 2 would be substituted into the equation for Z.
- Finally, there is the question of what value to insert into the formula for σ. Fortunately, the company had previously conducted a very similar study and in that study the standard deviation for the variable, average number of times visiting a fast food restaurant in the past 30 days, was 1.39 times. This is the best estimate of σ available. Therefore, a value of 1.39 would be substituted into the formula for the value of σ. The calculation follows.

$$n = \frac{Z^2 \sigma^2}{E^2}$$

$$n = \frac{2^2 (1.39)^2}{(0.10)^2}$$

$$n = \frac{4 (1.93)}{0.01}$$

$$n = \frac{7.72}{0.01}$$

$$n = 772$$

Based on this calculation, a simple random sample of 772 is necessary to meet the requirements outlined.

Problems Involving Proportions

Consider the problem of estimating the proportion of all fast food users who visit a fast food restaurant four or more times in an average month. The goal is to take a simple random sample from the population of all fast food users to estimate this proportion. A discussion of the determination of the appropriate values to substitute into the formula follows.

- As in the previous problem, involving the estimation of a population mean on the basis of sample results, the first task is to decide on an acceptable value for E. If, for example, it is decided that an error level of plus or minus 4 percent is acceptable, a value of .04 will be substituted into the formula for E.
- Next, assume that the researcher has determined a need to be 95 percent confident that the sample estimate is within plus or minus 4 percent of the true population proportion. As in the previous example, we would substitute a value of 2 into the equation for Z.
- Finally, in a study of the same issue conducted one year ago, the researcher found that 30 percent of all respondents indicated they had visited a fast food

restaurant four or more times in the previous month. We would substitute a value of .30 into the equation for P.

- The resulting calculations are as follows:

$$n = \frac{Z^2\,[P(1-P)]}{E^2}$$

$$n = \frac{2^2\,[.30(1-.30)]}{.04^2}$$

$$n = \frac{4\,(.21)}{.0016}$$

$$n = \frac{.84}{.0016}$$

$$n = 525$$

Given the requirements, a random sample of 525 respondents is needed. It should be noted that in comparison with the process of determining the sample size necessary to estimate a mean, the researcher has one major advantage when determining sample size necessary to estimate a proportion: if there is no basis for estimating P, you can make what is sometimes referred to as the *most pessimistic* or *worst case* assumption regarding the value of P. What value of P, given values of Z and E, will require the largest possible sample? A value of 0.50 will make the value of the expressions $P\,(1-P)$ larger than any other possible value of P. There is no corresponding most pessimistic assumption that the researcher can make regarding the value of σ in problems that involve determining sample size necessary to estimate a mean with given levels of Z and E.

Population Size and Sample Size

You may have noticed that none of the formulas for determining sample size takes into account in any way the size of the population. Students (and managers) frequently find this troubling. It seems to make sense that we should take a larger sample from a larger population. However, this is not true. Generally, there is no direct relationship between the size of the population and the size of the sample required to estimate a particular population parameter with a particular level of error and a particular level of confidence. In fact, the size of the population is of interest only in those situations in which the size of the sample is large in relation to the size of the population. One rule of thumb suggests that we need to make an adjustment in the sample size if the sample size is more than 5 percent of the size of the total population. The normal presumption is that sample elements are drawn independent of one another (independence assumption). This assumption is justified when the sample is small relative to the population. However, it is not appropriate when the sample is a relatively large (5 percent or more) proportion of the population. As a result, we must adjust the results obtained with the standard formulas. For example, the formula for the standard error of the mean, presented earlier, is

$$\sigma_{\overline{X}} = \frac{\sigma}{\sqrt{n}}$$

Adjusting for a sample that is 5 percent or more of the population and dropping the independence assumption, the correct formula is

$$\sigma_{\bar{x}} = \frac{\sigma}{\sqrt{n}} \sqrt{\frac{N-n}{N-1}}$$

finite population correction factor

An adjustment to the required sample size that is made in those cases in which the sample is expected to be equal to 5 percent or more of the total population.

The factor $(N-n)/(N-1)$ is referred to as the **finite population correction factor** (FPC).

In those situations in which the sample is large (5 percent or more) in relation to the population, the researcher can appropriately reduce the required sample size using the FPC. This calculation is made using the following formula:

$$n' = \frac{nN}{N+n-1}$$

where

n' = revised sample size
n = original sample size
N = population size

If the population has 2,000 elements and the original sample size is 400, then

$$n' = \frac{400(2{,}000)}{2{,}000 + 400 - 1} = \frac{800{,}000}{2{,}399}$$

$$n' = 333$$

Based on the FPC adjustment, we need a sample of only 333 rather than the original 400.

The key is not the size of the sample in relation to the size of the population, but whether the sample selected is truly representative of the population. Empirical evidence shows that relatively small but carefully chosen samples can quite accurately reflect characteristics of the population. Many well-known national surveys and opinion polls are based on samples of fewer than 2,000. The Gallup Poll, the Harris Poll, and the Nielsen Television Ratings are examples. These polls have shown that the behavior of tens of millions of people can be predicted quite accurately on the basis of samples that are minuscule in relation to the size of the population.

Determining Sample Size for Stratified and Cluster Samples

The formulas for sample size determination presented in this chapter apply only to simple random samples. There also are formulas for determining required sample size and sampling error for other types of probability samples such as stratified and cluster samples. Although many of the general concepts presented in this chapter apply to these other types of probability samples, the specific formulas are much more complicated.[3] In addition, these formulas require information that frequently is not available or difficult to obtain. For these reasons, sample size determination for other types of probability samples is beyond the scope of this introductory text. Those interested in pursuing the question of sample size determination for stratified and cluster samples are referred to advanced texts on the topic of sampling.

Summary

Determining sample size involves financial, statistical, and managerial considerations. Other things being equal, the larger the sample the less the sampling error. In turn, the cost of the research grows with the size of the sample.

There are several methods for determining sample size. One is the funds that are available. In essence, sample size is determined by the budget. Although seemingly unscientific, this is often a very real factor in the world of corporate marketing research. The second technique is the so-called rule of thumb approach. It is basically a determination of the sample size by a "gut feel" or common practice. Often samples of 300, 400, or 500 are listed in requests for proposals. Yet another technique for determining sample size is based on the number of subgroups to be analyzed. Generally speaking, the more subgroups that need to be analyzed, the larger is the required total sample size.

In addition to these factors, there are a number of traditional statistical techniques for determining sample size. Three pieces of data are required to make sample size calculations: an estimate of a population standard deviation, the level of sampling error that the researcher or client is willing to accept, and the desired level of confidence that the population value will fall within the acceptable limits.

Crucial to statistical sampling theory is the concept of the normal distribution. The normal distribution is bell-shaped and has only one mode. It also is symmetric about the mean. The standard normal distribution has the features of a normal distribution, however, the mean of the standard normal distribution is always equal to zero and the standard deviation is always equal to one. The transformation formula is used to transform any value X from any normal distribution to its equivalent value Z from a standard normal distribution. The central limit theorem states that the distribution of the means of a large number of random samples taken from virtually any population approaches a normal distribution with a mean equal to μ and a standard deviation equal to

$$S_{\bar{x}} = \frac{\sigma}{\sqrt{n}}$$

The standard deviation of a distribution of sample means is called the *standard error of the mean.*

When using the results of a sample to estimate a population mean, two kinds of estimates can be generated: point and interval estimates. For point estimates, the sample mean is the best estimate of the population mean. An interval estimate is an estimate regarding an interval or range of values of a variable that the researcher is attempting to estimate. Along with the magnitude of the interval, we also state the probability that the interval will take in the true value of the population mean; that is, the confidence level. The interval is the confidence interval.

The researcher who is interested in estimating proportions rather than means uses the sampling distribution of the proportion. The sampling distribution of the proportion is a relative frequency distribution of the sample proportions of a large number of samples of a given size drawn from a particular population. The standard error of a sampling distribution of proportion is computed as follows:

$$S_p = \sqrt{\frac{P(1 - P)}{n}}$$

The formula for calculating the required sample size for situations that involve the estimation of a mean is as follows:

$$n = \frac{Z^2 \sigma^2}{E^2}$$

To calculate sample size, the following are required: specification of the acceptable level of sampling error (E), specification of the acceptable level of confidence in standard errors or Z values, and an estimate of the population standard deviation. To calculate the required sample size for problems involving proportions, we use the following formula:

$$n = \frac{Z^2[P(1 - P)]}{E^2}$$

Key Terms

normal distribution
central limit theorem
standard normal distribution
standard deviation
population distribution
sample distribution
sampling distribution of the sample means
standard error of the mean
statistical features
point estimates
interval estimates
confidence level
sampling distribution of the proportion
allowable sampling error
population standard deviation
finite population correction factor

Review and Discussion Questions

1. Explain why the determination of sample size is a financial, statistical, and managerial issue.
2. Discuss and give examples of three methods for determining sample size.
3. A market researcher analyzing the fast food industry noticed the following. The average amount spent at a fast food restaurant in California was \$3.30, and the standard deviation was \$.40. Yet in Georgia, the average amount spent was \$3.25 with a standard deviation of \$.10. What do these statistics tell us about fast food consumption expenditures in these two states?
4. Distinguish between population, sample, and sampling distributions.
5. What is the finite population correction factor? Why is it used? When should it be used?
6. Assume that previous fast food research has shown that 80 percent of the consumers like curlicue french fries. The researcher wishes to have an error of 6 percent or less and be 95 percent confident of an estimate to be made about curlicue french fry consumption from a survey. What sample size is necessary?
7. A researcher at Disney World knows that 60 percent of the patrons like roller coaster rides. The researcher wishes to have an error of no more than 2 percent and to be 90 percent confident about attitudes toward a new roller coaster ride. What sample size is required?
8. You are in charge of planning a chili cook-off. You must make sure that there are plenty of samples for the patrons of the cook-off. The following standards have been set: a confidence level of 99 percent and an error of less than 4 ounces per cooking team. Last year's cook-off had a standard deviation in amount of chili cooked of 3 ounces. What would be the necessary sample size?
9. You are doing a survey of beer prices during spring break at Daytona Beach.

Last year the average price per six-pack for premium beer was $3.00 with a standard deviation of $.20. Your survey requires a 95 percent confidence level with an acceptable level of error of $.10 per six-pack. Calculate the required sample size.

10. Based on a client's requirements of a confidence interval of 99 percent and acceptable sampling error of 2 percent, a sample size of 500 was calculated. The cost to the client would be $20,000. The client replies that the budget for this project is $17,000. What are the alternatives?

CASE 14.1

Striplings Department Store

Striplings's target market is the middle- and upper-middle-income consumer, and the store is known primarily for having good, serviceable, yet not too fashionable lines of men's and women's clothing. It also carries popular names of perfumes, colognes, and so forth. Other departments in Striplings include carpeting, china, custom draperies, fashion jewelry, fine jewelry, a fur salon, glassware, and housewares. Several years ago Striplings gave up its major appliance business because of competition from the discounters.

Last year Striplings's management noticed a significant decrease in sales, much of which was in the areas of men's and women's apparel. Management was concerned that its target market customers were interested in more high-fashion merchandise. Thus, a market research study was commissioned to determine if Striplings should attempt to stock more designer clothing in the men's, women's, and children's departments.

The interviews were going to be conducted in the consumers' homes and probably would be rather lengthy, lasting more than an hour and 30 minutes. Striplings planned to show respondents a number of potential lines that could be added, including examples of the clothing and information about the designers themselves, thus accounting for the lengthy interview. The cost of the marketing research project also was of concern to management because of a relatively tight budget because of declining overall sales. Thus, management was concerned with the number of interviews to be taken because this naturally would affect the total cost of the project. Several scenarios were proposed to the market research service.

1. The estimated percentage of consumers who had shopped at Striplings in the past six months is 75 percent, the allowable error is ±10 percent, and the confidence level is 95 percent.
2. The estimated percentage of consumers who have shopped at Striplings in the past six months is 80 percent, the allowable error is ±10 percent, and the confidence level is 95 percent.
3. The estimated percentage of consumers who have shopped at Striplings in the past six months is 85 percent, the allowable error is ±10 percent, and the confidence level is 95 percent.

Management also was interested in the inferences that could be drawn from the sample after it had been taken. Management, therefore, asked for calculations of allowable errors under the following situations:

4. Given the sample size calculated in situation 2, a confidence level of 95 percent,

and a sample percentage of consumers who have shopped at Striplings in the past six months of 75 percent.

5. Given the sample size calculated in situation 3, a confidence level of 95 percent, and a sample percentage of consumers who have shopped at Striplings in the past six months of 80 percent.

After receiving the calculations, management planned to decide what sample size to take based on its budgetary restrictions and other information presented.

1. What sample sizes should have been calculated for situations 1, 2, and 3?
2. What allowable errors should have been calculated for situations 4 and 5?

CASE 14.2

Sky Kitchens

Sky Kitchens is the second largest airline caterer in the United States, providing nearly all the meals for passengers of three major airlines and several smaller commuter airlines. As part of a total quality management (TQM) program, its largest airline client, Continental Air, has recently met with representatives of Sky Kitchens to discuss a customer satisfaction program that it is planning to implement.

As part of its overall customer satisfaction program, Continental Airlines plans to interview a sample of its customers four times a year. As part of the survey, it intends to ask customers to rate the quality of meals provided. It intends to ask customers to rate meals on a 1 to 10 scale, where 1 means poor and 10 means excellent. It has just completed a benchmark study of 1,000 customers. In that study, meals received an average rating of 8.7 on the 10 point scale with a standard deviation of 1.65. Continental has indicated that it wants Sky Kitchens to guarantee a level of satisfaction of 8.5 in the first quarterly survey to be conducted in three months. For its quarterly surveys, it plans to use a sample size of 500. In the new contract with Sky Kitchens, Continental wants to write in a clause that will penalize Sky Kitchens $50,000 for each one-tenth of a point below an average 8.5 on the satisfaction scale on the next survey.

1. What is the 95 percent confidence interval for the estimated satisfaction level in the benchmark survey? What is the 99.5 percent confidence interval?
2. Assume that the upcoming first quarterly satisfaction survey shows an average rating on satisfaction with meals of 8.4. Compute the 95 percent confidence interval and the 99.5 confidence interval.
3. If you were negotiating for Sky Kitchens, how would you respond to Continental regarding the penalty clause?

ETHICAL DILEMMA

PART III

Dickson Research, Inc.

Dickson Research is a small, full-service custom marketing research firm in Burlington, Vermont. Last year Dickson's total revenues were only $85,000. This was barely enough for Richard Dickson, his secretary, and one assistant to survive and pay all the bills. It is now late September and this year has been kinder to the organization. Total revenues to date are $95,000. The company is completing a major research project for a national consumer goods manufacturer. Dickson conducted a total of 800 interviews in 10 locations in enclosed malls. The company charged the client $40 per interview for a total of $32,000. This will be paid on completion and presentation of the final report, which is due next week. The data have now been cleaned and tabulated and Richard has just glanced at the first printout. To his horror, he notes that only 760 questionnaires were completed. Further checking reveals that two field services did not complete their quotas. One service in San Francisco was 25 interviews short and a second firm in Albuquerque, New Mexico, was 15 interviews short. Because of the tight deadline, there is no time to return to the respective cities and get the 40 interviews required for the contract sample size of 800.

Richard's assistant notes that this is only about a 5 percent shortage from the total quota. He suggests that 40 questionnaires be randomly selected from the 760 interviews and simply replicated. He claims that replicating 40 interviews from a total of 760 is not going to have much impact on the total results. Besides, the responses are likely to be similar to what is already in the database. The client has demanded a full 800 interviews. Chances are that if the contract is not fully met, the firm will not pay for any of the survey. Not only will Dickson Research lose the $32,000 revenue, but also it will be out the expense to all of the field services.

1. You are Richard Dickson. Would you replicate the 40 interviews? Why or why not?
2. Given the time constraints, do you see any other alternatives that Richard might pursue?

PART IV

Data Analysis

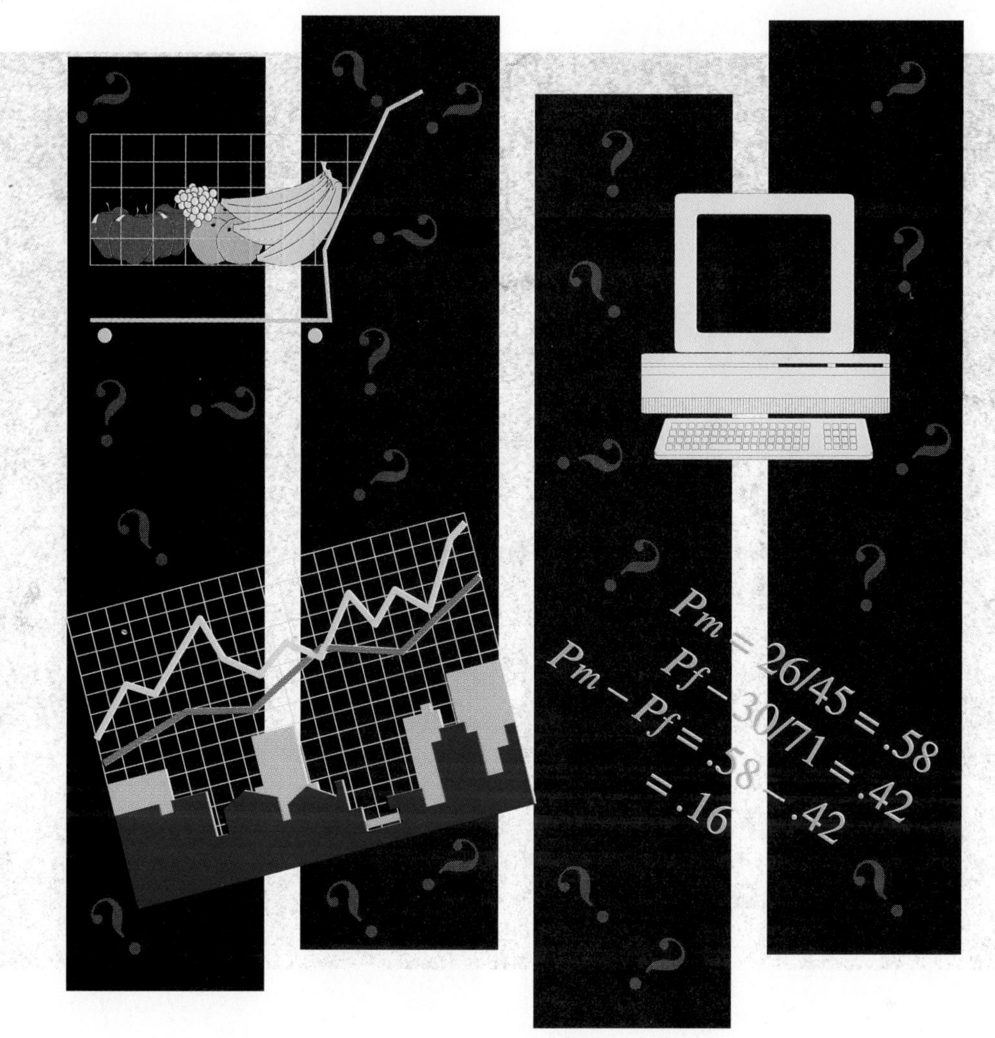

Pm = 26/45 = .58
Pf = 30/71 = .42
Pm − Pf = .58 − .42
= .16

CHAPTER 15

Data Processing and Fundamental Data Analysis

LEARNING OBJECTIVES

1. To develop an understanding of the importance and nature of quality control checks.
2. To understand the data entry process and data entry alternatives.
3. To learn how surveys are tabulated.
4. To learn how to set up and interpret crosstabulations.
5. To comprehend basic techniques of statistical analysis.

Jennifer Johnston is the marketing director for the Cleveland Ballet. For some time, she has been interested in developing a profile of ballet patrons. In addition, she wants to know what current patrons like and do not like about the company's selection of ballets and its artistic interpretation of those ballets. She needs the information for marketing planning purposes.

To answer these and other questions, she designed a survey instrument that was distributed at the door to attendees at a recent performance of the company. The form was brief and could be filled out in a few minutes. More than 1,100 completed questionnaires were returned to the boxes provided outside the performance hall. Although a seasoned marketing director in the arts, Jennifer has relatively little experience and training in marketing research. She is now confronted with the question of what to do with the completed questionnaires. She has read through a sample of more than 100 questionnaires and has gleaned some interesting information from them. How can she summarize the information provided on all the questionnaires? How can the responses to both the open- and closed-ended questions be summarized? ■

SOURCE: © Bob Daemmrick/Stock Boston.

The material in this chapter answers these and other questions. Consider Jennifer's problem after you have completed the chapter. At this point, all data collection has been completed and all completed questionnaires have been returned. The researcher is now confronted with a large stack of anywhere from a few hundred to several thousand interviews and each interview may range from a few pages to 20 or more pages. A recent study completed by the authors involved 1,300 10-page questionnaires. This amounted to a stack of paper nearly three feet high including 13,000 pages. How does the researcher transform all the information contained on the 13,000 pages of completed questionnaires into a form that will permit the summarization necessary for detailed analysis? At one extreme, the researcher could read all the interviews, make notes while reading them, and draw some kind of conclusions from this review of the questionnaires.

The folly of this approach is fairly obvious. Instead of this haphazard and inefficient approach, professional researchers follow a five-step procedure for data analysis.

1. Validation and editing (quality control)
2. Coding
3. Data entry
4. Machine cleaning
5. Tabulation and statistical analysis

Each of these five steps is discussed in detail in subsequent sections of this chapter.

Validation and Editing

validation

The process of ascertaining that interviews actually were conducted as specified.

editing

The process of ascertaining that questionnaires were filled out properly and completely.

The purpose of this step is to make sure that all the interviews actually were conducted as specified **(validation)** and that the questionnaires have been filled out properly and completely **(editing).**

Validation

The first step is to determine, to the extent possible, that each of the questionnaires to be processed represents a valid interview. Here we are using the term *valid* in a different sense from the way we used the term in Chapter 10. In Chapter 10, *validity* was defined as the extent to which a measurement measures what it is supposed to measure. A valid interview here is one that was conducted in the appropriate manner. In this context, no assessment is made regarding the extent to which the measurement measures what it purports to measure. The goal is to detect interviewer fraud or failure to follow key instructions.[1] With certain types of interviewing (e.g., door-to-door interviewing), there is no opportunity to observe or monitor the interviewing process as it actually takes place. In the various questionnaire examples presented throughout the text, you may have noticed that there is almost always a place to record the respondent's name, address, and telephone number. This information is ordinarily not used in any way in the analysis of the data. It is collected only to provide a basis for what marketing researchers call *validation.*

Professional researchers know that interviewer cheating is not uncommon.[2] Various studies have documented the existence and prevalence of interviewer falsification of various types. For this reason, validation is an integral and necessary step in the data processing stage of a marketing research project.

After all the interviews are completed, the research firm recontacts a certain percentage of the respondents surveyed by each interviewer. This applies to door-to-door, mall intercept, and telephone surveys. Normally this percentage ranges from 10 percent to 20 percent. If a particular interviewer surveyed 50 people and the research firm normally validates at a 10 percent rate, five respondents surveyed by that interviewer would be recontacted by telephone. Telephone validation typically covers five areas:

1. Was the person actually interviewed?

2. Did the person who was interviewed actually qualify to be interviewed according to the screening questions on the survey? For example, the interview may have required that the person being interviewed was from a family with an annual household income of $25,000 or more. On validation, the respondent would again be asked whether the annual household income for his family was $25,000 or more per year.
3. Was the interview conducted in the required manner? For example, a mall survey should have been conducted in the designated mall. Was this particular respondent actually interviewed in the mall, or was she interviewed at some other place such as a restaurant or a social gathering? The researcher needs to be sure that all data were collected in the prescribed manner.
4. Did the interviewer cover the entire survey? Sometimes interviewers recognize the respondent is in a hurry and does not have time to complete the entire survey. Respondents for the particular survey may be very difficult to find, so the interviewer may be motivated to ask this respondent a few questions at the beginning and a few questions at the end and then fill out the rest of the interview himself. Validation for this particular problem would involve asking respondents whether they were asked various questions from different points in the interview.
5. Finally, validation normally involves checking for other kinds of problems. Was the interviewer courteous? Did the interviewer speculate about the client's identity or the purpose of the survey? Was the interviewer neat in appearance? Does the respondent have any other negative comments about the interviewer or the interview experience?

The purpose of the validation process, as noted earlier, is to make sure that interviews were administered properly and in their entirety. Researchers must be sure that the research results on which they are basing their recommendations reflect the legitimate responses of target customers.

Editing

Whereas validation involves checking for interviewer cheating and failure to follow instructions, editing involves checking for interviewer and respondent mistakes. Questionnaires normally are edited at least twice before being submitted for data entry. First, they are edited by the field service firm that conducted the interviews, and then they are edited by the marketing research firm that hired the field service firm to do the interviewing. The editing process involves manual checking for a number of problems including the following:

1. *Determining whether the interviewer failed to ask certain questions or record answers for certain questions.* For example, in the questionnaire shown in Figure 15.1, no answer was recorded for question 19. According to the structure of the questionnaire, this question should have been asked of all respondents. However, no response has been recorded. Also note that in this case, the respondent's name does not give a clear indication of gender. The purpose of the first edit—the field edit—is to identify these types of problems at a point when there is still time to recontact the respondent and determine the appropriate answer for the question that was not asked.[3] This may also be done at the second edit—the edit by the marketing research firm—but in many

FIGURE 15.1 Sample Questionnaire

Consumer Survey
Cellular Telephone Survey Questionnaire

Long Branch—Asbury, N.J.
(1–3) 001

Date 1-05-93

Respondent Telephone Number 201-555-2322

Hello. My name is Sally with POST Research. May I please speak with the male or female head of the household?

IF INDIVIDUAL NOT AVAILABLE, RECORD NAME AND CALLBACK INFORMATION ON SAMPLING FORM.

(WHEN MALE/FEMALE HEAD OF HOUSEHOLD COMES TO PHONE): Hell, my name is ______________________, with POST Research. Your number was randomly selected and I am not trying to sell you anything. I simply want to task you a few questions about a new type of telephone service.

1. First, how many telephone calls do you make during a typical day? (04)
   - 0–2 1
   - 3–5 2
   - 6–10 .... ③
   - 11–15 4
   - 16–20 5
   - More than 20 6
   - Don't know 7

Now, let me tell you about a new service called cellular mobile telephone service, which is completely wireless. You can get either a portable model that may be carried in your coat pocket or a model mounted in any vehicle. You will be able to receive calls and make calls, no matter where you are. Although cellular phones are wireless, the voice quality is similar to your present phone service. This is expected to be a time saving convenience for household use.

This new cellular mobile phone service may soon be widely available in your area.

2. Now, let me explain to you the cost of this wireless service. Calls will cost 26 cents a minute plus normal toll charges. In addition, the monthly minimum charge for using the service will be $7.50 and rental of a cellular phone will be about $40. Of course, you can buy the equipment instead of leasing it. At this price, do you think you would be very likely, somewhat likely, somewhat unlikely, or very unlikely to subscribe to the new phone service? (05)
   - Very likely 1
   - Somewhat likely .... ②
   - Somewhat unlikely .... QUESTION 3
   - Very unlikely .... (GO TO QUESTION 16) 4
   - Don't know .... (GO TO QUESTION 16) 5

INTERVIEWER—IF "VERY UNLIKELY" OR "DON'T KNOW," GO TO QUESTION 16.

3. Do you think it is likely that your employer will furnish you with one of these phones for your job? (06)
   - No .... (GO TO QUESTION 5) 1
   - Don't know .... (GO TO QUESTION 5) 2
   - Yes .... (CONTINUE) .... ③

INTERVIEWER—IF NO OR DON'T KNOW, GO TO QUESTION 5; OTHERWISE CONTINUE.

4. If your employer did furnish you with a wireless phone, would you also purchase one for household use? (07)
   - Yes .... (CONTINUE) .... ①
   - No .... (GO TO QUESTION 16) 2
   - Don't Know .... (GO TO QUESTION 16) 3

FIGURE 15.1 Sample Questionnaire—*Continued*

5. Please give me your best estimate of the number of mobile phones your household would use (write in "DK" for Don't Know).

Number of Units ___01___ (08–09)

6. Given that cellular calls made or received will cost 26 cents a minute plus normal toll charges during weekdays, how many calls on the average would you expect to make in a typical weekday?

RECORD NUMBER ___06___ (10–11)

7. About how many minutes would the average cellular call last during the week?

RECORD NUMBER ___05___ (12–13)

8. Weekend cellular calls made or received will cost 08 cents per minute plus normal toll charges. Given this, about how many cellular calls on the average would you expect to make in a typical Saturday or Sunday?

RECORD NUMBER ___00___ (14–15)

9. About how many minutes would the average cellular call last on Saturday or Sunday?

RECORD NUMBER ______ (16–17)

10. You may recall from my previous description that two types of cellular phone units will be available. The vehicle phone may be installed in any vehicle. The portable phone will be totally portable—it can be carried in a briefcase, purse, or coat pocket. The totally portable phones may cost about 25 percent more and may have a more limited transmitting range in some areas than the vehicle phone. Do you think you would prefer portable or vehicle phones if you were able to subscribe to this service?

Portable 1
Vehicle .... ②
Both 3
Don't Know 4

11. Would you please tell me whether you, on the average, would use a mobile phone about once a week, less than once a week, or more than once a week from the following geographic locations.

	Less than Once a Week	Once a Week	More than Once a Week	Never	
Monmouth County, NJ (IF NEVER, SKIP TO QUESTION 12)	1	2	③	4	(19)
Sandy Hook	1	2	3	④	(20)
Keansburg	1	2	3	④	(21)
Atlantic Highlands	1	2	③	4	(22)
Matawan–Middletown	①	2	3	4	(23)
Redbank	①	2	3	4	(24)
Holmdel	1	2	③	4	(25)
Eatontown	1	②	3	4	(26)
Longbranch	1	2	3	④	(27)
Freehold	1	2	3	④	(28)
Manalapan	1	2	3	④	(29)
Cream Ridge	1	2	3	④	(30)
Belmar	1	2	3	④	(31)
Point Pleasant	1	2	③	4	(32)

I'm going to describe to you a list of possible extra features of the proposed cellular service. Each option I'm going to describe will cost not more than $3.00 a month per phone. Would you please tell me if you would be very interested, interested, or uninterested in each feature:

continues

FIGURE 15.1 **Sample Questionnaire—*Continued***

	Very Interested	Interested	Uninterested	
12. Call forwarding (ability to transfer any call coming in to your mobile phone to any other phone).	①	2	3	(33)
13. No answer transfer (if your phone is unanswered, this service redirects calls to another number).	1	2	③	(34)
14. Call waiting—signals you that another person is trying to call you while you are using your phone.	1	②	3	(35)
15. Voice mail box—permits calls to be transferred to a recording machine that will take the caller's message and relay it to you at a later time. This service will be provided at $5.00 per month.	1	2	③	(36)

16. What is your age group: (READ BELOW)

(37)
Under 25 1
25–44 . . . . ②
45–64 3
65 and over 4
Refused, no answer, or don't know 5

17. What is your occupation?

(38)
Manager, Official or Proprietor . . . . ①
Professional (Doctors, Lawyers, Architects, etc.) 2
Technical (Engineers, Computer Programmers, Draftsmen, etc.) . 3
Office Worker/Clerical 4
Sales 5
Skilled Worker or Foreman 6
Unskilled Worker 7
Teacher 8
Homemaker, Student, Retired 9
Not now employed X
Refused . . . . Y

18. Into which category did your total family income fall in 1992? Is it:

(39)
Under $15,000 1
$15,000–$24,999 2
$25,000–$49,999 3
$50,000–$74,999 4
$75,000 and over . . . . ⑤
Refused, no answer, don't know 6

19. (INTERVIEWER—RECORD SEX OF RESPONDENT):

(40)
Male 1
Female 2

20. May I have your name? My office calls about 10 percent of the people I talk with to verify that I have conducted the interview.

Gave name . . . . ①
Refused 2

Jordan Beasley
Name

Thank you for your time. Have a good day.

instances there may not be time to recontact the respondent, and the interview may have to be discarded.[4]

2. *Questionnaires are checked to make sure that skip patterns were followed.* For example, look at question 2 on the questionnaire shown in Figure 15.1. According to the **skip pattern,** if the answer to this question is "very unlikely" or "don't know," then the interviewer should skip to question 16. We need to make sure that the interviewer followed instructions. Sometimes, particularly during the first few interviews that they conduct on a particular study, interviewers may get mixed up and skip when they actually should not or fail to skip when they should.

skip pattern
Requirement to pass over certain questions in response to the respondent's answer to a previous question.

3. *Responses to open-ended questions are checked.* Marketing researchers and their clients usually are very interested in the responses to open-ended questions. The quality of the response, or at least what was recorded, is an excellent indicator of the competence of the interviewer who recorded the response. Interviewers normally are trained to record responses verbatim and not paraphrase or insert their own language in any way. They also are normally instructed to "probe" the initial response. Figure 15.2 shows examples of the various deficiencies just outlined. The first part of Figure 15.2 shows an example of interviewer paraphrasing and interpretation of a response to an open-ended question. The interviewer typically does not know the purposes of the study, know the sponsor of the study, or have the experience or training necessary to interpret respondent reactions.

   The second part of Figure 15.2 shows the result of interviewer failure to probe a response. The response is useless from a decision-making perspective. It comes as no surprise that the respondent goes to Burger King most often because he likes it.

   The third part of Figure 15.2 shows how this initial meaningless response can be expanded to something useful by means of proper probing. A proper probe to the answer "Because I like it" would be something like, "Why do

FIGURE 15.2 Recording of Open-Ended Questions

A. Example of Improper Interviewer Recording of Response to an Open-Ended Question.

Question: Why do you to to Burger King most often among fast-food/quick service restaurants? PROBE

Response recorded:

The consumer seemed to think Burger King had better tasting food and better quality ingredients.

B. Example of Interviewer Failure to Probe a Response.

Question: Same as Part A.

Response recorded:

Because I like it.

C. Example of Proper Recording and Probing.

Question: Same as Part A.

Response recorded:

Because I like it. (P)* I like it and I go there most often because it is the closet place to where I work. (AE)** No.

*(P) is interviewer mark indicating he or she has probed response.

**(AE) is interviewer shorthand for "anything else." This gives the respondent an opportunity to expand the original answer.

you like it?" or "What do you like about it?" Now the respondent indicates that he goes there most often because it is the most convenient fast food restaurant to his place of work.

The person doing the editing must make judgment calls in regard to substandard responses to open-ended questions. This individual will have to decide at what point particular answers are so limited as to be useless. Again, it may be possible to recontact respondents and reask those questions where responses are judged not to be useful.

The editing process is extremely tedious and time-consuming. Imagine for a moment reading through the 13,000 pages of interviews in the example cited earlier. However, editing is an important step in the processing stage.

Coding

Coding Defined

coding

The process of grouping and assigning numeric codes to the various responses to a question.

Coding refers to the process of grouping and assigning numeric codes to the various responses to a particular question.[5] Most questions on most surveys are closed-ended and precoded. This means that numeric codes have been assigned to the various responses on the questionnaire itself. All closed-ended questions should be precoded. For example, question 1 on the questionnaire in Figure 15.1 is this type of question. Note that each answer has a numeric code to the right. The answer "0–2" has the code "1," the answer "3–5" has the code "2," and so on. The interviewer would record the response by circling the numeric code next to the answer given by the respondent. In this case the respondent's answer was seven calls per day. The code "3" next to the category "6–10" calls is circled.

Open-ended questions are another matter. They were stated as open-ended questions because the researcher either had no idea what answers to expect or wanted a richer response than is possible with a closed-ended question. As with editing, the process of coding responses to open-ended questions is tedious and time-consuming. In addition, the procedure is to some degree subjective. For these reasons there is some tendency to avoid open-ended questions if at all possible.

The Coding Process

There are four steps in the process of coding responses to open-ended questions:[6]

1. *Listing responses.* Coders at the research firm prepare lists of the actual responses to each open-ended question on a particular survey. In studies of a few hundred respondents, all responses may be listed. With large samples, responses given by a sample of all respondents will be listed. The listing may be done as part of the editing process or as a separate step. It is often done by the same individuals who edited the questionnaires.
2. *Consolidating responses.* A sample list of responses to an open-ended question is provided in Table 15.1. Examination of this list indicates that a number of the responses can be interpreted to mean essentially the same thing; for example, the first three responses and probably the fourth. Therefore, they

TABLE 15.1 Sample of Responses to Open-Ended Question

Question: Why do you drink that brand of beer? (BRAND MENTIONED IN PREVIOUS QUESTION)

Sample Responses:

1. Because it tastes better.
2. It has the best taste.
3. I like the way it tastes.
4. I don't like the heavy taste of other beers.
5. It is the cheapest.
6. I buy whatever beer is on sale. It is on sale most of the time.
7. It doesn't upset my stomach the way other brands do.
8. Other brands give me headaches. This one doesn't.
9. It has always been my brand.
10. I have been drinking it for over 20 years.
11. It is the brand that most of the guys at work drink.
12. All my friends drink it.
13. It is the brand my wife buys at the grocery store.
14. It is my wife's/husband's favorite brand.
15. I have no idea.
16. Don't know.
17. No particular reason.

can be appropriately consolidated into a single category. After going through this process of consolidation, we end up with the list shown in Table 15.2. This is the final consolidated list of responses. A number of subjective decisions had to be made to derive this final list. For example, does response number 4 belong in category 1 or should it have its own category? These decisions normally are made by a qualified research analyst and frequently involve client input.

3. *Setting codes.* This is done after the final consolidated list of responses has been derived. Here numeric codes are assigned to each of the categories on the final consolidated list of responses. Code assignments for the sample beer study question are shown in Table 15.2.
4. *Entering codes.* After listing responses, consolidating responses, and setting codes, the final step involves the actual entry of codes. This involves several substeps:

TABLE 15.2 Consolidated Response Categories and Codes for Open-Ended Responses from Beer Study Introduced in Table 15.1

RESPONSE CATEGORY DESCRIPTOR	RESPONSE ITEMS FROM TABLE 15.1 INCLUDED	ASSIGNED NUMERIC CODE
Tastes better/like taste/tastes better than others	1, 2, 3, 4	1
Low/lower price	5, 6	2
Does not cause headache, stomach problems	7, 8	3
Long-term use, habit	9, 10	4
Friends drink it/influence of friends	11, 12	5
Wife/husband drinks/buys it	13, 14	6
Don't know	15, 16, 17	7

a. Read responses to individual open-ended questions on questionnaires.
b. Match individual responses with consolidated list of response categories developed in step 2.
c. Get the numeric code for the category into which you classified the particular response.
d. Write the numeric code in the appropriate place on the questionnaire for the response to the particular question (see Figure 15.3).

Coding Example

Consider the example shown in Tables 15.1 and 15.2 and Figure 15.3.

- The listing of responses is shown in Table 15.1.
- The consolidation and setting of codes is shown in Table 15.2.
- You have started entering codes. The first questionnaire has the response "Because it's cheaper" to the question shown in Table 15.1 (Why do you drink that brand of beer?).
- You compare this response to the consolidated response categories in Table 15.2 and decide that it fits into the "Low/lower price" category.
- The numeric code associated with this category is "2" (see Table 15.2).
- The code is entered in the appropriate place on the questionnaire (see Figure 15.3).

Data Entry

The questionnaires have now been validated, edited, and coded. We are ready for the next step in the process, data entry. The term *data entry* is used to refer to the process of converting information from a form that cannot be read by a computer to a form that can be read by a computer.[7] This process requires a data entry device and a storage medium. Data entry devices include computer terminals and personal computers. Storage media used in connection with the data entry include magnetic tape, floppy disks, and hard (magnetic) disks.

Intelligent versus Dumb Entry

intelligent data entry

The logical checking of information being entered into a data entry device by that machine or one connected to it.

Most data entry is done by means of intelligent entry systems. **Intelligent data entry** refers to the ability of the data entry devices to be programmed to do certain logical checking of the information being entered or their connection to computers that can do this checking. The data entry system can be programmed to

FIGURE 15.3 Example Questionnaire Setup for Open-Ended Questions

37. Why do you drink that brand of beer (BRAND MENTIONED IN PREVIOUS QUESTION)?

(48) 2

Because it's cheaper. (P) Nothing. (AE) Nothing.

to avoid certain types of errors at the point of data entry: entry of invalid or wild codes, and violation of skip patterns.

Consider question 2 on the questionnaire in Figure 15.1. The five valid answers have the associated numeric codes 1–5. An intelligent data entry system programmed for valid codes would permit the data entry operator to enter codes 1–5 only in the field reserved for the response to this question. If an attempt is made to enter a code other than the ones that have been defined as valid, the device will inform the data entry operator in some manner that there is a problem. The data entry device, for example, might beep and display a message on the screen that the code attempted is invalid. It also will not advance to the next appropriate field. Under this type of entry, of course, it is possible to incorrectly enter a "3" rather than the correct answer "2." Referring again to Figure 15.1, we see that if the answer to question 2 is "very unlikely" or "don't know," then the data entry operator should skip to question 16. An intelligent data entry device will make this skip automatically.

The Data Entry Process

The validated, edited, and coded questionnaires have now been given to a data entry operator seated in front of a personal computer or computer terminal. The data entry software system has been programmed for intelligent entry. The actual data entry process is ready to begin. Normally, the data will be entered directly from the questionnaires. Data normally are not transferred from questionnaires to computer coding sheets by professional marketing researchers because experience has shown that a large number of errors are made in the process of transposing data from the questionnaires to coding sheets. The process of going directly from the questionnaire to the data entry device and the associated storage medium has proven to be more accurate and efficient. To better understand the mechanics of the process, refer to the questionnaire in Figure 15.1. Consider the following points:

- In the upper right-hand corner of the questionnaire, the number 001 is written. This number uniquely identifies the particular questionnaire and this should be the first questionnaire in the stack that the data entry operator is preparing to enter. This code is an important point of reference because it will permit the data entry staff to refer back to the original input document if any errors are identified in connection with the data input for questionnaire number 001.
- Next to the handwritten number 001 is 1–3 in parentheses. This tells the data entry operator that 001 should be entered into fields 1–3 of the data record. Also note that throughout the questionnaire, the numbers in parentheses indicate the proper location on the data record for the circled code or answer to each question.
- Question 1 has the number 04 in parentheses associated with the codes for the answers to the question. The answer to this question would be entered in field 04 of the data record.
- In regard to open-ended questions, refer to Figure 15.3. Note the number 2 written in next to the number 48 in parentheses. As with closed-ended questions, the number in parentheses refers to the field on the data record where

Almost all data entry is done on personal computers today.

the code or codes written in for the response to this question should be entered. For example, a 2 should be entered in field 48 of the data record associated with this questionnaire.

This discussion illustrates the relationship between the layout of the questionnaire in terms of codes (numbers associated with different answers to questions) and field (place on data record where code for answer goes) assignments and the layout of the data record.

Optical Scanning

optical scanning

A data processing device that can "read" responses on questionnaires.

As all students know, **optical scanning** has been around for decades. It has been widely used in schools and universities as an efficient way to capture and score responses to multiple-choice questions. However, until recently, its use in marketing research has been limited. This limited use can be attributed to two factors: setup costs and the need to record all responses with a number 2 pencil. Setup costs include the need for special paper, special ink in the printing process, and very precise placement of the bubbles for recording responses. The break-even point, the point at which the savings in data entry costs exceeded the setup costs, was in the 10,000 to 12,000 survey range. Therefore, for most surveys, scanning was not feasible.

However, changes in scanning technology and the advent of personal computers have changed this equation. Now, questionnaires prepared with any one of a number of Windows word processing software packages and printed on a laser printer or through a standard printing process, using almost any type of paper, can be readily scanned using the appropriate software and a small scanner, costing about $2,000, attached to a personal computer. In addition, the latest technology permits respondents to fill out the survey using almost any type of writing implement (any pencil, ballpoint pen, roller ball, ink pen, and so on). This eliminates the need to provide respondents with a number 2 pencil and greatly simplifies the process for mail surveys. Finally, using the latest technology, it is not necessary for respondents to carefully shade in the entire circle or square next to their response choice. They can shade it in, put a check, put an *X*, or put any type of mark in the circle or square provided for their response choice.[8]

As a result of these developments, the use of scannable surveys is growing dramatically. When you expect more than 400 to 500 surveys to be completed, scannable surveys can be cost-effective.

Machine Cleaning of Data

At this point, the data from all questionnaires have been entered and stored in the computer that will be used to process them. It is time to do final error checking before proceeding to the tabulation and statistical analysis of the survey results. Most colleges have one or more statistical packages available for the tabulation and statistical analysis of data. You probably have access to SAS (Statistical Analysis System), SPSS (Statistical Package for the Social Sciences), or BMDP on a mainframe or minicomputer at your university. These have proven to be the most popular mainframe computer statistical packages. In addition, your college may have personal computer versions of SPSS or SAS. Furthermore a large number of personal computer statistical packages are available in addition to SAS and SPSS. The number of these other PC packages is large and growing and too extensive to list here. However, *STATISTICA*® is one highly rated example.[9]

Regardless of which computer package is used to tabulate the data, the first step is to do final error checking or what is sometimes referred to as **machine cleaning of data.** This may be done in one or both of two ways: error checking routines and marginal reports.

machine cleaning of data

A final computerized error check of data.

Some computer programs permit the user to write **error checking routines.** These routines include a number of statements to check for various conditions. For example, if a particular field on the data records for a particular study should only have a 1 or a 2 code, a logical statement can be written to check for the presence of any other code in that field. Some of the more sophisticated packages generate reports indicating how many times a particular condition was violated and list the data records on which it was violated. With this list the user can refer to the original questionnaires and determine the appropriate values.

error checking routines

Computer programs that accept instructions from the user to check for logical errors in the data.

Another approach to machine cleaning often used for error checking is the **marginal report** or one-way frequency table. A sample marginal report is shown in Table 15.3. The rows of this report are the fields of the data record. The columns show the frequencies with which each possible value was encountered in each field. For example, the first row in Table 15.3 shows that in field 1 (column 1) of the data records for this study there are 100 "1" punches, 100 "2" punches, 1 "3" punch, and 99 "10" punches. This report permits the user to determine whether inappropriate codes were entered and whether skip patterns were properly followed. If all the numbers are consistent, there is no need for further cleaning. However, if logical errors are detected, then the appropriate original questionnaires must be located and the corrections must be made in the computer data file.

marginal report

A computer-generated table of the frequencies of the responses to each question to monitor entry of valid codes and correct use of skip patterns.

TABLE 15.3 Sample Marginal Report (Marginal Counts of 300 Records)

COL	1	2	3	4	5	6	7	8	9	10	11	12	BL	TOT
111	100	100	1	0	0	0	0	0	0	99	0	0	0	300
112	30	30	30	30	30	30	30	30	30	0	0	0	0	300
113	30	30	30	30	30	30	30	30	30	30	0	0	0	300
114	67	233	0	0	0	0	0	0	0	0	0	0	0	300
115	192	108	0	0	0	0	0	0	0	0	0	0	0	300
116	108	190	0	0	0	0	0	0	0	0	0	2	0	300
117	13	35	8	0	2	136	95	7	2	0	0	0	2	298
118	0	0	0	0	0	0	0	0	0	0	0	2	298	2
119	29	43	12	1	2	48	50	6	4	1	0	0	104	196
1111	6	16	6	1	1	10	18	4	2	0	0	0	236	64
1113	3	4	1	1	0	1	2	0	1	0	0	0	288	12
1115	0	0	0	1	1	0	0	2	0	0	0	0	296	4
1117	24	2	22	0	1	239	9	2	0	0	0	0	1	299
1118	0	0	0	0	0	0	0	0	0	0	0	0	299	1
1119	4	49	6	0	0	81	117	5	2	0	0	0	36	264
1120	0	0	0	0	0	0	0	0	0	0	0	36	264	36
1121	5	60	6	0	0	84	116	4	3	1	0	0	21	279
1122	0	0	0	0	0	0	0	0	0	0	0	21	279	21
1123	118	182	0	0	0	0	0	0	0	0	0	0	0	300
1124	112	187	0	0	0	0	0	0	0	0	0	0	1	299
1125	47	252	0	0	0	0	0	0	0	0	0	1	0	300
1126	102	198	0	0	0	0	0	0	0	0	0	0	0	300
1127	5	31	5	1	0	33	31	9	1	0	0	0	184	116
1128	0	0	0	0	0	0	0	0	0	0	0	2	298	2
1129	0	3	1	0	0	4	8	2	1	0	0	0	281	19
1131	7	16	3	0	2	60	21	3	0	0	0	0	188	112
1133	1	3	1	0	0	2	3	1	0	0	0	0	289	11

This is the final error check in the process. When this step is completed, the computer data file should be "clean" and ready for tabulation and statistical analysis. Table 15.4 shows the data for the first 50 respondents out of a total of 400 for the study associated with the questionnaire shown in Figure 15.1. You might note that the apparent gaps in the data are a result of the skip called for in question 4. Also note that the gender data for respondent 001 has been filled in with a 2 for "female."

Tabulation of Survey Results

At this point the survey results are stored in a computer file and free of all logical data entry and interviewer recording error. By *logical errors* we mean violated skip patterns and impossible codes (a 3 was entered when 1 and 2 are the only possible codes). The procedures, described previously, cannot identify situations in which an interviewer or data entry operator entered a 2 for a "no" response instead of the correct 1 for a "yes" resposne.[10] The next step is to tabulate the survey results.

one-way frequency table

A table showing the number of responses to each answer of a survey question.

One-Way Frequency Tables

The most basic tabulation is the **one-way frequency table.** An example of this type of table is shown in Table 15.5. A one-way frequency table shows the num-

TABLE 15.4 **Printout of Data for the First 50 Respondents for Cellular Telephone Survey (See Figure 15.1)**

```
001323101060500  234431132444443132321521
00224                                 23412
00334                                 49622
00414                                 36221
00524                                 33312
00634                                 22612
00714                                 21321
008221 0204050310334232444434444222229321
00925                                 36311
01044                                 23311
01161310240050330134234444434443322330321
012622 0140072007334444444444444132330511
013221 0106030603231312333323322123216211
01424                                 29321
01514                                 40121
01624                                 22612
01774                                 20622
01854                                 34621
01924                                 25212
02024                                 23622
02114                                 16611
02214                                 36211
024131   00101004102213344444444442229611
02524                                 26621
026131 0101030203124221422244414223222611
02724                                 10122
02814                                 59622
02924                                 39622
03024                                 49611
03134                                 53621
03234                                 32622
03321    01         12444444444444211220211
03424                                 32622
035311 0410300430133131131113131211220121
03623230301050201334414433344244232320622
03724                                 37622
03814                                 40121
03934                                 30121
04024                                 16121
04124                                 26311
04264                                 26411
04324                                 20321
04414                                 26311
04524                                 19321
04634                                 19222
04724                                 29621
04824                                 31422
04924                                 33121
05014                                 21311
```

ber of respondents who gave each possible answer to each question. Table 15.5 shows that 144 consumers (48 percent) said they would choose a hospital in Saint Paul, 146 (48.7 percent) said they would choose a hospital in Minneapolis, and 10 people (3.3 percent) said they didn't know which one they would choose. A computer printout will be generated showing one-way frequency tables for every

TABLE 15.5 One-Way Frequency Table

Q.30 If you or a member of your family were to require hospitalization in the future, and the procedure could be performed in Minneapolis or St. Paul, where would you choose to go?

	TOTAL
Total	300 100%
To a hospital in St. Paul	144 48.0%
To a hospital in Minneapolis	146 48.7%
Don't know/No response	10 3.3%

question on the survey. In most instances, this will be the first summary of survey results seen by the research analyst.

In addition to frequencies, one-way frequency tables typically indicate the percentage of those responding to a question that gave each possible response.

Base for Percentages Another issue that must be dealt with at the time one-way frequency tables are run is the question of the base to be used for the percentages for each table. There are three choices:

1. *Total respondents.* If 300 people are interviewed in a particular study, and the decision is to use total respondents as the base for calculating percentages, then the percentages in each one-way frequency table will be based on 300 respondents.
2. *Number of people asked the particular question.* Because most questionnaires have skip patterns, not all respondents will be asked all questions. For example, question 4 on a particular survey might have asked whether the person owned a dog or cat. Assume that 200 respondents indicated they owned a dog or a cat. If questions 5 and 6 on the same survey should have been asked only of those individuals who own a dog or a cat, then question 5 and question 6 should have been asked of only 200 respondents. In most instances, it is appropriate to use 200 as the base for percentages associated with the one-way frequency tables for questions 5 and 6.
3. *Number answering.* Another alternative base for computing percentages in one-way frequency tables is the number of people who actually answered a particular question. Under this approach, if 300 people were asked a particular question but 28 indicated "don't know" or gave no response to the particular question, then the base for the percentages would be 272.

Ordinarily, the number of people who were asked a particular question is used as the base for all percentages throughout the tabulations, but there may be special cases in which other bases are judged appropriate. One-way frequency tables using the three different bases for calculating percentages are shown in Table 15.6.

Selecting the Base for One-Way Frequency Tables Showing Results from Multiple-Response Questions Some questions, by their nature, solicit more than one response from respondents. For example, con-

TABLE 15.6 **One-Way Frequency Table with Percents Shown for Total Respondents, Total Respondents Who Were Asked the Question, and Total Respondents Answering (gave response other than "don't know")**

Q.35 Why would you not consider going to St. Paul for hospitalization?

	TOTAL* RESPONDENTS	TOTAL ASKED	TOTAL ANSWERING
Total	300	64	56
	100%	100%	100%
They aren't good/service poor	18	18	18
	6%	28%	32%
St. Paul doesn't have the services/equipment that Minneapolis does	17	17	17
	6%	27%	30%
St. Paul is too small	6	6	6
	2%	9%	11%
Bad publicity	4	4	4
	1%	6%	7%
Other	11	11	11
	4%	17%	20%
Don't know/no response	8	8	
	3%	13%	

*A total of 300 respondents were surveyed. Only 64 answered the question because in the previous question they said they would not consider going to St. Paul for hospitalization.

sumers might be asked to name all the hospitals that come to mind. Most people will be able to name more than one hospital. Therefore, when these answers are tabulated, there will be more responses than people. If 200 consumers are surveyed and the average consumer names three hospitals, then the 200 respondents will have given 600 answers. The question is, Should percentages in frequency tables showing the results to these questions be based on the number of respondents or the number of responses? An example, showing percentages calculated both ways, is provided in Table 15.7. Common practice among marketing researchers is to compute percentages for multiple-response questions on the basis of the number of respondents. This is based on the logic that we primarily are interested in the proportion of people that gave a particular answer.

Crosstabulations

crosstabulation
Examination of the responses to one question relative to responses to one or more other questions.

Crosstabulations are likely to be the next step in analysis. They represent a simple to understand, yet powerful, analytical tool. Many marketing research studies, possibly most, go no further than crosstabulations in terms of analysis. The idea is to look at the responses to one question in relation to the responses to one or more other questions. Table 15.8 shows a simple crosstabulation. Here we are examining the relationship between cities consumers are willing to consider for hospitalization and their age. This crosstabulation shows frequencies and percentages, and the percentages are based on column totals. This table

TABLE 15.7 Percentages for a Multiple-Response Question Calculated on the Basis of Total Respondents and Total Responses

Q.34 To which of the following towns and cities would you consider going for hospitalization?

	TOTAL RESPONDENTS	TOTAL RESPONSES
Total	300 100%	818 100%
Minneapolis	265 88.3%	265 32.4%
St. Paul	240 80.0%	240 29.3%
Bloomington	112 37.3%	112 13.7%
Rochester	92 30.7%	92 11.2%
Minnetonka	63 21.0%	63 7.7%
Eagan	46 15.3%	46 5.6%

shows an interesting relationship between age and likelihood of choosing Minneapolis or St. Paul for hospitalization. Consumers in successively older age groups are increasingly likely to choose St. Paul and increasingly less likely to choose Minneapolis.

There are a number of considerations regarding the setup and percentaging of crosstabulation tables.[11] Some of the more important ones are summarized:

- The previous discussion regarding the selection of the appropriate base for percentages and the appropriate base for the percentaging of tables with multiple responses apply to crosstabulation tables as well.
- Three different percentages may be calculated for each cell in a crosstabulation table: column, row, and total percentages. Column percentages are computed on the basis of the column total, row percentages are based on the row

TABLE 15.8 Sample Crosstabulation

Q.30 If you or a member of your family were to require hospitalization in the future, and the procedure could be performed in Minneapolis or St. Paul, where would you choose to go?

		AGE			
	Total	*18–34*	*35–54*	*55–64*	*65 or Over*
Total	300 100%	65 100%	83 100%	51 100%	100 100%
To a hospital in St.. Paul	144 48.0%	21 32.3%	40 48.2%	25 49.0%	57 57.0%
To a hospital in Minneapolis	146 48.7%	43 66.2%	40 48.2%	23 45.1%	40 40.0%
Don't know/no response	10 3.3%	1 1.5%	3 3.6%	3 5.9%	3 3.0%

total, and total percentages are based on the total for the table. Table 15.9 shows a crosstabulation table with frequencies and all three of the percents shown for each cell in the table.

- A common way of setting up crosstabulation tables is to create a table in which the columns represent various factors such as demographics and lifestyle characteristics that are expected to be predictors of the state of mind, behavior, or intentions data that are shown as rows of the table. In such tables, percentages normally are calculated on the basis of column totals. This approach permits easy comparisons of the relationship between the state of mind, behavior, or intentions data and expected predictors such as sex or age. The question might be, How do people in different age groups differ in regard to the particular factor under examination? An example of this type of table is shown in Table 15.8.

Crosstabulations provide a powerful and easily understood approach to the summarization and analysis of survey research results. However, it is easy to become swamped by the sheer volume of computer printouts if a careful tabulation plan has not been developed. The crosstabulation plan should be developed with the research objectives and hypotheses in mind. The results of a particular survey might be crosstabulated in an almost endless number of ways. This is why it is important for the analyst to exercise some judgment and select from all possibilities those crosstabulations truly responsive to the research objectives of the project. A number of spreadsheet programs (Lotus 1–2–3, Excel, and Quattro Pro) and nearly all statistics packages (SAS, SPSS, SYSTAT, STATISTICA) can generate crosstabulations. In the next chapter we will discuss the chi-square test. This test can be used to determine whether the results in a particular crosstabulation table are significantly different from what we would expect due to chance.

TABLE 15.9 Crosstabulation Table with Row, Column, and Total Percentages*

Q.34 To which of the following towns and cities would you consider going for hospitalization?

	TOTAL	MALE	FEMALE
Total	300	67	233
	100%	100%	100%
	100%	22.3%	77.7%
	100%	22.3%	77.7%
St. Paul	265	63	202
	88.3%	94.0%	86.7%
	100%	23.6%	76.2%
	88.3%	21.0%	67.3%
Minneapolis	240	53	187
	80.0%	79.1%	80.3%
	100%	22.1%	77.9%
	80.0%	17.7%	62.3%
Bloomington	112	22	90
	37.3%	32.8%	38.6%
	100%	19.6%	80.4%
	37.3%	7.3%	30.0%

*Percentages listed are column, row, and total percentages, respectively.

In other words, are the response patterns of men significantly different from those of women? This statistical procedure enables us to determine whether the differences between two groups likely occurred because of chance or likely reflect real differences between the groups.

A more complex crosstabulation is shown in Table 15.10. It was generated using the UNCLE software package. UNCLE was designed with the special needs of marketing researchers in mind and is widely used in the marketing research industry. As indicated, this more complex table is sometimes referred to as a *stub and banner table*. The column headings are referred to as the *banner* and the row titles are referred to as the *stub*. In this single table, the relationship between marital status and seven other variables is explored.

Graphic Representations of Data

You have heard the saying, "One picture is worth a thousand words." Graphic presentation involves the use of "pictures" rather than tables to present research results. Results, particularly key results, can be presented more powerfully and efficiently by means of graphs. Crosstabulation and statistical analysis help us identify important findings. Graphs are the best way to present those findings to the consumers of our research.

Marketing researchers probably have always known that results could be best presented graphically. However, until recent years the preparation of graphs was tedious, difficult, and time-consuming. The advent of personal computers, coupled with graphics software and laser printers has changed all of this. All the major spreadsheet programs (Lotus 1–2–3, Excel, and Quattro Pro) have extensive graphics capabilities, particularly in their Windows versions. In addition, programs designed for creating presentations (PowerPoint, Freelance, Astound, and

TABLE 15.10 A More Complex Crosstabulation Table (sometimes referred to as a stub and banner table)

North Community College—Anywhere, U.S.A.
Q. 1c. Are you single, married, or formerly married?

		ZONES			GENDER		AGE			RACE			FAMILY PROFILE		VOTE HISTORY		REGISTERED VOTER	
	Total	*1*	*2*	*3*	*M*	*F*	*18–34*	*35–54*	*55 and Over*	*White*	*Black*	*Other*	*Child <18*	*Child >18*	*2x-3x*	*4x or more*	*Yes*	*No*
Total	300	142	103	55	169	131	48	122	130	268	28	4	101	53	104	196	72	228
	100%	100%	100%	100%	100%	100%	100%	100%	100%	100%	100%	100%	100%	100%	100%	100%	100%	100%
Married	228	105	87	36	131	97	36	97	95	207	18	3	82	39	80	148	58	170
	76%	74%	84%	65%	78%	74%	75%	80%	73%	77%	64%	75%	81%	74%	77%	76%	81%	75%
Single	5	1	2	2	4	1	2	1	2	5	–	–	–	–	2	3	1	4
	2%	1%	2%	4%	2%	1%	4%	1%	2%	2%	–	–	–	–	2%	2%	1%	2%
Formerly	24	11	10	3	12	12	3	9	12	18	6	–	5	6	10	14	3	21
married	8%	8%	10%	5%	7%	9%	6%	7%	9%	7%	21%	–	5%	11%	10%	7%	4%	9%
Refused	43	25	4	14	22	21	7	15	21	38	4	1	14	8	12	31	10	33
to answer	14%	18%	4%	25%	13%	16%	15%	12%	16%	14%	14%	25%	14%	15%	12%	16%	14%	14%

Harvard Graphics) permit the user to create a wide variety of high-quality graphics with ease. With these programs, it is possible to

- Quickly produce graphs.
- Display those graphs on the computer screen.
- Make desired changes and redisplay.
- Print final copies on a laser or dot matrix graphics printer.

All the graphs shown in this section were produced using a personal computer, laser printer, and a graphics software package.[12]

Line Charts

Line charts are perhaps the simplest form of graphs. They are particularly useful for presenting a particular measurement taken at a number of points over time. Monthly sales data for Just Add Water, a retailer of women's swimwear, are shown in Figure 15.4. The data are taken from Just Add Water's 1994 and 1995 sales records.

The results in Figure 15.4 show a very similar sales pattern for the two years with peaks in June and generally low sales in January through March and September through December. Just Add Water is evaluating the sales data to identify product lines that it might add to improve sales in the January through March and September through December periods.

Pie Charts

Pie charts are another frequently used type of graph. They are appropriate for displaying marketing research results in a wide range of situations. Results from a survey of residents of several gulf coast metropolitan areas in Louisiana, Mississippi, and Alabama regarding radio music preferences are displayed in Figure 15.5. Note the three-dimensional effect produced by the software.

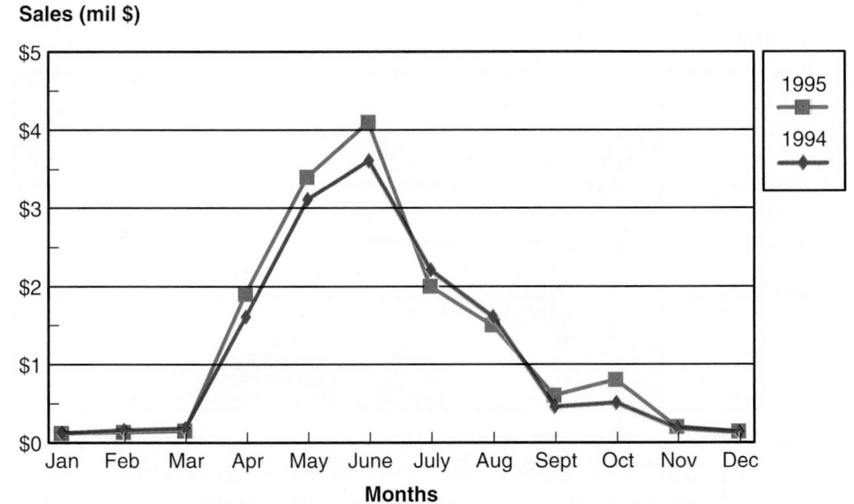

FIGURE 15.4

1994 and 1995 Sales for Just Add Water (Line Chart)

FIGURE 15.5

Type of Music Listened To Most Often (3-D Pie)

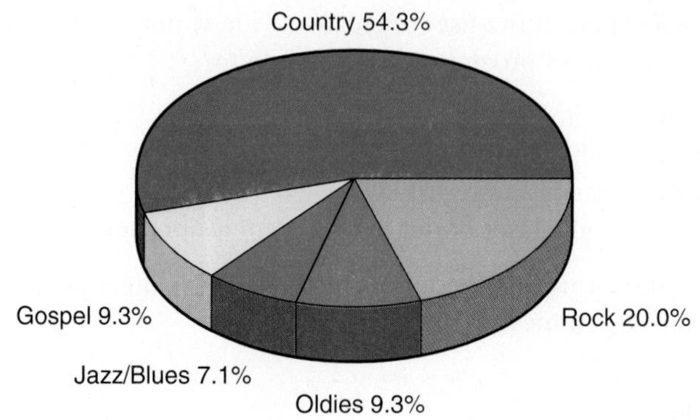

Bar Charts

Bar charts are the most flexible of the three types of graphs discussed in this section. Anything that can be shown in a line graph or a pie chart also can be shown in a bar chart. In addition, many things that cannot be shown, or effectively shown, with other types of graphs can readily be shown with bar charts. Four types of bar charts are discussed here.

1. *Plain bar chart.* As the name suggests, plain bar charts are the simplest form of bar chart. The same information displayed in the previous section in a pie chart is shown in a bar chart in Figure 15.6. Draw your own conclusions regarding whether the pie chart or the bar chart is the most effective way to present this information. Figure 15.6 is shown as a traditional two-dimensional chart. Many of the software packages available today can take the same information and present it with a three-dimensional effect. The same information is shown with this effect in Figure 15.7. Again, decide which approach is visually most appealing and interesting.
2. *Clustered bar charts.* Clustered bar charts represent the first of three type of bar charts that are useful for showing the results of crosstabulations. The music preference results crosstabulated by age are shown in Figure 15.8. The graph

FIGURE 15.6

Type of Music Listened To Most Often (Simple 2-D Bar)

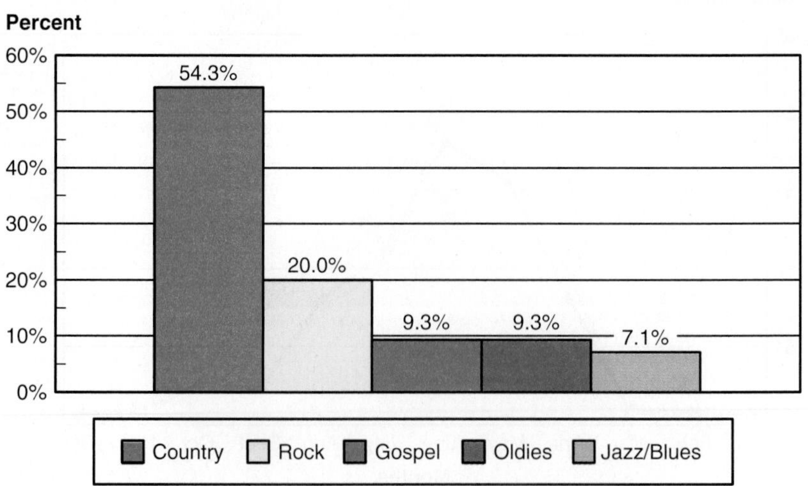

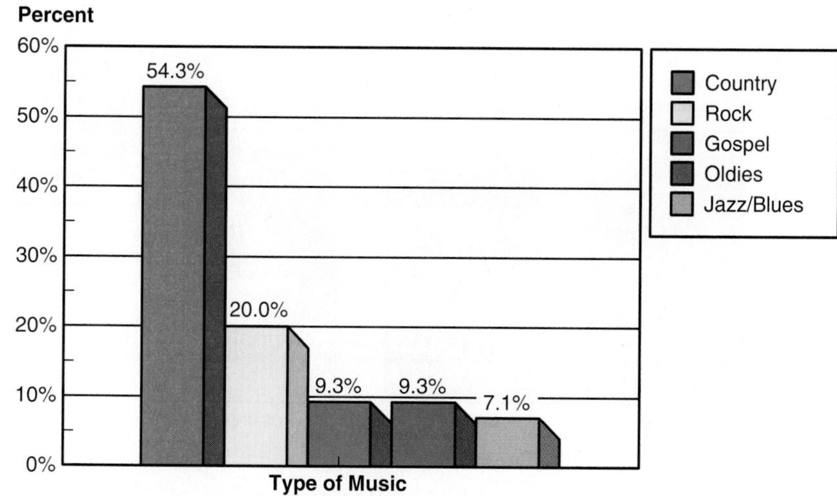

FIGURE 15.7

Type of Music Listened to Most often (Simple 3-D Bar)

shows that *country* is mentioned most often as the preferred radio music format by those over 35 and those 35 or under. However, the graph also shows that *rock* is a close second for those 35 or under and least frequently mentioned by those over 35. The results suggest that if the target audience is those in the 35 or under age group, then a mix of *country* and *rock* stations would be appropriate. A focus on country stations probably would be the most efficient approach for those over 35.

3. *Stacked bar charts.* The same information presented in Figure 15.8 is presented in the form of a stacked bar chart in Figure 15.9.
4. *Multiple row, three-dimensional bar charts.* This approach provides what we believe to be the most visually appealing way of presenting crosstabulation information. The same information displayed in Figures 15.8 and 15.9 is presented in a multiple row, three-dimensional bar chart in Figure 15.10.

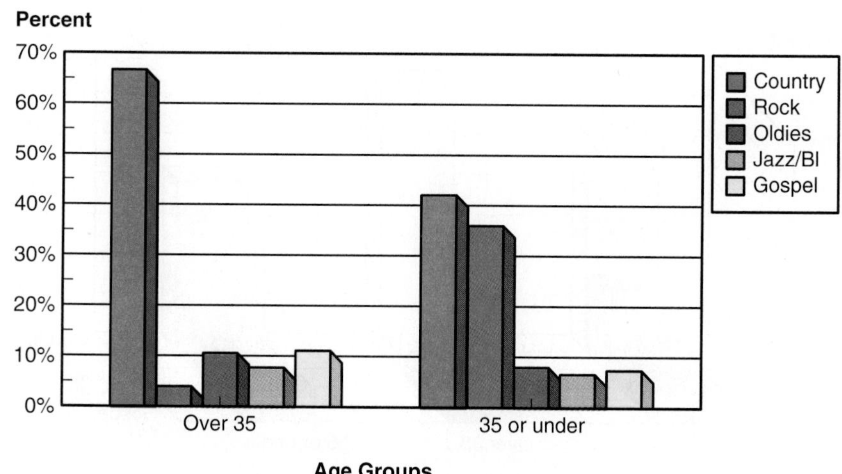

FIGURE 15.8

Type of Music Listened To Most often by Age (Clustered Bar)

FIGURE 15.9

Type of Music Listened to Most often by Age (Stacked Bar)

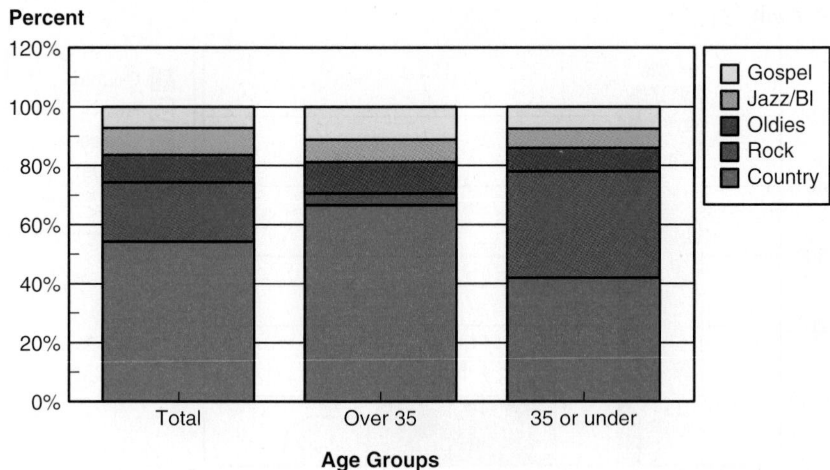

Descriptive Statistics

Descriptive statistics represent a more efficient means of summarizing the characteristics of large sets of data. In the case of statistical analysis, the analyst calculates one number or a few numbers that reveal something about the characteristics of large sets of data.

Measures of Central Tendency

There are three measures of central tendency: the arithmetic mean, median, and mode. Before beginning this section, it would be a good idea to review the types of data scales presented in Chapter 10. There are four basic types of scales: nominal, ordinal, interval, and ratio. Nominal and ordinal scales are sometimes referred to as *nonmetric scales,* whereas interval and ratio scales are referred to as *metric scales.*

FIGURE 15.10

Type of Music Listened to Most often by Age(Multiple Row 3-D Bar)

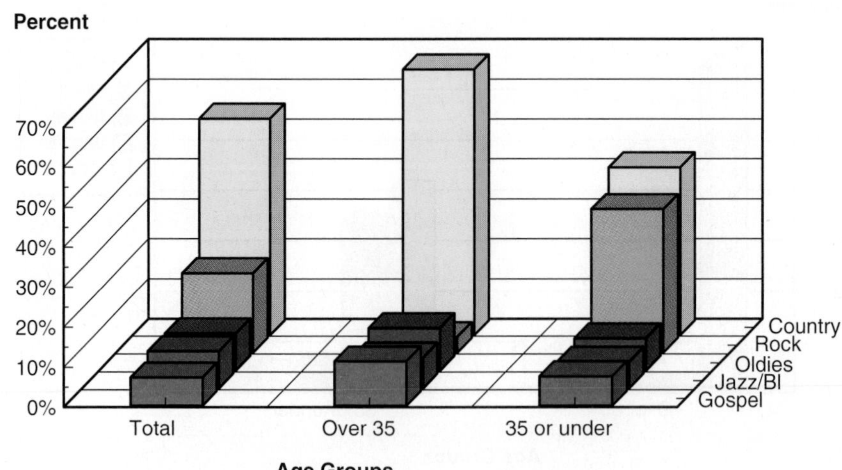

Many of the statistical procedures discussed in this section and in following sections require metric data, and others are designed for nonmetric data.

The arithmetic **mean** is properly computed only from interval or ratio scale (metric) data. It is computed by adding the values for all observations for a particular variable such as age and dividing the resulting sum by the number of observations. When working with survey data, the exact value of the variable may not be known but it may be known that the particular case falls in a particular category. For example, an age category on a survey might be 18–34 years of age. If a person falls in this particular category, we do not know the person's exact age, only that it is somewhere between 18 and 34. With grouped data, the midpoint of each category is multiplied by the number of observations in that category, the resulting totals are summed, and the total is divided by the total number of observations. This process is summarized in the following formula:

mean
The sum of the values for all observations of a variable divided by the number of observations.

$$\overline{X} = \frac{\sum_{i=1}^{h} f_i X_i}{n}$$

where

f_i = the frequency of the *i*th class
X_i = the midpoint of that class
h = the number of classes
n = the total number of observations

The **median** can be computed for all types of data except nominal data. It is calculated by finding the value below which 50 percent of the observations fall. If all the values for a particular variable were put in an array in either ascending or descending order, the median would be the middle value in that array. The median is often used to summarize variables such as income where the researcher is concerned that the arithmetic mean will be affected by a few extreme values and, therefore, will not accurately reflect the predominant central tendency of that variable for that group.

median
The observation below which 50 percent of the observations fall.

The **mode** can be computed with any type of data (nominal, ordinal, interval, ratio). It is determined by finding the value that occurs most frequently. In a frequency distribution, the mode is the value of the variable that has the highest frequency. One problem with the mode is that a particular data set may have more than one mode. If three different values occur with the same level of frequency and that frequency is higher than for any other value, then that data set has three modes. The mean, median, and mode for sample data on beer consumption are shown in Table 15.11.

mode
The value that occurs most frequently.

Measures of Dispersion

Frequently used measures of dispersion include the standard deviation, variance, and range. Whereas measures of central tendency indicate typical values for a particular variable, measures of dispersion indicate how "spread out" the data are. The dangers associated with relying only on measures of central tendency are suggested by the example shown in Table 15.12.

The formula for computing the **standard deviation** for a sample of observations is as follows:

standard deviation
A measure of dispersion calculated by subtracting the mean of a series from each value in a series, squaring each result, summing them, dividing the sum by the number of items minus 1, and taking the square root of this value.

TABLE 15.11 Mean, Median, and Mode

A total of 10 beer drinkers (drink one or more cans, bottles, or glasses of beer per day on the average) were interviewed in a mall intercept study. They were asked how many cans, bottles, or glasses of beer they drink in an average day. Their responses are summarized.

RESPONDENT	NUMBER OF CANS/ BOTTLES/GLASSES PER DAY
1	2
2	2
3	3
4	2
5	5
6	1
7	2
8	2
9	10
10	1

Mode = 2 cans/bottles/glasses
Median = 2 cans/bottles/glasses
Mean = 3 cans/bottles/glasses

$$S = \sqrt{\frac{\sum_{i=1}^{n}(X_i - \overline{X})^2}{n-1}}$$

where

S = sample standard deviation
X_i = the value of the ith observation
$\overline{X}$ = the sample mean
n = the sample size

variance
The sums of the squared deviations from the mean divided by the number of observations minus one.

range
The maximum value for a variable minus the minimum value for that variable.

The **variance** is calculated by using the same formula as for the standard deviation with the exception that the square-root sign is removed. Finally, the **range** is equal to the maximum value for a particular variable minus the minimum value for that variable.

Means, Percentages, and Statistical Tests

In terms of basic data analysis, the research analyst is faced with the decision of whether to use measures of central tendency (mean, median) or percentages (one-way frequency tables, crosstabulations). Responses to questions are either categorical or take the form of continuous variables. Occupation (coded 1 for professional/managerial, 2 for white collar, 3 for blue collar, and 4 for other) is an example of a categorical variable. The only thing that can be done with a variable of this type is to report the frequency and relative percentage with which each category was encountered. Variables such as age can be continuous or categorical, depending on how the information was obtained. For example, we can ask people their actual age or we can ask them which category (under 35, or 35 or older) includes their age. If actual age data are available, mean age can be readily com-

TABLE 15.12 **Measures of Dispersion and Measures of Central Tendency**

Consider the beer drinker example presented in Table 15.11. Assume that interviewing was conducted in two markets. The results for both markets are shown.

RESPONDENT	NUMBER OF CANS BOTTLES/GLASSES MARKET ONE	NUMBER OF CANS/ BOTTLES/GLASSES MARKET TWO
1	2	1
2	2	1
3	3	1
4	2	1
5	5	1
6	1	1
7	2	1
8	2	3
9	10	10
10	1	10
Mean	3	3
Standard deviation	2.7	3.7

NOTE: Average beer consumption is the same in both markets—3 cans/bottles/glasses. However, the standard deviation is larger in Market Two, indicating more dispersion in the data. Whereas the mean suggests the two markets are the same, the added information provided by the standard deviation tells us they are different.

puted. If categories are used, one-way frequency distributions and crosstabulations are the most obvious choices. However, continuous data can be put into categories, and means can be estimated for categorical data using the formula for computing a mean for grouped data presented earlier.

Finally, statistical tests are available that can tell us whether two means or two percentages differ to a greater extent than would be expected by chance (sampling error)—for example, average expenditures by men and average expenditures by women at fast food restaurants—or whether there is a significant relationship between two variables in a crosstabulation table. These tests are discussed in Chapter 16.

Summary

Once the questionnaires have been returned from the field, a five-step process takes place. These steps are (1) quality control checks, (2) coding, (3) data entry, (4) machine cleaning, and (5) tabulation and statistical analysis. The first step in the process is very critical. It is important to make sure that the data have integrity; otherwise the age-old adage is true, "garbage in, garbage out." Within the quality control process the first step is called *validation;* that is, determining as closely as possible that each questionnaire is, in fact, a valid interview. A valid interview in this sense is one that was conducted in an appropriate manner. The objective of validation is to detect interviewer fraud or failure to follow key instructions. Validation is accomplished by recontacting a certain percentage of the respondents surveyed by each interviewer. If inconsistencies are discovered in the validation process, then that interviewer's entire work will be validated and if, in fact, the interviews are fraudulent, those surveys will be eliminated from the database.

After the validation process is completed, editing begins. Editing involves checking for interviewer mistakes. This entails making certain that all questions that should be answered were, that skip patterns were followed properly, and that responses to open-ended questions were checked. Upon completion of editing, the next step is to code the data. Most questions on surveys are closed-ended and precoded. This means that numeric codes already have been assigned to the various responses on the questionnaire. With open-ended questions, the researcher has no idea in advance what the responses will be. Therefore, the coder must go back and establish numeric codes for response categories. This is accomplished by listing actual responses to open-ended questions, then consolidating those responses by assigning numeric codes to the consolidated categories. Once a coding sheet has been created, then all questionnaires are coded by following the coding sheet categories.

After validation, editing, and coding, the next step is data entry. Today, most data entry is done by means of intelligent entry systems that check the internal logic of the data. The data typically are entered directly from the questionnaires. New developments in optical scanning have made that more-automated approach to data entry cost-effective for smaller projects.

The final step in the process is tabulation of the data. The most basic tabulation is a one-way frequency table. A one-way frequency table indicates the number of respondents who give each possible answer to each question. One item that must be dealt with with one-way frequency tables is the basis for percentages. For example, are the percentages going to be calculated on total respondents, number of people asked a particular question, or the number answering a particular question? The next step in the analysis process is often crosstabulation: examination of the responses to one question in relation to the responses to one or more other questions. Crosstabulations are a very powerful and an easily understood approach of the summarization and analysis of survey research results.

Statistical measures are an even more powerful way to analyze data sets. Perhaps the most common statistical measures are those of central tendency: the arithmetic mean, the median, and the mode. The arithmetic mean is computed only from interval or ratio data by adding the values for all observations for a particular variable and dividing the resulting sum by the number of observations. The median can be computed for all types of data except nominal data by finding the value below which 50 percent of the observations fall. The mode can be computed with any type of data by simply finding the value that occurs most frequently. The arithmetic mean is, by far, the most commonly used measure of central tendency.

In addition to central tendency, researchers often want to have an indication of the dispersion of the data. Measures of dispersion include the standard deviation, variance, and range. The range is equal to the maximum value for a particular variable minus the minimum value for that variable.

Key Terms

validation
editing
skip pattern
coding
intelligent data entry
optical scanning

machine cleaning of data
error checking routines
marginal report
one-way frequency table
crosstabulation
mean
median
mode
standard deviation
variance
range

Review and Discussion Questions

1. What is the difference between measurement validity and interview validation?
2. Assume that Sally Smith, an interviewer, completed 50 questionnaires. Ten of the questionnaires were validated by calling the respondents and asking them one opinion question and two demographic questions over again. On one questionnaire, the respondent claimed that his age category was 30–40, and the age category marked on the questionnaire was 20–30. On a second questionnaire, the respondent was asked, "What is the most important problem facing our city government?" and the interviewer had written down, "The city council is too eager to raise taxes." When the interview was validated, the respondent said, "The city tax rate was too high." As a validator, would you assume that there were honest mistakes that were made and accept the entire lot of 50 interviews as valid? If not, what would you do?
3. What is meant by the editing process? Should editors be allowed to fill in what they think a respondent meant in open-ended questions if the information seems incomplete? Why or why not?
4. Give an example of a skip pattern on a questionnaire. Why is it important to always follow the skip patterns correctly?
5. It has been said that, to some degree, coding of open-ended questions is an art. Would you agree or disagree? Why? If, after coding a large number of questionnaires, the researcher notices that many responses end up in the "Other" category, what might this imply? What could be done to correct it?
6. Explain the difference between intelligent and dumb data entry. Why is data typically entered directly from the questionnaire into the data entry device?
7. What is the purpose of machine cleaning the data? Give some examples of how data can be machine cleaned. Do you think that machine cleaning is an expensive and unnecessary step in the data tabulation process? Why or why not?
8. It has been said that a crosstabulation of two variables gives the researcher much richer information than simply two one-way frequency tables. Why is this true? Give an example.
9. Illustrate the various alternatives for using percentages in one-way frequency tables. Explain the logic of using one alternative method over another.
10. Explain the difference between the mean, median, and mode. Give an example in which the researcher might be interested in each one of the alternative measures of central tendency.
11. Calculate the mean, median, mode, and standard deviation from the following data set:

Respondent	Times Visited whitehall Mall in Past Six Months	Times Visited Northpark Mall In Past Six Months	Times Visited Sampson Mall In Past Six Months
A	4	7	2
B	5	11	16
C	13	21	3
D	6	0	1
E	9	18	14
F	3	6	8
G	2	0	1
H	21	3	7
I	4	11	9
J	14	13	5
K	7	7	12
L	8	3	25
M	8	3	9

12. Using data from a newspaper or magazine article, create the following types of graphs:
   a. Line graph
   b. Pie chart
   c. Bar chart

CASE 15.1

Taco Bueno

Taco Bueno has recently opened its 15th store in Utah. Currently the chain offers tacos, enchiladas, and burritos. Management is considering offering a super taco that would be approximately two and a half times as large as a regular taco and contain 5 ounces of ground beef. The basic taco simply has spiced ground beef, lettuce, and cheese. Management feels that the super taco ought to have more toppings. Therefore, a market research study was undertaken to determine what those toppings should be. A key question on the survey was, "What, if anything, do you normally add to a taco that you have prepared at home besides meat?" The question is open-ended, and the coding categories that have been established for the question are shown in Table 15.13.

1. How would you code the following responses:

TABLE 15.13 Coding Categories

RESPONSE	CODE
Avocado	1
Cheese (Monterey Jack/cheddar)	2
Guacamole	3
Lettuce	4
Mexican hot sauce	5
Olive (black/green)	6
Onion (red/white)	7
Peppers (red/green)	8
Pimiento	9
Sour cream	0
Other	X

a. I usually add a green, avocado-tasting hot sauce.
b. I cut up a mixture of lettuce and spinach.
c. I'm a vegetarian; I don't use meat at all. My taco is filled only with guacamole.
d. Every now and then I use a little lettuce, but normally I like cilantro.

2. Is there anything wrong with having a great number of responses in the "Other" category? What problems does this present for the researcher?

CASE 15.2

Sunrise Mall

Sunrise Mall is an enclosed mall with more than 100 stores in Fort Lauderdale. Recently, management decided that it needed to know more about its target market and its competitors. A decision was made to conduct marketing research among both patrons and nonpatrons of Sunrise Mall. Management was interested in finding out why people did or did not shop at Sunrise, which stores were patronized most often, which ones were preferred, which ones were disliked, and how the image of Sunrise Mall compared with the image of competing malls. In addition, it wanted to know what promotions would be most effective in attracting both patrons and nonpatrons to Sunrise Mall. The questionnaire developed for the study is in the following survey.

Good ________, I'm __________________ of Americana Research, Inc. We are talking with people today about the shopping centers where they shop.

1. Are you 18 years of age or older? Yes ______ −1 No ______ −2 (TERMINATE)

2. What shopping center is more convenient for you to shop?

Sunrise	−1	Galleria	−5
Northwest Mall	−2	Other (SPECIFY)	
Park Plaza	−3	____________	−6
Oak City	−4	____________	−7
		Refused/DK	−0

3. In which shopping center do you do most of your shopping?

Sunrise	−1	Galleria	−5
Northwest Mall	−2	Other (SPECIFY)	
Park Plaza	−3	____________	−8
Oak City	−4	____________	−7
		Refused/DK	−0

4a. Do you presently shop at Sunrise Mall? Yes ______ −1 No ______ −2
(IF *YES*, GO TO Q. 5) (IF *NO*, ASK Q. 4b)

4b. Why do you not shop at Sunrise Mall? (PROBE) ______________________________

____

5. How often do you shop at Sunrise Mall?

More than once a week	−1
Once a week	−2
Twice a month	−3
Once a month	−4
Several times a year	−5
Refused	−0

6a. In Sunrise, which one store do you shop in most often? (MARK "1" FOR MOST)

6b. Which second most often? (MARK "2" FOR SECOND)

Stores/Places	6a	6b	7a
Adrien's	______	______	______
Bond's	______	______	______
Britt's	______	______	______
Craig's	______	______	______
Firestone	______	______	______
Graves	______	______	______
Joske's	______	______	______
Kresge's	______	______	______
Lerner's	______	______	______
Montgomery Ward	______	______	______
Oshman's	______	______	______
Piccadilly Cafeteria	______	______	______
The Woman's Shop	______	______	______
Thom McAn	______	______	______
Walgreen's	______	______	______
Weingarten's	______	______	______
Other: (SPECIFY)	______	______	______
______________	______	______	______
______________	______	______	______
______________	______	______	______
______________	______	______	______

NONE ( )
(GO to Q.8)

7a. Which store in the entire center do you least (MARK "L" FOR LEAST)

7b. Why do you like ________ the least? (PROBE) ______________________________

____

____

8. What changes of improvements could be made at Sunrise Mall? (PROBE)

____

____

____

____

9. What other type of store or other business (not in the center) would you like to see in Sunrise Mall? (PROBE)

____

____

____

10. Here is a list of various attributes of shopping centers. As I read each one, please tell me how you would rate Sunrise Mall in comparison with other shopping centers in Fort Lauderdale.

Would you say Sunrise Mall is *better than*, *the same as*, or *not as good* as other centers in regard to ______ (START WITH STARRED ATTRIBUTE AND ASK FOR ALL)?

Attributes	Better than	Same as	Not as Good
Selection of Merchandise	______	______	______
Parking at Center	______	______	______
Appearance/Atmosphere of Center	______	______	______
Appearance/Atmosphere of Stores	______	______	______
Special Prices	______	______	______
Center with Stores I Prefer	______	______	______
Variety of Eating Places	______	______	______
Housekeeping of Grounds	______	______	______
Housekeeping of Stores	______	______	______

Safe Place to Shop	______	______	______
Helpfulness of Salespeople	______	______	______
Good Eating Places	______	______	______
Special Promotions	______	______	______
Wide Range of Shopping Facilities	______	______	______
Hours Open to Shop	______	______	______
Convenience to Work	______	______	______
Convenience to Home			

11. What special events or promotions have you attended in Fort Lauderdale shopping centers in the past 12 months?

______

______

______

NONE ( ) (GO TO Q. 13)

12. What special event or promotion was your favorite?

______

______

13. What special event or promotion would you like to see sponsored by Sunrise Mall?

______

______

______

(GO TO DEMOGRAPHICS)

And now, a few questions for statistical classification.

14. Are you

Single	−1	Divorced	−4
Married	−2	Separated	−5
Widowed	−3	Refused	−0

15. In your home:
How many are adults age 18 and older?
How many are children under 18?
Total

16. In which of these brackets does your age fall?

18–24	−1	45–54	−4
25–34	−2	55–64	−5
35–44	−3	65 or over	−6

17. What is the last grade of school you completed?

None	−1	1–3 Years of College	−5
Some Grade School	−2	College Graduate	−6
Some High School	−3	Post Graduate	−7
Completed High School	−4		

18. Are you employed?
Yes −1 (ASK Q. 19)
No −2

18a. (IF MARRIED, ASK) is your (husband/wife) employed?
Yes −1 (ASK Q. 20)
No −2

19. What type of work do you do? (INDICATE IN GRID BELOW)

20. What type of work does your (husband/wife) do? (INDICATE IN GRID BELOW)

	Q. 19	Q. 20
Professional/Technical	−1	−1
Manager/Officials/Self-employed	−2	−2
Clerical or Sales	−3	−3
Skilled Worker	−4	−4
Service Worker	−5	−5
Unskilled laborer	−6	−6

Farm operator or rancher	−7	−7
Unemployed or student	−8	−8
Retired	−9	−9
Refused	−0	−0

21. Which Fort Lauderdale papers do you read? (DO NOT READ LIST)

Q. 21	READ
Globe	−1
Democrat	−2
Both	−3
Other (SPECIFY)	−4

22. What radio stations do you listen to?

MORNING	AFTERNOON	EVENING
________	________	________
________	________	________

23. Which TV station do you prefer for news?

Channel 2	−1	Channel 13	−4
Channel 8	−2	Channel 26	−5
Channel 11	−3	Channel 39	−6

24. Do you own or rent your home?

Own	−1
Rent	−2
Other	−3
Refused	−4

25. (IF LIVES IN SUNRISE MALL AREA, ASK) How long have you lived in this area?

Less than 1 year	−1	8 years to 10 years	−5
1 year to 3 years	−2	Over 10 years	−6
3 years to 6 years	−3	Refused	−4
6 years to 8 years	−4		

26. I'm going to read several income categories. Please tell me in which group your total family income falls.

Under $25,000	−1
$25,000–50,000	−2
Over $50,000	−3

1. You were in charge of specifying the crosstabulations for the study. Which questions would you crosstabulate?
2. Assume that you could only specify a total of 30 crosstabulations. Which 30 would you choose? (Crosstabbing one question by another question constitutes one crosstab. For example, crosstabbing "What shopping center is more convenient for you to shop?" by "Income of the Respondent" would count as one crosstab.)

CASE 15.3

Tan It All

Tan It All is a chain of 22 tanning salons in the Chicago metropolitan area. Business has been fairly flat for the past two years and the company believes that it needs a change in its pricing plan. Shannon Kelly, marketing director for Tan It All, met the marketing director for a chain of tanning salons in Cincinnati at an industry trade convention. The person she met told her about a new pricing plan

TABLE 15.14 Preference for Pricing Plans by Gender and Income

		GENDER		INCOME	
	Total	*Male*	*Female*	*≤$50K*	*>$50K*
Total	500	239	261	289	211
	100.0%	100.0%	100.0%	100.0%	100.0%
Prefer Plan A	201	112	89	147	54
	40.2%	46.9%	34.1%	50.9%	25.6%
Prefer Plan B	299	127	172	142	157
	59.8%	53.1%	65.9%	49.1%	74.4%

her company was using in Cincinnati that had proved, in her opinion, to be very effective. Shannon had just completed a survey of 500 target customers in the Chicago area. In that survey, her company described its current pricing (Plan A) plan and the pricing plan being used in Cincinnati (Plan B) and asked respondents which plan they preferred. In addition to the overall preference, Shannon is interested in adopting a plan that will be equally attractive to men and women and to those with incomes of more than $50,000 per year and those with incomes of $50,000 per year and less. Results, overall and by gender and income, are shown in Table 15.14.

1. Which plan appears to be most popular overall?
2. Is the plan preferred overall equally attractive to men and women?
3. What is the nature of the relationship between preference for pricing plans and income portrayed in the table?

CHAPTER 16

Data Analysis: Statistical Testing of Differences

LEARNING OBJECTIVES

1. To become aware of the nature of statistical significance.
2. To understand the concept of hypothesis development and the testing of hypotheses.
3. To understand the difference between Type I and Type II errors.
4. To describe several of the more common statistical tests of goodness of fit, hypotheses about one mean, hypothesis about two means, and hypotheses about proportions.
5. To learn about analysis of variance.

Kristine McKenzie is an ad executive with Gearhardt Advertising. She is responsible for the Taco Cabana account and is in the process of reviewing the results of a recent market survey conducted for Taco Cabana. She is concerned about two issues raised by the results. First, the survey indicates that women who eat at Taco Cabana eat there less often than do men. Is this difference something that she should take into consideration as she develops the new Taco Cabana campaign or could it be the result of sampling error? Second, the survey results show that older consumers eat at Mexican fast food restaurants less often, on average, than do younger consumers. The crosstabulations suggest that such a relationship exists, but Kristine needs to be more confident that these findings reflect actual consumer behavior. ■

SOURCE: Dallas Chang.

In this chapter, we will present some techniques that can be used to address these and similar questions.

Evaluating Differences and Changes

The notion of whether certain measurements are different from one another is central to many questions of critical interest to marketing managers. Some specific examples include the following:

- Our posttest measure of top-of-mind awareness is slightly higher than the level recorded in the pretest. Did top-of-mind awareness really increase, or is there some other explanation for the increase? Should we fire our agency or commend it?
- Our overall customer satisfaction score increased from 92 percent three months ago to 93.5 percent today. Did customer satisfaction really increase? Should we celebrate?

- Satisfaction with the customer service provided by our cable TV system in Dallas is, on average, 1.2 points higher on a 10-point scale than is satisfaction with the customer service provided by our cable TV system in Cincinnati. Are customers in Dallas really more satisfied? Should the customer service manager in Cincinnati be replaced? Should the Dallas manager be rewarded?
- In a recent product concept test, 19.8 percent of those surveyed said they were very likely to buy the new product they evaluated. Is this good? Is it better than the results we got last year for a similar product? What do these results suggest in terms of whether to introduce the new product?
- In a segmentation study, we find that those with incomes of more than $30,000 per year frequent fast food restaurants 6.2 times per month on average. Those with incomes of $30,000 or less go an average of 6.7 times. Is this difference real, is it meaningful?
- In an awareness test, 28.3 percent of those surveyed have heard of our product on an unaided basis. Is this a good result?

These are the eternal questions in marketing and marketing research. This is why, although considered boring by some, statistical hypothesis testing is important. This type of hypothesis testing helps us get closer to the ultimate answers to these questions. We say "closer" because we seldom achieve certainty in answering these questions in marketing research.

Statistical Significance

The basic motive for making statistical inferences is to be able to generalize from sample results to population characteristics. A basic tenet of statistical inference is that it is possible for numbers to be different in a mathematical sense but not significantly different in a statistical sense. For example, cola drinkers are asked to try two cola drinks in a blind taste test and indicate which they prefer. The results show that 51 percent prefer one test product and 49 percent prefer the other. There is a mathematical difference in the results, but the difference would appear to be minor and unimportant. The difference probably is well within the range of accuracy of our ability to measure taste preference, and the difference probably is not significant in a statistical sense. Three different concepts can be applied to the notion of differences.

- *Mathematical Differences.* By definition, if numbers are not exactly the same, they are different. This does not, however, suggest that the difference is either important or statistically significant.
- *Statistical Significance.* If a particular difference is large enough to be unlikely to have occurred because of chance or sampling error, then the difference is statistically significant.
- *Managerially Important Differences.* If results or numbers are different to the extent that the difference would matter from a managerial perspective, we can argue that the difference is important. For example, the difference in consumer response to two different packages in a test market might be statistically significant but yet so small as to have little practical or managerial significance.[1]

In this chapter, different approaches for testing whether results are statistically significant will be discussed.

Hypothesis Testing

A **hypothesis** can be defined as an assumption or guess that a researcher or manager makes about some characteristic of the population being investigated. The marketing researcher is often faced with the question of whether research results are different enough from the norm to conclude that some element of the firm's marketing strategy should be changed. Consider the following situations.

hypotheses
Assumptions or theories that a researcher or manager makes about some characteristic of the population under study.

- The results of a tracking survey show that awareness of the product is lower than it was in a similar survey conducted six months ago. Are the results significantly lower? Are the results sufficiently lower to call for a change in advertising strategy?
- A product manager believes that the average purchaser of his product is 35 years of age. A survey is conducted to test this hypothesis, and the survey shows that the average purchaser of the product is 38.5 years of age. Is the survey result enough different from the product manager's belief to conclude that the belief is incorrect?
- The marketing director of a fast food chain believes that 60 percent of her customers are female and 40 percent are male. She does a survey to test this hypothesis and finds that, according to the survey, 55 percent are female and 45 percent are male. Is this result sufficiently different from her original theory to permit her to conclude that her original theory was incorrect?

All these questions can be evaluated with some kind of statistical test. In hypothesis testing, the researcher determines whether a hypothesis concerning some characteristic of the population is likely given the evidence. A statistical hypothesis test allows us to calculate the probability of observing a particular result if the stated hypothesis is actually true.

There are two basic explanations for observing a difference between a hypothesized value and a particular research result: either the hypothesis is true and the

Cable TV viewers in Dallas on average had average satisfaction scores 1.25 points higher on a 10-point scale than did those in Cincinnati, are customers in Dallas really more satisfied? SOURCE: © Willie Hill/FPG.

observed difference is quite likely due to sampling error; or the hypothesis is most likely false and the true value is some other value.

Steps in Hypothesis Testing

Five basic steps are involved in testing a hypothesis. First, the hypothesis must be specified. Second, an appropriate statistical technique is selected to test the hypothesis. Third, a decision rule is specified as the basis for determining whether to reject or fail to reject (FTR) the null hypothesis H_0. Please note that we did not say "reject H_0 or accept H_0." Although a seemingly small distinction, it is an important one. The distinction will be discussed in greater detail later on. Fourth, calculate the value of the test statistic and perform the test. Fifth, state your conclusion from the perspective of the original research problem or question.

Stating the Hypothesis Hypotheses are stated using two basic forms: the null hypothesis H_0 and the alternative hypothesis H_a. The null hypothesis H_0 (sometimes called the *hypothesis of the status quo)* is the hypothesis that is tested against its complement, the alternative hypothesis, H_a (sometimes called the *research hypothesis of interest).* For example, the manager of Burger City believes that his operational procedures will guarantee that the average customer will have to wait two minutes in the drive-in window line. He conducts research based on the observation of 1,000 customers at randomly selected stores at randomly selected times. The average customer observed in this study spent 2.4 minutes in the drive-in window line. The null hypothesis and the alternative hypothesis might be stated as follows:

Null hypothesis H_0: Mean waiting time $= 2$ minutes.

Alternative hypothesis H_a: Mean waiting time $\neq 2$ minutes.

It should be noted that the null hypothesis and the alternative hypothesis must be stated in such a way that both cannot be true. The idea is to use the available evidence to ascertain which hypothesis is more likely to be true.

Choosing the Appropriate Test Statistic As you will see in the following sections of this chapter, the analyst must choose the appropriate statistical test given the characteristics of the situation under investigation. A number of different statistical tests and the situations where they are appropriate are discussed in this chapter. Table 16.1 provides a guide to selecting the appropriate test for various situations. All the tests discussed in this table are covered in detail later in this chapter.

Developing a Decision Rule Based on our previous discussions of distributions of sample means, you may recognize that it is very unlikely to get a sample result that is exactly equal to the value of the population parameter. The problem is one of determining whether the difference or deviation between the value of the actual sample mean and its expected value based on the hypothesis could have occurred by chance five times out of 100, for example, if the statisti-

TABLE 16.1 Statistical Tests Discussed in Chapter and Their Uses

AREA OF APPLICATION	SUBGROUPS OR SAMPLES	LEVEL SCALING	TEST	SPECIAL REQUIREMENTS	EXAMPLE
Hypotheses about about frequency distributions	One	Nominal	X^2	Random sample	Are observed differences in the numbers responding to three different promotions likely/not likely due to chance?
	Two or more	Nominal	X^2	Random sample, independent samples	Are differences in the numbers of men and women responding to a promotion likely/not likely due to chance?
	One	Ordinal	$K - S$	Random sample, natural order in data	Is the observed distribution of women preferring an ordered set of make-up colors (light to dark) likely/not likely due to chance?
Hypothesis about means	One (large sample)	Metric (interval or ratio)	Z-test for one mean	Random sample, $n \geqslant 30$	Is the observed difference between a sample estimate of the mean and some set standard or expected value of the mean likely/not likely due to chance?
	One (small sample)	Metric (interval or ratio)	t-test for one mean	Random sample, $n < 30$	Sample as for small sample
	Two (large sample)	Metric (interval or ratio)	Z-test for one means	Random sample, $n \geqslant 30$	Is the observed difference between the means for two subgroups (mean income for men and women) likely/not likely due to chance?
	Two (small sample)	Metric (interval or ratio)	One-way ANOVA	Random sample	Is the observed variation between means for three or more subgroups (mean expenditures on entertainment for high, moderate, and low-income people) likely/not likely due to chance?
Hypotheses about proportions	One (large sample)	Metric (interval or ratio)	Z-test for one proportion	Random sample, $n \geqslant 30$	Is the observed difference between a sample estimate of proportion (percentage who say they will buy) and some set standard or expected value likely/not likely due to chance?
	Two (large sample)	Metric (interval or ratio)	Z-test for two proportions	Random sample, $n \geqslant 30$	Is the observed difference between estimated percentages for two subgroups (percentage of men and women who have college degrees) likely/not likely due to chance?

cal hypothesis is true. A decision rule or standard is needed to determine whether to reject or fail to reject the null hypothesis. Statisticians state such decision rules in terms of significance levels.

The significance level (α) is critical in the process of choosing between the null and alternative hypotheses. The level of significance is the probability that is considered too low—.10, .05 or .01, for example—to justify acceptance of the null hypothesis.

Consider a situation in which we have decided that we want to test a hypothesis at the .05 level of significance. This means that we will reject the null hypothesis if the test indicates that the probability of occurrence of the observed result (e.g., difference between the sample mean and its expected value) because of chance or sampling error is less than 5 percent. Rejection of the null hypothesis is equivalent to supporting the alternative hypothesis.

Calculating the Value of the Test Statistic In this step we

- Use the appropriate formula to calculate the value of the statistic for the test chosen.
- Compare the value calculated (previously) to the critical value of the statistic (from the appropriate table) based on the decision rule chosen.
- Based on the comparison, state the result in terms of either rejecting or failing to reject the null hypothesis (H_0).

Stating the Conclusion Make a statement of your conclusion that summarizes the results of your test. State your conclusion from the perspective of the original research question.

Other Issues in Hypothesis Testing

Types of Errors in Hypothesis Testing

Type I error (α error)
Rejection of a null hypothesis when, in fact, it is true.

Type II error (β error)
Acceptance of a null hypothesis when, in fact, it is false.

Hypothesis tests are subject to two general types of errors: typically referred to as Type I error and Type II error.[2] A **Type I error** involves situations in which the researcher rejects the null hypothesis when it is, in fact, true. The researcher may reach this incorrect conclusion because the observed difference between the sample and population values is due to sampling error. The researcher must decide how willing she is to commit a Type I error. The probability of committing a Type I error is referred to as the *alpha (α) level.* Conversely, $1 - \alpha$ is the probability of making a correct decision if we do not reject the null hypothesis when, in fact, it is true.

Type II error involves situations in which the researcher fails to reject the null hypothesis when the null hypothesis actually is false. A Type II error is referred to as a *beta (β) error.* The value $1 - \beta$ reflects the probability of making a correct decision in rejecting the null hypothesis when, in fact, it is false. The various possibilities are summarized in Table 16.2.

As we consider the various types of hypothesis tests, keep in mind that when we reject or fail to reject the null hypothesis, this decision is never made with 100 percent certainty. There is a probability that our decision is correct and there is a probability that our decision is not correct. As noted earlier, the level of α is set

TABLE 16.2 Type I and Type II Errors

ACTUAL STATE OF THE NULL HYPOTHESIS	FAIL TO REJECT H_0	REJECT H_0
H_0 is true	Correct $(1 - \alpha)$ no error	Type I Error (α)
H_0 is false	Type II error (β)	Correct $(1 - \beta)$ no error

by the researcher. Although we say that "the level of α is set by the researcher," this is an oversimplification. In fact, the researcher must consult with his client, consider the resources available for the project, and consider the implications of making Type I and Type II errors. However, the estimation of β is more complicated and is beyond the scope of our discussion. Also, Type I and Type II errors are not complementary, $\alpha + \beta \neq 1$.

We would like to have control over n (the sample size), α (the probability of Type I error), and β (the probability of a Type II error) for any hypothesis test. Unfortunately, you can control only two of the three. For a given problem with a fixed sample size, n is fixed or controlled. Therefore, for α and β, you can control only one.

Assume that for a given problem you have decided to set $\alpha = .05$. As a result, the procedure you use to test H_0 versus H_a will reject H_0 when it is true (Type I error) 5 percent of the time. You could set $\alpha = 0$ so that you would never have a Type I error. The idea of never rejecting a correct H_0 sounds good. However, the downside is that β (the probability of Type II error) is equal to 1 in this situation. As a result, you will always fail to reject H_0 when it is false. For example, if we set $\alpha = 0$ in the fast food service time example where $H_0 = 2$ minutes, then the resulting test of H_0 versus H_a will automatically fail to reject H_0: (average waiting time $= 2$ minutes) whenever our estimated waiting time is any value other than 2 minutes. If, for example, we do a survey and determine that the mean waiting time for the people surveyed is 8.5 minutes, we would still fail to reject (FTR) H_0. As you can see, this is not a good compromise. As you also can see, we need a value of α that offers a more reasonable compromise between the probabilities of the two types of errors. Please note that in this situation in which $\alpha = 0$ and $\beta = 1$, $\alpha + \beta = 1$. As you will see later on, this is not true as a general rule.

The value of α selected should be a function of the relative importance of the two types of errors. Consider the following situation and associated hypotheses and decide if a Type I error or a Type II error would be more serious. You have just been subjected to a diagnostic test. The purpose of the test is to determine whether you have a particular medical condition that is fatal in most cases. If you have the disease, a treatment that is painless, inexpensive, and totally without risk will cure the condition 100 percent of the time. The hypotheses to be tested are

H_0: Test indicates that you do not have the disease.

H_a: Test indicates that you do have the disease.

$\alpha = P$ (rejecting H_0 when it is true) $= P$ (test indicates that you have the disease when you do not have it)

$\beta = P$ (FTR H_0 when in fact it is false) $= P$ (test indicates that you do not have the disease when you do have it)

When you think about it, you can see that a Type I error (measured by α) is not nearly as serious as a Type II error (measured by β). A Type I error is not serious because the test will not harm you if you are well. However, a Type II error means that you will not receive the treatment you need even though you are ill.

The value of β is never set in advance. If we make α smaller, β is larger. If you want to minimize Type II error, then you want β to be smaller and you choose a larger value for α. In most situations, the range of acceptable values for α is 0.01 to 0.1.

In the case of the diagnostic test situation, you might choose a value of α at or near 0.1 because of the seriousness of a Type II error in this situation. Conversely, if you are more concerned about Type I errors in a given situation, then a small value of α is appropriate. An example of this would be a situation in which you are testing commercials that were very expensive to produce and where there is a possibility of rejecting a commercial that is really effective. If there is no real difference between the effects of Type I and Type II errors, which is often the case, an α value of 0.05 is commonly used.

Accepting H_0 or Failing to Reject (FTR) H_0? Researchers often fail to make a distinction between accepting and failing to reject (FTR) H_0. However, there is an important distinction between these two decisions. When we test a hypothesis, H_0 is presumed to be true until it is demonstrated to likely be false. In any hypothesis testing situation, the only other hypothesis that can be accepted is the alternative hypothesis, H_a. There is either sufficient evidence to support H_a (reject H_0) or there is not (we fail to reject H_0). The real question is whether there is enough evidence in the data to conclude that H_a is correct. If we fail to reject H_0, we are saying that the data do not provide sufficient support of the claim made in H_a and not that we accept the statement made in H_0.

One-Tailed Test or Two-Tailed Test? The decision of whether to use a one-tailed test or a two-tailed test depends on the nature of the situation and what you are trying to demonstrate. For example, when the quality control department of a fast food organization receives a shipment of ground beef from one of its vendors and needs to determine whether the product meets specifications in regard to the fat content, a one-tailed test is appropriate. The ground beef shipment will be rejected if it does not meet specifications. On the other hand, the managers of the meat company that supplies the product should run two-tailed tests to determine two factors. First, they must make sure that the product meets the minimum specifications of their customer before they ship it. Second, they will want to determine whether the product exceeds specifications because this can be very costly to them. If they are consistently providing a product that exceeds the level of quality they have contracted to provide, this will increase their costs.

The classic example of a situation requiring a two-tailed test is the testing of electric fuses. A fuse must trip or break contact when it reaches a preset temperature or a fire may result. On the other hand, you do not want the fuse to break contact before it reaches the specified temperature or it will shut off the electricity unnecessarily. The test used in the quality control process for testing fuses must, therefore, be two-tailed.

Example: Performing a Statistical Test

Income is an important determinant of the sales of hot tubs. Tubs R Us (TRU) is a hot tub manufacturer in the process of developing sales estimates for one of its major markets in Southern California. According to the U.S. census of population, the average annual family income in the market is \$55,347. TRU has just completed a survey of 250 randomly selected households in the market to collect other data, not available in the census, necessary for its sales forecasting model. According to its survey, average annual family income in the market is \$54,323. The actual value of the population mean (μ) is unknown. We have two estimates of μ in the census result and the survey result. The difference between these two estimates makes a substantial difference in the estimate of hot tub sales produced by TRU's forecasting model. In the calculations, we treat the U.S. Census Bureau estimate as the best estimate of μ.

To evaluate the census estimate, TRU decides to statistically compare it with its survey result. The details regarding the sample are:

$$\bar{X} = \$54{,}323$$
$$S = \$4{,}323$$
$$n = 250$$

The following hypotheses are produced:

$$H_0 : \mu = \$55{,}347$$
$$H_a : \mu \neq \$55{,}347$$

The managers at TRU decide that they are willing to use a test that will reject H_0 when it is correct only 5 percent of the time ($\alpha = 0.05$). This is the significance level of the test. TRU will

- Reject H_0 if $|\bar{X} - \$55{,}347|$ is larger than can be explained by sampling error at $\alpha = .05$.
- Reject H_0 if $\left|\dfrac{\bar{X} - \$55{,}347}{S/\sqrt{n}}\right|$ is larger than can be explained by sampling error at $\alpha = .05$.

In the last expression we are standardizing the data so we can directly relate the result to Z-values in Table 2 in Appendix Two.

- This last expression can be rewritten as $\left|\dfrac{\bar{X} - \$55{,}347}{S/\sqrt{n}}\right| > k$

What is the value of k ? If H_0 is true, and the sample size is large (≥ 30), then (based on the central limit theorem) $\bar{X}$ approximates a normal random variable with

$$\text{mean} = \mu = \$55{,}347$$
$$\text{standard deviation} = \frac{S}{\sqrt{n}}$$

If H_0 is true, $(\bar{X} - \$55{,}347)/(S/\sqrt{n})$ approximates a standard normal variable, Z, for samples of 30 or larger with a mean equal to 0 and a standard deviation equal to 1.

We reject H_0 if $|Z| > k$. To find the value of k, consider Figure 16.1. When $|Z| > k$ then either $Z > k$ or $Z < -k$ as shown in Figure 16.1. Given that

$$P(|Z| > k) = .05,$$

then the total shaded area is .05 including .025 in each tail (two-tailed test). The area between 0 and k is .475. Referring to Table 2 in Appendix Two, we find that $k = 1.96$. Therefore the test is

$$\text{Reject } H_0 \text{ if } \left|\frac{\bar{X} - \$55{,}347}{S/\sqrt{n}}\right| > 1.96$$

FTR H_0 otherwise. Therefore,

$$\text{Reject } H_0 \text{ if } \left|\frac{\bar{X} - \$55{,}347}{S/\sqrt{n}}\right| > 1.96$$

or

$$\text{Reject } H_0 \text{ if } \left|\frac{\bar{X} - \$55{,}347}{S/\sqrt{n}}\right| < -1.96$$

The question is, is $\bar{X} = \$54{,}323$ far enough away from \$55,347 for TRU to reject H_0? The results show that

$$Z = \frac{\bar{X} - \$55{,}347}{S/\sqrt{n}}$$

$$Z = \frac{\$54{,}323 - \$55{,}347}{\$4{,}322/\sqrt{250}}$$

$$Z = -3.75$$

Because $-3.75 < -1.96$, we reject H_0. The conclusion is that on the basis of the sample results and $\alpha = .05$, the average household income in the market is not equal to \$55,347. If H_0 is true ($\mu = \$55{,}347$), then the value of $\bar{X}$ obtained from the sample (\$54, 323) is 3.75 standard deviations to the left of the mean using the normal curve for $\bar{X}$. A value of $\bar{X}$ this far away from the mean is very unlikely

FIGURE 16.1
Shaded Area Is Significance Level α

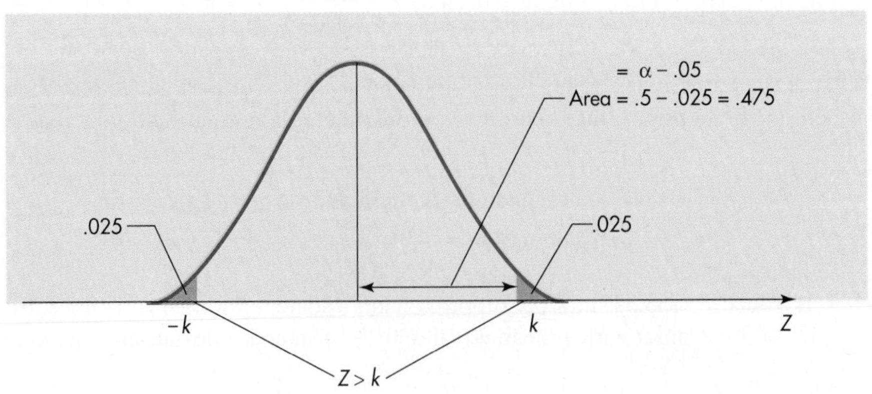

(probability is less than .05). As a result, we conclude that H_0 is not likely to be true and we reject it.

Hypothesis Tests

General Comments

A number of commonly used statistical hypothesis test of differences are presented in the following section. Many other statistical tests have been developed and are used, but a full discussion of all of them is beyond the scope of this text.

The distributions used in the following section for comparing the computed and tabular values of the statistics are the Z-distribution, the t-distribution, the F-distribution and the chi-square (χ^2) distribution. The tabular values for these distributions appear in Tables 2, 3, 4, and 5 of Appendix Two.

Independent versus Related Samples

In some cases one may need to test the hypothesis that the value of a variable in one population is equal to the value of that same variable in another population. The selection of the appropriate test statistic requires the researcher to consider whether the samples are independent or related. **Independent samples** involve situations in which measurement of the variable of interest in one sample has no effect on the measurement of the variable in the other sample. It is not necessary that there be two different surveys, only that the measurement of the variable in one population has no effect on the measurement of the variable in the other population. In the case of **related samples,** the measurement of the variable of interest in one sample may influence the measurement of the parameter of interest in another sample.

independent samples
Samples in which measurement of a variable in one population has no effect on the measurement of the variable in the other.

related samples
Samples in which the measurement of a variable in one population may influence the measurement of the variable in the other.

If, for example, men and women were interviewed in a particular survey regarding their frequency of eating out, there is no way that a man's response could affect or change the way a woman would respond to the question in this survey. This would be an example of independent samples. On the other hand, consider a situation in which the researcher needed to determine the effect of a new advertising campaign on consumer awareness of a particular brand. To do this, the researcher might survey a random sample of consumers before introducing the new campaign and survey the same sample of consumers 90 days after the new campaign was introduced. These samples are not independent. The measurement of awareness 90 days after the start of the campaign may be affected by the first measurement.

Degrees of Freedom

As you will see, many of the statistical tests discussed in this chapter require the researcher to specify degrees of freedom to find the critical value of the test statistic from the table for that statistic. Degrees of freedom are the number of observations in a statistical problem that are not restricted or are free to vary.

The number of degrees of freedom (d.f.) is equal to the number of observations minus the number of assumptions or constraints necessary to calculate a statistic. Consider the problem of adding five numbers when, for example, the mean of the five numbers is known to be 20. In this situation, only four of the five numbers are free to vary because once four of the numbers are known, the last value also is known (can be calculated) because the mean value must be 20. If we knew that four of the five numbers were 14, 23, 24, and 18, then the fifth number must be 21 to produce a mean of 20. We would say that the sample has $n-1$ degrees of freedom. It is as if the sample had one less observation. The inclusion of degrees of freedom in this calculation adjusts for this fact.

Goodness of Fit

Chi-Square

chi-square test

Test of the goodness of fit between the observed distribution and the expected distribution of a variable.

Data collected in surveys, as noted earlier in the text, are often analyzed by means of one-way frequency counts and crosstabulations. The purpose of crosstabulation is to study relationships among variables. The question is, Does the number of responses that fall into different categories differ from what one would expect? This could involve partitioning users into groups such as gender (male, female), age (under 18, 18–35, over 35), or income level (low, middle, high) and crosstabulating by the results to questions such as preferred brand or level of use. The **chi-square** (χ^2) **test** enables the research analyst to determine whether an observed pattern of frequencies corresponds to or fits an "expected" pattern.[3] It tests the "goodness of fit" of the observed distribution in relation to an expected distribution. In the following sections, we will describe the application of this technique to test distributions of crosstabulated categorical data for a single sample and for two independent samples.

Chi-Square Test of a Single Sample

Consider a situation in which the marketing manager of a retail electronics chain needs to test the effectiveness of three special deals (Deal 1, Deal 2, and Deal 3). Each deal will be offered for a month. The manager wants to measure the effect of each deal on the number of customers visiting a test store during the time the deal is on. The number of customers visiting the store under each deal was as follows:

DEAL	MONTH	CUSTOMERS PER MONTH
1	April	11,700
2	May	12,100
3	June	11,780
Total		35,580

The marketing manager needs to know whether there is a significant difference between the number of customers visiting the store during one time period covered by each deal. The chi-square (χ^2) one-sample test is the appropriate way to answer this question. This test would be applied as follows:

1. Specify the null and alternative hypotheses.

- Null hypothesis H_0: The number of customers visiting the store under the various deals is equal.
- Alternative hypothesis H_a: There is a significant difference in the number of customers visiting the store under the various deals.

2. Determine the number of visitors that would be expected in each category if the null hypotheses were correct (E_i). In the example, the null hypothesis is that there is no difference in the number of customers attracted by the different deals. Therefore, an equal number of customers would be expected under each deal. Of course, this assumes that no other factors influenced the number of visits to the store. Under the null (no difference) hypothesis, the expected number of customers visiting the store in each deal period would be 11,860, computed as follows:

$$E = \frac{TV}{N}$$

where

$$TV = \text{total number of visits}$$
$$N = \text{number of months}$$
$$E = \frac{35{,}580}{3}$$
$$E = 11{,}860$$

The researcher should check for cells in which small expected frequencies occur because they can distort χ^2 results. No more than 20 percent of the categories should have expected frequencies less than 5, and none should have an expected frequency less than 1. This is not a problem in this case.

3. Calculate the χ^2 value using the formula:

$$\chi^2 = \sum_{i=1}^{k} \frac{(O_i - E_i)^2}{E_i}$$

where

O_i = observed number in ith category
E_i = expected number in ith category
k = number of categories

For our example,

$$\chi^2 = \frac{(11{,}700 - 11{,}860)^2}{11{,}860} + \frac{(12{,}100 - 11{,}860)^2}{11{,}860} + \frac{(11{,}780 - 11{,}860)^2}{11{,}860}$$
$$= 7.55$$

4. Select the level of significance α. If the .05 (α) level of significance is selected, the tabular χ^2 value with 2 degrees of freedom ($k - 1$) is 5.99. (See Table 4 of Appendix Two.)
5. Because the calculated χ^2 value (7.55) is higher than the table value (see Table 4 in Appendix Two for $k - 1 = 2$ d.f., $\alpha = .05$), we would *reject the null hypothesis*. Therefore, we conclude with 95 percent confidence that customer response to the deals was significantly different. Unfortunately, this test tells us only that the overall variation among the cell frequencies is greater than would be expected by chance. It does not tell us whether any individual cell is significantly different from the others.

TABLE 16.3 Data for X^2 Two Independent Sample Test

VISITS TO CONVENIENCE STORE BY MALES				VISITS TO CONVENIENCE STORES BY FEMALES			
Number X_m	*Frequency f_m*	*Percent*	*Cumulative Percent*	*Number X_f*	*Frequency f_f*	*Percent*	*Cumulative Percent*
2	2	4.4	4.4	2	5	7.0	7.0
3	5	11.1	15.6	3	4	5.6	12.7
5	7	15.6	31.1	4	7	9.9	22.5
6	2	4.4	35.6	5	10	14.1	36.6
7	1	2.2	37.8	6	6	8.5	45.1
8	2	4.4	42.2	7	3	4.2	49.3
9	1	2.2	44.4	8	6	8.5	57.7
10	7	15.6	60.0	9	2	2.8	60.6
12	3	6.7	66.7	10	13	18.3	78.9
15	5	11.1	77.8	12	4	5.6	84.5
20	6	13.3	91.1	15	3	4.2	88.7
23	1	2.2	93.3	16	2	2.8	91.5
25	1	2.2	95.6	20	4	5.6	97.2
30	1	2.2	97.8	21	1	1.4	98.6
40	1	2.2	100.0	25	1	1.4	100.0

Total $n_m = 45$ $n_f = 71$

Mean number of visits by males, $\bar{X}_m = \frac{\sum X_m f_m}{45} = 11.49$

Mean number of visits by females, $\bar{X}_1 = \frac{\sum X_f f_f}{71} = 8.51$

Chi-Square Test of Two Independent Samples

Marketing researchers often need to determine whether there is any association between two or more variables. Questions such as, Are men and women equally divided into heavy-, medium-, and light-user categories? or Are purchasers and nonpurchasers equally divided into low-, middle-, and high-income groups? may need to be answered before formulation of a marketing strategy. The chi-square (χ^2) test for two independent samples is the appropriate test in this situation.

This technique is illustrated using the data from Table 16.3. A convenience store chain wants to determine the nature of the relationship, if any, between gender of customer and frequency of visiting stores in the chain. Frequency of visits has been divided into three categories: 1–5 visits per month (light user), 6–14 visits per month (medium user), and 15 and above visits per month (heavy user). The steps necessary for conducting this test follow.

1. State the null and alternative hypotheses.

   - Null hypothesis H_0: There is no relationship between gender and frequency of visit.
   - Alternative hypothesis H_a: There is a significant relationship between sex and frequency of visit.

2. Place the observed (sample) frequencies in a $k \times r$ table (crosstabulation or contingency table) using the k columns for the sample groups and the r rows for the conditions or treatments. Calculate the sum of each row and each column. Record those totals at the margins of the table (they are called *marginal totals).* Also, calculate the total for the entire table (N).

FREQUENCY OF VISITS	MALE	FEMALE	TOTALS
1–5	14	26	40
6–14	16	34	50
15 and Above	15	11	26
Totals	45	71	116

3. Determine the expected frequency for each cell in the contingency table by calculating the product of the two marginal totals common to that cell and dividing that value by N.

FREQUENCY OF VISITS	MALE	FEMALE
1–5	$\frac{45 \times 40}{116} = 15.52$	$\frac{71 \times 40}{116} = 24.48$
6–14	$\frac{45 \times 50}{116} = 19.40$	$\frac{71 \times 50}{116} = 30.60$
15 and Above	$\frac{45 \times 26}{116} = 10.09$	$\frac{71 \times 26}{116} = 15.91$

The χ^2 value will be distorted if more than 20 percent of the cells have an expected frequency of less than 5 or if any cell has an expected frequency of less than 1. The test should not be used under these conditions.

4. Calculate the value of χ^2 using

$$\chi^2 = \sum_{i=1}^{r} \sum_{j=1}^{k} \frac{(O_{ij} - E_{ij})^2}{E_{ij}}$$

where

O_{ij} = observed number in the ith row of the jth column
E_{ij} = expected number in the ith row of the jth column

For our example,

$$\chi^2 = \frac{(14 - 15.52)^2}{15.52} + \frac{(26 - 24.48)^2}{24.48} + \frac{(16 - 19.4)^2}{19.4} + \frac{(34 - 30.6)^2}{30.6} + \frac{(15 - 10.09)^2}{10.09} + \frac{(11 - 15.91)^2}{15.91}$$

$$\chi^2 = 5.12$$

5. The tabular χ^2 value at a .05 level of significance and $(r - 1)(k - 1) = 2$ degrees of freedom is 5.99 (see Table 4 of Appendix Two). Because the

calculated $\chi^2 = 5.12$ is less than the tabular value, we *fail to reject the null (FTR) hypothesis* and conclude that there is no significant difference between males and females in terms of frequency of their visits.

Kolmogorov-Smirnov Test

Kolmogorov-Smirnov test
Test of the goodness of fit between the observed distribution and the expected distribution using ordinal data.

The **Kolmogorov-Smirnov** (K-S) **test** is similar to the chi-square test of goodness of fit.[4] It is concerned with the degree of agreement between the distribution of observed values and some theoretical or expected distribution. However, the K-S test is appropriate if the researcher is dealing with ordinal data.

Compaq Computers is preparing to introduce a new line of computers designed for the home market. Focus group research has indicated that many potential new computer buyers in the home market are turned off by the colors traditionally used for computers in an office environment. Focus group participants were shown a wide range of colors, in addition to the traditional tans and grays used in an office environment, and expressed a preference for a brown

FIGURE 16.2
The Kolmogorov-Smirnov Test Can Be Applied to a Survey on Color Preference

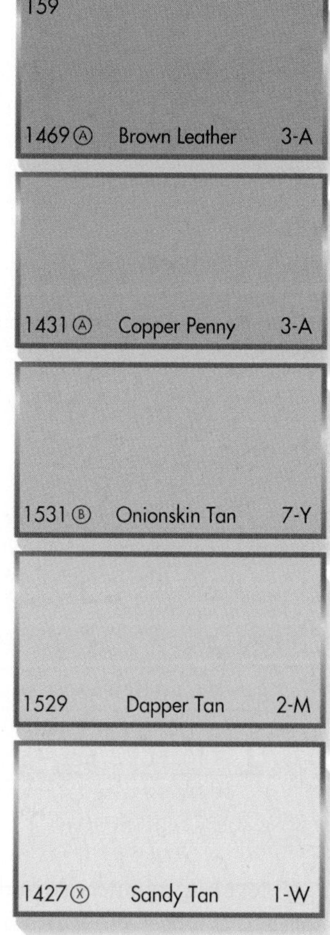

color. Compaq then surveyed 500 individuals who do not currently own computers but who indicated that they planned to buy a computer in the next six months. They were shown several shades of brown and asked to indicate their preference (see Figure 16.2). The survey results, in regard to color preference, are summarized in the following chart.

SHADES	NUMBER OF CONSUMERS PREFERRING A PARTICULAR SHADE
Very light	150
Light	170
Medium	80
Dark	45
Very Dark	55
Total	500

The manufacturer is interested in knowing whether these results might have occurred by chance or indicate a significant preference.

Because shade of color represents a natural ordering (ordinal data), the K-S test can be applied to test the preference hypothesis. The test involves specifying the cumulative frequency distribution that would be expected under the null hypothesis (theoretical distribution) and comparing it with the observed frequency distribution. The point at which the two distributions show the maximum deviation must be determined, and the value of this deviation is used as the test statistic. The magnitude of the test statistic (D) indicates whether such a

Compaq Computer used the Kolmogorov-Smirnov test to help determine the color shading of a new line of computers. SOURCE: Michael Newman/PhotoEdit.

divergence between the two distributions was likely to be due to chance or is indicative of a true preference.

The steps involved in the K-S test are as follows.

1. Specify the null and alternative hypotheses.

   - Null hypothesis H_0: There is no preference between the shades.
   - Alternative hypothesis H_a: There is a significant preference between the shades.

2. Establish the cumulative frequency distribution expected under the null hypothesis. The null hypothesis is that there is no difference in preference for the various shades of the new color. If this were true, the proportion of consumers preferring each shade would be equal to one-fifth or .20.
3. Calculate the observed cumulative frequency distribution from the sample.
4. Select the level of significance α. If the .05 (α) level of significance is selected, the critical value of D for large samples is given by $1.36/\sqrt{n}$, where n is the sample size. In our case, the critical value is $1.36/\sqrt{500}$.
5. Determine the K-S D statistic. D is equal to the largest deviation in absolute terms between the observed cumulative frequency proportions and the expected cumulative frequency proportions.

Table 16.4 provides the necessary data in tabular form. The largest absolute difference is .24, which is the Kolmogorov-Smirnov D value.

Because the calculated D (.24) exceeds the critical value (.06), *the null hypothesis of no preference among shades is rejected.*

Hypotheses About One Mean

Z-Test

***Z*-test**
Hypothesis test about a single mean if the sample is large enough and drawn from a normal population.

One of the most common problems in marketing research studies is the need to make some inference about the population mean. The appropriate test statistic for testing a hypothesis about a single mean is the ***Z*-test,** if the sample size is large enough ($n \geq 30$).[5] For small samples ($n < 30$), we should use the t-test with $n - 1$ degrees of freedom (n = sample size).

TABLE 16.4 Data for Kolmogorov-Smirnov Test

COLOR SHADE	OBSERVED NUMBER	OBSERVED PROPORTION	OBSERVED CUMULATIVE PROPORTION	NULL HYPOTHESIS PROPORTION	NULL CUMULATIVE PROPORTION	ABSOLUTE DIFFERENCE (OBSERVED AND NULL.)
Very Light	150	0.30	0.30	0.20	0.20	0.10
Light	170	0.34	0.64	0.20	0.40	0.24
Medium	80	0.16	0.80	0.20	0.60	0.20
Dark	45	0.09	0.89	0.20	0.80	0.09
Very Dark	55	0.11	1.00	0.20	1.00	0.00

Video Connection, a Dallas video store chain, recently completed a survey of 200 consumers in its market area. One of the questions was, "Compared to other video stores in the area, would you say Video Connection is much better than average, somewhat better than average, average, somewhat worse than average, or much worse than average?" Responses were coded as follows:

RESPONSE	CODE
Much better	5
Somewhat better	4
Average	3
Somewhat worse	2
Much worse	1

The mean rating of Video Connection is 3.4. The sample standard deviation is 1.9. How can the management of Video Connection be confident that its video stores' mean rating is significantly higher than 3 (average in the rating scale)? The Z-test for hypotheses about one mean is the appropriate test in this situation. The steps in the procedure follow.

1. Specify the null and alternative hypotheses.
   - Null hypothesis H_0: $M \leq 3$ (M = response on rating scale).
   - Alternative hypothesis H_a: $M > 3$.
2. Specify the level of sampling error (α) allowed. For $\alpha = .05$, the table value of Z (critical) = 1.64. (See Table 3 in Appendix Two for d.f. = ∞, .05 significance, one-tail. The table for t is used because $t = Z$ for samples greater than 30.) The need to be very confident that the mean rating is significantly higher than 3 is interpreted to mean that the management of Video Connection is willing to accept a chance of being wrong due to sampling error of no more than .05 (an α of .05).
3. The sample standard deviation (S) is given as $S = 1.90$.
4. Calculate the estimated standard error of the mean using the following formula:

$$S_{\bar{x}} = \frac{S}{\sqrt{n}}$$

where

$$S_{\bar{x}} = \text{the estimated standard error of the mean.}$$

Therefore,

$$S_{\bar{x}} = \frac{1.9}{\sqrt{200}} = 0.13$$

5. Calculate the test statistic:

$$Z = \frac{(\text{sample mean}) - \begin{pmatrix}\text{population mean specified} \\ \text{under the null hypothesis}\end{pmatrix}}{\text{estimated standard error of the mean}}$$

$$Z = \frac{3.4 - 3}{0.13}$$
$$= 3.07$$

The Null hypothesis can be rejected because the calculated Z-value (3.07) is larger than the critical Z-value (1.64). Management of Video Connection can now infer with 95 percent confidence that its video stores' mean rating is significantly higher than 3.

t-Test

***t*-test**
Hypothesis test about a single mean if the sample is too small to use the Z-test.

As noted earlier, for small samples ($n < 30$), the **t-test** with $n - 1$ degrees of freedom is the appropriate test for making statistical inferences. The *t*-distribution also is theoretically correct for large samples ($n \geq 30$). It approaches and becomes indistinguishable from the normal distribution for samples of 30 or more observations. Although we generally use the Z-test for large samples, some statistical packages (SAS, for example) use the *t*-test for all samples sizes.

To illustrate the application of the *t*-test, consider a soft drink manufacturer that plans to test market a new soft drink in Denver. Twelve supermarkets in that city are selected at random, and the new soft drink is offered for sale in these stores for a limited period. The company estimates that it must sell 1,000 cases per week in each store for the brand to be profitable enough to warrant large-scale introduction. Actual average sales per store per week for the test are shown in Table 16.5. The steps in the procedure for testing whether sales per store per week are more than 1,000 cases are

TABLE 16.5 Sales of Soft Drink in Denver

STORE	AVERAGE SALES PER WEEK (X_i)
1	870
2	910
3	1050
4	1200
5	860
6	1400
7	1305
8	890
9	1250
10	1100
11	950
12	1260

$$\text{Mean sales per week, } \overline{X} = \frac{\sum_{i=1}^{n} X_i}{n}$$

$$\overline{X} = 1087.1$$

1. Specify the null and alternative hypotheses.

   ■ Null hypotheses H_o: $M \leq 1000$ cases per store per week (M = average sales per store per week).
   ■ Alternative hypothesis H_a: $M > 1{,}000$ cases per store per week.

2. Specify the level of sampling error (α) allowed. For $\alpha = .05$, the table value of t (critical) = 1.796. (See Table 3 in Appendix Two for 12 − 1 = 11 d.f., α = .05, one-tail test.) The critical t-value is obtained from the t table with $n - 1 = 11$ degrees of freedom and $\alpha = .05$. Note that a one-tailed t-test is appropriate because the new soft drink will be introduced on a large scale only if sales per week are more than 1,000 cases.
3. Determine the sample standard deviation (S) as follows:

$$S = \sqrt{\frac{\sum_{i=1}^{n} (X_i - \bar{X})^2}{n - 1}}$$

   where

   X_i = observed sales per week in ith store
   $\bar{X}$ = average sales per week
   n = number of stores

4. Using the data from Table 16.5, S would be calculated as follows:

$$S = \sqrt{\frac{404095.8}{(12 - 1)}}$$
$$S = 191.6$$

5. Calculate the estimated standard error of the mean ($S_{\bar{X}}$) using the following formula:

$$S_{\bar{x}} = \frac{S}{\sqrt{n}} = \frac{191.6}{\sqrt{12}} = 55.31$$

6. Calculate the t-test statistic:

$$t = \frac{(\text{sample mean}) - \left(\begin{array}{c}\text{population mean}\\ \text{under the null hypothesis}\end{array}\right)}{\text{estimated standard error of the mean}}$$

$$t = \frac{1087.1 - 1000}{55.31}$$

$$t = 1.57$$

   The null hypothesis cannot be rejected because the calculated value of t is less than the critical value of t.

Although mean sales per store per week ($X = 1087.1$) are higher than 1,000 units, the difference is not statistically significant based on the 12 stores sampled. On the basis of this test and the decision criterion specified, the large-scale introduction of the new soft drink is not warranted.

Hypothesis About Two Means

Marketers are frequently interested in testing differences between groups. The following example shows how we would go about testing the differences between two means. The samples in our example are independent.

The management of the convenience store chain in our example is interested in differences between the store visit rates of men and women. It believes that men visit convenience stores more often than women and collected data on convenience store visits from 1,000 randomly selected consumers. Testing this hypothesis involves the following steps.

1. The null and alternative hypotheses are as follows.

   - Null hypothesis H_0: $M_m - M_f \leq 0$, the mean visit rate of men (M_m) is the same or less than the mean visit rate of women (M_f).
   - Alternative hypotheses H_a: $M_m - M_f > 0$, the mean visit rate of men (M_m) is higher than the mean visit rate of women (M_f). The observed difference in the two means (Table 16.3) is as follows:

   $$11.49 - 8.51 = 2.98$$

2. Set the level of sampling error (α). The managers decided that the acceptable level of sampling error for this test is $\alpha = .05$. For $\alpha = .05$, the table value of Z (critical) = 1.64. (See Table 3 in Appendix Two for d.f. = ∞, .05 significance, one-tail. The table for t is used because $t = Z$ for samples greater than 30.)
3. The estimated standard error of the differences between two means is calculated as follows:

   $$S_{X_{m-f}} = \sqrt{\frac{S_m^2}{n_m} + \frac{S_f^2}{n_f}}$$

   where

   S_m = estimated standard deviation of population m (men)
   S_f = estimated standard deviation of population f (women)
   n_m = sample size for sample m
   n_f = sample size for sample f

   Therefore,

   $$S_{X_{m-f}} = \sqrt{\frac{(8.16)^2}{45} + \frac{(5.23)^2}{71}}$$

   $$S_{X_{m-f}} = 1.37$$

Note that this formula is for those cases in which the two samples have unequal variances. A separate formula is used when two samples have equal variances. When you run this test in SAS and many other statistical packages, two *t*-values are provided – one for each variance assumption.

4. Calculate the test statistic. Z is calculated as follows:

$$Z = \frac{\begin{pmatrix}\text{difference between means}\\ \text{of first and second sample}\end{pmatrix} - \begin{pmatrix}\text{difference between means}\\ \text{under the null hypothesis}\end{pmatrix}}{\text{standard error of the differences between the two means}}$$

$$= \frac{(11.49 - 8.51) - (0)}{1.37}$$

$$= 2.18$$

5. The calculated value of Z, 2.18, is larger than the critical value (1.64). The *null hypothesis is rejected.* Management can conclude with 95 percent confidence ($1 - \alpha = .95$) that on the average, men visit convenience stores more often than do women.

Hypothesis About Proportions

In many situations, researchers are concerned with phenomena that are expressed as percentages.[6] For example, marketers might be interested in testing for the proportion of respondents who "prefer brand A" versus those who "prefer brand B" or those who are "brand loyal" versus those who are not.

Test of a Proportion, One Sample

A survey of 500 customers conducted by a major bank indicated that slightly more than 74 percent had family incomes of more than $50,000 per year. If this is true, the firm will develop a special package of services for this group.The management wants to determine whether the true percentage is greater than 60 percent before developing and introducing the new package of services. The survey results show that 74.29 percent of the bank's customers surveyed reported family incomes of $50,000 or more per year. The procedure for the **hypothesis test of proportions** follows:

hypothesis test of proportions
Test to determine whether the difference between proportions is greater than would be expected because of sampling error.

1. Specify the null and alternative hypotheses.

   - Null hypotheses H_0: $P \leq .60$.
   - Alternative hypothesis H_a: $P > .60$, where P = the proportion of customers with family incomes of $50,000 or more per year.

2. Specify the level of sampling error (α) allowed. For $\alpha = .05$, table value of Z (critical) = 1.64. (See Table 3 in Appendix Two for d.f. = ∞, .05 significance, one-tail. The table for t is used because $t = Z$ for samples greater than 30.)
3. Calculate the estimated standard error using the P-value specified in the null hypothesis:

$$S_p = \sqrt{\frac{P(1 - P)}{n - 1}}$$

where

P = proportion specified in the null hypothesis
n = sample size

Therefore

$$S_p = \sqrt{\frac{.6(1 - .6)}{35 - 1}}$$

$$= .084$$

4. Calculate the test statistic as follows:

$$Z = \frac{\text{(observed proportion} - \text{proportion under null hypothesis)}}{\text{estimated standard error } (S_p)}$$

$$= \frac{(0.7429 - 0.60)}{.084}$$

$$= 1.7$$

5. The *null hypothesis is rejected* because the calculated Z-value is larger than the critical Z-value. The bank can conclude with 95 percent confidence ($1 - \alpha = .95$) that more than 60 percent of its customers have family incomes of $50,000 or more. Management can introduce the new package of services targeted at this group.

Bank managers want to know the value of offering a special services package for customers with annual incomes over $50,000. They need to know the percentage of their customers with that income level. SOURCE: © Jim Pickerell/ Comstock.

Test of Differences Between Two Proportions, Independent Samples

In many instances, management is interested in the difference between the proportions of people in two different groups that engage in a certain activity or have a certain characteristic. For example, management of a convenience store chain had reason to believe, on the basis of a research study, that the percentage of men who visit convenience stores nine or more times per month (heavy users) was larger than the percentage of women who do so. The specifications required and the procedure for testing this hypothesis are as follows.

1. The null and alternative hypotheses are formally stated as follows:

   - Null hypothesis H_0: $P_m - P_f \leq 0$, the proportion of men (P_m) reporting nine or more visits per month is the same or less than the proportion of women (P_f) reporting nine or more visits per month.
   - Alternative hypothesis H_a: $P_m - P_f > 0$, the proportion of men (P_m) reporting nine or more visits per month is greater than the proportion of women (P_f) reporting nine or more visits per month.

   The sample proportions and the difference can be calculated from Table 16.3 as follows:

$$P_m = \frac{26}{45} = .58$$

$$P_f = \frac{30}{71} = .42$$

$$P_m - P_f = .58 - .42$$
$$= .16$$

2. Set the level of sampling error α at .10 (management decision). For $\alpha = .10$, the table value of Z (critical) = 1.28. (See Table 3 in Appendix Two for d.f. = ∞, .10 significance, one-tail. The table for t is used because $t = Z$ for samples greater than 30.)
3. The estimated standard error of the differences between the two proportions is calculated as follows:

$$S_{Pm-f} = \sqrt{P(1-P)\left(\frac{1}{n_m} + \frac{1}{n_f}\right)}$$

   where

$$P = \frac{n_m P_m + n_f P_f}{n_m + n_f}$$

P_m = proportion in sample m (men)
P_f = proportion in sample f (women)
n_m = size of sample m
n_f = size of sample f

   Therefore,

$$P = \frac{45(.58) + 71(.41)}{45 + 71}$$
$$= .48$$

and

$$S_{Pm-f} = \sqrt{.48(1 - .48)\left[\frac{1}{45} + \frac{1}{71}\right]}$$
$$= .10$$

4. Calculate the test statistic.

$$Z = \frac{\begin{pmatrix}\text{difference between}\\ \text{observed proportions}\end{pmatrix} - \begin{pmatrix}\text{difference between proportions}\\ \text{under the null hypothesis}\end{pmatrix}}{\text{estimated standard error of the differences between the two means}}$$

$$Z\,(\text{calculated}) = \frac{(.58 - .42) - (0)}{.10}$$

$$Z = 1.60$$

5. The *null hypothesis is rejected* because the calculated Z-value (1.60) is larger than the critical $Z =$ value (1.28 for $\alpha = .10$). Management can conclude with 90 percent confidence ($1 - \alpha = .90$) that the proportion of men who visit convenience stores nine or more times per month is larger than the proportion of women who do so.

It should be noted that if the level of sampling error α had been set at .05, the critical Z-value would equal 1.64. In this case, we would fail to reject (FTR) the null hypothesis because Z (calculated) is smaller than Z (critical).

Analysis of Variance (ANOVA)

analysis of variance (ANOVA)

Test for the differences among the means of two or more variables.

When there is a need to test the differences among the means of two or more independent samples, **analysis of variance (ANOVA)** is an appropriate statistical tool. Although it can be used to test differences between two means, ANOVA is more commonly used for hypothesis tests regarding the differences among the means of several (C) independent groups (where $C \geqslant 3$). It is a statistical technique that permits the researcher to determine whether the variability among or across the C sample means is greater than expected because of sampling error.

The Z- and t-tests described earlier normally are used to test the null hypothesis when only two sample means are involved. However, in situations in which there are three or more samples, it would be inefficient to test differences between the means two at a time. If there were five samples and associated means, 10 t-tests would be required to test all pairs of means. More important, the use of Z- or t-tests in situations involving three or more means increases the probability of a Type 1 error. These tests must be performed for all possible pairs of means. The more pairs tested, the more tests must be performed. The more tests performed, the more likely it is that tests of one or more pairs of means will show significant differences that are really due to sampling error. At an α of .05, this could be expected in one of 20 tests on average.

One-way ANOVA is often used to analyze experimental results. For example, the marketing manager for a chain of brake shops is considering three different services for a possible in-store promotion: wheel alignment, oil change, and tune-up. She is interested in knowing whether there are significant differences in potential sales of the three services.

Sixty similar stores (20 in each of three cities) were selected at random from among those operated by the chain. One of the services was introduced in each of three cities. Other variables such as price and advertising, under the firm's direct control, were kept at the same level during the course of the experiment. The experiment was conducted for a 30-day period and sales of the new services were recorded for the period.

Average sales for each shop are shown in Table 16.6. The question is, Are the differences among the means larger than would be expected due to chance?

1. The null and alternative hypotheses are formally stated as follows:
   - Null hypothesis H_0: $M_1 = M_2 = M_3$. Mean sales of the three items are equal.
   - Alternative hypothesis H_a: The variability in group means is greater than would be expected due to sampling error.
2. Sum the squared differences between each subsample mean ($\overline{X}_j$) and the overall sample mean ($\overline{X}_t$), weighted by sample size (n_j). This is called the *sum of squares among groups* or among group variation (SSA). SSA is calculated as follows:

$$SSA = \sum_{j=1}^{C} n_j (\overline{X}_j - \overline{X}_t)^2$$

TABLE 16.6 Average Sales per Day of the New Services in Each Test City

CHICAGO WHEEL ALIGNMENT		CLEVELAND OIL CHANGE		DETROIT TUNE-UP	
310	318	314	321	337	310
315	322	315	340	325	312
305	333	350	318	330	340
310	315	305	315	345	318
315	385	299	322	320	322
345	310	309	295	325	335
340	312	299	302	328	341
330	308	312	316	330	340
320	312	331	294	342	320
315	340	335	308	330	310
Mean $\overline{X} = 323$		$\overline{X} = 315$		$\overline{X} = 328$	

In our example, the overall sample mean is calculated from Table 16.6 as

$$\overline{X}_t = \frac{20(323) + 20(315) + 20(328)}{60}$$

$$\overline{X}_t = 322$$

$$\text{SSA} = 20(323 - 322)^2 + 20(315 - 322)^2 + 20(328 - 322)^2$$

$$= 1{,}720$$

The greater the differences among the sample means, the larger SSA will be.

3. Calculate the variation among group means as measured by the *mean sum of squares among groups* (MSA). MSA is calculated as follows:

$$\text{MSA} = \frac{\text{sum of squares among groups (SSA)}}{\text{degrees of freedom (d.f.)}}$$

$$\text{degrees of freedom} = \text{number of groups } (C) - 1$$

$$= 3 - 1$$

$$= 2$$

$$\text{MSA} = \frac{\text{SSA}}{\text{d.f.}}$$

$$= \frac{1{,}720}{2}$$

$$= 860$$

4. Sum the squared differences between each observation (X_{ij}) and its associated sample mean ($\overline{X}_j$), accumulated over all C levels (groups). This is called the *sum of squares within groups* or within group variation. It is generally referred to as the *sum of squared error* (SSE). SSE is calculated as follow:

$$\text{SSE} = \sum_{j=1}^{C} \sum_{i=1}^{n_j} (X_{ij} - \overline{X}_j)^2$$

$$\text{SSE} = (6{,}644) + (4{,}318) + (2{,}270)$$

$$= 13{,}232$$

5. Calculate the variation within the sample groups as measured by the mean sum of squares within groups. Referred to as *mean square error* (MSE), it represents an estimate of the random error in the data. MSE is calculated as follows:

$$\text{MSE} = \frac{\text{sum of squares within groups (SSE)}}{\text{degrees of freedom (d.f.)}}$$

Degrees of freedom is equal to the sum of the sample sizes for all groups minus the number of groups (C):

$$\text{d.f.} = \left(\sum_{j=1}^{K} n_j\right) - C = (20 + 20 + 20 - 3) = 57$$

$$\text{MSE} = \frac{\text{SSE}}{\text{d.f.}}$$

$$= \frac{13{,}232}{57}$$

$$= 232.14$$

As with the Z and t-distribution a sampling distribution known as the *F-distribution* permits the researcher to determine the probability that a particular calculated value of F could have occurred by chance rather than as a result of the treatment effect. The F-distribution, like the t-distribution, is really a set of distributions whose shape changes slightly depending upon the number and size of the samples involved. To use the ***F*-test,** it is necessary to calculate the degrees of freedom for the numerator and the denominator.

F-test
Test of the probability that a particular calculated value could have been due to chance.

6. Calculate the F-statistic as follows:

$$F = \frac{\text{MSA}}{\text{MSE}}$$

$$= \frac{860}{232.14}$$

$$= 3.70$$

The numerator is MSA and the degrees of freedom associated with it is 2 (Step 3). The denominator is MSE and the degrees of freedom associated with it is 57 (Step 5).

For an alpha of .05, the table value of F (critical) with 2 (numerator) and 57 (denominator) degrees of freedom is approximately 3.15. (See Table 5 in Appendix Two for d.f. for denominator = 5, for numerator = 2, .05 significance.) The calculated F-value (3.70) is greater than the table value (F = 3.15), and the *null hypothesis is rejected.* By rejecting the null hypothesis, we conclude that the variability observed in the three means is greater than expected due to chance.

The results of an ANOVA generally are displayed as follows:

SOURCE OF VARIATION	SUM OF SQUARES	DEGREES OF FREEDOM	MEAN SQUARE	F-STATISTIC
Treatments	1,720 (SSA)	2 ($C - 1$)	860 (MSA)	3.70 calculated
Error	13,232 (SSE)	57 ($n - C$)	232.14 (MSE)	
Total	14,592 (SST)	59 ($n - 1$)		

P-Values and Significance Testing

In the various tests discussed in this chapter, we established a standard—level of significance and associated critical value of the statistics—then calculated the value of the statistic to see whether it beat that standard. If the calculated value of the statistic exceeded the critical value, then the result being tested was said to be statistically significant at that level.

However, this approach did not tell us the exact probability of getting a computed test statistic that was largely due to chance. The calculations necessary to

***p*-value**

The exact probability of getting a computed test statistic that was largely due to chance. The smaller the *p*-value, the smaller the probability that the observed result occurred by chance.

compute this probability are tedious. Fortunately, they are easy for computers. This probability is commonly referred to as the ***p*-value.** The *p*-value is the most demanding level of statistical (not managerial) significance that can be met based on the calculated value of the statistic. You may see one of the following in output from various computer statistical packages:

- *p*-value
- ≤ PROB
- PROB =

These labels are used by various computer programs to identify the probability that such a large distance between the hypothesized population parameter and the observed test statistic could have occurred due to chance. The smaller the *p*-value, the smaller is the probability that the observed result occurred due to chance (sampling error).

An example of a computer output, showing a *p*-value calculation, is shown in Figure 16.3. This analysis shows the results of a *t*-test of the differences between means for two independent samples. In this case the null hypothesis (H_0) is that there is no difference between what men and women would be willing to pay for a new communications service. (The variable name is GENDER with the numeric codes of 0 for males and 1 for females. They were asked how much they would be willing to pay per month for a new wireless communications service that was described to them via a videotape. Variable ADDEDPAY is their response to the question.) The results show that women are willing to pay an average of $16.82 for the new service and men are willing to pay $20.04. Is this a significant difference? The calculated value of *t* of −1.328 indicates, via associated *P*-value of .185, that there is an 18.5 percent chance that the difference may be due to sampling. If, for example, the standard for the test had been set at .10 (willing to accept a 10 percent chance of incorrectly rejecting H_0), then the analyst would *fail to reject* H_0 in this case.

FIGURE 16.3
Sample STATISTICA *t*-Test Output

Stat. Basic Stats	Grouping: GENDER (pcs. sta) Group 1: G_1:1 Group 2: G_2:0						
Variable	Mean G_1:1	Mean G_2:0	*t*-value	df	P	Valid N G_1:1	Valid N G_2:0
ADDED PAY	16.82292	20.04717	-1.32878	200	.185434	96	106

Summary

The purpose of making statistical inferences is to generalize from sample results to population characteristics. Three important concepts relate to the notion of differences: mathematical differences, managerially important differences, and statistical significance.

A hypothesis is an assumption or theory that a researcher or manager makes about some characteristic of the population being investigated. By testing, the researcher determines whether a hypothesis concerning some characteristic of the population is valid. A statistical hypothesis test permits the researcher to calculate the probability of observing the particular result if the stated hypothesis actually were true. In hypothesis testing, the first step is to specify the hypothesis. Next, an appropriate statistical technique should be selected to test the hypothesis. Next, a decision rule must be specified as the basis for determining whether to reject or fail to reject the hypothesis. Hypothesis tests are subject to two types of errors called Type I (α error) and Type II (ß error). A Type I error involves rejecting the null hypothesis when it is, in fact, true. A Type II error involves failing to reject the null hypothesis when the alternative hypothesis actually is true. Finally, the value of the test statistic is calculated and a conclusion is stated that summarizes the results of the test.

Market researchers often develop crosstabulations, whose purpose usually is to uncover interrelationships among the variables. Usually the researcher needs to determine whether the number of subjects, objects, or responses that fall into some set of categories differ from chance. Thus, a test of "goodness of fit" of the observed distribution in relation to an expected distribution is appropriate. Two common tests of goodness of fit are chi-square and Kolmogorov-Smirnov.

Often market researchers need to make inferences about population mean. The appropriate test statistic for testing hypotheses about means is the Z -test if the sample size is equal to or greater than 30 and comes from a normal population. For small samples, researchers use the *t*-test with $n - 1$ degrees of freedom when making inferences (n is the size of the sample). In addition, researchers are often interested in testing differences between groups in regard to their response to marketing variables. Also, different responses to the same variable, such as advertising, by groups with different characteristics are frequently of interest. In this case, the researcher tests for differences between two means. A Z-value is calculated and compared to the critical value of Z. Based upon the comparison, the null hypothesis is either rejected or fails to be rejected. The Z-test also can be used to examine hypotheses about proportions from one sample or independent samples.

When a researcher needs to test for the differences between the means of three or more independent samples, analysis of variance is an appropriate statistical tool. It is often used for hypothesis tests regarding the differences between the means of several independent groups. It permits the researcher to test the null hypothesis that there are no significant differences among the population group means.

Key Terms

hypotheses
Type I error (α error)
Type II error (ß error)
independent samples
related samples
chi-square test
Kolmogorov-Smirnov test
Z-test
t-test
hypothesis test of proportions
analysis of variance (ANOVA)
F-test
p-values

Review and Discussion Questions

1. Explain the notions of mathematical differences, managerially important differences, and statistical significance. Can results be statistically significant and yet lack managerial importance? Explain your answer.
2. Describe the steps in the procedure for testing hypotheses. Discuss the difference between a null hypothesis and an alternative hypothesis.
3. Distinguish between a Type I error and Type II error. What is the relationship between the two?
4. What is meant by the terms *independent samples* and *related samples?* Why is it important for a researcher to determine whether a sample is independent?
5. Your university library is concerned about student desires for library hours on Sunday morning (9:00 A.M.–12:00 P.M.). It has undertaken a random sample of 1,600 undergraduate students (one-half men, one-half women) in each of four status levels (i.e., 400 freshmen, 400 sophomores, 400 juniors, 400 seniors). If the percentage of students preferring Sunday morning hours are those shown below, what conclusions can the library reach?

	SENIORS	JUNIORS	SOPHOMORES	FRESHMEN
Women	70	53	39	26
Men	30	48	31	27

6. A local car dealer is attempting to determine which premium will draw the most visitors to its showroom. An individual who visits the showroom and takes a test ride is given a premium with no obligation. The dealer chose four premiums and offered each for one week. The results are as follows.

WEEK	PREMIUM	TOTAL GIVEN OUT
1	Four-foot metal stepladder	425
2	$50 savings bond	610
3	Dinner for four at a local steak house	510
4	Six pink flamingos plus an outdoor thermometer	705

Using a chi-square test, what conclusions can be drawn regarding the premiums?

7. A market researcher has completed a study of pain relievers. The following table depicts the brand purchased most often broken down by men versus women. Perform a chi-square test on the data and determine what can be said regarding the crosstabulation.

PAIN RELIEVERS	MEN	WOMEN
Anacin	40	55
Bayer	60	28
Bufferin	70	97
Cope	14	21
Empirin	82	107
Excedrin	72	84
Excedrin PM	15	11
Vanquish	20	26

8. Five hundred women who use a particular type of makeup were interviewed regarding their preferences for six shades of the makeup. The results showing the number who preferred each shade follow. The results are listed in order from the darkest to the lightest shade in successively lighter shades.

	NUMBER PREFERRING
Shade 1 (darkest)	52
Shade 2	57
Shade 3	83
Shade 4	187
Shade 5	61
Shade 6 (lightest)	60

Using the Kolmogorov-Smirnov test, test the null hypothesis of no preference between shades. Based on the results of the test, does it make any difference which shade is used? Explain.

9. A child psychologist observed eight-year-old children behind a one-way mirror to determine how long they would play with a toy medical kit. The company that designed the toy was attempting to determine whether to give the kit a masculine or feminine orientation. The length of time (in minutes) the children played with the kits is shown in the following table. Calculate the value of Z and recommend to management whether the kit should have a male or female orientation.

BOYS	GIRLS	BOYS	GIRLS
31	26	67	9
12	38	67	9
41	20	25	16
34	32	73	26
63	16	36	81
7	45	41	20
		15	5

10. American Airlines is trying to determine which baggage handling system it will put in its new hub terminal at San Juan, Puerto Rico. One system is made by Jano Systems and a second baggage handling system is manufactured by Dynamic Enterprises. American has installed a small Jano system and a small Dynamic Enterprises system in two of its low-volume terminals. Both terminals handle approximately the same quantity of baggage each month. American has decided to select the system that will provide the minimum number of instances in which passengers disembarking must wait 20 minutes or longer for baggage. Analyze the data that follow and determine whether there is a significant difference at the .95 level of confidence between the two systems. If there is a difference, which one should American select?

MINUTES OF WAITING	JANO SYSTEMS (FREQUENCY)	DYNAMIC ENTERPRISES (FREQUENCY)
10–11	4	10
12–13	10	8
14–15	14	14

continues

Continued

MINUTES OF WAITING	JANO SYSTEMS (FREQUENCY)	DYNAMIC ENTERPRISES (FREQUENCY)
16–17	4	20
18–19	2	12
20–21	4	6
22–23	2	12
24–25	14	4
26–27	6	13
28–29	10	8
30–31	12	6
32–33	2	8
34–35	2	8
36 or more	2	2

11. Menu space is always limited in fast food restaurants. However, McDonalds has decided that it needs to add one more salad dressing to its menu for its garden salad and chef salad. It has decided to test market four flavors: Caesar, Ranch-style, Green Goddess, and Russian. Fifty restaurants were selected in the North-Central region to sell each new dressing. Thus, a total of 200 stores were used in the research project. The study was conducted for two weeks and the units of each dressing sold are shown in the following table. As a researcher, you want to know if the differences among the average daily sales of the dressings are larger than can be reasonably expected due to chance. If so, which dressing would you recommend be added to the inventory throughout the United States?

DAY	CAESAR	RANCH-STYLE	GREEN GODDESS	RUSSIAN
1	155	143	149	135
2	157	146	152	136
3	151	141	146	131
4	146	136	141	126
5	181	180	173	115
6	160	152	170	150
7	168	157	174	147
8	157	167	141	130
9	139	159	129	119
10	144	154	167	134
11	158	169	145	144
13	184	195	178	177
14	161	177	201	151

CASE 16.1

I Can't Believe It's Yogurt

Phil Jackson, research manager for I Can't Believe It's Yogurt (ICBIY), is trying to develop a more rational basis for evaluating alternative store locations. ICBIY has been growing rapidly, and, historically, the issue of store location has not been critical. It didn't seem to matter where it located its stores—all were successful. However, the yogurt craze has faded and some of its new stores and a few of its old ones were experiencing difficulties in the form of declining sales.

ICBIY wants to continue expanding, but it recognizes that it must be much more careful in selecting locations than it was in the past. It has determined that the percentage of individuals in an area who have visited a frozen yogurt store in the past 30 days is the best predictor of the potential for one of its stores—the higher that percentage, the better.

ICBIY wants to locate a store in Denver and has identified two locations that, on the basis of the other criteria, look good. It has conducted a survey of households in the areas that would be served from each location. The results of that survey are shown in Table 16.7.

1. Determine whether there is a significant difference at the .05 level between the two areas.
2. What would you recommend to ICBIY regarding which of the two areas it should choose for the new store based on this analysis? Explain your recommendation.

TABLE 16.7 Results of Surveys in the Two Areas

YOGURT STORE PATRONAGE	BOTH AREAS	AREA A	AREA B
Have patronized in past 30 days	465	220	245
Have not patronized	535	280	255

CASE 16.2

Ramada Inns

Ramada Inns is working on a new color scheme to be implemented in all its properties. In this phase of the process, it is trying to decide on the basic color for the walls in the rooms. After making that decision, it will make choices regarding furniture, fabrics, and accessories.

By talking to consumers and getting their reactions to different basic colors, it has decided on a peach color. Now it is trying to make a decision among 10 distinct shades of that color. It has completed mall intercept surveys with 1,000 people who fit the demographic profile of its target customer. The results, showing the number of people who prefer each shade of the color, are in Table 16.8.

1. Use the Kolmogorov-Smirnov test to determine whether the observed distribution of preferences is likely due to chance or indicate a significant preference for a particular shade or shades of the color.
2. Based on the results of the statistical test, what recommendation would you make to Ramada Inns regarding customer preference?

TABLE 16.8 Number of Consumers Who Said They Preferred Each Shade of the Test Color Scheme

FEATURE	CONSUMERS
Shade 1 – darkest	110
Shade 2	85
Shade 3	120
Shade 4	140
Shade 5	130
Shade 6	110
Shade 7	85
Shade 8	75
Shade 9	40
Shade 10 – lightest	105

CASE 16.3

Boggs Advertising

Mike Boggs, president of Boggs Advertising, is reviewing the results of awareness tracking research for Curry-in-a-Hurry, a chain of fast food Indian restaurants and one of the agency's largest clients. Boggs Advertising has just completed a 90-day television campaign for Curry-in-a-Hurry. The goal of the campaign was to increase awareness of these restaurants among target customers.

Before the beginning of the campaign, an awareness tracking study was completed among target customers. Five hundred randomly selected target customers were interviewed for the test. Immediately following the current campaign, another 500 target customers were interviewed (random sample) to again measure awareness and other factors. Mr. Patel, president of Curry-in-a-Hurry, told Boggs before the start of the campaign that if there was no significant increase in awareness, then he would move his account to another agency.

In the test conducted before the campaign began, 28.5 percent of the target customers surveyed were aware of Curry-in-a-Hurry. In the test completed after the end of the campaign, 32.4 percent were aware of the restaurants. Boggs has pointed out to Patel that awareness did increase by 1.6 percent. Patel knows enough about statistics to argue that it is possible that this increase is due to sampling error. He said that he wants to be 95 percent confident that the results did not occur due to sampling error and has asked Boggs to run the appropriate statistical test and report the results. Whether or not his account stays with Boggs rests on the outcome of the test.

1. Which statistical test, covered in the chapter, is appropriate for this problem? Why that test?
2. State the appropriate *null* and alternative hypotheses for this test.
3. Run the test. Show all your calculations.
4. Based on the criteria outlined by Patel, does your test show that the account will stay with Boggs or go somewhere else?

CHAPTER 

Data Analysis: Bivariate Correlation and Regression

LEARNING OBJECTIVES

1. To understand bivariate regression analysis.
2. To become aware of the coefficient of determination R^2.
3. To comprehend the nature of correlation analysis.

Chris Randle is the marketing director for the First Mart Supermarket chain. He is trying to convince the president of the chain, Brit Hawrylak, to decrease the overall price level of the chain, but Hawrylak is skeptical about reducing prices. He indicated in a recent meeting with Randle that he does not believe that reducing prices will increase sales for the chain.

SOURCE: © Jim McNee/FPG.

Randle has presented his problem to Amanda Henson, marketing research manager for First Mart, and has asked her to analyze past sales and pricing data to determine whether there is a relationship between pricing level and sales and, if there is, to measure the nature and extent of that relationship. Henson is currently considering the job that has been assigned to her. She is in the process of listing the options so that she might choose a statistical procedure that is appropriate to the problem. ■

Techniques that can be used to address the issue that Chris is confronting are presented in this chapter. After you finish the chapter, you will know how to analyze the relationship between price and sales in a powerful way. Reconsider the problem after you complete the chapter.

I Bivariate Analysis of Association

Bivariate Analysis Defined

bivariate techniques
Statistical methods of analyzing the relationship between two variables.

In many marketing research studies, the interests of the researcher and manager go beyond issues that can be addressed by the statistical testing of differences discussed in the previous chapter. They may be interested in the degree of association between two variables. Statistical techniques appropriate for this type of analysis are referred to as **bivariate techniques.**[1] When more than two variables are involved, the techniques employed are known as *multivariate techniques*. Multivariate techniques are discussed in the next chapter.

When analyzing the degree of association between two variables, the variables are classified as the *independent* (predictor) *variable* or the *dependent* (criterion)

variable. Independent variables are those that we believe affect the value of the dependent variable. Independent variables such as price, advertising expenditures, or number of retail outlets are often used to predict and explain sales or market share of a brand—the dependent variable. Bivariate analysis can help provide answers to questions such as, How does the price of our product affect sales? and What is the relationship between household income and expenditures on entertainment?

It must be noted that none of the techniques we will present can be used to prove that one variable caused some change in another variable. They can be used only to describe the nature of statistical relationships between variables.

Types of Bivariate Procedures

The analyst has a large number of bivariate techniques from which to choose. In this chapter we discuss two procedures that are appropriate for metric (ratio or internal) data, bivariate regression and Pearson product moment correlation, and one that is appropriate for ordinal (ranking) data, Spearman rank-order correlation. Other statistical procedures that can be used for analyzing the statistical relationship between two variables include

- Two group *t*-test.
- Chi-square analysis of crosstab or contingency tables.
- ANOVA (analysis of variance) for two groups.

All of these procedures were introduced and discussed in the previous chapter (Chapter 16).

Bivariate Regression

Bivariate Regression Defined

Bivariate regression analysis is a statistical procedure appropriate for anlayzing the relationship between two variables when one is considered the dependent variable and the other the independent variable. For example, we might be interested in analyzing the relationship between sales (dependent variable) and advertising (independent variable). If the relationship between advertising expenditures and sales can be estimated by regression analysis, the researcher can predict sales for different levels of advertising. When the problem involves using two or more independent variables (e.g., advertising and price) to predict the dependent variable of interest, multiple regression analysis (discussed in the next chapter) is appropriate.

bivariate regression analysis
Analysis of the strength of the linear relationship between two variables when one is considered the independent variable and the other the dependent variable.

Nature of the Relationship

To study the nature of the relationship between the dependent and the independent variables, the data can be plotted in a scatter diagram. The dependent variable Y is plotted on the vertical axis, while the independent variable X is plotted on the horizontal axis. By examining the scatter diagram, we can determine whether the relationship between the two variables, if any, is linear or curvilinear.

If the relationship appears to be linear or close to linear, linear regression is appropriate. If a nonlinear relationship is shown in the scatter diagram, curve-fitting nonlinear regression techniques are appropriate. These techniques are beyond the scope of this discussion.[2]

Figure 17.1 depicts several kinds of underlying relationships between the X and Y variables. Scatter diagrams A and B suggest a positive linear relationship between X and Y. However, the linear relationship shown in B is not as strong as that portrayed in A; there is more scatter in the data shown in B. Diagram C shows a perfect negative or inverse relationship between variables X and Y. Diagrams D and E show nonlinear relationships between the variables, and appropriate curve-fitting techniques should be used to mathematically describe these relationships. The scatter diagram in F shows no relationship between X and Y.

FIGURE 17.1

Types of Relationships Found in Scatter Diagrams

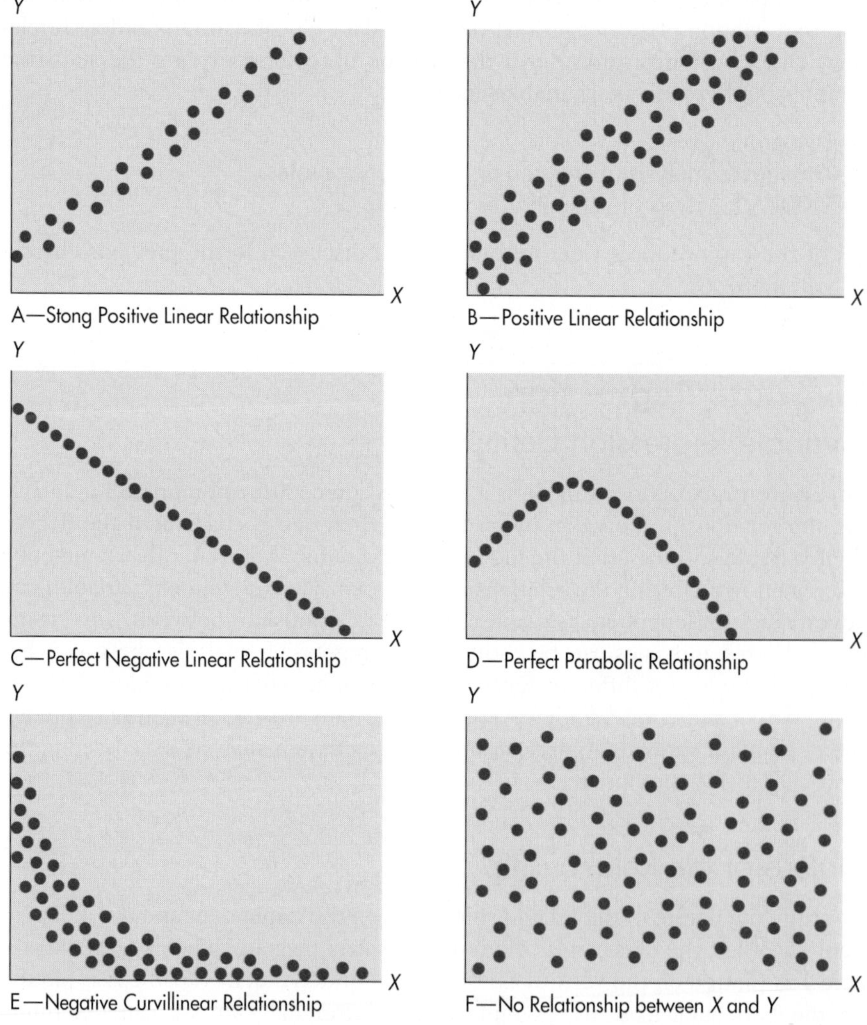

Bivariate Regression Example

Stop 'N Go recently conducted a research effort designed to measure the effect of vehicular traffic by a particular store location on annual sales at that location.

To do this properly, it identified 20 stores that were virtually identical on all other variables known to have a significant effect on store sales (e.g., square footage, amount of parking, demographics of the surrounding neighborhood, and so on). This particular analysis is part of an overall effort by Stop 'N Go to identify and quantify the effects of various factors that have an impact on store sales. Its ultimate goal is to develop a model that can be used to evaluate potential sites for store locations that will enable it to screen these sites and select the best ones, the ones that will produce the highest level of sales, for actual purchase and store construction.

After identifying the 20 sites, Stop 'N Go took daily traffic counts for each site over a 30-day period. In addition, from its own internal records, it obtained total sales data for each of the 20 tests stores for the preceding 12 months (see Table 17.1).

A scatter plot of the resulting data is shown in Figure 17.2. Visual inspection of the scatter plot suggests that total sales increase as the average daily vehicular traffic increases. The question now is how to characterize this relationship in a more explicit, quantitative manner.

TABLE 17.1 **Annual Sales and Average Daily Vehicular Traffic**

STORE NUMBER (i)	AVG. DAILY VEHICULAR COUNT IN THOUSANDS (X_i)	ANNUAL SALES IN THOUSANDS OF DOLLARS (Y_i)
1	62	1,121
2	35	766
3	36	701
4	72	1,304
5	41	832
6	39	782
7	49	977
8	25	503
9	41	773
10	39	839
11	35	893
12	27	588
13	55	957
14	38	703
15	24	497
16	28	657
17	53	1,209
18	55	997
19	33	844
20	29	883

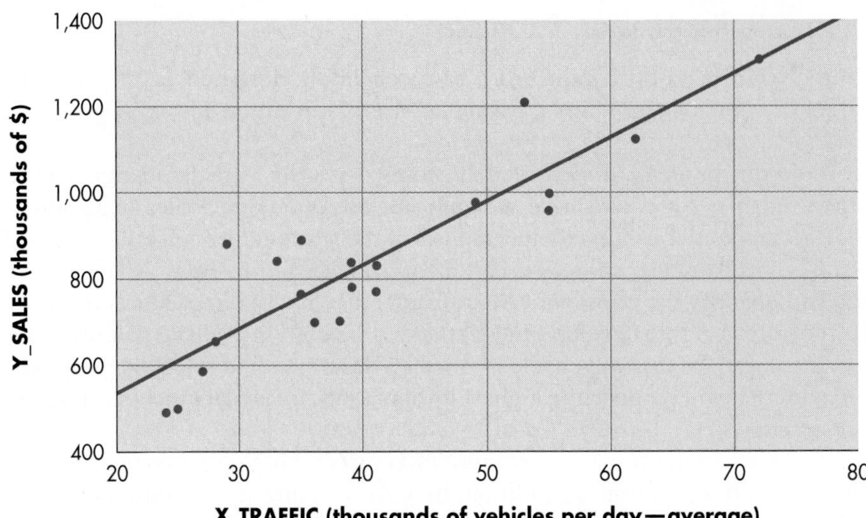

FIGURE 17.2
Scatter Plot of Annual Sales by Traffic

Least Squares Estimation Procedure

The least squares procedure is a fairly simple mathematical technique that can be used to fit a line to data for X and Y (see Figure 17.2) that best represents the relationship between the two variables. No straight line can perfectly represent every observation in the scatter plot. This is reflected in discrepancies between the actual values (dots on scatter diagram) and predicted values (value indicated by the line). Any straight line fitted to the data in the scatter plot will be subject to error. A number of lines could be drawn that would seem to fit the observations in Figure 17.2.

The least squares procedure results in a straight line that fits the actual observations (dots) better than any other line that could be fitted to the observations. Put another way, the sum of the squared deviations from this line (squared differences between dots and the line) will be less than for any other line that can be fitted to the observations.

The general equation for the line is $Y = a + bX$. The estimating equation for regression analysis is

$$Y = \hat{a} + \hat{b}X + e$$

where

Y = dependent variable—annual sales in thousands of dollars
$\hat{a}$ = estimated Y intercept for regression line
$\hat{b}$ = estimated slope of the regression line—regression coefficient
X = independent variable—average daily vehicular traffic in thousands of vehicles
e = error—difference between actual value and value predicted by regression line

Values for $\hat{a}$ and $\hat{b}$ can be calculated as follows:

$$\hat{b} = \frac{\sum X_i Y_i - n\overline{X}\overline{Y}}{\sum X_i^2 - n(\overline{X})^2}$$

$$\hat{a} = \overline{Y} - \hat{b}\overline{X}$$

where

$\overline{X}$ = mean value of X

$\overline{Y}$ = mean value of Y

n = sample size (number of units in the sample)

Using the data from Table 17.2, $\hat{b}$ is calculated as follows:

$$\hat{b} = \frac{734{,}083 - 20(40.8)(841.3)}{36{,}526 - 20(40.8)^2} = 14.72$$

The value of $\hat{a}$ is calculated as follows:

$$\hat{a} = \overline{Y} - \hat{b}\overline{X} = 841.3 - 14.72(40.8) = 240.86$$

Thus, our estimated regression function is given by

$$\hat{Y} = \hat{a} + \hat{b}X = 240.86 + 14.72(X)$$

TABLE 17.2 Least Squares Computation

STORE	X	Y	X^2	Y^2	XY
1	62	1,121	3,844	1,256,641	69,502
2	35	766	1,225	586,756	26,810
3	36	701	1,296	491,401	25,236
4	72	1,304	5,184	1,700,416	93,888
5	41	832	1,681	692,224	34,112
6	39	782	1,521	611,524	30,498
7	49	977	2,401	954,529	47,873
8	25	503	625	253,009	12,575
9	41	773	1,681	597,529	31,693
10	39	839	1,521	703,921	32,721
11	35	893	1,225	797,449	31,255
12	27	588	729	345,744	15,876
13	55	957	3,025	915,849	52,635
14	38	703	1,444	494,209	26,714
15	24	497	576	247,009	11,928
16	28	657	784	431,649	18,396
17	53	1,209	2,809	1,461,681	64,077
18	55	997	3,025	994,009	54,835
19	33	844	1,089	712,336	27,852
20	29	883	841	779,689	25,607
(sum)	816	16,826	36,526	15,027,574	734,083
(mean)	40.8	841.3			

Convenience store chains use regression analysis to predict sales for current and future sites.
SOURCE: Courtesy of Roger Gates.

where $\hat{Y}$ (Y hat) is the value of the estimated regression function for a given value of X.

According to the estimated regression function, for every additional 1,000 vehicles per day in traffic (X), total annual sales will increase by \$14,720 (estimated value of b). The value of a is 240.86. Technically, a hat is the estimated value of the dependent variable (Y or annual sales) when the value of the independent variable (X or average daily vehicular traffic) is zero.

The Regression Line

Predicted values for Y, based on calculated values for $\hat{a}$ and $\hat{b}$, are shown in Table 17.3. In addition, errors for each observation ($Y - \hat{Y}$) are shown. The regression line resulting from the $\hat{Y}$ values is shown in Figure 17.3.

FIGURE 17.3
Least Squares Regression Line Fitted to Sample Data

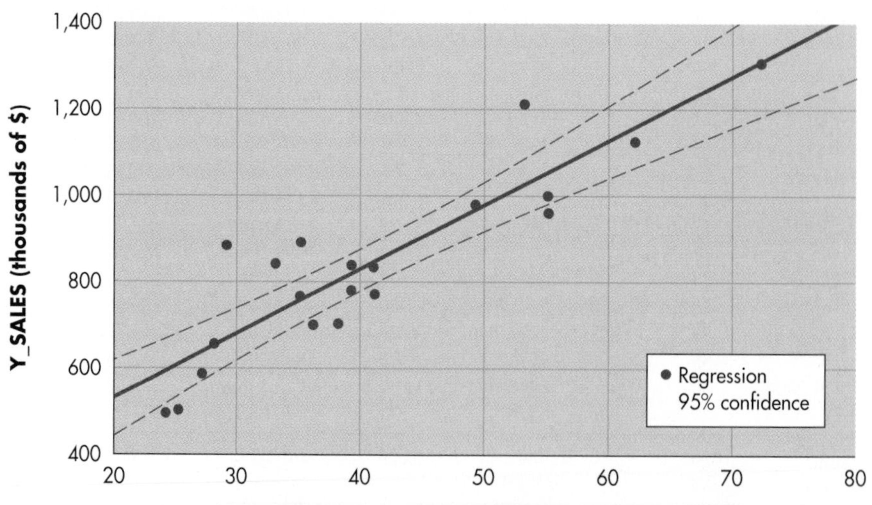

The Strength of Association—R^2

The estimated regression function describes the nature of the relationship between X and Y. In addition, we are interested in the strength of the relationship between the variables. How widely do the actual values of Y differ from the values predicted by our model?

The **coefficient of determination,** denoted by R^2, is the measure of the strength of the linear relationship between X and Y. The coefficient of determination measures the percent of the total variation in Y that is "explained" by the variation in X. The R^2 statistic ranges from 0 to 1. If there is a perfect linear relationship between X and Y, all the variation in Y is explained by the variation in X, then R^2 equals 1. At the other extreme, if there is no relationship between X and Y, then none of the variation in Y is explained by the variation in X and R^2 equals 0.

coefficient of determination
The percent of the total variation in the dependent variable explained by the independent variable.

The coefficient of determination of our example would be computed as follows. (See Table 17.3 for calculation of $(Y - \hat{Y})^2$ and $(Y - \bar{Y})^2$.)

$$R^2 = \frac{\text{explained variance}}{\text{total variance}}$$

$$\text{explained variance} = \text{total variance} - \text{unexplained variance}$$

$$R^2 = \frac{\text{total variance} - \text{unexplained variance}}{\text{total variance}}$$

$$R^2 = 1 - \frac{\text{unexplained variance}}{\text{total variance}}$$

$$R^2 = 1 - \frac{\sum_{i=1}^{n} (Y_i - \hat{Y}_i)^2}{\sum_{i=1}^{n} (Y_i - \bar{Y})^2}$$

$$R^2 = 1 - \frac{171{,}604.8}{871{,}860.2} = .803$$

Of the variation in Y (annual sales), 80 percent is explained by the variation in X (average daily vehicular traffic). There is a very strong linear relationship between X and Y.

Statistical Significance of Regression Results

In computing R^2, the total variation in Y was partitioned into two component sums of squares:

Total variation = explained variation + unexplained variation

The total variation is a measure of variation of the observed Y values around their mean $\bar{Y}$. It measures the variation of the Y values without any consideration of the X values.

Total variation, known as the *total sum of squares* (SST), is given by

$$\text{SST} = \sum_{i=1}^{n} (Y_i - \bar{Y})^2 = \sum_{i=1}^{n} Y_i^2 - \left(\frac{\sum_{i=1}^{n} Y_i^2}{n} \right)$$

TABLE 17.3 Predicted Values and Errors for Each Observation

STORE	X	Y	$\hat{Y}$	$Y - \hat{Y}$	$(Y - \hat{Y})^2$	$(Y - \bar{Y})^2$
1	62	1,121	1,153.3	-32.2951	1,043	78,232
2	35	766	755.9	10.05716	101	5,670
3	36	701	770.7	-69.6596	4,852	19,684
4	72	1,304	1,300.5	3.537362	13	214,091
5	41	832	844.2	-12.2434	150	86
6	39	782	814.8	-32.8098	1,076	3,516
7	49	977	962.0	15.02264	226	18,414
8	25	503	608.8	-105.775	11,188	114,447
9	41	773	844.2	-71.2434	5,076	4,665
10	39	839	814.8	24.19015	585	5
11	35	893	755.9	137.0572	18,785	2,673
12	27	588	638.2	-50.2088	2,521	64,161
13	55	957	1,050.3	-93.2779	8,701	13,386
14	38	703	800.1	-97.0931	9,427	19,127
15	24	497	594.1	-97.0586	9,420	118,542
16	28	657	652.9	4.074415	17	33,966
17	53	1,209	1,020.8	188.1556	35,403	135,203
18	55	997	1,050.3	-53.2779	2,839	24,242
19	33	844	726.5	117.4907	13,804	7
20	29	883	667.6	215.3577	46,379	1,739
(sum)	816	16,826	16,826.0		171,604.8	871,860.2
(mean)	40.8	841.3				

sum of squares due to regression

The variation explained by the regression.

The explained variation or the **sum of squares due to regression (SSR)** is given by

$$\text{SSR} = \sum_{i=1}^{n}(\hat{Y}_i - \bar{Y})^2 = a\sum_{i=1}^{n} Y_i + b\sum_{i=1}^{n} X_i Y_i - \frac{\left(\sum_{i=1}^{n} Y_i\right)^2}{n}$$

Figure 17.4 shows the various measures of variation (i.e., sum of squares) in a regression. SSR represents the differences between the $\hat{Y}_i$ (the values of Y predicted by the estimated regression equation) and Y (the average value of Y). In a well-fitting regression equation, the variation explained by regression (SSR) will represent a large portion of the total variation (SST). If $Y_i \equiv \hat{Y}_i$ at each value of X, then a perfect fit has been achieved. All the observed values of Y would then be on the computed regression line. Of course, in that case SSR $\equiv$ SST.

error sum of squares

The variation not explained by the regression.

The unexplained variation or **error sums of squares** (SSE) is obtained from

$$\text{SSE} = \sum_{i=1}^{n}(Y_i - \hat{Y}_i)^2 = \sum_{i=1}^{n} Y_i^2 - a\sum_{i=1}^{n} Y_i - b\sum_{i=1}^{n} X_i Y_i$$

From Figure 17.4 note that SSE represents the residual differences (error) between the observed and predicted Y values. Therefore, the unexplained variation is a measure of scatter around the regression line. If the fit were perfect, there would be no scatter around the regression line and SSE would be zero.

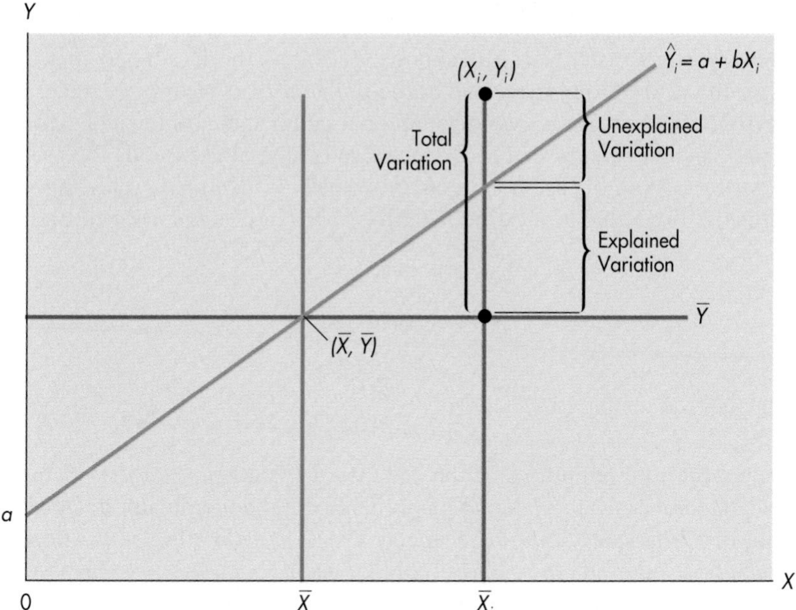

FIGURE 17.4
Measures of Variation in a Regression

Hypotheses Concerning The Overall Regression Here we are interested in hypotheses regarding the computed R^2 value for our problem. Is the amount of variance explained in our result (by our model) significantly greater than we would expect due to chance, or, as in the various statistical tests discussed in Chapter 16, to what extent can we rule out sampling error as an explanation of our results? Analysis of variance (F-test) is used to test the significance of the results.

The analysis of variance table would be set up as shown in Table 17.4. The computer output for our example is shown in Figure 17.5. The breakdowns of the total sum of squares and associated degrees of freedom are displayed in the form of an analysis of variance (ANOVA) table. We use the information in this table to test the significance of the linear relationship between Y and X. As noted previously, an F-test will be used for this purpose. Our hypotheses are

- Null hypothesis H_0: There is no linear relationship between X (average daily vehicular traffic) and Y (annual sales)

TABLE 17.4 **Analysis of Variance**

SOURCE OF VARIATION	DEGREES OF FREEDOM	SUM OF SQUARES	MEAN SQUARE	F-STATISTIC
Due to regression (explained)	1	SSR	$MSR = \frac{SSR}{1}$	$F = \frac{MSR}{MSE}$
Residual (unexplained)	$n-2$	SSE	$MSE = \frac{SSE}{n-2}$	
Total	$n-1$	SST		

- Alternative hypothesis H_a: There is a linear relationship between X and Y

As in other statistical tests, we must choose α. This is the likelihood that the observed result occurred due to chance or the probability of incorrectly rejecting the null hypothesis. In this case we decided on a rather standard level of significance or $\alpha = .05$. This means that if the calculated value of F exceeds the tabular value, we are willing to accept a 5 percent chance of incorrectly rejecting the null hypothesis. The value of F or the F-ratio is computed as follows (see Figure 17.5):

$$F = \frac{\text{MSR}}{\text{MSE}} = \frac{700{,}255.4}{9{,}533.6} = 73.45$$

We will reject the null hypothesis if the calculated F-statistic is greater than or equal to the table or critical F-value. The numerator and denominator degrees of freedom for this F-ratio are 1 and 18, respectively. As noted earlier, it was decided that an alpha level of .05 ($\alpha = .05$) should be used.

The table or critical value of F with 1 (numerator) and 18 (denominator) degrees of freedom at $\alpha = .05$ is 4.49 (see Table 5 in Appendix Two). Because the calculated value of F is greater than the critical value, we can reject the null hypothesis and conclude that there is a significant linear relationship between the average daily vehicular traffic (X) and annual sales (Y). This result is consistent with the high coefficient of determination R^2 discussed earlier.

Hypotheses About The Regression Coefficient (*b*) Finally, we may be interested in making hypotheses about b, the regression coefficient. As you may recall, b is the estimate of the effect of a one unit change in X on Y. The hypotheses are

- Null hypothesis H_0: $b = 0$
- Alternative hypothesis H_a: $b \neq 0$

The appropriate test is a t-test, and, as you can see from the last line of Figure 17.5, the computer program calculates the t-value (8.57) and the p-value (probability of incorrectly rejecting the null hypotheses of .0000). See Chapter 16 for a more detailed discussion of P-values. Given our α criterion of .05, we would reject the null hypothesis in this case.

FIGURE 17.5

***STATISTICA*® Regression Analysis Output**

STAT. MULTIPLE REGRESS.	Regression Summary for Dependent Variable: Y R=.89619973 R² =.80317395 Adjusted R²=.79223917 F(1,18)=73.451 p<.00000 Std. Error of estimate: 97.640					
N=20	BETA	St. Err. of BETA	B	St. Err. of B	t(18)	p-level
Intercpt			240.8566	73.38347	3.282164	.004141
X	.896200	.104570	14.7168	1.71717	8.570374	.000000

Correlation Analysis

Correlation for Metric Data—Pearson's Product Moment Correlation

Correlation is the measuement of the degree to which changes in one variable (the dependent variable) are associated with changes in another. If we are analyzing the relationship between two variables, the analysis is called simple or bivariate **correlation analysis.** The **Pearson's product moment correlation** approach is used if metric data are involved.

correlation analysis

Analysis of the degree to which changes in one variable are associated with changes in another.

Pearson's product moment correlation

Correlation analysis technique for use with metric data.

In bivariate regression, we discussed the coefficient of determination R^2 as a measure of the strength of the linear relationship between X and Y. Another descriptive measure, called the *coefficient of correlation* (R), is a measure of the degree of association between X and Y. It is the square root of the coefficient of determination with the appropriate sign (+ or −):

$$R = \pm\sqrt{R^2}$$

The value of R can range from −1 (perfect negative correlation) to +1 (perfect positive correlation). The closer R is to ±1, the stronger is the degree of association between X amd Y. If R is equal to zero, then there is no association between X and Y.

If we are not interested in estimating the regression function, R can be computed directly with the data from our convenience store example, using this formula:

$$R = \frac{n \sum XY - (\sum X)(\sum Y)}{\sqrt{[n \sum X^2 - (\sum X)^2]\,[n \sum Y^2 - (\sum Y)^2]}}$$

The correlation coefficient

$$R = \frac{20(734{,}083) - (816)(16{,}826)}{\sqrt{[20(36{,}526) - (816)^2][20(15{,}027{,}574) - (16{,}826)^2]}}$$

$$R = .896$$

This value of R indicates a positive correlation between the average daily vehicular traffic and annual sales. In other words, successively higher levels of sales are associated with successively higher levels of traffic.

Correlation Using Ordinal Data—Spearman's Rank-Order Correlation

Researchers often need to analyze the degree of association between two ordinally scaled variables. The authors recently worked with an ad agency that wanted to determine whether there was a correlation between a company's ranking on product quality and its market share rank. The agency did a small pilot study with users of the product category to obtain quality ranks for the 12 companies in the industry. Market share data for the 12 companies were estimated, and because the agency did not feel they were very accurate, the companies were ranked based on relative market shares. Please note that in the case of both quality rank and market share rank, a smaller number (higher rank) indicates a higher result. The resulting data are provided in Table 17.5. Three different conclusions are possible regarding the rankings:

1. They are positively correlated.
2. They are negatively correlated.
3. They are independent.

Spearman rank-order correlation

Correlation analysis technique for use with ordinal data.

The **Spearman rank-order correlation** coefficient, R_s, is the appropriate procedure for analyzing these data.[3] Spearman's rank correlation coefficient is defined by

$$R_s = 1 - \left(\frac{6\sum_{i=1}^{n} d_i^2}{n^3 - n} \right)$$

where

d_i = difference in ranks of the two variables
n = number of items ranked

Using the data from Table 17.5, R_s would be calculated as follows:

$$R_s = 1 - \left(\frac{6(44)}{(12)^3 - 12} \right)$$

$$R_s = .85$$

Based on this analysis, the two rankings are positively correlated. Higher rankings on one are associated with higher rankings on the other.

The value of the coefficient of rank correlation ($R_s = .85$) can be tested against the null hypothesis using a t-distribution for a given sample size ($n = 12$) as follows:

TABLE 17.5 Quality Image Rank versus Market Share Rank

	RANKS			
COMPANY	*Quality Rank* X	*Market Share Rank* Y	d_i	d
A	4	3	1	1
B	6	7	−1	1
C	9	5	4	16
D	7	6	1	1
E	1	2	−1	1
F	3	4	−1	1
G	11	12	−1	1
H	5	9	−4	16
I	8	8	0	0
J	12	10	2	4
K	10	11	−1	1
L	2	1	1	1
				$\sum_{i=1}^{n} d_i^2 = 44$

$$R_s = 1 - \frac{6(44)}{(12)^3 - 12} = 0.85$$

$$t = R_s\sqrt{\frac{n-2}{1-R_s^2}}$$

$$= .85\sqrt{\frac{12-2}{1-.85^2}}$$

$$= 5.1$$

The agency believes that there is a positive relationship between a company's quality image and its market share. The null and alternative hypotheses were formulated as:

- Null hypothesis $H_0{:}R_s = 0$
- Alternative hypothesis $H_a{:}R_s > 0$

The table value for t with 10 ($n - 2$) degrees of freedom is 2.23 (at $\alpha = .05$). Because the calculated t-value (5.1) is higher than the table or critical value (2.23), we reject the null hypothesis and conclude that there is a positive association between a company's quality image and it market share rank.

Spearman's coefficient of rank correlation (R_s), like the coefficient of correlation (R), has a lower limit of -1 and an upper limit of $+1$; that is, $-1 \leq R_s \leq 1$.

Summary

This chapter discusses the relationship between variables taken two at a time. The techniques used for this analysis are called *bivariate analyses*. Bivariate regression analysis is used so that a single dependent variable can be predicted from the knowledge about a single independent variable. One way to examine the underlying relationship between a dependent and an independent variable is to plot them on a scatter diagram. If the relationship appears to be linear, then linear regression analysis may be used. If it is curvilinear, then curve-fitting techniques should be applied. The general equation for a straight line fitted to two variables is given by the equation

$$Y = a + bX$$

where

Y = the dependent variable
X = the independent variable
a = Y intercept
b = the amount Y increases with each unit increase in X

Both a and b are unknown and must be estimated. This is known as *simple linear regression analysis*. Bivariate least squares regression analysis is a mathematical technique for fitting a line to measurements of the two variables X and Y. The line is fitted so that the algebraic sum of deviations of the actual observations from the line are zero and the sum of the squared deviations is less than they would be for any other line that might be fitted to the data.

The estimated regression function describes the nature of the relationship between X and Y. In addition, researchers want to know the strength of the relationship between the variables. This is measured by the coefficient of determination, denoted by R^2. The coefficient of determination measures the percent of the total variation in Y that is "explained" by the variation in X. The R^2 statistic ranges from 0 to 1. An analysis of variance (ANOVA) approach also can be used for regression analysis. The total variation is known as the *total sum of squares* (SST). The explained variation, or the sum of squares due to regression (SSR), represents the variability explained by the regression. The unexplained variation is called the *error sums of squares* (SSE).

Correlation analysis is the measurement of the degree to which changes in one variable are associated with changes in another. If the researcher is using ordinal data, then the appropriate technique is the Spearman rank-order correlation. Correlation analysis will tell the researcher whether the variables are positively correlated, negatively correlated, or independent.

Key Terms

bivariate techniques
independent variable
dependent variable
bivariate regression analysis
coefficient of determination
sum of squares due to regression
sum of squares due to residual
correlation analysis
Pearson's product moment correlation
Spearman rank-order correlation

Review and Discussion Questions

1. What are the primary differences between simple regression and correlation analysis?
2. A sales manager of a firm administered a standard multiple-item job satisfaction scale to a random sample of the firm's sales force. The manager then correlated the satisfaction scores with the years of school the salespeople had completed. The Pearson correlation between satisfaction and years of school turned out to be .15. On the basis of this evidence, the sales manager came to the following conclusions: "A salesperson's level of education has little to do with his or her job satisfaction. Furthermore, as education level rises, they continue to have the same average levels of job satisfaction." Would you agree or disagree with the sales manager's conclusions? Explain your answer.
3. What is the purpose of a scatter diagram?
4. Explain how a marketing researcher can use the coefficient of determination.
5. What is the difference between the Pearson correlation coefficient and the Spearman rank-order correlation coefficient?
6. Comment on the following: "When the AFC team has won the Super Bowl, the stock market has always risen in the first quarter of the year in every case except one; when the NFC has won the Super Bowl, the stock market has fallen in the first quarter in all cases except two."
7. The following table gives data collected for a convenience store chain for 20 of its stores. The data are

   - Column 1—ID number for each store.
   - Column 2—Annual sales for the store for the previous year in thousands of dollars.
   - Column 3—Average daily numbers of vehicles that pass the store each day based on actual traffic counts for one month.
   - Column 4—Total population that lives within a two-mile radius of the store based on 1990 census data.
   - Column 5—Median family income for households within a two-mile radius of the store based on 1990 census data.

STORE ID#	ANNUAL SALES ($000)	AVERAGE DAILY TRAFFIC	POPULATION IN TWO-MILE RADIUS	AVERAGE INCOME IN AREA
1	$1,121	61,655	17,880	$28,991
2	$ 766	35,236	13,742	$14,731
3	$ 595	35,403	19,741	$ 8,114
4	$ 899	52,832	23,246	$15,324
5	$ 915	40,809	24,485	$11,438
6	$ 782	40,820	20,410	$11,730
7	$ 833	49,147	28,997	$10,589
8	$ 571	24,953	9,981	$10,706
9	$ 692	40,828	8,982	$23,591
10	$1,005	39,195	18,814	$15,703
11	$ 589	34,574	16,941	$ 9,015
12	$ 671	26,639	13,319	$10,065
13	$ 903	55,083	21,482	$17,365
14	$ 703	37,892	26,524	$ 7,532
15	$ 556	24,019	14,412	$ 6,950
16	$ 657	27,791	13,896	$ 9,855
17	$1,209	53,438	22,444	$21,589
18	$ 997	54,835	18,096	$22,659
19	$ 844	32,916	16,458	$12,660
20	$ 883	29,139	16,609	$11,618

Answer the following:

a. Which of the other three variables is the best predictor of sales? Compute correlation coefficients to answer the question.

b. Do the following regressions:

1. Sales as a function of average daily traffic.
2. Sales as a function of population in two-mile radius.

c. Interpret the results of the two regressions.

8. Interpret the following:

a. $Y = .11 + .009X$, where Y is the likelihood of sending children to college and X is family income in thousands of dollars. Remember, it is family income in thousands.

1. According to our model, how likely is a family with an income of $30,000 to send their children to college?
2. What is the likelihood for a family with an income of $50,000?
3. What is the likelihood for a family with an income of $17,500?
4. Is there some logic to the estimates? Explain.

b. $Y = .25 - .0039X$, where Y is the likelihood of going to a skateboard park and X is age.

1. According to our model, how likely is a 10 year old to go to a skateboard park?
2. What is the likelihood for a 60 year old?
3. What is the likelihood for a 40 year old?
4. Is there some logic to the estimates? Explain.

9. The following ANOVA summary data are the result of a regression with sales per year (dependent variable) as a function of promotion expenditures per year (independent variable) for a toy company.

$$F = \frac{MSR}{MSE} = \frac{34{,}276}{4721}$$

The degrees of freedom are 1 for the numerator and 19 for the denominator. Is the relationship statistically significant at $\alpha = .05$? Comment.

CASE 17.1

The Carter Regional Blood Center

Before the 1960s, many small communities had their own blood program. It usually was organized by local hospital and civic leaders to meet the needs of the community. Physicians have conducted research into how to use blood efficiently and how to separate it into its various components. Today a patient is rarely given whole blood but receives only those components necessary for her well being.

Testing, processing, and separating blood into its components requires a specialized staff and equipment that are extremely costly for every community to duplicate. As a result, the nation's blood collection system is being regionalized. Blood is collected in small communities but transported to regional blood centers where it is processed. The blood is stored at these centers, with the quantities and types of blood needed returned to the small communities so that their supply is maintained. As a result of this centralization process, many small town blood programs are now part of larger regional programs.

Research has greatly improved our understanding of how disease is and is not transmitted through blood transfusions. As a result, individuals who were once rejected as blood donors can now donate. At one time, the average rejection rate for people willing to give blood was about 14 percent. Now, with new screening and diagnostic measures, less than 5 percent of those who come in are turned away. Typically, a person can donate blood approximately six times a year, but individuals who do donate in the United States usually do so less than once a year.

TABLE 17.6 Results of Carter Donor Survey

RESPONDENT #	PINTS DONATED	AGE	EDUCATION IN YEARS
1	10	42	19
2	1	21	16
3	2	24	12
4	2	27	14
5	1	23	10
6	7	39	16
7	5	35	16
8	4	38	14
9	3	33	12
10	2	30	13
11	5	36	16
12	6	37	17
13	2	22	12
14	8	40	16
15	1	24	16
16	7	36	18
17	1	22	11
18	2	25	12
19	2	26	13
20	3	29	16

The Carter Regional Blood Center is in Fort Worth, Texas. It is a regional center for six counties, including Tarrant (in which Fort Worth is located), Parker, Ellis, Collin, Erath, and Johnson. The center had an increased need for blood and blood components primarily because of the growing number of open heart and kidney transplant operations performed in the region. Also, regular transfusions of blood platelets are demanded by a growing number of patients undergoing chemotherapy for cancer or on the AIDS drug AZT. To meet the demand for blood and blood components, the administrators of the center decided that a marketing orientation was needed. The first step in this process was to gain some understanding of the target market. In particular, they were interested in the relationship between donations and age, and donations and income. They did a pilot study that involved collecting data from a random sample of 20 donors. The data are shown in Table 17.6:

- Column 1—ID number assigned to each donor.
- Column 2—Number of pints donated in past two years.
- Column 3—Age of donor in years.
- Column 4—Years of education for donor.

1. Which of the other two variables is the best predictor of donations? Compute correlation coefficients to answer the question.
2. Do the following regressions:
   a. Amount donated as a function of age.
   b. Amount donated as a function of education.
3. Interpret the results of the two regressions.

CASE 17.2

Selling Chevrolets to Female Car Buyers

Women are becoming increasingly important in America's car lots. Today they buy about 45 percent of all new cars sold in the United States, up from 23 percent in 1970. In addition, they influence 80 percent of all new car purchases. Most important for American manufacturers, among female car buyers, 76 percent bought domestic cars. If they choose an import, women are more likely to buy Japanese cars than are men, whereas men are more likely to buy European models. The most popular domestic line of cars among women is the Chevrolet; about 14 percent of female new-car buyers purchased Chevrolets in the late 1980s.

Chevrolet has been targeting the women's market since about 1985, making it the leader in this area among divisions of General Motors. Recently, Chevrolet launched an extensive direct mail and print campaign aimed exclusively at women. Secondary research by Chevrolet's market researchers has noted that women could account for up to 60 percent of new-car purchases by the year 2000. Additional secondary research has uncovered some interesting facets of the female automobile purchaser. Women are less comfortable than men are when dealing with the financial aspects of purchasing their car. Thus, it is likely that manufacturers and car dealerships that make women feel more comfortable with financial aspects can build a dominant market share among female purchasers. Also, women tend to be more brand loyal in car buying than men are. Women pick up on showroom details that men usually ignore. For example, they notice whether a showroom or service area is dirty or noisy. They are more aware of smells, decorative details, and overall environment.

The company decided to test these theories by means of empirical research:

- It randomly selected 25 dealerships from the population of all Chevrolet dealerships.
- During a one week period, 100 randomly selected women were interviewed at each dealership. Results of that study are summarized in Table 17.7.

The data include

- Column 1—ID number assigned to each dealership.
- Column 2—Percent of women who purchased a car from the particular dealership (they were tracked for 30 days after the interview).
- Column 3—Average rating assigned to overall decor of the dealership on a 10-point scale (10 = excellent and 1 = poor).
- Column 4—Average rating assigned to cleanliness of dealership (10 = extremely clean and 1 = extremely dirty).
- Column 5—Average age of the women interviewed in years.

TABLE 17.7 Results of Chevrolet Survey of Female Car Shoppers

DEALER ID#	PERCENT WHO PURCHASED	AVERAGE DECOR RATING	AVERAGE CLEANLINESS RATING	AVERAGE SIZE
1	11	6.2	8.7	39
2	30	9.2	9.4	44
3	20	8.4	7.3	22
4	9	5.9	6.9	29
5	5	5.2	5.5	34
6	6	6.0	8.8	45
7	5	6.6	6.8	53
8	14	7.1	8.2	21
9	12	6.8	6.9	26
10	7	5.9	4.9	35
11	3	5.1	6.6	27
12	4	8.3	6.3	72
13	5	6.3	7.3	44
14	14	7.8	7.1	39
15	12	7.0	9.1	47
16	4	4.9	7.0	44
17	3	5.2	5.4	34
18	9	6.7	7.3	44
19	8	6.5	8.2	58
20	4	5.9	6.2	62
21	6	6.1	6.3	37
22	11	7.0	7.9	48
23	19	8.8	8.9	41
24	21	9.1	9.4	22
25	22	8.8	8.3	55

1. Which of the other three variables is the best predictor of the percent who purchased? Use correlation analysis.
2. Do the following regressions:
   a. Percent who purchased as a function of decor rating.
   b. Percent who purchased as a function of cleanliness rating.
3. Interpret the results of the two regressions. Which rating has the largest effect on purchasing? Explain.
4. What do your results suggest that the effect of a one unit increase in decor rating on percent purchasing would be?
5. If you were a marketing manager for Chevrolet, what would you be inclined to do based on the statistical results? Explain.

CASE 17.3

Style and Quality in Athletic Shoes

Bill Sexton is the new product development manager for Road Runner Athletic Shoe Company. He recently has completed consumer testing of 12 new shoe models. As part of this test, a panel of consumers was asked to rank the 12 shoe concepts on two attributes, "overall quality" and "style." The panel of 20 met as a group and came up with the rankings as a group. Bill believes that there is a relationship between the style rankings and the overall quality rankings. He believes that shoes receiving higher rankings on style also will tend to receive higher rankings on overall quality. The ranking results for the 12 shoe concepts follow.

SHOE MODEL	STYLE RANK	QUALITY RANK
1	3	4
2	5	2
3	9	10
4	2	1
5	4	3
6	1	8
7	6	11
8	8	5
9	7	7
10	11	2
11	10	9
12	12	6

1. Which of the statistical procedures covered in this chapter is appropriate for addressing Bill's theory? Why would you choose that technique over the others?
2. Use the technique that you choose to determine whether Bill's theory is supported by the statistical evidence. State the appropriate null and alternative hypothses. Is Bill's theory supported by the statistical evidence? Why or why not?

CHAPTER 18

Multivariate Data Analysis

LEARNING OBJECTIVES

1. To define multivariate analysis.
2. To describe multiple regression analysis and multiple discriminate analysis.
3. To learn about factor analysis and cluster analysis.
4. To gain an appreciation of perceptual mapping.
5. To learn about conjoint analysis.

Chad Liggin is director of marketing for United Personal Communications (UPC). UPC recently won the right to provide wireless personal communications services (PCS) in the Rochester, New York, metropolitan area in an auction conducted by the Federal Communications Commission (FCC). PCS is the term used to refer to a new class of wireless communications services developed during the late 1980s and early 1990s. PCS is a digital technology and can be used as a platform to offer voice services similar to those currently offered via cellular technology and a range of new and enhanced digital communications including data and video transmission.

Chad has just completed a large market survey in the Rochester area that was designed to provide information for the development of a marketing program for UPC's PCS. Details regarding the questionnaire and the methodology employed are provided in the appendix to this chapter.

SOURCE: © R. Michael Stuckey/Comstock.

Chad is concerned about a number of issues addressed by the study. These issues are, to some degree, dealt with in the crosstabulation analysis. However, he is not totally pleased with that analysis. The crosstabulations suggest answers to some of his questions but lead to no clear conclusions. Specifically, he is concerned with the following:

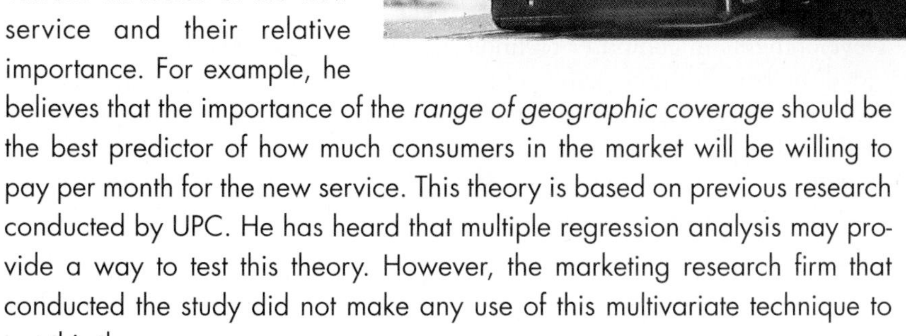

- First, he has certain theories regarding the importance of various attributes of the new service and their relative importance. For example, he believes that the importance of the *range of geographic coverage* should be the best predictor of how much consumers in the market will be willing to pay per month for the new service. This theory is based on previous research conducted by UPC. He has heard that multiple regression analysis may provide a way to test this theory. However, the marketing research firm that conducted the study did not make any use of this multivariate technique to test this theory.
- Second, he is interested in developing a better understanding of the factors associated with *having* or *not having cellular telephone service* at the current

time. A significant percentage of those surveyed in the recent study currently have cellular telephone service. He is interested in finding out how these individuals differ from those who do not currently have cellular service in regard to the importance they attach to various features of wireless telephone service. He believes that current cellular customers are likely to be good candidates for PCS because PCS offers a solution to some of the things that cellular subscribers complain about, such as static. Chad has heard that multiple discriminant analysis can be used to test these theories.

- Third, he believes that the market can be segmented on the basis of the importance that consumers in the market attach to different features of wireless communications services. If this is true, it will provide information that will be very useful in helping him decide how the new service should be positioned and who to target. Should it be positioned as a low-cost service, as a service that provides better sound quality than cellular, or in some other way? If the sizes of the groups that place highest importance on different features can be determined, the answers to these questions will be very straightforward.
- Finally, he believes that the way that consumers feel about some of the attributes of wireless service may be strongly coordinated with the way they feel about other attributes. If this is true, he may be able to build his positioning and communications strategy around clusters of product attributes or features that will naturally resonate with consumers. ■

These issues and questions are addressed in this chapter. Multivariate procedures are powerful tools for analyzing various types of marketing research data. They provide a basis for testing the types of questions being explored by Chad.

Multivariate Analysis

Developments in computer technology, both hardware and software, have provided the basis for remarkable advances in the use of powerful statistical procedures for the analysis of marketing research data. These developments have made it possible to analyze large amounts of complex data with relative ease. In particular, developments related to a group of analytical techniques known as *multivariate analysis* have been extremely significant in this data analysis revolution.

multivariate analysis
Statistical procedures that simultaneously analyze multiple measurements on each individual or object under study.

The term **multivariate analysis** is used to refer to a group of statistical procedures that simultaneously analyze multiple measurements on each individual or object being studied.[1] Some experts consider any simultaneous statistical analysis of more than two variables to be multivariate analysis. Multivariate procedures are extensions of the univariate and bivariate statistical procedures discussed in the previous chapters.

A number of techniques fall under the heading of multivariate analysis procedures. In this chapter we will consider six of these techniques:

- Multiple regression analysis
- Multiple discriminant analysis
- Cluster analysis
- Factor analysis
- Perceptual mapping
- Conjoint analysis

Most students have been exposed to multiple regression analysis in introductory statistics courses. The remaining procedures are newer and less widely studied. Summary descriptions of the techniques are provided in Table 18.1

Although awareness of multivariate techniques is still low, they have been around for decades and have been widely used for a variety of commercial purposes. Fair Isaac & Co. has built a $70-million business around the commercial use of multivariate techniques.[2] The firm and its clients have found that they can predict with surprising accuracy who will pay their bills on time, who will pay late, and who will not pay at all. The federal government uses secret formulas, based on the firm's analyses, to identify tax evaders. Fair Isaac has also shown that its multivariate analyses are good at identifying sales prospects.

Multiple Regression Analysis

Multiple Regression Analysis Defined

Multiple regression analysis is the appropriate multivariate technique if the researcher's goal is to examine the relationship between two or more metric predictor (independent) variables and one metric dependent (criterion) variable.[4] Under certain circumstances, described later in this section, nominal predictor variables can be used if they are recoded as binary variables.

multiple regression analysis
A procedure for predicting the level or magnitude of a dependent variable based on the levels of more than one independent variable.

Multiple regression analysis is an extension of bivariate regression discussed in Chapter 17. Instead of fitting a straight line to observations in a two-dimensional space, multiple regression analysis fits a plane to observations in a multidimensional space. The output obtained and the interpretation of multiple regression

TABLE 18.1 Brief Description of Multivariate Statistical Techniques Covered

- *Multiple regression analysis* enables the researcher to predict the level of magnitude of a dependent variable based on the levels of more than one independent variable.
- *Multiple discriminant analysis* enables the researcher to predict group membership on the basis of two or more independent variables.
- *Cluster analysis* is a procedure for identifying subgroups of individuals or items that are homogeneous within subgroups and different from other subgroups.
- *Factor analysis* permits the analyst to reduce a set of variables to a smaller set of factors or composite variables by identifying dimensions under the data.
- *Perceptual mapping* is appropriate when the goal is to analyze consumer perception of companies, products, brands, and so on.
- *Conjoint analysis* provides a basis to estimate the utility that consumers associate with different product features or attributes.

are essentially the same as for bivariate regression. The general equation for multiple regression is as follows:

$$Y = a + b_1X_1 + b_2X_2 + b_3X_3 + \ldots + b_nX_n$$

where

Y = dependent or criterion variable
a = estimated constant
b_{1-n} = coefficients associated with the predictor variables so that a change of one unit in X will cause a change of b_1 units in Y; the values for the coefficients are estimated from the regression analysis
X_{1-n} = predictor (independent) variables that influence the dependent variable

For example, consider the following regression equation (note that values for a, b_1, and b_2 have been estimated by means of regression analysis):

$$\hat{Y} = 200 + 17X_1 + 22X_2$$

where

$\hat{Y}$ = estimated sales in units
X_1 = advertising expenditures
X_2 = number of salespersons

This equation indicates that sales increase by 17 units for every one dollar increase in advertising and 22 units for every one unit increase in the number of salespersons.

Possible Applications of Multiple Regression

There are many possible applications of multiple regression analysis in marketing research:

- Estimating the effects various marketing mix variables have on sales or market share.
- Estimating the relationship between various demographic or psychographic factors and frequency of visiting fast food restaurants or other service businesses.
- Quantifying the relationship between various classification variables, such as age and income, and overall attitude toward a product or service.
- Determining which variables are predictive of sales of a particular product or service.

As just shown, multiple regression analysis can serve one or a combination of two basic purposes: prediction of the level of the dependent variable based on given levels of the predictor variables; or understanding the relationship between the independent variables and the dependent variable.

coefficient of determination

Measure of the percentage of the variation in the dependent variable explained by variations in the independent variables.

Multiple Regression Analysis Measures

In the earlier discussion of bivariate regression, a statistic referred to as the **coefficient of determination,** or R^2, was noted as one of the outputs of regression analysis. This statistic can assume values from 0 to 1 and provides a measure of the percentage of the variation in the dependent variable explained by variation in the independent variables. For example, if the R^2 in a given regression analysis was calculated to be .75, that means that 75 percent of the variation in the dependent variable is explained by variation in the independent variables. The analyst would prefer to have a calculated R^2 of close to 1. Frequently, variables are added to a regression model to see what effect they have on the R^2 value.

The b values, or **regression coefficients,** indicate the effect of the individual independent variables on the dependent variable. It is appropriate to determine the likelihood that each individual b value is the result of chance. This calculation is part of the output provided by virtually all statistical software packages. Normally, these packages compute the probability of incorrectly rejecting the null hypothesis of $b_n = 0$.

regression coefficients
Values that indicate the effect of the individual independent variables on the dependent variable.

Dummy Variables

In some situations, the analyst would like to include nominally scaled independent variables such as gender, marital status, occupation, or race in a multiple regression analysis. For this purpose, dummy variables can be created. Dichotomous nominally scaled independent variables can be transformed into dummy variables by coding one value (e.g., female) as 0 and the other (e.g., male) as 1. For nominally scaled independent variables that can assume more than two values, a slightly different approach is required. Consider a question regarding racial group with three possible answers: African American, Hispanic, or White. Binary or dummy variable coding of responses will require the use of two dummy variables, X_1 and X_2, that might be coded as follows:

	X_1	X_2
If person is African American	1	0
If person is Hispanic	0	1
If person is White	0	0

Potential Problems in Using and Interpreting Multiple Regression Analysis

We must be sensitive to certain problems that may be encountered in the use and interpretation of multiple regression analysis results. These problems are summarized in the following sections.

Collinearity One of the key assumptions of multiple regression analysis is that the independent variables are not correlated with each other.[5] If the independent variables are correlated, then the estimated b values (regression coefficients) will be biased and unstable. Conventional wisdom says that this is not a problem if the regression model is developed strictly for purposes of prediction. However, when the goal of the analysis is to determine how each of the predictor variables influences the dependent variable, the fact that the b values are biased due to **collinearity** is a serious problem.

collinearity
The correlation of independent variables with each other. Can bias estimates of regression coefficients.

The simplest way to check for collinearity is to examine the matrix showing the correlations between each variable in the analysis. One rule of thumb is to look for correlations between independent variables of .30 or greater. If correlations of this magnitude exist, then the analyst should check for distortions of the *b* values. One way to do this is to run regressions with the two or more collinear variables included and with each of them separately. The *b* values in the regression with all variables in the equation should be similar to the *b* values computed for the variables run separately.

There are a number of strategies for dealing with collinearity. First, if two variables are heavily correlated with each other, one of the variables can be dropped from the analysis. Second, the correlated variables can be combined in some fashion (e.g., an index) to form a new composite independent variable, and this variable can be used in subsequent regression analyses. These are two of the most commonly used strategies.

Causation Although regression analysis can show that variables are associated or correlated with each, it cannot prove **causation.** Causal relationships can be confirmed only by other means (see Chapter 9). A strong logical or theoretical basis must be developed to support the idea that there is a causal relationship between the independent variables and the dependent variable. However, even a strong logical base coupled with statistical results demonstrating correlation are only indicators of causation.

causation

The inference that a change in one variable is responsible for, or caused, an observed change in another variable.

Scaling of Coefficients The magnitude of the regression coefficients associated with the various independent variables can be compared directly only if they are scaled in the same units or if the data have been standardized. This point is illustrated in the following example:

$$\hat{Y} = 50 + 20X_1 + 20X_2$$

where

$\hat{Y}$ = estimated sales volume
X_1 = advertising expenditure in thousands of dollars
X_2 = number of salespersons

On initial examination it would appear that a dollar spent on advertising and an additional salesperson would have an equal effect on sales. However, on further consideration, this is false because X_1 and X_2 are measured in different kinds of units. If we want to make direct comparisons of regression coefficients, all independent variables must be measured in the same units (e.g., dollars or thousands of dollars) or the data must be standardized. Standardization is achieved by taking each number in a series, subtracting the mean of the series from the number, and dividing the result by the standard deviation of the series. The formula for this process is as follows:

$$\frac{X_1 - \bar{X}}{\sigma}$$

where

X_i = individual number from a series of numbers
$\bar{X}$ = mean of the series
σ = standard deviation of the series

Sample Size The value of R^2 is influenced by the number of predictor variables relative to sample size.[6] A number of different rules of thumb have been proposed and suggest that the number of observations should be equal to at least 10 to 15 times the number of predictor variables. This means that for the preceding example (sales volume is a function of advertising expenditures and number of salespersons), with two predictor variables, 20 to 30 observations are required as a minimum.

Regression Analysis Example

This sample problem and the others in this chapter use data from the research described in the appendix. Chad Liggin, the marketing director in the feature at the beginning of the chapter, believes that five variables are important in determining how much potential customers are willing to pay each month to receive *Wide Area Service* (brand name to be used for PCS). The five items are importance ratings of the following features of the service: *range of coverage, mobility, sound quality, ability to place and receive calls* when away from home, and *average monthly bill.* This hypothesis is based on the results of focus groups and other research conducted by UPC. All six variables (dependent variable and five independent and predictor variables) were measured in the survey. The five predictor variables were all measured on a nine-point scale where nine means the attribute is "very important" and one means the attribute is "very unimportant." The five predictors can be found under question 4 in the survey.

To test his hypothesis, the following model was estimated, using multiple regression analysis:

$$\hat{Y} = a + b_1X_1 + b_2X_2 + b_3X_3 + b_4X_4 + b_5X_5$$

where

Y = dependent variable—amount willing to pay each month to receive *Wide Area Service* (ADDED2)
a = constant term or Y axis intercept
b_{1-5} = regression coefficient to be estimated
X_1 = first independent variable—importance rating of range of coverage (RANGE)
X_2 = second independent variable—importance rating of mobility (MOBILITY)
X_3 = third independent variable—importance rating of sound quality (SOUND)
X_4 = fourth independent variable—importance rating or ability to place and receive calls when away from (PRECEIV)
X_5 = fifth independent variable—importance rating of average monthly telephone bill (AVGBILL)

The estimated regression equation is:

$$\hat{Y} = .82 + .44X_1 + .69X_2 + .21X_3 + .45X_4 + 1.44X_5$$

Complete regression results generated with the *STATISTICA*® software package are shown in Table 18.2. These results indicate that:

TABLE 18.2 Regression Summary for Dependent Variable: ADDED2

R = .86573182 R^2 = .74949158 Adjusted R^2 = .74303518
F (95,194) = 116.09 p<0.0000 Std. Error of estimate: 1.4863

	BETA	ST. ERR OF BETA.	B	ST. ERR. OF B	t(194)	p-LEVEL
Intercept			0.82	1.67	0.49	0.62
RANGE	0.21	0.05	0.44	0.10	4.25	0.00
MOBILITY	0.52	0.05	0.69	0.07	10.54	0.00
SOUND	0.07	0.04	0.21	0.13	1.67	0.10
PRECEIV	0.21	0.06	0.45	0.12	3.65	0.00
AVGBILL	0.32	0.04	1.44	0.17	8.33	0.00

- All the regression coefficients (b_1, b_2, and so on) have positive signs. This indicates that higher importance ratings on each of the five independent variables are associated with the willingness to pay more for *Wide Area Service.*
- The regression coefficient (b) shows the estimated effect of a one unit increase in each of the associated independent variables on the dependent variable. In these *STATISTICA*®results (Table 18.2), the estimated unstandardized coefficients are shown under the column labeled "B." The results show, for example, that a one-unit increase in the importance of RANGE will result in a 44-cent increase in the amount an individual is willing to pay per month for *Wide Area Service.* The column in Table 18.2 labeled "BETA" shows the regression coefficient computed with standardized data. According to these estimates, MOBILITY has a larger effect on the amount prospective customers are willing to pay for the service than any of the other four independent variables. AVGBILL is second in importance and RANGE and PRECEIV are tied for third place. Interestingly, according to the model, SOUND has the smallest relative effect on the amount prospective customers are willing to pay.
- The R^2 value or coefficient of determination is .743, indicating that 74.3 percent of the variation in the amount consumers are willing to pay for *Wide Area Service (Y)* is explained by the variation in the five independent or predictor variables.

Discriminant Analysis

Discriminant Analysis Defined

multiple discriminant analysis

A procedure for predicting group membership on the basis of two or more independent variables.

Multiple discriminant analysis is similar to multiple regression analysis;[7] however, there are important differences. First of all, in the case of multiple regression analysis, the dependent variable must be metric; in multiple discriminant analysis, the dependent variable is nominal or categorical in nature. For example, the dependent variable might be usage status for a particular product or service. A particular respondent who uses the product or service might be assigned a code of 1 for the dependent variable and a respondent who does not use it a code of 2. Independent variables might include various metric measures such as age, income, number of years of education, and so forth. The goals of multiple discriminant analysis are as follows:

- Determine if there are statistically significant differences between the average discriminant score profiles of the two or more groups (in this case users and nonusers).
- Establish a model for classifying individuals or objects into groups on the basis of their values on the independent variables.
- Determine how much of the difference in the average score profiles of the two or more groups is accounted for by each independent variable.

The general discriminant analysis equation follows:

$$Z = b_1X_1 + b_2X_2 + \ldots + b_3X_n$$

where

$$Z = \text{discriminate score}$$

$$b_{1-n} = \text{discriminant weights}$$

$$X_{1-n} = \text{independent variables}$$

The **discriminant score,** normally referred to as a *Z*-score, is the score derived for each individual or object by means of the equation. This score is the basis for predicting to which group the particular object or individual belongs. Discriminant weights, often referred to as **discriminant coefficients,** are computed by means of the discriminant analysis program. The size of the discriminant weight (or coefficient) associated with a particular independent variable is determined by the variance structure of the variables in the equation. Independent variables with large discriminatory power (large differences between groups) will have large weights, and those with little discriminatory power will have small weights.

discriminant score
The basis for predicting to which group a particular object or individual belongs.

discriminant coefficient
Estimate of the discriminatory power of a particular independent variable.

The goal of discriminant analysis is the prediction of a categorical variable. The analyst must decide which variables would be expected to be associated with the probability of an object or person falling into one of two or more groups or categories. The problem, in a statistical sense, of analyzing the nature of group differences is finding a linear combination of independent variables, the discriminant function, that shows large differences in group means.

Possible Applications of Discriminant Analysis

Discriminant analysis may be used to answer many questions in marketing research:

- How are consumers who purchase various brands different from those who do not purchase those brands?
- How do consumers who show a high probability of purchasing a new product differ in demographic and lifestyle characteristics from consumers with a low purchase probability?
- How do consumers who go to one fast food restaurant most frequently differ in their demographic and lifestyle characteristics from consumers who go to another fast food restaurant most frequently?
- How do consumers who have chosen indemnity insurance, HMO coverage, or PPO coverage differ from one another in regard to their health care use, perceptions, and attitudes?

Discriminant Analysis Example

The UPC marketing director also wants to predict whether or not the five importance ratings used in the regression analysis predict whether or not an individual currently has a cellular telephone. Cellular telephone ownership is captured by question 8 on the survey. Those who currently have cellular telephones were assigned a code of one and those who do not currently have cellular were assigned the code of zero. Previous research conducted by UPC suggested that the five independent variables (RANGE, MOBILITY, SOUND, PRECEIV, and AVGBILL) should be good predictors of cellular telephone ownership.

The following discriminant model was estimated to test this hypothesis:

$$Z = b_1X_1 + b_2X_2 + b_3X_3 + b_4X_4 + b_5X_5$$

where

Z = discriminant score
b_{1-5} = discriminant coefficients or weights
X_1 = first independent variable—importance rating of range of coverage (RANGE)
X_2 = second independent variable—importance rating of mobility (MOBILITY)
X_3 = third independent variable—importance rating of sound quality (SOUND)
X_4 = fourth independent variable—importance rating or ability to place and receive calls when away from (PRECEIV)
X_5 = fifth independent variable—importance rating of average monthly telephone bill (AVGBILL)

The discriminant analysis results are

$$Z = -.02X_1 + .22X_2 - .36X_3 + .55X_4 + .07X_5$$

The results show that the ability to place and receive calls when away from home (PRECEIV) is the most important variable and range of coverage (RANGE) is the least important variable in discriminating between those who currently have and do not have cellular telephone service.

Another important role of discriminant analysis is to classify objects or people. In this example, the goal was to correctly classify consumers into two groups—those who currently have cellular telephone service and those who do not have cellular telephone service. To determine whether the estimated discriminant model is a good predictor, the "confusion" or "classification matrix" is used. The classification matrix produced for this problem by the *STATISTICA*® discriminant analysis program is shown in Table 18.3. This table shows that the model correctly predicted 73.8 percent of the current cellular nonusers as nonusers. However, it incorrectly predicted that 33 or 26.2 percent of the nonusers are users. It shows that 71.6 percent of the current cellular users were predicted to be users but that 28.4 percent are predicted to be nonusers. Overall, the model correctly classified 73.0 percent of all respondents as cellular users or nonusers. This is far better than we would expect to do on a chance basis. The conclusion is that the five independent variables are significant predictors of whether or not a particular individual is a current cellular user. Statistical tests are available to

TABLE 18.3 Classification Matrix (pcstext.sta)

Rows: Observed classifications
Columns: Predicted classifications

	PERCENT CORRECT	G_1:0 p=.63000	G_2:1 p=.37000
G_1:0	73.8	93	33
G_2:1	71.6	21	53
Total	73.0	114	86

indicate whether the resulting classification is better than we would expect to get by chance. One simple approach is to use the proportional chance criterion when group sizes are unequal and our goal is to correctly predict membership in the two groups. The formula is

$$C_{\text{PRO}} = p^2 + (1 - p)^2$$

where

$$p = \text{proportion of individuals in group 1}$$
$$1 - p = \text{proportion of individuals in group 2}$$

In this case, group 1 (nonusers) includes 126 people or 63.0 percent of the total (126/200). Calculation of the proportional chance criterion follows:

$$\begin{aligned} C_{\text{PRO}} &= .63^2 + (1 - .63)^2 \\ &= .397 + .137 \\ &= .534 \text{ or } 53.4\% \end{aligned}$$

In the problem, we correctly classified 93 of the nonusers and 53 of the users for a total of 146 out of 200 or 73.0 percent correctly classified. This exceeds the proportional chance criterion of 53.4 percent by a wide margin and suggests our model did a better job than we would expect due to chance.

Cluster Analysis

Cluster Analysis Defined

The term **cluster analysis** refers to a group of techniques used to identify objects or people that are similar in regard to certain variables or measurements. The purpose of cluster analysis is to classify objects or people into some number of mutually exclusive and exhaustive groups, so that those within a group are as similar as possible to one another.[8] In other words, clusters should be very homogeneous internally (within cluster) and very heterogeneous externally (between clusters).

cluster analysis
Procedures for classifying objects or people into some number of mutually exclusive and exhaustive groups on the basis of two or more classification variables.

Procedures for Clustering

A number of different procedures are available for clustering people or objects, based on somewhat different mathematical and computer routines. However, the general approach underlying all these procedures is similar and involves measuring the similarity between people or objects in regard to their values on the variables used for clustering. Often, similarity among the people or objects being clustered is determined on the basis of some type of distance measure. This approach is best illustrated graphically. For example, you might want to group or cluster consumers on the basis of two variables: monthly frequency of eating out and monthly frequency of eating at fast food restaurants. Observations on the two variables are plotted on a two-dimensional graph in Figure 18.1. Each dot indicates the position of one consumer in regard to the two variables. The distance between any pair of points is positively related to how similar the corresponding individuals are when the two variables are considered together (the closer, the more similar). In the example, consumer *X* is more like consumer *Y* than either *Z* or *W*. Inspection of Figure 18.1 suggests the existence of three distinct clusters.

In this case, three clusters emerge on the basis of simultaneously considering frequency of eating out and frequency of eating at fast food restaurants:

- *Cluster 1.* This group or cluster includes those people who do not frequently eat out or frequently eat at fast food restaurants.
- *Cluster 2.* This cluster includes consumers who eat out frequently but seldom eat at fast food restaurants.
- *Cluster 3.* Here we have a cluster of people who eat out frequently and also eat at fast food restaurants frequently.

If this research was conducted by a fast food company, then the company can see that its customers are to be found among those who, in general, eat out frequently. To develop more insights, the analyst would probably want to develop demographic, psychographic, and behavioral profiles of consumers in cluster 3.

Clusters can be developed from scatter plots, as we have done in this case. However, this is a tedious, time-consuming, trial-and-error procedure. The

FIGURE 18.1

Cluster Analysis Based on Two Variables

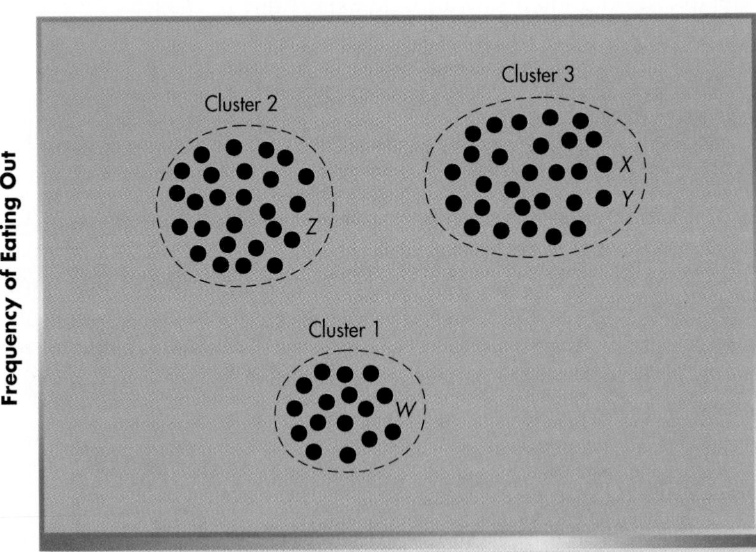

process becomes more tedious as the number of variables used to develop the clusters or the number of objects being clustered increases. You can readily visualize a problem, like the one shown in Figure 18.1 with two variables and fewer than 100 objects. When, for example, the number of variables is increased to three and the number of observations is increased to 500 or more, visualization becomes virtually impossible. Fortunately, computer algorithms are available for this purpose. The mechanics of these algorithms are complicated and beyond the scope of this discussion. The basic idea behind most of them is to start with some arbitrary cluster boundaries and modify the boundaries until a point is reached where the average interpoint distances within clusters are as small as possible relative to average distances between clusters.

Cluster Analysis Example

Again referring to the PCS example, UPC wants to explore the issue of market segmentation using the data from the Rochester consumer survey. It believes that the market can be segmented on the basis of the eight attribute importance responses (question 4) and that the resulting clusters or groups might be further described on the basis of demographic and usage data.

To address this issue, it ran a cluster analysis using the K-means procedure in *STATISTICA*®. Because cluster analysis does not produce a "best" solution, UPC experimented with a number of different solutions before choosing a three-cluster solution on the basis of the distinctness of the clusters. The sizes of the three clusters and the average ratings on the eight attribute importance questions for each cluster are summarized in Table 18.4. Average attribute ratings are also summarized in Figure 18.2. This solution has the following characteristics:

- *Cluster 3* is the largest with 83 respondents and *cluster 2* is the smallest with 55.
- In regard to attribute importance ratings, *cluster 2* and *cluster 3* are the most similar. They have almost identical average importance ratings on six of the eight attributes. They do differ significantly in regard to price sensitivity. Members of *cluster 3* assign a much higher importance to TELEPHON (price of the required equipment) and INSTALL (installation/activation charges).

TABLE 18.4 **Cluster Analysis Results with Cluster Size and Average Ratings on Attribute Importance Variable**

VARIABLE	CLUSTER 1 *(n = 62)*	CLUSTER 2 *(n = 55)*	CLUSTER 3 *(n = 83)*
RANGE	6.8	8.1	8.2
MOBILITY	4.5	8.1	8.2
SOUND	8.1	8.5	8.5
PLACE	6.7	8.3	8.7
PRECEIV	6.8	8.5	8.6
AVGBILL	8.6	8.4	8.8
TELEPHON	8.1	6.3	8.7
INSTALL	7.2	5.1	8.5

FIGURE 18.2
Average Attribute Ratings—3 Clusters

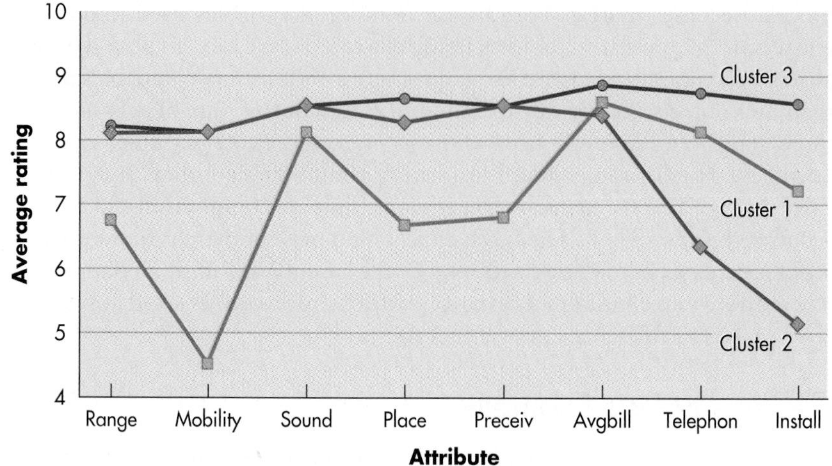

- *Cluster 1* differs markedly from *clusters 2* and *3*. In particular, members of this cluster view RANGE, MOBILITY, PLACE, and PRECEIV to be significantly less important than do the members of the other two clusters.
- Members of *clusters 2* and *3* are the best targets for the new PCS based on the importance they place on the RANGE, MOBILITY, PRECEIV, and PLACE variables. In the early stages of product introduction, *cluster 3* members represent the most attractive target because of their relative insensitivity to price. *Cluster 2* members might be targeted later, assuming that prices fall over time, which is the projected scenario.

The clusters also differ in regard to demographic and usage data. This issue was analyzed by crosstabulating cluster membership by the various demographic and usage measures available in the survey.

- *Cluster 1*. These individuals are the lightest users of all telephone services. They are about equally likely to be male or female, least likely to be married by a narrow margin, youngest, and come from households with the largest number of adults.
- *Cluster 2*. These individuals are the heaviest users of most telephone services. They are much more likely to be female and very similar to the members of *cluster 3* on most other demographic measures.
- *Cluster 3*. Of the three clusters, members of this cluster are in the middle in regard to usage of most telephone services. They are more likely to be male than female, most likely to be married of the three clusters, oldest, and willing to pay the highest amount, on average, for *Wide Area Service*.

UPC management is, as always, left with the question of what to do based on these findings. Preliminary analysis suggests that its initial target probably should be members of cluster 3 for reasons suggested here. Later, as prices fall, an appropriate strategy might be to expand its target to include the members of cluster 2. Members of cluster 1 should be targeted only after UPC has achieved saturation penetration levels among cluster 2 and cluster 3 members. This plan can be operationalized by more careful analysis of the demographic characteristics of the members of the three clusters and the implementation of a sales and media plan based on this analysis to maximize communication with the most likely prospects.

Factor Analysis[9]

Factor Analysis Defined

The purpose of **factor analysis** is data simplification.[10] The objective is to summarize the information contained in a large number of metric measures (e.g., rating scales) into a smaller number of summary measures, called *factors*. As with cluster analysis, there is no dependent variable.

factor analysis
Procedure for data simplification through reducing a set of variables to a smaller set of factors or composite variables by identifying dimensions underlying the data.

Many phenomena of interest to marketing researchers are actually composites or combinations of a number of measures. These concepts are often measured by means of a number of rating questions. For instance, in assessing consumer response to a new automobile, a general concept such as "luxury" might be measured by asking respondents to rate different cars on attributes such as "quiet ride," "smooth ride," or "plush carpeting." The product designer wants to produce an automobile that is perceived as luxurious but knows that a variety of features probably contribute to this general perception. Each attribute rated should measure a slightly different facet of luxury. The set of measures should provide a better representation of the concept than a single global rating of "luxury."

If there are several measures of a concept, they can be added together to develop a composite score or compute an average score on the concept. An example is

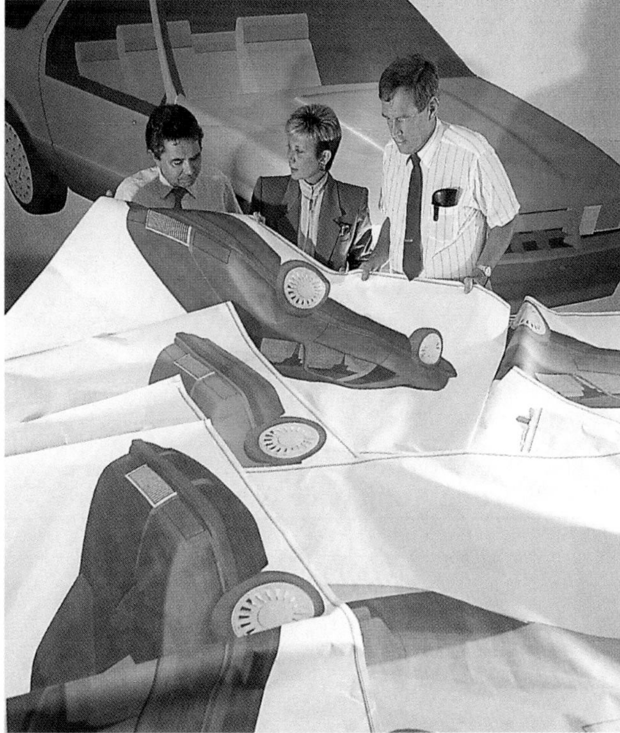

If product designers want to produce an automobile that is perceived as luxurious, they need to know what features contribute to a perception of luxury. SOURCE: Michael L. Abramson/Woodfin Camp & Associates.

TABLE 18.5 **Ratings of a Luxury Automobile Assigned by Six Subjects**

RESPONDENT	SMOOTH RIDE	QUIET RIDE	ACCELERATION	HANDLING
Bob	5	4	2	1
Roy	4	3	2	1
Hank	4	3	3	2
Janet	5	5	2	2
Jane	4	3	2	1
Ann	5	5	3	2
Average	4.50	3.83	2.33	1.50

shown in Table 18.5. Data for six subjects who each rated an automobile on four characteristics are shown in this table. One can see that those respondents who gave higher ratings on *Smooth Ride* also gave higher ratings on *Quiet Ride*. A similar pattern is evident between ratings of *Acceleration* and *Handling*. These four measures might be combined into two summary measures by averaging the pairs of ratings. The resulting summary measures might be called *Luxury* and *Performance* (see Table 18.6).

Factor Scores

Factor analysis produces one or more "factors" or composite variables when applied to a number of variables. A technical definition of a *factor* is "a linear combination of variables." A factor is simply a weighted summary score of a set of related variables. This is similar to the composite derived by averaging the measures. However, in factor analysis, each measure is first weighted according to how much it contributes to the variation of each factor.

With factor analysis, we can calculate a factor score on each factor for each subject in the data set. For example, in a factor analysis with two factors, the following equations would be used to determine factor scores:

$$F_1 = .40A_1 + .30A_2 + .02A_3 + .05A_4$$
$$F_2 = .01A_1 + .04A_2 + .45A_3 + .37A_4$$

where

$$F_{1-n} = \text{Factor scores}$$
$$A_{1-n} = \text{Attribute ratings}$$

TABLE 18.6 **Average Ratings of Two Constructs**

RESPONDENT	LUXURY	PERFORMANCE
Bob	4.5	1.5
Roy	3.5	1.5
Hank	3.5	2.5
Janet	5.0	2.0
Jane	3.5	1.5
Ann	5.0	2.5
Average	4.25	1.92

Using these formulas, two factor scores could be calculated for each subject by substituting their ratings on variables A_1 through A_4 into each equation. The coefficients in the equations (e.g., .40) are the factor scoring coefficients to be applied to each subject's ratings. For example, Bob's factor scores would be computed as

$$F_1 = .40(5) + .30(4) + .02(2) + .05(1) = 3.29$$
$$F_2 = .01(5) + .04(4) + .45(2) + .37(1) = 2.38$$

In the first equation, the factor scoring coefficients or weights for A_1 and A_2 (.40 and .30) are large whereas the weights for A_3 and A_4 are small. The small weights on A_3 and A_4 indicate that these variables contribute little to score variations on factor 1 (F_1). Regardless of the ratings a subject assigns to A_3 and A_4, they will have little effect on his score on F_1. In calculating the second factor score (F_2), variables A_3 and A_4 make a large contribution, whereas A_1 and A_2 have little effect. These equations also show that variables A_1 and A_2 are relatively independent of A_3 and A_4 because each variable takes on large values in only one scoring equation.

The relative sizes of the scoring coefficients are also of interest. Variable A_1 (with a weight of .4) is a more important contributor to factor 1 variation than is A_2 (with a smaller weight of .3). This finding may be very important to the product designer when examining the implications of various design changes. For example, the product manager might want to improve the perceived luxury of the car through product redesign or advertising. The product manager believes, based on other research, that a certain expenditure on redesign will result in an improvement of the average rating on *Smooth Ride* from 4.3 to 4.8. This research also shows that the same expenditure would also result in a one-half point improvement in rating on *Quiet Ride*. The factor analysis shows that perceived luxury would be enhanced to a greater extent by increasing ratings on *Smooth Ride* than by increasing ratings on *Quiet Ride* by the same amount.

Factor Loadings

The nature of the factors derived can be determined by examining the **factor loadings.** Using the scoring equations presented earlier, a pair of factors scores (F_1 and F_2) can be calculated for each respondent. Factor loadings are determined by calculating the correlation (can vary from +1.0 to −1.0) between each factor (F_1 and F_2) score and each of the original ratings variables. Each correlation coefficient represents the loading of the associated variable on the particular factor. If A_1 is closely associated with factor 1, the loading or correlation would be high. This analysis would produce a table like the one shown for our sample problem in Table 18.7. Because the loadings are correlation coefficients, values near +1 or −1 indicate a close positive or negative association. Variables A_1 and A_2 are closely associated (highly correlated) with scores on factor 1, and variables A_3 and A_4 are closely associated with scores on factor 2. Stated another way, variables A_1 and A_2 have "high loadings" on factor 1 and serve to "define" the factor.

factor loadings

The correlation between each factor score and each of the original variables.

Naming Factors

Having identified each factor's defining variables, the next step is to "name" the factors. This is a largely subjective step, combining intuition with an inspection

TABLE 18.7 Factor Loadings for Two Factors

VARIABLE	CORRELATION WITH	
	Factor 1	*Factor 2*
A_1	.85	.10
A_2	.76	.06
A_3	.06	.89
A_4	.04	.79

of the variables that have high loadings on each factor. More often than not, there is a certain consistency among the variables that load highly on a given factor. For instance, it is not surprising to see that the ratings on "smooth ride" and "plush carpeting" both load on the same factor. Although we have chosen to name this factor *luxury*, another analyst, looking at the same result, might decide to name the factor *prestige*.

How Many Factors?

In factor analysis we are also confronted with a decision regarding how many factors to retain. The final result could include from one factor up to as many factors as there are variables. The decision is often made by looking at the percent of the variation in the original data explained by each factor. In this case, we would definitely keep the first factor, explaining 55 percent of the variability (see Table 18.8) and probably the second factor. These two factors explain a total of 92.5 percent of the variability in the four measures. The last two factors explain only 7.5 percent of the variation and contribute little to our objective of data simplification.

There are many different decision rules for choosing the number of factors to retain. Probably the most appropriate decision rule is to stop factoring when additional factors no longer make sense. The first factors extracted are likely to exhibit logical consistency, later factors are usually harder to interpret because they are more likely to contain a large amount of random variation.

Factor Analysis Example

Once again, we refer to the UPC survey for an example of factor analysis. In this instance, UPC is interested in determining or identifying those attributes that are viewed in a similar fashion by target respondents. As suggested earlier, this will

TABLE 18.8 Percent of Variation in Original Data Explained by Each Factor

FACTOR	PERCENT OF VARIATION EXPLAINED
1	55.0
2	37.5
3	4.8
4	2.7

permit UPC to identify clusters of benefits that go together in the minds of target customers and to design market communications that logically appeal to one or more of the groups of related benefits. As you may recall, factors identified via factor analysis represent underlying constructs or supervariables that are made up of pieces of the original input variables.

In this instance, we used the *STATISTICA*® principal components procedure to identify these underlying factors or constructs. After experimenting with several different solutions, we settled on the three-factor solution as the "best" based on statistical and interpretability criteria. Factor analysis procedures produce a number of different types of output. One key type of output is the factor loadings. Factor loadings are the simple correlations between the original input variables and the factors or supervariable variables identified in the analysis. The factor loadings for the three-factor solution to this problem are shown in Table 18.9. Information on the proportion of the total variance in the original eight input variables explained by each factor is provided at the bottom of the table. These data show that the three factors explain 72 percent of the variance in the eight original input variables. The following is an interpretation of the factors.

- *Factor one.* Factor one loads heavily or correlates on the following input variables: RANGE, MOBILITY, PLACE, and PRECEIV. We conclude that this factor has something to do with "*staying in touch.*" As a result, we would assign this name to this factor. Obviously, different analysts might look at these results and come up with slightly different names for the factor. However, the fact that this factor loads on the four variables noted here suggests that it has something to do with the ability to reach and be reachable by other people at all times.
- *Factor two.* Factor two correlates or loads on the variables AVGBILL, TELEPHON, and INSTALL. A quick review indicates that all these variables have something to do with cost. Therefore, we might simply call this the "*cost*" factor.
- *Factor three.* Factor three correlates strongly with only one of the original input variables—SOUND. Therefore, we might call it the "*sound quality*" factor.

TABLE 18.9 Factor Loadings (Varimax raw) (pcstext.sta) Extraction: Principal Components

	FACTOR 1	FACTOR 2	FACTOR 3
RANGE	0.70	−0.10	0.39
MOBILITY	0.83	−0.09	0.07
SOUND	0.03	0.03	0.96
PLACE	0.85	0.19	−0.12
PRECEIV	0.91	−0.02	0.02
AVGBILL	−0.04	0.69	0.29
TELEPHON	−0.01	0.83	−0.11
INSTALL	0.06	0.77	0.02
Expl.Var	2.75	1.81	1.18
Prp. Totl	0.34	0.23	0.15

The analysis suggests, for example, that it is logical for consumers to receive information about RANGE, MOBILITY, PLACE, and PRECEIV issues together. This might well provide useful direction for the design of initial market communications.

Perceptual Mapping

Perceptual Mapping Defined

perceptual mapping

Visual representations of consumer perceptions of products, brands, companies, or other objects.

Perceptual mapping involves the production of perceptual maps. Perceptual maps are visual representations of consumer perceptions of a product, brand, company, or any other object in two or more dimensions. Ordinarily, these maps have the extremes of the dimensions on the ends of the *X* and *Y* axes of the map. Examples would be *fast service* and *slow service* at the extremes of the *X* axis and *good value for the money* and *poor value for the money* at the extremes of the *Y* axis. An example is provided in Figure 18.3.

Assuming that *good value* and *fast service* are features that target customers want in restaurants of this type, restaurant B is in the best position (high on *good value* and high on *fast service)* and restaurant D is in the worst position (*poor value* and *slow service).*

Producing Perceptual Maps

A number of different approaches are used to develop perceptual maps, including factor analysis, multidimensional scaling, discriminant analysis, and correspondence analysis. One approach, built around factor analysis, is discussed in the following section.[11]

FIGURE 18.3
Sample Perceptual Map

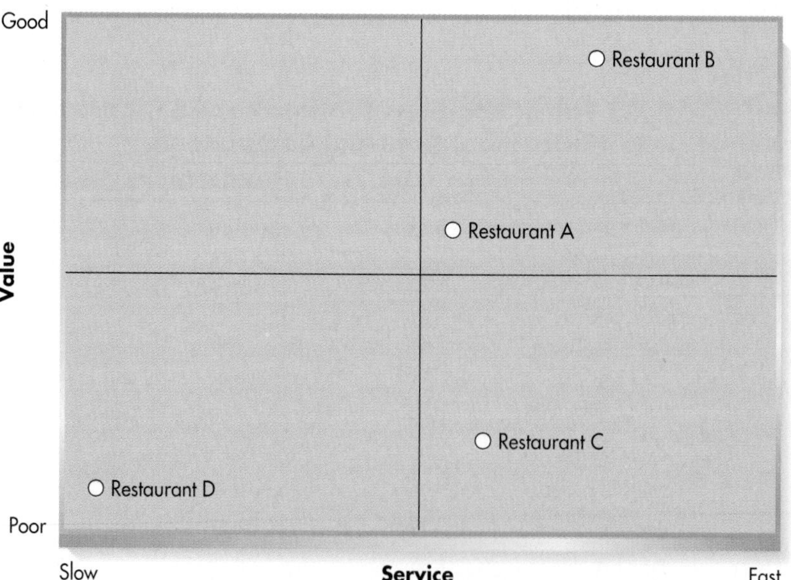

Clockwise from top left: 1995 Cadillac STS, 1995 Lincoln Continental, 1995 Chrysler New Yorker and 1995 BMW 535. Average factor scores for each automobile can be plotted in a perceptual map. Photos courtesy: Cadillac Motor Car Division of General Motors, Ford Motor Company, Chrysler Corporation, and BMW of North America.

In the factor analysis example discussed earlier, the results were based on a survey in which subjects rated only one automobile on a number of characteristics of interest. In many situations, the need is for ratings data on a competitive set of products. For example, each respondent might be asked to rate several different automobiles on a number of different attributes or characteristics.

The basic input for any factor analysis is a correlation matrix. This is a matrix that shows the correlation for each pair of variables. In the case of the problem presented in the previous section, the input would be a 4 by 4 matrix of correlations.

If ratings data were obtained for several automobiles, a separate set of factor scores could be calculated for each brand. A factor score could be calculated for each factor, each individual, each automobile rated. Averaging these factor scores across all individuals or a group of individuals would produce average scores for each product. These average factor scores represent the coordinate positions of the automobiles in a perceptual map.

Table 18.10 shows the average attribute ratings for four automobiles. Factor scores for each automobile, calculated with the scoring equations introduced earlier, are also shown in this table. The factor scores calculated in Table 18.10 can be plotted in a perceptual map like the one shown in Figure 18.4. This perceptual map is based on the average factor scores taken across all subjects. It shows

TABLE 18.10 Factor Scores for Four Automobile Concepts

ATTRIBUTE	CADILLAC SEVILLE	LINCOLN CONTINENTAL	BMW 535	CHRYSLER NEW YORKER
Smooth Ride	4.50	4.17	2.00	1.67
Quiet Ride	3.83	3.50	1.83	1.83
Acceleration	2.33	4.00	4.17	2.17
Handling	1.50	3.83	4.00	1.83
Score 1	3.07	2.87	1.53	1.22
Score 2	1.71	3.17	3.57	1.66

that the Lincoln Continental and the Cadillac Seville are seen as being more luxurious than the BMW 535 or the Chrysler New Yorker, and the Lincoln Continental and the BMW 535 are seen as offering a higher level of performance than the Chrysler New Yorker and the Cadillac Seville.

Conjoint Analysis

Overview of Conjoint Analysis

conjoint analysis
Procedure used to quantify the value that people associate with different levels of product/service attributes.

Conjoint analysis is a popular multivariate procedure used by marketers to determine what features a new product or service should have and how it should be priced. It can be argued that conjoint analysis has become popular because it is a more powerful, more flexible, and often less expensive way to address these important questions than the traditional concept testing approach.[12]

FIGURE 18.4 Perceptual Map—Average Factor Scores for Four Automobile Concepts

Conjoint analysis is not a completely standardized procedure.[13] A typical conjoint analysis application involves a series of steps covering a variety of procedures and is not a single procedure as is true in the case of, for example, regression analysis. Fortunately, conjoint analysis is not difficult to understand. The following section provides a basic idea of what can be accomplished with conjoint analysis.

Conjoint Analysis Example

Put yourself in the position of a product manager for Titelist, a major manufacturer of golf balls. You know from focus groups recently conducted, past research studies of various types, and your own personal experience as a golfer that golfers tend to evaluate golf balls in terms of three important features or attributes:

- Average driving distance
- Average ball life
- Price

The product manager also knows there is a range of feasible possibilities for each of these features or attributes as follows:

- Average driving distance:
  - 10 yards more than golfer's average
  - same as golfer's average
  - 10 yards less than golfer's average
- Average ball life:
  - 54 holes
  - 36 holes
  - 18 holes

Titelist can use conjoint analysis to produce the "best" golf ball taking into account business and consumer concerns. SOURCE: © Ed Bock/The Stock Market.

- Price
  - \$1.25
  - \$1.50
  - \$1.75.

From the perspective of potential purchasers, the "ideal" golf ball would probably have the following characteristics:

- Average driving distance—10 yards above average.
- Average ball life—54 holes.
- Price—\$1.25.

From the manufacturer's perspective, the ideal golf ball from the standpoint of manufacturing cost would probably have the following characteristics:

- Average driving distance—10 yards below average.
- Average ball life—18 holes.
- Price—\$1.75.

This golf ball profile is based on the fact that it costs less to produce a ball that travels a shorter distance and has a shorter life. The eternal marketing dilemma is suggested by the fact that the company would sell a lot of golf balls but go broke producing and selling the ideal ball from the golfer's perspective but sell very few balls if it produced and sold the ideal ball from the manufacturer's perspective. As always, the "best" golf ball from a business perspective lies somewhere between the two extremes.

Traditional Approach A traditional approach to this problem might produce information of the type displayed in Table 18.11. As you can see, the information in Table 18.11 does not provide new insights regarding which ball should be produced. The preferred driving distance is 10 yards above average and the preferred average ball life is 54 holes. These results are obvious without doing any additional research.

Considering Features Conjointly Instead of asking respondents to evaluate features individually, in conjoint analysis we ask them to evaluate features conjointly or in combination. The results of asking two different golfers to rank different combinations of *average driving distance* and *average ball life* conjointly are shown in Tables 18.12 and 18.13.

TABLE 18.11 Traditional Nonconjoint Rankings of Distance and Ball Life Attributes

AVERAGE DRIVING DISTANCE		AVERAGE BALL LIFE	
Rank	*Level*	*Rank*	*Level*
1	275 yards	1	54 holes
2	250 yards	2	36 holes
3	225 yards	3	18 holes

TABLE 18.12 **Conjoint Rankings of Combinations of Distance and Ball Life Considered Together for Golfer No. 1**

	BALL LIFE		
DISTANCE	*54 holes*	*36 holes*	*18 holes*
275 yards	1	2	4
250 yards	3	5	7
225 yards	6	8	9

TABLE 18.13 **Conjoint Rankings of Combinations of Distance and Ball Life Considered Together for Golfer No. 2**

	BALL LIFE		
DISTANCE	*54 holes*	*36 holes*	*18 holes*
275 yards	1	3	6
250 yards	2	5	8
225 yards	4	7	9

As expected, both golfers agree on the most and least preferred balls. However, by analyzing their ranks two through eight, it becomes clear that the first golfer is willing to trade off ball life for distance (accept a shorter ball life for longer distance), while the second golfer is willing to trade off distance for longer ball life (accept shorter distance if she can get longer ball life).

This sort of information is the essence of the important information that conjoint analysis produces that is not provided by traditional analysis. The technique permits marketers to see which attribute or feature potential customers are willing to trade off (accept less of) to obtain more of another attribute or feature. This is the sort of thing that we all do every day in our purchasing decisions (e.g., pay a higher price for a product at a convenience store for the convenience of shopping there).

Estimating Utilities The next step is to calculate a set of values, referred to as utilities or part worths, for the three levels of driving distance and the three levels of ball life in such a way that when they are added together for a particular combination of ball life and driving distance, they predict a particular golfer's rank orders. Such a set of utilities for golfer No. 1 is shown in Table 18.14. As you can readily see, this set of numbers perfectly predicts the original ranks. The relationship between these numbers or utilities is fixed though there is some arbitrariness in their magnitude. In other words, we can multiply or divide these utilities shown in Table 18.14 by any constant and obtain the same results.

The exact procedures for the estimation of these numbers or utilities are beyond the scope of this discussion. They are calculated by using various procedures related to regression, analysis of variance, or linear programming.

The trade-offs that golfer No. 1 is willing to make between *ball life* and *price* are shown in Table 18.15. This information can be used to estimate a set of utilities for *price* that can be added to those for *ball life*, discussed earlier, to predict the rankings for golfer No. 1 shown in Table 18.16.

TABLE 18.14 Ranks (in parentheses) and Combined Metric Utilities for Golfer No. 1—Distance and Ball Life

	BALL LIFE		
DISTANCE	*54 holes* 50	*36 holes* 25	*18 holes* 0
275 yards	(1)	(2)	(4)
100	150	125	100
250 yards	(3)	(5)	(7)
60	110	85	60
225 yards	(6)	(8)	(9)
0	50	25	0

TABLE 18.15 Conjoint Rankings of Combinations of Price and Ball Life Considered Together for Golfer No. 1

	BALL LIFE		
PRICE	*54 holes*	*36 holes*	*18 holes*
$1.25	1	2	4
$1.50	3	5	7
$1.75	6	8	9

TABLE 18.16 Ranks (in parentheses) and Combined Metric Utilities for Golfer No. 1—Price and Ball Life

	BALL LIFE		
PRICE	*54 holes* 50	*36 holes* 25	*18 holes* 0
$1.25	(1)	(2)	(4)
20	70	45	20
$1.50	(3)	(5)	(7)
5	55	30	5
$1.75	(6)	(8)	(9)
0	50	25	0

This step produces a complete set of utilities for all levels of the three features or attributes that successfully capture golfer No. 1's trade-offs. These utilities are shown in Table 18.17.

Simulating Buyer Choice For various technical reasons, the firm might be in a position to produce only two of the 27 golf balls that are possible with the three attributes, each with three levels. The possibilities are shown in Table 18.18. If we take the calculated utilities for golfer No. 1 and apply them to the two golf balls we are able to make, then we get the total utilities for the two balls shown in Figure 18.19. Based on these results, we would expect golfer No. 1 to prefer the ball with the longer life over the one with the greater distance because it has a higher total utility. We need only repeat this process for a representative sample of golfers to estimate potential market shares for the two balls. In addition, the analysis can be extended to cover other golf ball versions.

Summary The three steps discussed here—collecting trade-off data, using that data to estimate buyer preference structures, and predicting choice—are the basis of any conjoint analysis application. Tough the trade-off matrix approach, described here, is simple, useful for explaining conjoint analysis, and effective for dealing with problems with small numbers of attributes, this approach is not widely used today. It is easier and less time-consuming to collect conjoint data by having respondents rank or rate product descriptions on a paper questionnaire or by using PC-based interviewing software that applies certain rules to determine what questions and product profiles to present to each respondent based on his previous answers.

As suggested earlier, there is much more to conjoint analysis than has been discussed here. However, if you understand this simple example, then you understand the basic concepts behind conjoint analysis.

TABLE 18.17 **Complete Set of Estimated Utilities for Golfer No. 1**

DISTANCE		BALL LIFE		PRICE	
Level	*Utility*	*Level*	*Utility*	*Level*	*Utility*
275 yards	100	54 holes	50	$1.25	20
250 yards	60	36 holes	25	$1.50	5
225 yards	0	18 holes	0	$1.75	0

TABLE 18.18 **Ball Profiles for Simulation**

ATTRIBUTE	DISTANCE BALL	LONG-LIFE BALL
Distance	275	250
Life	18	54
Price	$1.50	$1.75

TABLE 18.19 **Estimated Total Utilities for the Two Sample Profiles**

	DISTANCE BALL		LONG-LIFE BALL	
ATTRIBUTE	*Level*	*Utility*	*Level*	*Utility*
Distance	275	100	250	60
Life	18	0	54	50
Price	$1.50	5	$1.75	0
Total utility	105	110		

Limitations

Like many research techniques, conjoint analysis suffers from a certain degree of artificiality. Respondents may be more deliberate in their choice processes in this context than they would be in a real situation. They may also have more product information provided in the survey than would be the case in a real market situation. Finally, it is important to remember that the advertising and promotion of any new product or service can lead to the creation of consumer perceptions that are different from those created via descriptions used in a survey.

Summary

Multivariate analysis refers to a group of statistical procedures that are used to simultaneously analyze multiple measurements on each individual or object being studied. Some of the more popular multivariate techniques include multiple regression analysis, multiple discriminant analysis, factor analysis, cluster analysis, perceptual mapping, and conjoint analysis.

Multiple regression enables the researcher to predict the magnitude of a dependent variable based upon the levels of more than one independent variable. Multiple regression fits a plane to observations in a multidimensional space. One statistic that results from multiple regression analysis is called the *coefficient of determination* or R^2. The value of this statistic ranges from 0 to 1. It provides a measure of the percentage of the variation in the dependent variable that is explained by variation in the independent variables. The b values, or regression coefficients, indicate the effect of the individual independent variable on the dependent variable.

Whereas multiple regression analysis requires the dependent variable to be metric, multiple discriminant analysis uses a dependent variable that is nominal or categorical in nature. Discriminant analysis can be used to determine if statistically significant differences exist between the average discriminant score profiles of two or more groups. The technique can also be used to establish a model for classifying individuals or objects into groups on the basis of their scores on several variables. Finally, discriminant analysis can be used to determine how much of the difference in the average score profiles of the two or more groups are accounted for by each independent variable. The discriminant score, called a Z-score, is derived for each individual or object by means of the discriminant equation.

Cluster analysis enables a researcher to identify subgroups of individuals or objects that are homogeneous within the subgroup yet different from other subgroups. Cluster analysis requires that all independent variables be metric, but there is no specification of a dependent variable. Cluster analysis is an excellent means for operationalizing the concept of market segmentation.

The purpose of factor analysis is to simplify massive amounts of data. The objective is to summarize the information contained in a large number of metric measures such as rating scales into a smaller number of summary measures called *factors*. Again, there is no dependent variable in factor analysis. Factor analysis produces factors, each of which is a weighted composite of a set of related variables. Each measure is weighted according to how much it contributes to variation of each factor. Another important concept is factor loadings. Factor loadings are determined by calculating the correlation coefficient between factor scores and the original input variables. By examining which variables load heavily on a given factor, the researcher can subjectively name that factor.

Perceptual maps can be produced by means of factor analysis, multidimensional scaling, discriminant analysis, or correspondence analysis. The maps provide a visual representation of how brands, products, companies, or other objects are perceived relative to each other on key features such as quality and value.All the approaches require, as input, consumer evaluations or ratings of the objects in question on some set of key characteristics.

Conjoint analysis is a technique that can be used to measure the trade-offs potential buyers make between different product or service offerings available to them on the basis of the features of each product or service. The technique permits the researcher to determine the relative value of each level of each feature. These estimated values are called *part worths* or *utilities* and can be used as a basis for simulating consumer choice.

Key Terms

multivariate analysis
multiple regression analysis
coefficient of determination
regression coefficients
collinearity
causation
multiple discriminant analysis
discriminant score
discriminant coefficient
cluster analysis
factor analysis
factor loadings
perceptual mapping
conjoint analysis

Review and Discussion Questions

1. Distinguish between multiple discriminant analysis and cluster analysis. Give several examples in which each might be used.
2. What purpose does multiple regression serve? Give an example of how it might be used in marketing research. How is the strength of multiple regression measures of association determined?
3. What is a dummy variable? Give an example using a dummy variable.
4. Describe the potential problem of collinearity and multiple regression. How might one test for collinearity? If collinearity is a problem, what should the researcher do?
5. A sales manager examined age data, education level, a personality measure that indicated introvertedness versus extrovertedness, and levels of sales attained by the company's 120-person sales force. The technique used was multiple regression analysis. After analyzing the data, the sales manager said, "It is apparent to me that the higher the level of education and the greater the degree of extrovertedness a salesperson has, the higher will be an individual's level of sales. In other words, a good education and being extroverted cause a person to sell more." Would you agree or disagree with the sales manager's conclusions? Why?
6. The factors produced and the result of the factor loadings from factor analysis are mathematical constructs. It is the task of the researcher to make sense out of what these factors really are. Listed in the following table are four factors produced from a study of cable TV viewers. What label would you put on each of these four factors? Why?

		FACTOR LOADING*
Factor 1	I don't like the way cable TV movie channels repeat the movies over and over.	.79
	The movie channels on cable need to spread their movies out (longer times between repeats)	.75
	I think the cable movie channels just run the same things over and over and over.	.73
	After a while, you've seen all the pay movies, so why keep cable service.	.53
Factor 2	I love to watch love stories.	.76
	I like a TV show that is sensitive and emotional.	.73
	Sometimes I cry when I watch movies on TV.	.65
	I like to watch "made for TV" movies.	.54
Factor 3	I like the religious programs on TV (negative correlation).	−.76
	I don't think TV evangelism is good.	.75
	I do not like religious programs.	.61
Factor 4	I would rather watch movies at home than go to the movies.	.63
	I like cable because you don't have to go out to see the movies.	.55
	I prefer cable TV movies because movie theaters are too expensive.	.46

*Factor loadings can be viewed as weightings that show the correlation between the individual statement(s) and the factors. The size of the factor loadings indicate the relative importance of each statement in making up the factor.

7. The following table is a discriminant analysis that examines data from cable TV users, former users, and people who have never used cable TV and their responses to various attitudinal questions. Looking at the various discriminate weights, what can you say about each of the three groups?

		DISCRIMINANT WEIGHTS		
		Users	*Formers*	*Nevers*
Users				
A19	Easygoing on repairs	−.40		
A18	No repair service	−.34		
A 7	Breakdown complainers	+.30		
A 5	Too many choices	−.27		
A13	Antisports	−.24		
A10	Antireligious	+.17		
Formers				
A4	Burned out on repeats		+.22	
A18	No repair service		+.19	
H12	Card/board game player		+.18	
H 1	High-brow		−.18	
H 3	Party hog		+.15	
A 9	VCR preference		+.16	
Nevers				
A 7	Breakdown complainer			−.29
A19	Easygoing on repairs			+.26
A 5	Too many choices			+.23
A13	Antisports			+.21
A10	Antireligious			−.19

8. The following table shows regression coefficients for two dependent variables. The first dependent variable is consumers' willingness to spend money for cable TV. The independent variables are responses to attitudinal statements. The second dependent variable is persons who would never allow cable TV in their homes. By examining the regression coefficients, what can you say about persons willing to spend money for cable TV and those who would not allow cable TV in their home?

	REGRESSION COEFFICIENTS
Willing to Spend Money for Cable TV	
Easygoing on cable repairs	−3.04
Cable movie watcher	2.81
Comedy watcher	2.73
Early to bed	−2.62
Breakdown complainer	2.25
Lovelorn	2.18
Burned out on repeats	−2.06
Never Allow Cable TV in Home	
Antisports	+1.37
Object to sex	+ .47
Too many choices	+ .88

CASE 18.1

Rose City Nursing Homes

The day when marketing can be overlooked or ignored in nursing home management is long passed. Nursing home administrators who do so will ultimately find themselves either out of business or facing an inadequate return on their investment. The importance of marketing has increased for several reasons: the spiraling cost of operation, the dwindling private market, and the increasing impact of competitors. Consequently, market segmentation research will aid management in identifying markets to be served, decision makers within those markets, decision influentials, and criteria about which nursing homes are evaluated.

The nursing home industry consists of over 23,000 firms, most of which enjoy only moderate levels of market concentration and penetration. Despite the continual replacement of "mom and pop" operations by chains of standardized units, the industry is still composed of a collection of localized markets. The effective market for a nursing home typically extends no more than a radius of 25 miles. Thus, for the most part, competition is characterized by a few nursing homes competing among themselves within a small geographic area. Traditionally, competition has been both price and nonprice oriented, and a primary form of product differentiation has been location.

The Rose City organization is composed of 20 individual nursing homes with headquarters in Lawrence, Kansas. The nursing home units are located in Kansas, Oklahoma, and Nebraska. Top management of the Rose City organization is more enlightened than most and strongly desires to implement the marketing concept within its organization.

Rose City management knows that the decision to place a loved one in a nursing home is often traumatic. The U.S. Department of Human Resources notes that the elderly view a nursing home with fear and hostility. Many of them believe that entry into a home is a prelude to death. The fear is not unfounded, because most persons entering a nursing home, in fact, will die there. The decision makers, in most cases, are the children or relatives of the potential residents. It is ironic that such individuals must select a service for those who are often frightened or hostile about receiving the service.

The time pressure to make a choice among the available nursing homes may be acute. Thus, a decision often must be made in a crisis environment by decision makers with little, if any, prior knowledge of the service. The influential role of "significant others" in the decision-making process is something that Rose City management wants to better understand. These "significant others" would include the judgment of physicians, social workers, hospital discharge planners, and ministers.

A large market research study was undertaken by Rose City to understand decision criteria in selecting a nursing home by four major groups: doctors, discharge planners, retirement home administrators, and responsible parties. Table 18.20 lists the average ratings of the importance of various criteria for each of the four groups. The questions are answered on a three-point scale of *Extremely Important* (3), *Somewhat Important* (2), and *Not Important* (1). To explore the commonalities among the response patterns of the various groups, a factor analysis was performed using the attribute variables as input. The factor loadings are shown in Table 18.21.

TABLE 18.20 Importance Ratings for Various Groups of Interest

	GROUP			
VARIABLE	*Doctors*	*Discharge Planners*	*Retirement Home Administrators*	*Responsible Parties*
Convenience to Home	2.000* (.000)	2.533 (.109)	1.940 (.151)	2.095 (.041)
Food and Special Diets	2.667 (.126)	2.400 (.091)	3.000 (.000)	2.861 (.024)
Outside View for Patient	1.333 (.119)	1.830 (.097)	2.000 (.114)	2.353 (.035)
Communal Dining Area	1.667 (.126)	2.000 (.107)	2.956 (.171)	2.309 (.036)
Medical Programs	2.730 (.118)	2.833 (.069)	2.556 (.166)	2.940 (.017)
Social Programs	2.130 (.091)	2.433 (.114)	2.556 (.166)	2.473 (.036)
Reputation of Center	2.200 (.017)	2.800 (.074)	2.778 (.101)	2.358 (.038)
Cost of Nursing Care	2.333 (.1236)	2.433 (.124)	2.389 (.164)	2.522 (.038)
Programs to Encourage Independence	2.533 (.133)	2.133 (.063)	2.389 (.118)	2.522 (.036)

*NOTE: Values reported are means with the standard errors given below in parentheses.

TABLE 18.21 Factor Analysis

DESCRIPTION	FACTOR 1	FACTOR 2
Convenience to Home	.0349	.7411
Food and Special Diets	.5108	−.1825
Outside View for Patient	.7446	−.0089
Communal Dining Area	.6643	.2201
Medical Programs	.5407	.0130
Social Programs	.6460	.2548
Reputation of Center	−.0640	.7660
Cost of Nursing Care	.2003	.3328
Programs to Encourage Independence	.4858	.1287

1. Describe qualitatively what you feel factors 1 and 2 represent.
2. If you were preparing a marketing presentation for each of the four groups, what factors would you stress with each group individually?
3. It was believed by the researchers that some additional decision-structure insight might be gained by presenting the results of the research in the form of a perceptual map. Examine the perceptual map in Figure 18.5 (on page 630) and explain what, if any, additional insight can be gained.

CASE 18.2

The Maine Power Company

The Maine Power Company had recently experienced difficulties with the Maine public utility commission in getting rate increases. Accordingly, management was concerned about the image of the organization among Maine residents. A decision was made to conduct a market research study that would examine the image of Maine Power. Table 18.22 (on page 631) reveals a factor analysis of the variables used to analyze the company's image.

1. How would you identify the four factors in the table?
2. How might this information help management in understanding and evaluating a semantic differential from which these variables were derived?

CASE 18.3

Acme Car Wash Systems

Acme Car Wash Systems franchises car washes throughout the United States. Currently 872 car washes franchised by Acme are in operation. As part of its service to franchisees, Acme runs a national marketing and advertising program.

Carl Bahn is the senior vice-president in charge of marketing for Acme. He is currently in the process of designing the marketing and advertising campaigns for the upcoming year. Bahn believes that it is time for Acme to take a more careful look at user segments in the market. Based on other analysis, he and his associates at Acme have decided that the upcoming campaign should target the heavy user market. Also, by reference to other research, Acme has defined *heavy car*

FIGURE 18.5
Perceptual Map of Attribute Importances for Four Respondent Groups

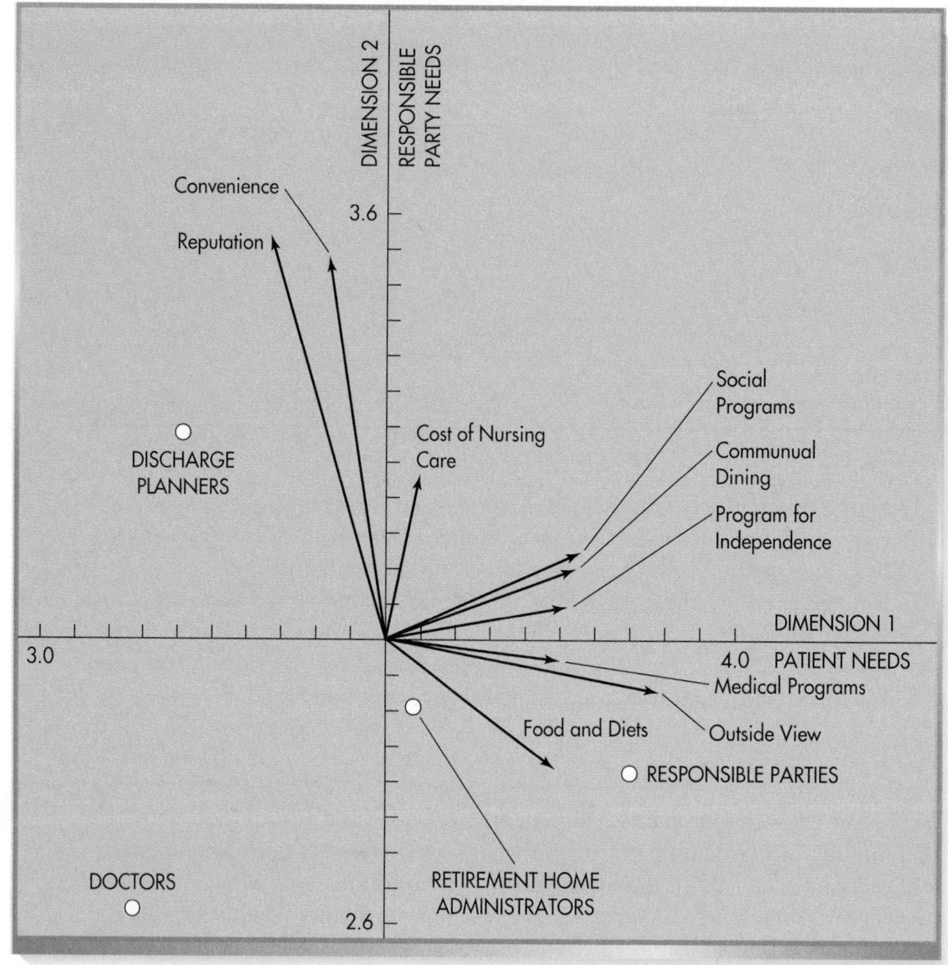

wash users as those individuals who have their cars washed at a car wash facility three or more times per month on average. *Light users* are defined as those who use such a facility less than three times a month but at least four times a year. *Nonusers* are defined as those who use such a facility less than four times per year. Bahn and his associates are currently in the process of attempting to identify those factors that discriminate between heavy and light users. In the first stage of this analysis, they conducted interviews with 50 customers at 100 of their locations for a total of 5,000 interviews. Crosstabulation of the classification variables by frequency of use suggests that four variables may be predictive of usage heaviness: vehicle owner age, annual income of vehicle owner, age of vehicle, and socioeconomic status of vehicle owner (based on an index of socioeconomic variables).

They retained a marketing research firm called Marketing Metrics to do fur-

TABLE 18.22 Maine Power Company's Image—Factor Loadings

Q#	DESCRIPTOR	FAC 1	FAC 2	FAC 3	FAC 4
Q18	Service and Information—Safety	0.82			
Q19	Service and Information—Efficiency	0.79			
Q16	Information from Maine Power—Safety	0.77			
Q15	Involvement of Personnel	0.74			
Q17	Information from Maine Power—Efficiency	0.74			
Q13	Speakers	0.74			
Q14	Safety Demonstrations	0.73			
Q12	Information about Classes	0.69			
Q8	Courtesy of Personnel		0.87		
Q7	Helpfulness of Personnel		0.87		
Q9	Responsiveness		0.75		
Q1	Maine Power Company		0.62		
Q6	Continuity of Service		0.57		
Q2	Overall Job		0.56		
Q3	Rates			0.81	
Q4	Rate Calculation			0.79	
Q5	Sources of Electricity			0.58	
Q11	Information on Bill				0.75
Q10	Way of Presenting Bill				0.78

ther analysis for them. Marketing Metrics evaluated the situation and decided to use multiple discriminant analysis to further analyze the survey results and identify the relative importance of each of the four variables in determining whether a particular individual is a heavy or light user. The firm obtained the following results:

$$Z = .18X_1 + .53X_2 - .49X_3 + .93X_4$$

where

X_1 = age of vehicle owner
X_2 = annual income of vehicle owner
X_3 = age of vehicle
X_4 = socioeconomic status of owner (measured by index where higher score = higher status)

1. What would you tell Bahn about the importance of each of the predictor variables?
2. What recommendations would you make to him about the type of people Acme should target based on its interest in communicating with heavy users?

APPENDIX A

Personal Communications Data Set

Introduction

This appendix includes a description of a data set obtained from an actual survey done for a client in the personal communications business. The client is referred to as JPC. You will also find descriptions of the research objectives, methodology used, and the physical layout of the data set.

Research Objectives

The objectives of the research were as follows:

- To determine the likelihood of purchasing the new wireless personal communications service at various monthly service charges and equipment costs.
- To measure the importance of various wireless communications service attributes.
- To determine expected usage patterns and usage heaviness for the new wireless service.
- To determine usage heaviness of existing residential and long-distance telephone services.
- To measure current expenditures on local and long-distance services.
- To determine, for purposes of market segmentation, the demographic characteristics of likely purchasers and nonpurchasers.

Methodology

A summary description of the methodology employed for this research follows:

- *Sample Size*—200 consumers were surveyed.

- *Qualified Respondents*—Individuals 18 years of age or older from households with annual incomes of $30,000 or more.
- *Sample Area*—Rochester, New York, metropolitan area.
- *Sample Type*—Random sample based on random digit dialing.
- *Sampling Error*—Plus or minus 7.1 percent with 95 percent confidence.
- *Data Collection Method*—All surveying was done by means of central location telephone interviewing using a computer assisted approach. Interviewing was supervised and unobtrusively monitored. All interviewing was conducted from a central location telephone interviewing facility.
- *Interview Length*—Surveys averaged 10 minutes in length.
- Survey Timing—All interviewing was conducted during February 1995.
- *Questionnaire*—A copy of the questionnaire employed for the study follows this methodology summary.

Description of the Data Set

The description of the data set is keyed to the questionnaire that follows. The data are available on diskette in two formats: ASCII and .dbf. The ASCII file has the name PCS.TXT and the other file has the name PSC.dbf. The PSC.dbf file can be directly imported into most statistical packages by using the import feature.

The locations of the numerical representations of the responses to each question for the ASCII file are shown in parentheses throughout the questionnaire. The variable names for the .dbf file are shown in the left margin in capital letters. If you employ the import feature of the statistical package you are using, these names should be correctly imported with the data and will appear at the top of the column containing the data for the particular question in the data set created.

PCS Survey

ADDED

1. Before we begin the next exercise, how much more would you be willing to pay each month to receive Wide Area Service? This is in addition to what you are currently paying for basic telephone service to your home. ENTER THE AMOUNT. TYPE "O" FOR NOTHING, "5" FOR $5, ETC.

   ___________ Additional amount willing to pay to receive Wide Area Service (4-6)

2. Considering the phone service that you currently have, please indicate the probability that you wil purchase one of the new wireless services presented as an **addition** to your existing service.

   Indicate your likelihood to purchase each wireless service on a 0 to 100 scale where 0 means you are not at all likely to purchase that telephone service and 100 means you are extremely likely to purchase that telephone service for your home.

W25100

2a. How likely would you be to purchase the new wireless service if your monthly service charge was $25 and the cost of the telephone was $100?

   ___________ Likelihood to purchase (7-9)

W500

2b. How likely would you be to purchase the new wireless service if your monthly service charge was $50 and the cost of the telephone was $0?

   ___________ Likelihood to purchase (10-12)

3. Now I would like for you to rate several attributes on their level of importance to you when selecting telephone service. For each factor, use a 9-point scale where 9 means the attribute is **"very important"** and 1 means the factor is **"very unimportant"** to you when selecting local telephone service. How important is . . . **READ LIST AND ROTATE**

	ATTRIBUTES	VI								VU	
RANGE	Range of coverage	9	8	7	6	5	4	3	2	1	(13)
MOBILITY	Mobility	9	8	7	6	5	4	3	2	1	(14)
SOUND	Sound Quality (Sound and Static)	9	8	7	6	5	4	3	2	1	(15)
PLACE	Ability to Place Calls When Away from Home	9	8	7	6	5	4	3	2	1	(16)
PRECEIV	Ability to Place and Receive Calls When Away from Home	9	8	7	6	5	4	3	2	1	(17)
AVGBILL	Average Monthly Telephone Bill	9	8	7	6	5	4	3	2	1	(18)
TELEPHON	Price of Telephone Equipment	9	8	7	6	5	4	3	2	1	(19)
INSTALL	Installation / Activation Charges	9	8	7	6	5	4	3	2	1	(20)

CAR

4. If you purchased Wide Area Service, what percentage of your calls (made and received) on the wireless service would be from your car? **ENTER A PERCENTAGE FROM 0 TO 100**

   ___________ Percentage of wireless calls from your call (21-23)

MET

5. What percentage of calls using Wide Area Service would be within the Washington/Baltimore/Annapolis metropolitan area?

   ___________ Percentage of wireless calls within metropolitan area (24-26)

HOME

6. And what percentage of your wireless calls would be made in and around your home or neighborhood?

   ___________ Percentage of wireless calls in and around the home (27–29)

And now, I have just a few questions concerning telephone usage in your household.

CELL

7. Do you own or use a cellular phone?

   (30)
   1 YES
   2 NO

MAKES

8. Considering the local telephone calls of all members of your household for a **typical day,** how many calls would you say your household MAKES in a typical day?

   ___________ Number of calls MADE by household per day (31–32)

RECV

9. How many calls would you say your household receives in a typical day?

   ___________ Number of calls RECEIVED by household per day (33-34)

LMAKE

10. Now considering the number of long-distance calls of all members of your household for a **typical week,** how many long-distance calls would you say your household MAKES in a typical week?

    ___________ Number of long-distance calls MADE by household per week (35–36)

LRECV

11. How many long-distance calls would you say your household receives in a typical week?

    ___________ Number of long-distance calls RECEIVED by household per week (37–38)

MONTHLY

12. How much is your average monthly telephone bill, including **local and long-distance charges?**

    ___________ Average monthly telephone bill (39–41)

PAYCALL

13. How often do you use a pay telephone for personal calls in a typical month?

    ___________ Number of pay telephone call per mo. (42–43)

GENDER 14. INDICATE GENDER BY OBSERVATION

(44)
1 MALE
2 FEMALE

MARRIED 15. Are you married?

(45)
1 YES
2 NO
3 RF

AGE 16. Which of the following categories includes your age?

(46)
1 18–24
2 25–34
3 35–44
4 45–54
5 55–64
6 65 and older
7 RF

ADULTS 17. How many adults age 18 and over are currently living in your household including yourself?

__________ Number of adults (47)

CHILDREN 18. Do you have any children age 18 and under currently living in your household?

(48)
1 YES
2 NO
3 RF

INCOME 19. Which of the following categories includes the total annual income of all members of your household before taxes?

(49)
1 Less than $35,000
2 $35,000 to $49,999
3 $50,000 to $74,999
4 $75,000 or more
5 DK/RF

Thanks for participating.

Name ____________________ Telephone __________

Address ______________________________

Interviewer # __________ Length of interview ____________________

PART IV

ETHICAL DILEMMA

General Electric's Americom Satellite Division

Barry Cook, director of marketing research for the NBC division of General Electric, was asked to conduct a market research study to provide a quantitative estimate of the market potential of a direct broadcast satellite business for GE's Americom satellite division, using Ku-band transmissions. (Ku band uses much higher frequencies than C band and requires a three-foot diameter dish-shaped antenna rather than the eight- to ten-foot dish for C band). This technology could be used as either an adjunct to cable or an alternative to cable, where subscribers throughout the United States could acquire the three-foot receiving dish and decoder, which would allow them to receive a number of channels of television programming. Several programming and pricing options were under consideration. A study had already been conducted using conjoint analysis to test a vast number of programming packages at various pricing options—and this study yielded estimates of high penetration rates for some of the packages (15 percent to 20 percent adoption).

This venture involved a large long-term investment, and management asked NBC's research department to design a study that would provide a valid estimate of the number of subscribers such a service would achieve. Management did not believe the conjoint study's estimates, and it wanted the researchers to conduct a study that it could believe.

Initially, Barry had two concerns: was it possible to do a study that produced estimates that he would believe of a future market for a nonexistent product? And even if he believed it, why should management believe it? The researchers who had conducted the conjoint analysis believed in what they were doing, but management doubted them.

To do a believable study, the method had to be based on clear reasoning and direct evidence. The logic of the method was shared with management before doing the study, and it was committed to a belief in the outcome before the study was even done.

But how can you estimate the market potential for a product that would not be available for years? The last refuge of a market researcher is consumer opinion. However, consumer opinion could be misused in so many ways in the service of predicting a market. Barry felt a lot more confident about measuring consumer *behavior* to predict consumer behavior than measuring consumer *opinion* to predict consumer behavior. How could he test consumer behavior relative to a product that does not exist?

You can describe the three-foot satellite dish to people and describe what kind of programming is available on the channels it receives—and people should be able to imagine what the product is. You can also describe the price to them, and people can certainly imagine a multi-hundred-dollar price tag. If you ask them if that dish is worth the money (plus the monthly charge for the decoder box), a certain percentage of people are going to say it is worth the money and the balance are not. Is this the percentage of people who will buy it?

When you ask consumers to help you predict a market for a product or service, they tell you what they think the market is going to be, or what they think other people will do, or what they think they will do. None of these pieces of information give you a market estimate. What you need to know is what consumers will actually do. Do not ask them to help predict a market; ask them to be a market.

What Barry really wanted to do was to test-market the dish and service. In a test market, you are not asking people to play what-if. You are telling them what, and they are telling you if. The percent who say yes *are* willing to spend their money on the product. That was the number GE needed to know. But GE did not have the dish and service yet, so Barry could not test-market it. Also, he needed to make an estimate for a very large geographical universe: those parts of the continental United States that are covered by a strong enough satellite signal for the three-foot dish to work (about 85 percent of the country). The cost of installing and servicing the dishes across the entire country is not a test market, it is the market. And GE wanted to test about ten options for pricing and programming. So those constraints pointed to a simulated test market with a telephone sampling frame.

What could be simulated? Telemarketing the sign-ups for this service, that is what. Here is the concept: a random sample of people throughout the potential coverage area of the satellite signal get a telephone call in which the interviewer gives them a sales pitch for the satellite dish, the channels it receives, what it costs, and how they could finance it. Then the interviewer pops the question: "Can we count on you to buy it?" The percentage of people who say "yes" is an estimate of the percentage of people who would say "yes" if the product were available today and it were marketed this way. That is not quite the same as the percentage of people who would say "yes" three years from now, especially if some unforeseen technology were also available to them that met similar needs.

So the approach is simulated test marketing through telemarketing. To tighten the estimate, Barry needed to find out who were the qualified prospects. Therefore, he also planned to collect qualification data from the respondents who said they would sign up in the interview. It was important to identify respondents who say yes but who already own the big dishes—because there may be a separate market for converters for big dishes. Also, he wanted to disqualify those with very low income—he did not expect many of them to say "yes." Barry also disqualified people who lived in apartments where the landlord would not let them put a TV aerial on the roof.

One more point: it is important to distinguish between people who can get cable and those who live in what are called nonpassed areas—places where cable is not available. The prime market for this device is probably in nonpassed areas, but no one had a list of people in nonpassed areas. Cable is available in 90 percent of the country, but there are little pockets where cable is not available. Barry wanted to test different options in passed versus nonpassed areas, so he needed to oversample nonpassed areas. He planned to start the interview with a screening question to identify people who could not get cable even if they wanted to, but it was going to be very expensive to screen for the required number of interviews in nonpassed areas given the low incidence. Barry decided to use a clustering approach rather than pure RDD: when he found a person who claimed to live in a nonpassed area, he made many more dialings in the same telephone exchange (with four digit random suffixes) and found that he could triple the yield of nonpassed homes over pure RDD using this enrichment technique.

So if GE does a research interview that sounds like a telemarketing sales pitch—but is really a research interview because nothing is being sold at the time, then Barry would get what he needs—real consumer behavior because respondents think they are buying when they answer the "Can we count on you to buy it" question.

The researchers start off by telling them that they are not selling anything but are doing a research study. This is the truth, although it happens to be the same wording that telemarketers use when they engage in deceptive practices. The researcher then asks them a couple of questions about their cable status and the availability of cable in their neighborhood if they are nonsubscribers. Then the interviewers launch into a big pitch about how wonderful this new dish is and all the great things they can receive on it. The interviewers say it costs only *X* hundred dollars to purchase the dish plus *Y* tens of dollars a month for the decoder box. Then the respondents are asked, "When this dish and service become available in your neighborhood, can we count on you to buy it?" At this point, respondents are placed in a situation that they are likely to perceive as a real purchase decision. The percent who say "yes" is the estimate of market penetration (less the disqualifications noted previously for low income, large dish ownership, and inability to install a dish).

Notice that the researcher is not asking them how likely they think they would be to purchase (definitely purchase, probably purchase, probably not purchase, or definitely not purchase). When you ask that kind of question, you then have to apply weights to the obtained percentages to discount some of the intended purchasers because this method produces estimates that past experience has shown to be too high. The past experience is with the question, not with the particular product or service. Do researchers really believe that a fixed percentage of people who hold an attitude will act on it—no matter what the attitude? And when you analyze the characteristics of those who hold the attitude, most of whom will not exhibit the behavior of interest, what are you learning about the characteristics of those who will exhibit the behavior? Certainly, you have a larger sample size of intended purchasers than purchasers, so you can attribute greater statistical significance to the analyses you do on the wrong people. The fundamental problem is that you have not asked people to make a purchase decision, you have asked them to sing the praises of your concept. Then, without the use of data from the market research, you, the market researcher, through your expertise alone, decide how many of the people who are gushing over the concept would actually purchase and how many of the people who are mildly interested in it will actually purchase. Why ask the wrong question and guess what percentage of the answer to believe, when you could have the information GE needs simply by asking the right question in the right context?

Recall that the key here was to produce an estimate that management could believe. To the extent that the respondents in the study believed that they were purchasing the dish, the clients for the study could believe the estimates of potential market.*

*This case was developed from Barry Cook, "Simulation of Purchase Decisions: Is It Unethical to Be Too Realistic?" *CASRO Journal* (1991), pp. 105–12.

1. Was Barry's research methodology unethical? Remember, respondents were told at the outset that it was not a sales call.
2. A pretest of twenty interviews was completed; sixteen out of the twenty people thought that they were making a commitment to purchase the dish. Does this information change your feelings about the ethical nature of the research?
3. Do you think that it is important to tell the respondents at the end of the interview that they didn't purchase anything and they could not have purchased anything because it is a research study? Why or why not?

PART V

Market Research in Action

CHAPTER 19

Communicating the Research Results

LEARNING OBJECTIVES

1. To gain an understanding of barriers to communication.
2. To become aware of the primary roles of a research report.
3. To understand how to organize a research report.
4. To learn how to prepare a research report.
5. To review pitfalls in marketing research reports.
6. To become acquainted with evaluating report drafts.
7. To learn about oral presentations.
8. To understand the effective use and communication of marketing research information.

With a core market of radiology departments in approximately 7,500 hospitals and clinics in the United States, GE Medical Systems Group has a small customer base relative to many industries. Soliciting the opinions of these customers who have made six- (or even seven-) figure investments in GE diagnostic imaging equipment is a high priority for GE Medical Systems.

Milwaukee-based GE Medical, a business group of the General Electric Co., uses two types of mailed surveys to encourage customers to voice their opinions. The first survey is called the postinstallation tracking study, which asks for customers' opinion of the sales process, preinstallation, delivery, installation, training, and product performance for their recent purchase. The second survey is the sales and service tracking study, which asks customers to evaluate GE Medical's total account management and service delivery performance. This survey is mailed to every GE medical customer annually.

The surveys achieved their initial goal—obtaining customer feedback—but GE Medical did not have an ongoing process to resolve the issues the surveys uncovered. In late 1991, GE Medical created a customer satisfaction department for this purpose, with the additional mission of raising overall customer satisfaction. The new department took on responsibility for the surveys.

Study results were distilled a variety of ways. Since the findings addressed the performance of several different departments at GE Medical, Kennedy Research tailored a potpourri of written reports to the specific needs of various departments, including a monthly one-page summary of key findings from each individual survey and a quarterly overview of the top five sources of satisfaction. "But as the study matured, it mushroomed in terms of the type of information we wanted from it," Dennis Cook, GE Medical customer satisfaction process manager, noted. "Each department was interested in a different aspect of the study, which meant that reporting the results became a fairly complicated process."[1] ■

What is the role of the research report? How can marketing researchers communicate more effectively? What constitutes a "good" report? What pitfalls should be avoided in writing a research report? We will address these questions in this chapter.

It should almost go without saying that no matter how appropriate the research design, how proper the statistical analyses, how representative the sample, how carefully worded the questionnaire, how stringent the quality control checks for field collection of the data, or how well matched the research was to the original research objectives, everything will be for naught if the researcher cannot communicate with the decision makers. Chapter 19 begins with a discussion of the communication process. Next, the roles of the research report are presented. From here, the chapter delves into the organization of the report and points out how findings are interpreted into conclusions and how conclusions are then formulated into recommendations. Next, the chapter turns to the actual writing of the report. Because oral presentations are common in marketing research, the chapter includes discussion of this aspect of reporting the results. We conclude with suggestions for getting managers to use the research recommendations.

Effective Communication

communication
The result of any action, physical, written, or verbal, that conveys meanings between two individuals.

Good **communication** is the result of any action, physical, written, or verbal, that conveys accurate meanings between two individuals. The essence of communication is shared meaning and mutual understanding. In other words, communication results in two or more individuals sharing the meaning of some concept such as an action, a word, or a symbol.

Perfect communication probably never occurs. Nonetheless, it is the goal of every marketing researcher writing a research report to present the information in as lucid a manner as possible. A number of factors have been identified to be deterrents or barriers to communication. Most of these factors are relevant to the marketing researcher attempting to communicate the research results to the decision makers.

Noise

noise
Anything that interferes with the audience receiving a message.

In communication theory, anything that interferes with the audience receiving a message is considered **noise.** This noise can be physical such as other people talking, a machine operating in the background, coughing, shuffling of the feet, or any other physical distraction that can be identified. Noise also can be of a psychological origin such as a distracting thought, some emotional turmoil in the mind of the receiver, or even a faulty mental process. The executive who listens to a marketing research presentation but is thinking about other company problems, such as how to improve production efficiency, is experiencing noise that interferes with the communication process.

Attention Span

attention span
The length of time a particular individual will concentrate on a particular subject at a particular time.

Every person has a limited **attention span.** Each individual's attention span is different, and it may be long or short, depending upon the person's interest or ego involvement with the topic, physical state, and mental capabilities. Marketing researchers constantly are encountering problems with the attention span of the decision makers in attempts to communicate the results of research. The marketing researcher is accustomed to working with large data sets, leafing through pages and pages of computer output, and compiling large tabular presentations of information. In other words, the marketing researcher has a very long attention span for a particular research study. However, the decision maker is much more accustomed to short periods of intense attention on a problem. Consequently, although the researcher must provide the findings, summaries, and whatever else are included in the research report, she constantly fights the battle of holding or restimulating the attention of the reader or listener.

Selective Perception

Research report writers must always be cognizant of **selective perception.** Managers and other users of research data tend to "see what they want to see." A new product manager may rejoice over a high rate of initial trial on a test market and ignore the low repurchase rate. Or, a manager may make an equivocal statement regarding a research project but ignore sampling limitations that greatly hamper the generalizability of the results. Subconsciously, individuals also filter out messages of low interest or for which they have preconceived notions. There is a human tendency to avoid opposing, disagreeable, and dissonant information. Alternatively, there exists a tendency to select specific pieces of information that supports a preconceived opinion or lend credence to a particular argument while ignoring or discounting information that does not support it.

selective perception
The ability of the listener or reader to filter out some information for conscious or subconscious reasons.

How does the marketing researcher overcome barriers of selective perception, attention span, and noise? Unfortunately, there are no easy answers to this question. There is no guaranteed way or combination of ways to effect complete and perfect communication. But, a number of guidelines can help overcome various parts of these communication barriers. These will be discussed after we describe the research report.

The Research Report

The marketing research report has three primary roles: to communicate findings, to serve as a reference document, and to provide credibility for the work accomplished.

1. *The marketing research report must communicate the study's specifics.* The marketing research report has the critical function of containing a complete and accurate description of the relevant findings of the marketing research project undertaken. That is, it must be detailed and communicate to the reader the following items:

   - The research objectives
   - Central background information
   - An overview of the research methods used
   - The findings displayed in tabular or visual format
   - Summary of the findings

- Conclusions
- Recommendations

2. *The research report must act as a reference document.* Once the research report has been duplicated and distributed to the relevant decision makers, it begins to live a life of its own. From that point on it serves as a valuable reference document. Most studies cover several objectives and contain a significant amount of information. Normally, it is impossible for a decision maker to retain this information in his memory for any length of time. Consequently, the marketing researcher will find that decision makers and others, perhaps those performing a secondary information search, will turn back to the report, rereading it to reacquaint themselves with the findings of the study. The findings may even serve as a baseline for a follow-up study. For example, a company's image may be measured yearly and changes in the strengths and weakness of the image can be examined by the decision makers.
3. *The research report must build and sustain the credibility of the study.* This third and final role of the marketing research report cannot be overemphasized. The marketing research report must communicate to the reader the degree of care and quality control that went into the marketing research project. The attention span and selective perception barriers operate against the marketing researcher in his capacity. In fact, it is not unusual for a manager to completely skip over the description of the research method and go directly to the findings, conclusions, or recommendations. Because this may be the case, the marketing researcher will find that the credibility of the study is greatly affected by the physical appearance of the research report itself. In other words, items such as typographical errors, poorly documented tables or figures, inconsistent margins, heading arrangements, or even the cover and binding of the report will affect the reader's evaluation of the credibility of the study. Such a situation is unfortunate, but it is a reality. The perceived quality of the research report by managers is a primary determinant of whether the managers will use the research findings.[2]

Organizing the Research Report

Physical Organization of the Report

Sometimes corporate policy or other factors may dictate the precise format of the research report. Nonetheless, every research report should have certain topics regardless of its specific format or physical appearance. The report must be structured and written in a manner that communicates timely, relevant, and succinct information to management decision makers. An important premise to recall in report writing is that people in middle and upper management often have extreme demands on their time. To help key people read the report, the writer must avoid jargon and structure the data presentation properly. The authors recommend that the following basic components be included:

1. Table of Contents
2. Objectives of the Research
3. Concise Statement of the Methodology
4. Brief Summary of the Findings
5. Conclusions and Recommendations

(Items 2–5: Executive Summary)

6. Detailed Introduction
7. Detailed Analysis and Findings
8. Detailed Conclusions
9. Detailed Methodology
10. Limitations
11. Appendices (if necessary)

Because a number of managers may be reading the report (many of whom were not present during the research request stage or the oral presentation), an executive summary is needed. The **executive summary** explains why and how the research was undertaken, what was found and what it means, and what action, if any, management should undertake. It is important to begin the summary with a statement of objectives. Why did the company spend the time and money and what was it trying to accomplish? This section places the remainder of the report in the proper perspective. It also allows management to review the findings and recommendations with a common frame of reference—the problem statement.

executive summary
The portion of a research report that explains why the research was done, what was found and what those findings mean, and what action, if any, management should undertake.

The objectives should be as explicit as possible, yet confined to one or two pages at most. The summary of findings also should be confined to one or two pages. Again, if the researcher wants management to read the work, the essential elements of the report (items 2–5) must be kept short. The conclusions and recommendations also should remain as brief as possible. Depending on circumstances, this section may run a few pages longer than the other essential elements. Excerpts from an actual executive summary are shown in the appendix to this chapter.

Obviously some managers, such as product managers, the director of marketing research, or others, want more information about the research. They will delve into the body of the report to examine the logic of the conclusions, to obtain a better understanding of key findings, to find nuances overlooked by the report writer, and to accept or reject the recommendations. The body of the report is written for these readers. But, it should not be a foregone conclusion that the detailed findings section of the report must be dull and boring. Proper use of summary tables and visual aids such as pie charts, bar graphs, and other tools will illustrate key points and provide additional clarity to the data. In the past, graphic displays of data were time-consuming and expensive to prepare. Personal computers and graphics software packages have solved this problem by providing a quick and low-cost means of preparing graphics of all types, from simple bar charts in black and white to sophisticated full-color graphics.

The appendix should be reserved for tables not included in the detailed findings section, a sample questionnaire, maps, and other material that is too complex, too specialized, or not directly relevant to the main body of the report. A suggested format for the research report is shown in Table 19.1.

Richard Kitaeff, manager of Marketing Research and Quality Measurements for AT&T, claims it is crucial that a transmittal letter addressed to the client accompany each report. The transmittal letter should include a short summary of the findings (sort of a highlight of the highlights) and the report's key recommendations. Often, Kitaeff notes, "that even if the report is never read by the decision makers—the transmittal letter will be."[3]

TABLE 19.1 Review of Windows Presentation Packages

- *Astound 1.5* Of the four Windows presentation packages reviewed, Astound is the least widely used. This is unfortunate because it has many outstanding features. Astound is particularly strong in areas related to adding animation and 3D features to charts. Astound is clearly the best of the packages in regard to its ability to control the perspective and rotation of 3D charts. It also permits the user to record and even edit audio narration and to add video clips to a presentation. If Astound has a weakness, it is in the area of working with text. Of the four packages, it is the most limited in regard to creating and editing bullet charts and text.
- *Freelance Graphics 2.1* This package is provided by Lotus Development Corporation. It can be purchased by itself or packaged with other Lotus programs (AmiPro, 123 and Organizer) in the Lotus SmartSuite. It is perhaps the easiest to use of the four packages and comes with more than 60 pre-designed templates for presentations. It is very strong in terms of creating bullet and other types of text charts and has strong organizational features. The built-in slide sorter displays slides as thumbnails and permits the user to move pages around by clicking and dragging, delete pages, and insert pages. Within the SmartSuite, this package permits you to include Freelance presentations in eMail messages and word processor documents. The package also includes an outliner and produces speakers notes and audience handouts if requested by the user.
- *Harvard Graphics 3.0* The Windows version of this venerable package from Software Publishing corrects many of the problems associated with difficulty of use found in older DOS versions of the program. The program uses a very simple step-by-step approach to creating presentations and includes standardized templates and other features that can be applied to an entire presentation. It also offers an outliner and a slide sorter.
- *PowerPoint 4.0* According to recent figures, this is the leading selling presentation package. It is included in the very popular Microsoft Office Suite of programs. It is comparable to Freelance in its ability to handle text and offers more than 100 chart types, a dramatic increase from previous versions. Of particular interests, the AutoContent Wizard asks the user a series of questions and prepares an outline of the presentation based on the answers given. Like Freelance, it also produces speaker and audience notes.

Presentation Software

presentation software

Personal computer software that provides easy-to-use platforms for creating effective reports and presentations.

Presentation software for personal computers is rapidly changing the nature of presentations and reports. The most recent Windows versions of the most popular and highly rated packages—Microsoft PowerPoint, Lotus Freelance Graphics, Harvard Graphics, and Astound—all provide easy-to-use platforms for creating reports and presentations that are more interesting, compelling, and effective than was possible just a few years ago. Descriptions of these packages are provided in Table 19.2. All these packages permit the user to:

- Create bullet charts using various font styles and sizes with bold, italicized and underlined text easily implemented by the user.
- Easily create dozens of different types of graphs and, with a few mouse clicks, experiment with different types of graphs (e.g., pie, bar, line, 3-D effects, etc.) that might be used to display a particular research finding.
- Apply various special effects, full-motion video, and sound when moving from page to page in an electronic presentation. It is becoming increasingly common for presentations to be presented using a personal computer attached to a color projection panel or a very large multisync monitor. The presenter con-

TABLE 19.2 Contents of Marketing Research Report

Title page

1. Title
2. Client
3. Research company
4. Date

Table of Contents

1. Section titles and subheadings with page numbers
2. Table of tables; titles and pages
3. Table of figures; titles and pages
4. Appendices; titles and pages

Executive Summary

1. Concise statement of objectives
2. Concise statement of methodoloy
3. Concise statement of major finding(s)
4. Concise statement of conclusions and recommendations
5. Other pertinent information as required (e.g., special techniques, limitations, or background information)

Introduction

1. Background of the research undertaken
2. People involved and positions held
3. Acknowledgments

Analysis and Findings

1. Types of analysis described in general terms
2. Tables and figures
3. Explanatory text

Conclusions and Recommendations

Research methodology

1. Type of study
2. Intent of study
3. Definition of population
4. Sample design and technique
   a. Definition of sampled unit
   b. Type of design (probability versus nonprobability; specific)
5. Data collection method (e.g., telephone, personal, mail, self-administered)
6. Questionnaire
   a. General description
   b. Discussion of "special" types of questions used
7. Special problems or considerations

Limitations

1. Sample size limitations
2. Sample selection limitations
3. Other limitations (frame error, timing, analysis, etc.)

Appendices

1. Questionnaire
2. Technical appendix; e.g., detailed explanation of a statistical tool such as conjoint analysis
3. Other appendices as necessary; e.g., a map of the area in which the survey took place

trols the presentation using a mouse and the software can be programmed to use various fades between slides in the presentation and to include video (e.g., focus group comments) and sound clips at various points in the presentation.

These software packages were developed for the purpose of constructing and making personal presentations. However, they have begun to affect the way that written reports are viewed and prepared. Increasingly, written reports are more like presentations than old-style written reports. In particular, the emerging style for reports:

- Minimizes the use of words.
- Feeds information to clients in what might be termed "sound bites."
- Makes extensive use of bullet charts.
- Makes extensive use of graphic presentation of results.

Examples of pages out of reports prepared using presentation software are provided in Figures 19.1 through 19.9.

Interpreting the Findings and Formulating Recommendations

Among the greatest difficulties faced by individuals who are writing a research report for the first time occurs in the interpretation of the findings to arrive at conclusions and using these conclusions to formulate recommendations. This difficulty is completely understandable given that the marketing researcher is often inundated with mounds of computer printouts, stacks of questionnaires, bundles of respondent contact and recontact sheets, and a scratch pad full of notes on the project. There is, however, a systematic method that the researcher can follow to draw conclusions. The overall guide comes from the research objectives stated very early in the marketing research process. These research objectives are stated as specifically as possible and perhaps even with an explicit priority rank for each objective. Also, the questionnaire was designed to touch facets of the objectives, but the specific bits of information for any one objective were spread across the questionnaire. The computer printouts often contain information in a statistical order rather than in the order in which managers will use the data. Consequently, the researcher's first task is to pull together all the printouts

FIGURE 19.1
Sample Bullet Chart

Executive Summary

- **Visit Information:**
  - **Overall.** 45.9% say they have visited a casino in the last 6 months.
  - **By market.** Visit rate is highest from Tampa (23.2%) and lowest from Panama City (4.1%).
  - **By demographics.** Those 54 and younger more likely to have visited than those 55+. Positive relationship with income. Those in $71K+ bracket most likely to have visited.
  - **No. of visits.** The average is just over 1.1 times across markets. Frequency highest for Miami (6.1) and lowest for Saint Petersburg (.39).

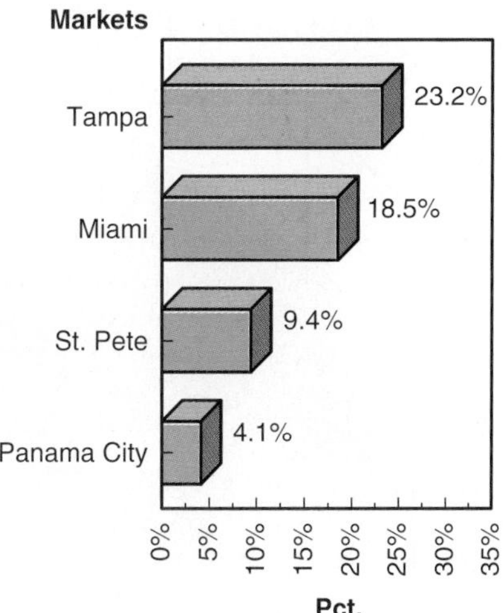

FIGURE 19.2
Text and 3-D Horizontal Bar Chart

and results pertaining to each of the various objectives. By focusing attention on the objectives one at a time, a system will evolve.

For example, assume that Burger King is considering its breakfast menu. An objective of its breakfast research study is "to determine the feasibility of adding (a) bagels and cream cheese, (b) a western omelette, or (c) french toast." All crosstabulations and one-dimensional tables referring to these food items should be brought together. Generally, the researcher first examines the one-dimensional tables to get the overall picture; that is, which of the three breakfast items was most preferred. Next, crosstabulations are analyzed to obtain a better

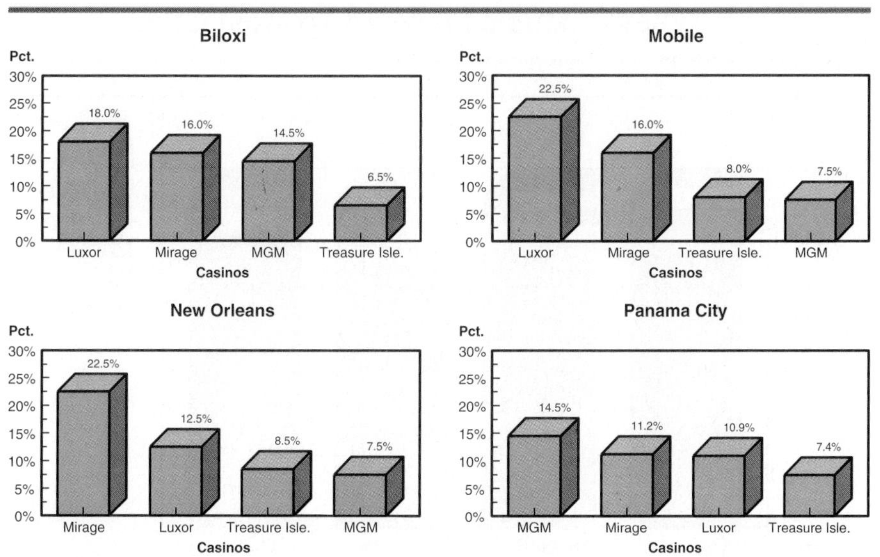

FIGURE 19.3
Multiple 3-D Bar Charts on Single Page

FIGURE 19.4
Area Chart for Summary Measures

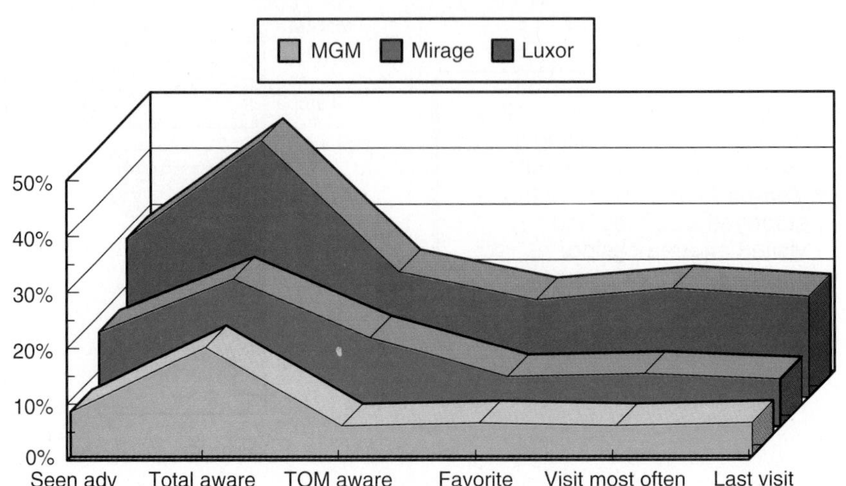

understanding of the overall data; that is, which age group was most likely to prefer french toast.

Conclusions are generalizations that answer the questions raised by the research objectives or otherwise satisfy the objectives. These conclusions are derived through the process of induction, which is the process of generalizing from small pieces of information. The researcher should try to combine the information and to paraphrase it in a few descriptive statements that generalize the results. In short, the conclusion or generalization would be a statement or series of statements that would communicate the results of the study to the reader but would not necessarily indicate the numbers derived from the statistical analysis.

FIGURE 19.5
Stacked Bar Chart with 3-D Effect

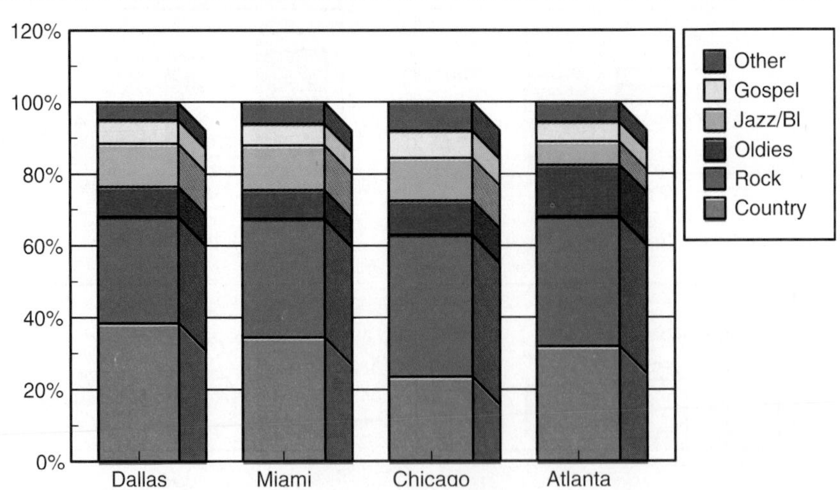

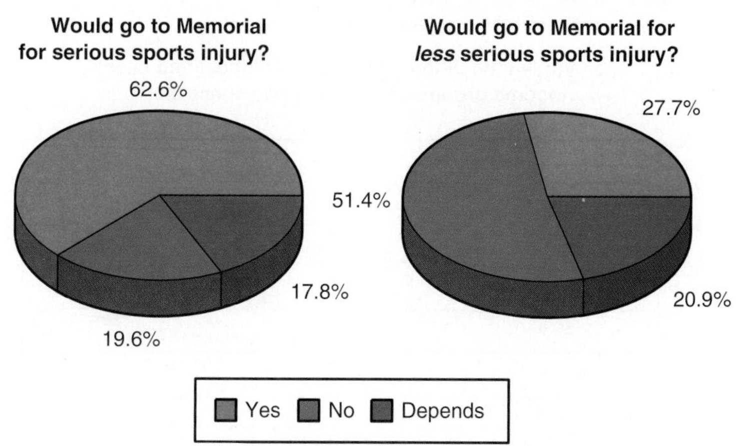

FIGURE 19.6
Pie Charts with 3-D Effect

Recommendations are gained from the process of deduction. The marketing researcher takes the conclusions to be specific areas of application for marketing strategy or tactics. A recommendation normally should focus on how the client can gain a differential advantage. A differential advantage is the true benefit offered by a potential marketing mix that the target market cannot obtain anywhere else, such as United Airlines having exclusive U.S. carrier landing rights at a foreign airport.

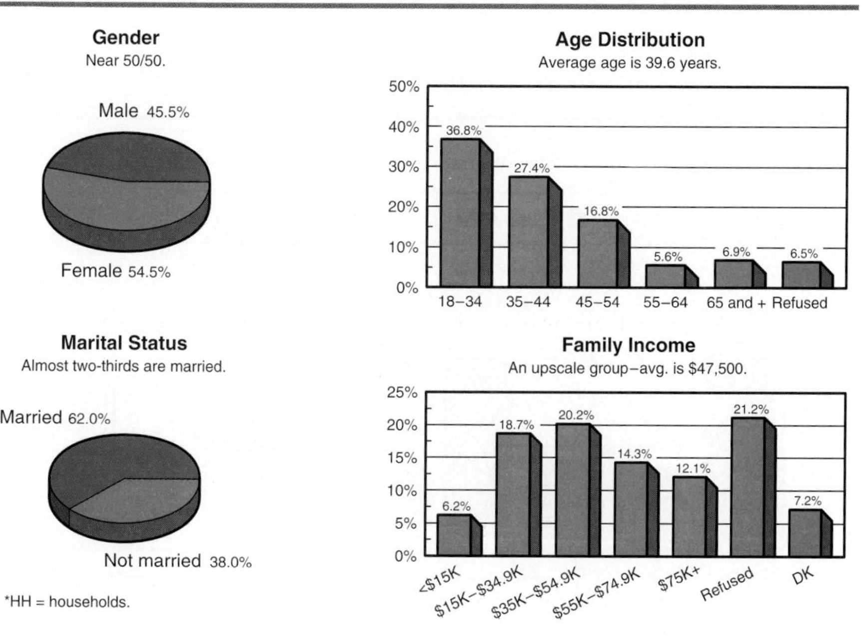

FIGURE 19.7
Mixing Pie and Bar Charts

FIGURE 19.8

Line Chart with Table Underneath

Likelihood to Choose Health Club Concepts at Various Membership Fee/Monthly Dues Levels by Income
(percent "very" or "somewhat" likely)

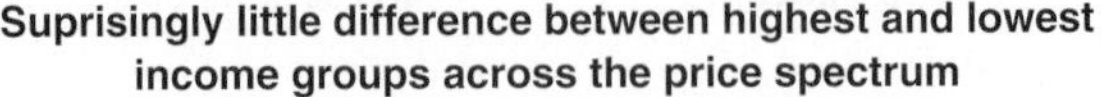

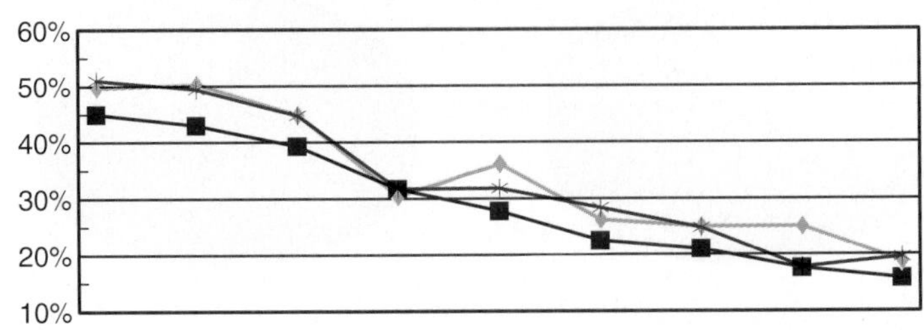

Income	$0/$5	$0/$10	$0/$15	$25/$5	$25/$10	$25/$15	$50/$5	$50/$10	$50/$15
Overall	45.0%	43.0%	39.3%	31.7%	27.8%	22.5%	21.0%	17.6%	15.8%
< $20K	49.3%	50.0%	44.5%	30.1%	35.8%	25.9%	24.7%	24.7%	18.5%
$40K+	50.8%	49.1%	44.5%	31.5%	31.6%	28.1%	24.6%	17.5%	19.3%

In some instances, a marketing researcher must refrain from making specific recommendations and fall back on general recommendations. These are cases in which the marketing researcher does not have sufficient information about the resource and experience base of the company or decision maker to whom the report is being directed or the researcher has been notified that the recommendations will be determined by the decision maker. Under these circumstances, the researcher offers conclusions and stops at that point.

FIGURE 19.9

XYZ Bar Chart with 3-D Effect

Preferred Hospital by County

Preferred hospitals vary dramatically across the five-county area.

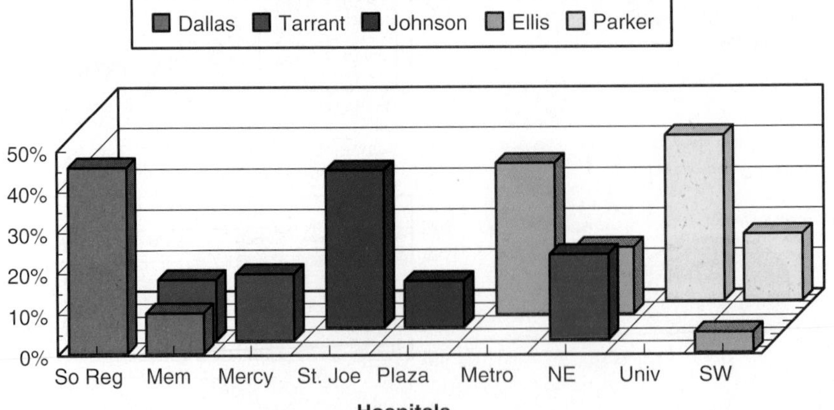

Preparing the Report

The final report, whether written, oral, or both, represents the culmination of the research effort. The quality of the report and its recommendations often determine whether a research user will return to a supplier. Within a corporation, an internal report prepared by a research department may have a smaller impact. If you want to think on a more selfish level, a history of excellent reports prepared by a research staff member may lead to merit salary increases and ultimately promotion.

Pitfalls in Marketing Research Reports

A number of common faults are encountered in writing research reports, and it is wise to keep them in mind throughout the report writing process.

Length Does Not Mean Quality One of the common misconceptions in marketing research is, "The longer the report, the better it is."[4] Often after working months on a project, a researcher is highly involved in a problem and wants to tell the reader everything known about the issue. All qualifications, implications, and hundreds of pages of computer printouts are included, resulting in noise sometimes referred to as "information overload." It is often difficult to convince a young researcher that most management people will not read the entire report. In fact, they may not read any of it if the report is not properly constructed. Research is not bought by the pound. Rather, quality, conciseness, and validity count.

Insufficient Explanation Some researchers simply repeat numbers from the tables without any attempt at interpretation. Although most people can read a table, it normally is the function of the writer to impart meaning to the data. Moreover, few things will "turn off" a reader more than page after page of statistics without an attempt at interpretation or explanation as to why the tables are there.

Failure to Relate to Objectives or Reality Reporting mounds of data without referring to the research objectives is another common pitfall of report writing. The reader wants to know what the survey results mean in terms of marketing goals. Are the goals now unattainable? Are additional resources needed? Should the product or service be repositioned?

Perhaps just as bad as failing to relate results to objectives is the unrealistic recommendation. Increasing promotional expenditures $10,000 per market may be beyond the financial capabilities of the firm. Or, if a product placement reveals that items "A" and "B" are perceived as parity products, a recommendation to produce both may be imprudent. A bank image study that recommends wholesale firing of loan officers undoubtedly would be considered impractical.

Indiscriminate Use of Quantitative Techniques Some report writers are guilty of the "snow job"; that is, writing a report in highly technical terms and using quantitative overkill. Sometimes extensive use of multivariate and other

A Professional Researcher's Perspective

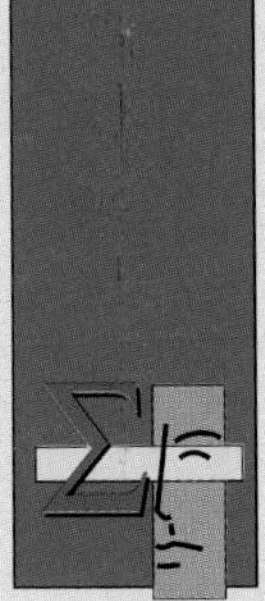

Howard Gordon, a principal of George R. Fredricks and Associates, A Chicago-based market research company, offers the following advice on preparing a good research report.

1. *Present tense works better.* Use present tense. Results and observations expressed in *now* terms sound better and are easier to read.

   Don's say: "The test panel liked the taste of the juice." Say: "People like the taste of the juice.

   We do studies for clients to help them make decisions today and tomorrow—not yesterday.
2. *Use active voice.* Use active voice where possible—which is in most cases. Passive voice doesn't swing. There is nothing wrong with saying: "We believe . . ." rather than, "It is believed that . . ."

   Passive voice is stilted. Use first person plural—not third person singular.

   Present tense and active voice make reports sound action oriented—businesslike.
3. *Use informative headlines—not label headlines.* Your reader will welcome this headline: "Convenience is the packaging's major benefit." Your reader will not generally welcome this headline: "Analysis of packaging." Nor this: "How people feel about packaging."
4. *Let your tables and charts work. Help them with words when needed.* Don't take a paragraph or a page to describe what a table already says. If there is nothing to say about a table or a chart, don't say it.

statistical techniques is a cover-up for ill-defined objectives and methodology. Little will cause a report to be rejected faster than writing that is not understandable by a nontechnical marketing manager. Overuse of statistics often raises legitimate questions of the quality of the research in the mind of the research user.

false accuracy

An unwarranted illusion of accuracy provided by details, such as statistics quoted to two decimal places.

False Accuracy Quoting statistics in two decimal places with a relatively small sample gives an unwarranted illusion of accuracy, or **false accuracy.** For example, a statement that our product was preferred by 68.47 percent of survey respondents tends to legitimize the statistic 68 percent. A reader may think that if the researcher can quote a number to .47 percent, then the 68 percent must be cast in concrete.

The Fallacy of Single-Number Research Some researchers place far too much emphasis on a single statistic to provide an answer to a client's decision. This tendency is prevalent in concept tests and product placements. The key question is purchase intent. If the "definitely will buy" and "probably will buy" do not add up to a predetermined standard, say, 75 percent, the concept or test product is dropped. But, a product placement questionnaire may contain 50 questions designed to ferret out positioning information, segmentation data, and perceived strengths and weaknesses; yet all this is totally subordinate to the pur-

The purpose of a table or a chart is to simplify. Use your words to point out significant items in the table—something that is not readily clear. Or use your words to offer interpretive comments. Use verbatims from sample respondents to support a point. But if you're simply going to repeat what's already in the chart, don't bother.

5. *Use the double-sided presentation whenever possible.* This format will reduce the verbiage in your report. It simply presents the table on the left side of the open report. Your informative headline and interpretive comments are on the right-hand page.

   Most people don't like research reports because they're wordy. Wordy reports offer little reader reward. They're right. Avoid wordy reports. Thin reports get taken home on weekends—and slide easily into briefcases for airplane and train reading.

6. *Make liberal use of verbatims.* Great nuggets of marketing wisdom have come from people's comments. Use **verbatims** if you have them.

   Sprinkle the verbatims throughout your report in appropriate places.

   Bulova Accutron was born from verbatims. So was man-size from Kleenex, Libby's bite-size fruit, United's friendly skies. They did not come from tables.

   Besides, verbatims help make research reports interesting and readable.

   People who think research reports are readable, interesting, rewarding, and useful usually ask for more research.[5] ■

chase intent question. There is no magic in any one question or predetermined cutoff standard. Overreliance on **single-number research** may result in missed opportunities or, in other situations, marketing the wrong product.

single-number research

Placing too much emphasis on a single statistic.

Inaccurate Data Interpretation It is the researcher's obligation to render objective interpretations; however, it is sometimes easy to slip into inaccurate interpretation. For example, scaling is a very common candidate for inaccurate data analysis. A researcher conducted a callback on a test coffee product placement with a Stapel scale devised to measure bitterness of coffees "A" and "B." The scale runs from "very bitter" to "no bitterness" with values of −2, −1, 0, +1, and +2. The average rating for "A" is 1.2 and for "B," 0.8. Subtracting one from another and calculating a simple percentage leads to the conclusion that "B" is perceived at 50 percent more bitter than "A."

But what if a different set of weights had been used? Assume a 1 to 5 scale of "very bitter" to "no bitterness" had been applied. "A" is rated 4.2 and "B" receives an average of 3.8. Using the same respondents, the same coffees, the same questionnaire, and a different rating scale yields a percentage difference of only 11.5 percent. Now test coffee "B" does not look so bad.

Now, take a third look at the same data. In this case, the researcher uses the 1 to 5 scale but reverses the adjectives. "No bitterness" is now 1 and "very bitter" equals 5. The mean ratings of 2.2 for coffee "B" and 1.8 for coffee "A," a percentage difference of 18.2 percent.

Accurate interpretation requires that the report writer have intimate knowledge of scaling assumptions, statistical methods, and the study's limitations.

The Gee-Whiz Chart A good picture is worth a thousand words, but a bad picture (chart) is not simply worthless, it is misleading. It may be artistic, colorful, and eye-catching but fail to fulfill its function. A chart dramatizes the facts, but many charts overdramatize them. These are called "gee-whiz" charts.[6]

Making a "gee-whiz" chart is simple. You draw a correct chart and cut off the bottom part, show a little job in the vertical scale on the left to indicate that the scale is incomplete, and voila! Any trend, up or down, will look much more impressive.

A "gee-whiz" chart similar to the one in Figure 19.10 ran in a respected business publication recently, depicting sales of an imported car. Compare that with the real chart showing the same data. A drop from 420 to 295 is a 30 percent decline. When charted, it should look like a 30 percent decline, not a 90 percent as in the "gee-whiz" chart. Sure, when we look at the numbers we realize that the decline is not 90 percent, but the whole point of a chart is to get away from looking at the numbers and to present their impact pictorially.

Evaluating the Report Drafts

The writing process is an art enhanced with communication effectiveness guidelines. With each written draft, the report writer should evaluate the quality of the work. The draft should be reviewed from the perspective of the client. Will she fully understand what this means? The writer also should become his own devil's advocate. If possible, a third party should critique the draft.

FIGURE 19.10

The Gee-Whiz Chart versus Reality

SOURCE: Thomas T. Semon, "A Bad Picture Is Worth Very Few Words," *Marketing News* (May 24, 1993), p. 11.

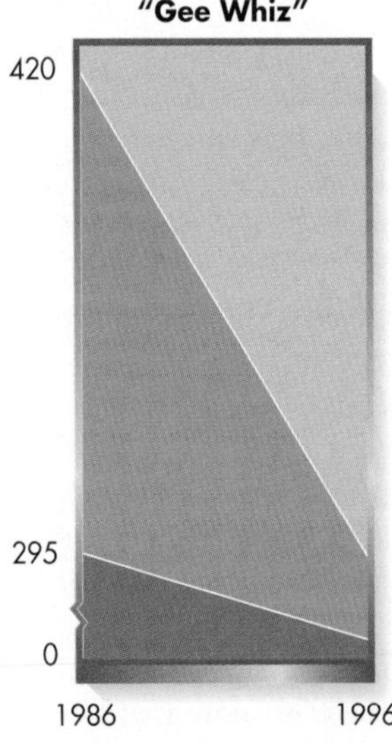

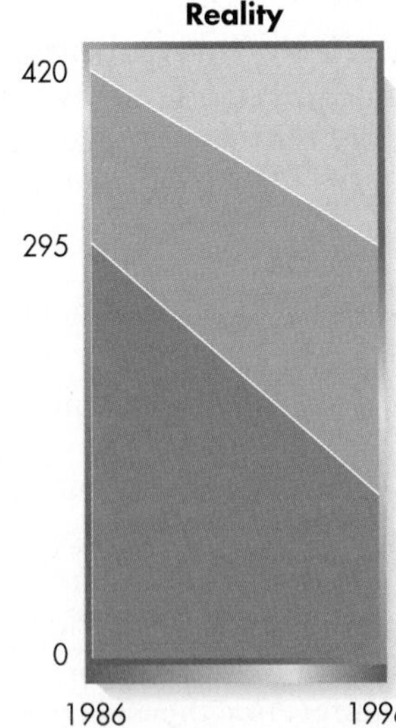

A Professional Researcher's Perspective

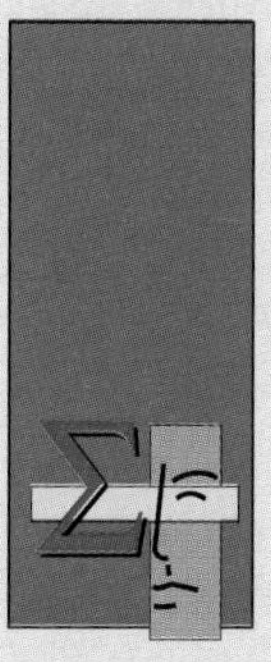

In determining the quality of a marketing research report, use these guidelines.

1. Does the report contain data from the pertinent survey exclusively, or does it also rely on other data, data from previous reports or external data, in order to gain more perspective and to control the validity of survey data through external data?
2. Does the report rely on the direct statements of respondents, taking them at face value? This could be called passing the investigation task on to the respondent. Or has more knowledge been brought to light by translating them into new questions, ideas, and new tests, as well as by applying mathematical-statistical analysis, than would have been obtained by direct questioning of the respondents and simply tallying up their responses?
3. Does the report contain surprising findings for you? Are these findings numerically established, crucial in providing an answer to the investigation task, and do they have an impact on the concrete conclusions you draw? Especially important, does the report contain results that common sense would not have expected?
4. Check the linguistic quality of both report and tables, and check in particular whether specific technical terms of your trade and your market are used, and used correctly. And conversely, how much superfluous jargon is used, befogging the text? Linguistic quality of text and tables (and particularly of tables) is like the tip of an iceberg. It reveals the overall quality of the work you receive.
5. Check whether the questions you want to find answered are clearly worded and answered in the report. Or is the report rather written in a fortune-telling style; that is, the assertions of one sentence nullify that of the other?
6. Check whether the report contains hints toward the practical significance of the results and consequences for their application. How well has the author of the report been able to immerse himself in your problems? And even if you draw your own conclusions, never leave out the opportunity of hearing the view of the report author.[7] ■

During the review process, the writer should refer to the research proposal. Did the report meet the objectives established in the proposal? Was the methodology outlined in the proposal followed? Are the conclusions based upon logical deductions from the data analysis? Do the recommendations seem prudent given the research conclusions?

Is the writing style crisp and lucid? The report should be as concise as possible. It should follow the format outlined earlier in the chapter so that salient findings and recommendations can be determined quickly and easily.

Although checklists often "overmechanize" an evaluation process, the points offered by Elizabeth Noelle-Neumann of the Institut for Demoskopie Allensbach, Frankfurt, Germany, in "A Professional Researcher's Perspective" feature on page 659 can be helpful in determining the quality of a marketing research report.

The Oral Presentation

Most clients expect an oral presentation of the research findings. This activity serves many purposes. It assembles the several interested parties together. It reacquaints them with the research objectives and method. Also, an oral presentation brings to light any unexpected events or findings. Most of all, it highlights the research conclusions. In fact, it is safe to say that for some decision makers in the company, the oral presentation will be their *only* exposure to the findings: they will never read the report. Other managers may only skim the written report, using it as a memory recall trigger for points made in the oral presentation. In short, effective communication in the oral presentation is absolutely critical.

SOURCE: Michael Krasowitz/FPG.

Materials for the Oral Presentation

We recommend four aids to be used in the oral presentation:

1. *Presentation outline.* Every audience member should be supplied a presentation outline that very briefly details the presentation flow (major parts) and significant findings. The outline should not contain statistics or tables, but it should have ample "white space" for the person to jot down notes or comments.
2. *Visuals.* The most commonly used visual device has been a projector. Either a slide projector or an overhead projector was common. Today, more and more researchers are using laptop personal computers coupled with an LCD panel and a high-intensity projector for visual presentations. Not only can traditional charts be shown but spreadsheets as well. The researcher can display "what if?" situations as questions arise from the audience. Summaries, conclusions, and recommendations also should be made with visuals.
3. *Executive summary.* Each audience member should have a copy of the executive summary (preferably several days in advance). This allows for a more fruitful discussion. It also enables managers to contemplate questions to ask in advance of the presentation.
4. *Copies of the final report.* The report serves as physical evidence of the research and should make clear that much detail has been omitted in the oral presentation. It should be made available to interested parties at the end of the presentation.

Making an Oral Presentation

Philip H. Abelson, a distinguished scientist and editor of *Science,* recently wrote a very blunt statement about the problem of communication in science and business: "When it comes to communicating, few researchers are skillful. The majority cannot even effectively convey scientific information to each other. This is true of verbal presentations, in which decade after decade most scientists use slides that cannot be read beyond the front row of the audience.[8] Some marketing researchers are guilty of inadequate oral presentations. Perhaps one reason for this is a lack of understanding of the barriers to effective communication outlined at the beginning of this chapter. A second factor is failure to recognize or admit that the purpose of many research reports is persuasion. This does not mean stretching or bending the truth but rather using research findings to reinforce the conclusions and recommendations of the researcher.

An effective oral presentation recognizes the nature of the audience. It is cognizant of the receiver's frame of reference, attitudes, prejudices, educational background, and time constraints. The speaker must select words, concepts, and illustrative figures to which an audience can relate. A good presentation also leaves time at the end for questions and discussion.

In preparing an oral presentation, the researcher should keep the following questions in mind:

- What do the data really mean?
- What impact do they have?
- What have we learned from the data?

Global Marketing Research

An American executive conducted an extensive marketing research study concerning the prospect of his company entering a strategic alliance with a Malaysian counterpart to market consumer products in Malaysia. Upon completing the study, he wrote a report that he would later present orally in Malaysia. The research results looked very promising, and the report was full of enthusiasm for the possibility of future success. Upon arriving in Malaysia to present the report to a Malaysian "top decision maker," the American was introduced to several Malaysian individuals, all with rather long and difficult names to pronounce. However, one distinguished-looking fellow had a name he could remember, namely—Rodger (or so he thought). Throughout his oral presentation, he addressed his finding to this man and, electing to take on an air of informality that often prevails in the United States, called him "Rog." Near the middle of his presentation, "Rodger" got up and left the room, apparently in a huff. The American's research presentation was immediately suspended, and the strategic alliance postponed. What had happened? Unfortunately, this well-meaning American did not know that, in Malaysia, while many states are headed by sultans, one is controlled by rajahs. Rajah is a title of nobility, not a personal name. The American not only insulted the "top decision maker" but sacrificed his joint venture. ■

- What do we need to do, given the information we now have?
- How can future studies of this nature be enhanced?
- What can make information such as this more useful?

Table 19.3 provides a few helpful hints that can increase the effectiveness of an oral presentation.

Getting Managers to Use the Research Information

A research study was conducted recently of Fortune 500 companies in the chemical, consumer packaged-goods, and telecommunications industries and also of 40 executives of large and medium-sized companies in different industries who are members of the Strategic Planning Institute, an international business think tank. The purpose of the research was to identify the key factors in the effective use of marketing research.[10] Those factors are:

1. *The perceived credibility and usefulness of the report to the users.* A good study "has data of recommendations that can be used to formulate a strategy." It "redirects activities, accentuates the positive, and corrects weaknesses." A good study also has a clearly defined scope, shows how the quantitative analysis meshes with the qualitative information, and contains no "big surprises" or radical recommendations. At the least, a good study "provides an understanding that wasn't there before."

TABLE 19.3 Eighteen Ways to Communicate Better

1. Prepare yourself by organizing primary and secondary data for your presentation.
2. Get to know your audience members and their interests before you make the presentation.
3. Know your objectives. Ask yourself: Why am I making the presentation? Develop a communicative strategy of how to combine the interest of your audience with your own goal. Practice the communication concept.
4. Use notes. Memorize the opening if you must.
5. Just be yourself. Nobody expects you to be Jay Leno, Bob Hope, or Billy Graham.
6. Start by outlining the entire presentation in the form of four or five key topics on the screen. It helps your audience see where things fit together and where the presentation is going.
7. Begin with your most dramatic and convincing point or quickly build up to a climax so that you receive the full attention of the audience from the start.
8. Think of your presentation as a service. Look at it from your audience members' viewpoints. Continuously ask yourself: How does the presentation help the audience? The organization? My own operation? What is in it for all? Establish mutual benefits. Think of the plus-plus relationship in transactional analysis.
9. Keep it simple and easy to understand. Use short sentences: subject, verb, object.
10. Do not discuss too many points and details; the main mission of your presentation may get lost.
11. Anticipate objections. Recognize them if you cannot fight them. Stating an objection calmly takes the emotion out of it. You also show that you are aware of it.
12. End with a positive note. Summarize what the listeners might lose and what they will gain.
13. Remember, a presentation is not a sermon. It is sharing ideas with your audience—ideas that may affect their jobs, their future.
14. Don't talk down to your audience. Use "we" instead of "I."
15. Talk directly to your audience. Don't lose personal contact by looking out of the window or at your shoes. Look people straight in the eyes.
16. Use charts and figures. Don't overload them. Keep them simple. A chart or figure shouldn't say all there is to say. It can later be distributed.
17. When you use charts or figures, talk to the audience, not to the chart or figure.
18. Look at your watch. Finish your presentation on time.

SOURCE: Adapted from: Hugh Kramer, "Communication Concept Would Offer Idea in Recipient's Terms," *Marketing News* (December 29, 1978), p. 4.

2. *The degree of client/researcher interaction.* Managers often assess a study's credibility or value even before the final presentation of findings. And this assessment often is based on their involvement (or lack thereof) with the study design and its conduct. "If involvement is low . . . then the lack of communication can cause surprises and the quality of the study becomes a moot point . . . because the study is likely to be shelved.
3. *The organizational climate for research.* Managers have to receive top management's approval for the use of research studies and consultants. One manager noted, "It's crucial to have signals from the top that encourage the use of outside help and openness to new ideas."
4. *The personality and job tenure of key users.* Some managers have a proinnovation bias and are willing to try almost anything. Other managers view outside information as threatening to their decision-making authority. Also, other research has shown that senior (longer-tenured) managers valued more sources of marketing research information and tended to use more "soft information" than did younger managers. Senior managers also tend to make more conservative decisions.[11] When managers have been in the same business for a long time, they naturally believe they "know the markets and customers in depth" and that marketing researchers are unlikely to offer any new information.

The Role of Trust Another recent study focused upon the importance of trust between the researcher and the decision maker.[12] Trust, in this case, simply means relying on one another. A survey of 779 researchers and research users found that trust was more a function of interpersonal factors than individual factors. The most important interpersonal factor was perceived integrity of the researcher. This was followed by the perceived willingness of the researcher to reduce research uncertainty for the users. This meant that researchers would use fewer data analysis skills and more data interpretation skills. In other words, "yes, the relationship is significant at the .05 level but what does this mean in the marketplace?" The researcher is being called upon to use her broad understanding of the marketplace and research insights to construct explanations about research findings. Other important determinants of trust were researcher confidentiality, level of expertise, and congeniality.[13]

Building Trust through Feedback Perhaps one of the most practical ways to build trust and therefore to get managers to use the research information is to use customer satisfaction research! AT&T marketing research, for example, put in a customer satisfaction tracking system to monitor its internal clients' perceptions on an ongoing basis.[14] The system consists of two separate questionnaires. One is a very general, short, high-level view and is completed periodically by marketing directors and other high-level executives (see Table 19.4). The executives rate the research department on five separate attributes, as well as overall support. The questionnaire is deliberately very short because of the respondents' limited exposure to research and the tremendous demands on their time.

The second questionnaire is more detailed and aimed at the specific client who requested the study. An example of a direct client questionnaire is shown in Table 19.5. The surveys provide AT&T researchers a good way to monitor how they are doing, build trust and confidence in the department, and provide useful, decision-making information for the corporation.

Doing "good research" per se does not guarantee that the findings will be used. The researcher must understand how managers think and must work with them to remove potential bias against using the research findings. Remember, marketing research has value only when it is considered and acted upon by management.

TABLE 19.4 AT&T's Executive Marketing Research Customer Satisfaction Survey

MARKET RESEARCH AND QUALITY MEASUREMENTS: PERIODIC SATISFACTION CALIBRATION

The purpose of this form is to obtain your input regarding marketing research and quality measurement performance on behalf of your Strategic Business Unit. The information will be used to measure your satisfaction and make improvements where needed. We appreciate your taking the time to respond.

Please circle your response for "importance" where "H" is high, "M" is medium, and "L" is low importance and for "rating" where "A" is extremely satisfied and "F" is extremely dissatisfied.

How Are We Doing?	*Importance*			*Rating*				
Overall support	H	M	L	A	B	C	D	F
Cost/value relationship	H	M	L	A	B	C	D	F
Advising on market research needs and setting up market research program	H	M	L	A	B	C	D	F
Responsiveness	H	M	L	A	B	C	D	F
Interpreting market research data for actionable decision making	H	M	L	A	B	C	D	F
Producing market	H	M	L	A	B	C	D	F

Comments:

SOURCE: AT&T.

TABLE 19.5 AT&T Internal Marketing Research Client Customer Satisfaction Survey

MARKET RESEARCH AND QUALITY MEASUREMENTS FEEDBACK REPORT

Product Name: ______________________ Name of Client: ______________________

MR & QM Market Intelligence Analyst: ______________________ Date: ______________

The purpose of this form is to provide feedback to marketing research and quality measurements on its overall performance in support of the process team. The information provided by this form is part of the MR & QM review process. Your thoughtful and honest responses to the following questions and explanatory comments are appreciated.

Please indicate your response to the following five questions

1. To what degree has MR & QM met your market intelligence needs? On a 10-point scale where 10 is "meets all needs" and 1 is "meets no needs," what score represents your response? (Please circle).

Meets no needs — *Meets all needs*

1 2 3 4 5 6 7 8 9 10

Comments:

2. To what degree do you feel MR & QM has a stake in the success of your product(s)? On a 10-point scale where 10 is "a great stake," what score represents your response?

No stake — *A great stake*

1 2 3 4 5 6 7 8 9 10

Comments:

3. To what degree is MR & QM seen as a credible provider of market intelligence products and services?

Not credible — *Very credible*

1 2 3 4 5 6 7 8 9 10

Comments:

4. To what degree do you feel MR & QM is your first-choice provider of market intelligence products and services?

Not first-choice provider — *First-choice provider*

1 2 3 4 5 6 7 8 9 10

Comments:

4a. What percent of the Market Research done in support of your products is conducted by MR & QM?

0%—25% 26%—50% 51%—75% 76%—99% 100%

5. To what degree did MR and QM research contribute to meeting your strategic product objectives?

No degree — *To a great degree*

1 2 3 4 5 6 7 8 9 10

Comments:

For the next five questions, please indicate the degree of your satisfaction with MR & QM performance

	Very dissatisfied	Somewhat dissatisfied	Neither satisfied nor dissatisfied	Generally satisfied	Very satisfied
6. Timeliness of information	1	2	3	4	5
7. Actionability of results	1	2	3	4	5
8. Cost/value relationship	1	2	3	4	5
9. Responsiveness	1	2	3	4	5
10. Overall satisfaction	1	2	3	4	5

Summary

The essence of communication is shared meaning. There are several barriers to effective communication, including noise, limited attention span, and selective perception.

The primary roles of the marketing research report are to communicate the findings, to serve as a reference document, and to provide credibility for the work that was accomplished. The basic components of a research report include beginning with an executive summary, followed by a detailed introduction, analysis of findings, conclusions, methodology, recommendations, and appendices, if necessary.

Typically, a research report should be in the present tense with use of the active voice whenever possible. Informative headlines are better than label headlines. Tables and charts should be used liberally in a report rather than several pages of verbiage. Also, the use of verbatims can make a research report come alive.

There are several pitfalls in marketing research reports. Length does not necessarily mean quality. Simply repeating numbers from tables without any attempt at interpretation degrades the quality of the research reports. Also, research reports should refer back to the research objectives from time to time. Care also must be taken to ensure adequate data interpretation. A number of factors are given in the chapter to help the reader evaluate the quality of the research report.

Oral presentations should include four aids: the presentation outline, visuals, the executive summary, and copies of the final report. An effective oral presentation recognizes the nature of the audience and attempts to meet the needs of that audience.

It is extremely important that marketing managers use marketing research information and use it appropriately. The marketing researcher needs to understand how managers think and the potential barriers to research information use. This task is complicated by the fact that different marketing managers use research information differently and value research information differently. The key determinants of whether marketing research data are used are the perceived credibility and usefulness to the users, the degree of client/researcher interaction, the organizational climate for research, and the personality and job tenure of key users. Trust also plays a key role in the use of marketing research information. Trust is derived from perceived integrity and the willingness of the researcher to help reduce uncertainty for the users. Other determinants of trust are researcher confidentiality, level of expertise, and congeniality. One good tool for building trust and credibility is a client-customer satisfaction survey.

Key Terms

communication
noise
attention span
selective perception
executive summary
presentation software
verbatims
false accuracy
single-number research

Review and Discussion Questions

1. What are the roles of the research report? Give examples.
2. What are some of the more common pitfalls in marketing research reports? Give examples of each pitfall.
3. Distinguish among findings, summaries, conclusions, and recommendations.
4. Should research reports contain executive summaries? Why or why not? If so, what should be contained in an executive summary?
5. Discuss the seven basic components of the research report. List several criteria that may be used to evaluate a research report and give examples of each.

6. What should be done to ensure the success of an oral report? Critique the following two paragraphs from a research report:

The trouble began when the Department of Agriculture published the hot dog ingredients—everything that may legally qualify—because it was asked by the poultry industry to relax the conditions under which the ingredients also might include chicken. In other words, can a chickenfurter find happiness in the land of the frank?

Judging by the 1,066 mainly hostile answers that the department got when it sent out a questionnaire on this point, the very thought is unthinkable. The public mood was most felicitously caught by the woman who replied, "I don't eat feather meat of no kind."

7. Develop one or more visual aids to present the following data. Indicate why you chose your particular form of visual aid.

CANDIDATE	LOCAL # EMPLOYEES	REVENUES (IN MILLIONS)	TARGET AS CHARTER OR AFFILIATE MEMBER	POTENTIAL MEMBERSHIP FEE
Mary Kay Cosmetics	958	$360	Charter	$50,000
Arrow Industries	950	50	Charter	20,000
NCH Corp.	800	427	Charter	50,000
Stratoflex, Inc.	622	81	Charter	25,000
BEI Defense Sys.	150	47	Affiliate	7,500
Atlas Match Corp.	150	82	Affiliate	7,500
Mangren R&D	143	20	Affiliate	7,500
Jet Research Ctr.	157	350	Affiliate	7,500

8. Explain why younger and older marketing managers might use marketing research data differently. Give some examples.
9. Discuss the key factors in the effective use of marketing research.

CASE 19.1

Sports Priority Research—The University of Georgia

The following report was given by a group of senior marketing research students at the University of Georgia. (Appendices referred to in the report are not reprinted here.)

SUMMARY

The purpose of this study is to determine student attitudes toward non-revenue-producing sports at the University of Georgia. Non-revenue-producing sports shall be defined as all varsity-level sports excluding men's football and basketball. To get additional insight into this problem, we spoke with Dr. Lee Cunningham, former University of Georgia head coach and current physical education academic adviser. The information we received from him, along with input from group members and additional secondary research, helped to formulate our hypotheses.

We chose a questionnaire as our data gathering tool. Given our time and costs restraints, this proved to be the most effective method. Each group member verbally administered the questionnaire to the respondents and recorded the responses.

In our study we used a stratified random sampling of 120 full-time University of Georgia students. This number of participants was chosen to achieve an equal number from each stratum.

There were several limitations present in our study. Time, cost, and a nonrepresentative sample were its inherent limitations.

The results of our study were tabulated using computer techniques. Specifically, the Statistical Package for the Social Sciences. The package calculated such analytical computations as frequency tables, crosstabulations, and discriminant analysis, which assisted in interpreting the results of our study.

The results of our study and any supportive recommendations will be discussed in the summary at the conclusion of our report.

INTRODUCTION

Because of recent legislation involving equality in men's and women's sports, there has been increased pressure within collegiate athletic departments to allocate funds proportionately to men's and women's sports programs. Consequently, the need has arisen to eliminate various non-revenue-producing sports so as to more equitably allocate funds. The problem arises when deciding which sports to eliminate and whether the athletic department should make this decision independently or whether it should consider student input in this decision-making process. This study is designed to probe student opinions concerning this controversy.

BACKGROUND

To broaden our knowledge about our topic, we decided to use various forms of secondary research. This explanatory research proved to be very useful to our study.

Our interview with Cunningham provided our group with the background information relevant to our project. The analysis of Title IX and other subject-related materials provided us added input.

The combination of these sources provided the framework for the design of our study.

BENEFITS

The benefit of conducting this study is to provide the University of Georgia Athletic Department with information concerning student attitudes toward sports priority evaluation. Ideally, the information we present will be useful to the athletic department when deciding which sport to eliminate. Student input should be a prime consideration in this decision.

OBJECTIVES

The primary objective is to determine student attitudes toward non-revenue, producing sports. Specifically

1. Criteria for ranking sports (won-lost, cost, revenue)
2. Percentage of attendance for each sport

3. Willingness to pay admission price

Secondary objectives include trying to determine whether a combination of additional revenue sources and more effective media usage would lead to retention of "minor" sports. (Minor sports shall now be referred to as sports other than football and men's basketball.)

METHODOLOGY

1. *Definition of Population.* A sample was selected of full-time undergraduate students attending the University of Georgia during fall quarter 1992. We have excluded students with fewer than 45 hours (freshmen) and also persons affiliated in any way with the UGA athletic department. These restrictions were to eliminate students who may have a limited knowledge and exposure to minor sports and also have those students who may exhibit a more extreme bias toward particular sports as a result of their affiliation with the athletic department.
2. *Sampling Frame.* In our study, we drew our sample from the full-time students at the University of Georgia during fall quarter 1992.
3. *Sampling Method.* Our sample consisted of 120 personal interviews. We stratified our sample according to sex and class standing. We used approximately 60 male and 60 female respondents. These two groups were further stratified into an equal number of sophomores, juniors, and seniors (20 from each stratum). We structured our personal interviews on the basis of a simple random sample, realizing the nonrepresentativeness of our sample.
4. *Sample Size.* Because of the various constraints imposed on our study, specifically time and cost, our sample size was limited to 120 students. This also enabled us to obtain an equal number of respondents in each stratum.
5. *Sampling Plan.* Various research areas were chosen on- and off-campus to conduct our interviews. These predetermined areas were chosen in an attempt to obtain as equal a representation as possible. These points also enabled us to obtain a reasonably equal number of students who line on- and off-campus. By using this method, our results were not overly biased in favor of any particular school or place of residence (see Appendix A).

HYPOTHESIS

The hypothesis of this study is that students are willing to support minor sports through attendance of these sports and a willingness to pay an admission fee to view these sports. Consequently, student input into the development of criteria for the evaluation of sports programs is significant and should be considered.

DATA COLLECTION TECHNIQUE

A personal interview was chosen as the best technique for gathering our information. We viewed this as our only choice considering the various constraints imposed on our study.

The first constraint was the need to use visual aids in our interview. This eliminated both the telephone interview and the mail questionnaire.

Another constraint was the considerable length of our interview. This also reduced our choices for data gathering because a long mail questionnaire typically has a low response rate. People also are less apt to complete lengthy telephone interviews.

QUESTIONNAIRE DESIGN

We designed our questionnaire based on the information acquired from our background research. We also used our own personal judgment when determining which type of questions might be the most applicable to the information we were trying to obtain.

In designing the format of our questionnaire, we used the standard procedure to formulate a questionnaire. We began with general questions and then became more specific as the questionnaire progressed, closing with several demographic questions.

The majority of our questions were dichotomous yes-no questions. There also were a few multichotomous questions, but they were not the dominant form. In one instance, we included along with the dichotomous design an aided and unaided response to determine student awareness of sports (see Appendix B).

PRETEST

A necessary pretesting of our questionnaire was conducted by each interviewer. We then gathered to discuss each interviewer's feelings about the questionnaire; how it could be improved, any oversights or inconsistencies, and the basic overall quality of the questionnaire. After discussing these areas, we revised our original questionnaire into a much more effective, comprehensive form.

This pretest proved to be very beneficial in eliminating many of the flaws in the questionnaire. After pretesting, a final questionnaire was written and approved.

COLLECTION PROCEDURES

Personal interviews were conducted using individual questionnaires for each respondent. The responses were recorded directly onto each questionnaire. Visual aids, in the form of cards, were used to assist the respondents when answering the questions. Skip patterns also were used when necessary (see Appendix C).

LIMITATIONS

Any research study is inevitably going to encounter some basic limitations. This also was the case in our study. Time seemed to be our most limited resource. To conduct a comprehensive research project in a 10-week period is difficult.

The absence of appropriate funding limited the extent of our study. With additional financial resources, the scope (sample size) of our study could have been enlarged, resulting in a more representative study.

Interviewer bias could not be avoided as in the case in many surveys. Open-ended questions involve the use of probing techniques that increase interviewer bias. However, as our study did not use any open-ended questions, the extent of this bias was reduced.

The major limitation inherent in our survey was a nonrepresentative sample. Given our time and cost limitations, it was necessary to limit our sample size. The limitation of the sample size reduced its representativeness.

PROGRAM EVALUATION AND REVIEW TECHNIQUE CHART

In order to use our resources as efficiently as possible, we formulated a PERT chart based upon our research project (see Appendix E).

ANALYSIS OF FREQUENCY DATA

The results of our frequency analysis revealed many enlightening facts. Out of our sample of 120 students, we found that 82.5 percent felt a well-rounded sports program was beneficial to their education.

In reference to our question of sport awareness, we found that women's volleyball and women's basketball were sports that were relatively unknown by the student body. The other 11 sports had a large following by the students.

Our analysis also shows that attendance for women's and men's cross-country, women's volleyball, and women's track were extremely low when contrasted with the attendance for men's tennis, men's baseball, and women's basketball. One could assume that lack of awareness has a definite effect on attendance for each sport.

Students showed strong support (willingness to pay) for men's and women's tennis, men's basketball, and men's and women's gymnastics. The other sports would be supported but to a much lesser degree. This analysis reveals that these sports possibly could become revenue-producing sports.

The most useful media form was friends; 49.2 percent of the students stated that they learned of the events, dates, and times through fellow students. Newspapers were the next largest category (28.3 percent), revealing that they were not as effective as would have been expected. The sports programs possibly could benefit from more intense advertising through this medium.

The students wanted to eliminate women's volleyball first, men's cross-country second, and women's cross-country third. The students evaluated sports programs first by won-lost record; next by attendance; then cost, revenue, and number of athletes participating.

ANALYSIS OF SAMPLE PLAN

Our sample size of 120 university students consisted of 48.3 percent men and 51.7 percent women. The class stratum was composed of 18.3 percent sophomores, 29.2 percent juniors, 35.8 percent seniors and 16.7 percent students with 180 hours or more. The sample residence consisted of 54.2 percent off-campus, 34.2 percent in dormitories, and 11.7 percent in fraternity or sorority houses.

1. Critique the report.
2. What could have been done to improve the quality of the research?

CASE 19.2

The United Way

The United Way was concerned about attitudes toward the organization by nondonors. Specifically, management was interested in why certain people did not give to the United Way. It also was interested in determining what factors might convert nondonors to donors. An executive summary of the research is presented here.

EXECUTIVE SUMMARY OBJECTIVES AND METHODOLOGY

- The general purposes of this study were to determine the attitudes of noncontributors toward the United Way, to assess the reasons for not contributing, and to ascertain factors that may influence nonparticipants to contribute.
- The study used primary data gathered through a self-administered questionnaire.
- Descriptive research design methods were used to examine the survey results for numerical comparison.
- The study employed nonprobability samples (e.g., convenience samples and judgment samples).
- Primary data were collected through a newly developed self-administered questionnaire administered to 134 respondents consisting of co-workers, friends, and students.

FINDINGS

- The percentage of the respondents having positive perceptions of the United Way was greater than those having negative perceptions; however, the majority of the respondents had no opinions concerning the United Way.
- Only 5.2 percent rated the United Way fair or poor in providing benefits to those in need.
- The United Way actually spends 9 percent to 10 percent of contributions on administrative costs, although 80.6 percent believed that the United Way used more than a 10 percent of its contributions on administrative costs.
- Primary reasons for not contributing were contribution to other charities or religious organizations, personal financial circumstances, lack of knowledge of how donated funds are used, personal beliefs, absence of favorite charities, pressure to contribute, and preference to donate time rather than money.
- Of those who were asked to contribute, pressure seemed somewhat important in influencing their decision not to contribute.
- Of those respondents who indicated that personal financial reasons influenced their decision not to give, 35.6 percent indicated they would give to the United Way if asked.
- Other charities and religious denominations appear to be in competition with the United Way for donated dollars.
- Many respondents indicated that they would contribute if they could specify the charity to receive their contribution, had more knowledge about the United Way and the charities it supports, were asked to give, had less pressure to give, had availability of payroll deduction, and had the option of spreading contributions over time.
- Of the respondents whose place of employment participated in the United

Way campaign, 79.6 percent had been asked to give but did not.

- Workplace campaigns reach a large number of executives and professional and administrative personnel in the higher-income brackets but do not reach a significant number of service personnel or lower-income households.

CONCLUSIONS

- Negative perceptions do not appear to be a major factor affecting reasons for not contributing; however, a positive perception does not necessarily translate into a contribution.
- Noncontributors lack sufficient information regarding the United Way to form a perception of the organization.
- There is a lack of knowledge concerning the United Way and the organizations to which it allocates contributions.
- Respondents believe that the United Way uses more for administrative costs than it actually does.
- The United Way is in competition for a limited number of charity dollars.

RECOMMENDATIONS

- Conduct additional research to determine noncontributor's level of knowledge of the United Way and the purpose that the United Way services, market penetration, and competitors.
- Increase education for potential contributors regarding the United Way's purpose, the organizations it supports, and the United Way's reasonable administrative costs.
- Expand the frequency of campaigns in the workplace and develop ways to increase awareness of the methods of contributing.
- Develop appropriate competitive marketing strategy to address the United Way's competitors.

1. Do you think that the executive summary provides guidance for decision-making information?
2. Are all elements present that should be included within an executive summary?
3. Based upon the objectives, do the findings, conclusions, and recommendations logically follow? Why or why not?

APPENDIX A

Sample Executive Summary

Objectives

The overall objective of the research was to determine to what extent consumer beliefs, attitudes, and information about electricity meter reading, rates, and bill determination vary by socioeconomic status. Items measured included the following:

- Attitudes, beliefs, and information about the reading of residential electricity meters.
- Attitudes, beliefs, and information about the method of determining electric bills.
- Attitudes and beliefs regarding differences or lack of differences between residential electric rates in different areas of the city.
- Whether consumers desire additional information regarding how their meter is read and the preferred means of receiving this information.
- Whether consumers would like to have additional information regarding how their bill is determined and the preferred means of receiving this information.
- Whether consumers would like to know when their meter is read.

Summary of the Methodology

Eight hundred telephone interviews were conducted in the greater Cleveland area from a central location telephone interviewing center. The sample was weighed in proportion to the number of households per telephone exchange. The last four digits of the telephone number were generated by a random digit dialing program. Only residential heads of household were interviewed.

Summary of Findings

- *Believe meter is read by the electric company.* Just over three-fourths of all consumers believe their meter is read by the electric company. This percentage did not vary significantly by socioeconomic group. It should be noted that 16.7 percent of all respondents "don't know" whether their meter is read by the electric company. This figure, also, did not vary significantly by socioeconomic group.
- *Method of determining electric bill.* Nearly three-fourths of all respondents said their electric bill is determined "by the amount of electricity used." Consumers in the high- and medium-socioeconomic groups were significantly more likely to give this response than those in the low socioeconomic status group. Eight percent of those in the low status group said they felt bills were determined "by the area of town," while only 4 percent of those in the high status group gave this response.
- *Treated as fairly.* Overall, three-fourths of all respondents felt that their meter reader treats them as fairly as others. Differences in this percentage by socioeconomic group were not statistically significant. It is interesting to note that nearly one-fourth of all respondents said "don't know" in response to this question.
- *Rates the same all over the city?* Just over one-half of all respondents said they believe that electric company rates are the same all over the city for residential consumers. However, those in the low-socioeconomic status group were significantly less likely to hold this belief than those in the high- and medium-status groups. Again, the percent of respondents who said "don't know" is of interest. Nearly 30 percent gave this response and the percentage giving this response did not vary by socioeconomic group.
- *Ever seen meter being read?* Over half of all respondents said they had never seen their meter being read. However, those in the low- and medium-socioeconomic status groups are more likely to have seen their meter being read than those in the high-status group.
- *How is bill determined?* About 70 percent of all respondents gave an answer that indicated that they had some reasonable idea about how their bill is determined. Thirty percent said "don't know" in response to this question. The percentage giving a "don't know" response was significantly higher in the low-status group.

Conclusions and Recommendations

The following conclusions were drawn from the research:

- *More information.* A large percentage of all consumers would like to have additional information regarding how their meter is read and how their bill is determined. Low-status consumers are significantly more likely to want this kind of information than medium- and high-status consumers. These high percentages suggest that there is a need for Standard Electric to communicate with all its residential customers regarding these issues. According to the survey, mail is the preferred means for receiving the information. However, the power of electronic media to more powerfully communicate this information should not be discounted. Along these same lines, it is interesting to note that over half of all respondents indicated they would like to know when their meter is read.

- *The Standard Electric public image is in good shape.* More than 81 percent of all Standard Electric customers interviewed felt that the electric company is "very committed" or "somewhat committed" to providing good service to them. It also is important to note that this percentage did not vary significantly by socioeconomic group. This finding suggests that Standard Electric has done a very good job of serving its customers and has effectively communicated this fact to them.

CHAPTER 20

Marketing Research in Practice

LEARNING OBJECTIVES

1. To understand the importance and types of strategic research.
2. To learn about product concept research.
3. To explore various types of promotion research.
4. To gain insight into satisfaction and quality measurement.

In 1990 Georgia-Pacific Corp. completed a $3.8-billion takeover of Great Northern Nekoosa Papers. The resulting merger meant that the Communication Papers Division of Atlanta-based Georgia-Pacific now had to work with its former competitor to incorporate product lines, sales forces, and customer bases. There actually were two units of Georgia-Pacific directly affected by the merger: the $1.2-billion Communication Papers Division, which produces a variety of uncoated, free-sheet business and writing papers, as well as the Hopper Paper Company, a G-P unit that produces cover, text, and specialty papers.

Immediately after the merger, it was decided that the best course of action for the time being was to maintain the status quo. Over time, however, it became evident that the redundancies caused by the merger needed to be addressed. A reorganization program was undertaken in early 1992, called Project Eagle. The focus of the project was the company's relationships with its merchant business distributors. After the merger, the company saw itself as a more comprehensive full-line, one-stop shopping supplier. Its merchant customers, however, saw it as a hodgepodge of brands and products that, in effect, meant poorer service.

SOURCE: Courtesy of Georgia Pacific Papers.

A three-pronged research plan was developed to determine how to structure the future operation of the two sides of the company: the premium papers side and the "everyday-use" papers side. Each of the three types of research focused on the value of various restructuring possibilities. Printers and designers, considered major users of Hopper and Nekoosa premium papers, participated in focus groups. Senior managers of key merchant distributors of Georgia-Pacific's papers were interviewed one-on-one, and, thirdly, office paper buyers, as well as printers and designers, were surveyed using quantitative studies.

The research results indicated that as a result of the merger, Georgia-Pacific Corp. had two different types of paper businesses, not just two paper businesses with different names. The two types were the premium cover and text papers used primarily by designers and specialty printers and the uncoated white-paper business that includes office copier paper and other such paper items. The sales dimensions and dynamics of the two are very different. As a result, the company decided to reorganize into two distinct business groups.

The second phase of the research focused on the positioning of these two newly identified businesses. Again, the research findings were clear, leading the company to leverage the Georgia-Pacific name and create "Georgia-Pacific Papers" as a superbrand. Customers for the everyday papers wanted to know there was a reputable company behind them. The research focused on the premium papers found that although the brands were viewed as solid and reputable, the product lines were in need of some vitality. Efforts to redesign the premium paper line have included color upgrading of products, making product lines compatible.

Yet another outcome of Project Eagle has been new packaging and a new logo for Georgia-Pacific and Hopper Papers. The goal of the packaging program was to make the two businesses appear to be part of the same company but to give each a different image. A final outcome was a reconstructing of the distribution system.

Market research was the driving force behind the major strategic moves made by Georgia-Pacific Papers. It provided a greater understanding of the marketplace, its standing in it, and a methodology for extending the appeal of its products and services. According to Frank Murray, marketing director for Georgia-Pacific's Communication Papers Division, "Through market research, we wanted to bring objectivity and remove emotional and historical baggage from business decisions that are going to affect how and with whom we do business in the future. We used market research as the equalizer in our decision-making processes." The final answer to whether this project was successful will not be known for several years, but to date the company feels positive about the progress it has made.[1] ■

Strategic marketing research, as illustrated by the Georgia-Pacific story, is one common type of marketing research. We will take an in-depth look at strategic research in Chapter 20. In addition, we will examine several other popular forms of marketing research: product, advertising, and quality, or satisfaction, research. Although these examples are in no way representative of all types of marketing research, they will provide you with a broad cross section of popular categories of marketing research.

This material was prepared with the assumption that you have covered the remainder of the text. Therefore, we make liberal use of terms and concepts previously covered. As important concepts and techniques are discussed, chapter references are provided. Chapter 20 will give you insight into how some of the techniques and procedures learned earlier can be applied in marketing research projects.

Strategic Research

The first step in the process of designing successful marketing programs is a thorough understanding of the structure of the market and the nature of competition in that market. It is hard to think of a situation in which decisions concerning marketing mix elements (products, price, promotion, and place) can be appropriately made without first understanding the market and the competition within it.

Strategic marketing research studies are undertaken to provide managers with the information they need to understand and deal with the current and future competitive environment in the marketplace. Two important types of strategic marketing research are positioning studies and market segmentation studies.

Product Positioning Research

product positioning research Used to determine how competitive brands are perceived relative to each other on key dimensions.

Product positioning research is strategic by nature and is undertaken for numerous reasons. One use of positioning research is to identify specific strengths, weaknesses, and points of difference for the brands in a category. Once identified, they can be leveraged, reinforced, or exploited. Another use of positioning research is to gain an understanding of the competitive structure of the market. This is done by determining which brands consumers perceive to be similar. Brands perceived to be similar to one another are considered substitutes. This information allows marketers to target certain brands to capture market share. Positioning also can provide information on why substitutes are considered interchangeable and what the important similarities and differences are at the point of purchase. Positioning research helps to assess the feasibility of trying to reach a certain position. It may be that a new position, although seemingly desirable, is too far removed from a brand's current position.[2]

Marketing managers use product positioning research to develop pictures or maps of the competitive structure or relations between brands in a particular market. These maps are developed using information from consumers regarding their perceptions of current brands in the market along a number of dimensions. A perceptual map for nonprescription pain relievers is provided in Figure 20.1.

FIGURE 20.1
Perceptual Map for Nonprescription Pain Relievers

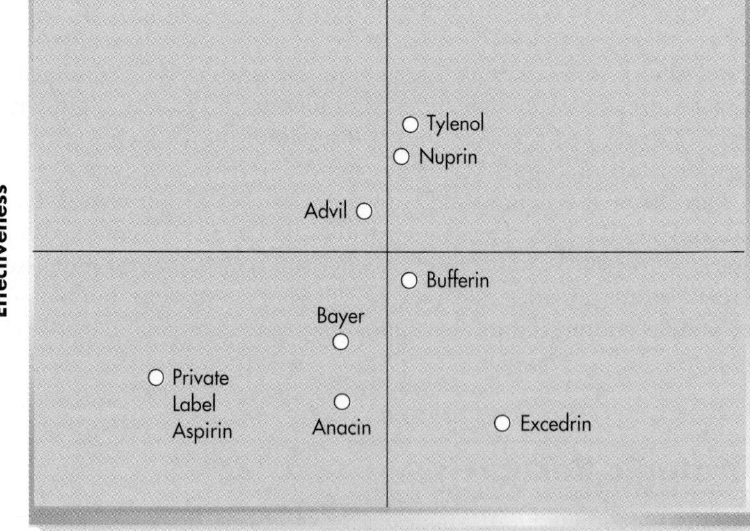

The analysis done to produce this map showed that consumers use two major attributes to classify nonprescription pain relievers in their minds: gentleness and effectiveness. Gentleness is measured on the vertical axis, with most gentle at the top and least gentle at the bottom. Effectiveness is measured on the horizontal axis, with most effective to the far right and least effective to the far left. Tylenol is perceived to be the most gentle product, followed by Nuprin and Advil. Tylenol is perceived to be more effective than private label aspirin, Bayer, or Anacin. However, it is perceived to be somewhat less effective than Bufferin or Excedrin. If you were developing a new brand of pain reliever, this information would provide valuable insights regarding how that product should be positioned.

These maps should be developed early in the marketing planning process so that they will be available later to help marketing managers make appropriate choices between alternative marketing programs. These maps can be used for a variety of purposes, including

- Developing and evaluating strategic plans
- Understanding the competitive structure of the market
- Tracking changes in the market over time
- Selecting the right competitive targets and learning their vulnerabilities
- Analyzing the effects of the film's marketing efforts on how the product is perceived
- Positioning or repositioning a brand to appeal to specific market segments
- Suggesting the likely success or failure of an extension into a new product category

Market Segmentation Research

Market segmentation divides consumers and potential customers into subgroups that exhibit differing sensitivities to one or more marketing mix variables. The idea of segmenting consumers, first introduced in 1956, was based on common knowledge among marketing management that different products generally are purchased by different groups of people. Take, for example, the wristwatch. Those who buy Swatches and those who buy Rolexes buy them for very different reasons. They are very different people and, therefore, belong to different segments.[4] Market segmentation research provides the foundation for a company's marketing strategy and the allocation of effort and resources among markets and products. By understanding and capitalizing on the heterogeneity among consumers in a market, managers can increase the effectiveness and profitability of the organization through market segmentation.

market segmentation
The process of dividing a total market into subgroups of consumers or potential customers who exhibit differing sensitivities to one or more marketing mix variables.

Market segmentation is a necessity for most companies in today's competitive environment; it is the opposite of a mass market approach. Under a mass market approach, the marketer assumes that consumer demand for the product category is driven primarily by price and supply. The assumption of mass marketing is that there is a single demand function that is uniform across all demographic and attitudinal consumer groups.

Through market segmentation, managers recognize that different consumer groups respond differently to product variations or have different demand responses to market variables such as product, price, place, and promotion. Green

Global Marketing Research

It may become necessary, for any number of reasons, to try to reposition an ailing brand once it has been on the market. This story demonstrates how innovative strategic research was designed and implemented, leading to actionable results.

A leading suntan oil company introduced its brand in Europe, using the same marketing, advertising, and promotional strategies that had been successful in the United States. The brand was a dismal failure and additional research was unable to determine why.

An American working in a French market research agency was consulted. It was his belief that European women and American women might have very different ideas about skin care, and to test this he used psychodrama, a technique adapted from the field of psychology. In psychodrama, subjects are asked how they would respond to hypothetical situations that are extreme but realistic.

The skin-care psychodrama asked the subjects to imagine that they were on a plane flying over the ocean. They are given a carry-on bag that contains various cosmetics and personal-care products, including an American brand of suntan lotion, a French brand of suntan lotion, other lotions, and moisturizing creams. The plane develops engine problems and has to land on the water near an island where they will be for at least five days. They are told they have 60 seconds to choose only a few of the items in their carry-on luggage. Virtually every French woman in the sample took all the moisturizing creams and lotions that were in the luggage, but very few took any of the suntan oil.

In exploring the reasons for their choices, it was discovered that loss of skin moisture is of primary concern to European women. The sun is seen as a main cause of moisture loss, which leads to skin deterioration and aging. In promoting the American brand of suntan oil, the focus had been on the tanning benefits with no mention of how it might prevent moisture loss. Furthermore, the product visuals and the advertising showed deeply tanned models. This was sending the message that the skin was being baked. One French respondent summed it up, "When my roast beef turns that color brown, I know it's done."

The insights gained from the innovative use of a psychological technique enabled the company to reposition the brand in Europe, where women have very different wants and needs regarding sun protection.[3] ■

and Tull define market segmentation as follows: "Market segmentation is concerned with individual or intergroup differences in response to marketing mix variables. The managerial presumption is that if these response differences exist, can be identified, are reasonably stable over time, and the segments can be efficiently reached the firm may increase its sales and profits beyond those obtained

Market segmentation is a necessity for companies in today's competitive market. Through market segmentation research, managers recognize that various consumer groups respond differently to product variations or have differing demand responses to marketing variables. SOURCE: Clockwise from top left, © Jim Cummins/FPG, © Arthur Tilley/FPG, Ron Chapple/FPG, © Robert Brenner/PhotoEdit.

by assuming market homogeneity."[5] In this definition you will note the four basic criteria for segmenting a market.

1. The segments must exist in the environment.
2. The segments must be identifiable.
3. The segments must be reasonably stable.
4. The segments must be efficiently reachable.

In today's marketplace, just about every product category market can be segmented. The major job of managers is to identify the most profitable segments on the basis of variations in consumer responses to alternative marketing strategies.

Market Segmentation Strategies

The objective of market segmentation research is to identify consumer groups that respond differently to product variations or have difference responses to marketing mix variables. Segmentation approaches can be based on one of three underlying strategies: a priori segmentation, post hoc segmentation, or unstructured segmentation.

a priori segmentation
The process of segmenting markets on the basis of hunches, assumptions, or custom. This type of segmentation is not empirically based.

In **a priori segmentation,** the segments are predefined according to specific criteria. Marketing researchers break out customer groups by some known and generally accepted classification scheme that is assumed or known to be related to variations in customer purchase or usage of the product or service category. The main objective of research is to see why the segments differ.

Marketing researchers approach this type of segmentation research with the belief that certain predefined groups may have varying demands for the product and varying response patterns to marketing mix variables. A priori segments that are not based on previous empirical research are seldom optimal and often are inefficient from a marketing perspective. This is because a priori segments are often based on convenience or tradition and not on thoughtful empirical research. For example, Happy Cat cat food traditionally has thought of its market as composed of two basic segments: those with pedigreed cats and those with nonpedigreed cats. This segmentation scheme was based on the assumption that consumers with pedigreed cats are more interested in pampering their cats and would be interested in a more expensive, higher-quality product. Based on this assumption, Happy Cat has a high-priced, higher-quality line targeted at pedigreed cat owners and a lower-priced, lower-quality line targeted at those with nonpedigreed cats. The media strategy for the higher-priced, higher-quality line traditionally has been based on the use of highly targeted print media that appealed to cat fanciers. However, Happy Cat found in a study that there was no difference between owners of pedigreed and nonpedigreed cats in regard to their desire to pamper their cats, the brands they purchase, or the amount they spend on cat food. As a result of the research, the company reevaluated its segmentation strategy.

post hoc segmentation
The process of segmenting a market or markets empirically.

In **post hoc segmentation,** or hypothesized segmentation, prior knowledge or research has suggested that certain segments exist. This type of research involves the identification of market segments empirically. Segments generated under a post hoc approach are formed by clustering respondents who respond similarly to sets of classification questions. These questions may cover product usage patterns, attitudes toward a product class, attitudes toward brands, brand switching behavior, or other related questions. For example, in a study of the fast food market, preferred fast food restaurants were analyzed by demographic characteristics using cluster analysis. Those who preferred McDonald's were more likely to be teenagers under the age of 16 or families with children under the age of 16. On the other hand, those who preferred Wendy's were more likely to be young adults between the ages of 18 and 25 and families without children.

unstructured segmentation
Process of segmenting a market using data collection and analysis when no prior ideas are held about number of segments, what they are, or how and why they are different.

There are four main objectives to the research in post hoc segmentation: (1) to confirm the segmentation; (2) to identify how the segments differ, (3) to discover why they differ; and (4) to determine their size.

The third underlying strategy on which segmentation approaches can be based is **unstructured segmentation,** in which no ideas are held about the number of

Cluster analysis was used to study the demographic characteristics of consumers frequenting fast food restaurants. Those who preferred McDonalds included families with young children while young adults preferred Wendy's. SOURCE: © Dennis Cody/FPG, © Mary Kate Denny/PhotoEdit.

segments, what they are, or how and why they are different. Data collection and analysis are carried out to identify segments.

There are several bases that can be used in segmentation:

1. Geographic (northern, southern, urban, rural, etc.)
2. Demographic (high/low income, life cycle, etc.)
3. Usage rate (consumption behavior, i.e., heavy users, light users, nonusers, etc.)
4. Benefits
5. Psychographics (lifestyle, attitudes, values, etc.)
6. Psychological[6]

Methodology for Post Hoc Market Segmentation Studies

All post hoc segmentation studies tend to have certain commonalities in methodology. These elements are described in the following paragraphs.

Research Strategy Post hoc segmentation is empirically derived. Segments are identified on the basis of a research study conducted for the specific purpose of segmenting the market.

Selecting Basis Variables The most important question facing the marketing researcher designing a post hoc segmentation study is the selection of "basis variables" for the segmentation. Basis variables are variables that are believed to be useful in identifying market segments. This problem is made more difficult because an almost limitless number of "basis variables" can be used. The researcher must call on his experience and theories about consumers and the market in selecting the appropriate basis variables for the particular segmentation. Some possible basis variables include

- Product purchase patterns
- Benefits sought from the product or service

- Sensitivity to price
- Socioeconomic status
- Lifestyle characteristics
- Product preference measures
- Product usage heaviness
- Brand preferences
- Purchase intent
- General attitudes and outlook on life
- Deal proneness (responsiveness to deals such as coupons)
- Combinations of the preceding basis variables

In addition to selecting the basis variables, marketing researchers also must select the descriptive variables. These are variables that researchers do not believe should be used as bases for segmentation but are needed to describe and help define the segments identified by using the segmentation basis variables. Descriptive variables generally fall into two categories: demographic variables (e.g., age, occupation, education, stage in the family life cycle, and many others) and media usage variables (e.g., television viewing habits, radio listening habits, magazine and newspaper readership). These variables will help marketing researchers and managers in developing marketing programs to effectively reach the targeted segments. For example, the research may reveal that heavy users of a new spicy cheese developed by Kraft General Foods watch *Monday Night Football.*

Data Collection Procedures Data for market segmentation studies must be collected by a sampling technique that provides a high-quality sample because of the need to accurately project the results to the total market. Given that interviewers seldom have to show anything to respondents in a market segmentation study, non-face-to-face survey methods are appropriate. These two considerations normally lead researchers to select central location telephone studies, ad hoc mail surveys, or mail panels.

Sampling Procedures It is critical that the results of market segmentation studies be projectable to the total target population. That is because we need to make accurate inferences about market segments that can be used for planning purposes. Researchers need to have accurate estimates of the sizes of particular segments. As a result, probability samples are required Simple random samples and stratified samples are used most often.

The Baseline Market Segmentation Study The first market segmentation study conducted by an organization is referred to as the **baseline market segmentation study**. The initial study should be preceded by a detailed review of secondary sources and previous research in the product category, both quantitative and qualitative. A baseline post hoc segmentation study should do the following:

baseline market segmentation study
The first market segmentation study conducted by an organization.

1. Deal with current and expected products.
2. Include both current and expected purchaser groups.
3. Given that the results will be used for strategic planning, ensure that senior management be involved from the beginning.

Marketing Research in Practice

The VALS (values and lifestyles) program originally was developed by SRI International as a basis for psychographic market segmentation. The original VALS, developed in the 1980s, began with a theory about psychographic segmentation and proceeded to collect the data to implement that theory. But VALS™2, developed in the 1990s, began with data and built a theory from it. The people who built VALS2 looked for specific relationships between attitudes and purchase behavior. VALS2 divides the American population into eight groups as defined by self-identity and resources. They range in affluence from Actualizers (upscale independent intellectuals) to Strugglers (mostly nostalgic, downscale elderly women). In between are the principle-oriented Fulfilleds and Believers, the status-oriented Achievers and Strivers, and the action-oriented Experiencers and Makers.

The advertising agency Della Femina of Pittsburgh used VALS2 to update the image of Iron City beer, says director of research John Mather. Iron City was a well-known brand in Pittsburgh, but it was losing sales. The core markets, Makers and Believers, were growing older and drinking less beer. Younger men were bypassing the brand.

Della Femina linked Simmons data to VALS types to show that Experiencers were the highest-volume beer consumers, followed by Strivers. Mather began interviewing men who fit these VALS types. He used a technique called *picture sorting* (Chapter 6) to get at Iron City's image problems. The technique involves giving focus group participants a deck of cards showing different kinds of people. The researcher then asks respondents to identify brand users and people most like themselves. The respondents pictured Iron City drinkers as "blue-collar steelworkers stopping at the local bar," Mather says. They portrayed themselves as hard working but also fun loving. Like the city, they were gaining economic strength and rejecting the heavy-industry image.

Della Femina designed ads that link Iron City beer to the changing self-image of the target group. The ads mix images of old Pittsburgh with images of the new, vibrant city and shots of young Experiencers and Strivers working hard at having fun. The soundtrack is the song "Working in a Coal Mine" with new lyrics—"working on a cold iron." The ads run on radio and TV programs popular with Strivers and Experiencers. After the first few months of the campaign, sales of Iron City went up significantly.

Transport Canada also scored with the new VALS. As the equivalent of the U.S. Department of Transportation, Transport Canada owns and operates about 140 airports. It attempted to use VALS several years ago, but many of the old questions ("Would you vote for a Communist to be mayor of your city?") were irrelevant to Canadians. However,

continues

after reviewing VALS2, the agency decided to use it.

Later, the agency did a VALS2 survey of 850 travelers who were passing through Vancouver's airport. The biggest share of respondents were Actualizers (37 percent), followed by Experiencers (20 percent). The surprising preponderance of Actualizers among travelers suggests that stores like Sharper Image or the Nature Company could do well at airports.

VALS2 has provided new insights into Canada's travelers. But this knowledge will not become useful until merchants, airport managers, and other government departments can be educated about the uses for the information. Understanding the VALS2 system is not easy; it takes time.[7] ■

FIGURE 20.2
VALS™2 Categories Used for Segmentation of the U.S. Population

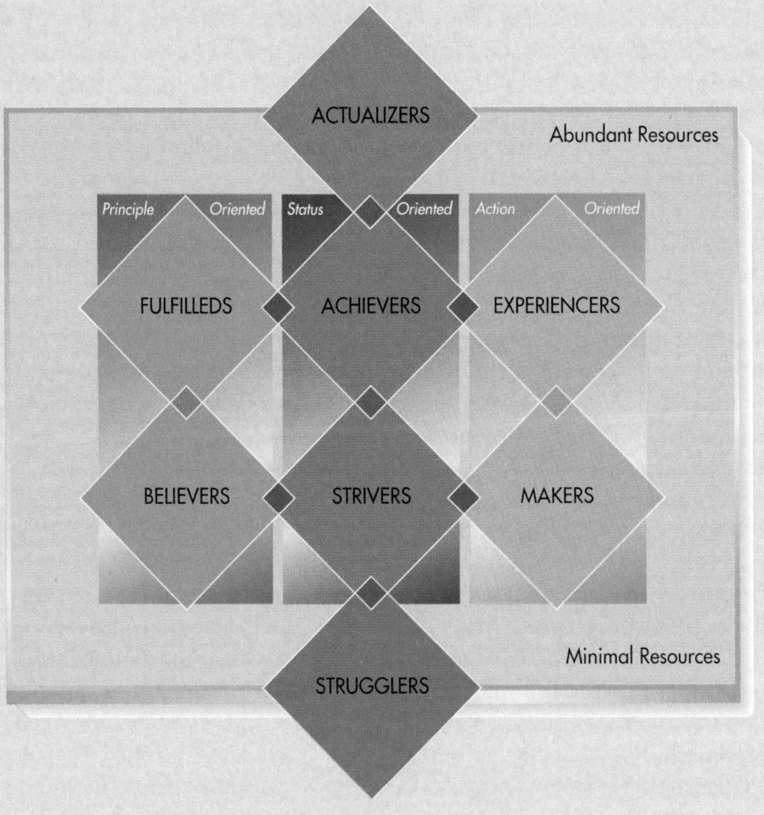

4. Use a large sample (sample size greater than 1,000) and a large number of variables to permit detailed analysis of alternative subgroups and segmentation approaches.
5. Include descriptive media usage variables to provide a basis for operationalizing a media plan that will efficiently reach the segments identified.
6. Devote a relatively large amount of time (several months) to the data analysis phase of the project because many approaches must be tried and reviewed with the client.

7. Ensure that management be prepared to spend the funds necessary to accomplish the baseline study objective. Costs exceeding $100,000 are not uncommon for national segmentation studies.

Segmentation Classification Schemes The results of all future marketing research studies should be reported by market segment after the completion of the baseline segmentation study. To operationalize this goal, it is necessary to develop a classification scheme from the baseline results. This scheme can be included in future studies by using a standard set of questions, which are used to classify future respondents into the appropriate market segment. The classification scheme provides the mechanism that will permit us to view future data from a consistent market segmentation perspective. From time to time the market segmentation scheme must be revised to take into account changes in the marketplace. For example, if a baseline study found that the only meaningful way to segment the fast food market was on the basis of age (those under 35 and those 35 years of age or older), then in all future studies, results would be analyzed separately for these two age groups.

Analysis A number of procedures, including cluster analysis, correspondence analysis, and *Q*-type factor analysis, are used to analyze the data produced in a market segmentation study (see Chapter 18). Cluster analysis has become the most commonly used segmentation analysis procedure. As you may recall, cluster analysis is a statistical procedure used to group together those respondents who give similar answers to the "basis questions." For example, a researcher may have determined through focus groups, previous research, and secondary sources that three factors are important in defining segments in the fast food market: age, income, and attitude toward nutrition. The next step would be to measure these three variables in a probability sample drawn from the target population. Cluster analysis would then be used to identify groups of people, out of the total number interviewed in the survey, who gave similar answers to the questions used to measure these three basic variables.

Product Research

Product is one of the four Ps of the marketing mix. Most marketing texts suggest that product and the other three Ps (price, place, and promotion) are equally important and must be determined simultaneously. Although this is true in theory, in practice the development of a marketing program usually begins with development of the product. As a result, product research is extremely important and one of the major areas of marketing research activity. There are many types of product research studies. Because of space limitations, we will discuss only a few of the most common types of product research.

Product Prototype Tests

product prototype tests

Tests conducted to obtain the reactions of target customers to early working versions of new products.

Product prototype tests seek consumer reactions to an actual early version of the product. This early version of the product (or prototype) ideally has been developed with the benefit of product concept screening and product concept evaluation tests. In prototype testing, the product is provided to consumers from

Marketing Research in Practice

Test marketing indicated that Frito-lay had another winner on its hands.

Frito-Lay is proving again that innovation drives growth in the multibillion-dollar salty-snack business. Sunchips, the marketer's multigrain salty snack, has been a smash hit but a long time in the making. After record test-market results and first-year sales in excess of $100 million, the chip product within five years could become Frito's sixth core brand behind its other powerhouses in the potato, corn tortilla, extruded, and pretzel segments.

"Sunchips is on its way to becoming a core brand," says Manny Goldman, analyst at Paine Webber. "It has the best of both worlds: very good taste and the positive image associated with a multigrain product. You start with taste and go from there. So you have the great taste, the right image, and Frito-Lay's distribution. There is the potential for a large number of variations on the theme—they will do more with Sunchips."

During its 10-plus years of development, Sunchips earned the code name *No. 6*, signaling the high hopes the company has had for the first multigrain snack in the $8.5-billion salty-snack market. Frito-Lay, PepsiCo's snack division, invested more then $30 million in marketing Sunchips on its national introduction in April 1991. In 1992, it spent $20 million more. "Sunchips is the first real substantial innovation in salty-snacks in 20 years," says Dwight Riskey, Frito-Lay marketing vice president. "We've had potato chips since the 1920s; corn chips since the early 1930s; and most recently tortilla chips in the mid-1960s with major growth in the 1980s. Innova-

the target group for in-home usage. After they have had an opportunity to use the product under actual market conditions for some period of time (often two weeks), follow-up interviews are conducted. The purpose of these interviews is to find out what consumers like and dislike about the product and their likelihood of purchase if it were available in the market. For example, when Kraft General Foods developed Cycle dog food, it tested several versions of the product with owners of various breeds of dogs.

Product Pricing Research

product pricing research
Research used to measure consumer sensitivity to different prices for a product.

Product pricing research is often conducted in conjunction with product research. The goal of many pricing studies is to measure consumer sensitivity to different prices that are being considered or to get consumer perceptions of the tion is what makes this business move."

Sunchips now sells in three flavors: original, French Onion, and Harvest Cheddar. The product is made from whole wheat, corn, other grains, and canola or sunflower oil; it offers a healthier alternative to heavy snackers and aging baby boomers.

By the early 1980s, Frito-Lay began to worry whether aging baby boomers would continue to eat salty snacks. The multigrain product seemed like an alternative for consumers who loved salty snacks but might cut back on consumption as they grew older. "The aging baby boomers were a very significant factor [in Sunchip's development]," says Riskey. "We were looking for new products that would allow them to snack. But we were looking for 'better-for-you' aspects in products and pushing against that demographic shift."

Working under the in-house code named *Harvest,* Frito-Lay in the late 1980s was poised to test its multigrain chip. Frito-Lay test-marketed Sunchips in Minnesota, North Dakota, South Dakota, and parts of Wisconsin and Iowa. "From the first day, it was the most successful test market we've ever seen," says Riskey. "Within four months, we had to cut the test market in half because we couldn't keep up with production." Even grocery store managers began getting complaints from consumers about not getting the product. "We learned repeat purchasing was at an awesome level," says Riskey. "We knew we had strong franchise within five months [of test marketing].

"Within six months, we started to make plans for expansion." Riskey points out that once people have tried the product, they continue to buy it, showing the best depth of repeat of any new Frito-Lay product.

A pleasant surprise for Frito-Lay is that Sunchips has turned out to be more "mainstream" than initial research suggested. The product has broad consumer appeal across all ages—a factor that gives Sunchips "megabrand" potential.[8] ■

appropriate price for the product. Single source research (see Chapter 8) provides an excellent vehicle for measuring price elasticity.

Packaging Tests

The package usually is considered to be part of the product. Packaging normally has two roles: to protect the product (e.g., keep it fresh) and to sell the product. The first role of the package is product related, whereas the second function serves primarily a promotional role. A number of aspects of packaging might be subjected to marketing research studies (i.e., **packaging tests**):

packaging tests
Tests used to gauge reactions to different packaging approaches.

- Which alternative color or graphic treatments are most effective in attracting consumer attention on the shelf?

Marketing Research in Practice

The Brawny paper towel brand that has been on the market since 1975 recently underwent numerous changes as a result of an in-depth research project. The brand's volume was fairly flat, and it had not really been advertised for two years. It was second position in the market along with ScotTowels. The James River Corporation, in conjunction with DDB Needham, New York, its advertising agency, developed a nine-month study that examined all aspects of the Brawny brand—its positioning, its identity and personality, packaging advertising, and the basic product itself.

Qualitative research was used to determine the strengths and weaknesses of the Brawny man. Both users and nonusers of the brand participated in focus groups. Role-playing and other techniques were used to explore Brawny's personality as well as the personality of the Brawny buyer. The results indicates that although consumers were not exactly sure what Brawny was, they found him kind and warm and, in general, an appealing character. The results of other qualitative exercises showed that Brawny was a pleasant conversationalist, well behaved, popular, a little shy, and, most important, dependable and reliable. Thus, Brawny's characteristics also could be applied to those of the paper towel: helpful, reliable, and willing to get the job done.

The company also wanted information on the value of the Brawny man logo. A quantitative study was done that looked at the various package designs as well as various representations of Brawny. The results indicated that the Brawny man symbol was almost universally recognized, more so than any other brand symbols they tested (see Tables 20.1 and 20.2).

Marketing research revealed that the Brawny man is perceived as helpful, reliable, and willing to get the job done.

- Which delivery approach is preferred by consumers who purchase this product (e.g., pop-top can, screw-off cap glass bottle, screw-off cap plastic bottle)?
- Which shape is preferred?

Product Concept Tests

product concept testing
The testing of new product ideas before they have been turned into prototypes.

Product concept testing is a popular type of product research. We use the term *product* in the broadest sense to refer to both physical products and services. This is consistent with current usage in that marketing managers in service industries

Using these research results, some alternative package designs were tested and several modifications were made to the Brawny package. Brawny's ax was removed and his size was shrunk about 10 percent so consumers could more easily see the decorative prints on the towels. His hairstyle was updated, the brand name was made more readable, and water droplets were added to communicate absorbency.

Additional qualitative research was done to determine consumers' needs and feelings on paper towels in general and Brawny in particular. The results showed that spills and absorbency were of prime importance and that consumers who had never tried Brawny towels before were impressed. Additional positioning tests showed opportunities for increasing Brawny's appeal and also purchases of the brand. A new positioning statement was developed, "Thirst Pockets for Spill Relief."

Using all these research results, DDB Needham began developing a new advertising campaign. More qualitative research was done to help develop a specific execution and the tone of the advertising. The resulting ad depicts a kindergarten teacher using Brawny towels for the messes created in her finger-painting class. When the advertising campaign began, a tracking study showed that awareness levels of Brawny were increasing significantly. This multifaceted research project had produced results that the James River Corporation then used to create a new package, new positioning, and a new advertising campaign.[9] ■

TABLE 20.1 Awareness Comparisons of Brands Based on Package Logos Only

Brawny paper towels	94%
Charmin bath tissue	92%
Bounty paper towels	90%
Quilted Northern bath tissue	80%
Viva paper towels	72%
Scott paper towels	63%

TABLE 20.2 Product Characteristics Associated with Brawny Name and Package

	SAW BRAWNY NAME ONLY	SAW BRAWNY PACKAGE
Purchase Intent	55%	65%
Thick	75%	83%
Absorbent	72%	82%
Strong	72%	81%

typically refer to their service offering as a "product." The single most important factor in marketing success is consumer acceptance of the product through purchase. The goal of product concept testing is to understand consumer perceptions of the product concept, perceived product benefits. The acceptance of the product by actual purchase is the ultimate goal. Product concept testing is a key element in the process of developing a successful marketing strategy.

A product concept is an idea for a new product or a significant modification of an existing product or service. The new product development process begins with the generation of ideas or concepts for new products. Normally, this process generates many more ideas for new products than possibly could be developed. As in any idea generation process, some of the ideas are good and others are not so good. To find out which ideas are worthy of further development, marketing researchers turn to the marketplace for evaluation. There are two types of concept tests.

The type of test just described is a concept screening test. The objective of concept screening tests is to identify those ideas or concepts, out of the large number generated, that have the greatest potential for successful development. In addition, marketing researchers also may use concept screening tests to rank those ideas that appear to have the potential for successful development. This type of concept test normally is conducted at an early stage in the new product development cycle. The objective is to eliminate concepts with limited potential for success before the firm has invested very much in them. For example, Frito-Lay often has more ideas for new products than it can possibly fund at a given time. It needs to know which of these ideas have adequate appeal in the marketplace and the relative appeal of each product idea or concept. With this information, it can make rational decisions regarding which concepts should move ahead in the development process, which concepts do not have adequate market appeal, and which concepts might be reserved for future development (have adequate appeal but not as much as the most attractive concepts).

The second type of product concept test is the concept evaluation test. At this stage, marketing researchers are working with a concept that has passed the initial screening. The goals of concept evaluation tests are to develop a better estimate of potential sales for the product, identify the characteristics of likely purchasers, determine the appropriate positioning for the product, and identify weaknesses in the concept so that they can be corrected.

The remainder of this section is devoted to concept evaluation tests.

Typical Methodology for Concept Evaluation Tests

Marketing researchers normally use several standard procedures for concept evaluation tests. These procedures relate to data collection, sampling, and analysis; they are described in the following paragraphs.

Data Collection Procedures Typically, in concept evaluation tests, researchers obtain consumer reactions to descriptions and visual representations of the proposed product. Figure 20.3 depicts an actual concept tested by a large pesticide manufacturer. The concept was thoroughly rejected. One respondent said, "I don't want dead flies all over my house." Others were concerned about children's safety.

In some cases, the data are collected using telephone interviews. Usually, however, researchers need to use a technique that enables them to get product descriptions and visual stimuli into the hands of target customers. Mall intercept and mail surveys frequently are used to achieve this goal. Mail intercept surveys have the advantage of enabling the researcher to present descriptions of the product concepts, test commercials, and other visual stimuli to target customers in a controlled environment. In some cases, mail surveys may be used alone or combined with telephone interviews. In the latter procedure, descriptions of product concepts and other visual stimuli are mailed to consumers and a telephone interview is conducted later.

FIGURE 20.3
The Daisy Fly-Bait Concept

Daisy Fly-Bait comes with a self-adhesive backing that can be attached to any window. Normally, flies migrate to the kitchen so this would be the most likely location for the Daisy. The Daisy contains a pheromone to attract the flies. The flies then eat the bait contained in the center of the Daisy. The bait contains a pesticide that kills the flies within 20 minutes.

Sampling Procedures An important issue in product concept evaluation research is the definition of the universe or population of interest for the study. The goal is to define the population to include those individuals believed to fall into the target group for the product. If the test is being conducted for a product that represents a new entry into an existing product category, the typical practice is to define the target market to include current users of brands in the category. For example, if a marketing researcher is testing a nonprescription cold-symptom relieving product, then the target market is defined to include those individuals who have purchased or used brands in that category with some level of frequency (e.g., three or more times) within some time frame (e.g., the past 90 days). This approach to sampling assumes that if a new entry into a product category is to be successful, it will have to garner significant sales from existing users of brands in the category. If mall intercept is used for data collection, the sample will be a convenience sample. On the other hand, if the test can be done as a telephone, mail, or mail-telephone survey, then the sample may be a probability sample.

General Categories of Questions Although every concept evaluation test has its own unique questions, several types of questions are found on almost every test. These concept evaluation questions fall into the following categories:

- *Purchase intent.* Usually the key question on any product concept test is whether the consumer will purchase the product (see Chapter 11). At some point in the interview, researchers describe the new product and ask something such as the following, "If this product were available in stores where you normally shop and sold for $9.95, how likely would you be to purchase it? Would you be very likely, somewhat likely, somewhat unlikely, or very unlikely?" Responses to this question provide the basis for making market share and sales estimates for the new product and serve as the basic classification variable for most of the remaining analysis.
- *Demographic characteristics.* Marketing researchers normally collect information on the demographic characteristics of respondents (e.g., age, income, education, and occupation). This information can be crosstabulated by the purchase

intent information to gain a better idea of the characteristics of likely purchasers. These data also are useful in the process of strategy development.

- *Category and brand usage.* Category usage questions are used to determine whether the particular individual falls into the population of interest or "target market." For those individuals who qualify based on their usage of the product category, we are interested in determining their frequency of purchase or use and their usage of various brands in the category. For example, assume that the researcher is interested in cold cereals and the respondent claims to eat cold cereal. The researcher will then ask, "Which cold cereals do you eat, Rice Krispies, Corn Flakes, Raisin Bran, or some other?" As in the case of demographics, marketing researchers normally analyze usage patterns by purchase intent for the product concept. Are we pulling from heavy users or from light users? This information will go into the model that we use to develop sales estimates for the product concept.
- *Attribute ratings.* We also may ask respondents to rate the importance of various product attributes and to rate the product concept on the same attributes. For example, we might ask respondents to rate a concept for a new car on styling, performance, and economy after having them rate the importance of those attributes.
- *Likes and dislikes.* Researchers would be remiss if they did not ask respondents what they particularly like about the product concept and what they particularly dislike. These questions are asked on an open-ended basis and may provide information that is useful in refining the concept.

Analysis Analysis of the results of our concept evaluation test can take many forms. However, there are several things that a researcher usually does as part of the analysis:

- *Develop sales estimates.* The marketing researcher will use the results of the purchase intent question and other questions to develop sales estimates for the product. The process of developing these estimates is described in the Videos to Go example, which follows. Sales estimates are used to decide whether to continue to develop the product concept.
- *Further define market segments.* By crosstabulating the results of the demographic and other classification questions by the responses to the purchase intent question, the researcher is able to better define the characteristics of likely purchasers and nonpurchasers of the proposed product.
- *Determine what likely purchasers particularly like and dislike about the concept.* This information provides guidance for improving the product concept. Researchers also may look at the likes and dislikes of people who are unlikely to purchase the new product. This also may provide clues for improving the product to make it more attractive to these individuals and, thereby, expand the market.

Concept Evaluation of Videos to Go

The Concept This is a concept evaluation test for a new video rental service. The features of the new service are:

- The name is Videos to Go.
- The service involves the use of kiosks in shopping center and mall parking lots, similar to those used by some film processing companies, to provide drive-up rental of videos.
- The stories will stock only the 100 leading videos based on industry sources that track video rental across the country.
- The titles carried will be changed once a month to keep up with the most recent top 100 list.
- Videos are rented for one night at a cost of two dollars. Additional days cost three dollars.
- Members will receive a plastic "credit card" with a magnetic strip that totally automates the rental transaction and, thus, speeds up the process so that waiting time is minimal.
- A list of current titles is mailed to members once a month.
- Members can expect to find a location within five minutes of their homes.

A rendering of the proposed units would be shown to respondents.

Research Objectives As we discussed earlier, the objectives of the research are the following:

- To develop an estimate of the number of people who will use the new service.
- To determine what potential purchasers like and dislike about the concepts so that the concept can be refined.
- To identify the characteristics of likely purchasers so that they can be more efficiently and effectively targeted in promotional programs for the new service.

A drive-through video rental shop similar to the Videos to Go store concept. SOURCE: Mimi Forsyth/Monkmeyer Press.

Methodology The test was conducted in Houston, Texas. Houston was chosen because, if the concept proved to be viable, the service would be launched in the Houston market. The mail-telephone approach, described earlier, was used for the test. The population was defined to include individuals 18 years of age or older who rent six or more videos in an average month. Potential respondents were contacted by telephone, screened for video rental qualifications, and asked whether they would be willing to participate in the mail survey portion of the study. They were offered a certificate good for three video rentals at a chain of Houston video rental stores for their participation. Six hundred qualified individuals were recruited; completed questionnaires were returned by 420. The questionnaire covered the research objectives, targeting reactions to each specific feature of the concept, and expected frequency of use of the new service.

Analysis The results of the concept test were subjected to extensive analysis. In this example, we focus on two facets of the analysis: market segmentation and developing a sales estimate.

Market segmentation focused on the results of the purchase intent question crosstabulated by age of the respondent, which are summarized in Table 20.3. Those under 35 years old are much more likely to use the new service. Of those under 35 years of age, 30.5 percent said they are "very likely" to use the new service compared with only 14.1 percent of those 35 years old and over. The difference between the two age groups is statistically significant by *t*-test or chi-square test. This suggests that the marketing strategy for the new service should be directed at those under 35 years of age. Also, the media strategy and the advertising message would be geared to the consumer 35 years old or younger. The researchers, of course, examined the results by other demographic characteristics to develop a more complete picture of the best target customers for the new service.

Using the survey results to develop an estimate of sales for the new concept required several steps:

1. *Adjust survey results.* First, the analysis needed to calculate a percentage that could be applied to the total target market, using the results from the pur-

TABLE 20.3 Videos to Go Concept Test Purchase Intent by Age (percentages are based on column totals)

	AGE GROUPS		
PURCHASE INTENT	*Totals (n = 420)*	*< 35 (n = 200)*	*35 or over (n = 220)*
Total	100%	100%	100%
Very likely	22.0%	30.5%	14.1%
Somewhat likely	30.0%	37.0%	23.9%
Somewhat unlikely	28.0%	20.0%	35.5%
Very unlikely	20.0%	12.5%	26.8%

chase intent question and deflation factors, sometimes referred to as *purchase intent adjustment factors* (see Chapter 11).[10] The question to be answered is, What percentages of those who said they were very likely, somewhat likely, somewhat unlikely, or very unlikely to use the new service would actually use it? By examining individuals who responded to purchase intent questions in tests done for similar services, researchers develop intent translation adjustment factors to apply to raw survey results. In other words, what percentages of people who said they were very likely, somewhat likely, somewhat unlikely, or very unlikely to purchase or use a new product actually did so after it was introduced? The company conducting this test had determined, in previous tests for similar services, that about 60 percent of those who said they were very likely to purchase or use the new service actually would use it after introduction. The comparable figures for the "somewhat likely" and "somewhat unlikely" categories are 30 percent and 5 percent, respectively. Based on the previous test, virtually none of those in the "very unlikely" category were expected to purchase. Applying these adjustment factors to the survey results provided the following estimate, which can be applied to the total target market:

LIKELIHOOD OF PURCHASE	SURVEY RESULT	ADJUSTMENT FACTOR	ADJUSTED RESULT
Very likely	22%	.60	13.2%
Somewhat likely	30%	.30	9.0%
Somewhat unlikely	28%	.05	1.4%
Very unlikely	20%	.00	.0%
Estimated percent purchasers			23.6%

2. *Apply the percentage developed in the previous step to the total target market.* Using the survey results and 1990 census data, approximately 327,000 people in the Houston metropolitan area were estimated to meet the target market characteristics (18 years of age or older and have rented six or more videos in the past 30 days). Multiplying the percentage calculated in Step 1 by 327,000 provides an estimated market size of 77,172.
3. *Estimate total annual video rental potential in the target market.* This figure was estimated by multiplying the total market size of 77,172 (obtained in the previous step) by the average number of rentals from the proposed store in an average month of 3.2. This result was obtained from a specific question in the survey. This calculation shows a monthly potential of 246,950 or an annual potential of 2,963,404 rentals.
4. *Prepare a financial analysis.* The projected number of annual rentals of 2,963,404, developed in the previous step, was multiplied by the expected rental rate of two dollars to obtain an expected annual revenue for the new service in the Houston market of $5,926,809. The volume estimate provides a basis for determining the number of locations and the required personnel at those locations. These figures, along with other estimated costs of doing business, provide a basis for estimating the total cost of serving this volume of business. This total cost figure would, of course, be subtracted from the total

projected revenue to arrive at an estimated profit-loss for the venture. Based on this analysis, the company should be in a position to make a final decision regarding whether to introduce the new service in the Houston market.

Using Research in the Product Development Process

A good example of the use of research in the product development process is provided by Samsonite's development of its Piggyback line of luggage (see Figure 20.4).[11] According to Bob Bengen, director, Direct Marketing & Research, Samsonite Corporation, Piggyback luggage, which includes a full-size model and a carry-on model, the top-selling style of Samsonite's hardside luggage. This was not achieved through luck, but rather through market segmentation research, concept research, and product research to listen to consumer concerns, act on them, and then determine whether these concerns were met.

Development of Piggyback luggage began when a qualitative study, called *luggage exploratory,* was conducted to focus on the issues that people have when they travel. Eleven focus groups were conducted with respondents who had previously completed a screening questionnaire so that each group represented a particular lifestyle segment.

The focus groups proceeded from a general discussion of travel-related problems to a more specific discussion of travel away from home, luggage used, packing, checking or carrying on luggage, luggage image, and ideal luggage. Both men and women said that any pleasure from traveling was diminished by, among other things, transporting luggage, especially in air travel, with long walks from car to gate.

Later, initial concept research was conducted to determine which direction to take a new product development. A total of 400 respondents, again prescreened and this time skewed toward women, were interviewed. Respondents viewed a

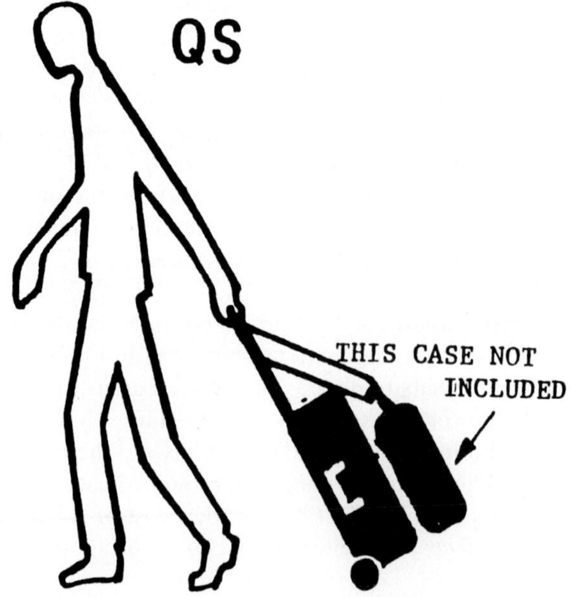

FIGURE 20.4

Concept Drawing for Samsonite's Piggyback Luggage

SOURCE: Direct Marketing and Research, Samsonite Corporation.

Marketing research played a critical role in developing Samsonite's line of Piggyback luggage. SOURCE: Courtesy of Samsonite Corporation.

series of black and white drawings with a brief description of each idea and then rated their interest in the ideas. One of the more appealing concepts was a "line of luggage that can be strapped together 'piggyback' fashion."

One of the designers, working in conjunction with marketing research, started development of a prototype of a revolutionary hard-side case with wheels. Most full-size luggage today, be it hard-side or soft-side, has wheels to aid in moving the case. What was so new about this luggage was that it had only two large wheels instead of the usual four and the wheels were on the side of the luggage rather than on the bottom. Obviously, this arrangement would be unstable without a handle for balance when pulling or pushing. In creating the handle, the designer also incorporated some untraditional ideas: a telescoping handle and a self-retracing strap. The patented handle, invisible when not in use, would incorporate a spring-loaded strap so that other items—briefcases, handbags, other luggage, and so forth—could be loaded atop the Piggyback and secured. In essence, the Piggyback had its own luggage carrier but without the extra weight and inconvenience of a separate piece.

In the midst of management's concern about the fate of hard-side luggage, a concept screening was conducted of the Piggyback, then labeled *Innovative Deluxe*. One hundred respondents were interviewed at a shopping mall for the screening. All respondents needed to be 16 to 60 years old and had to have purchased a travel bag in the past three years and used one in the past year. All interviews were conducted on a one-on-one basis so that any questions about operation could be answered and noted for future reference in preparing advertising and merchandising materials.

Respondents examined a series of rough drawings, outlining the features and use of the Piggyback concept, and then rated the product, both after concept exposure and after actual use, on a four-point purchase interest scale. Although about six out of 10 respondents liked the idea after concept exposure, after-use ratings increased to more than seven out of 10. The study concluded that "the purchase interest in the Piggyback case is consistently testing at a high level among the total population of luggage purchasers."

A production model of the Piggyback was tested, using one of Samsonite's unique testing methods, the "famed" parking lot test. Various Samsonite employees who were frequent travelers, from the president on down, tested the Piggyback on an outside obstacle course, rolling the product over curbs, into ditches, over gravel, and so on for the firm's own version of a *Consumer Reports* test. The testers included men and women and tall and short people. Everyone loved the Piggyback. The Piggyback was introduced in the 1988 Luggage Show, using a mock-up of the same obstacle course, and it received rave reviews from the attendees who gave it a "test drive."

However, Samsonite did not rest on its laurels. Earlier research had shown that, although some people check their luggage for air travel, many more carry on their luggage. Obviously, the original full-size Piggyback was not suitable for carry-on.

The Piggyback carry-on had special criteria. It had to have all the features of the large Piggyback (the wheels, the disappearing handle, and the automatic strap); it had to be small enough to wheel down an aisle and stow in most overhead compartments; yet it had to have sufficient space to carry adequate clothing.

In 1988, a prototype of the Piggyback carry-on was developed, and the company used both qualitative and quantitative consumer research to get the reactions of travelers. The qualitative research was done with two focus groups of flight attendants. Although flight attendants were seen as a target group, the main reason for wanting to talk to them was their vast experience with carry-on luggage, both personally and by observation. The objectives of the study were to understand carry-on usage, identify problems encountered with currently available carry-on luggage, and assess the appeal of the Piggyback carry-on.

The specific quantitative research on the Piggyback carry-on was designed to see how the Piggyback carry-on fared against other Samsonite luggage and competitive carry-ons. In this way, the appeal of the Piggyback carry-on could be assessed against the competition, and its cannibalization of other Samsonite products could be determined.

A total of 200 respondents took part in the study. The respondents examined both the exteriors and interiors of the carry-on luggage. The luggage, with retail prices attached, was displayed in two groups: one with merchandising materials and one without any materials. All the luggage could be wheeled, lifted, and carried to permit more realistic evaluation. Questioning focused on first and second choices, likes and dislikes, and reasons for choosing or not choosing the Piggyback carry-on.

The Piggyback carry-on was well received. The results showed the product's strength with frequent travelers, just the target Samsonite wanted to attract. With reactions so positive, the company made a few cosmetic changes and production began. In 1990, the Piggyback carry-on joined the full-sized Piggyback in luggage departments in stores throughout the United States. By 1992, the full Piggyback line was so successful that its sales, in effect, have been greater than those of some entire luggage companies.

Promotion Research

Promotion research probably is second to product research in frequency of use. The popularity of promotion research is due to the large amount of money spent on promotion and the many promotional alternatives from which to choose.

Ad Positioning Statement Testing

The objective of **ad positioning statement tests** is to obtain consumer reactions to positioning statements such as "At Ford, quality is job one." In the process of designing major ad campaigns, it is important to make sure that statements such as the preceding one are received positively by the target market and convey the message that the advertiser wishes to convey. Focus groups frequently are used for testing positioning statements in the early stages of campaign development.

ad positioning statement tests Tests used to obtain consumer reactions to positioning statements that are being considered for use in ads.

The use of research to develop basic positioning is illustrated in the "Marketing Research in Practice" example for Mr. Coffee.

Marketing Research in Practice

Most advertising, especially brand advertising, implicitly communicates a brand "persona" by nature of establishing what a brand stands for in very human terms. The recognition of the opportunity to explicitly personify that Mr. Coffee brand came from numerous focus groups held before development of a brand campaign itself.

Mr. Coffee regularly conducts focus groups as an initial exploratory step in new product development. In those group discussions with the target audience (primarily women, ages 25 to 59), there was a common thread in how respondents referred to Mr. Coffee. Although it seems obvious now, a "linguistic thread" was almost overlooked at the time.

The objectives of those focus groups dealt with new product development, and, consequently, they originally were analyzed in such a context. When the groups were revisited in the context of a brand message, a brand campaign, already latently understood and accepted, was discovered. Here are some of the consumer quotes referring to the brand: "He makes good coffee." "He's got a lot of different models and prices." "I would try the iced tea machine because I know he makes good coffee." "Why did he wait so long to make an iced tea machine?"

Quantitative and qualitative research identified the following factors as those most important in the purchase of small electric kitchen appliances:

- Good value for the price
- Good quality
- Lasts a long time
- Good taste (for beverage makers)

With these factors in mind, it was decided that "Mr. Coffee," the per-

continues

son, should be a practical, meticulous inventor. As a brand name *Mr. Coffee* denotes a narrow product scope. As a "practical inventor," expanded new product possibilities are much more acceptable. A meticulous nature implies quality products. To begin to develop other personality characteristics for the brand, the first primary research conducted specifically for the campaign was initiated.

To personify "Mr. Coffee," a detailed questionnaire was developed to help in defining nearly every aspect of "his" being, essentially creating both a personal and professional profile. All questions were open ended to allow for maximum latitude in each response. Specific questions included

- What kind of music does he listen to?
- Where does he shop for clothes?
- What type of car does he drive?
- Where was he born?
- Where did he go to college?
- What are his hobbies?

Using this questionnaire, a pilot study was conducted as a means of generating ideas. The results contained an unexpectedly high degree of consistency among the respondents on most questions. For example, when asked, "Which character or personality from TV or movies would he be most like?" respondents indicated Gregory Peck, Robert Young on *Father Knows Best*, and Andy Griffith. This demonstrated strong similarities in respondents' perceptions of "Mr. Coffee's" physical appearance and personality. Correspondingly, people associated "Mr. Coffee" as having a science or mathematics background, possessing an inventive spirit, and being practical or even prudent.

Subsequent to the pilot study, a general question asking respondents to describe "Mr. Coffee" was attached to a questionnaire for a product concept study being conducted for Mr. Coffee by NFO Research, Inc. This would provide national quantitative results that were considered to be requisite in validating the preliminary profile of "Mr. Coffee," which was compiled from the results of the pilot study. The profile that evolved from the quantitative study was surprisingly consistent with the results generated from the pilot study. Specifically, "Mr. Coffee" was perceived to be

married and in his mid-50s, with graying hair, not inordinately distinctive looking, having a scientific orientation, and an inventive yet practical bent.

The finished television advertising campaign featured four commercials: "Art Teacher," "Aunt Loreen," "Perfectionist," and "Hypnotic Suggestion." The documentary-style commercials are humorous reminiscences about inspirational moments in "Mr. Coffee's" career as an inventor, told in down-home, intimate chats with members of his family and friends. Wife, sister, parents, and elderly art teacher—each one gives the viewer some insight into why "Mr. Coffee" does what he does, and then they ponder the tag line for the campaign, "What'll he think of next?"

For example, the spot entitled "Art Teacher" is a monologue by "Mr. Coffee's" elementary school art teacher, Miss Finch. She shows the audience one piece of artwork after another, each one square, no matter what the assignment. "So in 1972 he comes out with a coffeemaker. Big surprise! Square," she sighs. The spot then introduces the new Accel coffeemaker, which has a more curved, sleek look than the traditional model. The spot closes with Miss Finch proclaiming, "Mister, you're making progress."

An advertising tracking study was then established that incorporated a number of brand attributes associated with the campaign through the "Mr. Coffee" character. The initial wave of the tracking study was conducted in early November 1991 before the rollout of the campaign in late November of that year. The study was conducted by the Maffett Research Group in Cleveland with a national sample of 1,000 respondents between the ages of 18 and 59. Along with typical awareness preference questions used in surveys of this type, respondents were asked to rate the Mr. Coffee brand on several attributes reflective of the "Mr. Coffee" character. These included

- Being innovative
- Being practical
- Being a brand you can trust
- Having highest quality overall

These questions enable the advertisers not only to establish a benchmark for the Mr. Coffee brand, but also to understand how effectively the brand image created by "Mr. Coffee" was being communicated.[12] ■

SOURCE: Courtesy of Meldrum & Fewsmith Communications.

Ad Concept Testing

ad concept testing

Testing used to obtain the reactions of target customers to preliminary, rough versions of alternative advertising approaches.

Ad concept testing usually follows positioning statement testing in the research process for developing an advertising campaign. At this point, the advertising agency has enough information to create preliminary versions of advertisements. Usually, the creative group produces a number of different campaign concept approaches, and there is a need to know which of these, if any, achieves the desired communications goals. Concepts for print, radio, or television advertisements may be the subject of this type of research. Regardless of the medium, the objective is to simulate the ad before going to the expense of producing a finished advertisement. Not only does this save on production costs, but it also helps avoid spending the money to place an ad in the particular medium without knowing whether it meets the campaign goals (e.g., increased consumer awareness). A variety of survey methods are used, but a face-to-face data collection procedure is the norm. This is because it is necessary to present the concepts to consumers and then measure their reactions. The mall intercept and focus groups are often used for ad concept testing. Print ads can easily be simulated with desktop publishing software or marker renderings. Radio ads also can be simulated by making a tape of the ad using nonprofessionals. Television ads are more difficult to simulate. They can be simulated, albeit crudely, by using storyboards and in a more realistic fashion using animatics. In the case of animatics, the agency films the frames of a storyboard on videotape and adds a sound track. The tape can then be played for respondents to get a fairly good idea of what the commercial will be like. Research also can be a source of ad concepts.

On-Air Testing

on-air testing

Testing used to measure the impact of television and radio ads after they have begun to run on the air.

On-air testing applies to television and radio advertising. The goal is to test ads after they actually have been produced and have begun to run on the air. The advertiser may be running the ads on a limited basis (i.e., test market), or the ads may be running regionally. The objective is to get a very early indication of whether the ad or ads are working so that they can be replaced with more effective ads before spending the entire budget. These studies usually are conducted by central location telephone interviewing. A typical approach is to call people the day after an ad ran and find out if they were watching television or listening to the radio at the time, whether they were watching or listening to the show when the ad ran, whether they recall the ad on an unaided basis, and, finally, whether they recall the ad on an aided basis. These results are then compared with the results for ads that were successful in the past to see how the ad being tested measures up.

The information in the "A Professional Researcher's Perspective" feature on pages 708 and 709 provides some useful insights on the testing of television commercials. A list of companies providing various types of advertising research is provided in Table 20.4.

Other Types of Promotion Research

In addition to the preceding, there are many other types of promotion research. In particular, an advertiser might be interested in testing a certain couponing approach, other types of promotional deals, premiums, contests, and the like. Often these programs are tested by experimental designs in which, for example,

TABLE 20.4 Ad Research Suppliers

SUPPLIER	MEDIUM	METHODS
ASI Market Research, Inc. New York, N.Y.	Television, print	Recall Persuasion
Bruzzone Research Co. Alameda, Calif.	Television	Recognition
Burke Marketing Research Cincinnati, Ohio	Television, print	Recall Persuasion In-market sales
Diagnostic Research, Inc. New York, N.Y.	Television, print, radio	Communications test
Gallup and Robinson, Inc. Princeton, N.J.	Television, print	Recall Persuasion
Information Resources, Inc. Chicago, Ill.	Television	In-market sales
Starch INRA Hooper, Inc. Mamaroneck, N.Y.	Print	Recognition

a researcher could test three different couponing offers by mailing them to three different matched sets of consumers and tracking the rates of redemption for the three groups. Differences in response rates can be tested statistically and the most effective couponing approach identified. Similar types of tests can be run for other promotional vehicles such as direct mail pieces, point-of-purchase displays, and premiums.

Ad Tracking Research

The purpose of concept evaluation testing is to aid in the development of a viable product. The research also may help in the development of an effective advertising approach. Once that approach has been chosen and implemented, management needs to know how well the communications strategy is working. The goal of **ad tracking research** is to take periodic measurements of variables indicative of how well the advertising campaign is achieving its promotional goals.

ad tracking research
Research used to make periodic measurements of the impact of ads over time.

Objectives of Ad Tracking Research The goal of most advertising campaigns is to increase the sales of the product. However, it is very difficult to assess the effectiveness of a particular advertising campaign based on the observed change in sales after introduction of the campaign. The problem is that many factors other than advertising can have an effect on sales. As a result, an observed change in sales may be due to the new advertising campaign, as well as the effects of all other sales determinants (e.g., price, competitors' advertising, economic conditions, and changing consumer tastes). As a result, it usually is impossible to determine how much of an observed change in sales is due to the new advertising approach and how much is due to these extraneous factors (a detailed discussion of extraneous factors or variables is provided in Chapter 9).

A Professional Researcher's Perspective

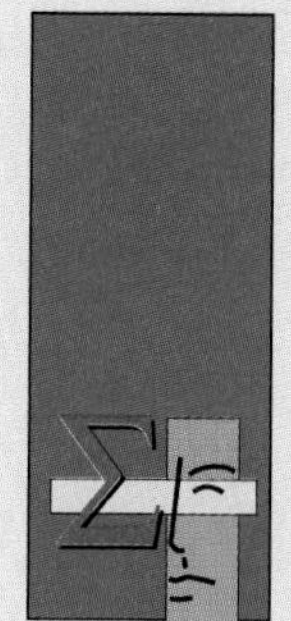

John Coulson, former vice president in charge of research at the Leo Burnett Agency, has some useful perspectives on the testing of television commercials:

1. No single set of measurements is appropriate for all commercials. A commercial is very complex with many different goals.
2. A key element in the results of a commercial test is the type of people on whom the commercial was tested. Some people are more receptive to a particular brand's advertising than are others. For example, product and brand users generally are more receptive to messages about that brand than are nonusers.
3. The most basic rule for achieving a successful commercial is that its viewers can readily identify the product and brand being advertised. It is not uncommon for a competitive brand to be identified as the advertiser.
4. A commercial's ability to generate brand or product recall is largely independent of its effect on the viewer's attitudes toward the brand or product. That is, high recall does not necessarily translate into a positive response.
5. One effective commercial format is to provide news that is relevant and important to viewers. Information about a product may be news to the public for a long time. Advertisers frequently feel that news is stale long before the public does.
6. When the objective of the commercial is to provide news, the news should be seen as important and relevant to the way consumers use the product. The news should be believable, and it should be unique to the brand being advertised. Otherwise, the commercial will be less effective.
7. The measurement of believabil-

Because of the difficulty of directly linking changes in sales to changes in advertising, advertisers tend to rely on the effects of advertising on other variables that can be measured. The variables and factors that typically are measured in ad tracking research include the following:

- *Unaided brand awareness.* In many product categories, advertising is used to maintain or increase top-of-mind awareness of the brand advertised. Advertisers want their brand to be one of those that consumers think of when they have a need for a particular type of product.
- *Aided brand awareness.* As a follow-up to the unaided awareness question, a researcher normally will ask respondents to indicate whether they are aware of various brands not mentioned in the unaided awareness question. The list of brands that is read will include the clients' brand and other major competitive brands. Obviously, aided awareness is not as powerful as unaided awareness as a future sales indicator. This is particularly true for new brands that may have very low initial awareness. For new brands, aided awareness is a significant precursor to the development of higher levels of unaided awareness.

ity is tricky. If there is no news in the commercial, it tends to be rated as believable. Also, the believability of the message in the commercial is not always important to the commercial's success. For example, if the product is relatively low in price, consumers may purchase it just to test the claim that they found hard to believe in the commercial.

8. A basic problem of advertising with the goal of providing news is trying to cover too many ideas. For example, it is more than twice as difficult to deliver two messages as to deliver one.
9. An attractive spokesperson who is appropriate for the product or brand attracts attention and makes the message more believable and compelling.
10. Viewers are wary about the use of celebrity spokespeople in advertising. If the spokesperson does not have characteristics appropriate to the commercial, viewers do not believe her and reject the entire message.
11. In addition to informative commercials, another widely used approach to television advertising is a mood or emotional commercial designed to create greater awareness of, and favorable reaction to, the product or brand. Many commercials successfully combine the two approaches.
12. When a commercial is delivering news of real interest to its viewers, liking the commercial or empathizing with its situation generally is not critical to its effectiveness; instead, clarity and simplicity are important. For mood commercials, on the other hand, likability and empathy are far more important than clarity and simplicity.
13. Appropriate music can enhance the mood of a commercial. Music can make a commercial more memorable and improve consumer attitudes toward the product.[13] ■

- *Advertising awareness.* Advertising awareness tests ask consumers whether they have seen or heard any advertising for brands in the product category of interest in the recent past (past 30 to 90 days). The researcher may ask about ad awareness on an unaided basis and an aided basis in a similar fashion to the way we ask about brand awareness. One of the companies used to conduct advertising brand awareness research is Burke Marketing Research. A description of the firm's DAR test is found in the "Marketing Research in Practice" on pages 710 and 711.
- *Playback.* Playback involves asking respondents to describe or "play back" what the advertising said or showed about the product. Those consumers who say they remember advertising for the product are asked to indicate what that advertising showed about the product. The question normally is asked and recorded as an open-ended response. The goal is to find whether the manufacturer is communicating what it is trying to communicate to target customers.
- *Proven recall.* Proven recall is the evaluation of all open-ended responses to the playback question and eliminating those that do not correctly describe some specific element of the ads for the company sponsoring the research.

Marketing Research in Practice

Burke conducts on-air testing day-after recall (DAR) tests. The In-View service of Gallup and Robinson is another recall test that measures how well ads capture and hold attention. In these recall tests, a finished commercial is run on network television during a regular prime-time program. The following night interviewers in several cities make random telephone calls until they have reached approximately 200 people who actually watched the program that carried the ad at the time the commercial appeared. When they locate one of these people, they ask a series of questions:

1. Do you recall seeing a commercial for any charcoal briquettes?
2. If the answer is no, they ask, do you remember seeing a commercial for Kingsford charcoal briquettes?
3. If the particular respondent gave a "yes" response to either question 1 or question 2, then they ask, what did the commercial say about the product? What did the commercial show about the product? Can you describe how the commercial looked? What ideas were covered in the commercial?

The first type of question is called *unaided recall* because the particular brand was not mentioned by the interviewer. The second question provides an example of an aided recall question because the name of a specific brand is mentioned. Verbatim responses are recorded for the third group of questions. The test requires that the consumer being interviewed tie a specific brand name, or specific product category, to a specific advertisement. If the advertisement fails to produce a direct connection between the brand name and the sales message, then the commercial will not get a high recall score.

There are a number of variations on this traditional approach.

1. In another testing approach, consumers are prerecruited to view a specific program and are contacted by telephone the following day. This approach is used because it reduces research costs and elimi-

Typical Ad Tracking Methodology

There are a number of approaches for the execution of an ad tracking test. Popular procedures that relate to general ad tracking research strategy, data collection, sampling, and analysis are described in the following paragraphs.

Ad Tracking Research Strategy Ad tracking research usually is based on the interrupted time series type of quasi-experimental design (see Chapter 9). This design might take the following form:

$$O_1 \; X_1 \; O_2 \; X_2 \; O_3 \; X_3 \; O_4$$

The *X*s in the expression indicate the introduction of advertising and *O*s indicate the taking of diagnostic measurements. The horizontal distance indicates the passage of time so that X_2 comes after X_1 in time and O_1 comes before X_1. The nates the need to make a large number of random telephone calls to find a given number of viewers who watched the program where the commercial of interest ran.

2. In another approach, consumers are exposed to commercials in a movie theater setting. They are then telephoned at home one to three days later.
3. Under a third approach, respondents are recruited to watch a telecast on a local cable television channel at a particular time. They are then contacted one to three days later and asked about recall for ads that ran in the program they were recruited to watch.

The last two methods have the added advantage that, because they do not use network television, they can be used to test rough, early versions of commercials.

The results of various types of recall tests also are analyzed by examining the verbatim responses to find out how many viewers remember specific features of the commercial. If the answer given to one of these questions suggests that the consumer is simply guessing or maybe recalling other advertising, then that individual is not counted toward the recall score. A few sample verbatims are provided. Which of them appear to indicate recall of the specific commercial being tested?

1. The man was in his backyard. I think he was cooking on his charcoal grill. I'm not really sure if he was.
2. The guy in the commercial was using Kingsford briquettes in his grill.
3. There were several grills in the commercial.
4. The commercial showed a bag of charcoal for most of the commercial. It was the kind that lights fast.
5. The commercial said that the charcoal would burn more even than other brands.

The average recall score for a 30-second commercial across all product categories is in the vicinity of 20 percent. This means that about one in five of the people exposed to a commercial can recall something about it the following day. Looking at individual cases, scores may range from 0 percent to 70 percent. ■

notation is the same as that introduced in the discussion of experimental design in Chapter 9. One issue that must be resolved is the decision regarding which measurements should be taken. Another issue is how frequently to take measurements. Advertising researchers want to take measurements frequently enough to measure the trend of change but also want enough time between measurements to give the advertising an opportunity to have an effect. For heavily advertised products such as soft drinks, measurements might be taken every 90 days or even more often. For less heavily advertised products, such as videotape, it may be appropriate to take measurements only once a year.

Data Collection Procedures Data for ad tracking studies normally are collected by central location telephone interviewing. All the types of information needed in this type of test can be collected by telephone interview. In addition, central location telephone interviewing permits the researcher to implement the type of high-quality sampling methodology required. The advertising researcher needs accurate measurements that can be appropriately compared over time and tested statistically for significance of difference.

Sampling Procedures If the researcher is to make comparisons of key measurements from advertising research wave to advertising research wave, including statistical testing of differences, it is important that a probability sampling procedure be used. In addition, it is important that the sampling procedures be consistent from wave to wave. Most ad tracking studies use simple random samples. The samples usually include a random digit dialing procedure. Where the necessary data are available, stratified samples may be used to achieve their greater statistical efficiency.

General Categories of Questions Most ad tracking studies will include some unique questions. However, several types of questions will be found on almost every ad tracking study. These general categories of questions include the following:

- *Screening questions.* The questionnaire will begin with appropriate screening questions. The purpose of these questions is to determine whether the individual contacted is part of the target group for the particular advertising campaign. For example, the researcher may have decided that the target for the advertising is those individuals who have purchased or used athletic shoes one or more times in the past 30 days. Questions designed to make this determination are asked at the very beginning of the interview. The interviewer continues the interview with those individuals who meet the qualifications that have been established and terminates the interview with those who do not meet these qualifications.
- *Brand awareness questions.* After the research determines that the individual falls into the target group, the interview moves to a series of questions designed to measure awareness of brands in the category. For example, in an ad tracking study for Reebok we would ask, "When you think of athletic shoes, which brands come to mind?" Respondents are given the opportunity to mention as many brands as they can think of, such as Puma, Reebok, and Nike. This is referred to as unaided, or top-of-mind, awareness. The researcher makes the measurement before and after the beginning of a campaign to see what effect the campaign had on top-of-mind awareness. After asking the ad awareness questions, the questionnaire moves to aided brand awareness. Here, the interviewer reads a list of brands not mentioned in unaided brand awareness and asks whether the respondent is aware of each of these brands. The list of brands used for the aided awareness question usually includes the advertiser's brand and other major competitive brands. These questions are asked after the ad awareness questions so as not to bias responses to the ad awareness.
- *Ad awareness questions.* These questions are designed to determine whether target customers actually have seen the advertiser's promotion. The researcher would ask, "Have you seen or heard any advertising for any brands of athletic shoes in the past 30 days?" If the respondent answers yes to this question, the interviewer asks, "What brands of athletic shoes have you seen or heard advertising for in the past 30 days?"

- *Ad playback questions.* This sequence of questions is designed to determine what message was imparted by the paste show polish advertising the respondent recalls. For each of the brands for which the respondent recalls advertising in the past 30 days, the interviewer asks, "What did the advertising for ___ say or show about the product?" This question is asked on an open-ended basis and verbatim responses are recorded. Responses regarding specific things shown or said about different brands are evaluated in relation to what actually was shown and said in the advertising for that brand. If a particular respondent gave an answer that correctly "plays back" some specific element of the advertising for the particular brand, then that respondent is recorded as having proven recall of the advertising for that brand.
- *Category-brand usage information.* This information is obtained for classification purposes. The researcher is interested in getting information about respondent's current athletic shoe ownership by brand (e.g., Nike, Reebok) and type (e.g., running shoes, tennis shoes, walking shoes). In the analysis phase, the researcher will be interested in evaluating responses to the advertising and brand awareness questions by the current athletic shoe preference as indicated by ownership.
- *Demographic and lifestyle information.* This information will be used for classification purposes. Various crosstabulations will be run to see how the diagnostic measures vary by different demographic and lifestyle subgroups.

Ad Tracking Research for Maxi Tan

The Problem Maxi Tan is a regional brand of suntan lotion. The product has distribution in Gulf Coast beach resort communities from Padre Island, Texas, to Naples, Florida. Two years ago, Maxi Tan began using television advertising on cable channels and in tourist-oriented publications in the beach resort communities where the product is sold. The manufacturer spent $4 million on this program the first year, $4.4 million the second year, and plans to spend $4.84 million this year. Before beginning the program in 1995, Maxi Tan's management decided that it wanted to conduct at least one ad tracking study each year to help assess the effectiveness of the campaign. The expected cost of the advertising campaign represented a major commitment for Maxi Tan; management wanted to have some indication of the effectiveness of the program so that, if it appeared to be ineffective, the program could be terminated before the end of the season. Management planned to run the campaign for six months each year, beginning in April and ending in September. It planned to take a measurement on April 1, 1996, for the beginning of the campaign and to take a second measurement on July 1, 1996, after the campaign was half over. This pattern was to be duplicated in subsequent years, if the program continued.

Methodology The advertising researchers chose five of the major markets in their total market area: Corpus Christi, Texas; Gulf Shores, Alabama; Pensacola, Florida; Panama City, Florida; and Saint Petersburg, Florida. The plan was to interview 200 qualified individuals from each of these five markets in each wave of research. Qualified individuals were defined as tourists 18 years of age or older who purchased a suntan product within the past year. The researchers explored various traditional data collection approaches and decided that, given the nature of their target market, none of the strategies would work. There was no way to reach target customers by telephone or mail. The researchers finally decided that they actually would have to locate and interview qualified individuals on the beach at the various locations. The research question was, How could they generate a probability sample based on interviewing people at the beach? The decision was to use a modified cluster sampling approach. The procedure they developed had the following elements:

- *Cluster maps of each beach.* First of all, the researchers hired two college students from the University of South Florida to travel to each of the five beach areas and develop maps of the beaches in those areas. In addition to developing the maps, the students were given the task of dividing each beach into 40 subareas of approximately equal size, using natural landmarks (e.g., lifeguard stands) as boundaries.
- *Number of interviews per cluster.* Given the goal of obtaining 200 interviews from each market and using the appropriate sample size calculation formula, it was decided to interview five people per cluster.
- *Timing of interviews.* To assure a representative mix of respondents, the times of day when interviews would be conducted in each cluster were selected at random. The appropriate hours of the day for interviewing were determined to be from 10:00 A.M. until 4:00 P.M. The day was divided into six one-hour segments. Multiplying the six one-hour segments by seven days per week provided 42 one-hour segments. A list of these 42 one-hour segments was developed, and a table of random numbers was used to choose two random numbers between 1 and 42. The days and times associated with these two random numbers were eliminated, leaving a total of 40 one-hour segments.
- *Association of each of the 40 beach areas with one of the 40 days and times.* The next step in the sample design was to link a particular area of beach (one of the 40 clusters) with a specific day and time. This was done by selecting a random number between 1 and 40 for each of the 40 areas of the beach. A computer program made sure that a number drawn did not duplicate a number previously drawn. At the end of the process, all 40 beach numbers had a unique number between 1 and 40 associated with it. These numbers were then associated with the 40 times of the day and week notated previously to associate a unique day and time with each of the 40 beach areas. Interviewing was conducted at the particular location at the particular time.
- *Choice of people to be interviewed from the cluster.* The final step was a set of detailed procedures to be used to decide who to interview from each cluster at the appointed day and time. This was done to take the choice of respondents away from the interviewers. A supervisor was to be present during the interviewing phase to be sure that procedures were followed. Given the setting in which the interviews were to be conducted, Maxi Tan knew that the interview would have to be very brief and that researchers would have to focus on the key measures.

The questionnaire was designed to be less than five minutes in length and covered the following areas:

- Screening question to make sure the individual was a tourist, over the age of 18 years, and a suntan lotion or oil purchaser.
- Unaided awareness of suntan brands.
- Awareness of suntan oil or lotion advertising.

- Aided awareness of suntan brands.
- If aware of Maxi Tan advertising, ability to describe what Maxi Tan advertising said or showed about the product.
- Demographic information including age, occupation, income, and city and state of residence.

Results and Analysis The plan for the research for the first three years can be stated as a quasi-experimental design as follows:

$$O_1 \; X_1 \; O_2 \; O_3 \; X_2 \; O_4 \; O_5 \; X_3 \; O_6$$

In this expression, the *O*s stand for research measurements and the *X*s stand for the introduction of the advertising campaign each year. For example, the pattern for the first year would be as follows: O_1 represents the research measurement taken before the advertising campaign begins, X_1 represents the introduction of the campaign for that year, and O_2 represents the research measurement taken in the middle of the campaign. This pattern was to be repeated in each of the three years in question. Detailed analysis was conducted. However, research focused on the top-of-mind or unaided awareness results for Maxi Tan. These results for the two years for which research has been completed follow. The percentages are the unaided awareness figures for Maxi Tan.

- April 1, 1995 (O_1—5.3%)
- July 1, 1995 (O_2—18.4%)
- April 1, 1996 (O_3—8.3%)
- July 1, 1996 (O_4—25.7%)

The results show a typical pattern for a product that is used and advertised on a seasonal basis. The results for 1995 show a large and significant increase in awareness between the premeasurement (before introduction of the advertising) and postmeasurement (after introduction of the advertising) testing. This is followed by a large and significant decline between July 1, 1995, and April 1, 1996. The 1996 results show a large and significant increase in top-of-mind awareness between the pre- and postmeasurements. The researcher might conclude from these findings that the advertising had a significant positive effect on top-of-mind awareness of the Maxi Tan brand. However, one should be careful in arriving at this conclusion because extraneous variables are at work. For example, because the sun is much hotter in July than in April, it might be a natural increase in interest in and purchase of suntan oils or lotions that has nothing to do with the Maxi Tan advertising.

Satisfaction Research

In recent years American business has become increasingly committed to the idea of customer satisfaction and product-service quality. Measurements of customer satisfaction and the link of these measurements to product-service attributes is the vehicle for developing a market-driven quality approach. In this section, we will discuss customer satisfaction research and provide an example of how this type of research might be operationalized.

customer satisfaction research
Research conducted to measure overall satisfaction with a product or service and satisfaction with specific elements of the product or service.

Customer satisfaction research has been around for a long time. However, it has become a fixture at most large corporations only in recent years.[14] The growth in the popularity of customer satisfaction research is, of course, a corollary to the quality movement in American business. You probably have heard of the Malcolm Baldridge National Quality Award and seen a number of companies advertising the fact that they have received this award (Cadillac, IBM, Xerox, Federal Express). The Malcolm Baldridge key award examination criteria are outlined in Table 20.5. Two of these criteria have particular relevance for the marketing research function. The first criterion is that quality is defined by the customer, the second is that decisions of the company need to be based upon facts and data.

The idea that the customer defines quality should not be new to marketers. However, its recognition in the Baldridge criteria has given this idea a credibility that was previously lacking. The notion of customer-drive quality is discussed at greater length in the application guidelines for the Malcolm Baldridge award:

> Quality is judged by the customer. All product and service attributes that contribute value to the customer, lead to customer satisfaction, and affect customer preference must be addressed appropriately in quality systems. Value, satisfaction, and preference may be influenced by many factors throughout the overall purchase, ownership, and service experiences of the customer. This includes the relation between the company and customers—the trust and confidence in products and services—that leads to loyalty and preference. This concept of quality includes not only the product and service attributes that meet basic requirements, it also includes those that enhance them and differentiate them from competing offerings.[15]

The guidelines also discuss the fact that customer-driven quality is a strategic concept. As such, it demands a high level of sensitivity to customers and quick

TABLE 20.5 Key Concepts in the Award Examination Criteria

Quality is defined by the customer.

The senior leadership of businesses needs to create clear quality values and build the values into the way the company operates.

Quality excellence derives from well-designed and well-executed systems and processes.

Continuous improvement must be part of the management of all systems and processes.

Companies need to develop goals, as well as strategic and operational plans, to achieve quality leadership.

Shortening the response time of all operations and processes of the company needs to be part of the quality improvement effort.

Operations and decisions of the company need to be based on facts and data.

All employees must be suitably trained and developed and involved in quality activities.

Design quality and defect and error prevention should be major elements of the quality system.

Companies need to communicate quality requirements to suppliers and work to elevate supplier quality performance.

SOURCE: The Malcolm Baldridge National Quality Award, *1991 Application Guidelines* (Gaithersburg, Md.: U.S. Department of Commerce, National Institute of Standards and Technology, 1991), p. 2. Photograph used with permission. Photograph by Steuben.

response to their changing requirements. The other major element that relates to marketing research is the notion that in meeting its quality improvement goals, the company must base its actions on reliable information, data, and analysis.[16]

Objectives of Satisfaction Research

Satisfaction research, like advertising tracking research, should be conducted at planned intervals so as to track satisfaction over time. Thus, satisfaction research can be put in the context of an interrupted time series quasi-experimental design. Over time, management will do various things to improve customer satisfaction, take measurements following these changes, and evaluate the results to see if the changes that were implemented had a positive effect on customer satisfaction. Normally, satisfaction research has four basic objectives:

1. *Identification of key satisfaction determinants.* Here the researcher is interested in identifying the specific elements of the product or service that drive overall customer satisfaction. For example, a fast food restaurant might find that three variables have a major effect on overall consumer satisfaction with the organization: satisfaction with quality of food, satisfaction with speed of service, and satisfaction with friendliness of employees. Procedures used to identify important satisfaction factors are discussed later.
2. *Measurement of current satisfaction levels.* After identifying key satisfaction factors, the next step is to measure current levels of customer satisfaction on each factor.
3. *Provision of recommendations to management.* After current satisfaction is measured on key factors, the researcher is in a position to make recommendations to management regarding the areas of service most in need of attention.
4. *Keeping track of satisfaction levels over time.* The company should continue to track satisfaction levels at periodic intervals. This provides an indication of the satisfaction trend and also provides a basis to evaluate the effectiveness of strategies adopted by management to improve service quality delivery.

Typical Methodology for Satisfaction Research

The major approaches to satisfaction research is widespread use in industry are discussed in the following paragraphs.

Research Strategy Before examining the details of the methodologies employed in customer satisfaction research, it is important to consider the basic research strategies issues that the research design must accommodate.

It is common practice in satisfaction research to develop models that can be used to estimate or derive the importance of satisfaction with different elements of a product or service in determining overall satisfaction with the product or service. The conceptual model is

$$S = f(X_1, X_2, X_3, \ldots, X_n)$$

where

S = overall satisfaction with product or service
X_{1-n} = satisfaction with individual product or service attributes

This model might be estimated using regression analysis. Using a regression approach, the researcher would estimate the following model:

$$S = a + b_1X_1 + b_2X_2 + b_3X_3 + \ldots + b_nX_n$$

where

a = estimated constant

b_{1-n} = regression coefficients associated with individual predictor variables (showing the effect of a one unit change in rating on the particular attribute on overall satisfaction)

Another issue relates to whether the researcher uses a gap analysis or more traditional approach to the measurement process. For a traditional approach, the researcher simply asks customers to rate the product or service on key satisfaction factors. For Wendy's these might be things such as speed of service, friendliness of employees, and quality of food. Consumers might be asked to indicate their satisfaction in each area on a scale of 1 to 10, where 10 is excellent and 1 is poor, or to indicate their degree of agreement (strongly agree, agree, disagree, or strongly disagree) with statements such as "Wendy's employees are courteous and friendly."

Under a gap analysis approach, the researcher needs to measure two things, customers' expectations and their perceptions of the firm's performance. In other words, what do they expect from fast food restaurants in a particular area and how do they believe Wendy's performed in that area. Expectations and perceptions of performance data are collected on some type of numeric scale, and we are interested in the difference between perceptions of performance and expectations in each area. If the performance exceeded the customers' expectations, the gap would be positive and the company is producing a satisfaction surplus on the particular area in question. On the other hand, if performance is lower than expectations, there is a satisfaction deficit. The gap analysis approach has a number of conceptual advantages and has been accepted by many practitioners as the appropriate way to conduct satisfaction research.

Data Collection Procedures The two major analytical steps in the process are to identify key satisfaction factors and to measure current satisfaction levels on these factors. Different research procedures are used for these two steps.

For identification of key satisfaction factors, focus groups and other qualitative research techniques are often used at this stage in the process. This qualitative research may be conducted with current customers, target customers who do not currently use or purchase the product or service, former customers, or some combination of these. The goal is to identify dimensions of the product or service that are important to customers.

After the researcher has identified the key satisfaction factors, the information is used to develop a questionnaire for a quantitative study to measure current satisfaction levels on these key factors. The questionnaire normally will be administered by mail, central location telephone, or via intercept at the place of business (e.g., a Wendy's restaurant).

Sampling Procedures The first step is to define the population or universe of interest. The specific way the researcher defines the population of interest for a given study is a function of the study's specific objectives. The

A Professional Researcher's Perspective

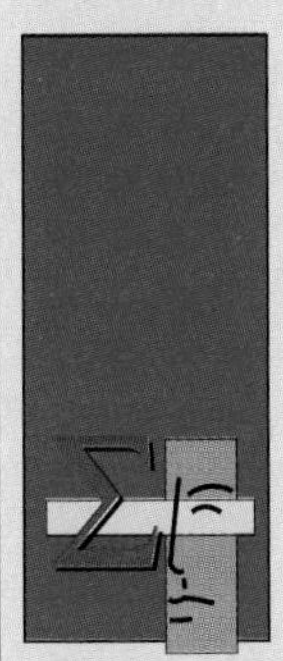

The Employee Benefits Division of the CIGNA Corporation, a Connecticut-based insurance and financial services firm, conducts an ongoing national survey of patients who belong to its network of health maintenance organizations. The network encompasses 43 HMOs in 24 states, staffed by 14,000 primary care physicians and 33,000 specialty care physicians in 1,000 hospitals.

The goal of the survey is to assess the members' satisfaction with their primary care physicians, say Sali Bonazelli, assistant director, customer satisfaction monitoring, CIGNA Employee Benefits Division. "The results are primarily for the health plans and also for the individual doctors. The doctors really like getting feedback on how their patients perceive them."

In a three- to five-minute interview, the patients give their impressions of several areas of their interaction with the doctor and his staff, including staff courtesy, doctor attentiveness to patient questions and needs, and clarity with which the doctor explains treatment options to the patient. The patients also express an overall satisfaction rating and indicate if they would recommend the service to a friend. The study interviews 12 patients per quarter for each doctor whose patient load meets the sample criteria.

Bonazelli says the patient satisfaction survey has been valuable because it provides CIGNA with tangible ways to improve service. "In one of the health plans, we found out that the members really wanted to be able to contact the health plan for help with administrative issues in the evening. We didn't have enough evening hours, so we put them in. In another case, we found out that both the patients and our providers found the explanation of benefits that accompanies reimbursement payments confusing. That lead to a work group that revised the explanation of benefits."

Because the survey is national and it encompasses all the CIGNA health plans, it assists the company in gearing service levels in the various regions of the country. "When you first organize a health plan network, you put in the same service standards across the board, but different regions have different expectations. You might find out, for instance, the people in the Midwest don't mind waiting 20 minutes to see the doctor, whereas someone in New York thinks waiting five minutes is horrendous. The research helps us see trends and patterns and that allows us to tailor service."

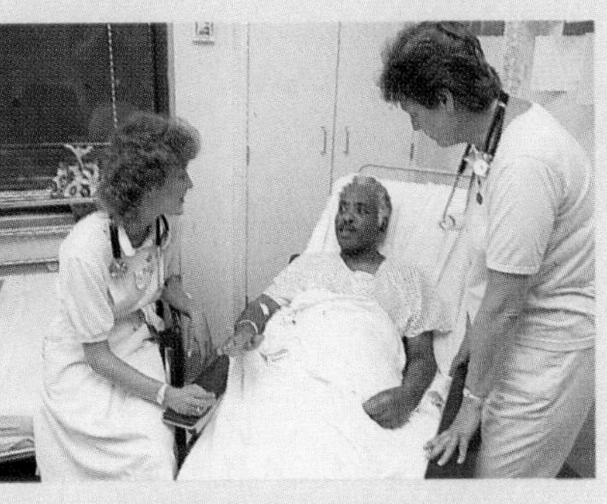

SOURCE: Mike Kagan/ Monkmeyer Press.

CIGNA sends written reports and tabulated results of the survey findings monthly to each of the health plans around the country, outlining how each plan scored on its own and in relation to others. After seeing early results, the physicians and HMOs came up with more service areas that they wanted the researcher to explore, Bonazelli says, citing an example of questions about appointment waiting time. "Initially, we asked the patients how satisfied they were with the amount of time spent waiting to see the doctor. That gave us a good gauge. But we weren't finding out how long the wait time is, so we added a question to do that."[17] ■

researcher may focus on only current customers (i.e., have patronized a Wendy's one or more times in the past 90 days) or may want to include target customers who are aware of Wendy's but have not patronized Wendy's in some period of time. The researcher also may want to include former customers. Regardless of the definition of the population, probability samples normally are used so that the results can be projected to the total population and inferences made about the population. To operationalize the sample, a customer list is needed or the interviewer will have to screen for qualified respondents in the general population. The latter approach is feasible only if the product is widely used.

General Categories of Questions Each customer satisfaction study uses questions that are, to some degree, unique. However, as in the other types of studies discussed in this chapter, certain general types of information are collected in most customer satisfaction studies:

- *Screening questions.* The questionnaire begins with screening questions to make sure that the person contacted falls into the target group. If the goal is to interview current customers and current customers are defined to include those individuals who have patronized Wendy's in the past 30 days, then the questionnaire will begin with a series of questions designed to determine whether the particular individual meets these requirements.
- *Overall ratings.* Some experts argue that it is important to get an overall satisfaction rating from respondents very early in the interview. This might be done by asking, "Please indicate your overall satisfaction with Wendy's on a scale of 1 to 10, where 1 is poor and 10 is excellent." This rating will be the dependent variable in the regression analysis described earlier.
- *Performance ratings.* The researchers are interested in measuring customer perceptions of Wendy's performance on a number of specific aspects of the product or service. The specific aspects are the key satisfaction factors discussed previously. The researcher will use a numeric rating scale (see Chapter 11) to gauge the satisfaction with each element.
- *Intent to use or purchase product or service in the future.* Satisfaction surveys usually include some measurement of customer likelihood to do business with the firm in the future. This provides a basis for determining whether the satisfaction levels being measured are predictive of future likelihood to purchase or use the product or service. The researcher would hypothesize that the higher is the satisfaction level, the higher is the likelihood to do business with the organization in the future.
- *Category or brand usage information.* This information will be used for classification purposes in cross-tabulation analysis. For example, does the respondent also patronize McDonald's, Burger King, Arby's, or Little Caesar's?
- *Demographic and lifestyle information.* This information also is used for classification purposes. The researcher is often interested in determining whether any particular demographic or lifestyle group is more or less satisfied than Wendy's average customer.

Analysis The analysis of the results will include all the traditional types of analysis, such as one-way frequency tables, crosstabulations, and descriptive statistics. Management is interested in knowing the average overall satisfaction level, the average satisfaction levels with specific elements of Wendy's services, and how these averages differ by demographic groups of customers. In addition, the researcher may do the type of regression modeling, discussed previously, to determine the importance of different elements of the product or service in determining overall customer satisfaction. These issues are discussed in greater detail in the following example.

Satisfaction Research for Pizza Pronto

The Problem Pizza Pronto is a regional chain of pizza restaurants operating in seven states in the Midwest. Pizza Pronto has adopted a Total Quality Management (or TQM) orientation. As part of this orientation, the firm is committed to the idea of market-driven quality. That is, it intends to go to the customers and find out what these customers want and expect in the way of quality. The company has decided to conduct a research project to address the issue of how its customers define quality.

Research Objectives The objectives of the proposed research are the following:

- To identify the key determinants of customer satisfaction
- To measure current customer satisfaction levels on those key satisfaction determinants
- To determine the relative importance of each of the key satisfaction determinants in driving overall satisfaction
- To provide recommendations to management regarding where to direct the company's efforts

Methodology The first objective was met by means of qualitative research. A series of focus groups were conducted with customers to determine which attributes of Pizza Pronto's products and services are most important to them. Based on this analysis, the following attributes were identified.

- Overall quality of food
- Variety of menu items
- Friendliness of Pizza Pronto's employees
- Providing a good value for the money
- Speed of service

In the second stage of the research, central location telephone interviews were conducted with 1,200 randomly selected individuals who had purchased or eaten at a Pizza Pronto restaurant (in the restaurant or take-out) in the past 30 days. Key information garnered in the survey included

- Overall rating of satisfaction with Pizza Pronto on a 10-point scale (= poor and 10 = excellent)
- Rating of Pizza Pronto on the five key satisfaction attributes identified in the qualitative research, using the same 10-point scale as for overall satisfaction
- Demographic characteristics

Results and Analysis Extensive crosstabulations and other traditional statistical analyses were conducted. A key part of the analysis was to estimate a regression model with overall satisfaction as the dependent variable and satisfaction with key product or service attributes as the predictors. The results of this analysis are

$$S = .48X_1 + 13X_2 + .27X_3 + .42X_4 + .57X_5$$

where

S = overall satisfaction rating
X_1 = rating of food quality
X_2 = rating of variety of menu
X_3 = rating of friendliness of employees
X_4 = rating of value
X_5 = rating of speed of service

Average ratings on the 10-point scale for overall satisfaction and the five key attributes are:

$S = 7.3$
$X_1 = 6.8$
$X_2 = 7.7$
$X_3 = 8.4$
$X_4 = 6.9$
$X_5 = 8.2$

The regression coefficients provide estimates of the relative importance of the different attributes in determining overall satisfaction. The results show that X_5 (rating of speed of service) is most important in determining overall satisfaction. The results indicate that a one-unit increase in average rating on speed of service will produce an increase of .57 in average satisfaction rating. For example, the current average rating on speed of service is 8.2. If, by providing faster service, Pizza Pronto could increase this rating to 9.2, then it would expect the average satisfaction rating to increase to 7.87. X_1 (rating of food quality) and X_4 (rating of value) are not far behind speed of service in their effect on overall satisfaction according to the regression estimates. At the other extreme, X_2 (rating of variety of menu) is least important in determining overall satisfaction and X_3 (rating of friendliness of employees) is in between in importance.

The performance ratings provide a different picture. According to the average ratings, customers believe Pizza Pronto is doing the best job on X_3 (friendliness of employees) and the worst job on X_1 (food quality). To simultaneously consider the importance estimates and the performance ratings we might use quadrant analysis. This technique is discussed in Figure 20.5. The results for Pizza Pronto, shown in Figure 20.6, indicate the most pressing problems for Pizza Pronto relate to food quality and value. Both of these attributes fell into the *threats* quadrant (high importance, low performance). On the other hand, Pizza Pronto has a very strong position in the minds of customers in regard to speed of service (*opportunities* quadrant). Speed of service is very important to customers, and Pizza Pronto is perceived to be doing a very good job in this area. Pizza Pronto also is perceived to be doing a good job in terms of variety of menu items and friendliness of employees (strengths). However, these items are somewhat less important to customers.

A major benefit of the statistical analysis is that it provides a basis for classifying needs in regard to their relative importance in driving overall satisfaction. Ratings from the survey provide the basis for quantifying performance on each of these needs. Together, the importance and performance estimates provide a basis for classifying needs in matrices.

SAMPLE MATRIX

Performance		Lowest Importance	Highest Importance
	High	Strengths	Opportunities
	Low	Weaknesses	Threats

FIGURE 20.5
Quadrant Analysis of Satisfaction Data

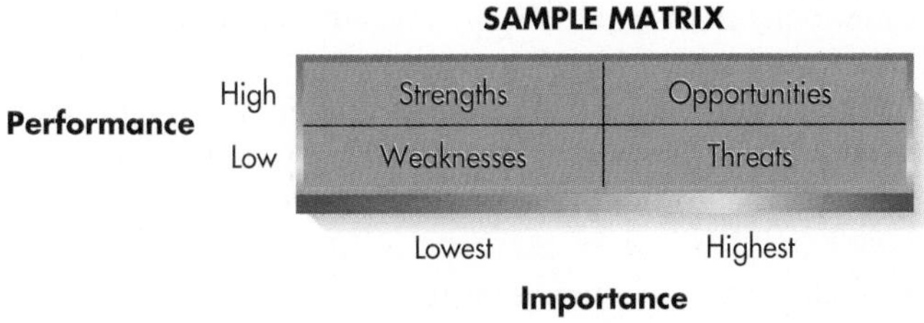

Opportunities (upper right-hand corner). These needs are highly important in determining overall customer satisfaction and the company received high performance ratings on them. The message here is keep it up and exploit these strong points.

Strengths (upper left-hand corner). These needs are somewhat less important in driving overall customer satisfaction and the company received high ratings.

Threats (lower right-hand corner). These needs are highly important in determining overall customer satisfaction and the company received low performance ratings. Improvements in performance on these items will produce the biggest improvements in overall customer satisfaction.

Weaknesses (lower left-hand corner). These needs are somewhat less important in driving overall customer satisfaction and the company received low performance ratings. The message is, look elsewhere for improvement.

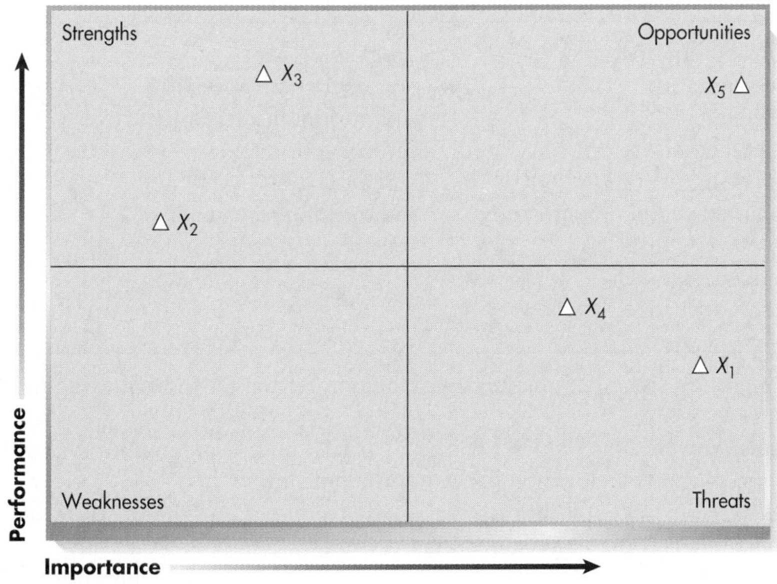

FIGURE 20.6
Quadrant Analysis of Pizza Pronto Satisfaction Data

Summary

The first step in designing a successful marketing program is to conduct strategic research. Strategic research is undertaken to aid managers in understanding the present and future competitive environment. Strategic studies focus on positioning and market segmentation. Positioning research develops perceptual maps of the competitive structure or relations between subgroups of customers and potential customers who exhibit differing sensitivities to one or more marketing mix variables.

The developing of a marketing program usually begins with the product. Managers cannot create distribution, pricing, and promotion strategies without a product. Therefore, product research typically precedes research on the remainder of the marketing mix. The first phase of product research is idea generation. Focus groups are used to generate product ideas. Other common types of product research are product prototype tests, product pricing research, and packaging tests.

There are many forms of promotion research; however, this chapter narrows the focus to advertising research. Before development of advertisements, researchers often conduct ad concept and ad positioning tests. After a commercial has been produced, a television advertiser may conduct on-air tests. One of the most important and common types of advertising research is ad tracking. The objective of ad tracking is to take periodic measurement of variables to determine how well the advertising campaign is achieving its promotional goals.

American business has become increasingly concerned with customer satisfaction and product or service quality. Part of this focus is due to the publicity generated by the Malcolm Baldridge National Quality Award. Satisfaction research may use the traditional approach whereby the researcher asks the customers to rate the product or service on key satisfaction variables. Conversely, the new approach is to use gap analysis. The researcher measures the gap between customer expectations and customer perceptions of the firm's performance.

Key Terms

product positioning research
market segmentation
a priori segmentation
post hoc segmentation
unstructured segmentation
baseline market segmentation study
product prototype tests
product pricing research
packaging tests
product concept testing
ad positioning statement tests
ad concept testing
on-air testing
ad tracking research
customer satisfaction research

Review and Discussion Questions

1. What might be some key market segmentation factors for the following new products:
   a. A solar-powered fan, which fits into a partially raised car window, that will help cool the vehicle when parked in the hot sun.
   b. A disposable travel toothbrush that applies toothpaste to the bristles when the handle is turned and squeezed.
   c. A bracelet that vibrates when the home unit is activated. Children would wear the bracelet so that parents could signal when it's time for dinner or to come home.
   d. A refrigerator with a CD player built into the door.
   e. A video telephone.
2. Explain the difference between a priori and post hoc market segmentation. Give examples of each.

3. What is meant by a baseline market segmentation study? Why is it so important?
4. Describe how you would conduct a product concept test for a new fast food restaurant at your university's or college's student center.
5. Why do managers pay for ad tracking studies? Why not simply observe sales volume?
6. Your company has just developed a new product prototype called the *weed sucker*, which looks something like a miniature steam shovel with a broom handle. It uses air pressure (created by squeezing a lever on the handle) to hydraulically dig into the lawn and remove a weed. Describe how you would conduct a product prototype test.
7. What do you see as the major problems in concept testing, if any?
8. Can industrial and institutional products manufacturers benefit from market segmentation research? If so, how? What are some bases for segmenting these markets?
9. Why is package testing important? Describe how you might conduct a packaging test for microwaveable french fries.
10. Why has American business become so focused on customer satisfaction or product quality research? Describe the procedures you would use and some questions you would ask in a satisfaction research project for your student center.

CASE 20.1

Total Research Corporation's EQUITREND[18]

Most consumers and researchers would agree that quality is an important factor in determining the products and services they use. Yet each consumer has a different definition of quality. For some, it is an automobile that gives years of trouble-free service. For others, it is a restaurant where the service is always fast and the food is always delicious. Quality is a complex issue with many different components.

Total Research Corporation's EQUITREND study is a step forward defining those components more clearly. Through telephone interviews with 2,000 men and women ages 15 and older, EQUITREND measures the perceived brand quality of 190 brands in 55 product and service categories (roughly one-third packaged goods, one-third durable goods, and one-third services) from long-distance service to candy bars.

Consumers are asked to respond to a list of brands in terms of their perception of each brand's quality. They also are asked about usage behavior and their level of satisfaction with the products and services. The EQUITREND study not only resulted in ranking brands based on consumer perceptions of quality, but it also allowed for the creation of a segmentation system based on those perceptions.

TEST THEORIES

John Morton, senior vice president and director of advanced statistical research for Total Research Corporation, says that the idea for creating the EQUITREND study came from the desire to test some theories that Total Research had about what could and could not be measured in consumer research. "Our experience has been that even if you're trying to understand consumers in a very deep and esoteric way, the simpler the questioning procedure and the more you use real concrete things as opposed to abstractions, the more useful your results will be. We wanted to develop a study that would be very germane to the whole issue of brand. We also wanted to develop a study that people would have no trouble responding to, that would elicit honest answers that had real meaning."

To react to each of the brand names read to them, respondents used a 10-point scale that had 10 as a measure of extraordinary quality, 5 quite acceptable, and 0 unacceptable. "One of the things about this scale is that 5 is quite acceptable and yet we give people five levels above quite acceptable to grade brands. The reason that we did that was that our past research had found that if you use 'excellent–good–fair–poor' or even 'excellent–very good–fair–poor' you get so many responses in the top two scale points that you haven't really gotten any information. Anybody who feels half decent about the brand would put it at the top of the scale or next to the top of the scale. So we were trying to develop a much more sensitive scaling procedure."

Total Research has identified seven primary factors of brand image that consumers use to evaluate a brand's quality. Each person weights these factors differently. The four most important factors include

- *Sophistication.* The more intellectual or sophisticated a brand appears to be, the higher is the quality.
- *Wholesomeness.* The brand has an image of being nurturing and caring; therefore, it is a quality brand.
- *Wide acceptance.* "There are a lot of people who believe that the brands that are the most widely accepted are the best brands, brands like Kodak, Campbell Soups, Hershey," Morton says.
- *Trendiness or stylishness.* The people who weight this factor the heaviest are the opposite of those who put a great deal of emphasis on a brand's level of acceptance, Morton says. "If something's been around a long time, they're not interested in it. They see quality as something that's constantly evolving."

The brands that scored the best in the EQUITREND study seem to blend sophistication and wholesomeness. "If you look at the brands that finished at the very top in perceived quality, they are the ones like Kodak film, which provides a technically sophisticated product but has a lot of wholesome imagery associated with it. CNN is another example. It has a kind of patriotic image because of the Gulf War coverage, but also it's a technically sophisticated product. IBM and AT&T are two other brands that combine these two traits."

On the other hand, two brands that scored in the top 20, Hallmark Cards and Mercedes-Benz, do very well with images that are dominated by only one factor, wholesomeness for Hallmark and sophistication for Mercedes-Benz. And the results show that brands can successfully combine factors other than wholesomeness or sophistication and still do well.

CROSS CATEGORY

Another goal of EQUITREND was to provide a way to compare several different brands, especially those in different industries and service categories. "The companies that make these brands have millions of dollars of research that looks at the brands versus their competitors. Our job wasn't to duplicate that work, it was to look at the brands in a cross-category context. For example, when we look at American Express card, we can certainly look at it versus MasterCard and Visa, but we're also very interested in American Express and its similarities and dissimilarities to all the other brands we tested."

Using perceptual maps, the brands are plotted according to consumer perceptions, providing a look at how the brands perform compared with many other brands, not just those in their product or service category. "You might expect that when you put brands from all these different categories into a perceptual map that you'd end up with all the candy bars together and all the sodas together and that there would be 34 little pockets of brands but it's not like that at all. Brands can be spread all over the place. For example, Pepsi has a much different market position than Coke does. Typically a brand is likely to be more similar to nonmembers of its category then members of its category in terms of its imagery and positioning."

From Total Research's point of view, this cross-category analysis allows marketers to see the big picture, to learn how their brand relates to competitors and brands outside of their specific product or service category—something that marketing research does not always allow, Morton says. "The trouble with 99.9 percent of market research is, it only looks at one category and it tries to figure out why people do what they do just based on exhaustive information about that one category. It takes consumers into levels of detail that are five quantum leaps beyond the level that they actually think at when they make their product selections.

"I might be the researcher on Maxwell House coffee, for example, and I'm spending 50 hours a week thinking about nothing but Maxwell House coffee. I develop this study where I ask consumers an hour's worth of questions about all the different coffee brands and get them rated on 10 occasions on 50 attributes by four different kinds of users. But the consumer's decision may be instantaneous, made without hardly any thought at all and is probably more a reflection of their general model as consumers than any kind of in-depth models that they have of the coffee market.

"The feeling that we have developed over a lot of these studies is that people don't have a separate decision model for each market that they have to make selections in. If they did it would be a nightmare to be a consumer. Most consumer choices are very casual. The overall model may be very well thought out in terms of a consumer saying, 'I'm primarily sophisticated but I also have a certain level of practicality to my choice and I certainly lean toward the trendy brand.' What we think is really exhaustive and stable is the person's overall model."

QUALITY = SALES

For those firms that still need convincing that the pursuit of quality makes more than just good public relations sense, EQUITREND results show the effect quality can have on a company's bottom line. "We've found in general that for any given brand, each step up the scale is associated with about a 30 percent increase in sales. So if a brand's overall score was 6.00 and it can move to 7.00, that's about a 30 percent increase in unit sales," Morton says.

1. Comment on the methodology used to measure brand quality. Do you see any problems with the methodology? If so, what? How else could one measure brand quality?

2. Who are the most likely customers for EQUITREND? Would a company need any additional quality or satisfaction research? If so, what kind?
3. Give other examples of products that would fit the seven primary factors that determine brand image.
4. Do you agree with Morton's comments about cross-category analysis? Why or why not?
5. How might you sue the EQUITREND data to convince top management to put more emphasis on product quality?

CASE 20.2

Racquet Tech

Racquet Tech is a new company started with capital from several major venture capital companies. The company has developed a new tennis racquet that uses high-tech alloys developed in the aerospace industry. Tests indicate that the new racquet promises to give serious players more power and control than conventional racquets. The approach requires the use of special equipment in retail outlets to measure the racquet head speed of an individual and to determine which of six different racquet stiffnesses will be best for that particular player.

The agreement with the venture capitalists requires Racquet Tech owners to show that there is adequate demand for the new racquets before they receive their next round of funding in the amount of $20,000,000. To demonstrate the sales potential for the new racquet they have agreed to conduct a standard product concept test. The test will seek a variety of information including purchase intent for the concept, demographic characteristics of purchasers and nonpurchasers, ratings of the new concept on a number of attributes, and likes and dislikes in regard to the new concept.

For purposes of this analysis, please focus on the purchase intent data. The target market for the new product is the serious amateur player. The serious amateur player is defined as an individual who plays tennis two or more times in an average week. In addition, given the relatively high projected retail cost of the proposed racquet, it has been decided that target customers should have a family income of at least $50,000 per year. Based on a survey conducted using a national mail panel, Racquet Tech estimates that approximately 375,000 people in the United States meet the income and frequency of play qualifications. It has just completed a product concept test with individuals that fit the target profile who were identified via the original mail panel screening. For purposes of this case, the key question on the product concept test is the likelihood of purchase question. Completed questionnaires were returned by 78 percent of the 1,000 individuals sampled. They were provided with a description of the concept including its advantages and cost and asked whether they would be very likely, somewhat likely, somewhat unlikely, or very unlikely to purchase the concept racquet in the next year. The results are as follows:

- Very likely—14.0 percent.
- Somewhat unlikely—39.0 percent.
- Somewhat unlikely—27.0 percent.
- Very unlikely—20.0 percent.

The researchers conducting the test indicate that in previous tests of other sporting goods concepts, they developed accurate estimates of the percent of a target group who actually would purchase a concept. They multiply the very likely responses times 0.6, the somewhat likely responses times 0.3, and the somewhat unlikely responses by 0.05 and sum the results. It is estimated that Racquet Tech must sell 70,000 racquets to achieve the financial results necessary to meet its goals.

1. Use the information provided in the case to develop a sales estimate for the Racquet Tech concept racquet.
2. On the basis of your estimate, will Racquet Tech be able to meet the necessary sales level?
3. If Racquet Tech plans to sell the racquets to distributors for $100, what will its revenues be for the first year?
4. Finally, if the firm's estimated fixed costs for the first year are $2,000,000 and its variable costs are expected to be $50 per unit, what is its projected first-year profit?

PART V

ETHICAL DILEMMA

KXXX Radio Research

Radio sweeps research is conducted four times per year by Arbitron Research. The ratings, as determined by Arbitron, mean hundreds of thousands of dollars of advertising revenue to the winners and similar losses to the losers.

KXXX decided to improve its ratings by sending out the following letter and questionnaire immediately before sweeps week (see Figure 20.7).

> Dear Radio Listener:
>
> We are conducting a research study on radio listening preferences in the Dallas–Fort Worth area, and we are requesting your participation. Your opinions will help shape the kind of music presented to the Dallas–Fort Worth radio audience.
>
> You have been carefully selected to represent a specific demographic segment of the general population. To obtain better information, each participant has been assigned a specific radio station. We would greatly appreciate your cooperation by listening to your assigned station for one hour and completing the brief survey card enclosed.
>
> The station you have been assigned is **KXXX,** which can be found at **100.5** on the **FM** dial. Please listen for at least one-half (1/2) hour, between 6:00 A.M. and 10:00 A.M. and another one-half (1/2) hour at any other time during the week, then, at your convenience, complete the enclosed survey card within the next week and return it to us. The postage is prepaid.
>
> Your opinions are very important. Please answer honestly. A donation will be made to a local charity when we receive your completed survey card. Thank you for your cooperation.
>
> Ken Jones
> Vice President, Research

1. Is the questionnaire simply a novel way to promote a radio station, or is it unethical?
2. If KXXX actually decided to use the research data, would its actions regarding the questionnaire be unethical?
3. What if the radio station conducted an extensive, in-depth research project immediately before the radio sweeps that asked people to listen to KXXX for a week in order to give meaningful replies to the questionnaire? Would management's actions be unethical?

FIGURE 20.7

KXXX Listener Questionnaire

YOUR OPINION COUNTS

Please answer all questions, detach the card, and mail it immediately.

Thank you for your help.

I listened to ***KXXX*** for at least one-half hour between 6 A.M. and 10 A.M. and another half hour at any other time during the week of ________, 1995.

I listened:
- ☐ EARLY MORNING (6–10 A.M.)
- ☐ MIDDAY (10 A.M.–P.M.)
- ☐ LATE AFTERNOON (2–6 P.M.)
- ☐ NIGHT (6 P.M.–6 A.M.)

(Check as many boxes as you wish)

I listened: ☐ at home ☐ at work ☐ in a car ☐ other place

I liked: The music played by ***KXXX***
☐ Yes ☐ No

The morning program
☐ Yes ☐ No

The on-air personalities
☐ Yes ☐ No

The uninterrupted music sets
☐ Yes ☐ No

Overall I would rate ***KXXX***: (circle one)

Really Dislike				Really Like
1	2	3	4	5

My other comments about ***KXXX*** music, artist, personalities, etc., are:

____

____

____

____

____

OPTIONAL

NAME ________________

ADDRESS ________________

CITY ________________

STATE _____ ZIP CODE ________

PHONE (   ) ________________

BIRTHDAY ________________

APPENDIX 1

Comprehensive Cases

A. Heritage Restaurants: The Screener Questionnaire
B. Heritage Restaurants: Concept Tests
C. Heritage Restaurants: Multivariate Analysis
D. Garcia's Supermarkets: Grocery Shopping Habits Survey
E. Rockingham National Bank: Visa Card

CASE A

Heritage Restaurants: The Screener Questionnaire with Data Disc

INTRODUCTION

BACKGROUND

Heritage Restaurants, a creator of "concept restaurants," is exploring various long-term growth strategies including new retail restaurant concepts. It has developed two complete restaurants concepts for testing, which are *Roxann's Cafe* and *Big Al's*.

PURPOSE

The purpose of this research is to provide Heritage Restaurants with consumer perceptions of the concepts and an evaluation of the viability of each concept. This information is to be used in the decision to select a concept for market testing.

OBJECTIVES

The objectives of this research are:

- *Store design concepts.* Assess consumer reactions to, and preferences for, each of a set of alternative store design concepts.
- *Interest in concept.* Gather reactions to, and identify preferences for, the store concepts, names, and logos from those who indicate an appropriate level of interest and likelihood to frequent the concept store.
- *Lifestyle.* Classify respondents into lifestyle groups based on classification schemes such as those used by PRIZM or VALS II to aid in determining appropriate lifestyle segmentation strategy (see Chapter 5).
- *Demographics.* Obtain detailed demographic data for each respondent.

METHODOLOGY

This quantitative research report is the result of telephone surveys that were conducted after the conclusion of focus groups.

- *Overview.* The research was based on a three-step data collection process:
  - *Initial telephone interview.* The first step in the process involved a random survey of consumers in 10 PRIZM lifestyle clusters.
  - *Mail out.* An organized package of store design, decor, product examples, and menus was sent to those who agreed to participate in the second survey. This package was sent so participants would receive it within three days of the date they were interviewed. A two-dollar cash incentive was included in the packet.
  - *Concept evaluation telephone interview.* Those who qualified for the concept evaluation interviews were again contacted by telephone after receiving the packet through the mail. This interview focused on identifying the best design for the retail concept.
- *PRIZM lifestyle clustering.* Respondent name lists for all phases of this research project were screened to include only members of 10 PRIZM lifestyle clusters. These clusters were selected by Heritage Restaurants to represent the target audience for the retail concepts tested. The 10 clusters are identified and discussed later. The lists included households with annual incomes of at least $25,000.
- *Initial telephone interview.* The initial telephone interview was designed to address objectives three and four. A copy of the survey instrument is provided later.

— *Sample size.* A total of 600 interviews was completed with respondents who agreed to receive the mail packet and respond to the second interview.
— *Stratification.* Approximately equal samples were taken from each of the 3 cities. Approximately equal samples were taken for each PRIZM cluster within those cities.
— *Sampling error.* Sampling error for a sample size of 600 is ± 4.1 percent at the 95 percent confidence level. This is based on the most pessimistic variance assumption (i.e., P = 0.5).

TEN PRIZM CLUSTERS SELECTED BY HERITAGE RESTAURANTS FOR SAMPLING

1. Money and Brains — Posh big-city enclaves of townhomes, condos, and apartments.

Statistics
- Percent of U.S. households—0.9 percent
- Primary age range—45–64
- Median household income—$45,798
- Median home value—$150,755

Demographics
- Posh in-town neighborhoods
- Single-unit housing
- Predominantly white families and singles
- College graduates
- White-collar workers

Sample Neighborhoods
- Georgetown, Washington, D.C.
- Grosse Pointe
- Palo Alto, California
- Princeton, New Jersey
- Park Cities, Dallas, Texas
- Coral Gables, Florida

2. Furs and Station Wagons — New money in metropolitan bedroom suburbs.

Statistics
- Percent of U.S. households—3.2 percent
- Primary age range—35–54
- Median household income—$50,086
- Median home value—$132,725

Demographics
- Executive bedroom communities
- Single-unit housing
- Predominately white families
- College educations
- White-collar jobs

Sample Neighborhoods
- Plano, Texas
- Reston, Virginia

- Glastonbury, Connecticut
- Needham, Massachusetts
- Pomona, California
- Dunwoody, Atlanta, Georgia

3. Urban Gold Coast — Upscale urban high-rise districts.

Statistics
- Percent of U.S. households—0.5 percent
- Primary age range—18–24 and 65+
- Median household income—$36,838
- Median home value—$200,000

Demographics
- Upscale urban enclaves
- High-rise housing
- Predominantly white singles
- College educations
- White-collar jobs

Sample Neighborhoods
- Upper East Side, Manhattan, New York
- Upper West Side, Manhattan, New York
- West End, Washington, D.C.
- Fort Dearborn, Chicago, Illinois
- Rincon East, San Francisco, California

4. Pools and Patios — Older, upper-middle class, suburban communities.

Statistics
- Percent of U.S. households—3.4 percent
- Primary age range—45–64
- Median household income—$35,895
- Median home value—$99,702

Demographics
- Aging, upper-middle-class suburbs
- Single-unit housing
- Predominantly white couples with grown children
- College graduates
- White-collar jobs

Sample Neighborhoods
- Fairfield, Connecticut
- Morton Grove, Chicago, Illinois
- Catonsville, Maryland
- Mission, Kansas City, Kansas
- La Crescenta, Los Angeles, California
- Kettering, Ohio

5. Young Influentials — Yuppie, fringe-city, condo and apartment developments.

Statistics
- Percent of U.S. households—2.9 percent
- Primary age range—18–34
- Median household income—$30,398
- Median home value—$106,332

Demographics
- Yuppie inner-ring suburbs
- Apartment and condo dwellings
- Predominantly white singles and childless couples
- College educations
- White-collar jobs

Sample Neighborhoods
- Glendale, Denver, Colorado
- North Side, Atlanta, Georgia
- Greenbelt, Maryland
- Redondo Beach, Los Angeles, California
- Westheimer, Houston, Texas
- Parkfairfax, Virginia

6. Young Suburbia — Child-rearing outlying suburbs.

Statistics
- Percent of U.S. households—5.3 percent
- Primary age range—25–44
- Median household income—$38,582
- Median home value—$93,281

Demographics
- Upper middle-class outlying suburbs
- Single-unit housing
- Predominately white families
- College educations
- White-collar jobs

Sample Neighborhoods
- Eagan, Minnesota
- Dale City, Virginia
- Pleasanton, California
- Smithtown, New York
- Ypsilanti, Michigan
- Lilburn, Georgia

7. God's Country — Upscale frontier boomtowns.

Statistics
- Percent of U.S. households—2.7 percent
- Primary age range—25–44
- Median household income–$36,728
- Median home value—$99,418

Demographics
- Upscale exurban boomtowns
- Single-unit housing
- Predominately white families
- College educations
- White-collar jobs

Sample Neighborhoods
- Woodstock, New York
- Plainsboro, New Jersey
- Corrales, Albuquerque, New Mexico
- Lake Arrowhead, California
- Aspen, Colorado
- Clancy, Montana

8. Blue-chip Blues — The wealthiest blue-collar suburbs.

Statistics
- Percent of U.S. households—6.0 percent
- Primary age range—25–44
- Median household income—$32,218
- Median home value—$72,563

Demographics
- Midscale working-class suburbs
- Single-unit dwellings
- Predominantly white families
- High school education
- Blue-collar jobs

Sample Neighborhoods
- Coon Rapids, Minnesota
- South Whittier, California
- Mesquite, Texas
- Ronkonkoma, New York
- St. Charles, St. Louis, Missouri
- Taylor, Detroit, Michigan

9. Black Enterprise — Predominately black, middle- and upper-class neighborhoods.

Statistics
- Percent of U.S. households—0.8 percent
- Primary age range—35–54
- Median household income—$33,149
- Median home value—$68,713

Demographics
- Middle-class inner suburbs
- Predominately black families
- Single-unit and duplex housing
- Some college educations
- White-collar jobs

Sample Neighborhoods
- Capitol Heights, Maryland
- Auburn Park, Chicago, Illinois
- Seven Oaks, Detroit, Michigan
- Mount Airy, Philadelphia, Pennsylvania
- South De Kalb, Atlanta, Georgia
- Cranwood, Cleveland, Ohio

10. New Beginnings — Fringe-city areas of single complexes, garden apartments, and trim bungalows.

Statistics
- Percent of U.S. households—4.3 percent
- Primary age range—18–34
- Median household income—$24,847
- Median home value—$75,364

Demographics
- Middle-class city neighborhoods
- Single and divorced apartment dwellers
- Some college educations
- White-collar jobs

Sample Neighborhoods

- Bloomington, Minnesota
- Northeast Phoenix, Arizona
- Reseda, Los Angeles, California
- Englewood, Denver, Colorado
- Parkmoor, San Francisco, California
- Park Place, Houston, Texas

RESTAURANT USAGE—SCREENER QUESTIONNAIRE

Hello, my name is ________________ with Ameridata Research, a marketing research firm. We are doing a study in your area about restaurant usage, and I would like to include your opinions. We are not trying to sell you anything, and my question will only take a few minutes of your time.

1. First, are you the male/female head of household?

1 YES **CONTINUE**
2 NO **ASK TO SPEAK TO APPROPRIATE PERSON AND ARRANGE CALLBACK IF NECESSARY**

2. Do you or does anyone in your immediate family work for an advertising agency, a marketing research firm, or own or manage a restaurant?

1 YES **THANK AND TERMINATE**
2 NO **CONTINUE**

3. In a typical week, do you normally make at least one purchase from a restaurant to either eat in the restaurant or carry out?

1 YES **CONTINUE**
2 NO **SKIP TO Q.8**
3 DK **SKIP TO Q.8**

4. In a typical week, approximately how many times do you purchase food from a restaurant to either eat in the restaurant or carry out in the following occasions or situations? **RECORD ANSWERS FOR 4a–4h BELOW 4h.**

4a. Breakfast?
4b. Lunch?
4c. Dinner?
4d. Other occasions, such as snacks?
4e. How many of your total (TOTAL VISITS FROM Q.4) restaurant visits, in a typical week, are to fast-food restaurants?
4f. How many of your total (TOTAL VISITS FROM Q.4) restaurant visits, in a typical week, involve taking food out rather than eating in the restaurant?
4g. How many of your (NUMBER FROM Q.4b) lunch visits, in a typical week, involve visits to delis or other nonhamburger restaurants that primarily serve sandwiches, soups, and salads?
4h. Thinking now of your (NUMBER FROM Q.4b) lunch visits, in a typical week, how much would you estimate that you spend on average per person?

	# of Visits		# of Visits
4a. Breakfast	_____	4e. Fast-food restaurants	_____
4b. Lunch	_____	4f. Taking food out	_____
4c. Dinner	_____	4g. Delis	_____
4d. Other	_____	4h. Approximate $	_____

5. Thinking now about selecting a restaurant for lunch or a light meal, how important are the following factors in choosing a restaurant when you are planning to **EAT AT THE RESTAURANT?** Please rate the importance of each item on a scale of 1 to 10, where "1" means very unimportant" and "10" means "very important." **READ AND ROTATE LIST. ENTER "11" IF DON'T KNOW (DK).**

______ Wide variety of menu items
______ Atmosphere
______ Convenience to home
______ Convenience to work
______ Attractiveness of interior decor
______ Having table service
______ Creative and different food items
______ Food that is a good value for the money
______ Use of fresh ingredients
______ Friendliness of employees
______ Speed of service
______ Having healthy items on the menu

6. Thinking now about selecting a restaurant for lunch or a light meal, how important are the following factors in choosing a restaurant when you are planning to **ORDER FOOD FOR TAKE-OUT?** Please rate the importance of each item on a scale of 1 to 10, where "I" means "very unimportant" and "10" means "very important." **READ AND ROTATE LIST. ENTER "11" IF DK.**

______ Wide variety of menu items
______ Atmosphere
______ Convenience to home
______ Convenience to work
______ Creative and different food items
______ Food that is a good value for the money
______ Use of fresh ingredients
______ Friendliness of employees
______ Speed of service
______ Having a drive-through window
______ Having healthy items on menu
______ Sturdy packaging materials
______ Attractiveness of packaging materials

7. In a typical month, how likely are you to try a new restaurant?
   1 Very likely
   2 Somewhat likely
   3 Neither likely nor unlikely
   4 Somewhat unlikely or
   5 Very unlikely
   6 DK/NS

Finally, I have just a few questions to help us classify your responses

8. **INDICATE GENDER OF RESPONDENT BY OBSERVATION:**
   1 MALE
   2 FEMALE
9. Could you please tell which of the following age categories you fall into? Are you between . . . **READ LIST**
   1 18–22
   2 23–30
   3 31–40
   4 41–50
   5 51–60 or
   6 Over 50
   7 RF
10. Are you currently . . . **READ ENTIRE LIST**
   1 Married
   2 Divorced/Separated

3 Widowed or
4 Single/Never married
5 RF

11. Do you currently have children under the age of 18 living with you?
1 YES **CONTINUE**
2 NO **SKIP TO Q.14**
3 RF **SKIP TO Q.14**

12. How many are . . . **READ LIST**
_____ Under 6
_____ 7–12
_____ 13–17

13. What is the highest level of education you have attained?
1 SOME HIGH SCHOOL
2 HIGH SCHOOL GRADUATE
3 SOME COLLEGE/TECHNICAL SCHOOL
4 COLLEGE GRADUATE
5 POSTGRADUATE WORK
6 RF

14. What is your racial or ethnic background? **DO NOT READ LIST**
1 WHITE/CAUCASIAN
2 AFRICAN/AMERICAN/BLACK
3 HISPANIC
4 ASIAN/ORIENTAL
5 OTHER
6 RF

15. And, could you tell me which of the following categories includes the total annual income of all members of your household before taxes for 1995? Was it . . .
1 Under $15,000
2 $15,000 but less than $25,000
3 $25,000 but less than $35,000
4 $35,000 but less than $50,000
5 $50,000 but less than $75,000
6 More than $75,000
7 DK
8 RF

Your answers to these questions have been very helpful. We would like to invite you to participate in the next phase of this research project, which will explore various new restaurant concepts. We would like to send you a booklet in the mail with specific information on new restaurant concepts. After you have received the booklet, we will call you back to ask you your opinions on the concepts. As a small token of our appreciation for your time and opinions, we will also include a $2.00 gratuity.

Can we count on you to help us out with this project?
1 YES **CONTINUE**
2 NO **THANK AND TERMINATE**

Now I will need your name and complete mailing address so that we can send the booklet to you. Your name and address will not be used for other purposes. **ASK FOR SPELLING—MUST BE CORRECT**

RESPONDENT'S NAME: ____
STREET ADDRESS: ____
CITY: ______________________ STATE: ________ ZIP: _________
TELEPHONE NUMBER: (______) _____ ________

You should receive the booklet within the next few days. Thank you very much for your assistance in this research project and we look forward to your opinions.

16. ENTER PRIZM CODE (2 DIGIT): _______

QUESTIONS FOR STUDENTS

1. Evaluate the research objectives.
2. Evaluate the research design in relation to the stated research objectives.
3. Use the computerized database to summarize the research results based on one-way frequency distributions. For questions 4 through 16, write a brief summary of the results.
4. Run crosstabulations for questions 4 through 7 against the demographics (questions 8 through 16). Are there any significant differences? If so, explain what they mean.

CASE B

Heritage Restaurants: Concept Tests with Data Disc

The restaurant concept tests for Roxann's Cafe and Big Al's were conducted with screener respondents who agreed to participate in a second survey.

- *Packet mailing.* Screener respondents received a packet within three days of their first interview. The packets contained color renderings of the store logos, designs, and decor.
- *Concept evaluation interview.* Telephone interviews were again conducted after the respondents received the mail packet, using the second questionnaire provided here. Interviews lasted from 35 minutes to 60 minutes. Respondent fatigue did not become a problem. We attribute this to the highly interactive nature of the interview and the color photographs respondents analyzed.
- *Sample size.* The second interview was completed with 400 respondents.
- *Sampling error.* Sampling error for a sample of this size is ± 5.0 percent at the 95 percent confidence level. This is based on the most pessimistic variance assumption (i.e., P = 0.5).

CONCEPT TEST—SECOND INTERVIEW

ASK FOR PERSON ON LIST.
Hello, I'm _____________ with Ameridata Research, a marketing research firm. A few days ago you spoke with one of our representatives and agreed to answer some questions about restaurant concepts.

1. Did you receive the packet we sent to you in the mail?
   1 YES **CONTINUE**
   2 NO **ARRANGE CALLBACK NEXT DAY.**
2. Do you have it in front of you? **IF NO:** Could you get your packet please? **WHEN RESPONDENT HAS PACKET:** I would like to go through the packet with you piece by piece and ask questions as we go.
3. Please turn to the first color picture. What does it say? **RECORD EITHER ROXANN'S OR BIG AL'S.**
   1 **ROXANN'S**
   2 **BIG AL'S**

Please turn the pages along with me, and I will ask questions that correspond with each page.

CONCEPT A (ROXANN'S)

The first page that you see has ROXANN'S CAFE DETROIT printed on it. This is a restaurant concept that is being presented. The name of each actual restaurant would reflect the particular city it is located in. The city of Detroit is being used for this example. Please go to the next page.

This page shows a view of the restaurant as it would appear when you enter through the front door. Notice on the left there is a cart with display of various products and to the right are "Roxann's" tables and chairs. Beyond the products is an easel on which the menu is displayed. Behind the curved wall is a serving line where you will receive your food. Tables are along the outside of the curved wall and booths are next to the windows.

On the next page there are some examples of the colors, textures, furniture, and accessories that would be part of the decor of Roxann's. The colors are subdued and the textures reflect natural wood and fibers.

4. Thinking about the serving line, do you believe there is room for a second serving line behind the curved wall, across from the existing service line?
   1 YES **CONTINUE**
   2 NO **SKIP TO Q.6**
   3. DK/RF **SKIP TO Q.6**
5. Would that be a good place for a desert bar?
   1 YES **SKIP TO Q.6**
   2 NO **CONTINUE**
   3 DK/RF **SKIP TO Q.6**

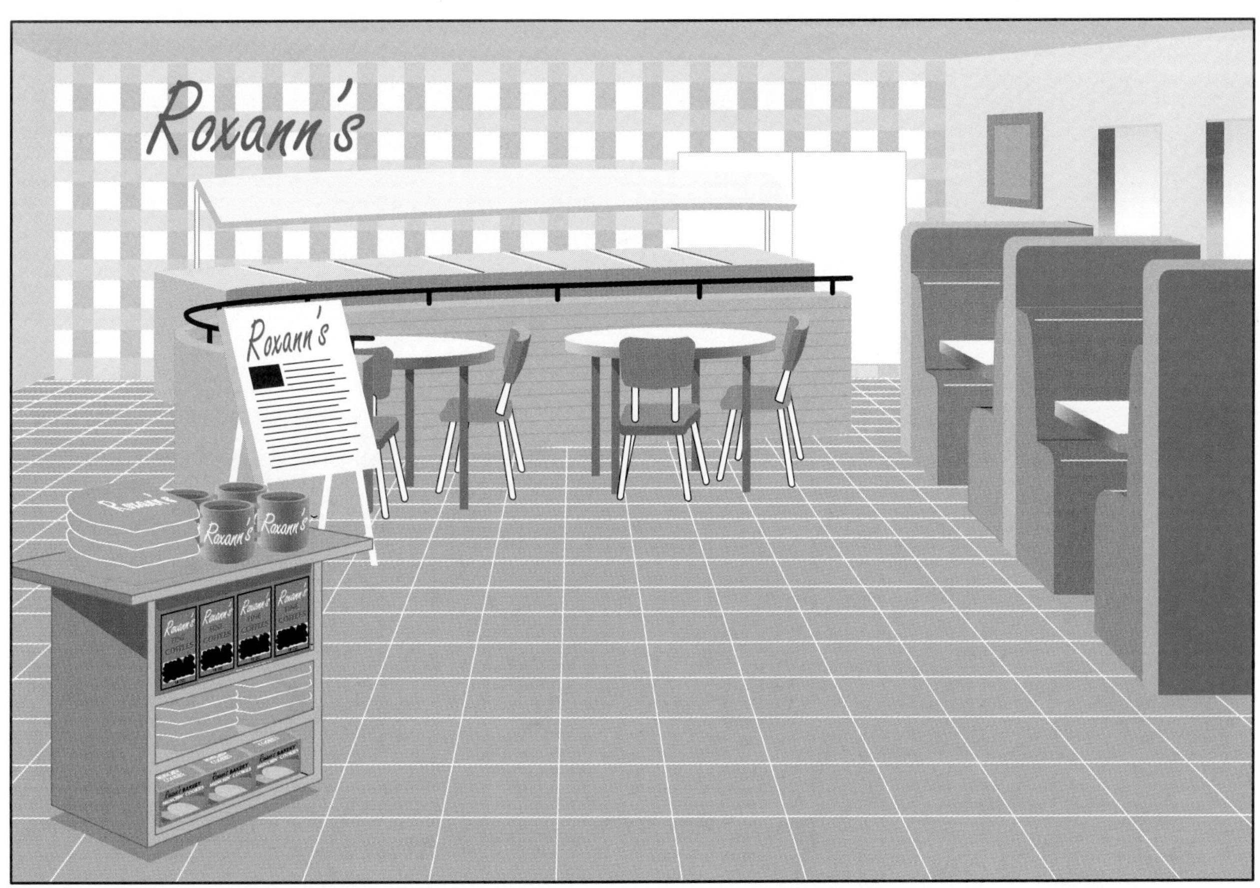

6. For the lunch shift, employees at Roxann's would wear khaki pants, a polo shirt, and loafers. For the dinner shift, the employees would wear black pants, black bowties, shirts, and white linen aprons. Would these uniforms change the mood of the restaurant?

1	YES	**CONTINUE**
2	NO	**SKIP TO DESCRIPTION**
3	DK/RF	**SKIP TO DESCRIPTION**

The last color page shows representations of the packaging and product lines that will be carried in the restaurant. These items include: gourmet coffees, coffee mugs, T-shirts and sweatshirts with the Roxann's logo emblazoned on the front, gift boxes, decorative jars of a variety of sauces, and cheese.

The next three pictures show what the front of the Roxann's restaurant might look like. (Pictures are not included in this text.) In the front window of each of the three pictures is a list of the various items that are sold inside. Please read the list of items in each of the three pictures.

7. Of these three pictures and the three lists of items written on the windows, which one is your first choice? **RECORD RESPONSE**

1 Roxann's Gourmet Coffee/Roxann's Baker/Roxann's soup, salad, sandwiches/Roxann's Desserts
2 Java Roast Fine Coffees/Roxann's Bakery/Roxann's soup, salad, sandwiches/Roxann's Frozen Yogurt
3 Java Coast Fine Coffees/Crumbles Bakery/Brio soup, salad, sandwiches/Roxann's Frozen Yogurt

8. Which is your second choice? **RECORD RESPONSE**

1 Roxann's Gourmet Coffee/Roxann's Bakery/Roxann's soup, salad, sandwiches/Roxann's Desserts
2 Java Coast Fine Coffees/Roxann's Bakery/Roxann's soup, salad, sandwiches/Roxann's Frozen Yogurt
3 Java Coast Fine Coffees/Crumbles Bakery/Brio soup, salad, sandwiches/Roxann's Frozen Yogurt

9. Would you ____________ that Roxann's is a restaurant for people like yourself? **READ LIST**

1 Strongly disagree
2 Disagree
3 Neither agree nor disagree
4 Agree or
5 Strongly agree
6 DK

10. What kind of restaurant does the name Roxann's convey? **DO NOT READ LIST**

1 Cafe
2 Deli
3 Sandwich shop
4 Coffee shop
5 Other
6 DK

11. Next, I am going to read you a list of descriptive terms. Please tell me to what extent you think each of these terms describes Roxann's. Please indicate whether you strongly agree, agree, neither agree nor disagree, disagree, or strongly disagree that these words describe Roxann's. **ROTATE LIST**

	SA	A	NAD	D	SD	DK
Fun	5	4	3	2	1	6
Casual	5	4	3	2	1	6
Traditional	5	4	3	2	1	6
Upscale	5	4	3	2	1	6
Unique	5	4	3	2	1	6
Elegant	5	4	3	2	1	6
Elite	5	4	3	2	1	6
Ordinary	5	4	3	2	1	6
Gourmet	5	4	3	2	1	6
Unusual	5	4	3	2	1	6
Contemporary	5	4	3	2	1	6
Relaxed	5	4	3	2	1	6
Intimate	5	4	3	2	1	6
Quiet	5	4	3	2	1	6
Noisy	5	4	3	2	1	6
Crowded	5	4	3	2	1	6
Expensive	5	4	3	2	1	6
Inexpensive	5	4	3	2	1	6

12. Of the following, which best describes the type of restaurant you would expect Roxann's to be? **READ LIST**

1 Lunch place
2 Dinner place
3 Lunch and dinner place
4 Dessert place
5 DK/RF

13. For which meals or for what occasions would you go to Roxann's? **DO NOT READ LIST—INDICATE ALL THAT APPLY**

1 Lunch
2 Dinner
3 Anytime
4 A night out
5 A family outing
6 A celebration
7 A party
8 A date
9 I WOULD NOT EAT THERE
10 DK/RF

14. How likely would you be to eat at a restaurant like Roxann's? Would you be . . . **READ LIST**

1 Very likely
2 Somewhat likely
3 Somewhat unlikely or
4 Very unlikely
5 DK/RF

15. If you went to Roxann's for lunch, who would you bring with you? Would you bring . . . **READ LIST—INDICATE ALL THAT APPLY**

1 Your family
2 A date
3 A friend or
4 Co-workers
5 I WOULD NOT EAT LUNCH THERE
6 Other
7 DK

16. If you went to Roxann's at night, who would you bring with you? Would you bring . . . **READ LIST—INDICATE ALL THAT APPLY**

1	Your family	**CONTINUE**
2	A date	**CONTINUE**
3	A friend or	**CONTINUE**
4	Co-workers	**CONTINUE**
5	I WOULD NOT EAT DINNER THERE	**SKIP TO Q.24**
6	Other	**CONTINUE**
7	DK	**SKIP TO Q.24**

17. How many people would typically be in your party when you go to Roxann's?

1 One
2 Two
3 Three or four
4 More than four
5 I WOULD NOT EAT THERE
6 DK/RF

18. Would you purchase food to go at Roxann's?

1 YES
2 NO
3 DK/RF

19. What kinds of sandwiches would you expect to find at Roxann's? **DO NOT READ LIST—INDICATE ALL THAT APPLY**

1 Reuben
2 Club
3 Ham & Cheese
4 Roast beef
5 Turkey
6 Muffuletta
7 Hamburgers/cheeseburgers
8 Other
9 DK

20. What kinds of desserts would you expect to find at Roxann's?

21. Would you expect to find **ITEMS NOT MENTIONED IN Q.20 . . .**

	Q.20 Unaided	Q.21 Aided
Frozen yogurt	1	2
Frozen yogurt pies	1	2
Candies	1	2
Cookies	1	2
Ice cream	1	2
Other (specify)	1	

22. What kind of beverages would you expect to find at Roxann's? **DO NOT READ LIST—INDICATE ALL THAT APPLY**

1 Sodas/Carbonated beverages (e.g., Coke, Pepsi, Sprite)
2 Coffee
3 Unusual bottled sodas
4 Sparking juices
5 Sparking flavored water
6 Tea
7 Other
8 DK

23. What kinds of take-home products would be sold at Roxann's? **READ LIST—INDICATE ALL THAT APPLY**

1 Coffee (beans or ground)
2 Cookies
3 Candy
4 Sauces
5 Cheeses
6 Other
7 DK

That concludes our questions for this concept. Now I would like you to turn to the next page.

CONCEPT B (BIG AL'S)

On the first page is the Big Al's logo.

On the next page you see a view of the restaurant as it would appear as you enter through the front door. Immediately to the left are shelves displaying various products. Beyond this display is the serving line behind which the menu is posted on boards along

BIG AL's
STOP
Fried Chicken
Broiled Halibut
Peas & Carrots
YIELD
BIG AL's All-You-Can-Eat Buffet
BIG AL's GOURMET COFFEE
BIG AL's SOUP
BIG AL's

BIG AL's FINE COFFEES
BIG AL's FINE COFFEES
BIG AL's
FINE COFFEES
BIG AL's
RESTAURANT
The Best Garage in Town!
BIG AL's DESSERTS
BIG AL's DESSERTS
BIG AL's DESSERTS
BIG AL's BAKERY MUNCHIN' COOKIES
BIG AL's BAKERY MUNCHIN' COOKIES

the wall. In front of the serving line and along the front wall are the tables and chairs. The front wall of the restaurant has garage doors that reveal large windows when opened. The decor depicts images of "Al's" garage.

The next page has an assortment of the colors, textures, furniture, and accessories that will be used in Big Al's. The colors are the natural brown of paper and navy blue. The pictures in the garage door windows depict fathers and their children. Some of the pictures used are of celebrity fathers and their children. The accessories and decor are an eclectic mix of sports equipment, cafe furniture, and items found in a garage.

24. On a scale of 1 to 5 where 5 is "strongly agree" and 1 is "strongly disagree," would you say the garage doors belong in a place like Big Al's? Do you . . . **READ LIST**

1 Strongly disagree
2 Disagree
3 Neither agree nor disagree
4 Agree or
5 Strongly agree
6 DK

On the last color page are representations of the packaging product lines that will be carried in the restaurant. These items include: gourmet coffees, coffee mugs, T-shirts, sweatshirts, shopping bags, decorative jars of a variety of sauces, cheeses, cartons of frozen yogurt desserts, and frozen yogurt bars, all with Big Al's logo emblazoned on the front.

The next three pictures show what the front of the Big Al's restaurant might look like. In the front window of each of the three pictures are various items that are sold inside. Please read the list of items in each of the three pictures.

25. Of these three pictures and the three lists of items written on the windows, which one is your first choice? **RECORD RESPONSE**

1 BIG AL'S Fine Coffee/BIG AL'S Bakery/BIG AL'S soup, salad, sandwiches/BIG AL'S Desserts
2 Java Coast Fine Coffees/BIG AL'S Bakery/BIG AL'S soup, salad, sandwiches/BIG AL'S Frozen Yogurt
3 BIG AL'S Frozen Yogurt/Java Coast Fine Coffees/Crumbles Bakery/Brio soup, salad, sandwiches

26. Which is your second choice? **RECORD RESPONSE**

1 BIG AL'S Fine Coffee/BIG AL'S Bakery/BIG AL'S Bakery/BIG AL'S soup, salad, sandwiches/BIG AL'S Frozen Yogurt
2 Java Coast Fine Coffees/BIG AL'S Bakery/BIG AL'S soup, salad, sandwiches/BIG AL'S Frozen Yogurt
3 BIG AL'S Frozen Yogurt/Java Coast Fine Coffees/Crumbles Bakery/Brio soup, salad, sandwiches.

27. Would you ____________ that Big Al's is a restaurant for people like yourself? **READ LIST**

1 Strongly disagree
2 Disagree
3 Neither agree nor disagree
4 Agree
5 Strongly agree
6 DK

28. What kind of restaurant does the name Big Al's convey? **DO NOT READ LIST**

1 Cafe
2 Deli
3 Sandwich shop
4 Coffee shop
5 Other

29. Next, I am going to read you a list of descriptive terms. Please tell me to what extent you think each of these terms describes Big Al's. Please indicate whether you strongly agree, agree, neither agree nor disagree, disagree, or strongly disagree that these words describe Big Al's. **ROTATE LIST**

	SA	A	NAD	D	SD	DK
Fun	5	4	3	2	1	6
Casual	5	4	3	2	1	6
Traditional	5	4	3	2	1	6
Upscale	5	4	3	2	1	6
Unique	5	4	3	2	1	6
Elegant	5	4	3	2	1	6
Elite	5	4	3	2	1	6
Ordinary	5	4	3	2	1	6
Gourmet	5	4	3	2	1	6
Unusual	5	4	3	2	1	6
Contemporary	5	4	3	2	1	6
Relaxed	5	4	3	2	1	6
Intimate	5	4	3	2	1	6
Quiet	5	4	3	2	1	6
Noisy	5	4	3	2	1	6
Crowded	5	4	3	2	1	6
Expensive	5	4	3	2	1	6
Inexpensive	5	4	3	2	1	6

30. Of the following, which best describes the type of restaurant you would expect Big Al's to be? **READ LIST**

1 Lunch place
2 Dinner place
3 Lunch and Dinner place
4 Dessert place
5 DK/RF

31. For which meals or for what occasions would you go to Big Al's? **DO NOT READ**

LIST—INDICATE ALL THAT APPLY

1 Lunch
2 Dinner
3 Anytime
4 A night out
5 A family outing
6 A celebration
7 A party
8 A date
9 I WOULD NOT EAT THERE
10 DK/RF

32. How likely would you be to eat at a restaurant like Big Al's? Would you be . . .
READ LIST

1 Very likely
2 Somewhat likely
3 Somewhat unlikely or
4 Very Unlikely
5 DK/RF

33. If you went to Big Al's for lunch, who would you bring with you? Would you bring . . . **READ LIST**

1 Your family
2 A date
3 A friend or
4 Co-workers
5 I WOULD NOT EAT LUNCH THERE
6 Other
7 DK

34. If you went to Big Al's at night, who would you bring with you? Would you bring . . .
READ LIST—INDICATE ALL THAT APPLY

1	Your family	**CONTINUE**
2	A date	**CONTINUE**
3	A friend or	**CONTINUE**
4	Co-workers	**CONTINUE**
5	I WOULD NOT EAT DINNER THERE	**SKIP TO Q.42**
6	Other	**CONTINUE**
7	DK	**SKIP TO Q.42**

35. How many people would typically be in your party when you go to Big Al's?

1 One
2 Two
3 Three or four
4 More than four
5 I WOULD NOT EAT THERE
6 DK/RF

36. Would you purchase food to go at Big Al's?

1 YES
2 NO
3 DK/RF

37. What kind of sandwiches would you expect to find at Big Al's? **DO NOT READ LIST—INDICATE ALL THAT APPLY**

1 Reuben
2 Club
3 Ham & Cheese

4 Roast beef
5 Turkey
6 Muffuletta
7 Hamburgers/cheeseburgers
8 Other
9 DK

38. What kinds of desserts would you expect to find at Big Al's?

39. Would you expect to find **ITEMS NOT MENTIONED IN Q.38 . . .**

	Q.38 Unaided	Q.39 Aided
Frozen yogurt	1	2
Frozen yogurt pies	1	2
Candies	1	2
Cookies	1	2
Ice cream	1	2
Other (specify)	1	

40. What kind of beverages would you expect to find at Big Al's? **DO NOT READ LIST—INDICATE ALL THAT APPLY**

1 Sodas/Carbonated beverages (e.g., Coke, Pepsi, Sprite)
2 Coffee
3 Unusual bottled sodas
4 Sparkling juices
5 Sparkling flavored water
6 Tea
7 Other
8 DK

41. What kinds of take-home products would be sold at Big Al's? **READ LIST—INDICATE ALL THAT APPLY**

1 Coffee (beans or ground)
2 Cookies
3 Candy
4 Sauces
5 Cheeses
6 Other
7 DK

Please look at the menus that are enclosed and read through both of them. **ONCE RESPONDENT HAS READ THE MENUS ASK:**

42. Which of these two menus do you prefer? **DO NOT READ LIST**

1 Traditional
2 Unique, upscale
3 DK/RF **SKIP TO Q.44**

43. Which of the two restaurant designs would you associate with the **(ANSWER TO Q.42)** menu? **DO NOT READ LIST**

1 ROXANN'S
2 BIG AL'S
3 NEITHER
4 BOTH
5 DK/RF

44. Thinking about your preferences while at restaurants, how do you prefer to be served soup and salad? Do you . . . **READ LIST**

1 Prefer to serve yourself
2 Prefer to be served by an attendant or
3 Have no preference

4 DK/RF

45. If you could select your seating and you were given a choice of a stool or a chair, which would you choose?

1	Chair	CONTINUE
2	Stool	CONTINUE
3	DK/RF	SKIP TO Q.47

46. How interested would you be in buying some of the products available at Roxann's or Big Al's to take home with you? Would you be . . . **READ LIST**

1 Very interested
2 Somewhat interested
3 Somewhat uninterested or
4 Very uninterested
5 DK/RF

47. Would you ever stop by Roxann's or Big Al's just to buy products to take home?

1 YES
2 NO
3 DK/RF

QUESTIONS FOR STUDENTS

1. What is the level of appeal of each concept?
2. Were the restaurants for people like themselves?
3. Describe the level of agreement with the concept statements for each restaurant.
4. Were respondents interested in take-home products?
5. Provide a demographic description of a person likely to eat at (a) Roxann's and (b) Big Al's two or more times per month.
6. Describe consumer expectations such as type of place; appropriate occasions; lunch companions; evening companions; size of party; and sandwiches, desserts, and beverages expected for Roxann's and Big Al's.
7. Which menu was preferred? Give a demographic description of the preferred menus.
8. Describe the preferred serving mode, employee attire, and type of seat preferences.
9. What written material was preferred on the window for Roxann's? For Big Al's?

TABLE B.1 Menus

TRADITIONAL SANDWICHES, SOUPS, AND SALADS YOU WOULD EXPECT FROM A RESTAURANT.

Breads like wheatberry, hearty rye and fresh-baked white.
Favorite cheeses like American, cheddar, Monterey Jack and mozzarella.
Examples include:

Reuben

- Turkey pastrami, piled high
- Melted, aged Swiss cheese
- Sauerkraut
- Mild mustard
- Toasted rye bread

Monday's Lunch

- Honey glazed ham, sliced
- Creamy mozzarella cheese
- Lettuce with tomato slices
- Spicy mustard
- Hearty rye bread

continues

Big Club

- Smoked chicken breast strips
- Bacon
- Ham
- Turkey
- Swiss and cheddar cheese
- Leaf lettuce with tomato slices
- Spicy mustard
- Three slices whole wheat toast

Best Roast Beef

- Roast beef (medium rare), piled high
- Mild Muenster cheese
- Red onion slices
- Spicy mustard
- Rye bread

UNIQUE AND UPSCALE SANDWICHES, SOUPS, AND SALADS WITH AN INTERNATIONAL FLAIR.

Gourmet breads, some flavored with dill or caraway seeds.
Spicy cheeses like Muenster, tangy provolone, and Monterey Jack.
Unusual sauces, spiced mustards, herbed mayonnaise.
Examples include:

The International Flair

- Mesquite-smoked ham
- Cotta salami
- Creamy mozzarella cheese
- Sharp provolone cheese
- Roasted red peppers
- Black olives
- Sun-dried tomatoes
- French baguette bread

Santa Fe Muffuletta

- Sliced turkey breast
- Hard and soft salamis
- Provolone and cheddar cheese
- Black olives
- Green chilies
- Cilantro
- Honey-wheat roll (soft)

A Lively Roast Beef

- Roast beef (medium rare)
- Mild Monterey Jack cheese
- Red leaf lettuce with tomato slices
- Red wine vinaigrette
- Creamy horseradish sauce
- Hearty rye bread

Turkey with a Twist

- Mesquite-smoked turkey slices (thin)
- Marinated artichoke hearts
- Leaf lettuce with tomato slices
- Uniquely spiced mayonnaise
- Seven-grain bread

CASE C

Heritage Restaurants: Multivariate Analysis with Data Disc

The final part of the concept questionnaire (see Heritage Restaurants—Concept Tests) contained conjoint analysis and perceptual mapping questions. These are shown here.

I am going to read you several questions concerning your preferences for restaurants. For each question, base your preferences on your lunchtime experiences. You will be given general price estimates that are based on the cost for a sandwich, a side order such as french fries, baked potato, etc., and a drink.

Before we begin, I want to explain two terms we will be using: Self-service and Assisted self-service.

> **SELF-SERVICE** is defined as a serving line where you would place your salad, soup, or dessert on the plate or bowl yourself.
>
> **ASSISTED SELF-SERVICE** is defined as a serving line where the attendant would place the salad, soup, or dessert on the plate or bowl and hand it to you.
>
> In both cases the restaurant employee would make your sandwich for you.

ACA (CONJOINT ANALYSIS) QUESTIONS

THE FOLLOWING ATTRIBUTES AND THEIR CORRESPONDING ATTRIBUTE LEVELS OR CATEGORIES WILL BE USED IN THE CONJOINT ANALYSIS

Concept—	Roxann's
	Big Al's
Service level—	Self-service
	Assisted self-service
Price—	$5
	$7
	$9
	$12
Seating—	Table for two
	Table for four
	Booth
	Counter

ACA-1. When considering a restaurant for lunch, which of the following would you prefer? **ASK FOR:**
Concept
Service level
Price
Seating—What would be your next choice? Your next choice?

ACA-2. Assuming everything else is equal, how important would the difference between your most preferred and least preferred option on each of the four attributes be to you when considering a restaurant for lunch? Would it be extremely important, very important, somewhat important, or not important at all? **ASK FOR EACH:**
Concept
Price
Service level
Seating

ACA-3. Based on what you have told me so far, the computer is going to create some different restaurants made up of two or three of these attributes. Two restaurants will be considered for each question. I would like you to tell me which of the two combinations of attributes you prefer and indicate whether you somewhat prefer or strongly prefer that combination. Assume any items not mentioned would be identified for both restaurants.

EXAMPLE

Which would you prefer

BIG AL's	ROXANN'S
Self-service	Assisted self-service
$5 per person	$7 per person

Is that strongly or somewhat?

Strongly prefer First	1	2	3	4	5	Strongly prefer Second

53. On a scale from 0 to 100, how likely are you to go to a restaurant like Big Al's if a sandwich, side order, and drink costs $5.50 per person, on average?
______ LIKELIHOOD TO VISIT

54. Using the same scale, how likely are you to go to a restaurant like Roxann's if a sandwich, side order, and drink costs $7.00 per person?
______ LIKELIHOOD TO VISIT

55. **IF LIKELIHOOD IS GREATER THAN 24, THEN ASK FOR EACH RESTAURANT:** How frequently would you eat at a restaurant like __________? Would you eat there . . .

1 Once a year
2 Once a month
3 Two or three times a month
4 Once a week, or
5 More than once a week
6 NEVER
7 DK/RF

AMP (PERCEPTUAL MAPPING) QUESTIONS

56. Please rate these four types of restaurants: fast food restaurants like McDonald's; Big Al's; full service restaurants like Benningans; and Roxann's on such items related to your dining experience. Considering each restaurant as a destination for a lunchtime meal, use a 9-point scale where 9 means it is "poor" and 1 means it is "excellent." How would you rate on . . . **READ LIST**

Item	Poor								Excellent
Wide variety of menu items	9	8	7	6	5	4	3	2	1
Atmosphere	9	8	7	6	5	4	3	2	1
Attractiveness of interior decor	9	8	7	6	5	4	3	2	1
Creative and different food items	9	8	7	6	5	4	3	2	1
Good value for the money	9	8	7	6	5	4	3	2	1
Use of fresh ingredients	9	8	7	6	5	4	3	2	1
Speed of service	9	8	7	6	5	4	3	2	1
Healthy menu items	9	8	7	6	5	4	3	2	1

That completes our interview. Thank you for your cooperation.

QUESTIONS FOR STUDENTS

1. The utilities for each level of each of the attributes discussed in the case are provided for each respondent in the database that accompanies this case. Analyze these utilities and answer the following questions:
   a. Which attributes are most important to customers? What levels of those attributes do they prefer?
   b. Cluster analyze the utilities and identify different customer segments on the basis of the features or benefits they want from the product. What are the segments? What do they want? How big is each segment.
   c. Continuing with the analysis you started in part b., do the segments have any distinct demographic characteristics? Explain the basis for your response. If they are distinct demographically, how are they distinct?
2. Break the estimated utilities down by gender and age using age groups 18–30 and 41–50. Interpret the results.
3. Use perceptual mapping to determine which attributes are most closely related.
4. Use perceptual maps to describe the image of each of the four restaurants.

CASE D

Garcia's Supermarkets: Grocery Shopping Habits Survey with Data Disk

INTRODUCTION

BACKGROUND

Garcia's Supermarkets is a local chain which caters to Hispanic customers. All stores are located in El Paso, Texas. *Garcia's* market share has stabilized in the past two years in a Hispanic market that is growing at four percent annually.

PURPOSE

The purpose of this research is to provide *Garcia's Supermarkets* with grocery shopping habits of El Paso consumers. This information will be used to alter *Garcia's* marketing mix to improve market share.

OBJECTIVES

- Determine the supermarket perceived to be most conveniently located.
- Determine the supermarket shopped most often (primary supermarket).
- Determine the secondary supermarket.
- Assess the percent of grocery expenditures and shopping frequency for primary and secondary supermarkets.
- Identify reasons for shopping the supermarkets.
- Identify supermarket-product category relationships.
- Identify specialty food store usage habits.
- Assess supermarket attribute importance and perceived performance ratings for Garcia's and major players in the market.

METHODOLOGY

- *Data collection.* All data were collected by means of central location telephone interviewing.
  - *Ameridata facility.* All interviews were conducted from the Ameridata central location telephone interviewing facility in Arlington, Texas.
  - *Experienced interviewers.* Experienced bilingual Ameridata interviewers conducted all of the interviews.
  - *CATI.* All interviewing conducted with software driven interfaces to virtually eliminate tabulation errors.
- *Quality control.* All interviewing was supervised and monitored by Ameridata personnel.
- *Geographic area covered.* El Paso, Texas.
- *Qualified respondents.* Individuals who make food purchasing decisions.
  - *Sample selection.* The sample was selected following the criteria for a simple random sample.
  - *Sample size.* 799 completed interviews.

QUESTIONNAIRE

Hello, my name is _________ I'm with Ameridata Research, an independent marketing research firm, and we're interested in your family's supermarket shopping habits. May I speak with the person who does most of the food buying in your household?

WHEN SPEAKING WITH PRIMARY FOOD SHOPPER: May I please take approximately 15 minutes of your time to ask you some questions about shopping in food stores?

1	YES	**CONTINUE**
2	NO	**ARRANGE CALLBACK**

S1. First of all, are any members of your household currently employed by a supermarket, a food wholesaler, or an advertising agency?

1	YES	**THANK AND TERMINATE**
2	NO	**CONTINUE**

1. What supermarket is closest to your home? **DO NOT READ LIST. ALLOW ONE RESPONSE.**

1	Garcia's
2	Tom Thumb
3	Food Lion
4	Minyard
5	Kroger
6	Albertson's
7	Winn-Dixie
8	Sack 'N Save
9	Jerry's
A	Other
B	NONE
C	DK

2. Out of your last five supermarket shopping trips, how many times did you shop . . . **READ LIST—TOTAL MUST = 5**

		# of Times
1	Garcia's	_________
2	Tom Thumb	_________
3	Food Lion	_________
4	Minyard	_________
5	Kroger	_________
6	Albertson's	_________
7	Winn-Dixie	_________
8	Sack 'N Save	_________
9	Jerry's	_________
A	Other	_________

3. At which one supermarket do you purchase most of your food needs? **DO NOT READ LIST. ALLOW ONE RESPONSE.**

1	Garcia's	
2	Tom Thumb	
3	Food Lion	
4	Minyard	
5	Kroger	
6	Albertson's	
7	Winn-Dixie	
8	Sack 'N Save	
9	Jerry's	
A	Other	
B	NONE	**THANK AND TERMINATE**
C	DK	**THANK AND TERMINATE**

4. Of the total amount of money you spend each week in food stores, supermarkets, meat markets, bakeries, produce markets, and the like, about what percent is spent at **(STORE MENTIONED IN Q.3)? READ LIST—ALLOW ONE RESPONSE.**

   1 0%–25%
   2 26%–50%
   3 51%–75%
   4 76%–100%
   5 DK

5. How often do you shop at **(STORE MENTIONED IN Q.3)?**

   1 Twice a week or more
   2 Weekly
   3 Twice a month
   4 Monthly
   5 Less than once a month
   6 DK

6. Why do you shop **(STORE MENTIONED IN Q.3)** most often? **DO NOT READ LIST. INDICATE ALL THAT APPLY. PROBE WITH "Any others" UNTIL UNPRODUCTIVE.**

1	Close or convenient location	H	Hispanic/ethnic food selection
2	Everyday prices	I	Hispanic/ethnic food quality
3	Special (advertised) prices/sales	J	Seafood
4	Meat prices	K	Bakery
5	Meat quality	L	Spanish-speaking store help
6	Meat variety	M	Large store
7	Produce variety	N	Coupons
8	Produce quality	O	Grocery department
9	Overall selection or variety	P	Dairy/frozen food departments
A	Overall quality	O	Has a pharmacy
B	Cleanliness	R	General merchandise
C	Fast checkout service	S	Deli
D	Overall service	T	Store layout
E	Store brands on private label	U	Store hours
F	Newly remodeled	V	Accept credit/debit cards
G	Friendly store help	W	Other
		X	Other

7. After **(STORE MENTIONED IN Q.3)**, at which one supermarket do you shop most often?

   1 Garcia's
   2 Tom Thumb
   3 Food Lion
   4 Minyard
   5 Kroger
   6 Albertson's
   7 Winn-Dixie
   8 Sack 'N Save
   9 Jerry's
   A Other
   B NONE **SKIP TO Q.11**
   C DK **SKIP TO Q.11**

8. Of the total amount of money you spend each week in food stores, supermarkets, meat markets, bakeries, produce markets, and the like, about what percent is spent at **(STORE MENTIONED IN Q.7)? READ LIST—ALLOW ONE RESPONSE.**

1 0%–25%
2 26%–50%
3 51%–75%
4 76%–100%
5 DK

9. How often do you shop at **(STORE MENTIONED IN Q.7)?**
1 Twice a week or more
2 Weekly
3 Twice a month
4 Monthly
5 Less than once a month
6 DK

10. Why do you shop **(STORE MENTIONED IN Q.7)** second most often? **DO NOT READ LIST. INDICATE ALL THAT APPLY. PROBE.**

1	Close or convenient location	H	Hispanic/ethnic food selection
2	Everyday prices	I	Hispanic/ethnic food quality
3	Special (advertised) prices/sales	J	Seafood
4	Meat prices	K	Bakery
5	Meat quality	L	Spanish-speaking store help
6	Meat variety	M	Large store
7	Produce variety	N	Coupons
8	Produce quality	O	Grocery department
9	Overall selection or variety	P	Dairy/frozen food departments
A	Overall quality	Q	Has a pharmacy
B	Cleanliness	R	General merchandise
C	Fast checkout service	S	Deli
D	Overall service	T	Store layout
E	Store brands or private label	U	Store hours
F	Newly remodeled	V	Accept credit/debit cards
G	Friendly store help	W	Other
		X	Other

11. Of all supermarkets in which you currently purchase food products, at which one supermarket do you shop most often for the following products? **READ LIST**

	GARCIA'S	TOM THUMB	FOOD LION	MINYARD	KROGER	ALBERTSON'S	WINN-DIXIE	SACK 'N SAVE	JERRY'S	OTHER	DK/NA
Fruits and vegetables	1	2	3	4	5	6	7	8	9	A	B
Meats	1	2	3	4	5	6	7	8	9	A	B
Seafood	1	2	3	4	5	6	7	8	9	A	B
Tortillas	1	2	3	4	5	6	7	8	9	A	B
Paper products like paper towels or napkins	1	2	3	4	5	6	7	8	9	A	B
Hispanic/ Ethnic foods	1	2	3	4	5	6	7	8	9	A	B
Private label or store brand products	1	2	3	4	5	6	7	8	9	A	B
Milk or dairy products	1	2	3	4	5	6	7	8	9	A	B

12. For each of the following statements, please tell me if you strongly agree, somewhat agree, somewhat disagree, or strongly disagree with each statement. **READ LIST. PROMPT WITH RESPONSES AS NECESSARY.**

	STRONGLY AGREE	SOMEWHAT AGREE	SOMEWHAT DISAGREE	STRONGLY DISAGREE	DON'T KNOW
I like to shop at a supermarket where other people are just like me.	1	2	3	4	5
I will search the newspapers to find the stores offering the lowest price on the items I want and will drive around to shop these different stores.	1	2	3	4	5
I prefer shopping at a supermarket where the clerks speak Spanish.	1	2	3	4	5
I hardly ever go to the supermarket without store coupons or manufacturers' coupons.	1	2	3	4	5
I typically buy store brands rather than national brands.	1	2	3	4	5
No supermarket in my area has the same selection or quality of ethnic foods or spices like smaller specialty food stores.	1	2	3	4	5
I will give my business to the store with the lowest prices.	1	2	3	4	5
I tend to do all my supermarket shopping at one store, rather than shopping many stores.	1	2	3	4	5
I prefer to shop supermarkets close to my house.	1	2	3	4	5
I like to shop at a supermarket where I can get in and out fast.	1	2	3	4	5

13. How many times, in an average week, does your family tend to dine together for dinner?

    _______ Number of times

14. Do you typically shop at any of the following specialty food stores? **READ LIST—IF NO TO ALL SPECIALTIES, SKIP TO Q.17.**

	YES	NO	DK
Meat markets or delis	1	2	3
Bakeries	1	2	3
Seafood markets	1	2	3
Produce markets	1	2	3
Spice shops	1	2	3
Hispanic/ethnic markets	1	2	3

15. How often do you shop at specialty food stores?

    1 Twice a week or more
    2 Weekly
    3 Twice a month

4 Monthly
5 Less than once a month
6 KD

16. Of the total amount of money you spend each week at food stores, about what percent is spent at specialty stores (produce or meat markets, bakeries, spice shops or Hispanic/ethnic markets)? **READ LIST. ALLOW ONE RESPONSE.**
1 0%–25%
2 26%–50%
3 51%–75%
4 76%–100%
5 DK

17. I would like you to tell me how important the following are to you in deciding where to shop for groceries. Please rank each item on a scale of 1 to 4 with 1 being least important and 4 being most important. How important is . . . **READ LIST.**
_______ Quality of fruits and vegetables
_______ Quality of meats
_______ Quality of seafood
_______ Quality of bakery

18. Again, using a scale of 1 to 4 with 1 being least important and 4 being most important, please rank each of the following items. **READ LIST.**
_______ Selection of fruits and vegetables
_______ Selection of meats
_______ Selection of seafood
_______ Selection of ethnic foods and products

19. Now, please rank the following items on a scale of 1 to 5 with 1 being least important and 5 being most important. How important is . . . **read list.**
_______ Fast checkouts
_______ Friendly employees
_______ Good security
_______ Easy to get in and out
_______ Clean store

20. Using the same 1 to 5 scale, please rank each of the following. **READ LIST.**
_______ Quality
_______ Best selection
_______ Lowest price
_______ Fast to get in and out
_______ Friendly shopping atmosphere

21. Of all the supermarkets in your area that you have heard about or shopped, in your opinion, who has . . . **READ LIST.**

	GARCIA'S	TOM THUMB	FOOD LION	MINYARD	KROGER	ALBERTSON'S	WINN-DIXIE	SACK 'N SAVE	JERRY'S OTHER	OTHER	DK/NA
The best produce	1	2	3	4	5	6	7	8	9	A	B
The best meats	1	2	3	4	5	6	7	8	9	A	B
The best seafood	1	2	3	4	5	6	7	8	9	A	B
The best deli	1	2	3	4	5	6	7	8	9	A	B
The largest selection of ethnic foods and products	1	2	3	4	5	6	7	8	9	A	B
The best bakery	1	2	3	4	5	6	7	8	9	A	B
The best overall selection	1	2	3	4	5	6	7	8	9	A	B
The best frozen foods department	1	2	3	4	5	6	7	8	9	A	B
The fastest checkouts	1	2	3	4	5	6	7	8	9	A	B

For classification purposes, I would like to ask a few questions about you and your household.

22. INDICATE GENDER OF RESPONDENT BY OBSERVATION:

1 MALE
2 FEMALE

23. How many people, including yourself, are currently living at home?

_______ Number of people

24. How many children under the age of 18 live in your household?

_______ Number of children

25. In an average week, how much does your household spend on groceries? READ LIST.

1 Less than $25
2 $26–$50
3 $51–$75
4 $76-$100
5 $101–$125
6 $126–$150
7 $151–$175
8 $176–$200
9 $201–$225
A $226–$250
B $251–$300
C Over $300
D DK
E RF

26. Which of the following categories includes your age? READ LIST.

1 18–24
2 25–34
3 35–44
4 45–54
5 55–64
6 65 or over
7 RF

27. Please tell me how many people in your household are employed outside the home.

\# of people

1 Full-time ________
2 Part-time ________

28. What is the primary language spoken in your home?

1 English
2 Spanish
3 Other, specify: __________________________
4 RF

29. Which of the following categories includes the total annual income of all members of your household?

1 Under $10,000
2 $10,000–$19,000
3 $20,000–$29,999
4 $30,000–$39,999
5 $40,000–$49,999
6 $50,000–$59,999
7 $60,000–$69,999
8 $70,000–$79,999
9 $80,000–$89,999
A $90,000–$99,999

B $100,000–$124,999
C $125,000–$149,999
D $150,000 or more
E RF

30. Which of the following best describes your racial or ethnic background? **READ LIST.**
    1 Anglo-American
    2 African American
    3 Asian American
    4 Mexican American
    5 Puerto Rican American
    6 Cuban American
    7 Hispanic American
    8 RF
31. Do you own or rent your home?
    1 Own
    2 Rent
    3 RF
32. How long have you lived in the United States?
    1 Less than five years
    2 5–10 years
    3 More than 10 years
    4 RF

That concludes our survey. Thank you very much for your time and participation.
RECORD RESPONDENT INFORMATION BELOW:
NAME: ______________________________
ADDRESS: ______________________________
TELEPHONE NUMBER: (_____) _________–______________
INTERVIEWER NUMBER: ______________

QUESTIONS FOR STUDENTS

1. Give a demographic profile of a typical respondent.
2. Compare a "typical" Garcia's shopper with one who shops elsewhere.
3. Why do consumers primarily patronize Kroger, Garcia's, and Jerry's?
4. Kroger is seen as "best" when shopping for what type of products? Garcia's?
5. Discuss quality, selection, and shopping experience attributes by persons who primarily patronize Kroger versus Garcia's. Analyze the attributes by demographics.
6. Create a perceptual map of the El Paso grocery market using patronage data and shopper motivations.

CASE E

Rockingham National Bank: Visa Card with Data Disc

BACKGROUND

Rockingham National Bank, located in Chicago, Illinois, is attempting to expand the market for its Visa card. It is examining certain target groups to determine the bank's ability to penetrate the credit card market with special offers.

PURPOSE

The purpose of this research is to evaluate how teachers in Illinois will respond to specific credit card promotional offers.

OBJECTIVES

The research was designed to achieve the following objectives:

- *Profile teachers.* Develop a demographic, psychographic, credit card ownership, and credit card usage profile of teachers.
- *Likelihood to respond.* Determine the likelihood of teachers to respond to several different concepts for a credit card offer.
- *Correlates of response likelihood.* Determine which demographic, psychographic, attitudinal, credit card ownership, and credit card usage variables are the best predictors of likelihood to respond to the concept credit card offers.
- *Level of response.* Make predictions regarding the likely level of response to a credit card offer to the teacher market.
- *Most attractive features.* Identify those features most likely to induce teachers to respond to a credit card offer.

METHODOLOGY

- *Data collection.* All data were collected by means of central location telephone intervening.
  - **Ameridata facility.** All interviews were conducted from the Ameridata central location telephone interviewing facility in Arlington, Texas.
  - **Experienced interviewers.** Experienced Ameridata interviewers conducted all the interviews.
  - **CATI.** All interviewing conducted with software driven interfaces to virtually eliminate tabulation errors.
- *Quality Control.* All interviewing was supervised and monitored by Ameridata personnel.
- *Geographic area covered.* State of Illinois.
- *Qualified respondents.* Individuals who are licensed teachers in Illinois.
  - **Sample selection.** The sample was selected following the criteria for a simple random sample.
  - **Sample size.** 400 completed interviews.

TEACHERS CREDIT CARD SURVEY

ASK TO SPEAK TO RESPONDENT LISTED ON THE SAMPLE SHEET. IF ANOTHER MEMBER OF THE HOUSEHOLD IS WILLING TO DO THE SURVEY, THANK THEM FOR THEIR WILLINGNESS, BUT EXPLAIN THAT WE NEED TO COMPLETE THE INTERVIEW WITH THE LISTED RESPONDENT.

Hello, my name is ____________ with Ameridata Research, an independent marketing research firm. I would like to ask you a few questions about credit card usage. First, let me assure you this is not a sales call, you will not be contacted again, and my questions will only take a few minutes of your time.

READ ONLY IF NEEDED: Let me assure you that this is not a sales call; we are only conducting research on credit card usage and are interested in your opinions about credit cards.

1. First of all, please tell me whether you strongly agree, agree, neither agree nor disagree, disagree, or strongly disagree with each of the following statements: **READ LIST AND ROTATE**

	SA	A	NAD	D	SD	DK
Money may not be everything, but it's got a big lead over whatever is second.	5	4	3	2	1	6
Money can't buy happiness.	5	4	3	2	1	6
It is important for me to be fashionable and chic.	5	4	3	2	1	6
I buy things even though I can't afford them.	5	4	3	2	1	6
I make only the minimum payments on my credit cards.	5	4	3	2	1	6
I sometimes buy things to make myself feel better.	5	4	3	2	1	6
Shopping is fun.	5	4	3	2	1	6
During the last three years, my financial situation has gotten worse.	5	4	3	2	1	6
I am satisfied with my present financial situation.	5	4	3	2	1	6
Buying things gives me a lot of pleasure.	5	4	3	2	1	6
You can tell a lot about people by the credit cards they use.	5	4	3	2	1	6
I attach great importance to money.	5	4	3	2	1	6
I attach great importance to credit cards.	5	4	3	2	1	6
I attach great importance to material possessions.	5	4	3	2	1	6
I generally read all offers that I receive through the mail just to know what they are about.	5	4	3	2	1	6

2. Please tell me which of the following credit cards you carry with you. Do you carry . . .
PROBE FOR VISA OR MASTERCARD.

1 Visa **ASK FOR NUMBER OF VISA CARDS:** ______
2 MasterCard **ASK FOR NUMBER OF MASTERCARDS:** _______
3 Discover
4 American Express
5 Optima
6 AT&T Universal
7 GM
8 Ford
9 NONE **SKIP TO Q.11**

3. Which card do you use the most often? **PROBE FOR ONE ANSWER ONLY; IF RESPONDENT IS UNABLE TO GIVE ONLY ONE RESPONSE, TAKE THE FIRST RESPONSE GIVEN.**

1 Visa
2 MasterCard
3 Discover
4 American Express
5 Optima
6 AT&T Universal
7 GM
8 Ford
9 DON'T KNOW **SKIP TO Q.11**

IF "VISA" OR "MASTERCARD" MENTIONED IN Q.3, ASK Q.4— OTHERWISE SKIP TO Q.11.

4. Which bank issued this Visa/MasterCard?
MASTERCARD ISSUERS

1 ASSOCIATES NATIONAL BANK
2 CHASE MANHATTAN
3 CITIBANK
4 CREDIT UNION ISSUED
5 FIRST CARD
6 HOUSEHOLD
7 MBNA
8 OTHER
9 DK

VISA ISSUERS

1 ASSOCIATES NATIONAL BANK
2 BANK OF AMERICA
3 CITIBANK
4 CREDIT UNION ISSUED
5 FIRST BANK
6 HOUSEHOLD
7 MBNA
8 OTHER
9 DK

5. Why do you use **ANSWERS FROM Q.3** most often?

1 Convenience
2 Only card owned/carried
3 Interest rate
4 Wide acceptance
5 Cash back
6 Cash rebate

7 Billing cycle/grace period
8 No annual fee
9 Issued by a local bank
10 Corporate/business card
11 Credit limit
12 Itemized bill
13 It's a Gold Card
14 Rebate toward automobile purchase
15 Relationship with organization sponsoring card. **IF YES:** Which organization?
16 Other

6. What is the interest rate on the balances that you carry on the card you use most often?
   1 Less than 8 percent
   2 8–8.9 percent
   3 9–9.9 percent
   4 10–10.9 percent
   5 11–11.9 percent
   6 12–12.9 percent
   7 13–13.9 percent
   8 14–14.9 percent
   9 15–15.9 percent
   10 16–16.9 percent
   11 17–17.9 percent
   12 18–18.9 percent
   13 19–19.9 percent
   14 20 percent or more
7. What is your credit limit on the card you can use the most?
   ______ credit limit
8. Is the card you use most often a Gold Card?
   1 YES
   2 NO
   3 DK
9. Does the card you use most often: **READ LIST**

	Yes	No	DK
Charge an annual fee	1	2	3
Offer cash rebates/cash back on purchases	1	2	3
Offer extended warranties on products you buy	1	2	3
Offer buyer protection policies on products you buy (to replace the product if damaged, lost or stolen)	1	2	3
Offer a photo credit card	1	2	3

10. Besides a lower interest rate, what feature or features would a new card need to have to convince you to obtain it?
    1 No annual fee
    2 Preapproved
    3 Rebate/cash back/free offers
    4 Business/corporate card
    5 Gold card
    6 High credit limit
    7 Wide acceptance
    8 Other
11. Have you received any credit card offers in the past year?
    1 YES CONTINUE

2 NO **SKIP TO Q.17**
3 DK **SKIP TO Q.17**

12. Approximately how many credit offers have you received in the past year?
_______ Number of offers received

13. Have you responded to any of these offers?
1 YES **CONTINUE**
2 NO **SKIP TO Q.16**
3 DK **SKIP TO Q.17**

14. To which offer or offers did you respond?
1 Visa
2 MasterCard
3 Discover
4 American Express
5 Optima
6 AT&T Universal
7 GM
8 Ford
9 Other

15. Why did you respond to this(these) offer(s)? **ASK FOR EACH RESPONSE IN Q.12**
1 No annual fee
2 Preapproved
3 Interest rate
4 Build credit rating
5 Convenience/Emergencies
6 Rebate/cash back/free offers
7 Business/corporate card
8 Gold Card
9 Credit limit
10 Travel
11 Grocery shopping
12 Wide acceptance
13 Other

SKIP TO Q.17

16. Why didn't you respond to any of the offers? **PROBE**
1 Interest rate too high
2 Have too many credit cards
3 Credit card balances too high
4 Credit limit
5 Interest rate confusing
6 Do not use credit cards
7 Do not need any more credit cards
8 Not preapproved or fear of being turned down
9 Other
10 DK

17. Have you closed or stopped using a credit card/cards in the past year?
1 YES **CONTINUE**
2 NO **SKIP TO Q.20**
3 DK **SKIP TO Q.20**

18. Which card/cards have you stopped using?
1 Visa
2 MasterCard
3 Discover

4 American Express
5 Optima
6 AT&T Universal
7 Other

19. Why have you stopped using this card? **ASK FOR EACH RESPONSE IN Q. 18**
1 Interest rate
2 Annual fee
3 Own too many credit cards
4 Balance too high
5 Billing problems
6 Never used it
7 Limited acceptance
8 Consolidation of debt
9 Other

20. Would you say that your attitudes toward the use of credit cards have changed in the past year?
1 YES **CONTINUE**
2 NO **SKIP TO Q.22**
3 DK **SKIP TO Q.22**

21. **IF "YES" IN RESPONSE TO Q.20:** How have your attitudes changed? **PROBE.** ______

22. In comparison with a year ago, would you say you are using your credit cards: **READ LIST**
1 Less often
2 About the same or
3 More often
4 DK

23. In comparison with a year ago, which of the following statements is true in regard to your total credit card balances? **READ LIST**
1 They are less
2 They are about the same or
3 They are greater
4 DK

24. Now, I would like to find out how you feel about a particular credit card offer. We are not making this offer to you today—we are only interested in how you feel about the offer. **READ LIST OF OFFER FEATURES. RESPONDENTS WILL BE ASKED ONE OF THE FOLLOWING, SCENARIOS—100 FOR EACH SCENARIO:**

	PREAPPROVED	APPLICATION
6.0% Intro APR		
9.9% Intro APR		

- You receive an application to apply for a Limited Edition Visa card (Preapproved);
- there is no annual fee;
- it has a 9.9 (6.0) percent initial APR through March 1997;
- after that the APR will be 16.9 percent;
- you can immediately transfer balances from other cards up to your credit limit—you can do this through March 1997 with no cash advance fees;
- it has a limit of up to $5,000.

25. On a scale of 0 to 100 where 0 is not at all likely and 100 is extremely likely, how likely would you be to respond to this offer?

______ **LIKELIHOOD**

26. What, if anything, do you particularly **LIKE** about this offer? **PROBE/ANYTHING ELSE?**
   1 NO ANNUAL FEE
   2 GOOD INTEREST RATE
   3 GOOD OFFER IN GENERAL
   4 FEATURES/BENEFITS
   5 ABILITY TO TRANSFER BALANCES
   6 CREDIT LIMIT
   7 APPEALING OFFER IN GENERAL
   8 ADVANTAGES OVER OTHER OFFERS
   9 MASTERCARD/VISA BRAND
   10 IDENTIFIES YOU AS A PROFESSIONAL
   11 PRESTIGE OF LIMITED EDITIONS NAME
   12 OTHER
27. What, if anything, do you particularly **DISLIKE** about this offer? **PROBE/ANYTHING ELSE?**
   1 INTEREST RATE TOO HIGH
   2 DON'T USE CREDIT CARDS
   3 INTEREST RATE CONFUSING
   4 NOT COMPETITIVE WITH CURRENT CARD
   5 INTEREST RATE CHANGE AFTER MARCH
   6 NO REASON
   7 OTHER
   8 DK
28. Is the interest rate in the Visa credit card offer clear and understandable?
   1 YES
   2 NO
   3 DK/NS
29. Using a scale of 1 to 10 where 1 is poor and 10 is excellent, please tell me how you would rate the following product features in the Visa credit card offer that was just described. **ROTATE TO REFLECT INTRODUCTORY PERCENTAGE RATE AND BEING PREAPPROVED/HAVING TO APPLY**
   ______ No annual fee
   ______ 9.9% (6.0) introductory rate through March 1997
   ______ 16.9% APR after March 1997
   ______ Being preapproved/received an application
   ______ Ability to transfer balances from other cards
   ______ Credit limit of up to $5,000
30. Do you consider this Visa credit card offer to be better than, about the same as, or worse than . . .

	Better	Same	Worse	DK
Discover Card	1	2	3	4
American Express Optima Card	1	2	3	4
AT&T Universal Card	1	2	3	4
GM or Ford Card	1	2	3	4
Other MasterCard/Visa for teaching professionals	1	2	3	4
Credit card you use most often	1	2	3	4

31. **IF BETTER OR WORSE IN Q.30:** Why do you feel that way? **PROBE.**
32. In evaluating a credit card offer, how important are the following things to you? Please use a 1 to 10 scale where 1 is very unimportant and 10 is very important. How important is ____________? **READ LIST AND ROTATE**
   ______ Being preapproved

_______ Interest rate
_______ Annual fee
_______ Credit limit
_______ Billing cycle/grace period
_______ Reputation of issuer
_______ Extended warranty/buyer protection
_______ No charges if monthly balance is paid
_______ Cash advance
_______ Financing payment plan
_______ 24-hour service for lost or stolen cards
_______ Ability to transfer balance from other card to it
_______ Rebates

Finally, just a few questions to help us classify your responses.

33. INDICATE SEX OF RESPONDENT:
1 MALE
2 FEMALE

34. Are you currently married or not married?
1 Married
2 Not married
3 RF

35. Which of the following categories include your age? Are you . . .
1 18–24
2 25–34
3 35–44
4 45–54
5 55–64
6 65 or over
7 RF

36. What is the highest level of education completed by the primary wage earner in your household?
1 Less than high school graduate
2 High school graduate
3 Some college
4 College graduate
5 Any postgraduate work
6 RF

37. What is your occupation? **PROBE FOR TYPE OF BUSINESS, ETC.**

____

38. IF MARRIED: What is your spouse's occupation? **PROBE FOR TYPE OF BUSINESS, ETC.**

____

39. Which of the following categories includes the total annual income of all the working members of your household before taxes?
1 Under $15,000
2 $15,000–$24,999
3 $25,000–$39,999
4 $40,000–$54,999
5 $55,000–$69,999
6 $70,000 or more
7 DK
8 RF

That concludes our survey and I would like to thank you for taking the time to assist us.
NAME ____

TELEPHONE (________) __________ ____
INTERVIEWER NUMBER ____

QUESTIONS FOR STUDENTS

1. Describe the credit cards carried most often, used most often, reasons used most often, features of credit card used most often, interest rate of the credit card used most often, credit limit of the respondents, and the main issuers of each credit card carried.
2. Give a demographic profile of the respondents.
3. Describe respondents' attitudes toward credit limits.
4. Discuss credit card offers and the teachers' responses. Also, discuss credit card closings.
5. How did respondents react to the new credit card proposals?
6. Use multivariate statistics to determine the strongest predictors to respond to the new credit card offers.

APPENDIX 2

Statistical Tables

1. Random Digits
2. Standard Normal Distribution—Z-values
3. t-Distribution
4. Chi-Square Distribution
5. F-Distribution

TABLE 1 Random Digits

63271	59986	71744	51102	15141	80714	58683	93108	13554	79945
88547	09896	95436	79115	08303	01041	20030	63754	08459	28364
55957	57243	83865	09911	19761	66535	40102	26646	60147	15702
46276	87453	44790	64122	45573	84358	21625	16999	13385	22782
55363	07449	34835	15290	76616	67191	12777	21861	68689	03263
69393	92785	49902	58447	42048	30378	87618	26933	40640	16281
13186	29431	88190	04588	38733	81290	89541	70290	40113	08243
17726	28652	56836	78351	47327	18518	92222	55201	27340	10493
36520	64465	05550	30157	82242	29520	69753	72602	23756	54935
81628	36100	39254	56835	37636	02421	98063	89641	64953	99337
84649	48968	75215	75498	49539	74240	03466	49292	36401	45525
63291	11618	12613	75055	43915	26488	41116	64531	56827	30825
70502	53225	03655	05915	37140	57051	48393	91322	25653	06543
06426	24771	59935	49801	11082	66762	94477	02494	88215	27191
20711	55609	29430	70165	45406	78484	31639	52009	18873	96927
41990	70538	77191	25860	55204	73417	83920	69468	74972	38712
72452	36618	76298	26678	89334	33938	95567	29380	75906	91807
37042	40318	57099	10528	09925	89773	41335	96244	29002	46453
53766	52875	15987	46962	67342	77592	57651	95508	80033	69828
90585	58955	53122	16025	84299	53310	67380	84249	25348	04332
32001	96293	37203	64516	51530	37069	40261	61374	05815	06714
62606	64324	46354	72157	67248	20135	49804	09226	64419	29457
10078	28073	85389	50324	14500	15562	64165	06125	71353	77669
91561	46145	24177	15294	10061	98124	75732	00815	83452	97355
13091	98112	53959	79607	52244	63303	10413	63839	74762	50289
73864	83014	72457	22682	03033	61714	88173	90835	00634	85169
66668	25467	48894	51043	02365	91726	09365	63167	95264	45643
84745	41042	29493	01836	09044	51926	43630	63470	76508	14194
48068	26805	94595	47907	13357	38412	33318	26098	82782	42851
54310	96175	97594	88616	42035	38093	36745	56702	40644	83514
14877	33095	10924	58013	61439	21882	42059	24177	58739	60170
78295	23179	02771	43464	59061	71411	05697	67194	30495	21157
67524	02865	39593	54278	04237	92441	26602	63835	38032	94770
58268	57219	68124	73455	83236	08710	04284	55005	84171	42596
97158	28672	50685	01181	24262	19427	52106	34308	73685	74246
04230	16831	69085	30802	65559	09205	71829	06489	85650	38707
94879	56606	30401	02602	57658	70091	54986	41394	60437	03195
71446	15232	66715	26385	91518	70566	02888	79941	39684	54315
32886	05644	79316	09819	00813	88407	17461	73925	53037	91904
62048	33711	25290	21526	02223	75947	66466	06332	10913	75336
84534	42351	21628	53669	81352	95152	08107	98814	72743	12849
84707	15885	84710	35866	06446	86311	32648	88141	73902	69981
19409	40868	64220	80861	13860	68493	52908	26374	63297	45052
57978	48015	25973	66777	45924	56144	24742	96702	88200	66162
57295	98298	11199	96510	75228	41600	47192	43267	35973	23152
94044	83785	93388	07833	38216	31413	70555	03023	54147	06647
30014	25879	71763	96679	90603	99396	74557	74224	18211	91637
07265	69563	64268	88802	72264	66540	01782	08396	19251	83613
84404	88642	30263	80310	11522	57810	27627	78376	36240	48952
21778	02085	27762	46097	43324	34354	09369	14966	10158	76089

TABLE 2 Standard Normal Distribution—Z-values

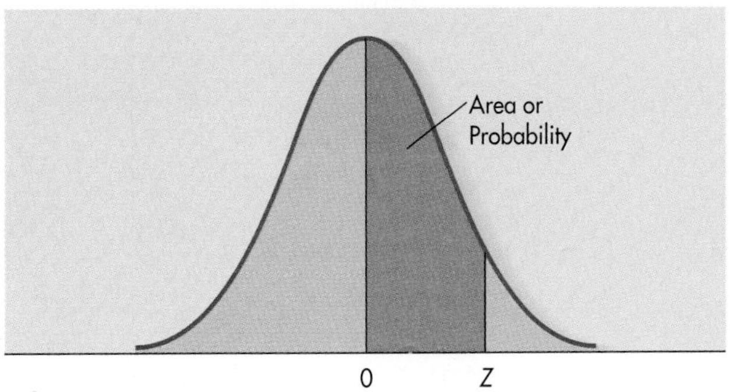

Entries in the table give the area under the curve between the mean and Z standard deviations above the mean. For example, for Z = 1.25, the area under the curve between the mean and Z is .3944.

Z	.00	.01	.02	.03	.04	.05	.06	.07	.08	.09
.0	.0000	.0040	.0080	.0120	.0160	.0199	.0239	.0279	.0319	.0359
.1	.0398	.0438	.0478	.0517	.0557	.0596	.0636	.0675	.0714	.0753
.2	.0793	.0832	.0871	.0910	.0948	.0987	.1026	.1064	.1103	.1141
.3	.1179	.1217	.1255	.1293	.1331	.1368	.1406	.1443	.1480	.1517
.4	.1554	.1591	.1628	.1664	.1700	.1736	.1772	.1808	.1844	.1879
.5	.1915	.1950	.1985	.2019	.2054	.2088	.2123	.2157	.2190	.2224
.6	.2257	.2291	.2324	.2357	.2389	.2422	.2454	.2486	.2518	.2549
.7	.2580	.2612	.2642	.2673	.2704	.2734	.2764	.2794	.2823	.2852
.8	.2881	.2910	.2939	.2967	.2995	.3023	.3051	.3078	.3106	.3133
.9	.3159	.3186	.3212	.3238	.3264	.3289	.3315	.3340	.3365	.3389
1.0	.3413	.3438	.3461	.3485	.3508	.3531	.3554	.3577	.3599	.3621
1.1	.3643	.3665	.3686	.3708	.3729	.3749	.3770	.3790	.3810	.3830
1.2	.3849	.3869	.3888	.3907	.3925	.3944	.3962	.3980	.3997	.4015
1.3	.4032	.4049	.4066	.4082	.4099	.4115	.4131	.4147	.4162	.4177
1.4	.4192	.4207	.4222	.4236	.4251	.4265	.4279	.4292	.4306	.4319
1.5	.4332	.4345	.4357	.4370	.4382	.4394	.4406	.4418	.4429	.4441
1.6	.4452	.4463	.4474	.4484	.4495	.4505	.4515	.4525	.4535	.4545
1.7	.4554	.4564	.4573	.4582	.4591	.4599	.4608	.4616	.4625	.4633
1.8	.4641	.4649	.4656	.4664	.4671	.4678	.4686	.4693	.4699	.4706
1.9	.4713	.4719	.4726	.4732	.4738	.4744	.4750	.4756	.4761	.4767
2.0	.4772	.4778	.4783	.4788	.4793	.4798	.4803	.4808	.4812	.4817
2.1	.4821	.4826	.4830	.4834	.4838	.4842	.4846	.4850	.4854	.4857
2.2	.4861	.4864	.4868	.4871	.4875	.4878	.4881	.4884	.4887	.4890
2.3	.4893	.4896	.4898	.4901	.4904	.4906	.4909	.4911	.4913	.4916
2.4	.4918	.4920	.4922	.4925	.4927	.4929	.4931	.4932	.4934	.4936
2.5	.4938	.4940	.4941	.4943	.4945	.4946	.4948	.4949	.4951	.4952
2.6	.4953	.4955	.4956	.4957	.4959	.4960	.4961	.4962	.4963	.4964
2.7	.4965	.4966	.4967	.4968	.4969	.4970	.4971	.4972	.4973	.4974
2.8	.4974	.4975	.4976	.4977	.4977	.4978	.4979	.4979	.4980	.4981
2.9	.4981	.4982	.4982	.4983	.4984	.4984	.4985	.4985	.4986	.4986
3.0	.4986	.4987	.4987	.4988	.4988	.4989	.4989	.4989	.4990	.4990

TABLE 3 *t*-Distribution

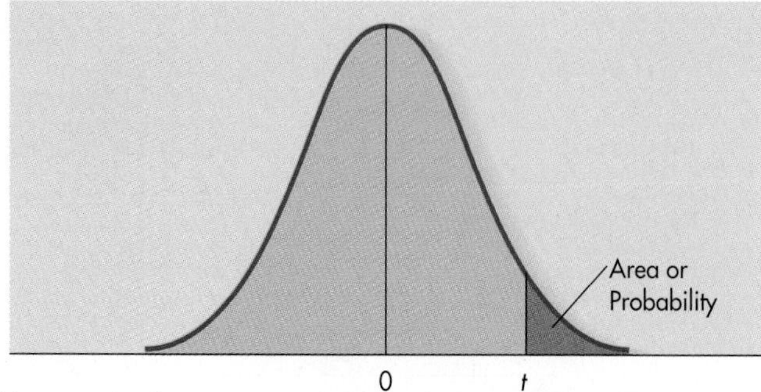

Entries in this table give *t*-values for an area or probability in the upper tail of the *t*-distribution. For example, with 10 degrees of freedom and a .05 area in the upper tail, $t_{.05} = 1.812$.

	AREA IN UPPER TAIL				
DEGREES OF FREEDOM	.10	.05	.025	.01	.005
1	3.078	6.314	12.706	31.821	63.657
2	1.886	2.920	4.303	6.965	9.925
3	1.638	2.353	3.182	4.541	5.841
4	1.533	2.132	2.776	3.747	4.604
5	1.476	2.015	2.571	3.365	4.032
6	1.440	1.943	2.447	3.143	3.707
7	1.415	1.895	2.365	2.998	3.499
8	1.397	1.860	2.306	2.896	3.355
9	1.383	1.833	2.262	2.821	3.250
10	1.372	1.812	2.228	2.764	3.169
11	1.363	1.796	2.201	2.718	3.106
12	1.356	1.782	2.179	2.681	3.055
13	1.350	1.771	2.160	2.650	3.012
14	1.345	1.761	2.145	2.624	2.977
15	1.341	1.753	2.131	2.602	2.947
16	1.337	1.746	2.120	2.583	2.921
17	1.333	1.740	2.110	2.567	2.898
18	1.330	1.734	2.101	2.552	2.878
19	1.328	1.729	2.093	2.539	2.861
20	1.325	1.725	2.086	2.528	2.845
21	1.323	1.721	2.080	2.518	2.831
22	1.321	1.717	2.074	2.508	2.819
23	1.319	1.714	2.069	2.500	2.807
24	1.318	1.711	2.064	2.492	2.797
25	1.316	1.708	2.060	2.485	2.787
26	1.315	1.706	2.056	2.479	2.779
27	1.314	1.703	2.052	2.473	2.771
28	1.313	1.701	2.048	2.467	2.763
29	1.311	1.699	2.045	2.462	2.756
30	1.310	1.697	2.042	2.457	2.750
40	1.303	1.684	2.021	2.423	2.704
60	1.296	1.671	2.000	2.390	2.660
120	1.289	1.658	1.980	2.358	2.617
∞	1.282	1.645	1.960	2.326	2.576

TABLE 4 Chi-Square Distribution

Entries in the table give X^2_α values, where α is the area or probability in the upper tail of the chi-square distribution. For example, with 10 degrees of freedom and a .01 area in the upper tail, $X^2_\alpha = 23.2093$.

DEGREES OF FREEDOM	AREA IN UPPER TAIL									
	.995	.99	.975	.95	.90	.10	.05	.025	.01	.005
1	$392{,}704 \times 10^{-19}$	$157{,}088 \times 10^{-9}$	$982{,}069 \times 10^{-9}$	$393{,}214 \times 10^{-8}$	.01570908	2.70554	3.84146	5.02389	6.63490	7.87944
2	.0100251	.0201007	.0506356	.102587	.210720	4.60517	5.99147	7.37776	9.21034	10.5966
3	.0717212	.114832	2.15795	.351846	.584375	6.25139	7.81473	9.34840	11.3449	12.8381
4	.206990	.297110	.484419	.710721	1.063623	7.77944	9.48773	11.1433	13.2767	14.8602
5	.411740	.554300	.831211	1.145476	1.61031	9.23635	11.0705	12.8325	15.0863	16.7496
6	.675727	.872085	1.237347	1.63539	2.20413	10.6446	12.5916	14.4494	16.8119	18.5476
7	.989265	1.239043	1.68987	2.16735	2.83311	12.0170	14.0671	16.0128	18.4753	20.2777
8	1.344419	1.646482	2.17973	2.73264	3.48954	13.3616	15.5073	17.5346	20.0902	21.9550
9	1.734926	2.087912	2.70039	3.32511	4.16816	14.6837	16.9190	19.0228	21.6660	23.5893
10	2.15585	2.55821	3.24697	3.94030	4.86518	15.9871	18.3070	20.4831	23.2093	25.1882
11	2.60321	3.05347	3.81575	4.57481	5.57779	17.2750	19.6751	21.9200	24.7250	26.7569
12	3.07382	3.57056	4.40379	5.22603	6.30380	18.5494	21.0261	23.3367	26.2170	28.2995
13	3.56503	4.10691	5.00874	5.89186	7.04150	19.8119	22.3621	24.7356	27.6883	29.8194
14	4.07468	4.66043	5.62872	6.57063	7.78953	21.0642	23.6848	26.1190	29.1413	31.3193

continues

TABLE 4 **Chi-Square Distribution—*Continued***

DEGREES OF FREEDOM	AREA IN UPPER TAIL									
	.995	.99	.975	.95	.90	.10	.05	.025	.01	.005
15	4.60094	5.22935	6.26214	7.26094	8.54675	22.3072	24.9958	27.4884	30.5779	32.8013
16	5.14224	5.81221	6.90766	7.96164	9.31223	23.5418	26.2962	28.8454	31.9999	34.2672
17	5.69724	6.40776	7.56418	8.67176	10.0852	24.7690	27.5871	30.1910	33.4087	35.7185
18	6.26481	7.01491	8.23075	9.39046	10.8649	25.9894	28.8693	31.5264	34.8053	37.1564
19	6.84398	7.63273	8.90655	10.1170	11.6509	27.2036	30.1435	32.8523	36.1908	38.5822
20	7.43386	8.26040	9.59083	10.8508	12.4426	28.4120	31.4104	34.1696	37.5662	39.9968
21	8.03366	8.89720	10.28293	11.5913	13.2396	29.6151	32.6705	35.4789	38.9321	41.4010
22	8.64272	9.54249	10.9823	12.3380	14.0415	30.8133	33.9244	36.7807	40.2894	42.7958
23	9.26042	10.19567	11.6885	13.0905	14.8479	32.0069	35.1725	38.0757	41.6384	44.1813
24	9.88623	10.8564	12.4011	13.8484	15.6587	33.1963	36.4151	39.3641	42.9798	45.5585
25	10.5197	11.5240	13.1197	14.6114	16.4734	34.3816	37.6525	40.6465	44.3141	46.9278
26	11.1603	12.1981	13.8439	15.3791	17.2919	35.5631	38.8852	41.9232	45.6417	48.2899
27	11.8076	12.8786	14.5733	16.1513	18.1138	36.7412	40.1133	43.1944	46.9630	49.6449
28	12.4613	13.5648	15.3079	16.9279	18.9392	37.9159	41.3372	44.4607	48.2782	50.9933
29	13.1211	14.2565	16.0471	17.7083	19.7677	39.0875	42.5569	45.7222	49.5879	52.3356
30	13.7867	14.9535	16.7908	18.4926	20.5992	40.2560	43.7729	46.9792	50.8922	53.6720
40	20.765	22.1643	24.4331	26.5093	29.0505	51.8050	55.7585	59.3417	63.6907	66.7659
50	27.9907	29.7067	32.3574	34.7642	37.6886	63.1671	67.5048	71.4202	76.1539	79.4900
60	35.5346	37.4848	40.4817	43.1879	46.4589	74.3970	79.0819	83.2976	88.3794	91.9517
70	43.2752	45.4418	48.7576	51.7393	55.3290	85.5271	90.5312	95.0231	100.425	104.215
80	51.1720	53.5400	57.1532	60.3915	64.2778	96.5782	101.879	106.629	112.329	116.321
90	59.1963	61.7541	65.6466	69.1260	73.2912	107.565	113.145	118.136	124.116	128.299
100	67.3276	70.0648	74.2219	77.9295	82.3581	118.498	124.342	129.561	135.807	140.169

Reprinted by permission of Biometrika Trustees from Table 8, Percentage Points of the X^{-} Distribution, by E. S. Pearson and H. O. Hartley, *Biometrika Tables for Statisticians*, Vol. 1, 3d. Edition, 1966.

TABLE 5 *F*-Distribution

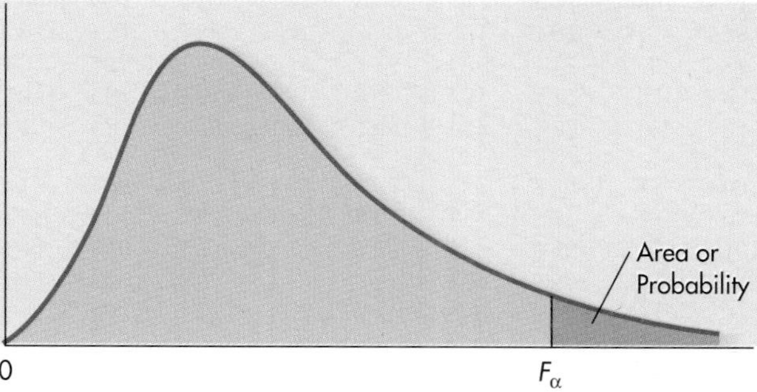

Entries in the table give F_α values, where α is the area or probability in the upper tail of the *F*-distribution. For example, with 12 numerator degrees of freedom, 15 denominator degrees of freedom, and a .05 area in the upper tail, $F_{.05} = 2.48$.

TABLE OF $F_{.05}$ VALUES

DENOMINATOR DEGREES OF FREEDOM	NUMERATOR DEGREES OF FREEDOM																		
	1	2	3	4	5	6	7	8	9	10	12	15	20	24	30	40	60	120	∞
1	161.4	199.5	215.7	224.6	230.2	234.0	236.8	238.9	240.5	241.9	243.9	245.9	248.0	249.1	250.1	251.1	252.2	253.3	254.3
2	18.51	19.00	19.16	19.25	19.30	19.33	19.35	19.37	19.38	19.40	19.41	19.43	19.45	19.45	19.46	19.47	19.48	19.49	19.50
3	10.13	9.55	9.28	9.12	9.01	8.94	8.89	8.85	8.81	8.79	8.74	8.70	8.66	8.64	8.62	8.59	8.57	8.55	8.53
4	7.71	6.94	6.59	6.39	6.26	6.16	6.09	6.04	6.00	5.96	5.91	5.86	5.80	5.77	5.75	5.72	5.69	5.66	5.63
5	6.61	5.79	5.41	5.19	5.05	4.95	4.88	4.82	4.77	4.74	4.68	4.62	4.56	4.53	4.50	4.46	4.43	4.40	4.36
6	5.99	5.14	4.76	4.53	4.39	4.28	4.21	4.15	4.10	4.06	4.00	3.94	3.87	3.84	3.81	3.77	3.74	3.70	3.67
7	5.59	4.74	4.35	4.12	3.97	3.87	3.79	3.73	3.68	3.64	3.57	3.51	3.44	3.41	3.38	3.34	3.30	3.27	3.23
8	5.32	4.46	4.07	3.84	3.69	3.58	3.50	3.44	3.39	3.35	3.28	3.22	3.15	3.12	3.08	3.04	3.01	2.97	2.93
9	5.12	4.26	3.86	3.63	3.48	3.37	3.29	3.23	3.18	3.14	3.07	3.01	2.94	2.90	2.86	2.83	2.79	2.75	2.71
10	4.96	4.10	3.71	3.48	3.33	3.22	3.14	3.07	3.02	2.98	2.91	2.85	2.77	2.74	2.70	2.66	2.62	2.58	2.54
11	4.84	3.98	3.59	3.36	3.20	3.09	3.01	2.95	2.90	2.85	2.79	2.72	2.65	2.61	2.57	2.53	2.49	2.45	2.40
12	4.75	3.89	3.49	3.26	3.11	3.00	2.91	2.85	2.80	2.75	2.69	2.62	2.54	2.51	2.47	2.43	2.38	2.34	2.30
13	4.67	3.81	3.41	3.18	3.03	2.92	2.83	2.77	2.71	2.67	2.60	2.53	2.46	2.42	2.38	2.34	2.30	2.25	2.21
14	4.60	3.74	3.34	3.11	2.96	2.85	2.76	2.70	2.65	2.60	2.53	2.46	2.39	2.35	2.31	2.27	2.22	2.18	2.13
15	4.54	3.68	3.29	3.06	2.90	2.79	2.71	2.64	2.59	2.54	2.48	2.40	2.33	2.29	2.25	2.20	2.16	2.11	2.07
16	4.49	3.63	3.42	3.01	2.85	2.74	2.66	2.59	2.54	2.49	2.42	2.35	2.28	2.24	2.19	2.15	2.11	2.06	2.01
17	4.45	3.59	3.20	2.96	2.81	2.70	2.61	2.55	2.49	2.45	2.38	2.31	2.23	2.19	2.15	2.10	2.06	2.01	1.96
18	4.41	3.55	3.16	2.93	2.77	2.66	2.58	2.51	2.46	2.41	2.34	2.27	2.19	2.15	2.11	2.06	2.02	1.97	1.92
19	4.38	3.52	3.13	2.90	2.74	2.63	2.54	2.48	2.42	2.38	2.31	2.23	2.16	2.11	2.07	2.03	1.98	1.93	1.88
20	4.35	3.49	3.10	2.87	2.71	2.60	2.51	2.45	2.39	2.35	2.28	2.20	2.12	2.08	2.04	1.99	1.95	1.90	1.84
21	4.32	3.47	3.07	2.84	2.68	2.57	2.49	2.42	2.37	2.32	2.25	2.18	2.10	2.05	2.01	1.96	1.92	1.87	1.81

continues

TABLE 5 ***F*-Distribution—*Continued***

TABLE OF $F_{.05}$ VALUES

DENOMINATOR DEGREES OF FREEDOM	NUMERATOR DEGREES OF FREEDOM																		
	1	2	3	4	5	6	7	8	9	10	12	15	20	24	30	40	60	120	∞
29	4.18	3.33	2.93	2.70	2.55	2.43	2.35	2.28	2.22	2.18	2.10	2.03	1.94	1.90	1.85	1.81	1.75	1.70	1.64
30	4.17	3.32	2.92	2.69	2.53	2.42	2.33	2.27	2.21	2.16	2.09	2.01	1.93	1.89	1.84	1.79	1.74	1.68	1.62
40	4.08	3.23	2.84	2.61	2.45	2.34	2.25	2.18	2.12	2.08	2.00	1.92	1.84	1.79	1.74	1.69	1.64	1.58	1.51
60	4.00	3.15	2.76	2.53	2.37	2.25	2.17	2.10	2.04	1.99	1.92	1.84	1.75	1.70	1.65	1.59	1.53	1.47	1.39
120	3.92	3.07	2.68	2.45	2.29	2.17	2.09	2.02	1.96	1.91	1.83	1.75	1.66	1.61	1.55	1.50	1.43	1.35	1.25
∞	3.84	3.00	2.60	2.37	2.21	2.10	2.01	1.94	1.88	1.83	1.75	1.67	1.57	1.52	1.46	1.39	1.32	1.22	1.00

TABLE OF $F_{.01}$ VALUES

DENOMINATOR DEGREES OF FREEDOM	NUMERATOR DEGREES OF FREEDOM																		
	1	2	3	4	5	6	7	8	9	10	12	15	20	24	30	40	60	120	∞
1	4,052	4,999.5	5,403	5,625	5,764	5,859	5,928	5,982	6,022	6,056	6,106	6,157	6,209	6,235	6,261	6,287	6,313	6,339	6,366
2	98.50	99.00	99.17	99.25	99.30	99.33	99.36	99.37	99.39	99.40	99.42	99.43	99.45	99.46	99.47	99.47	99.48	99.49	99.50
3	34.12	30.82	29.46	28.71	28.24	27.91	27.67	27.49	27.35	27.23	27.05	26.87	26.69	26.60	26.50	26.41	26.32	26.22	26.13
4	21.20	18.00	16.69	15.98	15.52	51.21	14.98	14.80	14.66	14.55	14.37	14.20	14.02	13.93	13.84	13.75	13.65	13.56	13.46
5	16.26	13.27	12.06	11.39	10.97	10.67	10.46	10.29	10.16	10.05	9.89	9.72	9.55	9.47	9.38	9.29	9.20	9.11	9.06
6	13.75	10.92	9.78	9.15	8.75	8.47	8.26	8.10	7.98	7.87	7.72	7.56	7.40	7.31	7.23	7.14	7.06	6.97	6.88
7	12.25	9.55	8.45	7.85	7.46	7.19	6.99	6.84	6.72	6.62	6.47	6.31	6.16	6.07	5.99	5.91	5.82	5.74	5.65
8	11.26	8.65	7.59	7.01	6.63	6.37	6.18	6.03	5.91	5.81	5.67	5.52	5.36	5.28	5.20	5.12	5.03	4.95	4.86
9	10.56	8.02	6.99	6.42	6.06	5.80	5.61	5.47	5.35	5.26	5.11	4.96	4.81	4.73	4.65	4.57	4.48	4.40	4.31
10	10.04	7.56	6.55	5.99	5.64	5.39	5.20	5.06	4.94	4.85	4.71	4.56	4.41	4.33	4.25	4.17	4.08	4.00	3.91
11	9.65	7.21	6.22	5.67	5.32	5.07	4.89	4.74	4.63	4.54	4.40	4.25	4.10	4.02	3.94	3.86	3.78	3.69	3.60
12	9.33	6.93	5.95	5.41	5.06	4.82	4.64	4.50	4.39	4.30	4.16	4.01	3.86	3.78	3.70	3.62	3.54	3.45	3.36
13	9.07	6.70	5.74	5.21	4.86	4.62	4.44	4.30	4.19	4.10	3.96	3.82	3.66	3.59	3.51	3.43	3.34	3.25	3.17
14	8.86	6.51	5.56	5.04	4.69	4.46	4.28	4.14	4.03	3.94	3.80	3.66	3.51	3.43	3.35	3.27	3.18	3.09	3.00
15	8.68	6.36	5.42	4.89	4.56	4.32	4.14	4.00	3.89	3.80	3.67	3.52	3.37	3.29	3.21	3.13	3.05	2.96	2.87
16	8.53	6.23	5.29	4.77	4.44	4.20	4.03	3.89	3.78	3.69	3.55	3.41	3.26	3.18	3.10	3.02	2.93	2.84	2.75
17	8.40	6.11	5.18	4.67	4.34	4.10	3.93	3.79	3.68	3.59	3.46	3.31	3.16	3.08	3.00	2.92	2.83	2.75	2.65
18	8.29	6.01	5.09	4.58	4.25	4.01	3.84	3.71	3.60	3.51	3.37	3.23	3.08	3.00	2.92	2.84	2.75	2.66	2.57
19	8.18	5.93	5.01	4.50	4.17	3.94	3.77	3.63	3.52	3.43	3.30	3.15	3.00	2.92	2.84	2.76	2.67	2.58	2.49
20	8.10	5.85	4.94	4.43	4.10	3.87	3.70	3.56	3.46	3.37	3.23	3.09	2.94	2.86	2.78	2.69	2.61	2.52	2.42
21	8.02	5.78	4.87	4.37	4.04	3.81	3.64	3.51	3.40	3.31	3.17	3.03	2.88	2.80	2.72	2.64	2.55	2.46	2.36
22	7.95	5.72	4.82	4.31	3.99	3.76	3.59	3.45	3.35	3.26	3.12	2.98	2.83	2.75	2.67	2.58	2.50	2.40	2.31
23	7.88	5.66	4.76	4.26	3.94	3.71	3.54	3.41	3.30	3.21	3.07	2.93	2.78	2.70	2.62	2.54	2.45	2.35	2.26
24	7.82	5.61	4.72	4.22	3.90	3.67	3.50	3.36	3.26	3.17	3.03	2.89	2.74	2.66	2.58	2.49	2.40	2.31	2.21

continues

TABLE 5 ***F*-Distribution—*Continued***

TABLE OF $F_{.01}$ VALUES

DENOMINATOR DEGREES OF FREEDOM	NUMERATOR DEGREES OF FREEDOM																		
	1	2	3	4	5	6	7	8	9	10	12	15	20	24	30	40	60	120	∞
22	4.30	3.44	3.05	2.82	2.66	2.55	2.46	2.40	2.34	2.30	2.23	2.15	2.07	2.03	1.98	1.94	1.89	1.84	1.78
23	4.28	3.42	3.03	2.80	2.64	2.53	2.44	2.37	2.32	2.27	2.20	2.13	2.05	2.01	1.96	1.91	1.86	1.81	1.76
24	4.26	3.40	3.01	2.78	2.62	2.51	2.42	2.36	2.30	2.25	2.18	2.11	2.03	1.98	1.94	1.89	1.84	1.79	1.73
25	4.24	3.39	2.99	2.76	2.60	2.49	2.40	2.34	2.28	2.24	2.16	2.09	2.01	1.96	1.92	1.87	1.82	1.77	1.71
26	4.23	3.37	2.98	2.74	2.59	2.47	2.39	2.32	2.27	2.22	2.15	2.07	1.99	1.95	1.90	1.85	1.80	1.75	1.69
27	4.21	3.35	2.96	2.73	2.57	2.46	2.37	2.31	2.25	2.20	2.13	2.06	1.97	1.93	1.88	1.84	1.79	1.73	1.67
28	4.20	3.34	2.95	2.71	2.56	2.45	2.36	2.29	2.24	2.19	2.12	2.04	1.96	1.91	1.87	1.82	1.77	1.71	1.65
25	7.77	5.57	4.68	4.18	3.85	3.63	3.46	3.32	3.22	3.13	2.99	2.85	2.70	2.62	2.54	2.45	2.36	2.27	2.17
26	7.72	5.53	4.64	4.14	3.82	3.59	3.42	3.29	3.18	3.09	2.96	2.81	2.66	2.58	2.50	2.42	2.33	2.23	2.13
27	7.68	5.49	4.60	4.11	3.78	3.56	3.39	3.26	3.15	3.06	2.93	2.78	2.63	2.55	2.47	2.38	2.29	2.20	2.10
28	7.64	5.45	4.57	4.07	3.75	3.53	3.36	3.23	3.12	3.03	2.90	2.75	2.60	2.52	2.44	2.35	2.26	2.17	2.06
29	7.60	5.42	4.54	4.04	3.73	3.50	3.33	3.20	3.09	3.00	2.87	2.73	2.57	2.49	2.41	2.33	2.23	2.14	2.03
30	7.56	5.39	4.51	4.02	3.70	3.47	3.30	3.17	3.07	2.98	2.84	2.70	2.55	2.47	2.39	2.30	2.21	2.11	2.01
40	7.31	5.18	4.31	3.83	3.51	3.29	3.12	2.99	2.89	2.80	2.66	2.52	2.37	2.29	2.20	2.11	2.02	1.92	1.80
60	7.08	4.98	4.13	3.65	3.34	3.12	2.95	2.82	2.72	2.63	2.50	2.35	2.20	2.12	2.03	1.94	1.84	1.73	1.60
120	6.85	4.79	3.95	3.48	3.17	2.96	2.79	2.66	2.56	2.47	2.34	2.19	2.03	1.95	1.86	1.76	1.66	1.53	1.38
∞	6.63	4.61	3.78	3.32	3.02	2.80	2.64	2.51	2.41	2.32	2.18	2.04	1.88	1.79	1.70	1.59	1.47	1.32	1.00

GLOSSARY

A. C. Nielsen Retail Index Audit of food, household supplies, beauty aids, etc., at the retail level.

ad agency marketing research departments Departments of advertising agencies that produce or oversee research to support the development and evaluation of advertising for the agency's clients.

ad concept testing Testing used to obtain the reactions of target customers to preliminary, rough versions of alternative advertising approaches.

ad hoc mail surveys Questionnaires sent to selected individuals with no prior contact by the researcher.

ad positioning statement tests Tests used to obtain consumer reactions to positioning statements that are being considered for use in ads.

ad tracking research Research used to make periodic measurements of the impact of ads over time.

affective component of attitudes An individual's feelings or emotional reactions about an object.

after-only with control group True experimental design that involves random assignment of subjects or test units to experimental and control groups but no premeasurement of the dependent variable.

allowable sampling error The amount of sampling error the researcher is willing to accept.

analysis of variance (ANOVA) Test for the differences among the means of two or more variables.

applied research Research aimed at solving a specific, pragmatic problem—better understanding of the marketplace, determination of why a strategy or tactic failed, reduction of uncertainty in management decision making.

appropriate time order of occurrence To be considered a likely cause of a dependent variable, a change in an independent variable must occur before an observed change in the dependent variable.

a priori segmentation The process of segmenting markets on the basis of hunches, assumptions, or custom. This type of segmentation is not empirically based.

attention span The length of time a particular individual will concentrate on a particular subject at a particular time.

attitude An enduring organization of motivational, emotional, perceptual, and cognitive processes with respect to some aspect of our environment.

audience data syndicated services Companies that collect, package, and sell general data on media audiences to many firms.

audit The examination and verification of the sale of a product.

balanced scales Scales with the same number of positive and negative categories.

baseline market segmentation study The first market segmentation study conducted by an organization.

basic research Research aimed at expanding the frontiers of knowledge rather than solving a specific, pragmatic problem.

before and after with control group True experimental design that includes random assignment of subjects or test units to experimental and control groups and premeasurement of both groups.

behavioral component of attitudes An individual's intentions to act in some manner based on attitudes about an object.

BehaviorScan A scanner-based research system that maintains a 3,000 household panel to record consumer purchases based upon manipulation of the marketing mix.

bibliographic database An index of published studies and reports, which may include explanation and analysis.

bivariate regression analysis Analysis of the strength of the linear relationship between two variables when one is considered the independent variable and the other the dependent variable.

bivariate techniques Statistical methods of analyzing the relationship between two variables.

call record sheets Interviewers' logs listing the number and results of a contact.

cartoon tests Tests in which the respondent fills in the dialogue of one character in a cartoon.

causal research Research designed to determine whether a change in one variable likely caused an observed change in another.

causal studies These studies examine whether one variable causes or determines the value of another variable.

causation The inference that a change in one variable is responsible for, or caused, an observed change in another variable.

census Data obtained from every member of the population of interest.

central limit theorem A distribution of a large number of sample means or sample proportions will approximate a normal distribution regardless of the actual distribution of the population from which they were drawn.

central location telephone interviewing Interviewers make calls from a marketing research facility to reach and interview respondents.

chi-square test Test of the goodness of fit between the observed distribution and the expected distribution of a variable.

clinical focus groups Focus groups that explore subconscious motivation.

closed-ended questions Questions that ask the respondent to choose from a list of answers.

cluster analysis Procedures for classifying objects or people into some number of mutually exclusive and exhaustive groups on the basis of two or more classification variables.

cluster samples Sampling approach used with door-to-door interviewing in which the sampling units are selected in groups to reduce data collection costs.

code of ethics Guidelines for making ethical decisions.

coding The process of grouping and assigning numeric codes to the various responses to a question.

coefficient of determination The percent of the total variation in the dependent variable explained by the independent variable.

cognitive component of attitudes An individual's knowledge and beliefs about an object.

collinearity The correlation of independent variables with each other. Can bias estimates of regression coefficients.

communication The result of any action, physical, written, or verbal, that conveys meanings between two individuals.

comparative scales A judgment comparing one object, concept, or person against another on a scale.

computer-assisted telephone interviewing Central location telephone interviewing in which the interviewer works with a computer survey and enters answers directly into a computer.

concomitant variation The degree to which a cause and effect occur or vary together.

concurrent validity The degree to which a variable, measured at the same point in time as the variable of interest, can be predicted by the measurement instrument.

confidence level The probability that a particular confidence interval will include the true population value.

conjoint analysis Procedure used to quantify the value that people associate with different levels of product/service attributes.

constant sum scales Scales that ask the respondent to divide a given number of points, typically 100, among two or more attributes based on their importance to the person.

constitutive definition Defines a concept with other concepts and constructs, establishing boundaries for the construct under study and stating the central idea or concept under study.

construct Specific types of concepts that exist at higher levels of abstraction.

construct validity The degree to which a measurement instrument represents and logically connects, via the underlying theory, the observed phenomenon to the construct.

consumer drawings Respondents draw what they are feeling or how they perceive an object.

consumer orientation Identification of and focus on the people or firms most likely to buy a product and production of a good or service that will meet their needs most effectively.

contamination The inclusion of a group of respondents in a test who are not normally there; for example, outside buyers who see an advertisement intended only for those in the test area and enter the area to purchase the product being tested.

content analysis A technique used to study written material (usually advertising copy) by breaking it into meaningful units, using carefully applied rules.

content validity The degree to which the instrument items represent the universe of the concept under study.

convenience samples Samples used primarily for reasons of convenience.

conventional morality Morality based on the expectations of society.

convergent validity The degree of association among different measurement instruments that purport to measure the same concept.

corporate marketing research departments Departments of major firms that produce or oversee collection and analysis of information relevant to marketing the firm's present or future products or services.

correlation analysis Analysis of the degree to which changes in one variable are associated with changes in another.

criterion-related validity The degree to which a measurement instrument can predict a variable that is designated a criterion.

crosstabulation Examination of the responses to one question relative to responses to one or more other questions.

custom, or ad hoc, marketing research firms Research companies that carry out customized marketing research to address specific projects for corporate clients.

customer satisfaction research Research conducted to measure overall satisfaction with a product or service and satisfaction with specific elements of the product or service.

database management software Computer programs for the retrieval and manipulation of data.

database management system The system in which data are captured on the computer, organized for effective use, updated, and maintained to provide information for decision making.

decision support systems (DSS) An interactive, personalized MIS, designed to be initiated and controlled by individual decision makers.

dependent variable A symbol or concept expected to be explained or caused by the independent variable.

depth interviews One-on-one interviews that probe and elicit detailed answers to questions, often using nondirective techniques to uncover hidden motivations.

descriptive function The gathering and presentation of statements of fact.

descriptive studies These studies answer the questions who, what, when, where, and how.

design control Use of the experimental design to control extraneous causal factors.

diagnostic function The explanation of data or actions.

dichotomous questions Questions that ask the respondent to choose between two answers.

direct computer interviewing Consumers are intercepted in a mall or other central location and interviewed by a computer that asks questions and accepts responses.

directory database Data available through directories or indexes of directory-type data.

discriminant coefficient Estimate of the discriminatory power of a particular independent variable.

discriminant score The basis for predicting to which group a particular object or individual belongs.

discriminant validity The lack of association among constructs that are supposed to be different.

discussion guide A written outline of topics to cover during a focus group discussion.

disguised observation The process of monitoring people, objects, or occurrences that do not know they are being watched.

disproportional or optimal allocation Sampling in which the number of elements taken from a given stratum is proportional to the relative size of the stratum and the standard deviation of the characteristic under consideration.

door-to-door interviewing Consumers are interviewed face to face in their homes.

editing The process of ascertaining that questionnaires were filled out properly.

electroencephalogram (EEG) A machine that measures the rhythmic fluctuations in electrical potential of the brain.

electronic data processing (EDP) systems Information systems that manipulate raw data with little intrinsic meaning to reflect transactional relationships, such as declarative and summary reports.

equivalent form reliability The ability to produce similar results using two instruments as similar as possible to measure the same object.

error checking routines Computer programs that accept instructions from the user to check for logical errors in the data.

error sum of squares The variation not explained by the regression.

ethics Moral principles or values generally governing the conduct of an individual or group.

evaluative research Research to determine the effectiveness and efficiency of specific programs.

executive interviewing The industrial equivalent of door-to-door interviewing.

executive summary The portion of a research report that explains why the research was done, what was found and what those findings mean, and what action, if any, management should undertake.

experiencing focus groups Focus groups that enable a client to observe and listen to how consumers think and feel about products and services.

experiment Research approach in which one variable is manipulated and the effect on another variable is observed.

experimental design A test in which the researcher has control over one or more independent variables and manipulates them.

experimental effect The effect of the treatment variable on the dependent variable.

experiments Research to measure causality in which one or more variables are changed while observing the effect of the change on another variable.

exploratory focus groups Focus groups that aid in the precise definition of the problem, in pilot testing, or in generating hypotheses for testing or concepts for further research.

exploratory research Preliminary research to clarify the exact nature of the problem to be solved.

external validity The extent to which causal relationships measured in an experiment can be generalized to outside persons, settings, and times.

F-test Test of the probability that a particular calculated value could have been due to chance.

face validity A measurement seems to measure what it is suppose to measure.

factor analysis Procedure for data simplification through reducing a set of variables to a smaller set of factors or composite variables by identifying dimensions underlying the data.

factor loadings The correlation between each factor score and each of the original variables.

false accuracy An unwarranted illusion of accuracy provided by details, such as statistics quoted to two decimal places.

field experiments Tests conducted outside the laboratory in an actual market environment.

field management companies Firms that provide support services such as questionnaire formatting, screener writing, and data collection to full-service research companies.

field service firms Companies that only collect survey data for corporate clients or research firms.

finite population correction factor An adjustment to the required sample size that is made in those cases in which the sample is expected to be equal to 5 percent or more of the total population.

focus group facility Facility consisting of conference or living room setting and a separate observation room. Facility also has audiovisual recording equipment.

focus group moderator The person hired by the client to lead the focus group. This person may need a background in psychology or sociology or, at least, marketing.

focus groups Groups of eight to 12 participants who are led by a moderator in an in-depth discussion on one particular topic or concept.

frame error Error resulting from an inaccurate or incomplete sample frame.

full text database Index containing the full text of source documents, such as articles.

galvanic skin response (GSR) The measurement of changes in the electric resistance of the skin associated with activation responses.

garbologists Researchers who sort through people's garbage to analyze household consumption patterns.

geographic information system A business tool for interpreting data that consists of a demographic database, digitized maps, a computer, and software.

goal orientation A focus on the accomplishment of corporate goals; a limit set on consumer orientation.

graphic rating scales Graphic continuums anchored by two extremes presented to respondents for evaluation of a concept or object.

group dynamics The interaction among people in a group.

history Things that happen or outside variables that change between the beginning and end of an experiment.

humanistic inquiry A research method in which the researcher is immersed in the system or group under study.

hypotheses Assumptions or theories that a researcher or manager makes about some characteristic of the population under study.

hypothesis test of proportions Test to determine whether the difference between proportions is greater than would be expected because of sampling error.

incidence rate The percentage of people or households in the general population that fit the qualifications to be sampled.

independent samples Samples in which measurement of a variable in one population has no effect on the measurement of the variable in the other.

independent variable The symbol or concept over which the researcher has some control or can manipulate to some extent and that is hypothesized to cause or influence the dependent variable.

InfoScan A scanner-based tracking service for consumer packaged goods.

instrument variation Differences or changes in measurement instruments (e.g., interviewers or observers) that explain differences in measurements.

intelligent data entry The logical checking of information being entered into a data entry device by that machine or one connected to it.

internal consistency reliability Ability to produce the similar results using different samples to measure a phenomenon during the same time period.

internal database Database developed from data within the organization.

internal validity The extent to which competing explanations for the experimental results observed can be avoided.

interrupted time-series design Research in which the treatment "interrupts" ongoing repeated measurements.

interval estimates Inferences regarding the likelihood that a population value will fall within a certain range.

interval scales Ordinal scales with equal intervals between points to show relative amounts; may include an arbitrary zero point.

interviewer error Error that results from conscious or unconscious bias in the interviewer's interaction with the respondent.

interviewer's instructions Written directions to the interviewer on how to conduct the interview.

itemized rating scales Scales in which the respondent selects an answer from a limited number of ordered categories.

judgment samples Samples in which the selection criteria are based on personal judgment that the element is representative of the population under study.

Kolmogorov-Smirnov test Test of the goodness of fit between the observed distribution and the expected distribution using ordinal data.

laboratory experiments Experiments conducted in a controlled setting.

Likert scale A scale in which the respondent specifies a level of agreement or disagreement with statements that express a favorable or unfavorable attitude toward the concept under study.

longitudinal study The same respondents are resurveyed over time.

low-ball pricing Offering an unrealistically low price to attract customers.

machine cleaning of data A final computerized error check of data.

mail panels Participants are precontacted and screened, then periodically sent questionnaires.

mall intercept interviewing Shoppers are intercepted in public areas of malls and interviewed face-to-face.

marginal report A computer-generated table of the frequencies of the responses to each question to monitor entry of valid codes and correct use of skip patterns.

marketing The process of planning and executing the conception, pricing, promotion, and distribution of ideas, goods, and services to create exchanges that satisfy individual and organizational objectives.

marketing concept A business philosophy based on consumer orientation, goal orientation, and systems orientation.

marketing information systems (MIS) These systems create rather than simply manipulate data, presenting data in a form useful to a variety of people within the organization.

marketing mix The unique blend of product pricing, promotion, offerings, and distribution designed to meet the needs of a specific group of consumers.

marketing research The planning, collection, and analysis of data relevant to marketing decision making and the communication of the results of this analysis to management.

market segmentation The process of dividing a total market into subgroups of consumers or potential customers who exhibit differing sensitivities to one or more marketing mix variables.

marketing strategy Guiding the long-run use of the firm's resources based on its existing and projected capabilities and on projected changes in the external environment.

maturation Changes in subjects that take place during the experiment that are not related to the experiment but may affect their response to the experimental factor.

mean The sum of the values for all observations of a variable divided by the number of observations.

measurement Process of assigning numbers or labels to things in accordance with specific rules to represent quantities or qualities of attributes.

measurement error Error that results from a variation between the information being sought and the information actually obtained by the measurement process.

measurement instrument bias Error that results from the design of the questionnaire or measurement instrument.

median The observation below which 50 percent of the observations fall.

methodological log A journal of detailed and time-sequenced notes on the investigative techniques used during a humanistic inquiry, with special attention to biases or distortions a given technique may have introduced.

mode The value that occurs most frequently.

modem A modulator-demodulator used to convert digital data to analog data so that the data can be transmitted over a telephone system.

morals Judgments concerning the goodness or badness of human action or character.

mortality Loss of test units or subjects during the course of an experiment. The problem is that those lost may be systematically different from those who stay.

multidimensional scaling Procedures designed to measure several dimensions of a concept or object.

multiple-choice questions Questions that ask a respondent to choose among a list of more than two answers.

multiple discriminant analysis A procedure for predicting group membership on the basis of two or more independent variables.

multiple regression analysis A procedure for predicting the level or magnitude of a dependent variable based on the levels of more than one independent variable.

multiple time-series design An interrupted time-series design with a control group.

multivariate analysis Statistical procedures that simultaneously analyze multiple measurements on each individual or object under study.

mystery shoppers People employed to pose as consumers and shop at the employer's competitors and their own stores to compare prices, displays, and the like.

noise Anything that interferes with the audience receiving a message.

nominal grouping session Qualitative research method in which consumers, brought together in small groups, independently generate ideas about a subject and then discuss the ideas.

nominal scales Scales that partition data into mutually exclusive and collectively exhaustive categories.

nonbalanced scales Scales weighted toward one end or the other.

noncomparative A judgment made without reference to another object, concept, or person.

nonprobability samples Subsets of a population in which little or no attempt is made to ensure a representative cross section.

nonresponse bias Error that results from a systematic difference between those who do and do not respond to the measurement instrument.

normal distribution A continuous distribution that is bell shaped and symmetrical about the mean—mean, median, and mode are equal. Sixty-eight percent of the observations fall within plus or minus one standard deviation of the mean, approximately 95 percent fall within plus or minus two standard deviations, and approximately 99.5 fall within plus or minus three standard deviations.

numeric database Database containing original survey data on a wide variety of general topics.

observation research Descriptive research that monitors respondents' actions without direct interaction.

on-air testing Testing used to measure the impact of television and radio ads after they have begun to run on the air.

on-line database A public information database accessible to anyone with proper communication facilities.

on-line vendor An intermediary that acquires databases from a variety of database creators.

one-group pretest-posttest design Preexperimental design with pre- and postmeasurements but no control group.

one-shot case study Preexperimental design with no control group and an after measurement only.

one-way frequency table A table showing the number of responses to each answer of a survey question.

one-way mirror observations The practice of watching unseen from behind a one-way mirror.

open-ended questions Questions that ask the respondent to reply in her own words.

open observation The process of monitoring people who know they are being watched.

operational definition Defines which observable characteristics will be measured and the process for assigning a value to the concept.

optical scanning A data processing device that can "read" responses on questionnaires.

ordinal scales Nominal scales that can order data.

packaging tests Tests used to gauge reactions to different packaging approaches.

paired comparison scales Scales that ask the respondent to pick one of two objects in a set based on some stated criteria.

part worths Estimates of the value or utility that people associate with different levels of product/service attributes.

Pearson's product moment correlation Correlation analysis technique for use with metric data.

people meter A microwave computerized rating system that transmits demographic information overnight to measure national TV audiences.

People Reader A machine that simultaneously records the respondent's reading material and eye reactions.

perceptual mapping Visual representations of consumer perceptions of products, brands, companies, or other objects.

philosophy A systematic attempt to understand individual and collective human experience.

photo sort Respondent sorts photos of different types of people, identifying those photos that respondent feels would use the specified product or service.

physical control Holding the value or level of extraneous variables constant throughout the course of an experiment.

point estimates Inferences regarding the sampling error associated with a particular estimate of a population value.

population distribution A frequency distribution of all the elements of a population.

population or universe The total group of people from whom information is needed.

population specification error Error that results from an incorrect definition of the universe, or population, from which the sample is chosen.

population standard deviation The standard deviation of a variable for the entire population.

postconventional morality Morality based on how one views and judges oneself in the long run.

post hoc segmentation The process of segmenting a market or markets empirically.

preconventional morality A childlike morality, based on immediate gratification or punishment.

predictive function Specification of how to use the descriptive and diagnostic research to predict the results of a planned marketing decision.

predictive validity The degree to which the future level of a criterion can be forecast by a current measurement scale.

preexperimental design A design that offers little or no control over extraneous factors.

presentation software Personal computer software that provides easy-to-use platforms for creating effective reports and presentations.

pretest A trial run of a questionnaire.

primary data New data gathered to help solve the problem at hand.

proactive management Management philosophy that involves continuously altering the marketing mix to fit emerging patterns in economic, social, and competitive environments.

probability samples Samples in which every element of the population has a known, nonzero probability of selection.

processing error Error that results from incorrect transfer of information from the data collection document to the computer.

product concept testing The testing of new product ideas before they have been turned into prototypes.

product movement data syndicated services Companies that collect, package, and sell retail and wholesale sales data to many firms.

product positioning research Research used to determine how competitive brands are perceived relative to each other on key dimensions.

product pricing research Research used to measure consumer sensitivity to different prices for a product.

product prototype tests Tests conducted to obtain the reactions of target customers to early working versions of new products.

programmatic research Research done to develop marketing options through market segmentation, market opportunity analysis, or consumer attitude and product usage studies.

projective techniques Ways of exploring respondents' deepest feelings by having them "project" those feelings into an unstructured situation.

proportional allocation Sampling in which the number of elements selected from a stratum is directly proportional to the size of the stratum relative to the population.

pupilometer A machine that measures changes in pupil dilation.

purchase intent scales Scales used to measure a respondent's intention to buy or not buy a product.

Q-sorting A sophisticated form of rank ordering using card sorts.

qualitative research Research data not subject to quantification or quantitative analysis.

quantitative research Studies that use mathematical analysis.

quasi-experiments Studies in which the researcher lacks complete control over the scheduling of treatment or must assign respondents to treatment in a nonrandom manner.

questionnaire A set of questions designed to generate the data necessary for accomplishing the objectives of the research project.

quota samples Samples in which quotas are established for population subgroups. Selection is by nonprobability means.

random digit dialing Method of generating lists of telephone numbers at random.

random error Error that affects measurement in a transient, inconsistent manner.

randomization The random assignment of subjects to treatment conditions to ensure equal representation of subject characteristics in all groups.

range The maximum value for a

variable minus the minimum value for that variable.

rank-order scales Scales in which the respondent compares one item with another or a group of items against each other and ranks them.

ratio scales Interval scales with a meaningful zero point so that magnitudes can be compared arithmetically.

regression coefficients Values that indicate the effect of the individual independent variables on the dependent variable.

regression to the mean Tendency for behavior of subjects to move toward the average for that behavior during the course of an experiment.

related samples Samples in which the measurement of a variable in one population may influence the measurement of the variable in the other.

reliability Measures that are consistent from one administration to the next.

research design The plan to be followed to answer the research objectives; the structure or framework to solve a specific problem.

research request Document used in large organizations that describes a potential research project, its benefits to the organization, and estimated costs. A project cannot begin until the research request has been formally approved.

response bias error that results from the tendency of people to answer a question falsely, through deliberate misrepresentation or unconscious falsification.

return on quality Management objective based on the principles that the quality being delivered is the quality desired by the target market and that quality must have a positive impact on profitability.

rule A guide, a method, or a command that tells a researcher what to do.

sample A subset of the population of interest.

sample distribution A frequency distribution of all the elements of an individual sample.

sampling distribution of sample means A frequency distribution of the means of many samples drawn from a particular population. It is normally distributed.

sampling distribution of the proportion A frequency distribution of the proportions of many samples drawn from a particular population. It is normally distributed.

sampling frame List of population elements from which we select units to be sampled.

scale A set of symbols or numbers so constructed that the symbols or numbers can be assigned by a rule to the individuals (or their behaviors or attitudes) to whom the scale is applied.

scaled-response questions Multiple-choice questions in which the choices are designed to capture the intensity of the respondent's answer.

scaling Procedures for assignment of numbers (or other symbols) to a property of objects to impart some of the characteristics of numbers to the properties in question.

scanners Devices that read the UPC codes on products and produce instantaneous information on sales.

screeners Questions used to screen for appropriate respondents.

secondary data Data that have been previously gathered.

selection bias Systematic differences between the test group and control group because of a biased selection process.

selection error Error that results from following incomplete or improper sampling procedures.

selective perception The ability of the listener or reader to filter out some information for conscious or subconscious reasons.

selective research Research to choose among several viable alternatives identified by programmatic research.

self-administered questionnaire A questionnaire filled out by the respondent with no interviewer involvement.

semantic differential A method of examining the strengths and weaknesses of a product or company versus the competition by having respondents rank it between dichotomous pairs of words or phrases that could be used to describe it; the mean of the responses is then plotted in a profile or image.

sentence and story completion tests Tests in which the respondents complete sentences or stories in their own words.

shopper patterns Drawings that record the footsteps of a shopper through a store.

simple random sample Sample selected in such a way that every element of the population has a known and equal probability of inclusion in the sample.

simulated test market (STM) Alternative to traditional test market; survey data and mathematical models are used to simulate test market results at a much lower cost.

single-number research Placing too much emphasis on a single statistic.

skip pattern Requirement to pass over certain questions in response to the respondent's answer to a previous question.

snowball samples Samples in which selection of additional respondents is based on referrals from the initial respondents.

Solomon four-group design Research using two experimental groups and two control groups to control for all extraneous variable threats.

Spearman rank-order correlation Correlation analysis technique for use with ordinal data.

specialized service or support firms Companies that handle a specific facet of research, such as data processing or statistical analysis, for many corporate clients.

split-half technique A method of assessing the reliability of a scale by dividing into two the total set of measurement items and correlating the results.

spurious association Another variable or variables may cause changes in the dependent variable.

stability Lack of change in results from test to retest.

standard deviation A measure of dispersion calculated by subtracting the mean of a series from each value in a series, squaring each result, summing them, dividing the sum by the number of items minus one, and taking the square root of this value.

standard error of the mean The standard deviation of a distribution of sample means.

standard normal distribution A normal distribution with a mean of zero and a standard deviation of one.

Stapel scale A scale, ranging from +5 to −5, that requires the respondent to rate how close and in what direction a descriptor adjective fits a given concept.

static-group comparison Preexperimental design that uses an experimental and a control group. However, subjects or test units are not randomly assigned to the two groups and no premeasurements are taken.

statistical control Adjusting for the effects of confounded variables by statistically adjusting the value of the dependent variable for each treatment condition.

strategic partnering Two or more marketing research firms with unique skills and resources form an alliance to offer a new service for clients, provide strategic support for each firm, or in some other manner create mutual benefits.

stratified samples Probability samples that force sample to be more representative.

structured observation A study in which the observer fills out a questionnairelike form or counts the number of times an activity occurs.

sum of squares due to regression The variation explained by the regression.

supervisor's instructions Written directions to the field service on how to conduct the survey.

surrogate information error Error that results from a discrepancy between the information needed to solve a problem and that sought by the researcher.

survey objectives The decision-making information sought through the questionnaire.

survey research Research in which an interviewer interacts with respondents to obtain facts, opinions, and attitudes.

syndicated service research firms Companies that collect, package, and sell the same general market research data to many firms.

systematic error Error that results from the research design or execution.

systematic sampling Probability sampling in which the entire population is numbered, and elements are drawn using a skip interval.

systems orientation Creation of systems to monitor the external environment and deliver the marketing mix to the target market.

telephone focus groups Focus groups that are conducted via conference calling.

temporal sequence Appropriate causal order of events.

testing effect An effect that is a by-product of the research process and not the experimental variable.

test market Testing of a new product or some element of the marketing mix using experimental or quasi-experimental designs.

test-retest reliability The ability of the same instrument to produce consistent results when used a second time under conditions as nearly the same as possible.

theory-construction diary A journal that documents in detail the thoughts, premises, hypotheses, and revisions in thinking of a humanistic researcher.

The Partners An expert software system designed to cut the mass of scanner data down to actionable pieces of information.

third-person techniques Ways of learning respondents' feelings by asking them to answer for a third party: "your neighbor," "most people."

traffic counters Machines used to measure vehicular flow over a particular stretch of roadway.

treatment The independent variable that is manipulated in an experiment.

true experimental design Research using an experimental group and a control group, and assignment of test units to both groups is randomized.

t-test Hypothesis test about a single mean if the sample is too small to use the Z-test.

two-way focus groups A target focus group observes another focus group, then discusses what it learned through observing.

Type I error (α error) Rejection of a null hypothesis when, in fact, it is true.

Type II error (ß error) Acceptance of a null hypothesis when, in fact, it is false.

unidimensional scaling Procedures designed to measure only one attribute of a respondent or object.

unstructured observation A study in which the observer simply makes notes on the behavior being observed.

unstructured segmentation Process of segmenting a market using data collection and analysis when no prior ideas are held about number of segments, what they are, or how and why they are different.

validation The process of ascertaining that interviews actually were conducted as specified.

validity Whether what we tried to measure was actually measured.

variance The sums of the squared deviations from the mean divided by the number of observations minus one.

virtual reality (VR) An artificial environment that is experienced through sensory stimuli provided by a computer; it is one of the latest technologies to be applied as a tool in experimentation.

voice pitch analysis The study of changes in the relative vibration frequency of the human voice to measure emotion.

word association tests Tests in which the interviewer says a word and the respondent must mention the first thing that comes to mind.

***Z*-test** Hypothesis test about a single mean if the sample is large enough and drawn from a normal population.

ENDNOTES

CHAPTER 1

1. John Wilke, "Beech's Sleekly Styled Starship Fails to Take Off with Corporate Customers," *Wall Street Journal* (September 29, 1993), pp. B1,B5.
2. "AMA Board Approves New Marketing Definitions,"*Marketing News* (March 1, 1985), p. 1.
3. "New Marketing Research Definition Approved," *Marketing News* (January 2, 1987), pp. 1, 14.
4. "Quality: How to Make It Pay," *Business Week* (August 8, 1994), pp. 54–59.
5. Ibid.
6. "Why Some Customers Are More Equal Than Others," *Fortune* (September 19, 1994), pp. 215–224.
7. Ibid.
8. Horst Stipp and Nicholas Schiavone, "Research at a Commercial Television Network: NBC 1990," *Marketing Research* (September 1990), pp. 3–10.
9. An excellent article on the value of marketing research is J. Walker Smith, "Beyond Anecdotes: Toward a Systematic Model of the Value of Marketing Research," *Marketing Research* (March 1991), pp. 3–14.
10. Christine Wright-Isak and David Prensky, "Early Marketing Research: Science and Application," *Marketing Research* (Fall 1993), pp. 16–23.
11. Percival White, *Market Analysis: Its Principles and Methods*, 2d ed. (New York: McGraw-Hill Book Co., 1921, 1925).
12. Much of this section is taken from David W. Stewart, "From Methods and Projects to Systems and Process: The Evolution of Marketing Research Techniques," *Marketing Research* (September 1991), pp. 25–34.
13. This case is adapted from Diane Crispell, "The Brave New World of Men," *American Demographics* (January 1992), pp. 38–43.
14. Theodore Dunn, "How Agencies Use Research," *Advertising Age* 45 (July 15, 1984), pp. 69–70.
15. The 3M story is from Joseph R. Kendall, "Corporate Marketing Research at 3M," *Marketing Research* (June 1991), pp. 4–6.
16. Richard Kitaeff, "Marketing Research As a Career: What to Tell the Junior Level Researcher," *Marketing Research* (March 1992), pp. 57–59.

CHAPTER 2

1. Terence P. Pare, "How to Find Out What They Want," *Fortune* (Autumn/Winter 1993), pp. 39–41.
2. Diane Schmalensee, "Establishing Objectives with the Client Is Vital to Success of Research Project," *Marketing News* (January 22, 1982), pp. 2–17.
3. Reprinted from the April 8, 1985 issue of *Business Week* by special permission. Copyright 1985 by McGraw Hill Companies.
4. This list is adapted from Paul Conner, "Research Request Step Can Enhance Use of Results," *Marketing News* (January 4, 1985), p. 41.
5. See Sil Seggev, "Listening Is Key to Providing Useful Marketing Research," *Marketing News* (January 22, 1982), p. 6.
6. Richard Kitaeff, "The Management of Project Management," *Marketing Research* (June 1991), pp. 57–58.
7. See "It's a Manager's Job to Be Responsible for Research," *Marketing News* (November 8, 1985), p. 22; and "Five Suggestions for Positioning a Department," *Marketing News* (January 4, 1988), pp. 39–40.
8. Seggev, "Listening Is Key to Providing Useful Marketing Research," p. 6.
9. Johnny K. Johansson and Ikujiro Nonaka, "Market Research the Japanese Way," *Harvard Business Review* (May/June 1987), pp. 16–18, 22.
10. Rohit Deshpande and Scott Jeffries, "Attitude Affecting the Use of Marketing Research in Decision Making: An Empirical Investigation," in *Educators' Conference Proceedings*, Series 47. Edited by Kenneth L. Bernhardt, et al. (Chicago: American Marketing Association, 1981), pp. 1–4.
11. Rohit Deshpande and Gerald Zaltman, "Factors Affecting the Use of Market Research Information: A Path Analysis," *Journal of Marketing Research* 19 (February 1982): 14–31; Rohit Deshpande [1984], "A Comparison of Factors Affecting Researcher and Manager Perceptions of Market Research Use," *Journal of Marketing Research* 21 (February 1989): 32–38; Hanjoon Lee, Frank Acito, and Ralph Day, "Evaluation and Use of Marketing Research by Decision Makers: A Behavioral Simulation," *Journal of Marketing Research* 24 (May 1987): 187–196; and Michael Hu, "An Experimental Study of Managers' and Researchers' Use of Consumer Market Research," *Journal of the Academy of Marketing Science* 14 (Fall 1986): 44–51.
12. Rohit Deshpande and Gerald Zaltman, "A Comparison of Factors Affecting Use of Marketing Information in Consumer and Industrial Firms," *Journal of Marketing Research* 24 (February 1987): 114–118.
13. "Numbers for the '90s," *Advertising Age* (September 12, 1994), p. 3.

CHAPTER 3

1. Joseph Rydholm, "Scanning the Seas," *Quirk's Marketing Research Review* (May 1993), pp. 6–7, 26–27.
2. Jack Honomichl, "Some Final Musings as Jack Writes Off into the Sunset," *Marketing News* (January 3, 1994), pp. 17, 20.

3. Ibid.
4. "Revenues Near $2 Billion, But Stormy Times Ahead," *Advertising Age* (June 3, 1991), p. 33.
5. Ibid.
6. Thomas Dupont, "A Word from the Chair: Is There a Future for Survey Research?" *CASRO Journal* (1993), pp. 5–6.
7. Jay Roth, "The Marketing Research Industry Monitor," *CASRO Journal* (1993), pp. 21–27.
8. Ibid.
9. Roger Hall, "Positioning Strategies: GPT Stromberg-Carlson Carves a Niche and Jumps Out," *Marketing Research* (June 1991), pp. 5–13.
10. Dennis Tootelian and Ralph Gaedeke, "Top Companies Keep Outside Researchers Looking In," *Marketing News* 20 (September 21, 1986), p. 4; Abdul Azhari and Joseph Kamen, "Marketing Research at Amoco Oil: The Culture, the Principles, and the Contributions," *Marketing Research* 1 (June 1989), pp. 3–10.
11. Jack Honomichl, "Prediction: Traditional Research Firms Will Vanish," *Marketing News* (February 3, 1992), p. 8.
12. Jack Honomichl, "Research Cultures Are Different in Mexico, Canada," *Marketing News* (May 10, 1993), pp. 12–13.
13. Lynn Lin, "BASES: Past, Present and Future," *CASRO Journal* (1991), pp. 19–21.
14. *Standard Directory of Advertising Agencies* (Skokie, Ill.: National Register Publishing Co., 1994).
15. James Donius, *Marketplace Measurement: Tracking and Testing* (New York: Association of National Advertisers, Inc., 1986), pp. 1–2.
16. Scott Hume, "Research Partnerships Here to Stay," *Advertising Age* (October 14, 1991), p. 33.
17. "Simmons Adopts Rival's Audience Methodology," *Advertising Age* (September 19, 1994), p. 5.
18. Hume, "Research Partnerships Here to Stay," p. 33.
19. Paul Boughton, "Marketing Research Partnerships: A Strategy for the '90s," *Marketing Research* (December 1992), pp. 8–12; also see "Maximizing the Client-Researcher Partnership," *Marketing News* (September 13, 1993), p. 38.
20. Phillip Barnard, "New Directions in World Research—Main Global Trends in Its Supply, Methods, Use, and Users," *CASRO Journal* (1993), pp. 37–46.
21. Laurie Ashcraft, "The Evolving Marketing Research Industry," *Marketing Research* (June 1991), pp. 27–29.
22. Bruce Knecht, "American Express to Try a Credit Card—Again," *Wall Street Journal* (September 6, 1994), pp. B1, B4.

CHAPTER 4

1. Richard Turner and John Emshwiller, "Movie-Research Czar Is Said to Sell Manipulated Findings," *Wall Street Journal* (December 17, 1993), pp. A1, A6.
2. Much of this section is based upon Edward Stevens, *Business Ethics* (New York: Paulist Press, 1979).
3. Steven Brenner and Earl Molander, "Is the Ethics of Business Changing?" *Harvard Business Review* (January–February 1977), p. 71.
4. Patrick Murphy and Gene Laczniak, "Emerging Ethical Issues Facing Marketing Researchers," *Marketing Research* (June 1992), pp. 6–10; also see Patrick Murphy and Gene Laczniak, "Traditional Ethical Issues Facing Marketing Researchers," *Marketing Research* (March 1992), pp. 6–21.
5. Richard Crosby, "Uniform Ethical Code Is Impractical Due to Shifting Marketing Research Circumstances," *Marketing News* (September 18, 1981), pp. 2–16.
6. Murphy and Laczniak, "Emerging Ethical Issues Facing Marketing Researchers," p. 7.
7. Cynthia Crossen, "Margins of Error: Studies Galore Support Products and Positions, But Are They Reliable?" *Wall Street Journal* (November 14, 1991), pp. A1, A7.
8. Stephen McDaniel, Perry Verille, and Charles Madden, "The Threats to Marketing Research: An Empirical Reappraisal," *Journal of Marketing Research* 22 (February 1985): 74–80.
9. "How Researchers Can Win Friends and Influence Politicians," *American Demographics* (August 1993), p. 9.
10. Ibid.
11. Stephen Schleifer, "Survey Participation Is Leaving a Sour Taste with Respondents, According to Image Study," *Marketing News* (February 15, 1985), p. 7.
12. See Ely Lurin, "Research and Lead Generation Are an Ethical Mix," *Marketing News* (January 2, 1987), p. 4; for a rebuttal, see "ARF Position Paper Phony or Misleading Polls," *Journal of Advertising Research* 26 (December 1986–January 1987): PRC–3–8.
13. Dick Whittington, "A Plea for Improving Respondent Satisfaction with the Interview Process: An Open Letter to My Research Colleagues," *CASRO Journal* (1993), pp. 122–124; and Richard Whittington, "It's Time to Apply Customer Satisfaction to Interviews," *Marketing News* (August 16, 1993), p. A14.
14. Shelby Hunt, Lawrence Chonko, and James Wilcox, "Ethical Problems of Marketing Researchers," *Journal of Marketing Research* 21 (August 1984): 314.
15. Robert Bezilla, Joel Haynes, and Clifford Elliott, "Ethics in Marketing Research," *Business Horizons* (April 1976), p. 84.
16. See Alice Tybout and Gerald Zaltman, "Ethics in Marketing Research: Their Practical Relevance," *Journal of Marketing Research* 11 (November 1974): 357–368; Robert Day, "A Comment on 'Ethics in Marketing Research,'" *Journal of Marketing Research* 12 (May 1975): 232–233; and Alice Tybout and Gerald Zaltman, "A Reply to Comments on Ethics in Marketing Research: Their Practical Relevance," *Journal of Marketing Research* 12 (May 1975): 234–237.
17. Cathy Goodwin, "Privacy: Recognition of a Consumer Right," *Journal of Public Policy and Marketing* 10 (Spring 1991): 150.
18. Mary Gardner Jones, "Privacy: A Significant Marketing Issue for the 1990s," *Journal of Public Policy and Marketing* 10 (Spring 1991): 133–148.
19. Judith Waldrop, "The Business of Privacy," *American Demographics* (October 1994), pp. 46–55.
20. "The Great Privacy Debate," *Superbrands 1991: A Supplement of Adweek's Marketing Week* (1991), p. 24.
21. Diane Bowers, "Privacy Concerns and the Research Industry," *Marketing Research* (Spring 1994), pp. 48–49.
22. Paul Bloom, George Milne, and Robert Adler, "Avoiding Misuse of New Information Technologies: Legal and Societal Considerations," *Journal of Marketing* (January 1994): 98–110.
23. "Marketing in Big Brother's Shadow," *Adweek's Marketing Week* (December 10, 1990), p. 25.

24. Diane Bowers, "The Privacy Challenge, Part I," *Marketing Research* (June 1991), pp. 59–62.
25. Ibid.
26. Waldrop, "The Business of Privacy," p. 50.
27. Ishmael Akaah and Edward Riordan, "Judgments of Marketing Professionals about Ethical Issues in Marketing Research: A Replication and Extension," *Journal of Marketing Research* 26 (February 1989): 112–120. For an interesting look at the scope of marketing research ethics, see Steven Skinner, Alan Dubinsky, and O. C. Ferrell, "Organizational Dimensions of Marketing Research Ethics," *Journal of Business Research* 16 (1988): 29–223; and Patrick Murphy and Gene Laczniak, "Traditional Ethical Issues Facing Marketing Researchers," *Marketing Research* (March 1992), pp. 8–21. Also see Patrick Murphy and Gene Laczniak, "Emerging Ethical Issues Facing Marketing Researchers," *Marketing Research* (June 1992), pp. 6–11.
28. Crossen, "Margins of Error," p. A1.
29. "Dial-in TV Polls Blasted as Junk," *Marketing News* (January 2, 1989), p. 30; also see Newton Frank, "900-Number Polls and the Marketing Research Community," *Marketing Research* (September 1991), pp. 3–4.
30. Diane Bowers, "Saga of a Sugger—Part I," *Marketing Research* (March 1990), pp. 68–72; and Diane Bowers, "Saga of a Sugger—Part II," *Marketing Research* (June 1990), pp. 64–67; also see: Diane Bowers, "Another Victory against Sugging," *Marketing Research* (September 1992), pp. 44–45.
31. Diane Bowers, "Promoting a Positive Image," *Marketing Research* (Winter 1993), pp. 40–42.
32. Diane Bowers, "CMOR: A Status Report," *Marketing Research* (Summer 1994), pp. 42–44.
33. These publications are available from ARF Information Center, 3 East 54th Street, New York, NY 10022.
34. Bruce Stern and Terry Crawford, "It's Time to Consider Certification of Researchers," *Marketing News* (September 12, 1986), pp. 20, 21; also see "Consensus Eludes Certification Issue," *Marketing News* (September 11, 1989), pp. 125, 127; Bruce Stern and Edward Grubb, "Alternative Solutions to the Marketing Research Industry's Quality Control Problem," in Robert King, ed., *Marketing: Toward the Twenty-First Century: Proceedings of the Annual Meeting of the 1992 Southern Marketing Association* (Richmond, Va.: Southern Marketing Association), pp. 225–229; and David Parmerlee, "Certification through Professional Development," *Marketing Research* (December 1991), pp. 63–65.
35. Stern and Crawford, p. 21.
36. Terri Rittenburg and Gene Murdock, "The Pros and Cons of Certifying Marketing Researchers," *Marketing Research* (Spring 1994), pp. 5–9; also see: Stephen McDaniel and Roberto Solano-Mendez, "Should Marketing Researchers Be Certified?" *Journal of Advertising Research* 33 (July/August 1993): 20–31.
37. Ralph Giacobbe and Madhav Segal, "Certifying Researchers: Segmentation by Attitudes," *Marketing Research* (Summer 1994), pp. 23–29.
38. Michael McDermott, "A Spy Tale: How RJR Smoked Philip Morris," *Brandweek* (June 20, 1994), p. 32.
39. This case was developed from Howard Schlossberg, "Court Allows Exxon to See Confidential Research Data," *Marketing News* (June 24, 1991), p. 1; and Howard Schlossberg, "Researcher in Exxon Case Develops System to Thwart Demands for Data," *Marketing News* (September 16, 1991), p. 7; also see: "Court Orders Researcher to Give Survey Materials to Exxon," *Marketing News* (August 16, 1993), p. 9.
40. The discussion of ethical relativism, utilitarianism, and Kantian formalism are adapted largely from Richard DeGeorge, *Business Ethics*, 2d ed. (New York: Macmillan, 1986).
41. The discussion of social Darwinism, Machiavellianism, and objectivism is adapted from Edward Stevens, *Business Ethics* (New York: Paulist Press, 1979).
42. Niccolo Machiavelli, *The Prince* (New York: Mentor Classics, 1952), p. 52.

CHAPTER 5

1. Robert Bengen, "Teamwork: It's in the Bag," *Marketing Research* (Winter 1993), pp. 30–33.
2. Joe Schwartz, "Databases Deliver the Goods," *American Demographics* (September 1989), p. 24.
3. "Interview with Mike Foytik, DSS Research," conducted by Roger Gates (November 29, 1994).
4. "A Potent New Tool for Selling: Database Marketing," *Business Week* (September 5, 1994), pp. 56–62.
5. "KGF Taps Data Base to Target Consumers," *Advertising Age* (October 8, 1990), pp. 3, 83.
6. "Coupon Clippers, Save Your Scissors," *Business Week* (June 20, 1994), pp. 164–166.
7. "Using Computers to Divine Who Might Buy a Gas Grill," *Wall Street Journal* (August 16, 1994), pp. B1, B6.
8. "Silicon and Software That Mine for Gold," *Business Week* (September 5, 1994), p. 62.
9. Scott, Hume, "McD's May Be Fried By Database Rental," *Advertising Age* (March 30, 1992), pp. 1, 58.
10. Peter Pae, "American Express Company Discloses It Gives Merchants Data on Cardholders' Habits," *Wall Street Journal* (May 14, 1992), p. A3.
11. For a rebuttal to some of the limitations of secondary data, see Tim Powell, "Despite Myths, Secondary Research Is a Valuable Tool," *Marketing News* (September 21, 1991), pp. 28, 33.
12. See David Steward, *Secondary Research: Information Sources and Methods* (Beverly Hills, Calif.: Sage Publications, 1984), pp. 23–33; also see "Prospecting for Marketing Treasures in Your Customer's Database," *Banker's Monthly* (June 1989), pp. 44–48.
13. "The Information Age in Charts," *Fortune* (April 4, 1994), p. 78.
14. Ibid., p. 53.
15. "How to Get Wired," *Business Week* (October 17, 1994), pp. 242–244.
16. "Companies Go On-Line to Chat, Spy and Rebut," *Wall Street Journal* (September 15, 1994), pp. B1, B6.
17. Ibid.
18. "All You Need to Go Online," *PC World* (June 1995), pp. 120–121; "Best Web Browsers," *PC World* (June 1995), pp. 141–152; and Jackson Morton, "Census On the Internet," *American Demographics* (March 1995), pp. 62–540.
19. "Many Software Programs Available, but Customized Often Yields Best Results," *Marketing News* (February 18, 1991), pp. 11, 22.
20. Ed Campbell, "CD-ROMs Bring Census Data In-House," *Marketing News* (January 6, 1992), pp. 12, 16.

21. "Mapping for Dollars," *Fortune* (October 18, 1993), pp. 91–96.
22. This application is from: Greg Lyles, "Getting Coffee to Go," *Marketing Tools—American Demographics* (September/October 1994), pp. 68–70.
23. Max Hopper, "Rattling SABRE—New Ways to Compete on Information," *Harvard Business Review* (May–June 1990), p. 125.
24. James Belohlav and Louis Raho, "Successful Planning in the Management Information Maze," *Managerial Planning* (May–June 1984), pp. 30–37; and Stephen Brown and Martin Goslar, "New Information Systems for Marketing Decision Making," *Business* (July–September 1988), pp. 18–24.
25. Trish Baumann, "How Quaker Oats Transforms Information into Market Leadership," *Sales and Marketing Management* (June 1989), p. 79.
26. Ibid.
27. "Hand-Held Computers Help Field Staff Cut Paper Work and Harvest More Data," *Wall Street Journal* (January 30, 1990), p. B1; and "How Software Is Making Food Sales a Piece of Cake," *Business Week* (July 2, 1990), pp. 54–56.
28. "Marketers Increasing Their Use of Decision Support Systems," *Marketing News* (May 22, 1989), p. 29; "More Marketers Are Going On-Line for Decision Support," *Marketing News* (November 12, 1990), p. 14; and Terrence O'Brien, "Decision Support Systems," *Marketing Research* (December 1990), pp. 51–55.
29. "Savin Replaces 'I Think' with 'I Know,'" *Sales and Marketing Management* (December 9, 1985), p. 74.
30. Neal Pruchansky, "Beware of Mentality That Puts Blame on Computers," *Marketing News* (November 7, 1985), p. 10; Robert Trippi and Tamer Salameh, "Strategic Information Systems: Current Research Issues," *Journal of Information Systems Management* (Summer 1989), pp. 30–35.
31. This case is taken from Jeffery Zbar, "Blockbuster's Database to Fuel Future Expansion," *Advertising Age* (July 18, 1994), p. 26.
32. This appendix was abstracted primarily from Jugoslav Milutinovich, "Business Facts for Decision Makers: Where to Find Them," *Business Horizons* (March–April 1985), pp. 63–80.
33. Partially abstracted from *Online Access Guide* (March–April 1987), pp. 64–88.

CHAPTER 6

1. Joseph Rydholm, "Dwelling on Satisfaction," *Quirk's Marketing Research Review* (October 1994), pp. 6–7, 32–33.
2. "The Qualitative vs. Quantitative Conflict Is a Futile One," *Marketing News* (August 29, 1988), p. 22; "Quantitative or Qualitative? That Is the Research Question," *Marketing News* (August 29, 1988), p. 46; Sonia Yuspeh, "Point of View: Dracula and Frankenstein Revisited," *Journal of Advertising Research* 28 (February–March 1988): 53–59.
3. Stephen Wells, "Wet Towels and Whetted Appetites or a Wet Blanket? The Role of Analysis in Qualitative Research," *Journal of the Marketing Research Society* 33 (January 1991): 39–40.
4. Thomas Dupont, "Exploratory Group Interview in Consumer Research: A Case Example," *Advances in Consumer Research* 4 (1976), pp. 431–433.
5. Danny N. Bellenger and Barnette A. Greenberg, *Marketing Research—A Management Information Approach* (Homewood, Ill.: Richard D. Irwin, 1978), pp. 169–170.
6. Wendy Sykes, "Taking Stock: Issues from the Literature on Validity and Reliability in Qualitative Research," *Journal of the Marketing Research Society* 33 (January 1991): 3–12.
7. Lewis Winters, "What's New in Focus Group Research," *Marketing Research* (December 1990), pp. 69–70.
8. Much of this section is taken from Bobby Calder, "Focus Groups and the Nature of Qualitative Marketing Research," *Journal of Marketing Research* 14 (August 1977): 353–364.
9. "Focus Groups Are Used as Bait in Trolling for Ideas," *Marketing News* (August 28, 1987), p. 48.
10. "Two Twists on Focus Groups: Off-the-Wall Respondents, Written Answers Work Best," *Marketing News* (August 29, 1988), p. 31.
11. Sid Shapiro, "Focus Groups: The First Step in Package Design," *Marketing News* (September 3, 1990), pp. 15, 17.
12. Jean Campbell, "Ease Anxieties of Elderly or Disabled Participants during Focus Groups," *Marketing News* (January 4, 1988), p. 2.
13. "Motives Are as Important as Words When Group Describes a Product," *Marketing News* (August 28, 1987), p. 49.
14. William McDonald, "Focus Group Research Dynamics and Reporting: An Examination of Research Objectives and Moderator Influences," *Journal of the Academy of Marketing Sciences* 21 (Spring 1993): 161–168.
15. Wendy Hayward and John Rose, "We'll Meet Again. . . . Repeat Attendance at Group Discussions—Does It Matter?" *Journal of the Market Research Society* (July 1990): 377–407.
16. "Marketing," The *Wall Street Journal* (January 13, 1992), p. B1.
17. Peter Tuckel, Elaine Leppo, and Barbara Kaplan, "Focus Groups under Scrutiny," *Marketing Research* (June 1992), pp. 12–17.
18. Martin Lautman, "Focus Groups: Theory and Method," *Advances in Consumer Research* 9 (October 1981), p. 54; and "Debriefing Sessions: The Missing Link in Focus Groups," *Marketing News* (January 8, 1990), pp. 20, 22.
19. B. G. Yovovich, "Focusing on Consumers' Needs and Motivations," *Business Marketing* (March 1991), pp. 41–43.
20. Thomas Greenbaum, "Observing a Focus Group Takes as Much Skill as Moderating It," *Marketing News* (August 29, 1994), p. 17.
21. Yovovich, "Focusing on Consumers' Needs and Motivations," p. 42.
22. Ibid.
23. Deborah Potts, "Bias Lurks in All Phases of Qualitative Research," *Marketing News* (September 3, 1990), pp. 12, 13.
24. Judith Langer, "18 Ways to Say 'Shut Up!'" *Marketing News* (January 6, 1992), p. FG-2; also, Stephanie Tudor, "Tips on Controlling Focus Group Crosstalk," *Quirk's Marketing Research Review* (December 1991), pp. 30–31.
25. "Feedback on the Phone," *Business Marketing* (March 1991), p. 46.
26. Michael Silverstein, "Two-Way Focus Groups Can Provide Startling Information," *Marketing News* (January 4, 1988), p. 31; also, "What the '90s Will Hold for Focus Group Research," *Advertising Age* (January 22, 1990), p. 267.
27. "Network to Broadcast Live Focus Groups," *Marketing News* (September 3, 1990), pp. 10, 47.
28. Barry Langford, "Nominal Grouping Sessions," *Marketing Research* (Summer 1994), pp. 16–21.

29. "Japanese Companies Import U.S. Trends," *USA Today* (March 21, 1990), p. 2B.
30. Hal Sokolow, "In-Depth Interviews Increasing in Importance," *Marketing News* (September 13, 1985), pp. 26, 31; Pamela Rogers, "One-on-Ones Don't Get the Credit They Deserve," *Marketing News* (January 2, 1989), pp. 9–10; Hazel Kahan, "One-on-One Should Sparkle Like the Gems They Are," *Marketing News* (September 3, 1990), pp. 8–9; Thomas Greenbaum, "Focus Groups vs. One-on-Ones: The Controversy Continues," *Marketing News* (September 2, 1991), p. 16.
31. "Projective Profiting Helps Reveal Buying Habits of Power Segments," *Marketing News* (August 28, 1987), p. 10.
32. Rebecca Piirto, "Measuring Minds in the 1990s," *American Demographics* (October 1990), pp. 31–35; also see: Doreen Mole, "Projective Technique to Uncover Consumers Attitudes," *Quirks Marketing Research Review* (March 1992), pp. 26–28.
33. "Putting a Face on the Big Brands," *Fortune* (September 19, 1994), p. 80.
34. Piirto, "Beyond Mind Games," p. 52.
35. Paul E. Green and Donald S. Tull, *Research for Marketing Decisions*, 5th ed. (Englewood Cliffs, N.J.: Prentice-Hall, 1988), pp. 156–157.
36. Joe Schwartz, "Marketing the Verdict," *American Demographics* (February 1993), pp. 52–54.

CHAPTER 7

1. Susan Krafft, "Who Slams the Door on Research?," *American Demographics* (September 1991), p. 14.
2. *Walker 1990 Industry Image Study* (Indianapolis: Walker Research, Incorporated), p. 3.
3. "Jackson, Michigan, Is Most Surveyed Market," *The Frame* (September 1994), pp. 1–2.
4. Patricia E. Moberg, "Biases in Unlisted Phone Numbers," *Journal of Advertising Research* 22 (August–September 1982): 55.
5. Thomas S. Gruca and Charles D. Schewe, "Researching Older Consumers," *Marketing Research* (September 1992), pp. 18–23.
6. Douglas Berdie, "Reassessing the Value of High Response Rates to Mail Surveys," *Marketing Research* (September 1989), pp. 52–63.
7. Thomas Danbury, "Current Issues in Survey Sampling," *CASRO Journal* (1991), p. 37.
8. *Walker 1990 Industry Image Study*, p. 3.
9. Ibid.
10. Cynthia Webster, "Consumer's Attitudes toward Data Collection Methods," in Robert King, ed., *1991 Southern Marketing Association Proceedings* (Richmond, Va.: University of Richmond Press, 1991), pp. 220–223.
11. Lynn Coleman, "Researchers Say Nonresponse Is Single Biggest Problem," *Marketing News* (January 7, 1991), pp. 32–33; and Subhash Jain, *International Marketing Management*, 3d ed. (Boston: PWS-Kent Publishing Company, 1990), pp. 338–339.
12. Jerry Rosenkranz, "Don't Knock Door-to-Door Interviewing," *CASRO Journal* (1991), p. 45.
13. Beth Schneider, "Using Interactive Kiosks for Retail Research," *Marketing News* (January 2, 1995), p. 5; Kelly Shermach, "Great Strides Made in P-O-P Technology," *Marketing News* (January 2, 1995), pp. 8–9; and Joseph Rydholm, "Keep the Kids Interested," *Quirk's Marketing Research Review* (February 1993), pp. 6–7, 37.
14. John P. Dickson and Douglas L. MacLachlan, "Fax Surveys?" *Marketing Research* (September 1992), pp. 26–30; Gary S. Vazzana and Duane Bachmann, "Fax Attracts," *Marketing Research* (Spring 1994); and "Fax-based Surveys Give *PC World* Magazine Flexibility and Quick Turnaround at a Low Cost," *Quirk's Marketing Research Review* (February 1994), pp. 7, 26–27.
15. Tibbett Speer, "Nickelodeon Puts Kids Online," *American Demographics* (the 1994 Directory), pp. 16–17; and Bill MacElroy and Bill Geissler, "Interactive Surveys Can Be More Fun Than the Traditional," *Marketing News* (October 24, 1994), pp. 4–5.
16. Barbara A. Schuldt and Jeff W. Totten, "Electronic Mail vs. Mail Survey Response Rates," *Marketing Research* (Winter 1994), pp. 36–39; and Bill MacElroy and Bill Geissler, "Interactive Surveys Can Be More Fun Than the Traditional."
17. For a discussion of voice mail and related technologies, see Peter J. DePaulo and Rick Weitzer, "Interactive Phone Technology Delivers Survey Data Quickly," *Marketing News* (January 3, 1994), p. 15; John R. Dickinson, A. J. Faria, and Dan Friesen, "Live vs. Automated Telephone Interviewing," *Marketing Research* (Winter 1994), pp. 28–34; and Tim Triplett, "Survey System Has Human Touch without the Human," *Marketing News* (October 24, 1994), p. 16.
18. Roger Gates and Paul Solomon, "Changing Patterns in Survey Research: Growth of the Mall Intercept," *Journal of Data Collection* 22 (Spring 1986): 3–8.
19. Cecil Phillips, "A View from All Sides," *Alert* 17 (September 1978), pp. 6–7.
20. Roger Gates and Bob Brobst, "RANDIAL: A Program for Generating Random Telephone Numbers in Interviewer Usable Form," *Journal of Marketing Research* 14 (May 1977): 240–242; also see Dianne Schmidley, "How to Overcome Bias in a Telephone Survey," *American Demographics* (November 1986), pp. 50–51; and Lewis Winters, "What's New in Telephone Sampling Technology," *Marketing Research: A Magazine of Management and Applications* (March 1990), pp. 80–82.
21. *Walker 1990 Industry Image Study*, p. 3.
22. Todd Remington, "Rising Refusal Rates: The Impact of Telemarketing," *Quirk's Marketing Research Review* (May 1992), pp. 8–15.
23. Kate Bertrand, "The Global Spyglass," *Business Marketing* (September 1990), pp. 52–56.
24. For a discussion of voice mail and related technologies, see Peter J. DePaulo and Rick Weitzer, "Interactive Phone Technology Delivers Survey Data Quickly," *Marketing News* (January 3, 1994), p. 15; John R. Dickinson, A. J. Faria, and Dan Friesen, "Live vs. Automated Telephone Interviewing," *Marketing Research* (Winter 1994), pp. 28–34; and Tim Triplett, "Survey System Has Human Touch without the Human," *Marketing News* (October 24, 1994), p. 16.
25. Tibbett Speer, "Nickelodeon Puts Kids Online."
26. Carl McDaniel and Roger Gates, "Personal vs. Computer Interviewing: Comparisons of Data Quality," *Journal of Data Collection* 22 (Fall 1982): 15–20.
27. Beth Schneider, "Using Interactive

Kiosks for Retail Research;" and Kelly Shermach "Great Strides Made in P-O-P Technology."

28. Charles D. Parker and Kevin F. McCrohan, "Increasing Mail Survey Response Rates: A Discussion of Methods and Induced Bias," in John Summey, R. Viswanathan, Ronald Taylor, and Karen Glynn, eds., *Marketing: Theories and Concepts for Era of Change* (Atlanta: Southern Marketing Association, 1983), pp. 254–256.
29. Douglas Berdie, "Reassessing the Value of High Response Rates to Mail Surveys," *Marketing Research* (September 1989), pp. 52–63; Jean Charles Chebat and Ayala Cohen, "Response Speed in Mail Surveys: Beware of Shortcuts," *Marketing Research* (Spring 1993), pp. 20–25; and Robert J. Sutton and Linda L. Zeits, "Multiple Prior Notifications, Personalization, and Reminder Surveys," *Marketing Research* (December 1992), pp. 14–21.
30. Joseph Rydholm, "Keep the Kids Interested."
31. Betsy Peterson, "Interviewers: The Vital Link to Consumer Cooperation," *Marketing Research* (Winter 1994), pp. 48–49.
32. Emanuel Demby, "ESOMAR Urges Changes in Reporting Demographics, Issues Worldwide Report," *Marketing News* (January 8, 1990), pp. 24–25.
33. "Marketing Research in Japan," *ESOMAR Newsbrief* (August 1994), p. 9.
34. N. Carroll Mohn, "Pacific Rim Prices," *Marketing Research* (Winter 1994), pp. 22–27.
35. The section on Russian marketing research is from William Wilson and Xiaoyan Zhao, "Perestroika and Research: Ivan's Opinion Counts," *CASRO Journal* (1991), pp. 29–30.
36. Jeffrey Pope, "International Research—It's a Different Game," *CASRO Journal* (1991), pp. 23–26.
37. This section was adapted from Phillip Cateora, *International Marketing*, 7th ed. (Homewood, Ill.: Richard D. Irwin, 1990), pp. 387–391.
38. Ibid.
39. This case was developed from Gail Tom, Michelle Dragics, and Christi Holderegger, "Using Visual Presentation to Assess Store Positioning: A Case Study of J. C. Penney," *Marketing Research* (September 1991), pp. 48–52.

CHAPTER 8

1. Michael J. McCarthy, "James Bond Hits the Supermarket: Stores Snoop on Shoppers' Habits to Boost Sales," *Wall Street Journal* (August 25, 1993), pp. B1, B8.
2. E. W. Webb, D. T. Campbell, K. D. Schwarts, and L. Sechrest, Unobtrusive *Measures: Nonreaction Research in the Social Sciences* (Chicago: Rand McNally, 1966), pp. 113–114.
3. Daniel Seymour, "Seeing Is Believing with Systematic Observation," *Marketing News* (August 28, 1987), p. 36.
4. "Any Way Out on the Leading Edge," *Fortune Special Edition* (Autumn/Winter 1993), p. 41; and "Researchers Go Under Cover to Learn About 'Laskerville,'" *Marketing News* (May 11, 1992), p. 8.
5. See Henry Krueckeberg, "Customer Observation: Procedures, Results, and Implications," *Quirk's Marketing Research Review* (December 1989), pp. 16–22, 42–43.
6. "The Spy Who Came in from the Cold Cuts," *Business Week* (July 20, 1987); "Who Was That Masked Customer?" *Chain Store Age Executive* November 1988), pp. 80–82; "Mystery Shoppers," *Restaurant Business* (February 10, 1989), pp. 38, 119; "There's No Mystery in How to Retain Customers," *Marketing News* (February 4, 1991), p. 10.
7. Ronald Milliman, "Using Background Music to Affect the Behavior of Supermarket Shoppers," *Journal of Marketing* 46 (Summer 1982): 86–91. Another interesting study on shopper research behavior in supermarkets is Cathy Cobb and Wayne Hoyer, "Direct Observation of Search Behavior in the Purchase of Two Nondurable Products," *Psychology and Marketing* (Fall 1985), pp. 161–179.
8. Ronald Milliman, "The Influence of Background Music on the Behavior of Restaurant Patrons," *Journal of Consumer Research* 13 (September 1986): 286–289.
9. Harold Kassarjian, "Content Analysis in Consumer Research, *Journal of Consumer Research* 4 (June 1977): 8–18. An excellent summary article on content analysis is: Richard Kolbe and Melissa Burnet, "Content-Analysis Research: An Examination of Applications with Directives for Improving Research Reliability and Objectivity," *Journal of Consumer Research* 18 (September 1991): 243–250. Other examples of content analysis are Mary Zimmer and Linda Golden, "Impressions of Retail Stores: A Content Analysis of Consumer Images," *Journal of Retailing* 64 (Fall 1988): 265–293; and Terence Shimp, Joel Urbany, and Sakeh Camlin, "The Use of Framing and Characterization for Magazine Advertising of Mass-Marketed Products," *Journal of Advertising* (January 1988): 23–30. Several good reference articles on content analysis are: Hans Kepplinger, "Content Analysis and Reception Analysis," *American Behavioral Scientist* (November/December 1989), pp. 21–38; Bradley Greenberg, "On Other Perspectives toward Message Analysis," *American Behavioral Scientist* (November/December 1989), pp. 39–51; Sonia Livingstone, "Audience Reception and the Analysis of Program Meaning," *American Behavioral Scientist* (November/December 1989), pp. 187–190; and Carl Roberts, "Other Than Counting Words: A Linguistic Approach to Content Analysis," *Social Forces* (September 1989), pp. 147–177.
10. John Healy and Harold Kassarjian, "Advertising Substantiation and Advertiser Response: A Content Analysis of Magazine Advertisements," *Journal of Marketing* 47 (Winter 1983): 107–117.
11. Anthony Ursic, Michael Ursic, and Virginia Ursic, "A Longitudinal Study of the Use of the Elderly in Magazine Advertising," *Journal of Consumer Research* 13 (June 1986): 131–133.
12. Much of this section is taken from Elizabeth Hirschman, "Humanistic Inquiry in Marketing Research: Philosophy, Method and Criteria," *Journal of Marketing Research* 23 (August 1986): 237–249. For more detailed information, see Yvonna Lincoln and Edward Guba, *Naturalistic Inquiry* (Beverly Hills, Calif.: Sage Publications, 1985).
13. A. C. Nielsen Retail Index Services (Northbrook, Ill.: A. C. Nielsen Company).
14. Ibid.

15. Johny Johanson and Ikujiro Nonaka, "Market Research the Japanese Way," *Harvard Business Review* (May–June 1987), pp. 16–22; an excellent article on Japanese observation research is Magoroh Maruyama, "International Proactive Marketing," *Marketing Research* (June 1990), pp. 36–49.
16. Werner Kroeber-Riel, "Activation Research: Psychological Approaches in Consumer Research," *Journal of Consumer Research* 6 (March 1979): 240–250.
17. Michael J. McCarthy, "Mind Probe," *Wall Street Journal* (March 22, 1991), p. B3.
18. S. Weinstein, C. Weinstein, and R. Drozdenko, "Brain Wave Analysis in Advertising Research: Validation from Basic Research and Independent Replications," *Psychology and Marketing* (Fall 1984), pp. 17–42.
19. See John Cacioppo and Richard Petty, "Physiological Responses and Advertising Effects," *Psychology and Marketing* (Summer 1985), pp. 115–126.
20. Ibid.
21. Tony Siciliano, "Europeans Discover T-Scope for Packaging Research," *Quirk's Marketing Research Review* (November 1993), pp. 8–9.
22. Michael Eysenck, "Arousal, Learning, and Memory," *Psychological Bulletin* 83 (1976), pp. 389–404.
23. James Grant and Dean Allman, "Voice Stress Analyzer Is a Marketing Research Tool," *Marketing News* (January 4, 1988), p. 22.
24. Glen Brickman, "Uses of Voice-Pitch Analysis," *Journal of Advertising Research* 20 (April 1980): 69–73.
25. Ronald Nelson and David Schwartz, "Voice-Pitch Analysis," *Journal of Advertising Research* 19 (October 1979): 55–59.
26. Nancy Nighswonger and Claude Martin, Jr., "On Using Voice Analysis in Marketing Research," *Journal of Marketing Research* 18 (August 1981): 350–355.
27. "Real-World Device Sheds New Light on Ad Readership Tests," *Marketing News* (June 5, 1987), pp. 1, 18.
28. Correspondence from Len Weinblatt, President of the PreTesting Company, March 13, 1995.
29. "Networks Urge Changes in People Meter System," *Marketing News* (January 22, 1990), pp. 6, 21; and "Nielsen's Magic Lantern Leaves the Networks Seeing Red," *Superbrands 1991: A Supplement of Adweek's Marketing Week*, p. 26.
30. "Nielsen, Sarnoff to Develop Passive People Meter," *Marketing News* (July 3, 1989), p. 7; and "People Meter Rerun," *Marketing News* (September 2, 1991), pp. 1, 44.
31. Rebecca Piirto, "Do Not Adjust Your Set," *American Demographics* (March 1993), p. 6; also see Laurence Gold, "Technology in Television Research: The Meter," *Marketing Research* (Winter 1994), pp. 57–58.
32. Laurence Gold, "The Coming of Age of Scanner Data," *Marketing Research* (Winter 1993), pp. 20–23.
33. J. Walker Smith, "The Promise of Single Source—When, Where, and How," *Marketing Research* (December 1990), pp. 3–5; another good article on the future of scanning is: Laurence Gold, "High Technology Data Collection for Measurement and Testing," *Marketing Research* (March 1992), pp. 29–38.
34. "IRI, Nielsen Slug It Out in Scanning Wars," *Marketing News* (September 2, 1991), p. 1. Three excellent summary articles on single-source systems are David Curry, "Single-Source Systems: Retail Management Present and Future," *Journal of Retailing* 65 (Spring 1989): 1–20; Melvin Prince, "Some Uses and Abuses of Single-Source Data for Promotional Decision Making," *Marketing Research* (December 1989), pp. 18–22; and "Futuristic Weaponry," Advertising Age (June 11, 1990), pp. 5–12.
35. The information on BehaviorScan is taken from a pamphlet from Information Resources, Incorporated entitled, "BehaviorScan." A good article that compares alternative single-source suppliers and their different methodologies is Leon Winters, "Home Scan vs. Store Scan Panels: Single Source Options for the 1990s," *Marketing Research* (December 1989), pp. 61–65.
36. Letter to authors from Robert Bregenzer, senior vice-president, Information Resources, Incorporated, dated October 20, 1994.
37. Speech given by Olan M. Fulgoni, president and CEO of Information Resources, Incorporated, delivered before the Advertising Research Foundation Annual Conference, March 4, 1987, New York City.
38. Bregenzer letter dated October 20, 1994.
39. "Rivals Duel Bitterly for Job of Supplying Market Information," *Wall Street Journal* (November 15, 1993), pp. A1, A9.
40. "Now It's Down to Two Equal Competitors," *Superbrands 1991: A Supplement to Adweek's Marketing Week*, p. 28.
41. "IRI, Nielsen Slug It Out in Scanning Wars," p. 47.
42. "Nielsen Weighs Assets," *Advertising Age* (August 12, 1991), p. 29.
43. "Information Resources Wires the Drugstores," *Adweek's Marketing Week* (May 27, 1991), p. 34.
44. "IRI Signs On to Track Household Goods Sales," *Advertising Age* (June 13, 1994), p. 37.
45. See, for example, William Moult, "Will Anybody Ever Link Survey Data to Scanner Data?" a paper delivered before the 1992 AMA Behavioral Research Conference, Scottsdale, Arizona.
46. James Sinkula, "Status of Company Usage of Scanner Based Research," *Journal of the Academy of Marketing Science* 14 (Spring 1986): 63–71.
47. "Merchandising Plays Effective? Scanners Know," *Marketing News* (January 4, 1985), p. 17.
48. Ibid.
49. Moult, "Will Anybody Ever Link Survey Data to Scanner Data?"
50. "Safeway Launches New StoreLab Testing Service," *Marketing News* (January 8, 1990), p. 45.
51. Undated speech entitled "New Technology Contributions to New Product and Advertising Strategy Testing: The ERIM Testsight System," by Laurence Gold, vice-president, Marketing, A. C. Nielsen Co.
52. Susan Caminiti, "A Star Is Born," *Fortune Special Edition* (Autumn/Winter 1993), pp. 44–47.

CHAPTER 9

1. Thomas D. Cook and Donald T. Campbell, *Experimentation: Design Analysis Issues for Field Settings* (Chicago: Rand McNally, 1979).

2. See Claire Selltiz et al., *Research in Social Relations*, rev. ed. (New York: Holt, Rinehart and Winston, 1959), pp. 80–82.
3. A good example of a laboratory experiment is described in Carroll Mohn, "Simulated-Purchase 'Chip' Testing vs. Trade-off Conjoint Analysis—Coca-Cola's Experience," *Marketing Research* (March 1990), pp. 49–54.
4. A. G. Sawyer, "Demand Artifacts in Laboratory Experiments in Consumer Research," *Journal of Consumer Research* 2 (March 1975): 181–201; and N. Giges, "No Miracle in Small Miracle: Story Behind Failure," *Advertising Age* (August 16, 1989), p. 76.
5. John Barry, "Keebler Springs to Life," *Adweek's Marketing Week* (January 6, 1992), pp. 19–20.
6. John G. Lynch, "On the External Validity of Experiments in Consumer Research," *Journal of Consumer Research* 9 (December 1982): 225–239.
7. For a more detailed discussion of this and other experimental issues, see Thomas D. Cook and Donald T. Campbell, "The Design and Conduct of Quasi-Experiments and True Experiments in Field Settings," in M. Dunnette, ed., *Handbook of Industrial and Organizational Psychology* (Skokie, Ill.: Rand McNally, 1978).
8. Ibid.
9. For a discussion of the characteristics of various types of experimental designs, see Donald T. Campbell and Julian C. Stanley, *Experimental and Quasi-Experimental Design for Research* (Chicago: Rand McNally, 1966); also see Richard Bagozzi and Youjar Yi, "On the Use of Structural Equation Models in Experimental Design," *Journal of Marketing Research* 26 (August 1989): 225–270.
10. Thomas D. Cook and Donald T. Campbell, *Quasi-Experimentation: Design and Analysis Issues for Field Settings* (Boston: Houghton-Mifflin, 1979) p. 56.
11. Alvin Achenbaum, "Market Testing: Using the Marketplace as a Laboratory," in Robert Ferber, ed., *Handbook of Marketing Research* (New York: McGraw-Hill, 1974), pp. 4–32; T. Karger, "Test Marketing as Dress Rehearsals," *Journal of Consumer Marketing* 2 (Fall 1985): 49–55; Tim Harris, "Marketing Research Passes Toy Marketer Test," *Advertising Age* (August 24, 1987), pp. 1, 8; and John L. Carefoot, "Marketing and Experimental Designs in Marketing Research: Uses and Misuses," *Marketing News* (June 7, 1993), p. 21.
12. Christopher Power, "Will It Sell in Podunk? Hard to Say," *Business Week* (August 10, 1992), pp. 46–47.
13. Jay Klompmaker, G. David Hughes, and Russell I. Haley, "Test Marketing in New Product Development," *Harvard Business Review* (May–June 1976), p. 129; and N. D. Cadbury, "When, Where and How to Test Market," *Harvard Business Review* (May–June 1985), pp. 97–98.
14. Joseph Rydholm, "To Test or Not to Test," *Quirk's Marketing Research Review* (February 1992), pp. 61–62.
15. "Test Marketing Is Valuable, But It's Often Abused," *Marketing News* (January 2, 1987), p. 40.
16. Joseph Rydholm, "To Test or Not to Test."
17. Benjamin Lipstein, "The Design of Test Market Experiments," *Journal of Advertising Research* (December 1965): 2–7; and Jeffery D. Zbar, "Blockbuster's CD-ROM Crash Course," *Advertising Age* (May 23, 1994), p. 18.
18. For a discussion of typical American cities and metropolitan areas, see Jane Rippeteau, "Where's Fort Wayne When You Need It?" *The Marketer* (July–August 1990), pp. 46–49; and Judith Waldrop, "All American Markets," *American Demographics* (January 1992), pp. 24–30.
19. Laurence N. Gold, "Virtual Reality Now a Research Reality," *Marketing Research* (November 1993), pp. 50–51.
20. Melvin Prince, "Choosing Simulated Test Marketing Systems," *Marketing Research* (September 1992), pp. 14–16.
21. G. L. Urban and G. M. Katz, "Pre-Test Market Models: Validation and Managerial Implications," *Journal of Marketing Research* (August 1983): 221–234; Standford Odesky and Richard Kerger, "Using Focus Groups for a Simulated Trial Process," *Quirk's Marketing Research Review* (April 1994), pp. 38–40,53; Frank Toboloski, "Package Design Requires Research," *Marketing News* (June 6, 1994), p. 4.
22. Adapted from "Test Marketing Is Valuable, but Its Often Abused," *Marketing News* (January 2, 1987), p. 40.
23. Christopher Power, "Will It Sell in Podunk? Hard to Say."
24. Adapted from *Laboratory Test Market* (New York: Yankelovich, Clancy, Shulman).

CHAPTER **10**

1. Tim Huberty, "Is It Live or Is It Gold'n Plump?" *Quirk's Marketing Research Review* (March 1994), pp. 6–7, 47–50.
2. Adapted from: Brian Toyne and Peter G.P. Walters, *Global Marketing Management: A Strategic Perspective* (Boston: Allyn & Bacon, 1989), p. 201.
3. F. N. Kerlinger, *Foundations of Behavioral Research*, 3d ed. (New York: Holt, Rinehart and Winston, Inc., 1986), p. 403; also see Mel Crask and R. J. Fox, "An Exploration of the Internal Properties of Three Commonly Used Research Scales," *Journal of the Marketing Research Society* (October 1987): 317–319.
4. These are adapted from Claire Selltiz, Laurence Wrightsman, and Stuart Cook, *Research Methods in Social Relations*, 3d ed. (New York: Holt, Rinehart and Winston, Inc., 1976), pp. 164–168.
5. Martin Weinberger, "Seven Perspectives on Consumer Research," *Marketing Research* (December 1989), pp. 9–17.
6. Raghav Singh, "Reliability and Validity of Survey Research in Marketing: The State of the Art," in Robert King, ed., *Marketing: Toward the Twenty-First Century, Proceedings of the 1991 Southern Marketing Association* (Richmond, Va.: University of Richmond, 1991), pp. 210–213; also see Paul Hensel, Gordon Bruner, and Calvin Berkey, "Toward the Compilation and Critical Assessment of Psychometric Scales Reported in Marketing Research," in Louis Capella et al., eds., *Progress in Marketing Thought, Proceedings of the 1990 Southern Marketing Association* (Houston: Houston Baptist College, 1990), pp. 330–334.
7. Andrew Erlich, "Dynamic Travel Trends in New Markets: Asians and Latinos," *Quirk's Marketing Research Review* (January 1994), pp. 16–17, 30.

CHAPTER **11**

1. Bickley Townsend, "Marketing Research That Matters," *American*

Demographics (August 1992), pp. 58–60.
2. George Day, *Buyer Attitudes and Brand Choice Behavior* (New York: Free Press, 1970).
3. See Brian Sternthal and C. Samuel Craig, *Consumer Behavior: An Information Processing Perspective* (Englewood Cliffs, N.J.: Prentice-Hall, 1982), pp. 157–162; also see Barbara Loken and Ronald Hoverstad, "Relationships between Information Recall and Subsequent Attitudes: Some Exploratory Findings," *Journal of Consumer Research* 12 (September 1985): 155–168.
4. Robert E. Smith and William Swinyard, "Attitude Behavior Consistency: The Impact of Product Trial versus Advertising," *Journal of Marketing Research* 20 (August 1983): 257–267.
5. This section is adapted from Del Hawkins, Robert Best, and Kenneth Coney, *Consumer Behavior: Implications for Marketing Strategy*, 3d ed. (Plano, Texas: Business Publications, 1986), pp. 455–462.
6. Michael Halberstam, "Understanding Inherent Differences in Asian-American Marketing Research," *Quirk's Marketing Research Review* (January 1994), pp. 8–9.
7. For an excellent discussion of the semantic differential, see Charles E. Osgood, George Suci, and Percy Tannenbaum, *The Measurement of Meaning* (Urbana: University of Illinois Press, 1957).
8. Ibid., pp. 140–153, 192, 193; also, William D. Barclay, "The Semantic Differential as an Index of Brand Attitude," *Journal of Advertising Research* 4 (March 1964): 30–33.
9. Theodore Clevenger, Jr., and Gilbert A. Lazier, "Measurement of Corporate Images by the Semantic Differential," *Journal of Marketing Research* 2 (February 1965): 80–82.
10. Sabra Brock, "Marketing Research in Asia: Problems, Opportunities, and Lessons," *Marketing Research: A Magazine of Management and Applications* (September 1989), pp. 44–51.
11. Michael J. Etzel, Terrell G. Williams, John C. Rogers, and Douglas J. Lincoln, "The Comparability of Three Stapel Forms in a Marketing Setting," in Ronald F. Bush and Shelby D. Hunt, eds., *Marketing Theory: Philosophy of Science Perspectives* (Chicago: American Marketing Association, 1982), pp. 303–306.
12. Adapted from Paul Green, Donald Tull, and Gerald Albaum, *Research for Marketing Decisions*, 5th ed. (Englewood Cliffs, N.J.: Prentice-Hall, 1988), pp. 305–306.
13. M. V. Kalwani and A. J. Silk, "On the Reliability and Prediction Validity of Purchase Intention Measures," *Marketing Science* 1 (Summer 1982): 243–287.
14. Glen Urban, John Hauser, and Nikhilesh Dholakia, *Essentials of New Product Management* (Englewood Cliffs, N.J.: Prentice-Hall, 1987), p. 145.
15. Tony Siciliano, "Purchase Intent: Separating Fact from Fiction," *Marketing Research* 21 (Spring 1993), p. 56.
16. M. M. Givon and Z. Shapira, "Response to Rating Scalings," *Journal of Marketing Research* (November 1984): 410–419; and D. E. Stem, Jr., and S. Noazin, "The Effects of Number of Objects and Scale Positions on Graphic Position Scale Reliability," in R. F. Lusch et al., *1985 AMA Educators' Proceedings* (Chicago: American Marketing Association, 1985), pp. 370–372.

CHAPTER **12**

1. Joseph Rydholm, "Here's Looking at You, Kid," *Quirk's Marketing Research Review* (March 1993), pp. 27–29.
2. Lewis Winters, "Innovations in Open-ended Questions," *Marketing Research* (June 1991), pp. 69–70.
3. Ibid.
4. Thomas Semon, "Asking Questions Is Too Limited," *Marketing News* (October 28, 1991), p. 19.
5. See S. L. Payne, *The Art of Asking Questions* (Princeton, N.J.: Princeton University Press, 1951). The entire book is highly recommended for any designer of questionnaires; also recommended is Seymour Sudman and Norman Bradburn, *Asking Questions* (San Francisco: Jossey-Bass, 1983).
6. Gary Mullet, "Back to Basics: Remember to Rotate," *Quirk Marketing Research Review* (January 1993), pp. 10–13.
7. Robert Peterson, Roger Kerin, and Mohammad Sabertehrani, "Question Understanding in Self-Report Data," in Bruce Walker et al., eds., *An Assessment of Marketing Thought and Practice—1982 AMA Educators' Conference Proceedings* (Chicago: American Marketing Association, 1982), pp. 426–429; also M. C. Macklin, "Do Children Understand TV Ads?" *Journal of Advertising Research* (February–March 1983): 63–70.
8. See Robert Greene and Ann Marie Thompson, "Sequential Position Bias: Is the Phenomenon for Real?" in John Crawford and Barbara Garland, eds., *Southwestern Marketing Association 1985 Proceedings* (Denton: North Texas State University), pp. 99–101.
9. Sandra M. J. Wong, "The Importance of Context in Conducting Asian Research," *Quirk's Marketing Research Review* (December 1993), pp. 24–27.
10. Charles F. Connell, Louis Oksenberg, and Jean M. Converse, "Striving for Response Accuracy: Experiments in New Interviewing Techniques, *Journal of Marketing Research* 14 (August 1977): 306–315; also see K. C. Schneider, "Uninformed Response Rates in Survey Research," *Journal of Business Research* 12 (April 1985): 153–162; G. F. Bishop, A. F. Tuchfarber, and R. W. Oldendick, "Opinions on Fictitious Issues," *Public Opinion Quarterly* 50 (Summer 1986), pp. 240–250; and D. I. Hawkins, K. A. Coney, and D. W. Jackson, Jr., "The Impact of Monetary Inducement on Uniformed Response Error," *Journal of the Academy of Marketing Science* 16 (Summer 1988): 30–35.
11. E. Scott Maynes, "The Anatomy of Response Errors: Consumer Saving," *Journal of Marketing Research* 2 (November 1965): 378–387; also see R. E. Goldsmith, "Personality and Uninformed Response Error," *Journal of Social Psychology* 126 (February 1986): 37–45; R. E. Goldsmith, J. D. White, and H. Walters, "Explanations for Spurious Response in Survey Research," *Business and Economic Review* 25 (Summer 1988): 93–104; and R. E. Goldsmith, "Spurious Response Error in a New Product Survey," *Journal of Business Research* 15 (December 1988): 271–281.
12. Kevin Walters, "Designing Screening Questionnaires to Minimize Dishonest Answers," *Applied Marketing Research* (Spring-Summer 1991), pp. 51–53.
13. Calvin Hodock, "The Decline and Fall of Marketing Research in Corporate America," *Marketing Research* (June 1991), pp. 12–22.
14. Susan Carroll, "Questionnaire Design Affects Response Rate," *Marketing News* (January 3, 1994), pp. 14, 23.
15. Joan Fredericks, "Observe These

Rules When Designing Questionnaires," *Marketing News* (January 22, 1982), pp. 2–18.

16. Shelby D. Hunt, Richard D. Sparkman, Jr., and James B. Wilcox, "The Pretest in Survey Research: Issues and Preliminary Findings," *Journal of Marketing Research* 19 (May 1982): 265–275.
17. This section is taken from: Pam Burns, "Field Management: A Better Mousetrap," *Quirk's Marketing Research Review* (June/July 1992), pp. 36–39.
18. Maura Isaacs, "Factors to Consider When Choosing Field Management Companies," *Quirk's Marketing Research Review* (June/July 1992), p. 39.

CHAPTER 13

1. For excellent discussions of sampling, see Seymour Sudman, *Applied Sampling* (New York: Academic Press, 1976); and L. J. Kish, *Survey Sampling* (New York: John Wiley and Sons, 1965).
2. For discussion of the debate surrounding the 1990 census, see Eugene Carlson, "Backers of an Adjusted Census Won't Take No for an Answer," *Wall Street Journal* (November 3, 1987), p. 35.
3. "George Gallup's Nation of Numbers," *Esquire* (December 1983), pp. 91–92.
4. J. A. Brunner and G. A. Brunner, "Are Voluntary Unlisted Telephone Subscribers Really Different?" *Journal of Marketing Research* 8 (February 1971): 121–124, 395–399.
5. G. J. Glasser and G. D. Metzger, "Random-Digit Dialing as a Method of Telephone Sampling," *Journal of Marketing Research* 9 (February 1972): 59–64.
6. S. Roslow and L. Roslow, "Unlisted Phone Subscribers Are Different," *Journal of Advertising* 12 (August 1972): 25–38.
7. Charles D. Cowan, "Using Multiple Sample Frames to Improve Survey Coverage, Quality, and Costs," *Marketing Research* (December 1991), pp. 66–69.
8. Kelley E. Fish, James H. Barnes, and Benjamin F. Banahan III, "Convenience or Calamity Pharmaceutical Study Explores the Effects of Sample Frame Error on Research Results," *Journal of Health Care Marketing* (Spring 1994): 45–49.
9. James McClove and P. George Benson, *Statistics for Business and Economics* (San Francisco: Dellen Publishing Co., 1988), pp. 184–185; and "Probability Sampling in the Real World," *CATI NEWS* (Summer 1993), pp. 1, 4–6.
10. R. J. Jaeger, *Sampling in Education and the Social Sciences* (New York: Longman, 1984), pp. 28–35.
11. Newton Frank, *CASRO Journal* (January 1991): 113–115.
12. Lewis C. Winters, "What's New in Telephone Sampling Technology?" *Marketing Research* (March 1990), pp. 80–82; and "A Survey Researcher's Handbook of Industry Terminology and Definitions," *Survey Sampling, Inc.* (Fairfield, Connecticut: 1992), pp. 3–20.
13. For discussions of related issues, see John E. Swan, Stephen J. O'Connor, and Seuug Doug Lee, "A Framework for Testing Sampling Bias and Methods of Bias Reduction in a Telephone Survey," *Marketing Research* (December 1991), pp. 23–34; and Charles D. Cowan, "Coverage Issues in Sample Surveys: A Component of Measurement Error," *Marketing Research* (June 1991), pp. 65–68.
14. For an excellent discussion of stratified sampling, see William G. Cochran, *Sampling Techniques*, 2d ed. (New York: John Wiley and Sons, 1963).
15. Sudman, *Applied Sampling*, pp. 110–121.
16. Ibid., pp. 110–112.
17. Earl R. Babbie, *The Practice of Social Research*, 2d ed. (Belmont, Calif.: Wadsworth Publishing, 1979), p. 167.
18. Adapted from "Probability Sampling: A Simplified Explanation," a brochure published by Opinion Research Corporation, Princeton, N.J., 1992.
19. L. J. Kish, *Survey Sampling* (New York: John Wiley and Sons, 1965).
20. "Convenience Sampling Outpacing Probability Sampling," *Survey Sampling, Inc.* (Fairfield, Connecticut: March 1994), p. 4.
21. Leo A. Goodman, "Snowball Sampling," *Annals of Mathematical Statistics* 32 (1961): 148–170.

CHAPTER 14

1. For excellent discussions of the various issues discussed in this chapter, see Seymour Sudman, *Applied Sampling* (New York: Academic Press, 1976); Morris Slonim, *Sampling in a Nutshell* (New York: Simon and Schuster, 1960); and Gerald Keller, Brian Warrach, and Henry Bartle, *Statistics for Management and Economics* (Belmont, Calif.: Wadsworth Publishing Company, 1990), p. 455.
2. Thomas T. Semon, "Save a Few Bucks on Sample Size, Risk Millions in Opportunity Loss," *Marketing News* (January 3, 1994), p. 19.
3. For discussions of these techniques, see Bill Williams, *A Sampler on Sampling* (New York: John Wiley and Sons, 1978) or Richard Jaeger, *Sampling in Education and the Social Sciences* (New York: Longmans, 1984).

CHAPTER 15

1. Harriet R. Beegle, "How Does the Field Rate?" *Advertising Age* (October 20, 1980), pp. S18–S26; "Need Honesty, Better Quality from Research Suppliers, Field Services, " *Marketing News* (September 18, 1981), p. 4.
2. Ibid.
3. D. W. Steward, "Filling the Gap: A Review of the Missing Data Problem," *An Assessment of Marketing Thought and Practice* (Chicago: American Marketing Association, 1982), pp. 395–399.
4. Ibid.
5. E. R. Morrissey, "Sources of Error in the Coding of Questionnaire Data," *Sociological Methods and Research* 1 (1982): 75–77; James McDonald, "Assessing Intercoder Reliability and Resolving Reliability and Discrepancies," *An Assessment of Marketing Thought and Practice* (Chicago: American Marketing Association, 1982), pp. 435–438; Joseph Rydholm, "Dealing with Those Pesky Open-Ended Responses," *Quirk's Marketing Research Review* (February 1994), pp. 70–69.
6. Raymond Raud and Michael A. Fallig, "Automating the Coding Process with Neural Networks," *Quirk's Marketing Research Review* (May 1993) pp. 14–16, 40–47. Eric DeRosia, "Data Processing Made Easy," *Quirk's Marketing Research Review* (February 1993), pp. 18, 34.
7. J. A. Sonquist and W. C. Dunkelberg, *Survey and Opinion Research: Procedures for Processing and Analysis* (Englewood Cliffs, N.J.: Prentice-Hall, 1977), pp. 100–105.

8. Joseph Rydholm, "Scanning the Seas: Scannable Questionnaires Give Princess Cruises Accuracy and Quick Turnaround," *Quirk's Marketing Research Review* (May 1993), pp. 6–7, 26–27; Norma Frendberg, "Scanning Questionnaires Efficiently," *Marketing Research* (Spring 1993), pp. 38–42.
9. Nancy J. Merritt and Cecile Bouchy, "Are Microcomputers Replacing Mainframes in Marketing Research Firms?" *Journal of the Academy of Marketing Science* 20 (Winter 1992): 81–85.
10. For a discussion of these issues, see Alan Roberts, "Understanding Data Requires Recognition of Types of Error," *Quirk's Marketing Research Review* (May 1987), pp. 20–59; Michael Sullivan, "Controlling Non-Response Bias and Item Non-Response Bias Using CATI Techniques," *Quirk's Marketing Research Review* (November 1991), pp. 10–49; Emmet J. Hoffman, "Continuing Analysis of Shopping Habits in San Diego," *Quirk's Marketing Research Review* (April 1987), pp. 10–25.
11. For a discussion of these issues, see Paul Green and Donald Tull, *Research for Marketing Decision*, 5th ed. (Englewood Cliffs, N.J.: Prentice-Hall, 1988), pp. 386–399.
12. For an excellent discussion on creating graphics presentations, see Gus Venditto, "Twelve Tips for Better Presentations," *PC Magazine* (January 28, 1992), pp. 253–260.

CHAPTER 16

1. Michael Baumgardner and Ron Tatham, "Statistical Significance Testing May Hinder Proper Decision Making," *Quirk's Marketing Research Review* (May 1987), pp. 16–19; Hank Zucker, "What Is Significance?" *Quirk's Marketing Research Review* (March 1994), pp. 12, 14; Gordon A. Wyner, "How High Is Up?" *Marketing Research* (Fall 1993), pp. 42–43; Gordon A. Wyner, "The 'Significance' of Marketing Research," *Marketing Research* (Winter 1993), pp. 43–45; Patrick M. Baldasare and Vikas Mittel, "The Use, Misuse, and Abuse of Significance," *Quirk's Marketing Research Review* (November 1994), pp. 16, 32.
2. Robert L. Zimmerman, "Spurious Enhancement of Statistical Significance," *Quirk's Marketing Research Review* (June/July 1987), pp. 20–55.
3. W.G. Cochran, "The X^2 Test of Goodness of Fit," *Annals of Mathematical Statistics* 23 (1952), pp. 315–345; Tony Babinec, "How to Think about Your Tables," *Quirk's Marketing Research Review* (January 1991), pp. 10–12; For a discussion of these issues, see Gopal K. Kanji, *100 Statistical Tests* (London: Sage Publications, 1993), pp. 75.
4. Jean Gibbons, *Nonparametric Statistical Inference*, 2d ed. (New York: Marcell Dekker, 1985).
5. For a good discussion of this test and those that follow, see Donald Harnett and James Murphy, *Introductory Statistical Analysis* 2d ed. (Reading, Mass.: Addison-Wesley, 1980); and Ronald Shiffler and Arthur Adams, *Introductory Business Statistics* (Boston: PWS-Kent, 1990).
6. Gary M. Mullet, "Correctly Estimating the Variances of Proportions," *Marketing Research* (June 1991), pp. 47–51.

CHAPTER 17

1. Joseph Hair, Rolph Anderson, and Ron Tatham, *Multivariate Data Analysis*, 3d ed. (New York: Macmillan, 1992), p. 4.
2. Robert Pindyck and Daniel Rubinfield, *Econometric Models and Economic Forecasts*, 2d ed. (New York: McGraw-Hill, 1981), pp. 273–312; Doug Grisaffe, "Appropriate Use of Regression in Customer Satisfaction Analyses: A Response to William McLauchlan," *Quirk's Marketing Research Review* (February 1993), pp. 10–17; Terry Clark, "Managing Outliers: Qualitative Issues in the Handling of Extreme Observations in Marketing Research," *Marketing Research* (June 1989), pp. 31–45.
3. Paul Green, Donald Tull, and Gerald Albaum, *Research for Marketing Decisions*, 5th ed. (Englewood Cliffs, N.J.: Prentice-Hall, 1988), pp. 460–462.

CHAPTER 18

1. For an excellent and highly understandable presentation of all the multivariate techniques presented in this chapter, see Joseph Hair, Rolph Anderson, Ron Tatham, and William Black, *Multivariate Data Analysis*, 3d ed. (New York: Macmillan, 1992); and also Charles J. Schwartz, "A Marketing Researcher's Guide to Multivariate Analysis," *Quirk's Marketing Research Review* (November 1994), pp. 12–14.
2. Joseph R. Garber, "Deadbeat Repellent," *Forbes* (February 14, 1994), p. 164.
3. John J. Yacono, "Anyone Can Be a Statistician," *Windows Magazine* (November 1994), 312–318; Steven Struhl, "Statistics Software Meets Windows," *Quirk's Marketing Research Review* (May 1993), pp. 8–9, 28–39; and Sheryl Canter, "Stat of the Art," *PC Magazine* (May 11, 1993), pp. 227–287.
4. For a thorough discussion of regression analysis, see Norman Draper and Harry Smith, *Applied Regression Analysis* (New York: John Wiley and Sons, 1966).
5. Charlotte H. Mason and William D. Perreault, Jr., "Collinear, Power and Interpretation of Multiple Regression Analysis," *Journal of Marketing Research* (August 1991): 268_280; Doug Grisaffe, "Appropriate Use of Regression in Customer Satisfaction Analyses: A Response to William McLauchlan," *Quirk's Marketing Research Review* (February 1993), pp. 10–17; and Terry Clark, "Managing Outliers: Qualitative Issues in the Handling of Extreme Observations in Marketing Research," *Marketing Research* (June 1989), pp. 31–45.
6. See Hair et al, *Multivariate Data Analysis*, p. 46.
7. William D. Neal, "Using Discriminant Analysis in Marketing Research: Part 1,"*Marketing Research* (September 1989), pp. 79–81; William D. Neal, "Using Discriminant Analysis in Marketing Research: Part 2," *Marketing Research* (December 1989), pp. 55–60; and Steven Struhl, "Multivariate and Perceptual Mapping with Discriminant Analysis," *Quirk's Marketing Research Review* (March 1993), 15–15, 43.
8. See Girish Punj and David Stewart, "Cluster Analysis in Marketing Research: Review and Suggestions for Application," *Journal of Marketing Research* 20 (May 1983): 134–148; and G. Ray Funkhouser, Anindya Chatterjee, and Richard Parker, "Segmenting Samples," *Marketing Research* (Winter 1994), pp. 40–46.
9. Based on material prepared by Glen Jar-

boe, University of Texas at Arlington.
10. See Paul Green, Donald Tull, and Gerald Albaum, *Research for Marketing Decision*, 5th ed. (Englewood Cliffs, N.J.: Prentice-Hall, 1988), pp. 553–573.
11. For a complete discussion of production of perceptual maps using factor analysis, see Glen Urban and John Hauser, *Design and Marketing of New Products*, 2d ed. (Englewood Cliffs, N.J.: Prentice-hall, 1993), pp. 233–241; in a more concise format, see Glen Urban, John Hauser, and Nikhilesh Dholakia, *Essential of New Product Management* (Englewood Cliffs, N.J.: Prentice-Hall, 1987), pp. 57–58, 105–119; and, for a humorous look at perceptual mapping, see "Company Brief: House of Windsor," *The Economist* (August 29, 1992), p. 53.
12. Dick Wittink and Phillipe Cattin, "Commercial Use of Conjoint Analysis: An Update," *Journal of Marketing* (July 1989): 91–96; also see Rajeev Kohli, "Assessing Attribute Significance in Conjoint Analysis: Nonparametric Tests and Empirical Validation," *Journal of Marketing Research* (May 1988): 123–133.
13. Examples of current issues and applications are provided in Richard Smallwood, "Using Conjoint Analysis for Price Optimization," *Quirk's Marketing Research Review* (October 1991), pp. 10–13; Paul E. Green, Abba M. Krieger, and Manoj K. Agarwal, "Adaptive Conjoint Analysis: Some Caveats and Suggestions," *Journal of Marketing Research* (May 1991): 215–222; Paul E. Green and V. Srinivasan, "Conjoint Analysis in Marketing: New Developments with Implications for Research and Practice," *Journal of Marketing* (October 1990): 3–19; Joseph Curry, "Determining Product Feature Price Sensitivities," *Quirk's Marketing Research Review* (November 1990), pp. 14–17; Gordon A. Wyner, "Customer-Based Pricing Research," *Marketing Research* (Spring 1993), pp. 50–52; Steven Struhl, "Discrete Choice Modeling Comes to the PC," *Quirk's Marketing Research Review* (May 1994), pp. 12–15, 36–41; Steven Struhl, "Discrete Choice Modeling: Understanding a Better Conjoint than a Conjoint," *Quirk's Marketing Research Review* (June/July 1994), pp. 12–15, 36–39; Bashir A. Datoo, "Measuring Price Elasticity," *Marketing Research* (Spring 1994), pp. 30–34; Gordon A. Wyner, "Uses and Limitations of Conjoint Analysis—Part I," *Marketing Research* (June 1992), pp. 42–44; and Gordon A. Wyner, "Uses and Limitations of Conjoint Analysis—Part II," *Marketing Research* (September 1992), pp. 46–47.

CHAPTER **19**

1. Jamal Din, "For GE Medical Systems, Each Customer Is . . . a market of One," *Quirk's Marketing Research Review* (October 1993), pp. 6–7, 30–31.
2. Rohit Deshpande and Gerald Zaltman, "A Comparison of Factors Affecting Researcher and Manager Perceptions of Market Research Use," *Journal of Marketing Research* 21 (February 1984): 37.
3. Richard Kitaeff, "Writing the Marketing Research Report," *Marketing Research* (Winter 1993), p. 4.
4. This section is partially taken from James H. Nelems, "Report Results, Implications, and Not Just Pounds of Data," *Marketing News* (January 12, 1979), p. 7.
5. Howard L. Gordon, "Eight Ways to Dress a Research Report," *Advertising Age* (October 20, 1980), pp. 5, 37. Reprinted with permission from Ad Age, October 20, 1980, copyright Crain Communications, Inc. All rights reserved.
6. Thomas T. Semon, "A Bad Picture Is Worth Very Few Words," *Marketing News* (May 24, 1993), p. 11.
7. Adapted from "Noelle-Neumann Blames Cost Cuts for Regression Research Quality," *Marketing News* (May 4, 1979), p. 5; also see Elizabeth H. Stephen and Beth Soldo, "How to Judge the Quality of a Survey," *American Demographics* (April 1990), pp. 42–43; and Randall Hansen, "Clear, Concise Writing Is Especially Important for Marketers," *Marketing News* (September 13, 1994), p. 20.
8. Philip H. Abelson, "Communicating with the Public," *Science* 194 (November 5, 1976), p. 565.
9. Peter Eder, "Merchandise All Research Results within Corporation," *Marketing News* (January 4, 1985), p. 40.
10. Anil Menon, "Are We Squandering Our Intellectual Capital?" *Marketing Research* (Summer 1994), pp. 18–22.
11. Steven Perkins and Ram Rao, "The Role of Experience in Information Use and Decision Making by Marketing Managers," *Journal of Marketing Research* 27 (February 1990): 1–10.
12. Christine Moorman, Rohit Deshpande, and Gerald Zaltman, "Factors Affecting Trust in Market Research Relationships," *Journal of Marketing* 57 (January 1993): 81–101.
13. Ibid.
14. Richard Kitaeff, "How Am I Doing?" *Marketing Research* (June 1992), pp. 38–39.

CHAPTER **20**

1. Joseph Rydhom, "On the Wings of an Eagle," *Quirk's Marketing Research Review* (April 1993), pp. 6–7, 26–31.
2. Gordon Wyner with Hilary Owen, "What's your Position?," *Marketing Research* (Winter 1994), pp. 54–56.
3. Tony Siciliano, Michael Amorosa "The Increasing Importance of Strategic Research," *CASRO Journal* (1993), pp. 65–68.
4. Peter Sampson, "People are People the World Over: The Case for Psychological Market Segmentation," *Marketing and Research Today*, (November 1992), pp. 236–244.
5. Paul Green and Donald Tull, *Research for Marketing Decisions*, 5th ed. (Englewood Cliffs, N.J.: Prentice-Hall, 1988), p. 687.
6. Jim Alleborn and John Morton, "A Cross Category Study of Brand Equity," *CASRO Journal* (1993), pp. 131–135; Phillip Kotler, *Marketing Management: Analysis Planning and Control*, (Englewood Cliffs, N.J.: Prentice-Hall, 1977), pp. 168–178; Peter Sampson, "People are People the World Over: The Case for Psychological Market Segmentation," *Marketing and Research Today* (November 1992), pp. 236–244; and Gordon A. Wyner, "Segmentation Design," *Marketing Research* (December 1992), pp. 38–41.
7. Rebecca Pierto, "VALS The Second Time," *American Demographics* (July 1991), p. 6. VALS is a trademark of SRI.
8. Jennifer Lawrence, "The Sunchip Also Rises," *Advertising Age*, (April 27, 1992),

pp. S–2, S–6.

9. Jack Weber, "Absorbing Some Changes: Brawny Takes a Giant Step Into Research," *Quirk's Marketing Research Review* (November 1994), pp. 6–8.
10. Glen Urban and John Hauser, *Design and Marketing of New Products* (Englewood Cliffs, N.J.: Prentice-Hall, 1990), pp. 281–285.
11. Bob Bengen, "Easy Travel Restrictions: Research with Travelers Helps Samsonite Develop a Convenient New Line of Luggage," *Quirk's Marketing Research Review* (February 1992), pp. 6–7, 26–27.
12. David Morawski and Lacey Zachary, "Making Mr. Coffee," *Quirk's Marketing Research Review* (March 1992), pp. 6–7, 29–33.
13. William Wells, John Burnett, and Sandra Moriarity, *Advertising Principles and Practices* (Englewood Cliffs, N.J.: Prentice-Hall, 1992), p. 618.
14. A. Parasuraman, Leonard Berry, and Valarie Zeithaml, "Guidelines for Conducting Quality Research," *Marketing Research* (December 1990), pp. 34–44.
15. The Malcom Baldridge National Quality Award, 1991 *Application Guidelines* (Gaithersburg, Md.: U.S. Department of Commerce, National Institute of Standards and Technology, 1991), p. 2.
16. A Parasuraman, Leonard Berry, and Valarie Zeithaml, "A Conceptual Model of Service Quality and Its Implications for Future Research," *Journal of Retailing* (Spring 1988), pp. 12–40.
17. "Regular Check Ups," *Quirk's Marketing Research Review* (November 1991), pp. 6–7, 50.
18. This case has been developed from Joseph Rydholm, "Study Seeks to Define Quality," *Quirk's Marketing Research Review* (October 1991), pp. 51–52.

INDEX

C

D

F

G

H

N

O

S

T

U